D0009401

Fundamental
accounting
principles

Fundamental accounting principles

WILLIAM W. PYLE
College of Business Administration
University of Hawaii

JOHN ARCH WHITE
Emeritus, Graduate School of Business
University of Texas

MICHAEL ZIN
Faculty of Business Administration
University of Windsor

Second Canadian edition

 1976

Irwin-Dorsey Limited   Georgetown, Ontario   L7G 4B3

© IRWIN-DORSEY LIMITED, 1972 and 1976

All rights reserved. No part of this publication may be
reproduced, stored in a retrieval system, or transmitted,
in any form or by any means, electronic, mechanical,
photocopying, recording, or otherwise, without the prior
written permission of the publisher.

Printed and published under Canadian license 1976.

Second Canadian Edition

First Printing, March 1976
Second Printing, September 1976

ISBN 0-256-01786-7

Printed in the United States of America

LEARNING SYSTEMS COMPANY—
a division of Richard D. Irwin, Inc.—has developed a
Programmed Learning AID
to accompany texts in this subject area.
Copies can be purchased through your bookstore
or by writing PLAIDS.
1818 Ridge Road, Homewood, Illinois   60430.

Preface

■ This Second Canadian Edition of *Fundamental Accounting Principles,* like the previous edition, is designed for use in the first accounting course at the university and college level. It describes how accounting data are accumulated and gives an understanding of the concepts necessary to use such data effectively. It maintains a balance between financial and managerial materials and thus meets the needs of students who will make accountancy a career, as well as students who will use accounting as a tool in other fields of specialization or in their personal affairs.

A new edition always offers an opportunity to reorganize, to rewrite, to condense, to expand, and to add new materials. In this edition many chapter sections were rewritten to increase ease of understanding, to update the materials, and to bring the discussions into line with recent pronouncements of the Canadian Institute of Chartered Accountants and with changes in legislation. The materials of several chapters were combined, and both chapters and topics were shifted to improve instructional efficiency. The condensation of purely procedural matters was continued to make room for the inclusion or expansion of topics such as capital budgeting, the interest method of amortizing bond premiums and discounts, present value concepts, and a new chapter on cost-volume-profit analysis.

Since the needs of students differ, the assignment flexibility of the previous edition was maintained. A minimum of time may still be devoted to Chapters 6 and 9, and almost any chapter beyond the fifth may be omitted, quickly covered, or taught out of sequence without detriment to an understanding of the materials that follow.

Again, an extensive set of supplementary materials accompanies the text. Available to students are a Workbook of Study Guides, two booklets of Working Papers, two Practice Sets, and a list of Problem Check Figures. A series of ten Achievement Tests and two Final Examinations plus comprehensive Solutions Manuals for the problems of the text, the practice sets, and the tests are available to the instructor.

Professionally manufactured transparencies are again free to adopters. These include a transparency solution to each problem in the text plus 24 additional transparencies designed to aid in teaching such subjects as the preparation of a work sheet, closing entries, the preparation of a break-even chart, and so on.

The two final examinations are new with this edition. The first covers Chapters 1 through 14 and the second Chapters 15 through 28. Each has 50 multiple-choice questions and problems and is designed to be graded either manually or electronically. If manually graded, the average grading time is less than two minutes per examination. To insure that the questions of the examinations are more than five-answer guessing games, the mistakes that students commonly make are anticipated, and the resulting wrong answers are included among the answer choices.

To present the usefulness of the computer in the accounting area, the Third Edition of *Accounting with the Computer: A Practice Case and Simulation* by Joseph Wilkinson of Arizona State University has been developed and keyed to the text. Professor Wilkinson's case builds on the material covered in Chapter 6, "Accounting Systems." A detailed Instructor's Manual, that assumes no expertise in the computer area, is available for adopters of the case.

Since the publication of the First Canadian Edition, many users have offered valuable suggestions for the improvement of this edition. The increased number of decision problems and the new "analytical and review problems" are among the suggestions that are reflected in this new edition.

The authors owe a special debt to a number of colleagues and associates who contributed significantly to the Second Canadian Edition and especially to W. P. Lam of the University of Windsor for his work on the new problem material.

February 1976   MICHAEL ZIN

Contents

1 *page 1*

**Accounting,
an introduction to
its concepts**

Why study accounting.
Accountancy as a profession.
The work of an accountant.
Accounting and bookkeeping.
Accounting statements. The
balance sheet equation.
Effects of transactions on
the accounting equation.

2 *page 25*

**Recording
transactions**

Business papers. Accounts.
Accounts commonly used.
The ledger. Debit and credit.
Mechanics of double-entry
accounting. Transactions
illustrating the rules of debit
and credit. The accounts and
the equation. Preparing a
trial balance. The proof
offered by a trial balance.
A standard account form.

Determining the balance of
an account. Need for a
journal. The General Journal.
Recording transactions in a
General Journal. Posting
transaction information.
Correcting errors.
Bookkeeping techniques.

3 *page 61*

**Adjusting the accounts
and preparing the
statements**

Need for adjustments before
the statements are prepared.
Adjusting the accounts. The
adjusted trial balance.
Preparing statements from
the adjusted trial balance.
Arrangement of the accounts
in the ledger. The adjustment
process. Matching revenues
and expenses. Cash and
accrual bases of accounting.
Disposing of accrued items.
Classification of balance
sheet items. Owner equity
on the balance sheet.
Arrangement of balance

sheet items. Classification
of income statement items.

4 *page 95*

**Balance column accounts,
the work sheet, and
closing the accounts**

Balance column account.
Need for a work sheet.
Preparing a work sheet. The
work sheet illustrated. Work
sheet and the financial
statements. Work sheet and
adjusting entries. Work sheet
and closing entries. Why
closing entries are made.
Closing entries illustrated.
Sources of closing entry
information. The accounts
after closing. The post-closing
trial balance. Matters of
terminology. The accounting
cycle. Accounting periods;
the natural business year.

5 *page 131*

**Accounting for a
merchandising concern**

Revenue from sales. Cost
of goods sold. Cost of goods

sold, periodic inventory system. Income statement of a merchandising concern. Work sheet of a merchandising concern. Preparing the statements; adjusting entries. Closing entries. Closing entries and the inventory. Dispensing with the Adjusted Trial Balance columns. Taking the ending inventory. Debit and credit memoranda. Code numbers as a means of identifying accounts. Trade discounts. Transportation charges.

6 *page 169*

Accounting systems

Reducing posting labour. Subsidiary ledgers. Posting the sales journal. Controlling accounts. Other columnar journals. Cash Receipts Journal. Posting the Cash Receipts Journal. Posting rule. Sales returns. Accounts payable. The Purchases Journal and its posting. The Cash Disbursements Journal and its posting. Identifying posted amounts. Purchases returns. Proving the ledgers. Sales taxes. Sales invoices as a Sales Journal. Purchase of assets used in the business. Speeding the data processing. Electric accounting machines. Electronic data processing.

7 *page 213*

Internal control

Internal control. Where internal control is needed.

Controlling purchases in a large store. The voucher system. The voucher. The voucher system and control. The Vouchers Payable account. The voucher system and expenses. Recording vouchers. Posting the voucher register. The unpaid vouchers file. The voucher system Cheque Register. Purchases returns. Other internal control procedures.

8 *page 243*

Cash and accounts receivable

Internal control for cash. The petty cash fund. Petty cash fund illustrated. Cash over and short. Reconciling the bank balance. Illustration of a bank reconciliation. **Accounts receivable.** Bad debts. Matching bad debt losses with sales. Allowance method of accounting for bad debts. Bad debt recoveries. Other bases for estimating bad debts. Aging accounts receivable. Direct write-off of bad debts.

9 *page 275*

Accounting for notes and interest

Promissory notes. Legal due dates. Calculating interest. Interest tables. **Notes payable.** Purchasing an asset with a note. Note given to secure an extension of time on an account. Recording a bank loan. **Notes receivable.** Recording the receipt of a

note. Dishonoured notes receivable. Discounting notes receivable. Payment of a discounted note by the maker. Dishonour of a discounted note. Discounting an interest-bearing note. Discounted interest-bearing note dishonoured at maturity. Collecting an out-of-town note. End-of-the-period adjustments.

10 *page 305*

Inventories and cost of goods sold

Matching merchandise costs with revenues. Assigning a cost to the ending inventory. Accounting for an inventory at cost. Consistency. Elements of inventory cost. Cost or replacement, the lower. Conservatism. Inventory errors. Perpetual inventories. Periodic and perpetual inventory systems. Estimated inventories.

11 *page 331*

Plant and equipment

Cost of plant and equipment. Nature of depreciation. Productive life of a plant asset. Salvage value. Allocating depreciation. Depreciation practice. Recording depreciation. Depreciation on the balance sheet. Balance sheet plant asset values. Recovering the cost of plant assets. Disposal of a plant asset. Depreciation for partial years. Plant asset records. Plant assets of low cost.

12 *page 361*

Plant and equipment; intangible assets

Accounting for small tools. Exchanging plant assets. Revising depreciation rates. Repairs and replacements. Betterments. Capital and revenue expenditures. Natural resources. Intangible assets.

13 *page 389*

Payroll accounting

Unemployment insurance. Withholding employees' income tax. The Canada Pension Plan. Workmen's compensation. Wages, hours, and union contracts. Other payroll deductions. Timekeeping. The Payroll Register. Recording the payroll. Paying the employees. Payroll bank account. Employee's Individual Earnings Record. Payroll taxes levied on the employer. Paying the payroll taxes. Accruing taxes and wages. Machine methods.

14 *page 411*

Accounting principles

Need for accounting principles. Nature of accounting principles. Accounting concepts. Accounting principles. Accounting principles and the public accountant.

15 *page 435*

Partnership accounting

Characteristics of a partnership. Advantages and disadvantages of a partnership. Partnership accounting. Nature of partnership earnings. Division of earnings. Earnings allocated on a stated fractional basis. Division of earnings based on the ratio of capital investments. Salaries and interest as aids in sharing. Partnership financial statements. Ending a partnership. Death of a partner. Liquidations.

16 *page 465*

Corporations: Organization and operation

Advantages of the corporate form. Disadvantages of the corporate form. Organizing a corporation. Minute book. Organization costs. Management of a corporation. Stock certificates and the transfer of stock. Corporation accounting. Corporation owner equity accounts illustrated. Authorization of stock. Selling stock for cash. Exchanging stock for assets other than cash. Stock subscriptions. Sale of stock through subscriptions, with collections in installments. Subscribed stock on the balance sheet. Cash dividends and retained earnings. Dividend policy. Rights of stockholders. Preferred stock. Why preferred stock is issued. Stock values.

17 *page 499*

Corporations: Additional stock transactions

Par value and minimum legal capital. Stock premiums and discounts. No-par stock. Treasury stock. Purchase of treasury stock. Reissuance of treasury stock. Retirement of stock. Donated treasury stock. Donations of capital by outsiders. Contributed capital in the accounts and on the statements. Contributed capital and dividends. Stock dividends. Stock splits. Accounting treatment for corporation income taxes.

18 *page 529*

Corporations: Retained earnings and consolidations

Retained earnings and dividends. Appropriation of retained earnings. Comprehensive treatment of equity items. Retained earnings statement. Extraordinary gains and losses. Normal corrections and adjustments. Earnings per share. Prior period adjustments. Comparative single-step income statement. Parent and subsidiary corporations. Consolidated balance sheets. Earnings of a subsidiary. Consolidated balance sheets at a date after acquisition. Other consolidated statements. Purchase versus a pooling of interests. Who uses consolidated statements.

19 *page 565*

Long-term liabilities and investments

Borrowing money with a mortgage. Borrowing money by issuing bonds. Characteristics of bonds. Why bonds are issued. Issuing bonds. Bonds sold between interest dates. Bond interest rates. Bonds sold at a discount. Bonds sold at a premium. Accrued bond interest expense. Sale of bonds by investors. Redemption of bonds. Convertible bonds. Bond sinking fund. Restriction on dividends due to outstanding bonds. The corporation balance sheet. **Stocks and bonds as investments.** Classifying investments. Accounting for stocks as investments. Accounting for bonds as investments.

20 *page 601*

Analyzing financial statements

Comparative statements. Analysis of working capital. Standards of comparison. Other balance sheet and income statement relations. The effect of price level changes.

21 *page 629*

Flow of funds: Flow of cash

Broad concept of financing and investing activities.

Nature of funds. Sources and uses of funds. Statement of changes in financial position. Broad concept of financing and investing. Preparing a statement of changes in financial position. Determining the change in working capital. Preparing the working paper. Analysis of working capital changes. Extraordinary gains and losses. **Cash flow.** Cash flow statement. Preparing a cash flow statement.

22 *page 665*

Departmental accounting; responsibility accounting

Basis for departmentalization. Departmental gross profits in a merchandising business. Securing departmental information. Income statement showing departmental gross profits. Allocating expenses. Bases for allocating expenses. Mechanics of allocating expenses. Allocating service department expenses. Departmental expense allocation sheet. Eliminating an unprofitable department. Departmental contributions to overhead. Controllable costs and expenses. Responsibility accounting. Joint costs.

23 *page 697*

Manufacturing accounting

Basic difference in accounting. Systems of accounting in manufacturing

concerns. Elements of manufacturing costs. Accounts unique to a manufacturing company. Income statement of a manufacturing company. Manufacturing statement. Work sheet for a manufacturing company. Preparing a manufacturing company's work sheet. Preparing statements. Adjusting entries. Closing entries. Inventory valuation problems of a manufacturer.

24 *page 725*

Cost accounting, job order and process

Job order cost accounting. Job cost sheets. The Goods in Process account. Accounting for materials under a job cost system. Accounting for labour in a job cost system. Accounting for overhead in a job cost system. Overapplied and underapplied overhead. Recording the completion of a job. Recording cost of goods sold. **Process cost accounting.** Assembling costs by departments. Charging costs to departments. Equivalent finished units. Process cost accounting illustrated.

25 *page 763*

Budgeting; standard costs

Other benefits from budgeting. The budget period. The budget committee. Preparing the budget. Accounting and budgeting. Preparing estimated statements. Fixed and variable budgets. **Standard costs.** Establishing standard costs. Variances. Isolating material and labour variances. Charging overhead to production. Establishing overhead standards. Overhead variances. Controlling a business through standard costs. Standard costs in the accounts.

26 *page 791*

Cost-volume-profit analysis

Cost behaviours. Cost assumptions. Break-even point. Break-even graph. Sales required for a desired net income. Margin of safety. Income from a given sales level. Other questions. Multi-product break-even point. Evaluating the results.

27 *page 811*

Capital budgeting; managerial decisions

Capital budgeting. Accepting additional business. Buy or make. Other costs. Scrap or rebuild defective units. Process or sell. Deciding the sales mix.

28 *page 835*

Tax considerations in business decisions

Tax planning. Tax evasion and tax avoidance. Provincial income taxes. History and objectives of the federal income tax. Synopsis of the federal income tax. Tax effects of business alternatives. Net income and taxable income. Capital cost allowances. Taxes and the distortion of net income. Entries for the allocation of taxes.

page 863

Appendix: The concept of present value

page 869

Index

1

Accounting, an introduction to its concepts

■ Accounting is a service activity the function of which is identifying, measuring, recording and communicating quantitative information, primarily financial in nature, about economic entities. If the entity for which the information is provided is a business, for example, the information is used by its management in making such decisions as: What are the resources of the business? What debts does it owe? Does it have earnings? Are expenses too large in relation to sales? Is too little or too much merchandise being kept? Are amounts owed by customers being collected rapidly? Will the business be able to meet its own debts as they mature? Should the plant be expanded? Should a new product be introduced? Should selling prices be increased? Also, grantors of credit such as banks, wholesale houses, and manufacturers use accounting information in answering such additional questions as: Are the customer's earning prospects good? What is his debt-paying ability? Has he paid his debts promptly in the past? Should he be granted additional credit?

Likewise, governmental units use accounting information in regulating businesses and collecting taxes; labour unions use it in negotiating working conditions and wage agreements; and investors make wide use of accounting data in investment decisions.

Why study accounting ■ Information for use in answering questions like those in the foregoing section is conveyed in accounting reports. If a business owner, manager, banker, lawyer, engineer, or other person is to use these reports effectively, he must have some understanding of how their data were gathered and the figures put together. He must appreciate the limitations of the data and the extent to which portions are based on estimates rather than precise measurements, and he must understand accounting terms and concepts. Needless to say, these understandings are gained in a study of accounting.

Another reason to study accounting is to make it one's lifework—to become a professional accountant. The work can be very interesting and highly rewarding.

Accountancy as a profession ■ Over the past half century, accountancy as a profession has attained a stature comparable with that of law or medicine. Provinces license public accountants just as they license doctors and lawyers, and for the same reason—to help ensure a high standard of professional service. Only individuals who have passed rigorous examinations of their accounting and related knowledge and met other requirements may be licensed.

In Canada, there are a number of accounting organizations providing education and professional training. These include the provincial Institutes of Chartered Accountants, the Certified General Accountants Associations, and the Societies of Industrial Accountants. Successful completion of the prescribed courses of instruction and practical experience lead to the following appellations:

Chartered Accountant (C.A.)
Certified General Accountant (C.G.A.)
Registered Industrial Accountant (R.I.A.)

Attitude toward an education for the accounting profession is undergoing a change. The change is not only in the body of knowledge deemed desirable for members of the profession but, probably more important, in the responsibility for the education. In general, accountancy is approaching the stage of maturity reached by the law profession a few years ago; that is, with universities responsible for education and the provincially chartered organizations responsible for certification.

Accountancy is the fastest growing of the professions. This growth is in response to the expansion and complexity of the economy, the increasing involvement of the accountant in the process of management decision making, and a growing number of financial reporting activities.

The work of an accountant ■ Accountants are commonly employed in one or the other of three main fields: (1) in public accounting, (2) in private business, or (3) in government.

Public accounting

A public accountant is one who offers his professional services and those of his employees to the public for a fee, in much the same manner as a lawyer or a consulting engineer.

AUDITING. The principal service offered by a public accountant is auditing. Limited companies, unless exempted, are required by law to have an annual audit of their accounting records by external public accountants. Proprietorships and partnerships, although not required by law, may have audits at the request of a major creditor, or as a matter of management policy.

The purpose of an audit is to enable the accountant making it to express the independent professional opinion whether he believes the audited company's financial reports fairly reflect its financial position and operating results. Banks, investors, and others rely on information in a company's financial reports in making loans, granting credit, and in buying and selling securities; and they rely on the independent public accountant's opinion that the reports fairly reflect the company's position.

In making an audit, a public accountant carefully examines the audited company's financial reports and the accounting records from which they are prepared, making such tests and checks of their information as he deems necessary in order to have a sound basis for his opinion, the accuracy of which determines his professional reputation.

MANAGEMENT ADVISORY SERVICES. In addition to auditing, accountants commonly offer management advisory services.

An accountant gains from an audit an intimate knowledge of the audited company's accounting procedures and its financial position, and thus is in an excellent position to offer constructive suggestions for improving the procedures and strengthening the position. Clients expect these suggestions as a useful audit by-product, and they also commonly engage public accountants to conduct additional investigations for the purpose of determining ways in which their operations may be improved. Such investigations and the suggestions growing from them are known as management advisory services.

Management advisory services include the design, installation, and improvement of a client's general accounting system and any system he may have for determining and controlling manufacturing and distributing costs. They also include the application of punched cards, electronics, and other modern machine methods to these systems, plus advice in financial planning, budgeting, forecasting, inventory control—in fact, in all phases of record keeping and related matters.

TAX SERVICES. In this day of increasing complexity in income and other tax laws and continued high rates, few important business decisions are made without consideration being given to their tax effect. A public accountant, through training and experience, is well qualified to render important service in this area. The service includes not only the preparation and filing of tax returns but also advice as to how transactions may be completed so as to incur the smallest tax allowed by law.

Private business

Many accountants are employed in private businesses. A small business may employ only one accountant or it may depend upon the services of a public accountant and employ none. A large business, on the other hand, may have more than a hundred employees in its accounting department, working under the supervision of a chief accounting officer, commonly called the *controller*. The title, controller, results from the fact that one of the chief uses of accounting data is to control the operations of a business.

The one accountant of the small business and the accounting department of a large concern do a variety of work, including general accounting, cost accounting, budgeting, and internal auditing.

GENERAL ACCOUNTING. Although it is hard to draw a line of demarcation, general accounting has to do primarily with recording transactions and preparing financial and other reports for the use of management, owners, creditors, and governmental agencies. The company accountant may design or help the public accountant design the system used in recording the transactions, and he will supervise the clerical or data processing staff in recording the transactions and preparing the reports.

COST ACCOUNTING. The phase of accounting that has to do with collecting, determining, and controlling costs, particularly costs of producing a given product or service, is called cost accounting. Since a knowledge of costs and controlling costs are vital to good management, a large company may have a number of accountants engaged in this activity.

BUDGETING. Planning business activities before they occur is called budgeting. The objective of budgeting is to provide management with an intelligent plan for future operations, and after the plan has been put into effect, to provide summaries and reports comparing actual accomplishments with the plan. Many large companies have within their accounting departments a number of people who devote all their time to this phase of accounting.

INTERNAL AUDITING. In addition to an annual audit by a firm of public accountants, some companies maintain a staff of internal auditors who constantly check the records prepared and maintained in each department or company branch. It is the responsibility of these internal auditors to make sure that established accounting procedures and management directives are being followed throughout the company.

Governmental accounting

Furnishing governmental services is a vast and complicated operation in which accounting is just as indispensable as in business. Elected and appointed officials must rely on data accumulated by means of accounting if they are to complete effectively their administrative duties. Accountants are responsible for the accumulation of these data. Accountants also check and audit the millions of income, payroll, and sales tax returns that accompany the tax payments upon which governmental units depend. And finally, federal and provincial agencies, such as the Securities Commissions, the Board of Transport Commissioners, Restrictive Trade Practices Commission, and so on, use accountants in many capacities in their regulation of business.

Accounting and book-keeping ■ Many people confuse accounting and bookkeeping and look upon them as one and the same—in effect they identify the whole with one of its parts. Actually, bookkeeping is only part of accounting, the record-making part. To keep books is to record transactions, and a bookkeeper is one who records transactions. The work is often routine and primarily clerical in nature. The work of an accountant goes far beyond this, as a rereading of the previous section will show.

Accounting statements ■ Accounting statements are the end product of the accounting process, but a good place to begin the study of accounting. They are used to convey to management and interested outsiders a concise picture of the profitability and financial position of a business. The two most important are the income statement and the balance sheet.

The income statement

A company's income statement (see Illustration 1–1) is perhaps more important than its balance sheet, since it shows whether or not the business achieved or failed to achieve its primary objective—earning a "profit" or net income. A net income is earned when revenues exceed expenses, and an income statement is prepared by listing the revenues earned during a period, listing the expenses incurred in earning the revenues, and subtracting the expenses from the revenues.

Coast Realty
Income Statement for Year Ended December 31, 19—

Revenues:		
Commissions earned	$18,450	
Property management fees	1,200	
Total revenues		$19,650
Operating expenses:		
Salaries expense	$ 3,600	
Rent expense	1,800	
Utilities expense	315	
Telephone expense	260	
Advertising expense	1,310	
Total operating expenses		7,285
Net Income		$12,365

Illustration
1–1

Revenues are inflows of cash or other properties received in exchange for goods or for services. Rents, dividends, and interest earned are also revenues. Coast Realty of Illustration 1–1 had revenue inflows from services which totaled $19,650.

Expenses are goods and services consumed in operating a business or other economic unit. Coast Realty consumed the services of its employees (salaries expense), the services of a telephone company, and so on.

The heading of an income statement tells the name of the business for which it is prepared and the time period covered by the statement. Both bits of information are important, but the time covered is extremely significant, since the items on the statement must be interpreted in connection with a period of time. For example, the item "Commissions earned, $18,450" on the income statement of Illustration 1–1 has little significance until it is known that the amount represents one year's commissions and not the commissions of a week or a month.

The balance sheet

The purpose of a balance sheet is to show the financial position of a business on a particular date, and it is often called a *position statement.* Financial position is shown by listing the *assets* of the business, its *liabilities* or debts, and the *equity of the owner or owners.* The name of the business and the date are given in the balance sheet heading, and it is understood that the item amounts shown are as of the close of business on that day.

Before a business manager, investor, or other person can make effective judgments based on balance sheet information, he or she must gain several concepts and understandings. Therefore, assume that on August 3, Joan Ball began a new business, called World Travel Agency, and during the day she completed these transactions in the name of the business.

Aug. 3   Invested $18,000 of her personal savings in the business.
     3   Paid $15,000 of the agency's cash for a small office building and the land on which it was built (cost of the building, $10,000, and cost of the land, $5,000).
     3   Purchased *on credit* from Office Equipment Company office equipment costing $2,000. (Purchased on credit means purchased with a promise to pay at a later date.)

A balance sheet reflecting the effects of these transactions appears in Illustration 1–2. It shows that after completing the transactions the agency has four assets, a $2,000 debt, and that its owner has an $18,000 equity in the business.

Observe that the two sides of the balance sheet are equal. This is where it gets its name. Its two sides must always be equal because one side shows the resources of the business and the other side shows who supplied the resources. For example, World Travel Agency has $20,000 of resources (assets) of which $18,000 were supplied by its owner and

$2,000 by its creditors. (Creditors are individuals and companies to whom the business owes debts.)

Illustration
1–2

World Travel Agency
Balance Sheet, August 3, 19—

ASSETS		LIABILITIES	
Cash	$ 3,000	Accounts payable	$ 2,000
Office equipment	2,000		
Building	10,000	OWNER EQUITY	
Land	5,000		
		Joan Ball, capital	18,000
Total Assets	$20,000	Total Equities	$20,000

Assets, liabilities, and owner equity

The assets of a business are, in general, the properties or economic resources owned by the business. They include cash, amounts owed to the business by its customers for goods and services sold to them on credit (called *accounts receivable*), merchandise held for sale by the business, supplies, equipment, buildings, and land. Assets may also include such intangible rights as those granted by a patent or copyright.

The liabilities of a business are its debts and include amounts owed to creditors for goods and services bought on credit (called *accounts payable*), salaries and wages owed employees, taxes payable, notes payable and mortgages payable.

Owner equity is the interest of the owner or owners of a business in its assets. When a business is owned by one man, his equity is shown on the balance sheet of the business by listing his name, followed by the word *capital,* and then the amount of the equity. The use of the word, capital, comes from the idea that the owner has furnished the business with resources or "capital" equal to his equity.

Liabilities are also sometimes called *equities*. An equity is a right, claim, or interest; and a liability represents a claim or right to be paid. Law recognizes this right; and if a business fails to pay its creditors, law gives the creditors the right to force the sale of the assets of the business to secure money to meet creditor claims. Furthermore, if the assets are sold, the creditors are paid first, with any remainder going to the business owner. Obviously, then, by law the creditor claims take precedence over those of a business owner.

Since creditor claims take precedence over those of an owner, owner equity in a business is always a residual amount. Creditors recognize this; and when they examine the balance sheet of a business, they are always interested in the share of its assets furnished by creditors and the share furnished by its owner or owners. The creditors' interest in the respective shares results from knowing that if the business must be liquidated and its assets sold, the shrinkage in converting the assets into cash must exceed the equity of the owner or owners before the creditors will lose.

In examining the Illustration 1–2 balance sheet, bear in mind that the $18,000 equity of Joan Ball in this business may not be all the assets she owns. In addition to her equity in the new business she may own a farm, a home, and many personal assets. However, these are not shown on the balance sheet of the business because if the personal property, affairs, and transactions of an owner are intermingled with those of her business, the records and statements of the business are misleading and fail their intended purpose, which is to show the financial position and operating results of the business.

Business entity concept

The idea discussed in the previous paragraph is known in accounting as the business entity concept. Under this concept it is assumed that a business is an entity that is separate and distinct from the person or persons who own it, and the business is treated as though it owns the business assets and in turn owes both the creditors and its owner or owners the amounts of their claims. Also, under this concept the resources and activities of the business are kept separate from those of its owner or owners.

Cost principle

In addition to the business entity concept, an accounting principle called the cost principle should be borne in mind when reading a balance sheet. Under this principle all transactions are recorded at cost and the goods and services purchased appear on the statements at cost. For example, if a business pays $50,000 for land to be used in carrying on its operations, the purchase should be recorded at $50,000. It makes no difference if the owner and several competent outside appraisers thought the land "worth" at least $60,000; it cost $50,000 and should appear on the balance sheet at that amount. Furthermore, if five years later, due to booming real estate prices, the land's fair market value has doubled, this makes no difference either. The land cost $50,000 and should continue to appear on the balance sheet at $50,000 even though its estimated market value is twice that.

Why are assets and services recorded at cost? The answer is that accounting must be factual and costs are factual. A buyer and a seller, each trying to strike the best bargain for himself, establish the costs; and these "bargained costs" are normally a fair measure of the goods and services acquired. If amounts other than costs were used, for example, amounts based on estimates, judgments, and appraisals, accounting records would lose much of their usefulness.

Going-concern concept

Why are balance sheet amounts not changed from time to time to reflect changing market values? The answer is that a balance sheet is prepared under the assumption that the business for which it is prepared is a *going concern,* and as a going concern its assets are not for sale, in fact, cannot be sold without disrupting the business. Therefore, since the assets are for use in the business and are not for sale, their current market values are generally not relevant.

The *going-concern concept* applies in most instances. However, if a business is about to be sold or liquidated, the going-concern concept and the cost principle do not apply in the preparation of its statements. In such cases amounts other than costs, such as current market values, are more useful and informative.

From the discussion of the cost principle and the going-concern concept it is obvious that in most instances a balance sheet does not show the amounts at which the listed assets can be sold or replaced. Nor does it show the "worth" of the business for which it was prepared, since some of the listed assets may be salable for much more or much less than their balance sheet amounts.

The balance sheet equation ■ A balance sheet is so called because its two sides must always balance; the sum of the assets shown on the balance sheet must equal liabilities plus owner equity. This equality may be expressed in equation form as follows:

$$\text{Assets} = \text{Liabilities} + \text{Owner Equity}$$

When balance sheet equality is expressed in equation form, the resulting equation is called the *balance sheet equation.* It is also known as the *accounting equation,* since all double-entry accounting is based on it. And, like any mathematical equation, its elements may be transposed and the equation expressed:

$$\text{Assets} - \text{Liabilities} = \text{Owner Equity}$$

The equation in this form illustrates the residual nature of owner equity; an owner's claims are secondary to those of his creditors.

Effects of transactions on the accounting equation ■ A business transaction is an exchange of goods or services, and business transactions affect the elements of the accounting equation. However, regardless of what transactions a business completes, its accounting equation always remains in balance and its assets always equal the combined claims of its creditors and its owner or owners. This may be demonstrated with the transactions of Owen Real Estate Agency which follow.

On the first day of July, Larry Owen invested $5,000 in a real estate agency and began business as a real estate agent. After the investment, the one asset of the new business and the equity of Owen in the one asset is shown by the following equation:

$$\underbrace{\text{Assets}}_{\text{Cash, \$5,000}} = \underbrace{\text{Owner Equity}}_{\text{Larry Owen, Capital, \$5,000}}$$

After its first transaction the Owen Real Estate Agency has one asset, cash, $5,000. It has no liabilities; therefore, the equity of Owen in this business is $5,000.

To continue the Owen Real Estate Agency illustration, after investing $5,000 cash, (1) Owen used $300 to pay the rent for three months in advance on an office, (2) $3,000 to buy an automobile that he planned to use only for business purposes, and (3) $1,000 to buy office furniture. The effects of these three transactions on the accounting equation are shown in Illustration 1–3. Observe that the equation remains in balance after each transaction.

	Cash	+	Prepaid Rent	+	Automobile	+	Office Equipment	=	Larry Owen, Capital
	$5,000								$5,000
(1)	−300		+$300						
	$4,700		$300						$5,000
(2)	−3,000				+$3,000				
	$1,700		$300		$3,000				$5,000
(3)	−1,000						+$1,000		
	$ 700	+	$300	+	$3,000	+	$1,000	=	$5,000

Illustration 1–3

The nature of the Owen Real Estate Agency assets was changed by the three transactions, the effects of which are shown in Illustration 1–3. After their completion only $700 of the concern's original $5,000 cash remains; however, in exchange for the cash the business acquired three new assets: (1) the right to occupy office space for three months, (2) an automobile, and (3) office furniture.

Continuing the illustration, assume that Owen found it necessary to have some additional equipment in his office. He felt that he should conserve the business cash; consequently, he purchased on credit or on account from Standard Supply Company office furniture costing $350 (transaction No. 4). The effects of this transaction on the agency assets and equities are shown in colour in Illustration 1–4. Note that the assets were increased by purchase of the additional office equipment; however, owner equity remained unchanged because Standard Supply

Company acquired a claim against the assets equal to the asset increase. The claim of or the amount owed Standard Supply Company is called an account payable.

		Assets			=	Liabilities	+	Owner Equity
	Cash +	Prepaid Rent +	Automobile +	Office Equipment	=	Accounts Payable	+	Larry Owen, Capital
	$5,000							$5,000
(1)	−300	+$300						
	$4,700	$300						$5,000
(2)	−3,000		+$3,000					
	$1,700	$300	$3,000					$5,000
(3)	−1,000			+$1,000				
	$ 700	$300	$3,000	$1,000				$5,000
(4)				+350		+$350		
	$ 700 +	$300 +	$3,000 +	$1,350	=	$350	+	$5,000

Illustration 1–4

At this stage assume that Larry Owen realized he had one piece of office equipment that did not fit his needs. Assume further that he was able to sell the equipment to Dale Hall for the $150 it cost. Mr. Hall paid $100 in cash on delivery and promised to pay the $50 balance at a later date. The effects of this transaction (No. 5) on the accounting equation are shown in colour in Illustration 1–5.

			Assets				=	Liabilities	+	Owner Equity
	Cash +	Accounts Receivable +	Prepaid Rent +	Auto-mobile +	Office Equipment	=	Accounts Payable	+	Larry Owen, Capital
	$5,000								$5,000
(1)	−300		+$300						
	$4,700		$300						$5,000
(2)	−3,000			+$3,000					
	$1,700		$300	$3,000					$5,000
(3)	−1,000				+$1,000				
	$ 700		$300	$3,000	$1,000				$5,000
(4)					+350		+$350		
	$ 700		$300	$3,000	$1,350		$350		$5,000
(5)	+100	+$50			−150				
	$ 800 +	$50 +	$300 +	$3,000 +	$1,200	=	$350	+	$5,000

Illustration 1–5

The sale of the unneeded office equipment was an exchange of office equipment for (1) cash, $100, and (2) a new asset, the right to collect $50 from Dale Hall at a future date. This new asset, the right to collect money from someone to whom goods or services have been sold on credit, is known as an account receivable.

A few days after the foregoing transaction, Dale Hall paid the amount owed (transaction No. 6); upon receipt of the money Larry Owen paid Standard Supply Company one half the amount owed to it (No. 7). The effect of these transactions is shown in Illustration 1–6. Note that the first, the receipt of cash from Dale Hall, is an exchange of assets; the second results in equal decreases in both assets and liabilities.

		Assets				=	Liabilities	+	Owner Equity
	Cash +	Accounts Receivable +	Prepaid Rent +	Auto-mobile +	Office Equip-ment	=	Accounts Payable	+	Larry Owen, Capital
	$5,000								$5,000
(1)	−300		+$300						
	$4,700		$300						$5,000
(2)	−3,000			+$3,000					
	$1,700		$300	$3,000					$5,000
(3)	−1,000				+$1,000				
	$ 700		$300	$3,000	$1,000				$5,000
(4)					+350		+$350		
	$ 700		$300	$3,000	$1,350		$350		$5,000
(5)	+100	+$50			−150				
	$ 800	$50	$300	$3,000	$1,200		$350		$5,000
(6)	+50	−50							
	$ 850	0	$300	$3,000	$1,200		$350		$5,000
(7)	−175						−175		
	$ 675 +	0 +	$300 +	$3,000 +	$1,200 =		$175	+	$5,000

Illustration 1–6

Important transaction effects

Look again at Illustration 1–6 and observe that (1) every transaction affected at least two items in the equation and (2) in each case, after the effects were entered in the columns, the equation remained in balance with the sum of the assets equaling the sum of the liabilities plus owner equity. The accounting system you are beginning to study is called a *double-entry system* and is based on the fact that every transaction affects two or more items in an accounting equation such as that in Illustration 1–6 and requires a "double entry" or, in other words, entries in two or more places. Also, the fact that the equation remained in balance after each transaction is important, for this is a proof of the accuracy with which the transactions were recorded.

Increasing owner equity

The primary objective of a business is to increase owner equity by earning a profit or a net income. The Owen Real Estate Agency will accomplish this objective by selling real estate on a commission basis for its clients. Of course, the business will accomplish this objective only if the commissions earned are greater than the expenses incurred in making the sales.

Commissions earned and expenses incurred affect the elements of an accounting equation. To illustrate their effect, assume that on July 12 Larry Owen sold a house for a client and collected an $850 commission for his services (No. 8). Also, on the last day of July he received the monthly telephone bill in the mail and issued a $20 cheque for its payment (No. 9). The effects of these two transactions are shown in Illustration 1-7.

	Cash +	Accounts Receivable +	Prepaid Rent +	Auto-mobile +	Office Equip-ment =	Accounts Payable +	Larry Owen, Capital
	$5,000						$5,000
(1)	−300		+$300				
	$4,700		$300				$5,000
(2)	−3,000			+$3,000			
	$1,700		$300	$3,000			$5,000
(3)	−1,000				+$1,000		
	$ 700		$300	$3,000	$1,000		$5,000
(4)					+350	+$350	
	$ 700		$300	$3,000	$1,350	$350	$5,000
(5)	+100	+$50			−150		
	$ 800	$50	$300	$3,000	$1,200	$350	$5,000
(6)	+50	−50					
	$ 850	0	$300	$3,000	$1,200	$350	$5,000
(7)	−175					−175	
	$ 675	0	$300	$3,000	$1,200	$175	$5,000
(8)	+850						+850
	$1,525	0	$300	$3,000	$1,200	$175	$5,850
(9)	−20						−20
	$1,505 +	0 +	$300 +	$3,000 +	$1,200 =	$175 +	$5,830

Illustration
1-7

Observe first the effects of the $850 commission. This commission is a revenue, an inflow of assets from the sale of services. However, note that the revenue not only increased the asset cash but also caused an $850 increase in owner equity. Owner equity increased because the transaction increased total assets without increasing liabilities.

Next observe the effects of the $20 telephone expense and note that they are opposite from those of a revenue. Expenses are goods and services consumed in the operation of a business. Owen Real Estate Agency consumed a service of the telephone company, and when the service was paid for, the Agency's assets were reduced. However, owner equity was also reduced because cash decreased without an increase in any other asset or a reduction in liabilities.

In concluding this chapter, note this about earning a net income. A business earns a net income when its revenues exceed its expenses, and the income increases both assets and owner equity. Assets are increased because more assets flow in from revenues than are consumed and flow out for expenses. Owner equity is increased because a net income increases *net assets*. Net assets are the excess of assets over liabilities.

Questions for class discussion

1. What is the nature of accounting and what is its function?
2. How does a businessowner use accounting information?
3. Why do provinces license public accountants?
4. Differentiate between a public accountant and an accountant employed in private business.
5. What accounting associations are found in Canada?
6. What is the purpose of an audit? What does a public accountant do when he makes an audit?
7. A public accountant may provide management advisory services. Of what does this consist?
8. What do the tax services of a public accountant include beyond preparing and filing tax returns?
9. What is a private accountant? A public accountant?
10. Differentiate between accounting and bookkeeping.
11. What does an income statement show?
12. As the word is used in accounting, what is a revenue? An expense?
13. Why is the period of time covered by an income statement of extreme significance?
14. What does a balance sheet show?
15. Define (a) asset, (b) liability, (c) equity, and (d) owner equity.
16. What is an account receivable?
17. What is the cost principle of accounting? Why is such a principle necessary?
18. A business shows office stationery on its balance sheet at its $50 cost, although the stationery can be sold for not more than $0.25 as scrap paper. What accounting principle and concept justify this?
19. What is the balance sheet equation? Why is it of importance to the accounting student?
20. Is it possible for a transaction to affect one asset item without affecting any other asset, liability, or owner equity item? Is it possible for a transaction to increase or decrease a single liability without affecting any other asset, liability, or owner equity item?

Exercise 1-1

Determine –

a. The equity of the owner in a business having $33,314 of assets and $8,203 of liabilities.

b. The liabilities of a business having $25,650 of assets and in which the owner has a $14,240 equity.

c. The assets of a business having $4,215 of liabilities and in which the owner has a $12,540 equity.

Exercise 1-2

Describe a transaction that will –

a. Increase an asset and decrease an asset.

b. Increase an asset and increase a liability.

c. Decrease an asset and decrease a liability.

d. Increase an asset and increase owner equity.

e. Decrease an asset and decrease owner equity.

Exercise 1-3

The effect of five transactions on the assets, liabilities, and owner equity of Gary Hall in his law practice are shown in the following equation with each transaction identified by a letter. Write a short sentence or phrase telling the probable nature of each transaction.

		Assets			= Liabilities +	Owner Equity
	Cash +	Accounts Receivable +	Law Library +	Office Equipment =	Accounts Payable +	Gary Hall, Capital
	$1,200		$1,500	$2,000		$4,700
a.	−100		+100			
	$1,100		$1,600	$2,000		$4,700
b.				+300	+300	
	$1,100		$1,600	$2,300	$300	$4,700
c.		+500				+500
	$1,100	$500	$1,600	$2,300	$300	$5,200
d.	−300				−300	
	$ 800	$500	$1,600	$2,300	$ 0	$5,200
e.	+500	−500				
	$1,300	$ 0	$1,600	$2,300	$ 0	$5,200

Exercise 1-4

Prepare a form with the following four columnar headings: (1) Transaction, (2) Assets, (3) Liabilities, and (4) Owner Equity. List each of the following transactions by letter on a separate line in the first column and indicate the effect of each on the assets, liabilities, and owner equity by writing in the proper columns a plus (+) sign to indicate an increase, a minus (−) sign to show a decrease, and a zero to indicate no effect.

a. An engineer invested cash and equipment in a consulting business.
b. Purchased additional equipment on credit for use in the business.
c. Completed a job for a client and immediately collected cash for the work done.
d. Paid for the equipment purchased in transaction (b).
e. Completed engineering work on credit for a client.
f. Paid the monthly telephone bill.
g. The client of transaction (e) paid for the work of that transaction.

Exercise 1-5

On October 1 of the current year Ottis Orr began the practice of law, and on October 31 his records showed the following asset, liability, and owner equity items including revenues earned and expenses. From the information, prepare an income statement for the month and a month-end balance sheet. Head the statements Ottis Orr, Lawyer. (The October 31, $2,500 amount for Ottis Orr's capital is the amount of his capital after it was increased and decreased by the October revenues and expenses shown.)

Cash	$ 600	Ottis Orr, capital	$2,500
Accounts receivable	200	Legal fees earned	1,200
Prepaid rent	300	Rent expense	300
Law library	1,500	Salaries expense	400
Accounts payable	100	Telephone expense	50

Problems   Problem 1-1

Roy Neal has just begun the practice of dentistry, and during a short period he completed the following transactions in the name of the practice:

a. Sold for $9,650 a personal investment in Xerox stock, which he had inherited, and deposited $9,000 of the proceeds in a bank account opened in the name of the practice.
b. Purchased for $20,000 a small building to be used as an office. He paid $5,000 in cash and signed a mortgage contract promising to pay the balance over a period of years.
c. Took dental equipment, which he had purchased while in college, from home for use in the practice. The equipment had a $300 fair market value.
d. Purchased dental supplies for cash, $100.
e. Purchased dental equipment from Dental Supply Company on credit, $3,000.
f. Completed dental work for Gary Gage and immediately collected $50 for the work done.
g. Paid the local newspaper $25 for a small advertisement announcing the opening of the practice.
h. Completed $100 additional work for Gary Gage, for which Mr. Gage paid $35 in cash and promised to pay the balance within a few days.

i. Paid Dental Supply Company a $500 installment on the amount owed.
j. Gary Gage paid a $30 installment on the balance due for the work of transaction *(h)*.
k. Paid the part-time dental assistant's wages, $75.
l. Roy Neal withdrew $100 from the bank account of the dental practice for personal living expenses.

Required:
1. Arrange the following asset, liability, and owner equity titles in an equation like Illustration 1–7: Cash; Accounts Receivable; Dental Supplies; Dental Equipment; Building; Accounts Payable; Mortgage Payable; and Roy Neal, Capital.
2. Show by additions and subtractions, as in Illustration 1–7, the effects of each transaction on the assets, liabilities, and owner equity. Show new totals after each transaction.

Problem 1–2

Paul Hill, a young lawyer, completed these transactions during a short period of time:
a. Began the practice of law by investing $2,000 in cash and a law library having a $600 fair value.
b. Paid cash for two months' rent in advance on suitable office space, $200.
c. Paid Office Suppliers $1,000 cash for several items of office equipment.
d. Completed legal work for John Thomas and collected $50 cash therefor.
e. Purchased office supplies, $50, and office equipment, $175, from Office Suppliers on credit.
f. Completed legal work for Security Bank on credit, $300.
g. Paid the salary of the legal secretary, $160.
h. Collected $300 from Security Bank for the legal work of transaction *(f)*.
i. Paid Office Suppliers for the items purchased in transaction *(e)*.
j. Completed additional legal work for Security Bank on credit, $150.
k. Paul Hill withdrew $100 from the bank account of the law practice to be used for personal living expenses.
l. Paid the monthly telephone bill, $25.
m. Purchased additional office supplies from Office Suppliers on credit, $35.

Required:
1. Arrange the following asset, liability, and owner equity titles in an equation like Illustration 1–7: Cash, Accounts Receivable; Prepaid Rent; Office Supplies; Office Equipment; Legal Library; Accounts Payable; and Paul Hill, Capital.
2. Show by additions and subtractions, as in Illustration 1–7, the effects of each transaction on the assets, liabilities, and owner equity of the law practice. Show new totals for all items after each transaction.

Problem 1–3

Betty Blake began the practice of law, and during October completed these transactions:
Oct. 1 Invested $1,000 in cash and a law library valued at $1,200 in the law practice.
1 Rented the furnished office of a lawyer who was retiring, and paid cash for three months' rent in advance, $450.

3   Purchased office supplies for cash, $50.

5   Completed legal work for a client and collected $100 cash for the work done.

8   Purchased law books on credit from Legal Publishing Company, $150.

10   Completed legal work for Guaranty Bank on credit, $400.

15   Paid the salary of the office secretary, $200.

17   Purchased additional office supplies on credit, $25.

20   Paid Legal Publishing Company for the books purchased on October 8.

21   Received $400 from Guaranty Bank for the work completed on October 10.

24   Completed legal work for The Fair Store on credit, $500.

31   Paid the monthly telephone bill, $15.

31   Paid the office secretary's salary, $200.

31   Recognized that one month's rent on the office had expired and had become an expense. (Reduce the prepaid rent and the owner's equity.)

31   Took an inventory of unused office supplies and determined that $20 of supplies had been used and had become an expense. (Reduce the asset and the owner's equity.)

Required:

1.   Arrange the following asset, liability, and owner equity titles in an equation like Illustration 1–7: Cash; Accounts Receivable; Prepaid Rent; Office Supplies; Law Library; Accounts Payable; and Betty Blake, Capital.

2.   Show by additions and subtractions the effects of each transaction on the items of the equation. Show new totals after each transaction.

3.   Prepare an October 31 balance sheet for the law practice. Head the statement Betty Blake, Lawyer.

4.   Analyze the increases and decreases in the last column of the equation and prepare an October income statement for the law practice.

Problem 1–4

The records of the architectural practice of George Thomas show the following assets and liabilities as of the ends of 1974 and 1975:

	December 31	
	1974	1975
Cash	$1,800	$ 600
Accounts receivable........................	6,000	9,000
Supplies.......................................	400	700
Furniture and equipment.................	4,000	6,000
Land		8,000
Building.......................................		22,000
Accounts payable	1,000	2,500
Mortgage payable		20,000

During the last week of December, 1975, Mr. Thomas purchased in the name of the architectural practice a small office building and moved the practice from rented quarters to the new building. The building and the land it occupied cost $30,000. The practice paid $10,000 in cash and assumed a mortgage liability for the balance. Mr. Thomas had to invest an additional $8,000 in the practice to enable it to pay the $10,000. The practice earned a satisfactory net income during 1975, which enabled Mr. Thomas to withdraw $1,000 per month from the business to pay his personal living expenses.

Required:
1. Prepare balance sheets for the business as of the ends of 1974 and 1975. Head the balance sheets George Thomas, Architect.
2. Calculate the amount of net income earned by the business during 1975. (Hint: reread the last paragraph in this chapter.)

Alternate problems

Problem 1–1A

Carl Cole recently began a cleaning and pressing business, and during a short period completed the following business transactions:
a. Sold a personal investment in General Motors stock for $8,450 and deposited $8,000 of the proceeds in a bank account opened in the name of the business.
b. Paid $300 cash in advance for two months' rent on the shop space.
c. Purchased for cash the cleaning equipment, $4,500, and cleaning supplies, $200, of a cleaning firm that was going out of business.
d. Removed the rear seat, added a rack for cleaning, and took his personal car for use as a delivery truck in the business. The car had a fair market value of $1,000. (In other words, he invested the car in the business.)
e. Purchased cleaning equipment, $500, and cleaning supplies, $100, for cash.
f. Delivered cleaning to customers and collected cash for the work done, $400.
g. Cleaned and delivered the draperies of Vale Hotel on credit, $50.
h. Purchased additional cleaning equipment from Cleaning Supply Company on credit, $350.
i. Collected the amount owed by Vale Hotel for the work of transaction *(g)*.
j. Paid the wages of the employees, $200.
k. Paid Cleaning Supply Company $200 of the amount owed to it.
l. Carl Cole wrote a $125 cheque on the bank account of the business to pay the rent on his personal apartment.

Required:
1. Arrange the following asset, liability, and owner equity titles in an equation like in Illustration 1–7: Cash; Accounts Receivable; Prepaid Rent; Cleaning Supplies; Cleaning Equipment; Delivery Equipment; Accounts Payable; and Carl Cole, Capital.
2. Show by additions and subtractions, as in Illustration 1–7, the effects of each transaction on the assets, liabilities, and owner equity. Show new totals after each transaction.

Problem 1–2A

Tom Hall owns and operates a radio and television repair shop. At the beginning of the current month the shop had the following assets: cash, $2,150;

repair supplies, $1,125; tools, $775; truck, $1,200. At that time the business owed Electronics Company an account payable, $135. During the month the business completed the following transactions:

a. Purchased repair supplies for cash, $10.
b. Gave tools carried in the accounting records at $75 plus $125 in cash for new tools priced at $200.
c. Purchased repair supplies from Electronics Company on credit, $105.
d. Paid the rent for two months in advance on the shop space, $150.
e. Paid Electronics Company the $135 owed to it at the beginning of the month.
f. Completed repair work for several customers and collected $450 cash for the work done.
g. Completed $45 of repair work for Gary Boyd on credit.
h. Gave the old company truck and $1,500 in cash for a new truck.
i. Collected the $45 owed by Gary Boyd for the work of transaction (g).
j. Paid $35 cash for advertising on a local radio station.
k. Traded repair supplies carried in the accounting records at $15 for tools.
l. Paid $20 cash for gas and oil placed in the trucks during the month.
m. Tom Hall wrote a $50 cheque on the business bank account to pay personal living expenses.

Required:
1. Arrange the following asset, liability, and owner equity titles in an equation like in Illustration 1–7: Cash; Accounts Receivable; Prepaid Rent; Repair Supplies; Tools; Trucks; Accounts Payable; and Tom Hall, Capital.
2. Enter the beginning-of-the-month assets and liability under the item names of the equation and determine the beginning owner equity and enter it.
3. Show by additions and subtractions the effects of the transactions on the equation. Show new totals after each transaction.

Problem 1–3A

On September 1 of the current year Betty Blake began the practice of law by investing $2,500 in the practice. She then completed these additional transactions:

Sept. 1 Rented the furnished office of a lawyer who was retiring, and paid cash for three months' rent in advance, $600.
1 Purchased the law library of the retiring lawyer for $1,500, paying $1,000 in cash and agreeing to pay the balance within one year.
2 Purchased office supplies for cash, $35.
5 Purchased law books on credit from Legal Book Company, $200.
7 Purchased additional office supplies on credit, $25.
10 Completed legal work for Walter Grimm and immediately collected $50 cash for the work done.
14 Completed legal work for Atlas Supply Company on credit, $450.
17 Paid for the supplies purchased on September 7.
21 Completed legal work for Rayco Company on credit, $600.
30 Paid the monthly telephone bill, $20.
30 Received $600 from Rayco Company for the work completed on September 21.
30 Paid the office secretary's salary, $425.
30 Recognized that one month's rent on the office had expired and had

become an expense. (Reduce the prepaid rent and the owner's equity.)

30 Took an inventory of the unused office supplies and determined that $15 of supplies had been used and had become an expense. (Reduce the asset and the owner's equity.)

Required:

1. Arrange the following asset, liability, and owner equity titles in an equation like Illustration 1–7: Cash; Accounts Receivable; Prepaid Rent; Office Supplies; Law Library; Accounts Payable; and Betty Blake, Capital.
2. Show by additions and subtractions the effects of each transaction on the items of the equation. Show new totals after each transaction.
3. Prepare a September 30 balance sheet for the law practice. Head the statement Betty Blake, Lawyer.
4. Analyze the increases and decreases in the last column of the equation and prepare a September income statement for the law practice.

Decision problem 1–1, Homecoming celebration

Joe Cook invested $500 in a short-term enterprise, the sale of soft drinks during the annual First of July homecoming celebration in his small town. He paid the town $100 for the exclusive right to sell soft drinks in the town park, the centre of the celebration, and constructed a stand from which to make his sales, at a cost of $25 for lumber and crepe paper, none of which would have any value at the end of the celebration. He bought ice for which he paid $35, and he purchased soft drinks costing $500. At this point he had only $340 in cash and could not pay in full for the drinks, but since his credit rating was good, the soft drink company accepted $300 in cash and the promise that he would pay the balance the day after the celebration. During the celebration he collected $900 in cash from sales and at the end of the day paid $15 to each of three boys he had hired to help with the sales. He also had soft drinks left over that had cost $50 and could be returned to the soft drink company. Prepare an income statement for Joe Cook for the day and a balance sheet as of the end of the celebration. (Hint: Use an equation to arrive at the end of the celebration amounts.)

Decision problem 1–2, Cycle Delivery Service

Carl Hale ran out of money during his sophomore year in college and had to go to work. He could not get a satisfactory job; and since he owned a Honda motorcycle having a $700 fair value, he decided to go into business for himself. Consequently, he began Cycle Delivery Service with no assets other than the motorcycle. He kept no accounting records and now, at the year-end, he has engaged you to determine the net income earned by the service during its first year. You find that the delivery service has a year-end bank balance of $730 plus $20 of undeposited cash; and a local store, The Broadway, owes it $125 for delivering packages during the past month. The service still owns the motorcycle, but from use it has depreciated $150 during the year. In addition to the motorcycle, the service has a new delivery truck that cost $3,500, has depreciated $200 since its purchase, and on which the service still owes the finance company $1,800. When the truck was purchased, Carl Hale borrowed $1,000 from his father to make the down payment. The loan was made to the delivery service, was interest free, and has not been repaid. Finally, since the service has been profitable from the beginning, Carl Hale has withdrawn $100 of its earnings each week (50 weeks) to pay his personal living expenses.

Determine the net income earned by the business during the year. Present figures to prove your answer. (Hint: Net income increases owner equity.)

Problem 1–1 A&R

Hugh Hope began his Auto-Repair Shop early this month. The balance sheet, prepared by an inexperienced part-time bookkeeper is shown below:

HOPE AUTO-REPAIR SHOP
Balance Sheet
November 30, 1975

ASSETS		LIABILITIES AND OWNER EQUITY	
Cash	$ 1,000	Parts and supplies	$ 3,000
Accounts payable	6,000	Accounts receivable	3,000
Building	4,000	Land	1,000
Hugh Hope, capital	3,000	Automotive equipment	2,000
		Mortgage payable	5,000
	$14,000		$14,000

Required:
1. Prepare a correct balance sheet.
2. Explain why the incorrect balance sheet can also be in balance.

Problem 1–2 A&R

An analysis of the cash, accounts payable, and capital accounts of Townsend Service for the month of October shows the following:

Cash accounts:
Beginning balance	nil
George Townsend, investment	$6,000
Rental payment for October	500
Automobile purchased	3,000
Services rendered	2,000
Wages paid	1,000
Payment to Townsend	200

Accounts payable account:
Beginning balance	nil
Office supplies purchased	$ 300

George Townsend capital:
Beginning balance .... nil
Investment $6,000
Services rendered 2,000
Wages paid 1,000
Withdrawal 200

Required:
1. Describe all the transactions that have occurred in the month of October for Townsend Service as described in the above accounts.
2. Compute the balance for *all* the accounts that should appear on the balance sheet at October 31.
3. Prepare a balance sheet as of October 31.

Problem 1–3 A&R

John Anderson is the owner of a television repair shop, Quick T-V Service, which has been in operation for some time. The following statements summarize the shop's operations for October, 1975.

QUICK T-V SERVICE
Income Statement
For the Month of October, 1975

Revenues:

Service fees	$6,000	
Accounts payable	2,000	
Accounts receivable	300	$8,300

Operating expenses:

Rent expense	$ 900	
Utility and telephone expense	200	
Repair parts and supplies	6,000	7,100
Net Income		$1,200

Balance Sheet
October 31, 1975

ASSETS		OWNER EQUITY	
Cash	$ 500	John Anderson	
Repair parts and supplies		capital	$4,600
expense	1,350		
Salaries expense	2,550		
Salaries payable	200		
	$4,600		$4,600

Required:
Prepare corrected income statement and balance sheet for October.

2

Recording transactions

■ Transactions are the raw material of the accounting process, a process which consists of identifying transactions, recording them, and summarizing their effects on periodic reports for the use of management and other decision makers.

Some years ago almost all concerns used pen and ink in recording transactions; but today only small concerns use this method, concerns small enough that their bookkeeping can be done by one person working as bookkeeper a part of his or her day. Larger, modern concerns use electric bookkeeping machines, punched cards, punched paper tape, and magnetic tape in recording transactions.

Nevertheless, most students begin their study of accounting by learning a double-entry accounting system based on pen and ink; and there are several reasons for this. First, since accounting reports evolved from and are based on double entry, the effective use of these reports requires some understanding of the system. Second, there is little lost motion from learning the system, since almost everything about it is applicable to machine methods. Primarily the machines replace pen and ink as the recording medium, taking the drudgery out of the recording process. And last, for the student who will start, manage, or own a small business, one small enough to use a pen-and-ink system, the system applies as it is taught.

Business papers ■ Business papers are evidence of transactions completed and are the basis for accounting entries to record the transactions. For example, when goods are sold on credit, two or more copies of an invoice or sales ticket are prepared. One copy is enclosed with the goods and is delivered to the customer and the other is sent to the accounting department where it becomes the basis for an entry to record the sale. Also, when goods are sold for cash, the sales are commonly "rung up" on a cash register that prints the amount of each sale on a paper tape locked inside the register. At the end of the day, when the proper key is depressed, the register prints on the tape the total cash sales for the day, after which the tape is removed and becomes the basis for an entry to record the sales. In addition to transactions involving sales, when an established business purchases assets, it normally buys on credit and receives an invoice that becomes the basis for an entry to record the purchase. Likewise, when the invoice is paid, a cheque is issued in its payment and the cheque or a carbon copy becomes the basis for an entry to record the payment. Obviously then, business papers are not only evidence of transactions completed but are also the starting point in the accounting process.

Accounts ■ The transactions of a business cause increases and decreases in its assets, its liabilities, and its owner equity; and a concern using an accounting system based on pen and ink or electric bookkeeping machines uses *accounts* in recording the increases and decreases. A number of accounts are normally required, with a separate account being used for summarizing the increases and decreases in each asset, liability, and owner equity item appearing on the balance sheet and of each revenue and each expense which appears on the income statement.

In its most simple form an account looks like the letter "T," is called a "T-account," and appears as follows:

(Place for the Name of the Item Recorded in This Account)	
(Left side)	(Right side)

Note that the "T" gives the account a left side, a right side, and a place for the name of the asset, liability, or owner equity item, the increases and decreases in which are recorded therein.

When a T-account is used in recording increases and decreases in an item, the increases are placed on one side of the account and the decreases on the other. For example, if the increases and decreases in the cash of Owen Real Estate Agency of the previous chapter are recorded in a T-account, they appear as follows:

Cash

Investment	5,000	Payment of rent	300
Sale of equipment	100	Purchase of automobile	3,000
Collection from Hall	50	Purchase of furniture	1,000
Receipt of commission	850	Payment on account payable	175
		Payment of telephone bill	20

The reason for putting the increases on one account side and the decreases on the other is that this makes it easy to add the increases, then add the decreases, and to subtract the sum of the decreases from the sum of the increases to learn how much of the item recorded in the account the company has, owns, or owes. For example, the increases in Owen Real Estate Agency's cash were:

Investment	$5,000
Sale of unneeded equipment to Dale Hall	100
Collection of balance owed by Hall	50
Receipt of a commission	850
Sum of the increases	$6,000

And the decreases were:

Payment of office rent	$ 300
Purchase of automobile	3,000
Purchase of furniture for cash	1,000
Payment on an account payable	175
Payment of telephone bill	20
Sum of the decreases	$4,495

And when the sum of the decreases is subtracted from the sum of the increases,

Sum of the increases	$6,000
Minus the sum of the decreases	4,495
Balance of cash remaining	$1,505

the subtraction thus shows that the Agency has $1,505 of cash remaining.

Balance of an account

When the increases and decreases recorded in an account are separately added, and the sum of the decreases is subtracted from the sum of the increases, the procedure is called determining the *balance* of an account. The balance of an account is the difference between its increases and decreases. It is also the amount of the item recorded in the account that the company has, owns, or owes at the time the balance is determined.

■ A business uses a number of accounts in recording its transactions. However, the specific accounts used vary from one concern to another, depending upon the assets owned, the debts owed, and the information to be secured from the accounting records. Nevertheless, although the specific accounts vary, the following are common.

Asset accounts

If useful records of a concern's assets are to be kept, an individual account is needed for the increases and decreases in each kind of asset owned. Some of the more common assets for which accounts are maintained are:

CASH. Increases and decreases in cash are recorded in an account called "Cash." The cash of a business consists of money or any media of exchange that a bank will accept at face value for deposit. It includes coins, currency, cheques, and postal and express money orders; and the balance of the Cash account shows both the cash on hand in the store or office and that on deposit in the bank.

NOTES RECEIVABLE. A formal written promise to pay a definite sum of money at a fixed future date is called a promissory note (see the illustration on page 276). When amounts due from others are evidenced by promissory notes, the notes are known as *notes receivable* and are recorded in a Notes Receivable account.

ACCOUNTS RECEIVABLE. Goods and services are commonly sold to customers on the basis of oral or implied promises of future payment. Such sales are known as "sales on credit" or "sales on account"; and the oral or implied promises to pay are known as accounts receivable. Accounts receivable are increased by sales on credit and are decreased by customer payments. Since it is necessary to know the amount currently owed by each customer, a separate record must be kept of each customer's purchases and payments. However, a discussion of the manner in which this separate record is kept is deferred until Chapter 6, and for the moment all increases and decreases in accounts receivable are recorded in a single account called Accounts Receivable.

PREPAID INSURANCE. Fire, liability, and other types of insurance protection are normally paid for in advance. The amount paid is called a "premium" and may give protection from loss for from one to five years. As a result, a large portion of each premium is an asset for a considerable time after payment. When insurance premiums are paid, the asset "prepaid insurance" is increased by the amount paid; and the increase is normally recorded in an account called "Prepaid Insurance." Day by day, insurance premiums expire. Consequently, at intervals the insurance policies are examined; the insurance that has expired is calculated; and the balance of the Prepaid Insurance account is reduced accordingly.

OFFICE SUPPLIES. Stamps, stationery, paper, pencils, and like items are known as office supplies. They are assets when purchased, and continue to be assets until consumed. As they are consumed, the amounts consumed become expenses. Increases and decreases in the asset "office supplies" are commonly recorded in an account called "Office Supplies."

STORE SUPPLIES. Wrapping paper, cartons, bags, string, and similar items used by a store are known as store supplies. Increases and decreases in store supplies are usually recorded in an account of that name.

OTHER PREPAID EXPENSES. Prepaid expenses are items that are assets at the time of purchase but become expenses as they are consumed or used. Prepaid insurance, office supplies, and store supplies are examples. Other examples are prepaid rent, prepaid taxes, and prepaid wages. Each type of prepaid expense is normally accounted for in a separate account which carries the name of the item, the increases and decreases of which are recorded therein.

EQUIPMENT ACCOUNTS. Increases and decreases in such things as typewriters, desks, chairs, and office machines having long lives are commonly recorded in an account called "Office Equipment." Likewise, changes in the amount of counters, showcases, shelves, cash registers, and like items used by a store are recorded in an account called "Store Equipment." And a company that owns and uses such things as lathes, drill presses, and the like records the increases and decreases in these items in an account called "Machinery and Equipment."

BUILDINGS. A building used by a business in carrying on its operations may be a store, garage, warehouse, or factory; but regardless of use, an account called "Buildings" is commonly employed in recording the increases and decreases in the buildings owned by a business and used in carrying on its operations.

LAND. An account called "Land" is commonly used in recording increases and decreases in the land owned by a business. Although land and the buildings placed upon it are inseparable in physical fact, it is usually desirable to account for land and its buildings in separate accounts, because buildings depreciate or wear out, but land does not.

Liability accounts

Most companies do not have as many liability accounts as asset accounts; however the following are common:

NOTES PAYABLE. Increases and decreases in amounts owed because of promissory notes given to creditors are accounted for in an account called "Notes Payable."

ACCOUNTS PAYABLE. An account payable is an amount owed to a creditor which resulted from an oral or implied promise to pay. Most accounts payable result from the purchase of merchandise, supplies, equipment, and services on credit. Since it is necessary to know the amount owed each creditor, an individual record must be kept of the purchases from and payments to each. However, a discussion of the manner in which this individual record is kept is deferred until Chapter

6, and for the moment all increases and decreases in accounts payable are recorded in a single Accounts Payable account.

OTHER SHORT-TERM PAYABLES. Wages payable, taxes payable, and interest payable are illustrations of other short-term liabilities for which individual accounts must be kept.

MORTGAGE PAYABLE. A mortgage payable is a long-term debt for which the creditor has a secured prior claim against some one or more of the debtor's assets. The mortgage gives its holder, the creditor, the right to force the sale of the mortgaged assets through a foreclosure if the mortgage debt is not paid when due. An account called "Mortgage Payable" is commonly used in recording the increases and decreases in the amount owed on a mortgage.

Owner equity accounts

Several kinds of transactions affect owner equity, including the investment of the owner, his withdrawals of cash and other assets for personal use, revenues earned, and expenses incurred. In the previous chapter all transactions affecting owner equity were entered in a column under the name of the owner. This simplified the material of the chapter, but made it necessary to analyze the items entered in the column in order to prepare an income statement. Fortunately such an analysis is not necessary. All that is required to avoid it is a number of accounts, a separate one for each owner equity item appearing on the balance sheet and a separate one for each kind of revenue and expense on the income statement. Then as each transaction affecting owner equity is completed, it is recorded in the proper account. Among the accounts required are the following:

CAPITAL ACCOUNT. When a person invests in a business of his own, his investment is recorded in an account carrying his name and the word "Capital." For example, an account called "Larry Owen, Capital" is used in recording the investment of Larry Owen in his real estate agency. In addition to the original investment, the Capital account is used for any permanent additional increases or decreases in owner equity.

WITHDRAWALS ACCOUNT. Usually a person invests in a business to earn a net income. However, income is earned over a period of time, say a year, and often during this period the business owner finds it necessary to withdraw a portion of the earnings to pay living expenses or for other personal uses. These withdrawals reduce both assets and owner equity; and to record them, an account carrying the name of the business owner and the word "Withdrawals" is used. For example, an account called "Larry Owen, Withdrawals" is used to record the withdrawals of cash and other assets by Larry Owen from his real estate agency. The Withdrawals account is also known as the "Personal" account or "Drawing" account.

An owner of a small unincorporated business like Owen Real Estate Agency often withdraws a fixed amount each week or month for personal living expenses, and often thinks of these withdrawals as a salary. However, in a legal sense they are not a salary because the owner of an unincorporated business cannot enter into a binding contract with himself to hire himself and pay himself a salary. Consequently, in law and custom it is recognized that withdrawals by the owner of an unincorporated business for personal living expenses are withdrawals in anticipation of the net income he expects his business to earn.

REVENUE AND EXPENSE ACCOUNTS. When an income statement is prepared, it is necessary to know the amount of each kind of revenue earned and each kind of expense incurred during the period covered by the statement; and to accumulate this information, a number of revenue and expense accounts are needed. However, all concerns do not have the same revenues and expenses. Consequently, it is impossible to list all revenue and expense accounts to be encountered. Nevertheless, Revenue from Repairs, Commissions Earned, Fees Earned, Rent Earned, and Interest Earned are common examples of revenue accounts; and Advertising Expense, Store Supplies Expense, Office Salaries Expense, Office Supplies Expense, Rent Expense, Utilities Expense, and Insurance Expense are common examples of expense accounts. It should be noted that the kind of revenue or expense recorded in each above-mentioned account is evident from its title. This is generally true of such accounts.

The ledger ■ A business may use from two dozen to several thousand accounts in recording its transactions, with each account placed on a separate page in a bound or loose-leaf book, or on a separate card in a tray of cards. If the accounts are kept in a book, the book is called a *ledger;* and if the accounts are kept on cards in a file tray, the tray of cards is a ledger. Actually, as used in accounting, the word ledger means a group of accounts.

Debit and credit ■ As previously stated, a T-account has a left side and a right side; however, in accounting the left side is called the *debit* side, abbreviated "Dr."; and the right side is called the *credit* side, abbreviated "Cr." Furthermore, when amounts are entered on the left side of an account, they are called *debits*, and the account is said to be *debited;* and when amounts are entered on the right side, they are called credits, and the account is said to be *credited.* Likewise, the difference between the total debits and the total credits recorded in an account is the account balance and may be either a *debit balance* or a *credit balance.* It is a debit balance when the sum of the debits exceeds the sum of the credits, and a credit balance when the sum of the credits exceeds the sum of the debits, and an account is said to be *in balance* when its debits and credits are equal.

The words "to debit" and "to credit" should not be confused with "to increase" and "to decrease." To debit means simply to enter an amount on the left side of an account, to credit means to enter an amount on the right side, and either may be an increase or a decrease. This may readily be seen by examining the way in which the investment of Larry Owen is recorded in his Cash and Capital accounts which follow:

Cash		Larry Owen, Capital	
Investment 5,000			Investment 5,000

When Owen invested $5,000 in his real estate business, both the business cash and Owen's equity were increased. Observe in the foregoing accounts that one increase, the increase in cash, is recorded on the left or debit side of the Cash account; while the other increase, the increase in owner equity, is recorded on the right or credit side. The transaction is recorded in this manner because of the mechanics of *double-entry accounting*.

Mechanics of double-entry accounting ■ The mechanics of double-entry accounting are such that every transaction affects and is recorded in two or more accounts with equal debits and credits. Transactions are so recorded because equal debits and credits offer a means of proving the recording accuracy. The proof is, if every transaction is recorded with equal debits and credits, then the sum of the debits in the ledger must equal the sum of the credits.

The person who first devised double-entry accounting based the system on the accounting equation, $A = L + OE$ (see discussion on pages 9 and 10), and he assigned the recording of increases in assets to the debit sides of asset accounts. He then recognized that the goal of equal debits and credits was possible only if increases in liabilities and owner equity were recorded on the opposite or credit sides of liability and owner equity accounts, or he recognized that if increases in assets were to be recorded as debits, then increases and decreases in all accounts would have to be recorded as follows:

Assets		=	Liabilities	+	Owner Equity	
Debit for Increases	Credit for Decreases		Debit for Decreases	Credit for Increases	Debit for Decreases	Credit for Increases

From the foregoing T-accounts it is possible to formulate rules for recording transactions under a double-entry system. The rules are:

1. Increases in assets are debited to asset accounts; consequently, decreases must be credited.
2. Increases in liability and owner equity items are credited to liability and owner equity accounts; consequently, decreases must be debited.

At this stage, the beginning student will find it helpful to memorize these rules. He should also note that there are four kinds of owner equity accounts: (1) the Capital account, (2) the Withdrawals account, (3) revenue accounts, and (4) expense accounts. Furthermore, in applying the rules of debit and credit for owner equity, the student should observe these additional points:

1. The original investment of the owner of a business plus any more or less permanent changes in the investment are recorded in his Capital account.
2. Withdrawals of assets for personal use, including cash to pay personal expenses, decrease owner equity and are debited to the owner's Withdrawals account.
3. Revenues increase owner equity and are credited in each case to a revenue account that shows the nature of the revenue earned.
4. Expenses decrease owner equity and are debited in each case to an expense account that shows the nature of the expense incurred.

In addition to the points outlined, the student should also recognize that after a number of transactions are completed, the owner equity of an owner in his business consists of the credit balance in his Capital account *minus* the debit balance of his Withdrawals account *plus* the credit balances in any revenue accounts and *minus* the debt balances in the expense accounts.

Trans- actions illustrating the rules of debit and credit

■ The following Owen Real Estate Agency transactions illustrate the application of debit and credit rules and show how transactions are recorded in the accounts. The number preceding each transaction is used throughout the illustration to identify the transaction as it appears in the accounts. Note that most of the transactions are the same ones used in Chapter 1 to illustrate the effects of transactions on the accounting equation.

1. Larry Owen invested $5,000 in a real estate agency.
2. He paid three months' office rent in advance, $300.
3. Paid $3,000 for a business automobile.
4. Purchased office equipment for cash, $1,000.
5. Purchased on credit from Standard Supply Company office supplies, $60, and office equipment, $350.
6. Sold unneeded office equipment to Dale Hall at its $150 cost, $100 cash and $50 to be paid at a later date.
7. Collected $50 from Dale Hall.
8. Paid Standard Supply Company $175 of the amount owed for supplies and equipment.
9. Sold a house and collected an $850 commission.
10. Paid the part-time secretary's salary for the first two weeks of the month, $100.

11. Signed a contract to manage an apartment building for $50 per month. Collected the management fee for the last half of July and the month of August, a month and a half, $75.
12. Paid the part-time secretary's salary for the second two weeks of July, $100.
13. Larry Owen withdrew $200 from the business for his personal use.
14. Paid the monthly telephone bill, $20.
15. Paid for gas and oil used in the agency car, $25.
16. Paid for newspaper advertising that had appeared, $60.

Before a transaction can be recorded, it must be analyzed into its debit and credit elements. The analysis consists of (1) determining what asset, liability, or owner equity items are increased or decreased by the transaction and then (2) applying the rules of debit and credit to determine the debit and credit effects of the increases or decreases. An analysis of each of the following transactions is given in order to demonstrate the process.

1. On July 1 of the current year, Larry Owen invested $5,000 in a real estate agency.

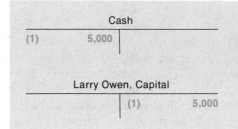

Cash		
(1)	5,000	

Larry Owen, Capital		
	(1)	5,000

Analysis of the transaction: The transaction increased the agency's cash and at the same time it increased the equity of Owen in the business. Increases in assets are debited, and increases in owner equity are credited. Consequently, to record the transaction, cash should be debited and Larry Owen, Capital should be credited for $5,000.

2. Paid the office rent for three months in advance, $300.

Cash			
(1)	5,000	(2)	300

Prepaid Rent		
(2)	300	

Analysis of the transaction: The asset prepaid rent, the right to occupy the office for three months, is increased; and the asset cash is decreased. Increases in assets are debited and decreases are credited. Therefore, to record the transaction, debit Prepaid Rent and credit Cash for $300.

3. Paid $3,000 for an automobile to be used for business purposes.

Cash

| (1) | 5,000 | (2) | 300 |
| | | (3) | 3,000 |

Automobile

| (3) | 3,000 | | |

Analysis of the transaction: The asset automobile is increased, and the asset cash is decreased. Debit Automobile and credit Cash for $3,000.

4. Purchased office equipment for cash, $1,000.

Cash

(1)	5,000	(2)	300
		(3)	3,000
		(4)	1,000

Office Equipment

| (4) | 1,000 | | |

Analysis of the transaction: The asset office equipment is increased; and the asset cash is decreased. Debit Office Equipment and credit Cash for $1,000.

5. Purchased office equipment, $350, and office supplies, $60, from Standard Supply Company on credit.

Office Equipment

| (4) | 1,000 | | |
| (5) | 350 | | |

Office Supplies

| (5) | 60 | | |

Accounts Payable

| | | (5) | 410 |

Analysis of the transaction: This transaction increased the assets office equipment and office supplies; but it also increased the liabilities by granting Standard Supply Company a claim against the business. Increases in assets are debits and increases in liabilities are credits; therefore, debit Office Equipment for $350 and Office Supplies for $60 and credit Accounts Payable for $410.

6. Sold unneeded office equipment to Dale Hall at its $150 cost; $100 in cash and $50 to be paid at a later date.

	Cash		
(1)	5,000	(2)	300
(6)	100	(3)	3,000
		(4)	1,000

	Accounts Receivable		
(6)	50		

	Office Equipment		
(4)	1,000	(6)	150
(5)	350		

Analysis of the transaction: The assets cash and the right to collect from Dale Hall (an account receivable) increased, and the asset office equipment decreased. Debit Cash and Accounts Receivable for the increases and credit Office Equipment for the decrease.

7. Collected $50 from Dale Hall.

	Cash		
(1)	5,000	(2)	300
(6)	100	(3)	3,000
(7)	50	(4)	1,000

	Accounts Receivable		
(6)	50	(7)	50

Analysis of the transaction: One asset was increased and the other decreased. Debit Cash for $50 to record the increase in cash, and credit Accounts Receivable $50 to record the decrease in the account receivable, or the decrease in the right to collect from Dale Hall.

8. Paid Standard Supply Company $175 of the amount owed.

	Cash		
(1)	5,000	(2)	300
(6)	100	(3)	3,000
(7)	50	(4)	1,000
		(8)	175

	Accounts Payable		
(8)	175	(5)	410

Analysis of the transaction: Payments to creditors decrease in like amounts both assets and liabilities. Decreases in liabilities are debited, and decreases in assets are credited. Debit Accounts Payable and credit Cash.

9. Sold a house and collected a commission, $850.

	Cash		
(1)	5,000	(2)	300
(6)	100	(3)	3,000
(7)	50	(4)	1,000
(9)	850	(8)	175

	Commissions Earned	
	(9)	850

Analysis of the transaction: This revenue transaction increased both assets and owner equity. Increases in assets are debits, and increases in owner equity are credits. Therefore, Cash is debited; and in order to show the nature of the increase in owner equity and at the same time accumulate information for the income statement, the revenue account Commissions Earned is credited.

10. Paid the part-time secretary's salary for the first two weeks in the month, $100.

	Cash		
(1)	5,000	(2)	300
(6)	100	(3)	3,000
(7)	50	(4)	1,000
(9)	850	(8)	175
		(10)	100

	Office Salaries Expense	
(10)	100	

Analysis of the transaction: The secretary's salary is an expense that decreased both assets and owner equity. Debit the account Office Salaries Expense to decrease owner equity and also to accumulate information for the income statement; and credit Cash to record the decrease in cash.

11. Signed a contract to manage an apartment building for $50 per month and collected the management fee for one and a half months in advance, $75.

	Cash		
(1)	5,000	(2)	300
(6)	100	(3)	3,000
(7)	50	(4)	1,000
(9)	850	(8)	175
(11)	75	(10)	100

	Unearned Management Fees	
	(11)	75

Analysis of the transaction: This transaction increased the asset cash and will result in an increase in owner equity as the fee is earned. However, acceptance of the fee in advance of its being earned created a liability for Owen Real Estate Agency, the liability or obligation to manage the apartment building for the next month and a half. Consequently, debit Cash and credit and increase the liability account Unearned Management Fees. (This transaction will be dealt with again in the next chapter.)

12. Paid the secretary's salary for the second two weeks of the month, $100.

Cash			
(1)	5,000	(2)	300
(6)	100	(3)	3,000
(7)	50	(4)	1,000
(9)	850	(8)	175
(11)	75	(10)	100
		(12)	100

Analysis of the transaction: An expense that decreased assets and owner equity. Debit Office Salaries Expense to accumulate information for the income statement and credit Cash.

Office Salaries Expense		
(10)	100	
(12)	100	

13. Larry Owen withdrew $200 for his personal use.

Cash			
(1)	5,000	(2)	300
(6)	100	(3)	3,000
(7)	50	(4)	1,000
(9)	850	(8)	175
(11)	75	(10)	100
		(12)	100
		(13)	200

Analysis of the transaction: This transaction reduced in equal amounts both assets and owner equity. Cash is credited to record the asset reduction; and the Larry Owen, Withdrawals account is debited for the reduction in owner equity.

Larry Owen, Withdrawals		
(13)	200	

14. Paid the monthly telephone bill, $20.
15. Paid for gas and oil used in the agency car, $25.
16. Paid for newspaper advertising that had appeared, $60.

Cash			
(1)	5,000	(2)	300
(6)	100	(3)	3,000
(7)	50	(4)	1,000
(9)	850	(8)	175
(11)	75	(10)	100
		(12)	100
		(13)	200
		(14)	20
		(15)	25
		(16)	60

Analysis of the transactions: These expense transactions are alike in that each decreased cash; they differ in each case as to the kind of expense involved. Consequently, in recording them, Cash is credited; and to accumulate information for the income statement, a different expense account, one showing the nature of the expense in each case, is debited.

Telephone Expense	
(14)	20

Gas, Oil, and Repairs	
(15)	25

Advertising Expense	
(16)	60

The accounts and the equation

■ In Illustration 2–1 which appears below the transactions of Owen Real Estate Agency are shown in the accounts, with the accounts brought together and classified under the elements of an accounting equation.

Assets	=	Liabilities	+	Owner Equity

Cash

(1)	5,000	(2)	300
(6)	100	(3)	3,000
(7)	50	(4)	1,000
(9)	850	(8)	175
(11)	75	(10)	100
		(12)	100
		(13)	200
		(14)	20
		(15)	25
		(16)	60

Accounts Receivable

(6)	50	(7)	50

Prepaid Rent

(2)	300	

Office Supplies

(5)	60	

Automobile

(3)	3,000	

Office Equipment

(4)	1,000	(6)	150
(5)	350		

Accounts Payable

(8)	175	(5)	410

Unearned Management Fees

	(11)	75

Larry Owen, Capital

	(1)	5,000

Larry Owen, Withdrawals

(13)	200	

Commissions Earned

	(9)	850

Office Salaries Expense

(10)	100	
(12)	100	

Telephone Expense

(14)	20	

Gas, Oil, and Repairs

(15)	25	

Advertising Expense

(16)	60	

Illustration 2–1

■ As previously stated, in a double-entry accounting system every transaction is recorded with equal debits and credits so that the equality of the debits and credits may be tested as a proof of the recording accuracy. This equality is tested at intervals by preparing a trial balance.

A trial balance is prepared by (1) determining the balance of each account in the ledger; (2) listing in their ledger order the accounts having balances, with the debit balances in one column and the credit balances in another (as in Illustration 2–2); (3) adding the debit balances; (4) adding the credit balances; and then (5) comparing the sum of the debit balances with the sum of the credit balances.

Owen Real Estate Agency
Trial Balance, July 31, 19 —

Cash	$1,095	
Prepaid rent	300	
Office supplies	60	
Automobile	3,000	
Office equipment	1,200	
Accounts payable		$ 235
Unearned management fees		75
Larry Owen, capital		5,000
Larry Owen, withdrawals	200	
Commissions earned		850
Office salaries expense	200	
Telephone expense	20	
Gas, oil, and repairs	25	
Advertising expense	60	
Totals	$6,160	$6,160

Illustration
2–2

Illustration 2–2 shows a trial balance of the Owen Real Estate Agency ledger. It was prepared from the accounts in Illustration 2–1. Note that its column totals are equal, or in other words, the trial balance is in balance. When a trial balance is in balance, debits equal credits in the ledger and it is assumed that no errors were made in recording transactions.

■ If when a trial balance is prepared it does not balance—the two columns are not equal—errors have been made either in recording transactions, in determining the account balances, in copying the balances on the trial balance, or in adding the trial balance columns. On the other hand, if a trial balance balances, it is assumed that no errors have been made. However, a trial balance that balances is not absolute proof of accuracy. Errors may have been made that did not affect the equality of its columns. For example, an error in which a correct debit amount is debited to the wrong account or a correct credit amount is credited to the wrong account will not cause a trial balance to be out of balance.

Likewise, an error in which a wrong amount is both debited and credited to the right accounts will not cause a trial balance to be out of balance. Consequently, a trial balance in balance is considered only presumptive proof of recording accuracy.

A standard account form

■ T-accounts like the ones just described are commonly used in teaching and are also commonly used by accountants in solving problems. In either case details are eliminated by their use and the student or accountant can concentrate on ideas. However, such accounts are not used in business for recording transactions. In business, accounts like the one of Illustration 2–3 may be used.

An examination of the Illustration 2–3 account will reveal it is like a T-account in that it has two sides and a place for the name of the item recorded therein. However, it differs in that each side is divided into columns for recording specific additional information, as indicated by the column headings.

		Cash								ACCOUNT NO. *1*	
DATE	EXPLANATION	FO-LIO		DEBIT		DATE	EXPLANATION	FO-LIO		CREDIT	
1975 July 1		1		5 000 00		*1975* July 1		1		30 00	
9				1 00 00		3		1		30 00 00	
		800.00		5 1 00 00		3		1		1 00 00 00	
										4 3 00 00	

Illustration 2–3

Determining the balance of an account

■ The basic procedures for determining the balance of an account were outlined earlier in this chapter; but when accounts like the one shown in Illustration 2–3 are used, these additional procedures are helpful. In determining the balance of an account—

1. Add the debits in the account and insert the total in small pencil figures just below the last entry in the Debit column. (Observe the placement of this pencil figure in Illustration 2–3 and note that it must be sufficiently small as not to be confused with an entry in the column.)
2. Add the credits in the account and insert the total in small pencil figures just below the last entry in the credit column.
3. Determine the account balance by subtracting the smaller pencil total from the larger. Then if a debit balance, enter it in the debit

Explanation column in line with the debit pencil total; and if a credit balance, enter it in the credit Explanation column in line with the credit total.

Need for a journal

■ It is possible to record transactions by entering debits and credits directly in the accounts, as was done earlier in this chapter. However, when this is done and an error is made, the error is difficult to locate, because even with a transaction having only one debit and one credit, the debit is entered on one ledger page or card and the credit on another, and there is nothing to link the two together.

Consequently, to link together the debits and credits of each transaction and to provide in one place a complete record of each transaction, it is the universal practice in pen-and-ink systems to record all transactions in a *journal* and then to copy the debit and credit information about each transaction from the journal to the ledger accounts. This debit and credit record of each transaction in a journal is important when errors are made, since the journal record makes it possible to trace the debits and credits into the accounts and to see that they are equal and properly recorded.

Each transaction entered in a journal is recorded with a separate *journal entry,* and the process of recording transactions in a journal is called *journalizing transactions.* Also, since transactions are recorded in a journal as the first or original step in their recording and their debit and credit information is copied from the journal to the ledger as a second or last step, a journal is called *a book of original entry* and a ledger *a book of final entry.*

The General Journal

■ The simplest and most flexible type of journal is a *General Journal.* It provides for each transaction places for recording (1) the transaction date, (2) the names of the accounts involved, (3) an explanation of the transaction, (4) the account numbers of the accounts to which the transaction's debit and credit information is copied, and (5) the transaction's debit and credit effect on the accounts named. A standard ruling for a general journal page with two of the transactions of Owen Real Estate Agency recorded therein is shown in Illustration 2–4.

The first entry in Illustration 2–4 records the sale of unneeded office equipment by Owen Real Estate Agency, and three accounts are involved. When a transaction involves three or more accounts and is recorded with a general journal entry, *a compound entry* is required. A compound entry is one involving three or more accounts. The second entry records the collection of $50 from Dale Hall.

DATE	ACCOUNT TITLES AND EXPLANATION	FO-LIO	DEBIT	CREDIT
1975 July 9	Cash		100.00	
	Accounts Receivable		50.00	
	Office Equipment			150.00
	Sold unneeded office			
	equipment at cost.			
11	Cash		50.00	
	Accounts Receivable			50.00
	In full of amount owed.			

Illustration
2–4

Recording trans- actions in a General Journal

■ To record transactions in a General Journal:

1. The year is written in small figures at the top of the first column.
2. The month is written on the first line in the first column. The year and the month are not repeated except at the top of a new page or at the beginning of a new month or year.
3. The day of each transaction is written in the second column on the first line of the transaction.
4. The names of the accounts to be debited and credited and an explanation of the transaction are written in the Account Titles and Explanation column. The name of the account debited is written first, beginning at the left margin of the column. The name of the account credited is written on the following line, indented about one inch. The explanation is placed on the next line, indented about a half inch from the left margin. The explanation should be short but sufficient to explain the transaction and set it apart from every other transaction.
5. The debit amount is written in the Debit column opposite the name of the account to be debited. The credit amount is written in the Credit column opposite the account to be credited.
6. A single line is skipped between each journal entry to set the entries apart.

At the time transactions are recorded in the General Journal, nothing is entered in the Folio column. However, when the debits and credits are copied from the journal to the ledger, the account numbers of the ledger accounts to which the debits and credits are copied are entered in the Folio column. The use of the Folio column is discussed in more detail later in this chapter.

Posting transaction information

■ The process of copying journal entry information and transferring it from the journal to the ledger is called *posting*. Normally, near the end of a day all transactions recorded in the journal that day are posted to the ledger. In the posting procedure, journal debits are copied and become ledger account debits and journal credits are copied and become ledger account credits.

The posting procedure for a journal entry is shown in Illustration 2–5, and it may be described as follows. To post a journal entry:

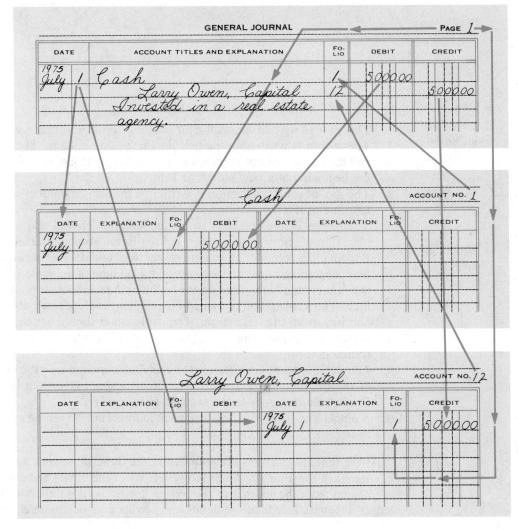

Illustration
2–5

For the debit:

1. Find in the ledger the account named in the debit of the entry to be posted.
2. Enter on the debit side of this account *(a)* the date of the entry as shown in the journal, *(b)* the page number of the journal from which the entry is being posted, and *(c)* the debit amount.
3. Enter in the Folio column of the journal the account number of the account to which the amount was posted.

For the credit:

Repeat the foregoing steps for the credit of the entry, with the exception that the entry date, journal page number, and credit amount are entered on the credit side of the account.

Observe that the last step (step 3) in the posting procedure for either the debit or the credit of an entry is to insert the account number in the Folio column of the journal. Inserting the account number in the journal Folio column serves two purposes: (1) The account number in the journal and the journal page number in the account act as a cross-reference when it is desired to trace an amount from one record to the other. And, (2) writing the account number in the journal as a last step in posting indicates that posting is completed. If posting is interrupted, the bookkeeper, by examining the journal Folio column, can easily see where posting stopped.

Account numbers and journal page numbers are often called *posting reference numbers*. The reason for this is obvious.

Correcting errors ■ When an error is discovered in either the journal or the ledger, it must be corrected. Such an error is never erased, for this seems to indicate an effort to conceal something. However, the exact method of correction will vary with the nature of the error and the stage in the accounting procedures at which it is discovered.

If an error is discovered in a journal entry before the error is posted, it may be corrected by ruling a single line through the incorrect amount or account name and writing in above the correct amount or account name. Likewise, a posted error or an error in posting in which only the amount is wrong may be corrected in the same manner. However, when a posted error involves a wrong account, it is considered best to correct the error with a correcting journal entry. For example, the following journal entry to record the purchase of office supplies was made and posted:

Oct.	14	Office Furniture and Fixtures.........................	15.00	
		Cash..		15.00
		To record the purchase of office supplies.		

Obviously, the debit of the entry is to the wrong account; consequently, the following entry is needed to correct the error:

Oct.	17	Office Supplies	15.00	
		Office Furniture and Fixtures.....................		15.00
		To correct the entry of October 14 in which		
		the Office Furniture and Fixtures account		
		was debited in error for the purchase of		
		office supplies.		

The debit of the second entry correctly records the purchase of supplies, and the credit cancels the error of the first entry. Note the full explanation of the correcting entry. The explanation of a correcting entry should always be full and complete so that anyone can see exactly what has occurred.

Book-
keeping
techniques

■ **Periods and commas in dollar amounts**

When amounts are entered in a journal or a ledger, commas to indicate thousands of dollars and periods to separate dollars and cents are not necessary because the ruled lines accomplish this purpose. However, when statements are prepared on unruled paper, the periods and commas are necessary.

Dollar signs

Dollar signs are not used in journals or ledgers, but they are required on the financial reports prepared on unruled paper. On the reports, a dollar sign is placed (1) before the first amount in each column of figures and (2) before the first amount appearing after a ruled line that indicates an addition or a subtraction. Examine Illustration 3–5 on page 76 for examples of the use of dollar signs on a financial report.

Omission of zeros in the cents columns

When an amount to be entered in a ledger or a journal is an amount of dollars and no cents, some bookkeepers will use a dash in the cents column in the place of two zeros to indicate that there are no cents. They feel that the dash is easier and more quickly made than the two zeros. This is a matter of choice in journal and ledger entries. However, on financial reports the two zeros are preferred because they are neater in appearance.

Often in this text, where space is limited, exact dollar amounts are used in order to save space. Obviously, in such cases, neither zeros nor dashes are used to show that there are no cents involved.

1. What is an account? What is a ledger?
2. What determines the number of accounts a business will use?
3. What are the meanings of the following words and terms: *(a)* debit, *(b)* to debit, *(c)* credit, and *(d)* to credit?
4. Does debit always mean increase and credit always mean decrease?
5. A transaction is to be entered in the accounts. How do you determine the accounts in which amounts are to be entered? How do you determine whether a particular account is to be debited or credited?
6. Why is a double-entry accounting system so called?
7. Give the rules of debit and credit for *(a)* asset accounts and *(b)* liability and owner equity accounts.
8. Why is the rule of debit and credit the same for both liability and owner equity accounts?
9. List the steps in the preparation of a trial balance.
10. What is the reason for preparing a trial balance?
11. Why is the trial balance considered to be only presumptive proof of recording accuracy? What types of errors are not revealed by a trial balance?
12. Is it possible to record transactions directly in the ledger accounts? What is gained by first recording transactions in a journal and then posting to the accounts?
13. In recording transactions in a journal, which is written first, the debit or the credit? How far is the name of the account credited indented? How far is the explanation indented?
14. What is a compound entry?
15. Are dollar signs used in journal entries? In the accounts?
16. If a period is not used in a journal debit to separate dollars from cents, what accomplishes this purpose?
17. Define or describe each of the following:
    a. Journal.   *e.* Folio column.
    b. Ledger.   *f.* Posting.
    c. Book of original entry.   *g.* Posting reference numbers.
    d. Book of final entry.
18. Entering in the Folio column of the journal the account number to which an amount was posted is the last step in posting the amount. What is gained by making this the last step?

Exercise 2–1

Place the following T-accounts on a sheet of ordinary notebook paper: Cash; Accounts Receivable; Office Supplies; Office Equipment; Accounts Payable; Ted Mohr, Capital; Revenue from Services; Utilities Expense. Then record the following transactions by entering debits and credits directly in the T-accounts. Use the transaction letters to identify the amounts in the accounts.

a. Ted Mohr began a service business, called Quick Service, by investing $1,000.
b. Purchased office supplies for cash, $50.
c. Purchased office equipment on credit, $300.

d. Earned revenue by rendering services for a customer for cash, $100.
e. Paid for the office equipment purchased in transaction *(c)*.
f. Earned revenue by rendering services for a customer on credit, $200.
g. Paid the monthly utility bills, $25.
h. Collected $150 of the amount owed by the customer of transaction *(f)*.

Exercise 2-2

After recording the transactions of Exercise 2-1, prepare a trial balance for Quick Service. Use the current date.

Exercise 2-3

On a sheet of ordinary notebook paper rule a general journal form like in Illustration 2-4 of your text. After completing the form, record the following transactions in the journal. Use the current year in the date.

Sept. 23 Roger Ross invested office equipment having a $1,000 fair value and $5,000 in cash in a new business.
   24 Purchased office equipment for cash, $500.

Exercise 2-4

Prepare a form on ordinary notebook paper with the following three column headings: (1) Error, (2) Amount Out of Balance, and (3) Column Having Larger Total. Then for each of the following errors: (1) list the error by letter in the first column, (2) tell the amount it will cause the trial balance to be out of balance in the second column, and (3) tell in the third column which trial balance column will have the larger total as a result of the error. If the error does not affect the trial balance, write "none" in each of the last two columns.

a. A $70 debit to Office Supplies was debited to Office Equipment.
b. A $90 credit to Office Equipment was credited to Sales.
c. A $60 credit to Sales was credited to the Sales account twice.
d. A $40 debit to Office Salaries was posted as a $45 debit.
e. A $35 debit to Office Salaries was not posted.
f. A $11 credit to Sales was posted as a $110 credit.

Exercise 2-5

FAST SERVICE COMPANY
Trial Balance, September 30, 19—

Cash	$ 2,550	
Accounts receivable		$ 3,175
Shop supplies	300	
Shop equipment	1,500	
Accounts payable	550	
Wages payable	50	
Joe Sims, capital	3,175	
Joe Sims, withdrawals	7,200	
Revenue from services		11,200
Rent expense		1,200
Advertising expense	125	
Totals	$15,450	$15,575

An inexperienced bookkeeper prepared the foregoing trial balance which does not balance, and you have been asked to prepare a corrected trial balance for the concern. In examining the records of the concern you discover the following: (1) The debits to the Cash account total $13,200 and the credits total $10,750. (2) A $75 receipt of cash from a customer in payment of his account was not posted to Accounts Receivable. (3) A $25 purchase of shop supplies on credit was entered in the journal but was not posted to any account. (4) Two digits in the balance of the Revenue from Services account, as shown on the trial balance of the bookkeeper, were transposed in copying the balance from the ledger to the trial balance. The correct amount is $12,100.

Problems **Problem 2-1**

Mary Hall began a new real estate agency called Sun Valley Realty, and during a short period completed these transactions:

a. Began business by investing the following assets at their fair values: cash, $3,500; office equipment, $1,500; automobile, $1,200; land, $5,000; and building, $12,000. The Security Bank held a $11,500 mortgage on the land and building.

b. Purchased office supplies, $50, and office equipment, $125, from Office Supply Company on credit.

c. Collected a $500 cash commission from the sale of property for a client.

d. Purchased additional office equipment from Office Supply Company on credit, $100.

e. Paid cash for advertising that had appeared in the local paper, $25.

f. Traded the company automobile and $2,500 in cash for a new automobile.

g. Paid the office secretary's $100 salary.

h. Paid Office Supply Company for the supplies and equipment purchased in transaction (b).

i. Completed a real estate appraisal for Robert Gregg, recorded the revenue earned, and sent him a bill for the service rendered, $150.

j. Paid Office Supply Company for the equipment purchased in transaction (d).

k. Received $50 cash and a letter from Robert Gregg in which he promised to pay the balance owed within a few days.

l. Paid the secretary's $100 salary.

m. Paid $50 cash for newspaper advertising that had appeared.

n. Mary Hall withdrew $250 from the business to be used for personal living expenses.

Required:

1. Open the following T-accounts: Cash; Accounts Receivable; Office Supplies; Office Equipment; Automobile; Land; Building; Accounts Payable; Mortgage Payable; Mary Hall, Capital; Mary Hall, Withdrawals; Commissions Earned; Appraisal Fees Earned; Office Salaries Expense; and Advertising Expense.

2. Record the transactions by entering debits and credits directly in the accounts. Use the transaction letters to identify each debit and credit amount.

3. Prepare a trial balance using the current date.

Problem 2–2

Kent Sims began a public accounting practice and completed these transactions during October of the current year:

Oct. 1 Invested $2,500 cash in a public accounting practice begun this day.
  1 Paid cash for three months' office rent in advance, $240.
  2 Purchased office supplies, $60, and office equipment, $750, from Office Supply Company on credit.
  3 Paid the premiums on two insurance policies, $75.
  8 Completed accounting work for Mary Hall and collected $80 cash therefor.
  13 Completed accounting work for Phoenix Company on credit, $150.
  15 Purchased additional office supplies on credit, $25.
  23 Received $150 from Phoenix Company for the work completed on October 13.
  25 Paid Office Supply Company $250 of the amount owed to it.
  30 Kent Sims wrote a $20 cheque on the bank account of the accounting practice to pay the electric bill of his personal residence.
  31 Completed accounting work for Evans Company on credit, $200.
  31 Paid the monthly utility bills of the accounting office, $15.

Required:
1. Open the following accounts: Cash; Accounts Receivable; Prepaid Rent; Office Supplies; Prepaid Insurance; Office Equipment; Accounts Payable; Kent Sims, Capital; Kent Sims, Withdrawals; Accounting Revenue; and Utilities Expense. Number the accounts beginning with 1.
2. Prepare general journal entries to record the transactions, post to the accounts, and prepare a trial balance. Head the trial balance Kent Sims, Public Accountant.

Problem 2–3

Ted Sears began business as an excavating contractor and during a short period completed these transactions:

a. Began business under the firm name of Glorious Dirt Movers by investing cash, $8,500; office equipment, $450; and excavating equipment, $12,500.
b. Paid $3,000 cash for land to be used as an office site and for parking excavating equipment.
c. Purchased for cash a small prefabricated building and moved it on to the land for use as an office. Total cost, $2,500.
d. Paid the premiums on a number of insurance policies, $200.
e. Completed an excavating job and collected $800 cash in payment therefor.
f. Purchased additional excavating equipment costing $5,000. Gave $1,000 in cash and signed a promissory note for the balance.
g. Completed excavating work for Western Contractors on credit, $1,100.
h. Purchased additional excavating equipment on credit, $350.
i. Completed an excavating job for Barry Fox on credit, $725.
j. Received and recorded as an account payable a bill for rent on a special machine used on the Barry Fox job, $100.
k. Received $1,100 from Western Contractors for the work of transaction *(g)*.
l. Paid the wages of the employees, $600.
m. Paid for the equipment purchased in transaction *(h)*.
n. Paid $150 cash for repairs to excavating equipment.

o. Ted Sears wrote a cheque on the bank account of the business for repairs to his personal automobile, $60. (The car is not used for business purposes.)

p. Paid the wages of the employees, $600.

q. Paid for gas and oil consumed by the excavating equipment, $125.

Required:

1. Open the following T-accounts: Cash; Accounts Receivable; Prepaid Insurance; Office Equipment; Excavating Equipment; Building; Land; Notes Payable; Accounts Payable; Ted Sears, Capital; Ted Sears, Withdrawals; Excavating Revenue; Equipment Repairs Expense; Wages Expense; Equipment Rentals Expense; and Gas and Oil Expense.

2. Record the transactions by entering debits and credits directly in the accounts, and prepare a trial balance. (Use the transaction letter to identify each amount in the accounts. Use the current date for the trial balance.)

Problem 2–4

Ann Evans completed these transactions during a short period:

Oct. 1 Began the practice of architecture by investing the following assets: cash, $1,200; drafting supplies, $50; and office and drafting equipment, $450.

1 Paid two months' rent in advance on suitable office space, $250.

2 Purchased drafting supplies, $100, and office and drafting equipment, $1,200, from West Company on credit.

2 Paid the premiums on several insurance policies taken out in the name of the practice, $50.

8 Delivered a set of plans to a contractor and collected $300 in full payment therefor.

15 Completed and delivered a set of plans to Phoenix Contractors on credit, $500.

15 Paid the salary of the draftsman, $180.

17 Paid West Company $300 of the amount owed to it.

18 Purchased drafting supplies, $50, and drafting equipment, $25, from West Company on credit.

24 Received $500 from Phoenix Contractors for the plans delivered on October 15.

26 Ann Evans withdrew $100 cash from the business for personal living expenses.

28 Paid for the supplies and equipment purchased on October 18.

29 Paid the salary of the draftsman, $180.

29 Completed architectural work for Mazer Realty on credit, $150.

31 Paid the monthly utility bills, $30.

31 Paid the blueprinting expense for the month of October, $40.

Required:

1. Open the following accounts, numbering them beginning with 1: Cash; Accounts Receivable; Prepaid Rent; Drafting Supplies; Prepaid Insurance; Office and Drafting Equipment; Accounts Payable; Ann Evans, Capital; Ann Evans, Withdrawals; Revenue from Services; Salaries Expense; Blueprinting Expense; and Utilities Expense.

2. Prepare general journal entries to record the transactions, post to the accounts, and prepare a trial balance. Use as the name of the business Ann Evans, Architect.

Problem 2-5

Tom Burns began a new business called A-1 Cabinet Shop, and during a short period he completed these transactions:

Oct. 2 Began business by depositing $5,000 in a bank account opened in the name of the business.

2 Paid three months' rent in advance on a shop building, $225.

2 Purchased shop machinery costing $2,500. Paid $1,000 in cash and signed a promissory note payable for the balance.

3 Purchased shop supplies costing $500 on credit.

5 Delivered cabinet work to a customer and collected $250 cash on delivery.

6 Delivered $300 of cabinet work to a customer, Tim Davis. Mr. Davis paid $100 in cash at delivery and promised to pay the balance within a few days.

10 Tom Burns took $25 of shop supplies home for use in repairing his personal residence.

15 Paid the employees' wages for the first half of the month, $350.

17 Completed and delivered cabinet work to Dale Cole on credit, $400.

17 Received a $200 cheque from Tim Davis for the balance due on the work delivered on October 6.

23 Purchased additional shop supplies on credit, $150.

27 Dale Cole paid for the work delivered to him on credit on October 17.

29 Tom Burns withdrew $100 from the business for personal living expenses.

31 Paid for the shop supplies purchased on October 3.

31 Paid the wages of the employees for the last half of the month, $350.

31 Paid the electric light and power bill, $40.

31 Paid Ace Delivery Service $35 for delivery services during October.

Required:

1. Open these accounts numbered beginning with 1: Cash; Accounts Receivable; Prepaid Rent; Shop Supplies; Shop Machinery; Notes Payable; Accounts Payable; Tom Burns, Capital; Tom Burns, Withdrawals; Revenue from Shop Work; Wages Expense; Delivery Expense; and Light and Power Expense.

2. Prepare general journal entries to record the transactions, post to the accounts, and prepare a trial balance.

Alternate problems

Problem 2-1A

a. Mary Hall began business as a real estate agent by investing $8,000 in cash and office equipment having a $2,500 fair value. She called her agency Surfside Realty.

b. Purchased land valued at $7,500 and a small office building valued at $15,000, paying $7,000 in cash and signing a mortgage contract to pay the balance over a period of years.

c. Purchased office supplies on credit, $75.

d. Took her personal automobile, which had a $3,000 fair value, for exclusive use in the business.

e. Purchased additional office equipment on credit, $300.

f. Collected a $650 cash commission from the sale of property for a client.

g. Paid the office secretary's $85 salary.

h. Paid cash for newspaper advertising that had appeared, $50.

i. Paid for the supplies of transaction *(c)*.

j. Gave a typewriter carried in the accounting records at $50 and $200 in cash for a new typewriter.

k. Completed an appraisal of real estate for Walter Kosh, recorded the revenue earned, and sent him a bill for the service rendered, $100.

l. Paid the secretary's $85 salary.

m. Received $100 cash from Walter Kosh for the services of transaction *(k)*.

n. Mary Hall wrote a $165 cheque on the bank account of the real estate agency to pay personal living expenses.

Required:

1. Open the following T-accounts: Cash; Accounts Receivable; Office Supplies; Office Equipment; Automobile; Land; Building; Accounts Payable; Mortgage Payable; Mary Hall, Capital; Mary Hall, Withdrawals; Commissions Earned; Appraisal Fees Earned; Office Salaries Expense; and Advertising Expense.

2. Record the transactions by entering debits and credits directly in the accounts. Use the transaction letters to identify each debit and credit amount.

3. Prepare a trial balance using the current date.

Problem 2–2A

Kent Sims, C.A., completed the following transactions during October of the current year:

Oct. 2 Began a public accounting practice by investing $1,000 in cash and office equipment having a $500 fair value.

2 Purchased office supplies, $50, and office equipment, $125, from Aloha Supply Company on credit.

2 Paid two months' rent in advance on suitable office space, $200.

5 Completed accounting work for Gary Thomas and collected $50 cash therefor.

9 Completed accounting work for Surfside Company on credit, $250.

12 Paid Aloha Supply Company $75 of the amount owed for the items purchased on October 2.

15 Paid the premium on an insurance policy, $60.

19 Received $250 from Surfside Company for the work completed on October 9.

25 Kent Sims withdrew $100 from the accounting practice for personal living expenses.

30 Completed accounting work for Wiltshire Company on credit, $150.

31 Paid the monthly utility bills, $20.

Required:

1. Open the following accounts: Cash; Accounts Receivable; Prepaid Rent; Office Supplies; Prepaid Insurance; Office Equipment; Accounts Payable; Kent Sims, Capital; Kent Sims, Withdrawals; Accounting Revenue; and Utilities Expense. Number the accounts beginning with 1.

2. Prepare general journal entries to record the transactions, post to the

accounts, and prepare a trial balance. Use the name Kent Sims, C.A., to head the trial balance.

Problem 2–3A

Ted Sears began a new business called Fast Dirt Movers, and during a short period completed these transactions:

a. Began business by investing $12,000 in cash and office equipment having a $500 fair value.
b. Purchased for $5,000 land to be used as an office site and for parking equipment. Paid $1,000 in cash and signed a promissory note for the balance.
c. Purchased excavating equipment costing $22,500. Paid $7,500 in cash and signed promissory notes for the balance.
d. Paid $1,500 cash for the erection of a quonset-type office building.
e. Paid the premiums on several insurance policies, $175.
f. Completed an excavating job and collected $825 cash in payment therefor.
g. Completed $1,200 of excavating work for Tri-City Contractors on credit.
h. Paid the wages of the equipment operators, $750.
i. Paid $225 cash for repairs to excavating equipment.
j. Received $1,200 from Tri-City Contractors for the work of transaction (g).
k. Completed $650 of excavating work for Ralph Sims on credit.
l. Recorded as an account payable a bill for rent of a special machine used on the Ralph Sims job, $75.
m. Purchased additional excavating equipment on credit, $850.
n. Ted Sears withdrew $50 from the business for personal use.
o. Paid the wages of the equipment operators, $800.
p. Paid the account payable resulting from renting the machine of transaction (l).
q. Paid for gas and oil consumed by the excavating equipment, $175.

Required:

1. Open the following T-accounts: Cash; Accounts Receivable; Prepaid Insurance; Office Equipment; Excavating Equipment; Building; Land; Notes Payable; Accounts Payable; Ted Sears, Capital; Ted Sears, Withdrawals; Excavating Revenue; Equipment Repairs Expense; Wages Expense; Equipment Rentals Expense; and Gas and Oil Expense.
2. Record the transactions by entering debits and credits directly in the T-accounts. Use the transaction letters to identify amounts in the accounts.
3. Prepare a trial balance using the current date.

Problem 2–4A

Ann Evans opened an office as an architect and completed these transactions during the month of October:

Oct. 2 Began the practice of architecture by opening a bank account in the name of the business, Ann Evans, Architect, and depositing $1,500 therein.

2 Rented office space, paying three months' rent in advance, $300.

2 Purchased drafting supplies for cash, $150.

3 Purchased $1,800 of office and drafting equipment under an agreement calling for a $500 down payment and the balance in monthly installments. Paid the down payment.

Oct. 9 Delivered a set of building plans to a contractor and collected $250 cash in full payment therefor.

10 Paid the premiums on fire and public liability insurance policies, $75.

11 Purchased additional drafting supplies, $25, and drafting equipment, $100, on credit.

16 Completed and delivered a set of plans to Lakeside Developers on credit, $450.

16 Paid the salary of the draftsman, $200.

22 Received $450 from Lakeside Developers for the plans delivered on October 16.

22 Paid for the supplies and equipment purchased on October 11.

26 Completed additional architectural work for Lakeside Developers on credit, $100.

28 Paid $50 cash for blueprinting expense.

30 Ann Evans withdrew $200 cash for personal living expenses.

31 Paid the monthly utility bills, $25.

31 Paid the salary of the draftsman, $200.

Required:

1. Open the following accounts numbered beginning with 1: Cash; Accounts Receivable; Prepaid Rent; Drafting Supplies; Prepaid Insurance; Office and Drafting Equipment; Accounts Payable; Ann Evans, Capital; Ann Evans, Withdrawals; Revenue from Services; Salaries Expense; Blueprinting Expense; and Utilities Expense.

2. Prepare general journal entries to record the transactions, post to the accounts, and prepare a trial balance.

Decision Problem 2–1, Summer Concession

Jack Neal has just completed the first summer's operation of a concession on a lake at which he rents boats and sells hamburgers, soft drinks, and candy. He began the summer's operation with $2,000 in cash and a five-year lease on a boat dock and small concession building on the lake. The lease calls for a $750 annual rental, although the concession is open only from May 15 to September 15. On opening day Jack paid the first year's rent and also purchased five boats at $150 each, paying cash. He estimated the boats would have a five-year life, after which he could sell them for $25 each.

During the summer he purchased food, soft drinks, and candy costing $3,450, all of which was paid for by summer's end, excepting food costing $150 which was purchased during the last week's operation. He also paid electric bills, $75, and the wages of a part-time helper, $800; and he withdrew $100 of the earnings of the concession each week for 16 weeks to pay personal living expenses.

He took in $1,250 in boat rentals during the summer and sold $7,400 of food and drinks, all of which was collected in cash, except $125 he had not collected from Apex Company for food and drinks for an employees' party.

When he closed for the summer, he was able to return to the soft drink company several cases of soft drinks for which he received a $50 cash refund. However, he had to take home for consumption by his family a number of candy bars and some hamburger and buns which cost $20 and could have been sold for $45.

Prepare an income statement for Summer Concession showing the results of the summer's operations and prepare a September 15 balance sheet. (T-accounts should prove helpful in organizing the data. To determine Jack Neal's end-of-the-period equity, apply the information in the last paragraph of the section titled "Mechanics of double-entry accounting."

Decision problem 2-2, Sparkle Glass Service

Ted Long began a window cleaning service by transferring $500 from his personal savings account to a current account opened in the name of the business, Sparkle Glass Service. From the amount invested, he made a $200 down payment on a secondhand truck priced at $800, and spent $150 for soap, sponges, and other supplies to be used in the business. He also paid $50 for newspaper advertising through which he gained a number of customers who together agreed to pay him approximately $200 per week for his services.

After six months, on June 30, 19—, Ted's records showed that he had collected $4,500 in cash from customers for services and that other customers owed him $300 for washing their windows. He had bought additional supplies for cash, $400, which brought the total supplies purchased during the six months to $550; however, supplies that had cost $100 were on hand unused at the period end. He had spent $150 for gas and oil used in the truck and through payments had reduced the balance owed on the truck to $300; but through use the truck had worn out and depreciated an amount equal to one fourth of its cost. Also, he had withdrawn sufficient cash from the business each week to pay his personal living expenses.

Under the assumption the business had a total of $400 of cash on hand and in the bank at the period end, determine the amount of cash Ted had withdrawn from the business. Prepare an income statement showing the net income earned by the business during the period and a balance sheet as of the period end. (T-accounts should prove helpful in organizing the data. To determine Ted Long's end-of-the-period equity, apply the information in the last paragraph of the section titled "Mechanics of double-entry accounting."

Decision problem 2-3, Robert Beach

Some weeks ago Robert Beach began a new business and he decided to keep his own accounting records. Several years ago, when he was a sophomore in college, he had a course in accounting, but he could not recall the exact procedural details. He remembered that assets had to equal liabilities plus owner equity, that accounts had an increases side and a decreases side, and that the increases side for liability and owner equity accounts was different from the increases side for asset accounts. However, he could not recall which was the increases side for either kind of accounts; so, being right-handed, he decided to enter increases in assets on the right side of asset accounts and increases in liability and owner equity on the left. He also dimly recalled that revenues increased and expenses decreased owner equity, so he decided to record these directly in his Capital account. And finally, he decided to dispense with a journal and to enter transactions directly in the accounts and thus avoid writing much the same thing in both a journal and the ledger.

After recording some two hundred transactions, he prepared a trial balance that would not balance and he has come to you for help. Explain the purpose of a journal record to Mr. Beach and list the changes you would make in his accounting procedures, telling why you would make each change.

Problem 2-1 A&R

The following T-accounts reflect all the business activities of David Lambert's realty operation for the month of November, 1975.

	Cash				Commissions Receivable		
Nov. 1	5,000	Nov. 15	1,000	Nov. 8	300	Nov. 15	300
15	300	18	100	30	500		
16	700	20	200		800		
	6,000	30	1,500				
			2,800				

	Accounts Payable				David Lambert, Capital		
Nov. 20	200	Nov. 1	200			Nov. 1	5,000
		10	500				
			700				

	Commissions Earned			Salaries Expense	
		Nov. 8	300	Nov. 15	1,000
		16	700	30	1,500
		30	500		2,500
			1,500		

	Office Expense	
Nov. 1	200	
10	500	
18	100	
	800	

Required:
1. Based on the above data, prepare journal entries (omit narratives) to record each of the transactions for November.
2. Assuming that all transactions for November are first summarized and then posted to the T-accounts, how do you summarize them in journal entry or entries? (Organize your approach so as to summarize the transactions before preparing the summary journal entry or entries.)
3. Open new T-accounts and post the summary journal entry or entries in (2) above to the T-accounts.

4. Is the summary approach in journalizing the entries and posting to the T-accounts less time consuming than the approach of journalizing the individual entries and posting them individually to the T-accounts? Why? Explain.

Problem 2-2 A&R

The following T-accounts show the October transactions of Pauline David's service business which was organized on the first day of October this year. Since the bookkeeper is very inexperienced, some dates and amounts are missing.

	Cash					Accounts Receivable	
Oct. 26	2,000	Oct. 2	3,000	Oct. 6	800		
		10	400				
		15	500				
		30	600				

Office Supplies	
Oct. 5 for cash	100

	Building			Land	
Oct. 2	6,000		Oct. 1	2,000	

Accounts Payable	
	300

	Wages Payable			Mortgage Payable	
	Oct. 31	200		Oct. 2	3,000

Pauline David's Capital	
Oct. 1	10,000

	Service Revenue			Wages Expense	
	Oct. 26	2,000	Oct. 15	500	
			30	600	

	Miscellaneous Expense	
Oct. 10	400	
24	300	

Required:
1. Prepare journal entries (omit narratives) to reconstruct all transactions for the month of October.
2. Identify the missing data.

Problem 2–3 A&R

Joy Cleaner Service, owned by Michael Joy, has been in operation for a few years. The transactions and trial balance for the month of November are presented below:

November	1	Received from Superior Hotel for cleaning work done in October, $600.
	2	Purchased cleaning supplies for cash, $300, to be used for the next three weeks.
	5	Bill Windsor Club for cleaning work completed on credit, $800.
	6	Cleaning services performed for customers and collected $100 in full payment therefore.
	16	Michael Joy invested an additional $2,000 cash in the business.
	22	Paid advertising, $150.
	28	Purchased cleaning supplies to be used for the next few days on credit, $50.
	29	Michael Joy withdrew $700 from the business.
	30	Paid telephone and utility expenses, $100.
	30	Paid employees' monthly salary, $500.
	30	Cleaning services completed and collected, $700.

JOY CLEANER SERVICE
Trial Balance
November 30, 1975

Cash	$1,800	
Accounts receivable	300	
Office supplies	100	
Land	5,000	
Accounts payable		$ 250
Mortgage payable		3,000
Michael Joy, capital		4,150
Michael Joy, withdrawals	700	
Cleaning service revenue		1,600
Salaries expense	500	
Cleaning supplies expense	350	
Advertising expense	150	
Telephone and utility expense	100	
	$9,000	$9,000

Required:

Assuming that Joy Cleaner Service's accounting period is a month and accordingly follows the practice of preparing financial statements monthly.

1. Open all necessary T-accounts and post the transactions directly to these T-accounts without preparing journal entries.
2. Compute the balance for all the accounts in (1) above.
3. Prepare a trial balance.
4. Compare the trial balance in (3) above with the trial balance presented in the problem, explain the differences between the two trial balances. (All information in the given trial balance is correct.)
5. Which types of accounts tend to have opening balances and why?

3

Adjusting the accounts and preparing the statements

■ The life of a business commonly spans a long interval of time, which for accounting purposes is divided into periods of equal length, called *accounting periods*. Accounting periods may be any length, such as a month, three months, or a year; but *annual accounting periods,* periods one year in length, are the most common. Accounting periods are made equal in length so that the revenues, expenses, and income earned by the business in one period may be compared with its revenues, expenses, and income in other periods.

For accounting purposes, each accounting period is an interval over which transactions are recorded; and at the end of which, after all transactions are recorded, an income statement and a balance sheet are prepared. The income statement should reflect as nearly as can be measured the revenues earned during the period and the amount of each kind of expense incurred in earning the revenues. The balance sheet should show the assets, liabilities, and owner's equity as of the close of business on the last day of the period.

Need for adjustments before the statements are prepared ■ Occasionally, at the end of a period, statements reflecting proper amounts can be prepared directly from the accounts just as soon as all transactions are recorded. However, this is unusual. Normally, several account balances as they appear on the end-of-the-period trial balance do not show proper statement amounts because of the expiration of costs brought about by the passage of time. For example, the second item on the trial balance of Owen Real Estate Agency, as prepared

Owen Real Estate Agency
Trial Balance, July 31, 19—

Cash	$1,095	
Prepaid rent	300	
Office supplies	60	
Automobile	3,000	
Office equipment	1,200	
Accounts payable		$ 235
Unearned management fees		75
Larry Owen, capital		5,000
Larry Owen, withdrawals	200	
Commissions earned		850
Office salaries expense	200	
Telephone expense	20	
Gas, oil, and repairs	25	
Advertising expense	60	
Totals	$6,160	$6,160

Illustration
3–1

first in Chapter 2 and reproduced again as Illustration 3–1, is "Prepaid rent, $300." This $300 represents the rent for three months paid in advance on July 1. On July 31, $300 is not the balance sheet amount for this asset because one month's rent, or $100, has expired and become an expense and only $200 remains as an asset. Likewise, a portion of the office supplies as represented by the $60 debit balance in the Office Supplies account has been used, and the automobile and office equipment have begun to wear out and depreciate. Obviously, then, the end-of-the-period balances of the Prepaid Rent, Office Supplies, Automobile, and Office Equipment accounts as they appear on the trial balance simply do not reflect the proper amounts for preparing the July 31 statements. The balance of each and also the balances of the Office Salaries Expense and Management Fees Earned accounts must be *adjusted* before they will show proper amounts for the July 31 statements.

Adjusting the accounts

■ Prepaid expenses

As the name implies, a prepaid expense is an expense that has been paid for in advance of its use. At the time of payment an asset is acquired that will be used or consumed and as it is used or consumed, it will become an expense. For example:

On July 1 Owen Real Estate Agency paid three months' rent in advance and thus obtained the right to occupy a rented office for the following three months. On July 1 this right was an asset valued at its $300 cost; but day by day the agency occupied the office; and each day a portion of the prepaid rent expired and became an expense. On July 31 one month's rent, valued at one third of $300, or $100, had expired.

Consequently, if the agency's July 31 accounts are to reflect proper asset and expense amounts, the following adjusting entry is required:

July	31	Rent Expense	100.00	
		Prepaid Rent		100.00
		To record the expired rent.		

Posting the adjusting entry has the following effect on the accounts:

	Prepaid Rent			Rent Expense	
July 1	300	July 31	100	July 31	100

After the entry is posted, the Prepaid Rent account with a $200 balance and the Rent Expense account with a $100 balance show proper statement amounts.

To continue, early in July, Owen Real Estate Agency purchased some office supplies and placed them in the office for use; and each day the secretary used a portion. The amount used or consumed each day was an expense that daily reduced the supplies on hand. However, the daily reductions were not recognized in the accounts because day-by-day information as to amounts used and remaining was not needed and because bookkeeping labour could be saved if only a single amount, the total of all supplies used during the month, was recorded.

Consequently, if on July 31 the accounts are to reflect proper statement amounts, it is necessary to record the office supplies used during the month. However, to do this, it is first necessary to learn the amount used; and to learn the amount used, it is necessary to count or inventory the unused supplies remaining and to deduct the amount remaining from the amount purchased. If, for example, $45 of unused supplies remain on hand in the office, then $15 ($60 − $45 = $15) of supplies have been used and have become an expense, and the following entry is required to record this:

July	31	Office Supplies Expense	15.00	
		Office Supplies		15.00
		To record the supplies used.		

The effect of the adjusting entry on the account is:

Office Supplies			Office Supplies Expense	
July 5	60	July 31 15	July 31	15

Often, unlike in the two previous examples, items that are prepaid expenses at the time of purchase are both bought and fully consumed within a single accounting period. For example, a company pays its rent in advance on the first day of each month. Each month the amount paid results in a prepaid expense that is entirely consumed before the month's end and before the end of the accounting period. In such cases, it is best to ignore the fact that an asset results from each prepayment. In such cases bookkeeping labour, an end-of-the-accounting-period adjustment, can be saved if each amount paid is recorded as an expense at the time of payment.

Other prepaid expenses that are handled in the same manner as prepaid rent and office supplies are prepaid insurance, store supplies, and factory supplies.

Depreciation

When a business buys a building or an item of equipment, it in effect buys a "quantity of usefulness"; and day by day as the asset is used in carrying on the business operations, a portion of this "quantity of usefulness" is consumed or expires. In accounting, this expiration of a plant asset's "quantity of usefulness" is known as *depreciation.*

Depreciation is an expense just like the expiration of prepaid rent is an expense. For example, if a company purchases a machine for $4,500 that it expects to use for four years, after which it expects to receive $500 for the machine in the form of a trade-in allowance on a new machine, the company has purchased a $4,000 quantity of usefulness ($4,500 − $500 = $4,000). Furthermore, this quantity of usefulness expires or the machine depreciates on a straight-line basis at the rate of $1,000 per year [($4,500 − $500) ÷ 4 years = $1,000]. Actually, when depreciation is compared to the expiration of a prepaid expense like rent or insurance, the primary difference is that since it is often impossible to predict how long a plant asset will be used or how much will be received for it at the end of its useful life, the amount it depreciates each accounting period is only an estimate.

Estimating and apportioning depreciation can be simple, as in the foregoing example, or it can become complex. A discussion of more complex situations is unnecessary at this point and is deferred to Chapter 11. However, to illustrate the recording of depreciation, assume that—

On July 31 Owen Real Estate Agency estimated its automobile had depreciated $35 and its office equipment $10 during July. In both cases the depreciation reduced the assets and increased expenses. To record the depreciation the following adjusting entries are required:

July	31	Depreciation Expense, Automobile................	35.00	
		Accumulated Depreciation, Automobile......		35.00
		To record the July depreciation.		
	31	Depreciation Expense, Office Equipment..........	10.00	
		Accumulated Depreciation, Office		
		Equipment..		10.00
		To record the July depreciation.		

The effect of the entries on the accounts is:

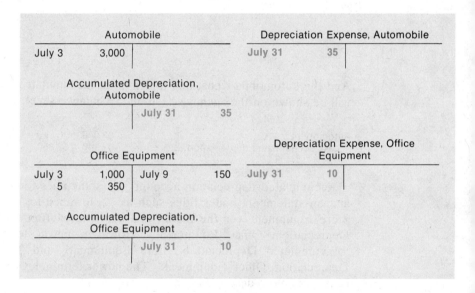

Carefully observe the accumulated depreciation accounts in the example just given. Normally, a decrease in an asset is recorded with a credit to the account in which the asset is recorded. However, note in the accounts just shown that this procedure is not followed in recording depreciation. Rather, depreciation is recorded in *contra accounts* such as the Accumulated Depreciation, Automobile and the Accumulated Depreciation, Office Equipment accounts. (A contra account is an account the balance of which is subtracted from the balance of an associate account to show a more proper amount for the items recorded in the associated account.)

There are two good reasons for using contra accounts in recording depreciation. First, at its best, depreciation is only an estimate; and, second, the use of contra accounts better preserves the facts in the lives of plant assets. For example, in this case the asset account, Automobile, preserves in the accounts a record of the auto's historical cost, and the Accumulated Depreciation, Automobile account shows its accumulated depreciation to date.

A better understanding of the latter point, along with an appreciation of why the word "accumulated" is used in the account name, can be gained when it is pointed out that depreciation is recorded at the end of each accounting period in a plant asset's life. As a result, at the end of the fourth month in the life of Owen Real Estate Agency's automobile, the Automobile account and its related accumulated depreciation account will look like this:

Automobile		Accumulated Depreciation, Automobile	
July 3	3,000	July 31	35
		Aug. 31	35
		Sept. 30	35
		Oct. 31	35

And the automobile's cost and four months' accumulated depreciation will be shown on the agency's October 31 balance sheet thus:

Automobile..	$3,000	
Less accumulated depreciation.....................	140	$2,860

Accumulated depreciation accounts are sometimes found in ledgers and on statements under titles such as "Allowance for Depreciation, Store Equipment" or the totally unacceptable caption, "Reserve for Depreciation, Office Equipment." However, newer terminology is "Accumulated Depreciation, Store Equipment" and "Accumulated Depreciation, Office Equipment." The newer terminology is better because it is more descriptive.

Accrued expenses

Most expenses are recorded during an accounting period at the time they are paid. However, when a period ends there may be a few expenses that have been incurred but have not been paid and recorded because payment is not yet due. These unpaid and unrecorded expenses for which payment is not due are called *accrued expenses*. Earned but unpaid salaries and wages are a common example. To illustrate:

Owen Real Estate Agency has a part-time secretary who is paid $10 per day or $50 per week for a week that begins on Monday and ends on Friday. Her wages are due and payable every two weeks on Friday night; and during July they were paid on the 12th and 26th and recorded as follows:

Cash			Office Salaries Expense		
July 12	100		July 12	100	
26	100		26	100	

If the calendar for July appears as illustrated and the secretary worked on Monday, Tuesday, and Wednesday, July 29, 30, 31, then at the close of business on Wednesday, July 31, she has earned three days' wages that are not paid and recorded because payment is not due. However, this $30 of earned but unpaid wages is just as much a part of the July expenses as the $200 of wages that have been paid. Furthermore, on July 31, the unpaid wages are a liability. Consequently, if the agency's accounts are to show the correct amount of secretary's wages for July and all liabilities owed on July 31, then an adjusting entry like the following must be made:

JULY						
S	M	T	W	T	F	S
	1	2	3	4	5	6
7	8	9	10	11	12	13
14	15	16	17	18	19	20
21	22	23	24	25	26	27
28	29	30	31			

July	31	Office Salaries Expense	30.00	
		Salaries Payable.......................................		30.00
		To record the earned but unpaid wages.		

The effect of the entry on the accounts is:

Office Salaries Expense			Salaries Payable		
July 12	100			July 31	30
26	100				
31	30				

Unearned revenues

An unearned revenue results when payment is received for goods or services in advance of their delivery. For instance, on July 16 Owen Real Estate Agency entered into an agreement to manage an apartment building for a $50 monthly fee, and on that date received $75 in advance for its services for the remainder of July and the month of August, which it recorded as follows:

July	16	Cash..	75.00	
		Unearned Management Fees		75.00
		Received a $75 management fee in advance.		

Acceptance of the fee in advance increased the agency's cash and created for it a liability, the obligation to manage the apartment building for the next month and a half. However, by managing the building July 16 through the 31st, the agency discharged $25 of the liability and earned that much revenue. Consequently, on July 31 the following entry is required to make the accounts show the proper statement amounts:

July	31	Unearned Management Fees..........................	25.00	
		Management Fees Earned........................		25.00
		To record the fees earned.		

Posting the entry has this effect on the accounts:

Unearned Management Fees				Management Fees Earned		
July 31	25	July 16	75		July 31	25

The effect of posting the entry is to transfer the $25 earned portion of the fees from the liability account to the revenue account. It reduces the liability and records as a revenue the $25 that has been earned.

Before proceeding, note that the advance payment of $75 to Owen Real Estate Agency for property management services was a prepaid expense to the apartment owner and would be treated as such in the accounting records of the apartment building.

Accrued revenues

An accrued revenue is a revenue that has been earned but has not been collected because payment is not due. For example, assume that on July 21 Owen Real Estate Agency signed an additional management contract and took over management of another apartment building for a $2 per day fee, payable at the end of each two months. Under this assumption, by July 31 the agency has managed the building for 10 days and has earned $20 for its services. Therefore, if its accounts are to show proper statement amounts, the following entry is required:

July	31	Accounts Receivable	20.00	
		Management Fees Earned........................		20.00
		To record accrued management fees.		

Posting the entry has this effect on the accounts:

Accounts Receivable				Management Fees Earned	
July 9	50	July 11	50	July 31	25
31	20			31	20

The **adjusted trial balance** ■ A trial balance prepared before adjustments is known as an *unadjusted trial balance,* or simply a trial balance. One prepared after adjustments is known as an *adjusted trial balance;* and a July 31 adjusted trial balance for Owen Real Estate Agency appears in Illustration 3–2.

Owen Real Estate Agency
Adjusted Trial Balance, July 31, 19 –

Cash	$1,095	
Accounts receivable	20	
Prepaid rent	200	
Office supplies	45	
Automobile	3,000	
Accumulated depreciation, automobile		$ 35
Office equipment	1,200	
Accumulated depreciation, office equipment		10
Accounts payable		235
Salaries payable		30
Unearned management fees		50
Larry Owen, capital		5,000
Larry Owen, withdrawals	200	
Commissions earned		850
Management fees earned		45
Office salaries expense	230	
Telephone expense	20	
Gas, oil, and repairs	25	
Advertising expense	60	
Rent expense	100	
Office supplies expense	15	
Depreciation expense, automobile	35	
Depreciation expense, office equipment	10	
Totals	$6,255	$6,255

Illustration 3–2

Preparing statements from the adjusted trial balance ■ An adjusted trial balance shows proper balance sheet and income statement amounts; and, consequently, may be used in preparing the statements. When it is so used, the revenue and expense items are arranged into an income statement as in Illustration 3–3 and the asset, liability, and owner equity items are arranged into a balance sheet as in Illustration 3–4.

When the statements are prepared from an adjusted trial balance, the income statement is normally prepared first because the net income, as

Owen Real Estate Agency
Adjusted Trial Balance, July 31, 19—

Cash	$1,095	
Accounts receivable	20	
Prepaid rent	200	
Office supplies	45	
Automobile	3,000	
Accumulated depreciation, automobile		$ 35
Office equipment	1,200	
Accumulated depreciation, office equipment		10
Accounts payable		235
Salaries payable		30
Unearned management fees		50
Larry Owen, capital		5,000
Larry Owen, withdrawals	200	
Commissions earned		850
Management fees earned		45
Office salaries expense	230	
Telephone expense	20	
Gas, oil, and repairs	25	
Advertising expense	60	
Rent expense	100	
Office supplies expense	15	
Depreciation expense, automobile	35	
Depreciation expense, office equipment	10	
Totals	$6,255	$6,255

PREPARING THE INCOME STATEMENT
FROM THE ADJUSTED TRIAL BALANCE

Owen Real Estate Agency
Income Statement for Month Ended July 31, 19—

Revenues:		
Commissions earned		$850
Management fees earned		45
Total revenues		$895
Operating expenses:		
Office salaries expense	$230	
Telephone expense	20	
Gas, oil, and repairs	25	
Advertising expense	60	
Rent expense	100	
Office supplies expense	15	
Depreciation expense, automobile	35	
Depreciation expense, office equipment	10	
Total operating expenses		495
Net Income		$400

Illustration
3–3

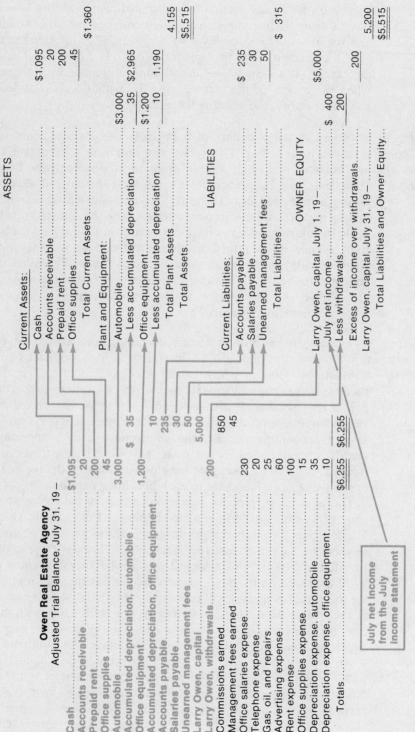

Owen Real Estate Agency
Adjusted Trial Balance, July 31, 19—

Cash	$1,095	
Accounts receivable	20	
Prepaid rent	200	
Office supplies	45	
Automobile	3,000	
Accumulated depreciation, automobile		$ 35
Office equipment	1,200	
Accumulated depreciation, office equipment		10
Accounts payable		235
Salaries payable		30
Unearned management fees		50
Larry Owen, capital		5,000
Larry Owen, withdrawals	200	
Commissions earned		850
Management fees earned		45
Office salaries expense	230	
Telephone expense	20	
Gas, oil, and repairs	25	
Advertising expense	60	
Rent expense	100	
Office supplies expense	15	
Depreciation expense, automobile	35	
Depreciation expense, office equipment	10	
Totals	$6,255	$6,255

Owen Real Estate Agency
Balance Sheet, July 31, 19—

ASSETS

Current Assets:			
Cash		$1,095	
Accounts receivable		20	
Prepaid rent		200	
Office supplies		45	
Total Current Assets			$1,360
Plant and Equipment:			
Automobile	$3,000		
Less accumulated depreciation	35	$2,965	
Office equipment	$1,200		
Less accumulated depreciation	10	1,190	
Total Plant Assets			4,155
Total Assets			$5,515

LIABILITIES

Current Liabilities:			
Accounts payable		$ 235	
Salaries payable		30	
Unearned management fees		50	
Total Liabilities			$ 315

OWNER EQUITY

Larry Owen, capital, July 1, 19—			$5,000
July net income	$ 400		
Less withdrawals	200		
Excess of income over withdrawals			200
Larry Owen, capital, July 31, 19—			5,200
Total Liabilities and Owner Equity			$5,515

July net income from the July income statement

Illustration
3–4

calculated on the income statement, is needed in completing the balance sheet's owner equity section. Observe in Illustration 3–4 how the net income from the income statement is combined with the withdrawals, and the excess of income over withdrawals, $200, is added to Owen's July 1 capital to show the amount of his July 31 equity. The income increased Owen's equity, and the withdrawals reduced it. Consequently, when the excess of the income over the withdrawals is added to the beginning equity, the result is the ending equity.

Arrangement of the accounts in the ledger

■ Normally the accounts of a business are classified and logically arranged in its ledger. This serves two purposes: (1) it aids in locating any account and (2) it aids in preparing the statements. Obviously, statements can be prepared with the least difficulty if accounts are arranged in the ledger in the order of their statement appearance. This arrangement causes the accounts to appear on the adjusted trial balance in their statement order, which in turn aids in rearranging the adjusted trial balance items into a balance sheet and an income statement. Consequently, the balance sheet accounts beginning with Cash and ending with the owner equity accounts appear first in the ledger. These are followed by the revenue and expense accounts in order of their income statement appearance.

The adjustment process

■ The adjustment process described in this chapter arises from recognition that the operation of a business results in a continuous stream of transactions, some of which benefit several accounting periods. And, the objective of the adjustment process is to allocate to each accounting period that portion of a transaction from which the period benefits. For example, if a revenue like a property management fee is earned over several accounting periods, the adjustment process apportions and credits to each period its fair share. Likewise, if an expense payment like that for rent or insurance benefits several periods, the adjustment process charges a fair share to each benefiting period.

The adjustment process also makes the information on accounting statements comparable from period to period. For example, Owen Real Estate Agency paid its rent for three months in advance on July 1 and debited the $300 payment to Prepaid Rent. Then at the end of July it transferred $100 of this amount to its Rent Expense account and the $100 appeared on its July income statement as the July rent expense. At the end of August it will transfer another $100 to rent expense and at the end of September it will transfer the third $100, with the result that the amounts shown for rent expense on its July, August, and September income statements will be comparable month by month.

An unsatisfactory alternate procedure would be to debit the entire $300 to Rent Expense at the time of payment and permit the entire amount to appear on the July income statement as rent expense for July. However, if this were done, the July income statement would show $300 of rent expense and the August and September statements would show none, and the income statements of the three months would not be comparable. In addition the July net income would be understated $200 and the net incomes of August and September would be overstated $100 each, and a person seeing only the fluctuations in net income might draw an incorrect conclusion.

Matching revenues and expenses

■ From the need for financial statement information that is comparable period after period has grown the *matching principle* of accounting. Under this principle, the revenues and expenses shown on an income statement must be matched. By this is meant that when an income statement is prepared at the end of an accounting period, it should show all revenues earned during the period, and matched against the revenues (deducted therefrom) should be all the expenses incurred in earning the revenues.

Cash and accrual bases of accounting

■ For income tax purposes certain individuals such as farmers and fishermen may report income on either a cash basis or an accrual basis. Under the cash basis no adjustments are made for prepaid, unearned, and accrued items. Revenues are reported as being earned in the accounting period in which they are received in cash; expenses are deducted from revenues in the accounting period in which cash is disbursed in their payment; and as a result, net income is the difference between revenue receipts and expense disbursements. Under the accrual basis, on the other hand, adjustments are made for accrued and deferred (prepaid and unearned) items. Under this basis revenues are credited to the period in which earned, expenses are matched with revenues, and no consideration is given to when cash is received and disbursed, with the result that net income is the difference between revenues earned and the expenses incurred in earning the revenues.

Needless to say, although the cash basis of accounting is satisfactory for individuals and small concerns in which accrued and deferred items are not important, it is not satisfactory for most concerns since it results in accounting reports that are not comparable from period to period. Consequently, most businesses keep their records on an accrual basis.

Disposing of accrued items

■ **Accrued expenses**

Several pages back the July 29, 30, and 31 accrued wages of Owen Real Estate Agency's secretary were recorded as follows:

July	31	Office Salaries Expense	30.00	
		Salaries Payable......................................		30.00
		To record the earned but unpaid wages.		

When these wages are paid on Friday, August 9, the following entry is required:

Aug.	9	Salaries Payable..	30.00	
		Office Salaries Expense	70.00	
		Cash..		100.00
		Paid two weeks' wages.		

The first debit in the second entry cancels the liability for the three days' wages accrued on July 31, and the second debit records the wages of August's first seven working days as an expense of the August accounting period. The credit records the amount paid the secretary.

Accrued revenues

On July 21 Owen Real Estate Agency entered into an agreement to manage an apartment building for $2 per day payable every two months, and on July 31 the following entry was made to record the first 10 days' revenue earned under this contract:

July	31	Accounts Receivable.....................................	20.00	
		Management Fees Earned.........................		20.00
		To record management fees that have accrued.		

On August 31 this additional entry will be made to record the 31 days' revenue earned during August:

Aug.	31	Accounts Receivable.....................................	62.00	
		Management Fees Earned.........................		62.00
		To record 31 days' accrued management fees.		

And when payment is received on September 21, the following entry will be made:

Sept.	21	Cash...	124.00	
		Accounts Receivable...............................		82.00
		Management Fees Earned.........................		42.00
		To record the receipt of management fees earned.		

The first credit in the September 21 entry records the collection of the fees accrued at the ends of July and August, and the second credit records as revenue the fees earned during the first 21 days of September.

Classification of balance sheet items ■ The balance sheets shown thus far have been simple ones with few items, and no attempt was made to classify the items. However, a balance sheet with a number of items becomes more useful when its assets and liabilities are classified into significant groups, because a reader of a *classified balance sheet* can better judge the adequacy of the different kinds of assets used in the business. He can also better estimate the probable availability of funds to meet the various liabilities as they become due.

Accountants are not in full agreement as to the best way in which to classify balance sheet items. As a result they are classified in several ways; but a common way classifies assets into (1) current assets, (2) long-term investments, (3) plant and equipment, and (4) intangible assets. It classifies liabilities into (1) current liabilities and (2) long-term liabilities.

Of the four asset classifications just listed, only two, current assets and plant and equipment, appear on the balance sheet of Valley Hardware Store, Illustration 3–5 on the next page, because the store is small and has no long-term investments and intangible assets.

Current assets

The assets listed on a balance sheet under the current asset caption are primarily those to which current creditors (current liabilities) may look for payment. As presently defined, current assets consist of cash and assets that are reasonably expected to be realized in cash or be sold or consumed within a short period, usually one year. The accounts and notes receivable of Illustration 3–5 are expected to be realized in cash, the merchandise (merchandise inventory) is expected to be sold, and the prepaid insurance and supplies are to be consumed.

Such things as prepaid insurance, office supplies, and store supplies are called prepaid expenses. They were purchased for use in the business and will be consumed within a relatively short period of time, and when consumed become expenses; but until consumed they are classified as current assets. The American Institute of Certified Public Accountants through one of its committees says: "Prepaid expenses are not current assets in the sense that they will be converted into cash but in the sense that, if not paid in advance, they would require the use of current assets during the operating cycle."[1] This means that if the prepaid expense items were not already owned, current assets would be required for their purchase during the operating cycle, which for most concerns is one year.

The prepaid expenses of a business, as a total, are seldom a major item on its balance sheet. As a result, instead of listing them individually, as in Illustration 3–5, they are commonly totaled and only the total is shown under the caption "Prepaid expenses."

Long-term investments

The second balance sheet classification is long-term investments. Stocks, bonds, and promissory notes that will be held for more than one

---

[1] *Accounting Research and Terminology Bulletins, Final Edition* (New York: American Institute of Certified Public Accountants, 1961), p. 20.

Valley Hardware Store
Balance Sheet, December 31, 1975

ASSETS

Current Assets:

Cash	$ 1,050	
Notes receivable	300	
Accounts receivable	3,961	
Merchandise inventory	10,248	
Prepaid insurance	109	
Office supplies	46	
Stores supplies	145	
Total Current Assets		$15,859

Plant and Equipment:

Office equipment	$ 1,500		
Less accumulated depreciation	300	$ 1,200	
Store equipment	$ 3,200		
Less accumulated depreciation	800	2,400	
Buildings	$25,000		
Less accumulated depreciation	7,400	17,600	
Land		4,200	
Total Plant and Equipment			25,400
Total Assets			$41,259

LIABILITIES

Current Liabilities:

Notes payable	$ 3,000	
Accounts payable	2,715	
Wages payable	112	
Total Current Liabilities		$ 5,827

Long-Term Liabilities:

First mortgage payable, secured by a mortgage on land and buildings	10,000	
Total Liabilities		$15,827

OWNER EQUITY

Samuel Jackson, capital, January 1, 1975		$23,721
Net income for the year	$ 7,711	
Less withdrawals	6,000	
Excess of income over withdrawals		1,711
Samuel Jackson, capital, December 31, 1975		25,432
Total Liabilities and Owner Equity		$41,259

Illustration
3–5

year appear under this classification. Also, such things as land held for future expansion but not now being used in the business appear here.

Plant and equipment

Plant assets are relatively long-lived assets of a tangible nature that are held for use in the production or sale of other assets or services, for example, items of equipment, buildings, and land. The key words in the foregoing sentence are "long-lived" and "held for use in the production or sale of other assets or services." Land held for future expansion, as mentioned in the previous paragraph, is not a plant asset because it is not being used to produce or sell other assets, goods, or services.

The words "Plant and equipment" are commonly used as a balance sheet caption; but more complete captions are "Property, plant, and equipment" and "Land, buildings, and equipment." However, all three captions are long and unwieldy; and as a result, items of plant and equipment will be called plant assets in this book.

The order in which plant assets are listed within the balance sheet classification is not uniform; however, it is often from the ones of least permanent nature to those of most permanent nature.

Plant assets, with the exception of land, wear out or depreciate through use and the passage of time; and as in Illustration 3–5, they are commonly shown on the balance sheet at cost less accumulated depreciation. The accumulated depreciation is the share of each asset's cost that has been charged off to depreciation expense or the amount the asset has been depreciated from the time of its purchase to the balance sheet date.

Intangible assets

Intangible assets are assets having no physical nature, their value being derived from the rights conferred upon their owner by possession. Goodwill, patents, and trademarks are examples.

Current liabilities

Current liabilities are debts or other obligations that must be paid or liquidated within a short time, usually one year, and whose payment or liquidation will require the use of current assets. Common current liabilities are notes payable, accounts payable, wages payable, taxes payable, interest payable, and unearned revenues. The order of their listing within the classification is not uniform. Often notes payable are listed as the first current liability because notes receivable are listed first after cash in the current asset section. (A note payable is an unconditional promise in writing to pay on demand or at a fixed or determinable future date a definite sum of money. They are discussed and described in more detail in Chapter 9.)

Unearned revenues, none of which are shown in Illustration 3–5, are normally the last items in the current liability section. They result from transactions in which money is received for goods or services to be delivered at a future date. Subscriptions received in advance by a publisher, rent received in advance by a landlord, and payments received for future delivery of merchandise or services are examples. Each is a liability, an obligation to deliver goods or services at a future date. Each is classified as a current liability because current assets will normally be required in its liquidation. For example, payments for future delivery of merchandise will be earned and the obligation for delivery will be liquidated by delivering merchandise, a current asset.

Long-term liabilities

The second main liability classification is long-term liabilities. Liabilities that are not due and payable for a comparatively long period, usually more than one year, are listed under this classification. Common long-term liability items are mortgages payable, bonds payable, and notes payable due more than a year after the balance sheet date.

Owner equity on the balance sheet

■ The terms owner equity, proprietorship, net worth, and capital are often used synonymously. All four indicate the equity, in the assets, of the owner or owners of a business. Of the four, owner equity, proprietorship, and capital are considered the better terms because the phrase "net worth" seems to indicate that the amount shown is the net or exact "worth" of the owner's equity. Actually the amount shown may or may not be the equity's "worth" because when assets are purchased, they are recorded at cost; and in most cases until sold or consumed in the business operations, cost remains the basis upon which they are accounted for even though their "worth" may change. Thus, if a building lot is bought for $20,000, its purchase is recorded at $20,000 and the lot remains on the records at that amount even though a year later it may be sold for $30,000. The lot remains on the records at $20,000 until sold; and the change in its "worth" along with the resulting change in its owner's "net worth" is not recorded until a sale is completed.

When a business is owned by one person, it is called a single proprietorship and the owner's equity may be reported on the balance sheet as follows:

OWNER EQUITY

James Gibbs, capital, January 1, 1975................		$13,152
Net income for the year................................	$3,753	
Withdrawals...	4,800	
Excess of withdrawals over earnings..............		1,047
James Gibbs, capital, December 31, 1975............		$12,105

The illustrated owner equity section from a balance sheet shows the increase and decrease resulting from earnings and withdrawals. Some accountants prefer to put these details on a supplementary schedule attached to the balance sheet and called a statement of owner equity. When such a supplementary statement is prepared, owner equity is shown on the balance sheet as follows:

OWNER EQUITY

James Gibbs, capital (see schedule attached)...... $12,105

■ The balance sheet of Illustration 1–2 in the first chapter, with the liabilities and owner equity placed to the right of the assets, is called an *account form balance sheet*. Such an arrangement emphasizes that assets equal liabilities plus owner equity. Account form balance sheets are often reproduced on a double page with the assets on the left-hand page and the liabilities and owner equity on the right-hand page.

The balance sheet of Illustration 3–5 is called a *report form balance sheet*. Its items are arranged vertically and better fit a single page. Both forms are commonly used, and neither is preferred.

■ An income statement, like a balance sheet, is more useful with its items classified. However, the classifications used depend upon the type of business for which the statement is prepared and the nature of its costs and expenses; consequently, a discussion of this is deferred to Chapter 5, after more income statement items are introduced.

1. Why must certain of the accounts of a business be adjusted at the end of an accounting period before statements are prepared?
2. A concern that operates with monthly accounting periods prepaid its rent for three months in advance on June 1, debiting the $450 paid to its Prepaid Rent account, and on June 30 it made an adjusting entry to record the expired rent. What effect did this adjusting entry have on the accounts?
3. A prepaid expense is an asset at the time of its purchase or prepayment. When is it best to ignore this and record the prepayment as an expense? Why?
4. What is a contra account? Give an example.
5. What contra account is used in recording depreciation? Why is such an account used?
6. What is an accrued expense? Give an example.
7. How does an unearned revenue arise? Give an example of an unearned revenue.
8. What is the balance sheet classification of an unearned revenue?
9. What is an accrued revenue? Give an example.
10. The adjustment process results from recognizing that some transactions benefit several accounting periods. What is the objective of the process?
11. When the statements are prepared from an adjusted trial balance, why should the income statement be prepared first?
12. Why should the income statements of a concern be comparable from period to period?
13. When are a concern's revenues and expenses matched?
14. Differentiate between the cash and the accrual bases of accounting.
15. What is the usual order in which accounts are arranged in the ledger?
16. What is a classified balance sheet?
17. What are the characteristics of a current asset? What are the characteristics of an asset classified as plant and equipment?
18. What are current liabilities? Long-term liabilities?

Exercise 3–1

A company has four shop employees who earn a total of $100 per day for a five-day week that begins on Monday and ends on Friday. They were paid for the week ended Friday, December 26, and all four worked full days on Monday, Tuesday, and Wednesday, December 29, 30, and 31. January 1 of the next year was an unpaid holiday and none of the employees worked, but all worked a full day on Friday, January 2. Give in general journal form the year-end adjusting entry to record the accrued wages and the entry to pay the employees on January 2.

Exercise 3–2

Give in general journal form the year-end adjusting entry for each of the following situations:
a. The Shop Supplies account had a $225 debit balance on January 1; $340 of supplies were purchased during the year; and a year-end inventory showed $120 of unconsumed supplies on hand.
b. The Prepaid Insurance account had a $765 debit balance at the end of the accounting period before adjustment for expired insurance. An examination of insurance policies showed $410 of insurance expired.
c. The Prepaid Insurance account had a $880 debit balance at the end of the accounting period before adjustment for expired insurance. An examination of insurance policies showed $315 of unexpired insurance.
d. Depreciation on shop equipment was estimated at $625 for the accounting period.
e. Three months' property taxes, estimated at $320, have accrued but are unrecorded at the accounting period end.

Exercise 3–3

Assume that the required adjustments of Exercise 3–2 were not made at the end of the accounting period and tell for each adjustment the effect of its omission on the income statement and balance sheet prepared at that time.

Exercise 3–4

Determine the amounts indicated by the question marks in the columns below. The amounts in each column constitute a separate problem.

	(a)	(b)	(c)	(d)
Supplies on hand on January 1	$235	$140	$375	$?
Supplies purchased during the year	450	530	?	630
Supplies remaining at the year-end	165	?	215	240
Supplies consumed during the year	?	480	670	560

Exercise 3–5

Realty Associates manages apartment buildings and credits the revenue earned for this service to an account called Management Fees Earned. On December 1 it received $450 from Gary Kellar, a client. The $450 paid in advance for three months' management of Kellar's apartment building and was credited to an account called Unearned Management Fees. Give, in general journal form, the entry to record receipt of the $450 on December 1 and the adjusting entry required on December 31, the end of the annual accounting period. Also tell how the $450 or portions of it would appear on the year-end statements.

Problems   **Problem 3–1**

The following information for adjustments was available on December 31, the end of a yearly accounting period. Prepare an adjusting journal entry for each unit of information.

a. The Store Supplies account had a $125 debit balance at the beginning of the year, $560 of supplies were purchased during the year, and an inventory of unused store supplies at the year-end totaled $135.

b. An examination of insurance policies showed three policies, as follows:

Policy No.	Date of Purchase	Life of Policy	Cost
123 54321	October 1 of previous year	3 years	$360
333 45454	April 1 of current year	2 years	240
010 99999	August 1 of current year	1 year	90

Prepaid Insurance was debited for the cost of each policy at the time of its purchase. Expired insurance was correctly recorded at the end of the previous year.

c. The company's two office employees earn $15 per day and $20 per day, respectively. They are paid each Friday for a five-day workweek that begins on Monday. This year December 31 falls on Tuesday and the employees both worked on Monday and Tuesday.

d. The company owns a building that it completed and occupied for the first time on June 1 of the current year. The building cost $144,000, has an estimated 40-year life, and is not expected to have any salvage value at the end of that time.

e. The company occupies most of the space in its building but it also rents space to two tenants. One tenant rented a small amount of space on September 1 at $60 per month. He paid his rent on the first day of each month September through November, and the amounts paid were credited to Rent Earned. However, he has not paid his rent for December, although he has said on several occasions that he would do so the next day. (f) The second tenant agreed on November 1 to rent a small amount of space at $50 per month, and on that date paid three months' rent in advance. The amount paid was credited to the Unearned Rent account.

Problem 3–2

A trial balance of the ledger of Waikiki Realty at the end of its annual accounting period appeared as follows:

WAIKIKI REALTY
Trial Balance, December 31, 19—

Cash	$ 2,940	
Prepaid insurance	315	
Office supplies	290	
Office equipment	3,250	
Accumulated depreciation, office equipment		$ 920
Automobile	3,780	
Accumulated depreciation, automobile		1,150
Accounts payable		125
Unearned management fees		420
Alice Hall, capital		4,845
Alice Hall, withdrawals	8,400	
Sales commissions earned		19,110
Office salaries expense	5,400	
Advertising expense	530	
Rent expense	1,500	
Telephone expense	165	
Totals	$26,570	$26,570

Required:
1. Open the accounts of the trial balance plus these additional ones: Accounts Receivable; Office Salaries Payable; Management Fees Earned; Insurance Expense; Office Supplies Expense; Depreciation Expense, Office Equipment; and Depreciation Expense, Automobile. Enter the trial balance amounts in the accounts.
2. Use the following information to prepare and post adjusting journal entries:
   a. An examination of insurance policies showed $285 of expired insurance.
   b. An inventory showed $75 of unused office supplies on hand.
   c. The year's depreciation on office equipment was estimated at $325 and (d) on the automobile at $600.
   e. and (f) Waikiki Realty offers property management services and has two contracts with clients. In the first contract (e) it agreed to manage an office building beginning on November 1. The contract called for a $140 monthly fee, and the client paid the fees for the first three months in advance at the time the contract was signed. The amount paid was credited to the Unearned Management Fees account. In the second contract (f) it agreed to manage an apartment building for a $50 monthly fee payable at the end of each quarter. The contract was signed on October 15, and two and a half months' fees have accrued.
   g. The one office employee is paid weekly, and on December 31 three days' wages at $20 per day have accrued.
3. After posting the adjusting entries prepare an adjusted trial balance, an income statement, and a classified balance sheet.

Problem 3–3
A trial balance of the ledger of Carefree Moving and Storage Service at the end of its annual accounting period carried these items:

CAREFREE MOVING AND STORAGE SERVICE
Trial Balance, December 31, 19—

Cash	$ 1,240	
Accounts receivable	590	
Prepaid insurance	1,280	
Office supplies	220	
Office equipment	1,650	
Accumulated depreciation, office equipment		$ 280
Trucks	14,200	
Accumulated depreciation, trucks		2,540
Buildings	38,000	
Accumulated depreciation, buildings		8,600
Land	7,500	
Accounts payable		580
Unearned storage fees		730
Mortgage payable		17,500
Ted Lee, capital		18,610
Ted Lee, withdrawals	8,400	
Revenue from moving services		47,860
Storage fees earned		3,190
Office salaries expense	5,400	
Truck drivers' wages	18,730	
Gas, oil, and repairs	2,680	
Totals	$99,890	$99,890

Required:
1. Open the accounts of the trial balance plus these additional ones: Wages Payable; Insurance Expense; Office Supplies Expense; Depreciation Expense, Office Equipment; Depreciation Expense, Trucks; and Depreciation Expense, Buildings. Enter the trial balance amounts in the accounts.
2. Use this information to prepare and post adjusting journal entries:
   a. An examination of insurance policies showed $870 of expired insurance.
   b. An inventory of office supplies showed $60 of unused supplies on hand.
   c. Estimated depreciation on office equipment, $140; *(d)* trucks, $3,000; and *(e)* buildings, $2,400.
   f. The company credits the storage fees of customers who pay in advance to the Unearned Storage Fees account. Of the $730 credited to this account during the year, $420 had been earned by the year-end.
   g. Accrued storage fees earned but unrecorded in the accounts and uncollected at the year-end totaled $160.
   h. There were $540 of accrued truck drivers' wages at the year-end.
3. After posting the adjusting journal entries, prepare an adjusted trial balance, an income statement, and a classified balance sheet.

Problem 3-4

Analyze the trial balance and adjusted trial balance of Rapid Delivery Service which follow and prepare the adjusting journal entries made by the concern.

Trial Balance and Adjusted Trial Balance, December 31, 19—

	Trial Balance		Adjusted Trial Balance	
Cash	$ 1,510	....	$ 1,510	....
Accounts receivable	540	....	600	....
Prepaid rent	125	....	....	....
Prepaid insurance	625	....	275	....
Office supplies	80	....	25	....
Office equipment	915	....	915	....
Accumulated depreciation, office equipment	....	$ 210	....	$ 320
Delivery equipment	9,280	....	9,280	....
Accumulated depreciation, delivery equipment	....	2,115	....	3,340
Accounts payable	....	245	....	245
Salaries and wages payable	....	....	....	110
Unearned delivery fees	....	450	....	235
Jerry Larr, capital	....	11,205	....	11,205
Jerry Larr, withdrawals	9,600	....	9,600	....
Delivery fees earned	....	21,650	....	21,925
Rent expense, office space	550	....	600	....
Office salaries expense	4,760	....	4,800	....
Telephone expense	185	....	185	....
Office supplies expense	....	....	55	....
Depreciation expense, office equipment	....	....	110	....
Rent expense, garage space	825	....	900	....
Truck drivers' wages	5,720	....	5,790	....
Gas, oil, and repairs	1,160	....	1,160	....
Insurance expense, delivery trucks	....	....	350	....
Depreciation expense, delivery equipment	....	....	1,225	....
Totals	$35,875	$35,875	$37,380	$37,380

Problem 3-5

After all its transactions were recorded at the end of an annual accounting period, the trial balance at the top of the next page was taken from the ledger of Sun Valley Trailer Park.

Required:

1. Open the accounts of the trial balance plus these additional ones: Accounts Receivable; Wages Payable; Property Taxes Payable; Interest Payable; Insurance Expense; Office Supplies Expense; Depreciation Expense, Office Equipment; Depreciation Expense, Buildings and Improvements.
2. Use the following information to prepare and to post adjusting journal entries:
   a. An examination of insurance policies showed $550 of insurance expired.
   b. An office supplies inventory showed $110 of unused supplies on hand.
   c. Estimated depreciation on office equipment, $125; and (d) on the buildings and improvements, $2,450.
   e. Sun Valley Trailer Park follows the practice of crediting the Unearned Rent account for rents paid in advance by tenants, and an examination

SUN VALLEY TRAILER PARK
Trial Balance, December 31, 19—

Cash	$ 3,540	
Prepaid insurance	825	
Office supplies	260	
Office equipment	1,450	
Accumulated depreciation, office equipment		$ 420
Buildings and improvements	72,000	
Accumulated depreciation, buildings and improvements		8,350
Land	85,000	
Accounts payable		185
Unearned rent		480
Mortgage payable		115,000
Judy Tarr, capital		28,360
Judy Tarr, withdrawals	10,500	
Rent earned		34,865
Wages expense	5,120	
Utilities expense	525	
Property taxes expense	2,115	
Interest expense	6,325	
Totals	$187,660	$187,660

        revealed that $360 of the balance of this account had been earned by year-end.

  f. A tenant is a month in arrears on his rent payments, and this $75 of accrued revenue was unrecorded at the time the trial balance was prepared.

  g. The one employee works a five-day week at $20 per day. He was paid last week but has worked three days this week for which he has not been paid.

  h. Three months' property taxes expense, totaling $700, has accrued but is unrecorded.

  i. One month's interest on the mortgage, $575, has accrued but is unrecorded.

3. After posting the adjusting journal entries prepare an adjusted trial balance, an income statement, and a classified balance sheet.

Alternate problems

Problem 3–1A

    The following information for adjustments was available on December 31, the end of an annual accounting period. Prepare an adjusting journal entry for each unit of information:

  a. The Office Supplies account showed the following items:

Office Supplies

Jan. 1	Balance	85.00
Feb. 9	Purchase	140.00
Oct. 4	Purchase	65.00

The year-end office supplies inventory showed $75 of unused supplies on hand.

b. The Prepaid Insurance account showed these items:

Prepaid Insurance

Jan. 1	Balance	140.00	
June 1		252.00	
Aug. 1		180.00	

The January 1 balance represents the unexpired premium on a one-year policy purchased on June 1 of the previous year. The June 1 debit resulted from paying the premium on a one-year policy, and the August 1 debit represents the cost of a three-year policy.

c. The company's three office employees earn $16, $20, and $24 per day, respectively. They are paid each Friday for a five-day workweek that begins on Monday. They were paid last week and have worked Monday, Tuesday, and Wednesday, December 29, 30, and 31, this week.

d. The company owns and occupies a building that was completed and occupied for the first time on March 1 of the current year. Previously the company had rented quarters. The building cost $180,000, has an estimated 40-year useful life, and is not expected to have any salvage value at the end of its life.

e. The company rents portions of the space in its building to two tenants. One tenant agreed beginning on September 1 to rent a small amount of space at $60 per month, and on that date he paid six months' rent in advance. The $360 payment was credited to the Unearned Rent account.

f. The other tenant pays $75 rent per month on the space he occupies. During the months May through November he paid his rent each month on the first day of the month and the amounts paid were credited to Rent Earned. However, he has recently experienced financial difficulties and has not as yet paid his rent for the month of December.

Problem 3–2A

The trial balance at the top of the next page was taken from the ledger of Lagoon Realty at the end of its annual accounting period.

Required:

1. Open the accounts of the trial balance plus these additional ones: Accounts Receivable; Office Salaries Payable; Management Fees Earned; Insurance Expense; Office Supplies Expense; Depreciation Expense, Office Equipment; and Depreciation Expense, Automobile. Enter the trial balance amounts in the accounts.

2. Use the following information to prepare and post adjusting journal entries:
   a. An examination of insurance policies showed $210 of expired insurance.
   b. An office supplies inventory showed $120 of unused supplies on hand.
   c. Depreciation for the year on the office equipment was estimated at $400 and (d) it was estimated at $650 on the automobile.
   e. The company offers property management services and has two clients under contract. It agreed to manage an apartment building for the first client for a $60 monthly fee payable at the end of each quarter. The

LAGOON REALTY
Trial Balance, December 31, 19__

Cash	$ 2,940	
Prepaid insurance	315	
Office supplies	290	
Office equipment	3,250	
Accumulated depreciation, office equipment		$ 920
Automobile	3,780	
Accumulated depreciation, automobile		1,150
Accounts payable		125
Unearned management fees		420
Alice Hall, capital		4,845
Alice Hall, withdrawals	8,400	
Sales commissions earned		19,110
Office salaries expense	5,400	
Advertising expense	530	
Rent expense	1,500	
Telephone expense	165	
Totals	$26,570	$26,570

contract with this client was signed on November 1, and two months' fees have accrued.

f. For the second client it agreed to manage an office building for a $70 monthly fee. The contract with this client was signed on October 15, and at that time the client paid six months' fees in advance, which were credited on receipt to the Unearned Management Fees account.

g. The office secretary is paid weekly, and on December 31 four days' wages at $22.50 per day have accrued.

3. After posting the adjusting entries prepare an adjusted trial balance, an income statement, and a classified balance sheet.

Problem 3–3A

At the end of its annual accounting period Hawaiian Moving and Storage Company prepared the trial balance at the top of the next page.

Required:

1. Open the accounts of the trial balance plus these additional ones: Wages Payable; Insurance Expense; Office Supplies Expense; Depreciation Expence, Office Equipment; Depreciation Expense, Trucks; and Depreciation Expense, Buildings. Enter the trial balance amounts in the accounts.

2. Use this information to prepare and post adjusting journal entries:

   a. An examination of insurance policies showed that $930 of insurance had expired.

   b. An inventory of office supplies showed $40 of unused supplies on hand.

   c. Estimated depreciation on office equipment, $170; *(d)* trucks, $4,200; and *(e)* buildings, $2,800.

   f. The company credits the storage fees of customers who pay in advance to the Unearned Storage Fees account. Of the $730 credited to this account during the year, $380 had been earned by the year-end.

HAWAIIAN MOVING AND STORAGE COMPANY
Trial Balance, December 31, 19—

Cash	$ 1,240	
Accounts receivable	590	
Prepaid insurance	1,280	
Office supplies	220	
Office equipment	1,650	
Accumulated depreciation, office equipment		$ 280
Trucks	14,200	
Accumulated depreciation, trucks		2,540
Buildings	38,000	
Accumulated depreciation, buildings		8,600
Land	7,500	
Accounts payable		580
Unearned storage fees		730
Mortgage payable		17,500
Ted Lee, capital		18,610
Ted Lee, withdrawals	8,400	
Revenue from moving services		47,860
Storage fees earned		3,190
Office salaries expense	5,400	
Truck drivers' wages	18,730	
Gas, oil, and repairs	2,680	
Totals	$99,890	$99,890

    g. Accrued storage fees earned but unrecorded in the accounts and un-collected at the year-end totaled $130.

    h. There were $490 of earned but unpaid truck drivers' wages at the year-end.

3. After posting the adjusting journal entries, prepare an adjusted trial balance, an income statement, and a classified balance sheet.

Problem 3–4A

ALA WAI REALTY
Income Statement for Year Ended December 31, 19—

Revenues:		
Commissions earned		$26,415
Property management fees		1,840
Total revenues		$28,255
Operating expenses:		
Office salaries expense	$8,125	
Office rent expense	1,650	
Advertising expense	855	
Utilities expense	320	
Telephone expense	435	
Gas, oil, and repairs	520	
Total operating expenses		11,905
Net Income		$16,350

88   Fundamental accounting principles

An inexperienced bookkeeper prepared the income statement on the previous page but he forgot to adjust the ledger accounts before its preparation. However the oversight was discovered and the following correct statement was prepared. Analyze the two statements and prepare the adjusting journal entries that were made between preparation of the two statements. Assume that one third of the additional property management fees resulted from recognizing accrued management fees and the other two thirds resulted from previously recorded unearned fees that were earned by the trial balance date.

ALA WAI REALTY

Income Statement for Year Ended December 31, 19__

Revenues:		
Commissions earned...		$26,415
Property management fees..		2,290
Total revenues...		$28,705
Operating expenses:		
Office salaries expense...	$8,170	
Office rent expense..	1,800	
Advertising expense	855	
Utilities expense...	320	
Telephone expense...	435	
Gas, oil, and repairs	520	
Office supplies expense	215	
Insurance expense...	310	
Depreciation expense, office equipment	285	
Depreciation expense, automobile...............................	640	
Property taxes expense	110	
Total operating expenses..		13,660
Net Income		$15,045

Decision problem 3–1, Scott Huff, realtor

Scott Huff sells real estate on a commission basis and manages apartment buildings for clients. He has always kept his accounting records on a cash basis, and at the end of 197B he prepared the following condensed income statement:

SCOTT HUFF, REALTOR

Income Statement for Year Ended December 31, 197B

Revenues..	$41,600
Expenses	22,400
Net Income...	$19,200

In preparing the statement, Scott Huff ignored the following amounts of accrued and deferred items at the ends of 197A and 197B:

	197A	197B
Unearned revenues	$1,780	$1,640
Accrued revenues	1,040	1,230
Prepaid expenses	1,240	870
Accrued expenses	2,410	3,100

Assume that all of Scott Huff's 197A prepaid and unearned items became expenses or were earned during 197B, that all ignored 197A accrued items were either received in cash or were paid during 197B, and prepare a new condensed 197B income statement for Scott Huff. (In other words, prepare an accrual basis income statement for him.)

Decision problem 3–2, We Fixit Shop

On January 1 of this year Fred Gage began a small business he calls We Fixit Shop. He has kept no formal accounting records, but he does file any unpaid invoices for things he has purchased by impaling them on a nail in the wall over his workbench. He has also kept a good cheque stub record of the year's cash receipts and payments, which shows the following:

	Receipts	Payments
Investment	$ 2,000	
Shop equipment		$ 1,500
Repair parts and supplies		2,940
Rent expense		1,300
Insurance premiums		340
Newspaper advertising		250
Utilities		180
Helper's wages		3,400
Fred Gage for personal use		7,200
Revenue from repairs	16,910	
Totals	$18,910	$17,110
Cash balance, December 31, 19__		1,800
	$18,910	$18,910

Mr. Gage wants to know how much his business actually earned during its first year's operations, and he would like for you to prepare an accrual basis income statement and a year-end classified report form balance sheet. You learn that the shop equipment has an estimated 10-year life, after which it will be worthless. There is a $330 unpaid invoice on the nail over Mr. Gage's workbench for supplies and parts that have been received, and an inventory shows a total of $410 of unused supplies on hand. The shop space rents for $100 per month on a five-year lease. The lease contract required payment of the first and last months' rents in advance, which were paid. The insurance premiums paid for two policies taken out on January 2. The first is a one-year policy that cost $70, and the second is a three-year policy that cost $270. There are $50 of accrued wages payable to the helper, and customers owe the shop $390 for services they have received.

Last September 1 Gary Cole purchased Vagabond Village, a mobile home park, and has operated it four months without keeping formal accounting records. However he has deposited all receipts in the bank and has kept an accurate cheque stub record of his payments, an analysis of which shows:

	Receipts	Payments
Investment..	$27,500	
Purchased Vagabond Village:		
Land.. $53,000		
Buildings and improvements.................... 45,000		
Office equipment................................. 1,200		
Total.. $99,200		
Less mortgage assumed.......................... 75,000		
Cash paid..		$24,200
Insurance premiums................................		960
Office supplies purchased.........................		120
Wages paid..		1,330
Utilities paid..		170
Property taxes paid.................................		1,260
Personal withdrawals of cash by owner........		2,400
Mobile home space rentals collected............	8,150	
Totals..	$35,650	$30,440
Cash balance, December 31.......................		5,210
Totals..	$35,650	$35,650

Mr. Cole wants you to prepare an accrual basis income statement for the village for the four-month period ended December 31. You ascertain the following:

The buildings and improvements were estimated to have a 30-year remaining useful life when purchased, and at the end of that time will be wrecked. It is estimated that the sale of salvaged materials will just pay the wrecking costs and the costs of clearing the site. The office equipment is in good condition, and at the time of purchase Mr. Cole estimated he would use it four years and would then trade it in on new equipment of a like kind. He thought $240 a fair estimate for what he would receive for the old equipment when traded in on new equipment at the end of the four-year period.

The $960 payment for insurance was for two policies taken out on September 1. One policy cost $150 and gives protection for one year; the other cost $810 and gives protection for three years. Mr. Cole estimates that one third of the office supplies purchased have been used. He also says that the one employee of the village earns $17.50 per day for a five-day week that ends on Friday. The employee was paid last week, but he has worked this week on Monday, Tuesday, Wednesday, and Thursday, December 28, 29, 30, and 31, for which he has not been paid. The property tax payment was for one year's taxes that were paid on October 1 for the tax year beginning September 1, the day Mr. Cole purchased Vagabond Village.

Included in the $8,150 of mobile home space rentals is $300 received from a tenant for six months' rent in advance beginning on November 1. Also, one tenant has not paid his December rent. The amount due is $50.

The mortgage requires the payment of 6% interest annually on the beginning principal balance and a $3,000 annual payment on the principal.

Prepare an accrual basis income statement for Vagabond Village for the four-month period ending December 31, and prepare a December 31 classified balance sheet.

Analytical and review problems

Problem 3–1 A&R

The Salaries Payable account of James Bay Company Limited appears below:

Salaries Payable			
Entries during 1975	74,560	Bal. Jan. 1, 1975	260
		Entries during 1975	74,420

The company records the salary expense and related liability at the end of each week and pays the employees on the first day of the fifth week.

Required:
Calculate:
1. Salary expense for 1975.
2. How much was paid to employees in 1975 for work done in 1974?
3. How much was paid to employees in 1975 for work done in 1975?
4. How much will be paid to employees in 1976 for work done in 1975?

Problem 3–2 A&R

The Prepaid Insurance account of Hobby Shops is reproduced below:

Prepaid Insurance			
Bal. Jan. 1, 1975	290	Entry Dec. 31, 1975	1,050
Entries during 1975	900		

Required:
Reconstruct the journal entries made by Hobby Shops in 1975.

Problem 3–3 A&R

Ida M. Smart, the accountant for Longview Company, believes that the need for adjusting entries at the end of the accounting period is caused by the lack of anticipation on the part of the accountant. She holds that if all transactions are recorded properly, with the year-end adjustments fully anticipated at the time the transactions occur, the need for year-end adjustments will be completely eliminated. To prove her point, she cites the following journal entries recorded in the books for the current year.

January 1	Insurance expense	120	
	Prepaid insurance	240	
	Cash..		360

To record the payment of a three-year insurance.

	1	Rent expense 1,200	
		Cash...	1,200
		One year's rent paid.	
	1	Depreciation expense 600	
		Accumulated depreciation	600
		One-year depreciation for office equipment costing $6,000 with an estimated useful life of 10 year and no salvage value.	
July	1	Cash... 1,000	
		Commission earned..................................	500
		Commission received in advance.................	500
		Receipt of 12 month's commissions.	
July	1	Office supplies used....................................... 200	
		Office supplies... 200	
		Accounts payable	400
		Purchase of office supplies, half of which will probably be used during the year.	

Required:

1. By anticipating year-end adjustments at the time the transactions are recorded, what problems or difficulties do you think Ms. Smart will most likely encounter at the year-end date?
2. Is it usually true that some adjustments are not susceptible to accurate anticipation? Explain and give examples to support your answer.
3. If you follow Ms. Smart's approach of anticipating adjustments at the time the transactions occur, what entries should you make at the beginning of year two, based on the entries recorded in year one?
4. What is to be gained by Ms. Smarts approach of anticipating adjustments? Explain.

Problem 3–4 A&R

Keith Robertson operates a management consulting firm and uses a cash basis for recording transactions. The trial balance presented below reflects the operations for the first year of business.

KEITH ROBERTSON, MANAGEMENT CONSULTANT
Trial Balance
December 31, 1975

Cash	$ 8,200	
Office equipment	6,000	
Keith Robertson, capital		$ 1,000
Management consulting fees..................................		36,000
Office salaries expense	18,000	
Telephone expense	1,000	
Office expense	3,000	
Office supplies expense	300	
Miscellaneous expense	500	
	$37,000	$37,000

Additional information:

1. Amount of office supplies still on hand at the end of the year was $50.
2. The office equipment was estimated to have a 10-year useful life with no salvage value.
3. Consulting services rendered for which no payment has been received amounted to $6,000.
4. Telephone bill for the month of December, 1975, was paid in January, 1976, $200.
5. Office expenses incurred but not yet paid for, $800.
6. Golden Ltd. paid $1,000 consulting fee for services to be performed in 1976.

Required:

1. Prepare all necessary adjusting entries (omit narratives) to reflect Robertson's operation on an accrual basis of accounting.
2. Prepare a trial balance on the accrual basis of accounting.
3. What is the difference in net income between the cash and the accrual bases of accounting for Robertson's business?
4. Which basis, in your opinion, more realistically reflects the operations of Robertson? Why?
5. What are the similarities and dissimilarities between the adjusting entries to convert a cash basis to an accrual basis and the adjusting entries for an accrual basis?

4

Balance column accounts, the work sheet, and closing the accounts

■ Since they have definite debit and credit sides, accounts like the ones in previous chapters help a beginning student to understand debits and credits. However, when such accounts are used and it becomes necessary to know the balance of an account, the balance must be calculated; and this is at times inconvenient. Consequently, since a student should by now have some understanding of debits and credits, it is time to introduce a more convenient and more commonly used kind of account, the *balance column account.*

Balance column account

■ Illustration 4–1 shows a balance column account. Such an account differs from the accounts in the previous chapters in that its debit and credit columns are placed side by side and a third or Balance column is provided for the account's current balance. In this Balance column the account's new balance is entered each time the account is debited or credited. For example, in Illustration 4–1 the account was debited to record the purchase of office equipment on July 3, and with this entry its balance became $1,000. On July 5 the account was debited again and its new $1,350 balance entered; and on July 9 it was credited for $150 and its balance reduced to $1,200. Obviously a Balance column is a convenience, since at any time it shows at a glance the current balance of the account.

DATE	EXPLANATION	FO-LIO	DEBIT	CREDIT	BALANCE
1975 July 3		1	1 000 00		1 000 00
5		1	350 00		1 350 00
9		1		150 00	1 200 00

Illustration
4–1

When a balance column account like that of Illustration 4–1 is used, the heading of the Balance column does not tell whether the balance is a debit balance as, for example, it would normally be for an asset account or a credit balance as it would normally be for a liability. However, this does not create a problem because an account is always assumed to have its normal kind of balance, unless the contrary is indicated in the account.

The normal balance of an account

Since its column headings do not tell the nature of an account's balance and the balance is always assumed to be the normal kind for that account, unless otherwise indicated, it follows that an accountant must know the normal balance of any account. Fortunately this is not difficult because the balance of an account normally results from recording in it a larger sum of increases than decreases. Consequently, if increases are recorded as debits, the account normally has a debit balance; and if increases are recorded as credits, the account normally has a credit balance. Or, increases are recorded in an account in each of the following classes as shown and its normal balance is:

Type of Account	Increases Are Recorded as–	And the Normal Balance Is–
Asset	Debits	Debit
Contra asset	Credits	Credit
Liability	Credits	Credit
Owner equity:		
Capital	Credits	Credit
Withdrawals	Debits	Debit
Revenue	Credits	Credit
Expense	Debits	Debit

An account with an opposite from normal kind of balance

When an unusual transaction causes an account to have a balance that is opposite from its normal kind of balance, this opposite from normal kind of balance is indicated in the account by entering it in red or by entering it in black and encircling the amount as in the customer account shown in Illustration 4–2.

The account of Illustration 4–2 is an account receivable, and when it has a balance, the balance is normally a debit. However, in this instance the customer made an error and overpaid the account, changing its normal debit balance to a $9 credit balance. Notice how this is shown by encircling the $9 amount. (Individual customer accounts or individual accounts receivable are discussed in more detail beginning in Chapter 6.)

F. M. Pope
1114 First Avenue, Portland, Oregon.   ACCOUNT NO.

DATE	EXPLANATION	FO-LIO	DEBIT	CREDIT	BALANCE
1975 May 4		16	123 00		123 00
14	Overpaid account	17		132 00	(9 00)

Illustration
4–2

An account without a balance

When a posting to a balance column account causes the account to have no balance, some bookkeepers place a –0– in the Balance column on the line of the posting. Other bookkeepers and bookkeeping machines write 0.00 in the Balance column to indicate the account does not have a balance.

Need for a work sheet

■ In the accounting procedures described in the previous chapter, at the end of an accounting period, as soon as all transactions were recorded, recall that (1) adjusting entries were entered in the journal and posted to the accounts and (2) then an adjusted trial balance was prepared and used in making an income statement and balance sheet. Furthermore, for a small business these are satisfactory procedures.

However, if a company has more than a very few accounts and adjustments, errors in adjusting the accounts and in preparing the statements are less apt to be made if an additional step is inserted in the procedures. The additional step is the preparation of a work sheet. A work sheet is a tool of the accountant upon which he (1) achieves the effect of adjusting the accounts before entering the adjustments in the accounts, (2) sorts the adjusted account balances into columns according to whether they are used in preparing the income statement or balance sheet, and (3) calculates and proves the mathematical accuracy of the net income.

A work sheet is prepared solely for the accountant's use. It is not given to the owner or manager of the business for which it is prepared but is retained by the accountant. Normally it is prepared with a pencil, which makes changes and corrections easy as its preparation progresses; and after it is completed, the accountant uses it in preparing the income statement and balance sheet and in making adjusting and closing entries. (Closing entries are discussed later in this chapter.)

Preparing a work sheet ■ Owen Real Estate Agency of the previous chapters does not have sufficient accounts or adjustments to warrant use of a work sheet. However, since its transactions and adjustments are familiar, they may be used to illustrate the preparation of a work sheet.

During July, Owen Real Estate Agency completed a number of transactions; and on July 31, after these transactions were recorded but **before any adjusting entries were prepared and posted,** a trial balance of its ledger appeared as in Illustration 4–3.

Owen Real Estate Agency
Trial Balance, July 31, 19—

Cash	$1,095	
Prepaid rent	300	
Office supplies	60	
Automobile	3,000	
Office equipment	1,200	
Accounts payable		$ 235
Unearned management fees		75
Larry Owen, capital		5,000
Larry Owen, withdrawals	200	
Commissions earned		850
Office salaries expense	200	
Telephone expense	20	
Gas, oil, and repairs	25	
Advertising expense	60	
Totals	$6,160	$6,160

Illustration 4–3

Notice that the illustrated trial balance is an **unadjusted trial balance.** The accounts have not been adjusted for expired rent, supplies consumed, depreciation, et cetera. Nevertheless, this unadjusted trial balance is the starting point in preparing a work sheet, and it is copied in the first two money columns of the work sheet form.

The work sheet illustrated ■ Note that the work sheet shown in Illustration 4–4 has five pairs of money columns and that the first pair is labeled "Trial Balance." In this first pair of columns is copied the unadjusted trial balance of Owen Real Estate Agency. Often when a work sheet is prepared, the trial balance is prepared for the first time in its first two money columns.

The second pair of work sheet columns is labeled "Adjustments," and the adjustments are entered in these columns. In the work sheet

Owen Real Estate Agency
Work Sheet for Month Ended July 31, 19--

ACCOUNT TITLES	TRIAL BALANCE Dr.	TRIAL BALANCE Cr.	ADJUSTMENTS Dr.	ADJUSTMENTS Cr.	ADJUSTED TRIAL BALANCE Dr.	ADJUSTED TRIAL BALANCE Cr.	INCOME STATEMENT Dr.	INCOME STATEMENT Cr.	BALANCE SHEET Dr.	BALANCE SHEET Cr.
Cash	1,085 00				1,085 00				1,085 00	
Prepaid rent	300 00			(a) 100 00	200 00				200 00	
Office supplies	60 00			(b) 15 00	45 00				45 00	
Automobile	3,000 00				3,000 00				3,000 00	
Office equipment	1,200 00				1,200 00				1,200 00	
Accounts payable		235 00				235 00				235 00
Unearned management fees		75 00	(f) 25 00			50 00				50 00
Gary Owen, capital		5,000 00				5,000 00				5,000 00
Gary Owen, withdrawals	200 00				200 00				200 00	
Commissions earned		850 00				850 00		850 00		
Office salaries expense	200 00		(e) 30 00		230 00		230 00			
Telephone expense	20 00				20 00		20 00			
Gas, oil and repairs	25 00				25 00		25 00			
Advertising expense	60 00				60 00		60 00			
	6,160 00	6,160 00								
Rent expense			(a) 100 00		100 00		100 00			
Office supplies expense			(b) 15 00		15 00		15 00			
Dep. expense, automobile			(c) 35 00		35 00		35 00			
Accum. depr., automobile				(c) 35 00		35 00				35 00
Dep. expense, office equip.			(d) 10 00		10 00		10 00			
Accum. depr., office equip.				(d) 10 00		10 00				10 00
Salaries payable				(e) 30 00		30 00				30 00
Management fees earned				(f) 45 00		45 00		45 00		
Accounts receivable			(f) 20 00		20 00				20 00	
			235 00	235 00	6,255 00	6,255 00	495 00	895 00	5,760 00	5,360 00
Net Income							400 00			400 00
							895 00	895 00	5,760 00	5,760 00

Illustration
4-4

shown in Illustration 4–4 the adjustments are, with one exception, the same as those for which adjusting journal entries were prepared and posted in the previous chapter, prior to the construction of the statements. The one exception is the last one, (*f*), in which the two adjustments affecting the Management Fees Earned account are combined into one compound adjustment, because both result in credits to the same account.

Note that the adjustments on the illustrated work sheet are keyed together with letters. When a work sheet is prepared, after it and the accounting statements are completed, the adjusting entries still have to be entered in the journal and posted to the ledger. At that time the key letters help identify each adjustment's related debits and credits. Explanations of the adjustments on the illustrated work sheet are:

Adjustment (a): To adjust for the rent expired.
Adjustment (b): To adjust for the office supplies consumed.
Adjustment (c): To adjust for depreciation of the automobile.
Adjustment (d): To adjust for depreciation of the office equipment.
Adjustment (e): To adjust for the accrued secretary's salary.
Adjustment (f): To adjust for the unearned and accrued revenue.

Each adjustment on the Owen Real Estate Agency work sheet required that one or two additional account names be written in below the original trial balance. These accounts did not have balances when the trial balance was prepared and, consequently, were not listed in the trial balance. Often, when a work sheet is prepared, the effects of the adjustments are anticipated; and any additional accounts required are provided without amounts in the body of the trial balance.

When a work sheet is prepared, after the adjustments are entered in the Adjustments columns, the columns are totaled to prove the equality of the adjustments.

The third set of work sheet columns is labeled "Adjusted Trial Balance." In preparing a work sheet each amount in the Trial Balance columns is combined with its adjustment in the Adjustments columns if there is an adjustment and is entered in the Adjusted Trial Balance columns. For example, in Illustration 4–4 the Prepaid Rent account has a $300 debit balance in the Trial Balance columns. This $300 debit is combined with the $100 credit in the Adjustments columns to give the Prepaid Rent account a $200 debit balance in the Adjusted Trial Balance columns. Rent Expense has no balance in the Trial Balance columns, but it has a $100 debit in the Adjustment columns. Therefore, no balance combined with a $100 debit gives Rent Expense a $100 debit in the Adjusted Trial Balance columns. Cash, Automobile, and several other accounts have trial balance amounts but no adjustments. As a result, their trial balance amounts are carried unchanged into the Adjusted Trial Balance columns. Notice that the result of combining the amounts in the Trial Balance columns with the amounts in the Adjustments columns is an adjusted trial balance in the Adjusted Trial Balance columns.

After the amounts in the Trial Balance columns are combined with the amounts in the Adjustments columns and carried to the Adjusted Trial Balance columns, the Adjusted Trial Balance columns are added to prove their equality. Then, after equality is proved, the amounts in these columns are sorted to the proper Balance Sheet or Income Statement columns according to the statement on which they will appear. This is an easy task that requires only two decisions: (1) is the item to be sorted a debit or a credit and (2) on which statement does it appear. As to the first decision, an adjusted trial balance debit amount must be sorted to either the Income Statement debit column or the Balance Sheet debit column and a credit amount must go into either the Income Statement credit or Balance Sheet credit column. In other words, debits remain debits and credits remain credits in the sorting process. As to the second decision, it is only necessary in the sorting process to remember that revenues and expenses appear on the income statement and assets, liabilities, and owner equity items go on the balance sheet.

After the amounts are sorted to the proper columns, the columns are totaled; and at this point, the difference between the debit and credit totals of the Income Statement columns is the net income or loss. The difference is the net income or loss because revenues are entered in the credit column and expenses in the debit column. If the credit column total exceeds the debit column total, the difference is a net income; and if the debit column total exceeds the credit column total, the difference is a net loss. In the illustrated work sheet, the credit column total exceeds the debit column total, and the result is a $400 net income.

On the Owen Real Estate Agency's work sheet, after the net income is determined in the Income Statement columns, it is added to the total of the Balance Sheet credit column. The reason for this is that with the exception of the balance of the Capital account, the amounts appearing in the Balance Sheet columns are "end-of-the-period" amounts. Therefore, it is necessary to add the net income to the Balance Sheet credit column total to make the Balance Sheet columns equal. Adding the income to this column has the effect of adding it to the Capital account.

Had there been a loss, it would have been necessary to add the loss to the debit column. This is because losses decrease owner equity, and adding the loss to the debit column has the effect of subtracting it from the Capital account.

Balancing the Balance Sheet columns by adding the net income or loss is a proof of the accuracy with which the work sheet has been prepared. When the income or loss is added in the Balance Sheet columns and the addition makes these columns equal, it is assumed that no errors were made in preparing the work sheet. However, if the addition does not make the columns equal, it is proof that an error or errors were made. The error or errors may have been either mathematical or an amount may have been sorted to a wrong column.

Although balancing the Balance Sheet columns with the net income or loss is a proof of the accuracy with which a work sheet was prepared, it is not an absolute proof. These columns will balance even when errors have been made if the errors are of a certain type. For example, an expense carried into the Balance Sheet debit column or an asset carried into the debit column of the income statement section will cause both of these columns to have incorrect totals. Likewise, the net income will be incorrect. However, when such an error is made, the Balance Sheet columns will balance, but with the incorrect amount of income. Therefore, when a work sheet is prepared, care must be exercised in sorting the adjusted trial balance amounts into the correct Income Statement or Balance Sheet columns.

Work sheet and the financial statements

■ As previously stated, the work sheet is a tool of the accountant and is not for management's use or publication. However, as soon as it is completed, the accountant uses it in preparing the income statement and balance sheet that are given to management. To do this he rearranges the items in the work sheet's Income Statement columns into a formal income statement and he rearranges the items in the Balance Sheet columns into a formal balance sheet.

Work sheet and adjusting entries

■ Entering the adjustments in the Adjustments columns of a work sheet does not get these adjustments into the ledger accounts. Consequently, after the work sheet and statements are completed, adjusting entries like the ones described in the previous chapter must still be entered in the General Journal and posted. The work sheet makes this easy, however, because its Adjustments columns provide the information for these entries, and all that is needed is an entry for each adjustment appearing in the columns.

As for the adjusting entries for the work sheet of Illustration 4–4, they are the same as the entries given in the previous chapter, with the exception of the entry for adjustment (f). Here a compound entry having a $25 debit to Unearned Management Fees, a $20 debit to Accounts Receivable, and a $45 credit to Management Fees Earned is used.

Work sheet and closing entries

■ In addition to adjusting entries, the work sheet is also an information source for *closing entries,* which are entries made to clear and close the revenue and expense accounts. These accounts are cleared in the sense that their balances are transferred to another account, and they are closed in the sense that they have zero balances after closing entries are posted.

Why closing entries are made

■ The revenue and expense accounts are cleared and closed at the end of each accounting period by transferring their balances to a summary account, called Income Summary, where the balances are summarized. Their summarized amount, which is the net income or loss for the period, is then transferred on to the owner's Capital account. These transfers are necessary because:

a. Revenues actually increase owner equity and expenses decrease it.
b. However, throughout an accounting period these increases and decreases are recorded in revenue and expense accounts rather than in the owner's Capital account.
c. As a result, closing entries are necessary at the end of each accounting period to transfer the net effect of these increases and decreases out of the revenue and expense accounts and on to the owner's Capital account.

In addition, closing entries also cause the revenue and expense accounts to begin each new accounting period with zero balances. This too is necessary because:

a. An income statement reports the revenues and expenses incurred during *one* accounting period and is prepared from information recorded in the revenue and expense accounts.
b. Consequently, these accounts must begin each new accounting period with zero balances if their end-of-the-period balances are to reflect just *one* period's revenues and expenses.

Closing entries illustrated

■ At the end of July, after its work sheet and statements were prepared and its adjusting entries posted but before its accounts were cleared and closed, the owner equity accounts of Owen Real Estate Agency had balances as shown in Illustration 4–5 on the next page. (An account's Balance column heading as a rule does not tell the nature of an account's balance. However, in Illustration 4–5 and in the illustrations immediately following, the nature of each account's balance is shown by means of a colour overprint. The authors feel the student needs this extra help until such time as he becomes more familiar with the normal balances of different accounts.)

Observe in Illustration 4–5 that Owen's Capital account shows only its $5,000 July 1 balance. This is not the amount of Owen's equity on July 31; closing entries are required to make this account show the July 31 equity.

Note also the third account in Illustration 4–5, the Income Summary account. This account is used only at the end of the accounting period in summarizing and clearing the revenue and expense accounts.

Closing revenue accounts

Before closing entries are posted, revenue accounts have credit balances; consequently, to clear and close a revenue account an entry debiting the account and crediting Income Summary is required. Owen

Larry Owen, Capital

Date		Explanation	Debit	Credit	Balance
July	1			5,000	5,000

Larry Owen, Withdrawals

Date		Explanation	Debit	Credit	Balance
July	26		200		200

Income Summary

Date	Explanation	Debit	Credit	Balance

Commissions Earned

Date		Explanation	Debit	Credit	Balance
July	12			850	850

Management Fees Earned

Date		Explanation	Debit	Credit	Balance
July	31			45	45

Office Salaries Expense

Date		Explanation	Debit	Credit	Balance
July	12		100		100
	26		100		200
	31		30		230

Telephone Expense

Date		Explanation	Debit	Credit	Balance
July	31		20		20

Gas, Oil, and Repairs

Date		Explanation	Debit	Credit	Balance
July	31		25		25

Advertising Expense

Date		Explanation	Debit	Credit	Balance
July	31		60		60

Rent Expense

Date		Explanation	Debit	Credit	Balance
July	31		100		100

Office Supplies Expense

Date		Explanation	Debit	Credit	Balance
July	31		15		15

Depreciation Expense, Automobile

Date		Explanation	Debit	Credit	Balance
July	31		35		35

Depreciation Expense, Office Equipment

Date		Explanation	Debit	Credit	Balance
July	31		10		10

Illustration
4–5

Real Estate Agency has two revenue accounts, and the compound entry to clear and close them is:

July	31	Commissions Earned.....................................	850.00	
		Management Fees Earned.............................	45.00	
		Income Summary		895.00
		To clear and close the revenue accounts		

Posting the entry has the effect shown in the accounts of Illustration 4–6.

Note that the entry (1) clears the revenue accounts of their balances, transferring the balances in total to the credit side of the In-

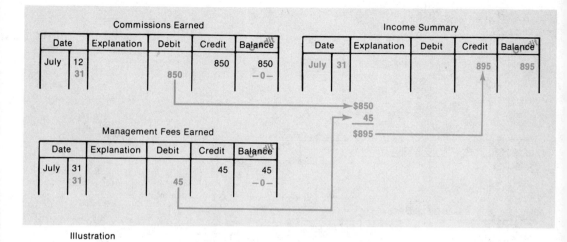

Illustration
4–6

come Summary account, and (2) it causes the revenue accounts to begin the new accounting period with zero balances.

Closing expense accounts

Before closing entries are posted, expense accounts have debit balances; consequently, to clear and close a concern's expense accounts a compound entry debiting the Income Summary account and crediting each individual expense account is required. Owen Real Estate Agency has eight expense accounts, and the compound entry to clear and close them is:

July	31	Income Summary...	495.00	
		Office Salaries Expense		230.00
		Telephone Expense.................................		20.00
		Gas, Oil, and Repairs................................		25.00
		Advertising Expense................................		60.00
		Rent Expense		100.00
		Office Supplies Expense		15.00
		Depreciation Expense, Automobile.............		35.00
		Depreciation Expense, Office Equipment		10.00
		To clear and close the expense accounts.		

Posting this entry has the effect shown in Illustration 4–7 on the next page. Note again that the effect is a dual one: (1) it clears the expense accounts of their balances by transferring balances in a total to the debit side of the Income Summary account, and (2) it causes the expense accounts to begin the new period with zero balances.

Office Salaries Expense

Date		Explanation	Debit	Credit	Balance
July	12		100		100
	26		100		200
	31		30		230
	31			230	-0-

Telephone Expense

Date		Explanation	Debit	Credit	Balance
July	31		20		20
	31			20	-0-

Gas, Oil, and Repairs

Date		Explanation	Debit	Credit	Balance
July	31		25		25
	31			25	-0-

Advertising Expense

Date		Explanation	Debit	Credit	Balance
July	31		60		60
	31			60	-0-

Rent Expense

Date		Explanation	Debit	Credit	Balance
July	31		100		100
	31			100	-0-

Office Supplies Expense

Date		Explanation	Debit	Credit	Balance
July	31		15		15
	31			15	-0-

Depreciation Expense, Automobile

Date		Explanation	Debit	Credit	Balance
July	31		35		35
	31			35	-0-

Depreciation Expense, Office Equipment

Date		Explanation	Debit	Credit	Balance
July	31		10		10
	31			10	-0-

Income Summary

Date		Explanation	Debit	Credit	Balance
July	31			895	895
	31		495		400

$230
20
25
60
100
15
35
10
$495

Illustration
4-7

Closing the Income Summary account

After a concern's revenue and expense accounts are cleared and their balances transferred to the Income Summary account, the balance of the Income Summary account is equal to the net income or loss. When revenues exceed expenses, there is a net income and the Income Summary account has a credit balance. On the other hand, when expenses exceed revenues, there is a loss and the account has a debit balance. But, regardless of the nature of its balance, the Income Summary account is cleared and its balance, the amount of the net income or loss, is transferred to the Capital account.

Owen Real Estate Agency earned $400 during July; consequently, after its revenue and expense accounts are cleared, its Income Summary account has a $400 credit balance, which is transferred to the Larry Owen, Capital account with an entry like this:

July	31	Income Summary...	400.00	
		Larry Owen, Capital..................................		400.00
		To clear and close the Income Summary account.		

Posting this entry has the following effect on the accounts:

	Income Summary					Larry Owen, Capital		
Date	Debit	Credit	Balance		Date	Debit	Credit	Balance
July 31		895	895		July 1		5,000	5,000
31	495		400		31		400	5,400
31	400		-0-					

Observe that the entry clears the Income Summary account, transferring the balance of the account, the amount of the net income in this case, to the Capital account.

Closing the Withdrawals account

At the end of an accounting period the debit balance of the Withdrawals account shows the amount the owner's equity was reduced during the period by withdrawals of cash and other assets for personal use, and this debit balance is transferred to the Capital account with an entry like this:

July	31	Larry Owen, Capital..	200.00	
		Larry Owen, Withdrawals		200.00
		To close the Withdrawals account.		

Posting the entry has this effect on the accounts:

Larry Owen, Withdrawals					Larry Owen, Capital			
Date	Debit	Credit	Balance		Date	Debit	Credit	Balance
July 26	200		200		July 1		5,000	5,000
31		200	-0-		31		400	5,400
					31	200		5,200

After the entry clearing and closing the Withdrawals account is posted, observe that the two reasons for making closing entries are accomplished: (1) all revenue and expense accounts have zero balances and (2) the net effect of the period's revenue, expense, and withdrawal transactions on the owner's equity is shown in his Capital account.

Sources of closing entry information ■ After adjusting entries have been posted, information for the closing entries may be taken from the individual revenue and expense accounts; however, the work sheet provides this information in a more convenient form. For example, if the Owen Real Estate Agency work sheet on page 99 is examined, it will be seen that every account having a balance extended into the Income Statement debit column has a debit balance in the ledger and must be credited in closing. Now compare the amounts in this column with the compound closing entry on page 105 and observe how the column amounts and their account titles are a source of information for the entry. Observe also that if the work sheet is used as an information source for the entry, it is not even necessary to add the entry's individual credit amounts in order to learn the amount of the debit — the debit amount can be taken from the work sheet column total.

In addition to the foregoing, observe also that the work sheet's Income Statement credit column is a convenient information source for the compound entry that clears and closes the revenue accounts.

The accounts after closing ■ At this stage, after both adjusting and closing entries have been posted, the Owen Real Estate Agency accounts appear as in Illustration 4–8 on this and the next several pages. Observe in the illustration that the asset, liability, and the owner's Capital accounts show their end-of-the-period balances. Observe also that the revenue and expense accounts have zero balances and are ready for recording the new accounting period's revenues and expenses.

Cash ACCOUNT NO. 1

DATE	EXPLANATION	FO-LIO	DEBIT	CREDIT	BALANCE
1975 July 1		1	5000 00		5000 00
1		1		300 00	4700 00
3		1		3000 00	1700 00
3		1		1000 00	700 00
9		1	100 00		800 00
11		1	50 00		850 00
11		1		175 00	675 00
12		2	850 00		1525 00
12		2		100 00	1425 00
16		2	75 00		1500 00
26		2		100 00	1400 00
26		2		200 00	1200 00
31		2		20 00	1180 00
31		2		25 00	1155 00
31		2		60 00	1095 00

Accounts Receivable ACCOUNT NO. 2

DATE	EXPLANATION	FO-LIO	DEBIT	CREDIT	BALANCE
1975 July 9		1	50 00		50 00
11		1		50 00	—0—
31		3	20 00		20 00

Prepaid Rent ACCOUNT NO. 3

DATE	EXPLANATION	FO-LIO	DEBIT	CREDIT	BALANCE
1975 July 1		1	300 00		300 00
31		3		100 00	200 00

Office Supplies ACCOUNT NO. 4

DATE	EXPLANATION	FO-LIO	DEBIT	CREDIT	BALANCE
1975 July 5		1	60 00		60 00
31		3		15 00	45 00

Illustration
4–8

Automobile ACCOUNT NO. 5

DATE	EXPLANATION	FO-LIO	DEBIT	CREDIT	BALANCE
1975 July 3		1	3 000 00		3 000 00

Accumulated Depreciation, Automobile ACCOUNT NO. 6

DATE	EXPLANATION	FO-LIO	DEBIT	CREDIT	BALANCE
1975 July 31		3		35 00	35 00

Office Equipment ACCOUNT NO. 7

DATE	EXPLANATION	FO-LIO	DEBIT	CREDIT	BALANCE
1975 July 3		1	1 000 00		1 000 00
5		1	350 00		1 350 00
9		1		150 00	1 200 00

Accumulated Depreciation – Office Equipment ACCOUNT NO. 8

DATE	EXPLANATION	FO-LIO	DEBIT	CREDIT	BALANCE
1975 July 31		3		10 00	10 00

Accounts Payable ACCOUNT NO. 9

DATE	EXPLANATION	FO-LIO	DEBIT	CREDIT	BALANCE
1975 July 5		1		410 00	410 00
11		1	175 00		235 00

Salaries Payable ACCOUNT NO. 10

DATE	EXPLANATION	FO-LIO	DEBIT	CREDIT	BALANCE
1975 July 31		3		30 00	30 00

Illustration
4–8
Continued

110 Fundamental accounting principles

Unearned Management Fees　　ACCOUNT NO. 11

DATE	EXPLANATION	FO-LIO	DEBIT	CREDIT	BALANCE
1975 July 16		2		75 00	75 00
31		3	25 00		50 00

Larry Owen, Capital　　ACCOUNT NO. 12

DATE	EXPLANATION	FO-LIO	DEBIT	CREDIT	BALANCE
1975 July 1		1		5000 00	5000 00
31		3		400 00	5400 00
31		3	200 00		5200 00

Larry Owen, Withdrawals　　ACCOUNT NO. 13

DATE	EXPLANATION	FO-LIO	DEBIT	CREDIT	BALANCE
1975 July 26		2	200 00		200 00
31		3		200 00	—0—

Income Summary　　ACCOUNT NO. 14

DATE	EXPLANATION	FO-LIO	DEBIT	CREDIT	BALANCE
1975 July 31		3		895 00	895 00
31		3	495 00		400 00
31		3	400 00		—0—

Commissions Earned　　ACCOUNT NO. 15

DATE	EXPLANATION	FO-LIO	DEBIT	CREDIT	BALANCE
1975 July 12		2		850 00	850 00
31		3	850 00		—0—

Management Fees Earned　　ACCOUNT NO. 16

DATE	EXPLANATION	FO-LIO	DEBIT	CREDIT	BALANCE
1975 July 31		3		45 00	45 00
31		3	45 00		—0—

Illustration
4–8
Continued

Office Salaries Expense ACCOUNT NO. 17

DATE	EXPLANATION	FO-LIO	DEBIT	CREDIT	BALANCE
1975 July 12		2	100 00		100 00
26		2	100 00		200 00
31		3	30 00		230 00
31		3		230 00	-0-

Telephone Expense ACCOUNT NO. 18

DATE	EXPLANATION	FO-LIO	DEBIT	CREDIT	BALANCE
1975 July 31		2	20 00		20 00
31		3		20 00	-0-

Gas, Oil, and Repairs ACCOUNT NO. 19

DATE	EXPLANATION	FO-LIO	DEBIT	CREDIT	BALANCE
1975 July 31		2	25 00		25 00
31		3		25 00	-0-

Advertising Expense ACCOUNT NO. 20

DATE	EXPLANATION	FO-LIO	DEBIT	CREDIT	BALANCE
1975 July 31		2	60 00		60 00
31		3		60 00	-0-

Rent Expense ACCOUNT NO. 21

DATE	EXPLANATION	FO-LIO	DEBIT	CREDIT	BALANCE
1975 July 31		3	100 00		100 00
31		3		100 00	-0-

Office Supplies Expense ACCOUNT NO. 22

DATE	EXPLANATION	FO-LIO	DEBIT	CREDIT	BALANCE
1975 July 31		3	15 00		15 00
31		3		15 00	-0-

Illustration
4–8
Continued

	Depreciation Expense, Automobile		ACCOUNT NO.	23		
DATE	EXPLANATION	FO-LIO	DEBIT	CREDIT	BALANCE	
1975 July 31		3	3 5 00		3 5 00	
31		3		3 5 00	—0—	

	Depreciation Expense, Office Equipment		ACCOUNT NO.	24		
DATE	EXPLANATION	FO-LIO	DEBIT	CREDIT	BALANCE	
1975 July 31		3	1 0 00		1 0 00	
31		3		1 0 00	—0—	

Illustration
4–8
Concluded

The post-closing trial balance

■ It is easy to make errors in adjusting and closing the accounts. Consequently, after all adjusting and closing entries are posted, a new trial balance is prepared to retest the equality of the accounts. This new, after-closing trial balance is called a *post-closing trial balance,* and for Owen Real Estate Agency appears as in Illustration 4–9.

Owen Real Estate Agency
Post-Closing Trial Balance, July 31, 19—

Cash	$1,095	
Accounts receivable	20	
Prepaid rent	200	
Office supplies	45	
Automobile	3,000	
Accumulated depreciation, automobile		$ 35
Office equipment	1,200	
Accumulated depreciation, office equipment		10
Accounts payable		235
Salaries payable		30
Unearned management fees		50
Larry Owen, capital		5,200
Totals	$5,560	$5,560

Illustration
4–9

Compare Illustration 4–9 with the accounts having balances in Illustration 4–8. Note that only asset, liability, and the owner's Capital accounts have balances in Illustration 4–8, and that these are the only accounts that appear on the post-closing trial balance of Illustration 4–9. The revenue and expense accounts have been cleared and have zero balances at this point.

■ **Temporary proprietorship accounts**

Revenue and expense accounts plus the Income Summary and Withdrawals accounts are called *temporary proprietorship accounts,* because in a sense the items recorded in these accounts are only temporarily recorded therein. To appreciate this, recall that all revenue, expense, and withdrawal transactions increase or decrease owner equity. However, the owner's Capital account is not debited and credited in recording such transactions. Rather, the debit and credit effects of these transactions are first accumulated in the revenue, expense, and withdrawals accounts, after which their summarized effect is transferred to the owner's Capital account. Consequently, the items recorded in these accounts are in a sense only temporarily recorded therein, because through closing entries their debit and credit effects are transferred out and on to the owner's Capital account at the end of each accounting period.

Real and nominal accounts

Balance sheet accounts are commonly called *real accounts,* presumably because the items recorded in these accounts exist in objective form. Likewise, income statement accounts are called *nominal accounts* because the items recorded in these accounts exist in name only.

Working papers

As an aid in their work, accountants prepare numerous memoranda, analyses, notes, and informal papers that serve as a basis for the more formal reports given to management or to their clients. These analyses, notes, and memoranda are called "working papers" and are invaluable tools of the accountant. The work sheet of this chapter is a so-called working paper. Others are discussed later in this text.

■ The life of a business is divided into accounting periods; and each period is a recurring accounting cycle, beginning with transactions recorded in a journal and ending with a post-closing trial balance. All steps in the cycle have now been discussed, and a knowledge of accounting requires that each step be understood and its relation to the others seen. The steps in the order of their occurrence are:

1. *Journalizing* .... Analyzing and recording transactions in a journal.
2. *Posting* .... Copying the debits and credits of journal entries into the ledger accounts.
3. *Preparing a trial balance* ...... Summarizing the ledger accounts and testing the recording accuracy.

4. *Constructing a work sheet* .... Gaining the effects of the adjustments before entering the adjustments in the accounts. Then sorting the account balances into balance sheet and income statement accounts and finally determining and proving the income or loss.

5. *Preparing the statements* .... Rearranging the work sheet information into a balance sheet and an income statement.

6. *Adjusting the ledger accounts* .... Preparing adjusting journal entries from information in the Adjustments columns of the work sheet and posting the entries in order to bring the account balances up to date.

7. *Closing the temporary proprietorship accounts* .... Preparing and posting entries to close the temporary proprietorship accounts and transfer the net income or loss to the Capital account.

8. *Preparing a post-closing trial balance* .... Proving the accuracy of the adjusting and closing procedure.

Accounting periods; the natural business year

■ In order to illustrate the entire accounting cycle, textbooks commonly have problems and illustrations in which a business operates with accounting periods one month in length, and the business is assumed to close its accounts and begin a new cycle of operations each month. In actual practice, however, few business concerns close their accounts each month; most operate with annual accounting periods and close their accounts once each year.

Any accounting period of 12 consecutive months is known as a *fiscal year*. A fiscal year or annual accounting period may coincide with the calendar year or it may follow the *natural business year*. The natural business year of a company begins and ends when the company's business activity is at its lowest point. For example, in the automobile sales business the natural business year begins October 1, just before the new models are brought out, and ends the following September 30. When accounting periods follow the natural business year, the books are closed when inventories are at their lowest point and business activity is at its lowest ebb.

1. A balance column account is more convenient than the kind of account described in earlier chapters. Why?
2. A work sheet is a tool of the accountant upon which he accomplishes three tasks. What are these tasks?
3. Is it possible to complete the statements and adjust and close the accounts without preparing a work sheet? What is gained by preparing a work sheet?
4. At what stage in the accounting process is a work sheet prepared?
5. From where are the amounts that are entered in the Trial Balance columns of a work sheet obtained?
6. Why are the adjustments in the Adjustments columns of a work sheet keyed together with letters?
7. What is the result of combining the amounts in the Trial Balance columns with the amounts in the Adjustments columns of a work sheet?
8. Why must care be exercised in sorting the items in the Adjusted Trial Balance columns to the proper Income Statement of Balance Sheet columns?
9. In extending the items in the Adjusted Trial Balance columns of a work sheet, what would be the result of extending: (a) an expense into the Balance Sheet debit column; (b) a liability into the Income Statement credit column; and (c) a revenue into the Balance Sheet debit column? Would each of these errors be automatically detected on the work sheet? Which would be automatically detected? Why?
10. Why are revenue and expense accounts called "temporary proprietorship accounts"?
11. What two purposes are accomplished by recording closing entries?
12. What accounts are affected by closing entries? What accounts are not affected?
13. Explain the difference between adjusting and closing entries.
14. What is the purpose of the Income Summary account?
15. Why is a post-closing trial balance prepared?

Class exercises

Exercise 4–1

A portion of the accounts of a small business follow. (a) Prepare the adjusting journal entries that have been posted to these accounts. (b) Prepare the journal entries needed to close the accounts. Use December 31 as the date.

Supplies		Accumulated Depreciation, Equipment	
140	180		810
90			415

Prepaid Insurance		Salaries Payable	
225	175		40
30			

Tim Gage, Withdrawals		Supplies Expense	
7,200		180	

Revenue from Services		Insurance Expense	
	14,200	175	

Salaries Expense		Depreciation Expense, Equipment	
5,450		415	
40			

Exercises 4–2

Following are the items and item amounts from a work sheet's Adjustments columns. From the information prepare adjusting journal entries. Use December 31 as the date.

	Adjustments			
	Debit		Credit	
Office supplies...		(a)	235
Prepaid insurance..		(b)	380
Accumulated depreciation, office equipment		(c)	265
Accumulated depreciation, delivery equipment.........		(d)	3,145
Office salaries expense.......................................	(e)	65	
Truck drivers' wages	(e)	210	
Office supplies expense	(a)	235	
Insurance expense, office equipment.....................	(b)	25	
Insurance expense, delivery equipment..................	(b)	355	
Depreciation expense, office equipment	(c)	265	
Depreciation expense, delivery equipment..............	(d)	3,145	
Salaries and wages payable.................................		(e)	275
Totals	4,300		4,300

Exercise 4–3

	Income Statement	
	Debit	Credit
Revenue from services		15,145
Wages expense	4,840	
Rent expense..	900	
Advertising expense..	265	
Insurance expense..	185	
Repair supplies expense	1,115	
Depreciation expense, repair equipment..........................	725	
	8,030	15,145
Net Income...	7,115	
	15,145	15,145

The foregoing items appeared in the Income Statement columns of a work sheet. Under the assumption the owner of the business for which the work sheet was prepared, Dale Evans, had withdrawn $6,000 from the business during the accounting period, prepare journal entries to close the revenue, expense, Income Summary, and withdrawals accounts of the business. Use December 31 as the date.

Exercise 4–4

Following is a list of trial balance accounts and their balances. All are normal balances. To save your time, the balances are in one- and two-digit numbers; however, to increase your skill in sorting adjusted trial balance amounts to the proper work sheet columns, the accounts are listed in alphabetical order.

TRIAL BALANCE ACCOUNTS AND BALANCES

Accounts payable	$2	Rent expense	$ 2
Accounts receivable	3	Revenue from repairs	18
Accumulated depreciation, shop		Robert Ross, capital	11
equipment	2	Robert Ross, withdrawals	2
Cash	5	Shop equipment	7
Notes payable	1	Shop supplies	4
Prepaid insurance	3	Wages expense	8

Required:
1. Prepare a work sheet form on ordinary notebook paper and enter the trial balance accounts and amounts on the work sheet in their alphabetical order.
2. Complete the work sheet using the following information:
   a. Estimated depreciation of shop equipment, $1.
   b. Expired insurance, $1.
   c. Unused shop supplies per inventory, $1.
   d. Earned but unpaid wages, $2.

Problems **Problem 4–1**

The trial balance of the ledger of Quick Repair Shop at the end of its annual accounting period carried the amounts shown at the top of the next page.

Required:
1. Enter the trial balance amounts in the Trial Balance columns of a work sheet and complete the work sheet using the following information:
   a. Expired insurance, $165.
   b. A repair supplies inventory showed $380 of unused supplies on hand.
   c. Estimated depreciation on repair equipment, $650.
   d. Wages earned by the one employee but unpaid on the trial balance date, $25.
2. From the work sheet prepare an income statement and balance sheet.

QUICK REPAIR SHOP
Trial Balance, December 31, 19—

Cash	$ 1,125	
Prepaid insurance	215	
Repair supplies	1,550	
Repair equipment	4,220	
Accumulated depreciation, repair equipment		$ 1,120
Accounts payable		250
Perry Winkle, capital		3,425
Perry Winkle, withdrawals	5,200	
Revenue from repairs		13,475
Wages expense	4,775	
Rent expense	960	
Advertising expense	225	
Totals	$18,270	$18,270

3. From the work sheet prepare adjusting journal entries and compound closing entries.

Problem 4-2

On October 1 of the current year Ted Nash opened Red Boot Repair Shop, and during the month he completed these transactions:

Oct. 1 Transferred $750 from a personal savings account to a current account opened in the name of the new business.

2 Signed a lease with Shoe Machinery Company for the installation and use of shoe repair equipment. The lease provided for a $60 monthly rental; Mr. Nash paid the first month's rent.

2 Paid Desert Realty $90, the rent on the shop space for the month of October.

3 Purchased shop furniture on credit from Store Fixtures, Ltd., $400.

4 Purchased shop supplies for cash, $125.

4 Paid the premium on a one-year insurance policy purchased on October 1, $60.

15 Cash shoe repair revenue for the first half of the month, $80.

20 Paid for advertising in a local newspaper, $25.

27 Paid Store Fixtures, Ltd., $100 on account.

31 Cash shoe repair revenue for the last half of the month, $135.

Required work for October:

1. Open the following accounts: Cash; Shop Supplies; Prepaid Insurance; Shop Furniture; Accumulated Depreciation, Shop Furniture; Accounts Payable; Ted Nash, Capital; Ted Nash, Withdrawals; Income Summary; Shoe Repair Revenue; Shop Rent; Equipment Rent; Advertising Expense; Shop Supplies Expense; Insurance Expense; and Depreciation Expense, Shop Furniture.

2. Prepare and post journal entries to record the October transactions.

3. Prepare a trial balance in the Trial Balance columns of a work sheet and complete the work sheet using the following information:

a. A shop supplies inventory showed $80 of unused shop supplies.
b. One month's insurance has expired.
c. Estimated depreciation of shop furniture, $10.
4. Prepare an October income statement and an October 31 balance sheet.
5. From the work sheet prepare and post adjusting and closing journal entries.
6. Prepare a post-closing trial balance.

During November Ted Nash completed the following additional business transactions:

Nov. 1 Paid Shoe Machinery Company the November rent on the shop equipment.
  1 Paid Desert Realty the November shop rent, $90.
  5 Purchased for cash $150 additional shop supplies.
  15 Cash shoe repair revenue for the first half of November, $265.
  15 Purchased on credit from Store Fixtures, Ltd., $200 additional shop furniture.
  23 Paid for newspaper advertising that had appeared, $35.
  26 Paid Store Fixtures, Ltd., $150 on account.
  28 Ted Nash withdrew $250 from the business for personal living expenses.
  30 Shoe repair revenue for the last half of the month, $300.

Required work for November:
1. Prepare and post journal entries to record the November transactions.
2. Prepare a trial balance in the Trial Balance columns of a work sheet and complete the work sheet using the following information:
   a. A shop supply inventory showed $125 of unused shop supplies.
   b. One month's insurance has expired.
   c. Estimated depreciation of shop furniture, $15.
3. Prepare a November income statement and a November 30 balance sheet.
4. Prepare and post adjusting and closing journal entries.
5. Prepare a post-closing trial balance.

Problem 4–3
(If the working papers that accompany this text are not used, omit this problem.)
   The ledger of Aloha Lanes, showing account balances as of December 31, the end of the current annual accounting period, appears in the booklet of working papers. All accounts with balances have normal kinds of balances.

Required:
1. Prepare a trial balance of the ledger in the Trial Balance columns of a work sheet form and complete the work sheet using the following information:
   a. Bowling supplies inventory, $590.
   b. Expired insurance, $395.
   c. Estimated depreciation of bowling equipment, $3,875.
   d. Salaries accrued but unpaid, $315.
   e. The lease contract on the building calls for an annual rental equal to 10% of the annual bowling revenue, with $200 payable monthly on the first day of each month. The $200 was paid each month and debited to the Rent Expense account.

f. Personal property taxes amounting to $85 have accrued on the bowling equipment but are unrecorded and unpaid.

g. The mortgage debt was incurred on June 1, and interest on the debt is at the rate of 6% per year or $50 per month. The mortgage contract calls for the payment of $150 interest each three months in advance. Interest payments of $150 each were made in advance and debited to the Interest Expense account on June 1, September 1, and December 1.

2. Prepare an income statement and a classified balance sheet.
3. Prepare and post adjusting and closing journal entries.
4. Prepare a post-closing trial balance.

Problem 4-4

At the end of its annual accounting period a trial balance of the ledger of Zippo Delivery Service appeared as follows:

ZIPPO DELIVERY SERVICE
Trial Balance, December 31, 19—

Cash	$ 2,880	
Accounts receivable	390	
Prepaid insurance	695	
Office supplies	230	
Office equipment	2,460	
Accumulated depreciation, office equipment		$ 470
Delivery equipment	10,790	
Accumulated depreciation, delivery equipment		3,150
Notes payable		1,500
Unearned delivery service revenue		450
Rose Moss, capital		8,645
Rose Moss, withdrawals	8,400	
Delivery service revenue		34,935
Office rent expense	600	
Telephone expense	185	
Office salaries expense	3,060	
Truck drivers' wages	16,320	
Gas, oil, and repairs	2,180	
Garage rent expense	960	
Totals	$49,150	$49,150

Required:

1. Copy the trial balance in the Trial Balance columns of a work sheet form and complete the work sheet using the following information:

   a. The delivery service entered into contracts with three stores during November and December in which it agreed to deliver packages for each store for a fixed fee. The contract of one store, signed on December 10, provides for a $90 monthly fee, payable on the 10th of each month after service is rendered. On December 31, $60, two thirds of the first month's fee, has been earned but is unrecorded. The other two stores made advance payments on their contracts, and the delivery service credited the amounts paid to its Unearned Delivery Service Revenue account. An examination of the contracts of these stores shows that $175 of the $450 paid has been earned by the accounting period end.

b. Insurance expired on the office equipment, $50; and on the delivery equipment, $510.

c. An inventory of office supplies shows $85 of unused office supplies on hand.

d. Estimated depreciation on office equipment, $150; and (e) on delivery equipment, $2,350.

f. Fifty dollars of office salaries and $300 of truck drivers' wages have accrued but are unrecorded.

2. Prepare an income statement and a classified balance sheet.

3. Prepare adjusting and closing journal entries.

Alternate problems

Problem 4–1A

At the end of its annual accounting period a trial balance of the ledger of Mr. Clean, Janitorial Service appeared as follows:

MR. CLEAN, JANITORIAL SERVICE
Trial Balance, December 31, 19—

Cash	$ 715	
Accounts receivable	180	
Prepaid insurance	565	
Cleaning supplies	840	
Prepaid rent	225	
Cleaning equipment	2,830	
Accumulated depreciation, cleaning equipment		$ 1,220
Trucks	6,690	
Accumulated depreciation, trucks		1,610
Accounts payable		135
Unearned janitorial revenue		180
Timothy Watts, capital		6,870
Timothy Watts, withdrawals	7,200	
Janitorial revenue		25,210
Wages expense	14,700	
Rent expense	600	
Gas, oil, and repairs	680	
Totals	$35,225	$35,225

Required:

1. Enter the trial balance amounts in the trial balance columns of a work sheet form and complete the work sheet using this information:

a. Expired insurance, $420.

b. A cleaning supplies inventory showed $135 of unused cleaning supplies on hand.

c. The cleaning service rents garage and equipment storage space. At the beginning of the annual accounting period three months' rent was prepaid as shown by the debit balance of the Prepaid Rent account. Rents for the months April through November were paid on the first day of each month and debited to the Rent Expense account. The December rent was unpaid on the trial balance date.

d. Estimated depreciation on cleaning equipment, $375; and *(e)* on the trucks, $900.

f. On November 1 the janitorial service contracted and began to clean the office of Waikiki Realty for $60 per month. The realty company paid in advance for three months' service, and the amount paid was credited to the Unearned Janitorial Revenue account. The janitorial service also entered into a contract and began cleaning the office of Ala Wai Realty on December 15. By the month-end a half month's revenue, $40, had been earned on this contract but was unrecorded.

g. Employees' wages amounting to $120 had accrued but were unrecorded on the trial balance date.

2. From the work sheet prepare an income statement and a classified balance sheet.

3. Prepare adjusting and closing journal entries from the work sheet.

Problem 4–3A

(If the working papers that accompany this text are not used, omit this problem.)

The ledger of Surfside Alleys, showing the account balances as of December 31, the end of the current annual accounting period, appears in the booklet of working papers. All accounts with balances have normal kinds of balances.

Required:

1. Prepare a trial balance of the ledger in the Trial Balance columns of a work sheet form and complete the work sheet using the following information:
   a. Bowling supplies inventory, $625.
   b. Expired insurance, $485.
   c. Estimated depreciation of bowling equipment, $3,850.
   d. Salaries accrued but unpaid on December 31, $240.
   e. The lease contract on the building calls for an annual rental equal to 8% of the annual bowling revenue, with $200 payable monthly on the first day of each month. The $200 was paid each month and debited to the Rent Expense account.
   f. On December 31 personal property taxes of $115 have accrued on the bowling equipment but are unrecorded and unpaid.
   g. Three months' interest, $150, has accrued on the mortgage.

2. Prepare an income statement and a classified balance sheet.

3. Prepare and post adjusting and closing journal entries.

4. Prepare a post-closing trial balance.

Problem 4–4A

Rapid Delivery Service operates with accounting periods that end each December 31, and on that date the following trial balance was taken from its ledger:

RAPID DELIVERY SERVICE
Trial Balance, December 31, 19—

Cash	$ 2,880	
Accounts receivable	390	
Prepaid insurance	695	
Office supplies	230	
Office equipment	2,460	
Accumulated depreciation, office equipment		$ 470
Delivery equipment	10,790	
Accumulated depreciation, delivery equipment		3,150
Notes payable		1,500
Unearned delivery service revenue		450
Rose Moss, capital		8,645
Rose Moss, withdrawals	8,400	
Delivery service revenue		34,935
Office rent expense	600	
Telephone expense	185	
Office salaries expense	3,060	
Truck drivers' wages	16,320	
Gas, oil, and repairs	2,180	
Garage rent expense	960	
Totals	$49,150	$49,150

Required:
1. Copy the trial balance in the Trial Balance columns of a work sheet form and complete the work sheet using the following information:
   a. Insurance expired on the office equipment, $60; and on the delivery equipment, $420.
   b. An inventory of office supplies shows $110 of unused office supplies on hand.
   c. Estimated depreciation on office equipment, $125; and *(d)* on delivery equipment, $2,125.
   e. Three stores entered into contracts with Rapid Delivery Service in which they agreed to pay a fixed fee for having packages delivered. Two of the stores made advance payments on their contracts, and the amounts paid were credited to Unearned Delivery Service Revenue. An examination of their contracts shows that $250 of the $450 they paid in advance was earned by the accounting period end. The contract of the third store provides for a $100 monthly fee to be paid at the end of each month's service. It was signed on December 15, and a half month's revenue has accrued but is unrecorded.
   f. Office salaries, $60, and truck drivers' wages, $320, have accrued.
2. Prepare an income statement and a classified balance sheet.
3. Prepare adjusting and closing journal entries.

Tom Barr's office secretary and bookkeeper was taken seriously ill during the first year-end closing of the accounts of Mr. Barr's law practice. He is sure she prepared a work sheet, income statement, and balance sheet, but he has only the income statement and cannot find either the work sheet or balance sheet. He does have a trial balance that he prepared from his ledger accounts, and he wants you to prepare adjusting and closing entries from the following trial balance and income statement so he can post them to the accounts. He also wants you to prepare a classified balance sheet. He says he has no legal work in process on which fees have accrued, and that the $600 of unearned fees on the trial balance represent a retainer fee paid by Security Bank. The bank had retained him on November 15 to do its legal work, agreeing to pay him $200 per month for his services.

TOM BARR, LAWYER
Trial Balance, December 31, 19 –

Cash	$ 1,250	
Legal fees receivable	1,500	
Office supplies	400	
Prepaid insurance	225	
Furniture and equipment	2,500	
Accounts payable		$ 200
Unearned legal fees		600
Tom Barr, capital		4,000
Tom Barr, withdrawals	12,000	
Legal fees earned		21,450
Rent expense	1,800	
Office salaries expense	6,425	
Miscellaneous office expenses	150	
Totals	$26,250	$26,250

TOM BARR, LAWYER
Income Statement for Year Ended December 31, 19 –

Revenue:		
Legal fees earned		$21,750
Operating expenses:		
Rent expense	$1,800	
Office salaries expense	6,500	
Miscellaneous office expenses	150	
Accrued property taxes expense	50	
Office supplies expense	225	
Insurance expense	125	
Depreciation expense, furniture and equipment	250	
Total operating expenses		9,100
Net Income		$12,650

Decision problem 4-2, Ted's Appliance Service

Ted Beal opened an appliance repair service on January 1 of this year; and now, at the year-end, he has asked you to determine his financial position. He says that business has been good all year, but the bank has begun to dishonour his cheques, his creditors are dunning him and he is unable to pay, and he just cannot understand why he is in such a position.

You find that Ted's wife, who has had no training in record keeping, has been keeping the "books" for the business, and she does not know what the problem is either. However, she has prepared for your inspection the following statement of cash receipts and disbursements:

TED'S APPLIANCE SERVICE
Cash Receipts and Disbursements
For Year Ended December 31, 19—

Receipts:

Investment	$ 5,000	
Received from customers	28,750	$33,750

Disbursements:

Rent expense	$ 1,625	
Repair equipment purchased	3,600	
Service truck expense	4,425	
Wages expense	18,200	
Insurance expense	300	
Repair parts and supplies	5,650	33,800
Bank overdraft		$ (50)

You find no errors in the statement and you learn these additional facts:

1. Mrs. Beal has a list of customers who owe a total of $400 for appliance repair work done on credit.
2. The lease contract for the shop space runs five years and requires rent payments of $125 per month. It also stipulates that rents for the first and last months of the lease must be paid in advance. All required payments were made on time.
3. The $3,600 of repair equipment has an estimated six-year life, after which it will be valueless.
4. The service truck expense consists of $3,800 paid for the truck on January 1, plus $625 paid for gas, oil, and minor repairs to the truck. Mr. Beal expects to use the truck for four years, after which he thinks he will get $1,000 for it as a trade-in on a new truck.
5. The wages expense consists of $7,800 paid the service's one employee plus $200 per week withdrawn by Mr. Beal for personal living expenses. In addition, $100 is owed the one employee on December 31 for wages earned since his last payday.
6. The $300 of insurance expense resulted from paying the premiums on two insurance policies on January 2. One policy cost $60 and gave protection for one year, and the other policy cost $240 for three years' protection.
7. In addition to the $5,650 of repair parts and supplies paid for during the year, Mr. Beal's creditors are dunning him for $475 for parts and supplies

purchased and delivered, but not paid for. Also, an inventory shows there are $1,350 of unused parts and supplies on hand.

Prepare an income statement showing the results of the first year's operations for Ted's Appliance Service and prepare a classified balance sheet showing its financial position as of the end of its first year.

Decision problem 4–3, Statewide Moving Service

A year ago on the death of his father, Fred Hall took over management of the family business, Statewide Moving Service. At the time he took over, Fred recognized he knew little about accounting, but he reasoned that if the cash of the business increased, it was doing OK. Therefore, he was pleased as he watched the balance of the concern's cash grow from $2,000 when he took over to $7,825 at the year end. Furthermore, at the year-end he reasoned that since he had withdrawn $1,000 per month from the business for personal living expenses, the business must have earned about $17,825 during the year. He arrived at this amount by adding the $5,825 increase in cash to the $12,000 he had withdrawn from the business, and he was more than shocked when he received the following income statement and learned the business had earned less than the amounts he had withdrawn.

STATEWIDE MOVING SERVICE
Income Statement for Year Ended December 31, 19—

Revenue from moving services		$45,850
Operating expenses:		
Salaries and wages expense	$24,650	
Gas, oil, and truck repairs	2,825	
Insurance expense	875	
Office supplies expense	150	
Depreciation expense, office equipment	200	
Depreciation expense, trucks	3,900	
Depreciation expense, buildings	3,600	
Total operating expenses		36,200
Net Income		$ 9,650

After mulling over the statement for several days, he has asked you to explain how in a year in which its cash increased almost $6,000 and he had withdrawn $12,000, the business could have earned only $9,650. In examining the accounts of the business, you note that there were no unpaid salaries and wages at the beginning of the year, but that $300 of the year's salaries and wages expense resulted from earned but unpaid salaries. Also, the balance of the Prepaid Insurance account decreased $125 between the beginning and the end of the year and the balance of the Office Supplies account decreased $50. However, except for these three changes, the change in cash, and the changes in the accumulated depreciation accounts, there were no other changes in the balances of the company's asset and liability accounts during the year. Back your explanation with a calculation accounting for the company's increase in cash.

Problem 4–1 A&R

Based on the data presented in the trial balance in Problem 2–3 of chapter 2; (a) prepare all necessary clearing or closing entries and explain (b) why certain types of accounts must always start with nil balance for a new accounting period, and (c) the objective of clearing or closing entries.

Problem 4–2 A&R

The following data are related to the operations of Suma Company:

SUMA COMPANY
Post-clearing Trial Balance
December 31, 1975

Cash	$1,000	
Prepaid rent	600	
Office supplies	400	
Office equipment	7,000	
Accumulated depreciation—office equipment		$2,000
Accounts payable		500
Office salaries payable		600
Unearned management fees		900
Larry Yorle, capital		5,000
	$9,000	$9,000

Clearing (Closing) entries for the year of 1975

(1)	Commissions revenue	2,500	
	Management fees revenue	27,500	
	Income summary		30,000
(2)	Income summary	16,000	
	Office salaries expense		11,000
	Telephone expense		200
	Advertising expense		600
	Depreciation expense		1,000
	Office supplies expense		200
	Rent expense		3,000
(3)	Income summary	14,000	
	Larry Yorle, capital		14,000
(4)	Larry Yorle, capital	12,000	
	Larry Yorle, withdrawals		12,000

Required:
1. Prepare a balance sheet and an income statement.
2. Identify the accounts to which adjusting entries must have been made and give reasons for your answer.
3. Identify the accounts to which adjusting entries probably have been made and give reasons for your answer.

Problem 4–3 A&R

Your examination of the books of Carzin Company revealed that the company followed the cash basis of accounting with respect to certain items. Further examination revealed the following matters had not been taken into account in computing net income of $10,000 for 1974 and a net loss of $5,000 for 1975:

	1974	1975
Office supplies on hand at the year-end	$400	$600
Wages expenses incurred during the year but neither paid nor recorded at the year-end	500	400
Advances from customers recorded as revenues but unearned at the year-end	650	700
Revenues earned during the year but not billed and not recorded at the year-end	550	400

Required:
Compute the correct net income or net loss for each year using the accrual basis of accounting. (Show all supporting calculations.)

Problem 4–4 A&R

The owner of Miracle Stores has come to you for assistance because his bookkeeper has just moved to another city. The following is the only information his bookkeeper left him.
(1) Balance sheets as at December 31, 1974 and 1975.

	1974	1975
Assets	$50,000	$40,000
Liabilities	$15,000	$10,000
Capital	35,000	30,000
	$50,000	$40,000

(2) The owner withdrew $25,000 in 1975 for his personal use.
(3) The business incurred total expenses of $40,000 for 1975, of which $30,000 was for wages and $10,000 for advertising.

Required:
1. Compute the total revenue and net income for 1975.
2. Prepare closing or clearing entries for 1975 (omit narratives).

5

Accounting for a merchandising concern

■ The accounting records and reports of Owen Real Estate Agency, as described in previous chapters, are those of a service enterprise. Other service enterprises are laundries, taxicab companies, barber and beauty shops, theaters, and golf courses. Each performs a service for a commission or fee, and the net income of each is the difference between fees or commissions earned and operating expenses.

A merchandising concern, on the other hand, whether a wholesaler or retailer, earns revenue by selling goods or merchandise, and a net income results when revenue from sales exceeds the cost of the goods sold plus operating expenses, as the following condensed income statement shows:

XYZ Store
Condensed Income Statement

Revenue from sales	$10,000
Less cost of goods sold	6,000
Gross profit from sales	$ 4,000
Less operating expenses	3,000
Net Income	$ 1,000

The store of the illustrated income statement sold for $10,000, goods that cost $6,000, and thereby earned a $4,000 gross profit from sales, from which it subtracted $3,000 of operating expenses to show a $1,000 net income.

Gross profit from sales, as shown on the illustrated income statement, is the "profit" before operating expenses are deducted; and accounting for the factors that enter into its calculation differentiates the accounting of a merchandising concern from that of a service enterprise.

Gross profit from sales is determined by subtracting the cost of whatever goods were sold from the revenue resulting from their sale; but before the subtraction can be made, both revenue from sales and cost of goods sold must be determined.

Revenue from sales ■ Revenue from sales consists of gross proceeds from merchandise sales less returns, allowances, and discounts. It is commonly reported on an income statement as follows:

Nelson Hardware Company
Income Statement for Year Ended December 31, 19—

Revenue from sales:		
Gross sales...		$78,750
Less: Sales returns and allowances................. $650		
Sales discounts 750		1,400
Net sales...		$77,350

Gross sales

The item, Gross sales, $78,750, on the illustrated partial income statement is the total cash and credit sales made by the company during the year. Cash sales were "rung up" on a cash register as each sale was completed, and at the end of each day the register total showed the amount of that day's cash sales, which was recorded with an entry like this:

Nov.	3	Cash..	205.00	
		Sales		205.00
		To record the day's cash sales.		

In addition an entry like this was used to record credit sales:

Nov.	3	Accounts Receivable	45.00	
		Sales		45.00
		Sold merchandise on credit.		

As a result, at the year-end the $78,750 credit balance of the company's Sales account showed the total of its cash and credit sales for the year.

Sales returns and allowances

In most stores a customer is permitted to return any unsatisfactory merchandise he has purchased; or he is sometimes allowed to keep the unsatisfactory goods and is given an allowance or an amount off its sales price. Either way, returns and allowances result from dissatisfied customers; consequently, it is important for management to know the amount of such returns and allowances and their relation to sales. Information as to returns and allowances is supplied by the Sales Returns and Allowances account when each return or allowance is recorded as follows:

Nov.	4	Sales Returns and Allowances.........................	20.00	
		Accounts Receivable (or Cash)..................		20.00
		Customer returned unsatisfactory merchandise.		

Sales discounts

When goods are sold on credit, the terms of payment are always made definite so there will be no misunderstanding as to the amount and time of payment. The terms normally appear on the invoice or sales ticket and are part of the sales agreement. Exact terms granted usually depend upon the custom of the trade. In some trades it is customary for invoices to become due and payable 10 days after the end of the month in which the sale occurred. Invoices in these trades carry terms, "n/10 EOM." In other trades invoices become due and payable 30 days after the invoice date and carry terms of "n/30." This means that the net amount of the invoice is due 30 days after the invoice date.

When credit periods are long, creditors usually grant discounts, called *cash discounts,* for early payments. This practice reduces the amount invested in accounts receivable and tends to decrease losses from uncollectible accounts. When discounts for early payment are granted, they are made part of the credit terms and appear on the invoice as, for example, "Terms: 2/10, n/60." Terms of 2/10, n/60 mean that the *credit period* is 60 days but that the debtor may deduct 2% from the invoice amount if payment is made within 10 days after the invoice date. The 10-day period is known as the *discount period.*

Since at the time of a sale it is not known if the customer will pay within the discount period and take advantage of a cash discount, sales discounts cannot be recorded until the customer pays. For example, on November 12, Nelson Hardware Company sold $100 of merchandise to a customer on credit, terms 2/10, n/60, and recorded the sale as follows:

Nov.	12	Accounts Receivable	100.00	
		Sales		100.00
		Sold merchandise, terms 2/10, n/60.		

At the time of the sale the customer had a choice. He could receive credit for paying the full $100 by paying Nelson Hardware Company $98 any time before November 22. Or he could wait 60 days, until January 11, and pay the full $100. If he elected to pay by November 22 and take advantage of the cash discount, Nelson Hardware Company would record the receipt of the $98 as follows:

Nov.	22	Cash...	98.00	
		Sales Discounts	2.00	
		Accounts Receivable		100.00
		Received payment for the November 12 sale less the discount.		

Sales discounts are accumulated in the Sales Discounts account until the end of an accounting period when their total appears on the income statement as a deduction from gross sales. This is logical, since a sales discount is an "amount off" the regular price of goods that is granted for early payment, and as a result reduces revenue from sales.

Cost of
goods sold
■ An automobile dealer or an appliance store, both of which make a limited number of sales each day, can easily refer to their records at the time of each sale and record the cost of the car or appliance sold. A drugstore, on the other hand, would find this difficult. For instance, if a drug or grocery store sells a customer a tube of toothpaste, a box of aspirin, and a magazine, it can easily record with a cash register the sale of these items at marked selling prices; but it would be difficult to maintain records that would enable it to also "look up" and record as "cost of goods sold" the costs of the items sold. As a result, stores such as drug, grocery, and others selling a volume of low-priced items make no effort to record the cost of the goods sold at the time of each sale. Rather, they wait until the end of an accounting period, take a physical inventory, and from the inventory and their accounting records determine at one time the cost of all goods sold during the period.

The end-of-the-period inventories taken by drug, grocery, hardware, or like stores in order to learn the cost of the goods they have sold are called *periodic inventories;* and the system used by such stores in accounting for cost of goods sold is known as a *periodic inventory system.* Such a system is described and discussed in this chapter. The system used by a car or appliance dealer to record the cost of each car or appliance sold depends on a *perpetual inventory record* of cars or appliances in stock, and as a result is known as a *perpetual inventory system of accounting for goods on hand and sold.* It is discussed in Chapter 10.

Cost of goods sold, periodic inventory system

■ As previously said, a store using a periodic inventory system makes no effort to determine and record the cost of items sold as they are sold. Rather, it waits until the end of an accounting period and determines at one time the cost of all the goods it sold during the period. And to do this, it must have information as to (1) the cost of the merchandise it had on hand at the beginning of the period, (2) the cost of the merchandise it purchased during the period, and (3) the cost of the unsold goods on hand at the period end. With this information a store can, for example, determine the cost of the goods it sold during a period as follows:

Cost of goods on hand at beginning of period..................	$ 2,000
Cost of goods purchased during the period	28,000
Goods available for sale during the period	$30,000
Unsold goods on hand at the period end	1,000
Cost of goods sold during the period	$29,000

The store of the calculation had $2,000 of merchandise at the beginning of the accounting period, and during the period it purchased an additional $28,000. Consequently, it had available and could have sold $30,000 of merchandise. However, $1,000 of this merchandise was on hand unsold at the period end; therefore, the cost of the goods it sold during the period was $29,000.

A reexamination of the foregoing calculation will show that three factors enter into calculating cost of goods sold: (1) the cost of the goods on hand at the beginning, (2) the cost of the goods purchased, and (3) the cost of the unsold goods on hand at the end. The sum of the first two is the amount of goods that were for sale, and by subtracting the last, the cost of the unsold goods on hand at the end, cost of goods sold is determined.

Merchandise inventories

The merchandise on hand at the beginning of an accounting period is called the *beginning inventory* and that on hand at the end is the *ending inventory*. Furthermore, since accounting periods follow one after another, the ending inventory of one period always becomes the beginning inventory of the next.

When a periodic inventory system is in use, cost of goods on hand at the end of an accounting period, the ending inventory, is determined by (1) counting the items on the shelves in the store and in the stock room, (2) multiplying the count for each kind of goods by its cost, and (3) adding the costs of the different kinds.

After the cost of the ending inventory is determined in this manner, it appears on the income statement as a subtraction in the cost of goods sold section. Also, by means of a closing entry, it is posted to an account called *Merchandise Inventory,* where it remains throughout the succeeding accounting period as a record of the inventory at the end of the period ended and the beginning of the succeeding period.

It should be emphasized at this point that entries are made in the Merchandise Inventory account only at the end of each accounting period; the entries are closing entries; and furthermore, since some goods are soon sold and other goods purchased, the account does not long show the amount of goods on hand. Rather, as soon as goods are sold or purchased, the account balance becomes a historical amount, the amount of goods that were on hand at the end of the last period and the beginning of the new period.

Cost of merchandise purchased

When a periodic inventory system is in use, cost of merchandise purchased is determined by subtracting from purchases any discounts, returns, and allowances and then adding any freight charges on the goods purchased. However, before examining this calculation it is best to see how the amounts involved are accumulated.

Under a periodic inventory system, when merchandise is bought for resale, its cost is debited to an account called *Purchases,* as follows:

Nov.	5	Purchases	1,000.00	
		Accounts Payable......................................		1,000.00
		Purchased merchandise on credit, terms 2/10, n/30.		

The Purchases account has as its sole purpose the accumulation of the cost of all merchandise bought for resale during an accounting period. The account does not at any time show whether the merchandise is on hand or has been disposed of through sale or other means.

If a credit purchase like that in the entry just given is subject to a cash discount, payment within the discount period results in a credit to *Purchases Discounts,* as in the following entry:

Nov.	12	Accounts Payable...	1,000.00	
		Purchases Discounts		20.00
		Cash..		980.00
		Paid for the purchase of November 5 less the discount.		

When purchase discounts are involved, it is important that every invoice on which there is a discount be paid within the discount period, so that no discounts are lost. On the other hand, good cash management requires that no invoice be paid until the last day of its discount period. Consequently, to ensure that no discount is lost for lack of payment within the discount period, but that no invoice is paid before the end of the discount period, every invoice must be filed in such a way that it automatically comes to the attention of the company treasurer or other disbursing officer on the last day of its discount period. A simple way to do this is to provide a file with 31 folders, one for each day in a month. Then after an invoice is recorded, it is placed in the file folder of the last day of its discount period. For example, if an invoice is dated November 2, with terms of 2/10, n/30, the last day of its discount period is November 12, and such an invoice would be filed in folder number 12. Then on November 12 this invoice, together with any other invoices in the same folder, would be removed and paid or refiled for payment on a later date.

Sometimes merchandise received from suppliers is not acceptable and must be returned or, if kept, is kept only because the supplier grants an allowance or reduction in its price. When merchandise is returned, the purchaser "gets his money back"; but from a managerial point of view more is involved. Buying merchandise, receiving and inspecting it, deciding that the merchandise is unsatisfactory, and returning it is a costly procedure that should be held to a minimum; and the first step in holding it to a minimum is to know the amount of returns and allowances. Therefore, to make this information available to management, returns and allowances on purchases are commonly recorded in an account called *Purchases Returns and Allowances,* as follows:

Nov.	8	Accounts Payable...................................	65.00	
		Purchases Returns and Allowances...........		65.00
		Returned defective merchandise.		

When an invoice is subject to a cash discount and a portion of the goods listed on the invoice is returned before the invoice is paid, the discount applies to just the goods purchased and kept. For example, if $500 of merchandise is purchased, terms 2/10, n/60, and $100 of the goods are returned before the invoice is paid, the discount applies only to the $400 of goods purchased and kept.

Sometimes a manufacturer or wholesaler pays freight, express, or other transportation costs on merchandise he sells and the total cost of the goods to the purchaser is the amount paid the manufacturer or wholesaler. Other times the purchaser must pay transportation costs; and when he does, such charges are a proper addition to the cost of the goods purchased and may be recorded with a debit to the Purchases account. However, more complete information is obtained if such costs are debited to an account called *Freight-In,* as follows:

Nov.	24	Freight-In	22.00	
		Cash		22.00
		Paid express charges on merchandise purchased.		

When an income statement is prepared at the end of an accounting period, the balances of the Purchases, Purchases Returns and Allowances, Purchases Discounts, and Freight-In accounts are combined on it as follows to show the cost of the merchandise purchased during the period:

Purchases..		$48,650
Less: Purchases returns and allowances $275		
Purchases discounts................................ 550	825	
Net purchases..		$47,825
Add: Freight-in...		1,100
Cost of goods purchased		$48,925

Cost of goods sold

The last item in the foregoing calculation is the cost of the merchandise purchased during the accounting period, and it is combined on the income statement with the beginning and ending inventories to arrive at cost of goods sold as follows:

Cost of goods sold:			
Merchandise inventory, January 1, 19–			$ 7,750
Purchases	$48,650		
Less: Purchases returns and allowances ... $275			
Purchases discounts 550	825		
Net purchases...	$47,825		
Add: Freight-in...	1,100		
Cost of goods purchased.................................		48,925	
Goods available for sale....................................		$56,675	
Merchandise inventory, December 31, 19–		8,950	
Cost of goods sold.......................................			$47,725

Inventory losses

Under a periodic inventory system the cost of any merchandise lost through shrinkage, spoilage, or shoplifting is automatically included in cost of goods sold. For example, assume a store lost $500 of merchandise to shoplifters during a year. This caused its year-end inventory to be $500 less than it otherwise would have been, since these goods were not available for inclusion in the year-end count. Consequently, since the year-end inventory was $500 smaller because of the loss, the cost of the goods the store sold was $500 greater.

Many stores are troubled with shoplifting; and although under a periodic inventory system the cost of such losses is automatically included in cost of goods sold, it is often important to know their extent.

Consequently, a way to estimate shoplifting losses is described in Chapter 10.

■ A classified income statement for a merchandising concern has (1) a revenue section, (2) a cost of goods sold section, and (3) an operating expenses section. The first two have already been discussed in this chapter, but note in Illustration 5–1 how they are brought together to show gross profit from sales.

Nelson Hardware Company
Income Statement for Year Ended December 31, 19–

Revenue:			
Gross sales			$78,750
Less: Sales returns and allowances		$ 650	
Sales discounts		750	1,400
Net sales			$77,350
Cost of goods sold:			
Merchandise inventory, January 1, 19–		$ 7,750	
Purchases	$48,650		
Less: Purchases returns and allowances $275			
Purchases discounts 550	825		
Net purchases	$47,825		
Add: Freight-in	1,100		
Cost of goods purchased		48,925	
Goods available for sale		$56,675	
Merchandise inventory, December 31, 19–		8,950	
Cost of goods sold			47,725
Gross profit from sales			$29,625
Operating expense:			
Selling expenses:			
Sales salaries expense	$ 8,200		
Rent expense, selling space	4,800		
Advertising expense	900		
Freight-out and delivery expense	1,350		
Store supplies expense	425		
Depreciation expense, store equipment	775		
Total selling expenses		$16,450	
General and administrative expenses:			
Office salaries expense	$ 3,100		
Rent expense, office space	600		
Insurance expense	65		
Office supplies expense	125		
Depreciation expense, office equipment	160		
Total general and administrative expenses		4,050	
Total operating expenses			20,500
Net Income			$ 9,125

Illustration
5–1

Observe also in Illustration 5–1 how operating expenses are classified as either "Selling expenses" or "General and administrative expenses." Selling expenses include expenses of storing and preparing goods for sale, promoting sales, actually making sales, and if there is not a delivery department separate from the selling departments, the expenses of delivering goods to customers. General and administrative expenses include the general office, accounting, personnel, and credit and collection expenses.

Sometimes an expenditure should be divided or prorated part to selling expenses and part to general and administrative expenses. Nelson Hardware Company divided the rent on its store building in this manner, as an examination of Illustration 5–1 will reveal. However, it did not prorate its insurance expense because the amount involved was so small the company felt the extra exactness did not warrant the extra work.

When an expense such as rent or heating and lighting is not prorated, it is a common practice to classify the expense as either a general and administrative expense or as a selling expense depending upon whether the office or the store occupies the greater amount of space. For example, if selling activities occupy more space than the office and rent is not prorated, it is only fair to classify it as a selling expense.

Work sheet of a merchandising concern

■ A concern selling merchandise, like a service-type company, uses a work sheet in bringing together the end-of-the-period information needed in preparing its income statement, balance sheet, and adjusting and closing entries. Such a work sheet, that of Nelson Hardware Company, is shown in Illustration 5–2.

Note in Illustration 5–2 that the merchandising accounts are stressed by the use of colour. This is done because the remainder of the accounts receive the same work sheet treatment as do the accounts of a service-type concern; and since this was fully discussed in Chapter 4, only the treatment of the merchandising accounts needs consideration here.

Trial Balance columns

The Trial Balance columns of the Nelson Hardware Company's work sheet, Illustration 5–2, show the balances of the company's accounts as of December 31, 19–. The account balances were taken from the company's ledger on that date and indicate that—

1. The January 1 beginning-of-the-year inventory was $7,750.
2. Sales totaling $78,750 were made during the year.
3. Customers returned $650 of goods they purchased.
4. Sales discounts totaling $750 were granted during the year.
5. The year's purchases of merchandise amounted to $48,650.
6. Merchandise purchases totaling $275 were returned.
7. Purchases discounts totaling $550 were taken during the year.
8. Freight charges totaling $1,100 were paid on goods purchased.

Adjustments columns and Adjusted Trial Balance columns

Generally none of the merchandising accounts require adjustments. Consequently, no adjustments appear opposite these accounts in the

Nelson Hardware Company
Work Sheet for Year Ended December 31, 19 —

Account Titles	Trial Balance Dr.	Trial Balance Cr.	Adjustments Dr.	Adjustments Cr.	Adjusted Trial Balance Dr.	Adjusted Trial Balance Cr.	Income Statement Dr.	Income Statement Cr.	Balance Sheet Dr.	Balance Sheet Cr.
Cash	2,400				2,400				2,400	
Accounts receivable	3,300				3,300				3,300	
Merchandise inventory	7,750				7,750		7,750	8,950	8,950	
Prepaid insurance	195			(a) 65	130				130	
Store supplies	590			(b) 425	165				165	
Office supplies	185			(c) 125	60				60	
Store equipment	7,910				7,910				7,910	
Accumulated depreciation, store equipment		3,200		(d) 775		3,975				3,975
Office equipment	1,590				1,590				1,590	
Accumulated depreciation, office equipment		250		(e) 160		410				410
Accounts payable		1,700				1,700				1,700
George Nelson, capital		14,095				14,095				14,095
George Nelson, withdrawals	4,800				4,800				4,800	
Sales		78,750				78,750		78,750		
Sales returns and allowances	650				650		650			
Sales discounts	750				750		750			
Purchases	48,650				48,650		48,650			
Purchases returns and allowances		275				275		275		
Purchase discounts		550				550		550		
Freight-in	1,100				1,100		1,100			
Sales salaries expense	8,200				8,200		8,200			
Rent expense, selling space	4,800				4,800		4,800			
Advertising expense	900				900		900			
Freight-out and delivery expense	1,350				1,350		1,350			
Office salaries expense	3,100				3,100		3,100			
Rent expense, office space	600				600		600			
	98,820	98,820								
Insurance expense			(a) 65		65		65			
Store supplies expense			(b) 425		425		425			
Office supplies expense			(c) 125		125		125			
Depreciation expense, store equipment			(d) 775		775		775			
Depreciation expense, office equipment			(e) 160		160		160			
			1,550	1,550	99,755	99,755	79,400	88,525	29,305	20,180
Net Income							9,125			9,125
							88,525	88,525	29,305	29,305

Illustration
5–2

Adjustments columns and the unadjusted trial balance amounts are carried directly into the Adjusted Trial Balance columns.

Income Statement columns

In any company the accounts that appear on its income statement are those the balances of which are carried into the Income Statement columns of its work sheet; and in a merchandising concern these are the (1) revenue, (2) cost of goods sold, and (3) operating expense accounts. (The work sheet treatment of the operating expense accounts was discussed in Chapter 4 and needs no further consideration here.)

REVENUE ACCOUNTS. The Sales account is the primary revenue account of a merchandising concern. It is credited throughout each accounting period for the selling price of goods sold, and always reaches the end of the period with a credit balance, which is carried into the work sheet's Income Statement credit column.

Sales returns and allowances and sales discounts are in effect negative sales; and although the Sales Returns and Allowances and Sales Discounts accounts are classified as revenue accounts, they are really negative revenue accounts. Throughout each accounting period they are debited for returns, allowances, and discounts and both reach the period end with debit balances which are carried into the Income Statement debit column, where in effect the returns, allowances, and discounts are subtracted from the sales when the debit column total is subtracted from the credit column total in arriving at net income.

COST OF GOODS SOLD ACCOUNTS. When a work sheet is prepared for a company selling merchandise, (1) the debit balances of its Merchandise Inventory, Purchases, and Freight-In accounts are carried into the Income Statement debit column; (2) the credit balances of the Purchases Returns and Allowances and Purchases Discounts accounts are carried into the Income Statement credit column; after which (3) the dollar amount of the ending inventory is entered directly in both the Income Statement credit column and Balance Sheet debit column.

It is easy to understand why the balances of the Merchandise Inventory, Purchases, and Freight-In accounts are carried into the Income Statement debit column—the balances are debit balances and they enter into the calculation of the net income. Likewise, it is easy to understand why the credit balances of the Purchases Returns and Allowances and Purchases Discounts accounts are carried into the Income Statement credit column—they are in effect subtractions from Purchases in the debit column. However, the reasons for the work sheet treatment of the ending inventory are not so apparent and require the following explanations:

First: Note that there are two inventories to be dealt with on the work sheet of a company selling merchandise—the beginning-of-the-period inventory and the end-of-the-period inventory.

Second: At the end of a period, before closing entries are posted, it is the beginning inventory amount that appears in the accounts as the debit balance of the Merchandise Inventory account; and it is this beginning inventory amount that is entered in the Trial Balance debit column opposite the account title, Merchandise Inventory, and is carried into the Adjusted Trial Balance and Income Statement debit columns.

Third: Before closing entries are posted, the dollar amount of the ending inventory does not appear in any account. As was explained earlier, the ending inventory is determined at the end of each period by counting the items of unsold merchandise on hand, multiplying the count for each kind by its cost, and adding the dollar amounts of the several kinds to determine the number of dollars of inventory.

Fourth: As soon as the number of dollars of ending inventory is determined, it is entered directly on the work sheet in both the Income Statement credit column and the Balance Sheet debit column. It is thus entered for three reasons: (1) After the other income statement items (including the operating expenses) have been carried into the Income Statement columns, it is necessary to enter the amount of the ending inventory if the difference between the two columns is to equal the net income or loss. (2) Entering the ending inventory in the Income Statement credit column puts this amount on the work sheet in position to become part of one of the closing entries and thus be taken into the accounts as the historical record of the inventory on hand at the end of the period. (Closing entries for a company selling merchandise are discussed in more detail later.) And finally, (3) since the amount of the ending inventory is an end-of-the-period asset, entering it in the Balance Sheet debit column puts this item in position to be added to the other end-of-the-period assets and to appear on the balance sheet.

Completing the work sheet

After the various income statement and balance sheet amounts of a company selling merchandise are sorted and entered in the proper columns of its work sheet, the columns are totaled and the work sheet is completed in the usual way.

Preparing the statements; adjusting entries

■ As in a service-type concern, the work sheet of a company selling merchandise is a tool for bringing together information needed in preparing the financial statements. The income statement is prepared from information in the Income Statement columns, the balance sheet from the Balance Sheet columns, and no essentially new techniques are required in the preparation of either.

Likewise, no new techniques are required in preparing and posting adjusting entries. Each adjustment in the work sheet's Adjustments columns requires an adjusting entry that is journalized and posted in the usual manner.

Closing entries ■ The Income Statement columns of its work sheet provide the information needed by a merchandising concern in making its closing entries, just as in a service enterprise. Furthermore, an examination of the following closing entries and the work sheet of Illustration 5–2, from which they were prepared, will show these closing entries are prepared in the same way as are those of a service-type company. In both types of companies the Income Summary account is debited for the work sheet's Income Statement debit column total and each account having an item in the column is credited. Then, each account having an item in the Income Statement credit column is debited and the Income Summary account is credited for the column total. And so on, as was explained in Chapter 4.

Dec.	31	Income Summary	79,400.00	
		Merchandise Inventory............................		7,750.00
		Sales Returns and Allowances...................		650.00
		Sales Discounts		750.00
		Purchases		48,650.00
		Freight-In		1,100.00
		Sales Salaries Expense............................		8,200.00
		Rent Expense, Selling Space....................		4,800.00
		Advertising Expense................................		900.00
		Freight-Out and Delivery Expense.............		1,350.00
		Office Salaries Expense		3,100.00
		Rent Expense, Office Space		600.00
		Insurance Expense..................................		65.00
		Store Supplies Expense...........................		425.00
		Office Supplies Expense		125.00
		Depreciation Expense, Store Equipment.....		775.00
		Depreciation Expense, Office Equipment		160.00
		To remove the beginning inventory from the accounts and to close the temporary proprietorship accounts having debit balances.		
	31	Merchandise Inventory..................................	8,950.00	
		Sales	78,750.00	
		Purchases Returns and Allowances.................	275.00	
		Purchases Discounts	550.00	
		Income Summary		88,525.00
		To put the ending inventory into the accounts and to close the temporary proprietorship accounts having credit balances.		
	31	Income Summary	9,125.00	
		George Nelson, Capital............................		9,125.00
		To close the Income Summary account.		

Dec.	31	George Nelson, Capital	4,800.00	
		George Nelson, Withdrawals		4,800.00
		To close the Withdrawals account.		

Closing
entries
and the
inventory

■ Although there is nothing essentially new about the closing entries of a merchandising concern, their effect on the Merchandise Inventory account should be observed.

Before closing entries were posted, the Merchandise Inventory account of Nelson Hardware Company showed in its $7,750 debit balance the amount of the company's beginning-of-the-period inventory,[1] as follows:

Merchandise Inventory				ACCOUNT NO. *114*	
DATE	EXPLANATION	FO-LIO	DEBIT	CREDIT	BALANCE
197A *Dec. 31*		*63*	7 7 5 0 00		7 7 5 0 00

Then, when the first closing entry was posted, its $7,750 credit to the Merchandise Inventory account had the effect of clearing the beginning inventory from the account, as follows:

Merchandise Inventory				ACCOUNT NO. *114*	
DATE	EXPLANATION	FO-LIO	DEBIT	CREDIT	BALANCE
197A *Dec. 31*		*63*	7 7 5 0 00		7 7 5 0 00
197B *Dec. 31*		*77*		7 7 5 0 00	—0—

After this, when the second closing entry was posted, its $8,950 debit to Merchandise Inventory put back into the account the amount of the ending inventory, as follows, where the amount remains throughout the succeeding year as the debit balance of the account and as a

---

[1] The date of the beginning inventory, 197A, is intended to convey the idea that the $7,750 beginning inventory amount was posted to this account at the end of the preceding year.

historical record of the amount of inventory on hand at the end of 197B and the beginning of 197C.

DATE	EXPLANATION	FO-LIO	DEBIT	CREDIT	BALANCE
197A Dec. 31		63	7 7 5 0 00		7 7 5 0 00
197B Dec. 31		77		7 7 5 0 00	-0-
31		77	8 9 5 0 00		8 9 5 0 00

Merchandise Inventory   ACCOUNT NO. *114*

Dispensing with the Adjusted Trial Balance columns ■ Thus far, because using such columns makes learning easier, all illustrated work sheets have had Adjusted Trial Balance columns. However, the experienced accountant commonly omits these columns from his work sheet in order to reduce the time and effort required in its preparation. When he does so, after he has entered the adjustments in the Adjustments columns, he combines the adjustment amounts with the trial balance amounts and sorts the combined amounts directly into the Income Statement and Balance Sheet columns in a single operation. In other words, he simply eliminates the adjusted trial balance from his work sheet.

Taking the ending inventory ■ As previously stated, when a periodic inventory system is in use, the dollar amount of the ending inventory is determined by (1) counting the items of unsold merchandise remaining in the store at the accounting period end, (2) multiplying the count for each kind of item by its cost, and (3) adding the costs for all the items. The first step, counting the items, is called taking an inventory.

Counting unsold merchandise at the end of an accounting period is often a difficult task; and unless great care is exercised, items may be omitted from the count or they may be counted more than once. Because of this, inventories are commonly taken at night, on holidays, and on weekends; or the store is closed for business in order to take the inventory.

A store's salesclerks who are familiar with the store and its merchandise are usually best equipped to make an inventory count. Before the count is started, the merchandise should be straightened and arranged in an orderly fashion on the shelves and in the showcases. Items are less apt to be counted twice or omitted if prenumbered inventory tickets like the one shown in Illustration 5-3 are used in making the count. If inventory tickets are used, at the start of the count a sufficient number of tickets, at least one for each type of product on hand, is issued to each department in the store. When the inventory count is made, a clerk counts the quantity of each product and from the count and the price tag attached to the merchandise fills in the information

Illustration
5-3

on the inventory ticket. He then initials the ticket and attaches it to the counted items. A department head or other responsible person usually examines and recounts a sufficient proportion of the items to ensure an accurate count. In each department, after the clerks complete the count, the department is examined for uncounted items. At this stage, inventory tickets are attached to all counted items. Consequently, any products without tickets attached are uncounted. After all items are counted and tickets attached, the tickets are removed and sent to the accounting department for completion of the inventory. To ensure that no ticket is lost or left attached to merchandise, all the prenumbered tickets issued are accounted for when the tickets arrive in the accounting department.

In the accounting department, the information on the tickets is copied on inventory summary sheets, and the sheets are completed by multiplying the number of units of each product by its unit cost. This gives the dollar amount of each product on hand, and the total for all products is the amount of the inventory.

Debit and credit memoranda ■ Merchandise purchased that does not meet specifications on delivery, goods received in damaged condition, goods received that were not ordered, goods received short of the amount ordered and billed, and invoice errors are matters for adjustment between the buyer and seller. In some cases the buyer can make the adjustment, and in others the adjustment is a subject for negotiation between the buyer and the seller. When there are invoice errors or when goods are received that were not ordered, the buyer may make the adjustment. If he does, he must notify the seller of his action, and commonly he does this by sending a *debit memorandum* or a *credit memorandum*.

For instance, in checking an invoice for merchandise purchased from Eugene Manufacturing Company, Salem Department Store discovered an invoice error, the correction of which reduced the invoice total from $85 to $75. Since an invoice error does not require negotiation, Salem Department Store notified Eugene Manufacturing Company of the error by mailing it the debit memorandum shown in Illustration 5–4. A debit memorandum was sent because correction of the error reduced the amount of Salem Department Store's debt to Eugene Manufacturing Company from $85 to $75, and to reduce an account payable a debit is required.

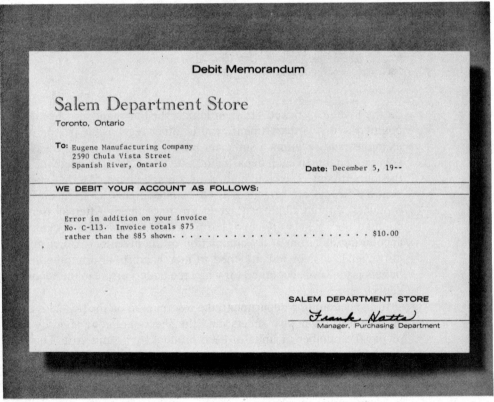

Debit Memorandum

Salem Department Store

Toronto, Ontario

To: Eugene Manufacturing Company
2590 Chula Vista Street
Spanish River, Ontario

Date: December 5, 19--

WE DEBIT YOUR ACCOUNT AS FOLLOWS:

Error in addition on your invoice
No. C-113. Invoice totals $75
rather than the $85 shown. $10.00

SALEM DEPARTMENT STORE

Frank Natts
Manager, Purchasing Department

Illustration
5–4

In recording this purchase, Salem Department Store could debit Purchases and credit Accounts Payable for $85 and then immediately record the debit memorandum by debiting Accounts Payable and crediting Purchases for $10. However, a better way would be to mark the correction on the invoice, attach a copy of the debit memorandum to show that Eugene Manufacturing Company had been notified, and then debit Purchases and credit Accounts Payable for the corrected amount of the invoice, $75.

Some adjustments, such as merchandise received in damaged condition or merchandise not meeting specifications, normally require negotiations between the buyer and seller. In such cases the buyer may debit Purchases for the full invoice amount and enter into negotiations with the seller for a return or a price adjustment. If the seller agrees to a return or adjustment, he notifies the buyer with a credit memorandum. This memorandum is a credit memorandum to the seller because the return or adjustment reduces the amount of his account receivable with the buyer. For example, Salem Department Store purchased a number of items from Novelty Supply Company, totaling $100. When the merchandise arrived, five ceramic figurines were found to have been improperly packed and were consequently damaged in transit. Salem Department Store recorded the full amount of the invoice by

CREDIT MEMORANDUM

Novelty Supply Company
WATERLOO, ONTARIO

NUMBER _L-364_
DATE _December 12, 19--_

TO_____Salem Department Store_____
_____1451 High Street_____
_____Toronto, Ontario_____

WE CREDIT YOUR ACCOUNT AS FOLLOWS

5 ceramic figurines damaged in transit and returned	$18.00

T. a. Briggs
Sales Manager

Illustration
5–5

debiting Purchases and crediting Accounts Payable for $100. It then entered into negotiations for an adjustment equal to the value of the broken figurines. Novelty Supply Company agreed to the adjustment and notified Salem Department Store with the credit memorandum shown in Illustration 5–5.

Since Salem Department Store debited Purchases and credited Accounts Payable for the full amount of the original invoice, it records the credit memorandum by a debit to Accounts Payable and a credit to Purchases Returns and Allowances for $18.

A debit or credit memorandum may originate with either party to a transaction. The memorandum gets its name from the action of the party originating it. If the originator debits, he sends a debit memorandum. If the originator credits, he sends a credit memorandum.

Code numbers as a means of identifying accounts

■ The account numbering scheme used in the chapters before this has been a simple one in which the accounts have been numbered consecutively. Such a scheme is satisfactory in a small business. However, in a larger more complicated accounting system, account numbers commonly become code numbers that not only identify accounts but also tell their statement classifications. For example, in one numbering system three-digit numbers with each digit having a significant meaning are used. In this system the first digit in each account number tells the major balance sheet or income statement classification of the account to which it is assigned. For example, account numbers with first digits of 1, numbers 111 to 199, are assigned to asset accounts, and liability accounts are assigned numbers with the first digits of 2, numbers 211 to 299. When this system is used, main balance sheet and income statement account classifications are assigned the following numbers:

111 to 199 are assigned to asset accounts.
211 to 299 are assigned to liability accounts.
311 to 399 are assigned to owner equity accounts.
411 to 499 are assigned to sales or revenue accounts.
511 to 599 are assigned to cost of goods sold accounts.
611 to 699 are assigned to operating expense accounts.
711 to 799 are assigned to other revenue and expense accounts.

When accounts are assigned code numbers having several digits, all of the digits have a significant meaning. In the system under discussion where the first digit indicates the main balance sheet or income statement classification, the second and third digits further classify the account. For example, the second digits under each of the following main classifications indicate the subclassification shown:

111 to 199. Asset accounts
    111 to 119. Current asset accounts (second digits of 1)
    121 to 129. Long-term investment accounts (second digits of 2)

131 to 139. Plant asset accounts (second digits of 3)
141 to 149. Intangible asset accounts (second digits of 4)

211 to 299. Liability accounts
211 to 219. Current liability accounts (second digits of 1)
221 to 229. Long-term liability accounts (second digits of 2)

611 to 699. Operating expense accounts
611 to 629. Selling expense accounts (second digits of 1 and 2)
631 to 649. Delivery expense accounts (second digits of 3 and 4)
651 to 669. General administrative expense accounts (second digits of 5 and 6)

The third digit in each number further classifies the account. For example, in the system under discussion, all selling expense accounts, which have account numbers with first digits of 6 and second digits of 1 and 2, are further classified as follows:

611 to 699. Operating expense accounts
611 to 629. Selling expense accounts
611. Sales salaries expense (third digit of 1)
612. Advertising expense (third digit of 2)
613. Depreciation expense, store equipment (third digit of 3)

Trade discounts ■ A trade discount is a deduction (often as much as 40% or more) from a list or catalogue price and is used in determining the actual price of the goods to which it applies. Such discounts are discussed here primarily to distinguish them from the cash discounts described earlier in this chapter.

Trade discounts are commonly used by manufacturers and wholesalers to avoid republication of catalogues when selling prices change. If selling prices change, catalogue prices can be adjusted by merely issuing a new list of discounts to be applied to the catalogue prices. Trade discounts are also used to offer different prices to different classes of customers. For example, a manufacturer might offer to sell to wholesalers at 40% off catalogue list prices and at the same time offer to sell to retailers at 30% off list prices.

Trade discounts are not entered in the accounts by either party to a sale. For example, if a manufacturer sells on credit an item listed in its catalogue at $100, less a 40% trade discount, it will record the sale as follows:

Dec.	10	Accounts Receivable	60.00	
		Sales		60.00
		Sold merchandise on credit.		

The buyer will also enter the purchase in his records at $60, and if a cash discount is involved, say 2% off for payment in 10 days, it applies only to the amount of the purchase, $60.

Transportation charges

■ When freight or express charges are involved in the sale and purchase of merchandise, it is important that the buyer and seller understand which party is responsible for the transportation costs. Normally, in quoting a price, the seller makes this clear. He may quote a price of, say $400, FOB factory. FOB factory means free on board or loaded on board the means of transportation at the factory free of loading charges, and the buyer pays transportation costs from there. Likewise, FOB destination means the seller will pay transportation costs to the destination of the goods.

Sometimes, when terms are FOB factory, the seller will prepay the transportation costs as a service to the buyer, adding the amount on the invoice and increasing its total. In such a case, if a cash discount is involved, the discount does not apply to the transportation charges.

Questions for class discussion

1. How does a merchandising concern earn revenue?
2. What is gross profit from sales?
3. What is a cash discount? If terms are 2/10, n/60, what is the length of the credit period? What is the length of the discount period?
4. How and when is cost of goods sold determined in a store using a periodic inventory system?
5. May a store sell goods at a price above their cost and still suffer a loss? How?
6. Why should a concern be interested in the amount of its sales returns and allowances?
7. Since total sales returns and allowances is subtracted from the balance of the Sales account on the income statement, why not save the effort of this subtraction by debiting each return or allowance to the Sales account?
8. If a concern may return for full credit all unsatisfactory merchandise purchased, why should it be interested in the amount returned?
9. Which of the following are debited to the Purchases account of a grocery store: *(a)* the purchase of a cash register; *(b)* the purchase of a roll of wrapping paper; *(c)* the purchase of advertising space in a newspaper; and *(d)* the purchase of a case of tomato soup?
10. At the end of an accounting period which inventory, the beginning inventory or the ending, appears on the trial balance?
11. Why is the amount of the ending inventory entered in the work sheet's Income Statement credit column? Why is it entered in the Balance Sheet debit column?
12. What effect do closing entries have on the Merchandise Inventory account?
13. Why are inventory tickets used in taking a physical inventory?
14. During a year a company purchased merchandise costing $22,000. What was the company's cost of goods sold if there were:
    a. No beginning or ending inventories?

b. A beginning inventory of $10,000 and no ending inventory?

c. A beginning inventory of $8,000 and an ending inventory of $9,500?

d. No beginning inventory and an ending inventory of $7,000?

15. In counting the merchandise on hand at the end of an accounting period, a clerk failed to count, and consequently omitted from the inventory, all the merchandise on one shelf. If the cost of the merchandise on the shelf was $100, what was the effect of the omission on *(a)* the balance sheet and *(b)* the income statement?

16. Suppose that the omission of the $100 from the inventory (Question 15) was not discovered. What would be the effect on the balance sheet and income statement prepared at the end of the next accounting period?

17. When a three-digit account numbering system like the one described in this chapter is in use, which digit of an account's number is the most significant?

18. When a debit memorandum is issued, who debits, the company originating the memorandum or the company receiving it.

19. Distinguish between cash discounts and trade discounts. Is the amount of a trade discount on merchandise purchased credited to the Purchases Discounts account?

20. When applied to transportation terms, what do the letters FOB mean? What does FOB destination mean?

Class exercises

Exercise 5–1

Hawaiian Shop purchased $1,000 of merchandise, terms 2/10, n/60, from Pacific Company and paid for the merchandise within the discount period. *(a)* Give without dates the journal entries made by Hawaiian Shop to record the purchase and payment and *(b)* give without dates the journal entries made by Pacific Company to record the sale and collection. *(c)* If Hawaiian Shop borrowed sufficient money at 6% interest on the last day of the discount period in order to pay this invoice, how much did it save by borrowing to take advantage of the discount?

Exercise 5–2

	Income Statement	
	Debit	*Credit*
Merchandise inventory...	18,000	20,000
Sales..		100,000
Sales returns and allowances	500	
Sales discounts	1,000	
Purchases	60,000	
Purchases returns and allowances............................		300
Purchase discounts...		1,200
Freight-in	800	
Selling expenses...	15,000	
General and administrative expenses........................	5,000	
	100,300	121,500
Net Income	21,200	
	121,500	121,500

The foregoing items, with expenses condensed to conserve space, appeared in the Income Statement columns of Campus Shop's December 31, 197B, work sheet. From the information prepare a 197B income statement for the shop.

Exercise 5-3

PART 1. Under the assumption that Campus Shop of Exercise 5-2 is owned by Mary Reed, prepare journal entries to close the shop's revenue, expense, and Income Summary accounts.

PART 2. Rule a balance-column Merchandise Inventory account on notebook paper, and under the date, December 31, 197A, enter the $18,000 beginning inventory of Exercise 5-2 as its balance. Then post to the account the portions of the closing entries that affect the account. (Post first the credit that removes the beginning inventory amount from the account.)

Exercise 5-4

Copy the following tabulation and fill in the missing amounts. Indicate a loss by placing a minus sign before the amount. Each horizontal row of figures is a separate problem situation.

Sales	Beginning Inventory	Purchases	Ending Inventory	Cost of Goods Sold	Gross Profit	Expenses	Net Income or Loss
80,000	50,000	40,000	?	65,000	?	20,000	?
95,000	35,000	?	45,000	50,000	?	25,000	20,000
120,000	50,000	?	40,000	?	55,000	35,000	20,000
?	40,000	70,000	35,000	?	40,000	35,000	?
110,000	40,000	65,000	?	60,000	?	25,000	?
70,000	30,000	?	35,000	40,000	?	?	10,000
?	40,000	50,000	30,000	?	40,000	?	−5,000
80,000	?	50,000	35,000	?	30,000	?	10,000

Exercise 5-5

Following is a list of trial balance accounts and their balances. To simplify the problem and to save time, the balances are in numbers of not more than two digits. However, in order to increase your skill in sorting adjusted trial balance amounts to the proper columns, the amounts are listed in alphabetical order.

TRIAL BALANCE ACCOUNTS AND AMOUNTS

Accounts payable	$2	Purchases	$12
Accounts receivable	3	Purchase discounts	1
Accumulated depreciation, store equipment	2	Salaries expense	4
Cash	3	Sales	31
Freight-in	1	Sales returns	1
Merchandise inventory	5	Samuel Smith, capital	19
Prepaid rent	6	Samuel Smith, withdrawals	4
Publicity expense	2	Store equipment	9
		Store supplies	5

Required:

Prepare a work sheet form on ordinary notebook paper and copy the trial balance accounts and amounts on the work sheet without changing their alphabetical arrangement. Then complete the work sheet using the following information:

a. Estimated depreciation of store equipment, $1.
b. Prepaid rent expired, $4.
c. Accrued salaries payable, $2.
d. Ending store supplies inventory, $2.
e. Ending merchandise inventory, $6.

Problems   **Problem 5–1**

Prepare general journal entries to record the following transactions:

Nov. 1   Purchased merchandise on credit, terms 1/10, n/30, $700.
      4   Sold merchandise for cash, $55.
      7   Purchased office equipment on credit, $300.
      8   Purchased merchandise on credit, terms 2/10, n/60, $645.
      8   Paid $30 cash for freight charges on the merchandise shipment of the previous transaction.
     11   Received a $45 credit memorandum for merchandise purchased on November 8 and returned for credit.
     12   Sold merchandise on credit, terms 2/10, 1/15, n/60, $500.
     15   Purchased office supplies on credit, $85.
     16   Sold merchandise on credit, terms 2/10, 1/15, n/60, $675.
     17   Received a credit memorandum for unsatisfactory office supplies purchased on November 15 and returned, $20.
     18   Issued a $25 credit memorandum to the customer who purchased merchandise on November 16 and returned a portion for credit, $25.
     18   Paid for the merchandise purchased on November 8, less the return and the discount.
     26   Received payment for the merchandise sold on November 16, less the return and applicable discount.
     27   The customer of November 12 paid for his purchase of that date, less the applicable discount.
     30   Paid for the merchandise purchased on November 1.

Problem 5–2

(If the working papers that accompany this text are not used, omit this problem.)

The work sheet of Beachside Shop completed through the Adjusted Trial Balance columns, is reproduced in the booklet of working papers.

Required:

1. Sort the work sheet's adjusted trial balance amounts into the proper In-

come Statement and Balance Sheet columns, enter the $15,875 ending inventory amount in the Income Statement credit and Balance Sheet debit columns, and complete the work sheet.
2. From the work sheet prepare an income statement that is complete through the calculation of gross profit from sales.
3. From the work sheet prepare compound closing entries.
4. Post those portions of the closing entries that affect the Merchandise Inventory account.

Problem 5-3

The following trial balance was taken from the ledger of The Tennis Shop at the end of its annual accounting period:

THE TENNIS SHOP

Trial Balance, December 31, 19—

Cash	$ 1,310	
Merchandise inventory	17,950	
Store supplies	875	
Prepaid insurance	335	
Store equipment	6,940	
Accumulated depreciation, store equipment		$ 2,780
Accounts payable		5,890
Jane Wells, capital		19,550
Jane Wells, withdrawals	6,000	
Sales		69,275
Sales returns and allowances	1,915	
Purchases	39,880	
Purchases returns and allowances		830
Purchases discounts		325
Freight-in	1,125	
Sales salaries expense	12,215	
Rent expense	9,000	
Advertising expense	465	
Utilities expense	640	
Totals	$98,650	$98,650

Required:
1. Copy the trial balance on a work sheet and complete the work sheet using this information:
   a. Store supplies inventory, $195.
   b. Expired insurance, $210.
   c. Estimated depreciation of store equipment, $825.
   d. Accrued sales salaries payable, $140.
   e. Ending merchandise inventory, $14,225.

2. Prepare an income statement complete through the calculation of gross profit from sales.
3. Prepare compound closing entries.
4. Open a Merchandise Inventory account and enter the $17,950 beginning inventory as its balance. Then post those portions of the closing entries that affect this account.

Problem 5-4

The following trial balance was taken from the ledger of The Man's Shop at the end of its annual accounting period:

THE MAN'S SHOP
Trial Balance, December 31, 19 —

Cash	$ 1,235	
Merchandise inventory	12,440	
Store supplies	815	
Office supplies	165	
Prepaid insurance	330	
Store equipment	9,125	
Accumulated depreciation, store equipment		$ 1,190
Office equipment	1,585	
Accumulated depreciation, office equipment		255
Accounts payable		2,670
Jerry Moore, capital		17,610
Jerry Moore, withdrawals	6,600	
Sales		75,215
Sales returns and allowances	735	
Sales discounts	975	
Purchases	41,050	
Purchases returns and allowances		370
Purchases discounts		640
Freight-in	840	
Sales salaries expense	11,175	
Rent expense, selling space	4,950	
Advertising expense	785	
Office salaries expense	4,160	
Rent expense, office space	550	
Telephone and utilities expense	435	
Totals	$97,950	$97,950

Required:
1. Enter the trial balance in the Trial Balance columns of a work sheet and complete the work sheet using the following information:
   a. Store supplies inventory, $165.
   b. Office supplies inventory, $60.
   c. Expired insurance, $180.

 d. Estimated depreciation on store equipment, $950; and *(e)* on office equipment, $150.

 f. Accrued sales salaries, $160; and accrued office salaries, $40.

 g. The Man's Shop allocates 10% of its rent to the office and the remainder to selling space. Rent for the year's first 11 months was paid and correctly recorded, but rent for December was unpaid and unrecorded on December 31.

 h. Ending merchandise inventory, $13,115.

2. Prepare a classified income statement.
3. Prepare compound closing entries.
4. Open a Merchandise Inventory account and enter the $12,440 beginning inventory as its balance. Then post those portions of the closing entries that affect this account.

Problem 5–5

The following trial balance was taken from the ledger of University Store at the end of its annual accounting period:

UNIVERSITY STORE
Trial Balance, December 31, 19–

Cash	$ 1,850	
Merchandise inventory	15,565	
Prepaid insurance	435	
Store supplies	1,175	
Office supplies	285	
Store equipment	14,140	
Accumulated depreciation, store equipment		$ 5,320
Office equipment	1,990	
Accumulated depreciation, office equipment		465
Notes payable		2,500
Accounts payable		2,145
Lois Dale, capital		20,770
Lois Dale, withdrawals	7,200	
Sales		79,145
Sales returns and allowances	1,135	
Purchases	42,170	
Purchases returns and allowances		610
Purchases discounts		880
Freight-in	885	
Sales salaries expense	12,540	
Rent expense, selling space	6,000	
Advertising expense	785	
Delivery expense	535	
Office salaries expense	4,130	
Rent expense, office space	600	
Telephone and utilities expense	415	
Totals	$111,835	$111,835

Required:

1. Enter the trial balance on a work sheet form and complete the work sheet using the following information:
   a. Expired insurance, $285.
   b. Store supplies inventory, $265, and *(c)* office supplies inventory, $130.
   d. Estimated depreciation of store equipment, $1,150, and *(e)* of office equipment, $210.
   f. Accrued but unpaid sales salaries, $240, and accrued office salaries, $70.
   g. Ending merchandise inventory, $16,140.
2. Prepare a classified income statement and a classified balance sheet.
3. Prepare adjusting and closing journal entries.
4. Open a Merchandise Inventory account and enter the $15,565 beginning inventory as its balance. Then post those portions of the closing entries that affect this account.

Alternate problems

Problem 5–1A

Prepare general journal entries to record the following transactions:

Nov. 1 Purchased merchandise on credit, terms 2/10, n/30, $800.
     1 Paid $35 cash for freight charges on the merchandise shipment of the previous transaction.
     4 Sold merchandise on credit, terms 2/10, 1/15, n/60, $500.
     7 Purchased on credit a new typewriter for office use, $300.
     9 Purchased merchandise on credit, terms 2/10, n/60, $580.
   11 Received a $30 credit memorandum for merchandise purchased on November 9 and returned for credit.
   13 Sold merchandise for cash, $65.
   15 Purchased office supplies on credit, $75.
   16 Received a credit memorandum for unsatisfactory office supplies purchased on November 15 and returned for credit, $15.
   17 Sold merchandise on credit, terms 2/10, 1/15, n/60, $540.
   18 Issued a $40 credit memorandum to the customer of November 17 who returned a portion of the merchandise he had purchased.
   19 Paid for the merchandise purchased on November 9, less the return and the discount.
   19 The customer who purchased merchandise on November 4 paid for his purchase of that date less the applicable discount.
   27 Received payment for the merchandise sold on November 17, less the return and applicable discount.
   30 Paid for the merchandise purchased on November 1.

Problem 5–3A

At the end of its annual accounting period the trial balance of The Racquet Shop carried these items:

THE RACQUET SHOP
Trial Balance, December 31, 19—

Cash	$ 1,310	
Merchandise inventory	17,950	
Store supplies	815	
Prepaid insurance	320	
Store equipment	7,980	
Accumulated depreciation, store equipment		$ 2,960
Accounts payable		2,640
Edith Holt, capital		14,880
Edith Holt, withdrawals	9,000	
Sales		74,990
Sales returns and allowances	535	
Sales discounts	615	
Purchases	36,860	
Purchases returns and allowances		355
Purchases discounts		710
Freight-in	585	
Sales salaries expense	11,460	
Rent expense	7,200	
Advertising expense	775	
Heating and lighting expense	1,130	
Totals	$96,535	$96,535

Required:
1. Copy the trial balance on a work sheet form and complete the work sheet using the following information:
    a. Store supplies inventory, $210.
    b. Expired insurance, $195.
    c. Estimated depreciation of store equipment, $850.
    d. Accrued sales salaries payable, $235.
    e. Ending merchandise inventory, $14,880.
2. Prepare an income statement complete through the calculation of gross profit from sales.
3. Prepare compound closing entries.
4. Open a merchandise inventory account and enter the $17,950 beginning inventory as its balance. Then post those portions of the closing entries that affect this account.

Problem 5–4A
    The following trial balance was taken from the ledger of Universal Sales at the end of its annual accounting period:

UNIVERSAL SALES
Trial Balance, December 31, 19—

Cash	$ 1,125	
Merchandise inventory	12,440	
Store supplies	845	
Office supplies	170	
Prepaid insurance	345	
Prepaid rent	550	
Store equipment	8,850	
Accumulated depreciation, store equipment		$ 3,115
Office equipment	1,280	
Accumulated depreciation, office equipment		380
Accounts payable		3,230
Ted West, capital		21,530
Ted West, withdrawals	6,000	
Sales		69,195
Sales returns and allowances	815	
Sales discounts	945	
Purchases	40,990	
Purchases returns and allowances		535
Purchases discounts		315
Freight-in	955	
Sales salaries expense	12,215	
Rent expense, selling space	5,445	
Advertising expense	810	
Office salaries expense	3,550	
Rent expense, office space	605	
Utilities expense	365	
Totals	$98,300	$98,300

Required:
1. Enter the trial balance on a work sheet form and complete the work sheet using the following information:
   a. Store supplies inventory, $135, and *(b)* office supplies inventory, $65.
   c. Expired insurance, $215.
   d. Universal Sales allocates 10% of its rent to the office and the remainder to selling space. Rent for January of the trial balance year had been prepaid on the previous December 28 and debited to the Prepaid Rent account; however, this prepayment, of course, had expired by the trial balance date.
   e. Estimated depreciation on store equipment, $1,050, and *(f)* on office equipment, $165.
   g. Accrued but unpaid sales salaries, $175, and accrued office salaries, $50.
   h. Ending merchandise inventory, $11,650.
2. Prepare a classified income statement.
3. Prepare compound closing entries.
4. Open a Merchandise Inventory account and enter the $12,440 beginning

inventory as its balance. Then post those portions of the closing entries that affect this account.

Last year Clyde Lamar retired from farming, sold his equipment, paid off his debts, and placed his remaining cash in a savings account. However, he soon became restless, and six months ago he opened a retail hardware store in his small rural community. At that time there was no such store in the community, and it appeared to Mr. Lamar that the venture would be profitable.

He began business by transferring $30,000 from his savings account to a current account opened in the store's name. He immediately bought for cash store equipment costing $4,000, which he expected to use for 10 years, after which it would be worn out and valueless, and a stock of merchandise costing $20,000. He also paid six months' rent in advance on the store building, $900.

He estimated that like stores in neighbouring communities marked their goods for sale at prices 40% above cost. In other words, an item costing $10 was marked for sale at $14. In order to get his store off to a fast start, he decided to mark his goods for sale at 35% above cost, and he thought this would still leave him a net income equal to 10% of the cost of goods sold.

Since he was in a rural farming community, Mr. Lamar granted liberal credit terms, telling his credit-worthy customers to pay "when the crops are in." His suppliers granted Mr. Lamar the normal 30-day credit period on his purchases.

Today, October 1, six months after opening his store, Mr. Lamar has come to you for advice. He thinks business has been excellent. He has paid his suppliers for all purchases when due and owes only for the purchases, $9,000, made during the last 30 days and for which payment is not due. He has replaced his original inventory three times during the last six months, and an income statement he has prepared shows a $21,000 gross profit and a $6,900 net income, which is a little better than he anticipated. He says he has a full stock of merchandise which cost $20,000 and his customers owe him $21,400. In addition to the rent paid in advance, he has paid all his other expenses, $13,200, with cash. However, you note on his income statement that he has not charged any depreciation on his store equipment.

Nevertheless, Mr. Lamar doubts the validity of his gross profit and net income figures, since he started business with $30,000 in cash and now has only $500 in the bank and also owes $9,000 for merchandise purchased on credit.

Did Mr. Lamar actually meet his profit expectations? If so, explain to him the apparent paradox of adequate income and a declining cash balance. Back your explanations with a statement accounting for the October 1 cash balance, a six months' income statement, and a September 30 balance sheet.

Part 1. In your initial audit of the records of Durham Sales you find the company never takes advantage of cash discounts, although it could earn a 2% discount on all purchases, since its suppliers all grant terms of 2/10, n/60. It does not take advantage of cash discounts because to do so it would, in the words of its owner, Carl Durham, "have to be constantly borrowing money from the bank," and he is opposed to this. The company's sales, purchases, and inventories remain at about the same levels throughout the year, and its typical annual income statement shows the following:

Sales... $270,000
Cost of goods sold 180,000
Gross profit on sales....................... $ 90,000
Operating expenses 70,000
Net Income .... $ 20,000

Can Durham Sales increase its annual net income by borrowing money from the bank at 7% per year to take advantage of all cash discounts? Back your answer with figures.

PART 2. Assume that Mr. Durham agrees that his concern should take advantage of all discounts. However, you discover that the concern's bookkeeper follows the practice of putting all invoices approved for payment in a file marked "To Be Paid." Then, each day she searches through the file to find invoices due for payment that day. You recognize that if discounts are to be taken on all invoices on the last day of the discount period, discounts are certain to be missed under such a filing system, because in searching through the file, invoices will occasionally be overlooked on the last day of the discount period. Consequently, describe a system for filing invoices that will reduce the chances of an invoice being overlooked on the last day of its discount period.

Decision problem 5–3, Colours Unlimited

Yesterday near closing time the accountant of Colours Unlimited finished the paint store's 197B financial statements and gave them to the store's owner, Carl Larson. Mr. Larson took the statements home with him last night to examine, but was unable to do so because of unexpected guests, and this morning he inadvertently left the 197B income statement at home when he came to work. However, he has the store's 197A and 197B balance sheets which show the following in condensed form:

	197A	197B
Cash..	$ 1,000	$ 3,200
Accounts receivable	7,500	8,400
Merchandise inventory..	9,000	8,000
Store equipment (net after depreciation).....................	5,000	4,500
Total assets...	$22,500	$24,100
Accounts payable (for merchandise)..........................	$ 6,200	$ 5,700
Accrued wages payable..	400	200
Carl Larson, capital...	15,900	18,200
	$22,500	$24,100

He also has the store's 197B cheque book record of cash receipts and disbursements which shows:

	Receipts	Payments
Collection of accounts receivable	$81,500	
Payment of accounts payable		$48,800
Wages and salaries		10,000
Other operating expenses		8,500
Carl Larson, withdrawals		12,000

Under the assumption that Colours Unlimited makes all purchases and sales of merchandise on credit, prepare a 197B accrual basis income statement for the store based on the information given.

Analytical and review problems

Problem 5–1 A&R

The partially completed work sheet of Incomplete Data Company appear below. Complete the work sheet using the following additional data:

a. Inventory December 31, 1975, $12.

b. Balance of Samuel Smith's Capital account as of December 31, 1975, $36.

Account Titles	Trial Balance Dr.	Trial Balance Cr.	Adjustments Dr.	Adjustments Cr.	Income Statement Dr.	Income Statement Cr	Balance Sheet Dr.	Balance Sheet Cr.
Cash	6.00							
Accounts receivable								
Store equipment	18.00							
Accumulated depreciation, store equipment		4.00						6.00
Inventory					10.00			
Supplies	10.00						4.00	
Prepaid rent	12.00						4.00	
Accounts payable		4.00						
Samuel Smith, capital		38.00						
Samuel Smith, withdrawals	8.00							
Purchases								
Purchase returns		2.00						
Freight-in	2.00							
Salaries expense	8.00				12.00			
Advertising expense	4.00				4.00			
Sales		62.00						
Sales returns	2.00							
		110.00						

Problem 5–2 A&R

The following selected data are related to Mystic Company:
1. Balance sheets

	December 31	
Assets	1975	1974
Cash..	$ 1,000	$ 2,000
Accounts receivable	3,000	2,000
Inventories	60,000	46,000
Land..	10,000	10,000
	$74,000	$60,000

Liabilities and Owner Equity		
Accounts payable	$14,000	$16,000
Mortgage payable	20,000	18,000
Michael McDonald, capital.................................	40,000	26,000
	$74,000	$60,000

2. Closing entries for sales, expenses, and withdrawals

Sales..	160,000	
Sales returns and allowances..........................		10,000
Income summary		150,000
Purchases returns and allowances........................	400	
Purchases discounts	600	
Income summary		1,000
Income summary	40,000	
Freight-in..		1,000
Sales salaries expense...................................		20,000
Rent expense		8,000
Delivery expense...		2,000
Advertising expense		9,000
Michael McDonald, capital.................................	11,000	
Michael McDonald, withdrawal......................		11,000

Required:
1. Compute the net income for 1975.
2. Compute the cost of goods sold and the amount of purchases for 1975.
3. Prepare the missing closing entry or entries.

Problem 5–3 A&R

The following are the selected data for Sunvalley Sales Company for the year 1975:
1. Selected closing entries

Income summary	148,000	
Purchases returns and allowances........................	1,500	
Purchases discounts	500	
Purchases..		100,000
Freight-in		2,000
Sales salaries expense....................................		20,000

Advertising expense......................................		10,000
Rent expense, office space............................		8,000
Delivery expense...		2,500
Office salaries expense.................................		6,000
Depreciation – office equipment......................		1,000
Miscellaneous expense.................................		500

To close expense and other nominal accounts.

George Lean, capital...	26,000	
George Lean, withdrawals............................		26,000

To close the withdrawals account.

2. George Lean follows the practice of withdrawing half of the annual net income from the business.
3. There were no sales returns and allowances for the year. However, sales discounts amounted to $1,000.
4. Inventories – December 31, 1974 20,000

    December 31, 1975 25,000

Required:
1. Compute the amount of net income for 1975.
2. Compute the amount of sales for 1975.
3. Prepare a classified income statement for 1975.

Problem 5–4 A&R

JOHN STONE
Balance Sheet
April 30, 1975

Current Assets:

			Liabilities:	
Cash	$ 20		Accounts Payable..............	$ 10
Accounts Receivable	30		Advance from customers.....	15
Merchandise inventory...........	25		Total Liabilities..............	$ 25
Prepaid insurance..................	16			
Total Current Assets	$ 91		*Owner Equity*	
			John Stone Capital.............	156

Fixed Assets:

Equipment	$96		
Accumulated depreciation-Equipment	6	90	
			Total Liabilities
Total Assets.............		$181	and Equity $181

May Transactions:

Sales on account	$100
Purchases on account.............	55
Collection of accounts receivable	95
Payment of accounts payable............................	40

Withdrawals by owner............	20
Sales returns........................	2
Purchases returns and allowances	1
Payment of wages during May...............................	10
Payment of other expenses..........................	8

Data for adjustment:
a. Accrued unpaid wages on May 31 amounted to $1.
b. A one-year insurance policy was purchased on January 1, 1975.
c. Equipment has an estimated service life of 4 years.
d. The necessary deliveries were made to all customers that had paid in advance.
e. A physical count of inventory was made on May 31, 1975 and its cost was determined as $20.

Required:
1. Journalize the May transactions.
2. Post to appropriate general ledger accounts. (T-accounts are acceptable.)
3. Take a trial balance (first two columns of work sheet).
4. Complete work sheet.
5. Prepare in good form the balance sheet and the income statement. (The fiscal period is May 1 to May 31) i.e. a monthly fiscal period.
6. Journalize the adjusting and closing entries.
7. Post the adjusting and closing journal entries.

(CGA adapted)

6

Accounting systems

■ An accounting system consists of the business papers, records, and reports plus the procedures that are used in recording transactions and reporting their effects. Operation of an accounting system begins with the preparation of a business paper, such as an invoice or cheque, and includes the capture of the data entered on this paper and its flow through the recording, classifying, summarizing, and reporting steps of the system. Actually an accounting system is a data processing system, and it is now time to introduce more efficient ways of processing data.

Reducing posting labour ■ The General Journal described in previous chapters is a flexible journal in which it is possible to record any transaction. However, since each debit and credit entered in such a journal must be posted individually, using a General Journal to record all the transactions of a business results in the expenditure of too much posting labour.

Several ways have been devised to reduce this labour. One takes advantage of the fact that like transactions always result in debits and credits to the same accounts. For example, all sales on credit are alike in that they result in debits to Accounts Receivable and credits to Sales. Consequently, if advantage is taken of this and a company's credit sales for, say, a month are recorded in a Sales Journal like Illustration 6-1, labour is saved by waiting until the end of the month, totaling the sales recorded in the journal, and debiting Accounts Receivable and crediting Sales for the total.

Sales Journal

Date		Account Debited	Invoice Number	F	Amount
Oct.	1	James Henry...	307	✓	200.00
	7	Albert Smith	308	✓	100.00
	12	John Wright...	309	✓	150.00
	15	Paul Roth	310	✓	225.00
	22	Sam Moore...	311	✓	125.00
	25	Frank Booth	312	✓	50.00
	28	Sam Moore...	313	✓	175.00
	31	Total—Accounts Receivable, Dr.; Sales, Cr....			1,025.00

Illustration
6-1

Only seven sales are recorded in the illustrated journal. However, if the seven sales are assumed to represent, say 700 sales, the labour saved by posting only one debit to Accounts Receivable and one credit to Sales for their total rather than 700 debits and 700 credits can better be appreciated.

The journal of Illustration 6-1 is called a *columnar journal* because it has columns for recording the date, the customer's name, invoice number, and the amount of each charge sale. Only charge sales can be recorded in it, and they are recorded daily with the information about each sale being placed on a separate line. Normally the information about each sale is taken from the sales ticket or invoice prepared at the time of the sale. However, before discussing the journal further, the subject of *subsidiary ledgers* first must be introduced to broaden your understanding.

Subsidiary ledgers

■ The one Accounts Receivable account used thus far does not readily tell how much each customer bought and paid for or how much each customer owes. As a result, a business selling on credit must maintain additional accounts receivable, one for each customer, to provide this information.

These individual customer accounts are in addition to the Accounts Receivable account used thus far and are normally kept in a book or file tray, called a *subsidiary ledger*, that is separate and distinct from the book or tray containing the financial statement accounts. Also, to distinguish the two, the book or tray containing the customer accounts is called the *Accounts Receivable Ledger,* while the one that contains the financial statement accounts is known as the *General Ledger.*

Posting the sales journal

■ When customer accounts are placed in a subsidiary ledger, a Sales Journal is posted as in Illustration 6–2. In the posting procedure the individual sales recorded in the journal are posted each day to the proper customer accounts in the Accounts Receivable Ledger. These daily postings keep the customer accounts up to date, which is important in granting credit. It is important because when a customer asks for credit, the person responsible for granting it should know the amount currently owed by the customer, as well as his promptness in meeting past obligations. The source of this information is the customer's account; and if the account is not up to date, an incorrect decision may be made.

Note the check marks in the Sales Journal's Folio column. They indicate that the sales recorded in the journal were individually posted to the customer accounts in the Accounts Receivable Ledger. Check marks rather than account numbers are used because the customer accounts commonly do not have numbers. Rather, as an aid in locating individual accounts, they are alphabetically arranged in the Accounts Receivable Ledger, with new accounts being added in their proper alphabetical positions as required. Consequently, numbering the accounts is impractical, since many numbers would have to be changed each time new accounts are added.

In addition to the daily postings to customer accounts, at the end of the month the Sales Journal's Amount column is totaled and the total is debited to Accounts Receivable and credited to Sales. The credit records the month's revenue from charge sales, and the debit records the resulting increase in accounts receivable.

Before going on, note again in Illustration 6–2 that the individual customer accounts in the subsidiary Accounts Receivable Ledger do not replace the Accounts Receivable account described in previous chapters but are in addition to it. The Accounts Receivable account of previous chapters must still be maintained in the General Ledger where it serves three functions: (1) it shows the total amount owed by all customers; (2) it helps keep the General Ledger a balancing ledger in which debits equal credits; and (3) it offers a means of proving the accuracy of the customer accounts in the subsidiary Accounts Receivable Ledger.

Controlling accounts

■ When a company maintains an Accounts Receivable account in its General Ledger and puts its individual customer accounts in a subsidiary ledger, the Accounts Receivable account is said to control the

Sales Journal

Date		Account Debited	Invoice Number	F	Amount
Oct.	1	James Henry.....................................	307	✔	200.00
	7	Albert Smith	308	✔	100.00
	12	John Wright.....................................	309	✔	150.00
	15	Paul Roth.....................................	310	✔	225.00
	22	Sam Moore.....................................	311	✔	125.00
	25	Frank Booth	312	✔	50.00
	28	Sam Moore.....................................	313	✔	175.00
	31	Total—Accounts Receivable, Dr.; Sales, Cr....			1,025.00
					(113/411)

Individual amounts are posted daily to the subsidiary ledger.

Total is posted at the end of the month to the general ledger accounts.

Accounts Receivable Ledger

Frank Booth

Date	Debit	Credit	Balance
Oct. 25	50.00		50.00

James Henry

Date	Debit	Credit	Balance
Oct. 1	200.00		200.00

Sam Moore

Date	Debit	Credit	Balance
Oct. 22	125.00		125.00
28	175.00		300.00

Paul Roth

Date	Debit	Credit	Balance
Oct. 15	225.00		225.00

Albert Smith

Date	Debit	Credit	Balance
Oct. 7	100.00		100.00

John Wright

Date	Debit	Credit	Balance
Oct. 12	150.00		150.00

General Ledger

Accounts Receivable   113

Date	Debit	Credit	Balance
Oct. 31	1,025.00		1,025.00

Sales   411

Date	Debit	Credit	Balance
Oct. 31		1,025.00	1,025.00

The double ruled lines around the accounts are meant to convey the idea that the customer accounts are in one ledger and the financial statement accounts are in a different ledger, kept in a different book or file tray.

Illustration
6–2
Posting the Sales Journal to the Accounts Receivable Ledger and to the General Ledger

subsidiary ledger and is called a *controlling account*. The extent of the control is such that after all posting is completed, if no errors were made, the sum of all of the customer account balances in the subsidiary Accounts Receivable Ledger will equal the balance of the Accounts Receivable controlling account in the General Ledger. This equality is also a proof of the customer account balances.

Other columnar journals ■ Only sales on credit may be recorded in a Sales Journal. As a result, if a merchandising company takes full advantage of the labour saving benefits of columnar journals, it must use several columnar journals in addition to a Sales Journal. These are a Cash Receipts Journal, a Purchases Journal, a Cash Disbursements Journal, and perhaps others. Also, and regardless of the columnar journals used, there are always a few miscellaneous transactions plus adjusting, closing, and correcting entries that cannot be recorded in any columnar journal, and for these a General Journal must be provided.

Cash Receipts Journal ■ A Cash Receipts Journal designed to save the maximum of posting labour through posting column totals must be a multicolumn journal. A multicolumn journal is necessary because although all cash receipts are alike in that they result in debits to Cash, they differ as to sources and, consequently, as to the accounts credited when cash is received from different sources. For example, if the cash receipts of a mercantile concern are classified as to sources, they normally fall into three groups: (1) cash from charge customers in payment of their accounts, (2) cash from cash sales, and (3) cash from miscellaneous sources. Note in the Cash Receipts Journal of Illustration 6–3 how a special column is provided for entering the credits resulting when cash is received from each of these sources. Also, note the special columns for the debits to Sales Discounts and to Cash.

Cash from charge customers

When cash received from a charge customer in payment of his account is recorded in a columnar Cash Receipts Journal like Illustration 6–3, the customer's name is entered in the Account Credited column; the amount credited to his account is entered in the Accounts Receivable credit column; and the debits to Sales Discounts and Cash are entered in the journal's last two columns.

Give close attention to the Accounts Receivable credit column. Observe that (1) only credits to customer accounts are entered in this column; (2) the individual credits are posted daily to the customer accounts in the subsidiary Accounts Receivable Ledger; and (3) the column total is posted at the month end to the credit of the Accounts Receivable controlling account. This is the normal recording and posting procedure when controlling accounts and subsidiary ledgers are used. When such accounts and ledgers are used, transactions are normally entered in a journal column, the individual amounts are posted to the

Cash Receipts Journal

Date	Account Credited	Explanation	F	Other Accounts Credit	Accts. Rec. Credit	Sales Credit	Sales Disc. Debit	Cash Debit
Oct. 6	Sales	Cash sales	✔			400.00		400.00
10	James Henry........	Invoice, 10/1	✔		200.00		4.00	196.00
13	Sales	Cash sales	✔			390.00		390.00
17	Albert Smith	Invoice, 10/7	✔		100.00		2.00	98.00
18	Notes Payable......	Note to bank	211	1,000.00				1,000.00
20	Sales	Cash sales	✔			450.00		450.00
20	John Wright	Invoice, 10/12......	✔		150.00		3.00	147.00
25	Paul Roth............	Invoice, 10/15......	✔		225.00		4.50	220.50
27	Sales	Cash sales	✔			398.50		398.50
31	Totals			1,000.00	675.00	1,638.50	13.50	3,300.00
				(✔)	(113)	(411)	(413)	(111)

Total is not posted.

Totals posted at the end of the month.

Individual amounts in the Other Accounts credit and Accounts Receivable credit columns are posted daily.

General Ledger

Cash 111

Date	Debit	Credit	Balance
Oct. 31	3,300.00		3,300.00

Accounts Receivable 113

Date	Debit	Credit	Balance
Oct. 31	1,025.00		1,025.00
31		675.00	350.00

Notes Payable 211

Date	Debit	Credit	Balance
Oct. 18		1,000.00	1,000.00

Sales 411

Date	Debit	Credit	Balance
Oct. 31		1,025.00	1,025.00
31		1,638.50	2,663.50

Sales Discounts 413

Date	Debit	Credit	Balance
Oct. 31	13.50		13.50

Accounts Receivable Ledger

James Henry

Date	Debit	Credit	Balance
Oct. 1	200.00		200.00
10		200.00	-0-

Paul Roth

Date	Debit	Credit	Balance
Oct. 15	225.00		225.00
25		225.00	-0-

Albert Smith

Date	Debit	Credit	Balance
Oct. 7	100.00		100.00
17		100.00	-0-

John Wright

Date	Debit	Credit	Balance
Oct. 12	150.00		150.00
20		150.00	-0-

Illustration
6–3
**Posting the Cash Receipts Journal
to the Accounts Receivable Ledger
and to the General Ledger**

subsidiary ledger accounts, and the column total is posted to the controlling account.

Cash sales

In an average company, cash sales are "rung up" each day on one or more cash registers and their total is recorded by means of a journal entry at the end of the day. All of these entries are alike; all have repetitive debits to Cash and repetitive credits to Sales.

When cash sales are recorded in a Cash Receipts Journal like that of Illustration 6–3, the repetitive debits to Cash are entered in the Cash debit column and a special column headed "Sales credit" is provided for the repetitive credits to Sales. By entering each day's cash sales in this column, the cash sales of a month may be posted at the month's end in a single amount, the column total. (Although cash sales are normally recorded daily from the cash register reading, the cash sales of Illustration 6–3 are recorded only once each week in order to shorten the illustration.)

At the time daily cash sales are recorded in the Cash Receipts Journal, some bookkeepers, as in Illustration 6–3, place a check mark in the Folio column to indicate that no amount is individually posted from that line of the journal. Other bookkeepers use a double check ($\nu\nu$) to distinguish amounts not posted from amounts posted to customer accounts.

Miscellaneous receipts of cash

Most cash receipts come from customer collections and cash sales. However, cash is occasionally received from other sources such as, for example, the sale for cash of an unneeded plant asset, or a promissory note is given to a bank in order to borrow money. For miscellaneous receipts such as these the Other Accounts credit column is provided in the Cash Receipts Journal.

Posting the Cash Receipts Journal

■ As previously stated, the individual items in the Cash Receipts Journal's Accounts Receivable column are posted daily as credits to the customer accounts named in the Account Credited column. These items must be posted daily so that the accounts receivable ledger accounts show for each customer the current amount owed.

In an average company, the items in the Other Accounts credit column are few and are posted to a variety of general ledger accounts. As a result, postings are less apt to be omitted if these items are also posted daily. Furthermore, if the individual items in both the Other Accounts and the Accounts Receivable columns are posted daily, only the column totals remain to be posted at the end of the month.

The amounts in the Accounts Receivable, Sales, Sales Discounts, and Cash columns are posted as column totals at the end of the month. However, since the transactions recorded in any journal must result in equal debits and credits to general ledger accounts, the debit and credit equality in a columnar journal such as the Cash Receipts Journal is proved by *crossfooting* or cross adding the column totals before they are posted at the end of the month.

To *foot* a column of figures is to add it; and to crossfoot the Cash Receipts Journal the debit column totals are added together, the credit column totals are added together, and the two sums are compared for equality. For example, if the debit column totals of the Cash Receipts Journal in Illustration 6–3 are added and the credit column totals are added, the two sums appear as follows:

Debit Columns		Credit Columns	
Sales discounts debit	$ 13.50	Other accounts credit	$1,000.00
Cash debit	3,300.00	Accounts receivable credit	675.00
		Sales credit	1,638.50
Total	$3,313.50	Total	$3,313.50

And since the sums are equal, the debits in the journal are assumed to equal the credits.

After the debit and credit equality is proved by crossfooting, the totals are posted. The Accounts Receivable column total is posted to the credit of the Accounts Receivable controlling account in the General Ledger; the Sales column total is posted to the credit of the Sales account; the Sales Discounts column total is posted to the debit of the Sales Discounts account; and the Cash column total is posted to the debit of the Cash account. Since individual items in the Other Accounts column are posted daily, this column total is not posted. This posting procedure is demonstrated in Illustration 6–3.

Posting items daily from the Other Accounts column of the Cash Receipts Journal with a delayed posting of the offsetting totals causes the General Ledger to be out of balance throughout the month. However, this is of no consequence because the offsetting totals are posted before a trial balance is prepared.

The Cash Receipts Journal's Folio column is used only for daily postings from the Other Accounts and Accounts Receivable columns. The account numbers appearing in the Folio column indicate items posted to the General Ledger from the Other Accounts column; and the check marks indicate either that an item like a day's cash sales was not posted or that an item was posted to the subsidiary Accounts Receivable Ledger. The total of the Other Accounts column is not posted. Note in Illustration 6–3 the check mark below this column. The check mark indicates that when the journal was posted, this column total was not posted. The account numbers of the accounts to which the Accounts Receivable, Sales, Sales Discounts, and Cash column totals of Illustration 6–3 were posted are indicated in parentheses below each column.

Posting rule ■ Posting to a subsidiary ledger and its controlling account from two journals has been demonstrated, and a rule to cover all such postings can now be given. The rule is: *In posting to a subsidiary ledger and its controlling account, the controlling account must be debited periodically for an amount or amounts equal to the sum of the debits to the subsidiary ledger and it must be credited periodically for an amount or amounts equal to the sum of the credits to the subsidiary ledger.*

The periodic postings to the controlling account bring its balance up to date and provide a proof of the subsidiary ledger accounts. The proof is that if no errors were made, after all posting is completed, the balance of the controlling account will equal the sum of the account balances in the subsidiary ledger.

Sales returns ■ A company having only a few such returns may record them in a General Journal with an entry like the following:

Oct.	17	Sales Returns and Allowances......................	412	17.50	
		Accounts Receivable – George Ball	113/✔		17.50
		Returned defective merchandise.			

The debit of the entry is posted to the Sales Returns and Allowances account; and the credit is posted to both the Accounts Receivable controlling account and to the customer's account. Note the account number and the check, 113/✔, in the Folio column on the credit line. This indicates that both the Accounts Receivable controlling account in the General Ledger and the George Ball account in the Accounts Receivable Ledger were credited for $17.50. Both were credited because the balance of the controlling account in the General Ledger will not equal the sum of the customer account balances in the subsidiary ledger unless both are credited.

Companies having sufficient sales returns can save posting labour by recording them in a special Sales Returns and Allowances Journal like that of Illustration 6–4. Note that this is in keeping with the generally

Sales Returns and Allowances Journal

Date		Account Credited	Explanation	Credit Memo No.	F	Amount
Oct.	7	Robert Moore...........	Defective mdse...........	203	✔	10.00
	14	James Warren	Defective mdse...........	204	✔	12.00
	18	T. M. Jones...............	Not ordered	205	✔	6.00
	23	Sam Smith...............	Defective mdse...........	206	✔	18.00
	31	Sales Returns and Allow., Dr.; Accounts Rec., Cr.				46.00
						412/113

Illustration
6–4

recognized idea that a company can design and use a special journal for any class of like transactions in which there are within the class sufficient transactions to warrant the journal. When a Sales Returns and Allowances Journal is used to record returns, the individual amounts entered in the journal are posted daily to the credit of each affected customer account. At the end of the month, the journal total is posted to both the debit of the Sales Returns and Allowances account and the credit of the Accounts Receivable controlling account.

Accounts payable ■ As with accounts receivable, the one Accounts Payable account used thus far does not show how much is owed each creditor. One way to secure this information is to maintain an individual account for each creditor in a subsidiary Accounts Payable Ledger controlled by an Accounts Payable controlling account in the General Ledger. If maintained, the controlling account, subsidiary ledger, and columnar journal techniques demonstrated thus far with accounts receivable apply to these accounts payable. The only difference is that a Purchases Journal and a Cash Disbursements Journal are used in recording most of the transactions affecting the accounts. However, this difference is not great, since these journals operate in the same manner as the journals described thus far.

The Purchases Journal and its posting ■ A one-column Purchases Journal is very similar to the Sales Journal previously described and operates in the same manner. The information recorded in the Purchases Journal usually includes the date of each entry, the creditor's name, the invoice date, terms, and the amount of the purchase. This information is recorded from approved purchase invoices; and its use, in the main, is apparent. The invoice date and the terms together indicate the date on which payment is due.

The one-column Purchases Journal is posted in the same manner as a Sales Journal: (1) the individual amounts in the Amount column are posted daily to the subsidiary Accounts Payable Ledger and (2) the column total is debited at the end of the month to the Purchases account and credited to the Accounts Payable controlling account. This posting is demonstrated in Illustration 6–5.

The Cash Disbursements Journal and its posting ■ The Cash Disbursements Journal, like the Cash Receipts Journal, has columns that make it possible to post repetitive debits and credits in column totals. The repetitive debits and credits of cash payments are debits to the Accounts Payable controlling account and credits to both Purchases Discounts and Cash. In most companies the purchase of merchandise for cash is not common; therefore, a Purchases column is not needed and a cash purchase is recorded as on line 2 of Illustration 6–6. However, although cash purchases are commonly treated as on line 2, it should be pointed out that any company having many such pur-

Purchases Journal

Date		Account Credited	Date of Invoice	Terms	F	Amount
Oct.	3	Horn Supply Company..............	10/2	n/30	✓	350.00
	5	Acme Mfg. Company	10/5	2/10, n/30	✓	200.00
	13	Wycoff & Company..................	10/10	n/30	✓	150.00
	20	Smith and Company.................	10/19	2/10, n/30	✓	300.00
	25	Acme Mfg. Company	10/24	2/10, n/30	✓	100.00
	29	H. A. Green Company...............	10/28	2/10, n/60	✓	225.00
	31	Total—Purchases, Dr.; Accounts Payable, Cr.				1,325.00

(511/212)

Individual amounts are posted daily.

Total is posted at the end of the month.

Accounts Payable Ledger

Acme Mfg. Company

Date	Debit	Credit	Balance
Oct. 5		200.00	200.00
15	200.00		-0-
25		100.00	100.00

H. A. Green Company

Date	Debit	Credit	Balance
Oct. 29		225.00	225.00

Horn Supply Company

Date	Debit	Credit	Balance
Oct. 3		350.00	350.00

Smith and Company

Date	Debit	Credit	Balance
Oct. 20		300.00	300.00

Wycoff & Company

Date	Debit	Credit	Balance
Oct. 13		150.00	150.00

General Ledger

Accounts Payable 212

Date	Debit	Credit	Balance
Oct. 31		1,325.00	1,325.00

Purchases 511

Date	Debit	Credit	Balance
Oct. 12	25.00		25.00
31	1,325.00		1,350.00

Illustration
6–5
Posting the Purchases Journal

Cash Disbursements Journal

Date		Ch. No.	Payee	Account Debited	F	Other Accounts Debit	Accts. Pay. Debit	Pur. Disc. Credit	Cash Credit
Oct.	3	105	L. & N. Railroad...	Freight-In	514	18.50			18.50
	12	106	East Sales Co	Purchases	511	25.00			25.00
	15	107	Acme Mfg. Co	Acme Mfg. Co	✔		200.00	4.00	196.00
	15	108	Jerry Hale	Salaries Expense...	611	86.00			86.00
	20	109	Horn Supply Co...	Horn Supply Co.....	✔		75.00		75.00
	29	110	Smith and Co	Smith and Co	✔		300.00	6.00	294.00
	31		Totals...........			129.50	575.00	10.00	694.50
						(✔)	(212)	(513)	(111)

Individual amounts in the Other Accounts debit column and Accounts Payable debit column are posted daily.

Totals posted at the end of the month.

Accounts Payable Ledger

Acme Mfg. Company

Date	Debit	Credit	Balance
Oct. 5		200.00	200.00
15	200.00		-0-
25		100.00	100.00

H. A. Green Company

Date	Debit	Credit	Balance
Oct. 29		225.00	225.00

Horn Supply Company

Date	Debit	Credit	Balance
Oct. 3		350.00	350.00
20	75.00		275.00

Smith and Company

Date	Debit	Credit	Balance
Oct. 20		300.00	300.00
29	300.00		-0-

Wycoff & Company

Date	Debit	Credit	Balance
Oct. 13		150.00	150.00

General Ledger

Cash   111

Date	Debit	Credit	Balance
Oct. 31	3,300.00		3,300.00
31		694.50	2,605.50

Accounts Payable   212

Date	Debit	Credit	Balance
Oct. 31		1,325.00	1,325.00
31	575.00		750.00

Purchases   511

Date	Debit	Credit	Balance
Oct. 12	25.00		25.00
31	1,325.00		1,350.00

Purchases Discounts   513

Date	Debit	Credit	Balance
Oct. 31		10.00	10.00

Freight-In   514

Date	Debit	Credit	Balance
Oct. 3	18.50		18.50

Salaries Expense   611

Date	Debit	Credit	Balance
Oct. 15	86.00		86.00

Illustration
6-6
Posting the Cash Disbursements Journal

chases would find it advantageous to place a Purchases column in its Cash Disbursements Journal.

Observe that the Cash Disbursements Journal of Illustration 6–6 has a column headed "Ch. No." In order to gain control over cash disbursements, all such disbursements (excepting petty cash disbursements, which are discussed in Chapter 8) should be made by cheque. The cheques should be prenumbered by the printer and they should be entered in the journal in numerical order with each cheque's number in the column headed "Ch. No." This makes it possible to scan the numbers in the column for omitted cheques. When a Cash Disbursements Journal has a column for cheque numbers, it is often called a Register.

A Cash Disbursements Journal or Cheque Register like Illustration 6–6 is posted as follows. The individual amounts in the Other Accounts column are posted daily to the debit of the general ledger accounts named in the Account Debited column; and the individual amounts in the Accounts Payable column are posted daily to the subsidiary Accounts Payable Ledger to the debit of the creditors named in the Account Debited column. At the end of the month, after the column totals are crossfooted to prove their equality, the Accounts Payable column total is posted to the debit of the Accounts Payable controlling account; the Purchases Discounts column total is posted to the credit of the Purchases Discounts account; and the Cash column total is posted to the credit of the Cash account. Since the items in the Other Accounts column are posted individually, this column total is not posted.

Identifying posted amounts

■ When several special journals are posted to ledger accounts, it is necessary to indicate in the account Folio column before each posted amount the journal as well as the page number of the journal from which the amount was posted. The journal is indicated by using its initial or initials. Because of this, items posted from the Cash Disbursements Journal carry the initial "D" before their journal page number in the Folio columns. Likewise, items from the Cash Receipts Journal carry the letter "R," those from the Sales Journal carry the initial "S," items from the Purchases Journal carry the initial "P," and from the General Journal, the letter "G."

Purchases returns

■ A company having sufficient purchases returns and allowances may use a Purchases Returns and Allowances Journal similar to the Sales Returns and Allowances Journal previously illustrated. However, if it has only a few such returns and allowances it will record them with a general journal entry like the following:

Oct.	8	Accounts Payable – Medford Mfg. Company	212/✓	32.00	
		Purchases Returns and Allowances	512		32.00
		Returned defective merchandise.			

■ Periodically, after all posting is completed, the General Ledger and the subsidiary ledgers are proved. The General Ledger is normally proved first by preparing a trial balance; and if the trial balance balances, the accounts in the General Ledger, including the controlling accounts, are assumed to be correct. The subsidiary ledgers are then proved, commonly by preparing schedules of accounts receivable and accounts payable. A schedule of accounts payable, for example, is prepared by listing with their balances the accounts in the Accounts Payable Ledger having balances. The balances are totaled; and if the total is equal to the balance of the Accounts Payable controlling account, the accounts in the Accounts Payable Ledger are assumed to be correct. Illustration 6–7 shows a schedule of the creditor accounts having balances in the Accounts Payable Ledger of Illustration 6–6. Note that the schedule total is equal to the balance of the Accounts Payable controlling account in the General Ledger of Illustration 6–6. A schedule of accounts receivable is prepared in the same way as a schedule of accounts payable; and if its total is equal to the balance of the Accounts Receivable controlling account, the accounts in the Accounts Receivable Ledger are also assumed to be correct.

Hawaiian Sales Company
Schedule of Accounts Payable, December 31, 19—

Acme Mfg. Company	$100
H. A. Green Company	225
Horn Supply Company	275
Wycoff & Company	150
Total Accounts Payable	$750

Illustration
6–7

Instead of a formal schedule to prove the accounts in a subsidiary ledger, an adding machine list may also be used. For example, the balances of the accounts in the Accounts Payable Ledger may be proved by listing on an adding machine the balance of each account in the ledger, totaling the list, and comparing the total with the balance of the Accounts Payable controlling account. A similar list may be used to prove the accounts in the Accounts Receivable Ledger.

Sales taxes ■ Most provinces require retailers to collect sales taxes from their customers and periodically remit these taxes to the provincial treasurer. When a columnar Sales Journal is used, a record of taxes collected can be obtained by adding special columns in the journal as shown in Illustration 6–8.

In posting a journal like Illustration 6–8, the individual amounts in the Accounts Receivable column are posted daily to customer accounts in the Accounts Receivable Ledger and the column total is posted at

Sales Journal

Date	Account Debited	Invoice Number	F	Accounts Receivable Debit	Sales Taxes Payable Credit	Sales Credit
Dec. 1	D. R. Horn..........	7-1698		103.00	3.00	100.00

Illustration
6–8

the end of the month to the Accounts Receivable controlling account. The individual amounts in the Sales Taxes Payable and Sales columns are not posted. However, at the end of the month the total of the Sales Taxes Payable column is credited to the Sales Taxes Payable account and the total of the Sales column is credited to Sales.

A concern making cash sales upon which sales taxes are collected may add a special Sales Taxes Payable column in its Cash Receipts Journal.

Sales invoices as a Sales Journal

■ To save labour, many companies do not enter charge sales in a Sales Journal. These companies post each sales invoice totally directly to the customer's account in a subsidiary Accounts Receivable Ledger. Copies of the invoices are then bound in numerical order in a binder; and at the end of the month, all the invoices of that month are totaled on an adding machine and a general journal entry is made debiting the Accounts Receivable account and crediting Sales for the total. In effect, the bound invoice copies act as a Sales Journal. Such a procedure eliminates the labour of entering each invoice in a Sales Journal and is known as direct posting of sales invoices.

Purchase of assets used in the business

■ When a Purchases Journal like the one described earlier is used, only purchases of merchandise may be recorded in it, because its column total is debited to the Purchases account and purchases of assets other than merchandise do not affect this account. However, every company must purchase assets for use in the business; and when these assets are no longer needed, they may be sold. If the purchase or sale is for cash, the transaction is recorded in one of the cash journals. But if the purchase or sale is on credit, the transaction must be recorded in either the General Journal or, in cases where assets are purchased and such a journal is used, a multicolumn Purchases Journal similar to that shown in Illustration 6–9.

The illustrated journal has one credit column and three debit columns; more debit columns could be added. The credit column is used to record the amounts credited to each creditor's account. These amounts are posted daily to the individual creditor accounts in the Accounts Payable Ledger, and the column total is credited to the controlling account at the end of the month. The items purchased are recorded in the debit

Purchases Journal

Date		Account Credited	F	Accts. Pay-able Credit	Pur-chases Debit	Store Sup-plies Debit	Office Sup-plies Debit
Oct.	2	Marsh Wholesale Company.........		154.10	154.10		
	2	Office Supply Company..............		18.75			18.75
	3	Dole and Dole...........................		127.60	99.50	28.10	

Illustration
6–9

columns and are posted in the column totals at the end of the month.

In companies using an ordinary one-column Purchases Journal rather than a multicolumn Purchases Journal, purchases of assets for use in the business are recorded in the General Journal with an entry like the following:

Oct.	29	Office Supplies..	119	23.75	
		Accounts Payable – Ace Supply Co............	212/✔		23.75
		Bought office supplies.			

Speeding the data processing

■ Columnar journals speed the processing of accounting data, and if a business is small, they may serve its needs very well. However, they are pen-and-ink records, and on a per transaction basis any pen-and-ink record is time consuming and costly. Consequently, when a business has sufficient transactions to warrant their use, it will employ electric accounting machines or computers to reduce unit costs and further speed the data processing.

Electric accounting machines

■ There are many electric accounting machines on the market, some designed for a single task and others for a multiplicity of tasks. No effort will be made to describe all the available machines. In fact only one machine will be discussed, and it for purposes of showing how such machines reduce labour and speed the processing of accounting data.

Illustration 6–10 shows an electric accounting machine which can be used for sales accounting, cash receipts, cash disbursements, accounts payable, payroll, and other accounting applications. No attempt will be made to describe the machine's operation in each of these applications. However, when used in sales accounting, as an example, the machine will produce the invoice for each charge sale, post to the customer's account, update the statement to be sent the customer at the end of the month, and enter the sale in the Sales Journal, all in one operation. Furthermore, it is as proficient in other applications.

In sales accounting the current page of the Sales Journal is placed in

Illustration
6–10

Courtesy National Cash Register Company

the machine at the time the operator begins processing a group of sales transactions. In Illustration 6–10 the Sales Journal sheet is on the tray at the back of the machine. Next, after putting the Sales Journal sheet in the machine, the operator will for each charge sale place in the machine's carriage a blank invoice form, the customer's account from the subsidiary Accounts Receivable Ledger, and the statement to be mailed to the customer at the end of the month. After this she picks up in the machine from the customer's account the amount of his previous balance. She then types the customer's name, address, terms, et cetera on the invoice. Then she types on the invoice the commodities sold. For each commodity this consists of a description, the number of units sold, and the unit price. After listing units and unit price for a commodity, the operator depresses a key and the machine multiplies units by unit price and prints the extension. After listing all items, the operator presses another key and the machine totals the invoice and prints the total on the invoice, makes the entry in the Sales Journal, and spaces over and enters the sale and the new balance on the customer's account and on the month-end statement. After this the carriage returns automatically and opens for the removal of the invoice, customer's account, and statement. It also spaces the Sales Journal sheet up one line and is ready for recording the next sale.

In addition, when the operator completes the processing of a day's sales, the machine will print out the dollar total of the invoices processed, which is the day's debit to the Accounts Receivable controlling account. Also, it will print out the total credit to Sales and, if any, the credit to Sales Taxes Payable. Furthermore, if the sales were entered in the machine by departments, it will break down the sales credit into totals by departments.

Electronic data processing

■ The phrase "processing data electronically" means using an electronic computer in processing data, with an electronic computer being one or more machines containing from several hundred to more than a thousand transistors and other electronic devices and being capable of, for example, from a few hundred to millions of additions, multiplications, divisions, and subtractions per second, all completed without computer error in a predetermined sequence according to instructions stored within the machine.

What a computer can do

Before explaining how a computer operates, it might be wise to convey some idea of what a computer can do. For example, before computers were used, a concern with, say, 10,000 or 12,000 employees required five or six days each pay period to complete its payroll records and prepare the pay cheques, even though a hundred or more people with desk calculators and other electric machines were used to speed the work. But, today, a computer can do all the calculations, complete the payroll records, and print the cheques in a matter of only three or four hours.

What a computer does

A computer is a machine, and as a machine it can do nothing without being given a detailed set of instructions called a *program*. However, with a properly prepared program, a computer is a complete data proc-

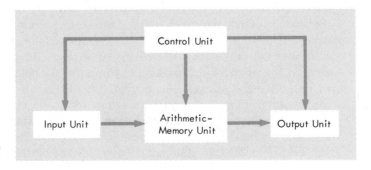

Illustration
6–11

essing system that will accept data through an *input unit*, store and process the data in an *arithmetic-memory unit*, and produce the processed results through an *output unit* in the form of, say, a printed balance sheet. To accomplish all of this and to control all its activities, a computer has a *control unit*. These units are diagrammed in Illustration 6–11.

How a computer operates

To understand how a computer operates, it is necessary to examine the function of each of its units and the computer program.

THE INPUT UNIT. The input unit provides a way to communicate with the computer; in other words, it provides a way to put data into the computer's arithmetic-memory unit and a way to tell the computer how to process the data. Communication may be through an electric typewriter connected to the computer, or by means of punched cards, punched paper tape, magnetic tape, or such things as bank cheques imprinted with magnetic ink. However, regardless of whether cards, tape, or other media, the media, through the input unit, transmit data and instructions to the computer's arithmetic-memory unit in the form of electrical impulses. The impulses are in a code language the computer can interpret.

The speed with which the various input media can enter data into the computer's memory varies from a character or two per second for the typewriter to hundreds of thousands of characters per second for magnetic tape.

THE ARITHMETIC-MEMORY UNIT. The arithmetic-memory unit should be viewed as having two sections: an arithmetic section and a memory section. The arithmetic section manipulates the data stored in the memory section. It performs addition, subtraction, multiplication, and division, and it makes simple yes-or-no decisions, such as: Are the two numbers equal? Has the end of the magnetic tape been reached? Does the card have an X punched in column 73? It performs these operations one at a time, storing the intermediate results in the memory section. And, depending upon the computer's size and cost, its arithmetic section performs these operations at a rate of from a few hundred operations per second for a small machine to several million per second for a large one.

The memory section of the arithmetic-memory unit serves the same purpose as a human's memory, a storage place for data and instructions. However, a computer's memory is more like a file of information than like a person's memory, since each bit of data stored in the computer's memory is stored in a specific location, just as in a file. Furthermore, for a computer to locate information in its memory, it must be told exactly where the information is stored.

Since a computer must be told where to find information in its memory, the memory is divided into cells, with each cell identified by a number, which is the cell's *address* within the memory unit. For example, if the memory unit has 4,000 cells for the storage of data, the cells are numbered from 0000 to 3999 and these numbers are the addresses of the cells.

Each cell in a computer's memory is capable of storing one bit of data, for example, one word or one number of up to, say, 10 digits. Likewise, depending upon its size, a computer may have storage capacity in its memory unit for from 1,000 bits of information for a small unit to 100,000 for a large one, and additional memory may be made available in auxiliary memory files.

THE OUTPUT UNIT. When processing of the data in the computer is finished, it is necessary for the machine to communicate the results. This may be done through various devices, such as an electric typewriter, a line printer, punched cards, magnetic tape, and punched paper tape. As an output device, a typewriter will type out a report at the rate of 10 characters per second, while a line printer, which prints a whole 120-character line of type in one operation, will print up to 800 lines per minute. The punched cards, magnetic tape, and punched paper tape, as output media, require further processing in, for example, a line printer.

THE CONTROL UNIT. The control unit controls the operations of all the computer units. It tells the input device what information or instructions to enter in memory and where (at what numbered addresses) to store the bits of information or instructions. It then reads the stored instructions one at a time and tells the arithmetic section what operation to perform, where in memory to find the required information, and where to store the results. And finally, it controls the output device, telling it what information to print out or punch out and where in memory to find the information, which all sounds fantastic. However, remember the control unit does nothing more than follow, step by step, a detailed set of instructions, called a program, that have been placed in the computer's memory unit.

THE PROGRAM. In processing data with a computer, both the data to be processed and the program for its processing are placed in the computer's memory section. The control unit then takes from the memory section the first instruction of the program plus the data needed in carrying out this instruction and places both in the arithmetic section. The arithmetic section executes the instruction, whether it be to add, multiply, divide, or compare two numbers for equality, and stores the results back in the memory section. The control unit then places the next instruction and the required data in the arithmetic section, and so on, until the program is completed and the data is processed, all at the rate of from a few hundred to millions of instructions per second.

At this point a typical computer program could be shown, but since a program consists of nothing more than a series of computer instructions expressed in code numbers, such a program would be quite incomprehensible to a beginning student. Furthermore, a typical program commonly contains hundreds or even thousands of individual instructions. Consequently, only a small portion of a program in which the instructions are in words rather than in code numbers is used to show the detail of such a program.

Assume a computer is processing a payroll and has computed and stored in its memory an employee's gross pay and the sum of his deductions for Canada Pension taxes, income taxes, hospital insurance, and so on. The next step would be to subtract the sum of the deductions from gross pay to arrive at net pay; but for the computer to do this, it must be instructed in detail. It must be told exactly where in memory the numbers representing gross pay and the sum of the deductions are stored and where the number representing net pay is to be stored. Assume the number representing gross pay is stored at memory address 1001, the sum of the deductions at memory address 1002, and net pay is to be stored at memory address 1003. Then, this portion of the program would have these three instructions:

1. Insert in the arithmetic section the number (gross pay) now stored in memory address 1001.
2. Subtract the number (sum of the deductions) stored in memory address 1002 from the contents of the arithmetic section.
3. Store the result of the subtraction (net pay) at memory address 1003.

These three instructions illustrate the detail of a computer program, and a program may contain hundreds or even thousands of such instructions. Nevertheless, a computer is able to execute such instructions in sequence, without error, at a rate of from a few hundred to millions of instructions per second.

At this point it might be asked how a computer can execute thousands or millions of instructions per second when the program it is processing has only a few hundred instructions. The answer is that the computer can be directed to repeat the same set of instructions over and over again, but each time with a new set of data. For example, in completing a payroll, the computer can be programmed to go through the same set of instructions over and over again, but each time with the hours, pay rate, and deductions of a different employee, until all the payroll is processed.

A computer requires a separate program for each job it is to do; and to change a computer from one job to another, it is only necessary to enter a new program in its memory, along with the data to be processed. For example, to change a computer from processing a payroll to processing inventory records, it is only necessary to feed the inventory program and the data of the inventory transactions into the computer's memory with the input device.

YES-OR-NO DECISIONS. One of the most important abilities of a computer is its ability to make yes-or-no decisions, such as, for example:

Has the employee's earnings reached the tax-exempt point for Canada Pension taxes? In processing a payroll, a computer can compare the amount of an employee's year-to-date earnings with the number of dollars representing the tax-exempt point and make a decision such as this. The importance of such a decision is obvious. If the earnings are below the tax-exempt point, the computer must calculate and deduct Canada Pension taxes; but if the earnings are beyond this point, the computer is programmed to omit this step.

The ability to compare numbers and make yes-or-no decisions makes it possible for a computer to process data containing exceptions, such as the Canada Pension tax example. However, it should be observed that the computer does not really make decisions. It only makes a comparison in each case, after which it processes the data one way or another, depending upon the result of the comparison. Also, for a computer to do this, a programmer must first design a program for the computer to follow. In designing the program, the programmer must determine in advance what exceptions can occur; he must then devise a set of yes-or-no questions that will isolate each exception, and he must tell the computer how to process each exception. Finally, after all this, the computer can follow through the program's maze of decisions and alternate instructions, rapidly and accurately. However, if it encounters an exception not anticipated in the program, it is helpless and can only process the exception incorrectly or stop.

IMPORTANCE OF THE COMPUTER PROGRAM. The ability to store a program in its memory section and then to race through the program's maze of yes-or-no decisions and alternate instructions is what distinguishes a computer from an electric calculator. To appreciate this, desk calculators exist that can do an addition, a multiplication, or division in one millionth of a second, in other words at about the speed of a fast computer. Yet, with all this speed, a calculator of this type cannot be operated much faster than an ordinary calculator, since without a program it must depend upon a person to push its keys telling it what to do.

In conclusion

Computers can process data with incredible speed and heretofore unobtainable accuracy. However, before a computer can do this, a human must think through the procedures the computer will use in processing the data, anticipate every processing exception, and then instruct the computer in great detail as to how to do its job. Consequently, computers are utterly dependent on humans; and rather than being giant brains are nothing but large, fast morons that can do nothing without first being told how. And, too, it always should be remembered that they are probably the fastest machines ever invented for turning out *wrong* answers when fed incorrect data or an inaccurate program.

1. How do columnar journals save posting labour?
2. How do columnar journals take advantage of the fact that for any single class of transactions either the debit or the credit of each transaction is always to the same account?
3. What functions are served by the Accounts Receivable controlling account?
4. Why should sales to charge customers and receipts of cash from charge customers be recorded and posted daily?
5. A company has the following numbers of accounts with balances:

   a. Asset accounts including the Accounts Receivable account
       but not the individual customer accounts............................ 25
   b. Customer accounts 500
   c. Liability accounts including the Accounts Payable account
       but not the individual creditor accounts............................. 10
   d. Creditor accounts 20
   e. Owner equity accounts including income statement
       accounts 20
                                                          Total 575

   How many items appear on the trial balance of this company? What in addition to a trial balance is used to prove the account balances of this company?
6. How is a schedule of accounts payable prepared? How is it used to prove the balances of the creditor accounts in the Accounts Payable Ledger? What may be substituted for a formal schedule?
7. How is the equality of a controlling account and its subsidiary ledger accounts maintained?
8. Describe how copies of a company's sales invoices may be used as a Sales Journal.
9. After all posting is completed, the balance of the Accounts Receivable controlling account does not agree with the sum of the balances in the Accounts Receivable Ledger. If the trial balance is in balance, where is the error apt to be?
10. How is a multicolumn journal crossfooted? Why is a multicolumn journal crossfooted?
11. How is it possible to tell from which journal a particular amount in a ledger account was posted?
12. When a general journal entry is used to record a returned charge sale, the credit of the entry must be posted twice. Does this cause the trial balance to be out of balance? Why or why not?
13. Both credits to customer accounts and credits to miscellaneous accounts are individually posted from a Cash Receipts Journal like that of Illustration 6–3. Why not place both kinds of credits in the same column and thus save journal space?

Exercise 6-1

A business uses a Cash Receipts Journal, Cash Disbursements Journal, Sales Journal, one-column Purchases Journal, and General Journal. List the following transactions by letter and opposite each letter give the name of the journal in which the transaction should be recorded:

a. Sale of merchandise on credit.
b. Purchase of office supplies on credit.
c. Purchase of merchandise on credit.
d. Purchase of office equipment for cash.
e. Sale of unneeded office equipment on credit.
f. Return of a charge sale.
g. Return of a cash sale.
h. Return of a credit purchase.
i. Payment of a creditor.
j. Adjusting entries.
k. Closing entries.

Exercise 6-2

At the end of November Pacific Company's Sales Journal showed the following credit sales:

SALES JOURNAL

Date		Account Debited	Invoice Number	F	Amount
Nov.	3	Dale Hall.......................................	123		250.00
	8	John Mohr.....................................	124		100.00
	19	Gary Roth......................................	125		225.00
	26	Dale Hall	126		300.00
	30	Total			875.00

The company's General Journal carried this entry:

Nov.	22	Sales Returns and Allowances..............	25.00	
		Accounts Receivable – Gary Roth...		25.00
		Customer returned merchandise.		

Required:

1. On a sheet of notebook paper open a subsidiary Accounts Receivable Ledger having a T-account for each of Dale Hall, John Mohr, and Gary

Roth. Post the sales journal entries to the customer accounts and also post the portion of the general journal entry that affects a customer's account.

2. Open a General Ledger having an Accounts Receivable controlling account, a Sales account, and a Sales Returns and Allowances account. Post the portions of the sales journal and general journal entries that affect these accounts.

3. Prove the subsidiary ledger accounts with a schedule of accounts receivable.

Exercise 6–3

Harbour Company, a company that posts its sales invoices directly and then binds the invoices to make them into a Sales Journal, had the following sales during October:

Oct.	3	Robert Hall	$ 500
	6	Carl Fetter	300
	11	Taylor Gordon	700
	18	Carl Fetter	200
	21	Taylor Gordon	800
	27	Walter Scott	400
		Total	$2,900

Required:

1. On a sheet of notebook paper open a subsidiary Accounts Receivable Ledger having a T-account for each customer with an invoice bound in the Sales Journal. Post the invoices to the subsidiary ledger.
2. Give the general journal entry to record the end-of-the-month total of the Sales Journal.
3. Open an Accounts Receivable controlling account and a Sales account and post the general journal entry.
4. Prove the subsidiary Accounts Receivable Ledger with a schedule of accounts receivable.

Exercise 6–4

A company that records credit sales in a one-column Sales Journal and records sales returns in its General Journal made the following errors. List each error by letter, and opposite each letter tell when the error will be discovered:

a. Recorded a $15 credit sale in the Sales Journal as a $150 sale.

b. Correctly recorded a $10 sale in the Sales Journal but posted it to the customer's account as a $100 sale.

c. Posted a sales return recorded in the General Journal to the Sales Returns and Allowances account and also to the Accounts Receivable account but did not post to the customer's account.

d. Made an addition error in determining the balance of a customer's account.

e. Posted a sales return to the Accounts Receivable account and to the customer's account but did not post to the Sales Returns and Allowances account.

f. Made an addition error in totaling the Amount column in the Sales Journal.

Exercise 6–5

Following are a merchandising concern's condensed journals, the column headings of which are incomplete in that they do not tell whether the columns are debit or credit columns.

SALES JOURNAL			PURCHASES JOURNAL	
Account	Amount		Account	Amount
Customer A	1,200		Company One..................	1,000
Customer B.................	1,400		Company Two	1,500
Customer C.................	1,600		Company Three	2,000
Total....................	4,200		Total	4,500

GENERAL JOURNAL

......	...	Sales Returns and Allowances................	400	
		Accounts Receivable – Customer B ...		400
		Customer returned merchandise.		
	...	Accounts Payable – Company Three........	200	
		Purchases Returns and Allowances ...		200
		Returned defective merchandise.		

CASH RECEIPTS JOURNAL

Account	Other Accounts	Accounts Receivable	Sales	Sales Discounts	Cash
Customer A...........	....	1,200	....	24	1,176
Customer B	....	500	....	10	490
Sales	....	....	1,250	....	1,250
Notes Payable........	5,000	....	....	....	5,000
Customer C...........	....	800	....	16	784
Sales	....	....	1,150	....	1,150
Totals.............	5,000	2,500	2,400	50	9,850

CASH DISBURSEMENTS JOURNAL

Account	Other Accounts	Accounts Payable	Purchases Discounts	Cash
Company Two......................	....	750	15	735
Salaries Expense..................	650	....	....	650
Company Three....................	....	1,000	20	980
Salaries Expense..................	650	....	....	650
Totals	1,300	1,750	35	3,015

Required:

1. Prepare T-accounts on a sheet of ordinary notebook paper for the following general ledger and subsidiary ledger accounts. Separate the accounts of each ledger into a group.

General Ledger Accounts	*Accounts Receivable Ledger Accounts*
Cash	Customer A
Accounts Receivable	Customer B
Notes Payable	Customer C
Accounts Payable	
Sales	*Accounts Payable Ledger Accounts*
Sales Returns and Allowances	Company One
Sales Discounts	Company Two
Purchases	Company Three
Purchases Returns and Allowances	
Purchases Discounts	
Salaries Expense	

2. Without referring to illustrations showing complete column headings, post the journal amounts to the proper T-accounts.

Problems   **Problem 6–1**

(If the working papers that accompany this text are not being used, omit this problem.)

Assume it is the last week of February and you have just been hired as bookkeeper for Cactus Sales Company. The previous bookkeeper has journalized the transactions for the first three weeks of the month and has posted those entry portions that would be posted as individual amounts. An examination of the company's journals and ledgers as they appear in the booklet of working papers will reveal this.

The company completed these transactions during the last week of the month:

Feb. 23 Sold merchandise on credit to George Mohr, Invoice No. 716, $565. The terms of all credit sales are 2/10, n/60.

23 Received merchandise and an invoice dated February 21, terms 2/10, n/60, from Southwest Wholesale Company, $550.

23 Issued a credit memorandum to Robert Johnson for $35 of merchandise sold on February 18 and returned for credit.

24 Issued Cheque No. 458 to Northern Insurance Company in payment of the premium on an insurance policy, $45.

24 Received a credit memorandum from Southwest Wholesale Company for defective merchandise purchased on February 17 and returned, $50.

25 Sold merchandise on credit to James Scott, Invoice No. 717, $445.

25 Issued Cheque No. 459 to Southwest Wholesale Company in payment of its February 15 invoice, less the return and discount.

26 Purchased store equipment on credit from Store Supply Company, $450.

26 Received payment from Albert Getty for the sale of February 16, less the discount.

27 Received merchandise and an invoice dated February 25, terms 2/10, n/60, Western Manufacturing Company, $630.

28 Received payment from Robert Johnson for the sale of February 18, less the return and the discount.

28 Issued Cheque No. 460 to Calgary Supply Company in payment of its February 18 invoice, less the discount.

28 Issued Cheque No. 461, payable to Payroll, in payment of sales salaries for the last half of the month, $315. The one employee had a small amount of overtime. Cash the cheque and paid the employee.

28 Cash sales for the last half of the month were $790.

Required:

1. Record the transactions for the last week of February.
2. Post to the customer and creditor accounts and also post any amounts that should be posted as individual amounts to the general ledger accounts. (Normally these postings would be made daily, but they are posted only twice during the month in this problem in order to simplify the problem.)
3. Foot and crossfoot the journals and make the month-end column total postings.
4. Prepare a trial balance to prove the general ledger accounts, and prepare schedules of accounts receivable and accounts payable to prove the subsidiary ledgers.

Problem 6-2

Pacific Company completed the following transactions during October:

Oct. 1 Issued Cheque No. 510 to Eastern Realty for the October rent on the store building, $650.

1 Purchased merchandise on credit from Lagoon Company, invoice dated September 28, terms 2/10, n/60, $850.

3 Purchased merchandise on credit from Palm Company, invoice dated October 1, terms 2/10, n/60, $1,100.

4 Purchased store equipment on credit from A-1 Supply Company, $475.

5 Received a $50 credit memorandum from Lagoon Company for unsatisfactory merchandise received on October 1 and returned.

8 Issued Cheque No. 511 to Lagoon Company in payment of its September 28 invoice less the return and discount.

9 Received a $75 credit memorandum from A-1 Supply Company for unsatisfactory store equipment purchased on October 4 and returned.

10 Issued Cheque No. 512 to Palm Company in payment of its October 1 invoice, less the discount.

10 Sold merchandise on credit to Walter Nash, Invoice No. 712, $650. The terms of all credit sales are 2/10, n/60.

13 Sold merchandise on credit to Gary Barr, Invoice No. 713, $550.

14 Purchased merchandise on credit from Harbour Company, invoice dated October 10, terms 1/10, n/30, $925.

15 Cash sales for the first half of the month, $2,345. (Cash sales are

normally recorded daily from the cash register readings; however, they are recorded only twice in this problem in order to shorten the problem.)

    15 *Make the individual postings from the journals. Normally items posted as individual amounts are posted daily; but since such items in this problem are few, you are asked to post them on only two occasions.*

    18 Sold merchandise on credit to John Dale, Invoice No. 714, $725.

    19 Sold merchandise on credit to Walter Nash, Invoice No. 715, $600.

    20 Received $637 from Walter Nash in payment for the October 10 sale, less the discount.

    23 Received $539 from Gary Barr in payment for the October 13 sale, less the discount.

    24 Sold $20 of store equipment at cost for cash.

    24 Purchased merchandise on credit from Palm Company, invoice dated October 21, terms 2/10, n/60, $800.

    25 Borrowed $2,500 from Guaranty Bank by giving a note payable.

    28 Sold merchandise on credit to Gary Barr, Invoice No. 716, $425.

Oct. 29 Received $588 from Walter Nash in payment of the October 19 sale, less discount.

    31 Issued Cheque No. 513 to Palm Company in payment of its October 21 invoice, less the discount.

    31 Issued Cheque No. 514, payable to Payroll, in payment of the monthly sales salaries, $1,200. Cashed the cheque and paid the employees.

    31 Cash sales for the last half of the month, $2,115.

    31 *Make the individual postings from the journals.*

    31 *Foot and crossfoot the journals and make the month-end postings.*

Required:

1. Open the following general ledger accounts: Cash; Accounts Receivable; Store Equipment; Notes Payable; Accounts Payable; Sales; Sales Discounts; Purchases; Purchases Returns and Allowances; Purchases Discounts; Sales Salaries Expense; and Rent Expense.
2. Open the following accounts receivable ledger accounts: Gary Barr; John Dale; and Walter Nash.
3. Open these accounts payable ledger accounts: A-1 Supply Company; Harbour Company; Lagoon Company; and Palm Company.
4. Prepare a Sales Journal, a one-column Purchases Journal, a Cash Receipts Journal, a Cash Disbursements Journal, and a General Journal.
5. Enter the transactions in the journals and post when instructed to do so.
6. Prove the general ledger with a trial balance and prepare schedules of accounts receivable and accounts payable to prove the subsidiary ledgers.

Problem 6–3

Marine Supply Company completed these credit transactions during November of the current year:

Nov. 3 Purchased merchandise from Cole Company, $1,125.

    6 Purchased store supplies, $135, and office supplies, $55, from Brill Company.

10 Purchased merchandise from Abbott Company, $930.
13 Purchased merchandise, $740, store supplies, $45, and office supplies, $30, from Brill Company.
16 Purchased merchandise, $585, from Cole Company.
21 Purchased store equipment from Dodge Company, $750.
26 Purchased office supplies from Brill Company, $35.
30 Purchased merchandise from Abbott Company, $545.

Required:
1. Prepare a General Journal and a multicolumn Purchases Journal like Illustration 6–8 and record the transactions in the journals.
2. Open the required general ledger and accounts payable ledger accounts and post the journals.

Problem 6–4

Lake Sales Company completed these transactions during November:

Nov. 2 Sold merchandise on credit to Paul Eddy, Invoice No. 933, $700. The terms of all credit sales are 2/10, n/60.
3 Purchased merchandise on credit from Hale Company, invoice dated October 31, terms 2/10, n/60, $1,385.
Nov. 5 Purchased merchandise on credit from Grady Company, invoice dated November 2, terms 1/10, n/30, $435.
6 Purchased store supplies on credit from Bodon Company, $165.
6 Borrowed $2,000 from Central Bank by giving a note payable.
7 Received an $85 credit memorandum from Hale Company for merchandise received on November 3 and returned.
10 Received a $40 credit memorandum from Bodon Company for unsatisfactory store supplies purchased on November 6 and returned.
10 Issued Cheque No. 989 to Hale Company in payment of its October 31 invoice, less the return and discount.
12 Sold merchandise on credit to David Case, Invoice No. 934, $785.
12 Received payment from Paul Eddy for the November 2 sale, less the discount.
13 Purchased merchandise on credit from Flint Company, invoice dated November 11, terms 2/10, n/60, $1,750.
15 Issued Cheque No. 990, payable to Payroll, for sales salaries for the first half of the month, $925. Cashed the cheque and paid the employees.
15 Cash sales for the first half of the month were $2,655. (Cash sales are usually recorded daily from the cash register readings; however, they are recorded only twice in this problem in order to shorten the problem.)
15 *Make the individual postings from the journals. (Normally such items are posted daily; but since they are so few in number in this problem, you are asked to post them on only two occasions.)*
16 Issued a $35 credit memorandum to David Case for defective merchandise sold on November 12 and returned for credit.
17 Purchased merchandise on credit from Flint Company, invoice dated November 14, terms 2/10, n/60, $1,500.
18 Sold merchandise to Paul Eddy on credit, Invoice No. 935, $650.

21 Issued Cheque No. 991 to Flint Company in payment of its November 11 invoice, less the discount.

21 Sold store supplies at cost for cash, $10.

22 Received payment from David Case for the November 12 sale, less the return and the discount.

24 Issued Cheque No. 992 to Flint Company in payment of its November 14 invoice, less the discount.

25 Sold merchandise on credit to David Case, Invoice No. 936, $885.

26 Sold merchandise on credit to A. J. Allen, Invoice No. 937, $745.

28 Issued Cheque No. 993 to *Daily Sun* for advertising expense, $295.

28 Received payment from Paul Eddy for the November 18 sale, less the discount.

30 Issued Cheque No. 994, payable to Payroll, in payment of the sales salaries for the last half of the month, $925. Cashed the cheque and paid the employees.

30 Cash sales for the last half of the month were $2,310.

30 *Make the individual postings from the journals.*

30 *Foot and crossfoot the journals and make the month-end postings.*

Required:

1. Open the following general ledger accounts: Cash; Accounts Receivable; Store Supplies; Notes Payable; Accounts Payable; Sales; Sales Returns and Allowances; Sales Discounts; Purchases; Purchases Returns and Allowances; Purchases Discounts; Advertising Expense; and Sales Salaries Expense.

2. Open the following accounts receivable ledger accounts: A. J. Allen; David Case; and Paul Eddy.

3. Open the following accounts payable ledger accounts: Bodon Company; Flint Company; Grady Company; and Hale Company.

4. Prepare a Sales Journal, a one-column Purchases Journal, a Cash Receipts Journal, a Cash Disbursements Journal, and a General Journal like the ones illustrated in this chapter.

5. Enter the transactions in the journals and post when instructed to do so.

6. Prove the general ledger accounts with a trial balance and prove the subsidiary ledgers with schedules of accounts receivable and accounts payable.

Problem 6–5

On the next page is a columnar journal of Very Different Company, a journal unlike any described in your text and designed to test your knowledge of the posting principles of columnar journals.

Required:

1. Open a General Ledger having T-accounts for Cash; Store Supplies; Accounts Payable; Purchases; Purchases Returns and Allowances; Purchases Discounts; Sales Salaries Expense; Advertising Expense; and Office Salaries Expense.

2. Open an Accounts Payable Ledger having these accounts: AAA Suppliers; Allen Company; Austin Sales Company; and Guelth Company.

3. Post the columnar journal, prepare a trial balance of the General Ledger, and prove the subsidiary ledger by preparing a schedule of accounts payable. (The Cash account will have a credit balance in the trial balance.)

Problem 6-5—Continued

CASH DISBURSEMENTS, PURCHASES, AND PURCHASES RETURNS JOURNAL

Sales Salaries Expense	Office Salaries Expense	Purchases	Accounts Payable	Other Accounts	Date	Account Titles and Explanations	Other Accounts	Accounts Payable	Pur. Discounts	Cash
		875.00			Nov. 2	Allen Company		875.00		
		1,450.00			4	Guelth Company		1,450.00		
			125.00		5	Allen Company – Purchases Returns	125.00			
			750.00		8	Allen Company			15.00	735.00
				145.00	10	Store Supplies – AAA Suppliers		145.00		
		2,400.00			11	Austin Sales Company		2,400.00		
			1,450.00		12	Guelth Company			29.00	1,421.00
925.00	450.00				15	First half of month's salaries				1,375.00
			2,400.00		17	Austin Sales Company			48.00	2,352.00
				100.00	23	Advertising Expenses				100.00
		565.00		85.00	25	Store Supplies – Allen Company		650.00		
			35.00		28	Allen Company – Store Supplies	35.00			
925.00	450.00				30	Last half month's salaries				1,375.00
1,850.00	900.00	5,290.00	4,760.00	330.00	30	Totals	160.00	5,520.00	92.00	7,358.00

Alternate problems

Problem 6–1A

(If the working papers that accompany this text are not being used, omit this problem.)

Assume it is the last week of February and you have just been hired as bookkeeper for Cactus Sales Company. The previous bookkeeper has journalized the transactions for the first three weeks of the month and has posted those entry portions that would be posted as individual amounts. An examination of the company's journals and ledgers as they appear in the booklet of working papers will show this.

The company completed these transactions during the last week of February:

Feb. 23 Received merchandise purchased on credit from Western Manufacturing Company. The invoice was dated February 20, terms 2/10, n/60, $615.

23 Purchased store supplies on credit from Store Supply Company, $55.

23 Sold merchandise on credit to Albert Getty, Invoice No. 716, $735. The terms of all credit sales are 2/10, n/60.

23 Received a credit memorandum from Southwest Wholesale Company for defective merchandise purchased on February 17 and returned, $100.

24 Issued a credit memorandum to Robert Johnson for $85 of merchandise sold on February 18 and returned for credit.

25 Issued Cheque No. 458 to Southwest Wholesale Company in payment of its February 15 invoice, less the return and the discount.

26 Sold merchandise on credit to George Mohr, Invoice No. 717, $695.

26 Received payment from Albert Getty for the sale of February 16, less the discount.

26 Kent Sears issued Cheque No. 459 payable to himself to withdraw $250 of cash for personal use.

27 Received merchandise purchased on credit from Southwest Wholesale Company. The invoice was dated February 25, terms 2/10, n/60, $975.

28 Received payment from Robert Johnson for the sale of February 18, less the return and the discount.

28 Issued Cheque No. 460 to Calgary Supply Company in payment of its February 18 invoice, less the discount.

28 Issued Cheque No. 461, payable to Payroll, in payment of sales salaries for the last half of the month, $300. Cashed the cheque and paid the employees.

28 Cash sales for the last half of the month were $845.

Required:

1. Record the transactions for the last week of February.
2. Post to the customer and creditor accounts and also post any amounts that should be posted as individual amounts to the general ledger accounts.
3. Foot and crossfoot the journals and make the month-end column total postings.

4. Prepare a trial balance to prove the general ledger accounts, and prepare schedules of accounts receivable and accounts payable to prove the subsidiary ledgers.

Problem 6–2A

Surfside Company completed these transactions during October:

Oct. 3 Sold merchandise on credit to John Dale, Invoice No. 615, $650. The terms of all credit sales are 2/10, n/60.

4 Purchased merchandise on credit from Harbour Company, invoice dated October 2, terms 2/10, n/60, $1,200.

6 Purchased store equipment on credit from A-1 Supply Company, $350.

6 Sold merchandise on credit to Walter Nash, Invoice No. 616, $700.

8 Borrowed $3,000 from Security Bank by giving a note payable.

9 Purchased merchandise on credit from Harbor Company, invoice dated October 6, terms 2/10, n/60, $1,150.

10 Issued Cheque No. 422 to Hilton Realty for one month's rent on the store building, $500.

11 Sold merchandise on credit to Gary Barr, Invoice No. 617, $900.

12 Received $637 from John Dale in payment of the October 3 sale, less the discount.

12 Issued Cheque No. 423 to Harbour Company in payment of its October 2 invoice, less the discount.

13 Purchased merchandise on credit from Lagoon Company, invoice dated October 10, terms 2/10, n/60, $1,375.

15 Cash sales for the first half of the month, $2,110. (Cash sales are normally recorded daily from the cash register readings; however, they are recorded only twice in this problem in order to shorten the problem.)

15 *Make the individual postings from the journals. Normally items posted as individual amounts are posted daily; but since such items in this problem are few, you are asked to post them on only two occasions.*

16 Received a $175 credit memorandum from Lagoon Company for unsatisfactory merchandise received on October 13 and returned for credit.

16 Issued Cheque No. 424 to Harbour Company in payment of its October 6 invoice, less the discount.

17 Sold merchandise on credit to John Dale, Invoice No. 618, $500.

20 Received $882 from Gary Barr in payment for the October 11 sale, less the discount.

20 Issued Cheque No. 425 to Lagoon Company in payment of its October 10 invoice, less the return and discount.

22 Sold $15 of unneeded store equipment at cost for cash.

25 Purchased merchandise on credit from Palm Company, invoice dated October 22, terms 2/10, n/60, $625.

27 Received $490 from John Dale in payment of the October 17 sale, less the discount.

27 Sold merchandise on credit to Gary Barr, Invoice No. 619, $350.

31 Issued Cheque No. 426, payable to Payroll, in payment of the monthly sales salaries, $1,000. Cashed the cheque and paid the employees.

Oct. 31 Cash sales for the last half of the month, $1,950.

    31 *Make the individual postings from the journals.*

    31 *Foot and crossfoot the journals and make the month-end postings.*

Required:

1. Open the following general ledger accounts: Cash; Accounts Receivable; Store Equipment; Notes Payable; Accounts Payable; Sales; Sales Discounts; Purchases; Purchases Returns and Allowances; Purchases Discounts; Sales Salaries Expense; and Rent Expense.
2. Open these accounts receivable ledger accounts: Gary Barr; John Dale; and Walter Nash.
3. Open the following accounts payable ledger accounts: A-1 Supply Company; Harbour Company; Lagoon Company; and Palm Company.
4. Prepare a Sales Journal, a one-column Purchases Journal, a Cash Receipts Journal, a Cash Disbursements Journal, and a General Journal.
5. Enter the transactions in the journals and post when instructed to do so.
6. Prove the general ledger accounts with a trial balance and prepare schedules of accounts receivable and accounts payable to prove the subsidiary ledgers.

Problem 6–3A

A company that uses a multicolumn Purchases Journal completed these credit transactions during October of the current year:

Oct. 5 Purchased merchandise from Abbott Company, $1,215.

    8 Purchased merchandise, $875, and store supplies, $115, from Brill Company.

  11 Purchased merchandise, $650, store supplies, $85, and office supplies, $50, from Cole Company.

  15 Purchased store equipment from Dodge Company, $550.

  17 Purchased store supplies, $60, and office supplies, $15, from Brill Company.

  24 Purchased merchandise, $1,035, from Abbott Company.

  27 Purchased merchandise from Cole Company, $745.

Required:

1. Prepare a General Journal and a multicolumn Purchases Journal like Illustration 6–8 and enter the transactions in the journals.
2. Open the required general ledger and accounts payable ledger accounts and post the journals.

Problem 6–4A

Island Sales Company completed these transactions during November:

Nov. 1 Purchased merchandise on credit from Grady Company, invoice dated October 29, terms 2/10, n/60, $2,100.

    2 Issued Cheque No. 915 to *Daily Clarion* for advertising expense, $115.

    2 Sold merchandise on credit to A. J. Allen, Invoice No. 821, $825. The terms of all credit sales are 2/10, n/60.

    3 Sold merchandise on credit to Paul Eddy, Invoice No. 822, $750.

    5 Purchased store supplies on credit from Hale Company, $185.

    8 Received a $20 credit memorandum from Hale Company for unsatisfactory store supplies purchased on November 5 and returned.

Nov. 8 Issued Cheque No. 916 to Grady Company in payment of its October 29 invoice, less the discount.

9 Issued a $75 credit memorandum to A. J. Allen for defective merchandise sold on November 2 and returned for credit.

10 Sold merchandise on credit to David Case, Invoice No. 823, $950.

11 Purchased merchandise on credit from Bodon Company, invoice dated November 8, terms 1/10, n/30, $465.

12 Received payment from A. J. Allen for the November 2 sale, less the return and discount.

13 Received payment from Paul Eddy for the November 3 sale, less the discount.

14 Sold merchandise on credit to A. J. Allen, Invoice No. 824, $650.

15 Issued Cheque No. 917, payable to Payroll, in payment of sales salaries for the first half of the month, $850. Cashed the cheque and paid the employees.

15 Cash sales for the first half of the month, $2,445. (Cash sales are usually recorded daily from the cash register readings; however, they are recorded only twice during the month in this problem in order to shorten the problem.)

15 *Make the individual postings from the journals. (Normally such items are posted daily; but since they are so few in number in this problem, you are asked to post them on only two occasions.)*

18 Purchased merchandise on credit from Flint Company, invoice dated November 15, terms 2/10, n/60, $1,350.

19 Sold store supplies at cost for cash, $15.

20 Received payment from David Case for the November 10 sale less the discount.

21 Purchased merchandise on credit from Bodon Company, invoice dated November 18, terms 1/10, n/30, $510.

22 Purchased merchandise on credit from Grady Company, invoice dated November 19, terms 2/10, n/60, $1,050.

23 Received a $150 credit memorandum from Flint Company for defective merchandise purchased on November 18 and returned.

24 Received payment from A. J. Allen for the November 14 sale, less the discount.

25 Issued Cheque No. 918 to Flint Company in payment of its November 15 invoice, less the return and discount.

27 Sold merchandise on credit to Paul Eddy, Invoice No. 825, $735.

28 Borrowed $5,000 from Security Bank by giving a note payable.

29 Issued Cheque No. 919 to Grady Company in payment of its November 19 invoice, less the discount.

30 Sold merchandise on credit to David Case, Invoice No. 826, $515.

30 Issued Cheque No. 920, payable to Payroll, in payment of the sales salaries for the last half of the month, $850.

30 Cash sales for the last half of the month were $2,685.

30 *Make the individual postings from the journals.*

30 *Foot and crossfoot the journals and make the month-end postings.*

Required:

1. Open the following general ledger accounts: Cash; Accounts Receivable; Store Supplies; Notes Payable; Accounts Payable; Sales; Sales Returns

and Allowances; Sales Discounts; Purchases; Purchases Returns and Allowances; Purchases Discounts; Advertising Expense; and Sales Salaries Expense.

2. Open these subsidiary accounts receivable ledger accounts: A. J. Allen; David Case; and Paul Eddy.
3. Open these accounts payable ledger accounts: Bodon Company; Flint Company; Grady Company; and Hale Company.
4. Prepare a Sales Journal, one-column Purchases Journal, Cash Receipts Journal, Cash Disbursements Journal, and a General Journal like the ones illustrated in this chapter.
5. Enter the transactions in the journals and post when instructed to do so.
6. Prepare a trial balance and prove the subsidiary ledgers by preparing schedules of accounts receivable and accounts payable.

Decision problem 6–1, Drywall Company

Today, November 16, is your first day on a new job in the accounting department of Drywall Company, and the first transaction you are called upon to analyze and record is based on the following information: On November 3 Drywall Company sent an order to Gypsum Products for merchandise having a $1,200 catalogue list price, less a 30% trade discount, FOB Gypsum Product's factory, 2/10, n/60. Gypsum Products shipped the entire order on November 6, prepaying and adding the freight charges, $80, to the invoice, since it was required on that class of freight. Drywall Company received and inspected the goods on November 8, finding that one fourth did not meet specifications. Nevertheless, it accepted and correctly recorded as a purchase the entire amount received and entered into negotiations to return the unsatisfactory portion. Gypsum Products agreed to the return with the understanding it would be responsible for and would give full credit for the goods returned and the freight charges on the return shipment plus one fourth the freight charges on the original shipment. The unsatisfactory goods were returned with freight charges of $22, which were prepaid by Drywall Company. Today, November 16, Drywall Company received a credit memorandum giving credit for the return and the freight charges as agreed, and it has mailed a cheque for the remaining amount owed. Determine the correct amount for that cheque. Back your answer with figures. Also, under the assumption the $22 of freight charges on the return shipment were debited to Gypsum Company's account when paid, give in general journal form the entry to record the November 16 cheque paying the balance owed on this purchase.

Decision problem 6–2, Corner Market

Robert Morris and his wife operate Corner Market, a small retail grocery for which Mrs. Morris keeps the books. The store's sales are mainly for cash, but some charge sales are made to select customers. In general, both Mr. and Mrs. Morris are happy with the store's accounting records. However, Mr. Morris feels some improvement in recording sales is possible.

Cash sales are "rung up" on cash registers, and each day's cash sales total is recorded in a Cash Receipts Journal from a summary of the cash register readings. The Cash Receipts Journal has columns headed Other Accounts, Cr.; Sales, Cr.; and Cash, Dr.; but it does not have an Accounts Receivable column because the store does not maintain individual customer accounts. Likewise, the store does not have a Sales Journal. However, it does have an account in its General Ledger titled Accounts Receivable, the use of which is explained later.

Credit sales are not numerous in relation to cash sales, and each credit sale is recorded on a sales ticket prepared in duplicate. The carbon copy is given to the customer at the time of the sale; the original copy is filed under the customer's name in a file tray; and no further record of a charge sale is made until a customer pays his account. When a customer pays his account, his sales tickets are totaled on an adding machine and surrendered to him as a receipt for his payment, and the total is at that time "rung up" on the cash register as though it were a cash sale.

In addition, in order to show all the assets on the balance sheet, at the end of each accounting period the amount of accounts receivable is determined by adding the unpaid sales tickets in the file tray of customer sales tickets; and an entry like the following is made in the General Journal to record these receivables:

| Dec. | 31 | Accounts Receivable........................ | 550.00 | |
| | | Sales .... | | 550.00 |

Then on the first day of the new accounting period the following entry is made to remove the effects of the foregoing entry from the books:

| Jan. | 1 | Sales .... | 550.00 | |
| | | Accounts receivable.................. | | 550.00 |

The second entry is made so that the practice of ringing up collections on the cash register may be continued in the new accounting period.

Although Mrs. Morris does not agree, Mr. Morris feels that some sales tickets are lost. If this happens, collections are not made on such lost tickets and, of course, the amounts of these tickets never find their way into the revenue account.

Prepare a report to Corner Market making such comments and recommendations as you feel justified about its systems for handling sales. Detail any improvements you would recommend.

Decision problem 6–3, Eastern Company, London Branch

Ted Hall went to work for Eastern Company as a salesman upon graduation from college, and at the beginning of last year he was appointed manager of the company's London Branch. He recognized his accounting knowledge was limited, but he reasoned that if the branch's Cash account grew, the branch was progressing satisfactorily. Consequently, he watched with enthusiasm the growth of the branch's cash balance from $2,000 when he took over to

$15,200 at the end of his first year as manager; and when he received the following income statement covering the year's operations, he was shocked to learn the branch had operated at a $1,000 loss.

EASTERN COMPANY, LONDON BRANCH
Income Statement for Year Ended December 31, 19—

Sales		$280,000
Cost of goods sold		190,000
Gross profit from sales		$ 90,000
Operating expenses:		
Salaries expense	$80,000	
Advertising expense	2,000	
Supplies expense	500	
Depreciation expense, equipment	2,500	
Depreciation expense, building	6,000	
Total operating expenses		91,000
Net Loss		$ (1,000)

As branch accountant, you have been called on to explain to Mr. Hall how it is possible for the branch to suffer a loss during a period in which there was such a gratifying increase in its cash. In your explanation, account for the change in the cash balance. Assume that the number of dollars the branch had invested in merchandise and supplies was the same at the beginning and end of the period. However, the accounts receivable decreased $6,500 and the accounts payable decreased $1,500 during the period. There were $200 of accrued salaries payable at the beginning of the period and $900 at the end. And finally, the advertising expense was incurred and paid for during the period.

Analytical and review problems

Problem 6–1 A&R

The following information is selected from the books and records of Gem Wholesaling Company:

1. Received a credit memorandum for office equipment purchased on credit and later returned.
2. Issued an invoice for merchandise sold to a charge customer.
3. The owner took home some office equipment for his personal use.
4. Returned to a supplier some unsatisfactory merchandise for credit.
5. The owner invested additional cash in the business.
6. A customer who had purchased some merchandise on credit returned some defective items to Gem Wholesaling.
7. Purchased merchandise for cash from a supplier.
8. A charge customer settled his account in full.
9. Received an invoice for merchandise bought on credit.
10. Issued a credit memorandum to a charge customer.
11. Paid salaries and wages to employees.
12. Sold merchandise to a customer on credit.
13. Wrote off a customer's long outstanding account as uncollectible.

14. Made an adjusting entry to set up this year's bad debts expense.
15. Made a year-end adjustment for accrued expenses.
16. Closed the Income Summary account to the Capital account.

Required:
Assuming that the company records its transactions in the following books of original entry:

Sales Journal
Purchases Journal
Cash Receipts Journal
Cash Disbursements Journal
Sales Returns and Allowances Journal
Purchases Returns and Allowances Journal
General Journal

1. Indicate the book of original entry in which you would record each of the above transactions.
2. Indicate which of the transactions or adjustments affect the accounts in the accounts receivable or accounts payable subsidiary ledgers.
   Suggested format for your answer:

Subsidiary Ledgers

Entry Number	Name of Journal	Accounts Receivable		Accounts Payable	
		Dr.	*Cr.*	*Dr.*	*Cr.*

Problem 6-2 A&R

The following general ledger and subsidiary ledger accounts show certain transactions in the month of October.
1. General ledger accounts:

Cash

Sept. 30 Balance 2,600	
Oct. 31 40,000	Oct. 31 12,400

Accounts Receivable

Sept. 30 Balance 12,000	
Oct. 31 80,000	Oct. 31 40,000

Accounts Payable

	Sept. 30 Balance 2,500
Oct. 31 12,400	Oct. 31 36,500

Sales

	Sept. 30 Balance 600,000
	Oct. 31 80,000

Purchases

Sept. 30 Balance 460,000	
Oct. 31 36,500	

2. Subsidiary ledger accounts:
   a. Accounts receivable

G. G. Jones			
Sept. 30 Balance	8,500		
Oct. 6	10,000	Oct. 10	6,000
10	6,000	Oct. 16	500

J. F. Parker			
Sept. 30 Balance	500		
Oct. 11	5,000	Oct. 30	5,500
26	14,000		

G. T. Neal			
Sept. 30 Balance	3,000		
Oct. 1	5,000	Oct. 20	3,000
16	8,000	Oct. 29	5,000
29	2,000		

H. W. Ford		
Oct. 2	9,000	Oct. 31 20,000
20	11,000	
31	10,000	

   b. Accounts payable

A. Ltd.			
		Sept. 30 Balance	1,000
Oct. 1 1,000		Oct. 1	8,000
Oct. 20 8,000		6	6,000

B. Ltd.			
		Sept. 30 Balance	500
Oct. 16 2,000		Oct. 2	1,500
		16	9,000

C. Ltd.			
		Sept. 30 Balance	400
Oct. 31 1,400		Oct. 10	1,000
		20	2,000

D. Ltd.		
	Sept. 30 Balance	600
	Oct. 19	3,000
	26	6,000

Required:
1. Prepare appropriate specialized journals to reconstruct the transactions for October based on the data presented in the general and subsidiary ledger accounts.

Problem 6–3 A&R

The following problem is designed to test your ability in the use of special journals and subsidiary ledgers. The special journals of Yorle Company are reproduced below, followed by a number of transactions which occurred during October. The money columns in the journals are numbered to minimize clerical work in recording each transaction.

Sales Journal			
Date	Account	F	Amount
			(1)

Purchases Journal			
Date	Account	F	Amount
			(2)

Cash Disbursements Journal

Date	Account	F	Sundry	✔	Accts. Pay	Cash
			(3)		(4)	(5)

Cash Receipts Journal

Date	Account	F	Sundry	✔	Accts. Rec.	Sales	Sales Disc.	Cash
			(6)		(7)	(8)	(9)	(10)

General Journal

Date	Account	F	Amount	Amount
			(11)	(12)

Oct. 4 Purchases on account from B. C. Company, $1,200   ( ) dr.
( ) cr.

6 Purchase of store equipment from Willis Company for cash   ( ) dr.
( ) cr.

6 Sales to Ted Fry cash $500 less 2% discount of $1,500   ( ) dr.
( ) cr.

8 Borrowed $3,000 from Guaranty Bank on note payable   ( ) dr.
( ) cr.

10 Ted Fry returned half of the goods and a credit memorandum ( ) dr.
was issued to him   ( ) cr.

12 Paid one month's rent on store building, $500   ( ) dr.
( ) cr.

12 Received a $980 cheque from Gary Ball in payment of the ( ) dr.
October 3 sale   ( ) cr.

15 Sold merchandise to P. Cherry on account, $800   ( ) dr.
( ) cr.

18 Purchased on account merchandise from D. Browning ( ) dr.
Company, $1,000   ( ) cr.

20 Cash sales to David Dufour, $1,800   ( ) dr.
( ) cr.

22 Received a $200 credit memorandum from D. Browning   ( ) dr.
( ) cr.

25 Issued cheque to B. C. Company for purchase of October 4   ( ) dr.
( ) cr.

27 Sales to Ann Musson on account, $800   ( ) dr.
( ) cr.

30 Purchased store supplies for cash, $200   ( ) dr.
                                                          ( ) cr.
31 Paid monthly utilities   ( ) dr.
                                                          ( ) cr.

Required:

1. Indicate the column number in the spaces provided after each transaction to identify the journal in which each transaction should be recorded. For example:

   October 3 Sales to Gary Ball, $1000, terms 2/10, n/30   (1) Dr.
                                                             (1) Cr.

2. Indicate how the data in the special journals are posted to various accounts by filling in the spaces provided with the following posting possibilities:
   A. Posted as a *debit* to some general ledger account.
   B. Posted as a *credit* to some general ledger account.
   C. Posted as a *debit* to some subsidiary ledger account.
   D. Posted as a *credit* to some subsidiary ledger account.
   E. Not posted.
   Note: The numbers in parenthesis are the identification numbers for the money columns of the special journals.
   For example: (1) Sales Journal money column.

			Posted as
a.	Total of column (1)	Example	(A,B)
b.	Detail items of column (2)		( )
c.	Total of column (3)		( )
d.	Detail items of column (5)		( )
e.	Total of column (2)		( )
f.	Detail items of column (6)		( )
g.	Detail items of column (1)		( )
h.	Total of column (4)		( )
i.	Total of column (11)		( )
g.	Detail items of column (8)		( )
k.	Total of column (9)		( )
l.	Total of column (10)		( )
m.	Detail items of column (12)		( )
n.	Detail items of column (7)		( )
o.	Total of column (6)		( )
p.	Total of column (5)		( )
q.	Detail items of column (4)		( )
	Total of column (8)		( )
r.	Total of column (7)		( )
s.	Detail items of column (9)		( )
t.	Detail items of column (3)		( )
u.	Detail items of column (10)		( )
v.	Total of column (12)		( )
x.	Detail items of column (11)		( )

7

Internal control

In a small business the owner-manager commonly controls the entire operation through his personal supervision and his direct participation in the affairs and activities of the business. For example, he commonly buys all the assets, goods, and services bought by the business, personally hires and closely supervises all employees, negotiates all contracts, and signs all cheques. As a result, when he signs cheques, for example, he knows from personal contact and observation that the assets, goods, and services for which the cheques are in payment were received by the business. However, as a business grows it becomes increasingly difficult to maintain this personal contact, and at some point it becomes necessary for a manager to delegate responsibilities and rely for control on *internal control procedures* rather than personal contact.

Internal control The methods and procedures adopted by a business to control its operations are collectively known as a *system of internal control*. In a properly designed system the procedures encourage adherence to prescribed managerial policies, promote operational efficiencies, protect the business assets from waste, fraud, and theft, and ensure accurate and reliable accounting data.

Internal control methods and procedures vary from company to company, depending on such factors as the nature of the business and its size. However, some broad principles of internal control are as follows:[1]

Responsibilities should be clearly established

Good internal control necessitates that responsibilities be clearly established. Furthermore, in a given situation or for a given task, one person should be made responsible. When responsibility is shared and something goes wrong, it is difficult to determine who was at fault. For example, when two salesclerks share the same cash drawer and there is a shortage, it is normally impossible to tell which clerk is at fault. Each will tend to blame the other, and neither can prove that the responsibility is not his. In such a situation each clerk should be assigned a separate cash drawer or one of the clerks should be given responsibility for making all change.

Adequate records should be maintained

Good records provide a means of control by placing responsibility for the care and protection of assets, but poor records invite laxity and often theft. When a company has poor accounting control over its assets, dishonest employees soon become aware of this and are quick to take advantage.

Assets should be insured and employees bonded

Assets should be covered by adequate casualty insurance, and employees who handle cash and negotiable assets should be bonded. Bonding not only provides a means for recovery if a loss occurs but it also tends to prevent losses, since a bonded employee is less apt to take assets for his personal use if he knows he must deal with a bonding company when the shortage is revealed.

Record keeping and custody should be separated

A fundamental principle of internal control requires that the person who has access to or is responsible for an asset should not maintain the accounting record for that asset. When this principle is observed, the custodian of an asset, knowing that a record of the asset is being kept by another person, is not apt to either misappropriate the asset or waste it; and the record keeper, who does not have access to the asset, has no reason to falsify his record. Furthermore, if the asset is to be misappropriated and the theft concealed in the records, collusion is necessary.

Responsibility for related transactions should be divided

Responsibility for a divisible transaction or a series of related transactions should be divided between individuals or departments in such a

---

[1] *Internal Control* (New York: American Institute of Certified Public Accountants, 1959), p. 6.

manner that the work of one acts as a check on that of another. This does not mean there should be duplication of work. Each employee or department should perform an unduplicated portion, but in such a manner that the work of one acts as a check on that of another. For example, responsibility for placing orders, receiving the merchandise, and paying the vendors should not be given to one individual or department. To do so is to invite laxity in checking the quality and quantity of goods received, and carelessness in verifying the validity and accuracy of invoices. It also invites the purchase of goods for an employee's personal use and the payment of fictitious invoices.

Personnel should be rotated

Whenever possible, employees should be rotated in their job assignments. This has a number of advantages. In the first place, an employee is less apt to be careless or to intentionally commit a wrong when he knows his action will likely be brought to light when job assignments are changed. Also, an employee who has handled a number of assignments in his department is usually more capable at any one job because he understands how that job fits into the work of the department. And finally, the work of a department does not cease when an employee who performs a key operation is ill or absent. Other employees can take his place.

Mechanical devices should be used whenever practicable

Cash registers, cheque protectors, time clocks, and mechanical counters are examples of control devices that should be used whenever practicable. A cash register with a locked-in tape makes a record of each cash sale, a cheque protector by perforating the amount of a cheque into its face makes it almost impossible to change the amount, and a time clock registers the exact time an employee arrived on the job and when he departed.

Employees should be informed

An internal control system will not function as it should unless the employees cooperate and perform their tasks competently and in the prescribed manner. When employees do not understand the need for certain procedures or feel the procedures cause them unnecessary work, they will often avoid the procedures and, thus, destroy the effectiveness of the entire system. Consequently, when an internal control system is installed, it should be designed to cause the employees the least amount of work and inconvenience, and the reasons for its prescribed procedures should be fully explained.

The system should be under constant review

An internal control system, no matter how well designed, cannot be expected to function properly without constant examination and review. An examination or audit may disclose that prescribed procedures are not being followed or that better control or better work at less cost will be gained with a change in the procedures. Large companies commonly maintain a staff of internal auditors who constantly review their company's internal control system to see that it is functioning properly and its procedures are being followed.

Where internal control is needed

■ Internal control procedures apply to all assets owned by a business and to every phase of its operations. However, such procedures are particularly important in transactions involving cash receipts and disbursements and in the purchase of assets, goods, and services. As a result, purchasing procedures and cash disbursements are used in this chapter to introduce the subject and controlling cash receipts is discussed in the next chapter.

To appreciate the need for control over purchasing procedures and cash disbursements, assume that every employee in a large store has and exercises the authority to buy merchandise for resale by the store and that no business forms and procedures are provided to keep a record of purchases. Under such conditions there would be nothing but confusion as to what had been ordered and received; and there would also be errors, duplications, shortages, and payments for goods not received, plus unlimited opportunities for fraud through kickbacks to dishonest employees and through the payment of fictitious invoices.

Controlling purchases in a large store

■ In a large store, due to the size of the task but also to gain control, it is necessary to divide the responsibilities connected with purchasing merchandise and other assets among several departments. These are commonly the departments requesting that merchandise or other assets be purchased, the purchasing department, the receiving department, and the accounting department. It is also necessary to coordinate and control the responsibilities of these departments with business papers, a list of which follows. An explanation of each paper with its use will show how a large concern may gain control over its purchases.

	Business Paper	Prepared by the—	Sent to the—
1.	Purchase requisition	Selling department manager desiring that merchandise be purchased	Purchasing department, with a copy to the accounting department
2.	Purchase order	Purchasing department	Vendor, with a copy to the accounting department
3.	Invoice	Company selling the merchandise	Accounting department
4.	Receiving report	Receiving department	Accounting department, with a copy to the purchasing and requisitioning departments
5.	Invoice approval form	Accounting department	Attached to invoice in the accounting department

Purchase requisition

A large store is normally divided into selling departments and service departments, with each department under the supervision of a manager. The selling departments sell different types of merchandise, and the service departments perform services for the selling departments; and in such a store the purchasing department is a service department responsible for buying for all departments.

In making purchases, the purchasing department generally cannot know firsthand the merchandise needs of all the selling departments; therefore, the responsibility for keeping an adequate supply of the right kinds of merchandise in each department is usually delegated to each department manager. However, the department managers cannot be permitted to purchase directly from supply sources because if each manager were permitted to deal directly with wholesalers and manufacturers, the amount of merchandise purchased and the resulting liabilities could not be controlled. Therefore, in order to gain control over purchases and resulting liabilities, department managers are commonly required to place all orders through the purchasing department. In such cases the function of the several department managers in the

TOPS—FORM 3243	Purchase Requisition	No. 2613

Date _____

Purchasing Department
Please purchase the following named items:

INDICATE SOURCE OF SUPPLY IF KNOWN

Quantity	Number	Description

Purpose or Use _____

To be filled in by Purchasing Dept.

Date ordered _____ Order No. _____

When wanted _____

From _____

For _____ Dept. Approved _____

Illustration
7–1

Courtesy Tops Business Forms

purchasing procedure is to inform the purchasing department of their needs. Each manager performs this function by preparing in triplicate a purchase requisition, Illustration 7–1, listing the merchandise desired. The original and a duplicate copy of the purchase requisition are sent to the purchasing department. The third copy is retained by the requisitioning department as a check on the purchasing department.

Purchase order

The purchase order is a business form used by the purchasing department in placing an order with a manufacturer or wholesaler. It authorizes the supplier to ship the merchandise ordered and takes the place of a typewritten letter placing the order. A sample purchase order is shown in Illustration 7–2.

		PURCHASE ORDER	NO.	4238

THE EUGENE MANUFACTURING COMPANY
2590 Chula Vista Street · Spanish River, Ontario

DATE
F.O.B.
SHIP BY
TERMS

TO

SHIP TO

PLEASE SHIP THE FOLLOWING   DATE REQUIRED

QUANTITY	✔	DESCRIPTION	PRICE	PER	AMOUNT

IMPORTANT
OUR ORDER NUMBER MUST APPEAR ON INVOICES AND PACKAGES. ACKNOWLEDGE IF UNABLE TO SHIP ON TIME.

ORDERED BY

Illustration
7–2

Courtesy Tops Business Forms

On receipt of a purchase requisition from a selling department, the purchasing department prepares four or more copies of the purchase order. The copies are distributed as follows:

Copy 1   Copy 1, the original copy, is sent to the supplier as a request to purchase and as authority to ship the merchandise listed.

Copy 2   Copy 2, with a copy of the purchase requisition attached, is sent to the accounting department where it will ultimately be used in approving the invoice of the purchase for payment.

Copy 3   Copy 3 is sent to the department issuing the requisition to acknowledge the requisition and tell the action taken.

Copy 4   Copy 4 is retained on file by the purchasing department.

Invoice

An invoice is an itemized statement of goods bought and sold. It is prepared by the seller or *vendor,* and to the seller it is a sales invoice. However, when the same invoice is received by the buyer or *vendee,* it becomes a purchase invoice to the buyer. Invoices used in manufacturing and wholesaling are of the general type shown in Illustration 7–3.

In the purchasing procedure, upon receipt of a purchase order, the

Illustration
7–3

Courtesy Tops Business Forms

manufacturer or wholesaler receiving the order ships the ordered merchandise to the buyer and mails a copy of the invoice covering the shipment. The goods are delivered to the buyer's receiving department, and the invoice is sent directly to the buyer's accounting department.

Receiving report

Most large companies maintain a special department assigned the duty of receiving all merchandise or other assets purchased. As each shipment is received, counted, and checked, the receiving department prepares four or more copies of a receiving report. On this report are listed the quantity, description, and condition of the items received. The original copy is sent to the accounting department; the second copy to the department that requisitioned the merchandise; the third copy is sent to the purchasing department; and the fourth copy is retained on file in the receiving department. The copies sent to the purchasing and requisitioning departments act as notification of the arrival of the goods. An example of a receiving report is shown in Illustration 7–4.

Received from	Receiving Report	No. 4383
		Date
		Purchase Order No.
		Supplier's Invoice No.
		Received via

Quantity	Description	Condition

Counted and inspected by

Courtesy Tops Business Forms

Illustration
7–4

Invoice approval form

When the receiving report arrives in the accounting department, the accounting department then has in its possession copies of the —

1. Requisition listing the items requisitioned.
2. Purchase order that lists the merchandise ordered.
3. Invoice showing quantity, description, unit price, and total of the goods shipped by the seller.
4. Receiving report that lists quantity and condition of the items received.

With the information on these papers, the accounting department is in position to approve the invoice for entry on the books and ultimate payment. In approving the invoice, the accounting department checks and compares the information on all the papers. To facilitate the checking procedure and to ensure that no step is omitted, an invoice approval form is commonly used. This may be a separate business paper that is attached to the invoice, or the information shown in Illustration 7–5 may be stamped directly on the invoice with a rubber stamp.

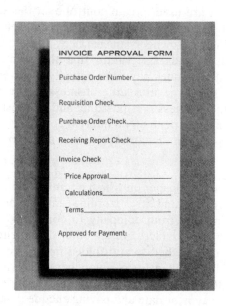

INVOICE APPROVAL FORM

Purchase Order Number_____

Requisition Check_____

Purchase Order Check_____

Receiving Report Check_____

Invoice Check

Price Approval_____

Calculations_____

Terms_____

Approved for Payment:

Illustration
7–5

As each step in the checking procedure is completed, the clerk making the check initials the invoice approval form. Initials in each space on the form indicate:

1. Requisition Check .... The items on the invoice agree with the requisition and were requisitioned.
2. Purchase Order Check .... The items on the invoice agree with the purchase order and were ordered.

3. Receiving Report Check...... The items on the invoice agree with the receiving report and were received.

4. Invoice Check:

    Price Approval .... The invoice prices are the agreed prices.

    Calculations .... The invoice has no mathematical errors.

    Terms .... The terms are the agreed terms.

Recording the Invoice

After the invoice is checked and approved, the purchase requisition, purchase order, receiving report, and the invoice approval form, if a stamp is not used, are attached to the invoice, and the invoice is then ready for final approval, recording, and payment. However, before going into this, a system for controlling cash disbursements, called a *voucher system,* should be discussed.

The voucher system

■ A voucher system consists of vouchers and the procedures built around vouchers that are used to gain control over the incurrence and payment of obligations that result in cash disbursements. In a small business, one in which the owner-manager signs all cheques and knows from personal contact and observation that the assets, goods, and services for which the cheques pay were actually received, such a system is not needed. However, in a large business this personal contact with all phases of the business is impossible; and as a result, the person who signs cheques must depend on an internal control system, such as a voucher system, to tell him that an obligation is a proper obligation and should be paid.

The voucher

■ A voucher is a business paper on which a transaction is summarized, its correctness certified, and its recording and payment approved. Vouchers vary somewhat from company to company; but in general are so designed that the invoice, bill, or other documents from which they are prepared are attached to and folded inside the voucher. This makes for ease in filing. The inside of a voucher is shown in Illustration 7–6 and the outside in Illustration 7–7. All information entered on a voucher except the payment date and paying cheque number is entered at the time the voucher is prepared. Information as to payment is written in later when the voucher is actually paid.

The voucher system and control

■ A voucher system gains control over cash disbursements by providing a routine which (1) permits only specific departments and individuals to incur obligations that will result in cash disbursements; (2) establishes procedures for incurring such obligations and for their verification, approval, and recording; and (3) permits cheques to be issued only in payment of properly verified, approved, and recorded

Voucher No. _767_

VALLEY SUPPLY COMPANY
Halifax, Nova Scotia

Date ___Oct. 1, 19--___
Pay to ___A.B. Seay Wholesale Company___
City ___Digby___   Province ___Nova Scotia___

For the following: (attach all invoices and supporting papers)

Date of Invoice	Terms	Invoice Number and Other Details	Amount
Sept. 30,19--	2/10,n/60	Invoice No. C-11756	800.00
		Less Discount	16.00
		Net Amount Payable	784.00

Payment Approved

N.O. Neal
Auditor

Illustration
7-6
**Inside of a
voucher**

obligations. Furthermore, every obligation must be recorded at the time it is incurred and every purchase is treated as an independent transaction, complete in itself, even though a number of purchases may be made from the same company during a month or other billing period.

When a voucher system is in use, control over cash disbursements begins with the incurrence of obligations that will result in cash disbursements. Only specified departments and individuals are authorized to incur such obligations, and the kind each may incur is limited. For example, only the purchasing department may incur obligations by purchasing merchandise, small assets, and supplies. Further control is gained by establishing a more or less inflexible routine to be followed in incurring each kind of obligation, providing within the routine for the production of business papers at each step, and providing a means of

ACCOUNTING DISTRIBUTION

Voucher No. _767_

Account Debited	Amount
Purchases	800.00
Freight-In	
Store Supplies	
Office Supplies	
Sales Salaries	

Due Date _____ October 10, 19-- _____

Pay to _A.B Seay Wholesale Co._
City _Digby_
Province _Nova Scotia_

Total Vouch. Pay.Cr.	800.00

Summary of Charges:
Total Charges _____ 800.00
Discount _____ 16.00
Net Payment _____ 784.00

Record of Payment:
Paid _____
Cheque No. _____

Illustration
7–7
**Outside of
a voucher**

bringing these papers together, checking them, and using them as a basis for approving the transaction for recording and payment.

Take the purchase of merchandise, for example, and recall how a department manager desiring the purchase of merchandise for his department must complete a purchase requisition and send it to the purchasing department. The purchasing department then issues a purchase order to a vendor who ships the merchandise to the purchaser's receiving department and mails an invoice to the accounting department. The receiving department counts and examines the merchandise and reports to the accounting department on a receiving report. The accounting department then has in its possession:

1. A copy of the requisition listing the items requested.

2. A purchase order listing the merchandise ordered.
3. An invoice showing the goods shipped by the seller.
4. A receiving report listing the items received.

With the information on these business papers the accounting department is in a position to approve the invoice for entry on the books and ultimate payment. In approving the invoice, clerks in the accounting department check and compare the information on these papers, noting the completion of each step on the invoice approval form. Then, after the checking and comparing procedure is completed, a voucher is prepared. This is a simple task requiring only that a clerk enter the required information in the proper blank spaces of a voucher form. The information is taken from the invoice and its supporting documents. After the voucher is completed, the invoice and its supporting documents are attached to and folded inside the voucher. The voucher is then sent to the desk of the chief clerk or auditor who makes an additional check, approves the accounting distribution (the accounts to be debited), and approves the voucher for recording.

After being approved and recorded a voucher is filed until its due date, when it is sent to the office of the company cashier or other disbursing officer for payment. Here the person responsible for issuing cheques depends upon the approved voucher and its supporting documents to tell him the obligation is a proper obligation, properly incurred, and should be paid. For example, the purchase requisition and purchase order attached to the voucher tell him the purchase was authorized, the receiving report tells him the items were received, and the invoice approval form tells him the invoice was checked for errors. Also, he knows there is little chance for fraud, unless all the documents were stolen and the signatures forged, or there was collusion.

The Vouchers Payable account

■ When a voucher system is in use, an account called Vouchers Payable replaces the Accounts Payable account discussed in previous chapters. As a result, when merchandise is purchased, the voucher covering the purchase is recorded and with a debit to Purchases and a credit to Vouchers Payable. Likewise, when a plant asset is purchased, a debit to the proper asset account and a credit to Vouchers Payable results. Furthermore, when any voucher is paid, its payment results in a debit to Vouchers Payable and a credit to Cash.

The voucher system and expenses

■ The substitution of the Vouchers Payable account for the Accounts Payable account, as described in the previous paragraph, is a small procedural change. However, the use of the new account in recording expenses, such as, for example, telephone expense, represents a somewhat greater change. To understand this change, recall that under a voucher system, in order to gain control over cash disbursements, every obligation that will result in a cash disbursement must be approved for payment and recorded as a liability (vouchers payable) at the time it is incurred. As a result, when the monthly telephone bill is received, it is verified and any long-distance calls are approved, a voucher is then prepared, and the telephone bill is attached to and folded inside the voucher. The voucher is then recorded in the same way as a voucher for the purchase of merchandise, with the only difference being that the recording entry results in a debit to Telephone Expense rather than to Purchases. A cheque is then issued in payment of the voucher.

Requiring that an expense payment be approved and recorded as a voucher payable at the time it is incurred helps ensure that every expense payment is approved when information for its approval is available. Often invoices, bills, and statements for such things as equipment repairs are received weeks after the work is done; and if no record of the repairs exist, it is difficult at that time to determine whether the invoice or bill is a correct statement of the amount owed. Also, if no records exist, it is possible for a dishonest employee to arrange with an outsider for more than one payment of an obligation, for payment of excessive amounts, and for payment for goods and services not received, all with kickbacks to the dishonest employee.

Recording vouchers ■ When a voucher system is in use, vouchers are recorded in a Voucher Register. Such registers vary somewhat; but a pen-and-ink version, Illustration 7–8 provides columns for the date, voucher number, payee, and a record of voucher payments. In addition, there is a Vouchers

Page 32   **Voucher**

Date 19–		Voucher No.	Payee	When and How Paid		Vouchers Payable Credit		Purchases Debit		Freight-in Debit		
				Date	Cheque No.							
Oct.	1	767	A. B. Seay Co.	10/9	753	800	00	800	00			1
	1	768	Daily Sentinel	10/9	754	53	00					2
	2	769	Seaboard Supply Co.	10/12	756	235	00	155	00	10	00	3
	6	770	George Smith	10/6	734	85	00					4
	6	771	Frank Jones	10/6	735	95	00					5
	6	772	George Roth	10/6	736	95	00					6
	30	998	First National Bank	10/30	972	505	00					33
												34
	30	999	Pacific Telephone Co.	10/30	973	18	00					35
	31	1000	Tarbell Wholesale Co.			235	00	235	00			36
	31	1001	Office Equipment Co.	10/31	974	195	00					37
	31		Totals			5,079	00	2,435	00	156	00	38
						(213)		(511)		(514)		39
												40
												41

Illustration
7–8

Payable credit column and several debit columns. Exact debit columns vary from company to company. However, in merchandising concerns a debit column is always provided for recording merchandise purchases; and in all companies, so long as space is available, special debit columns are provided in order that posting labour may be saved by posting column totals. In addition, an Other Accounts debit column is provided for those debits that do not occur often.

All information about each voucher that is entered in the register, with the exception of that entered in the columns used in recording the voucher's payment, is entered as soon as each voucher is approved for recording. The information as to payment date and the number of the paying cheque is entered later as each voucher is paid.

Posting the voucher register

■ A Voucher Register such as that shown in Illustration 7–8 is posted as follows. At the end of the month the columns are totaled and cross-footed to prove their equality. The Vouchers Payable column total is credited to the Vouchers Payable account; the Purchases, Freight-In, Sales Salaries Expense, Office Salaries Expense, Delivery Expense, and Advertising Expense column totals are debited to these accounts; and none of the individual amounts in these columns are posted. However, the individual amounts in the Other Accounts column are posted as debits to the accounts named and the column total is not posted.

Register							Page 32	
Sales Salaries Expense Debit	Adver- tising Expense Debit	Delivery Expense Debit	Office Salaries Expense Debit	Other Accounts Debit				
				Account Name	Folio	Amount Debit		
1								
2		53 00						
3					Store Supplies	117	70 00	
4				85 00				
5	95 00							
6	95 00							
33					Notes Payable	211	500 00	
34					Interest Expense	721	5 00	
35					Telephone Expense	655	18 00	
36								
37					Office Equipment	134	195 00	
38	740 00	115 00	358 00	340 00			935 00	
39	(611)	(612)	(615)	(651)			(✓)	
40								
41								

■ When a voucher system is in use, some vouchers are due and are paid as soon as they are recorded, while other vouchers must be filed until payment is due. As an aid in taking cash discounts, vouchers for which payment is not due are generally filed in an unpaid vouchers file under the dates on which they are to be paid.

As previously stated, when a voucher system is in use, a Vouchers Payable account is substituted for the Accounts Payable account. Likewise, the file of unpaid vouchers is substituted for and takes the place of the subsidiary Accounts Payable Ledger. Actually, the file of unpaid vouchers is a subsidiary ledger of creditors' accounts. Also, the Vouchers Payable account is in effect a controlling account controlling the unpaid vouchers file. Consequently, after posting is completed, the balance of the Vouchers Payable account should equal the sum of the unpaid vouchers in the unpaid vouchers file.

This equality is verified after posting is completed each month by preparing a schedule or adding machine list of the unpaid vouchers in the unpaid vouchers file and comparing its total with the balance of the Vouchers Payable account. Likewise, the unpaid vouchers in the file are compared with the unpaid vouchers shown in the Voucher Register's record of payments column. Since the number of each paying cheque and the payment date are entered in the Voucher Register's payments column as each voucher is paid, the vouchers in the register without cheque numbers and payment dates should be the same as those in the unpaid vouchers file.

■ Under a voucher system, cheques drawn in payment of vouchers are recorded in a Cheque Register that is nothing more than a simplified Cash Disbursement Journal. It is simplified because under a voucher system no obligation is paid until a voucher covering the payment is prepared and recorded, and no cheque is drawn except in payment of a specific voucher. Consequently, all cheques drawn result in debits to Vouchers Payable and credits to Cash, unless a discount must be recorded, and then there are credits to both Purchases Discounts and to Cash. As a result, a voucher system Cheque Register needs at most three money columns. It needs columns for debits to Vouchers Payable, credits to Purchases Discounts, and credits to Cash. Such a Cheque Register is shown in Illustration 7–9.

Not only is the design of a Cheque Register used with a voucher system simplified, its posting is also easier. No amounts are posted individually; all amounts are posted in column totals at the end of the month.

■ Occasionally an item must be returned after the voucher recording its purchase has been prepared and entered. In such cases the return may be recorded with a general journal entry similar to the following:

Cheque Register

Date		Payee	Voucher No.	Cheque No.	Vouchers Payable Debit	Purchases Discounts Credit	Cash Credit
19—							
Oct.	1	C. B. & Y. RR Co.	765	728	14.00		14.00
	3	Frank Mills	766	729	73.00		73.00
	3	Ajax Wholesale Co.	753	730	250.00	5.00	245.00
	4	Normal Supply Co.	747	731	100.00	2.00	98.00
	5	Thomas McGinnin	763	732	43.00		43.00
	6	Giant Equipment Co.	759	733	342.00		342.00
	6	George Smith	770	734	85.00		85.00
	6	Frank Jones	771	735	95.00		95.00
	30	First National Bank	998	972	505.00		505.00
	30	Pacific Telephone Co.	999	973	18.00		18.00
	31	Office Equipment Co.	1001	974	195.00		195.00
	31	Totals			6,468.00	28.00	6,440.00
					(213)	(512)	(111)

Illustration 7–9
The voucher system Cheque Register

Nov.	5	Vouchers Payable	15.00	
		Purchases Returns and Allowances...........		15.00
		Returned defective merchandise.		

In addition to the entry, a reference to the entry is made in the Payments columns of the Vouchers Register, on the upper half of the line for the voucher on which the return is made. The reference is made small enough so that the cheque number of the paying cheque and the date of the voucher's payment can be entered on the same line. Also, the amount of return is deducted on the voucher and the credit memorandum and other documents verifying the return are attached to the voucher. Then, when the voucher is paid, a cheque is drawn for its corrected amount.

Other internal control procedures

■ Internal control procedures apply to every phase of a company's operations from purchases through sales, cash receipts, cash disbursements, and the control of plant assets. Many of these procedures are discussed in later chapters. However, the way in which a company can gain control over purchases discounts should be discussed here.

Recall that thus far the following entries in general journal form have been used in recording the receipt and payment of an invoice for merchandise purchased:

Nov.	2	Purchases	1,000.00	
		Accounts (or Vouchers) Payable		1,000.00
		Purchased merchandise, terms 2/10, n/60.		
	12	Accounts (or Vouchers) Payable	1,000.00	
		Purchases Discounts		20.00
		Cash		980.00
		Paid the invoice of November 2.		

The invoice of these entries was recorded at its gross, $1,000, amount, and this is the way in which invoices are recorded in many companies. However, well-managed companies follow the practice of taking all offered cash discounts; and in many of these companies invoices are recorded at their net, after discount amounts. For example, if a company that records invoices at net amounts purchases merchandise having a $1,000 invoice price, terms 2/10, n/60, on receipt of the goods it deducts the offered $20 discount from the gross invoice amount and records the purchase in its Voucher Register with these debits and credits:

Nov.	1	Purchases	980.00	
		Vouchers Payable		980.00
		Purchased merchandise on credit.		

If the voucher for this purchase is paid within the discount period (all vouchers should be so paid), the cheque register entry to record the payment has a debit to Vouchers Payable and a credit to Cash for $980. However, if payment is not made within the discount period and the discount is lost, an entry like the following must be made in the General Journal when the voucher is paid:

Dec.	31	Discounts Lost	20.00	
		Vouchers Payable		20.00
		To record the discount lost.		

In addition to the last entry a notation is placed in the When and How Paid column of the Voucher Register on the line of the voucher on which the discount was lost. The notation might read "See G.J., P. 35" or something similar. It refers a person examining the records to the general journal entry recording the discount lost, and makes it easy to trace the entire transaction. Also, a notation of the discount lost is placed on the voucher and a cheque for the full $1,000 invoice amount is drawn in its payment and entered in the Cheque Register.

Advantage of the net method

When invoices are recorded at gross amounts, the amount of discounts taken is deducted from the balance of the Purchases account on the income statement to arrive at the cost of merchandise purchased. However, when invoices are recorded at gross amounts, if through oversight or carelessness discounts are lost, the amount of discounts lost does not appear in any account or on the income statement and may not come to the attention of management. On the other hand, when purchases are recorded at net amounts, the amount of discounts taken does not appear on the income statement; but the amount of discounts lost is called to management's attention through the appearance on the income statement of the expense account, Discounts Lost, as in the condensed income statement of Illustration 7–10.

<table>
<tr><td colspan="2" align="center">**XYZ Company**
Income Statement for Year Ended December 31, 19—</td></tr>
<tr><td>Sales</td><td>$100,000</td></tr>
<tr><td>Cost of goods sold</td><td>60,000</td></tr>
<tr><td>Gross profit from sales</td><td>$ 40,000</td></tr>
<tr><td>Operating expenses</td><td>28,000</td></tr>
<tr><td>Income from operations</td><td>$ 12,000</td></tr>
<tr><td>Other revenues and expenses:</td><td></td></tr>
<tr><td>Discounts lost</td><td>150</td></tr>
<tr><td>Net Income</td><td>$ 11,850</td></tr>
</table>

Illustration
7–10

Of the two methods, recording invoices at their net amounts probably supplies management with the more valuable information, the amount of discounts lost through oversight, carelessness, or other cause. It also gives management better control over the work of the people responsible for taking cash discounts; because if discounts are lost, someone must explain why. As a result, few discounts are lost through carelessness.

In passing it should be observed that when a voucher system is in use and invoices are recorded at net amounts, the Cheque Register needs only one money column. Only one money column is needed because discounts are not recorded and each cheque entered in the register results in a debit to Vouchers Payable and an equal credit to Cash. Therefore, the amount of each cheque may be entered in a register column and the total may be debited to Vouchers Payable and credited to Cash.

Questions for class discussion

1. Internal control procedures are important in every business, but at what stage in the development of a business do they become critical?
2. Name some of the broad principles of internal control.
3. Why should the person who keeps the record of an asset be a different person from the one responsible for custody of the asset?
4. Why should responsibility for a sequence of related transactions be divided among different departments or individuals?
5. In a small business it is sometimes impossible to separate the functions of

record keeping and asset custody, and it is sometimes impossible to divide responsibilities for related transactions. What should be substituted for these control procedures?

6. In purchasing merchandise in a large store, why are the department managers not permitted to deal directly with the sources of supply?

7. What are the duties of the selling department managers in the purchasing procedures of a large store?

8. Tell (*a*) who prepares, (*b*) who receives, and (*c*) the purpose of each of the following business papers:

a. Purchase requisition.   *d.* Receiving report.
b. Purchase order.   *e.* Invoice approval form.
c. Invoice.   *f.* Voucher.

9. Do all companies need a voucher system? At what approximate point in a company's growth would you recommend the installation of such a system?

10. When he issues a cheque in a large business, the disbursing officer usually cannot know from personal contact that the assets, goods, or services for which the cheque pays were received by the business or that their purchase was properly authorized. However, if the company has an internal control system, he can depend on the system. Exactly what documents does he depend on to tell him the purchase was authorized and properly made and the goods were actually received?

11. When a voucher system is installed, a Purchases Journal as described in the previous chapter is no longer used. What is substituted?

12. When a company installs a voucher system, it no longer uses an Accounts Payable Ledger. What is substituted?

13. When a voucher system is in use, why is a bill or statement for an expense verified and recorded in the same way as an invoice for the purchase of merchandise?

14. What valuable information becomes readily available to management when invoices are recorded at net amounts? Is this information readily available when invoices are recorded at gross amounts?

Class Exercises

Exercise 7-1

Give in general journal form the entries to record the following vouchers and voucher payments for a company that records invoices at gross amounts:

Nov. 10   Prepared Voucher No. 711 payable to Drylake Company for merchandise having a $750 invoice price, invoice dated November 8, terms FOB destination, 2/10, n/30.

10   Prepared Voucher No. 712 payable to Mountain Telephone Company for the monthly telephone bill, $45, and immediately issued Cheque No. 708 in its payment.

18   Issued Cheque No. 742 in payment of Voucher No. 711, less the discount.

Exercise 7-2

Prepare general journal entries to record the following transactions for a company that uses a voucher system in which invoices are recorded at gross amounts:

Nov. 14   Prepared Voucher No. 614 payable to Beta Company for merchandise having a $900 invoice price, invoice dated November 11, terms 2/10, n/60, FOB factory. Beta Company had prepaid the freight charges on the merchandise and had added the amount, $50, to the invoice, bringing its total to $950.

     19   Received a $100 credit memorandum from Beta Company for unsatisfactory merchandise from the November 14 purchase that was returned for credit after the voucher for the purchase was recorded.

     21   Mailed Cheque No. 610 to Beta Company in payment of the November 14 purchase, less the return and discount.

Exercise 7–3

A company completed these transactions:

Nov.   3   Prepared Voucher No. 433 payable to Alpha Company for merchandise having a $2,000 invoice price, invoice dated November 1, terms FOB destination, 2/10, n/30.

     8   Received a credit memorandum from Alpha Company for $300 (invoice price) of merchandise received on November 3 and returned for credit after its purchase was recorded. Recorded the memorandum, deducted the return on Voucher No. 433, and filed the voucher for payment, supposedly, on the last day of the discount period.

    18   Discovered that Voucher No. 433 had been filed in error for payment on this date, causing the discount to be lost. Refiled it for payment on the last day of the credit period.

Dec.   1   Issued a cheque in payment of Voucher No. 433.

Required:

Under the assumption that the invoice of Voucher No. 433 was recorded at its gross amount, prepare entries in general journal form to record the transactions.

Exercise 7–4

Assume that the company of Exercise 7–3 records invoices at net amounts and prepare a second set of entries in general journal form to record the transactions involving Voucher No. 433.

Exercise 7–5

Driftwood Company incurred $3,500 of operating expenses in October, a month in which its sales were $12,500. The company began October with a $6,500 merchandise inventory and ended the month with a $7,000 inventory, and during the month it purchased merchandise having an $8,000 invoice price, all of which was subject to a 2% discount for prompt payment. The company took advantage of the discounts on $5,500 of the purchases; but through an error in filing, it did not earn and could not take the discount on a $2,500 invoice paid on October 31.

Required:

1. Prepare an October income statement for the company under the assumption it records invoices at gross amounts.
2. Prepare a second income statement for the company under the assumption it records invoices at net amounts.

Problem 7-1

Eastern Company quoted Southland Company a $1,000 list price, less a 25% trade discount, FOB its factory, 2/10, n/60, for several items of merchandise. Southland Company accepted the offer and completed these transactions:

Nov. 11   Received the merchandise and an invoice dated November 9. Eastern Company had prepaid the freight charges, $60, as a service to Southland Company and had added the amount to the invoice. Southland Company prepared Voucher No. 652 authorizing payment of the invoice.

16   Received a $50 credit memorandum (invoice price) for merchandise from the Eastern Company shipment returned after the voucher was prepared. Recorded the memorandum, reduced the voucher total, attached the memorandum to the voucher, and refiled it for payment on the last day of the discount period.

19   Issued Cheque No. 649 in payment of Voucher No. 652.

Required:
1. Prepare general journal entries to record the transactions under the assumption Southland Company records invoices at gross amounts.
2. Prepare a second set of entries to record the transactions under the assumption the company records invoices at net amounts.
3. Assume that after the credit memorandum was recorded, rather than being filed for payment on the last day of the discount period, the voucher was filed in error for payment on the last day of the credit period, and give the entries to record payment of the invoice (*a*) when it is recorded at its gross amount and (*b*) when it is recorded at its net amount.

Problem 7-2

Hale Company had a $7,500 inventory on October 1 and a $7,000 inventory on October 31. During October it made $14,000 of sales, incurred $4,355 of operating expenses, and completed these transactions:

Oct. 3   Prepared Voucher No. 345 for the purchase of merchandise having a $2,750 invoice price, invoice dated October 1, terms 2/10, n/30.

8   Received a $250 credit memorandum for merchandise having that invoice price which was received on October 3 and returned after the voucher, No. 345, was recorded.

12   Prepared Voucher No. 351 for the purchase of merchandise having a $4,000 invoice price, invoice dated October 10, terms 2/10, n/30.

20   Issued Cheque No. 348 in payment of Voucher No. 351, less the discount.

21   Prepared Voucher No. 360 for the purchase of merchandise having a $1,250 invoice price, invoice dated October 19, terms 2/10, n/30.

29   Issued Cheque No. 358 in payment of Voucher No. 360.

31   Discovered that Voucher No. 345 had been filed in error for payment on this date. Issued Cheque No. 361 in its payment, making all necessary entries.

Required:
1. Under the assumption that Hale Company records invoices at gross

amounts, (a) prepare general journal entries to record the transactions and (b) prepare an October income statement for the company.

2. Under the assumption the company records invoices at net amounts, (a) prepare a second set of general journal entries to record the transactions and (b) prepare a second October income statement for the company.

Problem 7–3

Kenton Company completed these transactions affecting vouchers payable:

Oct. 2 Prepared Voucher No. 817 payable to Driftwood Company for merchandise having a $1,250 invoice price, invoice dated September 29, terms FOB destination, 2/10, n/30.

5 Prepared Voucher No. 818 payable to Surfside Company for merchandise having a $950 invoice price, invoice dated October 3, terms FOB shipping point, 2/10, n/60. The vendor had prepaid the freight charges, $40, adding the amount to the invoice and bringing its total to $990.

7 Received a credit memorandum for merchandise having a $250 invoice price. The merchandise was received on October 2, Voucher No. 817, and returned for credit.

10 Prepared Voucher No. 819 to Office Supply Co. for the purchase of office equipment having a $300 invoice price, terms n/10 EOM.

13 Issued Cheque No. 817 in payment of the invoice of Voucher No. 818, less the discount.

15 Prepared Voucher No. 820 payable to Payroll for sales salaries, $400, and office salaries, $200. Issued Cheque No. 818 in payment of the voucher. Cashed the cheque and paid the employees.

21 Prepared Voucher No. 821 payable to Valley Sales for Office supplies having a $150 invoice price, terms n/10 EOM.

23 Prepared Voucher No. 822 payable to Beachside Company for merchandise having a $750 invoice price, invoice dated October 22, terms FOB shipping point, 2/10, n/60. The vendor had prepaid the freight charges, $30, adding the amount to the invoice and bringing its total to $780.

29 Discovered that Voucher No. 817 had been filed in error for payment on the last day of its credit period rather than the last day of its discount period, causing the discount to be lost. Issued Cheque No. 819 in payment of the voucher, making all necessary entries. (Do not forget the return.)

Oct. 30 Prepared Voucher No. 823 payable to *The Daily Gazette* for advertising, $150. Issued Cheque No. 820 in payment of the voucher.

31 Prepared Voucher No. 824 payable to Payroll for sales salaries, $400, and office salaries, $200. Issued Cheque No. 821 in payment of the voucher. Cashed the cheque and paid the employees.

Required:

1. Prepare a Voucher Register, a Cheque Register, and a General Journal and record the transactions under the assumption Kenton Company records invoices at gross amounts.

2. Prepare a Vouchers Payable account and post those entry portions that affect the account.

3. Prove the balance of the Vouchers Payable account by preparing a schedule of unpaid vouchers.

Problem 7-4

Required:
1. Prepare a Voucher Register, a Cheque Register having one money column, and a General Journal and record the transactions of Problem 7-3 under the assumption Kenton Company records invoices at net amounts.
2. Prepare a Vouchers Payable account and post those entry portions that affect the account.
3. Prove the balance of the Vouchers Payable account by preparing a schedule of unpaid vouchers.

Problem 7-5

Hunter Company completed these transactions involving vouchers payable:

Nov. 1 Prepared Voucher No. 610 payable to Lake Realty for one month's rent, $500. Issued Cheque No. 610 in payment of the voucher.

2 Prepared Voucher No. 611 payable to Pine Company for merchandise having a $1,200 invoice price, invoice dated October 31, terms FOB shipping point, 2/10, n/30. Pine Company had prepaid the freight charges, $55, adding the amount to the invoice and bringing its total to $1,255.

5 Prepared Voucher No. 612 payable to West Company for merchandise having an $800 invoice price, invoice dated November 2, terms FOB shipping point, 2/10, n/30.

5 Prepared Voucher No. 613 payable to Coast Truck Lines for freight charges on the merchandise received from West Company, $35. Issued Cheque No. 611 in payment of the voucher.

7 Received a credit memorandum for merchandise having a $200 invoice price. The merchandise was received from Pine Company on November 2 and returned for credit. Recorded the memorandum, reduced the total of Voucher No. 611, attached the memorandum to the voucher, and filed the voucher, supposedly, for payment on the last day of its credit period.

9 Prepared Voucher No. 614 payable to *The Journal* for advertising, $75. Issued Cheque No. 612 in payment of the voucher.

12 Issued Cheque No. 613 in payment of the invoice of Voucher No. 612, less the discount.

14 Prepared Voucher No. 615 payable to Dale Company for store supplies, $60, terms n/10 EOM.

15 Prepared Voucher No. 616 payable to Payroll for sales salaries, $640, and office salaries, $265. Issued Cheque No. 614 in payment of the voucher. Cashed the cheque and paid the employees.

17 Prepared Voucher No. 617 payable to Beta Company for merchandise having a $900 invoice price, invoice dated November 15, terms FOB shipping point, 2/10, n/30. Beta Company had prepaid the freight charges, $45, adding the amount to the invoice and bringing its total to $945.

20 Prepared Voucher No. 618 payable to Office Supply Co. for office equipment, $350, terms n/10 EOM.

23 Prepared Voucher No. 619 payable to Blue Company for merchandise having a $1,500 invoice price, invoice dated November 21, terms FOB destination, 2/10, n/60.

25 Issued Cheque No. 615 in payment of the invoice of Voucher No. 617, less the discount.

30 Discovered that Voucher No. 611 had been filed in error for payment on this date rather than the last day of the discount period. Issued Cheque No. 616 in payment of the voucher, making all necessary entries. (Do not forget the return.)

30 Prepared Voucher No. 620 payable to Payroll for sales salaries, $640, and office salaries, $265. Issued Cheque No. 617 in payment of the voucher. Cashed the cheque and paid the employees.

Required:

1. Record the transactions in a Voucher Register, a Cheque Register, and a General Journal under the assumption Hunter Company records invoices at gross amounts.
2. Prepare a Vouchers Payable account and post the entry portions that affect the account.
3. Prove the balance of the Vouchers Payable account by preparing a schedule of unpaid vouchers.

Problem 7–6

Required:

1. Record the transactions of Problem 7–5 in a Voucher Register, a one-column Cheque Register, and a General Journal under the assumption that Hunter Company records invoices at net amounts.
2. Prepare a Vouchers Payable account and post those entry portions that affect the account.
3. Prove the balance of the Vouchers Payable account by preparing a schedule of unpaid vouchers.

Alternate problems

Problem 7–1A

Surfland Company placed an order for merchandise having a $1,500 list price, less a 40% trade discount, 2/10, n/60, FOB shipping point, and it completed these transactions involving the order:

Oct. 12 Received the merchandise and an invoice dated October 10. The vendor had prepaid the freight charges, $40, as a convenience to Surfland Company and had added the amount to the invoice. Surfland Company prepared Voucher No. 615 authorizing payment of the invoice and filed it for payment on the last day of the discount period.

15 Surfland Company received a $100 credit memorandum (invoice price) for merchandise from the foregoing shipment which was returned after the voucher was recorded. It recorded the memorandum, reduced the total of Voucher No. 615, attached the memorandum to the voucher, and filed it in error for payment on the last day of the invoice's credit period.

Dec. 9 Discovered the discount had been lost on the invoice of Voucher No. 615, made the necessary entry or entries, and mailed a cheque for the amount owed.

Required:

1. Prepare general journal entries to record the transactions under the assumption Surfland Company records invoices at gross amounts.
2. Prepare a second set of entries to record the transactions under the assumption the company records invoices at net amounts.
3. Under the contrary assumptions that Voucher No. 615 was correctly filed on October 15, was paid on October 20, and the discount earned, *(a)* give the entry to record payment under the assumption the company records invoices at gross amounts. Then *(b)* give the entry to record payment under the assumption the company records invoices at net amounts.

Problem 7–2A

On November 30 the credit balance of Huron Company's Sales account showed it had sold $15,000 of merchandise during the month. The company had begun November with a $9,000 merchandise inventory and ended it with an $8,250 inventory, and it had incurred $5,110 of operating expenses during the month. It had also recorded these transactions:

Nov 1   Prepared Voucher No. 333 for merchandise having a $3,000 invoice price, invoice dated October 29, terms 2/10, n/30.

5   Prepared Voucher No. 335 for merchandise having a $2,000 invoice price, invoice dated November 3, terms 2/10, n/30.

7   Received a $500 credit memorandum (invoice price) for merchandise received on November 1 and returned after Voucher No. 333 was prepared and recorded.

13   Issued Cheque No. 336 in payment of the invoice of Voucher No. 335, less the discount.

15   Prepared Voucher No. 338 for merchandise having a $3,500 invoice price, invoice dated November 12, terms 2/10, n/30.

22   Issued Cheque No. 339 in payment of the invoice of Voucher No. 338, less the discount.

28   Discovered that Voucher No. 333 had been filed in error for payment on this date. Issued Cheque No. 341 in its payment, making all necessary entries.

Required:

1. Assume that Huron Company records invoices at gross amounts and *(a)* prepare general journal entries to record the transactions. *(b)* Prepare a November income statement for the company.
2. Assume the company records invoices at net amounts and *(a)* prepare a second set of general journal entries to record the transactions. *(b)* Prepare a second November income statement for the company under this assumption.

Problem 7–3A

Valley Sales Company completed these transactions affecting vouchers payable:

Nov. 1   Prepared Voucher No. 810 payable to Gull Company for merchandise having a $1,500 invoice price, invoice dated October 30, terms FOB shipping point, 2/10, n/30. The vendor had prepaid the freight charges, $50, adding the amount to the invoice and bringing its total to $1,550.

4   Prepared Voucher No. 811 payable to Office Outfitters for the purchase of office equipment having a $250 invoice price, terms n/10 EOM.

6   Received a credit memorandum for merchandise having a $500 invoice price. The merchandise was received on November 1, Voucher No. 810, and returned for credit.

9   Prepared Voucher No. 812 payable to Kenton Company for merchandise having a $750 invoice price, invoice dated November 7, terms FOB shipping point, 2/10, n/60.

9   Prepared Voucher No. 813 payable to Western Truck Lines for freight charges on the shipment of Voucher No. 812, $50. Issued Cheque No. 810 in payment of the voucher.

14   Prepared Voucher No. 814 payable to Dale Sales Company for the purchase of office supplies having a $35 invoice price, terms n/10 EOM.

17   Issued Cheque No. 811 in payment of the invoice of Voucher No. 812, less the discount.

24   Prepared Voucher No. 815 payable to Driftwood Company for merchandise having an $850 invoice price, invoice dated November 22, terms FOB shipping point, 2/10, n/60. The vendor had prepaid the freight charges, $45, adding the amount to the invoice and bringing its total to $895.

29   Discovered that Voucher No. 810 had been filed in error for payment on this date rather than the last day of its discount period, causing the discount to be lost. Issued Cheque No. 812 in payment of the voucher, making all necessary entries. (Do not forget the return.)

30   Prepared Voucher No. 816 payable to *The Morning Star* for advertising, $80. Issued Cheque No. 813 in payment of the voucher.

30   Prepared Voucher No. 817 payable to Payroll for sales salaries, $800, and office salaries, $425. Issued Cheque No. 814 in payment of the voucher. Cashed the cheque and paid the employees.

Required:
1. Prepare a Voucher Register, a Cheque Register, and a General Journal and record the transactions under the assumption Valley Sales Company records invoices at gross amounts.
2. Prepare a Vouchers Payable account and post those entry portions that affect the account.
3. Prove the balance of the Vouchers Payable account by preparing a schedule of unpaid vouchers.

Problem 7–4A

Required:
1. Prepare a Voucher Register, a Cheque Register having one money column, and a General Journal and record the transactions of Problem 7–3A under the assumption Valley Sales Company records invoices at net amounts.
2. Prepare a Vouchers Payable account and post those entry portions that affect the account.
3. Prove the balance of the Vouchers Payable account by preparing a schedule of unpaid vouchers.

Gypsy Trailer Company, a manufacturer of travel trailers, began operations in a very small way 15 years ago and has since grown rapidly in size. Last year its sales were in excess of five million dollars. However, its purchasing procedures have not kept pace with its growth. When a plant foreman or other department head needs raw materials, plant assets, or supplies, he tells the purchasing department manager by phone or in person. The purchasing department manager prepares a purchase order in duplicate, sending one copy to the company selling the goods and keeping the other copy in his files. When the invoice arrives, it is sent directly to the purchasing department; and when the goods arrive, receiving department personnel count and inspect the items and prepare one copy of a receiving report which is sent to the purchasing department. The purchasing department manager attaches the receiving report and the retained copy of the purchase order to the invoice; and if all is in order, stamps the invoice "approved for payment" and signs his name. The invoice and its attached documents are then sent to the accounting department where a voucher is prepared, the invoice and its supporting documents are attached, and the voucher is recorded. On its due date the voucher and its supporting documents are sent to the office of the company treasurer where a cheque in payment of the voucher is prepared and mailed. The voucher is then stamped "paid," the number of the paying cheque is entered on it, and the paid voucher is returned to the accounting department for an entry to record its payment.

Do the present procedures of Gypsy Trailer Company make it fairly easy for someone in the company to institute the payment of fictitious invoices by the company? If so, who is this person and what would he have to do to receive payment for a fictitious invoice. What changes should be made in the company's purchasing procedures, and why should each change be made?

National Bridge Company fabricates structural steel beams to customers' specifications for bridges and buildings. It purchases flat rolled steel and angles from steel mills and places the steel in an enclosed storage area which is in charge of a storage area keeper. The company has a good system of internal control for purchases; and from invoices and receiving reports, its accounting department keeps a record of the number of tons of steel purchased and placed in the storage area. Also, when steel is needed for fabrication in the plant, a requisition must be prepared and signed by the plant superintendent or a foreman. The requisition shows the kinds and amounts of steel needed in the plant and the customer's job on which it is to be used. The steel is issued to the plant by the storage area keeper, but first it is weighed and its weight is entered on the requisition. The requisition is then sent to the accounting department where the cost of the steel is charged to the proper customer's job and the inventory record of steel in the storage area is reduced by the weight of the steel issued.

The steel issued to the plant is cut into proper shapes and to the proper size and is used in fabricating the beams specified in customers' orders. The plant superintendent is ultimately responsible for the cutting and for controlling waste. Studies in like plants have shown that an average of 6% of the steel issued for use in fabricating customers' orders is wasted due to cutting odd sizes and shapes. National Bridge Company accumulates this waste at the back door of its plant until the pile gets sufficiently large as to "get in the way." The plant superintendent then calls a local scrap dealer who hauls it away, weighs it, and mails a cheque payable to National Bridge Company, which is endorsed by the company treasurer and deposited in the company's bank account.

Records in the accounting department show that 24,500 tons of steel were issued to the plant for fabricating customers' orders. Freight records show that 22,220 tons of finished beams were shipped to customers, and records in the treasurer's office show the company received $42,560 from the sale of 1,520 tons of scrap steel.

Point out any poor internal control practices of the company and suggest corrective measures. Does there appear to be any discrepancy in the company's records? If so, how much money is involved and how could the discrepancy be explained?

Decision problem 7–3, Mesa Sales   Carl Nash felt something was amiss in the amount of purchases discounts appearing on the 197B income statement of Mesa Sales, a concern of which he is manager. He knew that every supplier from whom the concern purchased merchandise offered a 2% discount for payment within 10 days, and that it was the policy of the concern to pay every invoice within the discount period. Yet when he analyzed the relation between the amount of purchases discounts appearing on the concern's income statement, shown below in condensed form, and the amount of goods purchased during the year, he could see that purchases discounts were considerably less than 2% of purchases. He recognized that

MESA SALES
Income Statement for Year Ended December 31, 197B

Sales..		$425,000
Cost of goods sold:		
Merchandise inventory, January 1, 197B...........	$ 24,000	
Purchases $300,000		
Less purchases discounts............................ 4,000		
Cost of goods purchased	296,000	
Goods available for sale	$320,000	
Merchandise inventory, December 31, 197B......	25,000	
Cost of goods sold.......................................		295,000
Gross profit on sales....................................		$130,000
Operating expenses		100,000
Net Income...		$ 30,000

there is not a precise matching between purchases and purchases discounts due to the fact that some goods are purchased near the year-end and are not paid for until the next year, but he knew that this could not account for the discrepancy in this case. He also knew that the system used by Mesa Sales in recording purchase invoices and their payment showed only discounts taken during a year and not discounts missed and lost. He also dimly recalled from his one course in accounting that there was another system for recording invoices that would cause any discounts lost during an accounting period to appear on the income statement of that period as an expense.

Describe the system that Carl Nash dimly recalls, giving in general journal form the entries to record the purchase on October 10 of merchandise having a $500 invoice price, terms 2/10, n/60, and payment of the invoice on the last day of its discount period. Also give the entries required to pay the invoice under the assumption it was not paid until the end of the credit period. Then explain why this system offers better control over the people responsible for taking all offered cash discounts. Finally, prepare a condensed 197B income statement for Mesa Sales as it would appear if the company had recorded invoices at net amounts. In preparing the statement, assume that the difference between the amount of discounts taken by the concern in 197B and 2% of its 197B purchases represents discounts lost.

8

Cash and accounts receivable

■ Cash has universal usefulness, small bulk for high value, and no special identification marks by which its ownership may be established; consequently procedures for controlling cash transactions are very important to a business owner; but they are equally as important to the employees responsible for handling cash, since a good system of internal control enables the employees to prove their work was done accurately and honestly.

Internal control for cash

■ A good system of internal control for cash should provide adequate procedures for protecting both cash receipts and cash disbursements, and in these procedures three basic principles should always be observed. First, there should be a separation of duties so that the people responsible for handling cash and for its custody are not the same people who keep the cash records. Second, all cash receipts should be deposited in the bank, intact, each day. Third, all payments should be made by cheque. The one exception to the last principle is that small disbursements may be made in cash from the petty cash fund. The petty cash fund is discussed later in this chapter.

The reason for the first principle is that a division of duties necessitates collusion between two or more people if cash is to be embezzled and the theft concealed in the accounting records. The second, requiring that all receipts be deposited intact each day, prevents an employee from making personal use of the money for a few days before depositing it. And, requiring that all receipts be deposited intact and all payments be made by cheque provides a separate and external record of all cash transactions that may be used to prove the company's own records.

The exact procedures used to achieve control over cash vary from company to company and depend upon such things as company size, number of employees, cash sources, and so on; consequently, the procedures described below are only illustrative of some that are in use.

Cash sales

Cash from cash sales should be rung up on a cash register at the time of each sale. To help ensure that correct amounts are rung up, each cash register should be so placed that customers can see the amounts rung up, and the clerks should be required to ring up each sale before wrapping the merchandise. Also, each cash register should have a locked-in tape on which the amount of each sale and total sales are printed by the register.

Good cash control, as previously stated, requires a separation of custody for cash from record keeping for cash; and for cash sales this separation begins with the cash register. The salesclerk who has access to the cash in the register should not have access to its locked-in tape. At the end of each day the salesclerk is usually required to count the cash in his register and to turn the cash and its count over to an employee in the cashier's office. The employee in the cashier's office, like the salesclerk, has access to the cash and should not have access to the register tape or other accounting records. A third employee, commonly from the accounting department, removes the tape from the register, compares its total with the cash turned over to the cashier's office, and uses the tape's information as a basis for the entry recording cash sales.

Since the employee from the accounting department who has access to the register tape does not have access to cash, he cannot take any. Likewise, since the salesclerk and the employee from the cashier's office do not have access to the cash register tape, they cannot take cash without the shortage being revealed.

Control of cash received through the mail

Control of cash coming in through the mail begins with a mail clerk who opens the mail and makes a list in triplicate of the money received. The list should give each sender's name, the purpose for which the money was sent, and the amount. One copy of the list is sent to the cashier with the money, the second copy goes to the bookkeeper, and the third copy is kept by the mail clerk. The cashier deposits the money in the bank, and the bookkeeper uses his copy for entries in the Cash Receipts Journal. Then, if the bank balance is reconciled (discussed later) by a fourth person, errors or fraud by the mail clerk, the cashier, or bookkeeper will be detected. Errors will be detected because the cash deposited and the records of three people must agree; and fraud is impossible, unless there is collusion. The mail clerk must report all receipts or customers will question their account balances. The cashier must deposit all receipts because the bank balance must agree with the bookkeeper's cash balance. The bookkeeper and the person reconciling the bank balance do not have access to cash and, therefore, have no opportunity to withhold any.

Cash disbursements

To gain control over cash disbursements, all disbursements should be made by cheque, excepting those from petty cash. If authority to sign cheques is delegated to some person other than the business owner, that person should not have access to the accounting records. This helps prevent a fraudulent disbursement being made and concealed in the accounting records.

In a small business the owner-manager usually signs cheques and normally knows from personal contact and observation that the items for which the cheques pay were received by the business. However, this is impossible in a large business, and in a large business internal control procedures such as those described in the previous chapter should be used to tell the person who signs cheques that the obligations for which the cheques pay are proper obligations, properly incurred, and should be paid.

The petty cash fund
■ Petty cash payments are excluded from the all-payments-by-cheque rule because every business must make many small payments for items such as postage, express charges, collect telegrams, and small items of supplies. If each such payment is made by cheque, many cheques for immaterial amounts are written, which is both time consuming and expensive. Therefore, to avoid writing cheques for small amounts, a *petty cash fund* is established, and such payments are made from this fund.

When a petty cash fund is established, an estimate is made of the total small payments likely to be disbursed during a short period, usually not more than a month. A cheque is drawn and debited to the Petty Cash account for an amount slightly in excess of this estimate; the cheque is cashed; and the money is turned over to a member of the office staff who is designated *petty cashier* and who is responsible for the petty cash and for making payments therefrom.

The petty cashier usually keeps the petty cash in a locked box in the office safe. As each disbursement is made, a *petty cash receipt,* Illustration 8-1, is signed by the person receiving payment and is entered in the *Petty Cash Record* (Illustration 8-3) and then placed with the remaining money in the petty cashbox. Under this system, the petty cashbox should always contain paid petty cash receipts and money equal to the amount of the fund.

No. 1479 $ 1.65

RECEIVED. OF PETTY CASH

DATE Nov. 3   19 - -

FOR Collect telegram

CHARGE TO Miscellaneous General Expenses
                              ACCOUNT

APPROVED BY   RECEIVED BY
     CaB.   Bob Tone
TOPS—FORM 3008

Illustration 8–1

Courtesy Tops Business Forms

Each disbursement reduces the money and increases the sum of the receipts in the petty cashbox. When the money is nearly exhausted, the fund is reimbursed. To reimburse the fund, the petty cashier presents the paid petty cash receipts to the company cashier who stamps each receipt "paid" so that it may not be reused, retains the receipts, and gives the petty cashier a cheque for their sum. When this cheque is cashed and the proceeds returned to the petty cashbox, the money in the box is restored to its original amount and the fund is ready to begin anew the cycle of its operations.

Petty cash fund illustrated

■ To avoid writing numerous cheques for small amounts, a company established a petty cash fund, designating one of its office clerks, Alice Smith, petty cashier. A cheque for $20 was drawn, cashed, and the proceeds turned over to this clerk. The entry to record the cheque is shown in Illustration 8–2. The effect of the entry was to transfer $20 from the regular Cash account to the Petty Cash account.

Cash Disbursements Journal

Date	Ch. No.	Payee	Account Debited	F	Other Accts. Debit	Cash Credit
Nov. 1	58	Alice Smith, Petty Cashier	Petty Cash........		20.00	20.00

Illustration 8–2

The Petty Cash account is debited when the fund is established but is not debited or credited again unless the size of the fund is changed. If the fund is exhausted and reimbursements occur too often, the fund should be increased. This results in an additional debit to the Petty Cash account and a credit to the regular Cash account for the amount of the increase. If the fund is too large, part of its cash should be returned to general cash.

During the first month of the illustrated fund's operation, the following petty cash payments were made:

Nov. 3	Collect telegram	$ 1.65
7	Purchased paper clips	.50
12	Express on purchases	1.75
18	Postage on sale	1.80
19	Dinner for employee working overtime	1.60
20	Purchased postage stamps	5.00
21	Express on purchases	2.80
24	Cleaning windows	1.00
27	Repair of typewriter	2.50
	Total	$18.60

As each amount was disbursed, a petty cash receipt was signed by the person receiving payment. Each receipt was then recorded in the Petty Cash Record and placed in the petty cashbox. The Petty Cash Record with the paid receipts entered is shown in Illustration 8–3.

Commonly, as in this illustration, the Petty Cash Record is a supplementary record and not a book of original entry. A book of original entry is a journal or register from which postings are made. A supplementary record is one in which information is summarized but not posted. Rather, the summarized information is used as a basis for an entry in a regular journal or register, which is posted.

To continue the illustration, on November 27, after the last of the listed payments was made, only $1.40 in money remained in the fund. The petty cashier recognized that this would probably not cover another payment, so she gave her $18.60 of paid petty cash receipts to the company cashier in exchange for an $18.60 cheque to replenish the fund. On receiving the cheque, she ruled and balanced her Petty Cash Record (see Illustration 8–3), entered the amount of the replenishing cheque, cashed the cheque, and was ready to begin anew payments from the fund.

The reimbursing cheque was recorded in the Cash Disbursements Journal with the second entry of Illustration 8–4. Information for this entry was secured from a summarization of the entries in the Petty Cash Record. Commonly, as previously stated, the Petty Cash Record is a supplementary record and not a book of original entry; therefore, if petty cash payments are to get to the ledger accounts, an entry like the second one in Illustration 8–4 is required.

Observe the debits in the second entry in Illustration 8–4. All are to accounts affected by payments from the fund. Note that such an entry is necessary to get debits into the accounts for amounts paid from a petty cash fund. Consequently, petty cash must be reimbursed at the

Petty Cash Record

Date	Explanation	Receipt No.	Receipts	Payments	Postage	Freight-In	Misc. General Expense	Miscellaneous Payments Account	Amount
Nov. 1	Established fund (Ch. No. 58)		20.00						
3	Collect telegram	1		1.65			1.65		
7	Purchased paper clips	2		.50				Office supplies	.50
12	Express on purchases	3		1.75		1.75			
18	Postage on sale	4		1.80				Delivery expense	1.80
19	Overtime meals	5		1.60			1.60		
20	Purchased postage stamps	6		5.00	5.00				
21	Express on purchases	7		2.80		2.80			
24	Cleaning windows	8		1.00			1.00		
27	Repair of typewriter	9		2.50			2.50		
27	Totals		20.00	18.60	5.00	4.55	6.75		2.30
	Balance			1.40					
	Totals		20.00	20.00					
Nov. 27	Balance		1.40						
27	Replenished fund (Ch. No. 106)		18.60						

Illustration
8–3

Cash Disbursements Journal

Date	Ch. No.	Payee	Account Debited	F	Other Accts. Debit	Cash Credit
Nov. 1	58	Alice Smith, Petty Cashier	Petty Cash........		20.00	20.00
Nov. 27	106	Alice Smith, Petty Cashier	Postage		5.00	
			Freight-In.........		4.55	
			Misc. Gen. Expenses		6.75	
			Office Supplies..		.50	
			Delivery Expense		1.80	18.60

Illustration
8–4

end of each accounting period, as well as at any time the money in the fund is low. If the fund is not reimbursed at the end of each accounting period, the asset petty cash is overstated and the expenses and assets of the petty cash payments are understated on the financial statements.

Occasionally, at the time of a petty cash expenditure a petty cashier will forget to secure a receipt; and by the time the fund is reimbursed, she will have forgotten the expenditure. This causes the fund to be short. If at reimbursement time the petty cash fund is short and no errors or omitted entries can be found, the shortage is entered in the Petty Cash Record as a payment in the Miscellaneous Payments column. It is then recorded as an expense in the reimbursing entry with a debit to the Cash Over and Short account discussed in the next section.

Cash over and short ■ Regardless of care exercised in making change, customers are sometimes given too much change or are shortchanged. As a result, at the end of a day the actual cash from a cash register is commonly not equal to the cash sales "rung up" on the register. When this occurs and, for example, actual cash as counted is $557 but the register shows cash sales of $556, the entry in general journal form to record sales and the overage is:

Nov.	23	Cash..	557.00	
		Cash Over and Short.............................		1.00
		Sales		556.00
		Day's cash sales and overage.		

If, on the other hand, cash is short, less cash than the amount of sales shown on the register, the entry to record the sales and shortage is:

Nov.	24	Cash...	621.00	
		Cash Over and Short.....................................	4.00	
		Sales		625.00
		Day's cash sales and shortage.		

Over a period of time cash overages should about equal cash short-ages. However, customers are more prone to report instances in which they are given too little change; therefore, amounts of cash short are apt to be greater than amounts of cash over, and the Cash Over and Short account normally reaches the end of the accounting period with a debit balance. When it does so, the balance represents an expense, which may appear on the income statement, at the end, as one of the items in the other revenue and expense section. Or if the amount is small, it may be combined with other miscellaneous expenses and ap-pear as part of the item, miscellaneous expenses. When Cash Over and Short reaches the end of the period with a credit balance, the balance represents revenue and normally appears on the income statement as part of the item, miscellaneous revenues.

Reconciling the bank balance

■ Every month banks furnish each commercial depositor a statement of his account. The statement shows: (1) the amount on deposit at the beginning of the month, (2) cheques and any other amounts deducted from the account, (3) deposits and any other amounts added to the account, and (4) the account balance at the end of the month, accord-ing to the records of the bank. If all receipts are deposited and all pay-ments are made by cheque, the bank statement becomes a device for proving the depositor's cash records. A bank statement is shown in Illustration 8–5.

Banks commonly mail each depositor a bank statement soon after the end of each month. Included in the envelope with the statement are the depositor's *canceled cheques* and any debit or credit memo-randa that have affected the account. The cheques returned are the ones the bank has paid during the month. They are called "canceled cheques" because they are canceled by stamping or punching to show that they have been paid. During any month, in addition to the cheques the de-positor has drawn, the bank may deduct from the depositor's account amounts for service charges, printing cheques, items deposited that are uncollectible, and for errors. The bank notifies the depositor of each such deduction with a debit memorandum. A copy of the memorandum is always included with the monthly statement. The bank may also add amounts to the depositor's account for errors and for amounts collected for the depositor. A credit memorandum is used to notify of any such additions.

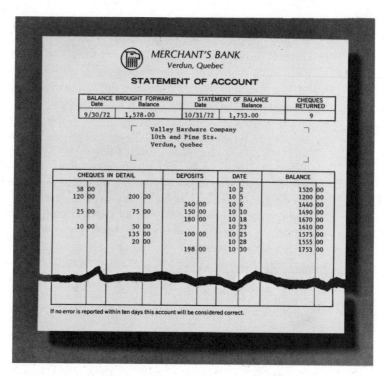

MERCHANT'S BANK
Verdun, Quebec

STATEMENT OF ACCOUNT

BALANCE BROUGHT FORWARD		STATEMENT OF BALANCE		CHEQUES RETURNED
Date	Balance	Date	Balance	
9/30/72	1,578.00	10/31/72	1,753.00	9

Valley Hardware Company
10th and Pine Sts.
Verdun, Quebec

CHEQUES IN DETAIL			DEPOSITS	DATE	BALANCE
58 00				10 2	1520 00
120 00	200 00			10 5	1200 00
			240 00	10 6	1440 00
25 00	75 00		150 00	10 10	1490 00
			180 00	10 18	1670 00
10 00	50 00			10 23	1610 00
	135 00		100 00	10 25	1575 00
	20 00			10 28	1555 00
			198 00	10 30	1753 00

If no error is reported within ten days this account will be considered correct.

Illustration
8-5

Need for reconciling the bank balance

Normally, when the bank statement arrives, the balance of cash as shown by the statement does not agree with the balance shown by the depositor's accounting records. Consequently, in order to prove the accuracy of both the depositor's records and those of the bank, it is necessary to reconcile and account for any differences between the two balances.

Numerous things may cause the bank statement balance to differ from the depositor's book balance of cash. Some are:

1. *Outstanding Cheques.* These are cheques that have been drawn by the depositor and deducted on the depositor's records but have not reached the bank for payment and deduction.
2. *Unrecorded Deposits.* Concerns often make deposits at the end of each business day, after the bank has closed. These deposits are made in the bank's night depository and are not recorded by the bank until the next business day. Consequently, if a deposit is placed in the night depository the last day of the month, it does not appear on the bank statement for that month.
3. *Charges for Service and Uncollectible Items.* A bank often deducts amounts from a depositor's account for services rendered and for items deposited that it is unable to collect. Insufficient funds cheques are the most common of the latter. The bank notifies the depositor of

each such deduction with a debit memorandum. If the item is material in amount, the memorandum is mailed to the depositor on the day of the deduction. Furthermore, in a well-managed company, each such deduction is entered in the Cash Disbursements Journal or the Voucher Register on the day the memorandum is received. However, occasionally there are unentered amounts near the end of the month.

4. *Collections.* Banks often act as collecting agents for their depositors, collecting for a small fee promissory notes and other items. When an item such as a promissory note is collected, the bank usually adds the proceeds to the depositor's account and sends a credit memorandum as notification of the transaction. As soon as the memorandum is received, an entry should be made in the Cash Receipts Journal. Occasionally, there are unentered amounts near the end of the month.

5. *Errors.* Regardless of care and systems of internal control for automatic error detection, both the bank and the depositor make errors that affect the bank balance. Occasionally, these errors are not discovered until the balance is reconciled.

Steps in reconciling the bank balance

The steps in reconciling the bank balance are:

1. Compare the deposits listed on the bank statement with deposits shown in the accounting records. Note any discrepancies and discover which is correct. List any errors or unrecorded items.

2. When canceled cheques are returned by the bank, they are in a stack in the order in which the bank paid them and also in the order of their listing on the bank statement. While the cheques are in this order, compare each with its bank statement listing. Note any discrepancies or errors.

3. Rearrange the returned cheques in numerical order, the order in which they were written. Secure the previous month's reconciliation and determine if any cheques outstanding at the end of the previous month are still outstanding. If there are any, list them. Also, see that any deposits that were unrecorded by the bank at the end of the previous month have been recorded.

4. Insert among the canceled cheques any bank memorandum according to their dates. Compare each cheque with its entry in the Cash Disbursements Journal or Cheque Register. Note for correction any discrepancies, and list any unpaid cheques or unrecorded memorandum.

5. Prepare a reconciliation of the bank statement balance with the book balance of cash. Such a reconciliation is shown in Illustration 8–6.

6. Determine if any debits or credits appearing on the bank statement are unrecorded in the books of account. Make journal entries to record them.

Valley Hardware Company
Bank Reconciliation as of October 31, 19___

Book Balance of Cash $1,370			Bank Statement Balance			$1,753
Add:			Add:			
Proceeds of note less			Deposit of 10/31 .... $120			
collection fee 198			Valley Haberdashery cheque			
$1,568			charged in error 25			145
						$1,898
Deduct:			Deduct:			
NSF cheque of Frank Jones 20			Outstanding cheques:			
			No. 124 .... $150			
			No. 126 200			350
Reconciled Balance $1,548			Reconciled Balance			$1,548

Illustration
8–6

Illustration of a bank reconciliation

■ To illustrate a bank reconciliation assume that Valley Hardware Company found the following when it attempted to reconcile its bank balance of October 31. The bank balance as shown by the bank statement was $1,753, and the cash balance according to the accounting records was $1,370. Cheque No. 124 for $150 and Cheque No. 126 for $200 were outstanding and unpaid by the bank. A $120 deposit, placed in the bank's night depository after banking hours on October 31, was unrecorded by the bank. Among the returned cheques was a credit memorandum showing the bank had collected a note receivable for the company on October 30, crediting the proceeds, $200 less a $2 collection fee, to the company account. Also returned with the bank statement was an NSF (not sufficient funds) cheque for $20. This cheque had been received from a customer, Frank Jones, on October 25, and had been included in that day's deposit. The collection of the note and the return of the NSF cheque were unrecorded on the company books. In addition, a cheque for $25 drawn by Valley Haberdashery was among the canceled cheques returned. This cheque had been charged in error to the account of Valley Hardware Company. The statement reconciling these amounts is shown in Illustration 8–6.

A bank reconciliation helps locate any errors made by either the bank or the depositor; discloses any items which have been entered on the company books but have not come to the bank's attention; and discloses items that should be recorded on the company books but are unrecorded on the date of the reconciliation. For example, in the reconciliation illustrated, the reconciled cash balance, $1,548, is the true cash balance. However, at the time the reconciliation is completed, Valley Hardware Company's accounting records show a $1,370 book balance. Consequently, entries must be made to adjust the book balance, increasing it to the true cash balance. This requires two entries, the first in general journal form is:

Nov.	2	Cash..	198.00	
		Collection Expense	2.00	
		Notes Receivable		200.00
		To record the proceeds and collection charge of a note collected by the bank.		

This entry is self-explanatory. The bank collected a note receivable, deducted a collection fee, and deposited the difference to the Valley Hardware Company account. The entry increases the amount of cash on the books, records the collection expense, and reduces notes receivable.

The second entry is:

Nov.	2	Accounts Receivable—Frank Jones.................	20.00	
		Cash...		20.00
		To charge back the NSF cheque received from Frank Jones.		

This entry records the NSF cheque returned as uncollectible. The cheque was received from Jones in payment of his account and was deposited as cash. The bank, unable to collect the cheque, deducted $20 from the Valley Hardware account, making it necessary for the company to reverse the entry made when the cheque was received. After recording the returned cheque, the company will endeavor to collect the $20 from Jones. If after all legal means of collection have been exhausted and the company is still unable to collect, the amount will be written off as a bad debt.

ACCOUNTS RECEIVABLE

■ Most of the problems encountered in recording transactions with customers have already been discussed. However, the matter of *bad debts* and a few miscellaneous matters need attention.

Bad debts ■ When goods and services are sold on credit, there are almost always a few customers who do not pay. The accounts of such customers are called bad debts and are a loss and expense of selling on credit.

It might be asked: Why do merchants sell on credit if bad debts result? The answer is, of course, that merchants sell on credit in order to increase total sales and profits. Merchants are willing to take a reasonable loss from bad debts in order to increase sales and profits. Therefore, bad debt losses are an expense of selling on credit, an expense incurred in order to increase sales. Also, if revenues and expenses are matched, bad debt losses must be matched against the sales they helped produce.

■ A bad debt loss results from an error in judgment, an error in granting credit and making a sale to a customer who will not pay. Consequently, a bad debt loss is incurred at the moment credit is granted and
a sale is made to such a customer. Of course the merchant making such a
sale does not know at the time of the sale that he has incurred a loss.
Actually, he normally will not be sure of the loss for as much as a year or
more, after he has exhausted every means of collecting. Nevertheless,
final recognition a year or so later does not change the time of the
loss — the loss occurred at the moment of the sale.

When it is recognized that a bad debt loss occurs at the moment of a
sale to a customer who will not pay and that a merchant cannot be sure
the customer will not pay until a year or more after the sale, it follows
that if bad debt losses are matched with the sales they helped produce,
they must be matched on an estimated basis. The allowance method of
accounting for bad debts does just that.[1]

■ Under the allowance method of accounting for bad debts, an estimate is made at the end of each accounting period of the total bad debts
that are expected to result from the period's sales, and an allowance is
provided for the resulting loss. This has two advantages: (1) the estimated loss is charged to the period in which the revenue is recognized,
and (2) the accounts receivable appear on the balance sheet at their
estimated realizable value, a more informative balance sheet amount.

Estimating bad debts

In making the year-end estimate of bad debts that are expected to
result from the year's sales, companies commonly assume that "history
will repeat." For example, over the past several years Alpha Company
has experienced bad debt losses equal to one half of 1% of its charge
sales, and during the past year its charge sales were $300,000. Conse-
quently, if history repeats, Alpha Company can expect $1,500 of bad
debt losses to result from the year's sales ($300,000 × 0.005 = $1,500).

Recording the estimated bad debts loss

Under the allowance method of accounting for bad debts, the estimated bad debts loss is recorded at the end of each accounting period
with a work sheet adjustment and an adjusting entry. For example,
Alpha Company will record its $1,500 estimated bad debts loss with a
work sheet adjustment and an adjusting entry like the following:

Dec.	31	Bad Debts Expense	1,500.00	
		Allowance for Doubtful Accounts...............		1,500.00
		To record the estimated bad debts.		

---

[1] *CICA Handbook* (Toronto: The Canadian Institute of Chartered Accountants),
p. 1061.

The debit of this entry causes the estimated bad debts loss to appear on the income statement of the year in which the sales were made; and as a result, the estimated $1,500 expense of selling on credit is matched with the $300,000 of revenue it helped to produce.

Bad debt losses normally appear on the income statement as an administrative expense rather than as a selling expense. They appear as an administrative expense because granting credit is usually not a responsibility of the sales department; and therefore since the sales department is not responsible for granting credit, it should not be held responsible for bad debt losses. The sales department is usually not given responsibility for granting credit because it is feared the sales department would at times be swayed in its judgment of a credit risk by its desire to make a sale.

Bad debts in the accounts

If at the time its bad debts adjusting entry is posted, Alpha Company has $20,000 of accounts receivable, its Accounts Receivable and Allowance for Doubtful Accounts accounts will show these balances:

Accounts Receivable		Allowance for Doubtful Accounts	
Dec. 31 20,000			Dec. 31 1,500

The bad debts adjusting entry reduces the accounts receivable to their estimated realizable value. However, note that the credit of the entry is to the contra account, Allowance for Doubtful Accounts, rather than to the Accounts Receivable controlling account.

It is necessary to credit the estimated bad debts loss to the contra account rather than the Accounts Receivable account because at the time of the adjusting entry it is not known for certain just which customers will fail to pay. (The total loss from bad debts can be estimated from past experience, but the exact customers who will not pay cannot be known until every means of collecting from each has been exhausted.) Consequently, since the bad accounts are not identifiable at the time the adjusting entry is made, they cannot be removed from the subsidiary Accounts Receivable Ledger; and the Allowance for Doubtful Accounts account must be credited instead of the controlling account. The allowance account must be credited because to credit the controlling account without removing the bad accounts from the subsidiary ledger would cause the controlling account balance to differ from the sum of the balances in the subsidiary ledger.

Allowance for doubtful accounts on the balance sheet

When the balance sheet is prepared, the balance of the Allowance for Doubtful Accounts account is subtracted thereon from the balance of the Accounts Receivable account to show the amount that is expected to be realized from the accounts, as follows:

ASSETS

Current Assets:

Cash		$11,300
Accounts receivable	$20,000	
Less allowance for doubtful accounts	1,500	18,500
Merchandise inventory		27,200
Prepaid expenses		1,100
Total Current Assets		$58,100

Writing off a bad debt

When an allowance for doubtful accounts is provided, accounts deemed uncollectible are written off against this allowance. For example, after spending a year trying to collect, Alpha Company finally concluded the $100 account of George Vale was uncollectible and made the following entry to write it off:

Jan.	23	Allowance for Doubtful Accounts	100.00	
		Accounts Receivable – George Vale		100.00
		To write off the uncollectible account of George Vale.		

Posting the entry had this effect on the accounts:

Accounts Receivable				Allowance for Doubtful Accounts			
Dec. 31	20,000	Jan. 23	100	Jan. 23	100	Dec. 31	1,500

Two points should be observed in the entry and accounts. First, although bad debts are an expense of selling on credit, the Allowance for Doubtful Accounts account rather than an expense account is debited in the write-off. The allowance account is debited because the expense was recorded at the end of the period in which the sale occurred. At that time, the loss was foreseen, and the expense was recorded in the estimated bad debts adjusting entry.

Second, although the write-off removed the amount of the account from the ledgers, it did not affect the estimated realizable amount of Alpha Company's accounts receivable, as the following tabulation shows:

	Before Write-off	After Write-off
Accounts receivable	$20,000	$19,900
Less allowance for doubtful accounts	1,500	1,400
Estimated realizable accounts receivable	$18,500	$18,500

Bad debts written off seldom equal the allowance provided

The uncollectible accounts from a given year's sales seldom, if ever, exactly equal the allowance provided for their loss. If accounts written off are less than the allowance provided, the Allowance for Doubtful Accounts account reaches the end of the year with a credit balance. On the other hand, if accounts written off exceed the allowance provided, the allowance account reaches the period end with a debit balance, which is then eliminated with the new bad debts adjusting entry. In either case no harm is done if the allowance provided is approximately equal to the bad debts written off and is neither continually excessive nor insufficient.

Often when the addition to the allowance for doubtful accounts is based on a percentage of sales, the passage of several accounting periods is required before it becomes apparent the percentage is either too large or too small. In such cases when it becomes apparent the percentage is incorrect, a change in the percentage should be made.

Bad debt recoveries ■ Frequently an error in judgment is made in regard to a customer's ability to pay his past-due account. As a result, accounts written off as uncollectible are later sometimes collected in full or in part. If an account is written off as uncollectible and later the customer pays part or all of the amount previously written off, the payment should be shown in the customer's account for future credit action. It should be shown because when a customer fails to pay and his account is written off, the customer's credit standing is impaired; and later when the customer pays the amount previously written off, the payment helps restore the credit standing. When an account previously written off as a bad debt is collected, two entries are made. The first reinstates the customer's account balance and has the effect of reversing the original write-off. The second entry records the collection of the reinstated account.

For example, if George Vale, whose account was written off by Alpha Company (page 257) on January 23, pays in full on August 15, the entries in general journal form to record the bad debt recovery are:

Aug.	15	Accounts Receivable—George Vale..................	100.00	
		Allowance for Doubtful Accounts..............		100.00
		To reinstate the account of George Vale written off on January 23.		
	15	Cash...	100.00	
		Accounts Receivable—George Vale...........		100.00
		In full of account.		

The cash collection just illustrated would normally be recorded in a Cash Receipts Journal. However, beginning at this point and continuing through the remainder of the text, almost all entries will be given in general journal form to simplify the illustrations. The student should realize that a company would make such entries in a Cash Receipts Journal or other appropriate journal if it made use of such.

Other bases for estimating bad debts ■ As previously explained, the relationship between charge sales and past bad debt losses is often used in estimating losses from uncollectible accounts. Too, when the proportion of credit sales to cash sales remains about the same, total sales rather than charge sales may be used. Likewise, in companies where about the same percentage of accounts receivable prove uncollectible each year, a percentage of the year-end balance of the Accounts Receivable account may be set up as the estimated bad debts expense.

Aging accounts receivable ■ In estimating bad debt losses, many companies age their accounts receivable. This consists of preparing a schedule of accounts receivable with the accounts listed and their balances entered in columns according to age. Such a schedule appears as in Illustration 8–7. After a schedule showing account ages is prepared, responsible and experienced executives of the sales and credit departments examine each account listed thereon and from experience and by judgment decide which are probably uncollectible. Normally, the majority of accounts appearing on the schedule are current and not past due; these are examined for possible losses but receive less scrutiny than past-due accounts. The older accounts are more apt to prove uncollectible; these receive the greatest attention. After decisions are made as to which accounts are probably uncollectible, the allowance for doubtful accounts is adjusted to provide for them.

Schedule of Accounts Receivable by Age					
Customer's Name	Not Due	1 to 30 Days Past Due	31 to 60 Days Past Due	61 to 90 Days Past Due	Over 90 Days Past Due
Charles Abbot	45.00				
Frank Allen	53.00				
George Arden			14.00		
Paul Baum					27.00

Illustration 8–7

To illustrate this adjustment, assume that a company has $60,000 of accounts receivable at the end of an accounting period and in aging these accounts its executives estimate that accounts totaling $1,950 are probably uncollectible. Assume further that the company has a $250 credit balance in its allowance account. Under these assumptions the company will make the following adjusting entry to increase the balance of the allowance account to the amount needed to provide for the estimated uncollectible accounts:

Dec.	31	Bad Debts Expense	1,700.00	
		Allowance for Doubtful Accounts...............		1,700.00
		To increase the allowance for doubtful accounts to $1,950.		

The $1,700 credit of the illustrated entry increases the balance of the allowance account to the $1,950 needed to provide for the estimated bad debts. If it had been assumed that the allowance account had a $150 debit balance before adjustment, rather than the assumed $250 credit balance, it would have been necessary to increase the entry amounts to $2,100 ($150 + $1,950) in order to bring the account balance up to the required amount.

Aging accounts receivable and increasing the allowance for doubtful accounts to an amount sufficient to provide for the accounts deemed uncollectible has two things in its favour. (1) When accounts receivable are aged, an excessive or an inadequate provision for bad debts in one period is automatically adjusted in the next; and as a result, the balance of the allowance account never builds up to an excessive amount, as sometimes happens when it is increased each period by a percent of sales. (2) The aging method also normally provides a better balance sheet figure than does the percent of sales method, a figure closer to realizable value. However, the aging method may not as closely match revenues and expenses as the percent of sales method.

Direct write-off of bad debts ■ Since the allowance method of accounting for bad debts results in a better matching of revenues and expenses, it is the method that should be used in most cases. However, under certain circumstances another method, called the *direct write-off method,* may be used. Under the direct write-off method, when it is decided that an account is uncollectible, it is written off directly to the Bad Debts Expense account with an entry like this:

Nov.	23	Bad Debts Expense	52.50	
		Accounts Receivable—Dale Hall		52.50
		To write off the uncollectible account of Dale Hall.		

The debit of the entry charges the bad debt loss directly to the current year's Bad Debts Expense account, and the credit removes the balance of the uncollectible account from the subsidiary ledger and controlling account.

If an account previously written off directly to the Bad Debts Expense account is later collected in full, the following entries in general journal form are used to record the bad debt recovery.

Mar.	11	Accounts Receivable—Dale Hall	52.50	
		Bad Debts Expense		52.50
		To reinstate the account of Dale Hall previously written off.		
	11	Cash	52.50	
		Accounts Receivable—Dale Hall		52.50
		In full of account.		

The entry to reinstate the Dale Hall account assumes collection in the year following the write-off and that the Bad Debts Expense account has a debit balance from other write-offs during the year. If the account has no balance from other write-offs and no write-offs are expected, the credit of the entry could be to a revenue account called, for example, Bad Debt Recoveries.

Direct write-off mismatches revenues and expenses

Since a bad debt loss occurs at the moment of a sale to a customer who will not pay but the bad debt cannot be identified until as much as a year or more later when every effort to collect has failed, it follows that the direct write-off method commonly mismatches revenues and expenses. It mismatches revenues and expenses because the revenue from a bad debt sale appears on the income statement of one year while the expense of the loss is deducted on the income statement of the following or a later year.

When direct write-off is permissible

Although the direct write-off method commonly fails in the matching process, it may still be used in situations where its use does not materially affect reported net income. For example, it may be used in a store where substantially all sales are for cash and bad debt losses from a few charge sales are immaterial in relation to total sales and net income. In such a store the use of direct write-off comes under *the accounting principle of materiality*. (Under the accounting principle of materiality it is held that a strict adherence to any accounting principle, in this case the matching principle, is not required when adherence is relatively difficult or expensive and the lack of adherence does not materially affect reported net income. Or in other words, failure to adhere is permissible when the failure does not produce an error or misstatement sufficiently large as to influence a financial statement reader's judgment of a given situation.)

1. Why should the bookkeeper of a company not be given the responsibility for receiving cash for the company nor the responsibility for signing cheques or making cash disbursements in any other way?
2. What is meant by the phrase "all receipts should be deposited intact"?
3. Why should all cash receipts be deposited intact on the day of receipt?
4. Why are some cash payments made from a petty cash fund? Why are not all payments made by cheque?
5. What is a petty cash receipt? When a petty cash receipt is prepared, who signs it?
6. Explain how a petty cash fund operates.
7. Why must a petty cash fund be reimbursed at the end of each accounting period?
8. What are two results of reimbursing the petty cash fund?
9. Is the Petty Cash Record a book of original entry?
10. What is a bank statement? What kind of information appears on a bank statement?
11. What is the meaning of the phrase "to reconcile"?
12. Why are the bank statement balance of cash and the depositor's book balance of cash reconciled?
13. What occurs when revenues and expenses are properly matched?
14. At what point in the selling-collecting procedures of a company does a bad debt loss occur?
15. Why does the direct write-off method of accounting for bad debt losses commonly fail in matching revenues and expenses?
16. George Jacks purchased $50 of merchandise from Company A and another $50 from Company B. He did not pay either company and one year later, on February 28, both wrote off his uncollectible accounts. Company A used the direct write-off method, and Company B used the allowance method. Give the write-off entries.
17. In estimating bad debt losses it is commonly assumed that "history will repeat." How is the assumption that "history will repeat" used in estimating bad debt losses? *Perc. of sales*
18. A company has charge sales for a year amounting to $484,000. What amount of bad debt losses may the company expect to experience from these sales if its past bad debt loss record shows losses equal to one fourth of 1% of charge sales? *1936*
19. What is a contra account? Why are estimated bad debt losses credited to a contra account rather than to the Accounts Receivable controlling account? *offeldd . cu not determine which acct Balance*
20. Classify the following accounts: (a) Accounts Receivable, (b) Allowance for Doubtful Accounts, and (c) Bad Debts Expense.

Class exercises

Exercise 8–1

A company established a $50 petty cash fund on September 23, appointing one of its office clerks, Mary Neal, petty cashier. The fund was reimbursed on October 18 for these expenditures: postage, $15; freight-in, $19.25; office supplies, $3.50; and miscellaneous expenses, $7.75. Give in general journal form the entry to establish the fund and the entry to reimburse it.

Exercise 8-2

Tackle Shop deposits all receipts intact each day and makes all payments by cheque; and on November 30, after all posting was completed, its Cash account had a $1,420 debit balance; but its November 30 bank statement showed only $1,295 on deposit in the bank on that day. Prepare a bank reconciliation for Tackle Shop, using the following information:

a. Outstanding cheques, $150.

b. The November 30 cash receipts, $315, were placed in the bank's night depository after banking hours on that date and were unrecorded by the bank.

c. Included with the November canceled cheques returned by the bank was an unrecorded $5 debit memorandum for bank services.

d. Cheque No. 815 for store supplies was correctly drawn for $127 and paid by the bank, but it was erroneously recorded in the Cash Disbursements Journal as though it were for $172.

Exercise 8-3

Prepare in general journal form any entries that Tackle Shop should make as a result of the preparation of the bank reconciliation of Exercise 8-2.

Exercise 8-4

On December 31, 1975, a company estimated it would lose as bad debts an amount equal to one fourth of 1% of its $724,000 of 1975 charge sales, and it provided an addition to its allowance for doubtful accounts equal to that amount. On the following March 27 it decided the $285 account of Arno Fall was uncollectible and wrote it off as a bad debt. On July 7 Arno Fall unexpectedly paid the amount previously written off. Give the required entries in general journal form to record these transactions.

Exercise 8-5

At the end of each year a company ages its accounts receivable and increases its allowance for doubtful accounts by an amount sufficient to provide for the estimated uncollectible accounts. At the end of last year it estimated it would not be able to collect $2,450 of its total accounts receivable. (a) Give the entry to increase the allowance account under the assumption it had a $125 credit balance before the adjustment. (b) Give the entry under the assumption the allowance account had a $150 debit balance before the adjustment.

Problems   **Problem 8-1**

The following transactions involving petty cash were completed during November of the current year:

Nov. 1 Drew Cheque No. 543 payable to Joan Hall to establish a $35 petty cash fund. Appointed Miss Hall petty cashier and delivered the cheque and the Petty Cash Record to her.

5 Purchased postage stamps with petty cash funds, $5.

8 Paid $6.50 express charges on merchandise purchased.

9 Paid for minor repairs to an office machine, $4.50.

12 Gave Mrs. Walter Nash, wife of the owner of the business, $5 for cab fare and other personal expenses.

14 Paid $2.50 from petty cash for the dinner of an employee working overtime.

19 Paid $1.75 for the delivery of a collect telegram.

23 Paid $3.50 express charges on merchandise purchased.

26 Purchased office supplies, $3.25.

26 Drew Cheque No. 614 to reimburse the petty cash fund for expenditures and a $1 shortage.

Required:

Prepare a Cash Disbursements Journal and a Petty Cash Record similar to those illustrated in this chapter and record the transactions. Balance and rule the Petty Cash Record before entering the replenishing cheque. Skip one line between the cash disbursements journal entries.

Problem 8-2

A company completed these transactions during a short period:

Oct. 4 Drew Cheque No. 214 to establish a $25 petty cash fund. Appointed Mary Wall, one of the office clerks, petty cashier. Delivered the cheque and Petty Cash Record to Miss Wall.

5 Paid $5 to have the office windows washed.

8 Purchased postage stamps, $10.

10 Paid $4.50 express on a shipment of merchandise purchased.

11 Purchased carbon paper and paper clips, $3.75.

11 Drew Cheque No. 235 to reimburse the petty cash fund, and because it had been so rapidly exhausted, made the cheque sufficiently large to increase the size of the fund to $50.

12 The proprietor of the company, Jay Cole, signed a petty cash receipt and took $1 from the petty cash fund for coffee money.

14 Paid $6.50 for minor repairs to a typewriter.

17 Paid $7.25 express charges on merchandise delivered by the express company.

23 Purchased postage stamps, $5.

26 Paid $7.50 to Ben Franklin Press for printing advertising circulars.

27 Paid a college student $5 to deliver the advertising circulars to prospective customers.

Nov. 3 Paid Cycle Delivery Service $4.50 to deliver merchandise to a customer.

7 Paid $8.50 express charges on a shipment of merchandise purchased.

9 Drew Cheque No. 250 to reimburse the petty cash fund. There was $4.25 in cash in the fund and the cashier could not account for the shortage.

Required:

Record the transactions in a Petty Cash Record and, where required, in a Cash Disbursements Journal. Balance and rule the Petty Cash Record at the time of each reimbursement. Skip a line between each entry in the Cash Disbursements Journal.

Problem 8-3

Leeward Store's October 31 bank statement showed $1,735.75 on deposit on the last day of the month. The store follows the practice of depositing all receipts intact and paying all obligations with cheques; and after all posting was completed on the last day of October, its Cash account showed a $1,577 balance. The following information was available to reconcile the two amounts:

a. Cheques No. 810 for $102.50 and No. 812 for $87.25 were outstanding on the September 30 bank reconciliation. Cheque No. 812 was returned with the October cheques, but Cheque No. 810 was not.

b. In comparing the October canceled cheques with the entries in the Cheque Register it was found that Cheque No. 848 was correctly drawn for $142 in payment for several items of office supplies but was entered in the Cheque Register as though it were for $124. Also, Cheque No. 885 for $71.25 and Cheque No. 886 for $32.50, both drawn on October 31, were not among the canceled cheques returned.

c. A debit memorandum with a $105.50 NSF cheque received from a customer, Dale Green, on October 27 and deposited was among the canceled cheques returned.

d. Also among the canceled cheques was a $4.75 debit memorandum for bank services.

e. A credit memorandum enclosed with the bank statement indicated the bank had collected a $500 noninterest-bearing note for Leeward Store, deducted a $3.50 collection fee, and credited the remainder to the store's account. None of the memoranda enclosed with the canceled cheques had been recorded.

f. The October 31 cash receipts of the store, $415.75, were placed in the bank's night depository after banking hours on October 31 and, consequently, did not appear on the bank statement as a deposit.

Required:

1. Prepare an October 31 bank reconciliation for Leeward Store.
2. Prepare in general journal form the entries the store would have to make to adjust its book balance of cash to the reconciled balance.

Problem 8–4

Seaside Company reconciled its bank balance on September 30 with two cheques, No. 710 for $165 and No. 711 for $240, outstanding. The following information was available for the company's October 31 bank reconciliation:

	Seaside Company *10 East 1st Street*		*Statement of account with* THE SECURITY BANK	
Date	Cheques and Other Debits		Deposits	Balance
Oct. 1	Balance brought forward			2,143.00
2	240.00			1,903.00
3	205.00		315.00	2,013.00
5	175.00		295.00	2,133.00
6	310.00			1,823.00
12	190.00		425.00	2,058.00
15	135.00	255.00	235.00	1,903.00
22	260.00		535.00	2,178.00
28	210.00	280.00	115.00	1,803.00
30			550.00	2,353.00
31	115.00 NSF	5.00 SC	398.00 CM	2,631.00
Code:	CM Credit memorandum DM Debit Memorandum		NSF Not sufficient funds cheque SC Service charge	

From the Cash Receipts Journal			From the Cheque Register		
Date		Cash Debit	Cheque No.		Cash Credit
Oct. 2		315.00	712		205.00
4		295.00	713		310.00
11		425.00	714		100.00
14		235.00	715		175.00
20		535.00	716		85.00
27		115.00	717		135.00
29		550.00	718		260.00
31		220.00	719		280.00
		2,690.00	720		255.00
			721		210.00
			722		105.00
					2,120.00

From the General Ledger
Cash

Date	Explanation	F	Debit	Credit	Balance
Sept. 30		✓			1,738.00
Oct. 31		R-9	2,690.00		4,428.00
31		D-8		2,120.00	2,308.00

The NSF cheque returned was received from Earl Black in payment of his account. The credit memorandum resulted from a $400 noninterest-bearing note, less a $2 collection fee, which the bank had collected for Seaside Company. None of the memoranda enclosed with the bank statement had been recorded.

Cheque No. 714 was correctly drawn for $190 in payment for office equipment. The bookkeeper had carelessly read the amount and had recorded the cheque in his Cheque Register as though it were for $100. The bank had paid and deducted the correct $190 amount.

Required:
1. Prepare an October 31 bank reconciliation for Seaside Company.
2. Prepare in general journal form the entries required to bring the company's book balance for cash into agreement with the reconciled balance.

Problem 8–5

A company's Allowance for Doubtful Accounts account had a $1,735 credit balance on January 1, 197A. During the year it completed these transactions:

Feb. 6   Wrote off the $155 uncollectible account of Roy Snell.

Mar. 14   Learned that Harry Vale had gone out of business, leaving no assets to attach. Wrote off his $385 uncollectible account as a bad debt.

May 11   Reinstated and recorded the collection of the $145 account of Larry West upon receipt of that amount from him. The account had been written off as a bad debt over a year ago.

Aug. 3 Learned of the bankruptcy of Walter Nash. Made a claim on his receiver in bankruptcy for $680 owed by Mr. Nash, and on October 5 received a $170 cheque from the receiver. A letter accompanying the cheque stated that the $170 was all that would be paid. Recorded receipt of the $170 and wrote off the remainder as uncollectible.

Nov. 27 Roy Snell whose account was written off on February 6 as uncollectible walked into the office today and paid $55 of the amount written off. He said that business had improved and that he would pay the balance within a short time.

Dec. 28 Made a compound entry to write off these accounts: Earl Hall, $365; Harry Kane, $215; and David Earl, $430.

31 Provided an addition to the allowance for doubtful accounts equal to one fourth of 1% of the $792,000 of 197A charge sales.

31 Closed the Bad Debts Expense account.

Required:

1. Open accounts for Allowance for Doubtful Accounts, Income Summary, and Bad Debts Expense; and enter the $1,735 balance in the Allowance for Doubtful Accounts account.

2. Prepare general journal entries to record the transactions and post the entry portions that affect the accounts opened.

3. Give the alternate bad debts adjusting entry that the company would make under the assumption that rather than provide an addition to its allowance for doubtful accounts equal to one fourth of 1% of its 197A charge sales, it aged its accounts, estimated that accounts totaling $2,045 were probably uncollectible, and increased its allowance for doubtful accounts to provide for them.

Alternate problems

Problem 8–1A

Robert Wren established a petty cash fund for his single proprietorship business and appointed June Hill, a clerk in the office, petty cashier. During the fund's first month's operation these transactions were completed:

Oct. 2 Drew a $50 cheque, No. 165, payable to June Hill, petty cashier, and delivered the cheque and Petty Cash Record to Miss Hill.

5 Paid $4.25 express on merchandise delivered by the express company.

6 Purchased postage stamps, $5.

8 Mrs. Wren, wife of the proprietor, was given $10 from the fund for cab fare and other personal expenses.

10 Purchased carbon paper and paper clips for office use, $4.65.

13 Paid a service station attendant $2 upon delivery to the office of Mr. Wren's personal car, which the attendant had washed.

15 Paid $5.50 express charges on merchandise purchased.

18 Paid $1.95 upon the delivery of a collect telegram.

21 Paid $5.60 for minor repairs to an office typewriter.

22 Prepaid the express charges on a special order of merchandise shipped to a customer, $6.15.

28 Paid Cycle Delivery Service $2.50 for the delivery of merchandise to a customer.

31   Drew Cheque No. 221 to reimburse the fund for expenditures and a $0.75 shortage.

Required:

Prepare a Petty Cash Record and a Cash Disbursements Journal similar to those illustrated in this chapter and record the foregoing transactions. Balance and rule the Petty Cash Record before entering the replenishing cheque. Skip a line between each cheque entered in the Cash Disbursements Journal.

Problem 8–2A

Valley Sales completed these petty cash transactions:

Nov. 25   Appointed one of its office clerks, Jane Cory, petty cashier. Drew Cheque No. 345 for $25 to establish a petty cash fund and delivered the cheque and the Petty Cash Record to Miss Cory.

     27   Paid $4.25 express charges on a purchase of merchandise delivered by the express company.

     29   Purchased carbon paper and thumb tacks for office use, $3.50.

     30   Purchased postage stamps, $10.

Dec.   3   Paid $5 to have the office windows washed.

      3   Drew Cheque No. 352 to reimburse the petty cash fund; and because the fund had been so rapidly exhausted, made the cheque sufficiently large to increase the size of the fund to $50.

      6   Paid Speedy Delivery Service $3.50 to deliver merchandise to a customer.

      9   Paid the delivery truck driver of Delux Cleaners $2.50 upon delivery of a suit Mr. Dale Mohr, owner of Valley Sales, had dropped off at the cleaners to be cleaned and pressed.

    14   Purchased postage stamps, $5.

    17   Paid $6.50 express charges on a purchase of merchandise delivered by the express company.

    20   Gave Mrs. Mohr, wife of the proprietor, $10 from petty cash for cab fare and other personal expenses.

    22   Paid $3.25 postage on a special order of merchandise mailed to a customer.

    27   Paid $6.75 for minor repairs to a typewriter.

    30   Paid $5.50 express charges on a purchase of merchandise delivered by the express company.

    31   Drew Cheque No. 380 to reimburse the petty cash fund at the end of the accounting period. There was $6.25 in cash in the fund, and the petty cashier could not account for the shortage.

Required:

Record the transactions in a Petty Cash Record and, where required, in a Cash Disbursements Journal. Balance the Petty Cash Record at the time of each reimbursement. Skip a line between each entry in the Cash Disbursements Journal.

Problem 8–3A

Hillside Shop follows the practice of depositing all receipts intact and making payments by cheque. After all posting was completed, the balance of its Cash account on October 31 was $2,104.75. However, its bank statement of that date showed a $2,220.25 ending balance. The following information was available to reconcile the two amounts:

a. The September bank reconciliation showed two cheques outstanding on September 30, No. 761 for $76.25 and No. 763 for $89.65. Cheque No. 763 was returned with the October bank statement but Cheque No. 761 was not.

b. In comparing the October canceled cheques with the entries in the Cheque Register, it was found that Cheque No. 799 was correctly drawn for $247 in payment for a new cash register. However, in recording this cheque in the Cheque Register the amount was transposed and it was recorded as though it were for $274.

c. It was also found that Cheques No. 842 for $35.75 and No. 847 for $103.25, both written and entered in the Cheque Register on October 28, were not among the canceled cheques returned.

d. Two debit memoranda and a credit memorandum were included with the returned cheques. None of the memoranda had been recorded at the time of the reconciliation. The first debit memorandum had a $65 NSF cheque written by a customer, Jay Neal, attached and had been used by the customer in paying his account. The second debit memorandum was a $3.25 memorandum for services charges. The credit memorandum was for $247 and represented the proceeds less a $3 collection fee from a $250 non-interest-bearing note collected for Hillside Shop by the bank.

e. The October 31 cash receipts, $305.50, had been placed in the bank's night depository after banking hours on that date; and, consequently, it did not appear on the bank statement.

Required:
1. Prepare an October 31 bank reconciliation for Hillside Shop.
2. Prepare general journal entries to record the information of the reconciliation.

Problem 8–4A

Bluelake Company reconciled its Cash account balance with its bank statement balance on October 31 with two cheques, No. 818 for $136 and No. 820 for $210, outstanding. The following information was available for the November 30 reconciliation:

Date	*Bluelake Company* *12 West 1st Street* Cheques and Other Debits		Statement of account with FIRST NATIONAL BANK Deposits	Balance
Nov. 1	Balance brought forward			2,215.00
2	210.00		295.00	2,300.00
3	175.00		244.00	2,369.00
5	240.00		178.00	2,307.00
9	562.00		270.00	2,015.00
12	84.00	97.00		1,834.00
14	42.00		127.00	1,919.00
18	135.00		255.00	2,039.00
21			365.00	2,404.00
28	334.00		125.00	2,195.00
29			245.00	2,440.00
30	125.00 NSF	4.00 SC	497.00 CM	2,808.00
Code: CM Credit memorandum DM Debit memorandum			NSF Not sufficient funds cheque SC Service charge	

From the Cash Receipts Journal		

Date		Cash Debit
Nov. 1		295.00
2		244.00
4		178.00
7		270.00
12		127.00
17		255.00
20		365.00
26		125.00
28		245.00
30		285.00
		2,389.00

From the Cheque Register		

Cheque No.		Cash Credit
821		175.00
822		240.00
823		84.00
824		42.00
825		562.00
826		97.00
827		124.00
828		185.00
829		334.00
830		105.00
		1,948.00

From the General Ledger

Cash

Date	Explanation	F	Debit	Credit	Balance
Oct. 31	Balance	✔			1,869.00
Nov. 30		R-8	2,389.00		4,258.00
30		D-9		1,948.00	2,310.00

Cheque No. 828 was correctly drawn for $135 in payment for store equipment; however, the bookkeeper misread its amount and entered it in his Cheque Register as though it were for $185. The bank paid and deducted the correct $135 amount.

The NSF cheque was received from a customer, Roy Hall, in payment of his account. The credit memorandum resulted from a $500 noninterest-bearing note collected for Bluelake Company by the bank. The bank deducted a $3 fee for collecting the note. None of the memoranda, including the $4 for bank services, had been recorded.

Required:
1. Prepare a November 30 bank reconciliation for Bluelake Company.
2. Prepare in general journal form the entries required to bring the company's book balance for cash into agreement with the reconciled balance.

Problem 8–5A

On January 1, 197A, a company's Allowance for Doubtful Accounts account had a $1,815 credit balance, and during the year it completed these transactions:

Feb. 18   Learned that Earl Kell had gone out of business leaving no assets to attached. Wrote off his $295 account as uncollectible.

Mar. 30   Wrote off the $345 uncollectible account of Gary East.

Apr. 15   Reinstated and recorded the collection of the $135 account of Jerry Kern upon the unexpected receipt of that amount from him. The account had been written off during the previous year.

June 12 Collected from his receiver in bankruptcy 15% of the $600 owed by Owen Price, and wrote off the remainder as uncollectible.

Oct. 22 Received $145 from Gary East in partial payment of the amount written off on March 30. Mr. East stated in the letter accompanying the payment that business had improved and he expected to pay the balance of his debt in the near future.

Dec. 29 Used a compound entry to write off the following accounts: Dale Todd, $560; and David Mays, $495.

31 Provided an addition to the allowance for doubtful accounts equal to one half of 1% of the $414,000 of 197A credit sales.

31 Closed the Bad Debts Expense account.

Required:

1. Open accounts for Allowance for Doubtful Accounts, Income Summary, and Bad Debts Expense; and enter the $1,815 balance in the Allowance for Doubtful Accounts account.
2. Prepare general journal entries to record the transactions and post the entry portions that affect the accounts opened.
3. Give the alternate bad debts adjusting entry the company would make under the assumption that rather than providing an addition to its allowance for doubtful accounts equal to one half of 1% of its 197A credit sales, it aged its accounts, estimated accounts totaling $1,945 would probably not be collected, and increased its allowance for doubtful accounts to provide for them.

Decision problem 8–1, Cinema East

 Ted Gage owns and operates Cinema East, acting as both manager and projectionist. The theater has not been too profitable of late; and this morning at breakfast, while discussing ways to cut costs, his wife suggested that he discharge the theater's doorman whose job is to collect and destroy the tickets sold by the cashier, and that he permit the cashier to collect an admission from each patron without issuing a ticket. This, Mrs. Gage pointed out, would result in a double savings, the wages of the doorman and, also, since there would be no one to take up tickets, rolls of prenumbered tickets would not have to be purchased. Mr. Gage said he could not do this unless Mrs. Gage would take over the cashier's job.

 Discuss the wife's suggestion and her husband's counter proposal from an internal control point of view. You may assume the cashier is a college student and that cashiers change frequently, since the job interferes with dating.

Decision problem 8–2, Miss Angela

 Miss Angela, the bookkeeper at Todd's Department Store, will retire next week after more than 40 years with the store, having been hired by the father of the store's present owner. She has always been a very dependable employee, and as a result has been given more and more responsibilities over the years. Actually, for the past 15 years she has "run" the store's office, keeping books, verifying invoices, and issuing cheques in their payment, which in the absence of the store's owner, Jack Todd, she could sign. In addition, at the end of each day the store's salesclerks turn over their daily cash receipts to Miss Angela, who after counting the money and comparing the amounts with the cash register tapes, which she is responsible for removing from the cash registers, makes the Cash Receipts Journal entry to record cash sales and then deposits the money in the bank. She also reconciles the bank balance each month with her book balance of cash.

Mr. Todd, the store's owner, realizes he cannot expect a new bookkeeper to accomplish as much in a day as Miss Angela does; and since the store is not large enough to warrant more than one office employee, he recognizes he must take over some of Miss Angela's duties when she retires. He already places all orders for merchandise and supplies and closely supervises all employees and does not want to add more to his duties than necessary.

Discuss the situation described here from an internal control point of view, setting forth which of Miss Angela's tasks should be taken over by Mr. Todd and which can be assigned to the new bookkeeper with safety.

Decision problem 8–3, Campus Jewels

Campus Jewels, a jewelry store, has been in operation five years. Three years ago the store liberalized its credit policy in an effort to increase sales. Sales have increased, but the store's owner, Ted Hall, is now concerned with the effects of the more liberal credit policy. Bad debts written off (the store uses the direct write-off method) have increased materially during the past two years, and now he wonders if the sales increase justifies the substantial bad debt losses which he is certain have resulted from the more liberal credit policy.

The store earns a 50% gross profit on sales; its operating expenses (excluding bad debts) are 40% of sales; and during the past five years it had the following credit sales and bad debts:

	1st Year	2d Year	3d Year	4th Year	5th Year
Credit sales	$100,000	$120,000	$150,000	$180,000	$200,000
Bad debts written off.........	100	600	750	3,240	3,400
Losses by year of sales......	500	720	2,850	3,060	3,600

The last line in the summary results from reclassifying bad debt losses by the years in which the merchandise was sold; consequently, the $3,600 of fifth-year losses includes $2,640 of estimated bad debts in present accounts receivable.

Prepare a schedule showing the following in columns by years: credit sales, cost of goods sold, gross profit on sales, operating expenses, income before bad debts, bad debts incurred (bad debts by year of sales), and net income. Then below the net income figures show for each year bad debts written off as a percentage of sales followed on the next line by bad debts incurred as a percentage of sales. Also, write a report to Mr. Hall answering his concern about the new credit policy and recommending any changes you consider desirable in his accounting for bad debts.

Problem 8-1 A&R

Your friend has just been employed by Coopers Co. and his first assignment is to reconcile the bank. To make sure his first job is free of errors, he has come to you for assistance and has provided you with the following information:
1. Balance per book (general ledger account), November 30, $1,600.
2. Cheque No. 603 for $100, listed as outstanding on October 31 bank reconciliation, was not returned with the canceled cheques that accompanied the November 30 bank statement.
3. All cheques issued in November except Cheque No. 806 for $200, were returned by the bank.
4. The November bank statement showed a deposit of $290 and a charge of $10, representing the proceeds of a note collected by the bank on behalf of Coopers. The collection had not been recorded by the company.
5. The company's November 30 deposit of $600 did not appear on the November bank statement.
6. A November Cheque No. 816, recorded erroneously by the company as $860, was cashed as $680, the correct amount. The cheque was for cash purchases.
7. Bank's regular monthly service charge was $20.
8. The bank deducted from the company's account a cheque of Copper Co. Ltd. for $500.
9. A cheque for $300 from a customer in settlement of his account balance was returned by the bank because of non-sufficient funds (NSF).

Required:
1. Indicate which of the above items should be added or deducted from the balance per book, without preparing a bank reconciliation.
2. Identify and explain the item or items which should not be added or deducted from the balance per book.
3. Prepare the necessary adjusting entries to bring the balance per book to the correct balance. (Omit narratives.)

Problem 8-2 A&R

The following information pertains to the accounts receivable and related accounts of Appollo Company for the current year.
1. Sales $1,088,600
   Sales returns and allowances 6,000
   Sales discounts.. 80,000
2. Accounts receivable aging schedule

Number of Days Outstanding	Amount	Probability of Collecting
1–30..........................	$ 50,000	100%
31–60	30,000	80%
61–90	20,000	60%
91 and over	6,000	50%
Total accounts receivable balance...................................	$106,000	

3. Allowance for doubtful accounts:

Allowance for Doubtful Accounts

		Opening balance	8210
March 31	660	Sept. 30	260
June 30	810		
		Ending balance	17,000

4. A recent study shows that the industry's bad debts expense over the past few years is approximately 1% of its total net sales. Appollo is considered as one of the most representative companies in the industry.

Required:
1. What method of estimating bad debt losses is employed by the company? Explain.
2. What is the amount of bad debts expense for the year?
3. Prepare an adjusting entry to record the bad debts expense for the year.
4. Would the entry be different from (3) above if an equally acceptable alternative method for estimating bad debt losses is used? What is the ending balance of the allowance account?

Problem 8–3 A&R

On July 7, 1975 when X Ltd.'s accounts receivable and allowance for doubtful accounts stood at $104,600 and $5,600, respectively, it wrote off one of its customer's accounts, Y company, having a $600 balance.

A few months later, when X Ltd.'s accounts receivable and allowance for doubtful accounts stood at $160,000 and $4,600, respectively, Y company paid its account in full.

Required:
1. Prepare the journal, entries for the write-off and the subsequent collection of Y company's account.
2. Compute the estimated realizable value of X Ltd.'s accounts receivable immediately prior to the write-off of the Y company account.
3. Compute the estimated realizable value of X Ltd.'s accounts receivable immediately after the write-off of the Y company account.
4. Compute the estimated realizable value of X Ltd.'s accounts receivable immediately after the collection of the Y company account.

Problem 8–4 A&R

The All Credit Sales Company recognizes revenues at the time of delivery. Uncollectible Accounts Receivable are expected to average 1% of sales. The information below is for the year ending December 31, 1975.

Accounts Receivable, Jan. 1, 1975	$250,000
Allowance for doubtful accounts, Jan. 1, 1975	12,500
Collection of accounts receivable during the year	800,000
Write-offs of uncollectible accounts	9,000
Accounts receivable, Dec. 31, 1975	270,000
Bad debt recoveries during the year	600

Required:
Prepare the adjusting entry as of December 31, 1975 to the Allowance for Doubtful Accounts account.

9

Accounting for notes and interest

■ Some companies sell merchandise on the installment plan and commonly take promissory notes from their customers. Others, such as dealers in farm machinery, likewise often take notes. However, when companies in which the credit period is long are excepted, note transactions in comparison to other transactions are not too numerous. Nevertheless, many companies in which such transactions are not common will at one time or another accept a note from a customer or will give a note to a creditor. Consequently, one interested in accounting must have some knowledge of promissory notes.

Promissory notes

■ A promissory note is an unconditional promise in writing to pay on demand or at a fixed or determinable future date a definite sum of money. In the note shown in Illustration 9–1 Hugo Brown promises to pay Frank Black or his order a definite sum of money at a fixed future date. Hugo Brown is the *maker* of the note; Frank Black is the *payee*. To Hugo Brown the illustrated note is a *note payable,* a liability; and to Frank Black the same note is a *note receivable,* an asset.

The illustrated Hugo Brown note bears interest at 6%. Interest is a charge for the use of money. To a borrower, interest is an expense; to a lender, it is a revenue. A note may be interest bearing or it may be noninterest bearing. If a note bears interest, the rate or the amount of

Illustration
9–1
**A Promissory
Note**

interest must be stated on the note. Interest is usually stated as a percentage of the note's *principal*. If a note is noninterest bearing, no interest is collected unless the note is not paid when due. If a non-interest-bearing note is not paid when due, interest at the full legal rate may be collected from the *legal due date* until the date of final payment. The legal due date is the date upon which a note is due and payable.

**Legal
due dates**

■ All notes, except notes payable on demand, are due and payable three days (called days of grace) after the time indicated in each note. The time of a note may be indicated in different ways. For example:

1. A note may read: "I promise to pay $500 on December 18." To determine the legal due date of this note, three days of grace are added to December 18 and the note is due on December 21.

2. A note dated June 10 may read: "Ninety days after date I promise to pay $1,000." In such a case exact days, not including the day of the note's date but including the day of its legal due date, are counted and this note is due on September 11, calculated as follows:

Number of days in June	30
Minus the date of the note, June 10	10
Gives the number of days the note runs in June	20
Add the number of days in July	31
Add the number of days in August	31
Total through August 31	82
Days needed in September to equal the time stated in the note plus 3 days of grace, a total of 93 days, and also the legal due date of the note, September 11	11
Total time the note runs in days	93

3. A note dated June 15 may read: "Four months after date I promise to pay $800." In such a case four months and three days (of grace) are added to June 15 and this note is due on October 18.

4. A note dated August 9, 1972, may read: "Four years after date I

promise to pay $5,000." Such a note is due on August 12, 1976, which is four years and three days after its date.

Some notes are payable on demand and read: "On demand, I promise to pay $1,500." Such a note is due on the day the payee demands payment and no days of grace are allowed.

Notes often fall due on a legal holiday or nonjudicial day, and such notes are due on the first business day thereafter. Saturdays, Sundays, New Year's Day, Good Friday, Easter Monday, Victoria Day, Dominion day, Labour Day, Rememberance Day, Thanksgiving Day, Christmas Day, and the birthday of the reigning sovereign are legal holidays or nonjudicial days throughout Canada. The Epiphany, Ascension Day, All Saints Day, and Conception Day are also legal holidays in Quebec. In addition, legal holidays that are observed only in that province or city may be proclaimed by the Lieutenant Governor or by a resolution of the municipal authority.

Calculating interest   ■ Unless otherwise stated, the rate of interest on a note is the rate charged for the use of the principal for one year of 365 days (366 days in a leap year); and the formula for calculating interest is:

$$\text{Principal of the Note} \times \text{Rate of Interest} \times \text{Time of the Note} = \text{Interest}$$

The time of a note always includes the days of grace and exact days are used in calculating interest. For example, the interest on a $1,000, 6%, one-year note is calculated as follows:

$$\$1,000 \times 0.06 \times \frac{368}{365} = \$60.49$$

And the interest on a $5,000, 7%, 90-day note is calculated:

$$\$5,000 \times 0.07 \times \frac{93}{365} = \$89.18$$

Also, interest on a note dated June 5 and reading: "Three months after date I promise to pay $1,000 with interest at 6%" is calculated:

1. First the legal due date of the note, September 8, is determined by adding three months plus three days of grace to June 5.
2. Next the time of the note is calculated as follows:

Number of days in June.. 30
Minus the date of the note, June 5............................. 5
Days the note runs in June 25
Days in July... 31
Days in August 31
Days the note runs in September.............................. 8
Total time the note runs in days 95

3. Then the interest on the note is calculated:

$$\$1,000 \times 0.06 \times \frac{95}{365} = \$15.62$$

Interest tables ■ Interest calculations are simplified by using tables such as those of Illustration 9–2. The tables of Illustration 9–2 show the amount of interest on $1 at selected per annum rates for varying periods of time.

Table of Simple Interest

$$\left(\$1 \times \text{Annual Interest Rate} \times \frac{\text{days}}{365}\right)$$

Days	1%	2%	3%	4%	5%	6%	7%	8%	9%	10%
1	.0000274	.0000548	.0000822	.0001096	.0001370	.0001644	.0001918	.0002192	.0002466	.0002740
2	.0000548	.0001096	.0001644	.0002192	.0002740	.0003288	.0003836	.0004384	.0004932	.0005479
3	.0000822	.0001644	.0002466	.0003288	.0004110	.0004932	.0005753	.0006575	.0007397	.0008219
4	.0001096	.0002192	.0003288	.0004384	.0005479	.0006575	.0007671	.0008767	.0009863	.0010959
5	.0001370	.0002740	.0004110	.0005479	.0006849	.0008219	.0009589	.0010959	.0012329	.0013699
6	.0001644	.0003288	.0004932	.0006575	.0008219	.0009863	.0011507	.0013151	.0014795	.0016438
7	.0001918	.0003836	.0005753	.0007671	.0009589	.0011507	.0013425	.0015342	.0017260	.0019178
8	.0002192	.0004384	.0006575	.0008767	.0010959	.0013151	.0015342	.0017534	.0019726	.0021918
9	.0002466	.0004932	.0007397	.0009863	.0012329	.0014795	.0017260	.0019726	.0022192	.0024658
10	.0002740	.0005479	.0008219	.0010959	.0013699	.0016438	.0019178	.0021918	.0024658	.0027397
11	.0003014	.0006027	.0009041	.0012055	.0015068	.0018082	.0021096	.0024110	.0027123	.0030137
12	.0003288	.0006575	.0009863	.0013151	.0016438	.0019726	.0023014	.0026301	.0029589	.0032877
13	.0003562	.0007123	.0010685	.0014247	.0017808	.0021370	.0024931	.0028493	.0032055	.0035616
14	.0003836	.0007671	.0011507	.0015342	.0019178	.0023014	.0026849	.0030685	.0034521	.0038356
15	.0004110	.0008219	.0012329	.0016438	.0020548	.0024658	.0028767	.0032877	.0036986	.0041096
16	.0004384	.0008767	.0013151	.0017534	.0021918	.0026301	.0030685	.0035068	.0039452	.0043836
17	.0004658	.0009315	.0013973	.0018630	.0023288	.0027945	.0032603	.0037260	.0041918	.0046575
18	.0004932	.0009863	.0014795	.0019726	.0024658	.0029589	.0034521	.0039452	.0044384	.0049315
19	.0005205	.0010411	.0015616	.0020822	.0026027	.0031233	.0036438	.0041644	.0046849	.0052055
20	.0005479	.0010959	.0016438	.0021918	.0027397	.0032877	.0038356	.0043836	.0049315	.0054794
21	.0005753	.0011507	.0017260	.0023014	.0028767	.0034521	.0040274	.0046027	.0051781	.0057534
22	.0006027	.0012055	.0018082	.0024110	.0030137	.0036164	.0042192	.0048219	.0054247	.0060274
23	.0006301	.0012603	.0018904	.0025205	.0031507	.0037808	.0044110	.0050411	.0056712	.0063014
24	.0006575	.0013151	.0019726	.0026301	.0032877	.0039452	.0046027	.0052603	.0059178	.0065753
25	.0006849	.0013699	.0020548	.0027397	.0034247	.0041096	.0047945	.0054794	.0061644	.0068493
26	.0007123	.0014247	.0021370	.0028493	.0035616	.0042740	.0049863	.0056986	.0064110	.0071233
27	.0007397	.0014795	.0022192	.0029589	.0036986	.0044384	.0051781	.0059178	.0066575	.0073973
28	.0007671	.0015342	.0023014	.0030685	.0038356	.0046027	.0053699	.0061370	.0069041	.0076712
29	.0007945	.0015890	.0023836	.0031781	.0039726	.0047671	.0055616	.0063562	.0071507	.0079452
30	.0008219	.0016438	.0024658	.0032877	.0041096	.0049315	.0057534	.0065753	.0073973	.0082192
31	.0008493	.0016986	.0025479	.0033973	.0042466	.0050959	.0059452	.0067945	.0076438	.0084931
32	.0008767	.0017534	.0026301	.0035068	.0043836	.0052603	.0061370	.0070137	.0078904	.0087671
33	.0009041	.0018082	.0027123	.0036164	.0045205	.0054247	.0063288	.0072329	.0081370	.0090411
34	.0009315	.0018630	.0027945	.0037260	.0046575	.0055890	.0065205	.0074521	.0083836	.0093151
35	.0009589	.0019173	.0028767	.0038356	.0047945	.0057534	.0067123	.0076712	.0086301	.0095890
36	.0009863	.0019726	.0029589	.0039452	.0049315	.0059178	.0069041	.0078904	.0088767	.0098630
37	.0010137	.0020274	.0030411	.0040548	.0050685	.0060822	.0070959	.0081096	.0091233	.0101370
38	.0010411	.0020822	.0031233	.0041644	.0052055	.0062466	.0072877	.0083288	.0093699	.0104109
39	.0010685	.0021370	.0032055	.0042740	.0053425	.0064110	.0074795	.0085479	.0096164	.0106849
40	.0010959	.0021918	.0032877	.0043836	.0054795	.0065753	.0076712	.0087671	.0098630	.0109589
41	.0011233	.0022466	.0033699	.0044931	.0056164	.0067397	.0078630	.0089863	.0101096	.0112329
42	.0011507	.0023014	.0034521	.0046027	.0057534	.0069041	.0080548	.0092055	.0103561	.0115068
43	.0011781	.0023562	.0035342	.0047123	.0058904	.0070685	.0082466	.0094247	.0106027	.0117808
44	.0012055	.0024110	.0036164	.0048219	.0060274	.0072329	.0084384	.0096438	.0108493	.0120548
45	.0012329	.0024658	.0036986	.0049315	.0061644	.0073973	.0086301	.0098630	.0110959	.0123287
46	.0012603	.0025205	.0037808	.0050411	.0063014	.0075616	.0088219	.0100822	.0113424	.0126027
47	.0012877	.0025753	.0038630	.0051507	.0064384	.0077260	.0090137	.0103014	.0115890	.0128767
48	.0013151	.0026301	.0039452	.0052603	.0065753	.0078904	.0092055	.0105205	.0118356	.0131507
49	.0013425	.0026849	.0040274	.0053699	.0067123	.0080548	.0093973	.0107397	.0120822	.0134246
50	.0013699	.0027397	.0041096	.0054794	.0068493	.0082192	.0095890	.0109589	.0123288	.0136986

Illustration
9–2

(Per annum means per year.) The tables are used as follows:

1. Determine the interest on a $1,000, 30-day, 6% note.
   a. With its days of grace, such a note runs for 33 days.

Table of Simple Interest

$$\left(\$1 \times \text{Annual Interest Rate} \times \frac{\text{days}}{365}\right)$$

Days	1%	2%	3%	4%	5%	6%	7%	8%	9%	10%
51	.0013973	.0027945	.0041918	.0055890	.0069863	.0083836	.0097808	.0111781	.0125753	.0139726
52	.0014247	.0028493	.0042740	.0056986	.0071233	.0085479	.0099726	.0113972	.0128219	.0142466
53	.0014521	.0029041	.0043562	.0058082	.0072603	.0087123	.0101644	.0116164	.0130685	.0145205
54	.0014795	.0029589	.0044384	.0059178	.0073973	.0088767	.0103562	.0118356	.0133151	.0147945
55	.0015068	.0030137	.0045205	.0060274	.0075342	.0090411	.0105479	.0120548	.0135616	.0150685
56	.0015342	.0030685	.0046027	.0061370	.0076712	.0092055	.0107397	.0122740	.0138082	.0153425
57	.0015616	.0031233	.0046849	.0062466	.0078082	.0093699	.0109315	.0124931	.0140548	.0156164
58	.0015890	.0031781	.0047671	.0063562	.0079452	.0095342	.0111233	.0127123	.0143014	.0158904
59	.0016164	.0032329	.0048493	.0064657	.0080822	.0096986	.0113151	.0129315	.0145479	.0161644
60	.0016438	.0032877	.0049315	.0065753	.0082192	.0098630	.0115068	.0131507	.0147945	.0164383
61	.0016712	.0033425	.0050137	.0066849	.0083562	.0100274	.0116986	.0133698	.0150411	.0167123
62	.0016986	.0033973	.0050959	.0067945	.0084931	.0101918	.0118904	.0135890	.0152877	.0169863
63	.0017260	.0034521	.0051781	.0069041	.0086301	.0103562	.0120822	.0138082	.0155342	.0172603
64	.0017534	.0035068	.0052603	.0070137	.0087671	.0105205	.0122740	.0140274	.0157808	.0175342
65	.0017808	.0035616	.0053425	.0071233	.0089041	.0106849	.0124657	.0142466	.0160274	.0178082
66	.0018082	.0036164	.0054247	.0072329	.0090411	.0108493	.0126575	.0144657	.0162740	.0180822
67	.0018356	.0036712	.0055068	.0073425	.0091781	.0110137	.0128493	.0146849	.0165205	.0183561
68	.0018630	.0037260	.0055890	.0074521	.0093151	.0111781	.0130411	.0149041	.0167671	.0186301
69	.0018904	.0037808	.0056712	.0075616	.0094520	.0113425	.0132329	.0151233	.0170137	.0189041
70	.0019178	.0038356	.0057534	.0076712	.0095890	.0115068	.0134246	.0153424	.0172603	.0191781
71	.0019452	.0038904	.0058356	.0077808	.0097260	.0116712	.0136164	.0155616	.0175068	.0194520
72	.0019726	.0039452	.0059178	.0078904	.0098630	.0118356	.0138082	.0157808	.0177534	.0197260
73	.0020000	.0040000	.0060000	.0080000	.0100000	.0120000	.0140000	.0160000	.0180000	.0200000
74	.0020274	.0040548	.0060822	.0081096	.0101370	.0121644	.0141918	.0162192	.0182466	.0202740
75	.0020548	.0041096	.0061644	.0082192	.0102740	.0123288	.0143836	.0164384	.0184931	.0205479
76	.0020822	.0041644	.0062466	.0083288	.0104109	.0124931	.0145753	.0166575	.0187397	.0208219
77	.0021096	.0042192	.0063288	.0084384	.0105479	.0126575	.0147671	.0168767	.0189863	.0210959
78	.0021370	.0042740	.0064110	.0085479	.0106849	.0128219	.0149589	.0170959	.0192329	.0213698
79	.0021644	.0043288	.0064931	.0086575	.0108219	.0129863	.0151507	.0173151	.0194794	.0216438
80	.0021918	.0043836	.0065753	.0087671	.0109589	.0131507	.0153425	.0175342	.0197260	.0219178
81	.0022192	.0044384	.0066575	.0088767	.0110959	.0133151	.0155342	.0177534	.0199726	.0221918
82	.0022466	.0044931	.0067397	.0089863	.0112329	.0134794	.0157260	.0179726	.0202192	.0224657
83	.0022740	.0045479	.0068219	.0090959	.0113698	.0136438	.0159178	.0181918	.0204657	.0227397
84	.0023014	.0046027	.0069041	.0092055	.0115068	.0138082	.0161096	.0184109	.0207123	.0230137
85	.0023288	.0046575	.0069863	.0093151	.0116438	.0139726	.0163014	.0186301	.0209589	.0232876
86	.0023562	.0047123	.0070685	.0094247	.0117808	.0141370	.0164931	.0188493	.0212055	.0235616
87	.0023836	.0047671	.0071507	.0095342	.0119178	.0143014	.0166849	.0190685	.0214520	.0238356
88	.0024110	.0048219	.0072329	.0096438	.0120548	.0144657	.0168767	.0192877	.0216986	.0241096
89	.0024384	.0048767	.0073151	.0097534	.0121918	.0146301	.0170685	.0195068	.0219452	.0243835
90	.0024658	.0049315	.0073973	.0098630	.0123287	.0147945	.0172603	.0197260	.0221918	.0246575
91	.0024931	.0049863	.0074794	.0099726	.0124657	.0149589	.0174520	.0199452	.0224383	.0249315
92	.0025205	.0050411	.0075616	.0100822	.0126027	.0151233	.0176438	.0201644	.0226849	.0252055
93	.0025479	.0050959	.0076438	.0101918	.0127397	.0152877	.0178356	.0203835	.0229315	.0254794
94	.0025753	.0051507	.0077260	.0103014	.0128767	.0154520	.0180274	.0206027	.0231781	.0257534
95	.0026027	.0052055	.0078082	.0104109	.0130137	.0156164	.0182192	.0208219	.0234246	.0260274
96	.0026301	.0052603	.0078904	.0105205	.0131507	.0157808	.0184109	.0210411	.0236712	.0263013
97	.0026575	.0053151	.0079726	.0106301	.0132877	.0159452	.0186027	.0212603	.0239178	.0265753
98	.0026849	.0053699	.0080548	.0107397	.0134246	.0161096	.0187945	.0214794	.0241644	.0268493
99	.0027123	.0054247	.0081370	.0108493	.0135616	.0162740	.0189863	.0216986	.0244109	.0271233
100	.0027397	.0054794	.0082192	.0109589	.0136986	.0164383	.0191781	.0219178	.0246575	.0273972

Illustration
9–2
Continued

$b.$ Consequently, go down the 6% column to the number opposite 33 days.

$c.$ Multiply this number, .0054247, by the principal of the note, $1,000, to determine the interest on $1,000 at 6% for 33 days. The answer is $1,000 × .0054247 = $5.42.

2.   Determine the interest on a $1,250, 60-day, $7\frac{1}{2}$% note.

$a.$ With its days of grace, such a note runs for 63 days.

$b.$ Since the table does not have a column for $7\frac{1}{2}$%, it is necessary to interpolate as follows:

Interest on $1 at 7% for 63 days is $0.01208220
Interest on $1 at $\frac{1}{2}$% for 63 days is 1/10 of the interest at 5% for 63 days or is (move the decimal point of the 5% number opposite 63 days one place to the left)............................ 0.00086301
Interest on $1 at $7\frac{1}{2}$% for 63 days is.................................. $0.01294521

$c.$ Then multiply the interpolated number, 0.01294521 by the principal of the note, $1,250, to determine the interest on $1,250 at $7\frac{1}{2}$% for 63 days. The answer is: $1,250 × 0.01294521 = $16.18.

The interest tables of Illustration 9–2 show interest amounts for 100 days only; therefore, if the tables are used to calculate interest on a note that runs for, say, 123 days, it is necessary to use the sum of the proper numbers opposite 100 days and opposite 23 days in making the calculation. Likewise, to calculate interest on a one-year note at, say, 6%, multiply the principal of the note by 6% and add to this the interest on the principal at 6% for the three days of grace.

NOTES PAYABLE

■ Notes payable result from the purchase of an asset with a note or from gaining an extension of time on an open account; and they frequently arise when money is borrowed from a bank.

Purchasing an asset with a note

■ Giving a note to purchase an asset is not a common transaction. Occasionally, when the purchase price is high or the credit period is long, a note is given instead of making the purchase on open account. The entry for such a transaction is:

Oct.	14	Store Equipment...	1,600.00	
		Notes Payable...		1,600.00
		Purchased display refrigerator with a one-year, 6% note.		

Usually, all notes payable are recorded in a single Notes Payable account. If several notes are issued, each may be identified in the account by writing the payee's name in the Explanation column on the line of the entry recording the note's issuance or payment. If a company issues many notes, an unusual situation, a supplementary record called a Notes Payable Register may be used for recording the details of each note.

Note given to secure an extension of time on an account ■ A note may be given to secure an extension of time on an open account. For example, George Brock cannot pay his open account with Ajax Company when it becomes due and the company agrees to accept Brock's 60-day, 6%, $350 note in settlement of the open account. Brock will record the transaction in his General Journal with the following entry:

Aug.	23	Accounts Payable – Ajax Company...................	350.00	
		Notes Payable..		350.00
		Gave a 60-day, 6% note in settlement of our open account.		

Observe that the note does not pay the debt; it merely changes its form from an account payable to a note payable. Ajax Company prefers the note to the open account because in case of default and a lawsuit to collect, the note improves its legal position, since the note is written evidence of the debt and its amount.

When the note becomes due, Brock gives Ajax Company a cheque for $353.62 and records the payment of the note and its interest with an entry as follows:

Oct.	25	Notes Payable...	350.00	
		Interest Expense	3.62	
		Cash...		353.62
		Paid our note with 63 days' interest.		

Recording a bank loan ■ In lending money, banks distinguish between *loans* and *discounts*. With either a loan or a discount, the bank lends money. However, in case of a loan, the bank collects interest when the loan is repaid; while in case of a discount, it deducts interest at the time the loan is made. To illustrate loans and discounts, assume that Henry Green wishes to borrow approximately $1,000 for 60 days at 6%.

A loan

In a loan transaction the bank will lend Green $1,000 in exchange for his signed promissory note. The note will read: "Sixty days after date I promise to pay $1,000 with interest at 6%," and Green will record the transaction as follows:

Sept.	10	Cash	1,000.00	
		Notes Payable		1,000.00
		Gave the bank a 60-day note.		

When the note and interest are paid, Green makes the following entry:

Nov.	12	Notes Payable	1,000.00	
		Interest Expense	10.36	
		Cash		1,010.36
		Paid our 60-day, 6% note.		

Observe in case of the loan transaction that interest is paid at the time the loan is repaid.

A discount

If, contrary to the situation described in the previous paragraphs, it is the practice of Green's bank to deduct interest at the time a loan is made, the bank will *discount* Green's $1,000 note. If it discounts the note at 6%, it will deduct from the face amount of the note 63 days' interest at 6%, which is $10.36, and will give Green the difference, $989.64. The $10.36 of deducted interest is called *bank discount,* and the $989.64 are the *proceeds* of the discounted note. Green will record the transaction as follows:

Sept.	10	Cash	989.64	
		Interest Expense	10.36	
		Notes Payable		1,000.00
		Discounted a $1,000 note at 6%.		

When the note matures, Green will pay the bank just the face amount of the note, $1,000, and will record the transaction like this:

Nov.	12	Notes Payable	1,000.00	
		Cash		1,000.00
		Paid our discounted note.		

Since interest is deducted in a discount transaction at the time the loan is made, the note used in such a transaction must state that only the principal amount is to be paid at maturity. Such a note may read: "Sixty days after date I promise to pay $1,000 with no interest," and is commonly called a noninterest-bearing note. However, banks are not in business to lend money interest free; and interest is paid in a discount transaction; but since it is deducted at the time the loan is made, the note used must state that no additional interest is to be collected at maturity. Of course it can be argued in the case of the discounted Green note that the bank collected $10.36 interest at maturity for the use of $989.64, and your authors would not disagree with this.

NOTES RECEIVABLE

■ With the exception of companies selling on the installment plan and other companies in which the credit period is long, notes receivable are not common. However, in enterprises in which the credit period is long, notes are preferred to open accounts because a note may be readily turned into cash before it is due by discounting or selling it to a bank. Notes are also preferred because a note represents a written acknowledgment by the debtor of both the debt and its amount. Also, notes are preferred because they generally earn interest.

Recording the receipt of a note

■ Notes receivable are recorded in a single Notes Receivable account. Each note may be identified in the account by writing the name of the maker in the Explanation column on the line of the entry recording its receipt or payment. Only one account is needed because the individual notes are on hand; and the maker, rate of interest, due date, and other information may be learned by examining each note. However, if note transactions are numerous, a supplementary record may be maintained to record the details of each note. This supplementary record is called a Notes Receivable Register, and as such does not change the regular journal and ledger record of notes.

A note received at the time of a sale is recorded as follows:

Dec.	5	Notes Receivable...	650.00	
		Sales		650.00
		Sold merchandise, terms six-months, 6% note.		

When a note is taken in granting an extension on a past-due open account, the creditor usually attempts to collect part of the past-due account in cash. This reduces the debt and requires the acceptance of a note for a smaller amount. For example, Symplex Company agrees to accept $232 in cash and a $500, 60-day, 6% note from Joseph Cook in settlement of his $732 past-due account. When Symplex receives the cash and note, the following entry is made:

Oct.	5	Cash..	232.00	
		Notes Receivable	500.00	
		Accounts Receivable–Joseph Cook............		732.00
		Received cash and a note in settlement of an account.		

Observe that the foregoing entry changes the form of $500 of the debt from an account receivable to a note receivable.

When Cook pays the note, this entry is made:

Dec.	7	Cash...	505.18	
		Notes Receivable		500.00
		Interest Earned		5.18
		Collected the Joseph Cook note.		

Dishonoured notes receivable

■ Occasionally, the maker of a note either cannot or will not pay his note at maturity. When a note's maker refuses to pay at maturity, the note is said to be *dishonoured*. Dishonouring a note does not relieve the maker of his obligation, and every legal means should be made to collect. However, collection may require lengthy legal proceedings.

The Notes Receivable account balance should show only the amount of notes that have not matured. Therefore, a dishonoured, past-due note is always removed from the Notes Receivable account and charged back to the account of its maker. For example, Symplex Company holds a $700, 6%, 60-day note of George Jones. At maturity, Mr. Jones dishonours the note. To remove the dishonoured note from its Notes Receivable account, the company makes the following entry:

Oct.	14	Accounts Receivable—George Jones	707.25	
		Interest Earned		7.25
		Notes Receivable		700.00
		To charge the account of George Jones for his dishonoured $700, 6%, 60-day note.		

Charging a dishonoured note back to the account of its maker serves two purposes. It removes the amount of the note from the Notes Receivable account, leaving in the account only notes that have not matured; and it records the dishonoured note in the maker's account. The second purpose is important because if in the future the maker of the dishonoured note again applies for credit, his account will show all past dealings, including the dishonoured note.

Observe in the foregoing entry, which charged back the dishonoured note of George Jones, that the Interest Earned account is credited for interest earned even though it was not collected. The reason for this is that George Jones owes both the principal and the interest, and his account should reflect the full amount owed.

Discounting notes receivable

■ Many concerns prefer a note receivable to an open account because a note may be discounted or sold to a bank. Discounting enables the businessman to turn a note into cash without waiting until it matures. To discount a note, the owner endorses and delivers the note to the bank in exchange for cash. The bank then collects the maturity value of the note from its maker at maturity.

If the credit reputation of a note's endorser is good, a bank is usually willing to accept and discount a note because the endorser, by his endorsement, agrees to pay the note at maturity if it is not paid by the maker. This means that the endorser makes himself *contingently liable* for payment of the note. His *contingent liability* depends upon the note's dishonour by its maker. If the maker pays, the endorser has no liability. However, if the maker dishonours the note, then the endorser's contingent liability becomes a real liability. Because contingent liabilities sometimes become actual liabilities, they may affect the credit standing of the one contingently liable. Consequently, when a note is discounted, the contingent liability should appear in the accounts and on the balance sheet of the person or company discounting the note.

Aside from recording the contingent liability, discounting a noninterest-bearing note receivable is similar to discounting one's own note payable. This is because the maker of a noninterest-bearing note is not required to pay interest on such a note. Consequently, the bank discounting a noninterest-bearing note collects only the amount of the note's principal at maturity; and as a result it bases the amount of its discount on the note's principal.

To illustrate, on April 6, Symplex Company received a noninterest-bearing, 60-day, $800 note, dated April 5, from Frank Brown in granting an extension on his account. The legal due date of this note is June 7, and if Symplex Company discounts the note at its bank on April 20, the bank must wait until June 7 to collect the $800 from Brown. This 48 days is called the *discount period*, and is calculated as follows:

```
Number of days in April ................................................ 30
Date of discount......................................................... 20
Days discounted in April ............................................. 10
Days note discounted in May........................................ 31
Days note discounted in June, including 3 days' grace......  7
    Days in discount period .......................................... 48
```

In this situation, the bank plans to collect $800 from Frank Brown in 48 days. Furthermore, if the bank's discount rate is 6%, it will deduct a $6.31 discount from the $800 maturity value of the note, and Symplex Company will receive $800 less $6.31, or $793.69, for the note. The $793.69 is called the *proceeds of the note*. The $6.31 discount is interest expense to Symplex Company. $800 \times 6\% \times \frac{48}{365}$

It records the transaction:

Apr.	20	Cash...	793.69	
		Interest Expense	6.31	
		Notes Receivable Discounted		800.00
		Discounted the Brown note.		

The foregoing credit to *Notes Receivable Discounted* records the contingent liability of Symplex. After the entry is posted, the Notes

Receivable and Notes Receivable Discounted accounts appear as follows:

Notes Receivable		Notes Receivable Discounted	
(Brown note) 800			(Brown note) 800
(Jones note) 500			

If a balance sheet is prepared before the maturity date of the foregoing discounted note, the balances of both the Notes Receivable and Notes Receivable Discounted accounts may appear on it as follows:

Current Assets:		
Cash		$2,500
Notes receivable...	$1,300	
Less notes receivable discounted	800	500
Accounts receivable		4,000
Merchandise inventory..		8,000
Total Current Assets		$15,000

Showing "Notes receivable discounted" on the balance sheet as a subtraction from "Notes receivable" indicates the contingent liability to a balance sheet reader. The contingent liability may also be shown by means of a balance sheet footnote. If Symplex Company followed this practice, it would show the amount of its notes receivable in the current asset section of its balance sheet at $500 followed by an asterisk or other indication of a footnote. It would then place a footnote at the bottom of the balance sheet saying, for example: "Symplex Company is contingently liable for $800 of notes receivable discounted."

Payment of a discounted note by the maker ■ When a note is discounted at a bank, the bank takes possession of the note in exchange for money. The bank will if possible collect the note from the maker at maturity. If the maker pays, it is only necessary for the one who discounted the note to remove the contingent liability from his books. If, for example, Frank Brown pays the note discounted by Symplex Company, Symplex will make the following entry:

June	7	Notes Receivable Discounted	800.00	
		Notes Receivable		800.00
		To remove the contingent liability of the Brown note.		

In this example, the effect of the entry is to balance the Notes Receivable Discounted account and to remove the amount of the paid $800 note from the Notes Receivable account as follows:

Notes Receivable		Notes Receivable Discounted	
(Brown note) 800	(Brown note) 800	(Brown note) 800	(Brown note) 800
(Jones note) 500			

■ If it is able to do so, a bank always collects a discounted note directly from the maker; and the one who discounted the note will not hear from the bank if the note is paid at maturity. However, if a discounted note is dishonored, the bank will notify at once the one who endorsed and discounted the note.

If the bank is unable to collect a discounted note from its maker at maturity, it will normally *protest* the note and look to the endorser or endorsers for payment. Protesting a dishonoured note fulfills one of the legal requirements necessary to hold endorsers liable. To protest a note, a *notice of protest* is prepared and mailed to each endorser. A notice of protest is a statement, usually attested by a notary public, that says the note was duly presented to the maker for payment and payment was refused. The cost of protesting a negotiable instrument is called a *protest fee.* The bank will look to the one who discounted a dishonoured note for payment of both its maturity value and the protest fee.

For example, suppose that instead of paying the $800 note previously illustrated, Frank Brown dishonours it. As soon as the note is dishonoured, the bank notifies Simplex Company by mailing a notice of protest and a letter asking payment of the note's maturity value and the protest fee. Symplex Company must pay both. If the protest fee is, say, $3, Symplex will pay the bank $803. In recording the payment, Symplex charges the note and protest fee back to the account of Frank Brown as follows:

June	8	Accounts Receivable – Frank Brown..................	803.00	
		Cash..		803.00
		To charge the account of Brown with his dishonoured note and the protest fee.		

The dishonour changed Symplex's contingent liability to a real liability; and upon payment of the dishonoured note both the real liaability and the contingent liability ended. The entry just given records the payment of the real liability. The following entry is made to remove the contingent liability from the books:

June	8	Notes Receivable Discounted	800.00	
		Notes Receivable		800.00
		To remove the contingent liability of the dishonoured Frank Brown note.		

Of course, upon receipt of the $803, the bank will deliver to Symplex the dishonoured note. Symplex Company will then make every legal effort to collect from Brown, not only the maturity value of the note and protest fee but also interest on the maturity value and protest fee from the date of dishonour until the date of final settlement. However, it may not be able to collect, and after exhausting every legal means to do so, it may have to write the account off as a bad debt. Normally in such cases no additional interest is taken onto the books before the write-off.

Discounting an interest-bearing note

■ Discounting an interest-bearing note receivable differs slightly from discounting a noninterest-bearing note. This is because when a bank discounts an interest-bearing note, it will collect from the maker at maturity both the note's principal and interest on the principal, which together are called the note's *maturity value*. As a result and as is customary, the bank bases its discount on this maturity value. For example, on September 19 Symplex Company discounts at 6% the $600, 4%, 90-day note of Carl Snow which is dated August 20.

The maturity value of this note is $606.12, calculated as follows:

Principal of the note	$600.00
Interest on $600 for 93 days at 4%	6.12
Maturity value	$606.12

If the bank discounts this note on September 19, it is discounting it for 63 days, calculated as follows:

Time of the note in days		93
Less time held by Symplex:		
Number of days in August	31	
Date of note	20	
Days held in August	11	
Days held in September	19	
Total days held		30
Discount period		63

This method of calculating the discount period differs from the one illustrated on page 285. However, either method gives the same result and is equally satisfactory.

Then since the bank bases the amount of its discount on the maturity value of the note, as is customary, and since its discount rate is 6%, it will in discounting the note deduct 63 days' interest at 6% from the maturity value of the note and will give Symplex Company the proceeds, $599.84. This is calculated:

Maturity value of the note	$606.12
Less interest on $606.12 at 6% for 63 days	6.28
Proceeds	$599.84

Note in this case that the proceeds are $0.16 less than the face amount of the note. Consequently, Symplex will record the transaction as follows:

Sept.	19	Cash	599.84	
		Interest Expense	.16	
		Notes Receivable Discounted		600.00
		Discounted the Carl Snow note for 63 days at 6%.		

In making the above entry, Symplex in effect offsets the $6.12 of interest it would have earned by holding the note to maturity against the $6.28 discount charged by the bank and records only the difference, the $0.16 éxcess of expense.

In the situation just described the proceeds of the discounted note were less than the principal, and the difference was recorded as interest expense. When the proceeds exceed the principal, the difference is credited to Interest Earned. For example, suppose that Symplex Company held the Carl Snow note and discounted it on October 19 rather than on September 19. If the note is discounted on October 19 at 6%, the discount period is 33 days, the discount is $3.29, and the proceeds of the note are $602.83, calculated as follows:

Maturity value of the note...	$606.12
Less interest on $606.12 at 6% for 33 days......................	3.29
Proceeds	$602.83

In this case the proceeds exceed the principal, and the transaction is recorded as follows:

Oct.	19	Cash..	602.83	
		Notes Receivable Discounted		600.00
		Interest Earned		2.83
		Discounted the Carl Snow note at 6% for 33 days.		

In either case, the bank collects the maturity value of the discounted note from Carl Snow at maturity. If within a day or so after the maturity date, Symplex does not receive notice of dishonour, it assumes that the note was paid and makes a general journal entry to cancel its contingent liability.

Discounted interest-bearing note dishonoured at maturity

■ If the Carl Snow note previously illustrated is dishonoured at maturity, the bank will demand payment from Symplex of—

The maturity value of the note:		
Principal	$600.00	
Interest..	6.12	$606.12
Protest fee (assumed amount)......................................		2.50
Total...		$608.62

Symplex must pay the $608.62. In recording the payment, it charges this amount to the account of Carl Snow in the manner shown on page 287; in addition, it should cancel its contingent liability.

When Symplex Company receives the dishonoured note from the bank, it should make every legal effort to collect its maturity value, the protest fee, and interest on both from the date of maturity. For example, if 30 days after the dishonour, Carl Snow pays the maturity value of the dishonoured note, the protest fee, and interest, he should pay:

Maturity value		....	$606.12	
Protest fee		....	2.50	
Interest on $608.62 at 4% for 30 days		....	2.00	
Total		....	$610.62	

This is recorded by Symplex Company:

Dec.	21	Cash...	610.62	
		Accounts Receivable—Carl Snow		608.62
		Interest Earned		2.00
		Dishonoured note and protest fee collected with interest.		

Interest on the dishonoured Carl Snow note illustrated is calculated at 4% from the date of maturity and is at the rate stated on the note. In some cases, regardless of the rate stated, interest at the maximum legal rate is collected on the maturity value and protest fee from the date of maturity.

Collecting an out-of-town note

■ A promissory note is a *negotiable instrument;* and a negotiable instrument is a document to which title is readily changed, usually by endorsement and delivery, but sometimes by delivery only. Negotiable instruments readily pass from hand to hand without question because negotiable instrument laws have been written to encourage this. No effort will be made here to go into the legal aspects of negotiable instruments. That is reserved for a course in business law. For the purpose of this discussion, it is sufficient to point out that a *holder in due course* of a negotiable instrument, or one who under certain circumstances receives a negotiable instrument from a holder in due course, has the legal right to collect the instrument without proving the existence of a debt. A holder in due course is one who gives something of value for a negotiable instrument before maturity without knowledge of defects in the title of previous holders.

These legal aspects sometimes cause a problem in collecting notes. The holder of a note will not part with it without receiving payment, since he does not wish to part with the evidence of indebtedness. Likewise, the maker will not pay his note without gaining possession of it, because he must pay again if the original holder transfers the note, even after receiving payment, to a holder in due course or to one with the same rights.

No problem is involved in collecting a note when both parties to the transaction live in the same city. The holder can present the note directly to its maker for payment. However, when the parties live in different cities, a problem does arise in the exchange of cash for possession of a note. This problem is usually overcome by using a bank as an agent to collect an out-of-town note. To illustrate, Symplex Company of Verdun, Quebec, holds the $1,000, 6%, 60-day note of Sam Small of Winnipeg, Manitoba. When the note nears maturity, Symplex delivers the note to its Verdun bank for collection. The Verdun bank forwards the note to a Winnipeg, Manitoba, correspondent bank, and the Winnipeg bank notifies Sam Small that it has the note for collection. When Small pays the Winnipeg bank, he receives possession of the note. The Winnipeg bank transmits the proceeds of the note to the Verdun bank, and the Verdun bank credits the proceeds, less a collection fee, to the Symplex Company bank account.

Only one entry is needed to record the collection of an out-of-town note through a bank. This is made when the bank notifies that it has credited the proceeds less the collection fee. No entry is made when the note is delivered to the bank for collection. At that time it is not known if the note will be paid or dishonoured. Until the note is paid, there is no change in the relationship of the parties. For example, when the Sam Small note is paid, the bank notifies Symplex that it has deposited the proceeds less the collection fee to Symplex's bank account. Symplex then makes the following entry:

Oct.	17	Cash	1,008.36	
		Collection Expense	2.00	
		Notes Receivable		1,000.00
		Interest Earned		10.36
		Proceeds of the Sam Small note less collection charge.		

End-of-the-period adjustments

■ **Accrued interest on notes payable**

Interest accrues daily on all interest-bearing notes; consequently, if any notes payable are outstanding at the end of an accounting period, their accrued interest should be calculated and recorded. For example, a company gave its bank a $5,000, 60-day, 6% note on December 13 to borrow that amount of money. If the company's accounting period ends on December 31, by then 18 days' or $14.79 interest has accrued on this note and may be recorded with a work sheet adjustment and the following adjusting entry:

Dec.	31	Interest Expense	14.79	
		Interest Payable		14.79
		To record accrued interest on a note payable.		

The adjusting entry causes the $14.79 accrued interest to appear on the income statement as an expense of the period benefiting from 18 days' use of the money. It also causes the interest payable to appear on the balance sheet as a current liability.

PAYING ACCRUED INTEREST THAT HAS BEEN RECORDED. When the foregoing note becomes due in the next accounting period, its payment may be recorded as follows:

Feb.	14	Notes Payable...................................	5,000.00	
		Interest Expense	36.99	
		Interest Payable	14.79	
		Cash.......................................		5,051.78
		Paid a $5,000 note and its interest.		

The foregoing $14.79 debit to Interest Payable records payment of the interest accrued at the end of the previous period.

Discount on notes payable

When a note payable is discounted at a bank, interest based on the principal of the note is deducted and this interest is normally recorded as interest expense. Furthermore, since most such notes run for 30, 60, or 90 days, the deducted interest is usually an expense of the period in which it is deducted. However, when the time of a note extends beyond a single accounting period, an adjusting entry is required. For example, on December 11, 197A, a company discounted at 6% its own $6,000, 60-day, noninterest-bearing note payable and recorded the transaction as follows:

197A				
Dec.	11	Cash..	5,937.86	
		Interest Expense	62.14	
		Notes Payable...............................		6,000.00
		Discounted our noninterest-bearing,		
		60-day note at 6%.		

If this company operates with accounting periods that end each December 31, 20 days' interest on this note, amounting to $19.73, is an expense of the 197A accounting period and 43 days' interest or $42.41 is an expense of 197B. Consequently, if revenues and expenses are matched, the company must make the following December 31, 197A, adjusting entry:

197A				
Dec.	31	Discount on Notes Payable	42.41	
		Interest Expense		42.41
		To set up as a contra liability the		
		interest applicable to 197B.		

The adjusting entry removes from the Interest Expense account the $42.41 of interest that is applicable to 197B, leaving in the account the $19.73 that is an expense of 197A. The $19.73 then appears on the 197A income statement as an expense, and the $42.41 is carried to the 197A balance sheet where, if this is the only note the company has outstanding, it is deducted from notes payable as follows:

Current Liabilities:
Notes payable ....,................................ $6,000.00
Less discount on notes payable 42.41 $5,957.59

Putting discount on notes payable on the balance sheet as a contra liability results in showing as a liability on the balance sheet date the amount of money received in discounting the note plus the accrued interest on the note to the balance sheet date. In this example $5,937.86 was received in discounting the note and the accrued interest on the note to December 31 amounts to $19.73, which together total $5,957.59, and which is the amount actually owed the bank on December 31.

The foregoing treatment of discount on notes payable is preferred by the authors. Nevertheless, a different treatment is occasionally encountered, one in which discount on notes payable is called "prepaid interest" and is placed on the balance sheet as a current asset. This treatment, however, cannot be justified in theory, for any attempt to prepay interest does nothing more than reduce the amount borrowed and increase the effective rate of interest on the loan.

ACCOUNTING FOR DISCOUNT ON NOTES PAYABLE IN THE NEW PERIOD. The $42.41 interest set out as discount on notes payable in the previous paragraphs becomes an expense early in 197B. Consequently, sooner or later it must be taken from the Discount on Notes Payable account and returned to the Interest Expense account. Some accountants make this return with a *reversing entry* that is made as the last step in the end-of-the-accounting-period work and is dated the first day of the new accounting period. Such a reversing entry appears as follows:

197B Jan.	1	Interest Expense .... Discount on Notes Payable .... To reverse the adjusting entry that set out discount on notes payable.	42.41	42.41

Observe that the foregoing reversing entry is debit for credit and credit for debit the reverse of the adjusting entry it reverses, and that is where it gets its name. Also, observe that it returns the $42.41 interest to the expense account so that it will appear on the 197B income statement as an expense without further ado.

Some accountants, rather than making a reversing entry, wait until the end of the new accounting period and handle a reversal like the above with a work sheet adjustment and an adjusting entry, as follows:

197B Dec.	31	Interest Expense .... Discount on Notes Payable .... To return to the expense account interest applicable to 197B.	42.41	42.41

Note that the reversing entry and the adjusting entry are identical, except as to their dates. Either may be used, since they both accomplish the same objective.

Accountants who make reversing entries normally prepare a work sheet, the year-end statements, adjusting and closing entries, and a post-closing trial balance. They then examine the work sheet and reverse any entries the reversal of which will expedite future accounting. In this case the reversal makes it unnecessary at the end of 197B for the accountant to search back through the records to see if the $42.41 of discount on notes payable has become an expense.

Accrued interest on notes receivable

Notes received from customers usually earn interest: and if any such notes are outstanding at the accounting period end, their accrued interest should be calculated and recorded. For example, on December 11 a company accepted a $3,000, 60-day, 6% note from a customer in granting an extension on a past-due account. If the company's accounting period ends on December 31, by then $9.86 interest has accrued on this note and should be recorded with a work sheet adjustment and the following adjusting entry:

Dec.	31	Interest Receivable...	9.86	
		Interest Earned		9.86
		To record accrued interest on a note receivable.		

The adjusting entry causes the interest earned to appear on the income statement of the period in which it was earned. It also causes the interest receivable to appear on the balance sheet as a current asset.

COLLECTING INTEREST PREVIOUSLY ACCRUED. When the foregoing note is collected, the transaction may be recorded as follows:

Feb.	12	Cash...	3,031.07	
		Interest Earned		21.21
		Interest Receivable....................................		9.86
		Notes Receivable		3,000.00
		Received payment of a note and its interest.		

The entry's credit to Interest Receivable records collection of the interest accrued at the end of the previous period.

Discount on notes receivable

When a bank discounts a customer's note, it deducts interest in advance; but since most such notes are short term, the interest is normally earned before the end of the accounting period. Consequently, when a customer's note is discounted, most banks credit the interest collected to Interest Earned, as follows:

197A				
Dec.	16	Notes Receivable	4,000.00	
		Interest Earned		41.42
		Cash...		3,958.58
		Discounted a customer's $4,000 note at 6% for 63 days.		

If the bank's accounting period ends on December 31, by that time $9.86 of the foregoing $41.41 interest has been earned and should appear on its 197A income statement as revenue, and $31.56 should be deferred until 197B. Consequently, the following adjusting entry is required:

197A				
Dec.	31	Interest Earned	31.56	
		Discount on Notes Receivable		31.56
		To remove the unearned interest from the revenue account.		

The foregoing entry causes $9.86 of the interest on the discounted note to appear on the bank's 197A income statement as revenue and $31.56 to appear on its balance sheet as a deduction from notes receivable.

Since the bank has many notes to account for, in a case such as this it will usually return the $31.56 to the Interest Earned account with a reversing entry.

Questions for class discussion

1. Define:
   a. Promissory note.
   b. Payee of a note.
   c. Maturity date.
   d. Dishonoured note.
   e. Notice of protest.
   f. Holder in due course.
   g. Discount period of a note.
   h. Maker of a note.
   i. Principal of a note.
   j. Maturity value.
   k. Contingent liability.
   l. Protest fee.
2. What distinction do banks make between discounts and loans?
3. Distinguish between bank discount and cash discount.
4. What are the legal due dates of the following notes:
   a. Sixty-day note dated June 14.
   b. Ninety-day note dated June 14.
   c. Three-month note dated June 14.
5. Calculate interest on the following notes:
   a. $5,000, 30-day, 7% note dated October 5.

b. $2,000, 90-day, 6% note dated November 6.

c. $2,000, 3-month, 6% note dated November 6.

6. James Thumb borrows from two different banks. From the first he borrows by giving his $1,000, 60-day, 6% note. From the second he borrows by discounting his $1,000, 60-day, noninterest-bearing note at 6%. (a) Give the entries in general journal form to record the two loans on the books of Thumb. (b) Give the entries in general journal form to record the payments of the loans. (c) How do the entries differ in the two situations? (d) Which method of making loans favours the bank?

7. B. A. Lee purchased $500 worth of merchandise from Mesa Manufacturing Company, terms 2/10, n/30. Lee could not pay the account when due and secured an extension of time from Mesa by giving a 60-day, 6% note in the amount of $500. Lee paid the note in full when due. Record this series of transactions in T-accounts (a) on the books of Lee and (b) on the books of Mesa.

8. On December 10, S. A. Starns received from a customer a $1,200, 60-day, 5% note dated December 8. On December 26, he discounted the note at 6%. The note was not protested at maturity. Give the required entries in general journal form on the books of Starns.

9. If the following accounts and balances appear in a ledger:

Notes Receivable		Notes Receivable Discounted	
Bal. 8,500			Bal. 5,200

a. How many dollars of notes receivable are in the hands of the company?

b. How many dollars of notes have been discounted?

c. What is the contingent liability of the company?

Class exercises

Exercise 9–1

Prepare entries in general journal form to record these transactions:

Nov. 4 Borrowed $4,000 from Guaranty Bank by giving a 60-day, 6% note payable.

Jan. 6 Paid the note given Guaranty Bank on November 4.

5 Borrowed money from Security Bank by discounting our own $4,000, noninterest-bearing note at 6% for 60 days.

Mar. 9 On its maturity date, paid the note discounted at Security Bank on January 5.

Exercise 9–2

Prepare entries in general journal form to record these transactions:

Aug. 5 Sold merchandise to Jay Hadley, $1,250, terms 2/10, n/60.

Oct. 6 Accepted $250 in cash and a $1,000, 60-day, 6% note dated October 4 in granting a time extension on the amount due from Jay Hadley.

22 Discounted the Jay Hadley note at the bank at 6%.

Dec. 9 Since notice protesting the Jay Hadley note had not been received, assumed it paid and canceled the discount liability.

Exercise 9-3

Prepare entries in general journal form to record these transactions:

Nov. 10 Accepted a $600, 6%, 60-day note dated this day from Dale West in granting a time extension on his past-due $600 account.

Jan. 12 Dale West dishonoured his note when presented for payment.

Dec. 28 After exhausting all legal means of collecting, wrote off the debt of Dale West against the allowance for doubtful accounts.

Exercise 9-4

Prepare entries in general journal form to record these transactions:

Aug. 23 Accepted a $2,400, 5%, 60-day note dated this day from Jerry Lane in granting a time extension on his past-due account.

29 Discounted the Jerry Lane note at the bank at 6%.

Oct. 26 Received notice protesting the Jerry Lane note. Paid the bank the maturity value of the note plus a $3 protest fee and canceled the discount liability.

Dec. 21 Received cheque from Jerry Lane paying the maturity value of his dishonoured note, the protest fee, and interest at 5% on both for 60 days beyond maturity.

Exercise 9-5

On August 15 Union Company sold Walter Collins merchandise having a $5,000 catalogue list price, less a 20% trade discount, 2/10, n/60. Collins was unable to pay and was granted a time extension on receipt of his 60-day, 6% note dated October 20. Union Company held the note until November 7, when it discounted it at its bank at 6%. The note was not protested.

Answer these questions:

1. How many dollars of trade discount were granted on this sale?
2. How many dollars of cash discount could Collins have received on the purchase?
3. What was the maturity date of the note?
4. How many days were in the discount period?
5. How much bank discount was deducted by the bank?
6. What were the proceeds of the note?
7. What was the last entry made by Union Company in recording the transactions growing out of this sale and collection?

Problems **Problem 9-1**

PART 1. Horton Company sold Jerry Barns $1,500 of merchandise, terms 2/10, n/60, on August 2. Mr. Barns could not pay the account when due, and on October 5 gave Horton Company $300 in cash and a 60-day, 6%, $1,200 note dated that day for the balance. Horton Company held the note until October 29 and then discounted it at 6% at its bank. The note was paid at maturity.

Required:

Prepare entries in general journal form to record these transactions first on the books of Horton Company and then on the books of Jerry Barns.

PART 2. Horton Company sold Ted Kane $1,000 of merchandise, terms 2/10, n/60, on December 7. Mr. Kane could not pay the account when due, and on February 10 gave Horton Company a 60-day, 6% note to gain an extension on the debt. When the note was presented for payment on April 14, it was dishonoured; and a year later, on April 15, after exhausting all legal means to collect, Horton Company wrote off the debt against its allowance for doubtful accounts.

Required:

Prepare entries in general journal form to record these transactions first on the books of Horton Company and then on the books of Ted Kane.

Problem 9-2

Prepare entries in general journal form to record these transactions:

July 5 Sold merchandise to Earl Gage, $2,210, terms 2/10, n/30.

Aug. 6 Received $410 in cash and accepted a $1,800, 60-day, 5% note dated this day from Earl Gage for the amount due on the July 5 sale.

12 Discounted the Earl Gage note at the bank at 6%.

Oct. 11 Since notice protesting the Earl Gage note had not been received, assumed it paid and canceled the discount liability.

11 Accepted a $900, 60-day, 6% note dated October 9 from Carl Lane in granting an extension on the due date of his account.

27 Discounted the Carl Lane note at the bank at 6%.

Dec. 12 Received notice protesting the Carl Lane note. Paid the bank the maturity value of the note plus a $3 protest fee. Canceled the discount liability.

29 Received a cheque from Carl Lane paying the maturity value of his dishonoured note, the protest fee, and interest on both at 6% for 18 days beyond maturity.

Jan. 5 Accepted a $1,000, 60-day, 6% note dated January 3 from Paul Nash in granting a time extension on his past-due account.

Feb. 28 Sent the Paul Nash note to Security Bank for collection.

Mar. 8 Security Bank returned the Paul Nash note. It had been dishonoured.

Dec. 31 Wrote off the Paul Nash account against the allowance for doubtful accounts.

Problem 9-3

Prepare entries in general journal form to record these transactions:

Dec. 3 Accepted a $1,600, 60-day, 6% note dated December 2 from John Oak in granting a time extension on his past-due account.

7 Borrowed money from Security Bank by discounting a $6,000 non-interest-bearing note payable at 6% for 60 days.

8 Accepted a $2,200, 60-day, 6% note dated December 7 from Ted Cole in granting a time extension on his past-due account.

14 Discounted the John Oak note at the bank at 6%.

16 Borrowed $3,600 from Guaranty Bank by giving a 60-day, 6% note.

31 Made an adjusting entry to record the accrued interest on the Ted Cole note.

Dec. 31   Made an adjusting entry to record the accrued interest on the Guaranty Bank note.

31   Made an adjusting entry to remove from the Interest Expense account the interest on the Security Bank note that is chargeable to the new accounting period.

31   Made a reversing entry dated January 1 to return to the Interest Expense account the interest on the Security Bank note chargeable to the new accounting period.

Feb. 4   Sent the Ted Cole note to Guaranty Bank for collection.

4   Received notice protesting the John Oak note. Paid the bank the maturity value of the note plus a $4 protest fee. Canceled the discount liability.

Feb. 8   Paid the note discounted at Security Bank on December 7.

10   Received a credit memorandum representing the proceeds of the Ted Cole note less a $3 collection charge.

17   Paid the note given Guaranty Bank on December 16.

28   Received a cheque from John Oak paying the maturity value of his dishonoured note, the protest fee, and interest on both at 6% for 24 days beyond maturity.

Problem 9–4

Prepare entries in general journal form to record these transactions:

Oct. 2   Borrowed from the bank by discounting our own noninterest-bearing, $3,500 note payable at 6% for 60 days.

4   Accepted a $1,600, 60-day, 6% note dated October 3 from Walter Kosh in granting a time extension on his past-due account.

13   Accepted a $2,400, 60-day, 5% note dated this day from Gary Nash in granting a time extension on his past-due account.

18   Discounted the Walter Kosh note at the bank at 6%.

19   Discounted the Gary Nash note at the bank at 6%.

24   Accepted a $800, 60-day, 6% note dated October 23 from Larry Neal in granting a time extension on his past-due account.

Dec. 4   Paid the note discounted on October 2.

6   Received notice protesting the Walter Kosh note discounted on October 18. Paid the bank the maturity value of the note plus a $3.50 protest fee and canceled the discount liability.

7   Borrowed $4,000 from the bank by giving a 60-day, 6% note payable.

17   Received a cheque from Walter Kosh paying the maturity value of his dishonoured note, the protest fee, and interest on both at 6% for 12 days beyond maturity.

19   Since notice protesting the Gary Nash note had not been received, assumed it paid and canceled the discount liability.

22   Delivered the Larry Neal note to Security Bank for collection.

27   Security Bank returned the Larry Neal note. It had been dishonoured.

31   Made an adjusting entry to record the accrued interest on the note given the bank on December 7.

Feb. 8   Paid the note given the bank on December 7.

Dec. 27   Wrote off the Larry Neal account against the allowance for doubtful accounts.

Problem 9-1A

PART 1. On August 5 Pacific Company sold Dale Best $1,600 of merchandise, terms 2/10, n/60. On October 7 it accepted Best's $1,200, 60-day, 6% note dated that day and $400 in cash in granting a time extension on the account. On October 19 Pacific Company discounted the Best note at 7%. The note was not protested at maturity.

Required:
Prepare general journal entries to record the transactions first on the books of Pacific Company and then on the books of Dale Best.

PART 2. On October 12 Pacific Company accepted a $2,400, 6%, 60-day note dated that day from Carl Zeff in granting a time extension on his past-due account. On October 18 Pacific Company discounted the note at 7%, and on December 15 received notice that it had been dishonoured. The concern paid the bank the maturity value of the note plus a $4 protest fee; and on December 31 it received a cheque from Carl Zeff paying the maturity value of the note, the protest fee, and interest at 6% on both for 17 days beyond maturity.

Required:
Prepare general journal entries to record the transactions first on the books of Pacific Company and then on the books of Carl Zeff.

Problem 9-2A

Prepare entries in general journal form to record these transactions:

Jan. 3 Sold merchandise to Fred Price, $1,800, terms 2/10, n/30.

Feb. 6 Accepted a $1,800, 60-day, 5% note dated this day in granting a time extension on the amount owed by Fred Price.

12 Discounted the Fred Price note at 6% at Guaranty Bank.

Apr. 12 Since notice protesting the Fred Price note had not been received, assumed it paid and canceled the discount liability.

12 Sold merchandise to Gary Cole, $1,200, terms 2/10, n/30.

May 18 Accepted a $1,200, 60-day, 6% note dated May 17 in granting a time extension on the amount owed by Gary Cole.

June 1 Discounted the Gary Cole note at 6% at Guaranty Bank.

July 20 Received notice protesting the Gary Cole note. Paid the bank the maturity value of the note plus a $2 protest fee and canceled the discount liability.

Aug 19 Received a cheque from Gary Cole paying the maturity value of his dishonoured note, the protest fee, and interest on both at 6% for 30 days beyond maturity.

Sept. 3 Sold merchandise to Dale Kirk, $2,000, terms 2/10, n/60.

Nov. 5 Accepted a $2,000, 6%, 30-day note dated November 3 from Dale Kirk in granting a time extension on the amount owed by him.

Dec. 4 Sent the Dale Kirk note to Guaranty Bank for collection.

5 Received a credit memorandum from Guaranty Bank which represented the proceeds of the Dale Kirk note less a $2 collection fee.

Problem 9-3A

Prepare entries in general journal form to record these transactions:

Nov. 8 Accepted a $1,500, 60-day, 6% noted dated this day from John Burns in granting a time extension on his past-due account.

18 Accepted a $2,000, 60-day, 6% note dated November 17 from Earl Hall in granting an extension on his past-due account.

26 Discounted the John Burns note at 6% at the bank.

29 Discounted the Earl Hall note at 6% at the bank.

Dec 7 Gave Security Bank a $4,000, 60-day, 6% note payable in borrowing that amount of money.

Dec. 11 Borrowed money from Guaranty Bank by discounting a $3,000 non-interest-bearing note payable for 60 days at 6%.

31 Made an adjusting entry to record the accrued interest on the note given Security Bank.

31 Made an adjusting entry to remove from the Interest Expense account the interest on the Guaranty Bank note that is applicable to the new accounting period.

31 Made an entry dated January 1 to return to the Interest Expense account the interest on the Guaranty Bank note that is applicable to the new accounting period.

Jan. 11 Received notice protesting the John Burns note. Paid the bank the maturity value of the note plus a $3 protest fee and canceled the discount liability.

22 Since notice protesting the Earl Hall note had not been received, assumed it paid and canceled the discount liability.

Feb. 8 Paid the note given Security Bank on December 7.

12 Paid the note discounted at Guaranty Bank on December 11.

12 Received a cheque from John Burns paying the maturity value of his dishonoured note, the protest fee, and interest at 6% on both for 30 days beyond maturity.

Problem 9-4A

Prepare entries in general journal form to record these transactions:

Oct. 12 Accepted $350 in cash and a $900, 60-day, 6% note dated this day from Paul Owen in granting a time extension on his past-due account.

14 Accepted a $750, 60-day, 6% note dated this day from Earl Potts in granting a time extension on his past due account.

18 Discounted the Paul Owen note at Security Bank at 7%.

Nov. 7 Discounted the Earl Potts note at Guaranty Bank at 6%.

25 Accepted a $1,200, 60-day, 6% note dated this day from Gary Nash in granting a time extension on his past-due account.

Dec. 17 Received a notice protesting the Earl Potts note discounted on November 7. Paid the bank the maturity value of the note plus a $2.50 protest fee and canceled the discount liability.

17 Since notice protesting the Paul Owen note had not been received, assumed it paid and canceled the discount liability.

16 Borrowed $5,000 from Guaranty Bank by giving a 60-day, 6% note payable.

29 Received payment from Earl Potts of the maturity value of his dishonoured note, the protest fee, and interest on both at 6% for 12 days beyond maturity.

Dec. 31 Made an adjusting entry to record the accrued interest on the Gary Nash note.

31 Made an adjusting entry to record the accrued interest on the note given Guaranty Bank on December 16.

Jan. 27 Gary Nash dishonoured his note when presented for payment.

Feb. 17 Paid the note given Guaranty Bank on December 16.

Dec. 31 Wrote off the Gary Nash note against the allowance for doubtful accounts.

Decision problem 9–1, Little Gem Company

Little Gem Company manufactures a corn picker which it sells through retail implement dealers. The company has not been in business too many years and is attempting to compete with larger and better established agricultural machinery manufacturers.

Little Gem Company's corn picker is somewhat less cumbersome and less complicated and, therefore, less expensive than those of its competitors. Nevertheless, the unit price is fairly substantial, and because of the custom in the industry, generous credit terms must be provided. Sales are made to dealers on credit at terms of 10% in cash, and the balance due three months after the date of sale. Dealers customarily give about the same terms to farmers, but since many credit extensions up to nine months are often given, the dealers must then also be given a longer period in which to pay Little Gem Company.

A number of other problems in financing have arisen. The company would like to schedule production uniformly over the year, but because of seasonal sales and the small cash inflow during certain months, it has had difficulty securing the necessary funds to operate uniformly over a 12-month period. Dealers also complain that customers should be given a longer credit period in order to meet competition. It is believed that sales could be increased 20% if credit terms were extended to nine months.

Sales for the past year were distributed as follows:

January......... $30,000	May $90,000	September....... $20,000
February....... 40,000	June 70,000	October 10,000
March........... 60,000	July........... 50,000	November....... 10,000
April 80,000	August....... 40,000	December 20,000

At a dealers' meeting in December Tom Burton, the founder and major owner of Little Gem Company, proposed the following plan:

1. Dealers ask customers to give noninterest-bearing notes for the amounts due after the 10% down payments. These notes would run for nine months from dates of sales.

2. Dealers would endorse to the manufacturer customer notes up to the amounts due the company on each month's sales beyond the 10% paid in cash.

3. The company could then discount these notes at its bank.

Prepare a report expressing your opinion of Tom Burton's proposal including the following:

1. Should dealers prefer the proposed credit plan over the current plan? Should the plan be acceptable to farmers? Should the bank be willing to discount the farmers' notes when presented by Little Gem Company?
2. Assume that sales will increase 20% under the new credit plan and that cash requirements to cover production and other cash operating costs are 60% of sales, how much cash will be needed each month if production is equalized over the year?
3. Would you recommend the adoption of Tom Burton's plan? Explain.

Analytical and review problem

Problem 9–1 A&R

The following information is obtained from the records of Mic Mac Company.

1. An analysis of the December 31, 1975, bank reconciliation shows:
    a. A bank debit memorandum for nonpayment of a customer's 90-day, 10% note discounted at the bank on November 2, 30 days after the date of the note. The amount of the debit memorandum was $10,260, of which $10 was for collection services rendered.
    b. A bank credit memorandum showing a 60-day, $6,000 noninterest bearing note from a customer, dated December 1 in settlement of his overdue account, was discounted at the bank on December 30.
    c. The bank charged a 12% for all notes discounted.
2. An analysis of the interest expense and income accounts shows the following:

Interest Expense		Interest Income	
Dec. 2 (interest expense for a noninterest bearing 60-day note payable discounted at the bank)	100	Nov. 2	45
Dec. 30	60		

3. The company and the bank both used a 360-day year to compute their interest expense and income.

Required:
Based on the above information, reconstruct all transactions in journal entries, including all necessary adjusting entries for a December 31 year-end.

10

Inventories
and
cost of goods
sold

■ A merchandising business earns revenue by selling merchandise, and for such a concern the phrase *merchandise inventory* is used to describe the aggregate of the items of tangible personal property it holds for sale. As a rule the items for sale are sold within one year; consequently, the inventory is a current asset, usually the largest current asset on a merchandising concern's balance sheet.

Matching merchandise costs with revenues

■ In accounting for inventories, the Canadian Institute of Chartered Accountants has said: "The method for determining cost should be one which results in the fairest matching of costs against revenues regardless of whether or not the method corresponds to the physical flow of goods."[1] The matching process referred to is one with which the student is already somewhat familiar. It consists of determining how much of the total cost of the goods that were for sale during a period should be deducted from the period's revenue from sales and how much should be carried forward as inventory to be matched against a future period's revenue.

The cost of the goods that were for sale during an accounting period may be determined from the accounting records by adding to the cost

---

[1] *CICA Handbook* (Toronto: The Canadian Institute of Chartered Accountants), p. 1083.

of the beginning inventory the net cost of the goods purchased during the period. But, since most concerns do not keep a record of the cost of the goods sold during a period, in most concerns cost of goods sold cannot be determined from accounting records but must be ascertained by separating *goods for sale* into *goods sold* and *goods unsold.*

In separating goods available for sale into its components of goods sold and goods not sold, the key problem is that of assigning a cost to the goods not sold or to the ending inventory. However, it should be constantly borne in mind that the procedures for assigning a cost to the ending inventory are also the means of determining cost of goods sold. Cost of goods sold and ending inventory are opposite sides of the same coin, because whatever portion of the cost of goods for sale is assigned to the ending inventory, the remainder goes into cost of goods sold.

Assigning a cost to the ending inventory

■ Assigning a cost to the ending inventory normally involves two problems: (1) determining the quantity of each product on hand and (2) pricing the products.

The quantity of unsold merchandise on hand at the end of an accounting period is usually determined by a physical inventory. Physical inventories and the way in which such inventories are taken were discussed in Chapter 5; consequently, it is only necessary to repeat that in a physical inventory the unsold merchandise is counted, weighed, or otherwise measured to determine the units, pounds, gallons, board feet, or other measure of each product on hand.

After an inventory is counted, weighed, or otherwise measured, the units are priced. Generally, inventories are priced at cost.[2] However, as previously stated, a departure from cost is sometimes necessary when goods have been damaged or have deteriorated. Likewise, a departure from cost is sometimes necessary when replacement costs for inventory items are less than the amounts actually paid for the items when they were purchased. This last point is discussed in more detail later in this chapter under the heading, "Cost or replacement, the lower."

Accounting for an inventory at cost

■ Pricing an inventory at cost is not difficult when costs remain fixed. However, when identical items were purchased during an accounting period at different costs, a problem arises as to which costs apply to the ending inventory and which apply to the goods sold. There are at least four acceptable ways of assigning costs to goods in the ending inventory and to goods sold. They are: (1) specific invoice prices; (2) weighted average cost; (3) first-in, first-out; and (4) last-in, first-out.

To illustrate the four, assume that a company has on hand at the end of an accounting period 12 units of Article X. Also, assume that the company began the year and purchased Article X during the year as follows:

---

[2] Ibid., p. 1081.

```
Jan.   1  Opening inventory......... 10 units @ $10.00  =  $100.00
Mar. 13  Purchased.................... 15 units @   11.50  =   172.50
Aug. 17  Purchased.................... 20 units @   12.50  =   250.00
Nov. 10  Purchased.................... 10 units @   12.00  =   120.00
              Total......................... 55 units                  $642.50
```

Specific invoice prices

When it is possible to identify each item in an inventory with a specific purchase and its invoice, specific invoice prices may be used to assign costs to the inventory and to the goods sold. For example, if for purposes of illustration it is assumed that 6 of the 12 remaining units of Article X were from the November purchase and 6 were from the August purchase, the costs are assigned to the inventory and goods sold by means of specific invoice prices as follows:

```
Total cost of 55 units available for sale.....................................      $642.50
Less final inventory priced by means of specific invoices:
    6 units from the November purchase at $12.00 each...............$72.00
    6 units from the August purchase at $12.50...........................  75.00
    12 units in ending inventory...............................................          147.00
Cost of goods sold................................................................      $495.50
```

Weighted average

Under this method prices for the units in the beginning inventory and in each purchase are weighted by the number of units in the beginning inventory and in each purchase and are averaged to find the weighted average cost per unit as follows:

```
10 units @ $10.00  =  $100.00
15 units @   11.50  =   172.50
20 units @   12.50  =   250.00
10 units @   12.00  =   120.00
55 units                  $642.50
$642.50  ÷  55  =  $11.682, weighted average cost per unit
```

After the average cost per unit is determined, this weighted average is used to assign costs to the inventory and the units sold as follows:

```
Total cost of 55 units available for sale ..................................... $642.50
Less ending inventory priced on a weighted average cost basis:
    12 units at $11.682 each ..................................................... 140.18
Cost of goods sold................................................................. $502.32
```

First-in, first-out

In a merchandising business clerks are usually instructed to sell the oldest merchandise first. Consequently, when this instruction is followed, merchandise tends to flow out on a first-in, first-out basis. When first-in, first-out is applied in pricing an inventory, it is assumed that costs also follow this pattern, and as a result, the cost of the last items received are assigned to the ending inventory and the remaining costs are assigned to goods sold. When first-in, first-out, or *Fifo* as it is often called from its first letters, is used, costs are assigned to the inventory and to the goods sold as follows:

Total cost of 55 units available for sale....................................... $642.50
Less ending inventory priced on a basis of Fifo:
  10 units from the November purchase at $12.00 each $120.00
   2 units from the August purchase at $12.50 each..................   25.00
  12 units in the ending inventory..   145.00
Cost of goods sold $497.50

Last-in, first-out

Under this method of inventory pricing, commonly called *Lifo*, the costs of the last goods received are matched with revenue from sales. The theoretical justification for this is that a going concern must at all times keep a certain amount of goods in stock; consequently, when goods are sold, replacements are purchased. Thus it is a sale that causes the replacement of goods; and if costs and revenues are matched, replacement costs should be matched with the sales that induced the acquisitions.

Under Lifo, costs are assigned to the 12 remaining units of Article X and to the goods sold as follows:

Total cost of 55 units available for sale....................................... $642.50
Less ending inventory priced on a basis of Lifo:
  10 units in the beginning inventory at $10.00 each................. $100.00
   2 units from the first purchase at $11.50 each 23.00
  12 units in the ending inventory..   123.00
Cost of goods sold $519.50

Notice that this method of matching costs and revenue results in the final inventory being priced at the cost of the oldest 12 units.

Comparison of methods

In a stable market where prices remain unchanged, the inventory pricing method is of little importance, because when prices are unchanged over a period of time, all methods give the same cost figures. However, in a changing market where prices are rising and falling, each method may give a different result. This may be seen by comparing the costs for the units of Article X sold as calculated by the several methods just discussed. These costs are:

Based on specific invoice prices.. $495.50
Based on weighted average invoice prices.............................. 502.32
Based on Fifo 497.50
Based on Lifo 519.50

All four pricing methods are used; and each under certain circumstances has its advantages. Specific invoice prices exactly match costs and revenue; average invoice prices tend to smooth out price fluctuations; Fifo tends to associate costs and the merchandising ideal of selling the oldest merchandise first; and when prices are rising, as in most of the years since World War II, Lifo has certain cost-revenue matching advantages. However, since the method used may affect the amounts of reported ending inventory and cost of goods sold, a company should show on its statements by means of footnotes or other manner the pricing method used. Also, accountants are of the opinion that a company should select for use the method that best reflects its periodic net income.

Consistency ■ Often a company's reported net income can be either increased or decreased simply by changing its method of inventory pricing. Consequently, although accountants hold that a company may use any accepted method that fairly reflects its periodic income, they insist that the company consistently follow the chosen method.

Often there are several acceptable ways of handling any transaction or accounting problem. Inventory pricing methods are one example, and the several methods of calculating depreciation as discussed in the next chapter are another. Accountants hold that when there are several acceptable methods or procedures that may be followed in a given situation, a concern may choose any one so long as the chosen method or procedure fairly reflects periodic income and is consistently followed thereafter. Consistency is a fundamental principle of accounting. Accountants strive for consistency so that there will be a high degree of comparability in the statements prepared period after period.

In their desire for consistency, however, accountants do not hold that a method once chosen can never be changed. Rather, they agree that if upon additional consideration it is decided that a different acceptable method from the one in use will better reflect periodic income, a change may be made. But in such a case accountants insist that adequate disclosure of the change and its effects be reported in the company's statements.

Elements of inventory cost ■ The Canadian Institute of Chartered Accountants has said: "In the case of inventories of merchandise purchased for resale or of raw materials, cost should be laid-down cost."[3] Therefore, the cost of an inventory item includes the invoice price, less the discount, plus any additional incidental costs necessary to put the goods into place and condition for sale. The additional incidental costs include import duties, freight and transportation, storage, insurance while being stored or transported, plus any other applicable costs, such as those incurred during an aging process.

If incurred, any of the foregoing enter into the cost of an inventory. However, in pricing an inventory, most concerns do not take into consideration the incidental costs of acquiring merchandise. They price

---

[3] Ibid., p. 1082

the inventory on the basis of invoice prices only, and treat all incidental costs of acquiring goods as expenses of the period in which incurred.

Although not correct in theory, treating incidental costs as expenses of the period in which incurred is commonly permissible and often best. In theory a share of each incidental cost should be assigned to every unit purchased, thus causing a portion of each to be carried forward in the inventory to be matched against the revenue of the period in which the inventory is sold. However, the expense of computing costs on such a precise basis usually outweighs any benefit from the extra accuracy. Consequently, when possible, most concerns take advantage of the accounting principle of materiality and treat such costs as expenses of the period in which incurred.

Cost or replacement, the lower ■ Over the years, the traditional rule for pricing an inventory has been "the lower of cost or replacement." This rule gained its wide acceptance because it placed an inventory on the balance sheet at a conservative figure — the lower of what the inventory cost or its replacement cost on the balance sheet date.

The argument advanced in support of this conservatism was that if the replacement cost of an inventory item had declined, then its selling price would probably have to be reduced, and since this might result in a loss, the loss should be anticipated and taken in the year of the price decline. It was a good argument; however, since selling prices do not always exactly and quickly follow cost prices, the application of the rule often resulted in misstating net income in the year of a price decline and again in the succeeding year. For example, suppose that a firm purchased merchandise costing $1,000; marked it up to a $1,500 selling price; and sold one half of the goods. The gross profit on the goods sold would be calculated as follows:

Sales	$750
Cost of goods sold	500
Gross profit	$250

However, if the $500 replacement cost of the unsold goods had declined to $450 on the inventory date, an income statement based upon the traditional application of cost or replacement would show:

Sales		$750
Cost of goods sold:		
Purchases	$1,000	
Less ending inventory	450	550
Gross profit		$200

The $450 would be a conservative balance sheet figure for the unsold goods. However, if these goods were sold at their full price early in the following year, the $450 inventory figure would have the erroneous effect of deferring $50 of income to the second year's income statement as follows:

Sales	$750
Cost of goods sold:	
Beginning inventory	450
Gross profit	$300

Merchants are prone to be slow in marking down goods; they normally try to sell merchandise at its full price if possible. Consequently, the illustrated situation was not uncommon. For this reason the lower of cost or replacement rule has been modified in recent years as follows for situations in which replacement costs are below actual costs.[4]

1. Goods should be placed on an inventory at cost, even though replacement cost is lower, if there has not been and there is not expected to be a decline in selling price.
2. Goods should at times be placed on an inventory at a price below their cost but above their replacement cost. For example, suppose the cost of an item that is normally bought for $20 and sold for $30 declines from $20 to $16, and its selling price declines from $30 to $27. The normal profit margin on this item is one third of its selling price. If this normal margin is applied to $27, the item should be placed on the inventory at two thirds of $27, or at $18. This is below cost but above replacement cost.
3. At times, goods should be placed on an inventory at a price below replacement cost. For example, assume that the goods described in the preceding paragraph can only be sold for $18.50 and that the disposal costs are estimated at $3. In this case the goods should be placed on the inventory at $15.50, a price below their replacement cost of $16.

Conservatism

■ Balance sheet conservatism was once considered one of the first principles of accounting. The objective of such conservatism was to place each item on the balance sheet at a conservative figure. This in itself was commendable; but it was often carried too far and resulted not only in the misstatement of asset values but also in unconservative income statements. For example, as shown in the foregoing paragraphs, when prices are falling, the blind application of the unmodified lower of cost or replacement rule to inventories may result in a conservative balance sheet figure for inventories; but it may also result in an improper deferring of net income and in inaccurate income statements. Likewise, the too rapid write-off of plant assets to depreciation, not uncommon in the past, in order to place these assets on the balance sheet at conservative figures resulted not only in the misstatement of the asset values but also in the overstatement of expenses and in misleading income statements. Consequently, accountants recognize that balance sheet conservatism does not outweigh other factors. Today, accountants favour practices that result in a fair statement of net income period after period.

---

[4] Ibid., p. 1083.

Inventory errors ■ An error in determining the end-of-the-period inventory will cause misstatements in cost of goods sold, gross profit, reported net income, the current assets, and owner equity. Also, since the ending inventory of one period is the beginning inventory of the next, the error will carry forward and cause misstatements in the succeeding period's cost of goods sold, gross profit, and reported net income. Furthermore, since the amount involved in an inventory is often large, the error and misstatements can be material without being readily apparent.

To illustrate the effects of an inventory error, assume that in each of the years 1975, 1976, and 1977 a company had $100,000 in sales. If the company maintained a $20,000 inventory throughout the period and made $60,000 in purchases in each of the years, its cost of goods sold each year was $60,000 and its annual gross profits were $40,000. However, assume the company incorrectly calculated its December 31, 1975, inventory at $18,000 rather than $20,000. The error would have the effects shown in Illustration 10–1.

	——1975——		——1976——		——1977——	
Sales...............................		$100,000		$100,000		$100,000
Cost of goods sold:						
Beginning inventory..............	$20,000		$18,000*		$20,000	
Purchases...........................	60,000		60,000		60,000	
Goods for sale	$80,000		$78,000		$80,000	
Ending inventory..................	18,000*		20,000		20,000	
Cost of goods sold		62,000		58,000		60,000
Gross profit		$ 38,000		$ 42,000		$ 40,000

*Should have been $20,000.

Illustration
10–1

Observe in Illustration 10–1 that the $2,000 understatement of the December 31, 1975, inventory caused a $2,000 overstatement in 1975 cost of goods sold and a $2,000 understatement in gross profit and net income. Also, since the ending inventory of 1975 became the beginning inventory of 1976, the error caused an understatement in the 1976 cost of goods sold and a $2,000 overstatement in gross profit and net income. However, by 1977 the error had no effect.

In Illustration 10–1 the December 31, 1975, inventory is understated. Had it been overstated, it would have caused opposite results – the 1975 net income would have been overstated and the 1976 income understated.

It is sometimes argued that a mistake in taking a year-end inventory is not too serious, since the error it causes in reported net income the first year is exactly offset by an opposite error in the second. However, such reasoning is unsound because it fails to consider that management, creditors, and owners base many important decisions on fluctuations in reported net income. Consequently, such mistakes should be avoided, and they may be avoided if care is exercised and procedures such as those outlined in Chapter 5 are used in taking an inventory.

Perpetual inventories ■ Concerns selling a limited number of products of relatively high value often keep perpetual or book inventories. Also, large concerns that process their accounting data electronically commonly keep such records.

A perpetual or book inventory based on pen and ink makes use of a subsidiary record card for each product in stock. On these individual cards, one for each kind of product, the number of units received is recorded as units are received; the number of units sold is recorded as units are sold; and after each receipt or sale, the balance remaining on hand is recorded. (An inventory record card for $\frac{1}{4}$H.P. Electric Motors is shown in Illustration 10–2.) At any time, each perpetual inventory card tells the balance on hand of any one product; and the total of all cards is the amount of the inventory.

Illustration 10–2 Inventory record card

Item ¼ H.P. Electric Motors			Location in stock room Bin 8					
Maximum 25			Minimum 5					

Date	Received			Sold			Balance		
	Units	Cost	Total	Units	Cost	Total	Units	Cost	Balance
1/1							10	10.00	100.00
1/5				5	10.00	50.00	5	10.00	50.00
1/8	20	10.50	210.00				{ 5	10.00	
							20	10.50	260.00 }
1/10				3	10.00	30.00	{ 2	10.00	
							20	10.50	230.00 }

The January 10 sale on the card of Illustration 10–2 indicates that the inventory of which this card is a part is kept on a first-in, first-out basis. Observe that this sale is recorded as being from the oldest units in stock. Perpetual inventories may also be kept on a last-in, first-out basis. When this is done, each sale is recorded as being from the last units received in stock, until these are exhausted, then sales are from the next to last, and so on.

When a concern keeps perpetual inventory records, it normally also makes a once-a-year physical count of each kind of goods in stock in order to check the accuracy of its book inventory records.

Perpetual inventories not only tell the amount of inventory on hand at any time but they also aid in controlling the total amount invested in inventory. Each perpetual inventory card may have on it the maximum and minimum amounts of that item that should be kept in stock. By keeping the amount of each item within these limits, an oversupply or an undersupply of inventory is avoided.

Periodic
and
perpetual
inventory
systems

■ A system of inventory accounting like that described in Chapter 5 is normally based upon periodic, physical inventories and is known as a periodic inventory system. As was explained in Chapter 5, cost of goods sold is determined under such a system by adding net cost of purchases to beginning inventory and subtracting the ending inventory. When such a system is used, an inventory is necessary in order to determine ending goods on hand and cost of goods sold.

Under a perpetual inventory system, cost of goods sold during a period, as well as the ending inventory, may be determined from the accounting records without a physical inventory. Under such a system an account called "Merchandise" takes the place of and is used for recording the information entered in the periodic inventory system accounts, "Purchases" and "Merchandise Inventory." The "Merchandise" account is a controlling account that controls the numerous perpetual inventory cards described in previous paragraphs.

When merchandise is purchased by a concern using a perpetual inventory system, the acquisition is recorded as follows:

Jan.	8	Merchandise..	210.00	
		Accounts Payable—Blue Company.............		210.00
		Purchased merchandise on credit.		

In addition to the entry debiting the purchase to the Merchandise account, entries are also made on the proper perpetual inventory cards in the Received columns to show the kinds of merchandise bought. (See Illustration 10–2.)

When a sale is made, since the inventory cards show the cost of each item sold, it is possible to record both the sale and the cost of the goods sold. For example, if goods that according to the inventory cards cost $30 are sold for $50, cost of goods sold and the sale may be recorded as follows:

Jan.	10	Accounts Receivable—George Black................	50.00	
		Cost of Goods Sold......................................	30.00	
		Sales		50.00
		Merchandise...		30.00
		Sold merchandise on credit.		

In addition to the credit in this entry to the Merchandise account for the cost of the goods sold, the costs of the items sold are also deducted in the Sold columns of the proper inventory cards.

Note the debit to the cost of Goods Sold account in the entry just given. If this account is debited at the time of each sale for the cost of the goods sold, the debit balance of the account will show at the end of the accounting period the cost of all goods sold during the period.

Note also the debit and the credit to the Merchandise account as they appear in the two entries just given. If this account is debited for the cost of merchandise purchased and credited for the cost of merchandise sold, at the end of an accounting period its debit balance will show the cost of the unsold goods on hand, the ending inventory.

Estimated inventories

■ **Retail method**

Good management requires that income statements be prepared more often than once each year, usually monthly or quarterly; and inventory information is necessary for these statements. However, taking a physical inventory in a retail store is both time consuming and expensive. Consequently, many retailers use the so-called *retail inventory method* to estimate inventories for monthly or quarterly statements. These monthly or quarterly statements are called *interim* or "in between" statements, since they are prepared in between the regular year-end statements.

ESTIMATING AN ENDING INVENTORY BY THE RETAIL METHOD. When the retail method is used to estimate an end-of-an-interim-period inventory, a store's records must show the amount of inventory it had at the beginning of the period both *at cost* and *at retail*. At cost for an inventory means just that, while "at retail" means the dollar amount of the inventory at the marked selling prices of the inventory items.

In addition to the beginning inventory, the records must also show the amount of goods purchased during the period both at cost and at retail plus the net sales at retail. The last item is easy; it is the balance of the Sales account less returns and discounts. Then, with this information the interim inventory is estimated as follows: (1) The amount of goods that were for sale during the period both at cost and at retail is first computed. Next, (2) "at cost" is divided by "at retail" to obtain a cost ratio. Then, (3) sales (at retail) are deducted from goods for sale (at retail) to arrive at the ending inventory (at retail). And finally, (4) the ending inventory at retail is multiplied by the cost ratio to reduce it to a cost basis. These calculations are shown in Illustration 10–3.

The essence of Illustration 10–3 is: (1) This store had $100,000 of goods (at marked selling prices) for sale during the period. (2) These goods cost 60% of the $100,000 total amount at which they were marked for sale. (3) The store's records (its Sales account) showed that $70,000 of these goods were sold, leaving $30,000 of merchandise unsold and presumably in the ending inventory. Therefore, (4) since cost in this

(1) Goods available for sale:	At Cost	At Retail
Beginning inventory..	$20,500	$ 34,500
Net purchases...	39,500	65,500
Goods available for sale.....................................	$60,000	$100,000
(2) Cost ratio: $60,000 ÷ $100,000 = 60%)		
(3) Deduct sales at retail		70,000
Ending inventory at retail		$ 30,000
(4) Ending inventory at cost ($30,000 × 60%)	$18,000	

Illustration
10–3

store is 60% of retail, the estimated cost of this ending inventory is
$18,000.

An ending inventory calculated as in Illustration 10–3 is an estimate
that is arrived at by deducting sales (goods sold) from goods for sale.
Inventories estimated in this manner are satisfactory for interim statements, but for year-end statements, or at least once each year, a store
should take a physical inventory.

USING THE RETAIL METHOD TO REDUCE A PHYSICAL INVENTORY
TO A COST BASIS. Items for sale in a retail store normally have price
tickets attached that show selling prices. Consequently, when a retail
store takes a physical inventory, it commonly takes the inventory at
the marked selling prices of the inventoried items. It then reduces the
dollar total of this inventory to a cost basis by applying its cost ratio.
It does this because the selling prices are readily available and the
application of the cost ratio eliminates the need to look up the invoice
price of each inventoried item.

For example, assume that the store of Illustration 10–3, in addition to
estimating its inventory by the retail method, also takes a physical
inventory at the marked selling prices of the inventoried goods. Assume
further that the total of this physical inventory is $29,600. Under these
assumptions the store may arrive at a cost basis for this inventory,
without having to look up the cost of each inventoried item, simply by
applying its cost ratio to the $29,600 inventory total as follows:

$$\$29,600 \times 60\% = \$17,760$$

The $17,760 cost figure for this store's ending physical inventory is a
satisfactory figure for year-end statement purposes.

INVENTORY SHORTAGES. An inventory determined as in Illustration
10–3 is an estimate of the amount of goods that should be on hand; but
since it is arrived at by deducting sales from goods for sale, it does not
reveal any actual shortages due to breakage, loss, or theft. However,
the amount of such shortages may be determined by first estimating an
inventory as in Illustration 10–3 and then taking a physical inventory
at marked selling prices.

For example, by means of the Illustration 10–3 calculations, it was
estimated the store of this discussion had a $30,000 ending inventory at

retail. However, in the previous section it was assumed that this same store took a physical inventory and had only $29,600 of merchandise on hand. Therefore, if this store should have had $30,000 of goods in its ending inventory as determined in Illustration 10–3, but had only $29,600 when it took a physical inventory, it must have had a $400 inventory shortage at retail or a $240 shortage at cost ($400 × 60% = $240).

MARKUPS AND MARKDOWNS. The calculation of a cost ratio is often not as simple as that shown in Illustration 10–3, because many stores not only have a *normal markup* (often called a *markon*) that they apply to items purchased for sale but also make *additional markups* and *markdowns*. A normal markup or markon is the normal amount or percentage that is applied to the cost of an item to arrive at its selling price. For example, if a store's normal markup is 50% on cost and it applies this normal markup to an item that cost $10, it will mark the item for sale at $15. Normal markups appear in the calculation of a store's cost ratio as the difference between net purchases at cost and at retail.

Additional markups are markups made in addition to normal markups. Stores commonly give goods of outstanding style or quality such additional markups, because they can get a higher than normal price for such goods. They also commonly mark down for a clearance sale any slow-moving merchandise.

When a store using the retail inventory method makes additional markups and markdowns it must keep a record of them. It then uses the information in calculating its cost ratio and in estimating an interim inventory as in Illustration 10–4.

Goods available for sale:	At Cost	At Retail
Beginning inventory	$18,000	$27,800
Net purchases	34,000	50,700
Additional markups		1,500
Goods available for sale	$52,000	$80,000
Cost ratio: $52,000 ÷ $80,000 = 65%		
Sales at retail		$54,000
Markdowns		2,000
Total sales and markdowns		$56,000
Ending inventory at retail ($80,000 less $56,000)		$24,000
Ending inventory at cost ($24,000 × 65%)	$15,600	

Illustration 10–4

Observe in Illustration 10–4 that the store's $80,000 of goods for sale at retail were reduced $54,000 by sales and $2,000 by markdowns, a total of $56,000. (To understand the markdowns, visualize this effect of a markdown: The store had an item for sale during the period at $25. The item did not sell, and to move it the manager marked its price down from $25 to $20. By this act he reduced the amount of goods for sale in the store at retail by $5, and by a number of such markdowns goods for sale at retail in the store of Illustration 10–4 were reduced $2,000.) Now back to Illustration 10–4. The store's $80,000 of goods for sale were reduced $54,000 by sales and $2,000 by markdowns, leaving an estimated $24,000 ending inventory at retail. Therefore, since "cost" is 65% of "retail," the ending inventory at "cost" is $15,600.

Observe also in Illustration 10–4 that markups enter into the calculation of the cost ratio, but markdowns do not. It has long been customary in using the retail inventory method to add additional markups but to ignore markdowns in computing the percentage relation between goods for sale at cost and at retail. The justification for this was and is that a more conservative figure for the ending inventory results, a figure that approaches "cost or replacement, the lower." A further discussion of this phase of the retail inventory method is reserved for a more advanced text.

Gross profit method

Often retail price information about beginning inventory, purchases, and markups is not kept. In such cases the retail inventory method cannot be used. However, if a company knows its normal gross profit margin; has information at cost in regard to its beginning inventory, net purchases, and freight-in; and knows the amount of its sales and sales returns, the company can estimate its ending inventory by the gross profit method.

For example, on March 27, the inventory of a company was destroyed by a fire. The company's average gross profit rate during the past five years has been 30% of net sales, and on the date of the fire the company's accounts showed the following balances:

Sales	$31,500
Sales returns	1,500
Inventory, January 1, 19–	12,000
Net purchases	20,000
Freight-in	500

Since the March 27 inventory was totally destroyed by fire, it was necessary for insurance purposes to estimate the inventory by the gross profit method as shown in Illustration 10–5.

To understand Illustration 10–5, recall that in a normal situation an ending inventory is subtracted from goods for sale to determine cost of goods sold. Then observe in Illustration 10–5 that the opposite subtraction is made. In Illustration 10–5 estimated cost of goods sold is subtracted from goods for sale to arrive at the ending inventory.

In addition to its use in insurance cases, as in this illustration, the gross profit method is also commonly used by accountants in checking on the probable accuracy of a physical inventory taken and priced in the normal way.

Goods available for sale:		
Inventory, January 1, 19—		$12,000
Net purchases..	$20,000	
Freight-in	500	20,500
Goods available for sale..		$32,500
Less estimated cost of goods sold:		
Sales	$31,500	
Sales returns	1,500	
Net sales...	$30,000	
Less estimated gross profit (30% of $30,000).............	9,000	
Estimated cost of goods sold		21,000
Estimated March 27 inventory		$11,500

Illustration 10–5

Questions for class discussion

1. Why may it be said that ending inventory and cost of goods sold are opposite sides of the same coin?
2. Give the meanings of the following when applied to inventory:
   - *a.* First-in, first-out.
   - *b.* Fifo.
   - *c.* Last-in, first-out.
   - *d.* Lifo.
   - *e.* Cost.
   - *f.* Replacement.
   - *g.* Cost or replacement, the lower.
   - *h.* Perpetual inventory.
   - *i.* Physical inventory.
   - *j.* Book inventory.
3. If prices are rising, will the "Lifo" or the "Fifo" method of inventory valuation result in the higher gross profit?
4. May a company change its inventory pricing method at will?
5. Why do accountants require consistency in the application of accounting methods?
6. What are the elements of an inventory cost?
7. Why are incidental costs commonly ignored in pricing an inventory?
8. What is meant when it is said that inventory errors "correct themselves"?
9. If inventory errors "correct themselves," why be concerned when such errors are made?
10. What is a "regular markup"? A "markdown"?

Class exercises

Exercise 10–1

A company began a year and purchased Article A as follows:

Jan.	1	Beginning inventory..................	100 units @ 53¢ =	$ 53
Jan.	5	Purchased.............................	300 units @ 51¢ =	153
May 21		Purchased.............................	200 units @ 55¢ =	110
Oct.	3	Purchased.............................	200 units @ 56¢ =	112
Dec.	7	Purchased.............................	200 units @ 61¢ =	122
		Total.............................. 1,000		$550

Required:

Under the assumption the ending inventory of Article A consisted of 100 units from each of the last three purchases, a total of 300 units, determine the share of the cost of the units for sale that should be assigned to the ending inventory and the share that should be assigned to goods sold under each of the following additional assumptions: *(a)* costs are assigned on the basis of specific invoice prices, *(b)* costs are assigned on a weighted average cost basis, *(c)* costs are assigned on the basis of Fifo, and *(d)* costs are assigned on the basis of Lifo.

Exercise 10-2

A company had $60,000 in sales during each of 197A, 197B, and 197C. It purchased merchandise costing $40,000 in each of the years and in addition maintained a $15,000 inventory from the beginning to the end of the three-year period. However, at the end of 197A it made an error that caused its December 31, 197A, inventory to appear on its income statement of that year at $17,000 rather than at the correct $15,000 amount. The error was not discovered.

Required:
1. State the actual amount of the company's gross profit in each of the years.
2. Prepare a comparative income statement like the one illustrated in this chapter, showing the effect of this error on the company's cost of goods sold and gross profit for each of the three years.

Exercise 10-3

A company sold $79,000 of merchandise at marked retail prices during an accounting period, and at the end of the period the following information was available from its accounting records:

	At Cost	At Retail
Beginning inventory	$10,500	$14,500
Net purchases	59,500	82,500
Additional markups		3,000
Markdowns		1,000

Required:
Use the retail method to estimate the company's ending inventory at cost.

Exercise 10-4

Assume that in addition to estimating its ending inventory by the retail method, the company of Exercise 10-3 also took a physical inventory at the marked selling prices of the inventory items. Assume further that the total of this physical inventory at marked selling prices was $19,600. Then *(a)* determine the dollar amount of this inventory at cost and *(b)* determine the company's inventory shrinkage from breakage, theft, or other cause at retail and at cost.

Exercise 10-5

A company that has averaged 30% gross profit on sales during the past five years had $100,000 of sales during the first half of this year. Use the gross profit method to prepare a calculation showing the estimated amount of the company's inventory at the end of the six months under the assumption it began the period with a $17,000 inventory, purchased $67,000 of merchandise, and paid $4,000 of freight on the purchases made during the period.

Problems   **Problem 10–1**

Mesa Company sold 880 units of its Product Z last year at $50 per unit, and it began the year and purchased the product as follows:

January 1, inventory......................... 100 units at $28 per unit
Purchases:
    February 12............................... 100 units at $30 per unit
    April 30.................................... 400 units at $32 per unit
    August 3 .... 300 units at $33 per unit
    December 15 .... 100 units at $35 per unit

Required:
Under the assumption the company incurred selling and administrative expenses of $10 per unit in marketing the 880 units of product, prepare three separate income statements for the company. In the first show last year's results with the ending periodic inventory priced on a Fifo basis, in the second use Lifo, and in the third use a weighted average cost basis in pricing the ending inventory.

Problem 10–2

A concern began an accounting period with 200 units of a product that cost $40 each, and it made successive purchases of the product as follows:

Jan. 10   500 units @ $50 each
Apr. 27   600 units @ $55 each
Aug. 22   300 units @ $60 each
Oct. 15   400 units @ $55 each

Required:
1. Prepare a calculation showing the number and total cost of the units for sale during the period.
2. Under the assumption the company had 500 units of the product in its December 31 end of the period periodic inventory, prepare calculations to show the portions of the total cost of the units for sale during the period that should be assigned to the ending inventory and to the units sold *(a)* first on a Fifo basis, *(b)* then on a Lifo basis, and *(c)* finally on a weighted average cost basis.

Problem 10–3

A company's inventory records for one of its products showed the following transactions:

Jan. 1 Beginning inventory: 15 units costing $35 each.
     10 Purchased 10 units at $40 each.
     16 Sold five units.
     18 Sold eight units.
     20 Purchased 10 units at $45 each.
     25 Sold 14 units.

Required:

1. Assume the company keeps its records on a Fifo basis and enter the transactions on a perpetual inventory record card. Use two or more lines to show units on hand at each price or units sold when units costing different amounts are on hand or sold.
2. Assume the company keeps its records on a Lifo basis and record the transactions on a second record card.
3. Assume the sale of January 25 was on credit to Ted Hall for $800 and prepare an entry in general journal form to record the sale and cost of goods sold on a Fifo basis.

Problem 10–4

A store has the following information from its accounting records and from a year-end physical inventory at marked selling prices:

	At Cost	At Retail
January 1 beginning inventory	$ 11,960	$ 15,220
Purchases	81,728	116,320
Purchases returns	1,820	2,600
Additional markups		2,300
Markdowns		840
Sales		114,150
Sales returns		1,500
December 31 physical inventory		17,300

The store reduces its year-end physical inventory taken at marked selling prices to a cost basis by an application of the retail inventory method. However, the store also always estimates its year-end inventory by the retail method and by a comparison determines the amount of inventory shortage, if any.

Required:

1. Prepare a calculation to estimate the dollar amount of the store's year-end inventory.
2. Use the store's cost ratio to reduce the dollar amount of its year-end physical inventory to a cost basis.
3. Prepare a calculation showing the amount of inventory shortage at cost and at retail.

Problem 10–5

Valley Sales Company sells candy and cigarettes to retailers; and during April of the current year the manager felt the inventory in the company's warehouse looked unusually low; consequently, on April 15 a surprise physical inventory was taken. It showed $17,110 of merchandise in the warehouse. Further investigation revealed that a new nightwatchman, who had been hired earlier in the year, had been systematically looting the warehouse. Fortunately the company bonds all its employees, so there would be no loss to the company; however, to collect from the bonding company it was necessary to establish the amount stolen. The following information was available:

1. Merchandise inventory on January 1, $33,150.
2. Purchases, January 1 through April 15, $92,215.
3. Purchases returns for the same period, $410.
4. Freight on purchase for the period, $1,285.
5. Sales from January 1 through April 15, $138,475.
6. Sales returns for the same period, $475.
7. Average gross profit margin for the past three years, 25%.

Required:
Prepare a statement showing the estimated amount of inventory that should have been in the warehouse on April 15 and the estimated amount of goods stolen.

Alternate problems

Problem 10–1A

Zest Company began last year and purchased Product X as follows:

January 1 inventory....................... 1,000 units @ $6.10 per unit
Purchases:
    February 5 .... 2,000 units @ $6.00 per unit
    June 3...................................... 3,000 units @ $6.30 per unit
    September 14........................... 3,000 units @ $6.40 per unit
    December 3 .... 1,000 units @ $6.60 per unit

Required:
Under the assumption the company incurred $20,000 of selling and administrative expenses last year in selling 8,500 units of the product at $10 per unit, prepare three separate income statements for the company. In the first use a periodic ending inventory based on Fifo, in the second an ending inventory based on Lifo, and in the third use a weighted average cost basis for the ending inventory.

Problem 10–2A

A company began an accounting period and made successive purchases of one of its products as follows:

Jan.   1 Beginning inventory....................... 200 units @ $75 per unit
Feb. 12 Purchased.................................... 300 units @ $90 per unit
Apr. 21 Purchased.................................... 400 units @ $100 per unit
June 14 Purchased.................................... 400 units @ $95 per unit
Aug. 30 Purchased.................................... 400 units @ $95 per unit
Nov. 27 Purchased.................................... 300 units @ $105 per unit

Required:
1. Prepare a calculation to show the number and total cost of the units for sale during the period.

2. Under the assumption the company had 400 units of the product in its end of the year inventory, prepare calculations to show the portions of the total cost of the units for sale during the period that should be assigned to the ending inventory and to the units sold *(a)* first on a Fifo basis, *(b)* then on a Lifo basis, and *(c)* finally on a weighted average cost basis.

Problem 10–3A

A company that keeps perpetual inventory records completed the following transactions involving one of its products:

Dec. 1 Beginning inventory: 12 units costing $6.25 each.
3 Received 10 units costing $6.50 each.
8 Sold five units.
12 Sold eight units.
18 Received 10 units costing $7 each.
22 Sold six units.
30 Sold eight units.

Required:
1. Under the assumption the company keeps its records on a first-in, first-out basis, record the transactions on a perpetual inventory record card. Use two or more lines to show units on hand at each price or units sold when units costing different amounts are on hand or sold.
2. Record the transactions on a second card under the assumption the company keeps its records on a last-in, first-out basis.
3. Under the assumption the December 30 sale was on credit to Dale West for $96, prepare a general journal entry to record the sale and the cost of the goods sold on a last-in, first-out basis.

Problem 10–4A

Tackle Shop takes a year-end physical inventory at marked selling prices and reduces the total to a cost basis for year-end statement purposes. It also uses the retail method to estimate the dollar amount of inventory it should have at the end of a year, and by comparison determines any inventory shortages due to shoplifting or other cause. At the end of the current year the following information was available to make the calculations:

	At Cost	At Retail
Sales...		$220,960
Sales returns		1,745
January 1 inventory...	$ 21,630	32,950
Purchases	146,400	219,735
Purchases returns...	980	1,470
Additional markups		5,785
Markdowns..		1,285
December 31 year-end physical inventory....................		35,800

Required:
1. Prepare a calculation to estimate the dollar amount of the store's year-end inventory, using the retail method.

2. Use the store's cost ratio to reduce the dollar amount of its year-end physical inventory to a cost basis.
3. Prepare a calculation showing the amount of inventory shortage at cost and at retail.

Problem 10–5A

On May 20 of the current year Dockside Store burned and everything excepting the accounting records, which were kept in a fireproof vault, was destroyed. The store's owner has asked you to prepare an estimate of the dollar amount of inventory in the store on the night of the fire, so he can file an insurance claim. The following information is available:

1. The store's accounts were closed on the previous December 31.
2. The store has earned an average 32% gross profit on sales for a number of years.
3. After all posting was completed, the store's account showed these May 20 balances:

Merchandise inventory (January 1 balance)........................	$ 42,850
Sales	188,950
Sales returns...	2,450
Purchases	123,900
Purchases returns..	1,250
Freight-in...	2,730

Required:
Prepare an estimate of the store's inventory at the time of the fire.

Decision problem 10–1, Kenton Company   The following preliminary income statement was prepared for the use of Kenton Company's management before the concern's accounts were closed for the year:

KENTON COMPANY
Income Statement for Year Ended December 31, 19—

Sales..			$274,550
Cost of goods sold:			
Merchandise inventory, January 1, 19—		$ 22,350	
Cost of goods purchased		184,600	
Goods available for sale...		$206,950	
Merchandise inventory, December 31, 19—		23,500	
Cost of goods sold			183,450
Gross profit on sales			$ 91,100
Operating expenses			62,000
Net Income			$ 29,100

There were no returns and allowances, but the following errors were discovered by the public accounting firm engaged to conduct the annual audit:

1. A $500 purchase invoice, dated December 27, was received on December 31 and recorded. The goods were shipped on the invoice date. Kenton Company was responsible for the freight charges which it had paid and recorded under a December 31 date. (Since both the invoice and the freight charges were recorded, their amounts are included in cost of goods purchased as listed in the preliminary income statement.) The goods were not included in the inventory, since they had not arrived on the inventory date.

2. A $350 purchase of merchandise was received on December 31 and included in the inventory. The invoice arrived on January 2, but had not been recorded. The seller was responsible for the freight charges.

3. A $750 purchase invoice, dated December 28, did not arrive until January 2 and had not been recorded. Kenton Company was responsible for and had paid and recorded the freight charges on the shipment of the invoice when it arrived on January 2. The goods were not included in the inventory, since they were in transit on the inventory date.

4. A sales invoice for $1,350, dated December 31, had been recorded. The terms of the sale required delivery of the goods to the buyer. The goods cost $900, had been set aside in the warehouse on December 31, and were excluded from the inventory, but had not been shipped.

5. A sales invoice for $1,200, dated December 31, had not been recorded. The merchandise was shipped on December 31 under terms requiring Kenton Company to deliver the goods to the buyer. Kenton Company had prepaid the freight charges on the shipment but had not recorded the payment. The goods cost $850, were excluded from the inventory, and were delivered to the buyer on January 2.

6. A $600 item of office equipment, received on December 31, was erroneously recorded as a purchase of merchandise and included in the inventory.

7. There was an error in totaling an inventory sheet, which caused a $200 understatement of the inventory total as given on the preliminary income statement.

Tell which of the invoice and error amounts should be included and which should be excluded from sales, purchases, and ending inventory. Tell how you would correct each error. Also, prepare a corrected income statement for the concern.

Decision problem 10–2, Fashion Bootery   Fashion Bootery suffered extensive damage from water and smoke and a small amount of fire damage on the night of October 25. The store carried adequate insurance, and next morning the insurance company's claims agent arrived to inspect the damage. After completing his survey, the agent agreed with Ned Ball, the store's owner, that the inventory could be sold to a company specializing in fire sales for about one fifth of its cost. The agent offered Mr. Ball $20,000 in full settlement for the damage to the inventory. He suggested that Mr. Ball accept the offer and said he had authority to deliver at once a cheque for the amount of the damage. He pointed out that a prompt settlement would provide funds to replace the inventory in time for the store to participate in the Christmas shopping season.

Mr. Ball felt the loss might exceed $20,000 but he recognized that a time-consuming physical count and inspection of each item in the inventory would be necessary to establish the loss more precisely; and he was reluctant to take the time for the inventory, since he was anxious to get back into business before the Christmas rush, the season making the largest contribution to his annual profit. Yet he was also unwilling to take a substantial loss on the insurance settlement; so he asked for and received a 24-hour period in which to consider the insurance company offer, and he immediately went to his records for the following information:

		At Cost	At Retail
a.	January 1 inventory	$ 23,480	$ 37,100
	Purchases, January 1 through October 25	181,900	288,700
	Net sales, January 1 through October 25		282,200

b. On March 1 the remaining inventory of winter footwear was marked down from $12,000 to $9,600, and placed on sale in the annual end-of-the-winter-season sale. Three fourths of the shoes were sold; the markdown on the remainder was canceled, and the shoes were returned to their regular retail price. (A markdown cancellation is subtracted from a markdown, and a markup cancellation is subtracted from a markup.)

c. In June a special line of imported Italian shoes proved popular, and 60 high-styled pairs were marked up from their normal $25 retail price to $30 per pair. Forty pairs were sold at this higher price, and on August 1 the markup on the remaining 20 pairs was canceled and they were returned to their regular $25 per pair price.

d. Between January 1 and October 25 markdowns totaling $1,500 were taken on several odd lots of shoes.

Recommend whether or not you think Mr. Ball should accept the insurance company's offer. Back your recommendation with figures.

Decision problem 10–3, Discount Furniture Centre

Discount Furniture Centre, a retail furniture store, has been in business for five years, during which it has earned a 35% average annual gross profit on sales. However, night before last, on May 29, it suffered a disastrous fire that destroyed its entire inventory; and Jed Adams, the store's owner, has filed a $56,000 inventory loss claim with the store's insurance company. When asked on what he based his claim, he replied that during the day before the fire he had marked every item in the store down 20% in preparation for the annual summer clearance sale, and during the marking-down process he had also taken an inventory of the merchandise in the store. Furthermore, he said, "It's a big loss, but every cloud has a silver lining, because I am giving you fellows (the insurance company) the benefit of the 20% markdown in filing this claim."

When it was explained to Mr. Adams that he had to back his loss claim with more than his word as to the amount of the loss, he produced the following information from his pre-sale inventory and his accounting records, which fortunately were in a fireproof vault and were not destroyed in the fire.

1. The store's accounts were closed on December 31, of last year.
2. After all posting was completed, the accounts showed these May 29 balances:

Sales	$189,860
Sales returns	4,760
Purchases	119,800
Purchases returns	1,450
Freight-in	3,140
Merchandise inventory (January 1, balance)	44,370

3. Mr. Adams's pre-fire inventory totaled $70,000 at pre-markdown prices.

From the information given, present figures to show the amount of loss suffered by Mr. Adams. Also, show how he arrived at the amount of his loss claim. Can his pre-sale inventory be used to substantiate the amount of his actual loss? If so, use the pre-sale inventory figure to substantiate the actual loss amount.

Analytical and review problems

Problem 10–1 A&R

The Lifo versus Fifo controversy has spanned a number of decades. Proponents of each of the inventory procedures attribute certain merits to each.

Required:
Identify the inventory procedure to which the following merits are attributed by writing either "Lifo" or "Fifo" opposite each of the letters (a) to (n).

Inventory procedure
a. ——————Matches actual physical flow of goods.
b. ——————Matches old costs with new prices.
c. ——————Costs inventory at approximate replacement cost.
d. ——————Matches new cost with new prices.
e. ——————Emphasizes balance sheet.
f. ——————Emphasizes income statement.
g. ——————Opens door for "profit manipulation."
h. ——————Understates the current ratio in a period by inflation.
i. ——————Overstates inventory turnover in a period of inflation.
j. ——————Gives higher profits in a period of inflation.
k. ——————Matches current costs with current revenues.
l. ——————More accurately reflects net income available to owners.
m. ——————Gives lower profits in a period of deflation.
n. ——————Results in a procession of costs in the same order as incurred.
(CGA adapted)

Problem 10–2 A&R

The following information is taken from the records of Nitram Company for four consecutive operating periods:

	Periods			
	1	*2*	*3*	*4*
Beginning inventory	$12,000	$18,000	$13,000	$16,000
Ending inventory	18,000	13,000	16,000	7,000
Net income................................	10,000	12,000	14,000	18,000

Assuming that the company made the errors below:

Period		Error in ending inventory	
1	Overstated	$3,000
2	Understated	2,000
3	Overstated	4,000

Required:
1. Compute the revised net income for each of the four periods.
2. Assuming that the company's ending inventory for period 4 is correct, how would these errors affect the total net income for the four periods combined? Explain.

Problem 10–3 A&R

The records of Philips Company as of December 31, 1975 show the following:

	Net Purchases	Net Income	Accounts Payable	Inventory
Balance per company's books...	$166,000	$ 14,500	$ 19,500	$ 39,000
(a)				
(b)				
(c)	_____	_____	_____	_____
Correct balances	=======	=======	=======	=======

The accountant of Philips Company discovers in the first week of January, 1974 that the following errors were made by his staff.
a. Goods costing $1,000 were in transit (FOB shipping point) and were not included in the ending inventory. The invoice had been received and the purchase recorded.
b. Damaged goods (cost $3,000) which were being held for return to the supplier were included in inventory. The goods had been recorded as a purchase and the entry for the return of these goods had also been made.
c. Inventory items costing $1,000 were incorrectly excluded from the final inventory. These goods had not been recorded as a purchase and had not been paid for by the company.

Required:
Using the format provided above, show the correct amount for net purchases, net income, accounts payable, and inventory for Philips Company as at December 31, 1975.

11

Plant
and
equipment

■ Assets that are used in the production or sale of other assets or services and that have a useful life longer than one accounting period are called *plant and equipment* or *fixed assets*. The phrase "fixed assets" has been used in accounting literature for many years in referring to items of plant and equipment, and it was once commonly used as a balance sheet caption. However, as a caption it is rapidly disappearing from published balance sheets, being replaced by the more descriptive "plant and equipment" or the more complete "property, plant, and equipment" or by "land, buildings, and equipment."

Its use in the production or sale of other assets or services is the characteristic that distinguishes a plant asset from an item of merchandise or an investment. An office machine or a factory machine held for sale by a dealer is merchandise to the dealer. Likewise, land purchased and held for future expansion but presently unused is classified as a long-term investment. Neither is a plant asset until put to use in the production or sale of other assets or services. However, standby equipment for use in case of a breakdown or for use during peak periods of production is a plant asset. Also, when equipment is removed from service and held for sale, it ceases to be a plant asset.

A productive or service life longer than one accounting period distinguishes an item of plant and equipment from an item of supplies.

An item of supplies may be consumed in a single accounting period; and if consumed, its cost is charged to the period of consumption. The productive life of a plant asset, on the other hand, is longer than one period. It contributes to production for several periods; and if revenues and expenses are matched, its cost must be allocated to these periods on some fair basis.

Cost of plant and equipment

■ The cost of an item of plant and equipment includes all normal and reasonable expenditures necessary to get the asset in place and ready to use. For example, the cost of a factory machine includes its invoice price, less any discount for cash, plus freight, unpacking, and assembling costs. Cost also includes any special concrete base or foundation, electrical or power connections, and adjustments needed to place the machine in operation. In short, the cost of a plant asset includes all normal, necessary, and reasonable costs incurred in getting the asset ready to produce.

A cost must be normal and reasonable as well as necessary if it is to be properly included in the cost of a plant asset. For example, if a machine is damaged by being dropped in unpacking, repairs should not be added to its cost but should be charged to an expense account. Likewise, a fine paid for moving a heavy machine on city streets without proper permits is not part of the cost of the machine; although if secured, the cost of the permits would be.

After being purchased but before being put to use, a plant asset must sometimes be repaired, reconditioned, or remodeled before it meets the needs of the purchaser. In such a case the repairing, remodeling, or reconditioning expenditures are part of its cost and should be charged to the asset account. Furthermore, depreciation charges should not begin until the asset is ready for use.

When a plant asset is constructed or manufactured by a concern for its own use, cost includes material and labour costs plus a reasonable amount of overhead or indirect expenses such as heat, lights, power, and depreciation on the machinery used in constructing or manufacturing the asset. Cost also includes architectural and design fees, building permits, and insurance during construction. Insurance during construction is included because it is necessary to get the asset ready to produce or be used. Needless to say, insurance on the same asset after it has been placed in production is an expense.

When land is purchased for a plant or building site, its cost includes the amount paid for the land plus real estate commissions, escrow and legal fees, fees for examining and insuring the title, and any accrued property taxes paid by the purchaser. Cost also includes expenditures for surveying, clearing, grading, draining, and landscaping. All are part of the cost of the land. Furthermore, any assessments incurred at the time of purchase or later for such things as the installation of streets, sewers, and sidewalks should be debited to the Land account since they add a more or less permanent value to the land.

Land purchased as a building site sometimes has an old building that must be removed. In such cases the entire purchase price, including the amount paid for the to-be-removed building, should be charged to the Land account. Also, the cost of removing the old building, less any amounts recovered through the sale of salvaged materials, should be charged to this account.

Land used as a building site is assumed to have an unlimited life and is therefore not subject to depreciation. However, buildings and land improvements such as driveways, parking lots, fences, and lighting systems are subject to depreciation. Consequently, land, building, and land improvement costs should not be recorded in the same account. At least two accounts should be used, one for land and a second for buildings and land improvements; but three accounts, one for land, a second for buildings, and a third for land improvements, would be better.

Often land, buildings, and equipment are purchased together for one lump sum. When this occurs, the purchase price must be apportioned among the assets on some fair basis, since some of the assets depreciate and some do not. A fair basis may be tax-assessed values or appraised values. For example, assume that land independently appraised at $30,-000 and a building appraised at $70,000 are purchased together for $90,000. The cost may be apportioned on the basis of appraised values as follows:

	Appraised Value	Percent of Total	Apportioned Cost
Land	$ 30,000	30%	$27,000
Building	70,000	70%	63,000
Totals	$100,000	100%	$90,000

Nature of depreciation ■ When a plant asset is purchased, in effect a quantity of usefulness that will contribute to production throughout the life of the asset is acquired. However, since the life of any plant asset (other than land) is limited, this quantity of usefulness is also limited and will in effect be consumed by the end of the asset's useful life. Consequently, depreciation, as the term is used in accounting, is nothing more than the expiration of a plant asset's quantity of usefulness, and the recording of depreciation is a process of allocating and charging the cost of this usefulness to the accounting periods that benefit from the asset's use.

For example, when a company purchases an automobile to be used by one of its salesmen, it in effect purchases a quantity of usefulness, a quantity of transportation for the salesman. The cost of this quantity of usefulness is the cost of the car less whatever will be received for it when sold or traded in at the end of its useful life. And, recording depreciation on the car is a process of allocating the cost of this usefulness to the accounting periods that benefit from the car's use. Note that it is not the recording of physical deterioration nor recording the decline in the car's market value.

The foregoing is in line with the pronouncements of the Canadian

Institute of Chartered Accountants which has defined depreciation as follows:

> An accounting procedure in which the cost or other recorded value of a fixed asset less estimated salvage (if any) is distributed over its estimated useful life in a systematic and rational manner. It is a process of allocation, not valuation.[1]

Productive life of a plant asset

■ The productive life of a plant asset is the period of time it will be used in producing or selling other assets or services. This may not be the same as the asset's potential life. For example, typewriters have a potential 10- or 12-year life; however, if a company finds from a production-cost view that it is wise to trade its old typewriters in on new ones every three years, in this company typewriters have a three-year productive or service life. Furthermore, in this business the cost of new typewriters less their trade-in value, in other words the cost of their quantity of usefulness should be charged to depreciation expense over this three-year period.

At the time of purchase a plant asset's productive life must be predicted so that its depreciation may be allocated to the several periods in which it will be used. Predicting or estimating service life is sometimes difficult because several factors are often involved. Wear and tear and the action of the elements determine the useful life of some assets. However, two additional factors, *inadequacy* and *obsolescence,* often need be considered. When a business acquires plant assets, it should acquire assets of a size and capacity to take care of its foreseeable needs. However, a business often grows more rapidly than anticipated; and in such cases plant assets may become too small for the productive demands of the business long before they wear out. When this happens, inadequacy is said to have taken place. Inadequacy cannot easily be predicted. Obsolescence, like inadequacy, is also difficult to foretell because the exact occurrence of new inventions and improvements normally cannot be predicted; yet new inventions and improvements often cause an asset to become obsolete and make it wise to discard the obsolete asset long before it wears out.

A company that has previously used a particular type of asset may estimate the service life of a new asset of like kind from past experience. A company without previous experience with a particular asset must depend upon the experience of others or upon engineering studies and judgment. Many businessmen refer to this information in estimating the life of a new asset.

---

[1] *Terminology for Accountants, Revised Edition* (Toronto: The Canadian Institute of Chartered Accountants, 1962), p. 25.

■ When a plant asset has a salvage value, the cost of its quantity of usefulness is the asset's cost minus its salvage value. The salvage value of a plant asset is the portion of its cost that is recovered at the end of its productive life. Some assets such as typewriters, trucks, and automobiles are traded in on similar new assets at the end of their service lives. The salvage values of such assets are their trade-in values. Other assets may have no trade-in value and little or no salvage value. For example, at the end of its service life, some machinery can be sold only as scrap metal.

When the disposal of a plant asset involves certain costs, as in the wrecking of a building, the salvage value is the net amount realized from the sale of the asset. The net amount realized is the amount received for the asset less its disposal cost.

Obviously, when a plant asset is purchased, its exact salvage value is difficult to estimate. Yet, salvage value must be estimated so that depreciation can be estimated and recorded.

■ Many methods of allocating a plant asset's total depreciation to the several accounting periods in its service life have been suggested and are used. Four of the more common are the *straight-line method*, the *units-of-production method*, the *declining-balance method*, and the *sum-of-the-years'-digits method*.

Straight-line method

When the straight-line method is used, the cost of the depreciating asset minus its estimated salvage value is divided by the estimated number of accounting periods in the asset's productive life. The result is the estimated amount the asset depreciates each period. For example, if a machine costs $550, has an estimated service life of five years, and an estimated $50 salvage value, its depreciation per year by the straight-line method is $100 and is calculated as follows:

$$\frac{\text{Cost} - \text{Salvage}}{\text{Service Life in Years}} = \frac{\$550 - \$50}{5} = \$100$$

Note that the straight-line method allocates an equal share of an asset's total depreciation to each accounting period in its life.

Units-of-production method

The primary purpose of recording depreciation is to charge each accounting period in which an asset is used with a fair share of its depreciation. The straight-line method charges an equal share to each period; and when plant assets are used about the same amount in each accounting period, this method rather fairly allocates total depreciation. However, in some lines of business the use of certain plant assets varies greatly from accounting period to accounting period. For example, a contractor may use a particular piece of construction equipment for a month and then not use it again for many months. For such an asset, since use and contribution to revenue may not be uniform from period to period, the units-of-production method often more fairly allocates depreciation than does the straight-line method.

When the units-of-production method is used in allocating depreciation, the cost of an asset's quantity of usefulness is divided by the estimated units of product it will produce during its entire service life. This division gives depreciation per unit of product. Then the amount the asset depreciates in any one accounting period is determined by multiplying the units of product produced in that period by depreciation per unit. Units of product may be expressed as units of product or in any other unit of measure such as hours of use or miles driven. For example, a delivery truck costing $4,800 is estimated to have an $800 salvage value. If it is also estimated that during the truck's service life it will be driven 50,000 miles, the depreciation per mile, or the depreciation per unit of product, is $0.08. This is calculated as follows:

$$\frac{\text{Cost } - \text{ Salvage Value}}{\substack{\text{Estimated Units of} \\ \text{Production}}} = \substack{\text{Depreciation per} \\ \text{Unit of Product}}$$

or

$$\frac{\$4,800 \ - \ \$800}{50,000 \text{ Miles}} = \$0.08 \text{ per Mile}$$

If these estimates are correct and the truck is driven 20,000 miles during its first year, depreciation for the first year is $1,600. This is 20,000 miles at $0.08 per mile. If the truck is driven 15,000 miles in the second year, depreciation for the second year is 15,000 times $0.08, or $1,200.

Declining-balance method

The declining-balance method is one of the depreciation methods which results in higher depreciation charges during the early years of a plant asset's life. Under the declining-balance method, depreciation of up to twice the straight-line rate, without considering salvage value, may be applied each year to the declining book value of a new plant asset having an estimated life of three years or more. If this method is followed and twice the straight-line rate is used, the amount charged each year as depreciation expense on a plant asset is determined by (1) calculating a straight-line depreciation rate for the asset without considering the asset's salvage value; (2) doubling this rate; and then (3) at the end of each year in the asset's life, applying this doubled rate to the asset's remaining book value. (The book value of a plant asset is its cost less accumulated depreciation; it is the value shown for the asset on the books.)

If this method is used to charge depreciation on a $10,000 new asset that has an estimated five-year life and no salvage value, these steps are followed: (Step 1) A straight-line depreciation rate is calculated by dividing 100% by five (years) to determine the straight-line annual depreciation rate of 20%. Next (Step 2) this rate is doubled; and then (Step 3) annual depreciation charges are calculated as in the following table:

Year	Annual Depreciation Calculation	Annual Depreciation Expense	Remaining Book Value
1st year	40% of $10,000	$4,000.00	$6,000.00
2d year	40% of 6,000	2,400.00	3,600.00
3d year	40% of 3,600	1,440.00	2,160.00
4th year	40% of 2,160	864.00	1,296.00
5th year	40% of 1,296	518.40	777.60

Under the declining-balance method the book value of a plant asset never reaches zero; consequently, when the asset is sold, exchanged, or scrapped, any remaining book value is used in determining the gain or loss on disposal.

In passing it should be observed that if an asset has a salvage value, the asset may not be depreciated beyond its salvage value. For example, if instead of no salvage value the foregoing $10,000 asset has an estimated $1,000 salvage value, depreciation for its fifth year is limited to $296, the amount required to reduce the asset's book value to its salvage value.

Declining-balance depreciation results in what is called *accelerated depreciation* or higher depreciation charges in the early years of a plant asset's life. The sum-of-the-years'-digits method has a like result.

Sum-of-the-years'-digits method

Under the sum-of-the-years'-digits method the years in an asset's service life are added and their sum becomes the denominator of a series of fractions used in allocating total depreciation to the periods in the asset's service life. The numerators of the fractions are the years in the asset's life in their reverse order.

For example, if the sum-of-the-years'-digits method is used in allocating depreciation on a machine costing $7,000, having an estimated five-year life and an estimated $1,000 salvage value, the sum of the years' digits in the asset's life is calculated:

$$1 + 2 + 3 + 4 + 5 = 15$$

and then annual depreciation charges are calculated as follows:

Year	Annual Depreciation Calculation	Annual Depreciation Expense
1st year	5/15 of $6,000	$2,000
2d year	4/15 of 6,000	1,600
3d year	3/15 of 6,000	1,200
4th year	2/15 of 6,000	800
5th year	1/15 of 6,000	400
Total depreciation		$6,000

When either declining-balance or sum-of-the-years'-digits depreciation is used and accounting periods do not coincide with the years in an asset's life, additional calculations are necessary if depreciation is to be properly charged. For example, assume that the machine for which sum-of-the-years'-digits depreciation was calculated above is placed in use on April 1 and the annual accounting periods of the company owning the machine end on December 31. Under these assumptions the machine will be in use three fourths of a year during the first accounting period in its life; and as a result, this period should be charged with $1,500 depreciation ($2,000 × $\frac{3}{4}$ = $1,500). Likewise, the second accounting period should be charged with $1,700 depreciation [($\frac{1}{4}$ × $2,000) + ($\frac{3}{4}$ × $1,600) = $1,700], and like calculations should be used for the remaining periods in the asset's life.

The reducing charge methods (both the declining-balance and the sum-of-the-years'-digits method) are advocated by many accountants who claim that their use results in a more equitable "use charge" for long-lived plant assets than other methods. These accountants point out, for example, that as assets grow older, repairs and maintenance increase. Therefore, when smaller amounts of depreciation computed by a reducing charge method are added to increasing repair costs, a more equitable total expense charge to match against revenue results. Also, they point out that as an asset grows older, in some instances its ability to produce revenue is reduced. For example, rentals from an apartment building are normally higher in the earlier years of its life but will decline as the building becomes less attractive and less modern. Certainly in such cases, a more reasonable allocation of cost would provide heavier depreciation charges in the earlier years and lighter charges in the later years of the asset's life.

The foregoing are sound reasons for the use under applicable conditions of reducing charge or accelerated depreciation. However, a tax reason rather than sound accounting theory is probably more responsible for the increase in their popularity. The tax reason may be described as follows: Accelerated depreciation normally results in the greatest amounts of depreciation expense during the early years of an asset's use. This in turn means smaller taxable incomes and taxes; and in effect it also means the interest-free use for a period of time of the amounts that would otherwise be paid in income taxes under, for example, a straight-line method. Of course, these interest-free amounts must in effect be repaid in higher income taxes during later years of the asset's use.

■ Since 1949 the Income Tax Act permitted the use of the declining-balance method for tax purposes. Depreciable assets are grouped into classes and depreciation (described in the Act as capital cost allowance) may be taken at rates prescribed by the income tax legislation. A taxpayer may take the maximum depreciation allowed or any part for tax purposes in any fiscal year. The amount of depreciation taken for tax purposes does not depend in any way on the amount of depreciation shown in the books or on the financial statements. Thus a taxpayer may record depreciation on his books using the straight-line method and claim, for tax purposes, depreciation based on the declining-balance method.

■ Depreciation on the several classes of a company's plant assets is recorded at the end of each accounting period by means of adjusting entries. This was discussed in an earlier chapter and needs no further amplification here.

■ In presenting information about the plant assets of a business, the cost of such assets and their accumulated depreciation should be shown on the balance sheet by major classes, and that a general description of the depreciation method or methods used be given in a balance sheet footnote or other manner. For example, the plant assets of a merchandising concern may be shown as follows:

Plant Assets:	Cost	Accumulated Depreciation	Book Value
Store equipment	$ 12,400	$1,500	$10,900
Office equipment	3,600	450	3,150
Building	72,300	7,800	64,500
Land	15,000	....	15,000
Totals	$103,300	$9,750	$93,550

When plant assets are thus shown and the depreciation methods described, a much better understanding can be gained by a balance sheet reader than if only information as to undepreciated cost is given. For example, $50,000 of assets with $40,000 of accumulated depreciation are quite different from $10,000 of new assets. Yet the net undepreciated cost is the same in both cases. Likewise, the picture is different if the $40,000 of accumulated depreciation resulted from the application of an accelerated depreciation method than if straight-line depreciation was used.

Financial statement readers who have never studied accounting sometimes mistakenly think that the amounts shown on a balance sheet as accumulated depreciation represent funds accumulated to buy new plant assets when present assets wear out and must be discarded. However, an informed reader recognizes that accumulated depreciation represents that portion of an asset's cost that has been charged off to depreciation expense during its life. He also knows that accumulated depreciation accounts are contra accounts having credit balances that cannot be used to buy anything. Furthermore, he knows that if a concern has cash with which to buy assets, it is shown on the balance sheet as a current asset "Cash."

Balance sheet plant asset values ■ From the discussion thus far the student should recognize that the recording of depreciation is not primarily a valuing process, rather it is a process of allocating the costs of plant assets to the several accounting periods that benefit from their use. Furthermore, he should recognize that because the recording of depreciation is an allocating process rather than a valuing process, balance sheets show for plant assets unallocated costs or undepreciated costs rather than market values.

The fact that balance sheets show undepreciated costs rather than market values seems to disturb many beginning accounting students. It should not. When a balance sheet is prepared, normally the company for which it is prepared has no intention of selling its plant assets; consequently, the market values of these assets are of no great significance. The student should recognize that when a balance sheet is prepared, it is under the assumption the company for which it is prepared is a going concern that will continue in business long enough to recover the costs of its plant assets through the sale of its products.

The assumption that a company is a going concern that will continue in business long enough to recover its plant asset costs through the sale of its products is known in accounting as the *going-concern concept*. It is a concept the student or any balance sheet reader should bear in mind as he reads a balance sheet.

Recovering the cost of plant assets ■ A company that earns a profit or breaks even (neither earns a profit nor suffers a loss) eventually recovers the cost of its plant assets through the sale of its products. This is best explained with a condensed income statement like that of Illustration 11–1.

Even Steven Company
Income Statement for Year Ended December 31, 19–

Sales		$100,000
Cost of goods sold	$60,000	
Rent expense	10,000	
Salaries expense	25,000	
Depreciation expense	5,000	
Total		100,000
Net Income		$ 0

Illustration 11–1

Even Steven Company broke even during the year of the illustrated income statement; but in breaking even it also recovered $5,000 of the cost of its plant assets through the sale of its products. It recovered the $5,000 because of the $100,000 that flowed into the company from sales only $95,000 flowed out to pay for goods sold, rent, and salaries. No funds flowed out for depreciation expense; and as a result, the company recovered this $5,000 portion of the cost of its plant assets through the sale of its products. Furthermore, if the company remains in business for the life of its plant assets, either breaking even or earning a profit, it will recover their entire cost in this manner.

At this point students commonly ask, "Where is the recovered $5,000?" The answer is that the company may have the $5,000 in the bank. If it does, its bank balance increased $5,000 during the year. However, the funds may also have flowed out to increase merchandise inventory, to buy additional equipment, to pay off a debt, or they may have been withdrawn for personal use by the business owner. In short, the funds may still be in the bank or they may have been used for any purpose for which a business uses funds, and only an examination of its balance sheets as of the beginning and end of the year will show this.

Disposal of a plant asset

■ Sooner or later a plant asset wears out, becomes obsolete, or becomes inadequate; and when this occurs, the asset is discarded, sold, or traded in on a new asset. The entry to record the disposal will vary with the nature of the disposal; however, in all cases the asset's cost and its accumulated depreciation are removed from the accounts.

Discarding a plant asset

When an asset's accumulated depreciation is equal to its cost, the asset is said to be fully depreciated; and if a fully depreciated asset is discarded, the entry to record the disposal is:

Jan.	7	Accumulated Depreciation, Machinery..............	1,500.00	
		Machinery		1,500.00
		Discarded a fully depreciated machine.		

Although often discarded, sometimes a fully depreciated asset is kept in use. In such situations the asset's cost and accumulated depreciation should not be removed from the accounts, but should remain on the books until the asset is sold, traded, or discarded. Otherwise the accounts do not show its continued existence. However, no additional depreciation should be recorded, since the reason for recording depreciation is to charge an asset's cost to depreciation expense, and in no case can the expense exceed the asset's cost.

Sometimes an asset is discarded before being fully depreciated. For example, suppose an error was made in estimating the service life of a $1,000 machine and it becomes worthless and is discarded after having only $800 of depreciation recorded against it. In such a situation there is a loss and the entry to record the disposal is:

Jan.	10	Loss on Disposal of Machinery........................	200.00	
		Accumulated Depreciation, Machinery..............	800.00	
		Machinery		1,000.00
		Discarded a worthless machine.		

Selling a plant asset

When a plant asset is sold, it may be sold at book value or at a gain or loss. If the selling price exceeds the asset's book value, there is a gain; and if the price is less than book value, there is a loss. To illustrate the possibilities, assume that a machine which cost $5,000 and which had been depreciated $4,000 is sold. If the machine is sold for its $1,000 book value, the entry to record the sale is:

Jan.	4	Cash..	1,000.00	
		Accumulated Depreciation, Machinery.............	4,000.00	
		Machinery		5,000.00
		Sold a machine at book value.		

If the machine is sold at a price in excess of its book value, say, for $1,200, there is a $200 gain and the entry to record the sale is:

Jan.	4	Cash..	1,200.00	
		Accumulated Depreciation, Machinery.............	4,000.00	
		Machinery		5,000.00
		Gain on the Sale of Plant Assets................		200.00
		Sold a machine at a price in excess of book value.		

However, if the machine is sold for $750, there is a $250 loss and the entry to record the sale is:

Jan.	4	Cash..	750.00	
		Loss on the Sale of Plant Assets.....................	250.00	
		Accumulated Depreciation, Machinery.............	4,000.00	
		Machinery		5,000.00
		Sold a machine at a price below book value.		

Discarding a damaged plant asset

Occasionally, before the end of its service life, a plant asset is wrecked in an accident or destroyed by fire; and in such cases a loss normally occurs. For example, if an uninsured machine that cost $900 and has been depreciated $400 is totally destroyed in an accident such as a fire, the entry to record the loss is:

Jan.	3	Loss from Fire	500.00	
		Accumulated Depreciation, Machinery.............	400.00	
		Machinery		900.00
		To record the accidental destruction of machinery.		

If the loss is partially covered by insurance, the money received from the insurance company is debited to Cash; the loss is less; and the entry to record the smaller loss is:

Jan.	3	Cash...	350.00	
		Loss from Fire	150.00	
		Accumulated Depreciation, Machinery............	400.00	
		Machinery		900.00
		To record the destruction of machinery and the receipt of insurance compensation.		

**Deprecia-
tion for
partial
years** ■ In the illustrations thus far it has been assumed that assets were purchased and discarded at either the beginning or end of an accounting period. This seldom occurs. Businessmen normally buy assets when needed and sell or discard these assets when they are no longer usable or needed; and the purchases and sales are normally made without regard for time. Because of this, depreciation must often be calculated for partial years. For example, a truck costing $2,600 and having an estimated five-year service life and a $600 estimated salvage value is purchased on October 8, 1971. If the yearly accounting period ends on December 31, depreciation for three months must be recorded on this truck on that date. Three months are three twelfths of a year. Consequently, the three months' depreciation is calculated:

$$\frac{\$2,600 - \$600}{5} \times \frac{3}{12} = \$100$$

In this illustration, depreciation is calculated for a full three months, even though the asset was purchased on October 8. Depreciation is an estimate; therefore calculation to the nearest full month is usually considered sufficiently accurate. This means that depreciation is usually calculated for a full month on assets purchased before the 15th of the month. Likewise, depreciation for the month in which an asset is purchased is normally disregarded if the asset is purchased after the middle of the month.

The entry to record depreciation for three months on the truck purchased on October 8 is:

Dec.	31	Depreciation Expense, Delivery Trucks.............	100.00	
		Accumulated Depreciation, Delivery Trucks.		100.00
		To record depreciation for three months on the delivery truck.		

On December 31, 1972, and at the end of each of the following three years, a journal entry to record a full year's depreciation on this truck is made. The entry is:

Dec.	31	Depreciation Expense, Delivery Trucks.............	400.00	
		Accumulated Depreciation, Delivery Trucks.		400.00
		To record depreciation for one year on the delivery truck.		

After the December 31, 1975, depreciation entry is recorded, the accounts showing the history of this truck appear as follows:

Delivery Trucks			Accumulated Depreciation, Delivery Trucks	
Oct. 8, '71	2,600		Dec. 31, '71	100
			Dec. 31, '72	400
			Dec. 31, '73	400
			Dec. 31, '74	400
			Dec. 31, '75	400

If this truck is disposed of during 1976, two entries must be made to record the disposal. The first records 1976 depreciation to the date of disposal, and the second records the actual disposal. For example, assume that the truck is sold for $900 on June 24, 1976. To record the disposal, depreciation for six months (depreciation to the nearest full month) must first be recorded. The entry for this is:

June	24	Depreciation Expense, Delivery Trucks.............	200.00	
		Accumulated Depreciation, Delivery Trucks.		200.00
		To record depreciation for one-half year on the delivery truck.		

After making the entry to record depreciation to the date of sale, a second entry to record the actual sale is made. This entry is:

June	24	Cash..	900.00	
		Accumulated Depreciation, Delivery Trucks	1,900.00	
		Delivery Trucks		2,600.00
		Gain on the Sale of Plant Assets................		200.00
		To record the sale of a delivery truck.		

Plant asset records ■ Business concerns commonly divide their plant assets into functional groups and provide separate asset and accumulated depreciation accounts for each group. For example, a store will normally provide an Office Equipment account and an Accumulated Depreciation, Office Equipment account, as well as a Store Equipment account and an Accumulated Depreciation, Store Equipment account. In short, the store will normally have a separate plant asset account and a separate accumulated depreciation account for each functional group of assets it owns. Furthermore, all transactions affecting any one of the functional groups are recorded in the asset and the accumulated depreciation accounts of that group. For example, the purchase, depreciation, exchange, or sale of all office equipment is recorded in the one office equipment and its related accumulated depreciation account.

Some years ago the functional general ledger plant asset accounts and their related accumulated depreciation accounts were often the only plant asset records maintained by any but larger concerns. However, today because of income tax regulations any business that reports a deduction from income for depreciation or reports a gain or loss on a plant asset sale must be able to substantiate such items with detailed records. No specific kind of records is required, but normally each general ledger plant asset account and its related accumulated depreciation account become controlling accounts controlling detailed subsidiary records. For example, the Office Equipment account and the Accumulated Depreciation, Office Equipment account control a subsidiary ledger having a separate record for each individual item of office equipment. Likewise, the Store Equipment account and its related Accumulated Depreciation, Store Equipment account become controlling accounts controlling a subsidiary store equipment ledger. Often these subsidiary ledger records are kept on plant asset record cards.

To illustrate these plant asset records, assume that a concern's office equipment consists of just one desk and a chair. The general ledger record of these assets is maintained in the Office Equipment controlling account and the Accumulated Depreciation, Office Equipment controlling account. Since in this case there are only two assets, only two subsidiary record cards are needed. The general ledger and subsidiary ledger record of these assets appear as in Illustration 11–2 below and on the following page.

Office Equipment   ACCOUNT NO. 132

DATE	EXPLANATION	FO-LIO	DEBIT	CREDIT	BALANCE
1973 July 2	Desk and chair	G-1	185 00		185 00

Accumulated Depreciation, Office Equipment   ACCOUNT NO. 132A

DATE	EXPLANATION	FO-LIO	DEBIT	CREDIT	BALANCE
1973 Dec. 31		G-23		4 50	4 50
1974 Dec. 31		G-42		9 00	13 50
1975 Dec. 31		G-65		9 00	22 50

Illustration
11–2

Plant Asset
No. 132-1

SUBSIDIARY PLANT ASSET AND DEPRECIATION RECORD

Item _Office chair_   General Ledger
                                             Account _Office Equipment_
Description _Office chair_
                                             Purchased
Mfg. Serial No. _____   from _Office Equipment Co._
Where Located _Office_
Person Responsible for the Asset _Office Manager_
Estimated Life _12 years_ Estimated Salvage Value _$4.00_
Depreciation per Year _$3.00_ per Month _$0.25_

Date	Explanation	F	Asset Record			Depreciation Record		
			Dr.	Cr.	Bal.	Dr.	Cr.	Bal.
July 2, '73		G1	40.00		40.00			
Dec. 31, '73		G23					1.50	1.50
Dec. 31, '74		G42					3.00	4.50
Dec. 31, '75		G65					3.00	7.50

Final Disposition of the Asset _____

Illustration
11-2
Continued

Plant Asset
No. 132-2

SUBSIDIARY PLANT ASSET AND DEPRECIATION RECORD

                                             General Ledger
Item _Desk_   Account _Office Equipment_
Description _Office desk_
                                             Purchased
Mfg. Serial No. _____   from _Office Equipment Co._
Where Located _Office_
Person Responsible for the Asset _Office Manager_
Estimated Life _20 years_ Estimated Salvage Value _$25.00_
Depreciation per Year _$6.00_ per Month _$0.50_

Date	Explanation	F	Asset Record			Depreciation Record		
			Dr.	Cr.	Bal.	Dr.	Cr.	Bal.
July 2, '73		G1	145.00		145.00			
Dec. 31, '73		G23					3.00	3.00
Dec. 31, '74		G42					6.00	9.00
Dec. 31, '75		G65					6.00	15.00

Final Disposition of the Asset _____

Illustration
11-2
Concluded

Observe at the top of the cards the plant asset numbers assigned to these two items of office equipment. In each case the assigned number consists of the number of the Office Equipment account, 132, followed by the asset's number. These numbers are stenciled on or otherwise attached to the items of office equipment as a means of identification and to increase control over the items. The remaining information on the record cards is more or less self-evident. Note how the balance of the general ledger account, Office Equipment, is equal to the sum of the balances in the asset record section of the two subsidiary ledger cards. The general ledger account controls this section of the subsidiary ledger. Observe also how the Accumulated Depreciation, Office Equipment account controls the depreciation record section of the cards. The disposition section at the bottom of the card is used to record the final disposal of the asset. When the asset is discarded, sold, or exchanged, a notation telling of the final disposition is entered here. The card is then removed from the subsidiary ledger and filed for future reference.

Plant assets of low cost ■ Because individual plant asset records are expensive to keep, many concerns establish a minimum, say $25, and do not keep such records for assets costing less than the minimum. Rather, they charge the cost of such assets directly to an expense account at the time of purchase; and if about the same amount is expended for such assets each year, this is an acceptable procedure.

Questions for class discussion

1. What are the characteristics of an asset classified as a plant asset?
2. What is the balance sheet classification of land held for future expansion? Why is such land not classified as a plant asset?
3. What in general is included in the cost of a plant asset?
4. A company asked for bids from several machine shops for the construction of a special machine. The lowest bid was $12,500. The company decided to build the machine for itself and did so at a total cash outlay of $10,000. It then recorded the machine's construction with a debit to Machinery for $12,500, a credit to Cash for $10,000, and a credit to Gain on the Construction of Machinery for $2,500. Was this a proper entry? Discuss.
5. As used in accounting, what is the meaning of the term depreciation?
6. Does the recording of depreciation cause a plant asset to appear on the balance sheet at market value? What is accomplished by recording depreciation?
7. Is it possible to keep a plant asset in such an excellent state of repair that recording depreciation is unnecessary?
8. A company has just purchased a machine that has a potential life of 15 years. However, the company's management believes that the development of a more efficient machine will make it necessary to replace the

machine in eight years. What period of useful life should be used in calculating depreciation on this machine?

9. A building estimated to have a useful life of 30 years was completed at a cost of $85,000. It was estimated that at the end of the building's life it would be wrecked at a cost of $1,000 and that materials salvaged from the wrecking operation would be sold for $2,000. How much straight-line depreciation should be charged on the building each year?

10. Define the following terms as used in accounting for plant assets:
    a. Trade-in value.   c. Book value.   e. Inadequacy.
    b. Market value.   d. Salvage value.   f. Obsolescence.

11. Does the balance of the account, Accumulated Depreciation, Machinery, represent funds accumulated to replace the machinery as it wears out? Tell in your own words what the balance of such an account represents.

12. What is the essence of the going-concern concept of a business?

13. Explain how a concern that breaks even recovers the cost of its plant assets through the sale of its products. Where are the funds thus recovered?

14. Straight-line depreciation assigns an equal share of the cost of a plant asset's amount of usefulness to each accounting period in which the asset is used. Describe a situation in which this might not be a fair basis of allocation. Name a more fair basis for the situation described.

Class exercises

Exercise 11–1

A machine was purchased for $3,000, terms 2/10, n/60, FOB shipping point. The invoice was paid within the discount period along with $140 of freight charges. The machine required a special concrete base and power connections costing $345. In moving the machine onto its new concrete base, it was dropped and damaged. The damage cost $65 to repair. After being repaired, $40 of raw materials were consumed in adjusting the machine so that it would produce a satisfactory product. The adjustments were normal for this type of machine and were not the result of its having been damaged. The product produced while the adjustments were being made was not salable. Prepare a calculation to show the cost of the machine for accounting purposes.

Exercise 11–2

Three machines were acquired in a lump-sum purchase for $5,490. The purchaser paid $200 to transport the machines to his factory. Machine No. 1 was twice as big and weighed twice as much as Machine No. 2, and Machines 2 and 3 were approximately equal in size and weight. The machines had the following appraised values and installation costs:

	Machine No. 1	Machine No. 2	Machine No. 3
Appraised values	$2,000	$4,000	$3,000
Installation costs	150	350	200

Determine the cost of each machine for accounting purposes.

Exercise 11-3

A machine was installed at a $3,600 cost. Its useful life was estimated at five years or 5,000 units of product with a $600 trade-in value. During its second year it produced 1,100 units of product. Determine the machine's second-year depreciation under each of the following assumptions. Depreciation was calculated on (a) straight-line basis, (b) units-of-production basis, (c) declining-balance basis at twice the straight-line rate, and (d) sum-of-the-years'-digits basis.

Exercise 11-4

A machine cost $1,600 installed and was estimated to have a four-year life and a $150 trade-in value. Use declining-balance depreciation at twice the straight-line rate to determine the amount of depreciation to be charged against the machine in each of the four years in its life.

Exercise 11-5

A machine was installed on January 5, 197A, at a $3,600 total cost. A full year's depreciation on a straight-line basis was charged against the machine on each December 31 of the years 197A, 197B, and 197C, under the assumption the machine would have a four-year life and no salvage value. The machine was disposed of on May 1, 197D. (a) Give the entry to record the partial year's depreciation on May 1, 197D, and give entries to record the disposal under each of the following unrelated assumptions: (b) the machine was sold for $750; (c) the machine was sold for $500; and (d) the machine was totally destroyed in a fire and the insurance company settled the loss claim for $400.

Problems **Problem 11-1**

PART 1. A secondhand machine was purchased on January 3, 197A, for $1,650. During the next week it was repaired and repainted at a cost of $265 and was installed on a new concrete base that cost $135. It was estimated the machine would have a three-year life and a $250 salvage value. Depreciation was charged against the machine on December 31, 197A; and on August 28, 197B, the machine was retired from service.

Required:
1. Prepare entries to record the purchase of the machine, the cost of repairing and repainting it, and its installation. Assume cash was paid in each case, with the repairing, painting, and concrete base costs being paid on January 10.
2. Give the entries to record the 197A and 197B depreciation on the machine on a straight-line basis.
3. Give the entries to record its retirement under each of the following unrelated assumptions: (a) The machine was sold for $1,200. (b) It was totally destroyed in a flood, and the insurance company paid $800 in full settlement of the loss claim.

PART 2. A machine costing $20,000 was installed in a factory. Its useful life was estimated at four years, after which it would have a $2,000 trade-in value. It was estimated the machine would produce 60,000 units of product during its life. It actually produced 12,000 units during its first year, 18,000 during the second, 20,000 during the third, and 10,000 during its fourth year.

Required:
1. Prepare a calculation to show the number of dollars of this machine's cost that should be charged to depreciation over its four-year life.
2. Prepare a form with the following column headings:

Year	Straight Line	Units of Production	Declining Balance	Sum of the Years' Digits

Then enter on the form the depreciation for each year and the total depreciation on the machine under each depreciation method. Use twice the straight-line rate for declining-balance depreciation.

Problem 11-2

Companies A and B are identical in almost every respect. Both began business during the first week of January last year with store equipment costing $20,000, having a 10-year life, and no salvage value; neither added to its equipment during the year; and both purchased merchandise as follows:

Jan.   5.................. 200 units @ $25
Mar. 12.................. 600 units @ $24
June 27.................. 400 units @ $27
Oct.   3.................. 400 units @ $28
Dec. 27.................. 200 units @ $30

At the year-end, before recording depreciation, their ledgers showed the following revenues and expenses:

	Company A	*Company B*
Sales...............................	$65,000	$65,000
Salaries expense..................	6,000	6,000
Rent expense.....................	2,400	2,400
Other expenses...................	400	400

However, at the year-end Company A decided to use declining-balance depreciation at twice the straight-line rate, while Company B chose straight-line depreciation. Likewise, Company A priced its 220-unit ending inventory on a Lifo basis, while Company B used Fifo for its 220-unit inventory.

Required:
1. Prepare an income statement for each company showing last year's results.
2. Prepare a schedule accounting for the difference in their net incomes.

Problem 11-3

A company purchased four machines during 197A and 197B. Machine No. 1 was placed in use on August 29, 197A. It cost $13,200, had an estimated eight-year life and a $1,200 salvage value, and was depreciated on a straight-line basis. Machine No. 2 was placed in use on October 2, 197A, and was depreciated on a units-of-production basis. It cost $11,800 and it was estimated that it would produce 50,000 units of product during its five-year life, after which it would have an $1,800 salvage value. It produced 3,000 units during 197A, 11,500 during 197B, and 12,000 during 197C. Machines 3 and 4 were purchased from a bankrupt firm at auction for $17,100 in cash on May 17, 197B, and were first placed in service on June 25 of that year. Additional information about the machines follows:

Machine Number	Appraised Value	Salvage Value	Estimated Life	Installation Cost	Depreciation Method
3	$ 8,000	$500	6 years	$250	Sum of the years' digits
4	10,000	800	10 years	500	Declining balance

Required:
1. Prepare a form with the following columnar headings:

Machine Number	Amount to Be Charged to Depreciation	197A Depreciation	197B Depreciation	197C Depreciation

Enter the machine numbers in the first column, complete the information opposite each machine number, and total the columns. Assume that twice the straight-line rate was used for the declining-balance depreciation.
2. Prepare entries to record payment for Machines 3 and 4 and for their installation. Assume cash was paid for the installation on the day the machines were placed in use.
3. Prepare an entry to record the 197C depreciation on the four machines.

Problem 11–4

Mesa Company completed these plant asset transactions:

197A

Dec. 28 Purchased on credit from Office Suppliers a Quicko calculator, serial number WM178, $870. The calculator's service life was estimated at eight years with a $150 trade-in value. Assigned plant asset number 123–1 to the calculator.

197B

Jan. 3 Purchased on credit from Speedy Typewriter Sales a Speedy typewriter, serial number M0778, $300. The machine's service life was estimated at five years with a $45 trade-in value. Assigned plant asset number 123–2 to the typewriter.

July 7 Purchased on credit from Zippo, Ltd., a Zippo adding machine, serial number 2X345, $290. The machine's service life was estimated at eight years with a $50 trade-in value. Assigned plant asset number 123–3 to the adding machine.

Dec. 31 Recorded the 197B straight-line depreciation on the office equipment.

197C

Oct. 23 Sold the Speedy typewriter to Mary Nash for $200 cash.

Oct. 25 Purchased on credit from Office Suppliers an Accurate typewriter, serial number MMM-123, $425. The typewriter's service life was estimated at five years with a $125 trade-in value. Assigned plant asset number 123–4 to the typewriter.

Dec. 31 Recorded the 197C depreciation on the office equipment.

Required:

1. Open Office Equipment and Accumulated Depreciation, Office Equipment accounts plus plant asset record cards as needed.
2. Prepare general journal entries to record the transactions and post to the general ledger accounts and plant asset record cards.
3. Prove the December 31, 197C, balances of the Office Equipment and Accumulated Depreciation, Office Equipment accounts by preparing a schedule showing the cost and accumulated depreciation on each plant asset owned on that date.

Problem 11–5

Assume you are making the first year-end audit of the records of a manufacturing company that was organized in January of the current year and you have discovered that the company's bookkeeper has debited an account called "Land, Buildings, and Machinery" for what he thought was the cost of the company's new factory. The account has a $744,650 debit balance made up of the following items:

Cost of land and an old building on the land purchased as the site of the company's new factory (appraised value of the land, $70,000, and of the old building, $10,000)	$ 75,000
Lawyer's fees resulting from the land purchase	750
Escrow fees resulting from the land purchase	500
Cost of removing old building from the plant site	2,500
Surveying and grading the plant site	1,800
Cost of retaining wall and drain tile placed on the site	900
Cost of new building (The contract price was $350,600; however, the contractor accepted $48,700 in cash and 30 bonds having a par value of $300,000. The company had purchased the bonds at the beginning of construction for $300,000. The market value of the bonds on the day they were given to the contractor was $301,900.)	348,700
Architect's fee for planning the building	21,400
Cost of paving parking lot	11,100
Lights for the parking lot	600
Landscaping	2,700
Machinery (including the $750 cost of a machine dropped and made useless while being unloaded from a freight car)	275,150
Fine and permit to haul heavy machinery on the city streets (The company was cited for hauling machinery without a permit. It then secured the permit. Fine, $275; cost of the permit, $25.)	300
Cost of hauling machinery from freight yard to factory	2,500
Cost of replacing damaged machine	750
Total	$744,650

In examining the company's other accounts it was discovered that the bookkeeper had credited the $400 proceeds from the sale of materials salvaged from the old building removed from the plant site to an account called "Miscellaneous Revenues." He had also credited this account for $75 from the sale of the wrecked machine.

An examination of the payroll records showed that an account called "Superintendence" had been debited for the plant superintendent's $10,800 salary for the nine-month period, April 1 through December 31. From April 1 through August 31 the superintendent had supervised construction of the factory building. During September and October he had supervised installation of the factory machinery. The factory began manufacturing operations on November 1.

Required:
1. Prepare a form having the following column headings: Land, Land Improvements, Buildings, and Machinery. List the items and sort their amounts to the proper columns. Show negative amounts in parentheses. Total the columns.
2. Under the assumption the company's accounts had not been closed, prepare an entry to remove any item amounts from the accounts in which they were incorrectly entered and record them in the proper accounts.
3. The company closes its books annually on December 31. Prepare the entry to record the partial year's depreciation on the plant assets. Assume the building and land improvements are estimated to have 30-year lives and no salvage values and that the machinery is estimated to have a 12-year life and a salvage value equal to 10% of its cost.

Alternate problems

Problem 11–1A

PART 1. A secondhand truck was purchased for $2,240 on April 4, 197A. The next day it was repainted and the company's name and business were lettered on its sides at a cost of $150. Also $140 was paid for a new set of tires. The tires were priced at $154, but a $14 trade-in allowance was received for the truck's old tires. Cash was paid in each instance.

At the time of purchase it was estimated the truck would be driven 25,000 miles, after which it would have a $530 trade-in value. The truck was driven 7,000 miles in 197A; and between January 1 and October 14, 197B, it was driven an additional 10,000 miles. On the latter date it was retired from service.

Required:
1. Prepare general journal entries to record the purchase of the truck, its repainting, the replacement of its tires, and the 197A and 197B depreciation.
2. Give the entries to record the retirement of the truck under each of the following unrelated assumptions: *(a)* It was sold for $1,000 on October 14, 197B. *(b)* It was totally destroyed in a wreck and the insurance company settled the loss claim on November 1, 197B, for $800.

PART 2. A machine costing $13,000 was installed in a factory. Its useful life was estimated at four years, after which it would have a $1,000 trade-in value; and it was estimated the machine would produce 30,000 units of product during its life. It actually produced 6,000 units during its first year, 9,000 during the second, 8,000 during the third, and 7,000 during its last year.

Required:
1. Prepare a calculation to show the number of dollars of this machine's cost that should be charged to depreciation over its four-year life.
2. Prepare a form with the following column headings:

Year	Straight Line	Units of Production	Declining Balance	Sum of the Years' Digits

Then show the depreciation for each year and the total depreciation for the machine under each depreciation method. Use twice the straight-line rate for the declining-balance method.

Problem 11–3A

A company purchased four machines during 197A and 197B, and it used four ways to allocate depreciation on them. Information about the machines follow:

Machine Number	Placed in Use on—	Cost	Estimated Life	Salvage Value	Depreciation Method
1	Oct. 29, 197A	$5,400	8 years	$600	Straight line
2	Nov. 27, 197A	3,650	4 years	650	Sum of the years' digits
3	Mar. 15, 197B	8,310	15,000 units	810	Units of production
4	Aug. 30, 197B	?	8 years	700	Declining balance

Machine No. 3 produced 2,500 units of product during 197B and 3,000 units in 197C. Machine No. 4 had a $5,600 invoice price, 2/10, n/60, FOB shipping point. The invoice was paid on the last day of its discount period, August 31, but the company had to borrow $5,000 in order to do so (90-day, 8% note). The loan was repaid on December 2. Freight charges on Machine No. 4 were $122, and the machine was placed on a special concrete base that cost $190. It was assembled and installed by the company's own employees. Their wages during the installation period were $200. Payment for the freight charges, the concrete base, and the employees' wages were made on August 31.

Required:
1. Prepare a form with the following columnar headings:

Machine Number	Amount to Be Charged to Depreciation	197A Depreciation	197B Depreciation	197C Depreciation

Enter the machine numbers in the first column and complete the information opposite each machine's number. Use twice the straight-line rate in depreciating Machine No. 4. Total all columns.
2. Prepare entries to record all transactions involving the purchase of Machine No. 4, including the note transactions.
3. Prepare an entry to record the 197C depreciation on the machines.

Problem 11-4A

Pine Market completed these plant asset transactions:

197A

Jan. 4 Purchased on credit from Alpha Equipment Company a Fair scale, serial number 00-123, $200. The scale's service life was estimated at 10 years with a $20 trade-in value. It was assigned plant asset number 123-1.

6 Purchased on credit from Alpha Equipment Company an Accurate cash register, serial number XX-1212, $320. The register's life was estimated at eight years with an $80 trade-in value. It was assigned plant asset number 123-2.

Feb. 28 Purchased on credit from Gamma Equipment Sales an Iceair refrigerated display case, serial number MM-777, $2,000. The asset's service life was estimated at 12 years with a $200 trade-in value. It was assigned plant asset number 123-3.

Dec. 31 Recorded the 197A depreciation on the store equipment.

197B

Aug. 24 Sold the Fair scale to Corner Market for $150.

26 Purchased a new Apex scale from Alpha Equipment Company on credit for $265. Its serial number was BB-321, and it was assigned plant asset number 123-4. The scale's service life was estimated at 10 years with a $25 trade-in value.

Dec. 31 Record the 197B depreciation on the store equipment.

Required:

1. Open a Store Equipment account and an Accumulated Depreciation, Store Equipment account plus subsidiary plant asset record cards as needed.
2. Prepare general journal entries to record the transactions. Post to the general ledger accounts and to the plant asset record cards.
3. Prove the December 31, 197B, balances of the Store Equipment and Accumulated Depreciation, Store Equipment accounts by preparing with totals a schedule showing the cost and accumulated depreciation on each plant asset owned on that date.

Problem 11-5A

Seal Rock Manufacturing Company was organized during the first week in January of the current year; and in making your audit of the company's records at the end of its first year, you have discovered that the company's bookkeeper has debited an account called "Land, Buildings, and Equipment" for what he thought was the cost of the company's new factory. The account had a $577,950 debit balance made up of the following items:

Cost of the land and an old building on the land purchased as the site of the company's
new plant (appraised value of the land $87,500, and of the old building, $12,500) ... $ 90,000
Lawyer's fee for a title search to assure a clear title to the land............................. 800
Cost of removing old building from site... 3,000
Cost of grading plant site.. 400
Architect's fee for planning new factory building 25,500
Cost of new building (Contract price, $255,300; but in lieu of cash, the contractor
accepted $7,200 in cash and 250 bonds the company had purchased as a temporary

investment while waiting for the completion of the building. The bonds cost $250,000 and had a $248,100 fair market value on the day they were given to the contractor.) 257,200
Cost of landscaping the plant site.. 4,500
Cost of new concrete walks and paving the parking lot 6,500
Cost of installing lights in the parking lot.. 700
Factory machinery and equipment (including the $650 cost of a machine dropped and made useless while being installed).. 166,125
Fine and permit for hauling heavy machinery on the city streets (The company was cited for hauling the machinery without a permit and it then secured the permit. The fine was $250 and the cost of the permit was $25.)..................................... 275
Cost of installing machinery 22,300
Cost of replacing the dropped and damaged machine............................ 650
    Total.. $577,950

An examination of the payroll records showed that an account called "Superintendence" had been debited for the plant superintendent's $12,000 salary for the 10-month period, March 1 through December 31. From March 1 through August 31 the superintendent had supervised construction of the factory building. During September, October, and November he had supervised installation of the factory machinery.

The bookkeeper had set up an account called "Miscellaneous Revenues" and had credited it for the $300 proceeds from the sale of materials salvaged from the old building removed from the plant site and for $50 from the sale of the wrecked machine.

Required:
1. Prepare a form having the following column headings: Land, Land Improvements, Buildings, and Machinery. List the items and sort their amounts to the proper asset columns under the assumption the company's manufacturing operations began on December 1. Show a negative item by enclosing it in parentheses. Total the columns.
2. Under the assumption the company's accounts had not been closed, prepare an entry to remove the item amounts from the accounts in which they were incorrectly recorded and enter them in the proper accounts.
3. Prepare an entry to record the depreciation expense for the partial year. Assume the building and land improvements have an estimated 30-year life and no salvage value and the machinery has a 12-year life and a salvage value equal to 10% of its cost.

Decision problem 11–1, Cactus Manufacturing Company
Cactus Manufacturing Company, a large corporation, is about to invest $120,000 in new machinery to add a new product to its line. The new machinery is expected to have a four-year life and an $8,000 salvage value; and you, the concern's accountant, have prepared the following statement showing the expected results from the sale of the product under the assumption the new machinery will be depreciated on a straight-line basis and that 50% of the income earned will have to be paid out in income taxes.

Expected Results from Sale of New Product

	1st Year	2d Year	3d Year	4th Year	Total
Sales	$200,000	$200,000	$200,000	$200,000	$800,000
All costs other than depreciation and income taxes	120,000	120,000	120,000	120,000	480,000
Income before depreciation and income taxes	$ 80,000	$ 80,000	$ 80,000	$ 80,000	$320,000
Depreciation of machinery	28,000	28,000	28,000	28,000	112,000
Income before taxes	$ 52,000	$ 52,000	$ 52,000	$ 52,000	$208,000
Income taxes	26,000	26,000	26,000	26,000	104,000
Net Income	$ 26,000	$ 26,000	$ 26,000	$ 26,000	$104,000

When the company president examined your statement, he said that he knew that regardless of how calculated, the company could charge off no more than $112,000 of depreciation on the new machinery during its four-year life. Furthermore, he said, as he could see, this would result in $208,000 of income before taxes for the four years, $104,000 of income taxes, and $104,000 of net income for the period, regardless of how depreciation was calculated. Nevertheless, he continued that he had been talking with a friend on the golf course a few days back and the friend had tried to explain the tax advantage of using declining-balance depreciation. He said he did not understand all the friend had tried to tell him; and as a result he would like for you to prepare an additional statement like the one already prepared, but based on the assumption that declining-balance depreciation at twice the straight-line rate would be used in depreciating the new machinery. He said he would also like a written explanation of the tax advantage gained through the use of declining-balance depreciation, with a dollar estimate of the amount the company would gain in this case. Prepare the information for the president. (In making your estimate, assume the company can earn a 5% after-tax return, compounded annually on any taxes that can be deferred from the early years of the machinery's life until later years. Also, to simplify the problem, assume that the taxes must be paid on the first day of January in the year following their incurrence.)

Decision problem 11–2, Junior Accountant I   You have just graduated from college and are working for a local accounting firm as a junior accountant; and in examining the plant asset accounts of a concern being audited by your firm, you find the following debits and credits in an account called Land and Buildings:

Debits

Jan. 4	Cost of land and buildings acquired for a new plant site	$ 65,000
5	Lawyer's fee for title search before buying land and buildings	400
21	Cost of wrecking old building on plant site	5,000
Feb. 1	Six months' liability and fire insurance on new building	1,800
June 30	Payment to building contractor on completion of building	258,500

June 30	Architect's fee for new building	15,000
July 10	City assessment for street improvement	4,100
15	Cost of landscaping new plant site..	2,500
		$352,300

Credits

Jan. 22	Proceeds from sale of salvaged materials from old building....................... $	2,000
July 3	Refund of one month's insurance on new building..................................	300
Dec. 31	One-half year's depreciation at 2½% per year..	4,375
31	Balance..	345,625
		$352,300

In consulting with the senior accountant in charge of the audit, you learn that 40 years is a reasonable life expectancy for a building of the type involved and that it is reasonable to assume that there will be no salvage value at the end of the building's life. He also tells you to prepare a schedule with columns headed Date, Description, Total Amount, Land, Buildings, and Other Accounts, and to enter the items found in the Land and Buildings account on the schedule, distributing the amounts to the proper columns. He suggests that you show credits on your schedule by enclosing them in parentheses; and finally he suggests that since the accounts have not been closed, you draft any required correcting entry or entries. Assume that an account called Depreciation Expense, Land and Buildings was debited in recording the $4,375 of depreciation.

Decision problem 11–3, Alpha and Beta Sales

Alpha Sales and Beta Sales are almost identical. Each began operations on January 2 of this year with $22,000 of equipment having an eight-year life and a $2,000 salvage value. Each purchased merchandise during the year as follows:

Jan.	2	100 units	@	$200 per unit
Mar.	11	200 units	@	$230 per unit
July	7	200 units	@	$250 per unit
Oct.	15	100 units	@	$260 per unit

And now, on December 31 at the end of the first year, each has 110 units of merchandise in its ending inventory. However, Alpha Sales will use straight-line depreciation in arriving at its net income for the year, while Beta Sales will use declining-balance depreciation at twice the straight-line rate. Also, Alpha Sales will use Fifo in costing its ending inventory and Beta Sales will use Lifo. The December 31 trial balances of the two concerns carried these amounts:

	Alpha Sales		*Beta Sales*	
Cash.....................................	$ 1,500		$ 1,500	
Accounts receivable	10,000		10,000	
Equipment.............................	22,000		22,000	
Accounts payable....................		$ 8,000		$ 8,000
Allen Alpha, capital.................		32,000		
Bruce Beta, capital..................				32,000
Sales......................................		170,000		170,000
Purchases..............................	142,000		142,000	
Salaries expense	15,000		15,000	
Rent expense	12,000		12,000	
Other expenses......................	7,500		7,500	
Totals	$210,000	$210,000	$210,000	$210,000

Prepare an income statement for each concern and a schedule accounting for the difference in their reported net incomes. Also tell which concern you think was the more profitable and why.

Analytical and review problems

Problem 11–1 A&R

The following diagram depicts the behaviour of three depreciation methods: *a, b,* and *c.*

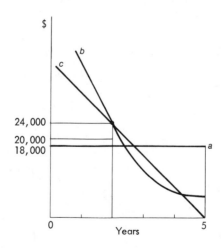

Required:
1. Identify the three methods used and construct a table showing the depreciation expense by each method for each year. Assume no salvage value.
2. Assuming that income before depreciation is $60,000 for each of the five years, show the amount of income after depreciation for the period covered by the assets. Briefly explain the impact which the depreciation method may have on reported net income for a business.

Problem 11-2 A&R

The opening balances in the Equipment account and the related Accumulated Depreciation-Equipment account were $6,000 and $2,220, respectively.

The depreciation expense for the year was $480 and equipment costing $1,800 was purchased during the year. The records also indicate that during the year equipment costing $1,200 was sold for $400, resulting in a loss on disposal of $220.

Required:

What are the correct ending balances in the Equipment and Accumulated Depreciation-Equipment accounts?

Problem 11-3 A&R

On January 2, the Red River Company purchased a truck for $6,800 cash. The company expected to sell the truck for $800 after using it for four years. After using the truck for three years the truck was sold for $2,500. Gain on disposal of the truck was recorded as $1,650.

Required:

Determine the depreciation method used by the company. Show supporting computations.

12

Plant and equipment; intangible assets

■ Some of the problems met in accounting for property, plant, and equipment were discussed in the previous chapter. Additional problems involving plant assets and some of the accounting problems encountered with intangible assets are examined in this chapter.

Accounting for small tools

■ Small tools such as hammers, wrenches, and drills which have low individual costs and are easily lost, broken, or stolen are normally either charged directly to an expense account at the time of purchase or are accounted for on an inventory basis. They are either expensed or accounted for on an inventory basis because it is impracticable to set up individual records and to account for such items on a depreciation basis. If small tools costing about the same amount are purchased each year to replace those lost, broken, or stolen, their costs may be charged directly to an expense account at the time of purchase. However, if the amounts purchased vary greatly from year to year, an inventory basis becomes a more equitable means of accounting for them.

When small tools are accounted for on an inventory basis, the cost of tools on hand at the beginning of a period is represented by a debit balance in the asset account, Small Tools; and as tools are purchased during the period, their cost is debited to this account. At the end of the period a physical inventory of usable tools on hand in the factory is taken; and the inventory amount is subtracted from the end-of-the-period balance of the Small Tools account to determine the cost of tools lost, broken, and stolen during the period. This cost is then charged to an expense account by a work sheet adjustment and an adjusting entry similar to the following:

Dec.	31	Small Tools Expense	200.00	
		Small Tools		200.00
		To record the cost of the tools lost, broken, and stolen.		

The debit of the foregoing entry records as an expense the cost of tools lost, broken, or stolen during the period. The credit reduces the balance of the Small Tools account to the cost of the usable tools on hand.

Since the lives of small tools are relatively short, when an inventory is taken at the end of an accounting period, normally all usable tools are placed on the inventory at cost.

Exchanging plant assets ■ Some plant assets are sold at the ends of their useful lives, but others such as some machinery, automobiles, and office equipment may be traded in on new, up-to-date assets of a like kind. No problems arise in recording such exchanges when the dealer's list price for the new asset is the same price for which the asset is sold for cash. In such a situation the dealer will grant a trade-in allowance equal to his estimate of the fair market value of the old asset, and the trade-in allowance is treated for accounting purposes as the selling price of the old asset, with any gain or loss being recorded.

For example, assume a company has a machine for which its accounting records show the following:

Cost	$4,500
Accumulated depreciation to date	3,000
Book value...	$1,500

Assume further that the company has been offered a $1,400 trade-in allowance on the old machine if traded in on a new machine of like nature having a $5,000 list price, which is also the lowest price for which the new machine can be bought for cash. If the company accepts the offer and pays the difference between the list price and the trade-in allowance in cash, it will record the transaction as follows:

Jan.	5	Machinery	5,000.00	
		Loss on Exchange of Plant Assets	100.00	
		Accumulated Depreciation, Machinery..............	3,000.00	
		Machinery		4,500.00
		Cash..		3,600.00
		Exchanged old machine and cash for a new machine of like kind.		

If in the foregoing exchange the trade-in allowance had been greater than the $1,500 book value of the old machine, the company would have recorded the difference as a gain.

Sometimes the list price of a new asset is not its lowest cash price. In the case of automobiles, for example, the list price is commonly set high so that a dealer can offer a customer a trade-in allowance far above the fair market value of the customer's trade-in. In such a situation the new asset should not be placed on the books at its list price; rather, its fair market value (cash price) should be ascertained, if possible, and it should be recorded at this price. For example, a company has a delivery truck for which its accounting records show the following:

```
Cost ........................................................................ $4,200
Accumulated depreciation to date ............................   3,200
Book value................................................................ $1,000
```

And a dealer has offered the company a $1,500 trade-in allowance on the old truck on a new truck having a $4,800 list price, but for which the dealer's lowest cash price is $4,350. In other words the dealer will exchange the new truck for the company's old truck and $3,300 in cash, or it will take $4,350 in cash for the truck with no trade-in. In this case the transaction should be recorded as follows:

Jan.	10	Delivery Equipment	4,350.00	
		Accumulated Depreciation, Delivery Equipment...	3,200.00	
		Delivery Equipment		4,200.00
		Gain on the Exchange of Plant Assets........		50.00
		Cash..		3,300.00
		Exchanged an old truck and cash for a new truck.		

Sometimes in an exchange it is impossible to ascertain either the fair market value (lowest cash price) of either the new asset or the asset being given in exchange. When this is the case, although the practice is a departure from the cost basis of accounting, it may be necessary to put the new asset on the books at its list price. However, if the list price is obviously inflated, a fairer basis of accounting for the new asset may be at the sum of the book value of the trade-in asset plus the cash given. In the exchange of the delivery equipment just described these were:

```
Book value of the old truck .................................................. $1,000
Cash given .........................................................................   3,300
Total ................................................................................... $4,300
```

And if the new asset is taken on the books at this amount, the transaction is recorded:

Jan.	10	Delivery Equipment	4,300.00	
		Accumulated Depreciation, Delivery		
		Equipment..	3,200.00	
		Delivery Equipment		4,200.00
		Cash...		3,300.00
		Exchanged an old truck and cash for a		
		new truck.		

When a plant asset is traded in on a new asset of like nature, a book gain or loss on the exchange usually results. However, accountants generally do not recognize such gains and losses and record the new asset at an amount equal to the book value of a traded-in asset plus the cash given. This practice is acceptable if such gains and losses are not material in amount. However, if a book gain or loss is material, the more theoretically accurate method in which the gain or loss is recorded is to be preferred.

Before turning to a new subject, it should be observed that whether a new asset is taken on the books at its list price, the lowest price for which it could have been bought for cash, or at an amount equal to the book value of a traded-in asset plus the cash given, the amount at which the new asset is taken on the books becomes the basis for calculating its depreciation and also any gain or loss on its sale or exchange.

Revising depreciation rates

■ An occasional error in estimating the useful life of a plant asset is to be expected. Furthermore, when such an error is discovered, it is normally corrected by spreading the cost of the asset's remaining quantity of usefulness over its remaining useful life. For example, seven years ago a machine was purchased at a cost of $12,500. At that time the machine was estimated to have a 10-year life and a $500 salvage value. Therefore, it was depreciated at the rate of $1,200 per year [($12,500 − $500) ÷ 10 = $1,200]; and it began its eighth year with a $4,100 book value calculated as follows:

Cost..	$12,500
Less seven years' accumulated depreciation	8,400
Book value	$ 4,100

If at the beginning of its eighth year the estimated number of years remaining in the machine's useful life is changed from three to five years, depreciation for each of the machine's remaining years is normally recalculated as follows:

$$\frac{\text{Book Value} \ - \ \text{Salvage Value}}{\text{Remaining Useful Life}} = \frac{\$4,100 \ - \ \$500}{5 \text{ Years}} = \$720 \text{ per Year}$$

And an entry like the following is then used to record depreciation at the end of the machine's eighth and each succeeding year to retirement:

Dec.	31	Depreciation Expense, Machinery.....................	720.00	
		Accumulated Depreciation, Machinery........		720.00
		To record depreciation at the revised rate.		

If depreciation is charged at the rate of $1,200 per year for the first seven years of this machine's life and $720 per year for the next five years, depreciation expense is overstated during the first seven years and understated during the next five. However, if a concern has many plant assets, the lives of some will be underestimated and the lives of others will be overestimated at the time of purchase; consequently, the errors will tend to cancel each other out with little effect on the income statement. As a result, accountants generally correct errors in estimating the lives of plant assets in the manner described.

Nevertheless, although the method described is generally used, in theory a more accurate way to handle such errors is to correct the misstatement of owner equity and adjust the accumulated depreciation account to the amount it would have contained had the revised estimates of the assets' useful lives been used from the beginning.

For instance, depreciation at $1,200 a year for its first seven years was charged on the machine of the foregoing example. The estimate of the machine's life was then changed from 10 years to 12. If the 12-year life had been used from the beginning, depreciation would have been charged at the rate of $1,000 per year for these seven years [($12,500 − $500) ÷ 12 years = $1,000 per year]. Consequently, the error in estimating the machine's life caused a $200 overstatement of depreciation expense each year and, by the end of seven years, a $1,400 overstatement of accumulated depreciation. However, the following entry will correct these overstatements:

Dec.	31	Accumulated Depreciation, Machinery..............	1,400.00	
		Correction of Prior Years' Errors, Depreciation		1,400.00
		To correct prior years' errors in recording depreciation and adjust accumulated depreciation on the basis of the current estimate of the asset's useful life.		

If the foregoing correcting entry is made, depreciation at $1,000 per year is recorded on the machine in the usual manner for the remaining five years of its life.

In the correcting entry just given, the debit is easy to understand. It removes from the Accumulated Depreciation, Machinery account the $1,400 overstatement that resulted from recording $200 too much depreciation each year for seven years. However, the credit needs additional explanation along these lines:

1. Charging depreciation on the machine of this illustration at the rate of $1,200 per year, instead of $1,000 per year, overstated depreciation expense $200 per year during each of the first seven years of its life.
2. The $200 per year overstatement of depreciation expense caused a $200 annual understatement of reported net income.
3. Consequently, in the year in which the error is corrected the credit balance of the account, Correction of Prior Years' Errors, Depreciation, is carried onto the income statement as in Illustration 12–1 where it results in a reduction of expenses and an increase in the year's net income figure by an amount equal to the seven annual $200 understatements, exactly offsetting them. In addition, the account's $1,400 credit balance is closed to Income Summary and on to the owner's capital account where it offsets the effects of the seven annual understatements of net income.

Northern Sales and Service
Income Statement for Year Ended December 31, 19–

Sales			$215,000
Cost of goods sold			129,000
Gross profit from sales			$ 86,000
Operating expenses:			
Depreciation expense, current period	$8,600		
Less: Depreciation expense overstatement of prior years	1,400	$7,200	
Total expenses			64,000
Net Income			$ 22,000

Illustration
12–1

CHOICE OF METHODS. Accountants generally correct an error in estimating the life of a plant asset by spreading the cost of its remaining quantity of usefulness over its remaining years, as was first explained in this section. However, sometimes this method of correction results in a material under- or overstatement of annual depreciation expense for the asset's remaining years. In such a case the more theoretically accurate adjustment of the accumulated depreciation account and correction of prior years' errors is to be preferred.

Repairs and replacements

■ Repairs and replacements fall into two groups: (1) ordinary repairs and replacements and (2) extraordinary repairs and replacements.

Ordinary repairs and replacements

Expenditures for ordinary repairs and replacements are necessary to maintain an asset in good operating condition. A building must be painted and its roof repaired or a machine must be reconditioned and small parts replaced. Any expenditures to maintain a plant asset in its normal good state of repair are considered ordinary repairs and replacements. Ordinary repairs and replacements are a current expense and should appear on the current income statement as a deduction from revenues.

Maintenance costs such as those for cleaning, lubricating, and adjusting machinery are also a current expense and are accounted for in the same way as ordinary repairs. Often such costs are combined with ordinary repairs for accounting purposes.

Extraordinary repairs and replacements

Extraordinary repairs and replacements are major repairs and replacements made, not to keep an asset in its normal good state of repair but to extend its useful life beyond that originally estimated. As a rule, the cost of such repairs and replacements should be debited to the repaired asset's accumulated depreciation account under the assumption they make good past depreciation, add to the asset's useful life, and benefit future periods. For example, a machine was purchased for $8,000 and depreciated under the assumption it would last eight years and have no salvage value. As a result, at the end of the machine's sixth year its book value is $2,000, calculated as follows:

```
Cost of machine ................................................ $8,000
Less six years' accumulated depreciation ............... 6,000
Book value ...................................................... $2,000
```

If at the beginning of the machine's seventh year it is given a major overhaul that extends its estimated useful life three years beyond the eight originally estimated, the $2,100 cost of the repairs should be recorded with an entry like the following:

Jan.	12	Accumulated Depreciation, Machinery	2,100.00	
		Cash (or Accounts Payable)		2,100.00
		To record extraordinary repairs to machinery.		

In addition, depreciation for each of the five years remaining in the machine's life should be calculated as follows:

```
Book value before extraordinary repairs ..................................................... $2,000
Extraordinary repairs ........................................................................... 2,100
    Total ..................................................................................... $4,100
Annual depreciation expense for remaining years ($4,100 ÷ 5 years) ........... $  820
```

And, if the machine remains in use for five years after the major overhaul, the five annual $820 depreciation charges will exactly write off its new book value, including the cost of the extraordinary repairs.

Betterments ■ A betterment may be defined as the replacement of an existing asset or asset portion with an improved or superior asset or portion, usually at a cost materially in excess of the replaced item. Replacing the manual controls on a machine with automatic controls, removing an old motor and replacing it with a larger, more powerful one, and replacing a wood shingle roof with a tile roof are illustrations of betterments. Usually a betterment results in a better, more efficient, or more productive asset, but not necessarily one having a longer life.

When a betterment is made, its cost should be debited to the improved asset's account and depreciated over the remaining service life of the asset. Also, the cost and applicable depreciation of the replaced asset or portion should be removed from the accounts. For example, if the motor on a machine is replaced with a faster more powerful one, the cost of the new motor should be debited to the Machinery account and the cost and applicable depreciation on the old motor should be removed from the accounts.

Capital and revenue expenditures ■ A *revenue expenditure* is one that should appear on the current income statement as an expense and a deduction from the period's revenues. Expenditures for ordinary repairs, rent, and salaries are examples.

Expenditures for betterments and for extraordinary repairs that lengthen the estimated life of an asset should appear on the balance sheet as increases in asset book values; and as a result, they are examples of what are called *capital expenditures* or balance sheet expenditures that benefit future periods.

Obviously, care must be exercised to distinguish between capital and revenue expenditures when transactions are recorded; for if errors are made, such errors often affect a number of accounting periods. For instance, an expenditure for a betterment initially recorded in error as an expense overstates expenses in the year of the error and understates net income. Also, since the cost of a betterment should be depreciated over the remaining useful life of the bettered asset, depreciation expense of future periods is understated and net income is overstated.

Natural resources ■ Natural resources such as standing timber, mineral deposits, and oil reserves are known as wasting assets. The distinguishing characteristic of wasting assets is that in their natural state they represent inventories that will be converted into a product by cutting, mining, or pumping. Standing timber, for example, is an inventory of uncut lumber. When it is cut and sawed, it becomes a product to be sold; and one of the costs of the product is the cost of the standing timber from which it was manufactured. However, until cut, it is a noncurrent asset commonly shown on the balance sheet under a caption such as "Timberlands." Or if a mineral deposit or oil reserve, it is commonly shown as "Mineral deposits" or "Oil reserves."

Natural resources are accounted for at cost, and appear on the balance sheet at cost less accumulated depletion. The amount such assets are depleted each year by cutting, mining, or pumping is commonly calculated on a "units-of-production" basis. For example, if a mine having an estimated 500,000 tons of available ore is purchased for $500,000, the depletion charge per ton of ore mined is $1. Furthermore, if 85,000 tons are mined during the first year, the depletion charge for the year is $85,000 and is recorded as follows:

Dec.	31	Depletion of Mineral Deposit............................	85,000.00	
		Accumulated Depletion, Mineral Deposit.....		85,000.00
		To record depletion of ore body resulting from mining 85,000 tons of ore.		

On the balance sheet prepared at the end of the first year the mine should appear at its $500,000 cost less $85,000 accumulated depletion. If all of the 85,000 tons of ore are sold by the end of the first year, the entire $85,000 depletion charge reaches the income statement as the depletion cost of the ore mined and sold. However, if a portion of the 85,000 tons remains unsold at the year-end, the depletion cost of the unsold ore is carried forward on the balance sheet as part of the cost of the unsold ore inventory, a current asset.

Often machinery must be installed or a building constructed in order to exploit a natural resource. The costs of such assets should be recorded in plant and equipment accounts, and should be depreciated over the life of the natural resource with annual depreciation charges that are in proportion to the annual depletion charges. For example, if a machine having a 10-year life is installed in a mine that will be depleted in six years, the machine should be depreciated over the six-year period. Furthermore, if one eighth of the mine's ore is removed during the first year, one eighth of the machine's total depreciation should be recorded as one of the costs of the ore mined.

Intangible assets ■ Intangible assets are assets having no intrinsic value, their value being derived from the rights conferred by ownership and possession. Patents, copyrights, leaseholds, goodwill, trademarks, and organization costs are examples. Notes and accounts receivable are also intangible in nature, but these appear on the balance sheet as current assets rather than under the intangible assets classification.

Intangible assets are accounted for at cost and should appear on the balance sheet in the intangible asset section at cost or at that portion of cost not previously written off. Normally the intangible asset section follows on the balance sheet immediately after the plant and equipment section. All intangibles are systematically amortized or written off to expense accounts over their estimated useful lives, which in no case should exceed 40 years. Amortization is a process similar to the recording of depreciation.

Patents

Patents are granted by the federal government to encourage the invention of new machines and mechanical devices. A patent gives its owner the exclusive right to manufacture and sell a patented machine or device for a period of 17 years. When patent rights to a previously developed successful machine or mechanical device are purchased, all costs of acquiring the rights may be debited to an account called "Patents." Also the costs of a successful lawsuit in defense of a patent may be debited to this account.

Although a patent gives its owner exclusive rights to the patented device for 17 years, its cost should be amortized or written off over a shorter period if its useful or economic life is estimated to be less than 17 years. For example, if a patent costing $25,000 has an estimated useful life of only 10 years, the following adjusting entry is made at the end of each year in the patent's life to write off one tenth of its cost.

Dec.	31	Patents Written Off...	2,500.00	
		Patents		2,500.00
		To write off one tenth of patent costs.		

The entry's debit causes $2,500 of patent costs to appear on the annual income statement as one of the costs of the patented product manufactured. The credit directly reduces the balance of the Patents account. Normally, patents are written off directly to the Patents account as in this entry.

Research and development costs

Many concerns maintain a research department charged with developing new products, testing raw materials, testing the company's own products and the products of competitors, and doing pure research. A cost incurred by such a department in testing and in pure research is an expense of the period in which it is incurred. Costs incurred in developing new products, on the other hand, may be capitalized in a Patents or like account or they may be charged to current expense accounts.

Some concerns charge all the costs of operating a research department to current expense accounts and thus expense all testing, research, and product development costs in the year in which the costs are incurred. They do this under the assumption that the costs of maintaining a research department are recurring costs that must be borne period after period if the company is to maintain its competitive position. Other companies use cost accounting to allocate research department costs to testing, to pure research, and to the several products under development. They then capitalize the costs that result in successful new products and write off as a current expense any testing, pure research, and unsuccessful new product costs. Either method is acceptable.

Copyrights

A copyright is granted by the federal government and gives its owner the exclusive right to publish and sell a musical, literary, or artwork. The right is for the lifetime of the author and 50 years after his death, subject to special qualifications in certain cases. Obviously, most copyrights have value for a much shorter time, and their costs should be amortized over the shorter period.

Leaseholds

Property is rented under a contract called a *lease.* The person or company owning the property and granting the lease is called the *lessor,* the person or company securing the right to possess and use the property is called the *lessee,* and the rights granted the lessee under the lease are called a *leasehold.*

Some leases require no advance payment from the lessee but do require monthly rent payments. In such cases a Leasehold account is not needed and the monthly payments are debited to a Rent Expense account. Sometimes a long-term lease is so drawn that the last year's rent must be paid in advance at the time the lease is signed. When this occurs, the last year's advance payment is debited to the Leasehold account where it remains until the last year of the lease, at which time it is transferred to Rent Expense.

Often a long-term lease, one running 20 or 25 years, becomes very valuable after a few years because its required rent payments are much less than current rentals for identical property. In such cases the increase in value of the lease should not be entered on the books since no extra cost was incurred in acquiring it. However, if the property is subleased and the new tenant makes a cash payment for the rights under the old lease, the new tenant should debit the payment to a Leasehold account and amortize or write it off as additional rent expense over the remaining life of the lease.

Leasehold improvements

Long-term leases often require the lessee to pay for any alterations or improvements to the leased property, such as new partitions and store fronts. Normally the costs of the improvements are debited to an account called Leasehold Improvements; and since the improvements become part of the property and revert to the lessor at the end of the lease, their cost should be amortized over the life of the lease or the life of the improvements, whichever is shorter. The amortization entry commonly has a debit to Rent Expense and a credit to Leasehold Improvements.

Goodwill

When a concern so conducts its affairs that its customers are convinced their future dealings with the company will be as completely satisfactory as in the past, when the customers always return to transact with the concern the kind of business it conducts, and when its customers' good reports tend to bring in new customers, that concern is said to have goodwill.

The foregoing is a common description of goodwill; but it is not sufficiently broad for accounting purposes. In accounting, *a business is said to have goodwill when its expected future earnings are greater than the earnings normally realized in its industry.* Above-average earnings and the existence of goodwill may be demonstrated as follows with Companies A and B, both of which are in the same industry:

	Company A	Company B
Net assets (other than goodwill)	$100,000	$100,000
Normal rate of return in this industry	10%	10%
Normal return on net assets	$ 10,000	$ 10,000
Actual net income earned	10,000	15,000
Earnings above average	$ 0	$ 5,000

Company B has above-average earnings for its industry and is said to have goodwill. Its goodwill, as with any concern, may be the result of excellent customer relations, the location of the business, manufacturing efficiency, monopolistic privileges, good employee relations, superior management, or a combination of these factors. However, regardless of what created the goodwill, a prospective investor would normally be willing to pay more for Company B than for Company A if he felt the extra earnings would continue. Thus, goodwill is an asset having value and it can be sold.

Accountants are in general agreement that goodwill should not be recorded unless it is bought or sold. This normally occurs only when a business is purchased in its entirety or when a new combination of partners takes over an existing partnership. When either of these events occur, the goodwill of a business may be valued in many ways. Examples of three follow:

1. The buyer and seller may place an arbitrary value on the goodwill of a business being sold. For instance, a seller may be willing to sell a business having above-average earnings for $115,000 and a buyer

may be willing to pay that amount; and if they both agree that the net assets of the business other than its goodwill have a $100,000 value, they are arbitrarily valuing the goodwill at $15,000.

2. Goodwill may be valued at some multiple of that portion of expected earnings which is above average. For example, if a company is expected to have $5,000 each year in above-average earnings, its goodwill may be valued at, say, four times that portion of its earnings which are above average or at $20,000. In this case it may also be said that the goodwill is valued at four years' above-average earnings; but regardless of how it is said, this too is placing an arbitrary value on the goodwill.

3. The portion of a concern's earnings which is above average may be capitalized in order to place a value on its goodwill. For example, if a business is expected to continue to have $5,000 each year in earnings that are above average and the normal rate of return on invested capital in its industry is 10%, the excess earnings may be capitalized at 10% and a $50,000 value may be placed on its goodwill ($5,000 ÷ 10% = $50,000). Note that this values the goodwill at the amount that must be invested at the normal rate of return in order to earn the extra $5,000 each year ($50,000 × 10% = $5,000). It is a satisfactory method if the extra earnings are expected to continue indefinitely. However, since this may not happen, the extra earnings are often capitalized at a rate higher than the normal rate of the industry, say in this case, at twice the normal rate or at 20%. If in this case the extra earnings are capitalized at 20%, the goodwill is valued at $25,000 ($5,000 ÷ 20% = $25,000).

There are other ways to value goodwill; but like the three just described, in a final analysis goodwill is always valued at the price a seller is willing to take and a buyer is willing to pay.

Trademarks and trade names

Proof of prior use of a trademark or trade name is sufficient under common law to prove ownership and right of use. However, both may be registered with the federal government at a nominal cost for the same purpose. The cost of developing a trademark or trade name through, say, advertising should be charged to an expense account in the period or periods incurred. However, if a trademark or trade name is purchased, its cost should be amortized as explained in the next section.

Amortization of intangibles

Some intangibles, such as patents, copyrights, and leaseholds, have determinable lives based on a law, contract, or the nature of the asset; and the costs of such assets should be amortized by systematic charges to income over the shorter of the term of their existence or the period expected to be benefited by their use. Other intangibles, such as goodwill, trademarks, and trade names, have indeterminable lives. However, since the value of any intangible will eventually disappear; a reasonable estimate of the period of usefulness of such assets should be made and their costs should be amortized to income by the straight-line method over the periods estimated to be benefited by their use, which in no case should exceed 40 years.[1]

[1]CICA Handbook (Toronto: The Canadian Institute of Chartered Accountants), p. 303.

Questions for class discussion

1. Why are small tools accounted for on an inventory basis?
2. When should a loss on the exchange of a plant asset be recorded? When is it permissible to absorb a loss into the cost basis of the new plant asset? Should a gain on a plant asset exchange be recorded as such?
3. When plant assets of like nature are exchanged, what determines the cost basis of the newly acquired asset?
4. What is the essence of the accounting principle of materiality?
5. If at the end of four years it is discovered that a machine that was expected to have a five-year life will actually have an eight-year life, how is the error corrected?
6. Distinguish between ordinary repairs and replacements and extraordinary repairs and replacements.
7. How should ordinary repairs to a machine be recorded? How should extraordinary repairs be recorded?
8. What is a betterment? How should a betterment to a machine be recorded?
9. Distinguish between revenue expenditures and capital expenditures.
10. What are the characteristics of an intangible asset?
11. In general, how are intangible assets accounted for?
12. Define (a) lease, (b) lessor, (c) leasehold, and (d) leasehold improvement.
13. In accounting, when is a business said to have goodwill?

Class exercises

Exercise 12-1

A machine that cost $4,000 and that had $2,800 of accumulated depreciation recorded against it was traded in on a new machine of like nature having a $4,500 cash price. A $1,000 trade-in allowance was received and the balance was paid in cash. Determine (a) the book value of the old machine, (b) the cash given in making the exchange, (c) the book loss on the exchange, (d) the annual straightline depreciation on the new machine under the assumption it will have an estimated six-year life and a $300 trade-in value.

Exercise 12-2

A machine that cost $3,500 and on which $2,000 of depreciation had been recorded was disposed of on January 2 of the current year. Give without explanations the entries to record the disposal under each of the following unrelated assumptions:

a. The machine was sold for $1,600 cash.
b. The machine was sold for $400 cash.
c. The machine was traded in on a new machine of like nature having a $4,000 cash price. A $1,600 trade-in allowance was received, and the balance was paid in cash. The gain or loss was considered immaterial in amount.
d. A $400 trade-in allowance was received for the machine on a new machine of like nature having a $4,000 cash price. The balance was paid in cash, and the gain or loss was considered material in amount.

Exercise 12–3

A machine that cost $8,000 was depreciated on a straight-line basis for 10 years under the assumption it would have a 12-year life and an $800 trade-in value. At that point it was recognized that the machine had four years of remaining useful life, after which it would still have an $800 trade-in value.

a. Determine the machine's book value at the end of its 10th year.
b. Determine the total depreciation to be charged against the machine during its remaining years of life.
c. Give the entry to record depreciation on the machine for its 11th year. (Assume that the correction did not result in a material difference in depreciation expense.)

Exercise 12–4

A company's building appeared on its balance sheet at the end of last year at its original $225,000 cost less $165,000 accumulated depreciation. The building had been depreciated on a straight-line basis under the assumption it would have a 30-year life and no salvage value. During the first week in January of the current year, major structural repairs were completed on the building at a $37,500 cost. The repairs did not improve the building's usefulness but they did extend its expected life for seven years beyond the 30 years originally estimated. *(a)* Determine the building's age on last year's balance sheet date. *(b)* Give the entry to record the cost of the repairs. *(c)* Determine the book value of the building after its repairs were recorded. *(d)* Give the entry to record the current year's depreciation.

Exercise 12–5

Five years ago a company purchased for $500,000 the mineral rights to an ore body containing 500,000 tons of ore. The company invested an additional $500,000 in mining machinery designed to exhaust the mine in 10 years. During the first four years the mine produced 200,000 tons of ore that were sold at a profit. During the fifth year 50,000 tons of ore were mined; but due to technological changes in the manufacturing processes of the customers to whom the ore was normally sold, there was little demand for the ore and it was sold at a $1 per ton loss.

Required:
Under the assumption that the remaining 250,000 tons of ore can be mined and sold at a $1 per ton loss during the next five years and there is no prospect of ever doing better, recommend whether the mine should be closed and the loss

stopped or it should be continued in operation at a loss. Cite figures to back your recommendation.

Problem 12-1

A company the accounting periods of which end each December 31 purchased, traded, and sold the following machines:

Machine No. 45 was installed on January 5, 1970, at a $9,000 cost. It was estimated the machine would produce 90,000 units of product, after which it would have a $450 salvage value. During its first year it produced 20,000 units of product, and on July 2, 1973, after producing a total of 80,000 units it was traded on Machine No. 81. A $1,200 trade-in allowance was received, and the loss was considered immaterial.

Machine No. 81 was purchased on July 2, 1973, at an installed cost of $10,-450, less the trade-in allowance received for Machine No. 45. It was estimated Machine No. 81 would have a four-year life and a $650 salvage value. Straight-line depreciation was recorded on each December 31 of this machine's life, and on January 5, 1977, it was sold for $1,500.

Machine No. 58 was purchased on January 7, 1971, for $8,000. Its useful life was estimated at five years, after which it would have a $2,000 trade-in value. Declining-balance depreciation at twice the straight-line rate was used in recording depreciation on this machine at the ends of 1971, 1972, and 1973, after which it was traded on Machine No. 87. A $2,400 trade-in allowance was received.

Machine No. 87 was purchased on January 5, 1974, at an installed cost of $8,500, less the $2,400 allowance received for Machine No. 58. It was estimated Machine No. 87 would have a five-year life and a $600 trade-in value. Sum-of-the-years'-digits depreciation was recorded on this machine at the ends of 1974, 1975, and 1976; and on January 11, 1977, it was sold for $2,500.

Required:

Prepare general journal entries to record (1) the purchase of each machine; (2) the depreciation recorded on the first December 31 of each machine's life; and (3) the disposal of each machine. Treat the entries for the first two machines as one series of transactions and those for the next two machines as an unrelated second series. Only one entry is needed to record the exchange of one machine for another.

Problem 12-2

Prepare general journal entries to record these transactions:

1971

Jan.   5   Purchased and placed in operation Machine No. 123-71 which was estimated to have an eight-year life and no salvage value. The machine and its special power connections cost $16,000.

Dec. 31   Recorded straight-line depreciation on Machine No. 123-71.

1972

Mar. 17   After a little over a year's operation Machine 123-71 was cleaned, oiled, and painted at a $195 cost.

Dec. 31   Recorded 1972 depreciation on Machine No. 123–71.

1973

July   6   Added a new device to Machine 123–71 at a $1,100 cost. The device materially increased the machine's output but did not increase its expected life and salvage value.

Dec. 31   Recorded the 1973 depreciation on Machine No. 123–71.

1974

Dec. 31   Recorded the 1974 depreciation on Machine No. 123–71.

1975

Jan. 10   Repaired and completely overhauled Machine No. 123–71 at a $3,-000 cost, of which $400 was for ordinary repairs and $2,600 was for extraordinary repairs that extended the service life of the machine an estimated two years beyond the eight originally expected.

Dec. 31   Recorded the 1975 depreciation on Machine No. 123–71.

1976

June 28   A tornado destroyed Machine No. 123–71, and the insurance company settled the loss claim for $7,500.

Problem 12–3

PART 1. On February 17 of the current year a company paid $640,000 for mineral land estimated to contain 800,000 tons of recoverable ore. It installed machinery costing $96,000, having a 12-year life and no salvage value, and capable of exhausting the mine in eight years. The machinery was paid for on June 26, three days after mining operations began. During the period, June 23 through December 31, the company mined 40,000 tons of ore.

Required:

Prepare entries to record (a) the purchase of the mineral land, (b) payment for the machinery, (c) the depletion of the land during the current year under the assumption it will be valueless after the ore is mined, and (d) the depreciation of the machinery.

PART 2. Eight years ago Joe Dean leased a store building for a period of 20 years. His lease contract calls for $9,000 annual rental payments to be paid on January 1 throughout the life of the lease, and it also provides that the leasee must pay for all additions and improvements to the leased property. The recent construction of a new shopping centre next door has made the location more valuable, and on January 1 Joe Dean subleased the building to Gary Nash for the remaining 12 years of the lease. Gary Nash paid Joe Dean $24,000 for the privilege of subleasing the property and in addition agreed to assume and pay the building owner the $9,000 annual rental charges. During the first 12 days of January Mr. Nash remodeled the store front on the leased building at a $7,200 cost. The store front is estimated to have a life equal to the remaining life of the building, 30 years, and was paid for on January 14, the day Mr. Nash opened his new store.

Required:

Prepare general journal entries to record: (a) Gary Nash's payment to sublease the building, (b) his payment of the annual rental charge to the building owner, and (c) payment for the new store front. Also, prepare the adjusting entries required at the end of the first year of the sublease to amortize *(d)* a proper share of the $24,000 cost of the sublease and *(e)* a proper share of the store front cost.

Problem 12–4

Prepare general journal entries to record the following transactions involving the purchase and operation of a secondhand truck:

197A

Jan. 6 Purchased a secondhand delivery truck for $2,660, with an estimated three years' of remaining useful life and a $650 trade-in value.

7 Paid Sunshine Garage for the following:

Repairs to the truck's motor.....................	$ 24
New tires for the truck...........................	216
Gas and oil	7
Total...	$247

Dec. 31 Recorded straight-line depreciation on the truck.

197B

Jan. 10 Installed a hydraulic loader on the truck at a cost of $350. The loader increased the truck's estimated salvage value to $700.

May 25 Paid Sunshine Garage for the following:

Minor repairs to the truck's motor............	$ 15
New battery for the truck	30
Gas and oil	6
Total...	$ 51

Nov. 4 Paid $45 for repairs to the hydraulic loader damaged when the driver backed into a loading dock.

Dec. 31 Recorded depreciation on the truck.

197C

Jan. 5 Paid Sunshine Garage $200 to overhaul the truck's motor, replacing its bearings and rings and extending the truck's life for one year beyond the original three years planned. However, it was also estimated that the extra year's operation would reduce the truck's trade-in value to $500.

Dec. 31 Recorded depreciation on the truck.

197D

June 29 Traded the old truck on a new one having a $4,200 cash price. Received a $1,000 trade-in allowance.

Problem 12–5

Dale Hern wishes to buy an established business and is considering Companies A and B, both of which have been in business exactly four years, during which time Company A has reported an average $10,790 net income and Company B has reported an average of $10,675. However the incomes are not comparable because the companies have not used the same accounting procedures. Current balance sheets of the companies show these items:

	Company A	*Company B*
Cash	$ 4,600	$ 5,100
Accounts receivable.......................................	42,300	46,600
Allowance for doubtful accounts.......................	-0-	(3,400)
Merchandise inventory....................................	52,400	47,900
Store equipment...	23,200	21,600
Accumulated depreciation, store equipment	(11,600)	(15,600)
Total Assets...	$110,900	$102,200
Current liabilities...	$ 41,400	$ 35,700
Owner equity..	69,500	66,500
Total Liabilities and Owner Equity...............	$110,900	$102,200

Company A has used the direct write-off method in accounting for bad debts but has been slow to write off bad debts, and an examination of its accounts shows $2,400 of accounts that are probably uncollectible. Company B, on the other hand, has used the allowance method and has added an amount equal to 1% of sales to its allowance for doubtful accounts each year. However, this seems excessive, since an examination shows only $1,600 of its accounts that are probably uncollectible.

During the past four years Company A has priced its inventory on a Fifo basis, and its ending inventory appears at approximately its replacement cost. During the same period Company B has used Lifo with the result that its ending inventory appears on its balance sheet at an amount that is $6,400 below its replacement cost.

Both companies have assumed eight-year lives and no salvage value in depreciating equipment; however, Company A has used straight-line depreciation, while Company B has used sum-of-the-years'-digits depreciation. Mr. Hern is of the opinion that straight-line depreciation has resulted in Company A's equipment appearing on its balance sheet at approximately its fair value, and that fair value would result from the use of the same method for Company B.

Mr. Hern is willing to pay what he considers fair value for the assets of either business, not including cash but including goodwill measured at four times average annual earnings in excess of 15% on the fair value of the net tangible assets. He defines net tangible assets as all assets, including cash and accounts receivable, minus liabilities. He will assume the liabilities of the business purchased, paying its owner the difference between total assets purchased and the liabilities assumed.

Required:
Prepare the following schedules: *(a)* a schedule showing net tangible assets of each company at their fair values according to Mr. Hern, *(b)* a schedule showing the revised net incomes of the companies based on Fifo inventories and straight-line depreciation, *(c)* a schedule showing the calculation of each company's goodwill, and *(d)* a schedule showing the amount Mr. Hern would pay for each business.

Problem 12–1A

The accounting periods of the company that owns the following machines end on December 31.

Ma-chine	Pur-chased	Cost	Estimated Useful Life	Estimated Salvage Value	Method of Depreciation	Disposal Date and Details
No. 1	21/4/69	$5,050	5 years	$550	Straight-line	Traded on Machine No. 2, 7/1/71 trade-in allow-ance, $3,500
No. 2	7/1/71	$6,450 less trade-in allowance	5 years	$600	Sum of the years' digits	Sold for $900 on 10/1/76
No. 3	11/1/71	$3,200	4 years	$300	Declining balance at twice the straight-line rate	Trade on Machine No. 4, 5/1/75 trade-in allow-ance, $150.
No. 4	5/1/75	$3,100 less trade-in allowance	60,000 units of product	$250	Units of production*	Sold for $2,500 on 8/3/76

* Asset No. 4 produced 10,200 units of product in 1975 and 4,000 more before its sale in 1976.

Required:

Prepare general journal entries to record: *(a)* the purchase of each machine: *(b)* the depreciation recorded on the first December 31 of each machine's life; and *(c)* the disposal of each machine. Assume that gain or loss on exchange of machines No. 1 and No. 3 was immaterial. (Treat the entries for the first two machines as one series of transactions and those for the next two machines as an unrelated second series. Only one entry is needed to record the exchange of one machine for another.)

Problem 12–2A

On May 4, 1970, a company purchased and placed in operation a machine that cost $12,000 and which was estimated to have an eight-year life and no salvage value. The machine was cleaned and inspected, and minor adjustments were made on October 10, 1971, by a factory expert called in for that purpose. This cost $180. On April 27, 1973, a $750 device that increased the machine's output by one fourth was added to the machine. During the first week in January, 1975, the machine was completely overhauled at a cost of $2,900 (completed and paid for on January 12). The overhaul increased the machine's remaining estimated useful life to a total of six years beyond the date of the overhaul but did not change its zero salvage value. On June 25, 1976, the machine was completely destroyed in a fire and the insurance company settled the loss claim for $5,000.

Required:

Prepare in general journal form all entries resulting from the purchase, operation, and destruction of this machine. Assume the machine was depreciated on a straight-line basis.

Problem 12–3A

PART 1. On January 12 of the current year a company paid $1,250,000 for land having an ore body estimated to contain 1,000,000 tons of ore. The company installed machinery costing $200,000, having an estimated 12-year life and no salvage value and designed to exhaust the mine in 10 years. The machinery was paid for on May 3. During the first year's operations, ending December 31, the company mined 60,000 tons of ore.

Required:

Prepare entries to record *(a)* the purchase of the mineral land, *(b)* installation of the machinery, *(c)* the first year's depletion under the assumption the land would be worthless after removal of the ore, and *(d)* the first year's depreciation on the machinery.

PART 2. On July 5, 1969, a company purchased and installed a machine at a total cost of $12,500, and depreciated it on a straight-line basis at the ends of 1969, 1970, 1971, 1972, and 1973 under the assumption the machine would have a 10-year life and a $2,500 salvage value. After more experience with the machine and before recording 1974 depreciation, the company revised its estimate of the machine's remaining useful life downward from five and one-half years to four years and revised the estimate of the machine's salvage value downward from $2,500 to $2,000. On August 27, 1975, after recording 1974 and a part of a year's depreciation in 1975, the company traded the machine on a new machine of like nature having a $14,200 cash price. A $3,000 trade-in allowance was received. The new machine was depreciated on a straight-line basis under the assumption it would have an eight-year life and a $2,200 salvage value.

Required:

Prepare entries in general journal form to record the purchase of the first machine and depreciation on it for 1969, 1970, and 1974. Also prepare entries to record the acquisition of the second machine and depreciation on it for 1975. Assume that revision of estimated useful life of the asset did not result in a material difference in depreciation expense, however, gain or loss on trade-in was material.

Problem 12–4A

PART 1. A company completed these transactions involving the purchase and operation of a secondhand truck:

197A

Jan.   9   Purchased a secondhand delivery truck for $2,465 cash. It was estimated the truck would be used for three years and would then have a $700 trade-in value.

9   Paid $165 for a new set of tires for the truck and $20 for minor repairs to its motor.

Dec. 31   Recorded straight-line depreciation on the truck.

197B

Jan. 5 Installed a hydraulic loader on the truck at a cost of $400. The loader increased the truck's salvage value by $100.

Dec. 31 Recorded depreciation on the truck.

197C

Oct. 2 Traded the secondhand truck on a new truck having a $4,650 cash price. A $1,200 trade-in allowance was received, and the balance was paid in cash. It was estimated the new truck would have a four-year life and an $850 trade-in value. Gain or loss on trade-in was not recognized.

Dec. 31 Recorded straight-line depreciation on the new truck.

Required:

Prepare entries to record the transactions and end-of-the-period adjustments.

PART 2. Five years ago George Green leased a store building for 15 years. The lease contract requires a $9,600 annual rental payment on each January 1 throughout the life of the lease, and it requires the lessee to pay for all improvements to the leased property. Due to traffic pattern changes the lease has become more valuable, and on January 1 of the current year Mr. Green subleased the property to High-Value Stores for the remaining period of the lease. High-Value Stores paid Mr. Green $15,000 for his rights under the lease and it also agreed to pay the annual rental charge directly to the building owner. In addition, during the first part of January it remodeled the store front on the leased building at an $8,500 total cost, paying the contractor on January 14. The remodeled store front was estimated to have a life equal to the remaining life of the leased building, 20 years.

Required:

Prepare general journal entries to record High-Value Stores' payment for the right to sublease the property, payment of the annual rental charge, and payment for the new store front. Also, prepare end-of-the-first-year adjusting entries to amortize portions of the sublease cost and the cost of the new store front.

Decision problem 12–1, Junior Accountant II

In helping to verify the records of a concern being audited by the public accounting firm for which you work as a junior accountant, you find the following entries:

1976				
July	12	Cash	10,000.00	
		Loss from Fire	6,000.00	
		Accumulated Depreciation, Machinery ...	12,000.00	
		Machinery		28,000.00
		Received payment of fire loss claim.		
Aug.	15	Cash	18,000.00	
		Factory Land		18,000.00
		Sold unneeded factory land.		

An investigation revealed that the first entry resulted from recording a $10,000 cheque received from an insurance company in full settlement of a loss claim resulting from the destruction of a machine in a small plant fire on June 30, 1976. The machine had originally cost $24,000, was put in operation on January 7, 1971, and had been depreciated on a straight-line basis at the ends of each of the first five years in its life under the assumption it would have a 10-year life and no salvage value. During the first week in January, 1976, the machine had been overhauled at a $4,000 cost. The overhaul did not increase the machine's capacity nor change its zero salvage value. However, it was expected the overhaul would lengthen the machine's service life 3 years beyond the 10 originally estimated.

The second entry resulted from recording a cheque received from selling a portion of a tract of land. The tract was adjacent to the company's plant and had been purchased on February 22, 1976. It cost $22,000, and $3,000 was paid for clearing and grading it. Both amounts were debited to the Factory Land account. The land was to be used for storing raw materials. However, after the grading was completed, it was obvious the company did not need the entire tract, and it was pleased when it received an offer from a purchaser who was willing to pay $12,000 for the east half or $18,000 for the west half. The company decided to sell the west half, and it recorded the receipt of the purchaser's cheque with the entry previously given.

Were any errors made in recording the transactions discussed here? If so, describe the errors and in each case give an entry or entries that will correct the account balances under the assumption the 1976 revenue and expense accounts have not been closed.

Decision problem 12–2, intangible assets

CASE 1. Tiptop Company has spent the last 10 years developing national recognition for its brand name coffee. It has used advertising and other public relations efforts in building the name. However, over the years it has made no effort to distinguish between advertising and public relations designed to build annual sales and those designed to build recognition for the brand name. Underhill Company, on the other hand, recently purchased the going business of a company distributing a nationally known brand of coffee. Included in the purchase price was the payment of $500,000 for the exclusive right to use the company's name for coffee.

What kind of an asset is involved in each case here? Assume that the assets described are of equal value. How will each company show the asset on its balance sheet? Will a statement reader find this confusing when he compares the balance sheets of the two companies? Discuss your response to the last question.

CASE 2. Harry Ball is negotiating for the purchase of a going business to which the following statistics apply:

Assets (exclusive of goodwill)	$135,000
Liabilities	55,000
Current and expected future annual earnings	12,000
Normal earnings rate on net assets for the industry	10%

Does this business have goodwill? If so, how much should Mr. Ball pay for the goodwill?

Decision problem 12–3, Ted Nash

Ted Nash plans to buy an established business, and he has narrowed his list to three choices, Companies A, B, and C. All three have been in business for exactly four years and have reported average annual net incomes as follows: Company A, $14,632; Company B, $12,245; and Company C, $22,590. However, since they have used different accounting procedures, their reported incomes are not comparable, nor are their current balance sheets which show these items:

	Company A	Company B	Company C
Cash	$ 10,200	$ 11,400	$ 18,700
Accounts receivable	85,600	94,300	98,200
Allowance for doubtful accounts	(6,200)	(2,100)	-0-
Merchandise inventory	95,800	74,900	93,600
Equipment	30,000	33,000	32,000
Accumulated depreciation, equipment	(17,712)	(20,400)	(12,800)
Building	100,000	96,000	108,000
Accumulated depreciation, building	(10,000)	(9,600)	-0-
Land	21,000	20,000	22,000
Goodwill			2,800
Total Assets	$308,688	$297,500	$362,500
Current liabilities	$ 80,000	$ 85,000	$ 90,000
Mortgage payable	70,000	75,000	80,000
Owner equity	158,688	137,500	192,500
Total Liabilities and Owner Equity	$308,688	$297,500	$362,500

Company A has added an amount to its allowance for doubtful accounts each year equal to one half of 1% of sales. These amounts seem to have been excessive, since an analysis shows just $2,000 of the company's accounts receivable that are probably uncollectible. Company B has been more conservative, and its allowance is approximately equal to its uncollectible accounts. Company C has used the direct write-off method in accounting for bad debts; but it has always been slow to recognize a bad debt, and an examination shows accounts totaling $8,600 that are probably uncollectible.

Company B has accounted for its inventories on a Lifo basis; and as a result its current inventory appears on its books as an amount that is $17,000 below replacement cost. Companies A and C have used Fifo, and their inventories are stated at amounts near replacement costs.

The three companies have not added to their plant assets since beginning operations, and all three have assumed 10-year lives and no salvage values in recording depreciation on equipment. However, Company A has used declining-balance depreciation at twice the straight-line rate, Company B has used sum-of-the-years'-digits depreciation, and Company C has used straight-line. The buildings of the companies are of concrete construction and are comparable in every respect, excepting as to cost. Companies A and B have recorded straight-line depreciation on their buildings, assuming 40-year lives and no salvage values. However, since its building is of concrete construction and "will last forever," Company C has taken no depreciation on its building. Mr. Nash is of the opinion that if all three companies had used straight-line depreciation for both buildings and equipment, the resulting book values would approximate market values.

The goodwill on Company C's balance sheet resulted from capitalizing advertising costs during the company's first year in business.

In buying a business, Mr. Nash will buy its tangible assets, including the accounts receivable, but not including cash; and he will pay what he thinks is fair market value. He will assume the liabilities of the business and will pay for goodwill measured at four times average annual earnings in excess of a 10% return on net tangible assets (including accounts receivable) based on first-in, first-out inventories and straight-line depreciation.

Determine the amount Mr. Nash would be willing to pay for each company. Base the amounts on the following schedules: *(a)* a schedule showing net tangible assets for each company, *(b)* a schedule showing revised and corrected average net incomes, *(c)* a schedule showing the calculation of each company's goodwill, and finally *(d)* a schedule showing the amounts Mr. Nash should pay for each of the three companies.

Problem 12–1 A&R

Your investigation of the books of Alarmed Company revealed that the "fired" bookkeeper, Mr. Notsowonderful, made a series of incorrect entries during the month of November (his period of employment). You further determined that the entries have already been posted to the ledger accounts and that the cash balance as reflected by the books is correct.

Required:
For each incorrect entry presented below prepare a journal entry to correct the error.

a. A three-year insurance policy dated November 15 was renewed. Payment for the insurance premium was not due until December:

Accounts Payable...................................... 1,080		
Insurance Expense		1,080

b. During September, one of the company's warehouses was damaged by a fire. The building was repaired during the first week of November at a cost of $4,200 and the amount was charged to Building Repairs and Maintenance account. On November 26 a cheque from the Insurance company for the amount was received and recorded as follows:

Cash 4,200		
Fire Losses		4,200

c. On November 23, $980 was accepted as full payment of an invoice dated November 15 covering a sale of $1,000 to Yorktown Limited:

Cash	980	
Accounts Receivable................................	20	
Sales Revenue		1,000

d. A typewriter was purchased on credit:

Office Expense...	450	
Accounts Receivable............................		450

e. Payment was made in full settlement of Red River's invoice of $800.

Accounts Receivable...................................	800	
Accounts Payable.................................		24
Cash		776

f. Because of problems encountered during inclement weather the warehouse roof was extended over the loading platform. The work was done by an outside contractor and payment was made in full.

Wages Expenses..	8,800	
Cash		8,800

Problem 12–2 A&R

The Machinery and the Accumulated Depreciation accounts in the ledger of Seneca Stamping Company contain the following entries:

Machinery account:

DEBITS

Prior to December 31, 1975, Machines	
No. 1, 2, 3 and 4 @ $6,000	$24,000
May 3, 1976, Machine No. 5	8,000
August 30, 1976, Machine No. 6	10,000

CREDITS

August 31, Machine No. 2..	3,600
September 30, Machine No. 4	3,200

Accumulated Depreciation-Machinery account:

DEBITS

No entries

CREDITS

Prior to December 31, 1975..	$10,200
May 3, 1976...	375
August 30, 1976	1,000
September 30, 1976..	1,125

The following events took place during 1976:

a. Machine No. 5 replaced Machine No. 1 which became obsolete and was re-moved from the premises at no cost to the company. Accumulated depreciation on Machine No. 1 on December 31, 1975 amounted to $2,800. Machine No. 5 was purchased for $8,000 cash.

b. Machine No. 2 was traded in on Machine No. 6 costing $10,000. The fair market value of Machine No. 2, on August 30, was $3,600 and the accumulated depreciation on December 31, 1975 amounted to $1,200.

c. Machine No. 4 was totally destroyed by fire on September 30. Accumulated depreciation on this machine on December 31, 1975 amounted to $2,000. The machine was insured and Seneca received $3,200 from the insurance company.

The company uses straight-line depreciation, four-year service life with no salvage value and computes depreciation to the nearest month.

Required:
a. Give the probable entries that were made by Seneca's accountant.
b. Give the entires that you would make (assume that all gains and losses are material).

Problem 12–3 A&R

The following data are taken from the financial statements of Superior Company, Limited:

	19X1	*19X2*	*19X3*	*19X4*
Total assets, December 31	$420,000	$440,000	$450,000	$550,000
Total liabilities, December 31 ...	60,000	80,000	70,000	105,000
Net income..........................	48,000	53,000	57,000	62,000

Additional information indicates that $100,000 was spent on a new plant completed in November of 19X4 and currently undergoing pre-production testing.

You have been asked by a client to determine the value of the business. Your investigation indicates that the asset values reflected in the statements are sound values and that the normal rate of earnings for the industry is 10%.

Required:
Determine the value of the business on the assumption that excess earnings are to be capitalized at 20%.

13

Payroll accounting

■ An understanding of payroll accounting and the design and use of payroll records, requires some knowledge of the laws and programs that affect payrolls. Consequently, the more pertinent of these are discussed in the first portion of this chapter before the subject of payroll records is introduced.

Unemployment insurance

■ To alleviate hardships caused by interruptions in earnings through unemployment, the federal government, with the concurrence of all provincial governments, implemented an employee-employer financed unemployment insurance plan in 1940. The 1940 Unemployment Insurance Act created a federal agency, the Unemployment Insurance Commission, which was charged with the administration of the Act. Under the Act, all employment in Canada was subjected to compulsory insurance unless specifically exempt by the legislation. Exempted classifications included employment as: (1) a member of the Canadian Forces; (2) a private duty nurse; (3) a teacher; (4) a farmer; (5) a hunter or trapper; (6) a domestic; (7) a permanent civil servant; (8) employee of husband, wife, et cetera; (9) a commission salesman of insurance, real estate, and securities; and (10) employment where annual remuneration was in excess of $7,800. In 1971 the then existing legislation was rescinded and the Unemployment Insurance Act of 1971 was passed. Under this Act compulsory unemployment insurance coverage was extended to all Canadian workers who are not self-employed. As of January 1, 1976, over 12 million employees, including teachers, hospital workers, and top-level executives were covered by the insurance plan.

The purpose of an unemployment insurance program is usually twofold:

1. To pay unemployment compensation for limited periods to unemployed individuals eligible for benefits.
2. To establish and operate employment facilities that assist unemployed individuals in finding suitable employment and assist employers in finding employees.

Such was the purpose of the original Unemployment Insurance Act from its passage to April 1, 1966. On that date the employment function was transferred to the Department of Manpower and Immigration. The Unemployment Commission continued the compensation function with responsibility for: (1) revenue collection and control and (2) administration of claims and benefits. On July 1, 1971, the collection function was assumed by the Department of National Revenue, Taxation Division.

The unemployment insurance fund from which benefits are paid is jointly financed by employees and their employers. Under the original act, equal contributions were made by each group. Under the current act, in 1975, an employer is required to deduct from his employees' wages 1.4% of insured earnings, to add his contribution of 1.4 times the amount deducted from his employees' wages, and remit both amounts to the Receiver General of Canada. Insured earnings refer to average weekly gross pay in the range of $35 to $185. In other words, no deduction is made if an employee's average weekly gross pay is less than $35 and maximum deduction is reached at average weekly gross pay of $185.

The Unemployment Insurance Act in addition to setting rates requires that an employer:

1. Withhold from the wages of each employee each payday an amount of unemployment insurance tax calculated at the current rate.
2. Pay an unemployment insurance tax equal to 1.4 times the amount withheld from the wages of all employees.
3. Periodically remit both the amounts withheld from employees' wages and the employer's tax to the Receiver General of Canada. (Remittance is discussed later in this chapter.)
4. Furnish each employee a certificate of separation on termination of employment indicating: (1) the number of weeks the employee was employed in the past 52-week period, (2) unemployment insurance deduction for the last 20 weeks, and (3) reason for termination of employment.
5. Keep a record for each employee that shows among other things

wages subject to unemployment insurance and taxes withheld. (The law does not specify the exact form of the record; but most employers keep individual employee earnings records similar to the one shown later in this chapter.)

Weekly unemployment benefits

The amount of weekly benefits received by an unemployed individual who qualifies is based on his average insurable weekly earnings. Benefits are paid at a rate of two thirds of the worker's average insurable earnings over his last eight weeks of employment. Unemployed individuals qualify for extended benefits if they have 20 weeks of work to their credit.

Withholding employees' income tax

■ With few exceptions, employers are required to calculate, collect, and remit to the Receiver General of Canada the income taxes of their employees. Historically, although the first federal income tax law became effective in 1917, it applied to only a few individuals having high earnings, and it was not until World War II that income taxes were levied on substantially all wage earners. At that time Parliament recognized that many individual wage earners could not be expected to save sufficient money with which to pay their income taxes once each year. Consequently, Parliament instituted a system of pay-as-you-go, withholding of taxes each payday at their source. This pay-as-you-go withholding of employee income taxes requires an employer to act as a tax collecting agent of the federal government.

The amount of income tax to be withheld from an employee's wages is determined by his wages and the amount of his exemptions. Each individual is entitled, in 1975, to the following exemptions (as applicable) at a minimum:

1. Basic exemption for a single person $1,878
2. Married or equivalent exemption, an additional 1,644
3. Exemption for each dependent child:
   Under 16 years of age...................................... 352
   Over 16 years of age.. 646

The $1,878 basic exemption of a single person exempts the first $1,878 of an employee's annual wages from income tax; and if entitled, an employee may claim the additional exemptions listed. Also, an employee may claim other exemptions, such as for a dependent parent, grandparent, or relative, or for seasonal or part-time employment.

Employers are responsible for determining and withholding each payday the required amount from each of their employee's pay for income taxes. However, to do so an employer must know the exemptions claimed by each of his employees. Consequently, every employee is required to file with his employer an Employee's Tax Deduction Return, Form TD1, on which he claims the exemption to which he is entitled, and he must file a revised Form TD1 each time his exemptions change during a year.

In determining the amounts of income taxes to be withheld from the wages of employees, employers normally use tax withholding tables provided by the Department of National Revenue. The tables indicate the tax to be withheld from any amount of wages and with any number of exemptions. The to-be-withheld amounts include both federal and provincial income taxes except for the province of Quebec. The province of Quebec levies and collects its own income tax and its own pension plan contributions. Employers in that province remit separately, to the respective authority, federal and provincial tax deductions.

In addition to determining and withholding income taxes from each employee's wages every payday, employers are required to:

1. Remit the withheld taxes to the Receiver General of Canada.
2. On or before the last day of February following each year, give each employee a T-4 statement which tells the employee *(a)* his total wages for the preceding year, *(b)* taxable benefits received from the employer, *(c)* income taxes withheld, *(d)* deductions for registered pension plan, *(e)* Canada Pension Plan contributions, and *(f)* unemployment insurance deductions.
3. On or before the last day of February following each year, forward to the District Taxation office copies of the employees' T-4 statements plus a T-4A form on which is summarized the information contained on the employees' T-4 statements.

The Canada Pension Plan

■ The Canada Pension Plan applies, with few exceptions, to everyone who is working. Every employee and the self-employed between the ages of 18 and 70 must make contributions in required amounts to the Canada Pension Plan. Self-employed individuals are required to remit periodically appropriate amounts to the Receiver General of Canada. Employee contributions are deducted by the employer from salary, wages, or other remuneration paid to the employee. Furthermore, each employer is required to contribute an amount equal to that deducted from his employees' earnings.

Contributions are based on earnings with the first $700 of each employee's annual earnings being exempt. On earnings above that amount, and up to the 1975 ceiling of $7,400 a year, the employee contributes at the rate of 1.8%. Thus, the total contribution from both employee and employer is 3.6% of earnings subject to the Canada Pension Plan tax. The ceiling on pensionable earnings has been raised in stages from the $5,400 in 1971 to $7,400 in 1975.

Employers are responsible for making the proper deductions from their employees' earnings. The employer remits these deductions each month, together with his own contributions, to the Receiver General of Canada.

Self-employed individuals pay the combined rate for employees and employers, or 3.6% on annual earnings between $700 and the tax-exempt ceiling, and are exempt from pension plan tax if their total annual earnings are less than $800. As for the $800 tax-exempt point, if a self-employed individual has total annual earnings of $799, he pays no tax. However, if he earns $801, he must pay a 3.6% tax on the $101 in excess of $700.

Most employers use wage bracket withholding tables similar to the one for 1975 shown in Illustration 13-1 in determining Canada Pension Plan and Unemployment Insurance to be withheld from employee's gross earnings.[1] The illustrated table is for a weekly pay period; different tables are provided for different pay periods. Somewhat similar tables are available for determining income tax withholdings.

CANADA PENSION PLAN CONTRIBUTIONS AND UNEMPLOYMENT INSURANCE PREMIUMS — COTISATIONS AU RÉGIME DE PENSIONS DU CANADA ET PRIMES D'ASSURANCE-CHÔMAGE   31

WEEKLY PAY PERIOD — *PÉRIODE HEBDOMADAIRE DE PAIE*
$133.19 — $518.17

Remuneration *Rémunération*		C.P.P. R.P.C.	U.I. Premium *Prime d'a.-c.*	Remuneration *Rémunération*		C.P.P. R.P.C.	U.I. Premium *Prime d'a.-c.*	Remuneration *Rémunération*		C.P.P. R.P.C.	U.I. Premium *Prime d'a.-c.*
From-*de*	To-*à*			From-*de*	To-*à*			From-*de*	To-*à*		
$133.19 -	133.73	2.16	1.87	$ 173.19 -	173.73	2.88	2.43	$ 213.19 -	218.17	3.64	2.59
133.74 -	134.29	2.17	1.88	173.74 -	174.29	2.89	2.44	218.18 -	223.18	3.73	2.59
134.30 -	134.84	2.18	1.88	174.30 -	174.84	2.90	2.44	223.19 -	228.17	3.82	2.59
134.85 -	135.40	2.19	1.89	174.85 -	175.40	2.91	2.45	228.18 -	233.18	3.91	2.59
135.41 -	135.95	2.20	1.90	175.41 -	175.95	2.92	2.46	233.19 -	238.17	4.00	2.59
135.96 -	136.51	2.21	1.91	175.96 -	176.51	2.93	2.47	238.18 -	243.18	4.09	2.59
136.52 -	137.07	2.22	1.92	176.52 -	177.07	2.94	2.48	243.19 -	248.17	4.18	2.59
137.08 -	137.62	2.23	1.92	177.08 -	177.62	2.95	2.48	248.18 -	253.18	4.27	2.59
137.63 -	138.18	2.24	1.93	177.63 -	178.18	2.96	2.49	253.19 -	258.17	4.36	2.59
138.19 -	138.73	2.25	1.94	178.19 -	178.73	2.97	2.50	258.18 -	263.18	4.45	2.59
138.74 -	139.29	2.26	1.95	178.74 -	179.29	2.98	2.51	263.19 -	268.17	4.54	2.59
139.30 -	139.84	2.27	1.95	179.30 -	179.84	2.99	2.51	268.18 -	273.18	4.63	2.59
139.85 -	140.40	2.28	1.96	179.85 -	180.40	3.00	2.52	273.19 -	278.17	4.72	2.59
140.41 -	140.95	2.29	1.97	180.41 -	180.95	3.01	2.53	278.18 -	283.18	4.81	2.59
140.96 -	141.51	2.30	1.98	180.96 -	181.51	3.02	2.54	283.19 -	288.17	4.90	2.59
141.52 -	142.07	2.31	1.99	181.52 -	182.07	3.03	2.55	288.18 -	293.18	4.99	2.59
142.08 -	142.62	2.32	1.99	182.08 -	182.62	3.04	2.55	293.19 -	298.17	5.08	2.59
142.63 -	143.18	2.33	2.00	182.63 -	183.18	3.05	2.56	298.18 -	303.18	5.17	2.59
143.19 -	143.73	2.34	2.01	183.19 -	183.73	3.06	2.57	303.19 -	308.17	5.26	2.59
143.74 -	144.29	2.35	2.02	183.74 -	184.29	3.07	2.58	308.18 -	313.18	5.35	2.59
144.30 -	144.84	2.36	2.02	184.30 -	184.84	3.08	2.58	313.19 -	318.17	5.44	2.59
144.85 -	145.40	2.37	2.03	184.85 -	185.40	3.09	2.59	318.18 -	323.18	5.53	2.59
145.41 -	145.95	2.38	2.04	185.41 -	185.95	3.10	2.59	323.19 -	328.17	5.62	2.59
145.96 -	146.51	2.39	2.05	185.96 -	186.51	3.11	2.59	328.18 -	333.18	5.71	2.59
146.52 -	147.07	2.40	2.06	186.52 -	187.07	3.12	2.59	333.19 -	338.17	5.80	2.59
147.08 -	147.62	2.41	2.06	187.08 -	187.62	3.13	2.59	338.18 -	343.18	5.89	2.59
147.63 -	148.18	2.42	2.07	187.63 -	188.18	3.14	2.59	343.19 -	348.17	5.98	2.59
148.19 -	148.73	2.⎵	2.08	188.19 -	188.73	3.15	2.59	348.18 -	35⎵		
168.⎵				188.74 -	189.29	3.⎵		353.19 -			
				⎵ -	189.84						

Illustration
13-1

Determining the amount of withholdings from an employee's gross wages is quite easy when withholding tables are used. First, the employee's wage bracket is located in the first two columns. Then the amounts to be withheld for Canada Pension Plan and Unemployment Insurance are found on the line of the wage bracket in the appropriate columns.

Workmen's compensation

■ Legislation is in effect in all provinces for payments to employees for an injury or disability arising out of or in the course of their employment. Under the provincial workmen's compensation acts, employers are in effect required to "insure" their employees against injury or disability that may arise as a result of employment. Premiums are normally based on: (1) accident experience of the industrial classification to which each business is assigned and (2) the total payroll.

Procedures for payment are as follows:

1. At the beginning of each year every covered employer is required to submit to the Workmen's Compensation Board an estimate of his expected payroll for the ensuing year.
2. Provisional premiums are then established by the Board by relating estimated requirements for disability payments to estimated payroll. Provisional premium notices are then sent to all employers.
3. Provisional premiums are normally payable in from three to six installments during the year.
4. At the end of each year actual payrolls are submitted to the Board and final assessments are made based on actual payrolls and actual payments. Premiums are normally between 1 and 2% of payrolls and are borne by the employer.

Wages, hours, and union contracts

■ All provinces have laws establishing maximum hours of work and minimum pay rates; and while the details vary with each province, generally, employers are required to pay an employee for hours worked in excess of 40 in any one week at the employee's regular pay rate plus an overtime premium of at least one half of his regular rate. This gives an employee an overtime rate of at least one and one-half times his regular hourly rate for hours in excess of 40 in any one week. In addition, employers commonly operate under contracts with their employees' union that provide even better terms. For example, union contracts often provide for time and one half for work in excess of eight hours in any one day, time and one half for work on Saturdays, and double time for Sundays and holidays. When an employer is under such a union contract, since the contract terms are better than those provided for by law, the contract terms take precedence over the law.

In addition to specifying working hours and wage rates, union contracts often provide for the collection of employees' union dues by the employer. Such a requirement commonly provides that the employer shall deduct dues from the wages of each employee and remit the amounts deducted to the union. The employer is usually required to

---

[1] The 1975 rates are used throughout this chapter. Because of a severe deficiency in the Unemployment Insurance Fund, unemployment insurance premiums are scheduled to increase by an average of 20% on January 1, 1976. Although the rates will change the method of using withholding tables will, however, remain the same.

remit once each month and to report the name and amount deducted from each employee's pay.

Other payroll deductions ■ In addition to the payroll deductions discussed thus far, employees may individually authorize additional deductions. Some examples of these might be:

1. Deductions to accumulate funds for the purchase of Government of Canada bonds.
2. Deductions to pay health, accident, hospital, or life insurance premiums.
3. Deductions to repay loans from the employer or the employees' credit union.
4. Deductions to pay for merchandise purchased from the company.
5. Deductions for donations to charitable organizations such as Boy Scouts, Girl Scouts, Community Fund, or Red Cross.

Timekeeping ■ Compiling a record of the time worked by each employee is called *timekeeping*. In an individual company the method of compiling such a record depends upon the nature of the business and the number of its employees. In a very small business timekeeping may consist of no more than pencil notations of each employee's working time made in a memorandum book by the manager or owner. On the other hand, in a larger company a time clock or several time clocks are often used to record on clock cards each employee's time of arrival and departure. When time clocks are used, they are placed at the entrances to the office, store, or factory, and a rack for clock cards is provided beside each clock. At the beginning of each payroll period a clock card for each employee similar to Illustration 13–2 is placed in the rack at the entrance to be used by the employee. Each day as the employee enters the plant, store, or office, he takes his card from the rack and places it in a slot in the time clock. This actuates the clock to stamp the date and arrival time on the card. The employee then returns the card to the rack and proceeds to his place of work. Upon leaving the plant, store, or office at noon or at the end of the day, the procedure is repeated. The employee takes the card from the rack, places it in the clock, and stamps the time of departure. As a result, at the end of the pay period the card shows the hours the employee was on the job.

The Payroll Register ■ Each pay period the information as to hours worked as compiled on clock cards or otherwise is summarized in a Payroll Register. A pen-and-ink form of such a register is shown in Illustration 13–3. A Payroll Register for use with a bookkeeping machine would be similar. The Illustration 13–3 register is for a weekly pay period and shows the payroll data for each employee on a separate line. The column headings and the data recorded in the columns are in the main self-explanatory.

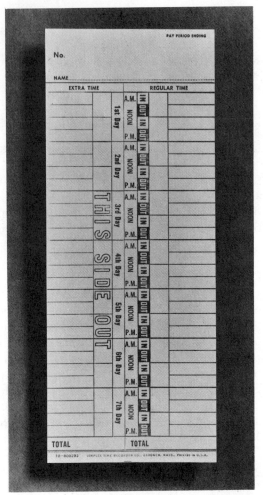

Illustration 13-2

Courtesy Simplex Time Recorder Co.

The columns under the heading "Daily Time" show hours worked each day by each employee. The total of each employee's hours is entered in the column headed "Total Hours." If hours worked include overtime hours, these are entered in the column headed "O.T. Hours."

The column headed "Reg. Pay Rate" is for the hourly pay rate of each employee. Total hours worked multiplied by the regular pay rate equals regular pay; overtime hours multiplied by the overtime premium rate equals overtime premium pay; and regular pay plus overtime premium pay is the gross pay of each employee.

Under the heading "Deductions," the amounts withheld from each employee's gross pay for unemployment insurance taxes are shown in the column marked "Unemployment Insurance." The amounts were determined by multiplying the gross pay of each employee, other than the next-to-last employee, by the 1.4% unemployment insurance rate. In the case of the next-to-last employee, maximum deduction of $2.59 per week is reached at gross weekly earnings of $185, thus only $185 of this employee's earnings are taxed and his tax deduction is $185 × 1.4% = $2.59.

As previously stated, the income tax withheld from the wages of each employee depends upon his gross pay and exemptions, and is commonly determined by using a tax table. When determined, it is entered in the column headed Income Taxes.

Deductions from employees' wages for Canada Pension Plan are entered in the column carrying that heading. In determining the amounts to be withheld, employers commonly use a tax table. Recall that the first $700 of an employee's earnings are exempt from pension plan tax. Likewise, earnings above a $7,400 ceiling in 1975 are also exempt. The table spreads the $700 exemption over the entire year for an employee having annual earnings less than $7,400; and if a weekly table, for example, allocates 1/52nd of the $700 or $13.46 to each week. As a result of the allocation the pension plan tax of the first employee of the Illustration 13-2 payroll is $120 gross pay minus $13.46 multiplied by 1.8% or is $1.92.

Observe in the "Canada Pension Plan" column of Illustration 13-2 that there is no deduction for the next-to-last employee, Robert Smith. This is because Smith's cumulative earnings for the year have previously passed the tax-exempt ceiling and his wages are no longer subject to tax.

The column headed "Hosp. Ins." shows the amounts withheld from employees' wages to pay hospital insurance premiums for the employees and their families. The total withheld from all employees is a current liability of the employer until paid to the insurance company.

Additional columns may be added to the Payroll Register for deductions that occur sufficiently often to warrant special columns. For example, a company that regularly deducts amounts from its employees' pay for Government of Canada bonds may add a special column for this deduction.

An employee's gross pay less his total deductions is his net pay and is entered in the column headed "Net Pay." The total of this column is the amount to be paid the employees. The numbers of the cheques in paying the employees are entered in the column headed "Cheque No."

The three columns under the heading "Distribution" are for sorting the various salaries into kinds of salary expense. Here each employee's gross salary is entered in the proper column according to the type of his work. The column totals then tell the amounts to be debited to the salary expense accounts.

Employee	Clock Card No.	Daily Time							Total Hours	O.T. Hours	Earnings			
		M	T	W	T	F	S	S			Reg. Pay Rate	Regular Pay	O.T. Premium Pay	Gross Pay
Robert Austin	105	8	8	8	8	8			40		3.00	120.00		120.00
Charles Cross	97	8	8	8	8	8	4		44	4	4.00	176.00	8.00	184.00
John Cruz	89	8	8	8	8	8			40		3.50	140.00		140.00
Howard Keife	112	8	8	0	0	0			16		3.50	56.00		56.00
Lee Miller	95	8	8	8	8	8			40		3.50	140.00		140.00
Dale Sears	53	8	8	8	8	8			40		3.00	120.00		120.00
Robert Smith	68	8	8	8	8	8	4		44	4	5.50	242.00	11.00	253.00
George Tucker	74	8	8	8	8	8			40		3.50	140.00		140.00
Totals														1,153.00

Illustration
13–3

Recording the payroll ■ Generally a Payroll Register such as the one shown in Illustration 13–3 is a supplementary memorandum record. As a supplementary record, its information is not posted directly to the accounts but is first recorded with a general journal entry, which is then posted. The entry to record the payroll shown in Illustration 13–3 is:

Nov.	18	Sales Salaries Expense	476.00	
		Office Salaries Expense	493.00	
		Delivery Salaries Expense	184.00	
		Unemployment Insurance Taxes Payable		15.20
		Employees' Income Taxes Payable		144.20
		Canada Pension Plan Taxes Payable		14.52
		Employees' Hospital Insurance Payable		19.50
		Accrued Payroll Payable		959.58
		To record the payroll of the week ended November 18.		

The debits of this entry are taken from the Payroll Register's distribution column totals, and they charge the employees' gross earnings to the proper salary expense accounts. The credits to Unemployment Insurance Taxes Payable, Employees' Income Taxes Payable, Canada Pension Plan Taxes Payable, and Employees' Hospital Insurance

Roll
November 18, 1975

Deductions					Payment		Distribution		
Unem-ployment Ins.	Income Taxes	Canada Pension Plan	Hosp. Ins.	Total Deduc-tions	Net Pay	Cheque No.	Sales Salaries	Office Salaries	Delivery Salaries
1.68	12.70	1.92	1.50	17.80	102.20	893		120.00	
2.58	25.00	3.07	3.00	33.65	150.35	894			184.00
1.96	18.20	2.28	1.50	23.94	116.06	895	140.00		
.79	0.00	.77	3.00	4.56	51.44	896	56.00		
1.96	9.90	2.28	3.00	17.14	122.86	897	140.00		
1.68	10.45	1.92	3.00	17.05	102.95	898		120.00	
2.59	49.75	0.00	3.00	55.34	197.66	899		253.00	
1.96	18.20	2.28	1.50	23.94	116.06	900	140.00		
15.20	144.20	14.52	19.50	193.42	959.58		476.00	493.00	184.00

Payable record these amounts as current liabilities. The credit to Accrued Payroll Payable records as a liability the amount to be paid the employees.

Paying the employees ■ Almost every business pays its employees by cheque. In a company having but few employees these cheques are often drawn on the regular bank account. When this is done, each cheque is recorded in either a Cheque Register or a Cash Disbursements Journal. Since each cheque results in a debit to the Accrued Payroll Payable account, posting labour may be saved by adding an Accrued Payroll Payable debit column to the Cheque Register or Cash Disbursements Journal. For example, assume that a firm uses a Cheque Register like that described in Chapter 6, before the introduction of the voucher system. If a firm uses such a register and adds an Accrued Payroll debit column, the entries to pay the employees of the Illustration 13–3 payroll will appear somewhat like those in Illustration 13–4.

Although not required by law, most employers furnish each employee an earnings statement each payday. The objective of such a statement is to inform the employee and give him a record of hours worked, gross pay, deductions, and net pay that may be retained. The statement usually takes the form of a detachable pay cheque portion that is removed before the cheque is cashed. A pay cheque with a detachable portion showing deductions is reproduced in Illustration 13–5.

Cheque Register

Date		Ch. No.	Payee	Account Debited	F	Sundry Accounts Debit	Accts. Pay. Debit	Accr. Payroll Debit	Pur. Dis. Credit	Cash Credit
Nov.	18	893	Robert Austin	Accrued Payroll				102.20		102.20
	18	894	Charles Cross	"				150.35		150.35
	18	895	John Cruz	"				116.06		116.06
	18	896	Howard Keife	"				51.44		51.44
	18	897	Lee Miller	"				122.86		122.86
	18	898	Dale Sears	"				102.95		102.95
	18	899	Robert Smith	"				197.66		197.66
	18	900	George Tucker	"				116.06		116.06

Illustration
13–4

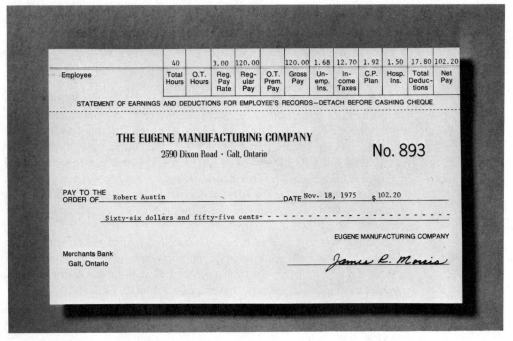

Illustration
13–5

■ A business with many employees normally makes use of a special payroll bank account in paying its employees. When such an account is used, one cheque for the amount of the payroll is drawn on the regular bank account and deposited in the special payroll bank account. Individual payroll cheques are then drawn on this special payroll account. Because only one cheque for the payroll is drawn on the regular bank account each payday, a special payroll bank account simplifies reconciliation of the regular bank account. It may be reconciled without considering the payroll cheques outstanding, and there may be many of these. Likewise, when the payroll bank account is separately reconciled, only the outstanding payroll cheques need be considered.

A company using a special payroll bank account completes the following steps in paying its employees:

1. First, it records the information shown on its Payroll Register in the usual manner with a general journal entry similar to the one illustrated on page 398. This entry causes the sum of the employees' net pay to be credited to the liability account Accrued Payroll Payable.
2. Next, a single cheque payable to Payroll Bank Account for the amount of the payroll is drawn and entered in the Cheque Register. This results in a debit to Accrued Payroll Payable and a credit to Cash.
3. Then this cheque is endorsed and deposited in the payroll bank account. This transfers cash equal to the payroll from the regular bank account to the special payroll bank account.
4. Last, individual payroll cheques are drawn on the special payroll bank account and delivered to the employees. These pay the employees and, as soon as all employees cash their cheques, exhaust the funds in the special account.

A special Payroll Cheque Register may be used in connection with a payroll bank account. However, most companies do not use such a register but prefer to enter the payroll cheque numbers in their Payroll Register, making it act as a Cheque Register.

■ An Employee's Individual Earnings Record, Illustration 13–6, provides for each employee in one record a full year's summary of his working time, gross earnings, deductions, and net pay. In addition it accumulates information that—

1. Serves as a basis for the employer's payroll tax returns.
2. Tells when an employee's earnings have reached the tax-exempt points for Canada Pension Plan and unemployment insurance taxes.
3. Supplies data for the Statement of Remuneration, Form T-4, which must be given to the employee at the end of the year.

The payroll information on an Employee's Individual Earnings Record is taken from the Payroll Register. The information as to earn-

EMPLOYEE'S INDIVIDUAL EARNINGS RECORD

Employee's Name _Robert Austin_   Soc. Ins. No. _307-003-195_   Employee No. _105_

Home Address _111 South Greenwood_   Notify in Case of Emergency _Margaret Austin_   Phone No. _964-9834_

Employed _6/7/65_   Date of Termination _____   Reason _____

Date of Birth _June 6, 1941_   Date Becomes 70 _June 6, 2011_   Male (x) Married ( ) Number of   Female ( ) Single (X) Exemptions _____   Pay Rate _$3.00 hr._

Occupation _Clerk_   Place _Office_

Date		Time Lost		Time Wk.		Reg. Pay	O.T. Prem. Pay	Gross Pay	U.I.	Income Taxes	C.P.P.	Hospital Insurance	Union Dues	Total Deduc- tions	Net Pay	Cheque No.	Cumu- lative Pay
Per. Ends	Paid	Hrs.	Reason	Total	O.T. Hours												
1/8	1/8			40		120.00		120.00	1.68	12.70	1.92	1.50		17.80	102.20	173	120.00
1/15	1/15			40		120.00		120.00	1.68	12.70	1.92	1.50		17.80	102.20	201	240.00
1/22	1/22			40		120.00		120.00	1.68	12.70	1.92	1.50		17.80	102.20	243	360.00
1/29	1/29	4	sick	36		108.00		108.00	1.32	9.55	1.70	1.50		14.07	93.93	295	468.00
2/5	2/5			40		120.00		120.00	1.68	12.70	1.92	1.50		17.80	102.20	339	588.00
2/12	2/12			40		120.00		120.00	1.68	12.70	1.92	1.50		17.80	102.20	354	708.00
2/19	2/19			40		120.00		120.00	1.68	12.70	1.92	1.50		17.80	102.20	397	828.00
2/26	2/26			40		120.00		120.00	1.68	12.70	1.92	1.50		17.80	102.20	446	948.00
11/18	11/18			40		120.00		120.00	1.68	12.70	1.92	1.50		17.80	102.20	893	5,420.00

Illustration
13–6

ings, deductions, and net pay is first recorded on a single line in the Payroll Register, from where it is posted each pay period to the earnings record.

Payroll taxes levied on the employer

■ Under the previous discussion of the Canada Pension Plan, it was pointed out that pension taxes are levied in like amounts on both employed workers and their employers. A covered employer is required by law to deduct from his employees' pay the amounts of their Canada Pension Plan taxes; but in addition, he must himself pay a tax equal to the sum of his employees' pension taxes. Commonly, the tax levied on the employer is recorded at the same time the payroll to which it relates is recorded. Also, since both the employees' taxes and employer's tax are reported on the same tax return and are paid in one amount, the liability for both is normally recorded in the same liability account, the Canada Pension Plan Taxes Payable account.

In addition to the pension plan tax, an employer is required to pay an unemployment insurance tax that is 1.4 times the sum of his employees' unemployment insurance deductions. Most employers record both of these payroll taxes with a general journal entry that is made at the time the payroll to which the taxes relates is recorded. For example, the entry to record the employer's payroll taxes on the payroll of Illustration 13–3 is:

Nov.	18	Payroll Taxes Expense....................................	35.80	
		Unemployment Insurance Taxes Payable....		21.28
		Canada Pension Plan Taxes Payable..........		14.52
		To record the employer's payroll taxes.		

The debit of the entry records as an expense the payroll taxes levied on the employer, and the credits record the liabilities for the taxes. The $21.28 credit to Unemployment Insurance Taxes Payable is 1.4 times the sum of the amounts deducted for this tax from the pay of the employees whose wages are recorded in the Payroll Register of Illustration 13–3, and the credit to Canada Pension Plan Taxes Payable is equal to the total of the employees' pension plan deductions.

In the illustration it was assumed that Hospital Insurance was shared equally by the employee and employer. A journal entry is, therefore, required to record the employer's portion of Hospital Insurance as follows:

Nov.	18	Hospital Insurance Expense	19.50	
		Employees' Hospital Insurance Payable......		19.50
		To record the employer's hospital insurance expense.		

Paying the payroll taxes
■ Income, Unemployment Insurance, and Canada Pension Plan taxes withheld each payday from the employees' pay plus the Unemployment Insurance and Canada Pension Plan taxes imposed on the employer are current liabilities until paid to the Receiver General of Canada. The normal method of payment is to pay the amounts due at any chartered bank or remit directly to the Receiver General of Canada. Payment of these taxes must be made before the 15th of the month following the month deductions were made from the earnings of the employees. Payment of these liabilities is recorded in the same manner as payment of any other liabilities.

Accruing taxes and wages
■ Payroll taxes are levied on wages actually paid; consequently, there is no legal liability for taxes on accrued wages. Nevertheless, both wages and the employer's payroll taxes on the wages are from a theoretical viewpoint expenses of the accounting period in which the wages are earned; and if the income statement is to show all expenses of an accounting period, both accrued wages and the accrued taxes on the wages should be recorded at the end of the period. However, the amounts by which such taxes differ from one accounting period to the next are commonly of little consequence. As a result, many accountants apply the rule of materiality and do not accrue payroll taxes.

Machine methods
■ Manually prepared pen-and-ink records like the ones described in this chapter are found in many small concerns, and very satisfactorily

meet their needs. However, concerns having many employees commonly use machines in their payroll work. The machines vary but are usually designed to take advantage of the fact that in each pay period much the same information must be entered for each employee in the Payroll Register, on his earnings record, and on his pay cheque. The machines take advantage of this and simultaneously print the information in all three places in one operation.

Questions for class discussion

1. Who pays taxes under the Canada Pension Plan?
2. Who pays premiums under the workmen's compensation laws?
3. What benefits are paid to unemployed workers from funds raised by the Federal Unemployment Insurance Act?
4. Who pays federal unemployment insurance taxes? What is the tax rate?
5. What are the objectives of unemployment insurance laws?
6. To whom and when are payroll taxes remitted?
7. What determines the amount that must be deducted from an employee's wages for income taxes?
8. What is a tax withholding table?
9. What is the Canada Pension Plan tax rate for self-employed individuals?
10. How is a clock card used in recording the time an employee is on the job?
11. How is a special payroll bank account used in paying the wages of employees?
12. At the end of an accounting period a firm's special payroll bank account has a $162.35 balance because the payroll cheques of two employees have not cleared the bank. Should this $162.35 appear on the firm's balance sheet? If so, where?
13. What information is accumulated on an employee's individual earnings record? Why must this information be accumulated? For what purposes is the information used?
14. What payroll taxes are levied on the employer? What taxes are deducted from the wages of an employee?

Class exercises

Exercise 13–1

William Smith, an employee of Crown Derby Company, received his notice of employment termination on May 19, 1975. The reason for dismissal was lack of work. Smith worked for the company for nearly a year and his rate of pay in 1975 was $4.50 per hour. During 1975 Smith did not miss a day of work and worked full 8-hour shifts, five days per week.

a. Calculate Smith's total contribution to the Unemployment Insurance Fund during 1975.
b. Calculate the company's related amount for the same period.
c. Calculate Smith's weekly Canada Pension Plan contribution.

Exercise 13–2

On January 6, at the end of its first weekly pay period in the year, the column totals of a company's Payroll Register showed that its sales employees had earned $1,200 and its office employees had earned $600. Withholdings from employees were as follows: Income taxes $185, unemployment insurance $25.20, union dues $45, hospital insurance $15, and Canada Pension Plan taxes of $30. Give the general journal entry to record the Payroll Register.

Exercise 13–3

Give the general journal entry to record the employer's payroll taxes resulting from the Exercise 13–2 payroll.

Exercise 13–4

The following information as to earnings and deductions for the pay period ended December 21 was taken from a company's payroll records:

Employees' Names	Gross Pay	Earnings to End of Previous Week	Income Taxes	Hospital Insurance Deductions
James Abbott..............	$135	$ 3,880	$10.30	$2.00
Jane Cotton.................	140	4,085	15.50	2.00
George Green.............	185	8,950	22.30	2.00
Jerry Hall...................	195	10,010	29.10	2.00
	$655		$77.20	$8.00

Required:
1. Calculate the employees' unemployment insurance withholdings.
2. Which employees have reached the tax-exempt point for Canada Pension Plan deduction?
3. Prepare a general journal entry to record the payroll information.
4. Prepare a general journal entry to record the employer's payroll taxes resulting from the payroll.
(Note: Use withholding table – Illustration 13–1).

Problems **Problem 13–1**

The column totals of a company's Payroll Register indicated its sales employees had earned $3,000 and its office employees $800 during the pay period ended January 6, and no employee had earned more than $185 or less than $35 during the period. Unemployment insurance taxes had been withheld from each employee's pay; and in addition, $60 of Canada Pension Plan taxes, $325 of income taxes, $110 of group insurance, and $50 of union dues had been withheld from the pay of all employees.

Required:
1. Calculate the total of the Unemployment Insurance column in the Payroll Register.
2. Prepare a general journal entry to record the payroll register information.
3. Prepare a general journal entry to record the employer's payroll taxes resulting from the payroll.

4. Under the assumption the company uses special payroll cheques and a payroll bank account in paying its employees. give the cheque register entry (Cheque No. 815) to transfer funds equal to the payroll from the regular bank account to the payroll bank account.
5. Answer this question: After the cheque register entry is made and posted, are additional debit and credit entries required to record the payroll cheques and pay the employees?

Problem 13–2

The following information was taken from a company's payroll records for the weekly pay period ended December 18:

Employees' Names	Clock Card No.	Daily Time							Pay Rate	Income Taxes	Medical Insurance	Earnings to End of Previous Week
		M	T	W	T	F	S	S				
Roy Andrews......	11	8	8	8	8	8	0	0	3.50	10.70	2.00	5,275
Jerry Dale	12	8	8	8	8	8	0	0	3.50	18.70	2.00	6,175
Ray Lewis.........	13	8	8	8	8	8	4	0	5.50	29.10	2.00	10,825
Walter Mohr.......	14	8	8	8	8	8	0	0	4.50	18.30	2.00	8,950
Mary Page.........	15	8	8	8	8	8	4	0	3.00	14.50	2.00	3,910

Required:
1. Enter the relevant information in the proper columns of a Payroll Register. The company pays time and one half for the hours over 40 in any one week. Calculate and enter the employees' unemployment insurance tax deductions (use 1975 rates). Calculate and enter pension plan deductions for the three employees whose wages have not reached the tax-exempt ceiling. (To do this subtract $13.46 from each employee's gross pay and multiply the remainder by the 1.8% tax rate.) Complete the register under the assumption the first two employees are salesmen, the third drives the delivery truck, and the last two work in the office.
2. Prepare a general journal entry to record the payroll register information.
3. Make the cheque register entry (Cheque No. 234) to transfer funds equal to the payroll from the regular bank account to the payroll bank account under the assumption that the company uses special payroll cheques and a payroll bank account in paying its employees. Assume the first payroll cheque is numbered 668 and enter the payroll cheque numbers in the Payroll Register.
4. Prepare a general journal entry to record the employer's payroll taxes resulting from the payroll.

Problem 13–3

A company that pays time and a half for hours in excess of 40 per week accumulated the following payroll information for the weekly pay period ended December 15:

Employees' Names	Clock Card No.	Daily Time							Pay Rate	Income Taxes	Canada Pension Plan	Medical Insur-ance
		M	T	W	T	F	S	S				
Paul Baer..........	22	8	8	8	8	8	0	0	5.90	29.50	4.00	2.00
Frank Clift.......	23	8	8	8	8	8	0	0	3.90	11.50	-0-	2.00
Dale Duff	24	0	0	8	8	8	0	0	4.50	5.70	1.69	2.00
June Nash.........	25	8	8	8	8	9	3	0	5.25	29.10	4.09	2.00
Lee Ross	26	8	8	8	9	9	0	0	5.50	31.50	-0-	2.00

Required:

1. Enter the relevant information in the proper columns of a Payroll Register. Calculate and enter the employees' unemployment insurance deductions. Complete the register. Assume the first two employees are salesmen, the second two work in the office and the last drives the delivery truck.
2. Prepare a general journal entry to record the payroll register information.
3. Make the cheque register entry to transfer funds equal to the payroll from the regular bank account to the payroll bank account (Cheque No. 567) under the assumption that the company uses special payroll cheques and a payroll bank account in paying its employees. Assume the first payroll cheque is numbered 444 and enter the payroll cheque numbers in the Payroll Register.
4. Prepare a general journal entry to record the employer's payroll taxes resulting from the payroll.

Problem 13–4

The All-salary Company computes its payroll on a monthly basis and gives its employees an advance on the 15th of the month for approximately one half of the net pay. On June 30 (after all entries pertaining to the June payroll were posted) the following account balances appeared in the company's ledger:
a. Unemployment Insurance Payable, $62.
b. Canada Pension Payable, $81.
c. Employees' Income Taxes Payable, $368.
d. Employees' Group Insurance Payable, $80.
e. Accrued Payroll Payable, $982. (The mid-month advance of $960 was debited to this account.)

Required:

1. General journal entry made by the company to record the payroll register information.
2. General journal entry made by the company to record the employer's payroll taxes.
3. Under the assumption the company uses a payroll bank account and special payroll cheques in paying its employees, give the cheque register entry (Cheque No. 747) to transfer funds equal to the balance of the payroll from the regular bank account to the payroll bank account.
4. Record the issuance of Cheque No. 812 to the Receiver General of Canada for the amount due on July 15, resulting from the June payroll.

Problem 13–1A

On January 7, at the end of the first weekly pay period of the year, the column totals of a company's Payroll Register indicated its sales employees had earned $1,800, its office employees had earned $900, and its delivery employees $800. Unemployment insurance had been withheld from each employee's wages and no employee had earned more than $185 or less than $35 during the period. In addition, $65 of Canada Pension Plan taxes, $390 of income taxes, $38 of hospital insurance, and $24 of union dues had been withheld from the pay of all employees.

1. Calculate the total of the Unemployment Insurance Taxes Payable column in the Payroll Register, and prepare a general journal entry to record the register information.
2. Prepare a general journal entry to record the employer's payroll taxes resulting from the payroll.
3. Under the assumption the company uses a payroll bank account and special payroll cheques in paying its employees, give the cheque register entry (Cheque No. 745) to transfer funds equal to the payroll from the regular bank account to the payroll bank account.
4. Answer this question: After the cheque register entry is made and posted, are additional debit and credit entries required to record the payroll cheque and pay the employees?

Problem 13–2A

A company's payroll records provided the following information for the weekly pay period ended December 20:

Employees' Names	Clock Card No.	Daily Time							Pay Rate	Income Taxes	Medical Insurance	Earnings to End of Previous Week
		M	T	W	T	F	S	S				
Dale Agnew.....	14	8	8	8	8	8	0	0	4.50	20.30	2.00	8,920
Mary Hall.......	15	8	8	8	8	8	4	0	4.00	29.50	2.00	8,140
John Koop	16	8	8	8	8	8	0	0	3.50	20.30	2.00	5,710
Carl Lee.........	17	8	8	8	8	8	0	0	5.50	32.30	2.00	5,325
Roy Page........	18	8	8	8	8	8	2	0	5.00	30.70	2.00	9,410

Required:
1. Enter the relevant information in the proper columns of a Payroll Register. The company pays time and one half for hours in excess of 40 in any one week. Calculate and enter the employees' unemployment insurance tax deductions (use 1975 rates). Calculate and enter pension plan deductions for the three employees whose wages have not reached the tax-exempt ceiling. (To do this subtract $13.46 from each employee's gross pay and multiply the remainder by the 1.8% tax rate.) Complete the register under the assumption that the first two employees work in the office, the next two are salesmen, and the last drives the delivery truck.

2. Prepare a general journal entry to record the payroll register information.
3. Assume the company uses special payroll cheques drawn on a payroll bank account in paying its employees, and make the cheque register entry (Cheque No. 202) to transfer funds equal to the payroll from the regular bank account to the payroll bank account. Also assume the first payroll cheque is No. 653 and enter the payroll cheque numbers in the Payroll Register.
4. Prepare a general journal entry to record the employer's payroll taxes resulting from the payroll.

Problem 13–3A

The following information for the weekly pay period ended December 17 was taken from the records of a company that pays time and one half for hours worked in excess of 40 per week:

| Employees' Names | Clock Card No. | Daily Time | | | | | | | Pay Rate | Income Taxes | Canada Pension Plan | Union Dues |
		M	T	W	T	F	S	S				
Mary Alt.............	21	8	8	8	8	8	0	0	4.50	19.10	3.00	-0-
Harry Bray..........	22	8	8	8	8	8	2	0	4.50	21.90	-0-	-0-
Jerry Hamm.........	23	8	8	8	8	8	0	0	5.80	36.50	3.91	4.50
Alex Hunt...........	24	8	8	8	8	8	0	0	5.80	30.70	3.91	4.50
Gary Sage	25	8	8	8	8	8	4	0	5.00	32.70	-0-	4.50

Required:
1. Enter the relevant information in the proper columns of a Payroll Register. Calculate and enter the employees' unemployment insurance deductions. Complete the register. Assume the first two employees work in the office, the next two are salesmen, and the last drives the delivery truck.
2. Prepare a general journal entry to record the payroll register information.
3. Make the cheque register entry (Cheque No. 789) to transfer funds equal to the payroll from the regular bank account to the payroll bank account. Assume the first payroll cheque is numbered 901 and enter the payroll cheque numbers in the Payroll Register.
4. Prepare a general journal entry to record the employer's payroll taxes resulting from the payroll. The company has a fully paid Hospital Insurance Plan. The company pays $1.50 per week for each employee.

Problem 13–4A

The Yukon Company computes its payroll on a monthly basis and gives its employees a mid-month advance for approximately one half of the monthly net pay. On June 30 (after all entries pertaining to the June payroll were posted) the following account balances appeared in the company's ledger:
a. Unemployment Insurance Payable, $320.
b. Canada Pension Payable, $384.
c. Employees' Income Taxes Payable, $984.
d. Employees' Group Insurance Payable, $140.
e. Accrued Payroll, $2,920. (The mid-month advance of $2,900 was debited to this month's account.)

Required:

1. General journal entry made by the company to record the payroll register information.
2. General journal entry made by the company to record the employer's payroll taxes.
3. Under the assumption the company uses a payroll bank account and special payroll cheques in paying its employees, give the cheque register entry (Cheque No. 642) to transfer funds equal to the balance of the payroll from the regular bank account to the payroll bank account.
4. Record the issuance of Cheque No. 706 to the Receiver General of Canada for amount due on July 15 resulting from the June payroll.

Decision problem 13–1, Plastic Toy Company

Plastic Toy Company manufactures a number of products from plastics. It has 300 full-time employees, all earning $6,000 or more per year.

Recently the company secured an order for Christmas toys from a large chain of department stores. The order should be very profitable and will probably be repeated each year. In filling the order Plastic Toy Company can stamp out the parts for the toys with its present machines and employees. However, it will have to add 50 women to its work force for 40 hours per week for 10 weeks to assemble the toys and pack them for shipment.

The company can hire these women and add them to its own payroll, or it can secure their services through Extra Hands, Ltd., a company in the business of supplying temporary help. If the temporary help is secured through Extra Hands, Ltd., Plastic Toy Company will pay Extra Hands, Ltd., $4.80 per hour for each hour worked by each person supplied. The people supplied will be employees of Extra Hands, Ltd., and it will pay their wages and all taxes on the wages. On the other hand, if Plastic Toy Company employs the women and places them on its payroll, it will pay them $4.00 per hour and will pay the usual payroll taxes and an estimated 50 cents per hour in addition to the regular rate for such things as the company's portion of medical insurance, workmen's compensation, vacation pay, etc. If the company secures the temporary help through Extra Hands, Ltd., it will save an estimated $800 in "want-ads" and in interviewing and selection costs. Also, it will not incur an estimated $300 per week in additional office expenses required to process the payroll, etc.

Should Plastic Toy Company place the temporary help on its own payroll or should it secure their services through Extra Hands, Ltd.? Justify your answer.

Analytical and review problem

Problem 13–1 A&R

Using current year's withholding tables for Canada Pension Plan, Unemployment Insurance, and Income Tax update the Payroll Register of Illustration 13–3. In computing income tax withholdings state *your* assumption as to each employee's personal deductions. Assume that Hospital Insurance deductions continue at the same amounts as in Illustration 13–3.

14

Accounting principles

■ Accounting is the art of accumulating and reporting financial information about an economic unit. If the information is to achieve its maximum usefulness, generally accepted accounting principles must be followed in accumulating the data and preparing the reports. A number of these principles have been discussed thus far; however, this seems an appropriate place to go further into the theoretical aspects of accounting.

Need for accounting principles ■ During the past century business enterprises have grown tremendously in size and complexity and commonly have become large corporations owned by thousands of stockholders and managed by professional managers. These managers have always been accountable to the enterprise owners (stockholders) who employ them. However, since control over a large company, like General Motors, carries with it much economic power and social responsibility, it is now generally recognized that managers are also accountable to employees, customers, creditors, potential investors, government, and the public.

The managers of a large company are known as "insiders," since they have ready access to the company's accounting records and make its decisions. The company's stockholders, customers, creditors, employees, and the general public are called "outsiders." Outsiders have to depend upon a company's published financial reports for information about the company and its activities; and unless these reports are prepared in conformity with generally accepted accounting principles, their content may be misleading and subject to manipulation.

Nature of
accounting
principles
■ Generally accepted accounting principles are broad rules adopted by the accounting profession as guides for use in recording and reporting the financial affairs and activities of a business to its stockholders, investors, creditors, and other outsiders. They are not natural laws in the sense of the laws of chemistry or physics, but are man-made rules designed to enhance the usefulness of accounting data. They have evolved from the combined thinking of members of the accounting profession and depend for their authority on their general acceptance by the accounting profession.

The Canadian Institute of Chartered Accountants (CICA), the professional association of chartered accountants, has long been influential in describing and defining general accepted accounting principles. In 1936 the Terminology Committee of the CICA was formed and asked to take steps to encourage greater uniformity in the use of accounting terms by its members. The year 1939 saw the establishment of a joint research program with Queen's University which in 1946 culminated in the creation of the Accounting and Auditing Research Committee. The aim of the committee was to improve both accounting and auditing practices, and to provide guidelines for communicating financial information and economic facts, and for auditing procedures and techniques.

For a number of years prior to 1968, the Research Committee issued bulletins on financial disclosure, accounting principles, terminology, reporting and auditing procedures. These bulletins were recognized as expression of generally accepted accounting principles. In 1968 the bulletins were consolidated to form a major part of the *CICA Handbook*.[1] Since 1968 the *Handbook* has been constantly updated by inclusion of approved exposure drafts on various current topics.

In 1973 the Accounting and Auditing Research Committee (ARC) and the Auditing Standards Committee (ASC) were established, replacing the Accounting and Auditing Research Committee. By far the most important responsibility of both committees is the issuance of *Accounting Recommendations* and *Auditing Recommendations* for the *CICA Handbook*. These pronouncements were given added importance by the requirement that "Where the accounting treatment does not follow the recommendations in the *Handbook*, the practice used should be explained in notes to the financial statements with an indication of the reasons why the recommendation was not followed."[2]

The American Accounting Association, an organization with strong academic ties, has also been influential in describing and defining generally accepted accounting principles. It has sponsored a number of re-

---

[1] *CICA Handbook* (Toronto: The Canadian Institute of Chartered Accountants).
[2] Ibid., p. 202.

search studies and has published many articles dealing with accounting principles. However, its influence has not been as great as the CICA in Canada and the AICPA (American Institute of Certified Public Accountants) in the United States, since it has no power to impose its views on the accounting profession, but must depend upon the prestige of its authors and the logic of their arguments.

Accounting
concepts

■ An understanding of accounting principles begins with the recognition of four broad concepts as to the nature of the economic setting in which accounting operates. The four do not include all aspects of the setting, but they are the more significant. They are (1) the entity concept, (2) the going-concern concept, (3) the stable dollar concept, and (4) the periodicity concept. Three have been discussed before, but further discussion is needed.

The business entity concept

Every business unit or enterprise is treated in accounting as a separate entity, with the affairs of the business and those of the owner or owners being kept entirely separate. Each unit is viewed as owning all resources committed to its purposes and in turn owing both its creditors and owners for having supplied the resources. Thus accounting is primarily concerned with the business unit and only secondarily interested in its owner or owners.

Corporations are in fact separate legal entities, but the separate existence of a single proprietorship or partnership is an arbitrary one derived solely for accounting purposes. Nevertheless, for accounting purposes, every business is treated as a separate entity, and all its records and reports are developed from this viewpoint. Furthermore, in carrying out the accounting function, the financial position and operating results of a business unit should never be distorted by including in its records and reports either the assets or transactions of another business or the personal assets and transactions of the owner or owners. For example, the personal automobile of a single proprietor or that of the president of a small family corporation should not be included among the business assets, nor should its gas, oil, and repairs be treated as a business expense, for to do so distorts the financial position and profitability reports of the business.

The going-concern concept

For accounting purposes, unless there is strong evidence to the contrary, it is assumed that a business will continue to operate as a going concern, earning a reasonable net income for a period longer than the life expectancy of any of its assets. In other words, it is assumed that a business will remain in operation long enough to recover the cost of its assets through the sale of its products or services.

The following income statement demonstrates the idea of recovering the cost of assets through product sales:

Excel Company
Income Statement for Year Ended December 31, 19—

Revenue...	$100,000
Cost of products sold, rent, wages, supplies, and other costs (including $5,000 depreciation on equipment)...	90,000
Net Income..	$ 10,000

During the year of the statement, Excel Company recovered all costs of selling its products with $10,000 left over. Included within the costs is $5,000 depreciation; and since none of the revenue that flowed into the company during the year flowed out for this expense, the company recovered $5,000 of the cost of its equipment through the sale of its products.

The going-concern concept provides the foundation for balance sheet preparation and periodic income measurement. For example, it provides the justification for carrying plant assets on the balance sheet at cost less accumulated depreciation, in other words at the share of their cost applicable to future periods. It is also the justification for carrying at cost such things as stationery imprinted with the company name, though salable only as scrap paper. In all such instances the intention is to use the assets in carrying on the business operations. They are not for sale, so it is pointless to place them on the balance sheet at market or realizable values, whether these values are greater or less than book values.

The going-concern concept puts emphasis on the income statement and on the proper matching of costs and revenues. Under it the balance sheet becomes secondary, as it probably should, since earning capacity is usually more important in judging the worth of a business or its debt-paying ability.

Although the going-concern concept is applicable in most accounting situations, it should be recognized that where a business is faced with liquidation, going-concern accounting is not applicable. In such a situation liquidation accounting and liquidation values apply.

The stable dollar concept

In our country all transactions are measured, recorded, and reported in terms of dollars; and in the measuring, recording, and reporting process the dollar is treated as a stable unit of measure, like a gallon, an acre, or a mile. However, unfortunately the dollar, like other currencies, is not a stable unit of measure. When the general price level (the average of all prices) changes, the value of money (its purchasing power) also changes. For example, during the past 15 years the general price level has approximately doubled, which means that over these years the purchasing power of the dollar has declined from 100 cents to approximately 50 cents.

Nevertheless, although the instability of the dollar is recognized, accountants in their reports continue to add and subtract items acquired in different years with dollars of different sizes. In effect they ignore changes in the size of the measuring unit. For example, assume a company purchased land some years ago for $10,000 and sold it today for $20,000. If during this period the purchasing power of the dollar declined from 100 cents to 50 cents, it can be said that the company is no better off for having purchased the land for $10,000 and sold it for $20,000, because the $20,000 will buy no more goods and services today than the $10,000 at the time of the purchase. Yet, using the dollar to measure both transactions, the accountant reports a $10,000 gain from the purchase and sale.

Since the instability of the dollar as a unit of measure is recognized, the question for accountants is should the amounts shown on financial statements be adjusted for changes in the purchasing power of the dollar. Techniques have been devised to convert the historical dollars of statement amounts into dollars of current purchasing power. Such statements are called *common-dollar statements*. However, their preparation requires subjective judgments as to the exact purchasing power of the dollar at various times and for various items. Also, the concept of common dollars as a measuring device is somewhat difficult for the general public to understand. Consequently, most accountants are of the opinion that the traditional statements based on the stable-dollar assumption and showing historical amounts are best for general publication.

Nevertheless, although the stable-dollar assumption helps to ensure objectivity in general-purpose financial statements, it does make an evaluation of financial position and operating results more difficult in times when the purchasing power of the dollar fluctuates. As a result, it has been recommended that supplementary statements which show the effects of price-level changes on reported net income and financial position be appended to the regular reports to stockholders. The CICA has acknowledged the usefulness of such statements and given its approval for their inclusion as a supplement to the regular financial statements, but it has expressed the belief that general price-level information is not required at this time for a fair presentation of financial position and operating results. However, the problem needs and will receive more attention in coming years.

The periodicity concept

Taxes based on annual earnings must be paid to governmental units; stockholders must receive annual reports and often quarterly ones; and some companies consider it necessary to divide operations into monthly periods for the preparation of internal reports for management. Consequently, the environment in which accounting operates — the business community and the government — requires that the life of a business be divided into relatively short periods and that changes in its wealth be measured over these short periods.

Yet, it is generally agreed that earnings cannot be measured precisely over a short period, that it is impossible to learn the exact earnings of a business until it has completed its last transaction and converted all its assets to cash. Therefore, it should be recognized that the financial statements of a business are tentative in nature and to an extent are based on assumptions and judgments. For example, assumptions as to inventory flows and judgments as to depreciation and the collectibility of accounts receivable.

Nevertheless, the environment in which accounting operates requires that the life of a business be divided into accounting periods of not more than a year in length and that test readings of the progress of the business be made at the end of each period. Furthermore, when acceptable accounting principles and procedures are used in assigning revenues and expenses to proper accounting periods, although judgments and opinions are involved, confidence in the short-term reports is justified.

Accounting principles

■ A common definition of the word *principle* is: "A broad general law or rule adopted or professed as a guide to action; a settled ground or basis of conduct or practice. . . ." Consequently, accounting principles may be described as broad rules adopted by the accounting profession as guides for use in accumulating and reporting financial data.

Brief discussions of some of the more significant principles follow.

The cost principle

Perhaps the basic principle underlying accounting records and reports is the cost principle. Under this principle it is held that cost is the appropriate basis for recording the acquisition of assets, services, and other factors of production and that cost is the basis for holding assets, services, and other factors of production in the accounts until sold, consumed, or otherwise disposed of by the business. The costs of properties, services, and other factors of production that are on hand at any particular time represent assets and are often referred to as "unexpired costs." When they are sold or consumed, they become "expired costs" or expenses.

Under the cost principle it is recognized that it is not the purpose of accounting to account for the "value" of the various factors of production committed to the business operations. Rather, it is to account for their acquisition at cost, to hold these costs in the accounts until the factors are sold, expire, or are consumed, and finally to match the costs of the sold, expired, or consumed factors and portions thereof against revenues.

Under the cost principle a balance sheet shows the "unexpired costs" of the various production factors committed to the business operations. It does not show their "value," for value like beauty can only be subjectively measured; and also the "value" (purchasing power) of the accountant's unit of measure is constantly, though gradually, changing.

In applying the cost principle, costs are measured on a cash or cash-equivalent basis. If the consideration given for a particular production factor is cash, the measure of the cost incurred is the entire cash outlay made to secure the factor and get it ready for use. If the consideration is other than cash, the measure of the consideration is the cash-equivalent value of the consideration, or the fair value (on a cash-equivalent basis) of the thing received, whichever is more clearly evident.

A deviation from cost is required for assets received by donation. Donated assets are recorded at their cash-equivalent value as of the donation date. This departure from cost is considered necessary because every business resource, regardless of its origin, should be properly accounted for, and only by charging a business with the acquisition cost or fair value of all its resources can the earning power of the enterprise be determined properly.

The cost principle is applicable in measuring equities, both owner and creditor, as well as assets. All three—assets, liabilities, and owner equities—should be recorded and reported in accordance with the cost principle.

The matching principle

This principle holds that a major objective of accounting is the determination of periodic net income by matching appropriate costs with revenues. The principle recognizes that streams of revenues continually flow into a business, and it requires that (1) there be a precise "cut off" in these streams at the end of an accounting period, (2) the inflows of the period be measured, (3) the costs incurred in securing the inflows be determined, and (4) the sum of the costs be deducted from the sum of the inflows to determine the period's net income.

As the terms are used here, costs include goods and services sold, goods and services consumed in the business operations, expired assets, and losses such as those from fire, storm, and the sale of capital assets. Revenues are inflows of assets from the sale of products and services and also the sale of assets other than stock in trade, such as unneeded equipment and investments. Revenues arise too from the advantageous settlement of liabilities. And, a net income results when the revenue inflows exceed the cost expirations and outflows plus casualty losses and losses from capital asset sales.

REVENUE RECOGNITION. The matching principle requires that a revenue be associated with an accounting period, and this in turn requires that the point or period in time at which revenue is realized be determined. Three commonly used bases for determining this point are

(1) the sales basis, (2) the cash basis, and (3) the percentage-of-completion basis.

Sales basis. The most commonly used basis for revenue recognition is the sales basis. Under this basis revenue is considered to be earned when a sale is completed, and a sale is completed when assets such as cash or a promise to pay cash are transferred from the buyer to the seller in exchange for title to goods or services.

Theoretically, revenue is earned throughout the whole business process, but its amount is not determinable until a price is agreed upon between a buyer and a seller and a legal sale is made. For example, a manufacturer earns part of his revenue upon completing each of these necessary business steps: (1) manufacturing goods for sale, (2) securing orders from customers, and (3) delivering the goods. Yet, until all steps are completed, there is no right to collect the sales price. The sales basis recognizes this, and under it revenue is not measured and reported until a sale is completed.

Cash basis. Where there is considerable doubt as to the amount which ultimately will be collected from a sale, it may be desirable to defer reporting revenue from the sale until collected in cash. Under the cash basis the desirability of this is perceived, and under the cash basis revenue is not recognized until collected in cash.

The cash basis for revenue recognition is often used in accounting for installment sales. Here the gross profit from a sale is held in suspense until collected in cash, at which point it is taken up as revenue. As a result, revenue from installment sales is recognized in the accounting periods in which the installment payments are collected in cash. For example, during its first year in business a home appliance store gained $70,000 of gross profit by selling on installment contracts for $200,000 appliances that cost $130,000. By the year's end it had incurred $20,000 of operating expenses and had collected $80,000 in cash on its installment contracts, which left it with $120,000 of installment accounts receivable. Since the store's gross profit rate is 35% ($70,000 ÷ $200,000 = 35%), if it recognizes revenue on a cash basis, it should hold in suspense until collected in cash the gross profit on its installment accounts receivable. If it does so, it will report $8,000 of net income for its first year, calculated as follows:

Installment sales	$200,000
Cost of goods sold	130,000
Gross profit on sales	$ 70,000
Less gross profit deferred (35% × $120,000)	42,000
Recognized gross profit	$ 28,000
Operating expenses	20,000
Net Income	$ 8,000

The cash basis is also commonly used by doctors, dentists, and others who perform professional services. Once doctors and dentists did not collect a large portion of fees billed, and the cash basis was justified in that it simplified accounting for uncollectible accounts. Today, its employment by professional people seems justifiable only on the basis of its simplicity, its long use, and the fact that it is acceptable for income tax purposes.

Percentage-of-completion basis. Sometimes the sales basis for taking up revenue fails even approximately to recognize revenue in the periods in which it is earned. For example, a contractor specializing in large construction jobs often finds the typical project requires two or more years for completion. If such a contractor has a three-year project and takes up revenue on a sales basis, he will recognize the revenue from this job and take up the earnings in the year of completion. Yet portions of the revenue and earnings are actually earned in each of the three years required for completion. Furthermore, if the contractor has only a few projects under construction at any one time, he may find that none or only a small portion are completed in a single year in spite of the year being one of heavy activity. In such cases a contractor may elect to take up revenue and earnings on his projects on a percentage-of-completion basis in order to allocate earnings to the periods in which earned.

To illustrate the percentage-of-completion basis for recognizing revenue, assume a contractor has under construction a large dam for which the total contract price is $80,000,000 and for which the estimated construction costs are $75,000,000. As construction progresses the costs incurred are accumulated. These costs include materials, labor, supplies, depreciation on equipment, insurance, and all other expenses related to the project. If at the end of the first accounting period in which this dam is under construction the total of the costs charged to the dam is $15,000,000, this amount is used to determine the period's revenue from the job. The $15,000,000 of costs are one fifth or 20% of the total estimated $75,000,000 cost of the job; consequently, $16,000,000 or one fifth ($80,000,000 $\times \frac{1}{5}$ = $16,000,000) of the total contract price is recognized as the year's revenue from this project.

At the end of the second year, the second year's costs and the same procedures are used to take up the second year's revenue; and this continues throughout the construction period until the last year, the year in which the job is completed, when any previously unrecognized revenue is taken into the accounts.

At times actual construction costs vary from estimates. When this occurs and the variation is material, an adjustment of the amount of revenue taken into the accounts may be necessary.

MEASURING AND MATCHING COSTS. In determining net income from business operations all costs which are *applicable* to the revenue of the period should be charged against that revenue. Costs are "applicable" if it is reasonably apparent that they represent resources and services consumed in the process of realizing that particular revenue.

Costs are applicable to the revenue of the period under each of the following circumstances:

1. If there is "a direct identification or association with the revenue of the period." Illustrations of costs directly associated with a period's revenue are cost of merchandise delivered to customers, sales commissions, etc.

2. If there is "an indirect association with the revenue of the period, as in the case of office salaries or rent."

3. Also, a commonly accepted accounting axiom holds that no income emerges until and unless capital is preserved intact. This is to say that there can be no gain on an investment where the investment is lost. For this reason, other measurable expirations of asset costs even though not associated with production of the period's revenue must be deducted from revenue before a final measurement of net income can be made. Thus losses from fire and storm, from the sale of capital assets, and from all other causes even though not related to ordinary business operations must be deducted from revenue before any beneficial net increase in business assets can be reported.

The measurement of "expired" costs (or the costs that should be deducted from a period's revenue) is in part precise and in part estimated through consistent application of definite methods. With reference to the period of expiration, expired costs are accounted for as follows:

1. *Costs of assets and services consumed in their entirety in one period*—the measure of these costs is precisely recorded in the accounts in accordance with the cost principle. Part of these costs (of assets and services consumed in their entirety) is normally applicable to the revenue of the current period and is so charged; part is also normally applicable to the future in that it is transformed by a manufacturing process into goods or services to be sold or used in the future. This latter portion is represented largely by inventories.

2. *Costs of assets and services consumed more or less gradually over two or more periods*—costs of this type are also recorded in the accounts in accordance with the cost principle, but it is necessary to arrive at a rational allocation of the total as between the current and future periods. This is done through the consistent application of methods found most useful in the industry, the methods being based on experience and expert opinion. In general the cost division is made by determining first the portion of cost which seems reasonably beneficial to future periods, and then subtracting these deferred costs from the total to determine the amount to be matched with current revenue.

"Applicable costs" are deducted from current revenue only when they are measurable "with reasonable approximation." It is important that all costs incurred in producing a period's revenue be matched against that revenue. However, when in the considered judgment of the accountant, material costs applicable to current revenue cannot be determined with sufficient accuracy to satisfy the accountant, he should not include these costs in the current income statement. For example, a company introduced a new machine in which it is felt that during the first year imperfections may be found by users which the company will feel obligated to remedy, perhaps at considerable cost. Yet, no experience is available by which to estimate this applicable cost "with reasonable approximation." In a case such as this the cost that cannot be measured with a reasonable approximation should be referred to by footnote or parenthetical notation on the income statement, pointing to the omission of the expected cost and thus emphasizing the provisional nature of the net income figure. Such a cost should be reported in a later statement when its amount is known. Of course, if the potential cost is so material as to make misleading any statement of net income, the revenue from the sale of the new product may have to be deferred until a more definite computation of applicable cost can be made.

The objectivity principle

This principle holds that changes in account balances should be supported to the fullest extent possible by objective evidence. Whims and fancies plus, for example, something like an opinion of management that "an asset is worth more than it cost" have no place in accounting. To be fully useful, accounting information must, as nearly as possible, be based on objective evidence.

Bargained transactions supported by verifiable business documents originating outside the business are the best objective evidence obtainable; and whenever possible, accounting data should be supported by such documents. However, at times it is necessary to rely on an opinion or an estimate, for example, in determining depreciation or bad debts; but here also objective evidence should be used to the fullest extent possible. After all, bad debt losses of previous years are a form of objective evidence.

At times a dependable estimate cannot be made for lack of objective evidence. When this happens the estimate should not be entered in the accounts; but if pertinent, it should be disclosed by means of a balance sheet or income statement footnote.

The consistency principle

In many cases two or more methods or procedures have been derived in accounting practice to accomplish a particular accounting objective.

For example, there are several methods of computing depreciation, and more than one method has been found satisfactory in arriving at the cost of inventory. In each case one method may be considered more useful for one enterprise, while another may be more satisfactory for a concern operating under different circumstances.

Nevertheless, while recognizing the validity of different methods under varying circumstances, it is still necessary in order to ensure a high degree of comparability in any concern's accounting data to insist on a consistent application in the company of any given accounting method, period after period. It is also necessary to insist that any departures from this doctrine of consistency be fully disclosed on the financial statements and the effects thereof on the statements fully described.

As a result of this consistency principle, in the absence of clear indications to the contrary, a reader of a company's accounting statements is able to assume that in the preparation of the statements generally accepted accounting principles have been followed in a manner consistent with previous years. Only on the basis of this assumption can meaningful comparisons of the information in a company's statement be made year after year.

As a final point, it should be observed that the principle of consistency applies to a single accounting entity and does not require that all companies, even those in the same industry, use the same accounting procedures. Consequently, in comparing the financial statements of different companies, it is important to look for and determine the effects of differences in the accounting procedures of the companies.

The full-disclosure principle

Under this principle it is held that financial statements and their accompanying footnotes and other explanatory materials should disclose fully and completely all relevant data of a material nature relating to the financial position and operating results of the company for which they are prepared. This does not necessarily mean that the information should be detailed, for details can at times obscure. It simply means that all information necessary to an appreciation of the company's position be reported in a readily understandable manner and that nothing of a significant nature be withheld.

Full disclosure is not limited to information in the ledger accounts. For example, any of the following would be considered relevant and should be disclosed by means of footnotes or explanatory paragraphs attached to the statements:

LONG-TERM COMMITMENTS UNDER A CONTRACT. If the company has signed a long-term lease requiring a material annual payment, this should be disclosed even though the liability does not appear in the accounts. Also, if the company has pledged certain of its assets as security for a loan, this should be revealed.

CONTINGENT LIABILITIES. A company that is contingently liable due to possible additional tax assessments, note endorsements, pending lawsuits, or product guarantees should disclose this on its statements.

ACCOUNTING METHODS USED. Whenever there are several acceptable accounting methods that may be followed, a company should report in each case the method used, especially when a choice of methods can materially affect reported net income. For example, a company should report by means of footnotes or notes accompanying its statements the inventory method or methods used, depreciation methods, treatment of research and development costs, and the like.[3]

CHANGES IN ACCOUNTING METHODS. Under the accounting principle of consistency it is held that a company should consistently follow the same accounting methods period after period, but may change if it is decided that a different acceptable method will better reflect periodic net income. When such a change is made, for example, a change in depreciation method for assets acquired in a previous period, the nature of the change, justification for the change, and the effect of the change on current net income should be disclosed in notes accompanying the statements. Also, the cumulative effect of the change on the income of prior periods, net of taxes, should be added or subtracted on the current income statement at a point immediately before the amount described as the current period's net income.[4]

EVENTS SUBSEQUENT TO THE DATE OF THE STATEMENTS. An event such as a major casualty loss, settlement of a legal action, sale of a major asset, in fact any and all significant events occurring after the balance sheet date but before the statements are released should be disclosed if the events are expected to materially affect the company's future.

The principle of conservatism

Decisions based on estimates and opinions as to future events affect financial statements. Financial statements are also affected by the selection of accounting procedures. The principle of conservatism holds that the accountant should be prudent in his estimates and opinions and in his selection of procedures, choosing those that neither unduly understate nor overstate the situation.

It is generally conceded that business executives tend toward the optimistic side in their appraisal of a business situation and that they need a counterweight of caution if a proper balance in the judgment of future prospects and unresolved risks is to be attained. Under the principle of conservatism it is held that the accountant should supply this counterweight, that in all judgment situations he should take an analytical, conservative, "show me" attitude.

---

[3] Ibid., pp. 211–12.
[4] Ibid., p. 212.

Something called balance sheet conservatism was once considered the "first" principle of accounting, the objective being to place every item on the balance sheet at a conservative figure. This in itself was commendable; but it commonly resulted in overconservatism, which in turn resulted in (1) an understatement of asset and equity amounts, (2) an overstatement of costs in the year the assets were first understated, and (3) an understatement of costs on each income statement thereafter throughout the lives of the understated assets. Today, accountants recognize that balance sheet conservatism is not desirable when it misrepresents true situations; and they recognize that full and fair disclosure is a more important accounting objective.

The principle of materiality

Under this principle it is held that a strict adherence to accounting principles is not required for items of little significance because accounting must be practical. Consequently, the accountant must always weigh the costs of complying with an accounting principle against the extra accuracy gained thereby; and in those situations where the cost is relatively great and the lack of compliance will have no material effect on the financial statements, compliance is not necessary. For example, if a wastepaper basket is purchased for $2.50, its cost might better be charged to an expense account in the period of purchase than be depreciated over the asset's estimated five-year life, because the extra accuracy gained from depreciating is not worth its cost.

There is no clear-cut distinction between material and immaterial items, and no item is material or immaterial by itself. Each situation must be individually judged, and an item is material or immaterial as it relates to other items. For example, a $1,000 item on an income statement showing a $1,000,000 net income might not be significant; but it would be significant if the net income were, say, $10,000. Generally, an item is considered significant if it is sufficiently large as to influence a statement reader's judgment of a situation.

Accounting principles and the public accountant

■ Transactions are recorded and financial statements are usually prepared by the employees of the company issuing the statements; and as employees they must do the company's bidding, as a rule, or seek employment elsewhere. Consequently, agreements as to generally accepted accounting principles are of no value unless there is some way of assuring outsiders that the principles were faithfully followed. In other words, outsiders need an independent representative who will examine the company's records and certify that its reported income is fairly stated, that its balance sheet carries an all-inclusive list of its assets and liabilities, that owner equity is fairly stated, and that all is in accordance with generally accepted accounting principles.

The public accountant fills this roll; and his importance is evidenced by the fact that for a corporation to sell its stock on a major stock exchange, and in some cases over the counter, its records must be audited by an independent public accountant before the stock is sold and annually thereafter. Also, in securing a loan and in fulfilling the requirements of corporate bylaws, such an audit is commonly required.

An audit of a business enterprise consists of a critical review and exploration of its internal controls and accounting records made to enable the auditor to express an opinion as to the accuracy and fairness of the concern's financial statements. Upon its completion, the auditor issues a report which the audited concern attaches to or publishes as a part of its financial statements. A typical report will read:

To the Shareholders of _____

We have examined the balance sheet of _____
as at _____, 19__ and the statements of income, retained earnings and source and application of funds for the year then ended. Our examination included a general review of the accounting procedures and such tests of accounting records and other supporting evidence as we considered necessary in the circumstances.

In our opinion these financial statements present fairly the financial position of the company as at _____, 19__ and the results of its operations and the source and application of its funds for the year then ended, in accordance with generally accepted accounting principles applied on a basis consistent with that of the preceding year.

(signed) _____

Chartered Accountants

City
Date

Note in the report that the auditors made such tests of the accounting records as they considered necessary under the circumstances. In making an audit, auditors normally examine only a portion of the audited concern's transactions, the size of the sample being dependent upon how much the auditors feel they can rely on the audited concern's internal control systems.

If the auditor takes exception to any of the audited concern's accounting or internal control practices, he must either withhold his report until the condition is corrected or he must place a qualification in the report.

Questions for class discussion

1. Who are the insiders of a corporation? Who are its outsiders?
2. What are accounting principles? Why are they needed?
3. What is the essence of the business entity concept?
4. What is the essence of the going-concern concept?
5. Explain how a business just breaking even (no profit or loss) will recover the cost of its plant assets over a period of years through the sale of its products.

6. Do the dollar amounts shown on a balance sheet for assets represent the value of these assets?
7. What is the essence of the periodicity concept?
8. A company constructed a machine for itself after a local shop submitted a low bid of $15,000 for building it. It cost the company $10,000 to build the machine, and in recording the acquisition the company debited Machinery for $15,000 and took up a $5,000 profit on the deal. Was this a correct treatment for the transaction? What accounting principle governs in this situation?
9. An automobile dealer offers a customer $800 cash for his used car. However, if the customer will buy a new car for $4,000, he will allow the customer a $1,000 trade-in on his old car. (a) If the customer accepts the offer for trading in his old car, what is the cost of the new car to the customer? (b) What is the dealer's revenue from the sale of the new car?
10. When is revenue recognized under the (a) sales basis, (b) cash basis, and (c) percentage-of-completion basis?
11. What is the essence of the objectivity principle?
12. What is the best objective evidence upon which to base an accounting entry?
13. May a concern change its inventory costing method at will? If it does so, what accounting principle is violated?
14. If a company changed its accounting methods at will, what would be lost?
15. What is the essence of the full-disclosure principle?
16. Under what accounting principle does an accountant justify charging the cost of a pencil sharpener to an expense account in the year of purchase, rather than to an asset account the balance of which will be depreciated over the pencil sharpener's life?
17. What determines the number of transactions an auditor will examine in making his annual audit of a company's records?

Class exercises

Exercise 14–1

The going business of Zoom Company has just been sold at a price twice the amount shown on its latest balance sheet for its owners' equity. The company was organized 10 years ago and has always followed generally accepted accounting principles in keeping its accounting records. Its accounts were audited just prior to the sale, and the auditor stated that in his opinion the company's balance sheet of that date presented fairly the financial position of the business. Explain fully why in a case such as this the sale price of a business may differ so greatly from the equity of its owners.

Exercise 14–2

A mail-order company, the accounting periods of which end each October 31, sends out its general catalogue at the end of August each year; and its customers order from this catalogue for a year until a new catalogue arrives on about September 1 of the next year. Last August it cost $1,500,000 to print and mail the catalogue, and the company followed its usual practice and charged the entire cost to an expense account on the day the catalogues were mailed. Did the company violate generally accepted accounting principles? Would you suggest an alternate treatment for the printing and mailing costs? State your position and defend it.

Exercise 14–3

A company purchased a site for a new factory for $400,000 cash; but due to changes in competitive conditions, the factory was not built; and 10 years later the site was sold for $500,000. The company reported a $100,000 gain on the transactions and paid $25,000 of income taxes on the gain. Did the company report the gain according to generally accepted accounting principles? If the purchasing power of the dollar declined from 100 cents on the day of the purchase to 80 cents on the day of the sale, what was the company's gain or loss in purchasing power as a result of the purchase and sale?

Exercise 14–4

A company sells on an installment basis for $100 per unit a machine that costs $60 per unit. Last year it sold 2,000 of the machines, incurred $25,000 of operating expenses, and collected $85,000 in cash from the year's installment sales. Prepare calculations to show the company's income before taxes with revenue recognized (a) on a sales basis and (b) on a cash basis.

Exercise 14–5

A company contracted to build a shopping centre for $2,640,000. It estimated the centre would cost $2,400,000 to build. The job was begun in 197A and completed in 197B. Construction costs in 197A were $840,000, and they were $1,575,000 in 197B. Determine the revenue the company will recognize each year if it recognizes revenue (a) on a sales basis and (b) on a percentage of completion basis.

Problems **Problem 14–1**

A change in the purchasing power of the monetary unit used in recording and reporting accounting data causes problems in interpreting financial statement information. Based on what you have learned thus far in this course, discuss the nature of such problems as related to inventories, to plant and equipment, and to long-term debt.

Problem 14–2

In each of the following unrelated cases one or more accounting principles may have been ignored. In each case in which you think a principle may have been ignored, name the principle and write a sentence or so telling what should have been done. In any case in which you think generally accepted principles were followed, write a sentence or so defending the action taken.
a. Early this year High Flyer Company acquired the plant, equipment, and other assets of a company that had experienced a number of financial and operating problems during recent years. High Flyer Company paid for the assets acquired with 100,000 shares of its own stock, and in addition it agreed to pay $250,000 of delinquent property taxes on the acquired plant and equipment. Upon completion of the purchase, the High Flyer account-

ant took the plant, equipment, and other assets purchased into his company's accounts at an amount equal to the book value of the 100,000 shares of stock given, which was some 20% under their market value on the day of the purchase. He also recorded the cheque for the delinquent property taxes with a debit to Property Taxes Expense.

b. On January 10, 197B, a company's plant was struck by a tornado that caused $500,000 of damage to the plant. The company's insurance was adequate to pay for the physical damage to the plant, but it made no provision for the loss that would result from the one-month shutdown while repairs were being made. The company had expected to show a $1 per share profit during the first three months of 197B; however, as a result of the shutdown, it could expect to no more than break even. Nevertheless, since the wind damage occurred after the close of business on December 31, 197A, and did not affect the amount of the company's assets of that date, the company mailed its 197A statements to its stockholders without further accounting action.

c. The purchase of a stapler was recorded with a debit to the Office Equipment account for its $8 cost. The stapler was expected to have a 10-year life and no salvage value. As a result, a subsidiary plant asset record card was set up and $0.80 depreciation was recorded on the stapler at the ends of each of the first four years of its life. During the fifth year it disappeared from the office and the loss was recorded with a debit to an account called Miscellaneous Expenses and Losses.

d. A company opened a new branch in a leased building. The lease contract ran for 25 years, required no payment at the time the lease was signed, but did provide for a $36,000 annual rental charge, a material amount. The rental payment was recorded each year with a debit to Rent Expense, and no further accounting action was taken.

e. A company had a bad year during 197A; as a result, its president ordered a clerk in the accounting department to keep the Sales account open during the first two weeks of 197B and to record the sales of that period as though they had occurred during the 197A period, which ended on December 31. The clerk, fearful for his job, followed the president's orders.

f. A company changed its inventory costing method from Fifo to Lifo during 197A. The change made a material difference in its reported 197A net income. However, the year-end balance sheet and the 197A income statement both referred to the change by means of a footnote which told of the change, the reasons therefor, and restated the 197A income on the basis of Fifo, and restated the reported incomes of the previous five years on the basis of Lifo.

Problem 14–3

PART 1. Last year a company earned a 30% gross profit on $196,500 of sales. Its operating expenses totaled $35,300 and its sales by types were:

Cash sales	$ 44,200
Sales on 30-day accounts	68,300
Installment sales (two years to pay; collections during the year, $22,500)	84,000
Total sales	$196,500

Required:
Prepare a calculation *(a)* to show the company's income before taxes under the assumption it recognizes revenue on a sales basis and *(b)* prepare a second calculation to show its income before taxes under the assumption it recognizes revenue from cash sales and 30-day accounts on a sales basis and revenue from installment sales on a cash basis.

PART 2. A construction company began three jobs during 197A and 197B. Job No. 1 was completed during 197B, and Jobs Nos. 2 and 3 were completed in 197C. Following are the contract prices, estimated costs, and yearly costs for the jobs:

Job No.	Contract Prices	Estimated Costs	197A Costs	197B Costs	197C Costs
1	$3,945,000	$3,600,000	$1,200,000	$2,415,000	
2	4,860,000	4,400,000	440,000	3,300,000	$ 658,000
3	3,080,000	2,800,000		350,000	2,455,000

Required:
Determine the revenue the company will recognize in each of the three years if *(a)* it recognizes revenue on a sales basis and *(b)* it recognizes revenue on a percentage-of-completion basis.

Problem 14–4

Ted Weeks has been in the construction business for three years, building commercial buildings on a contract basis. During the three years he has recognized revenue on a sales basis but is unhappy with the results, since his construction income each year bore no relation to the year's construction activity. He began and completed three jobs during the period. Job No. 1 was begun and completed in 197A, his first year in business. Job No. 2 was begun in 197A and completed in 197B, and Job No. 3 was begun in 197B and completed in 197C. The following information as to contract prices and costs is available:

Job No.	Contract Prices	Estimated Costs	197A Costs	197B Costs	197C Costs
1	$ 302,500	$ 276,400	$ 274,300		
2	464,000	424,800	106,200	$ 320,100	
3	496,500	453,000		151,000	$ 304,800
	$1,263,000	$1,154,200	$ 380,500	$ 471,100	$ 304,800

Required:
1. Prepare a comparative income statement showing in the first three columns the revenue, costs, and construction income for each year, plus the combined figures for the three years in the fourth column, with revenue recognized on a sales basis.
2. Prepare a second columnar statement showing the same information with revenue recognized on a percentage-of-completion basis.

Problem 14–5

Warehouse Furniture Sales has been in business for three years, selling furniture for cash and on an installment basis. Condensed income statements for the three years show these results:

	197A	197B	197C
Cash sales	$166,700	$201,700	$205,700
Installment sales	208,300	263,300	270,800
Total sales	$375,000	$465,000	$476,500
Cost of goods sold	228,750	274,350	285,900
Gross profit from sales	$146,250	$190,650	$190,600
Operating expenses	118,100	142,300	143,950
Net Income	$ 28,150	$ 48,350	$ 46,650

The company collected the following amounts from its installment sales during the three-year period:

	197A	197B	197C
Collected from 197A sales	$ 52,300	$105,000	$ 51,000
Collected from 197B sales		65,800	131,500
Collected from 197C sales			67,300

Required:
Prepare income statements in columnar form that show the company's net income for each of the years with revenue recognized on a cash basis. (To simplify the problem it is assumed there were no bad debts or repossessions.)

Alternate problems

Problem 14–2A

In each of the following unrelated cases one or more accounting principles may have been ignored. In each case in which you think a principle may have been ignored, name the principle and write a sentence or so telling what should have been done. In any case in which you think generally accepted principles were followed, write a sentence or so defending the action taken.

a. Walter Kraft, his wife, and son own all the stock in Walter Kraft, Ltd., a manufacturing concern. Mr. Kraft is president and manages the company; the son is in college; and Mrs. Kraft takes no part in the management or other affairs of the company. However, during the past year the company leased an Oldsmobile 98 which was turned over to Mrs. Kraft for her personal use. She was also given a credit card, issued to the company, for use in charging gas, oil, and repairs to the car.

b. Some 10 years ago a company purchased for $15,000 a tract of land adjacent to its plant. From the time of its purchase until this year the land was carried at cost in an account, Long-Term Investment in Land. In March of this year the land was appraised by an independent appraiser and assigned a $50,000 current market value. In June it was graded and paved for an employees' parking lot at a $40,000 cost for the grading and paving, and the company recorded the transaction as follows:

June	27	Land Improvements.......................	90,000.00	
		Long-Term Investment in Land ...		15,000.00
		Gain on Investments.................		35,000.00
		Cash		40,000.00

c. A company received as a gift from the local chamber of commerce a plot of land having a $5,000 fair market value; but to secure and clear title to the land, the company had to pay $450 in delinquent taxes plus transfer and other fees totaling $50. As a result, the bookkeeper recorded the land's acquisition at cost with a $500 debit to Land and a $500 credit to Cash.

d. Zeel Company was sued for $1,000,000 in August, 197A, by a competitor who claimed patent infringements. The company took no accounting action as a result of the suit during 197A and 197B because it was not scheduled for trial until 197C, and besides the company's directors were of the opinion that the competitor had no basis for the suit and could not win.

e. To reduce accounting costs, a company follows the practice of charging directly to an expense account at the time of purchase any machine or piece of equipment having an invoice price of $100 or less.

f. The factory building of Tiptop Company, carried in its accounts at its $200,000 cost less $75,000 accumulated depreciation, was appraised for insurance purposes and found to have a $300,000 replacement cost and to be one third depreciated. Upon receipt of the appraisal, the company president ordered a clerk in the accounting department to write up the value of the building and to credit Gain from Appraisal. The clerk, meek fellow that he was, swallowed twice and complied.

Problem 14–3A

PART 1. A company has been in business for one year selling on an installment basis for $500 each a machine that costs $325. At the year-end the following sales information is available:

Sales (all on installment basis)...	$500,000
Installment accounts receivable...	280,000
Sales commissions (10% of selling price on each machine).............	50,000
Other expenses	35,000

Required:
Prepare (a) a calculation showing the company's income before taxes under the assumption it recognizes revenue on a sales basis and (b) prepare a second calculation showing income before taxes under the assumption it recognizes revenue on a cash basis and matches sales commissions with revenue.

PART 2. A construction company began three jobs during 197A. It completed Jobs Nos. 1 and 2 in 197B and Job No. 3 in 197C. Following are the contract prices, estimated costs, and yearly costs for the jobs:

Job No.	Contract Prices	Estimated Costs	197A Costs	197B Costs	197C Costs
1	$2,040,000	$1,800,000	$1,500,000	$ 295,500	
2	1,788,000	1,500,000	500,000	997,300	
3	2,640,000	2,400,000	400,000	800,000	$1,211,000

Required:
Determine the revenue the company will recognize in each of the three years if it (a) recognizes revenue on a sales basis and (b) recognizes revenue on a percentage-of-completion basis.

Problem 14–4A

Island Construction Company has recognized revenue on a sales basis during the three years it has been in business. However, it is unhappy with the results, since its construction income for each of the years bears no relation to construction activity. The company began and completed Job No. 1 in 197A, the first year it was in business. It began Job No. 2 in 197A and completed it in 197B, and it began Job No. 3 in 197A and completed it 197C. The following information as to contract prices and costs is available:

Job No.	Contract Prices	Estimated Costs	197A Costs	197B Costs	197C Costs
1	$ 277,000	$ 242,000	$ 240,500		
2	492,000	445,000	89,000	$ 357,500	
3	513,000	468,000	46,800	234,000	$ 189,000
	$1,282,000	$1,155,000	$ 376,300	$ 591,500	$ 189,000

Required:
1. Prepare a comparative income statement showing in the first three columns the revenue, costs, and construction income for each year, plus the combined figures for the three years in the fourth column, with revenue recognized on a sales basis.
2. Prepare a second columnar statement showing the same information with revenue recognized on a percentage-of-completion basis.

Problem 14–5A

Easy Furniture Company has been in business selling furniture for cash and on an installment basis for three years. The following statistics show the results of its operations:

	197A	197B	197C
Cash sales	$152,700	$168,000	$183,500
Installment sales	195,600	227,500	263,500
Cost of furniture sold	226,395	264,985	295,020
Operating expenses	69,775	70,325	83,730
Collected from 197A installment sales	48,800	97,600	49,200
Collected from 197B installment sales		56,500	114,000
Collected from 197C installment sales			65,500

Required:

1. Under the assumption the company recognized revenue on a sales basis, prepare a columnar income statement showing in columns for each of the three years sales, cost of goods sold, gross profit from sales, operating expenses, and net income.
2. Prepare a similar columnar statement showing the results of each year's operations with revenue recognized on a cash basis. (To simplify the problem it is assumed there were no bad debts or repossessions.)

Decision problem 14–1, Junior Accountant III

You are a new junior accountant, and in completing the training program of your firm you have been asked to write brief answers to the following problems:

PROBLEM 1. On December 10, last year, Zoom Company purchased the entire inventory of a bankrupt competitor, paying $25,000. The goods would have cost $40,000 if purchased through normal sources; and as a result, the company recorded the purchase as follows:

Dec.	10	Purchases..	40,000.00	
		Gain on Purchase of Inventory.......		15,000.00
		Cash		25,000.00

The goods were marked for sale as if they had cost $40,000; none were sold during the year of purchase; but all were sold without markdowns during the following year. The company's accounting year ends on December 31.

Discuss the accounting principles violated in recording the purchase and tell how the transaction should have been recorded.

PROBLEM 2. Valley Tractor Sales sells farm machinery, taking in used equipment on many of its deals. Any new equipment the company sells has a definite cost and suggested selling price set by its manufacturer; but the amount a farmer is given on a trade-in depends entirely on the farmer's bargaining ability.

Last week the company traded for some land a used tractor and two used corn pickers it had taken in on trades.

Discuss the determination of the cost of this land for accounting purposes.

PROBLEM 3. Mesa Construction Company specializes in building large bridges, most of which require 15 months to 3 years to complete. The company uses the sales basis of revenue recognition, but the accuracy of this is under question.

Discuss the company's revenue recognition problem, giving the conditions under which you would recommend a change to the percentage-of-completion basis.

Problem 14–1 A&R

Interprovincial Oil Company drilled 10 oil wells at an average cost of $2,500,000 each. Four of the oil wells were found to be "producers," with estimated total reserves of 10,000,000 barrels, while the remaining six were "dry." Interprovincial's experience was representative of the industry. The same year 1,000,000 barrels of crude were pumped.

Accountant A argues that the following entries are proper for the recording of the above:

Oil wells...	25,000,000	
Cash (or Payables)......................................		25,000,000
Depletion expense..	2,500,000	
Accumulated depletion—oil wells		2,500,000

Accountant B argues that the entries should be:

Oil wells...	10,000,000	
Loss on drilling of dry wells...............................	15,000,000	
Cash (Payables)...		25,000,000
Depletion expense..	1,000,000	
Accumulated depletion—oil wells		1,000,000

Required:
You have been asked to arbitrate the case. Present your supported views.

15

Partnership accounting

■ The provincial Partnership Acts and the Civil Code, with minor variation, defined a partnership as: "Partnership is the relation which subsists between persons carrying on a business in common with a view of profit; but the relationship between members of any company or association incorporated under the provisions of any Act of the legislature is not a partnership within the meaning of the Act." A partnership has been further defined as "an association of two or more competent persons under a contract to combine some or all their property, labour, and skills in the operation of a business." And although both of these definitions tell something of its legal nature, a better understanding of a partnership as a form of business organization may be gained by examining some of its characteristics.

Characteristics of a partnership

■ A voluntary association

A partnership is a voluntary association into which a person cannot be forced against his will. This is because a partner is responsible for the business acts of his partners, when the acts are within the scope of the partnership; and too, a partner is unlimitedly liable for the debts of his partnership. Consequently, partnership law recognizes it is only fair that a person be permitted to select the people he wishes to join in a partnership, and normally a person will select only financially responsible people in whose judgment he has respect.

Based on a contract

One advantage of a partnership as a form of business organization is the ease with which it may be begun. All that is required is that two or more legally competent people agree to be partners. Their agreement becomes a contract and should be in writing, with all anticipated points of future disagreement covered. However, it is just as binding if only orally expressed.

Limited life

The life of a partnership is always limited. Death, bankruptcy, or anything that takes away the ability of one of the partners to contract automatically ends a partnership. In addition, since a partnership is based on a contract, if the contract is for a definite period, the partnership ends with the period's expiration. If the contract does not specify a time period, the partnership ends when the business for which it was created is completed. Or, if no time is stated and the business for which it was created cannot be completed but goes on indefinitely, the partnership may be terminated at will by any one of the partners.

Mutual agency

Normally there is mutual agency in a partnership. This means that under normal circumstances every partner is an agent of his partnership and can enter into and bind the partnership to any contract within the apparent scope of its business. For example, a partner in a trading business can bind his partnership to contracts to buy merchandise, lease a store building, borrow money, or hire employees, since these are all within the scope of a trading firm. On the other hand, a partner in a law firm, acting alone, cannot bind his partners to a contract to buy merchandise or rent a store building, since these are not within the normal scope of a law firm's business.

Partners among themselves may agree to limit the right of any one or more of the partners to negotiate certain contracts for the partnership. However, although such an agreement is binding on the partners and on outsiders who know of the agreement, it is not binding on outsiders who are unaware of its existence. Outsiders who are unaware of anything to the contrary have a right to assume that each partner has the normal agency rights of a partner.

Mutual agency offers an important reason for care in the selection of partners. Good partners benefit all; but a poor partner can do great damage. Mutual agency plus unlimited liability are the reasons most partnerships have only a few members, with two, three, or four being common numbers of partners.

Unlimited liability

When a partnership is unable to pay its debts, the creditors may satisfy their claims from the personal assets of the partners. Furthermore, if the personal property of a partner is insufficient to meet his share, the creditors may turn to the assets of the remaining partners who are able to pay. Thus, a partner may be called on to pay all the debts of his partnership and is said to have unlimited liability for its debts.

Unlimited liability may be illustrated as follows: Albert and Bates each invested $1,000 in a store to be operated as a partnership venture, under an agreement to share losses and gains equally. Albert has no property other than his $1,000 investment; Bates owns his own home, a farm, and has sizable savings in addition to his investment. The partners rented store space and bought merchandise and fixtures costing $10,000, paying $2,000 in cash and promising to pay the balance at a later date. However, the night before the store opened the building in which it was located burned and the merchandise and fixtures were totally destroyed. There was no insurance, all the partnership assets were lost, and Albert has no other assets. Consequently, the partnership creditors may collect the full $8,000 of their claims from Bates, although Bates may look to Albert for payment of half at a later date, if Albert ever becomes able to pay.

Advantages and disadvantages of a partnership

■ Limited life, mutual agency, and unlimited liability are disadvantages of a partnership. Yet, a partnership has advantages over both the single proprietorship and corporation forms of organization. A partnership has the advantage of being able to bring together more money and skills than a single proprietorship, and is much easier to organize than a corporation. Also, it does not have the corporation's governmental supervision nor its extra burden of taxation, and partners may act freely and without the necessity of stockholders' and directors' meetings, as in a corporation.

Partnership accounting

■ Partnership accounting is exactly like that of a single proprietorship except for transactions affecting owner equity. Here, because ownership rights are divided between two or more partners, there must be:

1. A Capital account for each partner.
2. A Withdrawals account for each partner.
3. An accurate measurement and division of earnings among the partners.

As for the separate Capital and Withdrawals accounts, each partner's Capital account is credited, and asset accounts showing the nature of the assets invested are debited in recording the investment of each partner. Likewise, a partner's withdrawals are debited to his Withdrawals account, and in the end-of-the-period closing procedure the Capital account is credited for a partner's share of the net income. Obviously, these procedures are not new, only the added accounts are new, and they need no further consideration here. However, the matter of dividing earnings among partners does need additional discussion.

Nature of partnership earnings

■ Because, as a member of his partnership, a partner cannot enter into an employer-employee contractural relationship with himself, a partner, like a single proprietor, cannot legally hire himself and pay himself a salary. Law and custom recognize this. Furthermore, law and custom recognize that a partner works for partnership profits and not a salary, and law and custom recognize that a partner invests in a partnership for earnings and not for interest.

Nevertheless, although partners have no legal right to interest on their partnership investments or salaries in payment for their partnership services, it should be recognized that partnership earnings do include a return for services, even though the return is contained within the earnings and is not a salary in a legal sense. Likewise, partnership earnings include a return on invested capital, although the return is not interest in the legal sense of the term.

Furthermore, if partnership earnings are to be fairly shared, it is often necessary to recognize that the earnings do include a return for services and a return on investments. For example, if one partner contributes five times as much capital as another, it is only fair that this be taken into consideration in the method of sharing. Likewise, if the services of one partner are much more valuable than those of another, it is only fair that some provision be made for the unequal service contributions.

Division of earnings

■ The law provides that in the absence of a contrary agreement, all partnership earnings are shared equally. This means that if partners do not agree in advance as to the method of sharing, each partner receives an equal share. Partners may agree in advance to any method of sharing; and if they agree as to the method of sharing earnings but say nothing of losses, losses are shared in the same way as earnings.

Several methods of sharing partnership earnings are employed. All attempt in one way or another to recognize differences in service contributions or in investments, when such differences exist. The following three methods will be discussed here:

1. On a stated fractional basis.
2. Based on the ratio of capital investments.
3. Salary and interest allowances and the remainder in a fixed ratio.

Earnings allocated on a stated fractional basis

■ The easiest way to divide partnership earnings is to give each partner a stated fraction of the total. A division on a fractional basis may provide for an equal sharing if service and capital contributions are equal. An equal sharing may also be provided when the greater capital contribution of one partner is offset by a greater service contribution of another. Or, if the service and capital contributions are unequal, a fixed ratio may easily provide for an unequal sharing. All that is necessary in any case is for the partners to agree as to the fractional share to be given each.

For example, the partnership agreement of Morse and North may provide that each partner is to receive half the earnings; or the agreement may provide for two thirds to Morse and one third to North; or it may provide for three fourths to Morse and one fourth to North. Any fractional basis may be agreed upon as long as the partners feel earnings are thereby fairly shared. For example, assume the agreement of Morse and North provides for a two-thirds and one-third sharing, and earnings for a year are $18,000. After all revenue and expense accounts are closed, if earnings are $18,000, the partnership Income Summary account has an $18,000 credit balance. It is closed, and the earnings are allocated to the partners with the following entry:

Dec.	31	Income Summary	18,000.00	
		A. P. Morse, Capital.................................		12,000.00
		R. G. North, Capital		6,000.00
		To close the Income Summary account and allocate the earnings.		

Division of earnings based on the ratio of capital investments

■ If the business of a partnership is of a nature that earnings are closely related to money invested, a division of earnings based on the ratio of partner's investments offers a fair sharing method. To illustrate this method, assume that Chase, Davis, and Fall have agreed to share earnings in the ratio of their investments. If these are Chase $50,000, Davis $30,000, and Fall $40,000, and if the earnings for the year are $24,000, the respective shares of the partners are calculated as follows:

Step 1: Chase, capital.. $ 50,000
Davis, capital.. 30,000
Fall, capital 40,000
Total invested... $120,000

Step 2: Share of earnings to Chase $\frac{\$50,000}{\$120,000}$ × $24,000 = $10,000

Share of earnings to Davis $\frac{\$30,000}{\$120,000}$ × $24,000 = $6,000

Share of earnings to Fall $\frac{\$40,000}{\$120,000}$ × $24,000 = $8,000

The entry to allocate the earnings to the partners is then:

Dec.	31	Income Summary	24,000.00	
		T. S. Chase, Capital.................................		10,000.00
		S. A. Davis, Capital.................................		6,000.00
		R. R. Fall, Capital		8,000.00
		To close the Income Summary account and allocate the earnings.		

■ Sometimes partners' capital contributions are unequal; and sometimes one partner devotes full time to partnership affairs and the other or others devote only part time. Too, in partnerships in which all partners devote full time, the services of one partner may be more valuable than the services of another. When these situations occur and, for example, the capital contributions are unequal, the partners may allocate a portion of their net income to themselves in the form of interest, so as to compensate for the unequal investments. Or when service contributions are unequal, they may use salary allowances as a means of compensating for unequal service contributions. Or when investment and service contributions are both unequal, they may use a combination of interest and salary allowances in an effort to share earnings fairly.

For example, Hill and Dale are partners in a business in which Hill has had experience and could command a $9,000 annual salary working for another firm of like nature. Dale is new to the business and could expect to earn not more than $6,000 working elsewhere. Furthermore, Hill has invested $15,000 in the business and Dale has invested $5,000. Consequently, the partners have agreed that in order to compensate for the unequal service and capital contributions, they will share losses and gains as follows:

1. A share of the profits equal to interest at 8% is to be allowed on the partners' initial investments.
2. Annual salary allowances of $9,000 per year to Hill and $6,000 per year to Dale are to be allowed.
3. The remaining balance of income or loss is to be shared equally.

Under this agreement a year's $17,700 net income would be shared:

	Share to Hill	Share to Dale	Income Allocated
Total net income..			$17,700
Allocated as interest:			
Hill (8% on $15,000)	$ 1,200		
Dale (8% on $5,000)		$ 400	
Total allocated as interest.........................			1,600
Balance of income after interest allowances..........			$16,100
Allocated as salary allowances:			
Hill..	9,000		
Dale		6,000	
Total allocated as salary allowances			15,000
Balance of income after interest and salary allowances..			$ 1,100
Balance allocated equality:			
Hill..	550		
Dale		550	
Total allocated equally			1,100
Balance of income.................................			-0-
Shares of the Partners..	$10,750	$6,950	

Illustration
15–1

After the shares in the $17,700 net income are determined, the following entry may be used to close the Income Summary account and carry the net income shares to the partners' Capital accounts. Observe in the entry that the credit amounts may be taken from the first two column totals of the computation of Illustration 15–1.

Dec.	31	Income Summary	17,700.00	
		Robert Hill, Capital..................................		10,750.00
		William Dale, Capital		6,950.00
		To close the Income Summary account and allocate the earnings.		

In a legal sense, a partner does not work for a salary, nor does he invest in a partnership to earn interest; he invests and works for earnings. Consequently, when a partnership agreement provides for salaries and interest, the partners should understand that the salaries and interest are not really salaries and interest but are only a means of sharing losses and gains.

In the illustration just completed the $17,700 net income exceeded the salary and interest allowances of the partners; but Hill and Dale would use the same method to share a net income smaller than their salary and interest allowances, or to share a loss. For example, assume that Hill and Dale earned only $6,600 in a year. A $6,600 net income would be shared by the partners as in Illustration 15–2.

	Share to Hill	Share to Dale	Income Allocated
Total net income..			$ 6,600
Allocated as interest:			
Hill (8% on $15,000).....................................	$ 1,200		
Dale (8% on $5,000)		$ 400	
Total allocated as interest.........................			1,600
Balance of income after interest allowances..........			$ 5,000
Allocated as salary allowances:			
Hill...	9,000		
Dale		6,000	
Total allocated as salary allowances			15,000
Balance of income after interest and salary allowances (a negative amount)			($10,000)
Balance allocated equally:			
Hill...	(5,000)		
Dale		(5,000)	
Total allocated equally			(10,000)
Balance of income...............................			-0-
Shares of the Partners..	$ 5,200	$1,400	

Illustration
15–2

The Illustration 15-2 items enclosed in parentheses are negative items. It is common practice in accounting to show negative items in red or to show them enclosed in parentheses as in this illustration.

A net loss would be shared by Hill and Dale in the same manner as the foregoing $6,600 net income; the only difference being that the loss-and-gain-sharing procedure would begin with a negative amount of income, in other words a net loss, and the amount allocated equally would be a larger negative amount.

Partnership financial statements ■ The balance sheet and the income statement of a partnership are like those of a single proprietorship. However, one additional statement, that of the partners' capital accounts is normally prepared. A typical statement of partners' capital accounts is shown below. Note that the details of partners' income sharing computation are presented in a separate schedule such as in Illustration 15-2.

Carter and Lam
Statement of Partners' Capital Accounts for Year Ended December 31, 19—

		Carter		Lam
		Carter		Lam
Capital account balances Jan. 1, 19—........		$22,000		$18,000
Add: Investment during year....................	$10,000		$ 6,000	
Share of net income (per schedule)........	8,250		6,650	
	$18,250		$12,650	
Less: Drawings....................................	5,200	13,050	5,200	7,450
Capital account balances Dec. 31, 19—......		$35,050		$25,450

Illustration
15-3

Ending a partnership ■ Often a partnership is terminated by the retirement of a partner. When a partner retires, he may sell his partnership interest to an outsider or to one or more of his partners, or he may withdraw his equity in the form of cash or other assets.

Sale of a partnership interest

Assume that Abbott, Burns, and Camp are equal partners in a $15,000 partnership that has no liabilities and the following assets and equities:

ASSETS		EQUITIES	
Cash......................................	$ 3,000	Abbott, capital........................	$ 5,000
Merchandise..........................	8,000	Burns, capital.........................	5,000
Store equipment.....................	4,000	Camp, capital.........................	5,000
Total Assets.....................	$15,000	Total Equities..................	$15,000

Camp's equity in this partnership is $5,000. If Camp sells this equity to Davis for $7,000, he is selling his $5,000 interest in the partnership assets. The entry on the partnership books to transfer the equity is:

Feb.	4	Camp, Capital..	5,000.00	
		Davis, Capital...		5,000.00
		To transfer Camp's equity in the partnership assets to Davis.		

After this entry is posted, the accounting equation that shows the assets and equities of the new partnership is:

ASSETS		EQUITIES	
Cash	$ 3,000	Abbott, capital........................	$ 5,000
Merchandise	8,000	Burns, capital........................	5,000
Store equipment....................	4,000	Davis, capital	5,000
Total Assets	$15,000	Total Equities..................	$15,000

Two points should be noted in regard to this transaction. First, the $7,000 Davis paid Camp is not recorded in the partnership books. Camp sold and transferred his $5,000 equity in the partnership assets to Davis. The entry that records the transfer is a debit to Camp, Capital and a credit to Davis, Capital for $5,000. Furthermore, the entry is the same whether Davis pays Camp $7,000 or $70,000. The amount is paid directly to Camp. It is a side transaction between Camp and Davis and does not affect partnership assets.

The second point to be noted is that Abbott and Burns must agree to the sale and transfer if Davis is to become a partner. Abbott and Burns cannot prevent Camp from selling his interest to Davis. On the other hand, Camp cannot force Abbott and Burns to accept Davis as a partner. If Abbott and Burns agree to accept Davis, a new partnership is formed and a new contract with a new loss-and-gain-sharing ratio must be drawn. If Camp sells to Davis and either Abbott or Burns refuses to accept Davis as a partner, under the common law the old partnership must be liquidated and Davis receives only the liquidation rights of Camp. However, under some Partnership Acts this situation may be treated differently, but a discussion of this is left to a more advanced text.

Withdrawal of a partner

The best practice in regard to withdrawals is for partners to provide in advance, in their partnership contract, the procedure to be followed when a partner withdraws from the partnership. When such a procedure is agreed on in advance, it commonly provides for an audit of the accounting records and a revaluation of the partnership assets. The revaluation just prior to a retirement is very desirable because it places all assets on the books at current values and causes the retiring partner's Capital account to reflect the current value of his equity. Often, if a partnership agreement provides for an audit and asset revaluation when a partner retires, it also provides that the retiring partner is to withdraw assets equal to the book amount of his revalued equity.

For example, assume that Blue is retiring from the partnership of Smith, Blue, and Short. The partners have always shared losses and gains in the ratio of Smith, one half; Blue, one fourth; and Short, one fourth. Their partnership agreement provides for an audit and asset revaluation upon the retirement of a partner, and their balance sheet just prior to the audit and revaluation shows the following assets and equities:

ASSETS			EQUITIES	
Cash..........................		$11,000	Smith, capital........................	$22,000
Merchandise inventory		16,000	Blue, capital..........................	10,000
Building....................	$20,000		Short, capital	10,000
Less accum. depr	5,000	15,000		
Total Assets..........		$42,000	Total Equities..................	$42,000

The audit and appraisal indicate the merchandise inventory is overvalued by $4,000 and that due to market changes the partnership building should be valued at $25,000 with accumulated depreciation of $8,000. The entries to record these revaluations are:

Oct.	31	Smith, Capital...	2,000.00	
		Blue, Capital...	1,000.00	
		Short, Capital	1,000.00	
		Merchandise Inventory............................		4,000.00
		To revalue the inventory.		
	31	Building	5,000.00	
		Accumulated Depreciation, Building		3,000.00
		Smith, Capital...		1,000.00
		Blue, Capital...		500.00
		Short, Capital		500.00
		To revalue the building.		

Note in the illustrated entries that losses and gains are shared in the partners' loss-and-gain-sharing ratio. Losses and gains from asset revaluations are always shared by partners in their loss-and-gain-sharing ratio, and the fairness of this is easy to see when it is remembered that if the partnership did not terminate, such losses and gains would sooner or later be reflected on the income statement.

After the entries revaluing the partnership assets are recorded, a balance sheet will show these revalued assets and equities for Smith, Blue, and Short:

ASSETS			EQUITIES	
Cash..........................		$11,000	Smith, capital........................	$21,000
Merchandise inventory		12,000	Blue, capital..........................	9,500
Building....................	$25,000		Short, capital	9,500
Less accum. depr	8,000	17,000		
Total Assets..........		$40,000	Total Equities..................	$40,000

After the revaluation, if Blue withdraws from the partnership and takes assets equal to his revalued equity, the entry to record his withdrawal is:

Oct.	31	Blue, Capital..	9,500.00	
		Cash...		9,500.00
		To record the withdrawal of Blue.		

In withdrawing, Blue does not have to take cash in settlement of his equity. He may take any combination of assets to which the partners agree, or he may take the new partnership's promissory note. Also, the withdrawal of Blue creates a new partnership; and consequently, a new partnership contract and a new loss-and-gain-sharing ratio are required.

Partner withdraws taking assets of less value than his book equity

Sometimes when a partner retires, the remaining partners may not wish to have the assets revalued and the new values recorded. In such cases the partners may agree, for example, that the assets are overvalued; and due to the overvalued assets, the retiring partner should in settlement of his equity take assets of less value than the book value of his equity. Sometimes, too, when assets are not overvalued, the retiring partner may be so anxious to retire that he is willing to take less than the current value of his equity just to get out of the partnership or out of the business.

When a partner retires taking assets of less value than his equity, he is in effect leaving a portion of his book equity in the business. In such cases, the remaining partners divide the unwithdrawn equity portion in their loss-and-gain-sharing ratio. For example, assume that Black, Brown, and Green are partners sharing gains and losses in a 2:2:1 ratio. Their assets and equities are:

ASSETS		EQUITIES	
Cash	$ 5,000	Black, capital	$ 6,000
Merchandise.........................	9,000	Brown, capital.......................	6,000
Store equipment....................	4,000	Green, capital	6,000
Total Assets....................	$18,000	Total Equities..................	$18,000

Brown is so anxious to withdraw from the partnership that he is willing to retire if permitted to take $4,500 in cash in settlement for his equity. Black and Green agree to the $4,500 withdrawal, and Brown retires. The entry to record the retirement is:

Mar.	4	Brown, Capital...	6,000.00	
		Cash...		4,500.00
		Black, Capital		1,000.00
		Green, Capital..		500.00
		To record the withdrawal of Brown.		

In retiring, Brown did not withdraw $1,500 of his book equity. This is divided between Black and Green in their loss-and-gain-sharing ratio. The loss-and-gain-sharing ratio of the original partnership was Black, 2; Brown, 2; and Green, 1. Therefore in the original partnership, Black and Green shared in a 2 to 1 ratio; and the unwithdrawn book equity of Brown is shared by Black and Green in this ratio.

Partner withdraws taking assets of greater value than his book equity

There are two common reasons for a partner receiving upon retirement assets of greater value than his book equity. First, certain of the partnership assets may be undervalued; and second, the partners continuing the business may be so anxious for the retiring partner to withdraw that they are willing for him to take assets of greater value than his book equity.

When assets are undervalued or unrecorded and the partners do not wish to change the recorded values, the partners may agree to permit a retiring member to withdraw assets of greater value than his book equity. In such cases the retiring partner is, in effect, withdrawing his own book equity and a portion of his partners' equities. For example, assume that Jones, Thomas, and Finch are partners sharing gains and losses in a 3:2:1 ratio. Their assets and equities are:

ASSETS		EQUITIES	
Cash	$ 5,000	Jones, capital	$ 9,000
Merchandise	10,000	Thomas, capital	6,000
Equipment	3,000	Finch, capital	3,000
Total Assets	$18,000	Total Equities	$18,000

Finch wishes to withdraw from the partnership; Jones and Thomas plan to continue the business. The partners agree that certain of their assets are undervalued, but they do not wish to increase the recorded values. They further agree that if current values were recorded, the asset total would be increased $6,000 and the equity of Finch would be increased $1,000. Therefore, the partners agree that $4,000 is the proper value for Finch's equity and that he may withdraw that amount in cash. The entry to record the withdrawal is:

May	7	Finch, Capital	3,000.00	
		Jones, Capital	600.00	
		Thomas, Capital	400.00	
		Cash		4,000.00
		To record the withdrawal of Finch.		

Death of a partner ■ A partner's death automatically dissolves and ends a partnership, and his estate is entitled to receive the amount of his equity. The partnership contract should contain provisions for settlement in case a partner dies, and one provision should provide a method for ascertaining the current value of the deceased partner's equity. This requires at least: (a) an immediate closing of the books to determine earnings since the end of the previous accounting period and (b) a method for determining and recording current values for the assets. Upon a partner's death and after the current value of the deceased partner's equity is determined, the remaining partners and the deceased partner's estate must agree to a disposition of the equity. They may agree to its sale to the remaining partners or to an outsider, or they may agree to the withdrawal of assets in settlement. Entries for both of these procedures have already been discussed.

Liquidations ■ When a partnership is liquidated, its business is ended, the assets are converted into cash, the creditors are paid, the remaining cash is distributed to the partners, and the partnership is dissolved. Although many combinations of circumstances occur in liquidations, only three are discussed here.

All assets realized before a distribution, assets are sold at a profit

A partnership liquidation under this assumption may be illustrated with the following example. Ottis, Skinner, and Parr have operated a partnership for a number of years, sharing losses and gains in a 3:2:1 ratio. Due to several unsatisfactory conditions, the partners decide to liquidate as of December 31. On that date the books are closed, the income from operations is transferred to the partners' Capital accounts, and the condensed balance sheet shown in Illustration 15–4 is prepared.

In any liquidation the business always ends and the assets are sold. Normally, either a gain or a loss results from the sale of each group of assets. These losses and gains are called "losses and gains from realization" and are shared by the partners in their loss-and-gain-sharing ratio.

Ottis, Skinner, and Parr
Balance Sheet, December 31, 19__

ASSETS		EQUITIES	
Cash	$10,000	Accounts payable	$ 5,000
Merchandise inventory	15,000	Ottis, capital	15,000
Other assets	25,000	Skinner, capital	15,000
		Parr, capital	15,000
Total Assets	$50,000	Total Equities	$50,000

Illustration
15–4

If Ottis, Skinner, and Parr sell their merchandise inventory for $12,000 and their other assets for $34,000, the sales and the gain allocation are recorded as follows:

Jan.	12	Cash...	12,000.00	
		Loss or Gain from Realization	3,000.00	
		Merchandise Inventory.............................		15,000.00
		Sold the inventory at a loss.		
	15	Cash...	34,000.00	
		Other Assets..		25,000.00
		Loss or Gain from Realization		9,000.00
		Sold the other assets at a profit.		
	15	Loss or Gain from Realization	6,000.00	
		Ottis, Capital..		3,000.00
		Skinner, Capital		2,000.00
		Parr, Capital		1,000.00
		To allocate the net gain from realization to the partners in their 3:2:1 loss-and-gain-sharing ratio.		

Careful notice should be taken of the last journal entry. In a partnership termination when assets are sold at a loss or gain, the loss or gain is allocated to the partners in their loss-and-gain-sharing ratio. Often students, in solving liquidation problems, attempt to allocate the assets to the partners in their loss-and-gain-sharing ratio. Obviously this is not correct; it is not assets but losses and gains that are shared in the loss-and-gain-sharing ratio.

After partnership assets are sold and the gain or loss allocated, the partnership cash exactly equals the combined equities of the partners and creditors. This point is illustrated for Ottis, Skinner, and Parr in the balance sheet of Illustration 15-5.

After partnership assets are realized and the gain or loss shared, entries are made to distribute the realized cash to the proper parties. Since creditors have first claim, they are paid first. After the creditors are paid, the remaining cash is divided among the partners. Each partner has the right to cash equal to his equity or, in other words, cash equal to

Ottis, Skinner, and Parr
Balance Sheet, January 15, 19__

ASSETS		EQUITIES	
Cash	$56,000	Accounts payable	$ 5,000
		Ottis, capital	18,000
		Skinner, capital	17,000
		Parr, capital	16,000
Total Assets	$56,000	Total Equities..................	$56,000

Illustration
15-5

the balance of his Capital account. The entries to distribute the cash of Ottis, Skinner, and Parr are:

Jan.	15	Accounts Payable...	5,000.00	
		Cash...		5,000.00
		To pay the claims of the creditors.		
	15	Ottis, Capital..	18,000.00	
		Skinner, Capital	17,000.00	
		Parr, Capital	16,000.00	
		Cash...		51,000.00
		To distribute the remaining cash to the partners according to their Capital account balances.		

Notice that after losses and gains are shared and the creditors are paid, each partner receives liquidation cash equal to the balance remaining in his Capital account. The partners receive these amounts because a partner's Capital account balance shows his equity in the one partnership asset, cash.

All assets realized before a distribution, assets sold at a loss, each partner's Capital account is sufficient to absorb his share of the loss

In a partnership liquidation, the assets are sometimes sold at a net loss. For example, if contrary to the assumptions of the previous illustration, the merchandise inventory of Ottis, Skinner, and Parr is sold for $9,000 and the other assets for $13,000, the entries to record the sales and loss allocation are:

Jan.	12	Cash..	9,000.00	
		Loss or Gain from Realization	6,000.00	
		Merchandise Inventory..............................		15,000.00
		Sold the inventory at a loss.		
	15	Cash..	13,000.00	
		Loss or Gain from Realization	12,000.00	
		Other Assets...		25,000.00
		Sold the other assets at a loss.		
	15	Ottis, Capital..	9,000.00	
		Skinner, Capital	6,000.00	
		Parr, Capital	3,000.00	
		Loss or Gain from Realization		18,000.00
		To allocate the loss from realization to the partners in their loss-and-gain-sharing ratio.		

After these entries are recorded, a new partnership balance sheet appears as in Illustration 15–6. The balance sheet shows the equities

Ottis, Skinner, and Parr
Balance Sheet, January 15, 19__

ASSETS		EQUITIES	
Cash	$32,000	Accounts payable	$ 5,000
		Ottis, capital	6,000
		Skinner, capital	9,000
		Parr, capital	12,000
Total Assets	$32,000	Total Equities	$32,000

Illustration
15–6

in the partnership cash, and the following entries are required to distribute the cash to the proper parties:

Jan.	15	Accounts Payable	5,000.00	
		Cash		5,000.00
		To pay the partnership creditors.		
	15	Ottis, Capital	6,000.00	
		Skinner, Capital	9,000.00	
		Parr, Capital	12,000.00	
		Cash		27,000.00
		To distribute the remaining cash to the partners according to the balances of their Capital accounts.		

Notice again that after realization losses are shared and creditors are paid, each partner receives cash equal to his Capital account balance.

All assets realized before a distribution, assets sold at a loss, a partner's Capital account is not sufficient to cover his share of the loss

Sometimes a partner's share of realization losses is greater than the balance of his Capital account. In such cases the partner whose share of losses is greater than his capital balance must, if he can, cover the deficit by paying cash into the partnership. For example, assume contrary to the previous two illustrations that Ottis, Skinner, and Parr sell their merchandise for $3,000 and the other assets for $4,000. The entries to record the sales and the loss allocation are:

Jan.	12	Cash	3,000.00	
		Loss or Gain from Realization	12,000.00	
		Merchandise Inventory		15,000.00
		Sold the inventory at a loss.		
	15	Cash	4,000.00	
		Loss or Gain from Realization	21,000.00	
		Other Assets		25,000.00
		Sold the other assets at a loss.		

Jan.	15	Ottis, Capital..	16,500.00		
		Skinner, Capital	11,000.00		
		Parr, Capital	5,500.00		
		Loss or Gain from Realization		33,000.00	
		To record the allocation of the loss from realization to the partners in their loss-and-gain-sharing ratio.			

After the entry allocating the realization loss is posted, the Capital account of Ottis has a $1,500 debit balance and appears as follows:

Ottis, Capital

Date		Explanation	F	Debit	Credit	Balance
Dec.	31	Balance				15,000.00
Jan.	15	Share of loss from realization		16,500.00		(1,500.00)

Since the partnership agreement provides that Ottis is to take one half the losses or gains, and since his Capital account balance is not large enough to absorb his loss share in this case, he must, if he can, pay $1,500 into the partnership to cover his full share of the losses. If he is able to pay, the following entry is made:

Jan.	15	Cash...	1,500.00	
		Ottis, Capital...		1,500.00
		To record the additional investment of Ottis to cover his share of realization losses.		

After the $1,500 is received from Ottis, the partnership has $18,500 in cash; and the following entries are made to distribute it to the proper parties:

Jan.	15	Accounts Payable...	5,000.00	
		Cash..		5,000.00
		To pay the partnership creditors.		
	15	Skinner, Capital	4,000.00	
		Parr, Capital	9,500.00	
		Cash..		13,500.00
		To distribute the remaining cash to the partners according to the balances of their Capital accounts.		

Often when a partner's share of partnership losses exceeds his Capital account balance, he is unable to make up the deficit. In such cases, since each partner has unlimited liability, the deficit must be borne by the remaining partner or partners. For example, assume that contrary to the previous illustration, Ottis is unable to pay in the $1,500 necessary to cover the deficit in his Capital account. If Ottis is unable to pay, the deficit that he is unable to make good must be shared by Skinner and Parr in their loss-and-gain-sharing ratio. In the original loss-and-gain-sharing agreement, the partners shared losses and gains in the ratio of Ottis, 3; Skinner, 2; and Parr, 1. Therefore, Skinner and Parr shared in a 2 to 1 ratio; and the $1,500 that Ottis's share of the losses exceeded his Capital account balance is apportioned between them in this ratio. Normally the defaulting partner's deficit is transferred to the Capital accounts of the remaining partners. This is accomplished for Ottis, Skinner, and Parr with the following entry:

Jan.	15	Skinner, Capital	1,000.00	
		Parr, Capital	500.00	
		Ottis, Capital...		1,500.00
		To transfer the deficit of Ottis to the Capital accounts of Skinner and Parr.		

After the deficit is transferred, the Capital accounts of the partners appear as in Illustration 15–7.

Ottis, Capital

Date		Explanation	F	Debit	Credit	Balance
Dec.	31	Balance				15,000.00
Jan.	15	Share of loss from realization		16,500.00		(1,500.00)
	15	Deficit to Skinner and Parr			1,500.00	-0-

Skinner, Capital

Date		Explanation	F	Debit	Credit	Balance
Dec.	31	Balance				15,000.00
Jan.	15	Share of loss from realization		11,000.00		4,000.00
	15	Share of Ottis's deficit		1,000.00		3,000.00

Parr, Capital

Date		Explanation	F	Debit	Credit	Balance
Dec.	31	Balance				15,000.00
Jan.	15	Share of loss from realization		5,500.00		9,500.00
	15	Share of Ottis's deficit		500.00		9,000.00

Illustration 15–7

After the deficit is transferred, the $17,000 of liquidation cash is distributed with the following entries:

Jan.	15	Accounts Payable...	5,000.00	
		Cash..		5,000.00
		To pay the partnership creditors.		
	15	Skinner, Capital	3,000.00	
		Parr, Capital	9,000.00	
		Cash..		12,000.00
		To distribute the remaining cash to the partners according to their Capital account balances.		

It should be understood that the inability of Ottis to meet his loss share at this time does not relieve him of liability. If at any time in the future he becomes able to pay, Skinner and Parr may collect from him the full $1,500. Skinner may collect $1,000 and Parr, $500.

The sharing of an insolvent partner's deficit by the remaining partners in their original loss-and-gain-sharing ratio is generally regarded as equitable. In England, however, in the case of *Garner* v. *Murray*, Judge J. Joyce ruled that the debit balance of the insolvent partner's Capital account is a personal debt due to the other partners and to be borne by them in the ratio of their Capital account balances immediately prior to liquidation.

While the *Garner* v. *Murray* decision still appears to be good law, it is considered by most to be inequitable. The decision applies only when the partnership agreement does not cover this situation and, although rendered in 1904, has not been applied in Canada. It is common practice to provide in the partnership agreement for the sharing of a partner's debit balance by the remaining partners in their loss-and-gain-sharing ratio.

Questions for class discussion

1. Hill and Dale are partners. Hill dies and his son claims the right to take his father's place in the partnership. Does he have this right? Why?
2. Ted Hall cannot legally enter into a contract. Can he become a partner?
3. If a partnership contract does not state the period of time the partnership is to exist, when does the partnership end?
4. What is the meaning of the term "mutual agency" as applied to a partnership?
5. Jack and Jill are partners in the operation of a store. Jack without consulting Jill enters into a contract for the purchase of merchandise for resale by the store. Jill contends that he did not authorize the order and refuses to take delivery. The vendor sues the partners for the contract price of the merchandise. Will the firm have to pay? Why?
6. Would your answer to Question 5 differ if Jack and Jill were partners in a public accounting firm?
7. May partners limit the right of a member of their firm to bind their partner-

ship to contracts? Is such an agreement binding *(a)* on the partners and *(b)* on outsiders?

8. What is the meaning of the term "unlimited liability" when it is applied to members of a partnership?

9. Kennedy, Porter, and Foulke have been partners for three years. The partnership is dissolving, Kennedy is leaving the firm, and Porter and Foulke plan to carry on the business. In the final settlement Kennedy places a $30,000 salary claim against the partnership. His contention is that since he devoted all of his time for three years to the affairs of the partnership, he has a claim for a salary of $10,000 for each year. Is his claim valid? Why?

10. The partnership agreement of Martin and Tritt provides for a two-thirds, one-third sharing of income but says nothing of losses. The operations for a year result in a loss. Martin claims the loss should be shared equally since the partnership agreement said nothing of sharing losses. Do you agree?

11. A, B, and C are partners with Capital account balances of $6,000 each. D gives A $7,500 for his one-third interest in the partnership. The bookkeeper debits A, Capital and credits D, Capital for $6,000. D objects. He wants his Capital account to show a $7,500 balance, the amount he paid for his interest. Explain why D's Capital account is credited for $6,000.

12. After all partnership assets are converted to cash and all creditor claims paid, the remaining cash should equal the sum of the balances of the partners' Capital accounts. Why?

13. J, K, and L are partners. In a liquidation J's share of partnership losses exceeds his Capital account balance. He is unable to meet the deficit from his personal assets, and the excess losses are shared by his partners. Does this relieve J of liability?

Class exercises

Exercise 15–1

Able and Cole began a partnership by investing $12,000 and $8,000, respectively, and during its first year the partnership earned $24,000.

Required:

1. Prepare a schedule with the following columnar headings:

Ways of Sharing	Able's Share	Cole's Share

2. List the following ways of sharing income by letter on separate lines in the first column and then opposite each letter show the share of each partner in the $24,000 net income.

    a. The partners could not agree on a method of sharing income.

    b. The partners agreed to share income in their investment ratio.

    c. The partners agreed to share income by giving a $9,000 per year salary allowance to Able, a $12,000 per year salary allowance to Cole, 10% interest on their investments, and the balance equally.

Exercise 15-2

Assume the partners of Exercise 15-1 agreed to share losses and gains by allowing salary allowances of $9,000 per year to Able and $12,000 per year to Cole, 10% interest on investments, and the balance equally.

a. Determine the share of Able and the share of Cole in a $6,000 first-year net income.

b. Determine the partners' shares in a $4,000 first-year net loss.

Exercise 15-3

Burns, Cook, and Dole have equities of $5,000 each in a partnership. With the consent of Cook and Dole, who have agreed to accept Earl as a partner, Burns is about to sell his equity in the partnership to Earl for a cup of coffee and $10 in cash. Give the entry to record the sale on the partnership books.

Exercise 15-4

Fall is retiring from the partnership of Fall, Ginn, and Hart. The partners have always shared losses and gains in a 2:2:1 ratio; and on the date of Fall's retirement they have the following equities in the partnership: Gary Fall, $8,000; Dale Ginn, $10,000; and Tom Hart, $6,000.

Required:

Using the current date, give entries in general journal form for the retirement of Fall under each of the following unrelated assumptions:

a. Fall retires, taking $8,000 in partnership cash for his equity.

b. Fall retires, taking $9,500 in partnership cash for his partnership rights.

c. Fall retires, taking $7,100 in partnership cash.

Exercise 15-5

Ives, Jones, and Kelly entered into a partnership. Ives invested $4,000, Jones invested $8,000, and Kelly invested $12,000. They agreed to share losses and gains equally. They lost heavily, and at the end of the first year decided to liquidate. After converting all partnership assets to cash and paying all creditor claims, $9,000 in partnership cash remained.

Required:

Under a December 31 date, give the general journal entry to record the distribution of the correct shares of cash to the partners in final liquidation of their business.

Problems   **Problem 15-1**

Ted Allen, John Bell, and Gary Cole invested $12,000, $9,000, and $6,000, respectively, in a partnership. During its first year the partnership earned $31,500.

Required:

1. Prepare entries dated December 31 to close the Income Summary account and to allocate the net income to the partners under each of the following assumptions:

a. The partners could not agree on a method of sharing earnings.

b. The partners agreed to share earnings in the ratio of their beginning investments.

c. The partners agreed to share income by allowing annual salary allowances of $8,000 to Allen, $7,200 to Bell, and $10,000 to Cole; allowing a share of the income equal to 10% interest on the partners' investments; and sharing any remainder equally.

2. Prepare the section of the partners' first year income statement showing the allocation of the income to the partners under assumption *(c)*.

Problem 15–2

The partnership agreement of Ash, Elm, and Oak provides that losses and gains be shared by allowing annual salary allowances of $7,200 to Ash, $9,600 to Elm, and $8,400 to Oak; interest on the partners' investments at the rate of 8% annually; and sharing any remaining balance equally. The partners' investments are Ash, $20,000; Elm, $25,000; and Oak, $10,000.

Assume that the current year's operations produced the following incomes or losses: *(a)* a $34,700 net income, *(b)* a $27,500 net income, *(c)* a $1,900 net loss, and *(d)* a $9,100 net loss.

Required:
1. Prepare a schedule with the following columnar headings:

Net Income or Loss	Share to Ash	Share to Elm	Share to Oak

2. List the amounts of income or loss on separate lines in the first column. Then enter the amount of each partner's share under his name in the proper column.

Problem 15–3

Dodd, Evon, and Falk are partners sharing losses and gains in a 2:1:2 ratio. Dodd plans to withdraw from the partnership, and on the date of his withdrawal the equities of the partners are: Ivan Dodd, $12,000; John Evon, $10,000; and Carl Falk, $12,000.

Required:
Under a March 12 date give in general journal form the entries for the withdrawal of Dodd under each of the following unrelated assumptions:

a. Dodd sells his interest to Roy Gill, taking $9,000 in cash and a second-hand car. Evon and Falk agree to accept Gill as a partner.

b. With the agreement of Evon and Falk to accept the son as a partner, Dodd gives his partnership interest to his son, Paul.

c. Dodd withdraws, taking $12,000 of partnership cash for his equity.

d. Dodd withdraws, taking $10,500 of partnership cash for his equity.

e. Dodd withdraws, taking $10,000 in partnership cash and delivery equipment carried on the partnership books at $3,500, less $900 accumulated depreciation.

f. Dodd withdraws, taking $3,000 in partnership cash and a $7,500 note payable of the new partnership for his equity.

Problem 15–4

Mead, Nash, and Owen, who have always shared losses and gains in a 4:2:1 ratio, are liquidating their partnership. Just prior to the first asset sale their balance sheet appeared as follows:

MEAD, NASH, AND OWEN
Balance Sheet, June 30, 19 —

Cash	$ 2,000	Accounts payable	$15,000
Other assets	48,000	John Mead, capital	10,000
		Dale Nash, capital	20,000
		Gary Owen, capital	5,000
Total Assets	$50,000	Total Equities	$50,000

Required:

Under the assumption the other assets are sold and the cash is distributed to the proper parties on July 5, give the entries to record the sale, the loss or gain allocation, and the distribution under each of the following unrelated assumptions:

a. The other assets are sold for $51,500.

b. The other assets are sold for $41,000.

c. The other assets are sold for $27,000, and the partner with a deficit pays in the amount of his deficit.

d. The other assets are sold for $20,000, and the partners have no assets other than those invested in the business.

Problem 15–5

Long, Macy, and Nunn share partnership losses and gains in a 3:1:1 ratio, since Long devotes full time to partnership affairs and Macy and Nunn give little time to the business. Recently the business has not prospered and the partners plan to liquidate. Just prior to the first asset sale a partnership balance sheet appeared as follows:

LONG, MACY, AND NUNN
Balance Sheet, January 31, 19 —

Cash		$ 4,000	Accounts payable	$ 8,000
Accounts receivable		12,000	Robert Long, capital	8,000
Merchandise inventory		24,000	James Macy, capital	20,000
Equipment	$20,000		George Nunn, capital	20,000
Accumulated depreciation	4,000	16,000		
Total Assets		$56,000	Total Equities	$56,000

The assets were sold, the creditors were paid, and the remaining cash was distributed to the partners on the following dates:

Feb. 2 The accounts receivable were sold for $7,200.

    5 The merchandise inventory was sold for $16,000.

    8 The equipment was sold for $11,800.

    9 The creditors were paid in full.

    9 The remaining cash was distributed to the partners.

Required:

1. Give the entries to record the sale of the assets, the allocation of the losses, and the payment of the creditors.
2. Under the assumption the partner with a deficit pays in the amount of his deficit, give the entries to record the receipt and the payment of cash to the remaining partners.
3. Under the assumption the partner with a deficit cannot pay, give the entry to allocate his deficit to the remaining partners and the entry to pay the partners to whom cash is due.

Alternate problems

Problem 15–1A

During its first year, ending December 31, the partnership of Nash, Orr, and Price earned $31,800.

Required:

1. Prepare entries to close the Income Summary account and to allocate the net income to the partners under each of the following assumptions:
    a. The partners could not agree on a method for sharing earnings.
    b. The partners had agreed to share earnings in the ratio of their investments which were Gary Nash, $12,000; Walter Orr, $16,000; and Ted Price, $20,000.
    c. The partners had agreed to share earnings by allowing annual salary allowances of $8,400 to Nash, $9,600 to Orr, and $6,000 to Price, plus interest at 10% annually on investments, and any remainder equally.
2. Prepare the income statement section showing the allocation of the year's income to the partners under assumption *(c)*.

Problem 15–2A

Abel, Barr, and Cobb have investments of $15,000, $12,000, and $8,000, respectively, in a partnership. Their partnership contract provides that losses and gains be shared by allowing annual salary allowances of $7,000 to Abel, $10,000 to Barr, and $7,000 to Cobb; interest at 10% annually on investments; and any balance equally.

Required:

1. Prepare a schedule with the following columnar headings:

Net Income or Loss	Share to Abel	Share to Barr	Share to Cobb

2. Assume that the current year's operations produced in turn the following incomes or losses: *(a)* a $33,200 net income, *(b)* a $21,500 net income, *(c)* a $2,500 net loss, and *(d)* a $7,600 net loss, and list the amounts of income or loss on separate lines in the first column. Then enter the amount of each partner's share under his name in the proper column.

Problem 15–3A

Earl Dunn is retiring from the partnership of Dunn, Ely, and Farr. The partners have always shared losses and gains in a 2:3:1 ratio; and on Dunn's retirement date they have the following Capital account balances: Earl Dunn, $14,000; Alan Ely, $16,000; and Ray Farr, $10,000.

Required:

Under a February 3 date give in general journal form the entries for the withdrawal of Dunn under each of the following unrelated assumptions:

a.   Dunn withdraws, taking $14,000 of partnership cash for his equity.

b.   Dunn withdraws, taking $15,000 of partnership cash for his equity.

c.   Dunn withdraws, taking $10,000 in partnership cash and machinery carried on the partnership books at $3,600, less $1,600 of accumulated depreciation.

d.   Dunn withdraws, taking $1,600 of partnership cash and a $12,000 note payable of the new partnership of Ely and Farr.

e.   With the consent of Ely and Farr, Dunn sells his interest to Ted Gill, taking from Gill $6,000 in cash and Gill's personal note for $10,000.

f.   Dunn transfers his interest to Ely and Farr, taking Ely's $9,000 personal note for 60% of his equity and Farr's $6,000 personal note for 40%.

Problem 15–4A

Davis, Eaton, and Farley are about to liquidate their partnership. They have always shared losses and gains in a 3:2:1 ratio, and just prior to the liquidation their balance sheet appeared as follows:

DAVIS, EATON, AND FARLEY
Balance Sheet, October 31, 19—

Cash	$ 3,000	Accounts payable	$12,000
Other assets	69,000	Carl Davis, capital	15,000
		Dale Eaton, capital	35,000
		John Farley, capital	10,000
Total Assets	$72,000	Total Equities	$72,000

Required:

Prepare general journal entries to record the sale of the other assets and the distribution of the cash to the proper parties under each of the following unrelated assumptions:

a.   The other assets were sold for $72,000.

b.   The other assets were sold for $45,000.

c.   The other assets were sold for $36,000, and the partner with a deficit was able to pay in the amount of his deficit.

d.   The other assets were sold for $21,000, and none of the partners had any personal assets from which to make good a deficit.

Problem 15–5A

Until April 3 of the current year Judd, Kern, and Lee were partners sharing losses and gains in a 2:2:1 ratio. On that date Judd was drowned in a boating accident. Kern and Lee immediately ended the business operations and prepared the following adjusted trial balance:

JUDD, KERN, AND LEE
Adjusted Trial Balance April 3, 19—

Cash	$ 5,200	
Accounts receivable	11,800	
Allowance for doubtful accounts		$ 600
Merchandise inventory	30,000	
Store equipment	15,000	
Accumulated depreciation, store equipment		7,500
Land	10,000	
Building	50,000	
Accumulated depreciation, building		10,000
Accounts payable		4,400
Mortgage payable		16,500
Earl Judd, capital		26,000
Ted Kern, capital		28,000
Gary Lee, capital		14,000
Revenues		50,000
Expenses	35,000	
Totals	$157,000	$157,000

Required:

1. Prepare entries to close the revenues, expenses, and income summary accounts of the partnership.

2. Assume that the estate of Judd agreed to accept the land and building and assume the mortgage in full settlement of its claim against the partnership, and that Kern and Lee planned to continue the business and rent the building from the estate. Give under an April 30 date the entry to transfer the land, building, and mortgage and to settle with the estate.

3. Make the contrary assumption that the estate of Judd demanded a cash settlement and the business had to be sold to a competitor who gave $72,200 for the noncash assets and assumed the mortgage but not the accounts payable. Give the entry to transfer the assets and mortgage to the competitor, the entry to allocate the loss to the partners, and the entries to distribute the partnership cash to the proper parties. Date the entries April 30.

Decision problem 15–1, partnership decisions

PART 1. On January 10 of this year Ted Gage and Dale Hall formed a partnership to operate a delivery service. Ted invested $6,000 in the business and Dale invested $4,000, and the partners agreed to share all losses and gains equally. Business has been bad; the partners have been unable to make any withdrawals; and now, after six months, they have decided to end all operations and liquidate their partnership, the assets of which now consist of $3,000 in cash and a delivery truck that both partners agree is worth $3,000. In discussing the liquidation, Dale Hall says that he is willing to take either the cash or the delivery truck for his partnership rights, and he also says he is willing to flip a coin to see which partner takes the cash and which takes the truck. Ted Gage is unsure of who should take what and why, and he has come to you for advice. Advise him, giving reasons for your advice.

PART 2. The partnership agreement of Moe and Roe provides that losses and gains be shared by allowing salary allowances of $8,000 per year to Moe and $10,000 per year to Roe and then sharing any remaining balance equally. At the end of the first year in business, when a work sheet was prepared, it was discovered that the partnership had earned $10 during the year. As a result, Moe suggested that the $10 be given to the office secretary as a bonus, thereby increasing the expenses of the year and causing the partnership to exactly break even. He further suggested that the partnership could then forget the sharing of losses and gains for the first year, since there would be none. If Moe's suggestions are followed, who gains most and how much does this person gain?

Decision problem 15–2, Sports Centre

Sports Centre, a sporting goods store, is owned and operated by Roy Mann and Jack Lee as a partnership enterprise. Mann has a $43,000 equity in the business, and Lee has a $20,000 equity. Annual salary allowances of $12,000 to Mann and $10,000 to Lee are used in sharing losses and gains, with any balance after salary allowances being shared 60% to Mann and 40% to Lee.

Ted Mann, Roy Mann's only son, has been working for the firm on a salary basis. Ted was an outstanding high school and college athlete and has maintained his contacts with coaches and athletes since graduating from college, and thus attracts a great deal of business to the firm. Actually, 30% of the past three years' sales can be traced directly to Ted's association with the business, and it is reasonable to assume he was instrumental in attracting some of the balance.

Ted is paid $8,000 per year, but feels this is not sufficient to induce him to remain with the firm as an employee. However, he likes the work and would like to remain in the sporting goods business. What he really wants is to become a partner in the business.

His father is anxious for him to remain in the business and has proposed the following:

a. That Ted be admitted to the partnership with a 20% equity in the partnership assets.

b. That he, Roy Mann, transfer from his Capital account to that of Ted's one half of the 20% interest Ted would receive; that Ted contribute to the firm's assets a 6% note for the other half; and that he, Roy Mann, will guarantee payment of the note and its interest.

c. That losses and gains be shared by continuing the $12,000 and $10,000 salary allowances of the original partners and that Ted be given an $8,000 salary allowance, after which any remaining loss or gain would be shared 40% to Roy Mann, 40% to Jack Lee, and 20% to Ted Mann.

Prepare a report to Mr. Lee on the advisability of accepting Mr. Mann's proposal. Under the assumption that net incomes for the past three years have been $36,000, $38,000, and $40,000, respectively, prepare schedules showing (a) how net income was allocated during the past three years and (b) how it would have been allocated had the proposed agreement been in effect. Also, (c) prepare a schedule showing the partners' capital interests as they would be immediately after the admission of Ted.

Cole and Dean are partners sharing losses and gains as follows:

a.   Annual salary allowances of $12,000 to Cole and $14,000 to Dean are allowed.

b.   Interest at 6% on the excess of his Capital account balance over that of his partner is allowed to the partner having the larger Capital account balance as of the beginning of the year.

c.   Any remainder is divided equally between the partners.

The partnership earned $40,000 last year, and the partners began the year with Capital account balances of $50,000 for Cole and $40,000 for Dean.

Although the partners consider last year a successful one, Dean is unhappy with his share of the net income. He feels he should have a larger share, since he spends twice as much time on partnership affairs as Cole. Cole agrees that Dean spends double the time he spends on partnership business and also that Dean is primarily responsible for the 10% compound annual increase in partnership earnings for the past several years. Consequently, he suggests that the partners change their loss-and-gain-sharing plan. He knows that Dean has $30,-000 in a savings account on which he earns interest at 5% annually, so he suggests the following:

a.   Dean is to invest an additional $30,000 in the business.

b.   Interest at 8% is to be allowed the partners on the full amounts invested, which are to be Cole, $50,000 and Dean, $70,000.

c.   Each partner is to get a $5,000 increase in his salary allowance, with the allowances becoming: Cole, $17,000; and Dean, $19,000.

d.   Any remaining balance after salary and interest allowances is to be given in full to Dean.

Dean is interested in earning 8% on the $30,000 he now has in the bank, is pleased with the $5,000 increase in his salary allowance, and is impressed with Cole's generosity in giving him any balance over the partners' salary and interest allowances. However, before accepting the offer, he has come to you for advice. Advise Dean, backing your advice with income-sharing schedules where desirable.

Problem 15–1 A&R

D P AND L

Balance Sheet, October 31, 1975

Cash	$ 4,000	Accounts payable.................	$12,000
Other assets	62,000	Duke, capital.......................	25,000
		Prince, capital	23,000
		Lord, capital	6,000
	$66,000		$66,000

On November 1, 1975 the assets were sold, the creditors were paid and the remaining cash was distributed to the partners as follows:

Duke $16,000, Prince $14,000 and Lord 0.

Required:
Present the partnership liquidation entries.

Problem 15–2 A&R

SUPERIOR, ERIE AND ONTARIO
Balance Sheet, January 31, 1976.

Cash	$ 2,000	Accounts payable	$ 8,000
Other Assets	46,000	Superior	25,000
		Erie	10,000
	$48,000	Ontario	5,000
			$48,000

Superior, Erie and Ontario shared profit and losses in the ratio of 5:3:2, respectively. On February 1, 1976, the partners decided to liquidate. The assets were sold, the creditors were paid and the remaining cash was distributed to the partners as follows:

Superior	$32,500
Erie	14,500
Ontario	8,000

Required:
Present the partnership liquidation entries.

Problem 15–3 A&R

The Trunk and Field Company, a partnership, was organized on January 1, 1975 with each partner investing $25,000 in cash. The partners failed to provide for an adequate system of records, and when called on to present statements as of December 31, 1975, were unable to do so. You were called in to prepare the required statements. Your investigation of available data and your discussions with the partners revealed the following:

1. Total cash receipts (including partners' investment) from January 1 to December 31, 1975 was $109,840. Included in receipts was a bank loan of $2,000 on which $120 of interest had accrued on December 31, 1975.
2. An analysis of cash disbursements showed the following:

Payment for land ($5,000) and building ($30,000)	$35,000
Payment for furniture and fixtures	8,000
Payment of salaries and wages	2,850
Payment of other expenses	825
Payment of accounts payable	51,165

3. On December 31 you ascertained the following account balances:

Accounts payable	$ 2,160
Accounts receivable	5,680
Inventory	8,920
Prepaid expenses	180
Accrued expenses other than interest	210

4. You also learned that, during the year, goods costing $500 were purchased and paid for by the company but were found to be for the personal use of Field who had not reimbursed the company.
5. You determined that recognition of the following was required:
   a. Depreciation of building at a rate of 10%.
   b. A depreciation of furniture and fixtures at a rate of 20%.
   c. Estimated uncollectible accounts receivable $350.

Required:
Prepare, in good form;
1. A balance sheet as of December 31, 1975.
2. An income statement for the year ended December 31, 1975.
3. A statement of the partners' capital accounts.

(CGA adapted)

16

Corporations: Organization and operation

■ The three common types of business organizations are single proprietorships, partnerships, and corporations.[1] Of the three, corporations are fewer in number; yet in dollar volume, they transact more business than do the other two combined. Thus, because of their business volume and also because almost every person reading this paragraph will at some time either work for or own an interest in a corporation, an understanding of corporations and their accounting is important. And, a start on this understanding may well be made by examining some of the advantages and disadvantages of the corporate form of business organization.

Advantages
of the
corporate
form

■ Separate legal entity

From Chief Justice John Marshall's long ago (1819) definition and description of a corporation as "an artificial being, invisible, intangible, and existing only in the contemplation of the law" has grown the doctrine that a corporation is a legal entity, separate and distinct from the persons who own it. The owners are called *stockholders or shareholders;* they own the corporation, but they are not the corporation. The

---

[1] The terms "Corporation" and "Capital Stock" are used rather than "Limited Company" and "Share Capital" because of their general acceptance and common usage. The terms "Stockholder(s)" and "Shareholder(s)" are used interchangeably.

corporation in a legal sense is an artificial person, separate and distinct from its owners.

Separate legal entity is the most important characteristic of a corporation, since it gives a corporation all the rights and responsibilities of a person except those only a natural person may exercise, such as the right to vote or marry. Because of its separate legal entity, a corporation may buy, own, and sell property in its own name. It may sue and be sued in its own name. It may enter into contracts with both outsiders and its own shareholders. In short, through its agents, a corporation may conduct its affairs as a legal person with the rights, duties, and responsibilities of a person.

Lack of stockholders' liability

As a separate legal entity a corporation is responsible for its own acts and its own debts, and its shareholders have no liability for either. From the viewpoint of an investor, this is perhaps the most important advantage of the corporate form.

Ease of transferring ownership rights

Ownership rights in a corporation are represented by shares of stock. And all that is necessary to convey these rights is a transfer of ownership of the shares. Furthermore, since a corporation is a legal entity, the transfer has no effect on the corporation, and a stockholder generally may transfer and dispose of his stock at will.

Continuity of life

The death, incapacity, or sale of a stockholder's interest does not affect the life of a corporation. A corporation's life depends on its charter, and may continue for the time stated in the charter. Furthermore, this period may be of any length permitted by the laws of the jurisdiction in which the corporation is organized; and at the expiration of the stated time, the charter may normally be renewed and the period extended. Thus, a perpetual life is possible for a successful corporation.

No mutual agency

Mutual agency does not exist in a corporation. A corporation stockholder, acting as a stockholder, has no power to bind the corporation to contracts. His participation in the affairs of the corporation is limited to the right to vote in the stockholders' meetings. Consequently, stockholders need not exercise the care of partners in selecting people with whom they associate themselves in the ownership of a corporation.

Ease of capital assembly

Lack of stockholders' liability, lack of mutual agency, and the ease with which an interest may be transferred make it easy for a corporation to assemble large amounts of capital from the combined investments of many stockholders. Actually, a corporation's capital-raising ability is as a rule limited only by the profitableness with which it can employ the funds of its stockholders. This is very different from a partnership. In a partnership, capital-raising ability is always limited by the number of partners and their individual wealth; and the number of partners is in turn usually limited by mutual agency and unlimited liability.

Disadvantages of the corporate form

■ Governmental control and supervision

Corporations are created by fulfilling the requirements of federal or provincial corporation laws. Because of this, corporations are said to be "creatures of the state," and as such are subject to much closer governmental control and supervision than are single proprietorships and partnerships.

In addition, the rights, powers, and duties of corporations, their stockholders, and officials are derived from corporation laws. There would be no objection to this if the laws were simple and easy to understand; but unfortunately, they are notoriously diverse, complicated, and in some cases vague; and as a result the exact rights, duties, and responsibilities of corporations, their directors, and shareholders vary from state to state and are often difficult to define precisely.

Taxation

The greatest disadvantage of the corporate form is usually considered its extra burden of taxes. Corporations as business units are subject to all the taxes of single proprietorships and partnerships; and in addition, they are subject to several not levied on either of the other two. The most important of these are provincial and federal income taxes which together commonly exceed 50% of a corporation's income. However, insofar as the owners of a corporation are concerned, the burden does not end here. The income of a corporation is taxed twice: first as corporation income and again as personal income when distributed to the stockholders as dividends. This differs from single proprietorships and partnerships, which as business units are not subject to income taxes, and whose income is taxed only as the personal income of their owners.

Organizing a corporation

■ A corporation is created by securing a charter from one of the 10 provinces or the federal government. Certain corporations, such as those engaged in railroading, banking, insurance, and telegraphy and which seek powers of a different kind from those granted to ordinary business corporations, are incorporated under special acts of the Canadian Parliament or provincial legislatures.

Corporations intending to operate in several provinces or in foreign countries may find it advantageous to secure a federal charter, since such a charter carries the right to operate in any province. However, the corporation laws of the several provinces differ from each other and from the federal statutes; consequently, it is at times advantageous to secure a provincial charter and operate under the laws of one of the provinces. Also, provincial incorporation may be less expensive than federal incorporation and it is normally more convenient to deal with local rather than federal officials. Too, a company incorporated in one province may normally (through registration) carry on its business activities in other provinces.

Requirements for incorporation vary somewhat in each jurisdiction, but in general call for a filing of an application for a charter. Normally, the application must be signed by three or more incorporators and contain such information as the following:

1. The proposed corporate name, the last word of which, depending on the jurisdiction of incorporation, must be Limited, Incorporated or Corporation including their French equivalents or the abbreviation thereof.
2. The purposes for which incorporation is sought.
3. The place within Canada (federal incorporation) or within the province (provincial incorporation) where the head office of the corporation is to be located.
4. The number of shares authorized and their par value, if any.
5. If there is to be more than one kind or class of shares, the number of each as well as the restrictive rights, restrictions, conditions, and limitations attaching to each class.
6. The name, address, and occupation of each of the applicants.
7. The names of the applicants, not less than three (federal legislation provides for incorporation by one or more incorporators), who are to be directors until the initial meeting of the shareholders.

Upon the approval of the application and payment of incorporation fees, the charter is issued. In any case, the corporation comes into existence with the issuance of its charter.

In a number of provincial jurisdictions incorporation may take the form of either a private company or a public company. A private company is a corporation with essentially the same characteristics as a public corporation except: (1) the number of its shareholders may not exceed 50, exclusive of its present and former employees; (2) the right to transfer shares is restricted; and (3) it is prohibited from making a public offering of its shares or debentures. Also, private companies are subject to less rigid regulatory legislation than are public companies.

After a corporation comes into existence, usually at the first meeting of its shareholders, bylaws to govern the conduct of its affairs are adopted. Bylaws normally include among other things:

1. The method or plan for alloting shares to shareholders.
2. The time, place, manner of calling, and rules for conducting meetings of the shareholders and directors.
3. The number, qualifications, duties, powers, and length of office of the directors.
4. The appointment, duties, compensation, and length of office of the corporation officers other than directors.
5. The conduct in all other particulars of the affairs of the corporation.

The bylaws together with the charter give the basic rules for conducting the corporation affairs. It is important that all acts of the shareholders, directors, and officers conform with the regulations in both.

Minute book ■ A corporation is required to maintain a record of all actions taken by the shareholders and directors at their meetings. The record is kept in narrative form by the secretary of the corporation in a book called a minute book.

The minute book is a source of information for both the company's accountant and the public accountant. For example, certain resolutions passed by the board have financial implications and reference to the minute book may be necessary to obtain information for journal entries. Auditors refer to the minute book in order to validate amounts of dividends declared, valuation of assets acquired in exchange for the company's own shares, amounts of officers' salaries, et cetera. The minute book also contains the bylaws of the corporation.

Organization costs ■ The costs of organizing a corporation, such as legal fees, promoters' fees, and amounts paid the provincial or federal government to secure a charter, are called organization costs and are debited on incurrence to an account called Organization Costs. Theoretically, the sum of these costs represents an intangible asset from which the corporation will benefit throughout its life. However, the life of a corporation is always indeterminable; consequently, the period over which it will benefit from being organized is indeterminable. Nevertheless, a corporation should make a reasonable estimate of the benefit period and write off its organization costs over this period. Although not necessarily related to the benefit period, income tax rules permit a corporation to write off 50% of the post-1972 organization costs as a tax-deductible expense at an annual 10% rate on a diminishing balance basis. Consequently, some corporations adopt the tax period over which to write off such costs. There is no theoretical justification for this, but it is generally accepted in practice because organization costs are usually immaterial in amount and the write-off eliminates an unnecessary balance sheet item.

Management of a corporation ■ Although ultimate control of a corporation rests with its stockholders, this control is exercised indirectly through the election of the board of directors. The individual stockholder as a stockholder does not actively participate in management. His right as a stockholder to participate begins and ends with his vote in the stockholders' meeting, where he has one vote for each share of stock owned.

Normally a corporation's stockholders meet once each year to elect directors and transact such other business as is provided in the corporation's bylaws. Theoretically, stockholders owning or controlling the votes of 50% plus one share of a corporation's stock can elect the board and control the corporation. Actually, because many stockholders do not attend the annual meeting, a much smaller percentage is frequently sufficient for control. Commonly, stockholders who do not attend the annual meeting delegate to an agent their voting rights. This is done by signing a legal document called a *proxy,* which gives the agent the right to vote the stock.

A corporation's board of directors is responsible and has final authority for the direction of corporation affairs; but it may act only as a collective body — an individual director, as a director, has no power to transact corporation business. And, as a rule, although it has final authority, a board will limit itself to establishing policy, delegating the day-by-day direction of corporation business to the corporation's administrative officers whom it selects and elects.

A corporation's administrative officers are commonly headed by a president who is normally the chief executive officer and is directly responsible to the board for managing, controlling, and supervising the corporation's business. To aid the president, many corporations have one or more vice presidents who are vested with specific managerial powers and duties by the president and the directors. In addition, the corporation secretary keeps the minutes of the meetings of the stockholders and directors, and in a small corporation may also be responsible for keeping a record of the stockholders and the changing amounts of their stock interests. The treasurer is custodian of corporation funds.

Illustration 16–1 shows the organizational chart of a corporation. Note how the chart's lines of authority extend from the stockholders through the board and on to the administrative officers.

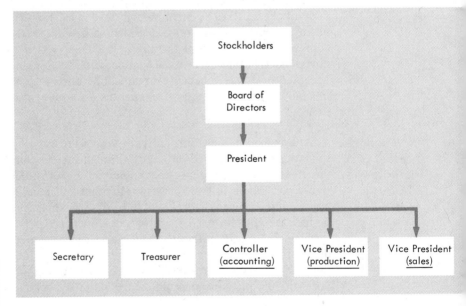

Illustration
16–1
**Organization
chart of a
corporation**

■ A person invests in a corporation by buying its stock; and when he does so, he receives a stock certificate as evidence of the shares purchased. Usually in a small corporation only one certificate is issued for each block of stock purchased, the one certificate may be for any number of shares. For example, the certificate of Illustration 16–2 is for 50 shares. Large corporations commonly use preprinted 100-share denomination certificates in addition to blank certificates that may be made out for any number of shares.

INCORPORATED UNDER THE LAWS
OF THE
PROVINCE OF ONTARIO

C9800

-50-

WESTFIELD PUBLISHING COMPANY, LTD.

THIS CERTIFIES that   ROBERT WETZEL   is the owner of

—— FIFTY ——
FULLY PAID AND NON-ASSESSABLE NO-PAR-VALUE SHARES OF COMMON STOCK OF THE
WESTFIELD PUBLISHING COMPANY, LTD. transferable on the books of the Corporation in person or by duly authorized attorney upon surrender of this Certificate properly endorsed. This Certificate is not valid unless countersigned by the Transfer Agent and registered by the Registrar.
WITNESS the facsimile seal of the Corporation and the facsimile signatures of its duly authorized officers.
Dated: March 10, 1958

SEAL

SECRETARY   PRESIDENT

Registrar
Authorized Signature
Registered:
By Southern Trust Company

Countersigned:
By
Transfer Agent
Authorized Signature

Illustration
16–2

Observe that the certificate of Illustration 16–2 is for *50 shares of no-par-value common stock.* When a corporation issues only one kind of stock, it is called common stock. (A corporation may issue more than one kind or class of stock, as will be explained later.) If Robert Wetzel of Illustration 16–2 invested $5,000 in Westfield Publishing Company by paying the corporation $100 per share for 50 shares of its common stock ($100 × 50 = $5,000), the investment increased the corporation's assets by $5,000 and it increased owner equity or stockholders' equity in the corporation by the same amount.

An owner of stock may transfer at will either part or all the shares represented by a stock certificate. To do so he completes the endorsement on the reverse side of the certificate and sends the certificate to the corporation secretary in a small corporation or to the corporation's transfer agent in a large one. For example, assume that Robert Wetzel, the owner of the certificate for 50 shares shown in Illustration 16–2 sells 10 of the shares to William Morris. To transfer the stock Wetzel completes the endorsement on the back of the certificate, as shown in Illustration 16–3, signs his name, and sends it to the corporation secretary or transfer agent. The old certificate is canceled and retained, and two new certificates are issued in its place. One for 10 shares is sent to Morris, and the other for 40 shares is sent to Wetzel.

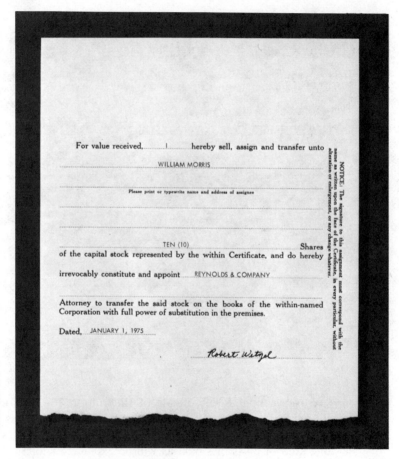

Illustration
16–3
**Stock certificate
(reverse side)
showing
endorsement for
transferred
stock**

Stock certificate book

When it is organized, a corporation must have a supply of stock certificates printed. In a small corporation the certificates often have stubs attached, and the certificates and stubs are bound in a Stock Certificate Book in the manner of a cheque book. As each stock certificate is issued, the name of its owner, the number of shares, and the date of issuance are entered on a blank certificate, and the certificate is signed by the proper corporation officials. At the same time, the name and address of the stock owner, the number of shares, and the date are entered on the certificate stub. The certificate is then removed and delivered to its owner.

When the stock is returned for transfer, the old certificate is marked canceled, attached to its stub in the Stock Certificate Book, and one or more new certificates are issued in its place. Consequently, as a result of these procedures, the Stock Certificate Book of a small corporation contains a current record of the shares owned by each stockholder.

If a small corporation issues more than one kind or class of stock, it uses separate stock certificate books as well as separate stock accounts for each.

Transfer agent and registrar

A large corporation, one whose stock is listed on a major stock exchange, must have a registrar and a transfer agent who are assigned the responsibilities of transferring the corporation's stock, keeping its stockholder records, and preparing the official lists of stockholders for stockholders' meetings and for payment of dividends.

Assigning the duties of transferring stock and keeping stockholder records to a transfer agent and a registrar helps ensure that only the proper amount of stock is issued and that the stock records are honestly and accurately kept. Usually registrars and transfer agents are large trust companies.

When the owner of stock in a corporation having a registrar and a transfer agent wishes to transfer his stock to a new owner, he completes the endorsement on the back of his certificate and, usually through a stockbroker, sends the certificate to the transfer agent. The transfer agent cancels the old certificate and issues one or more new certificates which he sends to the registrar. The registrar enters the transfer in the stockholder records and sends the new certificate or certificates to the proper owners.

Trust companies acting as registrars and transfer agents commonly so act for a number of corporations; and consequently are in a position to make use of punched card and electronic equipment in keeping stockholder records for each.

Corporation accounting ■ A corporation's accounting differs from that of an equal-size single proprietorship or partnership only for transactions directly affecting its stockholder equity accounts. Here a difference results because a distinction is always made in corporation accounting between invested capital and capital from earnings retained in the business.

No such distinction is made in a single proprietorship or partnership where an owner's investment and changes in his equity resulting from gains and losses are recorded in the same account, the owner's Capital account. However, in a corporation the distinction is made and two kinds of owner equity accounts, (1) *contributed capital accounts* and (2) *retained earnings accounts,* are used in preserving the distinction. The contributed capital accounts, such as the Common Stock account, show amounts invested in or contributed to the corporation by stockholders or others. The retained earnings accounts show earnings retained in the business. The distinction between contributed capital and retained earnings is necessary because in most jurisdictions a corporation cannot pay a legal dividend except from retained earnings.

Corporation owner equity accounts illustrated

■ To demonstrate the use of separate accounts for contributed capital and retained earnings as found in corporation accounting and to contrast their use with the single capital account in a sole proprietorship, assume that on January 5, 1975, a single proprietorship and a corporation having five stockholders were formed. Assume further that $25,000 was invested in each. In the sole proprietorship the owner, John Ohm, invested the entire amount; and in the corporation five stockholders each bought 500 shares of its $10 par value common stock at $10 per share. Without dates and explanations, general journal entries to record the investments are:

Single Proprietorship		Corporation	
Cash......................... 25,000		Cash......................... 25,000	
John Ohm, Capital	25,000	Common Stock.....	25,000

And after the entries were posted, the owner equity accounts of the two concerns appeared as follows:

Single Proprietorship				Corporation			
John Ohm, Capital				Common Stock			
Date	Dr.	Cr.	Bal.	Date	Dr.	Cr.	Bal.
Jan. 5, '75		25,000	25,000	Jan. 5, '75		25,000	25,000

To continue the illustration, in a single proprietorship when the Income Summary account is closed, the amount of net income or loss is transferred from the Income Summary account to the owner's Capital account. In a corporation this differs; in a corporation the net income or loss is carried to the Retained Earnings account. For example, if in the two concerns under discussion, each earned $8,000 during the first year and retained the earnings for use in carrying on their operations, after the Income Summary accounts were closed, the owner equity of each appeared in its accounts as follows:

Single Proprietorship John Ohm, Capital				Corporation Common Stock			
Date	Dr.	Cr.	Bal.	Date	Dr.	Cr.	Bal.
Jan. 5, '75		25,000	25,000	Jan. 5, '75		25,000	25,000
Dec. 31, '75		8,000	33,000				

Retained Earnings			
Date	Dr.	Cr.	Bal.
Dec. 31, '75		8,000	8,000

And the owner equity of each appeared on its balance sheet as follows:

Single Proprietorship OWNER EQUITY	Corporation STOCKHOLDERS' EQUITY

John Ohm, capital, January 1
  1975.................................. $25,000
Add net income...................... 8,000
John Ohm, capital, December
  31, 1975............................. $33,000
	Common stock, $10 par
	  value, authorized and
	  issued 2,500 shares $25,000
	Retained earnings 8,000
	Stockholders' equity.............. $33,000

To continue the illustration, assume that the concerns each lost $11,000 during their second year. If there were no withdrawals in the single proprietorship or additional investments in either concern, the owner equity accounts of each appeared at the end of the second year as follows:

Single Proprietorship John Ohm, Capital				Corporation Common Stock			
Date	Dr.	Cr.	Bal.	Date	Dr.	Cr.	Bal.
Jan. 5, '75		25,000	25,000	Jan. 5, '75		25,000	25,000
Dec. 31, '75		8,000	33,000				
Dec. 31, '76	11,000		22,000				

Retained Earnings			
Date	Dr.	Cr.	Bal.
Dec. 31, '75		8,000	8,000
Dec. 31, '76	11,000		3,000

Observe that the Retained Earnings account of the corporation has a $3,000 debit balance. A corporation is said to have a *deficit* when it has a debit balance in its Retained Earnings account, as in this illustration. A deficit is in effect a negative amount of retained earnings, and in most jurisdictions a corporation with a deficit cannot pay a legal dividend.

At the end of the second year the owner equity sections on the balance sheets of the two concerns appeared as follows:

Single Proprietorship	Corporation
OWNER EQUITY	STOCKHOLDERS' EQUITY
John Ohm, capital, January 1, 1976 .... $33,000	Common stock, $10 par value, 2,500 shares authorized and issued.......... $25,000
Deduct: Net loss...................... (11,000)	Deduct: Deficit........................ (3,000)
John Ohm, capital, December 31, 1976 .... $22,000	Stockholders' equity $22,000

During their second year both the corporation and the proprietorship suffered losses, which in each case reduced the equities of their owners to $22,000. Notice in the illustration just given how the $22,000 equity in the corporation is shown by listing the amount of stock and deducting therefrom the $3,000 deficit.

Authorization of stock

■ When a corporation is organized, it is authorized in its charter to issue a certain amount of stock. The stock may be of one kind, common stock, or both common and preferred stock may be authorized. (Preferred stock is discussed later in this chapter.) However, regardless of whether one or two kinds of stock are authorized, the corporation may issue no more than the amount of each authorized by its charter.

Often a corporation will secure an authorization to issue more stock than it plans to sell at the time of its organization. This enables it to expand at any time in its future through the sale of the additional stock, and without the need of applying to the government for the right to issue more. For example, a corporation needing $300,000 to begin its operations may secure the right to issue $500,000 of stock, but then issue only $300,000, keeping the remainder until a future date when it may wish to sell the stock and expand without applying to the government for the right to issue more stock.

At the time a corporation receives its charter, it is common practice to write or type across the top of each stock account the amount of stock authorized. For example, if 5,000 shares of $100 par value common stock are authorized, the memorandum written across the top of the Common Stock account might read: "Authorized on June 1, 19—, to issue 5,000 shares of $100 per value common stock." If preferred stock is also authorized, a similar memorandum telling the number of preferred shares authorized would be written across the top of the Preferred Stock account.

■ When stock is sold for cash and immediately issued, an entry in general journal form like the following is commonly used to record the sale and issuance:

June	5	Cash	300,000.00	
		Common Stock		300,000.00
		Sold and issued 3,000 shares of $100 par value common stock.		

After authorized stock has been sold and issued, it is a common practice to show on the balance sheet both the amount of stock authorized and the amount issued (see bottom of page 479).

■ Corporations often accept assets other than cash in exchange for their stock. When they do so, the transaction is recorded in somewhat the following manner:

Apr.	3	Machinery	10,000.00	
		Buildings..	25,000.00	
		Land...	5,000.00	
		Common Stock....................................		40,000.00
		Exchanged 400 shares of common stock for machinery, buildings, and land.		

Or another example: A corporation may give shares of its stock to its promoters in exchange for their services in getting the corporation organized. In such a case the corporation receives the intangible asset of being organized in exchange for its stock, and the transaction is recorded as follows:

Apr.	5	Organization Costs................................ ...	5,000.00	
		Common Stock.................................... ...		5,000.00
		Gave the promoters shares of common stock in exchange for their services in getting the corporation organized.		

When a corporation accepts assets other than cash for its stock, it is the duty of the board of directors to place a fair value on the assets; and if the assets are fairly valued, such transactions are perfectly proper.

■ Often corporations sell their stock for cash and immediately issue the stock. Often, too, when stock is first sold, especially in organizing a new corporation, it is sold by means of *subscriptions*. When stock is sold by means of subscriptions, a person wishing to become a stockholder signs a subscription blank or a subscription list on which he subscribes to a certain number of shares and agrees to pay for the stock either in one amount or in installments. When the subscription is accepted by the corporation, it becomes a contract.

When a prospective stockholder signs a corporation's subscription list or one of its subscription blanks and the corporation accepts the subscription, the corporation acquires an asset, the right to receive payment from the subscriber; and at the same time, its stockholder equity is increased by the amount the subscriber agrees to pay. The increase in assets is recorded in an account for common stock, called *Subscriptions Receivable, Common Stock;* and the increase in stockholder equity is recorded in an account for common stock, called *Common Stock Subscribed.* Both accounts are of a temporary nature. The subscriptions receivable will be turned into cash when the subscriber pays for his stock. Likewise, when payment is completed, the subscribed stock will be issued and will become outstanding stock. Under federal legislation subscribed stock is not issued until paid for.

If a corporation receives subscriptions to both common and preferred stock, separate subscriptions receivable and stock subscribed accounts must be kept for each. If the number of subscribers becomes large, the subscriptions receivable accounts often become controlling accounts that control subsidiary Subscribers' Ledgers having an account with each subscriber. The controlling account for each class of subscriptions receivable and its Subscribers' Ledger operate in the same manner as, for example, the Accounts Receivable controlling account and the Accounts Receivable Ledger discussed in a previous chapter.

When unpaid subscriptions exist on the balance sheet date, the intention is normally to collect the amounts within a relatively short period. Therefore, unpaid subscriptions normally appear on the balance sheet as current assets under the title "Subscriptions Receivable, Common Stock" or "Subscriptions Receivable, Preferred Stock."

Sale of stock through subscriptions, with collections in installments

■ Corporations selling stock through subscriptions may collect the subscriptions in one amount or in installments. To illustrate the sale of stock through subscriptions collected in installments, assume that on June 7, 19–, Northgate Corporation accepted subscriptions to 5,000 shares of its $10 par value common stock at par, under subscription contracts calling for a 10% down payment to accompany the subscriptions and the balance in two equal installments due in 30 and 60 days.

The subscriptions were recorded with the following entry:

June	7	Subscriptions Receivable, Common Stock........	50,000.00	
		Common Stock Subscribed.......................		50,000.00
		Accepted subscriptions to 5,000 shares of common stock at par.		

Receipt of the down payments and the two installment payments were recorded with these entries:

June	7	Cash..	5,000.00	
		Subscriptions Receivable, Common Stock ...		5,000.00
		Collected the down payments on the common stock subscribed.		
July	6	Cash..	22,500.00	
		Subscriptions Receivable, Common Stock ...		22,500.00
		Collected the first installment payments on the common stock subscribed.		
Aug.	5	Cash..	22,500.00	
		Subscriptions Receivable, Common Stock ...		22,500.00
		Collected the second installment payments on the common stock subscribed.		

When stock is sold through subscriptions, the stock is paid for as soon as the subscriptions are paid in full; and as soon as the subscriptions are paid, the stock is issued. The entry to record the issuance of the Northgate common stock appeared as follows:

Aug.	5	Common Stock Subscribed............................	50,000.00	
		Common Stock..		50,000.00
		Issued 5,000 shares of common stock sold through subscriptions.		

Most subscriptions are collected in full, although not always. Sometimes a subscriber fails to pay; and when this happens, the subscription contract must be canceled. In such a case, if the subscriber has made a partial payment on his contract, the amount paid may be returned. Or, a smaller amount of stock than that subscribed, an amount equal to the partial payment, may be issued. Or, in some jurisdictions the subscriber's partial payment may be kept by the corporation to compensate for any damages suffered.

Subscribed stock on the balance sheet

■ In many jurisdictions a subscriber to stock gains all the rights of a stockholder upon acceptance of his signed subscription contract by the corporation to whose stock he is subscribing. Also, acceptance of such contracts increase a corporation's assets and the equity of the subscribers in the corporation. Consequently, if a corporation prepares a balance sheet after accepting subscriptions to its stock but before the stock is issued, it shows both its issued stock and its subscribed stock on the balance sheet as follows:

STOCKHOLDERS' EQUITY

Common stock, $10 par value, 25,000 shares authorized, 15,000 shares issued $150,000
Unissued common stock subscribed, 5,000 shares 50,000
Total common stock issued and subscribed $200,000

■ A dividend is a distribution made to its stockholders by a corporation. Dividends are declared or voted by the board of directors, and courts have generally held that the board is final judge of when if at all a dividend should be paid. Dividends may be distributed in cash, other assets, or in a corporation's own stock. Cash dividends are the most common, and are normally stated in terms of so many dollars or cents per share of stock. For example, a corporation may declare a dividend of $1 per share on its outstanding common stock. If it does so, an owner of 100 shares will receive $100.

Since a corporation's stockholders change, a dividend is normally declared on one date to be paid on a future date to the *stockholders of record* (stockholders according to the corporation's records) of a specified third date. For example, a board of directors may declare a dividend on December 28, to be paid on January 25 to the stockholders of record of January 20. Of the three dates involved here, December 28 is called the *date of declaration*, January 20 is the *date of record*, and January 25 is the *date of payment*. Declaring a dividend on one date to be paid on a future date gives new purchasers of the stock an opportunity to have their ownership recorded in time to receive the dividend.

A stockholder has no right to a dividend until it is declared by the board of directors. However, as soon as a cash dividend is declared, it becomes a liability of the corporation, normally a current liability, and must be paid. Furthermore, the stockholders have the right to sue and force payment of a cash dividend once it is declared. Since dividends are normally declared on one date to be paid on a future date, two entries are used to record the declaration and payment of each dividend. The first entry, which is made at the time of the declaration, reduces the stockholders' equity and records the liability for the dividend; and the second records its payment. The two entries commonly appear as follows:

Dec.	28	Dividends (closed to Retained Earnings)...........	25,000.00	
		Common Dividend Payable		25,000.00
		To record the declaration of a $1 per share dividend on the 25,000 shares of outstanding common stock.		
Jan.	25	Common Dividend Payable	25,000.00	
		Cash...		25,000.00
		To record payment of the dividend declared on December 28.		

■ Since a corporation is a legal entity, its earnings belong to the corporation. The stockholders own the corporation; but they have no legal right to its earnings until the board declares a dividend; and the board is the final judge of when such a dividend should be declared. In deciding upon a dividend, the board normally considers both its legality and the wisdom of its declaration. Although the answers vary from jurisdiction to jurisdiction, generally a legal dividend may be declared if a corporation has retained earnings from which to pay the dividend. (Laws governing the payment of dividends normally make directors personally liable for repayment to the corporation of a dividend declared and paid in violation of the laws. A director who votes against such a dividend is not held liable; consequently, directors are usually careful not to vote for an illegal dividend.)

As to the wisdom of a dividend, the directors must decide whether the corporation can spare the cash needed for its payment, or when cash is available, if the cash cannot be used to better advantage in expanding the corporation's operations for greater profits in the future. Many large corporations follow the policy of paying out in dividends around 60% of earnings and retaining the balance to finance expansion and growth.

Rights of stockholders

■ If a corporation issues only one kind of stock, the stock is known as *common stock*. When individuals buy such stock, they acquire all the specific rights granted by the corporation's charter to its common stockholders; and they also acquire the general rights granted stockholders by the laws of the jurisdiction in which the corporation is organized. The laws vary, but in general all common stockholders have the following rights:

1. The right to vote in the stockholders' meetings.
2. The right to sell or otherwise dispose of their stock.
3. The right to share pro rata with other common stockholders in any dividends declared.
4. The right to share in any assets remaining after creditors are paid if the corporation is liquidated.

In addition if desired the articles of incorporation may provide additional rights. For example, the articles may specifically provide for the *preemptive right*. This right holds that no shares of a class shall be issued unless the shares have first been offered to the shareholders holding shares of that class, and that those shareholders have a first opportunity to acquire the offered shares in proportion to their holdings of the shares of that class, at such a price and on such terms as those shares are to be offered to others.

Preferred stock

■ A corporation may issue more than one kind or class of stock. If two classes are issued, one is generally known as common stock and the other as *preferred stock*. Preferred stock is so called because of the preferences granted its owners. These commonly include a preference as to payment of dividends, and may include a preference as to the return of the stock's par value in a liquidation.

A preference as to dividends does not give an absolute right to dividends. Rather if dividends are declared, it gives the preferred stock-holders the right to receive their preferred dividend before the common stockholders are paid a dividend. In other words, if dividends are declared, a dividend must be paid the preferred stockholders before a dividend may be paid to the common stockholders. However, if the directors are of the opinion that no dividends should be paid, then neither the preferred nor the common stockholders receive a dividend.

Dividends on the majority of preferred stocks are limited to a fixed maximum amount. For example, a share of $100 par value, 6%, non-participating preferred stock has a preference each year to a dividend equal to 6% of its par value, or $6; but the dividend is limited to that amount.

Although dividends on the majority of preferred stocks are limited in amount, dividends on a corporation's common stock are unlimited, except by the earning power of the corporation and the judgment of its board of directors.

While dividends on most preferred stocks are limited to a fixed basic percentage or amount, some preferred stocks have the right under certain circumstances to dividends in excess of a fixed basic percentage or amount. Such preferred stocks are called *participating preferred stocks*. Participating preferred stocks may be fully participating, or their participation may be limited to a fixed amount, depending in each case on the exact terms set forth in the corporation's charter. For example, if a corporation issues fully participating, 6%, $100 par value, preferred stock and $50 par value common stock, the owners of the preferred stock have a preference to a 6% or $6 per share dividend each year. Then, each year, after the common stockholders have received a 6% or $3 per share dividend, the preferred stockholders have a right to participate with the common stockholders in any additional dividends declared. The participation is usually on the basis of the same additional per cent-on-par-value-per-share dividend to each kind of stock. For instance, if in this case the common stockholders are paid an additional 2% or $1 per share dividend, the preferred stockholders should receive an additional 2% or $2 per share dividend.

Often when preferred stock is participating, participation is limited. For example, a $100 par value, 5%, preferred stock may be issued with the right to participate in dividends to 10% of its par value. Such a stock has a preference to dividends of 5% each year. It also has a right after the common stockholders receive a 5% dividend to participate in additional dividends until it has received 10%, or $10, per share. Its participation rights end at this point.

In addition to being participating or nonparticipating, preferred stocks are either *cumulative* or *noncumulative*. A cumulative preferred stock is one on which any undeclared dividends accumulate each year until paid. A noncumulative preferred stock is one on which the right to receive dividends is forfeited in any year in which dividends are not declared.

The accumulation of dividends on cumulative preferred stocks does not guarantee their payment. Dividends cannot be guaranteed because earnings from which they are paid cannot be guaranteed. However, when a corporation issues cumulative preferred stock, it does agree to pay its cumulative preferred stockholders both their current dividends and any unpaid back dividends, called *dividends in arrears,* before it pays a dividend to its common stockholders.

In addition to the preferences it receives, preferred stock carries with it all the rights of common stock, unless such rights are specifically denied in the corporation charter. Commonly, preferred stock is denied the right to vote in the stockholders' meetings, as in the example in a following section that tells why preferred stock is issued.

Preferred dividends in arrears on the balance sheet date

A liability for a dividend does not come into existence until the dividend is declared by the board of directors; and unlike interest, dividends do not accrue. Consequently, if on the dividend date a corporation's board fails to declare a dividend on its cumulative preferred stock, the dividend in arrears is not a liability and does not appear on the balance sheet as such. However, if there are preferred dividends in arrears, this information should appear on the balance sheet, and normally such information is given in a balance sheet footnote. For example, if three years' dividends have been missed, such a footnote might read, "Dividends for the current and two past years are in arrears on the preferred stock." When a balance sheet does not carry such a footnote, a balance sheet reader has the right to assume that all current and back dividends on the preferred stock have been paid.

Why preferred stock is issued ■ Two common reasons why preferred stock is issued can best be shown by means of an example. Suppose that three men with a total of $100,000 to invest wish to organize a corporation requiring $200,000 capital. If they sell and issue $200,000 of common stock, they will have to share control with other stockholders. However, if they sell and issue $100,000 of common stock to themselves and sell to outsiders $100,000 of 6%, cumulative preferred stock having no voting rights, they can retain control of the corporation for themselves.

Also, suppose the three promoters expect their new corporation to earn an annual after-tax return of $20,000. If they sell and issue $200,000 of common stock, this will mean a 10% return; but if they sell and issue $100,000 of each kind of stock, retaining the common for themselves, they can increase their own return to 14%, as follows:

Net after-tax income	$20,000
Preferred dividends at 6%	6,000
Balance to common stockholders (equal to 14% on their $100,000 investment)	$14,000

This is an example of what is known as securing a *leverage* on an investment. The common stockholders secure a leverage, or greater return, on their investment because the dividends on the preferred stock are less than the amount that can be earned through the use of the preferred stockholders' money.

In the example the preferred stock carries a cumulative preference as to dividends. The exact preferences granted in this and every other case always depend on what must be granted to sell the stock. As a rule, nothing is granted beyond what is necessary.

Stock values ■ Several values apply to stock. For instance, a stock may have a par value, a book value, a market value, and a redemption value.

Par value

Par value is the arbitrary value established for a share of stock in the charter of its issuing corporation and is printed on the face of each stock certificate. Par value does not establish worth, and its main significance is a legal one that is discussed in the next chapter.

Book value

The book value of a share of stock measures the equity of one share of the stock in the assets of its issuing corporation. If a corporation has only one kind of stock, common stock, and all of its authorized shares are outstanding, the book value of all the shares is equal to the sum of the corporation's contributed and retained capital, and the book value of one of the shares is equal to the sum of the contributed and retained capital divided by the number of shares outstanding. For example, consider a corporation that has the following contributed and retained capital:

Common stock, $25 par value, 1,000 shares authorized and issued............. $25,000
Retained earnings... 6,100
    Total Stockholders' Equity.. $31,100

The book value of one share of the corporation's common stock is $31,100 divided by 1,000 shares, or $31.10 per share.

When a corporation issues both common and preferred stock and the book value of each is to be determined, it is first necessary to allocate total stockholders' equity between the two classes of stock. Then the equity allocated to the preferred stock is divided by the preferred shares involved and the equity allocated to the common stock is divided by the common shares involved to determine the book value of each.

The allocation of total stockholders' equity between the two classes of stock may be simple or complex, depending upon the liquidation rights granted the preferred stockholders. Preferred stockholders are commonly given a preference in a liquidation to the return of the par value of their shares plus any dividends in arrears. For example, assume a corporation has the following capitalization:

Preferred stock, $100 par value, 7% cumulative and nonparticipating,
  1,000 shares authorized and outstanding... $100,000
Common stock, $10 par value, 20,000 shares authorized and outstanding 200,000
Retained earnings... 40,000
    Total Stockholders' Equity... $340,000

If in this case the preferred stockholders are granted a preference in a liquidation to the par value of their shares plus dividends in arrears and there are no dividends in arrears, the total stockholders' equity is divided as follows:

Total stockholders' equity... $340,000
Less equity allocated to preferred stockholders:
  Par value of outstanding preferred shares 100,000
Equity of common stockholders $240,000

And the book value of each is:

     Preferred stock: $100,000 ÷ 1,000 shares = $100 per share
     Common stock: $240,000 ÷ 20,000 shares = $12 per share

When there is a deficit or dividends in arrears, the allocation procedure is the same but the results differ. For example, assume there are two years' dividends in arrears on the preferred stock of a corporation having the following stockholders' equity:

Preferred stock, $100 par value, 7½% cumulative and nonparticipating, 1,000
  shares authorized and outstanding.. $100,000
Common stock, $10 par value, 50,000 shares authorized and outstanding 500,000
Deficit .... (25,000)
    Total Stockholders' Equity... $575,000

If in this case the preferred stockholders have a preference in a liquidation to the par value of their shares plus dividends in arrears, total stockholders' equity is allocated as follows:

Total stockholders' equity $575,000
Less equity allocated to preferred stockholders:
  Par value of outstanding preferred shares.......................... $100,000
  Dividends in arrears.. 15,000   115,000
Equity of common stockholders... $460,000

And the book value per share is:

     Preferred stock: $115,000 ÷ 1,000 shares = $115 per share
     Common stock: $460,000 ÷ 50,000 shares = $9.20 per share

Corporations in their annual reports to their shareholders often point out the increase that has occurred in the book value of the corporation's shares during a year or other period of time. Book value is also of significance in many contracts. For example, a stockholder may enter into a contract to sell his shares at their book value at some future date.

However, book value should not be confused with *liquidation value,* because if a corporation is liquidated, its assets will probably sell at prices quite different from the amounts at which they are carried on the books. Also, book value is only one of several factors that affect the market value of stock; and dividends, earning capacity, and future prospects are usually of much more importance. For instance a common stock having a $11 book value may sell for $25 per share if its earnings, dividends, and prospects are good; but it may sell for $5 per share if these factors are unfavorable.

Market value

The market value of a share of stock is the price at which a share can be bought or sold. Market values are influenced by earnings, dividends, future prospects, book value, and general market conditions.

Redemption value

Redemption values apply to preferred stocks. Often corporations issuing preferred stock reserve the right to redeem the stock by paying the preferred stockholders the par value of their stock plus a premium. The amount a corporation agrees to pay to redeem a share of its preferred stock is called the "redemption value" of the stock. Normally, a corporation reserves the right to either redeem or permit the stock to remain outstanding, as it chooses.

Questions for class discussion

1. List *(a)* the advantages and *(b)* disadvantages of the corporation form of business organization.
2. A corporation is said to be a separate legal entity. What is meant by this?
3. What effect does a separate legal existence have upon the ability of a corporation to enter into contracts with its stockholders? What effect does a corporation's separate legal existence have on the liability of its stockholders for the corporation's debts?
4. What is a proxy?
5. What are organization costs? List several.
6. What are the duties and responsibilities of a corporation's registrar and transfer agent?
7. Why is a corporation whose stock is sold on a stock exchange required to have a registrar and transfer agent? Why is such a corporation required to have both a registrar and a transfer agent?
8. List the rights of common stockholders.
9. What is the preemptive right of common stockholders?
10. What are the balance sheet classifications of the accounts: *(a)* Subscriptions Receivable, Common Stock and *(b)* Common Stock Subscribed?
11. What two kinds of proprietary accounts are used in corporation accounting? Why are the two kinds used?
12. In corporation accounting, what is a deficit?
13. What are the meanings of the following when applied to preferred stock:

(a) preferred, (b) participating, (c) nonparticipating, (d) cumulative, and (e) noncumulative?

14. What are the meanings of the following terms when applied to stock: (a) par value, (b) book value, (c) market value, and (d) redemption value?

Exercise 16–1

A corporation has 10,000 shares of $10 par value common stock outstanding. Last year the corporation earned $39,000, after taxes; and on January 10 of this year its board of directors voted a $1 per share dividend on the stock, payable on February 5 to the January 31 stockholders of record. Give the entries to (a) close the corporation's Income Summary account at the end of last year and to record (b) the dividend declaration and (c) its payment. (d) Name and give the three dates involved in the dividend declaration and payment.

Exercise 16–2

A corporation has outstanding 1,000 shares of $100 par value, 7% cumulative and nonparticipating preferred stock and 8,000 shares of $25 par value common stock; and during the first four years in its life it paid out the following amounts in dividends: first year, nothing; second year, $8,000; third year, $24,000; and fourth year, $30,000. Determine the total dividends paid to each class of stockholders each year.

Exercise 16–3

Determine the total dividends paid each class of stockholders of the previous exercise under the assumption that rather than being cumulative and nonparticipating, the preferred stock is noncumulative and nonparticipating.

Exercise 16–4

A corporation has outstanding 1,000 shares of $100 par value, 7% cumulative and fully participating preferred stock and 20,000 shares of $10 par value common stock. It has regularly paid all dividends on the preferred stock. This year the board of directors voted to pay out a total of $28,500 in dividends to the two classes of stockholders. Determine the per cent on par to be paid each class of stockholders and the dividend per share to be paid each class.

Exercise 16–5

The stockholders' equity section from a corporation's balance sheet appeared as follows:

STOCKHOLDERS' EQUITY

Preferred stock, 7% cumulative and nonparticipating,
$10 par value, 10,000 shares issued and outstanding $100,000
Common stock, $5 par value, 50,000 shares issued and outstanding 250,000
Retained earnings 85,000
Total Stockholders' Equity $435,000

Required:

1. Determine the book value per share of the preferred stock and of the common stock under the assumption there are no dividends in arrears on the preferred stock.
2. Determine the book value per share for each kind of stock under the assumption that two years' dividends are in arrears on the preferred stock.

Exercise 16-6

Corporations A, B, and C have outstanding 20,000 shares of common stock each. Following is additional information as to each corporation's assets, liabilities, and stockholders' equity:

	Corporation A	*Corporation B*	*Corporation C*
Assets	$325,000	$262,000	291,000
Liabilities	79,000	32,000	$ 61,000
Common stock	250,000	100,000	200,000
Retained earnings or deficit	(20,000)	130,00	30,00

Required:
Under the assumption the book values of the corporations' common stocks are the same, determine the missing amounts indicated by the question marks.

Problems   **Problem 16-1**

Twin Lake Corporation received a charter granting the right to issue 1,000 shares of $100 par value, 7% cumulative and nonparticipating preferred stock and 50,000 shares of $5 par value common stock. It then completed these transactions:

Jan. 26 Sold and issued 20,000 shares of common stock for cash.

29 Accepted subscriptions to the 1,000 shares of preferred stock at par. The subscription contracts were accompanied by 10% down payments.

Feb. 12 Exchanged 15,000 shares of common stock for land having a $25,000 fair market value and a building having a $50,000 fair value.

15 Gave the corporation's promoters 1,000 shares of common stock for their services in getting the corporation organized. The services were valued by the board of directors at $5,000.

28 Collected the balance due on the January 29 subscriptions and issued the stock.

28 Accepted subscriptions to 5,000 shares of common stock at par. Twenty percent down payments accompanied the subscription contracts.

Required:
Prepare general journal entries to record the transactions and prepare a February 28 classified balance sheet for the corporation.

Problem 16–2

A corporation received a charter granting the right to issue 50,000 shares of $10 par value common stock. It then completed these transactions:

197A

Feb. 17 Sold and issued 15,000 shares of common stock at par for cash.

20 Gave the corporation's promoters 1,000 shares of common stock for their services in getting the corporation organized. The directors valued the services at $10,000.

25 Exchanged 25,000 shares of common stock for the following assets at fair market values: land, $25,000; buildings, $100,000; and machinery, $125,000.

Dec. 10 Accepted subscriptions to 2,000 shares of common stock at par. Ten percent down payments accompanied the subscription contracts.

Dec. 31 Closed the Income Summary account. A $17,500 loss was incurred.

197B

Jan. 10 Received payment of the balance due on the December 10 subscriptions and issued the stock.

Dec. 31 Closed the Income Summary account. A $34,800 net income was earned.

197C

Jan. 8 The board of directors declared $0.20 per share dividend on the outstanding common stock, payable on February 10 to the January 31 stockholders of record.

Feb. 10 Paid the previously declared dividend.

Required:
1. Prepare general journal entries to record the transactions.
2. Prepare the stockholders' equity section of the corporation's December 31, 197A, balance sheet.
3. Prepare a second stockholders' equity section as of the close of business on February 10, 197C.

Problem 16–3

Bluelake Corporation has outstanding 10,000 shares of $10 par value, 6%, preferred stock and 20,000 shares of $10 par value common stock. During a seven-year period the company paid out the following amounts in dividends: 197A, nothing; 197B, $24,000; 197C, nothing; 197D, $20,000; 197E, $18,000; 197F, $30,000; and 197G, $36,000.

Required:
1. Prepare three schedules with columnar headings as follows:

Year	Amount Distributed in Dividends	Total to Preferred	Balance Due Preferred	Total to Common	Dividend per Share Preferred	Dividend per Share Common

2. Complete a schedule under each of the following assumptions, showing for each year the total dollars paid the preferred stockholders, balance due the

preferred stockholders, etc. There were no dividends in arrears for the years prior to 197A.

a. The preferred stock is noncumulative and nonparticipating.

b. The preferred stock is cumulative and nonparticipating.

c. The preferred stock is cumulative and fully participating.

Problem 16–4

PART 1. Following are the stockholder equity sections from the balance sheets of three corporations. From the information given prepare a schedule showing the book value per share of the preferred and of the common stock of each corporation.

1. Stockholders' Equity:

Seven percent cumulative and nonparticipating, $10 par value, preferred stock, authorized and issued 10,000 shares	$ 100,000
Common stock, $5 par value, authorized and issued 100,000 shares	500,000
Retained earnings	148,000
Total Stockholders' Equity	$ 748,000

2. Stockholders' Investment:

Cumulative and nonparticipating, $100 par value, 6%, preferred stock, 10,000 shares issued and outstanding	$1,000,000*
Common stock, $25 par value, 100,000 shares issued and outstanding	2,500,000
Retained earnings	85,000
Total Stockholders' Investment	$3,585,000

* One year's dividends are in arrears on the preferred stock.

3. Stockholders' Equity:

Preferred stock, $100 par value, 7% cumulative and nonparticipating, 5,000 shares issued and outstanding	$ 500,000*
Common stock, $1 par value, 500,000 shares issued and outstanding	500,000
Total contributed capital	$1,000,000
Deficit	(40,000)
Total Stockholders' Equity	$ 960,000

* Two years' dividends are in arrears on the preferred stock.

PART 2. A corporation's common stock is selling on the stock exchange today at $12.50 per share, and a just published balance sheet shows the stockholders' equity in the company as follows:

STOCKHOLDERS' EQUITY

Preferred stock, $100 par value, 7% cumulative and nonparticipating, issued and outstanding 2,500 shares	$250,000
Common stock, $10 par value, issued and outstanding 50,000 shares	500,000
Total contributed capital	$750,000
Retained earnings	63,000
Total Stockholders' Equity	$813,000

Required:

Answer these questions: (1) What is the market value of the corporation's common stock? (2) What are the par values of its *(a)* preferred stock and *(b)* common stock? (3) If there are no dividends in arrears, what are the book values of the *(a)* preferred stock and *(b)* common stock? (4) If two years' dividends are in arrears on the preferred stock, what are the book values of the *(a)* preferred stock and the *(b)* common stock?

Problem 16–5

A corporation has outstanding 25,000 shares of $10 par value common stock, all owned by five men who are the corporation's board of directors. The corporation is in a position to expand; but to do so it needs $250,000 additional capital which its owners are unable to supply. Consequently, they are considering the issuance of 2,500 shares of $100 par value, 7%, cumulative and nonparticipating, preferred stock to gain the needed capital, and they have asked you to prepare a report showing the return to the two classes of stockholders from the following amounts of before-tax earnings.

a. $25,000 or a 5% before-tax return on the $500,000 invested.
b. $50,000 or a 10% before-tax return on the $500,000 invested.
c. $100,000 or a 20% before-tax return on the $500,000 invested.
d. $125,000 or a 25% before-tax return on the $500,000 invested.

Required:
1. Prepare a form with columnar headings as follows:

Before-Tax Earnings	Income Taxes	After-Tax Earnings		Preferred Dividends		Common Dividends	
		Amount	Per cent Return on Investment	Total Paid to Preferred	Per cent Return on Investment	Total Paid to Common	Per cent Return on Investment

2. Enter the amounts of before-tax earnings in the first column.
3. Calculate the federal income tax applicable to each level of earnings and enter in the second column. (Assume that this corporation qualifies for a 25% tax rate on taxable income up to $100,000 and 50% on amounts in excess.)
4. Complete the form under the assumption that all after-tax earnings are paid out in dividends.
5. Explain why at the $100,000 and $125,000 pretax levels the after-tax rate of return to the common stockholders is greater than the after-tax rate earned by the corporation as a whole.
6. Prepare a calculation to account for the difference between the rate of return to the corporation as a whole at the $100,000 level and the return to the common stockholders at this level.

Problem 16–1A

Deeplake Corporation received a charter granting the right to issue 1,000 shares of $100 par value, 7% cumulative and nonparticipating preferred stock and 20,000 shares of $10 par value common stock. It then completed these transactions:

Jan. 10 Sold and issued 5,000 shares of common stock at par for cash.

11 Gave the corporation's lawyers 200 shares of common stock for their services in securing the corporation's charter. The services were valued at $2,000.

14 Exchanged 1,000 shares of preferred stock for assets having the following fair market values: land, $10,000; buildings, $30,000; and machinery, $60,000.

15 Accepted subscriptions to 8,000 shares of common stock at par. The subscriptions contracts were accompanied by 20% down payments.

30 Collected the balance due on the stock subscriptions of January 15 and issued the stock.

31 Accepted subscriptions to 2,000 shares of common stock at par. The subscriptions contracts were accompanied by 20% down payments.

Required:
Prepare general journal entries to record the transactions and prepare a January 31 classified balance sheet for the corporation.

Problem 16–2A

A corporation received a charter granting it the right to issue 50,000 shares of $5 par value common stock. It then completed these transactions:

197A

Mar. 17 Sold and issued 8,000 shares of common stock at par for cash.

20 Issued 1,000 shares of common stock to the corporation's lawyers for their services in getting the corporation organized. The directors placed a $5,000 value on the services.

31 Exchanged 30,000 shares of common stock for the following assets at their fair market values: land, $25,000; buildings, $75,000; and machinery, $50,000.

Dec. 20 Accepted subscriptions to the remaining unissued common stock at par. Down payments of 20% accompanied the subscription contracts.

31 Closed the Income Summary account. There was a $9,250 net loss.

197B

Jan. 19 Collected the balance due on the December 20 subscriptions and issued the stock.

Dec. 31 Closed the Income Summary account. There was a $31,500 net income.

197C

Jan. 10 The board of directors declared a $0.25 per share dividend on the outstanding common stock, payable on February 10 to the January 31 stockholders of record.

Feb. 10 Paid the dividend previously declared.

Required:
1. Prepare general journal entries to record the transactions.
2. Prepare the stockholders' equity section of the corporation's December 31, 197A, balance sheet.
3. Prepare a second stockholders' equity section as of the close of business on February 10, 197C.

Problem 16–3A

A corporation has outstanding 10,000 shares of $10 par value, 7% preferred stock and 30,000 shares of $10 par value common stock. During a seven-year period it paid out the following amounts in dividends: 197A, $5,000; 197B, nothing; 197C, $7,000; 197D, $22,000; 197E, $22,000; 197F, $28,000; and 197G, $52,000. There were no dividends in arrears for the years before 197A.

Required:
1. Prepare three schedules with columnar headings as follows:

Year	Amount Distributed in Dividends	Total to Preferred	Balance Due Preferred	Total to Common	Dividend per Share Preferred	Dividend per Share Common

2. Complete a schedule under each of the following assumptions, showing for each year the total dollars paid the preferred stockholders, balance due the preferred stockholders, etc.
   a. The preferred stock is noncumulative and nonparticipating.
   b. The preferred stock is cumulative and nonparticipating.
   c. The preferred stock is cumulative and participating to 10% of its par value.

Problem 16–4A

PART 1. The stockholder equity section from a corporation's balance sheet appeared as follows:

STOCKHOLDERS' EQUITY

Seven per cent cumulative and nonparticipating, $100 par value, preferred stock, authorized and issued 1,000 shares... $100,000
Common stock, $25 par value, 10,000 shares authorized and issued 250,000
Retained earnings.. 18,000
    Total Stockholders' Equity.. $368,000

Required:
Prepare a schedule showing the book values per share of the preferred and common stocks under each of the following assumptions:
1. There are no dividends in arrears on the preferred stock.
2. One year's dividends are in arrears on the preferred stock.
3. Three years' dividends are in arrears on the preferred stock.

PART 2. A corporation has had outstanding since its organization 25,000 shares of $10 par value, 7%, preferred stock and 100,000 shares of $10 par value common stock. The current year's and two prior years', a total of three years', dividends are in arrears on the preferred stock. However, the company has recently prospered and the board of directors wants to know how much cash will be required for dividends if a $1 per share dividend is paid on the common stock.

Required:

Prepare a schedule showing the amounts of cash required for dividends to each class of stockholders under each of the following assumptions:

a.   The preferred stock is noncumulative and nonparticipating.
b.   The preferred stock is cumulative and nonparticipating.
c.   The preferred stock is cumulative and fully participating.
d.   The preferred stock is cumulative and participating to 9%.

Problem 16–5A

A corporation has outstanding 8,000 shares of $25 par value common stock, all owned by four men who are also the corporation's board of directors. The company needs $200,000 additional capital for expansion purposes, which its owners are unable to supply. Consequently, they are considering the issuance of 2,000 shares of $100 par value, 7%, cumulative and nonparticipating preferred stock to gain the additional capital, and they have asked you to prepare a report showing the return to the two classes of stockholders from the following amounts of before-tax earnings.

a. $20,000 or a 5% before-tax return on the $400,000 invested.
b. $40,000 or a 10% before-tax return on the $400,000 invested.
c. $60,000 or a 15% before-tax return on the $400,000 invested.
d. $80,000 or a 20% before-tax return on the $400,000 invested.

Required:

1.   Prepare a form with columnar headings as follows:

		After-Tax Earnings		Preferred Dividends		Common Dividends	
Before-Tax Earnings	Income Taxes	Amount	Per cent Return on In-vestment	Total Paid to Preferred	Per cent Return on In-vestment	Total Paid to Common	Per cent Return on In-vestment

2.   Enter the amounts of before-tax earnings in the first column.
3.   Calculate the federal income tax applicable to each level of earnings and enter in the second column. (Assume that this corporation qualifies for a 25% tax rate on taxable income up to $100,000 and 50% on amounts in excess.)
4.   Complete the form under the assumption that all after-tax earnings are paid out in dividends.

5. Explain why at the pretax levels of $60,000 and $80,000 the after-tax rate of return to the common stockholders is greater than the after-tax rate earned by the corporation as a whole.
6. Prepare a calculation to account for the difference between the rate of return to the corporation as a whole at the $60,000 level and the return to the common stockholders at this level.

Decision problem 16–1, Knothole Supply Company, Inc.

Edwin Brand and Dennis Cahill have operated a building supply firm, Knothole Suppliers, for a number of years as partners sharing losses and gains in a 3 to 2 ratio. They have entered into an agreement with John Decker to reorganize their firm into a corporation and have just received a charter granting their corporation, Knothole Supply Company, Inc., the right to issue 20,000 shares of $5 par value common stock. On the date of the reorganization, March 3 of the current year, a trial balance of the partnership ledger appears as follows:

KNOTHOLE SUPPLIERS
Trial Balance, March 3, 19—

Cash	$ 3,100	
Accounts receivable	11,300	
Allowance for doubtful accounts		$ 350
Merchandise inventory	42,250	
Store equipment	9,800	
Accumulated depreciation, store equipment		2,100
Buildings	50,000	
Accumulated depreciation, buildings		10,000
Land	12,500	
Accounts payable		5,550
Mortgage payable		35,000
Edwin Brand, capital		45,250
Dennis Cahill, capital		30,700
Totals	$128,950	$128,950

The agreement between the partners and Decker carries these provisions:

1. The partnership assets are to be revalued as follows:
   a. The $300 account receivable of Valley Contractors is known to be uncollectible and is to be written off as a bad debt, after which (b) the allowance for doubtful accounts is to be increased to 5% of the remaining accounts receivable.
   c. The merchandise inventory is to be written down to $40,000 to allow for damaged and shopworn goods.
   d. Insufficient depreciation has been taken on the store equipment; consequently, its book value is to be decreased to $6,500 by increasing the balance of the accumulated depreciation account.
   e. The building is to be written up to its replacement cost, $60,000, and the balance of the accumulated depreciation account is to be increased to show the building to be one-fifth depreciated.

2. After the partnership assets are revalued, the assets and liabilities are to be transferred to the corporation in exchange for its stock, with each partner accepting stock at par value for his equity in the partnership.
3. John Decker is to buy any remaining stock for cash at par value.

After reaching the agreement outlined, the three men hired you as book-keeper for the new corporation. Your first task is to determine the amount of stock each man should receive, and to prepare entries on the corporation's books to record the issuance of stock in exchange for the partnership assets and liabilities and the issuance of stock to Decker for cash. In addition prepare a balance sheet for the corporation as it should appear after all its stock is issued.

Decision problem 16–2, Ted and Ned

Ted Gulley recently received a patent on a gadget on which he has spent his spare time for several years. He is certain the gadget has tremendous market potential, but as a school teacher he has never been able to save much money and does not have the capital to manufacture and sell it. Consequently, last night he approached Ned Paine, a long-time friend who recently inherited several hundred thousand dollars from his father, for a $10,000 loan. Before asking for the loan, Ted demonstrated the gadget to Ned. Ned immediately became excited about its possibilities and agreed to make the loan. However, Ned pointed out that $10,000 would hardly get the item into production and it would take as much or more for a marketing campaign.

After discussing production and marketing needs for some time, Ned suggested that instead of a loan he should go into business with Ted. He suggested that he furnish the necessary capital for the business and that Ted transfer his patent rights to the business. Ted accepted the offer, and after more discussion it was agreed that Ted would resign his teaching job at the end of the school year, a month away, and devote full time to organizing and managing the new business. It was also agreed that although Ned would furnish all the capital needed by the business, he could devote no time to its affairs. Both men agreed that the marketing campaign should be turned over to professionals, but they did not agree as to the form of business organization for their new venture.

Write a report to Ted and Ned discussing the factors they should consider in choosing between a partnership form of organization for their business or a corporation form.

Decision problem 16–3, Gary Ashby

Gary Ashby recently inherited $15,000 from the estate of his father and is involved in its investment. He is looking with interest at two stocks: the preferred stock of Dunhill Company and the common stock of Wayside Industries. The companies are in the same industry, and both are young in years. Dunhill

Company was organized six years ago, and Wayside Industries began business one year later. The stockholder equity sections from the latest balance sheets of the two corporations show the following information:

DUNHILL COMPANY

Preferred stock, $100 par value, 6% cumulative and
  nonparticipating, 1,000 shares authorized and issued................ 100,000*
Common stock, $25 par value, 100,000 shares authorized,
  80,000 shares issued.. $200,000
Retained earnings 11,000
    Total Stockholders' Equity $311,000

* Three years' dividends are in arrears on the preferred stock.

WAYSIDE INDUSTRIES

Common stock, $10 par value, 50,000 shares authorized,
  25,000 shares issued $250,000
Retained earnings 50,000
    Total Stockholders' Equity... $300,000

The Dunhill Company preferred stock is selling for $98 per share, while the common stock of Wayside Industries is selling for $15 per share; and as a result, Mr. Ashby favors the Dunhill Company stock as an investment. He feels this stock is a real bargain since it is not only selling below its par value but also $20 below its book value, and as he put it, "Since it is preferred stock, the dividends are guaranteed." On the other hand, he feels the common stock of Wayside Industries, selling at 25% above book value and 50% above its par value, is overpriced.

a. Is the preferred stock selling at a price $20 below its book value, and is the common stock selling at a price 50% above its par value and 25% above its book value? *(b)* From an analysis of the stockholder equity sections, express your opinion of the two stocks as investments and give the reason for your opinion.

Analytical and review problem

Problem 16–1 A&R

Until March 2 of the current year Knox, Lacy and Mann were partners sharing losses and gains in their capital ratio. On that date they received their certificate of incorporation of KLM Company, Limited. All the assets liabilities of the partnership were taken over by the new corporation.

The Trial Balance of the Partnership just before the transfer and the opening Trial Balance of the corporation appear on the following page:

Knox, Lacy and Mann
Post Closing Trial Balance, March 2, 19—

Cash	$ 4,500	
Accounts receivable	10,500	
Allowance for doubtful accounts		$ 500
Merchandise inventory	23,000	
Store equipment	13,500	
Accumulated depreciation, store equipment		3,500
Land	4,500	
Building	50,000	
Accumulated depreciation, building		9,500
Accounts payable		5,500
Mortgage payable		12,000
John Knox, capital		30,000
Robert Lacy, capital		30,000
George Mann, capital		15,000
	$106,000	$106,000

KLM Company, Limited
Trial Balance, March 2, 19—

Cash	$ 4,500	
Accounts receivable	10,500	
Allowance for doubtful accounts		$ 500
Merchandise inventory	17,000	
Store equipment	12,500	
Land	16,000	
Building	56,700	
Accounts payable		5,500
Mortgage payable		12,000
Share capital, common, no par value		99,200
	$117,200	$117,200

Required:

1. Journal entries to close the books of the partnership and to open the books of the corporation.
2. What is the value of shares received by each of the three shareholders?

17

Corporations: Additional stock transactions

■ The organization of a corporation and a number of transactions involving the issuance of stock by a corporation were discussed in the previous chapter. In this chapter additional transactions involving stock are introduced. Although the Canada Business Corporations Act, 1975, eliminated the concept of par value, the provincial jurisdictions continue to allow both par and no-par-value stock. Thus, it is necessary to introduce such consequences of par value as interpretation of minimum legal capital and the nature of stock premiums and discounts.

Par value and minimum legal capital

■ As previously stated, par value is an arbitrary value a corporation places on a share of its stock at the time it seeks authorization of the stock. Normally a corporation may choose a par value of any amount for its stock; but par values of $100, $50, $25, $10, $5, and $1 are common. Early corporation laws required all stocks to have a par value; but today, all jurisdictions permit the issuance of stock having no par value.

When a corporation issues par value stock, the par value is printed on each certificate and is used in accounting for the stock. Also, in many jurisdictions when a corporation issues par value stock, it establishes for itself a *minimum legal capital* equal to the par value of the issued stock. For example, if a corporation issues 1,000 shares of $100 par value stock, it establishes for itself a minimum legal capital of $100,000.

Laws establishing minimum legal capital normally require stockholders to invest in a corporation, assets equal in value to minimum legal capital or be liable to the corporation's creditors for the deficiency. In other words, these laws require stockholders to give a corporation par value for its stock or be liable for the deficiency. In addition, when corporation laws set minimum legal capital requirements, they normally also make illegal any payments to stockholders for dividends or their equivalent when these payments reduce stockholder equity below minimum legal capital.

Corporation laws governing minimum legal capital were written in an effort to protect corporation creditors. The authors of these laws reasoned somewhat as follows: A corporation's creditors may look only to the assets of the corporation for satisfaction of their claims. Consequently, when a corporation is organized, its stockholders should provide it with a fund of assets equal to its minimum legal capital. Thereafter, this fund of assets should remain with the corporation and should not be returned to the stockholders in any form until all creditor claims are paid.

Although par value helps establish minimum legal capital and is used in accounting for par value stock, it does not establish a stock's worth nor the price at which a corporation must issue the stock. If purchasers are willing to pay more than par, a corporation may sell and issue its stock at a price above par. Likewise, in some jurisdictions, if purchasers will not pay par, a corporation may issue its stock at a price below par. Normally a corporation's potential earning power and the supply of investment funds determine whether purchasers will pay par, less than par, or more than par.

Stock premiums and discounts

■ **Premiums**

When a corporation sells and issues stock at a price above its par value, the stock is said to be issued at a *premium*. A premium is an amount in excess of par paid by the purchasers of newly issued stock. For example, if a corporation sells and issues its $100 par value stock for $125 per share, the $25 in excess of par is called a "premium." And, although a premium is an amount in excess of par paid by purchasers of newly issued stock, it is not considered a profit to the issuing corporation. Rather a premium is part of the investment of the stockholders who pay more than par for their stock. When stock is issued at a premium, stockholders invest more than the legal minimum of capital; consequently since premiums are amounts in excess of minimum legal capital, they should be accounted for separately from the par value of the stock to which they apply.

Some jurisdictions permit the payment of a "dividend" from amounts received as stock premiums. Nevertheless, and regardless of legality, accountants are opposed to calling such a distribution a "dividend," because it is obviously a return of invested capital and should be labeled clearly as such. Calling it a "dividend" might lead an uninformed person to believe the payment was from earnings.

Entries for stock sold at a premium

When, for example, common stock is sold at a premium and the stock is immediately issued, the transaction may be recorded as follows:

Dec.	1	Cash	110,000.00	
		Common Stock		100,000.00
		Premium on Common Stock		10,000.00
		To record the sale of 10,000 shares of $10 par value common stock at $11 per share.		

If subscriptions are taken for stock at a premium, the subscriptions collected, and the stock issued, the following entries are used:

Dec.	2	Subscriptions Receivable, Common Stock	11,000.00	
		Common Stock Subscribed		10,000.00
		Premium on Common Stock		1,000.00
		Accepted subscriptions to 1,000 shares of $10 par value common stock at $11 per share.		
Jan.	2	Cash	11,000.00	
		Subscriptions Receivable, Common Stock		11,000.00
		Collected subscriptions in full.		
	2	Common Stock Subscribed	10,000.00	
		Common Stock		10,000.00
		Issued stock to fully paid subscribers.		

Notice that the subscriptions receivable account is debited at the time the subscription is accepted for the sum of the stock's par value and premium; this is the amount the subscribers agree to pay. Notice, too, that the stock subscribed account is credited for par value and that the premium is credited to a premium account at the time the subscriptions are accepted.

When stock is issued for assets other than cash, the board of directors is responsible for placing a fair value on the assets; and if this value exceeds the par value of the stock, a premium is recorded. In cases where the board fails to place a value on such assets, a price established by recent sales of the stock may be used to value both the stock and the assets accepted in exchange for it.

Stock premiums on the balance sheet

Stock premiums help to measure the capital contributions of stockholders, and on the balance sheet they are commonly added to the par value of the stock to which they relate, as in Illustration 17–1.

SHAREHOLDERS' EQUITY

Preferred stock, $100 par value, 7% cumulative and nonparticipating,		
2,500 shares authorized, 1,500 shares issued	$150,000	
Add premium on preferred stock	7,500	
Amount paid in		$157,500
Common stock, $10 par value, 25,000 shares authorized, 20,000		
shares issued	$200,000	
Unissued common stock subscribed, 5,000 shares	50,000	
Total common stock issued and subscribed	$250,000	
Add premium on common stock	20,000	
Amount paid in and subscribed		270,000
Total contributed capital		$427,500
Retained earnings		122,300
Total Shareholders' Equity		$549,800

Illustration
17–1

Discounts

Stock issued at a price below par is said to be issued at a discount. For example, if a corporation sells and issues its $100 par value stock at $90 per share, the stock is issued at a discount. The discount is not considered a loss to the issuing corporation, rather the corporation's shareholders are investing less than par value and in some jurisdictions less than minimum capital. For this reason in most provinces it is illegal for corporations to issue other than mining stock at a discount.[1] Furthermore, in those jurisdictions where stock may be issued at a discount certain provisions must be complied with, otherwise the stockholders may become contingently liable to the corporation's creditors for the amount of the discount.

A similar practice of issuing stock at a discount is to pay the purchaser of the stock a commission. For example, I, an investor, purchases from C, the corporation, 100 shares of stock for $1,000. C then pays a $200 commission to I for purchasing the stock. Payment of a commission normally up to 20% to the purchasers of stock is provided for in all Canadian jurisdictions.

Issuing stock at a discount, or paying a commission to purchasers of the stock is a questionable practice. However, if a corporation issues stock at a discount, or pays a purchaser of the stock a commission, the discount is debited to a discount account and the commission is debited to a commission account. The balances of these accounts should be subtracted on the balance sheet from the par value of the stock to which they apply.

---

[1] Issuance of stock at a price below par value is permitted in the following jurisdictions provided the prescribed statutory provisions are followed: Companies incorporated in New Brunswick and mining companies incorporated in Alberta, British Columbia, Manitoba, Ontario, Quebec, and Saskatchewan.

No-par stock ■ At one time all stocks were required to have a par value; but today all jurisdictions permit the issuance of so-called no-par stocks or stocks without par value with the Canada Business Corporations Act, 1975, requiring that all stock be of no par value. The primary advantages claimed for no-par stock are:

1. Since no-par stock does not have a par value, it may be issued at any price without a discount liability attaching.
2. Printing a par value, say $100, on a stock certificate may cause a person lacking in knowledge to believe a share of the stock to be worth $100, when it actually may be worthless. Therefore, eliminating the par value figures helps force such a person to examine the factors that give a stock value, which are earnings, dividends, and future prospects.
3. The use of no-par shares results in more realistic values being placed on noncash assets acquired in exchange for stock. When par value stock is issued, the law in many instances says the stock may not be issued for less than par value. However, the law can easily be circumvented by issuing the stock in exchange for property other than cash and placing an inflated value on the property, a value equal to the par value of the stock. The use of no-par stock makes such a subterfuge unnecessary and results in more realistic values being placed on assets taken in exchange for stock.

When no-par-value stock is issued, the issuance may be recorded in one of two ways. The choice depends upon the laws of the jurisdiction of incorporation and the wishes of the board of directors. The most recent legislations require that a corporation must credit the entire proceeds from the sale of no-par stock to a no-par stock account. In some jurisdictions, however, when no-par stock is issued, the board may choose to place a *stated value* on the stock. When a stated value is placed on no-par stock and the stock is sold for more than stated value, the no-par stock account is credited for stated value and the remainder is credited to a contributed capital account called, for instance, "Contributed Capital in Excess of Stated Value of No-Par Stock," or, "Distributable Surplus." To illustrate the two methods of recording no-par stock, assume that a corporation sells and issues 1,000 shares of its authorized no-par common stock at $42 per share.

If the corporation is organized in a jurisdiction in which the entire amount received from the sale of no-par stock must be credited to a no-par stock account, it will record the sale as follows:

Sept.	20	Cash...	42,000.00	
		No-Par Common Stock............................		42,000.00
		Sold and issued 1,000 shares of no-par common stock at $42 per share.		

If the corporation is organized in a jurisdiction in which the directors may place a stated value on no-par stock, accounting for its sale is similar to accounting for par value stock. For example, if the directors place a stated value of $35 per share on the foregoing stock, its sale and issuance are recorded as follows:

Sept.	20	Cash..	42,000.00	
		No-Par Common Stock.............................		25,000.00
		Contributed Capital in Excess of Stated Value, No-Par Common Stock................		17,000.00
		Sold at $42 per share 1,000 shares of no-par stock having a $35 per share stated value.		

From the entries it is apparent that when a stated value is placed on no-par stock, the accounting treatment for such stock is similar to that for par value stock. However, a sharp distinction should be made between a par value and a stated value; they are not synonymous. A par value is more formal than a stated value. A par value is established by a corporation at the time of its organization. It appears in the corporation's charter and normally can be changed only by a vote of the stockholders and approval of the jurisdiction of incorporation. A stated value is more flexible. The directors of a corporation establish a stock's stated value by resolution. Normally, at any time, they may also change it by passing an additional resolution.

As to minimum legal capital requirements for corporations issuing no-par stock, legislation varies. For example, the Canada Business Corporations Act, 1975, requires the entire amount received by a corporation from the sale of its no-par stock be considered as stated and minimum legal capital and as such be made unavailable for dividend payments. A few jurisdictions permit a corporation issuing no-par stock to establish its minimum legal capital at the stock's stated value which is below the amount received by the corporation, and to pay out as "dividends" any amount above stated value received from the sale of such stock.

Treasury stock   ■ In some jurisdictions corporations may reacquire shares of their own stock.[2] Sometimes a corporation will purchase its own stock on the open market to be given to employees as a bonus. Sometimes shares are bought in order to maintain a favorable market for the stock. Occasionally a corporation in a poor financial position will receive shares of its own stock as a gift from its stockholders. Regardless, if a corporation reacquires shares of its own stock, such stock is known as *treasury stock*. Treasury stock is a corporation's own stock that has

---

[2] Both Ontario and British Columbia corporations may reacquire shares of their own stock and reissue these shares at a future date. The Canada Business Corporations Act, 1975, requires that shares issued by a corporation and purchased, redeemed, or otherwise acquired by it shall be canceled or, if the articles limit the number of authorized shares, shall be restored to the status of authorized but unissued shares.

been issued and then reacquired either by purchase or gift and not canceled. Notice that the stock must be the corporation's own stock; the acquisition of stock of another corporation does not create treasury stock. Furthermore, the stock must have been once issued and then reacquired and held for future reissue; only stock issued and reacquired qualifies as treasury stock. The last point distinguishes treasury stock from unissued stock, and the distinction is important because stock once issued at par or above and then reacquired as treasury stock may be legally reissued at a discount without discount liability.

As just pointed out, treasury stock differs from unissued stock in that it may be sold at a discount without discount liability. Additionally the reissue of treasury stock is normally not subject to the rigid security issue legislation as the issue of unissued shares. However, in other respects it has the same status as unissued stock. Both are equity items rather than assets. Both are subtracted from authorized stock to determine outstanding stock when such things as book values are calculated. Neither receives cash dividends nor has a vote in the stockholders' meetings.

Purchase of treasury stock[3] ■ When a corporation purchases its own stock, it reduces in equal amounts both its assets and its stockholders' equity. To illustrate this, assume that on May 1 of the current year the condensed balance sheet of Curry Corporation appears as in Illustration 17–2.

Curry Corporation
Balance Sheet, May 1, 19—

ASSETS		CAPITAL	
Cash	$ 30,000	Common stock, $100 par value, authorized and issued 1,000 shares	$100,000
Other assets	95,000	Retained earnings	25,000
Total Assets	$125,000	Total Capital	$125,000

Illustration 17–2

If on May 1 Curry Corporation purchases 100 shares of its outstanding stock at $115 per share, the transaction is recorded as follows:

May	1	Treasury Stock, Common	11,500.00	
		Cash		11,500.00
		Purchased 100 shares of treasury stock at $115 per share.		

---

[3]There are several ways of accounting for treasury stock transactions. This text will discuss the so-called cost basis or single transaction method. This method is recommended by the CICA.

The debit in the foregoing entry records a reduction in the equity of the stockholders; and the credit to Cash records a reduction in assets. Both are equal to the cost of the treasury stock; after the entry is posted, a new balance sheet will show the reductions as in Illustration 17–3.

Notice in the second balance sheet that the cost of the treasury stock appears in the stockholders' equity section as a deduction from common stock and retained earnings. In comparing the two balance sheets, notice that the treasury stock purchase reduces both assets and stockholders' equity by the $11,500 cost of the stock.

Curry Corporation
Balance Sheet, May 1, 19—

ASSETS		CAPITAL	
Cash....................................	$ 18,500	Common stock, $100 par value, authorized and issued 1,000 shares of which 100 are in the treasury	$100,000
Other assets.........................	95,000	Retained earnings of which $11,500 is restricted by the purchase of treasury stock	25,000
		Total.............................	$125,000
		Less cost of treasury stock	11,500
Total Assets	$113,500	Total Capital...............	$113,500

Illustration
17–3

Notice also on the second balance sheet that the dollar amount of issued stock remains at $100,000 and is unchanged from the first balance sheet. The amount of *issued stock* is not changed by the purchase of treasury stock. However, the purchase of treasury stock does reduce *outstanding stock*. In Curry Corporation, the purchase reduced the outstanding stock from 1,000 to 900 shares.

There is a distinction between issued stock and outstanding stock. Issued stock is stock that has been sold, it may or may not be outstanding. For example, treasury stock is issued stock but not outstanding stock. Outstanding stock is stock that has been issued and is owned by persons or institutions other than the issuing corporation itself. Only outstanding stock is effective stock, receives cash dividends and is given a vote in the meetings of stockholders.

Restricting retained earnings by the purchase of treasury stock

When a corporation purchases treasury stock, the effect on its assets and total stockholders' equity is the same as a cash dividend. When a corporation purchases treasury stock or declares a cash dividend, it transfers corporation assets to its stockholders and thereby reduces both its assets and its stockholders' equity. Consequently, since the effect is the same, corporation laws place limitations upon treasury stock purchases just as they place limitations on dividends. These limitations usually provide that a corporation may purchase treasury stock only to the extent of retained earnings available for dividend charges, after which the retained earnings become restricted and legally unavailable for dividends. This means that (1) only a corporation with retained earnings available for dividends may purchase treasury stock; and (2) it may either purchase treasury stock to the extent of such earnings or it may use the earnings as a basis for dividends, but it may not do both. In other words, a corporation may not purchase treasury stock to the extent of its retained earnings available for dividend charges and then use the same retained earnings again as a basis for the declaration of dividends. Or again, it may not by the purchase of treasury stock transfer corporation assets to its stockholders to the extent of retained earnings available for dividends and then transfer more assets by means of cash dividends.

Notice in Illustration 17–3 how the restriction of retained earnings is shown on the balance sheet. It may also be shown by means of a balance sheet footnote.

In addition to showing such a restriction on the balance sheet, some corporations also show the restriction in the accounts. This is not required because if retained earnings are legally restricted, the earnings are restricted whether the accounts show the restriction or not. Nevertheless, to show such a restriction in the accounts, an entry is made transferring the restricted portion of retained earnings from the Retained Earnings account to an account called, for instance, Retained Earnings Restricted by the Purchase of Treasury Stock. If such an entry is made by Curry Corporation, it appears as follows:

May	1	Retained Earnings...	11,500.00	
		Retained Earnings Restricted by the		
		Purchase of Treasury Stock		11,500.00
		To record the restriction of retained		
		earnings.		

When treasury stock is sold and retained earnings are no longer restricted because of its purchase, the restricted portion of retained earnings is returned to the Retained Earnings account.

Reissuance of treasury stock

■ When treasury stock is reissued, it may be reissued at cost, above cost, or below cost.

Reissuance at cost

When treasury stock is reissued at cost, the entry to record the transaction is the reverse of the one used to record its purchase. For example, assume that Curry Corporation sells at cost 10 of the 100 treasury shares, the purchase of which at $115 per share was previously illustrated. The entry to record the sale is:

May	27	Cash..	1,150.00	
		Treasury Stock, Common.........................		1,150.00
		Reissued 10 shares of treasury stock at its		
		$115 per share cost price.		

Notice that the sale of the 10 shares at cost restores to the corporation the same amount of assets and stockholder equity taken away when these shares were purchased.

Reissuance at a price above cost

Although treasury stock may be sold at cost, it is commonly sold at a price either above or below cost. When sold above cost, the amount received in excess of cost is commonly credited to a contributed capital account called "Contributed Capital, Treasury Stock Transactions." For example, assume that Curry Corporation sells for $120 per share an additional 10 shares of the treasury stock purchased at $115. The entry to record the transaction appears as follows:

June	3	Cash..	1,200.00	
		Treasury Stock, Common.........................		1,150.00
		Contributed Capital, Treasury Stock		
		Transactions...		50.00
		Sold at $120 per share treasury stock that		
		cost $115 per share.		

Reissuance at a price below cost

When treasury stock is reissued at a price below cost, the entry to record the sale normally depends upon whether there is contributed capital from previous transactions in treasury stock. If a corporation has such contributed capital, a "loss" on the sale of treasury stock may be debited to the account of this capital. For example, assume that after having sold 10 of its 100 treasury shares at $115 and 10 at $120, Curry Corporation sells 10 shares at $110. The entry to record the transaction is:

July	7	Cash..	1,100.00	
		Contributed Capital, Treasury Stock		
		Transactions...	50.00	
		Treasury Stock, Common.........................		1,150.00
		Sold at $110 per share 10 shares of		
		treasury stock purchased at $115.		

If a corporation selling treasury stock below cost does not have sufficient contributed capital from previous treasury stock transactions to absorb the "loss," the "loss" in excess of contributed capital from previous treasury stock sales is normally debited to Retained Earnings. For example, if Curry Corporation sells its remaining 70 shares of treasury stock at $110 per share, the following entry is made to record the transaction:

July	10	Cash..	7,700.00	
		Retained Earnings...	350.00	
		Treasury Stock, Common...........................		8,050.00
		Sold treasury stock purchased at $115 per share for $110 per share.		

Retirement of stock

■ A corporation may purchase shares of its own stock which are not to be held as treasury stock but for immediate retirement, with the shares being permanently canceled upon receipt. Such action is permissible if the interests of creditors and other stockholders are not jeopardized.

When stock is purchased for retirement, all capital items related to the shares being retired are removed from the accounts; and if there is a "gain" on the transaction, it should be credited to contributed capital. On the other hand, if there is a "loss," it should be debited to Retained Earnings.

For example, assume a corporation originally issued its $10 par value common stock at $12 per share, with the premium being credited to an account called Premium on Common Stock. If the corporation later purchased for retirement 1,000 shares of this stock at the price for which it was issued, the entry to record the retirement is:

Apr.	12	Common Stock..	10,000.00	
		Premium on Common Stock	2,000.00	
		Cash..		12,000.00
		Purchased and retired 1,000 shares of common stock at $12 per share.		

If on the other hand the corporation paid $11 per share instead of $12, the entry for the retirement at a "gain" is:

Apr.	12	Common Stock..	10,000.00	
		Premium on Common Stock	2,000.00	
		Cash..		11,000.00
		Contributed Capital from the Retirement		
		of Common Stock		1,000.00
		Purchased and retired 1,000 shares of common stock at $11 per share.		

Or if the corporation paid $15 per share, the entry for the purchase and retirement is:

Apr.	12	Common Stock..	10,000.00	
		Premium on Common Stock	2,000.00	
		Retained Earnings.......................................	3,000.00	
		Cash..		15,000.00
		Purchased and retired 1,000 shares of common stock at $15 per share.		

If the redeemed shares were of no-par value, the debit to the stated capital account is the product of the number of shares redeemed multiplied by the amount per share invested by shareholders.

Donated treasury stock
■ Sometimes when a corporation is in financial difficulty and its stock is owned by a relatively few people, the stockholders will vote to return to the corporation as a gift a portion of their shares, with the donated shares to be resold to provide the corporation with additional assets. When this happens, the stock is secured by the corporation without cost. As a result, since the acquisition does not decrease the corporation's assets or increase its liabilities, it has no effect on stockholders' equity. On the other hand, although the acquisition of donated treasury stock has no effect on assets and equities, its sale increases both. These points may be demonstrated with Bell Corporation.

On June 1 Bell Corporation, having experienced a series of losses, finds itself in the need of additional assets to carry on its operations. In order to secure the assets the company's stockholders decide to donate to the corporation a portion of their stockholdings which are to be sold to outsiders for cash. The corporation's balance sheet before the donation appears as in Illustration 17–4.

Bell Corporation
Balance Sheet, June 1, 19—

ASSETS		CAPITAL	
Cash.....................................	$ 1,000	Common, stock, $10 par value, authorized and issued 10,000 shares	$100,000
Other assets..........................	103,000	Retained earnings.................	4,000
Total Assets	$104,000	Total Capital...................	$104,000

Illustration 17–4

If Bell Corporation stockholders donate pro rata 1,000 shares of stock, the donation may be recorded in the General Journal with a memorandum entry like that immediately below Illustration 17–4.

June	1	Received on this date from the stockholders as a donation 1,000 shares of $10 par value common stock.		

Such an entry cannot be posted in the sense that dollar amounts are entered in the accounts. However, when treasury stock is received as a donation, a treasury stock account is opened in the ledger and the number of shares received is shown in the account by means of a memorandum. This memorandum is in effect a posting of the journal memorandum recording the receipt of the stock.

After Bell Corporation receives the foregoing shares from its stockholders, a new balance sheet showing its financial position appears as in Illustration 17–5. A comparison of the balance sheets prepared before and after the donation shows that the donation did not affect either total assets nor the amount of stockholders' equity.

Bell Corporation
Balance Sheet, June 1, 19—

ASSETS		CAPITAL	
Cash.................................	$ 1,000	Common stock, $10 par value, authorized and issued 10,000 shares of which 1,000 are donated shares and are in the treasury.................	$100,000
Other assets........................	103,000	Retained earnings................	4,000
Total Assets	$104,000	Total Capital..................	$104,000

Illustration
17–5

Although the receipt of donated treasury stock does not increase or decrease assets and stockholders' equity, its sale increases both. For example, if Bell Corporation sells its 1,000 shares of donated treasury stock for $9.20 per share, both assets and the stockholders' equity are increased $9,200, and the transaction is recorded:

June	7	Cash..	9,200.00	
		Contributed Capital, Sale of Donated Treasury Stock....................................		9,200.00
		Sold 1,000 shares of donated treasury stock at $9.20 per share.		

After the treasury stock is sold and the transaction recorded, a balance sheet showing the new financial position of Bell Corporation appears as in Illustration 17–6.

Bell Corporation
Balance Sheet, June 7, 19—

ASSETS		CAPITAL	
Cash	$ 10,200	Common stock, $10 par	
Other assets	103,000	value authorized and	
		issued 10,000 shares	$100,000
		Contributed capital, sale of	
		donated stock	9,200
		Retained earnings	4,000
Total Assets	$113,200	Total Capital	$113,200

Illustration
17–6

Observe in the balance sheet prepared after the sale that both assets and stockholders' equity are increased $9,200 by the sale. The increase in assets is in cash; the increase in stockholders' equity appears as contributed capital from the sale of donated stock.

Donations of capital by outsiders

■ Sometimes a corporation will receive a gift or a donation from some person or persons other than its stockholders. For example, as an inducement to locate a plant in a particular city, a corporation may receive a plant site as a gift. Such a donation increases both assets and stockholders' equity by the fair market value of the contributed asset. The increase in stockholders' equity is contributed capital, capital contributed by others than the stockholders.

For example, assume that as an inducement to locate a plant in Circle City, the Circle City Chamber of Commerce donated a plant site to a corporation. The corporation recorded the donation as follows:

Apr.	17	Land	22,000.00	
		Contributed Capital from Donated Plant Site		22,000.00
		To record the donation of land by Circle City		
		Chamber of Commerce.		

Contributed capital in the accounts and on the statements

■ From the discussion thus far it is obvious that numerous accounts are required in recording contributed capital transactions. Actually a separate account is needed for each kind or source of contributed capital. Furthermore, in addition to separate accounts, each kind of contributed capital may be shown on the balance sheet as in Illustration 18–2 on page 533.

Contributed capital and dividends

■ Under the laws of some jurisdictions, contributed capital may not be returned to stockholders as dividends. However, one reason for separate contributed capital accounts is that under the laws of some jurisdictions, dividends may be debited or charged to certain contributed capital accounts. Dividends may not be charged against the par or stated value of the outstanding stock; however, the exact contributed capital accounts to which a corporation may charge dividends depend upon the laws of the jurisdiction of its incorporation. For this reason it is usually wise for a board of directors to secure competent legal advice before voting to charge dividends to any contributed capital account.

Stock dividends ■ A stock dividend is a distribution by a corporation of shares of its own common stock to its common stockholders without any consideration being given in return therefor. Usually the distribution is prompted by a desire to give the stockholders some evidence of their interest in retained earnings without distributing cash or other corporation assets which the board of directors thinks it wise to retain in the business. A clear distinction should be made between a cash dividend and a stock dividend. Cash is distributed in a cash dividend; and as was pointed out in a previous section, such a dividend reduces both assets and stockholders' equity. A stock dividend differs in that shares of the corporation's own stock rather than cash are distributed; and such a dividend has no effect on assets, total capital, or the amount of any stockholders' equity.

A stock dividend has no effect on corporation assets, total capital, and the amount of any stockholders' equity because such a dividend involves nothing more than a transfer of retained earnings to contributed capital. To illustrate this assume that Northwest Corporation has the following capital stock and retained earnings:

CAPITAL STOCK AND RETAINED INCOME

Common stock, $100 par value, authorized 1,500 shares, issued and outstanding 1,000 shares	$100,000
Premium on common stock	8,000
Total contributed capital	$108,000
Retained earnings	35,000
Total contributed capital and retained earnings	$143,000

Assume further that on December 28 the directors of Northwest Corporation declared a 10% or 100-share stock dividend distributable on January 20 to the January 15 stockholders of record.

If the fair market value of Northwest Corporation's stock on December 28 is $150 per share, the following entries may be made to record the dividend declaration and distribution:

Dec.	28	Retained Earnings	15,000.00	
		Common Stock Dividend Distributable		10,000.00
		Premium on Common Stock		5,000.00
		To record the declaration of a 100-share common stock dividend.		
Jan.	20	Common Stock Dividend Distributable	10,000.00	
		Common Stock		10,000.00
		To record the distribution of a 100-share common stock dividend.		

Note that the entries change $15,000 of the stockholders' equity from retained earnings to contributed capital, or as it is commonly said, $15,000 of retained earnings are capitalized. Note also that the retained earnings capitalized are equal to the fair market value of the 100 shares issued ($150 × 100 shares = $15,000).[4]

As previously pointed out, a stock dividend does not distribute funds from retained earnings to the stockholders, nor does it affect in any way the corporation assets. Likewise, it has no effect on total capital and on the individual equities of the stockholders. To illustrate these last points, assume that Johnson owned 10 shares of Northwest Corporation's stock prior to the dividend. The corporation's total contributed and retained capital before the dividend and the book value of Johnson's 10 shares were as follows:

Common stock (1,000 shares) $100,000
Premium on common stock 8,000
Retained earnings 35,000
   Total contributed and retained capital $143,000

$143,000 ÷ 1,000 Shares Outstanding = $143 per Share Book Value
 $143 × 10 = $1,430 for the Book Value of Johnson's 10 Shares

A 10% stock dividend gives a stockholder one new share for each 10 shares previously held. Consequently, Johnson received one new share; and after the dividend, the contributed and retained capital of the corporation and the book value of Johnson's holdings are as follows:

Common stock (1,100 shares) $110,000
Premium on common stock 13,000
Retained earnings 20,000
   Total contributed and retained capital $143,000

$143,000 ÷ 1,100 Shares Outstanding = $130 per Share Book Value
 $130 × 11 = $1,430 for the Book Value of Johnson's 11 Shares

Before the stock dividend, Johnson owned 10/1,000 or 1/100 of the Northwest Corporation stock and his holdings had a $1,430 book value. After the dividend, he owned 11/1,100 or 1/100 of the corporation and his holdings still had a $1,430 book value. In other words, there was no effect on his equity other than that it was repackaged from 10 units into 11. Likewise, the only effect on corporation capital was a permanent transfer to contributed capital of $15,000 in retained earnings. Consequently, insofar as both the corporation and Johnson are concerned, there was no shift in equities or corporation assets.

Why stock dividends are distributed

If a stock dividend has no effect on corporation assets and stockholders' equities other than to repackage the equities into more units, why are such dividends declared and distributed?

---

[4] As an alternative, either par value or simply an amount determined by the board of directors may be capitalized.

Among the reasons cited for a stock **dividend are the follow**

1. ". . . . such action is prompted mainly by a desire to give cipient shareholders some ostensibly separate evidence of a part of their respective interests in accumulated corporate earnings without distribution of cash or other property which the board of directors deems necessary or desirable to retain in the business."[5]
2. Shareholders may benefit from a small stock dividend, although they own no greater share in the issuing corporation after the dividend than before. They may benefit because, in the short run, a small stock dividend has little or no effect on the per share market price of the issuing corporation's stock. Consequently, since each shareholder has more shares after the dividend, if the price is unchanged, the total market value of his holdings is increased.

Strong sentiments are also voiced against stock dividends. The most frequent are:

1. Stock dividends are undesirable because they may be considered as income to the recipient and subject to income tax.
2. Also, to make shareholders believe they got something in a stock dividend that they did not have before is to prey on the ignorance of shareholders and others, and is therefore wrong.

Regardless of the merit of such arguments, most shareholders welcome stock dividends.

Stock dividends on the balance sheet

Since a stock dividend is "payable" in stock rather than in assets, it is not a liability to its issuing corporation. Therefore, if a balance sheet is prepared between the declaration and distribution dates of a stock dividend, the amount of the dividend distributable should appear thereon in the contributed capital section. (See Illustration 18–2 on page 533.)

Stock splits ■ Sometimes, when a corporation's stock is selling at a high price, the corporation will call it in and issue two, three, four, five, or more new shares in the place of each old share previously outstanding. For example, a corporation having outstanding $100 par value stock selling for $375 a share may call in the old shares and issue to the stockholders 2 shares of $50 par, or 4 shares of $25 par, or 10 shares of $10 par, or any number of shares of no-par stock in exchange for each $100 share formerly held. This is known as a *stock split* or a *stock split-up,* and its usual purpose is to cause a reduction in the market price of the stock and, consequently, to facilitate trading in the stock.

A stock split has no effect on total stockholders' equity, the equities of the individual stockholders, or on the balances of any of the contrib-

---

[5]*Accounting Research and Terminology Bulletins, Final Edition* (New York: American Institute of Certified Public Accountants, 1961), p. 49.

uted or retained capital accounts. Consequently, all that is required in recording a stock split is a memorandum entry in the stock account reciting the facts of the split. For example, such a memorandum might read, "Called in the outstanding $100 par value common stock and issued 10 shares of $10 par value common stock for each old share previously outstanding." Also, there would be a change in the description of the stock on the balance sheet.

Accounting treatment for corporation income taxes

■ As previously stated, of the three common types of business organizations, the corporation alone as a business unit is subject to federal and provincial income taxes. Single proprietorships and partnerships as business units are not required to pay income taxes. Insofar as tax laws are concerned, the income of single proprietorships and partnerships is taxed as the personal income of the single proprietor or the partners.

Federal and provincial income taxes are an expense of doing business as a corporation. However, as a rule, no attempt is made to classify the expense on the income statement; rather it is commonly listed at the end of the statement as in Illustration 17–7.

On the work sheet prepared for a corporation, provincial and federal income taxes are commonly treated in the nature of an adjustment in the

The Excel Manufacturing Company, Ltd.
Income Statement for Year Ended December 31, 19—

Revenue from sales:
Sales $310,000

Income before provincial and federal income taxes .... $ 78,700
Less provincial and federal income taxes 32,600
Net Income... $ 46,100

Illustration
17–7

Adjustment columns as on the work sheet on pages 704 and 705; and after the work sheet is completed an adjusting entry like the following is used to record the taxes:

Dec.	31	Provincial and Federal Income Taxes Expense...	32,600.00	
		Provincial and Federal Income Taxes Payable..		32,600.00
		To record the liability for income taxes.		

Questions for class discussion

1. Laws place no limit on the amounts partners may withdraw from a partnership. On the other hand, laws regulating corporations place definite limits on the amounts corporation owners may withdraw from a corporation in dividends. Why is there a difference?

2. What is a stock premium? What is a stock discount?
3. Differentiate between discount on stock and discount on a note given to a bank in order to borrow money.
4. Does a corporation earn a profit by selling its stock at a premium? Does it incur a loss by selling its stock at a discount?
5. Why do corporation laws make purchasers of stock at a discount contingently liable for the discount? To whom are such purchasers contingently liable?
6. What is the main advantage of no-par stock?
7. What is treasury stock? How is it like unissued stock? How does it differ from unissued stock? What is the legal significance of this difference?
8. General Plastics Corporation bought 1,000 shares of Capital Steel Corporation stock and turned it over to its treasurer for safekeeping. Is this treasury stock? Why or why not?
9. What is the effect of a treasury stock purchase in terms of assets and stockholders' equity? What is the effect on a corporation's assets and stockholders' equity of a treasury stock donation?
10. Distinguish between issued stock and outstanding stock.
11. Why do corporation laws place limitations on the purchase of treasury stock?
12. What are the effects in terms of assets and stockholders' equity of the declaration and distribution of *(a)* a cash dividend and *(b)* a stock dividend?
13. What is the difference between a stock dividend and a stock split?
14. If a balance sheet is prepared between the date of declaration and the date of distribution of a dividend, how should the dividend be shown if it is to be distributed in *(a)* cash and *(b)* stock?

Class exercises

Exercise 17–1

On March 3 a corporation accepted subscriptions to 10,000 shares of its $5 par value common stock at $5.50 per share. The subscription contracts called for one fifth of the subscription price to accompany each contract as a down payment and the balance to be paid on April 2. Give the entries to record *(a)* the subscriptions, *(b)* the down payments, *(c)* receipt of the remaining amounts due on the subscriptions on April 2, and *(d)* issuance of the stock.

Exercise 17–2

A corporation sold and issued 2,000 shares of its no-par common stock for $27,500 on March 6. *(a)* Give the entry to record the sale under the assumption the board of directors did not place a stated value on the stock. *(b)* Give the entry to record the sale under the assumption the board placed a $10 per share stated value on the stock.

Exercise 17–3

On February 5 the stockholders' equity section of a corporation's balance sheet appeared as follows:

STOCKHOLDERS' EQUITY

Common stock, $10 par value, 25,000 shares authorized and issued $250,000
Retained earnings.. 65,000
    Total Stockholders' Equity.. $315,000

On the date of the equity section the corporation purchased 1,000 shares of treasury stock at $13.50 per share. Give the entry to record the purchase and prepare a stockholders' equity section as it would appear immediately after the purchase.

Exercise 17–4

On February 15 the corporation of Exercise 17–3 sold 400 shares of its treasury stock at $14 per share, and on March 10 it sold the remaining treasury shares at $12.75 per share. Give the entries to record the sales.

Exercise 17–5

The stockholders' equity section of a corporation's balance sheet appeared as follows on April 1:

STOCKHOLDERS' EQUITY

Common stock, $5 par value, 250,000 shares authorized, 200,000 shares issued...... $1,000,000
Premium on common stock 200,000
    Total contributed capital $1,200,000
Retained earnings 270,000
    Total Stockholders' Equity $1,470,000

On that date, when the stock was selling for $7.50 per share, the corporation's directors voted a 5% stock dividend distributable on May 15 to the May 1 stockholders of record. The dividend's declaration and distribution had no apparent effect on the market price of the shares, since they were still selling at $7.50 per share as of the close of business on May 15.

Required:
1. Give the entries to record the declaration and distribution of the dividend.
2. Under the assumption that Jessie Bork owned 1,000 shares of the stock on April 1 and received the proper number of dividend shares on May 15, prepare a schedule showing the numbers of shares held by this stockholder on April 1 and May 15, with their total book values and total market values.

Problems   **Problem 17–1**

A corporation was organized to construct a shopping centre. Its charter granted it the right to issue 2,000 shares of $100 par value, 7% cumulative and nonparticipating, preferred stock and 100,000 shares of $10 par value common stock. It then completed these transactions:

Jan. 27   Accepted subscriptions to 50,000 shares of common stock at $11.50 per share. Down payments equal to 20% of the subscription price accompanied each subscription.

     31   Gave the corporation's promoters 1,000 shares of common stock for their services in getting the corporation organized. The board valued the services at $11,500.

Feb.   3   Accepted subscriptions to 1,500 shares of preferred stock at $110 per share. The subscriptions were accompanied by 50% down payments.

     26   Collected the balance due on the January 27 common stock subscriptions and issued the stock.

     28   Accepted subscriptions to 500 shares of preferred stock at $108 per share. The subscriptions were accompanied by 50% down payments.

Mar.   5   Collected the balance due on the February 3 preferred stock subscriptions and issued the stock.

Required:

1. Prepare general journal entries to record the transactions.
2. Prepare the stockholders' equity section of the corporation's balance sheet as of the close of business on March 5.

Problem 17–2

A corporation received a charter granting the right to issue 50,000 shares of $5 par value common stock. It then completed these transactions.

a. Accepted subscriptions to 25,000 of its common shares at $6 per share.
b. Exchanged 20,000 of its common shares for the following assets: machinery, $25,000; factory building, $80,000; and land, $15,000.
c. Collected the subscriptions of the first transaction and immediately issued the stock to the paid-up subscribers.
d. Paid $100,000 for additional machinery.
e. Sold $640,000 of products for cash during its first year and paid $550,000 of operating expenses.
f. Recorded depreciation on machinery, $10,000, and depreciation on factory building, $3,000. (Debit Operating Expenses Controlling.)
g. Made an entry to record income taxes payable, $25,000.
h. Made an entry to close the Sales, Operating Expenses Controlling, Income Taxes Expense, and Income Summary accounts.
i. Purchased 2,000 shares of treasury stock at $5.50 per share.
j. Sold 1,000 of the treasury shares at $6 per share.
k. Declared a $0.25 per share dividend on the outstanding common stock.
l. Paid the $25,000 income taxes payable.
m. Paid the cash dividend previously declared.
n. The local chamber of commerce purchased and gave the corporation a plot of land having a $12,000 fair market value. The land was to be used in expanding the factory and its payroll.
o. On a day the stock was selling for $6.25 per share, the board of directors declared a 10% stock dividend on the corporation's outstanding shares.
p. Distributed the stock dividend.

Required:

1. Open the following T-accounts: Cash; Subscriptions Receivable Common Stock; Machinery and Equipment; Accumulated Depreciation, Machinery and Equipment; Building; Accumulated Depreciation, Building; Land; Income Taxes Payable; Cash Dividend Payable; Common Stock; Premium on Common Stock; Common Stock Subscribed; Contributed Capital, Treasury Stock Transactions; Contributed Capital, Plant Site Donation; Retained Earnings; Stock Dividend Distributable; Treasury Stock; Income Summary; Sales; Operating Expenses Controlling; and Income Taxes and State and Federal Income Taxes Expense.
2. Record the transactions directly in the accounts, using the transaction letters to identify the amounts.
3. Prepare the stockholders' equity section of a balance sheet reflecting the transactions.

Problem 17–3

The equity sections from a corporation's 197A and 197B balance sheets appear as follows:

SHAREHOLDERS' EQUITY
(as of December 31, 197A)

Common stock, $10 par value, 150,000 shares authorized, 100,000 shares issued	$1,000,000
Premium on common stock	150,000
Total contributed capital	$1,150,000
Retained earnings	655,500
Total Shareholders' Equity	$1,805,500

SHAREHOLDERS' EQUITY
(as of December 31, 197B)

Common stock, $10 par value, 150,000 shares authorized, 104,900 shares issued of which 2,000 are in the treasury	$1,049,000
Premium on common stock	203,900
Total contributed capital	$1,252,900
Retained earnings of which $41,000 is restricted by the purchase of treasury stock	665,820
Total	$1,918,720
Less cost of treasury stock	41,000
Total Shareholders' Equity	$1,877,720

On March 15, June 12, September 17, and again on December 14, 197B, the corporation's board of directors declared $0.20 per share dividends on the outstanding stock. The treasury stock was purchased on July 20. On September 17, when the stock was selling at $21 per share, the corporation declared a 5% stock dividend on its outstanding shares. The new shares were issued on October 20.

Required:

Under the assumption there were no transactions affecting retained earnings other than the ones given, determine the corporation's net income. Present calculations to prove your net income figure.

Problem 17-4

On September 30, 197A, stockholders' equity in a corporation consisted of the following:

Common stock, $10 par value, 50,000 shares authorized, 40,000 shares
    issued.. $400,000
Premium on common stock.. 20,000
    Total contributed capital.. $420,000
Retained earnings... 192,000
      Total Stockholders' Equity... $612,000

On October 1, 197A, the corporation's board of directors declared a $0.10 per share cash dividend payable on October 25 to the October 20 stockholders of record. On November 1 the board declared a 25% stock dividend distributable on November 25 to the November 20 stockholders of record. The stock was selling at $16 per share on the day of the declaration, and the board voted to use that price in recording the dividend. The corporation earned $40,000, after taxes, during 197A, and on January 2, 197B the board voted to split the stock two for one by calling in the old shares and issuing each stockholder two shares of $5 par value common stock for each $10 share previously held. The stockholders voted to approve the split and the authorization of the necessary 100,000 new shares; all legal requirements were fulfilled; and the split was completed on January 30.

Required:

1. Prepare general journal entries to record the transactions and to close the Income Summary account.
2. Under the assumption that Ted Gage owned 400 shares of the corporation's stock on September 30 and neither bought nor sold any shares during the next six months, prepare a schedule showing the book value per share of the corporation's stock in one column and the book value of all of Gage's shares in a second column at the close of business on September 30, October 1, October 25, October 31, November 25, January 1, and January 30.
3. Prepare the stockholders' equity section of the corporation's balance sheet as of the close of business on December 31, and prepare another equity section as of the close of business on January 30.

Problem 17-5

On March 15 stockholder equity in a corporation consisted of the following:

STOCKHOLDERS' EQUITY

Preferred stock, $100 par value, 7% cumulative and
    nonparticipating, 2,000 shares authorized, 1,500 shares issued.......... $150,000
Common stock, $10 par value, 100,000 shares authorized,
    45,000 shares issued.. $450,000
Premium on common stock 45,000
Amount paid in by common stockholders... 495,000
    Total contributed capital $645,000
Retained earnings 138,500
      Total Stockholders' Equity $783,500

The corporation completed these transactions:

Mar. 16 The directors voted the regular semiannual $3.50 per share pre-ferred dividend and a $0.40 per share common dividend, both payable on April 15 to the April 10 stockholders of record.

Apr. 15 Paid the dividends declared on March 16.

May 1 Accepted subscriptions to 5,000 shares of common stock at $15 per share. One-third down payments accompanied the subscription contracts.

31 Received the balance due on the May 1 subscriptions and issued the stock.

Sept. 9 Declared the regular semiannual $3.50 per share preferred dividend and a $0.40 per share dividend on the common stock.

Oct. 14 Paid the October 9 stockholders of record the dividends declared on September 9.

Nov. 15 Declared a 10% common stock dividend distributable on December 20 to the December 15 common stockholders of record. The market quotation for the company's stock on November 15 was $15 per share, and the directors voted to use this price in recording the dividend.

Dec. 20 Distributed the stock of the November 15 dividend.

Required:

1. Prepare general journal entries to record the transactions.
2. Under the assumption that Joan Hall owned 100 shares of the corporation's common stock on December 15 and participated in the stock dividend, prepare a three-column schedule with headings as follows: Shares Held, Book Value, and Market Value. Then show in the schedule the shares held by Joan Hall and their total book and market values before and after the dividend. In calculating market values assume the stock dividend did not affect the market price of the stock and that it was still selling at $15 per share on December 20.
3. Prepare the stockholders' equity section of the corporation's balance sheet as of the close of business on December 20.

Problem 17–6

Surfside Corporation declared its regular semiannual $0.20 per share com-mon dividend on December 24, 197A. The dividend was payable on January 22 to the January 15 stockholders of record and, consequently, was unpaid on December 31, 197A, when the stockholders' equity in the corporation appeared as follows:

STOCKHOLDERS' EQUITY

Common stock, $5 par value, 200,000 shares authorized, 80,000 shares issued and outstanding	$400,000
Premium on common stock	20,000
Total contributed capital	$420,000
Retained earnings	202,000
Total Stockholders' Equity	$622,000

During 197B the corporation completed these transactions:

Jan. 22 Paid the dividend declared on the previous December 24.

Feb. 28 Accepted subscriptions to 20,000 shares of common stock at $8 per share. Twenty-five per cent down payments accompanied the subscription contracts.

Mar. 30 Received the balance due on the common stock subscriptions and issued the stock.

June 21 Declared the regular 20 cents per share semiannual dividend on the common stock.

July 23 Paid the July 16 stockholders of record the dividend declared on June 21.

Oct. 21 Declared a 20% stock dividend distributable on November 20 to the November 14 stockholders of record. The stock was selling at $7.50 per share, and the directors voted to use this amount in recording the dividend.

Nov. 20 Distributed the stock of the dividend declared on October 21.

Dec. 21 Declared the regular 20 cents per share semiannual dividend on the common stock.

31 Closed the Income Summary account with a $72,000 after-tax net income.

Required:

1. Prepare general journal entries to record the transactions.
2. Dale Roth owned 400 shares of Surfside Corporation stock on December 31, 197A, and during 197B he neither bought nor sold any stock. Prepare a schedule showing in one column the book value per share of the company's stock at the close of business on December 31, 197A, February 27, March 30, June 20, July 23, October 20, and November 20, 197B, and in the second column the book value of Roth's entire holdings on the same dates.
3. Prepare the stockholders' equity section of the corporation's balance sheet as of December 31, 197B.

Alternate problems

Problem 17–1A

A corporation was organized to buy and expand an existing manufacturing company. Upon receipt of its charter, which gave it the right to issue 2,000 shares of $100 par value, 7½% cumulative and nonparticipating preferred stock and 200,000 shares of $5 par value common stock, it completed these transactions:

Feb. 2 Exchanged 100,000 shares of common stock for land valued by the board of directors at $25,000, buildings valued at $125,000, and machinery valued at $375,000.

3 Accepted subscriptions to 50,000 shares of common stock at $5.25 per share. The subscription contracts were accompanied by 10% down payments.

5 Accepted subscriptions and $21,000 in down payments on 1,000 shares of preferred stock at $105 per share.

7 Gave the corporation's attorneys $1,000 in cash and 400 shares of common stock for their services in securing the corporation charter. The services were valued by the board of directors at $3,100.

Mar. 5 Collected the balance due on the February 3 common stock subscriptions and issued the stock.

Mar. 7 Collected the balance due on the preferred stock subscriptions and issued the stock.

   31 Accepted subscriptions accompanied by 10% down payments to 10,000 shares of common stock at $5.50 per share.

Required:
1. Prepare general journal entries to record the transactions.
2. Prepare the stockholders' equity section of the corporation's balance sheet as of the close of business on March 31.

Problem 17–2A

A corporation received a charter granting the right to issue 50,000 shares of $10 par value common stock, after which it completed these transactions.

a. Accepted subscriptions to 20,000 of its common shares at $12 per share.
b. Collected the subscriptions of the previous transaction and issued the stock.
c. Accepted a plant site having a $20,000 fair market value from Lakeview Chamber of Commerce in return for locating its plant on the site.
d. Gave a contractor $84,000 cash and 500 shares of common stock for erecting a factory building. The contract price for the building was $90,000; but the contractor had agreed to accept the cash and stock in full settlement.
e. Paid $150,000 for factory machinery.
f. During its first year the company sold $615,000 of products for cash and paid $525,000 of operating expenses.
g. Made an entry to record depreciation on the machinery, $8,000, and depreciation on the factory building, $2,000. (Debit Operating Expenses Controlling.)
h. Made an entry to record state and federal income taxes payable, $30,000.
i. Closed the Sales, Operating Expenses Controlling, Income Taxes Expense, and Income Summary accounts.
j. Declared a $0.25 per share quarterly cash dividend.
k. Paid the income taxes payable.
l. Paid the cash dividend previously declared.
m. Purchased 2,000 shares of treasury stock at $12.50 per share.
n. Sold 1,000 of the treasury shares at $13.50 per share.
o. Declared a $0.25 per share quarterly cash dividend.
p. Declared a 10% stock dividend on the corporation's outstanding shares on a day when the stock was selling at $13 per share.

Required:
1. Open the following T-accounts: Cash; Subscriptions Receivable Common Stock; Machinery and Equipment; Accumulated Depreciation, Machinery and Equipment; Building; Accumulated Depreciation, Building; Land; Income Taxes Payable; Cash Dividend Payable; Common Stock; Premium on Common Stock; Common Stock Subscribed; Contributed Capital, Treasury Stock Transactions; Contributed Capital, Plant Site Donation; Retained Earnings; Stock Dividend Distributable; Treasury Stock; Income Summary; Sales; Operating Expenses Controlling; and Income Taxes Expense.
2. Record the transactions directly in the accounts, using the transaction letters to identify the amounts.

3. Prepare the stockholders' equity section of a balance sheet reflecting the transactions.

Problem 17-4A

On October 31, 197A, stockholders' equity in a corporation consisted of the following:

Common stock, $25 par value, 10,000 shares authorized, 8,000 shares issued $200,000
Premium on common stock 20,000
    Total contributed capital $220,000
Retained earnings 132,000
      Total Stockholders' Equity $352,000

During the succeeding three months the corporation completed these transactions:

Nov. 1   Declared a $0.25 per share dividend on the common stock, payable on November 28 to the November 20 stockholders of record.

      28   Paid the dividend declared on November 1.

Dec. 3   Declared a 25% stock dividend, distributable on December 29 to the December 21 stockholders of record. The stock was selling for $45 per share, and the directors voted to use that amount in recording the dividend.

      29   Distributed the stock dividend previously declared.

      31   Closed the Income Summary account on a $30,000 after-tax income for the year.

Jan. 5   The board of directors voted to split the corporation's stock 2½ for 1 by calling in the old stock and issuing 25 shares of $10 par value common stock for each 10 of the old $25 par value shares held. The stockholders voted approval of the split and authorization of the required 25,000 new shares; all legal requirements were met; and the split was completed on February 1.

Required:
1. Prepare general journal entries to record the transactions and to close the Income Summary account at the year-end.
2. Under the assumption Ted Hall owned 200 of the $25 par value shares on October 31 and neither bought nor sold any shares during the three-month period, prepare a schedule showing in one column the book value per share of the corporations stock and in a second column the book value of Hall's shares at the close of business on each of October 31, November 1, November 28, December 2, December 29, December 31, and February 1.
3. Prepare the stockholders' equity section of the corporation's balance sheet as of December 31, 197A, and prepare a second stockholder's equity section as of February 1, 197B.

Problem 17-5A

A corporation received a charter granting it the right to issue 25,000 shares of $10 par value common stock and 1,000 shares of $100 par value, 7% cumulative and nonparticipating, preferred stock on which a $3.50 dividend is payable semiannually. On May 31 of the year in which the charter was granted, 20,000 shares of the common stock were subscribed at $12 per share. One fourth of that amount accompanied the subscription contracts, and all subscribers paid their remaining balances 30 days thereafter, on which date the stock was issued. The preferred stock was issued at par for cash on the same day. The company prospered from the beginning and paid all dividends on its preferred stock plus dividends on its common stock.

On October 10 of its fourth year when the corporation had a $43,500 balance in its Retained Earnings account and its common stock was selling at $16 per share, the board of directors voted a 5% common stock dividend which was distributed on November 20 to the November 15 stockholders of record.

One year later, on November 20, when the corporation had a $52,000 balance in its Retained Earnings account, the common stock was split two for one by calling in the old $10 par value shares and issuing two $5 par value shares for each old share held.

Near the end of the fifth year, on November 27, the corporation declared the regular $3.50 per share semiannual dividend on its preferred stock and a $0.10 per share dividend on its common stock, payable on December 31 to the December 20 stockholders of record.

Required:
1. Prepare general journal entries to record:
    a. The sale and issuance of the original common stock through subscriptions.
    b. The sale and issuance of the preferred stock.
    c. The declaration and distribution of the common stock dividend.
    d. The declaration and distribution of the fifth-year cash dividends.
2. Dale Nash owned 100 shares of the corporation's common stock on the record date of the fourth-year common stock dividend. Under the assumption the market value of the stock was not affected by the stock dividend and was still $16 per share on the day the dividend was distributed and that Nash neither bought nor sold any shares during the year, prepare a schedule showing the shares held by Nash, their total book value, and their total market value on the day the dividend was declared and on the day it was distributed. (Remember preferred dividends do not accrue.)
3. Prepare the stockholders' equity section of the corporation's balance sheet as of the close of business on the day the $5 par value shares were distributed. (Assume that 50,000 of these shares were authorized.)

Decision problem 17–1, Apache Corporation

The stockholders' equity section of Apache Corporation's December 31, 197A, balance sheet carried these items:

Common stock, $10 par value, 50,000 shares authorized, 40,000 shares issued.......... $400,000
Premium on common stock... 100,000
Retained earnings... 276,000
   Total Stockholders' Equity.. $776,000

During 197B the following events took place in the sequence given:
a. A $0.50 per share cash dividend was declared and paid.
b. A 5% stock dividend was declared and the stock was issued. The stock was selling at $25 per share on the date the dividend was declared, and this price was used in recording the dividend.
c. Three thousand shares of treasury stock were purchased at $28 per share.
d. One thousand of the treasury shares were sold at $30 per share.
e. The 8,000 shares of authorized but unissued stock were sold and issued at $32 per share.
f. The 50,000 shares of $10 par value common stock were called in, and the stock was split two for one by issuing two shares of $5 par value common stock for each $10 share in the treasury and outstanding.
g. The company earned $93,200 during 197B.

Prepare a calculation to show the total stockholders' equity as of December 31, 197B, and prepare the stockholders' equity section of the corporation's balance sheet as of that date. Then answer these questions: *(a)* How many shares of the corporation's stock were issued on December 31, 197B? *(b)* How many were outstanding? *(c)* What was the book value per share?

Decision problem 17–2, Peoria Corporation

On October 25 the stockholders' equity in Peoria Corporation consisted of the following:

Common stock, $5 par value, 500,000 shares authorized, 400,000 shares issued......	$2,000,000
Premium on common stock	200,000
Retained earnings	2,024,000
Total Stockholders' Equity	$4,224,000

On the equity section date, when the stock was selling at $12 per share, the corporation's directors voted a 20% stock dividend, distributable on November 30 to the November 20 stockholders of record. The directors also voted a $0.45 per share annual cash dividend payable on December 15 to the December 1 stockholders of record. The amount of the latter dividend was a disappointment to some stockholders, since the company had paid a $0.50 per share annual cash dividend for a number of years.

Walter Nash owned 1,000 shares of Peoria Corporation stock on October 25, which he had purchased a number of years previously, and as a result he received his dividend shares. He continued to hold all of his shares until after he received the December 15 cash dividend. However, he did note that his stock had a $12 per share market value on October 25, a market value it held until the close of business on November 20, when the market value declined to $10.50 per share.

Give the entries to record the declaration and payment of the dividends involved here, and answer these questions:
a. What was the book value of Nash's total shares on October 25, and what was the book value on November 30, after he received his dividend shares?

b. What fraction of the corporation did Nash own on October 25, and what fraction did he own on November 30?

c. What was the market value of Nash's total shares on October 25, and what was the market value at the close of business on November 20?

d. What did Nash gain from the stock dividend?

Decision problem 17–3, Hopi Corporation

On January 1, 197A, the stockholders' equity in Hopi Corporation consisted of the following items:

Common stock, $10 par value, 250,000 shares authorized,
200,000 shares issued and outstanding.................................. $2,000,000
Premium on common stock.. 250,000
Retained earnings.. 560,000
     Total Stockholders' Equity $2,810,000

On June 30, 197A, at a time when its stock was selling at $17.50 per share, Hopi Corporation declared a 10% stock dividend which was distributed one month later. On May 27, 197B, the corporation doubled the number of its authorized shares, changing their par value to $5 per share, and issued two of the new shares for each of the $10 shares previously outstanding. On April 30, 197C, the corporation purchased 10,000 shares of treasury stock at $9 per share. The shares were in the treasury at the end of 197C.

Throughout the three-year period the corporation prospered, declared dividends, and the book value of its shares changed. On December 31, 197A, the book value was $13.50 per share; on December 31, 197B, it was $7.20; and on December 31, 197C, it was $7.70 per share.

Based on the information given, prepare calculations to show the amounts of the corporation's retained earnings at the ends of 197A, 197B, and 197C. Also prepare the stockholder equity sections of the corporation's balance sheets as they should have appeared at the end of each of these years.

Analytical and review problem

Problem 17–1 A&R

Section 39 of the Canada Business Corporations Act states in part:

"The directors acting in good faith and with a view to the best interests of a corporation may authorize the corporation to pay a commission to any person in consideration of his purchasing or agreeing to purchase shares of the corporation from the corporation. . . ."

Required:

Draft a letter to the minister in charge of administering the Act, criticising the provision with respect to accounting implications.

18

Corporations: Retained earnings and consolidations

■ Retained earnings, as the name implies, is stockholders' equity that has arisen from retaining assets from earnings in the business. The retained income includes earnings from normal operations as well as gains from such transactions as the sale of plant assets or investments.

The often-held notion that retained earnings represent cash is without substance. Cash is an asset and appears, with other assets, on the asset side of the balance sheet; retained earnings, on the other hand, are a shareholder equity item and show the source of a portion of the total assets. To view retained earnings as a balancing amount is equally erroneous, for retained earnings are nothing more than the net accumulation, after deducting dividends, of income less losses arising from operation of the business.[1] Furthermore, since the Retained Earnings account is both a summary of past operating results and a balance sheet account, it should be viewed as the connecting link between the periodic balance sheets and income statements.

Retained earnings and dividends

■ In most jurisdictions a corporation must have retained earnings in order to pay a cash dividend. However, the payment of a cash dividend reduces in equal amounts both cash and stockholders' equity. Consequently, in order to pay a cash dividend, a corporation must have not only a credit balance in its Retained Earnings account but also cash with

---

[1] *CICA Handbook* (Toronto: The Canadian Institute of Chartered Accountants), p. 1552.

which to pay the dividend. If cash or assets that will shortly become cash are not available, a borad may think it wise to forgo the declaration of a dividend, even though retained earnings exist. Often the directors of a corporation having a large amount of retained earnings will not declare a dividend because all current assets are needed in the operation of the business.

In considering the wisdom of a dividend, a board must recognize that earnings are a source of assets, and while some assets from earnings should probably be paid out in dividends, some should be retained for emergencies, for distribution as dividends in years in which earnings are not sufficient to pay normal dividends, and for use in expanding operations. The last reason is an important one. If a corporation is to expand and grow, it may sell additional stock to secure the assets needed in expansion; however, it may also expand by using assets acquired through earnings. Ford Motor Company is a good example of a company that has made use of the latter method. Less than $100,000 was originally invested in Ford Motor Company, and it has grown to its present size primarily from retaining in the business assets from earnings.

Appropriation of retained earnings

■ When a corporation expands by retaining assets from earnings, the earnings are invested in plant, equipment, merchandise, et cetera, and are not available for dividends. Many stockholders do not understand this; and upon seeing a large amount of retained earnings reported on the balance sheet, agitate for dividends that cannot be paid because the assets from earnings are invested in the business. Consequently, although the practice is not now as common as it once was, some corporations earmark or appropriate retained earnings as a means of informing their stockholders that assets from earnings equal to the appropriations are unavailable for dividends. Retained earnings are appropriated by a resolution passed by the board of directors; and the appropriations are recorded in the accounts and may be reported on the balance sheet as in Illustration 18–1.

STOCKHOLDERS' EQUITY			
Common stock, $1 par value, 5,000,000 shares authorized and issued..................................			$5,000,000
Retained earnings:			
Appropriated retained earnings:			
Appropriated for plant expansion.................	$200,000		
Appropriated for working capital..................	250,000		
Appropriated for bonded indebtedness.........	75,000		
Total appropriated retained earnings.........		$525,000	
Unappropriated retained earnings...................		350,000	
Total retained earnings			875,000
Total contributed and retained capital			$5,875,000

Illustration
18–1

Appropriations of retained earnings are sometimes called "reserves of retained earnings" and may appear on the balance sheet under captions such as "Reserve for plant expansion," "Reserve for working capital," and "Reserve for bonded indebtedness." Such terminology, since it seems to imply that something is held in reserve, should not be used.

Voluntary and contractual appropriations

Appropriations of retained earnings may be voluntarily made or they may be required by contract. Retained earnings appropriated for plant expansion or for working capital are examples of voluntary appropriations. The first is made to show that assets from earnings are being kept in the business for use in expanding the plant, and the second to show that the company is supplying a portion of its working capital or current asset needs from earnings. Both are known as discretionary appropriations, since they are made at the discretion of the board of directors. Also, since they are voluntary and discretionary, the board may at any time reverse its judgment and return these or any like appropriations to unappropriated retained earnings.

Illustration of a retained earnings appropriation

To illustrate an appropriation of retained earnings, assume the directors of Deeplake Corporation recognize that in five years their plant will need to be expanded by the construction of a $1,000,000 addition. To finance the expansion, the board discusses the possibility of waiting until the addition is needed and then securing the required funds through the sale of additional stock. They also discuss the possibility of financing the expansion through the annual retention for each of the next five years of $200,000 of assets from earnings. Income in excess of this amount is expected to be earned each year, and the directors decide this is the better plan.

In order each year to retain in the business $200,000 of assets from earnings, the directors recognize it is only necessary to refrain from paying out earnings equal to this amount in dividends. However, the board also recognizes that if earnings are retained, the Retained Earnings account and the amount reported on the balance sheet under the caption "Retained earnings" will grow each year and will create a demand by some stockholders for more dividends. Consequently, the board decides that in addition to retaining the assets from earnings, it will at the end of each of the succeeding five years vote an appropriation and transfer of $200,000 of retained earnings from the Retained Earnings account to the Retained Earnings Appropriated for Plant Expansion account. Also, it will show the appropriations on the balance sheet.

If the board follows through on this plan and votes the yearly appropriations, the entry to record each appropriation is:

Dec.	28	Retained Earnings	200,000.00	
		Retained Earnings Appropriated for		
		Plant Expansion		200,000.00
		To record the appropriation of retained		
		earnings.		

When a retained earnings appropriation is recorded, a portion of the balance of the Retained Earnings account is transferred to the proper appropriated retained earnings account, as in the illustrated entry. This reduces the balance of the Retained Earnings account but does not reduce total retained earnings. It merely changes a portion from free, unappropriated retained earnings to appropriated retained earnings.

Before going on, it should be observed in this situation that the transfer of $200,000 each year from the Retained Earnings account to the Retained Earnings Appropriated for Plant Expansion account does not provide funds for the expansion. Earnings provided the funds; the appropriations do nothing more than inform the stockholders of the board's intention to retain in the business assets from earnings equal to the amount appropriated.

Disposing of an appropriation of retained earnings

The purpose for which an appropriation of retained earnings was made is at times accomplished or passes, and there is no longer a need for the appropriation. When this occurs, the appropriated retained earnings should be returned to the (unappropriated) Retained Earnings account. For example, when bonds mature and are paid and there is no longer a need for an appropriation of retained earnings for bonded indebtedness, the balance of the Retained Earnings Appropriated for Bonded Indebtedness account should be returned to the Retained Earnings account.

Comprehensive treatment of equity items

■ In this and previous chapters there have been a number of illustrations showing the balance sheet treatment of stockholder equity items. Rarely, if ever, will all the illustrated items appear on a single balance sheet. However, Illustration 18–2 at the top of page 533 shows a rather comprehensive stockholder equity section as an aid to the student in dealing with whatever equity items he is called upon to handle.

In Illustration 18–2 the second item is "Capital contributed by preferred stockholders in excess of the par value of their shares, $4,000." This item resulted from preferred stock premiums. At the time the amounts originated they were probably credited to an account called "Premium on Preferred Stock." However, as in Illustration 18–2, it is common practice to show an item such as this on the balance sheet under a more descriptive caption than the name of the account in which it is recorded.

STOCKHOLDERS' EQUITY

Preferred stock, $100 par value 7% cumulative and nonparticipating, 2,000 shares authorized, 1,000 shares issued and outstanding	$100,000	
Capital contributed by preferred stockholders in excess of the par value of their shares	4,000	
Total contributed by preferred stockholders		$104,000
Common stock, $10 par value, 50,000 shares authorized, 20,000 shares issued of which 1,000 are in the treasury	$200,000	
Common stock subscribed, 5,000 shares	50,000	
Common stock dividend distributable, 1,900 shares	19,000	
Total common stock issued and to be issued	$269,000	
Capital contributed by common stockholders in excess of the par value of their shares	52,000	
Less discount on common stock issued	(6,000)	
Total contributed and subscribed by common stockholders		315,000
Total capital contributed for shares		$419,000
Other contributed capital:		
Contributed capital from plant site donation	$ 40,000	
Contributed capital from treasury stock transactions	2,000	42,000
Total contributed capital		$461,000
Retained earnings:		
Appropriated for plant expansion	$175,000	
Restricted by the purchase of treasury stock	15,000	
Free and unappropriated	115,000	
Total retained earnings		305,000
Total contributed capital and retained earnings		$766,000
Less cost of treasury stock		(15,000)
Total Stockholders' Equity		$751,000

Illustration
18–2

Retained earnings statement

■ The financial statements prepared for a corporation at the end of each accounting period include a balance sheet, an income statement, a statement of changes in financial position (discussed in Chapter 21), and a statement of retained earnings. On the retained earnings statement are reported the changes in the corporation's retained earnings during the year. Illustration 18–3 shows the retained earnings statement of Westwood Corporation. It was prepared from information in the corporation's accounts shown below and on top of page 534.

Retained Earnings

Date	Explanations	Debit	Credit	Balance
Jan. 1, '75	Balance			180,250
Mar. 24, '75	Quarterly dividend	3,000		177,250
June 21, '75	Quarterly dividend	3,000		174,250
Sept. 27, '75	Quarterly dividend	3,000		171,250
Dec. 20, '75	Quarterly dividend	3,000		168,250
Dec. 20, '75	Stock dividend	20,000		148,250
Dec. 20, '75	Appropriation for plant expansion	25,000		123,250
Dec. 31, '75	Net income after taxes		53,400	176,650

Retained Earnings Appropriated for Plant Expansion

Date	Explanations	Debit	Credit	Balance
Dec. 22, '74			25,000	25,000
Dec. 20, '75			25,000	50,000

When the retained earnings statement of Illustration 18–3 is compared with the information shown in the corporation's Retained Earnings and Retained Earnings Appropriated for Plant Expansion accounts, it is apparent the statement is nothing more than a report of the changes recorded in the accounts.

Westwood Corporation
Statement of Retained Earnings
For Year Ended December 31, 1975

Unappropriated retained earnings:
Unappropriated retained earnings, January 1, 1975................ $180,250
   Additions:
      Net income... 53,400
      Total.. $233,650
Deductions and appropriations:
   Quarterly cash dividends.. $12,000
   Dividend in common stock... 20,000
   Retained earnings appropriated for plant expansion........ 25,000
      Total deductions and appropriations....................... 57,000
Unappropriated retained earnings, December 31, 1975.......... $176,650

Appropriated retained earnings:
Appropriated for plant expansion, balance, January 1, 1975 ... $25,000
Appropriated during 1975 25,000
Appropriated for plant expansion, December 31, 1975 50,000
Total Retained Earnings as of December 31, 1975 .... $226,650

Illustration
18–3

Extraordinary gains and losses

■ Extraordinary gains and losses are material gains and losses which (1) do not typically result from a company's normal business activities, (2) are not expected to occur regularly over a period of years, and (3) are not recurring factors in any evaluation of the ordinary operations of the business. Such gains and losses include gains and losses from:

a. The sale or abandonment of a plant or a significant segment of the business;
b. The sale of investments not acquired for resale;
c. The expropriation of properties;
d. A material revaluation of a foreign currency; and
e. An income tax reduction realized on the carry-forward of a loss.

Prior to 1969 there was a lack of uniformity in our country in the treatment of extraordinary gains and losses. In the annual reports of some companies such items were placed on the income statement and entered into the determination of the net income figure for the year in which they occurred. In other companies the income statement was bypassed and such items were reported on the retained earnings statement. Obviously this resulted in the reporting of significantly different net income figures for companies that had experienced the same gains and losses.

For example, assume that in 1968 each of two companies earned $1,000,000 from normal business activities. However, each also had a plant expropriated by an emerging nation with a resulting $1,500,000 extraordinary loss. Assume further that one company reported its extraordinary loss on its 1968 income statement, while the other bypassed its income statement and reported the loss as a deduction on its retained earnings statement. Under these assumptions the company reporting the extraordinary loss on its income statement showed a $500,000 net loss for 1968, while the company that bypassed its income statement in reporting the extraordinary loss showed a $1,000,000 net income.

As a result of this lack of uniformity, the Research Committee of the Canadian Institute of Chartered Accountants concluded in 1969 that an income statement said to present fairly the results of operations for a period should reflect all gains and losses recognized during the period, whether ordinary or extraordinary in nature.[2] It also concluded that extraordinary items should be disclosed separately on an income statement, with their related income tax effects, so that a user of the statement could determine the extent to which the ordinary income of the business was affected by extraordinary items. Illustration 18–4 shows such a statement.

Observe in Illustration 18–4 that income before extraordinary gains and losses is set out as a separate amount each year. These are the amounts of income earned by Dale Limited from ordinary operation, and from these amounts are added or deducted the extraordinary items, net of applicable income tax, to arrive at each year's net income.

Normal corrections and adjustments ■ In concluding that extraordinary items should be set out separately on the income statement, as in Illustration 18–4, the Research Committee also concluded that certain items, even though material in amount and caused by unusual circumstances, are not extraordinary items, as defined above, "since they are of a character typical of the customary activities of the enterprise." These items are called normal corrections and adjustments and include:

a. Adjustments arising from changes in the estimated useful lives of plant assets;
b. Unusual bad debt losses;
c. Unusual inventory losses; and
d. Write-off of development costs.

---

[2] Ibid., pp. 2001–3.

Dale Limited
Income Statement for Years Ended December 31, 1975 and 1976

	1976	1975
Net sales	$8,500,000	$7,600,000
Other revenue	8,000	9,000
Total revenue	$8,508,000	$7,609,000
Cost and expenses:		
Cost of goods sold	$6,000,000	$5,400,000
Selling, general and administrative expenses	500,000	450,000
Interest expense	10,000	10,000
Other deductions	8,000	7,000
Income tax	940,000	842,000
Total cost and expenses	$7,458,000	$6,709,000
Income before extraordinary gains and losses	$1,050,000	$ 900,000
Extraordinary gains and losses:		
Gain on sale of investments not held for resale net of applicable income tax of $14,000		50,000
Loss from abandonment of plant assets net of applicable income tax of $11,000	(25,000)	
Net Income	$1,025,000	$ 950,000
Earnings per common share:		
Income before extraordinary items	$4.10	$3.60
Net income	4.00	3.80

Illustration
18–4

As a result such items should be deducted on the income statement in arriving at "Income before extraordinary gains and losses." For example, if a company experiences an unusual bad debt loss due to the bankruptcy of an important customer, the amount of such loss should be added to the normal losses from bad debts and deducted as a general and administrative expense. Likewise, if a company suffers an unusual inventory loss, it should be deducted in arriving at "gross profit from sales." However, in both cases and in all such cases, if the amount of the unusual loss is material, it may be set out separately or it may be explained by means of a footnote.

Earnings per share

■ Earnings per share data are among the most commonly quoted figures on the financial pages of daily newspapers. Such data are used by investors in evaluating the past performance of a business, in projecting its future earnings, and in weighing investment opportunities. As a result, the CICA concluded that earnings per share or net loss per share data should be shown on the face of a published income statement. Also, if there are extraordinary items per share amounts should be shown (a) for income before extraordinary items and (b) for the final net income figure. As an alternative it may be desirable to present per share data for the extraordinary items.

The importance of presenting per share data for income before extraordinary items, as well as for the final income figure, is demonstrated in Illustration 18–4. Note that Dale Limited earned $0.20 per share more in 1976 than in 1975, but its 1976 earnings from normal operations increased $0.50 per share. In judging a company's earnings trend in a situation such as this, earnings from normal operations are usually more important than the final income figure, since the extraordinary items that contribute to the final figure are nonrecurring.

In Illustration 18–4 it is assumed that Dale Limited had 250,000 common shares outstanding during the two-year period and no preferred stock. Consequently, its earnings per share data were determined by dividing each earnings item by 250,000. Had there been preferred stock outstanding, it would have been necessary to subtract the preferred dividend requirements from the income from ordinary operations and from the final income figure before making the divisions.

Some corporations have a simple capital structure consisting only of common stock. Other corporations have outstanding not only common stock but also preferred stock and bonds that under certain circumstances may be converted to common stock with a resulting increase in the number of common shares outstanding. When such convertible preferred stock and bonds are outstanding, it is recognized that if the stock and bonds were converted, the issuing corporation's earnings would be spread over more shares of common stock and would, therefore, be diluted by the conversion. Consequently, where a corporation has outstanding convertible preferred stock or bonds in addition to common stock, it should treat the convertible stock or bonds as the equivalent of common stock in calculating earnings per share, and unless an increased amount results, it should report as earnings per share an amount based on the assumption that the convertible stock or bonds had been converted to common stock.

For companies with complex capital structures, such as convertible preferred shares or convertible debt, dual disclosure of earnings per share is recommended. The first type is referred to as *basic earnings per share* and is the same for all companies regardless of whether the capital structure is simple or complex. The second type is referred to as *fully-diluted earnings per share* and applies only to companies with complex capital structures. The calculation of fully-diluted per share earnings is somewhat complex and beyond the scope of this book.

Prior period adjustments

■ In establishing the treatment for extraordinary items and for normal corrections and adjustments, the Accounting Research Committee recognized that certain items, which it called "prior period adjustments," are neither extraordinary items nor normal corrections and adjustments. The Committee concluded that these prior period adjustments are limited to material adjustments which have all four of these characteristics:[3]

a. Are specifically identified with and directly related to the business activities of a particular prior period;

b. Are not attributable to economic events, including obsolescence, occurring subsequent to the date of the financial statements for such prior period;

c. Depend primarily on decisions or determinations by persons other than management or owners; and

d. Could not reasonably be estimated prior to such decisions or determinations.

Examples of prior period adjustments (provided they have all four characteristics) might be:

a. Nonrecurring adjustments or settlements of income taxes; and

b. Settlements of claims resulting from litigation.

The Committee concluded that such prior period adjustments with any related income tax effect should be shown on the retained earnings statement as an adjustment of the opening balance of retained earnings, as in Illustration 18–5.

Smythe Company, Ltd.
Statement of Retained Earnings
For Year Ended December 31, 1976

Retained earnings, January 1, 1976	$89,000
Adjustments of prior years' income:	
Settlement of lawsuit arising from 1973 accident	(32,000)
Retained earnings as restated	$57,000
Net income for the year	26,000
Total	$83,000
Dividends declared in 1976	(10,000)
Retained Earnings, December 31, 1976	$73,000

Illustration
18–5

Comparative single-step income statement

■ Return again to the income statement of Illustration 18–4 and note that this is a *comparative single-step income statement*. It is a comparative statement because it shows the operating results of two periods in columns side by side. This is a desirable feature that makes it easy for a statement reader to compare the results of the two periods. It is also a single-step income statement because all normal costs and expenses are deducted on it in one step. The income statements illustrated in

---

[3] Ibid., pp. 2201–2202.

previous chapters have been multiple-step statements on which cost of goods sold was deducted in a first step, then operating expenses in a second step, and then income taxes. This treatment for costs and expenses is satisfactory, but the multiple deductions do imply a preferential order for their recovery, when actually there is no preferential order. Consequently, to avoid the implication of a preferential order for the recovery of costs and expenses, the single-step income statement is being used more and more in published reports. Such statements may show considerable detail, but generally when published for the use of stockholders and the public, they are condensed as in Illustration 18–4.

Parent and subsidiary corporations

■ Corporations commonly own and control other corporations. For example, if Corporation A owns more than 50% of the voting stock of Corporation B, Corporation A can elect Corporation B's board of directors and thus control its activities and resources. In such a situation the controlling corporation, Corporation A, is known as the *parent company* and Corporation B is called a *subsidiary*.

When a corporation owns all the outstanding stock of a subsidiary, it can take over the subsidiary's assets, cancel its stock, and fuse the subsidiary into the parent company. However, there are often financial, legal, and tax advantages in operating a large business as a parent company controlling one or more subsidiaries rather than as a single corporation. Actually, most large companies are parent corporations owning one or more subsidiaries.

When a business is operated as a parent company with subsidiaries, separate accounting records are kept for each corporation. Also, from a legal viewpoint the parent and each subsidiary is a separate entity with all the rights, duties, and responsibilities of a separate corporation. Nevertheless, if a parent and its subsidiaries are engaged in the same business under a unified management, the corporations are for all practical purposes a single enterprise. Therefore, it is often desirable to develop for a parent and its subsidiaries a set of *consolidated statements* in which the assets and liabilities of all the affiliated companies are combined on a single balance sheet and their revenues and expenses are combined on a single income statement, as though the business were in fact a single company.

Consolidated balance sheets

■ **Principles of consolidation**

When parent and subsidiary balance sheets are consolidated, duplications in items are eliminated so that the combined figures do not show more assets and equities than actually exist. For example, a parent's investment in a subsidiary is evidenced by shares of stock which are carried as an asset in the parent company's records. However, these shares actually represent an equity in the subsidiary's assets. Consequently, if the parent's investment in a subsidiary and the subsidiary's assets were both shown on the consolidated balance sheet, the same resources would be counted twice. To prevent this, the parent's investment and the subsidiary's capital accounts are offset and eliminated in preparing a consolidated balance sheet.

Likewise, a single enterprise cannot owe a debt to itself. This would be analogous to a student borrowing $20 for a date from funds he has saved for next semester's expenses and then preparing a balance sheet showing the $20 as both receivable from himself and payable to himself. To prevent such a double showing, intercompany debts and receivables are also eliminated in preparing a consolidated balance sheet.

Balance sheets consolidated at time of acquisition

When a parent and subsidiary's assets are combined in the preparation of a consolidated balance sheet, a work sheet is normally used to effect the consolidation. Illustration 18–6 shows such a work sheet. It was prepared to consolidate the accounts of Parent Company and its subsidiary, called Subsidiary Company, on January 1, 197A, the day Parent Company acquired Subsidiary Company through the purchase for cash of all its outstanding no-par-value common stock. The stock

Parent Company and Subsidiary Company
Work Sheet for a Consolidated Balance Sheet, January 1, 197A

	Parent Company	Subsidiary Company	Eliminations Debit	Eliminations Credit	Consolidated Amounts
ASSETS					
Cash...........................	5,000	15,000			20,000
Notes receivable	10,000			(a) 10,000	
Accounts receivable, net.....	20,000	13,000			33,000
Inventories	45,000	22,000			67,000
Investment in Subsidiary Company......................	115,000			(b) 115,000	
Buildings and equipment, net..............	100,000	74,000			174,000
Land............................	25,000	8,000			33,000
	320,000	132,000			327,000
EQUITIES					
Accounts payable.............	15,000	7,000			22,000
Notes payable..................		10,000	(a) 10,000		
Common stock	250,000	100,000	(b) 100,000		250,000
Retained earnings............	55,000	15,000	(b) 15,000		55,000
	320,000	132,000	125,000	125,000	327,000

Illustration
18–6

had a book value of $115,000 or $11.50 per share, which in this first illustration is the amount Parent Company is assumed to have paid for it. Explanations of the work sheet's two eliminating entries follow:

ENTRY (a). On the day it acquired Subsidiary Company, Parent Company lent Subsidiary Company $10,000 for use in the subsidiary's operations, taking the subsidiary's note as evidence of the transaction. Since this intercompany debt was in reality a transfer of funds within the organization and did not increase the total assets and total liabilities of the affiliated companies, it is eliminated by means of Entry (a). To understand this entry, recall that the subsidiary's promissory note is represented by a $10,000 debit in the Parent Company's Notes Receivable account. Then observe that the first credit in the Eliminations column exactly offsets and eliminates this item. Next, recall that the subsidiary's note appears as a credit in its Notes Payable account, and observe that the $10,000 debit in the Eliminations column completes the elimination of this intercompany debt.

ENTRY (b). When a parent company invests in a subsidiary by buying the subsidiary's stock, the parent company exchanges cash for an equity in the subsidiary's assets; and the amount given appears on the parent company's balance sheet as an asset, "Investment in subsidiary." Therefore, in consolidating the assets of a parent and its subsidiary, the parent company's investment in the subsidiary must be eliminated, because to show on the consolidated balance sheet both the subsidiary's assets and the amount of the parent's investment (an equity in these assets) would be to show more resources than actually exist. Also, not only does the parent's investment in the subsidiary represent an equity in the subsidiary's assets, but so do the stockholder equity accounts of the subsidiary. Consequently, in consolidating the balance sheets of a parent and its subsidiary, the amount of the parent's investment in the subsidiary is offset against the subsidiary's stockholder equity accounts and both are eliminated.

After the intercompany items are eliminated on a work sheet like Illustration 18–6, the assets of the parent and its subsidiary are combined and carried into the work sheet's last column. Next, the equities in these assets are combined and carried into the column, after which the amounts in the column are used to prepare a consolidated balance sheet like Illustration 18–7.

Parent company does not buy all of subsidiary's stock and does not pay book value

In the situation just described, Parent Company purchased 100% or all of its subsidiary's stock, paying book value for it. Often a parent company purchases less than 100% of a subsidiary's stock, and commonly pays a price either above or below the stock's book value. To illustrate such a situation, assume the parent company of the previous illustration purchased for cash only 80% of its subsidiary's stock, rather

Parent Company and Subsidiary
Consolidated Balance Sheet, January 1, 197A

ASSETS

Current Assets:
Cash .... $ 20,000
Accounts receivable, net 33,000
Inventories.. 67,000
   Total Current Assets $120,000
Plant and Equipment:
Buildings and equipment, net.. $174,000
Land 33,000
   Total Plant and Equipment 207,000
   Total Assets $327,000

LIABILITIES AND STOCKHOLDERS' EQUITY

Liabilities:
Accounts payable .... $ 22,000
Stockholders' Equity:
Common stock.. $250,000
Retained earnings 55,000
   Total Stockholders' Equity... 305,000
   Total Liabilities and Stockholders' Equity........................... $327,000

Illustration
18–7

than 100%, and that it paid $13 per share, a price $1.50 above the stock's book value.

These new assumptions result in a more complicated work sheet entry to eliminate the parent's investment and the subsidiary's stockholder equity accounts. The entry is complicated by (1) the minority interest in the subsidiary and (2) the excess over book value paid by the parent company for the subsidiary's stock.

MINORITY INTEREST. When a parent buys a controlling interest in a subsidiary, the parent company is the subsidiary's majority stockholder. However, when the parent owns less than 100% of the subsidiary's stock, the subsidiary has other stockholders who own a minority interest in its assets and share its earnings. Consequently, when there is a minority interest and the stockholder equity accounts of the subsidiary are eliminated on a consolidated work sheet, the interest of the minority stockholders must be set out as on the last line of Illustration 18–8. In this case the minority stockholders have a 20% interest in the subsidiary; consequently, 20% of the balances of the subsidiary's common stock and retained earnings accounts [($100,000 + $15,000) × 20% = $23,000] is set out on the work sheet as the minority interest.

EXCESS OF INVESTMENT COST OVER BOOK VALUE. At the time Parent Company purchased 80% of Subsidiary Company's stock, the subsidiary had outstanding 10,000 shares of no-par-value common stock with a book value of $11.50 per share.

Parent Company and Subsidiary Company
Work Sheet for a Consolidated Balance Sheet, January 1, 197A

	Parent Company	Subsidiary Company	Eliminations		Consolidated Amounts
			Debit	Credit	
ASSETS					
Cash.............................	16,000	15,000			31,000
Notes receivable	10,000			(a) 10,000	
Accounts receivable, net.....	20,000	13,000			33,000
Inventories	45,000	22,000			67,000
Investment in Subsidiary Company.......................	104,000			(b) 104,000	
Buildings and equipment, net..............	100,000	74,000			174,000
Land.............................	25,000	8,000			33,000
Excess of cost over book value			(b) 12,000		12,000
	320,000	132,000			350,000
EQUITIES					
Accounts payable..............	15,000	7,000			22,000
Notes payable..................		10,000	(a) 10,000		
Common stock	250,000	100,000	(b) 100,000		250,000
Retained earnings.............	55,000	15,000	(b) 15,000		55,000
Minority interest...............				(b) 23,000	23,000
	320,000	132,000	137,000	137,000	350,000

Illustration
18–8

Parent Company paid $13 per share for 8,000 of the shares; consequently, the cost of these shares exceeded their book value by $12,000, calculated as follows:

Cost of stock (8,000 shares at $13 per share)............. $104,000
Book value (8,000 shares at $11.50 per share)............ 92,000
Excess of cost over book value............................ $ 12,000

Now observe how this excess of cost over book value is set out on the work sheet in eliminating the parent's investment in the subsidiary and how it is carried into the Consolidated Amounts column as an asset.

After its completion, the consolidated amounts in the last column of the work sheet of Illustration 18–8 were used to prepare the consolidated balance sheet of Illustration 18–9. Note the treatment of the minority interest in the stockholders' equity section of the balance sheet. The minority stockholders have a $23,000 equity in the consolidated assets of the affiliated companies, and the balance sheet shows this.

Next observe that the $12,000 excess over book value paid by the parent company for the subsidiary's stock appears on the consolidated

Parent Company and Subsidiary
Consolidated Balance Sheet, January 1, 197A

ASSETS

Current Assets:
Cash .... $ 31,000
Accounts receivable, net 33,000
Inventories... 67,000
    Total Current Assets $131,000
Plant and Equipment:
Buildings and equipment, net.. $174,000
Land 33,000
    Total Plant and Equipment 207,000
Goodwill from consolidation.. 12,000
    Total Assets $350,000

LIABILITIES AND STOCKHOLDERS' EQUITY

Liabilities:
Accounts payable.. $ 22,000
Minority interest... 23,000
Stockholders' Equity:
Common stock $250,000
Retained earnings.. 55,000
    Total Stockholders' Equity 305,000
    Total Liabilities and Stockholders' Equity $350,000

Illustration
18–9

balance sheet as the asset, "Goodwill from consolidation." When a parent company purchases an interest in a subsidiary, it may pay more than book value for its equity because (1) it believes that certain of the subsidiary's assets are carried on the subsidiary's books at less than their fair value or (2) it believes the subsidiary's earnings prospects are good enough to justify paying more than book value. In this illustration it is assumed that Parent Company believed Subsidiary Company's expected earnings justified paying $104,000 for an 80% equity in the subsidiary's assets.

The CICA has ruled that in cases where a parent company pays more than book value for an equity in a subsidiary because it believes expected earnings justify the price, the excess over book value should appear on the consolidated balance sheet as goodwill from consolidation.[4] A justification for this is that a business is assumed in accounting to have goodwill when its expected earnings are greater than normal for its industry. The CICA has also ruled that where a company pays more than book value because it believes certain of the subsidiary's assets are undervalued, the amounts at which the undervalued assets are placed on the consolidated balance sheet should be revised upward to the extent of the excess over book value paid. And, it has ruled that

[4] Ibid., pp. 292–304.

where elements of both factors exist, the excess over book value should be allocated between the factors.[5]

Occasionally a parent company pays less than book value for its interest in a subsidiary. In such a case, since a "bargain" purchase is very unlikely, the logical reason for a price below book value is that certain of the subsidiary's assets are carried on its books at amounts in excess of fair value. In such a situation the amounts at which the overvalued assets are placed on the consolidated balance sheet should be reduced accordingly.

Earnings of a subsidiary

■ In the years following acquisition, if the operations of a subsidiary are profitable, its net assets and retained earnings increase; and if it pays dividends, the dividends are paid to the parent company and any minority stockholders in proportion to the stockholdings of each. Furthermore, the subsidiary records the transactions that result in earnings, closes its Income Summary account, and records the declaration and payment of dividends just like any other corporation.

Accounting for a subsidiary's earnings

A parent company should use the *equity method* in accounting for its share of a subsidiary's earnings and dividends. Under this method it is recognized that a subsidiary's earnings not only increase the subsidiary's net assets but also increase the equity of the parent company in the assets. Consequently, under this method, when the subsidiary closes its books and reports the amount of its earnings, the parent company takes up its share in its account, Investment in Subsidiary Company. For example, assume the subsidiary previously described earned $12,500 during the first year in which 80% of its stock was owned by Parent Company. When the subsidiary closes its books and reports its net income, Parent Company records its share as follows:

Dec.	31	Investment in Subsidiary Company	10,000.00	
		Earnings from Investment in Subsidiary......		10,000.00
		To take up 80% of the $12,500 net income of Subsidiary Company.		

The illustrated entry's debit records the increase in Parent Company's equity in the subsidiary. The credit causes 80% of the subsidiary's net income to appear on Parent Company's income statement as earnings from the investment, and Parent Company closes the earnings to its Income Summary account and on to its Retained Earnings account just as it would close earnings from any investment.

If instead of a net income a subsidiary incurs a loss, the parent company debits the loss to an account called Loss from Investment in Sub-

---

[5] Ibid., p. 299.

sidiary and credits and reduces its Investment in Subsidiary Company account. It then carries the loss to its Income Summary account and on to its Retained Earnings account.

Accounting for a subsidiary's dividends

Dividends paid by a subsidiary decrease the subsidiary's assets and retained earnings and also decrease the parent company's equity in the subsidiary. For example, assume that the subsidiary previously described paid a $7,500 dividend at the end of the first year after coming under the control of Parent Company. Upon receipt of its share, Parent Company makes this entry:

Dec.	31	Cash..	6,000.00	
		Investment in Subsidiary Company		6,000.00
		To record receipt of 80% of the $7,500 dividend paid by Subsidiary Company.		

Notice that the credit of the entry reduces the amount at which the parent company carries its investment in the subsidiary.

Consolidated balance sheets at a date after acquisition

■ From the discussion thus far it can be seen that the earnings and dividends of a subsidiary not only affect the balance of the subsidiary's Retained Earnings account but also result in changes in the parent company's account, Investment in Subsidiary. As a result, in the years following acquisition, when consolidated balance sheets are prepared, the amounts eliminated from these accounts change as the account balances change.

For example, Subsidiary Company of this illustration earned $12,500 during the first year after being acquired by Parent Company, and paid out $7,500 in dividends. The earnings less the dividends caused the subsidiary's Retained Earnings account to increase from $15,000 at the beginning of the year to $20,000 at the year-end. Consequently, $20,000 of retained earnings are eliminated on the year-end work sheet to consolidate the balance sheets of the companies (see Illustration 18–10). In examining the work sheet, also observe that the earnings of the subsidiary, less its dividend ($12,500 – $7,500), resulted in a $5,000 increase in the subsidiary's net assets. (To simplify the illustration, it is assumed that the liabilities of both the parent company and the subsidiary were unchanged and that the subsidiary had not paid the note given to Parent Company. It is also assumed that Parent Company earned $31,000 during the year, including the $10,000 from its investment in Subsidiary Company; and that it paid out $22,000 in dividends and retained the balance for use in expanding its operations. As a result, Parent Company's net assets and Retained Earnings increased $9,000 during the year, as shown in the first column of the illustration.)

Parent Company and Subsidiary Company
Work Sheet for a Consolidated Balance Sheet, December 31, 197A

| | Parent Company | Subsidiary Company | Eliminations | | Consolidated Amounts |
			Debit	Credit	
ASSETS					
Cash..............................	14,000	10,000			24,000
Notes receivable	10,000			(a) 10,000	
Accounts receivable, net.....	27,000	14,000			41,000
Inventories	50,000	29,000			79,000
Investment in Subsidiary Company......................	108,000			(b) 108,000	
Buildings and equipment, net..............	95,000	76,000			171,000
Land.............................	25,000	8,000			33,000
Excess of cost over book value			(b) 12,000		12,000
	329,000	137,000			360,000
EQUITIES					
Accounts payable..............	15,000	7,000			22,000
Notes payable...................		10,000	(a) 10,000		
Common stock	250,000	100,000	(b) 100,000		250,000
Retained earnings.............	64,000	20,000	(b) 20,000		64,000
Minority interest................				(b) 24,000	24,000
	329,000	137,000	142,000	142,000	360,000

Illustration
18–10

To continue the explanation, Parent Company paid $104,000 for 80% of Subsidiary Company's stock and debited that amount to its Investment in Subsidiary Company account. During the year Parent Company increased this account $10,000 by taking up 80% of the subsidiary's earnings and decreased it $6,000 upon receipt of its share of the subsidiary's dividend. As a result, the account had a $108,000 year-end balance, which is the amount eliminated on the work sheet.

Two additional items in Illustration 18–10 require explanations. First, the minority interest set out on the year-end work sheet is greater than on the beginning-of-the-year work sheet (Illustration 18–8). The minority stockholders have a 20% equity in Subsidiary Company, and the $24,000 shown on the year-end work sheet is 20% of the year-end balances of the Subsidiary's Common Stock and Retained Earnings accounts. This $24,000 is $1,000 greater than the beginning-of-the-year minority interest because the subsidiary's retained earnings increased $5,000 during the year and the minority stockholder's share of the increase is 20% or $1,000. Second, the $12,000 amount set out as the excess cost of Parent Company's investment over its book value is, in this illustration, the same on the end-of-the-year work sheet as on the work sheet at the beginning. The CICA has ruled that such excess cost or "goodwill" should be amortized by systematic charges to income over the accounting periods estimated to be benefited.[6] Amortization is not illustrated here because a discussion of the required procedures is beyond the scope of this introduction to consolidations.

After its completion the work sheet of Illustration 18–10 is used to prepare the year-end consolidated balance sheet of the parent company and its subsidiary.

Other con-
solidated
statements

■ Consolidated income statements and consolidated retained earnings statements are also prepared for affiliated companies. However, preparation of these require procedures a discussion of which must be deferred to an advanced accounting course. Nevertheless, a knowledge of the procedures is not necessary to an understanding of such statements. A reader needs only to recognize that all duplications in items and all profit arising from intercompany transactions are eliminated in their preparation.

Purchase
versus a
pooling of
interests

■ In the discussion thus far it has been assumed that Parent Company acquired its interest in a subsidiary by purchasing the subsidiary's stock for cash. This often happens, but more often a parent company acquires an interest in a subsidiary by exchanging shares of its own stock for the outstanding stock of the subsidiary. In such cases, where stock is exchanged, financial statements may be consolidated using the *purchase method* illustrated thus far or, if certain requirements are met, by the *pooling-of-interests method.* Under the purchase method it is assumed that the subsidiary's stockholders sold their interest in the subsidiary, taking either cash or shares of the parent company's stock in payment. Under the pooling-of-interests method it is assumed that no sale occurred and that the stockholders of the parent and subsidiary companies pooled or combined their interests to form the consolidated company.

Three important differences in the two methods are:

1. Under the purchase method the parent company records its investment in the subsidiary at the amount of cash given or at the market value of the shares of its stock exchanged for the shares of the subsidiary; but under the pooling-of-interests method the parent company records its investment in the subsidiary at the book value of the subsidiary's net assets, regardless of the market value of the shares given.
2. Under the purchase method only that portion of the subsidiary's net income earned in the year of acquisition after the acquisition date becomes part of the consolidated earnings for the year; but under the pooling-of-interests method the subsidiary's earnings for the

---

[6] Ibid., pp. 302–4.

entire year in which it was acquired become part of the consolidated earnings for the year, even though the subsidiary was acquired late in the year.

3. Under the purchase method the subsidiary's retained earnings as of the date of acquisition do not become part of the consolidated retained earnings; but under the pooling-of-interests method the retained earnings do become part of the consolidated retained earnings.

Due to the first difference, when a parent company pays more than book value for an interest in a subsidiary and afterwards prepares consolidated statements by the purchase method, it must either revalue the subsidiary's assets upward or show goodwill from consolidation on the consolidated balance sheet. If the assets are revalued upward, more depreciation must be deducted from revenues on the consolidated income statement; and if goodwill is shown, it must be amortized. Consequently, under the purchase method either the extra depreciation or the amortization of the goodwill result in less consolidated net income than would result with the pooling-of-interests method, under which neither goodwill nor higher asset values are required. Likewise, since a subsidiary's net income is consolidated from the beginning of the year of acquisition rather than from the date of acquisition, consolidation by the pooling-of-interests method commonly results in more consolidated net income in the year of acquisition. Therefore, it can be seen that significantly different balance sheet and income statement amounts can result from the two methods of consolidation. Nevertheless, the CICA has ruled that both methods are acceptable in accounting for business combinations, although not as alternatives in accounting for the same combination.[7] It has further established specific conditions that, if met, require accounting by the pooling-of-interests method, and it has ruled that all other business combinations should be accounted for by the purchase method.[8]

No effort will be made here to discuss further or to illustrate the preparation of financial statements by the pooling of interest method. Time and a lack of space require that some things be deferred to an advanced accounting course.

Who uses consolidated statements

■ Consolidated statements are of no interest to minority stockholders. Their interests normally go no further than the statements of the subsidiary in which they own stock. Likewise, creditors of a subsidiary and people looking to their legal rights find little of interest in consolidated statements.

On the other hand, the stockholders of the parent company, its management, and its board of directors have a very real interest in con-

---

[7] Ibid., pp. 291–95.
[8] Ibid., pp. 294–95.

solidated statements. The parent company's stockholders benefit from earnings, an increase in assets, and financial strength anywhere in the organization. They likewise suffer from a loss or any weakness. And, the managers and directors of the parent company are responsible for all the resources under their control.

Questions for class discussion

1. While examining a corporation balance sheet, a businessman observed that the various items in the stockholders' equity section really showed sources of assets. Was this observation correct?
2. Explain how earnings increase a corporation's assets and stockholders' equity.
3. Why do accountants feel that the word "surplus" should not be used in published balance sheets as a term to describe a portion of the stockholders' equity?
4. Why are retained earnings sometimes appropriated?
5. Does the appropriation and transfer of retained earnings to retained earnings appropriated for plant expansion provide funds for the expansion? How do such appropriations aid in accumulating funds for a plant expansion?
6. How does a corporation dispose of a retained earnings appropriation such as retained earnings appropriated for plant expansion?
7. What are (a) a parent company, (b) a subsidiary, and (c) a consolidated balance sheet?
8. When a work sheet for consolidating the balance sheets of a parent company and its subsidiaries is prepared, intercompany debts are eliminated on the work sheet. Why?
9. A consolidated balance sheet shows as an asset the item "Goodwill from consolidation." What does this item represent?
10. A consolidated balance sheet shows the item "Minority interest." What does this item represent?

Class exercises

Exercise 18–1

1. On a sheet of notebook paper open the following T-accounts: Cash; Accounts Receivable; Equipment; Notes Payable; Common Stock; Retained Earnings; Income Summary; Revenue from Services; and Operating Expenses.
2. Record directly in the T-accounts these transactions of a corporation.
   a. Sold and issued $10,000 of common stock for cash.
   b. Purchased $9,000 of equipment for cash.
   c. Sold and delivered $25,000 of services on credit.
   d. Collected $22,000 of accounts receivable.
   e. Paid $20,000 of operating expenses.
   f. Purchased $5,000 of additional equipment, giving $3,000 in cash and a $2,000 promissory note.

g. Closed the Revenue from Services, Operating Expenses, and Income Summary accounts.

3. Answer these questions:
   a. Does the corporation have retained earnings?
   b. Does it have any cash?
   c. If the corporation has retained earnings, why does it not also have cash?
   d. Can the corporation declare a legal cash dividend?
   e. Can it pay the dividend?
   f. In terms of assets, what does the balance of the Notes Payable account represent?
   g. In terms of assets, what does the balance of the Common Stock account represent?
   h. In terms of assets, what does the balance of the Retained Earnings account represent?

Exercise 18–2

On December 27 of last year the directors of a corporation voted to appropriate and place in Retained Earnings Appropriated for Plant Expansion, $100,000. This was the fifth of such appropriations and brought the balance of the Retained Earnings Appropriated for Plant Expansion account up to $500,000. On January 17 of this year the corporation entered into a contract for the construction of the plant addition for which the earnings were appropriated; and on November 10, upon completion of the addition, the contractor was paid $495,000, the contract price. Give the December 27 entry to record the appropriation and the November 10 entry to pay the contractor.

Exercise 18–3

At the end of the current year the Retained Earnings account of Driftwood Corporation appeared as follows. From the information in the account, prepare a retained earnings statement for the company.

Retained Earnings

June 15	Semiannual cash dividend	5,000	Jan. 1	Balance	80,000
Dec. 12	Semiannual cash dividend	5,000	Dec. 31	Net income	27,000
12	Stock dividend	15,000			

Exercise 18–4

On January 2 Company B had the following stockholders' equity:

Common stock, no-par value, 10,000 shares authorized and outstanding....... $100,000
Retained earnings 20,000
   Total Stockholders' Equity.. $120,000

a. Under the assumption that Company A purchased all of Company B's stock on January 2, paying $12 per share, and that a work sheet to consolidate the two companies' balance sheet was prepared, give the entry made on this work sheet to eliminate Company A's investment and Company B's stockholders' equity accounts.

b. Make the contrary assumption that Company A purchased only 90% of Company B's stock, paying $14 per share, and give the entry to eliminate Company A's investment and Company B's stockholder equity accounts.

Exercise 18–5

Assume again that Company A of Exercise 4 purchased for cash 90% of Company B's stock, paying $14 per share. Also assume that Company B earned $10,000 during the year following its acquisition, paid out $8,000 of these earnings in dividends, and retained the balance for use in its operations. (a) Give the entry made by Company A to take up its share of Company B's earnings. (b) Give the entry made by Company A to record its share of the $8,000 in dividends paid by Company B. (c) Give the work sheet entry made to eliminate Company A's investment and Company B's stockholders' equity accounts at the end of the year following acquisition.

Problems   Problem 18–1

On December 23 of last year the directors of a corporation voted to appropriate $50,000 of retained earnings and to retain in the business assets equal to the appropriation for use in expanding the corporation's plant. This was the fifth of such appropriations; and after it was recorded the corporation had contributed and retained capital as follows:

Common stock, no-par value, 250,000 shares authorized,
    200,000 shares issued and outstanding.................................. $2,000,000
Retained earnings appropriated for plant expansion.................... 250,000
Unappropriated retained earnings 185,000
    Total Stockholders' Equity $2,435,000

On January 9 of the current year the corporation entered into a contract for the construction of the plant addition for which the retained earnings were appropriated; and on October 3, upon completion of the addition the contractor was paid $246,500, the contract price.

At their December 22 meeting the directors voted to return the balance of the Retained Earnings Appropriated for Plant Expansion account to unappropriated retained earnings. They also voted a 20,000 share stock dividend distributable on January 20 to the January 15 stockholders of record. The company's stock was selling for $12.75 per share on December 22.

Required:
1. Prepare entries to record the December 23 appropriation, the payment of the contractor, the return of the appropriated retained earnings to unappropriated retained earnings, the declaration of the stock dividend, and the distribution of the dividend.
2. Prepare the stockholders' equity section of the corporation's balance sheet as it would appear after the transactions were recorded.

Problem 18–2

On January 1, 197A, stockholders' equity in Easton Corporation consisted of the following items:

Common stock, no-par value, 10,000 shares authorized, 8,000
    shares issued and outstanding $240,000
Retained earnings 85,000
      Total Stockholders' Equity.. $325,000

During 197A the company completed these transactions affecting its stockholders' equity:

Apr. 10   The directors voted a $0.50 per share cash dividend payable on May 15 to its May 10 stockholders of record.

May 15   Paid the previously declared cash dividend.

June 3   Received as a donation a plot of land adjacent to the company's plant. The land was given by Easton Chamber of Commerce, had a $20,000 fair market value, and was to be used to expand the plant and its payroll.

Aug. 21   Purchased 500 shares of treasury stock at $40 per share.

Oct. 11   The directors voted a $0.50 per share cash dividend payable on November 15 to the November 10 stockholders of record.

Nov. 15   Paid the previously declared cash dividend.

     25   Sold the 500 treasury shares at $45 per share.

Dec. 12   The directors voted a 5% stock dividend distributable on January 15 to the January 10 stockholders of record. The stock was selling at $45 per share.

     31   Closed the Income Summary account and carried the company's $32,000 net income to Retained Earnings.

Required:

1. Prepare general journal entries to record the transactions.
2. Prepare a retained earnings statement for the year and the stockholders' equity section of the corporation's year-end balance sheet.

Problem 18–3

Pinetop Corporation's December 31, 197A, balance sheet carried the following stockholders' equity section:

STOCKHOLDERS' EQUITY

Common stock, no-par value, 100,000 shares authorized, 75,000
    issued of which 2,000 are in the treasury $800,000
Retained earnings of which $24,000 is restricted by the purchase
    of treasury stock 175,000
      Total contributed and retained capital $975,000
Deduct cost of treasury stock... (24,000)
      Total Stockholders' Equity... $951,000

The treasury stock was sold at $13.50 per share during the first week in January, 197B. The company neither declared nor paid any dividends during

197A, but quarterly cash dividends at $0.10 per share were declared in March, June, and September, 197B, and were paid in each case during the following month. On December 22, 197B, the directors declared the fourth $0.10 per share quarterly dividend for the year, to be paid the following January 30 to the January 20 stockholders of record.

On December 31, 197B, the company treasurer prepared the following income statement for his own use:

PINETOP CORPORATION

Income Statement for Year Ended December 31, 197B

Sales...		$980,000
Gain on sale of unused factory land, net of		
$1,700 of applicable income taxes........................		6,000
Gain on sale of treasury stock...................................		3,000
		$989,000
Less:		
Cost of goods sold	$650,000	
Selling and administrative expenses........................	187,000	
Loss from flood, net of a $6,000 reduction		
in applicable income taxes.................................	9,000	
Dividends paid	22,500	
Interest expense	5,000	
Income taxes expense...	57,000	930,500
Net Income		$ 58,500

Required:

Prepare for the corporation *(a)* a 197B single-step income statement showing earnings per share data, *(b)* a retained earnings statement, and *(c)* the stockholders' equity section of the corporation's December 31, 197B, balance sheet.

Problem 18–4

Green Valley Corporation's December 31, 197A, balance sheet carried this stockholders' equity section.

STOCKHOLDERS' EQUITY

Common stock, no-par value, 100,000 shares		
authorized, 40,000 shares issued of which 2,000		
are in the treasury	$460,000	
Retained earnings:		
Appropriated for plant expansion............................	$150,000	
Appropriated and restricted by the purchase of		
treasury stock...	24,500	
Free and unappropriated	123,500	
Total retained earnings.....................................		298,000
Total contributed capital and retained earnings.............		$758,000
Less cost of treasury stock		24,500
Total Stockholders' Equity		$733,500

At the end of 197B the corporation's unappropriated Retained Earnings account showed these amounts:

Date		Explanation	Debit	Credit	Balance
Jan.	1	Balance			123,500
May	5	Treasury stock appropriation		24,500	148,000
June	15	Cash dividend (payable July 20)	6,000		142,000
	15	Stock dividend (distributable July 20)	28,000		114,000
Dec.	14	Cash dividend (payable January 21)	6,300		107,700
	14	Stock dividend (distributable January 21)	29,400		78,300
	14	Appropriated for plant expansion	25,000		53,300
	31	Net income		98,700	152,000

The treasury stock was sold on May 5, 197B, at $13.75 per share, and the June 15 cash dividend was paid on July 20. One new share of stock was distributed on July 20 for each 20 shares held and one new share will be distributed on January 21 for each 20 held on the record date.

Required:
1. Prepare entries to record the transactions reflected in the Retained Earnings account, and also prepare entries to record the sale of the treasury stock and the payment and distribution of the June 15 dividends.
2. Prepare a 197B retained earnings statement for the company and also the stockholders' equity section of its December 31, 197B balance sheet.

Problem 18–5

The following items appeared in the first two columns of a work sheet prepared to consolidate the balance sheets of Company A and Company B on the day Company A acquired control of Company B by purchasing for cash 8,500 shares of its $10-par-value common stock at $13 per share:

ASSETS	*Company A*	*Company B*
Cash	$ 9,500	$ 9,000
Accounts receivable	39,000	21,000
Allowance for doubtful accounts	(3,000)	(2,000)
Inventories	40,000	32,000
Investment in Company B	110,500	
Equipment	85,000	80,000
Accumulated depreciation, equipment	(14,000)	(5,000)
Buildings	90,000	
Accumulated depreciation, buildings	(12,000)	
Land	15,000	
	$360,000	$135,000

EQUITIES		
Accounts payable	$ 27,000	$ 15,000
Note payable	10,000	
Common stock	250,000	100,000
Retained earnings	73,000	20,000
	$360,000	$135,000

Included in the items is a $5,000 debt of Company B to Company A for the sale and delivery of some equipment at cost on the day Company A acquired control of Company B. The sale was an open account (account receivable). Management of Company A believed Company B's earnings prospects justified the $13 per share paid for its stock.

Required:
1. Enter the items on a work sheet and consolidate them for preparation of a consolidated balance sheet.
2. Prepare a consolidated balance sheet for Company A and its subsidiary.
3. Under the assumption that Company B earned $10,000 during the first year after it was acquired by Company A, paid out $6,000 of the earnings in dividends, and retained the balance in its operations, give in general journal form the entries made by Company A *(a)* to take up its share of Company B's earnings and *(b)* to record receipt of its share of the dividends paid by Company B. Also *(c)* give the entry to eliminate Company A's investment in Company B and Company B's stockholder equity accounts on the end-of-the-first-year work sheet to consolidate the balance sheets of the two companies.

Alternate problems

Problem 18–1A

At the end of 197A a corporation's balance sheet showed the following stockholders' equity:

Common stock, no-par-value, 500,000 shares authorized, 350,000 shares issued.....................		$1,750,000
Retained earnings:		
Appropriated for plant expansion $240,000		
Free and unappropriated..................................... 178,000		418,000
Total Stockholders' Equity...........................		$2,168,000

During 197B the corporation completed these transactions:

Jan. 11 The directors voted to appropriate and transfer an additional $60,000 from unappropriated retained earnings to retained earnings appropriated for plant expansion.

Nov. 5 Upon completion of the addition to the plant (buildings) for which the retained earnings were appropriated, the corporation paid the contractor $292,500, the contract price of the addition.

20 The directors voted to return the balance of the Retained Earnings Appropriated for Plant Expansion account to (unappropriated) Retained Earnings. They also voted a stock dividend requiring the capitalization at $7.50 per share (the market price of the stock) of an amount of retained earnings equal to that returned to unappropriated retained earnings through the elimination of the plant expansion appropriation.

Dec. 30 Distributed the shares of the stock dividend declared on November 20.

Required:
1. Prepare general journal entries to record the transactions.
2. Prepare the stockholders' equity section of the corporation's balance sheet as it would appear after the distribution of the stock dividend.

Problem 18–2A

On January 1, 197A, stockholder equity in Weston Corporation consisted of these items:

Common stock, no-par value. 50,000 shares authorized, 40,000
    shares issued and outstanding $460,000
Retained earnings 120,000
      Total Shareholders' Equity.. $580,000

During 197A the company completed these transactions affecting stockholders' equity:

Mar. 10   Received as a gift from Weston Chamber of Commerce a plot of land adjacent to the company's plant. The land had a $10,000 fair market value and was to be used to expand the company's plant and payroll.

Apr. 4   Purchased 1,000 shares of treasury stock at $14 per share.

June 20   The board of directors voted a $0.25 per share cash dividend payable on July 15 to the July 10 stockholders of record.

July 15   Paid the dividend declared in June.

    22   Sold 500 of the treasury shares at $17 per share.

Oct. 12   Sold the remaining treasury shares at $13 per share.

Dec. 18   The board of directors voted a $0.25 per share cash dividend and a 5% stock dividend payable on January 15 to the January 10 stockholders of record. The stock was selling at $12.50 per share.

    31   Closed the Income Summary account and carried the company's $28,000 net income to Retained Earnings.

Required:
1. Prepare general journal entries to record the transactions.
2. Prepare a retained earnings statement for the year and the stockholders' equity section of the company's year-end balance sheet.

Problem 18–3A

Pacific Corporation's December 31, 197A, balance sheet carried the following stockholder equity items:

Common stock, no-par value, 100,000 shares authorized,
    80,000 shares issued of which 5,000 are in the corporation
    treasury $420,000
Retained earnings of which $30,000 is restricted by the purchase
    of treasury stock 115,000
Cost of treasury stock .... (30,000)
      Total Stockholders' Equity... $505,000

The treasury stock was sold for $7 per share during the first week of January, 197B. Quarterly cash dividends at $0.10 per share were declared during March,

June, and September and were paid in each case during the following month. On December 20, 197B, the directors voted a $0.10 per share cash dividend plus a 2% stock dividend, payable and distributable the following January 31 to the January 21 stockholders of record. The stock was selling at $7.50 per share on December 20.

On December 31, 197B, the company treasurer prepared the following income statement for his own use:

PACIFIC CORPORATION
Income Statement for Year Ended December 31, 197B

Sales	$600,000	
Gain on sale of unused factory land, net of		
$4,000 of applicable income taxes	12,000	
Gain on sale of treasury stock	5,000	$617,000
Less:		
Cost of goods sold	$380,000	
Selling and administrative expenses	115,000	
Loss from earthquake, net of a $5,000 reduction		
in applicable income taxes	8,000	
Dividends in cash and stock	44,000	
Interest expense	5,000	
Income taxes expense	44,000	596,000
Net Income		$ 21,000

Required:
Prepare (a) a single-step income statement for the corporation showing earnings per share data, (b) a retained earnings statement. and (c) the stockholders' equity section of its December 31, 197B, balance sheet.

Problem 18–5A

The following items appeared in the first two columns of a work sheet prepared to consolidate the balance sheets of Company X and Company Y on the day Company X gained control of Company Y by purchasing for cash 8,000 shares of its $10 par value common stock at $12 per share.

ASSETS

	Company X	Company Y
Cash	$ 7,000	$ 12,000
Note receivable, Company Y	5,000	
Accounts receivable, net	32,000	28,000
Inventories	45,000	30,000
Investment in Company Y	96,000	
Equipment, net	75,000	60,000
Buildings, net	80,000	
Land	20,000	
	$360,000	$130,000

EQUITIES

Accounts payable...	$ 28,000	$ 10,000
Note payable, Company X..................................		5,000
Common stock..	250,000	100,000
Retained earnings..	82,000	15,000
	$360,000	$130,000

At the time Company X acquired control of Company Y it took Company Y's note in exchange for $5,000 in cash and it sold and delivered to it $3,000 of equipment at cost on open account (account receivable). Both transactions are reflected in the foregoing accounts. Management of Company X believed that Company Y's earnings prospects justified the $12 per share paid for its stock.

Required:
1. Prepare a work sheet for consolidating the balance sheets of the two companies and prepare a consolidated balance sheet.
2. Under the assumption Company Y earned $11,000 during the first year after it was acquired by Company X, paid out $6,000 of the earnings in dividends, and retained the balance in its operations, give in general journal form the entries made by Company X *(a)* to take up its share of Company Y's earnings and *(b)* to record the receipt of its share of the dividends paid by Company Y. Also *(c)* give the entry to eliminate Company X's investment in Company Y and Company Y's stockholder equity accounts on the end-of-the-first-year work sheet to consolidate the balance sheets of the two companies.

Decision problem 18–1, McGregor Stores, Ltd.

McGregor Stores, Ltd., operates six clothing stores in a large eastern city and its suburbs. Stockholder equity in the corporation consists of 50,000 shares of no-par-value common stock, all owned by Ira McGregor, his wife, and only son, and approximately $800,000 of retained earnings. Mr. McGregor began the business 32 years ago with one store, and the business has grown to its present size primarily from the retention of assets from earnings. The company has no long-term debt and only normal amounts of accounts payable, short-term bank loans, and accrued payables. It has an excellent reputation with its creditors and has always paid its debts on time.

An opportunity to expand the number of the company's stores from six to eight has recently arisen, but the expansion will make it necessary to borrow $300,000 by issuing a 10-year mortgage note. The company has never before borrowed to an extent that made the issuance of financial statements to outsiders necessary. Actually, since all the company's stock is owned by the three members of the McGregor family and Ira McGregor has always been most secretive about his business affairs, the only people who have ever seen the company's financial statements are the family members, a very few employees, and some income tax people. Consequently, when Ira McGregor was told by the company's bank that it could not consider the loan unless it was provided with detailed financial statements for the past five years and audited statements for the most recent year, he was ready to call off the expansion. However, after additional consideration he changed his position to a willingness to have the audit and to provide the balance sheets for the most recent five years, but he was unwilling to provide income statements or retained earnings statements.

If the balance sheets are detailed and the last one is audited, what information will they give the bank? Will this information be sufficient to justify the loan? If you were the bank's loan officer and sought to compromise with Mr. McGregor in order to secure more financial information without receiving summarized or complete income statements and retained earnings statements, what information would you seek?

Decision problem 18–2, Electro-Dynamics, Ltd.

Each year for a number of past years the directors of Electro-Dynamics, Ltd., have appropriated and placed in retained earnings appropriated for plant expansion an amount of retained earnings equal to half the year's net income, and the total of these appropriations has grown to $2,000,000. During these years the actual process of expanding and modernizing the plant has been going on; and expenditures for this purpose, financed in part by borrowing, have totaled $3,500,000. However, over the years no entries have been made in the Retained Earnings Appropriated for Plant Expansion account other than to record the appropriations. Consequently, at the last board meeting, following a statement by the company treasurer regarding the need to borrow $1,000,000 to finance a proposed new expansion, one of the company's directors stated that he could not understand why the company needed to borrow funds for expansion purposes when its latest balance sheet showed it had $2,000,000 of retained earnings appropriated for that purpose. The company treasurer blinked twice, swallowed hard, and said he would prepare a written statement explaining the nature of the retained earnings appropriated for plant expansion and why the company needed to borrow money. He then returned to his office and assigned the job of preparing the statement to you. Prepare it.

Decision problem 18–3, Alpha Company

On May 10 of the current year Alpha Company gained control of Beta Company through the purchase of 85% of Beta Company's 20,000 outstanding no-par-value common stock at $6.50 per share. On that date Beta Company owed Alpha Company $4,000 for merchandise purchased on credit and $10,000 it had borrowed by giving a promissory note. The condensed May 10 balance sheets of the two companies follow:

ALPHA AND BETA COMPANIES
Balance Sheets, May 10, 19—

ASSETS

	Alpha Company	Beta Company
Cash	$ 6,500	$ 10,500
Note receivable, Beta Company	10,000	
Accounts receivable, net	29,000	24,500
Inventories	42,000	35,000
Investment in Beta Company	110,500	
Equipment, net	80,000	70,000
Buildings, net	85,000	
Land	20,000	
Total Assets	$383,000	$140,000

EQUITIES

	Alpha Company	Beta Company
Note payable, Alpha Company		$ 10,000
Accounts payable	$ 20,000	10,000
Common stock	250,000	100,000
Retained earnings	113,000	20,000
Total Equities	$383,000	$140,000

Prepare a consolidated balance sheet for Alpha Company and its subsidiary, and write a short explanation of why consolidated statements are prepared and explain the principles of consolidation.

Analytical and review problems

Problem 18–1 A&R

Early in January you assumed your new post of controller of Eastern Sales Limited. Your predecessor prepared the following *preliminary* financial statements:

EASTERN SALES LIMITED
Income Statement
For the Year Ended December 31, 1975

Sales		$586,700
Cost of Goods Sold	$362,300	
Depreciation	5,400	
Wages and salaries	68,000	
Interest, insurance and property taxes	11,600	
Advertising and promotion	35,000	482,300
		$104,400
Income taxes		26,100
Income before extraordinary items		$ 78,300

Extraordinary items (net of tax):
Settlement of lawsuit .... $ 25,000
Sales office relocation expenses 20,000   45,000
Net Income .... $ 33,300

EASTERN SALES LIMITED
Statement of Retained Earnings
For the Year Ended December 31, 1975

Retained earnings January 1, 1975 .... $158,200
Add: Net income less dividends of $20,000   13,300
                                                                                                    $171,500
Less: Loss on disposal of manufacturing division net of tax   50,000
Retained earnings December 31, 1975 .... $121,500

In the course of examining the records you discover the following:
a. A $1,000 purchase invoice, dated December 27, was received December 31, and recorded. The goods were in transit and were not included in the inventory.
b. A $700 purchase of merchandise was received on December 31, and included in the inventory. The invoice did not arrive until after the trial balance was drawn and therefore was not recorded in the December purchases.
c. A sales invoice for $2,700 dated December 31, had been recorded. The goods which cost $1,800 had not been shipped and were included in inventory.
d. A $1,200 item of office equipment, received on December 31, was erroneously recorded as a purchase of merchandise. The company depreciates office equipment on a straight-line basis over a five-year service life.
e. The $68,000 of wages and salaries represented debits to this account during the year. Your predecessor failed to recognize $800 of accrued wages and salaries expense at December 31, 1974 and $1,200 at December 31, 1975.
(Assume that all purchases are FOB destination.)

Required:
1. Determine the correct cost of goods sold (periodic inventory method was used).
2. Determine the correct depreciation expense.
3. Determine the correct wages and salaries expense.
4. Determine the correct sales.
5. Prepare, in proper form, a corrected income statement. Income tax on normal income is 25%.
6. Prepare, in proper form, a corrected retained earnings statement.

(CGA adapted)

Problem 18–2 A&R

The following are partial balance sheets of W&T Limited as at December 31, 1975 and 1976:

W&T LIMITED
Partial Balance Sheet
As at December 31, 1975

Shareholders' Equity
Capital Stock—authorized 100,000, no par
 value shares — issued and outstanding 10,000 shares ... $100,000
Retained Earnings
 Free $50,000
 Appropriated Reserve for Plant Expansion 40,000   90.000
                            $190,000

W&T LIMITED
Partial Balance Sheet
As at December 31, 1976

Shareholders' Equity
Capital Stock—authorized 100,000 $10 par
 value shares — issued and outstanding 11.000 shares ... $118,000
Retained Earnings
 Free $68,000
 Appropriated Reserve for Plant Expansion................. 50,000   118,000
                            $236,000

Additional Information:
1. On June 1, 1976 the company declared a stock dividend of 10% when the shares had a fair market value of $18. The dividend was distributed August 15, 1976.
2. On December 15, 1976, the directors declared a cash dividend of 50 cents per share to be paid on January 15, 1977 to all shareholders on record as at December 31, 1976.
3. On September 30, 1976, the company paid a lawsuit of $25,000 pending since 1970. The amount was not determinable until September 30, 1976.
4. On November 1, 1976, the company which had plant facilities in Toronto and Windsor sold the Toronto plant at a gain of $25.000.
5. The only expenses that the company incurred for 1976 were

Cost of Goods Sold... $200,000
Selling Expenses... 25,000
Administrative Expenses.. 40,000
Income Tax Expense (of which $5.000 related to the gain on
 the sale of the Toronto plant)... 20,000

Required.
1. Prepare a classified income statement for the year ended December 31, 1976.
2. Reconstruct the closing (clearing) journal entries (omit narratives) as at December 31, 1976, which the company has already recorded in its books.

Problem 18–3 A&R

The president of Stingie Company. Limited, received the following letter following the declaration of the semiannual dividend:

Dear President Cruke:

It is with utter amazement and disgust that I read your message to the share-holders. In case you have forgotten, I will remind you that you stated that the company had a very good year with net income of some $10 million. Then you went on to state that the company will continue to pay the same dividend of 10 cents per share for a total pay-out of $2 million. This is the same dividend the company has paid for the last five years.

Now, Mr. President, I am a widow dependent on dividend income for my livelihood and with the kind of dividends you pay in this period of rapidly rising prices I am bordering on bread and water. I believe many other people feel the same way because the stock is selling for about half of what it used to. So you see I cannot sell the stock because I would lose so much.

Your excuse for not increasing the dividend is that heavy expenditures will be made in the future to modernize plant and equipment necessitated by competition and government requirements with regard to pollution control equipment.

I have no quarrel with the policy of modernization to improve the company's future position. However, does it have to be at the shareholders' expense, especially widows like myself? Why don't you spend some of the reserves, surpluses and retained earnings you have accumulated over the years? A quick check of these indicates that they total in excess of $100 million, certainly ample, if not a few times over, for the necessary present and future needs. So why don't you pay out the whole $10 million earned this past year?

I am spending my "mad money" to get me to the annual meeting and you better have some good answers.

Yours in great expectation of an increased dividend,

Phyllis Driller

Required:
President Cruke asks you to draft a reply that he can use at the annual meeting.

19

Long-term liabilities and investments

■ When a business borrows money that is not to be repaid for a relatively long period of time, 10, 20, or more years, it may borrow by means of a mortgage or by issuing bonds.

Borrowing money with a mortgage

■ A business may borrow by placing a mortgage on some or all of its plant assets. A mortgage actually involves two legal documents. The first is a kind of promissory note called a *mortgage note,* which is secured by a second legal document called a *mortgage* or a *mortgage contract.* In the mortgage note the mortgagor, the one who mortgages property, promises to repay the money borrowed. The mortgage or mortgage contract commonly requires the mortgagor to keep the mortgaged property in a good state of repair, carry adequate insurance, pay the interest on the mortgage note, and, often, make payments to reduce the mortgage liability. In addition it normally grants the mortgage holder the right to foreclose in case the mortgagor fails in any of the required duties. In a foreclosure a court takes possession of the mortgaged property for the mortgage holder and may order its sale. If the property is sold, the proceeds go first to pay court costs and the claims of the mortgage holder, after which any money remaining is paid to the former owner of the property.

Borrowing money by issuing bonds

■ Borrowing money by issuing bonds is similar to borrowing by giving a mortgage. Actually in many cases the only real difference is that a number of bonds, often in denominations of $1,000, are issued in the place of a single mortgage note. For all practical purposes each bond is a promissory note, promising to pay a definite sum of money to its holder, or owner of record, at a fixed future date. Like promissory notes, bonds bear interest; and like a mortgage note, they are often secured by a mortgage. However, since bonds may be owned and transferred during their lives by a number of people, they differ from promissory notes in that they do not name the lender.

When a company issues bonds secured by a mortgage, it normally sells the bonds to an investment firm, known as the *underwriter,* which in turn resells the bonds to the public. In addition to the underwriter, the company issuing bonds selects a trustee to represent the bondholders. In most cases the trustee is a large bank or trust company to whom the company issuing the bonds executes and delivers the mortgage contract which acts as security for the bonds. It is the duty of the trustee to see that the company fulfills all the pledged responsibilities of the mortgage contract, or as it is often called the *deed of trust.* It is also the duty of the trustee to foreclose if any pledges are not fulfilled.

Characteristics of bonds

■ Over the years corporation lawyers and financiers have created a wide variety of bonds, each with different combinations of characteristics. For example, bonds may be *serial bonds* or *sinking fund bonds.* When serial or term bonds are issued, portions of the issue become due and are paid in installments over a period of years, as in the case of a corporation that issues $5,000,000 of serial bonds with the provision that $500,000 of the bonds become due and are to be paid each year until all are paid. Sinking fund bonds differ in that they are paid at maturity from a sinking fund created for that purpose. Sinking funds are discussed in more detail later in this chapter.

Bonds may also be either *registered bonds* or *coupon bonds.* Ownership of registered bonds is registered or recorded with the issuing corporation, which offers some protection from loss or theft. Title to such bonds is transferred in much the same manner as title to stock is transferred. Interest payments are usually made by cheques mailed to the registered owners. Coupon bonds secure their name from the interest coupons attached to each bond. Each coupon calls for payment on the interest payment date of the interest due on the bond to which it is attached. The coupons are detached as they become due and are deposited with a bank for collection. Often ownership of a coupon bond is not registered. Such unregistered bonds are payable to bearer or are bearer paper, and ownership is transferred by delivery. Sometimes bonds are registered as to principal with interest payments by coupons.

Bonds also may be secured or unsecured. Unsecured bonds are called *debentures* and depend upon the general credit standing of their issuing corporation for security. Only financially strong companies are able to sell unsecured bonds. When bonds are secured, they are normally secured by a mortgage or lien on some or all of their issuing company's plant assets.

Why bonds are issued ■ A corporation in need of long-term funds may secure the funds by issuing additional common stock, issuing preferred stock, or by selling bonds. Each has advantages and disadvantages. Stockholders are owners, and issuing additional common stock spreads ownership, control of management, and earnings over more shares. Bondholders, on the other hand, are creditors and do not share in either management or earnings. However, bond interest must be paid whether there are any earnings or not; otherwise the bondholders may foreclose and take the assets pledged for their security. Nevertheless, when long-term funds are needed, bonds are often issued because they offer the common stockholders of the issuing company a leverage on their investment.

For example, a corporation with 200,000 shares of $10 par value common stock outstanding needs $2,000,000 to expand. Management of the corporation estimates that after the expansion the company can earn $800,000 annually before bond interest and income taxes, and has proposed three plans for securing the needed funds. Plan No. 1 calls for the issuance of $2,000,000 of common stock, which would increase the total number of common shares outstanding to 400,000. Plan No. 2 calls for the issuance of $2,000,000 of 7½% preferred stock, and plan No. 3 calls for the sale at par of $2,000,000 of 7% bonds. Illustration 19–1 shows how each of these plans will affect the earnings of the corporation's common stockholders.

Notice the effect on the three methods of financing of the assumed 50% income tax rate. Bond interest expense is a deductible expense in arriving at income subject to income taxes, but dividends are a sharing of earnings and are not tax deductible. As a result the tax savings from issuing bonds greatly increases their leverage, as in this example.

	Plan 1	Plan 2	Plan 3
Earnings before bond interest and income taxes	$800,000	$800,000	$800,000
Deduct bond interest expense			140,000
Income before taxes	$800,000	$800,000	$660,000
Deduct income taxes	400,000	400,000	330,000
Net income	$400,000	$400,000	$330,000
Deduct preferred dividends		150,000	
Income available for dividends on common stock	$400,000	$250,000	$330,000
Income per share of common stock	$1.00	$1.25	$1.65

Illustration
19–1

Income per share of common stock is determined in each case in Illustration 19–1 by dividing the income available to the common stockholders by the number of common shares outstanding. Plan No. 1 calls for the issuance of 200,000 additional common shares, bringing the total of these shares to 400,000. Therefore, the income per common share under this plan will be: $400,000 \div 400,000 = \$1$. Under each of the other plans there will be only 200,000 common shares outstanding and the earnings per share will be greater.

Issuing bonds

■ A decision to issue bonds rests with a corporation's board of directors, but corporation bylaws commonly require that the decision must be approved by the stockholders. When a resolution authorizing a bond issue is passed by a board of directors and approved by the stockholders, the bonds are printed and the deed of trust is drawn and deposited with the trustee of the bondholders. At that point a memorandum describing the bond issue is commonly entered in the Bonds Payable account. Such a memorandum might read, "Authorized to issue $1,000,000 of 7%, 20-year bonds dated January 1, 1976, and with interest payable semiannually on each July 1 and January 1." As in this case, bond interest is usually payable semiannually.

After the deed of trust is deposited with the trustee of the bondholders, all or a portion of the bonds may be sold. If all are sold at their par value, also called their *face amount,* an entry like this is made to record the sale:

Jan.	1	Cash	1,000,000.00	
		Bonds Payable		1,000,000.00
		Sold bonds at par on their interest date.		

When the semiannual interest is paid on these bonds, the transaction is recorded as follows:

July	1	Bond Interest Expense	35,000.00	
		Cash		35,000.00
		Paid the semiannual interest on the bonds.		

And when the bonds are paid at maturity, an entry like this is made:

Jan.	1	Bonds Payable	1,000,000.00	
		Cash		1,000,000.00
		Paid bonds at maturity.		

■ Sometimes bonds are sold on their date of issue, which is also their interest date, as in the previous illustration. More often they are sold after their date of issue and between interest dates. In such cases, when bonds are sold between interest dates, it is customary to charge and collect from the purchasers the interest that has accrued on the bonds since the previous interest payment and to return this accrued interest to the purchasers on the next interest date. For example, assume that on March 1, a corporation sold at par $100,000 of 7½% bonds on which interest is payable semiannually on each January 1 and July 1. The entry to record the sale between interest dates is:

Mar.	1	Cash	101,250.00	
		Bond Interest Expense.....................		1,250.00
		Bonds Payable		100,000.00
		Sold $100,000 of bonds on which two months' interest has accrued.		

At the end of four months, on the July 1 semiannual interest date, the purchasers of these bonds are paid a full six months' interest. This payment includes four months' interest earned by the bondholders after March 1 and the two months' accrued interest collected from them at the time the bonds were sold. The entry to record the payment is:

July	1	Bond Interest Expense..........................	3,750.00	
		Cash		3,750.00
		Paid the semiannual interest on the bonds.		

After both of these entries are posted, the Bond Interest Expense account has a $2,500 debit balance and appears as follows:

Bond Interest Expense

July 1 (Payment)	3,750.00	Mar. 1 (Accrued interest)	1,250.00

The $2,500 debit balance is the interest on the $100,000 of bonds at 7½% for the four months from March 1 to July 1.

Beginning students often think it strange to charge bond purchasers for accrued interest when bonds are sold between interest dates, and to return this accrued interest in the next interest payment. However, this is the custom, all bond transactions are "plus accrued interest"; and there is a good reason for the practice. For instance, if a corporation sells portions of a bond issue to different purchasers on different dates during an interest period without collecting the accrued interest, it must keep records of the purchasers and the dates on which they bought bonds. Otherwise it cannot pay the correct amount of interest to each. However, if it charges each buyer for accrued interest at the time of his purchase, it need not keep records of the purchasers and their purchase dates, since it can pay a full period's interest to all purchasers for the period in which they bought their bonds and each receives the interest he has earned and gets back the accrued interest paid at the time of his purchase.

Bond interest rates

■ **At this point the student who is unfamiliar with the concept of present value should turn to the Appendix at the back of this book and familiarize himself with this concept before attempting to go further into this chapter.**

A corporation issuing bonds specifies in the deed of trust and on each bond the interest rate it will pay. This rate is called the *contract rate*. It is usually stated on an annual basis, although bond interest is normally paid semiannually; and it is applied to the par value of the bonds to determine the dollars of interest the corporation will pay. For example, a corporation will pay $70 each year in two semiannual installments of $35 each on a $1,000, 7% bond on which interest is paid semiannually.

Although the contract rate establishes the amount of interest a corporation will pay, it is not necessarily the rate of interest the corporation will incur in issuing bonds. The rate of interest it will incur depends upon what lenders consider their risks to be in lending to the corporation and upon the current *market rate* for bond interest. The market rate for bond interest is the rate borrowers are willing to pay and lenders are willing to take for the use of money at the level of risk involved. It fluctuates from day to day at any level of risk as the supply and demand for loanable funds fluctuate. It goes up when the demand for bond money increases and the supply decreases, and it goes down when the supply increases and the demand decreases.

A corporation issuing bonds usually offers a contract rate of interest equal to what it estimates the market will demand on the day the bonds are to be issued. If its estimate is correct, and the contract rate and market rate coincide on the day the bonds are issued, the bonds will sell at par and the corporation will record the sale as shown on page 568. However, since bonds must be printed and a deed of trust drawn, a number of days always elapse between the day the interest rate estimate is made and the day the bonds are sold. Consequently, when bonds are sold, their contract rate seldom coincides with the market rate; and as a result, bonds usually sell either at a premium or at a discount.

Bonds sold at a discount

■ When a corporation offers to sell bonds carrying a contract rate below the prevailing market rate, the bonds will sell, but only at a discount. Investors can get the market rate of interest elsewhere for the use of their money, so they will buy the bonds only at a price that will yield the prevailing market rate on the investment. What price will they pay and how is it determined? The price they will pay is the *present value* of the expected returns from the investment and is determined by discounting these returns at the current market rate for bond interest.

To illustrate how bond prices are determined, assume that on a day when the market rate for bond interest is 8%, a corporation offers to sell and issue bonds having a $100,000 par value, a 10-year life, and on which interest is to be paid semiannually at a 7% annual rate.[1] In exchange for current dollars a buyer of these bonds will gain two monetary rights:

1. The right to receive $100,000 at the end of the bond issue's 10-year life.
2. The right to receive $3,500 in interest at the end of each 6-month interest period throughout the 10-year life of the bonds.

Since both are rights to receive money in the future, to determine their present value, the amounts to be received are discounted at the prevailing market rate of interest. If the prevailing market rate is 8% annually, it is 4% semiannually; and in 10 years there are 20 semi-annual periods. Consequently, using the last number in the 4% column of Table 1 in the Appendix to discount the first amount and the last number in the 4% column of Table 2 to discount the series of $3,500 amounts, the present value of the rights and the price an informed buyer will offer for the bonds is:

Present value of $100,000 to be received 20 periods hence, discounted
  at 4% per period ($100,000 × 0.4564) $45,640
Present value of $3,500 to be received periodically for 20 periods,
  discounted at 4% ($3,500 × 13.590) 47,565
Present value of the bond investment... $93,205

If the corporation accepts the $93,205 offer for its bonds and sells them on their date of issue, it will record the sale with an entry like this:

Jan.	1	Cash	93,205.00	
		Discount on Bonds Payable.........................	6,795.00	
		Bonds Payable		100,000.00
		Sold bonds at a discount on their date of issue.		

If the corporation prepares a balance sheet on the day the bonds are sold, it may show the bonds in the long-term liability section as follows:

Long-Term Liabilities:
  First mortgage, 7% bonds payable, due January 1, 1986......... $100,000
    Less unamortized discount based on the 8% market rate
    for bond interest prevailing on the date of issue.............. 6,795 $93,205

---

[1] The spread between the contract rate and the market rate of interest on a bond issue is seldom more than a fraction of a per cent. However, a spread of a full per cent is used here to simplify the illustrations.

On a balance sheet any unamortized discount on a bond issue is deducted from the par value of the bonds to show the amount at which the bonds are carried on the books, called the *carrying amount*.

Amortizing the discount

The corporation of this discussion received $93,205 for its bonds, but in 10 years it must pay the bondholders $100,000. The difference, the $6,795 discount, is a cost of using the $93,205 that was incurred because the contract rate of interest on the bonds was below the prevailing market rate. It is a cost that must be paid when the bonds mature. However, since each semiannual interest period in the life of the bond issue benefits from the use of the $93,205, it is only fair that each should bear a fair share of this cost.

The accounting procedure for dividing a discount and charging a fair share to each period in the life of the applicable bond issue is called *amortizing* a discount. A simple method of amortizing a discount is the *straight-line method,* a method in which an equal portion of the discount is amortized each interest period. If this method is used to amortize the $6,795 discount of this discussion, the $6,795 is divided by 20, the number of interest periods in the life of the bond issue, and $339.75 ($6,795 ÷ 20 = $339.75) of discount is amortized at the end of each interest period with an entry like this:

July	1	Bond Interest Expense.............................	3,839.75	
		Discount on Bonds Payable		339.75
		Cash..		3,500.00
		To record payment of six months' interest and amortization of $\frac{1}{20}$ of the discount.		

The amortization of $339.75 of discount each six months will completely write off the $6,795 of discount by the end of the issue's 10-year life. It also increases the amount of bond interest expense recorded each six months to the sum of the $3,500 paid the bondholders and the discount amortized.

Straight-line amortization is easy to understand and has long been used. However, it may be used only in situations where the results do not materially differ from those obtained through use of the so-called interest method described in the following paragraphs. The interest method is to be favoured because it results in a constant rate of interest on the carrying amount of a bond issue, while the straight-line method results in a decreasing rate when a discount is amortized and an increasing rate when a premium is amortized.

When the interest method is used in amortizing a bond discount, the interest expense to be recorded each period is determined by applying a constant rate of interest to the beginning-of-the-period carrying amount of the bonds. The constant rate applied is the market rate prevailing at the time the bonds were issued. The amount of discount amortized each period is then determined by subtracting the amount of interest to be paid the bondholders from the interest expense to be recorded. Illustration 19–2, with amounts rounded to full dollars, shows

Period	Beginning-of-Period Carrying Amount	Interest Expense to Be Recorded	Interest to Be Paid the Bondholders	Discount to Be Amortized	Unamortized Discount at End of Period	End-of-Period Carrying Amount
1	$93,205	$3,728	$3,500	$228	$6,567	$93,433
2	93,433	3,737	3,500	237	6,330	93,670
3	93,670	3,747	3,500	247	6,083	93,917
4	93,917	3,757	3,500	257	5,826	94,174
5	94,174	3,767	3,500	267	5,559	94,441
6	94,441	3,778	3,500	278	5,281	94,719
7	94,719	3,789	3,500	289	4,992	95,008
8	95,008	3,800	3,500	300	4,692	95,308
9	95,308	3,812	3,500	312	4,380	95,620
10	95,620	3,825	3,500	325	4,055	95,945
11	95,945	3,838	3,500	338	3,717	96,283
12	96,283	3,851	3,500	351	3,366	96,634
13	96,634	3,865	3,500	365	3,001	96,999
14	96,999	3,880	3,500	380	2,621	97,379
15	97,379	3,895	3,500	395	2,226	97,774
16	97,774	3,911	3,500	411	1,815	98,185
17	98,185	3,927	3,500	427	1,388	98,612
18	98,612	3,944	3,500	444	944	99,056
19	99,056	3,962	3,500	462	482	99,518
20	99,518	3,982*	3,500	482	-0-	100,000

*Adjusted to compensate for accumulated rounding of amounts.

Illustration
19–2

the interest expense to be recorded, the discount to be amortized, et cetera, when the interest method of amortizing a discount is applied to the bond issue of this discussion. In examining Illustration 19–2, note these points:

1. The bonds were sold at a $6,795 discount, which when subtracted from their face amount gives a beginning of Period 1 carrying amount of $93,205.
2. The interest expense amounts result from multiplying each beginning-of-the-period carrying amount by the 4% market rate prevailing when the bonds were issued. For example, $93,205 × 4% = $3,728 and $93,433 × 4% = $3,737.
3. Interest to be paid bondholders each period is determined by multiplying par value of the bonds by the contract rate of interest.

4. The discount to be amortized each period is determined by subtracting the amount of interest to be paid the bondholders from the amount of interest expense.
5. The unamortized discount at the end of each period is determined by subtracting the discount amortized from the unamortized discount at the beginning of the period.
6. The end-of-the-period carrying amount for the bonds is determined by subtracting the end-of-the-period amount of unamortized discount from the face amount of the bonds. For example, at the end of Period 1: $100,000 − $6,567 = $93,433.

When the interest method is used in amortizing a discount, the periodic amortizing entries are like the entries used with the straight-line method, excepting as to the amounts. For example, the entry to pay the bondholders and amortize a portion of the discount at the end of the first interest period of the issue of Illustration 19–2 is:

July	1	Bond Interest Expense...................................	3,728.00	
		Discount on Bonds Payable		228.00
		Cash..		3,500.00
		To record payment of the bondholders and amortization of a portion of the discount.		

Similar entries, differing only in the amounts of interest expense recorded and discount amortized, are made at the end of each interest period in the life of the bond issue.

Bonds sold at a premium ■ When a corporation offers to sell bonds carrying a contract rate of interest above the prevailing market rate for the risks involved, the bonds will sell at a premium. Buyers will bid up the price of the bonds, going as high, but no higher than a price that will return the current market rate of interest on the investment. What price will they pay? They will pay the present value of the expected returns from the investment, determined by discounting these returns at the prevailing market rate for bond interest. For example, assume that on a day the current market rate for bond interest is 6%, a corporation offers to sell bonds having a $100,000 par value and a 10-year life with interest to be paid semiannually at a 7% annual rate. An informed buyer of these bonds will discount the expectation of receiving $100,000 in 10 years and the expectation of receiving $3,500 semiannually for 20 periods at the current 6% market rate as follows:

Present value of $100,000 to be received 20 periods hence, discounted
  at 3% per period ($100,000 × 0.5537) .... $ 55,370
Present value of $3,500 to be received periodically for 20 periods,
  discounted at 3% ($3,500 × 14.878)... 52,073
Present value of the bond investment $107,443

And the informed investor will offer the corporation $107,443 for its bonds. If the corporation accepts and sells the bonds on their date of issue, say, May 1, 1976, it will record the sale as follows:

May	1	Cash	107,443.00	
		Premium on Bonds Payable...................		7,443.00
		Bonds Payable		100,000.00
		Sold bonds at a premium on their date of issue.		

It may then show the bonds on a balance sheet prepared on the day of the sale as follows:

Long-Term Liabilities:
  First mortgage, 7% bonds payable, due May 1, 1986 .... $100,000
    Add unamortized premium based on the 6% market rate
      for bond interest prevailing on the date of issue............   7,443 $107,443

On a balance sheet any unamortized premium on bonds payable is added to the par value of the bonds to show the carrying amount of the bonds, as illustrated.

Amortizing the premium

Although the corporation discussed here received $107,443 for its bonds, it will have to repay only $100,000 to the bondholders at maturity. The difference, the $7,443 premium, represents a reduction in the cost of using the $107,443, which should be amortized over the life of the bond issue in such a manner as to lower the recorded bond interest expense. If the $7,443 premium is amortized by the interest method, Illustration 19–3 shows the amounts of interest expense to be recorded each period, the premium to be amortized, et cetera.

Observe in Illustration 19–3 that the premium to be amortized each period is determined by subtracting the interest to be recorded from the interest to be paid the bondholders.

Based on Illustration 19–3, the entry to record the first interest payment and premium amortization is:

Nov.	1	Bond Interest Expense....................................	3,223.00	
		Premium on Bonds Payable	277.00	
		Cash..		3,500.00
		To record payment of the bondholders and amortization of a portion of the premium.		

Note how the amortization of the premium results in a reduction in the amount of interest expense recorded. Similar entries having decreasing amounts of interest expense and increasing amounts of premium amortized are made at the ends of the remaining periods in the life of the bond issue.

Pe-riod	Beginning-of-Period Carrying Amount	Interest Expense to Be Recorded	Interest to Be Paid the Bondholders	Premium to Be Amortized	Unamortized Premium at End of Period	End-of-Period Carrying Amount
1	$107,443	$3,223	$3,500	$277	$7,166	$107,166
2	107,166	3,215	3,500	285	6,881	106,881
3	106,881	3,206	3,500	294	6,587	106,587
4	106,587	3,198	3,500	302	6,285	106,285
5	106,285	3,189	3,500	311	5,974	105,974
6	105,974	3,179	3,500	321	5,653	105,653
7	105,653	3,170	3,500	330	5,323	105,323
8	105,323	3,160	3,500	340	4,983	104,983
9	104,983	3,149	3,500	351	4,632	104,632
10	104,632	3,139	3,500	361	4,271	104,271
11	104,271	3,128	3,500	372	3,899	103,899
12	103,899	3,117	3,500	383	3,516	103,516
13	103,516	3,105	3,500	395	3,121	103,121
14	103,121	3,094	3,500	406	2,715	102,715
15	102,715	3,081	3,500	419	2,296	102,296
16	102,296	3,069	3,500	431	1,865	101,865
17	101,865	3,056	3,500	444	1,421	101,421
18	101,421	3,043	3,500	457	964	100,964
19	100,964	3,029	3,500	471	493	100,493
20	100,493	3,007*	3,500	493	-0-	100,000

*Adjusted to compensate for accumulated rounding of amounts.

Illustration
19–3

Accrued bond interest expense

■ Often when bonds are sold the bond interest periods do not coincide with the issuing company's accounting periods. In such cases it is necessary at the end of each accounting period to make an adjustment for accrued interest. For example, it was assumed that the bonds of Illustration 19–3 were issued on May 1, 1976, and interest was paid on these bonds on November 1 of that year. If the accounting periods of the corporation issuing these bonds end each December 31, on December 31, 1976, two months' interest has accrued on these bonds, and the following adjusting entry is required:

Dec.	31	Bond Interest Expense....................................	1,071.67	
		Premium on Bonds Payable	95.00	
		Bond Interest Payable..............................		1,166.67
		To record two months' accrued interest and amortize one third of the premium applicable to the interest period.		

Two months are one third of a semiannual interest period; consequently, the bond interest and premium amortized in the entry are each one third of the amounts applicable to the second interest period in the life of the bond issue. Similar entries will be made on each December 31 throughout the life of the issue; however, the amounts will differ, since in each case they will apply to a different interest period.

When the interest is paid on these bonds on May 1, 1977, an entry like this is required:

May	1	Bond Interest Expense...................................	2,143.33	
		Bond Interest Payable....................................	1,166.67	
		Premium on Bonds Payable	190.00	
		Cash..		3,500.00
		Paid the interest on the bonds, a portion of which was previously accrued, and amortized four months' premium.		

Sale of bonds by investors ■ A purchaser of a bond may not hold it to maturity but may sell it after a period of months or years to a new investor at a price which is determined by the market rate for bond interest on the day of the sale. The current market rate for bond interest determines the price because the new investor can get the current rate elsewhere for the use of his money. Therefore, he will discount the right to receive the bond's face amount at maturity and the right to receive its interest for the remaining periods in its life at the current market rate to determine the price he will pay for the bond. As a result, since bond interest rates may vary greatly over a period of months or years, a bond that originally sold at a premium may later sell at a discount, and vice versa.

Redemption of bonds ■ Bonds are commonly issued with the provision that they may be redeemed at the issuing corporation's option, usually upon the payment of a redemption premium. Such bonds are known as *callable bonds*. Corporations commonly insert redemption clauses in deeds of trust because if interest rates decline, it may be advantageous to call and redeem outstanding bonds and issue in their place new bonds paying a lower interest rate.

Not all bonds have a provision giving their issuing company the right to call. However, even though the right is not provided, a company may secure the same effect by purchasing its bonds on the open market and retiring them. Often such action is wise when a company has funds available and its bonds are selling at a price below their carrying amount. For example, a company has outstanding on their interest date $1,000,000 of bonds on which there is $12,000 unamortized premium. The bonds are selling at $98\frac{1}{2}\%$ of par value, and the company decides to buy and retire one tenth of the issue. The entry to record the purchase and retirement is:

Apr.	1	Bonds Payable	100,000.00	
		Premium on Bonds Payable.........................	1,200.00	
		Gain on the Retirement of Bonds		2,700.00
		Cash..		98,500.00
		To record the retirement of bonds.		

The retirement resulted in a $2,700 gain in this instance because the bonds were purchased at a price $2,700 below their carrying amount.

Back a paragraph the statement was made that the bonds were selling at 98½% of par value. Bond quotations are commonly made in this manner. For example, a bond may be quoted for sale at 101¼. This means the bond is for sale at 101¼% of its par value, plus accrued interest, of course, if applicable.

Convertible bonds ■ To make an issue more attractive, bond owners may be given the right to exchange their bonds for a fixed number of shares of the issuing company's common stock. Such bonds are known as convertible bonds. They offer investors initial investment security and, if the issuing company prospers, an opportunity to share in the prosperity by converting their bonds to stock. Conversion is always at the bondholders' option and is not exercised except when to do so is to their advantage.

When bonds are converted into stock, the conversion changes creditor equity into ownership equity. The generally accepted rule for measuring the contribution for the issued shares is that the carrying amount of the converted bonds becomes the book value of the capital contributed for the new shares. For example, assume that (1) a company has outstanding $1,000,000 of bonds upon which there is $8,000 unamortized discount; (2) the bonds are convertible at the rate of a $1,000 bond for 90 shares of $10 par value common stock; and (3) $100,000 in bonds have been presented on their interest date for conversion. The entry to record the conversion is:

May	1	Bonds Payable	100,000.00	
		Discount on Bonds Payable		800.00
		Common Stock.....................................		90,000.00
		Premium on Common Stock		9,200.00
		To record the conversion of bonds.		

Note in this entry that the bonds' $99,200 carrying amount sets the accounting value for the capital contributed. Usually when bonds have a conversion privilege, it is not exercised until the stock's market value and normal dividend payments are sufficiently high to make the conversion profitable to the bondholders.

Bond sinking fund ■ Because of their fixed return and greater security, bonds appeal to a portion of the investing public. Security is usually important to bond investors. A corporation issuing bonds may offer investors a measure of security by placing a mortgage on certain of its assets. Often it will give additional security by agreeing in its deed of trust to create a *bond sinking fund,* which is a fund of assets accumulated to pay the bondholders at maturity.

When a corporation issuing bonds agrees to create a bond sinking fund, it normally agrees to create the fund by making periodic cash deposits with a sinking fund trustee. It is the duty of the trustee to safeguard the cash, to invest it in good sound securities, and to add the interest or dividends earned to the sinking fund. Generally, when the bonds become due, it is also the duty of the sinking fund trustee to sell the sinking fund securities and to use the proceeds to pay the bondholders.

When a sinking fund is created, the amount that must be deposited periodically in order to provide enough money to retire a bond issue at maturity will depend upon the net rate of compound interest that can be earned on the invested funds. The rate is a compound rate because earnings are continually reinvested by the sinking fund trustee to earn an additional return, and it is a net rate because the trustee commonly deducts the fee for its services from the earnings.

To illustrate the operation of a sinking fund, assume a corporation issues $1,000,000 of 10-year bonds and agrees to deposit with a sinking fund trustee at the end of each year in the issue's life sufficient cash to create a fund large enough to retire the bonds at maturity. If the trustee is able to invest the funds in such a manner as to earn a 5% net return, $79,504 must be deposited each year and the fund will grow to maturity (in rounded dollars) as shown in Illustration 19–4.

End of Year	Amount Deposited	Interest Earned on Fund Balance	Balance in Fund after Deposit and Interest
1	$79,504	-0-	$ 79,504
2	79,504	$ 3,975	162,983
3	79,504	8,149	250,636
4	79,504	12,532	342,672
5	79,504	17,134	439,310
6	79,504	21,966	540,780
7	79,504	27,039	647,323
8	79,504	32,366	759,193
9	79,504	37,960	876,657
10	79,504	43,839*	1,000,000

Illustration
19–4

* Adjusted for rounding.

When a sinking fund is created by periodic deposits, the entry to record the amount deposited each year appears as follows:

Dec.	31	Bond Sinking Fund	79,504.00	
		Cash..		79,504.00
		Deposited cash with sinking fund trustee.		

Each year the sinking fund trustee invests the amount deposited, and each year it collects and reports the earnings on the investments. The earnings report results in a journal entry to record the sinking fund income. For example, if $79,504 is deposited at the end of the first year in the sinking fund, the accumulation of which is shown in Illustration 19–4, and 5% is earned, the entry to record the sinking fund earnings at the end of the second year is:

Dec.	31	Bond Sinking Fund	3,975.00	
		Sinking Fund Earnings		3,975.00
		To record the sinking fund earnings.		

Sinking fund earnings appear on the income statement as financial revenue in the "other revenues and expenses section."

The assets resulting from sinking fund earnings, as well as sinking fund deposits and sinking fund investments, in other words, the items making up a sinking fund, are the property of the company creating the fund and should appear on its balance sheet in the long-term investments section, as in Illustration 19–5.

When bonds mature, it is usually the duty of the sinking fund trustee to convert the fund's investments into cash and pay the bondholders. Normally the sinking fund securities, when sold, produce either a little more or a little less cash than is needed to pay the bondholders. If more cash than is needed is produced, the extra cash is returned to the corporation; and if less cash is produced than is needed, the corporation must make up the deficiency. For example, if the securities in the sinking fund of a $1,000,000 bond issue produce $1,001,325 when converted to cash, the trustee will use $1,000,000 to pay the bondholders and will return the extra $1,325 to the corporation. The corporation will then record the payment of its bonds and the return of the extra cash with an entry like this:

Jan.	3	Cash..	1,325.00	
		Bonds Payable	1,000,000.00	
		Bonds Sinking Fund		1,001,325.00
		To record payment of our bonds and the return of extra cash from the sinking fund.		

Best Limited
Balance Sheet, December 31, 19—

ASSETS

Current Assets:

Cash			$ 15,000
Able Corporation common stock			5,000
Accounts receivable		$ 50,000	
Less allowance for doubtful accounts		1,000	49,000
Merchandise inventory			115,000
Subscriptions receivable, common stock			15,000
Prepaid expenses			1,000
Total Current Assets				$200,000

Long-Term Investments:

Bond sinking fund		$ 15,000	
Toledo Corporation common stock		5,000	
Total Long-Term Investments			20,000

Plant Assets:

Land		$ 28,000	
Buildings	$190,000		
Less accumulated depreciation	30,000	160,000	
Store equipment	$ 85,000		
Less accumulated depreciation	20,000	65,000	
Total Plant Assets			253,000

Intangible Assets:

Goodwill		23,000

Deferred Charges:

Unamortized moving costs		4,000
Total Assets		$500,000

LIABILITIES

Current Liabilities:

Notes payable		$ 10,000	
Accounts payable		24,000	
Income taxes payable		16,000	
Total Current Liabilities			$ 50,000

Long-Term Liabilities:

First 6% real estate mortgage bonds, due in 1990		$100,000	
Less unamortized discount based on the 7% market rate for bond interest prevailing on the date of issue		2,000	98,000
Total Liabilities			$148,000

SHAREHOLDERS' EQUITY

Contributed Capital:

Common stock, $100 par value per share, authorized 2,500 shares, issued 2,000 shares		$200,000	
Unissued common stock subscribed, 250 shares		25,000	
Capital contributed by the shareholders in excess of the par value of their shares		33,000	
Total Contributed Capital			$258,000

Retained Earnings:

Appropriated retained earnings:

Appropriated for bonded indebtedness	$15,000		
Appropriated for plant expansion	10,000	$ 25,000	
Unappropriated retained earnings		69,000	
Total Retained Earnings			94,000
Shareholders' Equity			352,000
Total Liabilities and Shareholders' Equity			$500,000

Illustration
19–5

Restriction on dividends due to outstanding bonds

■ If a corporation disburses in dividends all assets acquired each year through earnings and pays out still more assets in sinking fund deposits, it may find itself within a few years without sufficient assets, particularly current assets, to operate and unable either to pay dividends or make sinking fund deposits. To prevent this, a deed of trust may restrict the dividends a corporation may pay while its bonds are outstanding. Commonly the restriction provides that the corporation may pay dividends in any year only to the extent that the year's earnings exceed sinking fund requirements.

The corporation balance sheet

■ Corporation balance sheets are normally longer and more complicated than those of either single proprietorships or partnerships. In this and the three previous chapters a number of isolated corporation balance sheet sections have been illustrated. In order to bring all of these together, the balance sheet of Best Limited is shown in Illustration 19–5.

Observe the treatment of the bond sinking fund in Illustration 19–5. A bond sinking fund belongs to the corporation creating such a fund and appears on its balance sheet as a long-term investment. Observe also the treatment of the unamortized discount on the bonds payable. When a balance sheet is prepared, discount on outstanding bonds is subtracted thereon from the par value of the bonds. Had there been a premium on these bonds, it would have been added to the par value.

STOCKS AND BONDS AS INVESTMENTS

■ The stock and bond transactions illustrated thus far have been transactions in which a corporation sold and issued its own stocks and bonds. Such transactions represent only a very small portion of the daily transactions in stocks and bonds. The great daily volume of security sales are transactions between investors, some investors selling and other investors buying, with the transactions taking place through brokers who charge a commission for their services.

Brokers acting as agents for their customers buy and sell stocks and bonds on stock exchanges such as the Toronto Stock Exchange. Five million or more shares of stock and several thousand bonds are bought and sold each day, and each day the prices at which sales occurred are published on the financial pages of many newspapers. Stock prices are quoted on the basis of dollars and $\frac{1}{8}$ dollars per share. For example, a stock quoted at $46\frac{1}{8}$ sold for $46.125 per share, and stock quoted at $25\frac{1}{2}$ sold for $25.50 per share. Bonds are normally issued in $1,000 denominations, but their prices are quoted on a percentage basis. For example, a $1,000 bond quoted at $98\frac{1}{8}$ sold at $98\frac{1}{8}\%$ of $1,000, or $981.25, and a $1,000 bond quoted at $86\frac{1}{4}$ sold for $862.50.

A corporation issuing bonds normally sells them to an underwriter who bids a price based on the present value of the bond returns. The underwriter then offers the bonds to the public at a markup and at a price usually quoted at a percentage of the par value of the bonds.

Classifying investments

■ Stocks and bonds should be classified as current assets only if capable of reasonably prompt liquidation. Such investments appear on the balance sheet under the caption of *temporary investments* or *marketable securities*. They may be held for a number of years, but this is not important. The important point is that in case of need they may quickly be turned into cash without interfering with the normal operations of the business. Such investments appear on the balance sheet immediately following cash. Temporary investments are normally carried at cost with disclosure of their market value. Where the market value has declined below the carrying value by a significant amount, the securities should be carried at market value.

Investments that are not intended as a ready source of cash in case of need are classified as *long-term investments*. They include funds earmarked for special purposes, such as bond sinking funds, as well as land or other assets owned but not employed in the regular operations of the business. They also include shares of stock held for purpose of controlling another corporation or for maintaining good customer relations, or for any other reason that would make their sale inadvisable.

Long-term investments appear on the balance sheet in a classification of their own titled "Long-term investments," which is placed immediately following the current asset section, as in Illustration 19–5. Since there is no intention to sell, long-term investments are normally carried at cost, or in case of bonds, at cost adjusted for premium or discount amortized and temporary declines below the carrying value are ignored. If a loss in value of an investment is other than a temporary decline, the investment should be written down to recognize the loss.

Accounting for stocks as investments

■ When a corporation purchases sufficient outstanding voting shares of another corporation to effectively influence or control its operations, the equity method should be used in accounting for the investment. This method of accounting for an investment was described in Chapter 18; consequently, attention is given here to investments which do not result in effective control of another corporation. Investments of this nature are designated by the CICA as "Portfolio Investments."

When a corporation's voting stock is purchased as either a short- or long-term investment, the purchase is recorded at total cost, which includes the commission paid the broker. For example, 1,000 shares of Canadian Sales Corporation common stock were purchased as an investment at $23\frac{1}{4}$ plus a $300 broker's commission. The entry to record the transaction is:

Sept.	10	Canadian Sales Corporation Stock...................	23,550.00	
		Cash..		23,550.00
		Purchased 1,000 shares of stock for $23,250 plus a $300 broker's commission.		

Observe that nothing is said about a premium or a discount on the Canadian Sales Corporation stock. Nothing is said because stock premiums and discounts apply only when stock is first issued. They do not apply to sales and purchases between investors.

When a portfolio investment of a corporation's voting stock is held as either a short- or long-term investment and a dividend is received on the stock, an entry similar to the following is made:

Oct.	5	Cash...	1,000.00	
		Dividends Earned....................................		1,000.00
		Received a $1 per share dividend on the Canadian Sales Corporation stock.		

Dividends on stocks do not accrue; consequently, an end-of-the accounting-period entry to record accrued dividends is never made. However, if a balance sheet is prepared after a dividend is declared but before it is paid, an entry debiting Dividends Receivable and crediting Dividends Earned should be made.

A dividend in shares of stock is not income, and a debit and credit entry recording it should not be made. However, a memorandum entry or a notation as to the additional shares should be made in the investment account. Also, receipt of the stock does affect the per share cost basis of the old shares. For example, if a 20-share dividend is received on 100 shares originally purchased for $1,500 or at $15 per share, the cost of all 120 shares is $1,500 and the cost per share is $12.50 ($1,500 ÷ 120 shares = $12.50 per share).

When an investment of a corporation's stock is sold, normally a gain or a loss is incurred. If the amount received is greater than the original cost of the investment plus the commission on the sale and other costs, there is a gain. For example, if the 1,000 shares of Canadian Sales Corporation common stock, the purchase of which at $23,550 was previously recorded, are sold at 25¾ less a commission and taxes on the sale amounting to $315, there is a $1,885 gain, and the transaction is recorded:

Jan.	7	Cash...	25,435.00	
		Canadian Sales Corporation Stock..............		23,550.00
		Gain on the Sale of Investments		1,885.00
		Sold 1,000 shares of stock for $25,750 less a $315 commission and other costs.		

If the net amount received for these shares had been less than their $23,550 cost, there would have been a loss on the transaction.

Accounting for bonds as investments

■ Bonds like stocks are purchased as investments, but they differ in that interest accrues on bonds and must be accounted for. Earlier in this chapter it was pointed out that all bond transactions are "plus accrued interest." Consequently, when a bond is quoted between interest dates at $101\frac{1}{2}$, it means the bond is for sale at $101\frac{1}{2}$ plus accrued interest. The purchaser pays accrued interest to the seller, and if he in turn sells between interest dates, he collects accrued interest from the next buyer.

Bonds as short-term investments

Bonds purchased as short-term investments are accounted for at cost, which includes any commission paid a broker. Also, generally there is accrued interest to be accounted for as a separate item. For example, if six Zoom Corporation, $1,000, $7\frac{1}{2}\%$ bonds paying interest on each January 1 and July 1 are purchased as a temporary investment on May 1 at $102\frac{1}{2}$ plus a $15 commission and accrued interest, the cost of the bonds is $6,165 [($1,025 \times 6) + $15 = $6,165], and the four months' accrued interest amounts to $150 ($6,000 \times .075 \times 4/12 = $150). Consequently the entry to record the purchase is:

May	1	Zoom Corporation Bonds..............................	6,165.00	
		Bond Interest Earned..	150.00	
		Cash...		6,315.00
		Purchased six bonds at $102\frac{1}{2}$ plus accrued interest and a $15 commission.		

Observe in the entry that the premium on the bonds, which includes the commission, is not treated as a separate item but is included in the debit to the bond investment account. However, the accrued interest is accounted for as a separate item.

On July 1, if the purchaser of the previous entry still holds these bonds, he will collect six months' interest on them, of which $150 is a return of the interest paid the previous holder when the bonds were bought and $75 is interest earned since their purchase. The receipt of the six months' interest is recorded as follows:

July	1	Cash..	225.00	
		Bond Interest Earned..............................		225.00
		Received six months' interest on the Zoom Corporation bonds.		

The net effect of the illustrated two entries on the Bond Interest Earned account is a $75 credit, which is the amount of interest earned by the buyer during the two months he has held the bonds.

Observe in the last entry that in accounting for the interest on the Zoom Corporation bonds the premium on their purchase is ignored. This is the common practice. When bonds are purchased as a short-term investment, since they are not to be held to maturity, the discount or premium on their purchase is seldom amortized.

If the buyer of these bonds holds them until August 1 and then sells them at 101½, plus accrued interest and less a $15 commission, the entry for the sale is:

Aug.	1	Cash..	6,112.50	
		Loss on Sale of Investments...........................	90.00	
		Bond Interest Earned...............................		37.50
		Zoom Corporation Bonds..........................		6,165.00
		Sold six bonds at 101½ plus accrued interest and less a $15 commission.		

At 101½, less the commission, the bonds sold for $6,090 less $15, or for $6,075, net; consequently, there was $90 loss on their sale. Also, one month's interest, $37.50, had accrued and was collected from the new purchaser. If the amount received for the bonds had been greater than $6,165, there would have been a gain on the transaction.

Bonds as long-term investments

Bonds may be purchased as a long-term investment; and when they are, they are accounted for in the same manner as bonds bought for a short-term investment, with one exception. The exception has to do with accounting for interest earned. Here, since the bonds may be held to maturity, a portion of the premium or discount, if material, is amortized at the time of each interest receipt.

For example, 10 Zest Corporation, $1,000, 6.6% bonds were purchased on their interest date, January 1, 197A, five years before maturity. The market rate for bond interest on that date was 7%, and the bonds were bought at 98 plus $35 of commission and other costs. At 98 plus the other costs, the bonds cost $9,835 [(10 × $980) + $35 = $9,835]; and since the bonds were purchased on their interest date, there was no accrued interest. Consequently, the entry to record the purchase is:

Jan.	1	Zest Corporation Bonds................................	9,835.00	
		Cash..		9,835.00
		Purchased 10 bonds on their interest date at 98 plus $35 of commission and other costs.		

Note that the bond investment account is debited for the cost of the bonds and the discount is not treated as a separate item.

As previously stated, bonds differ from stocks in that sooner or later they mature and are normally redeemed at par. Consequently, if the Zest Corporation bonds are held to maturity and are redeemed at par, they will produce 6.6% interest each year plus the $165 difference between their cost and maturity value. In accounting for these bonds as a long-term investment, the $165 difference, although a combination of discount, commission, and other costs, is called a discount and is amortized over the remaining life of the bonds as an adjustment of the bond interest earned. If it is amortized by the interest method, the entry to record the interest received and the discount amortized at the time of the first semiannual interest receipt is:

July	1	Cash..	330.00	
		Zest Corporation Bonds................................	14.00	
		Bond Interest Earned................................		344.00
		Received the semiannual interest on the Zest Corporation bonds and amortized a portion of the discount.		

The entry's $14 debit to the bond investment account increases the carrying amount of the bonds, and after it is posted the bond investment account appears as follows:

Zest Corporation Bonds

Date	Explanation	Debit	Credit	Balance
Jan. 1, 197A	Purchase	9,835.00		9,835.00
July 1, 197A	Discount amortization	14.00		9,849.00

If the correct amounts are amortized each interest period and the bonds are held to maturity, when they mature, they will appear in the bond investment account at their full $10,000 maturity value.

Bonds purchased as long-term investments may be sold before maturity. If the Zest Corporation bonds are held three years and then sold, the bond investment account just prior to the sale will show a $9,928 carrying amount for the bonds and will appear as follows:

Zest Corporation Bonds

Date	Explanation	Debit	Credit	Balance
Jan. 1, 197A	Purchase	9,835.00		9,835.00
July 1, 197A	Discount amortization	14.00		9,849.00
Jan. 1, 197B	Discount amortization	15.00		9,864.00
July 1, 197B	Discount amortization	15.00		9,879.00
Jan. 1, 197C	Discount amortization	16.00		9,895.00
July 1, 197C	Discount amortization	16.00		9,911.00
Jan. 1, 197D	Discount amortization	17.00		9,928.00

If the bonds are sold after three years for $9,975 less $35 of commission and other costs, the entry to record the sale is:

Jan.	1	Cash..	9,940.00	
		Zest Corporation Bonds............................		9,928.00
		Gain on Sale of Investments......................		12.00
		Sold Zest Corporation bonds at 99¾ less		
		$35 of commission and other costs.		

Bonds may be purchased as a long-term investment at a cost greater than their maturity value. In such a case the bonds are recorded at cost and the difference between cost and maturity value, called a premium, is commonly treated as an adjustment to the interest earned and amortized over the remaining life of the bonds.

Questions for class discussion

1. What two legal documents are involved when a company borrows by giving a mortgage? What is the purpose of each?
2. What is the primary difference between a share of stock and a bond?
3. What is a deed of trust? What are some of the provisions commonly contained in a deed of trust?
4. Define or describe: (a) registered bonds, (b) coupon bonds, (c) serial bonds, (d) sinking fund bonds, (e) callable bonds, (f) convertible bonds, and (g) debenture bonds.
5. Why does a corporation issuing bonds between interest dates charge and collect accrued interest from the purchasers of the bonds?
6. As it relates to a bond issue, what is the meaning of the phrase "contract rate of interest"? As it relates to bonds, what is the meaning of the phrase "market rate for bond interest"?
7. What determines bond interest rates?
8. Convertible bonds are very popular with investors. Why?
9. If a $1,000 bond is sold at 98¼, at what price is it sold? If a $1,000 bond is sold at 101½, at what price is it sold?
10. If the quoted price for a bond is 97¾, does this include accrued interest?
11. What purpose is served by creating a bond sinking fund?
12. How are bond sinking funds classified for balance sheet purposes?
13. What is the balance sheet classification of securities purchased as (a) a short-term investment and (b) a long-term investment? What are the characteristics of (c) a short-term investment in securities and of (d) a long-term investment in securities?
14. What is a common difference in accounting for bonds as a short-term investment and accounting for bonds as a long-term investment?

Class exercises

Exercise 19-1

On May 1, 197A, a corporation sold at par plus accrued interest $1,000,000 of its 7.2% bonds. The bonds were dated January 1, 197A, and paid interest on each July 1 and January 1. *(a)* Give the entry to record the sale. *(b)* Give the entry to record the first interest payment. *(c)* Set up a T-account for Bond Interest Expense and post the portions of the entries that affect the account. Answer these questions: *(d)* How many months' interest were accrued on these bonds when they were sold? *(e)* How many months' interest were paid on July 1? *(f)* What is the balance of the Bond Interest Expense account after the entry recording the first interest payment is posted? *(g)* How many months' interest does this balance represent? *(h)* How many months' interest did the bondholders earn during the first interest period?

Exercise 19–2

On March 1, 197A, a corporation sold $1,000,000 of its 6.8%, 10-year bonds. The bonds were dated March 1, 197A, and paid interest on each September 1 and March 1. *(a)* Give the entries to record the sale at $98\frac{1}{4}$ and the first semiannual interest payment under the assumption $475 of discount was amortized. *(b)* Give the entry to record the sale at 101 and the first semiannual interest payment under the assumption $400 of premium was amortized.

Exercise 19–3

On January 1, 197A, a corporation sold $1,000,000 of its 7%, 10-year bonds at $99\frac{1}{2}$. The bonds were dated January 1, 197A, and paid interest on each July 1, and January 1. On January 1, five years later, after the bond interest for the period had been paid and after 40% of the total discount on the issue had been amortized, the corporation purchased $100,000 of the bonds on the open market at $98\frac{1}{4}$ and retired them. Give the entry to record the retirement.

Exercise 19–4

Assume that the bonds of Exercise 19–3 could be converted into the issuing company's $10 par value common stock at the rate of 90 shares of stock for each $1,000 bond. Also, assume that on January 1, five years after the bonds were issued and after 40% of the discount had been amortized, bondholders converted $100,000 of their bonds to common stock. Give the entry to record the conversion.

Exercise 19–5

Prepare general journal entries to record these transactions:

Jan. 12 Purchased 500 shares of West Corporation $10 par value common stock, paying $21\frac{1}{2}$ plus a $110 commission.

Mar. 15 Received a $0.25 per share dividend on the West Corporation stock.

June 18 Received a 100-share stock dividend on the West Corporation stock.

20 Sold the 100 shares of West Corporation stock received as a dividend on June 18, receiving $20\frac{1}{2}$ less a $20 commission.

Exercise 19–6

Prepare general journal entries to record these transactions:

Feb. 1 Purchased as a short-term investment six East Corporation, $1,000, 7%, 20-year bonds on which interest is payable each January 1 and July 1. The purchase price was $98\frac{1}{2}$ plus one month's accrued interest and a $15 commission.

July 1 Received the semiannual interest on the East Corporation bonds.

Oct. 1 Sold the East Corporation bonds at $100\frac{1}{2}$ plus three months' accrued interest and less a $15 commission.

Exercise 19–7

Prepare general journal entries to record these transactions:

197A

July 1 Purchased as a long-term investment 10 Boat Corporation, $1,000, 7½% 20-year bonds on their interest date five years before maturity, paying 101¾ plus a $30 commission, a total price that would return 7% on the investment.

197B

Jan. 1 Received the semiannual interest on the Boat Corporation bonds and amortized $18 of the purchase premium.

July 1 After receiving and recording the semiannual interest and amortizing $18 of the purchase premium, changed the investment policy toward the Boat Corporation bonds and sold them at 101 less a $30 commission.

Problems **Problem 19–1**

A corporation is presently earning a 20% before-tax return on its stockholders' equity, which is:

STOCKHOLDERS' EQUITY

Common stock, $10 par value, 200,000 shares authorized, 100,000 shares issued	$1,000,000
Premium on common stock	250,000
Retained earnings	550,000
Total Stockholders' Equity	$1,800,000

The corporation's directors are of the opinion that if an additional $2,000,000 were invested in the business, it could earn not only a 20% return on its present stockholders' equity but also a 20% return on the additional $2,000,000, before any bond interest or income taxes, of course. Furthermore, the directors are considering three plans to secure the $2,000,000. They are:

Plan 1. Issue the corporation's 100,000 shares of authorized but unissued $10 par value common stock at $20 per share.

Plan 2. Secure an authorization and issue 20,000 shares of $100 par value, 7½% cumulative and nonparticipating, preferred stock.

Plan 3. Sell $2,000,000 of 7%, 20-year bonds at par.

Required:

1. Prepare a calculation to show the earnings per share that will accrue to the corporation's present stockholders under each plan. (Assume a 50% income tax rate.)

2. In the situation described here the total earnings available to the common stockholders are $80,000 greater each year if bonds rather than preferred stock are issued. Explain why the total earnings available to the common stockholders are $80,000 greater each year when the difference between the bond interest and the preferred dividends is only $10,000 annually.

Problem 19–2

PART 1. A corporation completed these bond transactions:

197A

Jan. 1 Sold $1,000,000 of its own 6.8%, 10-year bonds dated January 1, 197A, with interest payable on each June 30 and December 31. The bonds sold for $985,808 cash, a price that would yield the buyers a 7% annual return on their investment.

June 30 Paid the semiannual interest on the bonds and amortized a portion of the discount calculated by the interest method.

Dec. 31 Paid the semiannual interest on the bonds and amortized a portion of the discount calculated by the interest method.

Required:

Prepare general journal entries to record the transactions. Round the discount amortized each interest period to the nearest whole dollar.

PART 2. A corporation completed these bond transactions:

197A

Apr. 1 Sold $1,000,000 of its own 7.2%, 10-year bonds dated April 1, 197A, with interest payable on each October 1 and April 1. The bonds sold for $1,014,232 cash, a price to yield the buyers a 7% annual return.

Oct. 1 Paid the semiannual interest on the bonds and amortized $502 of the premium.

Dec. 31 Made an adjusting entry to record the accrued interest on the bonds and amortize a portion of the premium. (Assume that $520 of premium is applicable to the entire second interest period of this bond issue.)

197B

Apr. 1 Paid the semiannual interest on the bonds and amortized a portion of the premium.

Required:

Prepare general journal entries to record the transactions.

Problem 19–3

On July 15, 197A, a corporation deposited a deed of trust with the trustee of its bondholders that authorized it to issue $1,000,000 of 7½%, 10-year convertible bonds dated August 1, 197A, with interest payable each February 1 and August 1. The conversion clause in the deed of trust granted the bondholders the right to convert their bonds into shares of the company's common stock at the rate of 80 shares of $10 par value stock for each $1,000 bond. The corporation then completed these transactions:

197A

Aug. 1 Sold the entire issue to an underwriter for $966,000 cash, a price that would yield the buyer an 8% annual return on the investment.

Dec. 31 Made an adjusting entry to record the accrued interest on the bonds and to amortize five sixths of the discount applicable to the first semiannual interest period. The interest method was used in amortizing the discount.

197B

Feb. 1 Paid the semiannual interest on the bonds and amortized the remainder of the discount applicable to the first semiannual interest period.

Aug. 1 Paid the semiannual interest on the bonds and amortized the discount applicable to the second interest period.

197E

Feb. 1 After recording the entry paying the semiannual interest on the bonds on this date and amortizing a portion of the discount, the bonds were carried on the books at $975,000. At this point the corporation purchased on the open market and retired bonds having a $100,000 par value. The total cash outlay was $96,750.

1 On the same day it purchased and retired $100,000 of its outstanding bonds, the corporation converted bonds having a $100,000 par value to common stock.

Required:

Prepare general journal entries to record the transactions. Round amounts of bond interest expense recorded to the nearest whole dollar.

Problem 19–4

A corporation deposited a deed of trust with the trustee of its bondholders on December 12, 197A, which authorized it to issue $1,000,000 of 6.8%, four-year bonds dated January 1, 197B, with interest payable annually on each December 31 throughout the life of the issue. (Four years are an unrealistically small number of years for a bond issue, and annual interest payments are not common; however, by using a four-year life and annual interest payments, all entries for a bond issue and a bond sinking fund may be required without the necessity of many repetitive entries.)

In the deed of trust the corporation agreed to create a bond sinking fund by depositing with a trustee $228,600 at the end of each year in the life of the bond issue. It was assumed the sinking fund investments would earn approximately 6% net and the fund would grow to maturity as follows:

End of—	Amount Deposited	Interest Earned on Fund Balance	Balance in Fund after Deposit and Interest
197B	$228,600	–0–	$ 228,600
197C	228,600	$13,710	470,910
197D	228,600	28,240	727,750
197E	228,600	43,650	1,000,000

After depositing the deed of trust, the corporation completed these transactions:

197B

Jan. 1 Sold the entire issue to an underwriter for $993,230 cash, a price that would yield the buyer a 7% annual return on the investment.

Dec. 31 Paid the annual interest on the bonds and amortized a portion of the discount based on the following information:

	197B	197C	197D	197E
Beginning-of-period carrying amount......	$993,230	$994,756	$996,389	$ 998,136
Interest expense to be recorded............	69,526	69,633	69,747	69,864
Interest to be paid bondholders.............	68,000	68,000	68,000	68,000
Discount to be amortized.....................	1,526	1,633	1,747	1,864
End-of-period carrying amount	994,756	996,389	998,136	1,000,000

31 Made the first annual sinking fund deposit.

197C

Dec. 31 Paid the annual interest on the bonds and amortized a portion of the discount.

31 Received the sinking fund trustee's report showing the sinking fund had earned $13,710 during the year.

31 Made the second annual sinking fund deposit.

197D

Dec. 31 Paid the interest on the bonds and amortized a portion of the discount.

31 Received the sinking fund trustee's report showing the sinking fund had earned $28,315. (This is slightly more than was anticipated the fund would earn. However, it is not enough to warrant a change in the deposit required of the corporation.)

31 Made the third annual sinking fund deposit.

197E

Dec. 31 Paid the interest on the bonds and amortized a portion of the discount.

31 Received the sinking fund trustee's report showing the sinking fund had earned $43,625.

31 Made the fourth annual sinking fund deposit.

197F

Jan. 10 Received a report from the sinking fund trustee showing the bonds had been paid in full. Attached to the report was a cheque for the excess earnings in the sinking fund.

Required:
Prepare general journal entries to record the transactions.

Problem 19-5

Prepare general journal entries to record these transactions:

197A

Feb. 1 Purchased as a long-term investment to yield a 7% annual return 10 Morgan Corporation, $1,000, 7½%, 20-year bonds on their interest date five years before maturity, the total purchase price was $10,200.

11 Purchased as a temporary investment 1,000 shares of Gage Corporation, $5 par value common stock, paying 11⅛ plus a $106 commission. The purchase represented less than 1% of the corporation's voting shares.

Mar. 19 Received a $0.20 per share quarterly dividend on the Gage Corporation common stock.

May 15 Received a 100-share common stock dividend from Gage Corporation.

18 Sold the 100 shares of Gage Corporation common stock received as a dividend in the previous transaction, receiving 10¾ less a $11 commission.

June 10 Sold the remaining Gage Corporation common stock at $10\frac{1}{4}$ less a $100 commission.

Aug. 1 Received a cheque for the semiannual interest on the Morgan Corporation bonds and amortized $18 of the premium.

Oct. 1 Purchased as a temporary investment 10 Dale Corporation, $1,000, 6.6%, 25-year bonds on which interest is payable each June 1 and December 1. The purchase price was $97\frac{1}{2}$ plus a $25 commission and four months' accrued interest.

Dec. 1 Received the semiannual interest on the Dale Corporation bonds.

197B

Feb. 1 After receiving the semiannual interest and amortizing $19 of the purchase premium, change the investment policy toward the Morgan Corporation bonds and sold them at $101\frac{3}{4}$ less a $25 commission.

Apr. 1 Sold the Dale Corporation bonds at 99 less a $25 commission and plus four months' accrued interest.

15 Purchased as a long-term investment 500 shares of Surf Corporation common stock at $22\frac{1}{2}$ plus a $115 commission.

May 12 Received a $0.25 per share regular quarterly dividend on the Surf Corporation common stock.

Problem 19–1A

Stockholders' equity in Valley Corporation consists of these items:

Common stock, no par value, 200,000 shares authorized,
  100,000 shares issued and outstanding $750,000
Retained earnings 115,000
    Total Stockholders' Equity... $865,000

The corporation needs $1,000,000 to expand, and it estimates that after the expansion it can earn $400,000 per year before bond interest, if any, and income taxes; and its board of directors is considering three plans for securing the $1,000,000. They are:

Plan 1. Issue 100,000 additional shares of no-par common stock at $10 per share.

Plan 2. Issue 10,000 shares of $100 par value, $7\frac{1}{2}$% cumulative and nonparticipating preferred stock at par.

Plan 3. Sell $1,000,000 of 6.8%, 20-year bonds at par.

Required:

1. Prepare a calculation to show the earnings per share that will accrue to the corporation's present stockholders under each plan. (Assume a 50% income tax rate.)

2. In the situation described here the total earnings available to the common stockholders are $41,000 greater each year if bonds rather than preferred stock are issued. Explain why the total earnings available to the common stockholders are $41,000 greater each year when the difference between the bond interest and the preferred dividends is only $7,000 annually.

Problem 19-2A

PART 1. Prepare general journal entries to record these bond transactions of a corporation:

197A

Nov. 1 Sold and issued $1,000,000 par value, 7.8%, 10-year bonds dated November 1, 197A, with interest payable on each May 1 and November 1. The bonds sold for $986,410 cash, a price to yield the buyers an 8% annual return on their investment.

Dec. 31 Made an adjusting entry to record the accrued interest on the bonds and to amortize a portion of the discount calculated by the interest method. (Round each interest period's interest to be recorded to the nearest full dollar.)

197B

May 1 Paid the semiannual interest on the bonds and amortized the remainder of the discount applicable to the first interest period.

Nov. 1 Paid the semiannual interest on the bonds and amortized a portion of the discount.

PART 2. Prepare general journal entries to record these bond transactions of a corporation.

197A

Apr. 1 Sold and issued $1,000,000 par value, $7\frac{1}{2}\%$, 10-year bonds dated April 1 197A, with interest payable each October 1 and April 1. The bonds sold for $1,035,550 cash, a price to yield the buyers a 7% annual return.

Oct. 1 Paid the semiannual interest on the bonds and amortized a portion of the premium calculated by the interest method. (Round each interest period's interest to be recorded to the nearest full dollar.)

Dec. 31 Made an adjusting entry to record the accrued interest on the bonds and to amortize a portion of the discount.

197B

Apr. 1 Paid the semiannual interest on the bonds and amortized a portion of the discount.

Problem 19-3A

On October 12, 197A, a corporation deposited a deed of trust with the trustee of its bondholders that authorized it to issue $1,000,000 of 8.1%, 10-year, convertible bonds dated November 1, 197A, with interest payable each May 1 and November 1. The conversion clause in the deed of trust granted the bondholders the right to convert their bonds into shares of the company's common stock at the rate of 85 shares of $10 par value stock for each $1,000 bond. The corporation then completed these transactions:

197A

Nov. 1 Sold the entire issue to an underwriter for $1,006,800 cash, a price that would yield an 8% annual return on the investment.

Dec. 31 Made an adjusting entry to record the accrued interest and to amortize the applicable portion of the premium on the bonds.

197B

May 1 Paid the semiannual interest on the bonds and amortized the applicable portion of the premium.

Nov. 1 Paid the semiannual interest on the bonds and amortized the applicable portion of the premium.

197E

May 1 Payment of the semiannual interest on the bonds on this date and amortization of the applicable premium reduced the carrying amount of the bonds to $1,005,000, which enabled the corporation to purchase one tenth of the issue on the open market for $98,750 and retire the purchased bonds at a gain.

   1 On the same day it purchased and retired one tenth of its outstanding bonds, the corporation converted bonds having a $100,000 par value to common stock.

Required:

Prepare general journal entries to record the transaction. Use the interest method in calculating amounts of premium to be amortized and round all amounts to the nearest full dollar.

Problem 19–4A

A corporation deposited a deed of trust with the trustee of its bondholders on December 18, 197A, authorizing a $2,000,000, 7.2%, four-year bond issue dated January 1, 197B, with interest payable annually on each December 31 throughout the life of the issue. (Four years are an unrealistically small number of years for a bond issue and annual interest payments are not common; however, by using a four-year life and annual interest payments, all entries for a bond issue and a bond sinking fund may be required without too many repetitive entries.)

In the deed of trust the corporation agreed to create a bond sinking fund by depositing with a trustee $457,200 at the end of each year in the life of the bond issue. It was assumed the sinking fund investments would earn approximately 6% net and would grow to maturity as follows:

End of—	Amount Deposited	Interest Earned on Fund Balance	Balance in Fund after Deposit and Interest
197B	$457,200	–0–	$ 457,200
197C	457,200	$27,420	941,820
197D	457,200	56,480	1,455,500
197E	457,200	87,300	2,000,000

After depositing the deed of trust, the corporation completed these transactions:

197B

Jan. 1 Sold the entire issue for $2,013,550 cash, a price that would yield the buyers a 7% annual return on the investment.

Dec. 31 Paid the annual interest on the bonds and amortized a portion of the discount based on the following information:

	197B	197C	197D	197E
Beginning-of-period carrying amount	$2,013,550	$2,010,499	$2,007,234	$2,003,740
Interest to be paid the bondholders.........	144,000	144,000	144,000	144,000
Interest expense to be recorded..............	140,949	140,735	140,506	140,260
Premium to be amortized	3,051	3,265	3,494	3,740
End-of-period carrying amount..............	2,010,499	2,007,234	2,003,740	2,000,000

Dec. 31 Made the first annual sinking fund deposit.
197C
Dec. 31 Paid the annual interest on the bonds and amortized a portion of the premium.

31 Received the sinking fund trustee's report showing the sinking fund had earned $27,420 during the year.

31 Made the second annual sinking fund deposit.
197D
Dec. 31 Paid the interest on the bonds and amortized a portion of the premium.

31 Received the sinking funds trustee's report showing the fund had earned $56,425. This is slightly less than was anticipated the fund would earn. However, it is not enough to warrant a change in the deposit required of the corporation.

31 Made the third annual sinking fund deposit.
197E
Dec. 31 Paid the interest on the bonds and amortized a portion of the premium.

31 Received the sinking fund trustee's report showing the fund had earned $88,250.

31 Made the fourth annual sinking fund deposit.
197F
Jan. 8 Received a report from the sinking fund trustee showing the bonds had been paid in full. Attached to the report was a cheque for the excess earnings of the sinking fund.

Required:
Prepare general journal entries to record the transactions.

Problem 19–5A

Prepare general journal entries to record these transactions:

Mar. 1 Purchased as a temporary investment six $1,000 Beach Corporation, 6½%, 20-year bonds on which interest is payable semiannually on each January 1 and July 1. The purchase price was 98¼ plus two months' accrued interest and a $15 commission.

July 1 Received the semiannual interest on the Beach Corporation bonds.

Nov. 1 Sold the Beach Corporation bonds at 99½ plus four months' accrued interest and less a $15 commission.

Dec. 1 Purchased as a long-term investment ten $1,000 Surf Corporation 6.8%, 20-year bonds on their interest date six years before maturity. The purchase price was 98¾ plus a $25 commission, a price that would yield a 7% annual return on the investment.

June 1 Received the semiannual interest on the Surf Corporation bonds and amortized $7 of the discount.

Dec. 1 Received the semiannual interest on the Surf Corporation bonds and amortized $7 of the discount.

1 Changed the investment policy toward the Surf Corporation bonds and sold them at 100½ less a $25 commission.

5 Purchased as a temporary investment 100 shares of Blue Corporation common stock at 83¼ plus an $83.50 commission.

Jan. 3 Received the regular $0.75 per share quarterly dividend on the Blue Corporation stock.

Feb. 1 Sold the Blue Corporation stock at 91½ less a $92 commission.

Mar. 6 Purchased as a long-term investment 500 shares of Gold Corporation $25 par value common stock at 62½ plus a $310 commission. The 500 shares represented less than 1% of the corporation's voting stock.

Apr. 28 Received the regular $0.50 per share quarterly dividend on the Gold Corporation stock.

May 20 Received a 100-share common stock dividend from Gold Corporation.

21 Sold the 100 shares of Gold Corporation stock received as a dividend in the previous transaction, receiving $5,500 less a $55 commission.

Decision problem 19–1, Harbour Corporation

Stockholders' equity in Harbour Corporation consists of the following:

No-par common stock, stated value $7.50 per share, 300,000
    shares authorized, 200,000 shares issued............................... $1,500,000
Retained earnings.. 425,000
    Total Stockholders' Equity $1,925,000

For several years the company has earned only about 5% on its stockholders' equity, which its directors consider unsatisfactory. Consequently, they are planning an expansion that will require $1,000,000 of additional capital to be acquired in one of the following ways:

1. Issuing the remaining authorized common stock at $10 per share.
2. Securing an authorization and issuing 10,000 shares of $100 par value, 7½% cumulative and nonparticipating preferred stock.
3. Selling at par $1,000,000 of 7%, 20-year bonds.

The company's accounting department has prepared the following estimates of income before bond interest and taxes for the next 10 years under the assumption the expansion program will be carried out: Year 1, $270,000; Year 2, $318,000; Year 3, $354,000; Year 4, $390,000; Year 5, $432,000; Year 6, $480,000; Year 7, $528,000; Year 8, $582,000; Year 9, $642,000; Year 10, $708,000. Income taxes will take 50% of the company's before-tax income each year.

The company directors want to finance the expansion in the manner that will serve the best interests of present stockholders and they have asked you to determine this for them. In your report to the directors express an opinion as to the relative merits and disadvantages of each of the contemplated plans. Attach to your report a schedule showing annual expected earnings per share of the common stockholders under each plan.

Decision Problem 19–2, Bishop Corporation Bishop Corporation is considering a change in its capital structure to eliminate its outstanding 8% preferred stock. The company's capital structure consists of the following:

Preferred stock, $100 par value, 8% cumulative and nonparticipating, 20,000 shares authorized and issued, callable at par plus dividends due...	$2,000,000
Preferred stock, $50 par value, 7% cumulative and nonparticipating, 40,000 shares authorized and issued, callable at par plus dividends due...	2,000,000
Common stock, $10 par value, 500,000 shares authorized, 200,000 shares issued	2,000,000
Retained earnings...	1,250,000
Total..	$7,250,000

During the past five years the company's annual income has averaged $1,200,000 per year before income taxes; and considering the inelasticity of its operations, it can be assumed there will be little change.

Two alternatives have been suggested for securing the funds to call the 8% preferred stock. They are (1) issue at par $2,000,000 of 7½%, 20-year bonds and (2) offer the common stockholders the right to purchase one new share of common stock at par for each share now held.

The directors have asked you to prepare a statement showing the effect of the proposed changes on earnings applicable to the company's outstanding common stock, including earnings per share. If they are satisfied that either of the proposed changes is to the advantage of the common stockholders, they will call the necessary stockholders' meetings and seek authorization to proceed with the better of the suggested changes.

Prepare the statement requested by the directors. Also explain why the replacement of a $160,000 annual payment to the preferred stockholders with a $150,000 annual payment to bondholders, which amounts to a $10,000 savings or $0.05 per common share, can result in a $0.425 per share increase in the earnings of the common stockholders. You may assume that the company's income taxes will continue to take 50% of its before-tax income.

Analytical and review problems **Problem 19–1 A&R**

The accounts of Clues Company Limited showed the following balances as of December 31, 1975:

Bonds Payable...	$1,000,000
Bond Discount	25,750

The 8% 10-year bonds dated August 1, 1974 were issued on November 1, 1974 and the cash proceeds were $990,750. Interest is payable semiannually.

Required:
Reconstruct the entries pertaining to the bond issue that were made on the company's books. Assume that the company's fiscal year coincides with the calendar year.

Problem 19–2 A&R

On December 31, 1975 the accounts of Riskey Venture Company Limited showed a balance in the Bond Premium account of $51,500. The 12% 10-year bonds dated August 1, 1974 were issued on December 1, 1974 at 105.8. Interest is payable semiannually.

Required:
Reconstruct the entries pertaining to the bond issue that were made on the company's books. The company's fiscal year coincides with the calendar year.

Problem 19–3 A&R

The following are three methods of accounting for long-term investments:
a. Cost.
b. Equity.
c. Consolidation.

Required:
1. Briefly describe the nature of each of these three methods.
2. Explain the conditions or circumstances under which the three methods may be used, support your answer with appropriate examples.

20

Analyzing financial statements

■ The financial statements of a business are analyzed to determine its overall position and also to find out about certain aspects of that position, such as earnings prospects and debt-paying ability. In making the analysis, individual statement items are in themselves generally not too significant, but relationships between items and groups of items plus changes that have occurred are significant. As a result, financial statement analysis requires that relationships between items and groups of items and changes in items and groups of items be seen.

Compara-tive statements

■ Changes in financial statement items can usually best be seen when item amounts for two or more successive years are placed side by side in columns on a single statement. Such a statement is called a *comparative statement,* and may be a comparative balance sheet or a comparative income statement or a portion of either.

In its most simple form a comparative balance sheet consists of the item amounts from two or more of a company's successive balance sheets arranged side by side, so that changes in amounts may be seen. However, since the average person often has difficulty grasping significant changes, such a statement can be improved by also showing in both dollar amounts and in percentages the changes that have occurred. When this is done, as in Illustration 20–1, large dollar and large percentage changes become more readily apparent to the statement reader.

Anchor Supply Company, Ltd.
Comparative Balance Sheet
December 31, 1975, and December 31, 1976

	Years Ended December 31		Amount of Increase or (Decrease) during 1976	Per cent of Increase or (Decrease) during 1976
	1976	1975		
ASSETS				
Current Assets:				
Cash	$ 18,000	$ 90,500	$ (72,500)	(80.1)
Accounts receivable, net	68,000	64,000	4,000	6.3
Merchandise inventory	90,000	84,000	6,000	7.1
Prepaid expenses	5,800	6,000	(200)	(3.3)
Total Current Assets	$181,800	$244,500	$ (62,700)	(25.6)
Long-Term Investments:				
Real estate	$ -0-	$ 30,000	$ (30,000)	(100.0)
Apex Company 6% bonds	-0-	50,000	(50,000)	(100.0)
Total Long-Term Investments	$ -0-	$ 80,000	$ (80,000)	(100.0)
Plant and Equipment:				
Office equipment, net	$ 3,500	$ 3,700	$ (200)	(5.4)
Store equipment, net	17,900	6,800	11,100	163.2
Buildings, net	176,800	28,000	148,800	531.4
Land	50,000	20,000	30,000	150.0
Total Plant and Equipment	$248,200	$ 58,500	$189,700	324.3
Total Assets	$430,000	$383,000	$ 47,000	12.3
LIABILITIES				
Current Liabilities:				
Notes payable	$ 5,000	$ -0-	$ 5,000	
Accounts payable	43,600	55,000	(11,400)	(20.7)
Taxes payable	4,800	5,000	(200)	(4.0)
Wages payable	800	1,200	(400)	(33.3)
Total Current Liabilities	$ 54,200	$ 61,200	$ (7,000)	(11.4)
Long-Term Liabilities:				
Mortgage payable	$ 60,000	$ 10,000	$ 50,000	500.0
Total Liabilities	$114,200	$ 71,200	$ 43,000	60.4
CAPITAL				
Common stock, $10 par value	$250,000	$250,000	$ -0-	-0-
Retained earnings	65,800	61,800	4,000	6.5
Total Capital	$315,800	$311,800	$ 4,000	1.3
Total Liabilities and Capital	$430,000	$383,000	$ 47,000	12.3

Illustration
20–1

A comparative income statement is prepared in the same manner as a comparative balance sheet. Income statement amounts for two or more successive periods are placed side by side, with dollar and percentage changes in additional columns. Such a statement is shown in Illustration 20–2.

Anchor Supply Company, Ltd.
Comparative Income Statement
Years Ended December 31, 1975 and 1976

	Years Ended December 31		Amount of Increase or (Decrease) during 1976	Per cent of Increase or (Decrease) during 1976
	1976	1975		
Gross sales...	$973,500	$853,000	$120,500	14.1
Sales returns and allowances	13,500	10,200	3,300	32.4
Net sales	$960,000	$842,800	$117,200	13.9
Cost of goods sold	715,000	622,500	92,500	14.9
Gross profit from sales...............................	$245,000	$220,300	$ 24,700	11.2
Operating expenses:				
Selling expenses:				
Advertising expense.............................	$ 7,500	$ 5,000	$ 2,500	50.0
Sales salaries expense	113,500	98,000	15,500	15.8
Store supplies expense	3,200	2,800	400	14.3
Depreciation expense, store equipment ..	2,400	1,700	700	41.2
Delivery expense	14,800	14,000	800	5.7
Total selling expenses.......................	$141,400	$121,500	$ 19,900	16.4
General and administrative expenses:				
Office salaries expense	$ 41,000	$ 40,050	$ 950	2.1
Office supplies expense	1,300	1,250	50	4.0
Insurance expense................................	1,600	1,200	400	33.3
Depreciation expense, office equipment..	300	300	-0-	-0-
Depreciation expense, buildings	2,850	1,500	1,350	90.0
Bad debts expense	2,250	2,200	50	2.3
Total general and admin. expenses	$ 49,300	$ 46,500	$ 2,800	6.0
Total operating expenses	$190,700	$168,000	$ 22,700	13.5
Operating income..	$ 54,300	$ 52,300	$ 2,000	3.8
Less interest expense	2,300	1,000	1,300	130.0
Income before taxes	$ 52,000	$ 51,300	$ 700	1.4
Income taxes	19,000	18,700	300	1.6
Net Income..	$ 33,000	$ 32,600	$ 400	1.2

Illustration
20–2

Analyzing and interpreting comparative statements

In analyzing and interpreting comparative data, it is necessary for the analyst to select for study any items showing significant dollar or percentage changes, to determine the reasons for each change, and to determine if possible whether they are favourable or unfavourable. For example, in the comparative balance sheet of Anchor Supply Company, Illustration 20–1, the first item, "Cash," shows a large decrease, and at first glance this appears unfavourable. However, when the decrease in "Cash" is considered with the decrease in "Investments" and the increase in "Store equipment," "Buildings," and "Land," plus the increase in "Mortgage payable," it becomes apparent the company has materially increased its plant assets between the two balance sheet dates. Further study reveals the company has apparently constructed a new building on land it has held as an investment until needed in this expansion. Also, it seems the company has paid for its new plant assets by reducing cash, selling its Apex Company bonds, and issuing a $50,000 mortgage.

As an aid in controlling operations, a comparative income statement is usually more valuable than a comparative balance sheet. For example, in Illustration 20–2, "Gross sales" increased 14.1% and "Net sales" increased 13.9%. At the same time, "Sales returns" increased 32.4%, or at a rate more than twice that of gross sales. Returned sales represent wasted sales effort and indicate dissatisfied customers; consequently, such an increase in returns should be investigated, and the reason therefor determined if at all possible. Also, in addition to the large increase in the "Sales returns," it is significant that the rate of increase in "Cost of goods sold" is greater than that of "Net sales." This is an unfavourable trend and should be remedied if at all possible.

In attempting to account for Anchor Supply Company's increase in sales, the increases in advertising and in plant assets merit attention. It is reasonable to expect an increase in advertising to increase sales. It is also reasonable to expect an increase in plant assets to result in a sales increase in a merchandising company or a decrease in cost of goods sold in a manufacturing company.

Calculating percentage increases and decreases

When percentage increases and decreases are calculated for comparative statements, the increase or decrease in an item is divided by the amount shown for the item in the base year. No problems arise in these calculations when positive amounts are shown in the base year. However, when no amount is shown or a negative amount is shown in the base year, a percentage increase or decrease cannot be calculated. For example, in Illustration 20–1 there were no notes payable at the end of 1975 and a percentage change for this item cannot be calculated.

Trend percentages

Trend percentages or index numbers are useful in comparing data from a company's financial statements covering a number of years, since trend percentages emphasize changes that have occurred during the period. They are calculated as follows:

1. A base year is selected, and each item amount on the base year statement is assigned a weight of 100%.
2. Then each item from the statements for the years after the base year is expressed as a percentage of its base year amount. To determine these percentages, the item amounts in the years after the base year are divided by the amount of the item in the base year.

For example, if 1971 is made the base year for the following data, the trend percentages for "Sales" are calculated by dividing by $210,000

	1971	1972	1973	1974	1975	1976
Sales	$210,000	$204,000	$292,000	$284,000	$310,000	$324,000
Cost of goods sold	145,000	139,000	204,000	198,000	218,000	229,000
Gross profit	$ 65,000	$ 65,000	$ 88,000	$ 86,000	$ 92,000	$ 95,000

the amount shown for "Sales" in each year after the first. The trend percentages for "Cost of goods sold" are found by dividing by $145,000 the amount shown for "Cost of goods sold" in each year after the first. And, the trend percentages for "Gross profit" are found by dividing the amounts shown for "Gross profit" by $65,000. When these divisions are made, the trends for these three items appear as follows:

	1971	1972	1973	1974	1975	1976
Sales	100	97	139	135	148	154
Cost of goods sold	100	96	141	137	150	158
Gross profit	100	100	135	132	142	146

It is interesting to note in the illustrated trends that while after the second year the sales trend is upward, the cost of goods sold trend is upward at a slightly more rapid rate. This indicates a contracting gross profit rate and should receive attention.

It should be pointed out in a discussion of trends that the trend for a single balance sheet or income statement item is seldom too informative. However, a comparison of trends for related items often tells the analyst a great deal. For example, a downward sales trend with an upward trend for merchandise inventory, accounts receivable, and loss on bad debts would generally indicate an unfavourable situation. On the other hand, an upward sales trend with a downward trend or a slower upward trend for accounts receivable, merchandise inventory, and selling expenses would indicate an increase in operating efficiency.

Common-size comparative statements

The comparative statements shown thus far do not show proportional changes in items except in a general way. Changes in proportions are often shown and emphasized by *common-size comparative statements*.

A common-size statement is so called because its items are shown in common-size figures, figures that are fractions of 100%. For example, on a common-size balance sheet (1) the asset total is assigned a value of 100%; (2) the total of the liabilities and owner equity is also assigned a value of 100%; and then (3) each asset, liability, and owner equity item is shown as a fraction of one of the 100% totals. When a company's balance sheets for more than one year are shown in this manner, see Illustration 20–3, proportional changes are emphasized.

A common-size income statement is prepared by assigning net sales a 100% value and then expressing each income statement item as a per cent of net sales. Such a statement is an informative and useful tool, because when the 100% sales amount is assumed to represent one sales dollar, then the remaining income statement items show how each sales

Anchor Supply Company, Ltd.
Common-Size Comparative Balance Sheet
December 31, 1975, and December 31, 1976

	Years Ended December 31		Common-Size Percentages	
	1976	1975	1976	1975
ASSETS				
Current Assets:				
Cash..	$ 18,000	$ 90,500	4.19	23.63
Accounts receivable, net..............	68,000	64,000	15.81	16.71
Merchandise inventory	90,000	84,000	20.93	21.93
Prepaid expenses	5,800	6,000	1.35	1.57
Total Current Assets..............	$181,800	$244,500	42.28	63.84
Long-Term Investments:				
Real estate...............................	$ -0-	$ 30,000		7.83
Apex Company 6% bonds.............	-0-	50,000		13.05
Total Long-Term Investments..	$ -0-	$ 80,000		20.88
Plant and Equipment:				
Office equipment, net..................	$ 3,500	$ 3,700	0.81	0.97
Store equipment, net..................	17,900	6,800	4.16	1.78
Buildings, net............................	176,800	28,000	41.12	7.31
Land..	50,000	20,000	11.63	5.22
Total Plant and Equipment	$248,200	$ 58,500	57.72	15.28
Total Assets	$430,000	$383,000	100.00	100.00
LIABILITIES				
Current Liabilities:				
Notes payable............................	$ 5,000	$ -0-	1.16	
Accounts payable	43,600	55,000	10.14	14.36
Taxes payable	4,800	5,000	1.12	1.31
Wages payable	800	1,200	0.19	0.31
Total Current Liabilities..........	$ 54,200	$ 61,200	12.61	15.98
Long-Term Liabilities:				
Mortgage payable.......................	$ 60,000	$ 10,000	13.95	2.61
Total Liabilities...................	$114,200	$ 71,200	26.56	18.59
CAPITAL				
Common stock, $10 par value..........	$250,000	$250,000	58.14	65.27
Retained earnings.........................	65,800	61,800	15.30	16.14
Total Capital.........................	$315,800	$311,800	73.44	81.44
Total Liabilities and Capital..	$430,000	$383,000	100.00	100.00

Illustration
20–3

dollar was distributed to costs, expenses, and profit. For example, on the comparative income statement shown in Illustration 20–4, the 1975 cost of goods sold consumed 73.86 cents of each sales dollar. In 1976 cost of goods sold consumed 74.48 cents from each sales dollar. While this increase is apparently small, if in 1976 the proportion of cost of goods sold had remained at the 1975 level, almost $6,000 additional

Anchor Supply Company, Ltd.
Common-Size Comparative Income Statement
Years Ended December 31, 1975 and 1976

	Years Ended December 31		Common-Size Percentages	
	1976	1975	1976	1975
Gross sales..	$973,500	$853,000	101.41	101.21
Sales returns and allowances............................	13,500	10,200	1.41	1.21
Net sales...	$960,000	$842,800	100.00	100.00
Cost of goods sold...	715,000	622,500	74.48	73.86
Gross profit from sales	$245,000	$220,300	25.52	26.14
Operating expenses:				
Selling expenses:				
Advertising expense	$ 7,500	$ 5,000	0.78	0.59
Sales salaries expense...............................	113,500	98,000	11.82	11.63
Store supplies expense...............................	3,200	2,800	0.33	0.33
Depreciation expense, store equipment.........	2,400	1,700	0.25	0.20
Delivery expense.....................................	14,800	14,000	1.54	1.66
Total selling expenses	$141,400	$121,500	14.72	14.41
General and administrative expenses:				
Office salaries expense.............................	$ 41,000	$ 40,050	4.27	4.75
Office supplies expense.............................	1,300	1,250	0.14	0.15
Insurance expense	1,600	1,200	0.17	0.14
Depreciation expense, office equipment	300	300	0.03	0.04
Depreciation expense, buildings..................	2,850	1,500	0.30	0.18
Bad debts expense...................................	2,250	2,200	0.23	0.26
Total general and administrative expenses..	$ 49,300	$ 46,500	5.14	5.52
Total operating expenses.......................	$190,700	$168,000	19.86	19.93
Operating income	$ 54,300	$ 52,300	5.66	6.21
Less interest expense..................................	2,300	1,000	0.24	0.12
Income before taxes.....................................	$ 52,000	$ 51,300	5.42	6.09
Income taxes...	19,000	18,700	1.98	2.22
Net Income..	$ 33,000	$ 32,600	3.44	3.87

Illustration
20–4

gross profit would have been earned; and if carried through to net income, this would have been a significant amount.

Common-size percentages point out efficiencies and inefficiencies that are otherwise difficult to see, and for this reason are a valuable management tool. To illustrate, sales salaries of Anchor Supply Company took a higher percentage of each sales dollar in 1976 than in 1975. On the other hand, office salaries took a smaller percentage of each 1976 sales dollar. Furthermore, although the loss from bad debts was greater in 1976 than in 1975, loss from bad debts took a smaller proportion of each sales dollar in 1976 than in 1975.

Analysis of working capital ■ The term *working capital* is used to denote the excess of a company's current assets over its current liabilities; and when balance sheets are analyzed, working capital always receives close attention. This is as it should be. Adequate working capital enables a company to carry sufficient inventories, meet current debts, take advantage of cash discounts, and extend favourable terms to customers. These are desirable. A company that is deficient in working capital and unable to do these things is in a poor competitive position. Its survival chances are normally small, unless its working capital position is improved. Inadequacy of working capital has ended the business lives of many companies whose total assets were far in excess of liabilities.

As previously said, a company's working capital should be sufficient to enable it to carry adequate inventories, meet current debts, and take advantage of cash discounts. However, the amount of working capital a company has is not a measure of these abilities, and this may be demonstrated as follows with Companies A and B:

	Company A	Company B
Current assets	$100,000	$20,000
Current liabilities	90,000	10,000
Working capital	$ 10,000	$10,000

Companies A and B have the same amounts of working capital. However, Company A's current liabilities are nine times its working capital, while Company B's current liabilities and working capital are equal. As a result, if liabilities are to be paid on time, Company A must experience much less shrinkage and delay in converting its current assets to cash than Company B. Obviously then, as the example shows, the amount of a company's working capital is not a measure of its working capital position, but the relation of its current assets to its current liabilities is.

Current ratio

The relation of a company's current assets to its current liabilities is known as its *current ratio*. The current ratio of the foregoing Company B is calculated as follows:

$$\frac{\text{Current Assets, \$20,000}}{\text{Current Liabilities, \$10,000}} = 2$$

A current ratio is calculated by dividing current assets by current liabilities. After the division is made, the relation is expressed as, for example, Company B's current assets are two times its current liabilities, or Company B has $2 of current assets for each $1 of current liabilities, or simply Company B's current ratio is 2 to 1.

The current ratio is the relation of current assets and current liabilities expressed mathematically. A high current ratio indicates a large proportion of current assets to current liabilities. The higher the ratio, the more liquid is a company's current position, and normally the better it can meet current obligations.

For many years bankers and other credit grantors measured a credit-seeking company's debt-paying ability by whether or not it had a 2 to 1 current ratio. Today most credit grantors realize that the 2 to 1 rule of thumb is not an adequate test of debt-paying ability. They realize that whether or not a company's current ratio is good or bad depends upon at least three factors:

1. The nature of the company's business.
2. The composition of its current assets.
3. The turnover of certain of its current assets.

The nature of a company's business has much to do with whether or not its current ratio is adequate. A public utility or a railroad which has no inventories other than supplies and which grants little or no credit can operate on a current ratio less than 1 to 1. On the other hand, because a misjudgment of style can make an inventory of goods for sale almost worthless, a company manufacturing articles in which style is the important sales factor may find a current ratio of much more than 2 to 1 to be inadequate. Consequently, when the adequacy of working capital is studied, consideration must be given to the type of business under review.

Also, in an analysis of a company's working capital, the composition of its current assets should be considered. Normally a company with a high proportion of cash to accounts receivable, merchandise inventory, and other current assets is in a better position to meet quickly its current obligations than is a company with most of its current assets tied up in accounts receivable and merchandise. The company with cash can pay its current debts at once, while the company with accounts receivable and merchandise must often turn these items into cash before it can pay.

Acid-test ratio

An easily calculated check on current asset composition is the *acid-test* ratio, which is also called the *quick ratio* because it is the ratio of "quick assets" to current liabilities. "Quick assets" are cash, notes receivable, accounts receivable, and marketable securities. They are the current assets that can quickly be turned into cash. An acid-test ratio of 1 to 1 is normally considered satisfactory. However, this is a rule of thumb and should be applied with care. The acid-test ratio of Anchor Supply Company as of the end of 1976 is calculated as follows:

Quick Assets:		Current Liabilities:	
Cash	$18,000	Notes payable	$ 5,000
Accounts receivable	68,000	Accounts payable	43,600
		Taxes payable	4,800
		Wages payable	800
Total	$86,000	Total	$54,200

Acid-test ratio is: $86,000 ÷ $54,200 = 1.59$ or is 1.59 to 1

Turnover of accounts receivable

Certain current asset turnovers affect working capital requirements. For example, assume Companies A and B sell the same amounts of merchandise on credit each month. However, Company A grants 30-day terms to its customers, while Company B grants 60 days. Both collect their accounts at the end of the credit periods granted. But as a result of the difference in terms, Company A turns over or collects its accounts twice as rapidly as does Company B. Also, as a result of the more rapid turnover, Company A requires only one half the investment in accounts receivable that is required of Company B and can operate with a smaller current ratio.

Accounts receivable turnover is calculated by dividing net sales for a year by the year-end accounts receivable, and Anchor Supply Company's accounts receivable turnovers for 1975 and 1976 are calculated as follows:

		1976	1975
a.	Net sales for year..	$960,000	$842,800
b.	Year-end accounts receivable	68,000	64,000
	Times accounts receivable were turned over (a ÷ b)..........	14.1	13.2

The turnover of 14.1 times in 1976 in comparison to 13.2 in 1975 indicates the company's accounts receivable were collected more rapidly in 1976.

The year-end amount of accounts receivable is commonly used in calculating accounts receivable turnover. However, if year-end accounts receivable are not representative, an average of the year's accounts receivable by months should be used. Also, credit sales rather than the sum of cash and credit sales, and accounts receivable before subtracting the allowance for doubtful accounts should be used. However, information as to credit sales is seldom available in a published balance sheet, and many published balance sheets report accounts receivable at their net amount. Consequently, total sales and net accounts receivable must often be used.

Days' sales uncollected

Accounts receivable turnover is one indication of the speed with which a company collects its accounts. *Days' sales uncollected* is another indication of the same thing. To illustrate the calculation of days' sales uncollected, assume a company had charge sales during a year of $250,-000, and that it has $25,000 of accounts receivable at the year-end. In other words, one tenth of its charge sales, or the charge sales made during one tenth of a year, or the charge sales of 36.5 days ($\frac{1}{10} \times 365$ days in a year = 36.5 days) are uncollected. This calculation of days' sales uncollected in equation form appears as follows:

$$\frac{\text{Accounts Receivable, \$25,000}}{\text{Charge Sales, \$250,000}} \times 365 = 36.5 \text{ Days' Sales Uncollected}$$

Days' sales uncollected takes on more meaning when credit terms are known. According to a rule of thumb, a company's days' sales uncollected should not exceed one and one-third times the days in its credit period when it does not offer discounts and one and one-third times the days in its discount period when it does. If the company, whose days' sales uncollected is calculated in the illustration just given, offers 30-day terms, then 36.5 days is within the rule-of-thumb amount. However, if its terms are 2/10, n/30, its days' sales uncollected seem excessive.

Turnover of merchandise inventory

A company's merchandise turnover is the number of times its average inventory is sold during an accounting period, and a high turnover is considered an indication of good merchandising. Also, from a working capital point of view, a company with a high turnover requires a smaller investment in inventory than one producing the same sales with a low turnover. Merchandise turnover is calculated by dividing cost of goods sold by average inventory. Cost of goods sold is the amount of merchandise at its cost price that was sold during an accounting period; average inventory is the average amount of merchandise, at its cost price, on hand during the period. The 1976 merchandise turnover of Anchor Supply Company is calculated as follows:

$$\frac{\text{Cost of Goods Sold, \$715,000}}{\text{Average Merchandise Inventory, \$87,000}} = \text{Merchandise Turnover of 8.2 Times}$$

The cost of goods sold is taken from the company's 1976 income statement. The average inventory is found by dividing by two the sum of the $84,000, January 1, 1976, inventory and the $90,000, December 31, 1976, inventory. In a company in which beginning and ending inventories are not representative of the inventory normally on hand, a more accurate turnover may be secured by using the average of all the 12 month-end inventories rather than just the beginning- and end-of-the-year inventories.

Standards of comparison

■ When financial statements are analyzed by computing ratios and turnovers, the analyst must determine whether the ratios and turnovers obtained are good, bad, or just average; and in making the decision he must have some basis for comparison. The following are available:

1. A trained analyst may compare the ratios and turnovers of the company under review with his own mental standards acquired from past experiences.
2. An analyst may calculate for purposes of comparison the ratios and turnovers of a selected group of competitive companies in the same industry as the one whose statements are under review.
3. Published ratios and turnovers such as those put out by Dun & Bradstreet may be secured for comparison.
4. Some local and national trade associations' gather data from their members and publish standard or average ratios for their trade or industry. These offer the analyst a very good basis of comparison when available.
5. Rule-of-thumb standards may be used as a basis for comparison.

Of these five standards, the ratios and turnovers of a selected group of competitive companies normally offer the best basis for comparison. Rule-of-thumb standards should be applied with care if erroneous conclusions are to be avoided.

Other balance sheet and income statement relations

■ Several balance sheet and income statement relations in addition to those having to do with working capital are important to the analyst. Some of the more important are:

Capital contributions of owners and creditors

The share of a company's assets contributed by its owners and the share contributed by creditors are always of interest to the analyst. The owner and creditor contributions of Anchor Supply Company are calculated as follows:

		1976	1975
a.	Total liabilities	$114,200	$ 71,200
b.	Total owner equity	315,800	311,800
c.	Total liabilities and owner equity	$430,000	$383,000
	Creditors' equity (a ÷ c)	26.6%	18.6%
	Owner equity (b ÷ c)	73.4%	81.4%

Creditors like to see a high proportion of owner equity because owner equity acts as a cushion in absorbing losses. The greater the equity of the owners in relation to that of the creditors, the greater the losses that can be absorbed by the owners before the creditors begin to lose.

From the creditors' standpoint a high percentage of owner equity is desirable. However, if an enterprise can earn a return on borrowed capital that is in excess of the capital's cost, then a reasonable amount of creditor equity is desirable from the owners' viewpoint, with the amount depending upon the stability of the earnings.

Pledged plant assets to long-term liabilities

Companies commonly borrow by issuing a note or bonds secured by a mortgage on certain of their plant assets. The ratio of pledged plant assets to long-term debt is often calculated to measure the security granted to mortgage or bondholders by the pledged assets. This ratio is calculated by dividing the pledged assets' book value by the liabilities for which the assets are pledged. It is calculated for Anchor Supply Company as of the ends of 1975 and 1976 as follows:

		1976	1975
	Buildings, net	$176,800	$28,000
	Land	50,000	20,000
a.	Book value of pledged plant assets	$226,800	$48,000
b.	Mortgage payable	$ 60,000	$10,000
	Ratio of pledged assets to secured liabilities (a ÷ b)	3.8 to 1	4.8 to 1

The usual rule-of-thumb minimum for this ratio is 2 to 1. However, the ratio needs careful interpretation because it is based on the *book value* of the pledged assets, and book value may bear little or no relation to the amount that would be received for the assets in a foreclosure or a liquidation. As a result, estimated liquidation values or foreclosure values are normally a better measure of the protection offered bond or mortgage holders by pledged assets. Too, in a situation in which assets are pledged, the long-term earning ability of the company whose assets are pledged is usually more important to long-term creditors than the pledged assets' book value.

Times fixed interest charges were earned

The number of times fixed interest charges were earned is often calculated to measure the security of the return offered to bondholders or a mortgage holder. To make this calculation, the fixed interest charges are added to income before taxes to determine the amount of income before fixed interest charges and income taxes. This amount is available to pay the fixed interest charges and is divided by the amount of the fixed interest charges to determine the number of times the charges were earned. Often the return to a company's long-term creditors is considered secure if the company consistently earns its fixed interest charges two or more times each year.

Rate of return on total assets employed

The return earned on total assets employed is a measure of management's performance. Assets are used to earn a profit, and management is responsible for the way in which they are used; consequently, the return on assets employed is a measure of management's performance.

The return figure used in this calculation should be after-tax income plus interest expense. Interest expense is included because it is a return paid creditors for assets they have supplied. Likewise, if the amount of assets has fluctuated during the year, an average of the beginning- and end-of-the-year assets employed should be used.

The rates of return earned on the average total assets employed by Anchor Supply Company during 1975 and 1976 are calculated as follows:

		1976	1975
	Net income after taxes	$ 33,000	$ 32,600
	Add interest expense	2,300	1,000
a.	Net income plus interest expense	$ 35,300	$ 33,600
b.	Average total assets employed	$406,500	$380,000
	Rate of return on total assets employed (a ÷ b)	8.68%	8.84%

In the case of Anchor Supply Company the change in the rates is not too significant, and it is impossible to tell whether the returns are good or bad without some basis of comparison. The best comparison would be the returns earned by similar-size companies engaged in the same kind of business, or a comparison could be made with the returns earned by this company in previous years. Neither of these is available in this case.

Rate of return on common stockholders' equity

A primary reason for the operation of a corporation is to earn a net income for its common stockholders; and the rate of return on the common stockholders' equity is a measure of the success achieved in this area. Usually an average of the beginning- and end-of-the-year equities is used in calculating the return, and for Anchor Supply Company the 1975 and 1976 calculations are as follows:

		1976	1975
a.	Net income after taxes	$ 33,000	$ 32,600
b.	Average stockholders' equity	313,800	309,000
	Rate of return on stockholders' equity (a ÷ b)	10.52%	10.55%

In the two calculations just illustrated, compare the returns on stockholders' equity with the returns on total assets employed and note that the return on the stockholders' equity is greater in both years. The greater returns resulted from leverage gained by using borrowed money.

When there is preferred stock outstanding, the preferred dividend requirements must be subtracted from net income to arrive at the common stockholders' share of income to be used in calculating the rate of return on common stockholders' equity.

Earnings per share of common stock

Earnings per share data are commonly used by investors in evaluating the past performance of a company, in projecting its future earnings, and in weighing investment opportunities. Consequently, the CICA has recommended that per share amounts (a) for income before extraordinary items and (b) for the final net income figure should be shown on the face of a company's published income statement or in a note to the financial statements cross-referenced to the income statement. It also held that it may be desirable to present per share amounts for the extraordinary items. All of this and the manner in which earnings per share data are calculated was discussed in Chapter 18 and needs no additional discussion here. However, Anchor Supply Company has 25,000 common shares, but no preferred stock outstanding; consequently, its 1975 earnings per common share were $1.30 ($32,600 ÷ 25,000 = $1.30) and its 1976 earnings per share were $1.32, a very small increase for 1976.

Price-earnings ratio

Price-earnings ratios are commonly used in comparing investment opportunities. A price-earnings ratio is calculated by dividing market price per share by earnings per share. For example, if Anchor Supply

Company's common stock sold at $16 per share at the end of 1976, the stock's end-of-the-year price-earnings ratio is calculated:

$$\frac{\$16 \text{ Market Price per Share}}{\$1.32 \text{ Earnings per Share}} = 12.1$$

After the calculation is made, it may be said that the stock had a 12 to 1 price-earnings ratio at the end of 1976, or it may be said that $12 was required at that time to buy $1 of this company's 1976 earnings.

In comparing price-earnings ratios it must be remembered that such ratios vary from industry to industry. For example, in the steel industry a 10 or 12 to 1 price-earnings ratio is normal, while in growth industries, such as the photography or electronics industries, 30 to 1 or higher ratios are not uncommon.

The effect of price level changes

■ When financial statements for a period of several years are analyzed, the analyst must keep in mind the effect on the statements of *price level changes*. Price level changes are changes in the purchasing power of money. Often, if price level changes are ignored, incorrect conclusions may be drawn. For example, during the last 10 years many companies showed a large dollar increase in sales when their physical volume of sales actually remained unchanged or increased only a small amount. In these companies the increase in dollar sales volume was caused by the decrease in the purchasing power of the dollar. During these years a dollar purchased a smaller amount of goods each year; or, in other words, during each of these years it required an increasing number of dollars to buy the same amount of goods.

Price level changes affect income statement items, but their effect is not limited to such items. They also affect the balance sheet. For example, many companies are operating today with plant assets, the replacement costs of which are several times their reported balance sheet amounts. This is particularly true of buildings purchased or constructed some years ago.

No effort will be made here to enter into an exhaustive discussion of the effect of price level changes on financial statements. Such a discussion is reserved for a more advanced course. However, the student should be aware of this phenomenon.

Questions for class discussion

1. Why does a comparative balance sheet often have columns showing increases and decreases in both dollar amounts and percentages?
2. When trends are calculated and compared, what item trends should be compared with the trend of sales?
3. Why are common-size statements so called?
4. What items are assigned a value of 100% *(a)* on a common-size balance sheet and *(b)* on a common-size income statement?
5. Define the term working capital.

6. For the following transactions tell which increase working capital, which decrease working capital, and which have no effect on working capital:
   a. Collected accounts receivable.
   b. Borrowed money from the bank by giving a 90-day interest-bearing note.
   c. Declared a cash dividend.
   d. Paid a cash dividend previously declared.
   e. Sold plant assets at their book value.
   f. Sold merchandise at a profit.
7. Why is adequate working capital of importance to a business?
8. List several factors that have an effect on working capital requirements.
9. A company has a 2 to 1 current ratio. List several reasons why this ratio may not be adequate.
10. Tell the significance of each of the following ratios and turnovers and tell how each is calculated:
    a. Current ratio.
    b. Acid-test ratio.
    c. Turnover of accounts receivable.
    d. Turnover of merchandise inventory.
    e. Rate of return on common stockholders' equity.
    f. Ratio of pledged plant assets to long-term liabilities.
11. How are days' sales uncollected calculated? What is the significance of the number of days' sales uncollected?
12. Why do creditors like to see a high proportion of owner equity?
13. What is the ratio of pledged plant assets to long-term liabilities supposed to measure? Why must this ratio be interpreted with care?
14. What does the rate of return on assets employed tell about management?
15. What are price level changes? Why must the effect of price level changes be considered when statements covering a period of years are analyzed?

Class exercises

Exercise 20–1

Where possible calculate percentages of increase and decrease for the following unrelated items. The parentheses indicate deficit items.

	1976	1975
Buildings, net	$75,000	$60,000
Investments	-0-	20,000
Notes payable	5,000	-0-
Retained earnings	(4,500)	15,000
Cash	12,000	(1,500)

Exercise 20–2

Calculate trend percentages for the following items and tell whether the situation shown by the trends if favourable or unfavourable.

	1974	1975	1976
Sales	$150,000	$169,500	$178,500
Merchandise inventory	30,000	36,000	39,600
Accounts receivable	18,000	23,040	24,300

Exercise 20–3

Express the following income statement information in common-size percentages and tell whether the situation shown is favourable or unfavourable.

HILLTOP SALES COMPANY
Comparative Income Statement
Years Ended June 30, 1975, and 1976

	1976	1975
Sales...	$100,000	$90,000
Cost of goods sold	67,500	60,390
Gross profit from sales.........................	$ 32,500	$29,610
Operating expenses	25,300	22,860
Net Income	$ 7,200	$ 6,750

Exercise 20–4

The 197A statements of Pacific Sales Company, Ltd. follow:

PACIFIC SALES COMPANY, LTD.
Income Statement for Year Ended December 31, 197A

Sales..		$365,000
Cost of goods sold:		
Merchandise inventory, January 1, 197A	$ 29,400	
Purchases	241,200	
Goods for sale..	$270,600	
Merchandise inventory, December 31, 197A	30,600	
Cost of goods sold		240,000
Gross profit on sales...		$125,000
Operating expenses		106,200
Operating income...		$ 18,800
Interest expense		3,000
Income before taxes		$ 15,800
Income taxes..		3,300
Net Income		$ 12,500

PACIFIC SALES COMPANY, LTD.
Balance Sheet, December 31, 197A

Cash	$ 6,500	Accounts payable........................	$ 20,000
Accounts receivable, net...............	22,500	Mortgage payable secured by a	
Merchandise inventory	30,600	lien on the plant assets	50,000
Prepaid expenses.........................	400	Common stock $10 par value	100,000
Plant assets, net	140,000	Retained earnings........................	30,000
Total Assets	$200,000	Total Equities	$200,000

Required:
Calculate the following: *(a)* current ratio, *(b)* acid-test ratio, *(c)* days' sales uncollected, *(d)* merchandise turnover, *(e)* capital contribution of the owners

expressed as a percent, (f) ratio of pledged plant assets to long-term liabilities, (g) return on total assets employed, (h) return on stockholders' equity, and (i) earnings per share. (Assume all sales were on credit, the stockholders' equity was $120,000 on January 1, 197A, and total assets has not fluctuated during the year.)

Exercise 20–5

Common-size and trend percentages for a company's sales, cost of goods sold, and expenses follow:

COMMON-SIZE PERCENTAGES	197A	197B	197C	TREND PERCENTAGES	197A	197B	197C
Sales	100	100	100	Sales	100	110	120
Cost of goods sold.........	68	67	65	Cost of goods sold.........	100	108	115
Expenses	22	24	27	Expenses	100	120	147

Required:
Present statistics to prove whether the company's net income increased, decreased, or remained unchanged during the three-year period.

Problems   **Problem 20–1**

The condensed 197A statements of Surf Corporation follow:

SURF CORPORATION
Income Statement for Year Ended December 31, 197A

Sales..		$365,000
Cost of goods sold:		
Merchandise inventory, January 1, 197A	$ 41,500	
Purchases, net..	257,000	
Goods for sale...	$298,500	
Merchandise inventory, December 31, 197A............	38,500	
Cost of goods sold		260,000
Gross profit on sales...		$105,000
Operating expenses		75,500
Operating income...		$ 29,500
Interest expense		2,500
Income before taxes..		$ 27,000
Income taxes		6,000
Net Income		$ 21,000

618   Fundamental accounting principles

SURF CORPORATION
Balance Sheet, December 31, 197A

Cash	$ 7,750	Accounts payable	$ 17,500
Accounts receivable, net..............	18,250	Income taxes payable...................	2,500
Merchandise inventory	38,500	Mortgage payable, secured by a	
Prepaid expenses........................	1,500	lien on land and building...........	40,000
Equipment, net...........................	78,000	Common stock, $10 par value	125,000
Building, net	84,000	Retained earnings	55,000
Land	12,000		
Total Assets	$240,000	Total Equities	$240,000

Required:

Under the assumption the previous year's balance sheet showed total assets at $230,000 and stockholders' equity at $170,000, calculate the following: (1) current ratio; (2) acid-test ratio; (3) days' sales uncollected; (4) accounts receivable turnover; (5) merchandise turnover; (6) earnings per share; (7) rate of return on total assets employed; (8) rate of return on stockholders' equity; (9) percent of capital contributed by the owners; and (10) pledged plant assets to long-term liabilities.

Problem 20-2

Following are data from the statements of two competing companies:

Data from the Current December 31 Balance Sheets

	Company A	Company B
Cash	$ 8,000	$ 10,000
Notes receivable	3,500	4,000
Accounts receivable, net....................................	32,000	44,000
Merchandise inventory	28,500	40,500
Prepaid expenses...	1,500	1,000
Plant assets, net	139,500	165,500
Total Assets	$213,000	$265,000
Current liabilities...	$ 30,000	$ 40,000
Long-term liabilities	50,000	50,000
Common stock, $10 par value	100,000	100,000
Retained earnings	33,000	75,000
Total Liabilities and Capital	$213,000	$265,000

Data from the Current Yearly Income Statements

Sales	$288,000	$380,000
Cost of goods sold..	191,700	254,600
Interest expense...	3,000	3,000
Net income	13,200	16,900

Beginning of the Year Data

Merchandise inventory	$ 25,500	$ 37,500
Total assets	207,000	255,000
Stockholders' equity	127,000	169,000

Required:
1. Calculate current ratios, acid-test ratios, merchandise turnovers, and days' sales uncollected for the two companies. Then state which company you think is the better short-term credit risk and why.
2. Calculate earnings per share, rate of return on total assets employed, and rate of return on stockholders' equity. Then under the assumption that each company's stock could be purchased at book value, state which company's stock you think is the better investment and why.

Problem 20–3

Pine Corporation's 1974, 1975, and 1976 income statements carried the following information (in thousands of dollars):

	1976	1975	1974
Sales	$14,000	$12,000	$10,000
Cost of goods sold	10,150	8,580	7,000
Gross profit from sales	$ 3,850	$ 3,420	$ 3,000
Selling expenses	$ 1,975	$ 1,680	$ 1,400
Administrative expenses	1,165	1,080	1,000
Interest expense	50	50	50
Total expenses	$ 3,190	$ 2,810	$ 2,450
Income before taxes	$ 660	$ 610	$ 550
Income taxes	330	305	275
Net Income	$ 330	$ 305	$ 275

Its balance sheets for the same period carried this information (in thousands of dollars):

ASSETS

	1976	1975	1974
Current assets	$ 900	$ 700	$ 1,000
Plant and equipment	4,600	4,400	4,000
Total Assets	$ 5,500	$ 5,100	$ 5,000

LIABILITIES AND CAPITAL

	1976	1975	1974
Current liabilities	$ 360	$ 410	$ 400
Long-term liabilities	1,000	1,000	1,000
Common stock, $25 par value	2,800	2,500	2,500
Other contributed capital	260	200	200
Retained earnings	1,080	990	900
Total Liabilities and Capital	$ 5,500	$ 5,100	$ 5,000

Required:
1. Express the income statement items in common-size percentages.
2. Express the balance sheet items in trend percentages, using 1974 as the base year.
3. Comment on the trends and relations shown by your calculations.

Problem 20–4

The condensed comparative statements of High Flyer Company, Ltd. follow:

HIGH FLYER COMPANY, LTD.
Comparative Income Statements
Years Ended December 31, 1971–76
(in thousands of dollars)

	1971	1972	1973	1974	1975	1976
Sales	$500	$625	$735	$890	$930	$975
Cost of goods sold	350	441	511	637	672	714
Gross profit from sales	$150	$184	$224	$253	$258	$261
Operating expenses	100	124	146	181	190	202
Income before taxes	$ 50	$ 60	$ 78	$ 72	$ 68	$ 59

HIGH FLYER COMPANY, LTD.
Comparative Balance Sheets
As of December 31, 1971–76
(in thousands of dollars)

ASSETS

	1971	1972	1973	1974	1975	1976
Cash	$ 20	$ 21	$ 19	$ 13	$ 11	$ 9
Accounts receivable, net	50	58	56	92	97	99
Merchandise inventory	100	106	112	186	194	204
Long-term investments	30	30	30			
Plant and equipment, net	300	297	306	465	468	462
Total Assets	$500	$512	$523	$756	$770	$774

LIABILITIES AND CAPITAL

	1971	1972	1973	1974	1975	1976
Current liabilities	$ 50	$ 53	$ 58	$ 96	$107	$114
Long-term liabilities	60	60	60	165	165	165
Common stock	270	270	270	345	345	345
Retained earnings	120	129	135	150	153	150
Total Liabilities and Capital	$500	$512	$523	$756	$770	$774

Required:
1. Express the data of the statements in trends percentages.
2. Analyze and comment on any situations shown in the statements.

Problem 20–5

A company had $120,000 of current assets, a 2.4 to 1 current ratio, and a 1.2 to 1 acid-test ratio before completing these transactions:

a. Wrote off against the allowance for doubtful accounts an $800 uncollectible account receivable.
b. Sold for $5,000 a plant asset having a $6,000 book value.
c. Sold for $10,000 temporary investments that cost $15,000.
d. Sold for $15,000 merchandise that cost $10,000.
e. Borrowed $10,000 by giving the bank a 60-day note payable.
f. Declared a $0.50 per share dividend on the 10,000 outstanding shares of common stock.
g. Paid the dividend declared in transaction (f).
h. Borrowed $20,000 by placing a 6%, 20-year mortgage on the plant.
i. Declared a 1,000-share common stock dividend on a day when the stock was selling at $12.50 per share.
j. Distributed the stock of the dividend declared in transaction (i).

Required:
Prepare a three-column schedule showing in columns the company's current ratio, acid-test ratio, and working capital after each of the transactions.

Alternate problems

Problem 20–1A

The condensed statements of Douglas Corporation follow. Calculate the following ratios and turnovers for 1976: (1) current ratio; (2) acid-test ratio; (3) days' sales uncollected; (4) accounts receivable turnover; (5) merchandise turnover; (6) earnings per share; (7) rate of return on total assets employed; (8) rate of return on stockholders' equity; (9) per cent of capital contributed by owners; and (10) ratio of pledged plant assets to long-term liabilities (assume both building and equipment are mortgaged).

DOUGLAS CORPORATION
Comparative Balance Sheet
December 31, 1975, and 1976

	1976	1975
Cash	$ 6,000	$ 8,000
Accounts receivable, net	16,000	14,000
Merchandise inventory	32,000	28,000
Building and equipment, net	186,000	180,000
Total Assets	$240,000	$230,000
Current liabilities	$ 20,000	$ 15,000
Mortgage payable	80,000	85,000
Common stock, $10 par value	100,000	100,000
Retained earnings	40,000	30,000
Total Equities	$240,000	$230,000

Douglas Corporation
Comparative Income Statement
Years Ended December 31, 1975, and 1976

	1976	1975
Sales, all on credit	$200,000	$180,000
Cost of goods sold	120,000	109,000
Gross profit on sales	$ 80,000	$ 71,000
Operating expenses	49,000	45,000
Operating income	$ 31,000	$ 26,000
Interest expense	5,000	5,500
Income before taxes	$ 26,000	$ 20,500
Income taxes	6,000	5,500
Net Income	$ 20,000	$ 15,000

Problem 20–2A

Pinetop Corporation's condensed 1975 and 1976 statements follow:

Pinetop Corporation
Comparative Income Statements
Years Ended December 31, 1975, and 1976

	1976	1975
Sales	$900,000	$800,000
Cost of goods sold	559,200	488,500
Gross profit from sales	$340,800	$311,500
Selling expenses	$161,500	$144,500
Administrative expenses	85,500	81,500
Total expenses	$247,000	$226,000
Income before taxes	$ 93,800	$ 85,500
Income taxes	46,900	42,750
Net Income	$ 46,900	$ 42,750

Pinetop Corporation
Comparative Balance Sheets
As of December 31, 1975, and 1976

ASSETS

	1976	1975
Cash	$ 24,000	$ 24,000
Accounts receivable	50,000	56,000
Merchandise inventory	84,000	64,000
Plant assets, net	167,000	168,000
Total Assets	$325,000	$312,000

LIABILITIES AND CAPITAL

	1976	1975
Current liabilities	$ 50,000	$ 50,000
Long-term liabilities	60,000	60,000
Common stock	150,000	150,000
Retained earnings	65,000	52,000
Total Liabilities and Capital	$325,000	$312,000

Required:

1. Express the income statement data in common-size percentages and calculate the current ratio, acid-test ratio, merchandise turnover, and days' sales uncollected for each year. Assume the January 1, 1975, inventory was $58,000.
2. Comment on the situations shown by your calculations.

Problem 20–3A

The condensed statements of Sandy Corporation follow:

SANDY CORPORATION
Comparative Income Statements
Years Ended December 31
(in thousands of dollars)

	1976	1975	1974
Sales	$13,000	$12,000	$10,000
Cost of goods sold	8,995	8,260	6,800
Gross profit on sales	$ 4,005	$ 3,740	$ 3,200
Selling expenses	$ 2,120	$ 1,970	$ 1,600
Administrative expenses	1,120	1,110	1,000
Interest expense	25		
Total expenses	$ 3,265	$ 3,080	$ 2,600
Income before taxes	$ 740	$ 660	$ 600
Income taxes	370	330	300
Net Income	$ 370	$ 330	$ 300

SANDY CORPORATION
Comparative Balance Sheets
As of December 31
(in thousands of dollars)

ASSETS

	1976	1975	1974
Current assets	$ 750	$ 600	$ 800
Plant assets, net	4,000	3,520	3,200
Total Assets	$ 4,750	$ 4,120	$ 4,000

LIABILITIES AND CAPITAL

	1976	1975	1974
Current liabilities	$ 250	$ 295	$ 250
Long-term liabilities	500		
Common stock	2,500	2,500	2,500
Retained earnings	1,500	1,325	1,250
Total Liabilities and Capital	$ 4,750	$ 4,120	$ 4,000

Required:

1. Express the income statement items in common-size percentages.
2. Express the balance sheet items in trend percentages, using 1974 as the base year.
3. Comment on the trends and relations shown by your calculations.

Problem 20–5A

A company had $250,000 of current assets, a $2\frac{1}{2}$ to 1 current ratio, and a $1\frac{1}{4}$ to 1 acid-test ratio. It then completed these transactions:
a. Collected a $1,500 account receivable.
b. Sold for $35,000 a short-term investment carried on the books at its $25,000 cost.
c. Wrote off a $500 bad debt against the allowance for doubtful accounts.
d. Declared a $0.10 per share cash dividend on the 100,000 shares of common stock.
e. Paid the cash dividend declared in transaction (d).
f. Borrowed $10,000 by issuing a 60-day, 6% note payable.
g. Declared a 5,000-share stock dividend. The stock was selling for $12 per share on the day of the declaration.
h. Distributed the stock dividend of transaction (g).
i. Sold for $15,000 merchandise that cost $10,000.
j. Purchased $10,000 of merchandise on credit. The company uses a perpetual inventory system.

Required:
Prepare a three-column schedule showing the company's current ratio, acid-test ratio, and working capital after each transaction.

Decision problem 20–1, Pueblo Limited

As controller of Pueblo Company, Limited you have calculated the following ratios, turnovers. and percentages to aid you in answering questions the directors will ask at their next meeting.

	1976	1975	1974
Current ratio	2.8 to 1	2.4 to 1	2.2 to 1
Acid-test ratio	0.9 to 1	1.1 to 1	1.4 to 1
Merchandise turnover	7 times	8 times	9 times
Accounts receivable turnover	6 times	7 times	8 times
Return on stockholders' equity	6.8%	6.9%	7.1%
Return on total assets employed	6.2%	6.3%	6.4%
Sales to plant assets	4.1 to 1	3.9 to 1	3.4 to 1
Sales trend	132	121	100
Selling expenses as a percentage of sales	15.1%	15.5%	16.1%

Use the controller's statistics to answer the following questions, explaining in each case how you arrived at your answer.
a. Is it becoming easier for the company to pay its current debts on time and take advantage of all cash discounts?
b. Is the company collecting its accounts receivable more rapidly?
c. Are dollars of accounts receivable increasing?
d. Is the investment in inventory increasing?
e. Are plant facilities expanding?
f. Were dollars of selling expense greater in 1976 than in 1974?
g. Is the stockholders' investment becoming more profitable?
h. Is the company using debt leverage to the advantage of its stockholders?

Hill Company and Dale Company are competitors; both were organized 10 years ago; and both have seen their sales increase tenfold during the 10-year period. However, the tenfold increase is not as good as it sounds, because both companies' costs and selling prices have doubled during the same period. Nevertheless, the sales of both companies have and are increasing. Both offer the same credit terms; age their accounts receivable to allow for bad debts; and collect their accounts in about the same length of time. Actually about the only real difference in their accounting procedures is that Hill Company since its organization has used Fifo in costing its goods sold and Dale Company has used Lifo.

The current ratios of the two companies for the past four years were:

	Hill Company	Dale Company
December 31, 197A	5.2 to 1	3.3 to 1
December 31, 197B	5.6 to 1	3.1 to 1
December 31, 197C	5.9 to 1	2.8 to 1
December 31, 197D	6.0 to 1	3.0 to 1

You are the loan officer of a bank, and both companies have come to your bank for 90-day loans. In addition to the current ratios, you note that Dale Company has turned its inventory more than two and one half times as fast as Hill Company in each of the last four years. You also discover that for each $10,000 of current liabilities the companies have the following amounts of inventory:

	Hill Company	Dale Company
December 31, 197A	$41,000	$21,000
December 31, 197B	47,000	20,000
December 31, 197C	50,000	18,000
December 31, 197D	52,000	18,000

Which company do you think is the better short-term credit risk? Back your opinion with computations showing why. Are the inventory turnovers of the two companies comparable? Explain. Which company seems to have the better inventory turnover?

Jerry Bean has an opportunity to invest in either Company X or Company Y. The stock of either company can be bought at its book value, and he is undecided which is the better managed company and which is the better investment. Following are data from the financial statements of the companies:

DATA FROM THE CURRENT YEAR-END BALANCE SHEETS

	Company X	Company Y
Cash	$ 12,000	$ 14,500
Accounts receivable, net	30,000	40,000
Merchandise inventory	44,000	54,800
Prepaid expenses	1,200	1,200
Plant and equipment, net	165,800	174,500
Total Assets	$253,000	$285,000
Current liabilities	$ 40,000	$ 50,000
Mortgage payable	50,000	50,000
Common stock, $10 par value	100,000	100,000
Retained earnings	63,000	85,000
Total Liabilities and Capital	$253,000	$285,000

DATA FROM THE CURRENT YEAR'S INCOME STATEMENTS

	Company X	Company Y
Sales	$597,000	$696,000
Cost of goods sold	430,500	502,200
Gross profit on sales	$166,500	$193,800
Operating expenses	142,000	167,000
Operating income	$ 24,500	$ 26,800
Interest expense	3,000	3,500
Income before taxes	$ 21,500	$ 23,300
Income taxes	4,700	5,200
Net Income	$ 16,800	$ 18,100

BEGINNING-OF-THE-YEAR DATA

	Company X	Company Y
Merchandise inventory	$ 38,000	$ 53,200
Total assets	247,000	277,000
Stockholders' equity	157,000	177,000

Prepare a report to Jerry Bean stating which company you think is the better managed and which company's stock you think is the better investment. Back your report with any ratios, turnovers, and other analyses you think pertinent.

Analytical and review problems

Problem 20-1 A&R

RATIO DATA COMPANY, LTD.
Balance Sheet
As at June 1, 1975

Cash	$_____	Current Liabilities	$_____
Accounts Receivable	_____	Long-Term Debt @ 10%	_____
Inventory	_____	Shareholders' Equity	_____
Fixed Assets	_____		
	$_____		$_____

Required:

Using the format shown above complete the balance sheet for Ratio Data Company Ltd., from the following ratios (Round items to the nearest thousand dollars).

Net Income	$ 1,200,000
Sales	15,000,000
Current Ratio	2 to 1
Debt to Total Assets	50%
Inventory Turnover	10 times
Average (Collection Period (based on 360 days)	100 days
Fixed Asset Turnover	5 times
Total Asset Turnover	1.5 times
Expenses (including Income Tax @ 50%)	$ 3,800,000

(CGA adapted)

Problem 20–2 A&R

On the basis of the information given, complete the balance sheet.

RATIO COMPANY LIMITED
December 31, 1975

Cash	$_____	Current liabilities	$_____	
Accounts receivable	_____	8% Bonds payable	_____	
Inventory	_____	Shareholders' Equity	_____	
Fixed assets	_____			
	$_____		$_____	

Sales (all credit)	$10,000
Cost of goods sold	6,000
Expenses	2,000
Income taxes	1,000
Net income	1,000

Net income/shareholders' equity	25%
Bonds payable/shareholders' equity	1 to 2
Inventory turnover	4 times
Accounts receivable collection period (360-day year)	72 days
Current ratio	2.5 to 1
Total asset turnover	1.25 times
Rate of return (after taxes) on total investment	12.5%

(CGA adapted)

21

Flow of funds:
Flow of cash

■ At the end of an accounting period when financial statements are prepared, the income statement shows whether or not a business earned a net income during the period, the retained earnings statement summarizes the changes in its retained earnings, and the balance sheet shows its end-of-the-period financial position. However, for a better understanding of all of this, more information is needed; and this is supplied by a *statement of changes in financial position,* which as its name implies, summarizes the changes that have occurred in the financial position of the business during the period.

A statement of changes in financial position aids in understanding the financial position of a business by supplying answers to such questions as: How many dollars of funds flowed into the business from earnings and how were these funds used? What was the source of the funds used to finance the new plant? For what were the proceeds of the bond issue used? Why were there fewer current assets and more current liabilities at the end of the period than at the beginning? The statement supplies answers to such questions by showing from where a business got funds and how it used them. For this reason it is sometimes called a *statement of sources and uses of funds,* or a *statement of sources and applications of funds,* or simply a *funds statement;* however, the CICA recommends that the title "Statement of Changes in Financial Position" be used for published statements.

Broad
concept of
financing
and
investing
activities

■ The CICA, in 1974, also recommended that a statement of changes in financial position should be based on a broad concept of the financing and investing activities of a business and it should disclose all important aspects of such activities even though elements of working capital are not directly affected.[1] For example, the acquisition of a building in exchange for a mortgage or the conversion of bonds to stock are transactions that do not directly affect elements of working capital. However, such transactions should be disclosed on the statement of changes in financial position even though working capital is not directly involved. For example, if a building is acquired by issuing a mortgage, the issuance of the mortgage should be disclosed on the statement of changes in financial position as a source of funds, "Mortgage issued to acquire building." Likewise the acquisition of the building should appear as a use of funds, "Building acquired by issuing a mortgage."

■ The general public uses the word "funds" to mean cash, but businessmen apply a broader meaning. They use the word to describe working capital or, in other words, the excess of a concern's current assets over its current liabilities. Businessmen give the term this broader meaning because the current assets and current liabilities of a business constantly circulate. Short-term credit is used to buy merchandise, which is sold and turned into accounts receivable, which are collected and turned into cash, which is used to pay bills so that short-term credit can be used again to buy more merchandise, and so on. Therefore, since current assets and current liabilities are constantly circulating, it is only normal to think of that portion of the current assets not immediately needed to pay current debts as liquid resources or available funds. However, businessmen recognize that only a portion of these funds can be drawn off at any one time to pay dividends, buy plant assets, pay long-term debt, or for other like purposes. Only a portion can be used because a large share must remain in circulation.

■ Transactions that increase working capital are called *sources of funds,* and transactions that decrease working capital are *uses of funds.* If the working capital of a company increases during an accounting period, more funds are generated by its transactions than are used; and if working capital decreases, more funds are used than are generated.

Sources of funds

Some of the more common sources of funds are:

CURRENT OPERATIONS. Funds in the form of cash and accounts receivable flow into a business from sales; and funds flow out for expenses and goods sold. Consequently, funds are increased as a result of normal

---

[1] *CICA Handbook* (Toronto: The Canadian Institute of Chartered Accountants), pp. 281–82.

operations if the inflow from sales exceeds the outflow for expenses and goods sold.

In an analysis of a concern's funds the income statement shows how many dollars of funds were generated by operations. However, although the net income reported on the income statement is the amount revenues exceeded expenses, the net income figure does not generally represent the amount of funds from this source, because some expenses listed on an income statement, such as depreciation, depletion, and bond discount did not cause a funds outflow in the period of the statement.

For example, Rexel Sales Company, Illustration 21–1, experienced a $50,000 funds inflow from sales during the year. It also experienced outflows of $30,000 for goods sold, $8,000 for salaries, and $1,200 for rent; but there was no funds outflow for the depreciation expense. Consequently, during this period the company gained funds equal to the sum of its reported net income plus recorded depreciation, or it gained $9,800 plus $1,000 or $10,800 of funds from operations.

Illustration
21–1

Rexel Sales Company
Income Statement for Year Ended December 31, 19—

Sales..		$50,000
Cost of goods sold		30,000
Gross profit from sales		$20,000
Operating Expenses:		
Sales salaries expense	$8,000	
Rent expense...	1,200	
Depreciation expense, equipment	1,000	10,200
Net income		$ 9,800

Businessmen often speak of depreciation as a source of funds, but it is not. Look again at Illustration 21–1. Sales are the source of funds on this statement. No funds flowed into this company from recording depreciation. However, of the funds that flowed in from sales, none flowed out for depreciation. In this case, as with every business, the revenues are the source of funds from operations; but since depreciation, unlike most expenses, did not and does not cause a funds outflow in the current period, it must be added to the net income to determine funds from operations.

LONG-TERM LIABILITIES. Transactions that increase long-term liabilities increase working capital or are so treated and, therefore, are sources of funds regardless of whether long-term notes, mortgages, or bonds are involved. On the other hand, short-term credit, whether obtained from banks or other creditors, is not a source of funds because short-term credit does not increase working capital. For example, if $10,000 is borrowed for a short period, say six months, both current assets and current liabilities are increased; but since both are increased the same amount, total working capital is unchanged.

SALE OF NONCURRENT ASSETS. When a plant asset, long-term investment, or other noncurrent asset is sold for cash or receivables, working capital is increased by the amount of the sale; therefore, such sales are sources of funds.

SALE OF CAPITAL STOCK. The issuance of stock for cash or current receivables increases current assets; and as a result, such sales are sources of funds. Likewise, an additional investment of current assets by a single proprietor or partner is also a source of funds.

Uses of funds

Transactions that decrease working capital use funds. A list includes:

PURCHASE OF NONCURRENT ASSETS. When noncurrent assets such as plant and equipment or long-term investments are purchased, working capital is reduced; consequently, such purchases are uses of funds.

PAYMENT OF NONCURRENT LIABILITIES. Payment of a long-term debt such as a mortgage, bonds, or a long-term note reduces working capital and is a use of funds. Likewise, a contribution to a debt retirement fund, bond sinking fund, or other special noncurrent fund is also a use of funds.

CAPITAL REDUCTIONS. The withdrawals of cash or other current assets by a single proprietor, the purchase of treasury stock, or the purchase of stock for retirement reduce working capital and are uses of funds.

DECLARATION OF A DIVIDEND. The declaration of a dividend which is to be paid in cash or other current assets reduces working capital and is a use of funds. Note that it is the declaration that is the use. The declaration creates a current liability, dividends payable, and therefore reduces working capital as soon as it is voted by the board of directors. The final payment of a dividend previously declared does not affect working capital because it reduces current assets and current liabilities in equal amounts.

Statement of changes in financial position

■ A primary reason for preparing a statement of changes in financial position is to explain the increase or decrease in a concern's working capital. This is done by (1) listing on the statement all sources of new working capital, (2) listing the uses made of working capital, and then (3) setting out the difference, which is the net increase or decrease in working capital. Such a statement is shown in Illustration 21–2. Note that it covers a period of time and accounts for the increase or decrease in working capital during the period. It also summarizes the financing and investing activities of the business during the period, with the most important item being the amount of working capital generated by operations.

The ability of an enterprise to provide working capital through its operations is a most important factor in judging its success or lack of success. Consequently, the CICA has held that, as in Illustration 21–2, a concern's statement of changes in financial position should begin with

Illustration
21–2

Delta Company, Ltd.
Statement of Changes in Financial Position
For Year Ended December 31, 1976

Sources of working capital:
  Current operations:
    Net income for 1976.. $12,200
    Add expenses not requiring outlays of working
      capital in the current period:
    Depreciation of buildings and equipment............... 4,500
        Working capital provided by operations.............. $16,700
  Other sources:
    Mortgage issued to acquire land............................. $ 5,000
    Sale of common stock.. 12,500
                                                                                    17,500
        Total new working capital...................................... $34,200
Uses of working capital:
    Purchase of office equipment....................................... $ 500
    Purchase of store equipment..................................... 6,000
    Addition to building.. 15,000
    Reduction of mortgage debt...................................... 2,500
    Declaration of dividends.. 3,100
    Land acquired by issuing a mortgage......................... 5,000
        Total uses of working capital.................................... 32,100
Net Increase in Working Capital....................................... $ 2,100

the amount of its net income or loss for the period, before extraordinary items. To this should be added or deducted any items recognized in determining the income or loss, which did not require outlays of working capital. The resulting amount should then be appropriately described as, for example, "Working capital provided by operations" or "Working capital used in operations." (A net loss that exceeds the items not requiring working capital results in "Working capital used in operations.") Before going on, observe how the terminology of the statement avoids leaving the impression that depreciation is a source of funds.

Preparing a statement of changes in financial position

■ A statement of changes in financial position could be prepared by searching through a concern's current asset and current liability accounts for the transactions that increased or decreased its working capital. However, this would be time consuming because almost every transaction completed by a concern affected these accounts and only a very few of the transactions either increased or decreased its working capital. Therefore, in preparing a statement of changes in financial position, it is not the current asset and current liability accounts that are examined for working capital changes, but rather the noncurrent accounts. (The noncurrent accounts are the accounts other than the current asset and current liability accounts.) The noncurrent accounts are examined because (1) only a few transactions affected these accounts and (2) almost every one either increased or decreased working capital.

Normally, in making an audit of a company's records, as he examines the noncurrent accounts, the auditor makes a list of the transactions that

Delta Company, Ltd.
Comparative Balance Sheet
December 31, 1976, and December 31, 1975

ASSETS

	1976	1975
Current Assets:		
Cash	$ 7,500	$ 4,800
Accounts receivable, net	8,000	9,500
Merchandise inventory	31,500	32,000
Prepaid expenses	1,000	1,200
Total Current Assets	$ 48,000	$ 47,500
Plant and Equipment:		
Office equipment	$ 3,500	$ 3,000
Accumulated depreciation, office equipment	(900)	(600)
Store equipment	26,200	21,000
Accumulated depreciation, store equipment	(5,200)	(4,200)
Buildings	95,000	80,000
Accumulated depreciation, buildings	(10,600)	(8,200)
Land	30,000	25,000
Total Plant and Equipment	$138,000	$116,000
Total Assets	$186,000	$163,500

LIABILITIES

	1976	1975
Current Liabilities:		
Notes payable	$ 2,500	$ 1,500
Accounts payable	16,700	19,600
Dividends payable	1,000	700
Total Current Liabilities	$ 20,200	$ 21,800
Long-Term Liabilities:		
Mortgage payable	$ 22,500	$ 20,000
Total Liabilities	$ 42,700	$ 41,800

STOCKHOLDERS' EQUITY

	1976	1975
Common stock, $10 par value	$115,000	$100,000
Premium on common stock	8,500	5,000
Retained earnings	19,800	16,700
Total Stockholders' Equity	$143,300	$121,700
Total Liabilities and Stockholders' Equity	$186,000	$163,500

Illustration
21–3

affected these accounts during the period under review. He then uses this list along with company's balance sheets as of the beginning and end of the period to prepare the statement of changes in financial position. The comparative balance sheet of Illustration 21–3 and the following list of transactions that affected the noncurrent accounts of Delta Company were used in preparing the funds statement of Illustration 21–2.

a. Purchased office equipment costing $500 during the year.
b. Purchased store equipment that cost $6,000.

c. Discarded and junked fully depreciated store equipment that cost $800 when new.
d. Added a new addition to the building that cost $15,000.
e. Earned a $12,200 net income during the year.
f. Delta Company deducted on its 1976 income statement $300 of depreciation on office equipment, (g) $1,800 on its store equipment, and (h) $2,400 on its building.
i. Made a $2,500 payment on the mortgage.
j. Declared a 5% stock dividend at a time when the company's stock was selling for $12 per share.
k. Sold and issued 1,000 shares of common stock at $12.50 per share.
l. Declared cash dividends totaling $3,100 during the year.
m. Issued a $5,000 mortgage in exchange for land.

Steps in preparing a statement of changes in financial position

Three steps are involved in preparing a statement of changes in financial position. They are:

1. Determine the increase or decrease in working capital for the period of the statement.
2. Prepare a working paper to account for the changes in the company's noncurrent accounts and in the process set out on the working paper the period's sources and uses of working capital.
3. Use the working paper to prepare the formal statement of changes in financial position.

Determining the change in working capital ■ The 1976 change in Delta Company's working capital is calculated in Illustration 21–4. The calculation is a simple one requiring nothing more than a determination of the amounts of working capital at the beginning and at the end of the period and a subtraction to arrive at the increase or decrease in working capital.

Working capital, December 31, 1976:		
Current assets	$48,000	
Current liabilities	20,200	
Working capital		$27,800
Working capital, December 31, 1975:		
Current assets	$47,500	
Current liabilities	21,800	
Working capital		25,700
Increase in Working Capital		$ 2,100

Illustration 21–4

Preparing the working paper ■ Delta Company's sources and uses of funds resulted from simple transactions, and a statement of changes in financial position could be prepared for the company without a working paper. However, the working paper brings together in an orderly way the information needed

Delta Company, Ltd.
Working Paper for Statement of Changes in Financial Position
For Year Ended December 31, 1976

	Account Balances 12/31/75	Analyzing Entries Debit	Analyzing Entries Credit	Account Balances 12/31/76
Debits:				
Working capital..................................	25,700			27,800
Office equipment...............................	3,000	(a) 500		3,500
Store equipment	21,000	(b) 6,000	(c) 800	26,200
Buildings...	80,000	(d) 15,000		95,000
Land	25,000	(m) 5,000		30,000
Totals..	154,700			182,500
Credits:				
Accumulated depreciation, office equipment........	600		(f) 300	900
Accumulated depreciation, store equipment.........	4,200	(c) 800	(g) 1,800	5,200
Accumulated depreciation, buildings..................	8,200		(h) 2,400	10,600
Mortgage payable...............................	20,000	(i) 2,500	(m) 5,000	22,500
Common stock..................................	100,000		(j) 5,000 / (k) 10,000	115,000
Premium on common stock..........................	5,000		(j) 1,000 / (k) 2,500	8,500
Retained earnings	16,700	(j) 6,000 / (l) 3,100	(e) 12,200	19,800
Totals...	154,700			182,500
Sources of working capital:				
Current operations:				
Net income...............................		(e) 12,200		
Depreciation of office equipment		(f) 300		
Depreciation of store equipment..................		(g) 1,800		
Depreciation of buildings		(h) 2,400		
Other sources:				
Mortgage issued to acquire land..................		(m) 5,000		
Sale of stock..		(k) 12,500		
Uses of working capital:				
Purchase of office equipment..........................			(a) 500	
Purchase of store equipment...........................			(b) 6,000	
Addition to building......................................			(d) 15,000	
Reduction of mortgage			(i) 2,500	
Declaration of dividends			(l) 3,100	
Land acquired by issuing a mortgage..............			(m) 5,000	
Totals		73,100	73,100	

Illustration
21–5

for the statement and also offers a proof of the accuracy of the work.

The working paper for Delta Company's statement of changes in financial position is shown in Illustration 21–5. Such a working paper is prepared as follows:

1. First, the amount of working capital at the beginning of the period under review is entered on the first line in the first money column

and the amount of working capital at the end is entered in the last column.

2. Next, the noncurrent balance sheet amounts are entered on the working paper, the amounts or account balances as of the beginning of the period are entered in the first money column and those of the end in the last. Observe that debit items are listed first and are followed by credit items. This is a convenience that places the accumulated depreciation items with the liability and capital amounts.

3. After the noncurrent account balances are entered, the working capital amount and debit items in each column are added; then the credit items are added to be certain that debits equal credits.

4. After the items are added to see that debits equal credits, the phrase "Sources of working capital:" is written on the line following the total of the credit items. Sufficient lines are then skipped to allow for listing all possible fund sources and then the phrase "Uses of working capital:" is written.

5. Next, analyzing entries are entered in the second and third money columns. These entries do two things: (1) they account for or explain the amount of change in each noncurrent account and (2) they set out the sources and uses of working capital. (The analyzing entries on the illustrated working paper are discussed later in this chapter.)

6. After the last analyzing entry is entered, the working paper is completed by adding the Analyzing Entries columns to determine their equality. The information on the paper as to sources and uses of working capital is then used to prepare the formal statement of changes in financial position.

In passing it should be observed that a funds statement working paper is prepared solely for the purpose of bringing together information as to sources and uses of working capital and its analyzing entries are never entered in the accounts.

Analyzing entries

As previously stated, in addition to setting out sources and uses of funds, the analyzing entries on a funds statement working paper also account for or explain the amount of change in each noncurrent account. The change in each noncurrent account is explained with one or more analyzing entries because every transaction that caused an increase or decrease in working capital also increased or decreased a noncurrent account. Consequently, when all increases and decreases in noncurrent accounts are explained by means of analyzing entries, all sources and uses of working capital are set out on the working paper.

The analyzing entries on the working paper of Illustration 21–5 account for the changes in Delta Company's noncurrent accounts and set out its sources and uses of working capital. Explanations of the entries follow:

a. During the year Delta Company purchased new office equipment that cost $500. This required the use of working capital and also caused a $500 increase in the balance of its Office Equipment account. Consequently analyzing entry (a) has a $500 debit to Office Equipment and a like credit to "Uses of working capital: Purchase of office equipment." The debit accounts for the change in the Office Equipment account and the credit sets out the use of working capital.

b. Delta Company purchased $6,000 of new store equipment during the period. This required the use of $6,000 of working capital and the use is set out with analyzing entry (b). However, note that the $6,000 debit of the entry does not fully account for the change in the balance of the Store Equipment account. Analyzing entry (c) is also needed.

c. During the period under review Delta Company discarded and junked fully depreciated store equipment that, when new, had cost $800, and the entry made at that time to record the disposal decreased the company's Store Equipment and related accumulated depreciation accounts by $800. However, the disposal had no effect on the company's working capital. Nevertheless, analyzing entry (c) must be made to account for the changes in the accounts, otherwise all changes in the company's noncurrent accounts will not be explained; and unless all changes are explained, the person preparing the working paper cannot be certain that all sources and uses of funds have been set out on the working paper.

d. Delta Company used $15,000 to increase the size of its building. The cost of the addition was debited to the Buildings account and analyzing entry (d) sets out this use of funds.

e. Delta Company reported a $12,200 net income for 1976, and the income was a source of funds. In the end-of-the-year closing procedures the amount of this net income was transferred from the company's Income Summary account to its Retained Earnings account and helped change the balance of the latter account from $16,700 at the beginning of the year to $19,800 at the year-end. Observe the analyzing entry that sets out this source of funds on the working paper. The entry's debit sets out the net income as a source of funds and the credit helps explain the change in the Retained Earnings account.

f. (g), and (h) On its 1976 income statement Delta Company deducted $300 of depreciation expense on its office equipment, $1,800 on its store equipment, and $2,400 on its building. As previously explained, although depreciation is a rightful deduction from revenues in arriving at net income, any depreciation so deducted must be added to net income in determining working capital from operations. The debits of entries (f), (g), and (h) show the depreciation taken by the company as part of the working capital generated by operations, and the credits of the entries either account for or help account for the changes in the accumulated depreciation accounts.

i. On June 10 Delta Company made a $2,500 payment on the mortgage on its plant and equipment. The payment required the use of funds and it reduced the balance of the Mortgage Payable account by $2,500. Entry *(i)* sets out this use of funds and accounts for the change in the Mortgage Payable account.

j. At the September board meeting the directors of the company declared a 5% or 500 share stock dividend on a day the company's stock was selling at $12 per share. The declaration and later distribution of this dividend had no effect on the company's working capital. However, it did decrease Retained Earnings $6,000 and increase the Common Stock account $5,000 and Premium on Common Stock $1,000. Entry *(j)* accounts for the changes in the accounts resulting from the dividend.

k. In October the company sold and issued 1,000 shares of its common stock for cash at $12.50 per share. The sale was a source of funds that increased the balance of the company's Common Stock account $10,000 and increased the balance of its Premium on Common Stock account $2,500. Entry *(k)* sets out this source of funds and completes the explanation of the changes in the stock and premium accounts.

l. At the ends of each of the first three quarters in the year the company declared a $700 quarterly cash dividend, and on December 22 it declared a fourth $1,000 dividend, payable on the following January 15. The fourth dividend brought the total cash dividends declared the year to $3,100. Each declaration required the use of working capital and each reduced the balance of the Retained Earnings account. On the working paper the four dividends are combined and one analyzing entry is made for the $3,100 use of funds. The entry's debit helps account for the change in the balance of the Retained Earnings account and its credit sets out the use of funds.

m. During the year Delta Company issued a $5,000, 8% mortgage in exchange for land. Although the transaction does not directly affect working capital, consistent with the CICA recommendation, this financing activity is shown as a source of $5,000 and as a use of $5,000.

After the last analyzing entry is entered on a funds statement working paper, an examination is made to be certain that all changes in the noncurrent accounts listed on the paper have been explained with analyzing entries. To make this examination, the debits and credits in the Analyzing Entries columns opposite each beginning account balance are added to or are subtracted from the beginning balance, and the result must equal the ending balance. For example, the $3,000 beginning debit balance of office equipment plus the $500 debit of analyzing entry *(a)* equals the $3,500 ending amount of office equipment. Likewise, the $21,000 beginning balance of store equipment plus the $6,000 debit and minus the $800 credit equals the $26,200 ending balance for this asset, and so on down the working paper until all changes are accounted for. Then if in every case the debits and credits opposite each beginning balance explain the change in the balance, all sources and uses of working capital have been set out on the working paper and the working paper is completed by adding the amounts in its Analyzing Entries columns.

Preparing the statement of changes in financial position from the working paper

After the working paper is completed, the sources and uses of working capital set out on the bottom of the paper are used to prepare the formal statement of changes in financial position. This is a simple task that requires little more than a relisting of the sources and uses of funds on the formal statement, as a comparison of the items appearing on the statement of Illustration 21–2 with the items at the bottom of the working paper of Illustration 21–5 will show.

A net loss on the working paper

When a concern incurs a net loss, the amount of the loss is debited to its Retained Earnings account in the end-of-the-period closing procedures. Then, when the working paper for a statement of changes in financial position is prepared, the words "Net loss" are substituted for "Net income" in its sources of working capital section, and the amount of the loss is debited to Retained Earnings and credited to "Net loss" on the working paper. After this the loss is placed on the formal statement of changes in financial position as the first monetary item and the expenses not requiring outlays of working capital are deducted therefrom. If the net loss is less than these expenses, the resulting amount is working capital provided by operations. If the net loss exceeds these expenses, the result is working capital used in operations.

Analysis of working capital changes

■ A statement of changes in financial position accounts for the increase or decrease in a company's working capital by showing sources and uses of working capital. The usefulness of such a statement is enhanced if it is accompanied by a tabulation on which the changes in the various elements of the company's working capital are analyzed in appropriate detail. Such a tabulation for Delta Company is shown in Illustration 21–6. Note how the tabulation's final figure ties back to the final figure in Illustration 21–2.

An analysis of changes in working capital items may be attached to the statement of changes in financial position that it accompanies. Many concerns place the analysis on the same sheet of paper immediately after the statement of changes in financial position.

Information for preparing the analysis of changes in working capital is taken from balance sheets as of the beginning and end of the period

Delta Company, Ltd.
Analysis of Changes in Working Capital Items
For Year Ended December 31, 1976

Current Assets:	Dec. 31, 1976	Dec. 31, 1975	Working Capital Increases	Working Capital Decreases
Cash	$ 7,500	$ 4,800	$ 2,700	
Accounts receivable, net	8,000	9,500		$ 1,500
Merchandise inventory	31,500	32,000		500
Prepaid expenses	1,000	1,200		200
Total Current Assets	$48,000	$47,500		
Current Liabilities:				
Notes payable	$ 2,500	$ 1,500		1,000
Accounts payable	16,700	19,600	2,900	
Dividends payable	1,000	700		300
Total Current Liabilities	$20,200	$21,800		
Working Capital	$27,800	$25,700		
			$ 5,600	$ 3,500
Net Increase in Working Capital				2,100
			$ 5,600	$ 5,600

Illustration
21–6

under review. (Compare the information in Illustration 21–6 with that in Illustration 21–3.) The current asset and current liability items on the analysis and the preparation of the analysis need little discussion. However, students sometimes have difficulty understanding how, for example, an increase in a current liability results in a decrease in working capital. They should not, because a moment's thought will reveal that when a current liability increases, a larger amount is subtracted from current assets in determining working capital.

Extraordinary gains and losses

■ Extraordinary gains and losses are set out as special items on a company's income statement as was explained in Chapter 18, and they require special treatment on the statement of changes in financial position and on the working paper for such a statement. For example, Beta Company sold land that it had purchased some years before to expand its plant, but had not used for that or any other purpose. The land cost $15,000 and was sold for $25,000. The company paid $2,500 of income taxes on the sale and reported the $7,500 net gain on its income statement as shown in Illustration 21–7.

Since Beta Company, as is common, carried this land as a long-term investment, a noncurrent asset, the sale increased its working capital $22,500 (sale price of land less applicable income taxes). The sale also reduced by $15,000 the balance of the account, Land Held for Expansion; and it resulted in a $7,500 after-tax, extraordinary gain that was closed to Income Summary and included in the $39,500 net income carried to Retained Earnings at the end of the accounting period.

Beta Company, Ltd.
Income Statement for Year Ended December 31, 19—

Revenue:
Net sales $500,000
Cost and expenses:
Cost of goods sold $300,000
Selling and administrative expenses other than
depreciation.. 141,000
Depreciation expense, plant and equipment........ 9,000
Income taxes 18,000   468,000
Income before extraordinary gain........................... $ 32,000
Gain on sale of land held for expansion, net of $2,500 of
applicable income taxes..............................   7,500
Net Income .... $ 39,500

Illustration
21–7

	Analyzing Entries	
	Debit	Credit
Land held for expansion....................................		(a) 15,000
Accumulated depreciation, plant and equipment...........		(b) 9,000
Retained earnings..		(a) 39,500
Sources of working capital:		
Current operations:		
Income before extraordinary item...................	(a) 32,000	
Depreciation expense, plant and equipment	(b) 9,000	
Extraordinary item:		
Sale of land held for expansion.....................	(a) 22,500	
Other sources:		

Illustration
21–8

Sources of working capital:
Current operations:
Net income of 197A, exclusive of extraordinary item $32,000
Add expenses not requiring outlays of working capital
in the current period:
Depreciation expense, plant and equipment 9,000
Working capital provided by operations, exclusive
of extraordinary item... $41,000
Extraordinary item:
Sale of land held for expansion, net of $2,500 of
applicable income taxes.. 22,500
Other sources:

Illustration
21–9

As a result, the analyzing entries of Illustration 21–8 are required on the company's funds statement working paper to set out working capital generated by the land sale and by normal operations.

The working capital generated by the land sale is then shown on the formal statement of changes in financial position as an extraordinary item immediately after the amount of working capital provided by normal operations, as shown in Illustration 21–9.

CASH FLOW

■ Since the word "funds" in the phrase "funds flow" does not mean "cash," it follows that "funds flow" and "cash flow" are different. While funds flow refers to the flow of working capital, cash flow relates to the inflow and outflow of cash only.

Planning and controlling cash flow, or managing money, is an important phase of management's work. However, cash flow is also important to creditors, stockholders, and investors because cash flow affects ability to meet liabilities, pay dividends, replace plant assets, and to expand and grow.

Cash flow statement

■ A cash flow statement covers a period of time and accounts for the increase or decrease in a company's cash by showing where the company got cash and the uses it made of cash during the period. For example, Royal Supply Company of Illustration 21–10 began the period of the statement with $2,200 of cash. This beginning balance was increased $22,000 by cash from operations and $4,500 by cash from the sale of investments; and it was decreased $12,000 by the withdrawals of the business owner and $6,500 by the purchase of plant assets. Or there was an $8,000 net increase in cash during the period.

Royal Supply Company
Cash Flow Statement for Year Ended December 31, 19—

Cash balance, January 1, 19—		$ 2,200
Sources of cash:		
Cash generated by operations	$22,000	
Sale of investments	4,500	
Total sources of cash		$26,500
Uses of cash:		
Withdrawals of owner	$12,000	
Purchase of plant assets	6,500	
Total uses of cash		18,500
Increase in cash		8,000
Cash Balance, December 31, 19—		$10,200

Illustration
21–10

A work sheet similar to that utilized in preparing a statement of changes in financial position is commonly used to analyze the changes in a company's noncash accounts and to bring together the data needed to prepare a cash flow statement. A discussion of this work sheet is deferred to a more advanced text, and a simple analysis based on the difference between the cash basis and the accrual basis of accounting is used here to introduce the subject of cash flow. However, before beginning the analysis a review of the difference between the cash and the accrual bases of accounting is in order.

Under the cash basis of accounting a revenue appears on the income statement of the period in which it is collected in cash, regardless of when earned. For example, if a sale of merchandise is made in November, 197A, but the customer does not pay for the goods until January, 197B, under the cash basis of accounting the revenue from the sale appears on the 197B income statement. Likewise, under the cash basis of accounting an expense appears on the income statement of the period in which cash is disbursed in its payment, regardless of which accounting period benefited from its incurrence. Consequently, under the cash basis the gain or loss reported for an accounting period is the difference between cash received from revenues and cash disbursed for expenses. The difference is also the amount of cash generated by operations during the period.

Under the accrual basis of accounting all of this differs. Under the accrual basis revenues are credited to the period in which they are earned regardless of when cash is received and expenses are matched with revenues regardless of when cash is disbursed. As a result, under the accrual basis the gain or loss of an accounting period is the difference between revenues earned and the expenses incurred in earning the revenues. Most enterprises of any size use the accrual basis of accounting, and all accounting demonstrated thus far in this text has been accrual basis accounting.

Preparing a cash flow statement

■ Reexamine the cash flow statement of Illustration 21–10 and note that the cash inflow shown thereon from the sale of investments and the outflow for withdrawals and to buy plant assets need no explanations. However, the inflow of cash from operations does.

Cash flows into a company from sales and it flows out for goods sold and expenses; and although cost of goods sold and expenses are deducted from sales on an accrual basis income statement, the resulting net income figure does not show the amount of cash generated by operations. To determine cash from operations, it is necessary to convert the item amounts on a company's income statement from an accrual basis to a cash basis.

Royal Supply Company's accrual basis income statement appears in Illustration 21–11, and the statement amounts are converted from an accrual basis to a cash basis in Illustration 21–13. The conversion is

Royal Supply Company
Income Statement for Year Ended December 31, 19—

Sales, net...		$90,000
Cost of goods sold:		
Inventory, January 1, 19—.................................	$10,000	
Purchases, net	55,000	
Goods for sale...	$65,000	
Inventory, December 31, 19—............................	11,000	
Cost of goods sold		54,000
Gross profit from sales...		$36,000
Operating expenses:		
Depreciation expense..	$ 3,400	
Bad debts expense	300	
Salaries and wages expense.............................	12,500	
Other expenses	3,300	
Total operating expenses.................................		19,500
Net Income		$16,500

Illustration
21–11

Condensation of Royal Supply Company's Cash Account

(Debits)		(Credits)	
Balance, January 1	2,200	Cash purchases of merchandise.....	200
Cash sales	40,000	Payments to creditors for	
Accounts receivable collections	50,500	merchandise purchased	52,800
Sale of investments.......................	4,500	Salary and wage payments	12,100
		Payments for other expenses.........	3,400
		Plant asset purchases	6,500
		Withdrawals by owner...................	12,000
		Balance, December 31	10,200
Total	97,200	Total	97,200

Illustration
21–12

based on the information in the company's condensed Cash account which is shown in Illustration 21–12. Explanations of the conversion follow.

a. Cash flowed into Royal Supply Company from sales; but the $90,000 sales figure on the company's income statement was not the amount. Rather, cash from goods sold consisted of cash sales, $40,000, plus collections from customers, $50,500, or a total of $90,500, as shown in the condensed Cash account of Illustration 21–12. Consequently, since cash from goods sold was $500 greater than the income statement sales figure, $500 is added to convert the sales figure from an accrual basis to a cash basis.

b. Likewise, the $54,000 cost of goods sold figure on the income statement is not the amount of money that flowed out to pay for goods sold. Rather, the actual cash outflow for merchandise amounted to

Royal Supply Company
Conversion of Income Statement Amounts from an Accrual to a Cash Basis
For Year Ended December 31, 19—

	Accrual Basis Amounts	Add (Deduct)	Cash Basis Amounts
Sales, net...	$90,000	$ 500	$90,500
Cost of goods sold...	54,000	(1,000)	53,000
Gross profit from sales	$36,000		$37,500
Operating expenses:			
Depreciation expense......................................	$ 3,400	(3,400)	$ -0-
Bad debts expense..	300	(300)	-0-
Salaries and wages expense	12,500	(400)	12,100
Other expenses..	3,300	100	3,400
Total operating expenses.............................	$19,500		$15,500
Net Income..	$16,500		
Cash Generated by Operations............................			$22,000

Illustration
21–13

$53,000, $200 for cash purchases plus $52,800 paid to creditors for merchandise, as shown in the condensed Cash account. Since the cash outflow for the purchase of merchandise was $1,000 less than the accrual basis cost of goods sold figure, $1,000 is subtracted in converting cost of goods sold from an accrual to a cash basis.

c. Since depreciation and bad debts expense did not take cash, the amounts for these items are deducted in converting the income statement amounts to a cash basis.

d. And since the cash paid by Royal Supply Company for salaries and wages was $400 less than the accrual basis income statement amount for this expense and cash disbursed for "other expenses" was $100 more, $400 is deducted and $100 is added in converting these expenses to a cash basis.

The last figure in Illustration 21–13, the $22,000 of cash generated by operations, is the amount Royal Supply Company would have reported as net income had it kept its books on a cash basis rather than an accrual basis. The $22,000 is also the amount of cash the company got from its operations and the amount that appears on its Illustration 21–10 cash flow statement as cash from this source.

Questions for class discussion

1. When the word "funds" is used in connection with a funds statement, what are "funds"?
2. List several sources of funds. For what may a company use funds?
3. People in the field of finance often speak of depreciation as a source of funds. Is depreciation a source of funds?

4. Explain why such expenses as depreciation, amortization of patents, and of bond discount are added to the net income in order to determine funds provided by operations.

5. On December 12 a company borrowed $20,000 by giving its bank a 60-day, interest-bearing note. Was this transaction a source of working capital?

6. A company began an accounting period with a $45,000 merchandise inventory and ended it with a $40,000 inventory. Was the decrease in inventory a source of funds?

7. What is shown on a statement of changes in financial position?

8. Why are the noncurrent accounts examined for sources of funds?

9. When a working paper for the preparation of a statement of changes in financial position is prepared, all changes in noncurrent balance sheet accounts are accounted for on the working paper. Why?

10. A company discarded and wrote off fully depreciated store equipment. What account balances appearing on the funds statement working paper were affected by the write-off? What analyzing entry was made on the working paper to account for the write-off? If the write-off did not affect working capital, why was the analyzing entry made on the working paper?

11. Explain why a decrease in a current liability results in an increase in working capital.

12. How is the amount of cash generated by a company's operations determined?

Class exercises

Exercise 21–1

From the following income statement of Seaside Corporation list and total the amounts of working capital the company gained from current operations.

SEASIDE CORPORATION
Income Statement for Year Ended December 31, 19—

Sales..		$750,000
Cost of goods sold		525,000
Gross profit from sales		$225,000
Operating expenses:		
Salaries and wages..	$115,000	
Depreciation expense	20,000	
Advertising expense	5,000	
Patent costs written off...	2,000	
Bad debts expense	3,000	145,000
Operating income..		$ 80,000
Bond interest expense (including $6,000 accrued interest payable and $500 of bond discount amortized)...		12,500
Net Income		$ 67,500

Exercise 21–2

Ridgeway Corporation's 1975 and 1976 year-end balance sheets carried these debit and credit amounts:

Debits	1976	1975
Cash..	$ 4,000	$ 3,000
Accounts receivable, net	8,000	10,000
Merchandise inventory.................................	22,000	20,000
Equipment...	19,000	15,000
Totals	$53,000	$48,000

Credits		
Accumulated depreciation, equipment..............	$ 5,000	$ 4,000
Accounts payable...	4,000	6,000
Taxes payable	2,000	1,000
Common stock, no par value	28,000	25,000
Retained earnings..	14,000	12,000
Totals	$53,000	$48,000

Required:

Prepare a working paper for 1976 statement of changes in financial position, using the following information from the company's 1976 income statement and accounts:

a. The company's income statement showed an $8,000 net income for 1976.
b. The company's equipment was depreciated $2,000 during the year.
c. Equipment costing $5,000 was purchased.
d. Fully depreciated equipment that cost $1,000 was discarded, and its cost and accumulated depreciation were removed from the accounts.
e. Two hundred shares of the company's common stock were sold and issued at $15 per share.
f. Dividends totaling $6,000 were declared and paid during the year.

Exercise 21–3

From the working paper prepared for Exercise 21–2 prepare a statement of changes in financial position for Ridgeway Corporation.

Exercise 21–4

From the information supplied in Exercise 21–2 prepare an analysis of changes in Ridgeway Corporation's working capital items for the year ended December 31, 1976.

Exercise 21–5

Following is the 197A income statement of Hillside Company and an analysis of the items in its Cash account:

HILLSIDE COMPANY

Income Statement for Year Ended December 31, 197A

Sales, net		$80,000
Cost of goods sold:		
Merchandise inventory, January 1, 197A	$10,000	
Purchases, net	52,000	
Goods for sale	$62,000	
Merchandise inventory, December 31, 197A	12,000	
Cost of goods sold		50,000
Gross profit on sales		$30,000
Operating expenses:		
Salaries and wages expense	$10,000	
Rent expense	6,000	
Depreciation expense, equipment	3,000	
Bad debts expense	1,000	20,000
Net Income		$10,000

Cash Account Analysis

Cash balance, January 1, 197A		$ 5,000
Debits:		
Cash sales	$25,000	
Accounts receivable collections	50,000	
Bank loan	3,000	78,000
Total		$83,000
Credits:		
Payments to creditors for merchandise	$51,000	
Salary and wage payments	9,700	
Rent payments	6,000	
Payment for new equipment purchased	3,800	
Personal withdrawals of proprietor	8,000	78,500
Cash Balance, December 31, 197A		$ 4,500

Required:

1. Prepare a statement converting the company's income statement amounts from an accrual basis to a cash basis.
2. Prepare a cash flow statement for the company.

Problems   **Problem 21–1**

A comparative balance sheet of Southern Company, Ltd., carried these items:

SOUTHERN COMPANY, LTD.
Comparative Balance Sheets
December 31, 1975 and 1976

ASSETS

Current Assets:	1976	1975
Cash	$ 12,700	$ 11,800
Accounts receivable, net	34,900	33,400
Merchandise inventory	85,900	86,700
Prepaid expenses	2,000	1,800
Total Current Assets	$135,500	$133,700
Plant and Equipment:		
Office equipment	$ 5,400	$ 6,100
Accumulated depreciation, office equipment	(2,500)	(2,400)
Store equipment	31,700	27,800
Accumulated depreciation, store equipment	(7,400)	(6,500)
Total Plant and Equipment	$ 27,200	$ 25,000
Total Assets	$162,700	$158,700

LIABILITIES

Current Liabilities:		
Accounts payable	$ 19,500	$ 20,200
Notes payable	4,500	5,000
Income taxes payable	3,500	3,300
Total Liabilities	$ 27,500	$ 28,500

STOCKHOLDERS' EQUITY

Common stock, $5 par value	$105,000	$100,000
Premium on common stock	8,500	5,500
Retained earnings	21,700	24,700
Total Stockholders' Equity	$135,200	$130,200
Total Liabilities and Stockholders' Equity	$162,700	$158,700

An examination of the company's 1976 income statement and accounting records revealed this additional information:

a. A $15,000 net income was earned in 1976.
b. Depreciation charged on office equipment, $600; and on store equipment, $1,500.
c. Office equipment that cost $700 and had been depreciated $500 was sold to an employee for its book value.
d. Store equipment that cost $4,500 was purchased during 1976.
e. Fully depreciated store equipment that cost $600 was discarded, and its cost and accumulated depreciation were removed from the accounts.
f. Cash dividends totaling $10,000 were declared during the year.
g. A 5% stock dividend was declared and distributed during the year at a time when the company's stock was selling at $8 per share.

Required:
Prepare (1) a working paper for a 1976 statement of changes in Southern

Company, Ltd.'s financial position and (2) a statement of changes in the company financial position. Also, (3) prepare an analysis of changes in the company's working capital items.

Problem 21-2

Vale Corporation's 1975 and 1976 comparative balance sheet carried these items:

ASSETS

	December 31	
	1976	1975
Cash	$ 10,400	$ 11,500
Accounts receivable, net	26,600	27,300
Merchandise inventory	68,700	64,200
Prepaid expenses	1,100	800
Office equipment	6,100	6,200
Accumulated depreciation, office equipment	(2,100)	(1,900)
Store equipment	39,900	39,800
Accumulated depreciation, store equipment	(10,900)	(7,600)
	$139,800	$140,300

LIABILITIES AND STOCKHOLDERS' EQUITY

Notes payable	$ 5,000	$ 2,500
Accounts payable	17,300	17,600
Common stock, $5 par value	105,000	100,000
Premium on common stock	5,500	4,000
Retained earnings	7,000	16,200
	$139,800	$140,300

The company's 1976 income statement and accounting records revealed the following:

a. A $700 net loss for 1976.
b. Depreciation on office equipment, $600; and on store equipment, $3,800.
c. Office equipment costing $300 was purchased during the year.
d. Fully depreciated office equipment that cost $400 was discarded, and its cost and accumulated depreciation were removed from the accounts.
e. Store equipment that cost $800 and had been depreciated $500 was traded in on new equipment having a $1,000 cash price. A $400 trade-in allowance was received.
f. A 1,000-share stock dividend was declared and distributed while the stock was selling at $6.50 per share.
g. Cash dividends totaling $2,000 were declared and paid during the year.

Required:
Prepare a working paper for a statement of changes in financial position and a statement of changes in financial position.

Problem 21-3

Sunshine Corporation's 1976 comparative balance sheet carried these items:

ASSETS

	December 31,	
	1976	1975
Cash	$ 14,800	$ 18,600
Accounts receivable, net	15,800	16,200
Merchandise inventory	73,500	72,400
Other current assets	1,100	1,400
Office equipment	4,500	4,700
Accumulated depreciation, office equipment	(1,900)	(1,600)
Store equipment	22,000	15,500
Accumulated depreciation, store equipment	(4,600)	(4,200)
Building	85,000	-0-
Accumulated depreciation, building	(2,000)	-0-
Land	20,000	-0-
Totals	$228,200	$123,000

EQUITIES

Notes payable	$ 7,500	$ -0-
Accounts payable	29,200	28,400
Other current liabilities	1,800	2,100
Mortgage payable	60,000	-0-
Common stock	105,000	75,000
Retained earnings	24,700	17,500
Totals	$228,200	$123,000

The company's 1976 income statement and accounting records showed the following:

a. A 1976 net income of $13,200.
b. Depreciation on office equipment, $500; on store equipment, $1,600; and on the building, $2,000.
c. Fully depreciated office equipment that cost $200 was discarded, and its cost and accumulated depreciation were removed from the accounts.
d. Store equipment that cost $8,000 was purchased during the year.
e. Store equipment that cost $1,500 and had been depreciated $1,200 was sold to an employee for its book value.
f. The mortgage was incurred in purchasing for $105,000 the land and building previously rented by the company.
g. One thousand shares of common stock were sold and issued at $30 per share.
h. Cash dividends totaling $6,000 were declared and paid during the year.

Required:
Prepare a working paper for a statement of changes in financial position and a statement of changes in financial position. Also prepare an analysis of changes in working capital items.

Problem 21–4
Alpha Corporation's 1976 comparative balance sheet carried these items:

ASSETS

	December 31, 1976	1975
Cash	$ 20,200	$ 15,400
Accounts receivable, net	33,200	32,100
Inventories	60,700	56,400
Prepaid expenses	2,000	1,700
Bond sinking fund	8,000	-0-
Land held for expansion	-0-	10,000
Machinery	126,600	92,800
Accumulated depreciation, machinery	(39,700)	(33,700)
Buildings	194,500	112,500
Accumulated depreciation, buildings	(25,000)	(20,200)
Factory land	30,000	30,000
Totals	$410,500	$297,000

EQUITIES

Accounts payable	$ 21,400	$ 23,600
Wages payable	2,900	2,800
Income taxes payable	5,100	4,200
Bonds payable	100,000	-0-
Discount on bonds payable	(1,800)	-0-
Common stock, $10 par value	210,000	200,000
Premium on common stock	22,500	20,000
Retained earnings	50,400	46,400
Totals	$410,500	$297,000

At the end of 1976 the company's noncurrent accounts showed these amounts:

Bond Sinking Fund

Date	Explanation	Debit	Credit	Balance
1976 Dec. 31	First annual deposit	8,000		8,000

Land Held for Expansion

Date	Explanation	Debit	Credit	Balance
1976 Jan. 1	Balance			10,000
May 7	Sold		10,000	-0-

Machinery

Date	Explanation	Debit	Credit	Balance
1976 Jan. 1	Balance			92,800
23	Purchase	38,100		130,900
July 8	Discarded machinery		4,300	126,600

Accumulated Depreciation, Machinery

Date	Explanation	Debit	Credit	Balance
1976				
Jan. 1	Balance			33,700
July 8	Discarded machinery	4,300		29,400
Dec. 31	Year's depreciation		10,300	39,700

Buildings

Date	Explanation	Debit	Credit	Balance
1976				
Jan. 1	Balance			112,500
8	Building addition	82,000		194,500

Accumulated Depreciation, Buildings

Date	Explanation	Debit	Credit	Balance
1976				
Jan. 1	Balance			20,200
Dec. 31	Year's depreciation		4,800	25,000

Factory Land

Date	Explanation	Debit	Credit	Balance
1976				
Jan. 1	Balance			30,000

Bonds Payable

Date	Explanation	Debit	Credit	Balance
1976				
Jan. 1	Issued 7½% 10-year bonds		100,000	100,000

Bond Discount

Date	Explanation	Debit	Credit	Balance
1976				
Jan. 1	Discount on issuance	2,000		2,000
June 30	Amortization		100	1,900
Dec. 31	Amortization		100	1,800

Common Stock, $10 Par Value

Date	Explanation	Debit	Credit	Balance
1976				
Jan. 1	Balance			200,000
Dec. 1	Stock dividend		10,000	210,000

Premium on Common Stock

Date	Explanation	Debit	Credit	Balance
1976				
Jan. 1	Balance			20,000
Dec. 1	Stock dividend		2,500	22,500

Retained Earnings

Date	Explanation	Debit	Credit	Balance
1976				
Jan. 1	Balance			46,400
June 9	Cash dividend	16,000		30,400
Dec. 1	Stock dividend	12,500		17,900
31	Net income		32,500	50,400

The land held for expansion was not used in the expansion and was sold for $16,700. The company paid $1,700 of income taxes on the transaction and included the $5,000 net gain as an extraordinary item in the $32,500 net income it reported for the year.

Required:

Use the information supplied to prepare a working paper for a statement of changes in financial position, a statement of changes in financial position, and an analysis of changes in working capital items.

Problem 21–5

The income statement of The Tackle Shop and an analysis of its Cash account for the year of the income statement follow:

THE TACKLE SHOP

Income Statement for Year Ended December 31, 19—

Sales, net..		$258,400
Cost of goods sold:		
Merchandise inventory, January 1, 19—	$ 52,200	
Purchases, net	174,500	
Goods for sale..	$226,700	
Merchandise inventory, December 31, 19—	53,800	
Cost of goods sold		172,900
Gross profit on sales...		$ 85,500
Operating expenses:		
Salaries and wages expense	$ 48,600	
Rent expense	15,000	
Depreciation expense	3,200	
Bad debts expense	1,200	
Store supplies expense...	1,000	
Other operating expenses	1,800	
Total operating expenses.....................................		70,800
Operating income..		$ 14,700
Interest expense		100
Net Income		$ 14,600

Analysis of Cash Account

Cash balance, January 1, 19–		$ 10,200
Debits:		
Cash sales	$ 62,500	
Accounts receivable collections...........................	196,500	
Bank loan	5,000	
Sale of unneeded equipment at book value	300	264,300
Total...		$274,500
Credits:		
Creditor payments for merchandise purchased	$175,300	
Rent payments	16,250	
Creditor payments for store supplies bought.............	800	
Salary and wage payments....................................	48,100	
Other operating expense payments.........................	1,700	
New equipment purchased....................................	10,000	
Personal withdrawals by proprietor	12,000	264,150
Cash Balance, December 31, 19–		$ 10,350

Required:

Prepare a statement converting the company's income statement amounts from an accrual basis to a cash basis and prepare a cash flow statement for the company.

Alternate problems

Problem 21–2A

Fred Craft operates South Beach Shop as a single proprietorship, and the store's 1976 comparative balance sheet carried these amounts:

ASSETS

	1976	1975
Cash	$ 5,200	$ 4,400
Accounts receivable, net...	15,100	15,600
Merchandise inventory...	30,300	31,200
Prepaid expenses..	1,100	900
Office equipment..	2,800	2,600
Accumulated depreciation, office equipment...................	(900)	(800)
Store equipment...	14,900	12,500
Accumulated depreciation, store equipment	(4,700)	(3,800)
Totals...	$63,800	$62,600

LIABILITIES AND OWNER EQUITY

Notes payable..	$ 4,000	$ 5,000
Accounts payable..	16,000	14,500
Fred Craft, capital..	43,800	43,100
Totals...	$63,800	$62,600

The store's 1976 balance sheet summarized the change in owner equity as follows:

Fred Craft, capital, January 1, 1976		$43,100
Net income for the year	$10,300	
Less withdrawals..	9,600	
Excess of income over withdrawals		700
Fred Craft, capital, December 31, 1976		$43,800

The accounts showed that during 1976: (1) Office equipment that cost $400 and had been depreciated $200 was traded on office equipment having a $500 cash price. A $100 trade-in allowance was received, and the income tax method was used to record the transaction. (2) Store equipment costing $3,000 was purchased. (3) Fully depreciated store equipment that cost $600 when new was discarded. (4) The 1976 income statement showed depreciation expense on office equipment, $300; and on store equipment, $1,500.

Required:
Prepare a working paper for a 1976 statement of changes in the store's financial position and a statement of changes in financial position.

Problem 21–3A

The 1976 comparative balance sheet of Dockside Corporation carried these items:

ASSETS

	December 31, 1976	December 31, 1975
Cash..	$ 19,100	$ 22,300
Accounts receivable, net	16,200	15,600
Merchandise inventory...	50,200	51,400
Prepaid expenses	1,300	1,100
Land held for new store building	-0-	15,000
Office equipment...	4,400	4,200
Accumulated depreciation, office equipment	(1,400)	(1,300)
Store equipment..	26,000	24,300
Accumulated depreciation, store equipment................	(5,200)	(3,600)
Store building...	100,000	-0-
Accumulated depreciation, store building	(1,200)	-0-
Land...	20,000	-0-
Totals	$229,400	$129,000

EQUITIES

Accounts payable..	$ 17,300	$ 18,700
Income taxes payable	4,400	4,100
Mortgage payable..	65,000	-0-
Common stock, no par value.....................................	104,000	80,000
Retained earnings..	38,700	26,200
Totals	$229,400	$129,000

The company's 1976 income statement and accounting records showed:

a. The company sold for $19,000 the land it had held for the construction of a new store building. It paid $1,000 of applicable income taxes on the transaction and included the $3,000 net gain as an extraordinary item in its $18,500 reported net income for the year.

b. It then purchased for $120,000 the land and building it had occupied as a rental for a number of years, giving $55,000 in cash and issuing a mortgage for the balance.

c. Office equipment that cost $500 and had been depreciated $300 was traded in on new office equipment priced at $800. A $300 trade-in allowance was received.

d. Store equipment that cost $2,500 was purchased during the year.

e. Fully depreciated store equipment that cost $800 was discarded, and its cost and accumulated depreciation were removed from the accounts.

f. The office equipment was depreciated $400, the store equipment $2,400, and the building $1,200 during the year.

g. Two thousand shares of common stock were sold and issued at $12 per share.

h. Cash dividends totaling $6,000 were declared and paid during the year.

Required:

Prepare (1) a working paper for a statement of changes in financial position, (2) a statement of changes in financial position, and (3) an analysis of changes in the company's working capital items.

Problem 21–5A

The income statement of The Deep Sea Shop and an analysis of its Cash account for the year of the income statement follow:

THE DEEP SEA SHOP
Income Statement for Year Ended December 31, 19—

Sales, net		$121,400
Cost of goods sold:		
Merchandise inventory, January 1, 19— $22,400		
Purchases, net.. 77,100		
Goods for sale $99,500		
Merchandise inventory, December 31, 19— 21,300		
Cost of goods sold...		78,200
Gross profit on sales		$ 43,200
Operating expenses:		
Salaries and wages expense $30,300		
Rent expense... 9,000		
Depreciation expense 2,400		
Bad debts expense 600		
Store supplies expense... 1,200		
Total operating expenses......................................		43,500
Operating loss...	$	(300)
Interest expense		200
Net Loss...	$	(500)

Analysis of Cash Account

Cash balance, January 1, 19–		$ 6,200
Debits:		
Cash sales	$26,400	
Accounts receivable collections..............................	97,100	
Sale of unneeded equipment at book value.................	200	
Bank loan...	5,000	128,700
Total		$134,900
Credits:		
Payments to creditors for merchandise	$78,400	
Payments for store supplies....................................	1,400	
Salary and wage payments	30,200	
Rent payments	8,250	
Purchase of equipment	1,500	
Personal withdrawals of proprietor	7,200	126,950
Cash Balance, December 31, 19–		$ 7,950

Required:

Prepare a statement converting the company's income statement amounts from an accrual basis to a cash basis and prepare a cash flow statement for the company.

Decision problem 21–1, Mesa Company, Ltd.

The presidents of Mesa Company, Ltd., and Chandler Company are on very good terms, since Chandler Company makes components for Mesa Company. They often play golf together, and today on the golf course the president of Mesa Company bragged that his company had purchased $2,500,000 of new equipment during 1975 and 1976 without incurring any long-term debt or issuing any additional stock. The president of Chandler Company wondered how this was done, but did not ask. However, on returning to his office he got out the financial statements of Mesa Company, and they provided him with the following information:

	In Thousands of Dollars		
	1976	*1975*	*1974*
Net income after taxes...	$390	$360	$320
Depreciation on plant and equipment.......................	420	360	300
Dividends declared and paid	150	150	150

Included in the 1976 net income was a $10,000 extraordinary net-of-tax gain from the sale of land originally purchased for an expansion. The land had cost $50,000 and was sold for $60,000, net of taxes. The company's balance sheet provided this information:

MESA COMPANY, LTD.
Comparative Balance Sheets
December 31, 1974, 1975, and 1976
(in thousands of dollars)

ASSETS

	1976	1975	1974
Cash	$ 790	$ 660	$ 510
Temporary investments	-0-	1,100	1,500
Accounts receivable, net	840	790	820
Inventories	960	1,020	930
Land held for expansion	-0-	50	50
Plant and equipment	7,000	5,300	4,500
Accumulated depreciation, plant and equipment	(1,990)	(1,570)	(1,210)
Total Assets	$7,600	$7,350	$7,100

EQUITIES

	1976	1975	1974
Accounts payable	$ 960	$ 970	$ 940
Other short-term payables	830	810	800
Common stock	3,500	3,500	3,500
Retained earnings	2,310	2,070	1,860
Total Equities	$7,600	$7,350	$7,100

Explain how Mesa Company, Ltd. was able to purchase $2,500,000 of plant and equipment during 1975 and 1976. Back your explanation with figures and a statement of changes in financial position covering that period.

Decision problem 21-2, Tackle Shop

Ted Blake owns Tackle Shop, a sporting goods store; and during 1976 he remodeled and replaced $18,000 of the store's fully depreciated equipment with new equipment costing $22,000. However, by the year-end he was having trouble meeting the store's current expenses and had to secure a $5,000 short-term bank loan. As a result he asked his accountant to prepare some sort of a report showing what had happened to the store's funds during the year. The accountant analyzed the changes in the store's 1976 accounts and produced the following funds statement at the top of the next page.

On reading the report, Mr. Blake was dumbfounded by the $2,700 increase in funds in a year he knew his store's bank balance had decreased by $8,500. Also, he could not understand how depreciation was a source of funds, but the $5,000 bank loan was not. Explain these points to Mr. Blake, and attach to your explanation any additional or different statement from that prepared by the accountant that you think helps make your explanation clear.

TACKLE SHOP
Statement of Sources and Uses of Funds
Year Ended December 31, 1976

Sources of funds:
  Current operations:
    Net income earned in 1976 .... $17,200
    Add expenses not requiring the use of funds:
      Depreciation of store equipment   4,500
        Total funds from operations $21,700
  Other sources:
    Mortgage on new store equipment 15,000
      Total new funds $36,700
Uses of funds:
  Purchase of new equipment $22,000
  Personal withdrawals of proprietor 12,000
    Total uses of funds   34,000
Net Increase in Funds .... $ 2,700

The following post-closing trial balances were used by the accountant in preparing the store's statement of changes in financial position or funds statement.

TACKLE SHOP
1975–76 Post-Closing Trial Balances

	Dec. 31, 1976		Dec. 31, 1975	
Cash	$ 2,900		$11,400	
Accounts receivable	17,900		13,900	
Allowance for doubtful accounts		$ 500		$ 400
Merchandise inventory	27,400		17,200	
Prepaid expenses	800		500	
Store equipment	39,000		35,000	
Accumulated depr., store equipment ...		10,500		24,000
Notes payable		5,000		
Accounts payable		8,800		10,400
Accrued payables		500		700
Mortgage payable		15,000		
Ted Blake, capital		47,700		42,500
Totals	$88,000	$88,000	$78,000	$78,000

Decision problem 21–3, Blue Lake Store   At the end of 1976 the accountant of Blue Lake Store prepared the following income statement, the statement of changes in financial position, and the analysis of changes in working capital items for Blue Lake Store's owner, Jerry Lake.

When Mr. Lake saw the income statement, he was pleased to learn that his net income had increased 25% in 1976, but he could not understand how this could happen in a year in which his cash had declined to the point that he had found it necessary in late December to secure a $5,000 short-term bank loan in order to meet his current expenses. His accountant pointed to the statement of changes in financial position by way of explanation, but this statement only confused Mr. Lake further. He could not understand how depreciation could be a source of funds, while a bank loan was not, and he could not understand how his funds could increase $3,000 at a time when his cash decreased $11,700.

BLUE LAKE STORE
Comparative Income Statement
Years Ended December 31, 1975–76

	1976		1975	
Sales.....................................		$250,000		$230,000
Cost of goods sold:				
Inventory, January 1	$ 25,000		$ 28,000	
Purchases............................	160,000		137,000	
Goods for sale......................	$185,000		$165,000	
Inventory, December 31	35,000		25,000	
Cost of goods sold		150,000		140,000
Gross profit on sales.................		$100,000		$ 90,000
Operating expenses:				
Salaries and wages	$ 63,000		$ 60,000	
Depreciation of plant assets.....	10,000		8,500	
Insurance and supplies............	2,000		1,500	
Total operating expenses......		75,000		70,000
Net Income		$ 25,000		$ 20,000

BLUE LAKE STORE
Statement of Changes in Financial Position
Year Ended December 31, 1976

Sources of working capital:
Current operations:
Net income for 1976.. $25,000
Add expenses not requiring working capital outlays
in the current period:
Depreciation of plant assets 10,000
Total new working capital............................... $35,000
Uses of working capital:
Purchase of new plant assets.................................... $17,000
Reduction of mortgage 3,000
Personal withdrawals of proprietor............................ 12,000
Total uses of working capital................................. 32,000
Net Increase in Working Capital.................................... $ 3,000

BLUE LAKE STORE
Analysis of Changes in Working Capital Items
Year Ended December 31, 1976

	Dec. 31, 1976	Dec. 31, 1975	Working Capital Increase	Working Capital Decreases
Current Assets:				
Cash	$ 3,500	$15,200		$11,700
Accounts receivable, net	36,000	30,000	$ 6,000	
Merchandise inventory.................................	35,000	25,000	10,000	
Prepaid expenses	500	800		300
Total Current Assets	$75,000	$71,000		
Current Liabilities:				
Notes payable	$ 5,000			5,000
Accounts payable (for merchandise)	20,000	$23,000	3,000	
Salaries and wages payable	1,000	2,000	1,000	
Total Current Liabilities.........................	$26,000	$25,000		
Working Capital...	$49,000	$46,000		
			$20,000	$17,000
Net Increase in Working Capital......................				3,000
			$20,000	$20,000

Explain the points Mr. Lake finds confusing. Attach to your explanation a 1976 cash flow statement and a 1976 cash basis income statement for Blue Lake Store. (In preparing the income statement, cash basis sales are determined as follows:

Accounts receivable, January 1, 1976	$ 30,000
Accrual basis sales	250,000
Total..	$280,000
Less accounts receivable, December 31, 1976............	36,000
Cash basis sales	$244,000

Use similar calculations to determine the cash basis amounts for cost of goods sold and each of the operating expenses.)

Analytical and review problem

Problem 21–1 A&R

A company began the month of May with $200,000 of current assets, a $2\frac{1}{2}$ to 1 current ratio, and a $1\frac{1}{4}$ to 1 acid-test (quick) ratio. During the month it completed the following transactions:

	Current Ratio		No Change	Working Capital		No Change
	Inc.	Dcr.	Change	Inc.	Dcr.	Change
a. Bought $20,000 of merchandise on account (The company uses a perpetual inventory system)						
b. Sold for $10,000 merchandise that cost $5,000						
c. Collected a $2,500 account receivable.....						
d. Paid a $10,000 account payable						
e. Wrote off a $1,500 bad debt against the allowance for doubtful accounts						
f. Declared a $1 per share cash dividend on the 10,000 shares of outstanding common stock						
g. Paid the dividend declared in (f)............						
h. Borrowed $10,000 by giving the bank a 60-day, 10% note						
i. Borrowed $25,000 by placing a 10-year mortgage on the plant..........................						
j. Used the $25,000 proceeds of the mortgage to buy additional machinery...................						

Required:
1. Indicate the affect on *(i)* current ratio and *(ii)* working capital of each transaction. Set up a chart in your answer similar to that shown above and use check marks to indicate your answers. (Working capital is defined as "current assets minus current liabilities.")
2. At the end of May the
    a. Current ratio was _____
    b. Acid-test ratio was _____
    c. Working capital was _____

(CGA adapted)

22

Departmental accounting; responsibility accounting

■ A business is departmentalized or divided into departments for managerial purposes, with each department commonly being placed in charge of a manager who under perfect circumstances is responsible for both the output of the department and the resources expended in attaining that output. Output may be in units of product manufactured, dollars of sales achieved, or services performed; and resources expended may be goods sold, raw materials consumed, wages paid, depreciation, heat, lights, et cetera. And, ideally the optimum output should be obtained with the most reasonable expenditure of resources.

When a business is divided into departments, if management is to know how well each department is performing, it is necessary for the accounting system to supply information by departments as to resources expended and outputs achieved, and this requires that revenue and expense information be measured and accumulated by departments. However, before going further it should be observed that such information is generally not made public, since it might be of considerable benefit to competitors. Rather, it is for the use of management in controlling operations, appraising performances, allocating resources, and in taking remedial actions. For example, if one of several departments is particularly profitable, perhaps it should be expanded. Or if a department is showing poor results, information as to its revenues, costs, and expenses may point to a proper remedial action.

Basis for departmentalization

■ In every departmentalized business there are two basic kinds of departments, *productive departments* and *service departments*. In a factory the productive departments are those engaged directly in manufacturing operations, and in a store they are the departments making sales. Departmental divisions in a factory are commonly based on manufacturing processes employed or products or components manufactured. The division in a store is usually based on kinds of goods sold, with each selling or productive department being assigned the sale of one or more kinds of merchandise. In either type of business the service departments assist or perform services for the productive departments and are such departments as the general office, advertising, purchasing, payroll, and personnel departments.

In addition to dividing a business into productive departments and service departments, it is also recognized that certain departments are *cost centres* and others are *profit centres*. A cost centre is a unit of the business that incurs costs (or expenses) but does not directly generate revenues. The productive departments of a factory and such service departments as the general office, advertising, and purchasing departments are cost centres. A profit centre differs from a cost centre in that it not only incurs costs but also generates revenues. The selling departments of a store are profit centres. In judging departmental efficiencies in the two kinds of centres, the manager of a cost centre is judged on his ability to control costs and keep his costs within a satisfactory range. The manager of a profit centre, on the other hand, is judged on his ability to generate earnings, which are the excess of revenues over costs.

Departmental gross profits in a merchandising business

■ In a merchandising concern the managers of the sales departments constantly make decisions that affect the gross profits of their departments, always with the intention of maximizing such profits. Of course they do not ignore operating expenses, since their ultimate objective is net income; but the factors of gross profit receive a great deal of attention, probably because gross profit is subject to considerable managerial control. It at times can be increased by lowering prices and increasing the volume of goods sold. At other times a larger margin on a smaller volume will increase gross profit.

A departmental gross profit is the function of (1) the number of dollars of goods sold and (2) the markup on the goods. Therefore, management of departmental gross profits begins with the accumulation of information as to sales, purchases, and inventories by departments, so that departmental gross profits may be calculated. The information is gathered in a number of ways; and normally a store's size, the goods it sells, and the number of its departments determine the methods and procedures used. For instance, a store may provide a separate set of merchandising accounts for each of its departments or it may use analysis sheets to accumulate the information necessary to determine gross profits by departments.

If separate merchandising accounts are provided, separate Sales, Sales Returns, Purchases, Purchases Returns, and Merchandise Inventory accounts are provided for each department. However, unless the store has a very limited number of departments, this causes its ledger to become large and awkward and complicates its end-of-the-period closing procedures. Consequently, rather than separate departmental accounts, many stores use a single store-wide account each for sales, sales returns, purchases, purchases returns, and merchandise inventory; but in addition accumulate a separate supplementary record of sales, purchases, and inventories by departments. This separate supplementary record may be accumulated with electronic equipment on magnetic tapes or analysis sheets may be used.

Analysis sheets

When a store uses departmental analysis sheets, it provides only one undepartmentalized general ledger account for sales, another account for sales returns, another for purchases, and another for purchases returns; and it records its transactions and posts to these accounts as though it were not departmentalized. But in addition to this, each day it also summarizes its merchandise transactions by departments and records the summarized amounts on analysis sheets. For example, a concern using analysis sheets, in addition to recording sales in its usual manner, will total each day's sales by departments and enter the daily totals on a sales analysis sheet like Illustration 22–1. As a result, at the end of a month or other period the column totals of the analysis sheet will show total sales by departments and the grand total of all the sheet's columns should equal the balance of the Sales account.

Departmental Sales Analysis Sheet

Date		Men's Wear Dept.	Boys' Wear Dept.	Shoe Dept.	Leather Goods Dept.	Women's Wear Dept.
May	1	$357.15	$175.06	$115.00	$ 75.25	$427.18
	2	298.55	136.27	145.80	110.20	387.27

Illustration 22–1

When a store uses departmental analysis sheets, it uses one analysis sheet to accumulate sales figures, another analysis sheet for sales returns, another for purchases, and still another for purchases returns; and at the end of the period the several analysis sheets show the store's sales, sales returns, purchases, and purchases returns by departments. If the store then takes inventories by departments, it can calculate gross profits by departments.

■ Modern cash registers enable even a small store to accumulate daily totals for sales and sales returns by departments. Such a store can also use analysis sheets to sort information as to purchases and purchases returns by departments. Larger stores use electric bookkeeping machines, punched cards, and cash registers that feed information directly into the store's computer. Short descriptions of how these devices operate follow:

Electric bookkeeping machines

Illustration 6–10 on page 185 shows a modern electric bookkeeping machine. It was explained beginning on page 184 that this machine could be used for sales accounting, purchases, cash receipts, or any other accounting application; and it was also explained how the machine could, for example, for each charge sale produce the customer's invoice, post to the customer's account, update the customer's month-end statement, and enter the sale in the Sales Journal. In addition to this, if the machine is properly set and the right keys are depressed in the sales invoice preparation procedure, the machine will accumulate information as to sales by departments and will print out departmental sales totals after the last sales invoice is prepared each day. When used for recording purchases or returns, it will also accumulate departmental totals for these transactions. Such machines are commonly used by wholesale firms.

Punched cards

Illustration 22–2 shows a type of pin-punched price tag used by many large department stores. Such tags show the price of an item of merchandise and are an essential part of the inventory control system in a store using them—an inventory control system that makes it easy to accumulate information as to sales and returns by items, colours, sizes,

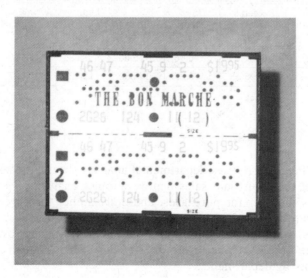

Illustration
22–2

manufacturers, et cetera, as well as in dollar amounts by departments.

Pin-punched price tags get their name from the pin-size holes punched in the tags. These holes carry information in the code arrangement of their punching as to an item's price, size, colour, and so on. The machine used to punch the holes also prints the punched information on the tag for visual reading.

When an item of merchandise is sold, the lower half of the tag is removed by the salesperson and placed on a spindle beside the cash register, and the upper half is left attached to the item sold. At the end of each day the spindled tag portions are taken to the accounting department and run through a tag converter, a machine that electronically repunches each tag's information into a regular full-size punched card or into paper or magnetic tape. The information on the cards or tape is then fed into a computer that sorts it and produces reports as to sales by departments plus information for inventory control and for updating the inventory records.

When merchandise is returned, the customer is instructed to return with the merchandise the price tag portion left attached at the time of sale. These returned portions are spindled until the end of each day when they too are run through the tag coverter to produce the cards or tapes used in accumulating information about returns.

Punched paper tape

Some stores use punched paper tape in recording information about sales as to departments, prices, items, et cetera. The punched paper tape, which is approximately one inch in width, is produced by the cash registers on which salespeople "ring up" sales. A sample of this tape is shown in Illustration 22–3.

In producing such paper tape, all that is required of the salesperson is that he depress the proper cash register keys in "ringing up" a sale, causing the register to punch the sale information into the tape as to the department of the sale, the item sold, its colour, size, price, et cetera.

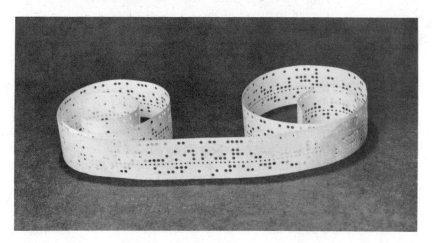

Illustration
22–3

At the end of each day or other period the tape produced in each register is sent to the store's computer department or to an outside computer centre, such as those operated by National Cash Register Company, where the information punched into the tapes is entered in a computer that sorts it and produces the desired reports and summaries.

Some cash registers capture data on magnetic tape rather than on paper tape, and in large stores the registers are often connected to and enter information directly into the store's computer. Also, all such modern cash registers are capable of doing much more than accumulating sales totals. For example, if a charge sale is to be recorded with such a register, the salesperson uses the customer's plastic credit card to print the customer's name on a blank sales ticket. He then places the sales ticket in the Forms Printer of the cash register and records the sale in the same way as a cash sale. The register prints all pertinent information on the sales ticket and totals it. Then in order to finalize the sale, controls within the register require that the salesperson depress the proper register keys to record the customer's account number, and by this final act the salesperson, in effect, posts the sale to the customer's account. He does not actually post to the account. Rather, from the information punched into or entered on the register's paper or magnetic tape, the store's computer will update the customer's account and produce his month-end statement, ready for mailing without further bookkeeping labour.

Income statement showing departmental gross profits

■ Accumulating information and arriving at a gross profit figure for each selling department in a departmentalized business is not too difficult, as the discussion thus far reveals. However, to go beyond this and arrive at useful net income figures by departments is not so easy; consequently, many concerns make no effort to calculate more than gross profits by departments. Illustration 22–4 shows an income statement prepared for such a concern. The statement sets out departmental gross profits and combines these figures to arrive at a combined gross profit figure, a figure from which the unallocated operating expenses are deducted to arrive at the store's net income.

Observe in Illustration 22–4 that in addition to showing gross profits in dollar amounts, gross profits are also expressed as percentages of net sales. These percentages make departmental comparisons easier.

Allocating expenses

■ If a concern goes beyond the calculation of departmental gross profits and attempts to arrive at a net income figure for each selling department, it must charge each department with its *direct expenses* and allocate to the departments any *indirect expenses*. The direct expenses of a department are those incurred for the sole benefit of that department; for example, the salary of an employee who works in only one department is a direct expense of that department. Indirect expenses are expenses incurred for the joint benefit of more than one department, for example, rent, heat, and lights. The entire amount of a direct expense may be charged directly to the department benefited by its incurrence.

Valley Haberdashery
Income Statement
For Year Ended December 31, 19—

	Men's Clothing	Boys' Clothing	Shoes	Combined
Revenue from sales:				
Sales..................	$46,000	$34,000	$20,000	$100,000
Less returns......	750	425	350	1,525
Net sales	$45,250	$33,575	$19,650	$ 98,475
Cost of goods sold:				
Inventory, Jan. 1 ...	$ 7,400	$ 4,200	$ 3,350	$14,950
Purchases............	30,000	21,700	11,800	63,500
Freight-in	150	125	75	350
Goods for sale	$37,550	$26,025	$15,225	$78,800
Inventory, Dec. 31..	8,100	3,500	4,150	15,750
Cost of goods sold....	29,450	22,525	11,075	63,050
Gross profits...........	$15,800	$11,050	$ 8,575	$ 35,425
Gross profit percentages	(34.9%)	(32.9%)	(43.5%)	(36.0%)

Operating expenses:

Selling expenses:		
Sales salaries...	$7,000	
Sales commissions	5,000	
Advertising..	550	
Sales supplies used	200	
Depreciation of store equipment	700	
Total selling expenses....................................		$13,450
General and administrative expenses:		
Office salaries	$3,800	
Office supplies used	250	
Expired insurance	300	
Bad debts	210	
Depreciation of office equipment	150	
Depreciation of building......................................	1,200	
Property taxes...	900	
Total general and administrative expenses.......................		6,810
Total operating expenses		20,260
Net Income..		$ 15,165

Illustration
22–4

However, an indirect expense can only be allocated on some fair basis such as, for example, the amount of floor space occupied, as in the allocation of janitorial expenses.

When an indirect expense is allocated, portions are assigned to each department, preferably on the basis of benefits received. For example, a jewelry store purchases janitorial services from an outside firm and allocates the cost among its three departments according to the floor space occupied. If the cost of janitorial services for a short period is $280 and the amounts of floor space occupied are:

Jewelry department..	250 sq. ft.
Watch repair department	125
China and silver department.......................................	500
Total...	875 sq. ft.

The departmental shares of the janitorial expense are:

Jewelry Department: $\dfrac{250}{875} \times \$280 = \$80$

Watch Repair Department: $\dfrac{125}{875} \times \$280 = \$40$

China and Silver Department: $\dfrac{500}{875} \times \$280 = \$160$

Bases for allocating expenses

■ In the following paragraphs, bases for allocating a representation of indirect expenses are discussed. In the discussions no hard-and-fast rules are given because several factors are often involved in an expense allocation, and the importance of the factors vary from situation to situation. Also, judgment rather than hard-and-fast rules is required, and often accountants of equal ability and experience will not agree as to the proper basis for allocating an expense.

Wages and salaries

An employee's wages may be either a direct or an indirect expense. If an employee spends all of his time in one department, his wages are a direct expense of the benefited department; but if an employee works in more than one department, his wages become an indirect expense that may be allocated between or among the benefited departments. Normally, working time spent in each department is a fair basis for allocating wages.

A supervisory employee at times supervises more than one department, and in such cases the time spent in each department is usually a fair basis for allocating his salary. However, since a supervisory employee is frequently on the move from department to department, the time spent in each is often difficult to measure. Consequently, some companies allocate the salary of such an employee to his departments on the basis of the number of employees in each department, while others make the allocation on the basis of the supervised departments' sales. When a supervisor's salary is allocated on the basis of employees, it is assumed that he is supervising people and the time spent in each department is related to the number of employees in each. When a supervisory employee's salary is allocated on the basis of sales, it is assumed that the time devoted to each department is related to the department's productiveness.

Rent

Rent expense is normally allocated to benefited departments on the basis of the amount and value of the floor space occupied by each. Furthermore, since all customers who enter a store must pass the departments by the entrance and only a fraction of these people go beyond the first floor, ground floor space is more valuable for retail purposes than is basement or upper floor space, and space near the entrance is more valuable than is space in an out-of-the-way corner. Yet since there is no exact measure of floor space values, all such values and the allocations of rent based on such values must depend on judgment. Nevertheless, if good judgment, statistics as to customer traffic, and the opinions of experts who are familiar with current rental values are used, fair allocations can be made.

Advertising

When a store advertises a department's products, if the advertising is effective, people come into the store to buy the products. However, at the same time they also often buy other unadvertised products. Consequently, advertising benefits all departments, even those the products of which are not advertised; and as a result, many stores treat advertising as an indirect expense and allocate it on the basis of sales. When advertising costs are allocated on a sales basis, a department producing one fifteenth of the total sales is charged with one fifteenth of the advertising cost and a department producing one sixth of the sales is charged with one sixth.

Although in many stores advertising costs are allocated to departments on the basis of sales, in others advertising is treated as a direct expense and charged directly to the departments. When advertising is charged directly, each advertisement is analyzed and the cost of the column inches of newspaper space or minutes of TV or radio time devoted to the products of a department is charged to the department.

Since advertising is treated by some stores as a direct expense and by others as an indirect expense, both treatments appear in the illustrations that follow.

Depreciation

Depreciation on equipment used solely in one department is a direct expense of that department; and if adequate plant asset records are kept, the depreciation applicable to each department may be learned by examining the records. Where adequate records are not maintained, depreciation must be treated as an indirect expense and allocated to the departments on the basis of the value of the equipment in each. When the building is owned, building depreciation is normally allocated like rent.

Taxes and insurance

Taxes and insurance are indirect expenses and are allocated to departments on the basis of the insured and taxable property in each. Taxes and insurance on the building are allocated like rent.

Heating and lighting expense

Heating and lighting expense is usually allocated on the basis of floor space occupied under the assumption that the amount of heat and the number of lights, their wattage, and the extent of their use are uniform throughout the store. Should there be a material variation in lighting, however, further analysis and a separate allocation may be advisable.

Delivery expense

The cost of delivering packages depends upon the number, size, and weight of the packages. Usually, it is impossible to consider all three factors in a single allocation basis. Consequently, the most important one is often used. Sometimes all three factors, number, size, and weight, are ignored, and delivery expenses are allocated on a sales basis. Often, too, where the number, size, and weight of packages are closely related to sales, such a basis is fair.

Mechanics of allocating expenses ■ It would be possible in most cases to analyze each indirect expense incurred and to allocate and charge portions to several departmental expense accounts at the time of incurrence or payment. However, this is seldom done because it involves too many allocations and too much work. Instead, expense amounts paid or incurred, both direct and indirect, are commonly accumulated in undepartmentalized expense accounts until the end of a period, when a *departmental expense allocation sheet* is used to allocate and charge each expense to the benefited departments. A departmental expense allocation sheet is shown in Illustration 22-5 and is discussed in more detail later in this chapter.

Allocating service department expenses ■ In order that they may sell their products, selling departments must have the services provided by the service departments just as they must have building space, heat, and lights. Therefore, service department operating expenses are in effect indirect expenses of the selling departments; and if net incomes are calculated, the cost of operating each service department should be allocated to the selling departments it serves. The following list shows commonly used bases for these allocations:

Departments	Expense Allocation Bases
General office department	Number of employees in each department or sales.
Personnel department	Number of employees in each department.
Payroll department	Number of employees in each department.
Advertising department	Sales or amounts of advertising charged directly to each department.
Purchasing department	Dollar amounts of purchases or number of purchase invoices.
Cleaning and maintenance department	Square feet of floor space occupied.

Departmental expense allocation sheet ■ As previously stated, expenses are commonly accumulated in undepartmentalized expense accounts until the end of an accounting period when a departmental expense allocation sheet is used, not only to allocate the accumulated expenses to the benefited departments but also to allocate to the productive departments the costs of operating the service departments, Illustration 22-5 shows such an allocation sheet.

Tempe Hardware Company
Departmental Expense Allocation Sheet
Year Ended December 31, 19—

Undepartmentalized Expense Accounts and Service Departments	Bases of Allocation	Expense Account Balances	Allocations of Expenses to Departments					
			General Office Dept.	Purchasing Dept.	Cleaning and Maintenance	Hardware Dept.	Housewares Dept.	Appliances Dept.
Salaries expense	Direct, payroll records	$39,050	$7,250	$6,400	$3,000	$10,200	$ 4,800	$ 7,400
Rent expense	Amount and value of space	7,200	360	360	40	3,200	814	2,426
Advertising expense	Sales	2,070				920	460	690
Insurance expense	Insured property	320	50	30	12	132	24	72
Depreciation expense, equipment	Direct, property records	1,200	200	125	50	350	175	300
Lighting expense	Wattage of lights	226	18	18	5	90	40	55
Heating expense	Floor space	960	48	48	8	424	144	288
Supplies expense	Direct, requisitions	625	102	63	125	133	54	148
Total expenses by departments		$51,651	$8,028	$7,044	$3,240	$15,449	$ 6,511	$11,379
Allocation of service department expenses:								
General office department	Sales		8,028			3,568	1,784	2,676
Purchasing department	Purchases			7,044		3,166	1,761	2,117
Cleaning and maintenance	Floor space				3,240	1,605	545	1,090
Total Expenses Applicable to Selling Departments		51,651				$23,788	$10,601	$17,262

Illustration
22–5

To prepare an expense allocation sheet, the account names of the to-be-allocated expenses are entered in the sheet's first column along with the names of the service departments. Next, the bases of allocation are entered in the second column, and the account balances are entered in the third. Then, each expense account balance is allocated according to the basis shown, and the allocated portions are entered in the departmental columns. After this the departmental columns are totaled and the service department column totals are allocated in turn to the productive departments.

Upon completion, the amounts in the columns of an expense allocation sheet are available for preparing departmental income statements showing net incomes by departments. Such a statement for the appliance department of the firm of Illustration 22–5 is shown in Illustration 22–6.

Tempe Hardware Company
Appliance Department Income Statement
For Year Ended December 31, 19—

Sales..		$84,464
Cost of goods sold		59,321
Gross profit from sales		$25,143
Operating expenses:		
Sales salaries expense....................................	$7,400	
Rent expense..	2,426	
Advertising expense	690	
Insurance expense	72	
Depreciation expense, equipment	300	
Lighting expense...	55	
Heating expense	288	
Supplies expense..	148	
General office department expense................	2,676	
Purchasing department expenses	2,117	
Cleaning and maintenance expenses..............	1,090	
Total operating expenses............................		17,262
Appliance Department Net Income		$ 7,881

Illustration 22–6

Eliminating an unprofitable department

■ The management of a store in which departmental net incomes are calculated is often confronted with a situation in which one or more departments shows a loss. When this occurs, consideration is often given to eliminating the unprofitable department or departments; and when such consideration is given, what are known as escapable and inescapable expenses are encountered. Escapable expenses are those that would end with an unprofitable department's elimination; inescapable expenses are those that would continue even though the department were eliminated. For example, Joe M. Hardt Company is contemplating the elimination of its Department A. The company's income statement for the past year, see Illustration 22–7, shows that Department A incurred a $415 net loss for the year. However, an examination of its expenses reveals the following escapable and inescapable expenses:

	Escapable Expenses	Inescapable Expenses
Sales salaries expense	$ 8,200	
Advertising expense	1,225	
Store supplies expense	225	
Depreciation expense, store equipment		$ 320
Rent expense		2,800
Insurance expense (merchandise and equipment)	215	85
Bad debts expense	325	
Share of the general office expenses	550	3,220
Totals	$10,740	$6,425

If Department A is discontinued, its $6,425 of inescapable expenses will have to be borne by Department B; thus until Department A's annual loss exceeds $6,425, Joe M. Hardt Company is better off continuing the unprofitable department.

In considering the elimination of an unprofitable department, aside from the fact that some of its expenses cannot be escaped, such a department is often continued because it brings business to other profitable departments. Also, the solution is often one of substituting a more profitable department or endeavor for the unprofitable department.

Joe M. Hardt Company
Income Statement for Year Ended December 31, 19—

	Department A	Department B	Combined
Sales	$63,150	$94,725	$157,875
Cost of goods sold	46,400	56,550	102,950
Gross profit on sales	$16,750	$38,175	$ 54,925
Operating expenses:			
Selling expenses:			
Sales salaries expense	$ 8,200	$12,400	$ 20,600
Advertising expense	1,225	1,580	2,805
Store supplies expense	225	420	645
Depreciation expense, store equipment	320	630	950
Rent expense	2,800	3,200	6,000
Total selling expenses	$12,770	$18,230	$ 31,000
General and administrative expenses:			
Insurance expense	$ 300	$ 425	$ 725
Bad debts expense	325	435	760
Share of the general office expenses	3,770	5,655	9,425
Total general and administrative expenses	$ 4,395	$ 6,515	$ 10,910
Total operating expenses	$17,165	$24,745	$ 41,910
Net Income or (Loss)	$ (415)	$13,430	$ 13,015

Illustration
22–7

Departmental contributions to overhead

■ Many people, particularly department heads whose efficiencies are judged and whose salaries depend on the amounts of "net income" earned by their departments, are critical when such net income figures are used in making decisions as to departmental efficiencies. Their critical attitude arises from the fact that departmental net income figures are always affected by the assumptions made in allocating expenses. Such people often suggest the substitution of what are known as *departmental contributions to overhead* when decisions are to be made as to the efficiencies with which departments have been operated. A department's contribution to overhead is the amount its revenues exceed its direct costs and expenses. Illustration 22–8 is a departmental income statement showing contributions to overhead.

Smithfield Men's Store
Income Statement Showing Departmental Contributions
Year Ended December 31, 19—

	Men's Department	Boys' Department	Shoe Department	Combined
Revenue from sales...	$100,000	$ 40,000	$ 30,000	$170,000
Cost of goods sold...	62,000	24,000	17,000	103,000
Gross profit on sales.......................................	$ 38,000	$ 16,000	$ 13,000	$ 67,000
Direct expenses:				
Sales salaries expense	$ 16,500	$ 7,500	$ 6,000	$ 30,000
Advertising expense......................................	900	500	400	1,800
Depreciation expense...................................	700	400	500	1,600
Supplies expense..	300	200	100	600
Total direct expenses..............................	$ 18,400	$ 8,600	$ 7,000	$ 34,000
Departmental contribution to overhead..............	$ 19,600	$ 7,400	$ 6,000	$ 33,000
Contribution percentages	19.6%	18.5%	20.0%	19.4%
Indirect expenses:				
Rent expense..				$ 6,000
Heating and lighting expense				800
Taxes and insurance expense............................				1,200
Expenses of the general office............................				9,400
Total Indirect Expenses............................				$17,400
Net Income				$15,600

Illustration
22–8

Controllable costs and expenses

■ Net income figures and contributions to overhead are used in judging departmental efficiencies; but is either a good index of how well a department manager has performed? Many people hold that neither is. These people say that since many expenses entering into the calculation of a department's net income or into its contribution to overhead are beyond the control of the department's manager, neither net income nor contribution to overhead should be used in judging how well the department has operated. These people are of the opinion that only a departments *controllable costs and expenses* should be used in judging a department's performance.

A department's controllable costs and expenses are those over which the department's manager has control as to the amounts expended. They are not the same as direct costs and expenses. Direct costs and expenses are those chargeable directly to a department, the amounts expended may or may not be under the control of the manager. For example, a manager often has little or no control over the amount of equipment assigned to his department and the resulting depreciation expense, but he commonly has some control over the employees and the amount of work they do. Also, he normally has some control over supplies used in his department, but no control over the amount of his own salary.

When controllable costs and expenses are used in judging a department's efficiency, statistics are prepared showing the department's output and its controllable costs and expenses. The statistics of the current period are then compared with prior periods and with planned levels of output and planned costs and the manager's performance is judged.

When costs are examined, it is generally recognized that all costs are controllable at some level of management and at some point in time. For example, a cost such as property insurance may not be controllable at the level of a department manager, but it is subject to control by the executive who is responsible for obtaining insurance coverage for the concern. Likewise the executive responsible for obtaining insurance coverage may not have any control over insurance expense resulting from insurance contracts presently in force; but when a contract expires, he is free to renegotiate and thus has control over the long run. Consequently, it is recognized that all costs are subject to the control of some manager at some point in time. Revenues are likewise subject to the control of some manager.

Responsibility accounting

■ The concept of controllable costs and expenses leads naturally to the idea of responsibility accounting. In responsibility accounting:

a. A determination is made of the person responsible for each activity carried on by the business and the controllable costs and expenses of each activity are assigned to the person responsible for the activity. Responsibility assignments are normally made at the lowest possible managerial level, under the assumption that the manager nearest the action is in the best position to control its costs. For example, a factory foreman is made responsible for the raw materials and supplies used in his department.

b. The accounting system is then designed to accumulate costs and expenses in such a way that timely reports can be made to each manager of the costs for which he is responsible. Each manager is then judged on his ability to control his costs and keep them within a budgeted range, and no manager is held responsible for a cost over which he has no control. Furthermore, prorations and arbitrary allocations of costs are not made because it is recognized that responsibilities cannot be allocated.

At the lowest levels of management, responsibilities and costs over which control is exercised are limited. Consequently, cost reports to this management level cover only a few costs, usually just those costs over which a manager exercises control. Moving up the management hierarchy, responsibilities and control broaden, and reports to a higher level manager are broader and cover a wider range of costs. However, reports to a higher level manager normally do not contain the details reported to his subordinates. Rather, the details reported to a lower level manager are normally summarized on the report to his superior. The details are summarized for two reasons: (1) the lower level manager is primarily responsible and (2) too many details can confuse. If the higher manager's report contains too much detail, he may have difficulty "seeing the woods because of the trees."

In conclusion it should be said that our ability to produce vast amounts of raw figures mechanically and electronically has far outstripped our ability to use the figures. What is needed is the ability to select those figures that are meaningful for planning and control. This is recognized in responsibility accounting, and every effort is made to get the right figure to the right person at the right time, and the right person is the person who can control the cost or revenue.

Joint costs ■ Joint costs are encountered in some manufacturing concerns and are introduced here because they have much in common with indirect expenses. A joint cost is a single cost incurred to secure two or more essentially different products. For example, a meat-packer incurs a joint cost when he buys a pig from which he will get bacon, hams, shoulders, liver, heart, hide, pig feet, and a variety of other products in portions which he cannot alter. Likewise, a sawmill incurs joint costs when it buys a log and saws it into unalterable portions of Clears, Select Structurals, No. 1 Common, No. 2 Common, and other grades of lumber. In both cases, as with all joint costs, the problem is one of allocating the costs to the several joint products.

A joint cost may be, but is not commonly, allocated on some physical basis, such as the ratio of pounds, square feet, or gallons of each joint product to total pounds, square feet, or gallons of all joint products flowing from the cost. The reason this method is not commonly used is that the cost allocations resulting from its use may be completely out of keeping with the market values of the joint products, and thus may cause certain of the products to sell at a profit while other products always show a loss. For example, a sawmill bought for $30,000 a number of logs which when sawed produced a million board feet of lumber in the grades and amounts shown in Illustration 22–9.

Observe in Illustration 22–9 that the logs produced 200,000 board feet of No. 3 Common lumber and that this is two tenths of the total lumber produced from the logs. If the No. 3 lumber is assigned two tenths of the $30,000 cost of the logs, it will be assigned $6,000 of the cost ($30,000 $\times$ $\frac{2}{10}$ = $6,000); and since this lumber can be sold for only $4,000, the assignment will cause this grade to show a loss. As a result, as in this situation, to avoid always showing a loss on one or more of the

Grade of Lumber	Production in Board Feet	Market Price per 1,000 Board Feet	Market Value of Production of Each Grade	Ratio of Market Value of Each Grade to Total
Structural............................	100,000	$120	$12,000	12/50
No. 1 Common	300,000	60	18,000	18/50
No. 2 Common	400,000	40	16,000	16/50
No. 3 Common	200,000	20	4,000	4/50
	1,000,000		$50,000	

Illustration
22–9

products flowing from a joint cost, such costs are commonly allocated to the joint products *in the ratio of the market values of the joint products at the point of separation.*

The ratios of the market values of the joint products flowing from the $30,000 of log cost are shown in the last column of Illustration 22–9, and if these ratios are used to allocate the $30,000 cost, the cost will be apportioned between the grades as follows:

$$\begin{aligned}
\text{Structural:} \quad & \$30,000 \times 12/50 = \$ 7,200 \\
\text{No. 1 Common:} \quad & \$30,000 \times 18/50 = 10,800 \\
\text{No. 2 Common:} \quad & \$30,000 \times 16/50 = 9,600 \\
\text{No. 3 Common:} \quad & \$30,000 \times 4/50 = \underline{2,400} \\
& \underline{\$30,000}
\end{aligned}$$

Observe that if the No. 3 Common is allocated a share of the $30,000 joint cost based on market values by grades, it is allocated $2,400 of the $30,000. Furthermore, when the $2,400 is subtracted from the grade's $4,000 market value, $1,600 remains to cover other after-separation costs and provide a profit.

Questions for class discussion

1. Why is a business divided into departments?
2. Differentiate between productive departments and service departments.
3. Name several of a department store's service departments.
4. What are the productive departments of (a) a factory and (b) a store?
5. What is the purpose of a departmental sales analysis sheet? How is a sales analysis sheet used in determining sales by departments?
6. What is a pin-punched price tag? How is such a tag used in determining sales by departments?
7. How is punched paper tape used in determining sales by departments?
8. Differentiate between direct and indirect expenses.
9. Suggest a basis for allocating each of the following expenses to departments: (a) salary of a supervisory employee, (b) rent, (c) heat, (d) electricity used in lighting, (e) janitorial services, (f) advertising, (g) expired insurance, and (h) taxes.

10. How is a departmental expense allocation sheet used in allocating expenses to departments?
11. How reliable are the amounts shown as net incomes for the various departments of a store when expenses are allocated to the departments?
12. As the terms are used in departmental accounting, what are (a) escapable expenses and (b) inescapable expenses?
13. How is a department's contribution to overhead measured?
14. What are a department's controllable costs and expenses?
15. In responsibility accounting, who is the right person to be given timely reports and statistics on a given cost?
16. What is a joint cost? How are joint costs normally allocated?

Class exercises

Exercise 22-1

A company rents for $30,000 per year all the space in a building, which is assigned to its departments as follows:

Department	Location	Floor Space
A	Basement	1,500 sq. ft.
B	Basement	1,500 sq. ft.
C	1st floor	600 sq. ft.
D	1st floor	800 sq. ft.
E	1st floor	1,600 sq. ft.
F	2nd floor	2,000 sq. ft.
G	2nd floor	1,000 sq. ft.

The company allocates 20% of the total rent to the basement, 50% to the first floor, and 30% to the second floor; and it then allocates the rent of each floor to the departments on that floor. Determine the rent expense to be allocated to each department.

Exercise 22-2

A company rents for $10,000 per year all the space in a small building, and it occupies the space as follows:

Department A: 1,000 sq. ft. of first-floor space
Department B: 3,000 sq. ft. of first-floor space
Department C: 4,000 sq. ft. of second-floor space

Determine the rent expense to be allocated to each department under the assumption that in the city in which this building is located, second-floor space rents on an average for two thirds as much as first-floor space.

Exercise 22-3

Excel Company has a general office department, a purchasing department, and two sales departments, A and B. During the past year the departments had the following direct expenses: general office, $3,600; purchasing department,

$2,900; Department A, $12,000; and Department B, $9,000. The departments occupy the following square feet of floor space: office, 600; purchasing, 300; A, 1,500; and B, 1,200. Department A had twice as many dollars of sales during the year as did Department B. During the year the purchasing department processed three purchase orders for Department A for every two processed for Department B.

Required:

Prepare an expense allocation sheet for Excel Company on which the direct expenses are entered by departments, the year's $7,200 of rent expense is allocated to the departments on the basis of floor space occupied, office department expenses are allocated to the sales departments on the basis of dollars of sales, and purchasing department expenses are allocated on the basis of purchases orders processed.

Exercise 22–4

Sport Shop is departmentalized, and Ted Lee works as a salesclerk in both the men's shoe department and the men's clothing department. His work consists of waiting on customers in turn as they enter either department, and also of straightening and rearranging merchandise in either department as needed after the merchandise has been shown to customers.

The shop divides Lee's $6,000 annual salary between the two selling departments in which he works, and last year the division was based on a sample of the time Lee spent working in the two departments. To gain the sample, observations were made on several days throughout the year of the manner in which he spent his time while at work. Following are the results of these observations:

Observed Manner in Which Employee Spent His Time	*Elapsed Time in Minutes*
Selling in men's clothing department	2,100
Straightening and rearranging merchandise in men's clothing department	300
Selling in shoe department	1,450
Straightening and rearranging merchandise in shoe department	150
Doing nothing while waiting for a customer to enter one or the other of the selling departments	400

Required:

Prepare a calculation showing the shares of the employee's salary to be allocated to the selling departments.

Exercise 22–5

A real estate agent bought four acres of hilly land at $5,000 per acre, spent $36,000 putting in a street and sidewalks, and divided the land into 12 lots of equal size. However, since some of the lots sloped downhill and some sloped uphill and some had trees and some did not, the lots were not of equal value. Therefore two lots were marked for sale at $5,000 each, five at $6,000 each, and five at $8,000 each.

Required:

Under the assumption that land and development costs are assigned to the lots as joint costs, determine the share of costs to be assigned to a lot in each price class.

Problem 22-1

Sterling Department Store occupies all the space in a building having two floors with 10,000 square feet of usable floor space on each floor. The company maintains an account in its ledger called Building Occupancy Expenses, and it debited the following to the account last year:

Building depreciation...	$ 7,200
Mortgage interest, building.....................................	17,500
Taxes, building and land...	6,500
Heating and cooling expenses.................................	2,400
Lighting expense	1,100
Cleaning and maintenance expenses........................	9,500
Total...	$44,200

At the end of the year the company divided the $44,200 account total by the number of square feet in the building, 20,000, and charged each department with building occupancy expenses at the rate of $2.21 per square foot occupied.

Joe Kelly manages a department for the company that occupies 3,000 square feet of second-floor space, and he feels his department was charged with an unfair share of the building occupancy expenses. Furthermore, in a discussion with a friend in the real estate business he learned that first-floor space comparable to that occupied by Sterling Department Store is renting for $2 to $2.50 per square foot and that like second-floor space is renting for $1.20 to $1.50 per square foot, including heating and cooling.

Required:

Prepare a computation showing the amount of building occupancy expenses that should have been charged to Joe Kelly's department last year.

Problem 22-2

Dockside Sales has three selling departments, 1, 2, and 3, and two service departments, general office and purchasing. It treats salaries, supplies expense, and depreciation as direct departmental expenses; and its payroll, requisition, and plant asset records showed the following amounts of these expenses by departments for the year ended December 31:

	Salaries Expense	Supplies Expense	Depreciation Expense
General office......................................	$ 8,200	$146	$ 350
Purchasing department..........................	5,900	128	180
Department 1.......................................	14,280	290	900
Department 2.......................................	3,900	112	650
Department 3.......................................	3,350	158	420
Totals	$35,630	$834	$2,500

The concern incurred these indirect expenses: rent expense, $8,500; advertising expense, $7,440; insurance expense, $500; heating and lighting expenses, $1,710; and janitorial expenses, $1,800; and it allocates its indirect expenses as follows:

a. Rent expense on the basis of the amount and value of the space occupied. The general office and purchasing departments occupy space at the rear of the store which is not as valuable as space in the front; and as a result the store's executives feel that $500 of the rent expense should be allocated to these two departments in proportion to the space occupied and the balance to the sales departments in proportion to the space occupied. The five departments occupy the following amounts of space: General Office, 600 square feet; Purchasing Department, 400 square feet; Department 1, 4,000 square feet; Department 2, 2,500 square feet; and Department 3, 1,500 square feet.

b. Advertising expense on the basis of sales.

c. Insurance expense on the basis of equipment book values, and the book values of the equipment in the departments are: General Office, $3,500; Purchasing Department, $1,800; Department 1, $10,000; Department 2, $6,000 and Department 3, $3,700.

d. Heating and lighting and janitorial expenses on the basis of floor space occupied.

The company also allocates its general office department expenses to its selling departments on the basis of sales, and it allocates the purchasing department expenses on the basis of dollars of purchases. Sales and purchases for the year were:

	Dept. 1	Dept. 2	Dept. 3	Totals
Sales	$108,500	$31,000	$46,500	$186,000
Purchases	72,300	13,200	24,500	110,000

Required:
Prepare a departmental expense allocation sheet for the company.

Problem 22–3

Pine Company began operations one year ago with two selling departments and an office department. The year's results appear on page 686.

The company plans to open a third selling department, Department C, which it estimates will produce $80,000 in sales with a 35% gross profit margin and will require the following direct expenses: sales salaries, $10,000; store supplies, $800; and depreciation of equipment, $1,000.

When the company began business, it had to rent store space in excess of its requirements. The extra space was assigned to and used by Departments A and B; but when the new department, Department C, is open, it will take one third of the space presently assigned to Department A and one sixth of the space assigned to Department B.

The company allocates its general office department expenses to its selling departments on the basis of sales, and it expects the new department to cause a $1,900 increase in these expenses.

The company expects Department C to bring new customers into the store who in addition to buying goods in the new department will also buy sufficient

PINE COMPANY
Income Statement for Year Ended December 31, 19—

	Dept. A	Dept. B	Combined
Sales...	$150,000	$120,000	$270,000
Cost of goods sold	90,000	78,000	168,000
Gross profit on sales	$ 60,000	$ 42,000	$102,000
Direct expenses:			
Sales salaries..	$ 19,200	$ 15,000	$ 34,200
Store supplies expense............................	1,500	1,000	2,500
Depreciation expense, equipment	2,600	1,200	3,800
Total direct expenses...........................	$ 23,300	$ 17,200	$ 40,500
Indirect expenses:			
Rent expense	$ 12,000	$ 6,000	$ 18,000
Heating and lighting expenses	1,200	600	1,800
Share of the office department expenses......	9,000	7,200	16,200
Total indirect expenses........................	$ 22,200	$ 13,800	$ 36,000
Total expenses	$ 45,500	$ 31,000	$ 76,500
Net Income	$ 14,500	$ 11,000	$ 25,500

merchandise in the two old departments to increase the sales of Department A by 4% and Department B by 5%. And although the old departments' sales are expected to increase, their gross profit percentages are not expected to change. Likewise, their direct expenses, other than supplies, are not expected to change. The supplies used will increase in proportion to sales.

Required:
Prepare a departmental income statement showing the company's expected operations with three selling departments.

Problem 22–4

Zephyr Sales is considering the elimination of its unprofitable Department 1, which lost $405 last year as the income statement at the top of page 687 shows:

If Department 1 is eliminated:
1. Its advertising, store supplies, and bad debts expenses will be eliminated. Also, two thirds of its insurance expense, the portion on its merchandise, and 20% of the miscellaneous office expenses presently allocated to Department 1 will be eliminated.
2. The company has one office clerk and four salesclerks who each earn $100 per week or $5,200 per year. At present the salaries of two and one-half salesclerks are allocated to Department 2 and one and one-half salesclerks to Department 1. Management feels that two salesclerks may be dismissed if Department 1 is eliminated, leaving two full-time salesclerks in Department 2, and making up the difference by assigning the office clerk to part-time sales work in the department. Management feels that if the office clerk

ZEPHYR SALES
Income Statement for Year Ended December 31, 19—

	Dept. 1	Dept. 2	Combined
Sales	$58,500	$97,600	$156,100
Cost of goods sold	43,800	59,100	102,900
Gross profit on sales	$14,700	$38,500	$ 53,200
Operating expenses:			
Direct expenses:			
Advertising expense	$ 1,225	$ 1,650	$ 2,875
Store supplies expense	350	425	775
Depreciation expense, equipment	950	1,200	2,150
Total direct expenses	$ 2,525	$ 3,275	$ 5,800
Indirect expenses:			
Sales salaries expense	$ 7,800	$13,000	$ 20,800
Rent expense	2,000	2,800	4,800
Bad debts expense	250	375	625
Office salaries expense	2,080	3,120	5,200
Insurance expense	150	225	375
Miscellaneous office expenses	300	450	750
Total indirect expenses	$12,580	$19,970	$ 32,550
Total operating expenses	$15,105	$23,245	$ 38,350
Net Income (Loss)	$ (405)	$15,255	$ 14,850

devotes the same amount of time to selling in Department 2 as she has to the office work of Department 1, this will be sufficient to carry the load.

3. The lease on the store is long term and cannot be changed; therefore, the space presently occupied by Department 1 will have to be used by and charged to Department 2.

4. One half of Department 1's store equipment can be sold at its book value, and this will eliminate one half of the department's depreciation expense. However, Department 2 will have to make whatever use it can of the other half of the department's equipment and be charged with the depreciation, since it has little or no sale value.

Required:

1. List in separate columns and total the amounts of Department 1's escapable and inescapable expenses.

2. Under the assumption that Department 2's sales and gross profit will not be affected by the elimination of Department 1, prepare an income statement showing what the company can expect to earn from the operation of Department 2 after the elimination of Department 1.

Problem 22–5

Ted Orchard marketed a half million pounds of apples last year, and he prepared the following income statement to show the results:

Ted Orchard
Income from the Sale of Apples
Year Ended December 31, 19—

	Results by Grades			Combined
	No. 1	No. 2	No. 3	
Sales by grades:				
No. 1, 200,000 lbs. @ $0.10 per lb	$20,000			
No. 2, 200,000 lbs. @ $0.06 per lb		$12,000		
No. 3, 100,000 lbs. @ $0.03 per lb			$ 3,000	
Combined sales.......................................				$35,000
Costs:				
Tree pruning and orchard care @ $0.0147 per lb......................................	$ 2,940	$ 2,940	$ 1,470	$ 7,350
Fruit picking, grading, and sorting @ $0.0175 ...	3,500	3,500	1,750	8,750
Marketing @ $0.0064 per lb..........................	1,280	1,280	640	3,200
Total costs..	$ 7,720	$ 7,720	$ 3,860	$19,300
Net Income or (Loss)	$12,280	$ 4,280	$ (860)	$15,700

Upon completing the statement, Mr. Orchard thought a wise course of future action might be to leave the No. 3 apples on the trees to fall off and be plowed under when he cultivated between the trees, and thus avoid the loss from their sale. However, before doing so he consulted you.

When you examined the statement, you recognized that Mr. Orchard had divided all his costs by 500,000 and allocated them on a per pound basis. You asked him about the marketing costs and learned that $3,040 of the $3,200 was incurred in placing the No. 1 and No. 2 fruit in boxes and delivering them to the warehouse of the fruit buyer. The cost for this was the same for both grades. You also learned that the remaining $160 was for loading the No. 3 fruit on the trucks of a cider manufacturer who bought this grade of fruit in bulk at the orchard for use in making apple cider.

Required:
Prepare an income statement that will reflect better the results of producing and marketing the apples.

Alternate problems

Problem 22–1A

Broadway Department Store occupies all of a building having selling space on three floors, basement, street floor, and second floor; and it has in its ledger an account called Building Occupancy to which it debited the following last year:

Building depreciation..	$ 6,000
Mortgage interest, building....................................	18,000
Taxes and insurance, building...............................	6,500
Heating and cooling expenses...............................	1,900
Lighting expense	1,500
Cleaning and maintenance expenses.......................	10,500
Total	$44,400

The building has 4,000 square feet of floor space on each of its three floors, a total of 12,000 feet; and the bookkeeper divided the $44,400 of building occupancy costs by 12,000 and charged the selling departments on each floor with $3.70 of building occupancy costs for each square foot of space occupied.

When the manager of a basement department saw the $3.70 per square foot of building occupancy costs charged to his department, he complained and cited a recent study by the local real estate board which showed average rental charges for like space, not including lights and janitorial service, but including heating and cooling, as follows:

Basement level space .... $2 per sq. ft.
Street level space................................ $4 per sq. ft.
Second-floor level space........................ $3 per sq. ft.

Required:
Prepare computations to show the amount of building occupancy costs you think should be charged to the selling departments per square foot of space occupied on each floor.

Problem 22–2A

Valley Sales carries on its operations in three selling departments, A, B, and C, and two service departments, general office and purchasing. The concern incurred these expenses last year:

Salaries expense $39,036
Rent expense 9,500
Advertising expense 4,400
Insurance expense.. 600
Heating and lighting expense............................. 1,900
Depreciation expense, equipment........................ 2,700
Supplies expense... 940
Janitorial expense.. 1,500
    Total.. $60,576

And its sales and purchases by departments were:

	Dept. A	Dept. B	Dept. C	Combined
Sales.....................................	$143,400	$34,500	$42,100	$220,000
Purchases.............................	82,900	23,700	28,400	135,000

Required:
Prepare a departmental expense allocation sheet for the company using the following information:
a. The company treats salaries, supplies used, and depreciation of equipment as direct departmental expenses. The payroll, requisition, and plant asset records show the following amounts of these expenses by departments:

	Salaries Expense	Supplies Expense	Depr. of Equipment
General office	$ 9,846	$176	$ 390
Purchasing department	6,050	122	200
Department A	15,130	320	1,100
Department B	4,400	104	600
Department C	3,610	218	410
	$39,036	$940	$2,700

b. The company treats the remainder of its expenses as indirect and allocates them as follows:
   (1) Rent expense on the basis of the amount and value of floor space occupied. The general office occupies 600 square feet, and the purchasing department 400 square feet on a balcony at the rear of the store. This space is not as valuable as space on the main floor; therefore, the store allocates $500 of its rent to these two departments on the basis of space occupied and allocates the remainder of the rent to the selling departments on the basis of the space they occupy. The selling departments occupy the following amounts of space on the main floor: Department A, 4,500 square feet; Department B, 3,000 square feet; and Department C, 1,500 square feet.
   (2) Advertising expense on the basis of sales.
   (3) Insurance expense on the basis of book value of equipment in each department, which is: general office, $4,200; purchasing, $2,100; Department A, $12,400; Department B, $7,000; and Department C, $4,300.
   (4) Heating and lighting and janitorial expense on the basis of floor space occupied.
c. The company allocates general office department expenses to the selling departments on the basis of sales; and it allocates purchasing department expenses on the basis of purchases.

Problem 22-4A

The income statement at the top of page 691 reflects last year's results for High Tide Sales.

As a result of its loss, the concern's management is considering the elimination of its Department B, and it has an offer from a noncompeting business to sublease the department's space and half of its equipment for $3,500 per year on a long-term lease.

An analysis of the operating expenses indicates:
a. If Department B is discontinued, its advertising, store supplies, and bad debts expenses will be eliminated. Also, the two sales employees assigned to the department may be terminated and their $13,260 salaries eliminated.
b. The Department B equipment that will be leased along with its space accounts for one half the depreciation presently charged to the department.

Income Statement for Year Ended December 31, 19—

	Dept. A	Dept. B	Combined
Sales...	$152,000	$93,000	$245,000
Cost of goods sold	93,500	69,600	163,100
Gross profit on sales	$ 58,500	$23,400	$ 81,900
Operating expenses:			
Direct expenses:			
Advertising expense .... $	2,350	$ 1,770	$ 4,120
Store supplies expense........................	650	425	1,075
Depreciation expense, equipment	1,800	1,000	2,800
Total direct expenses..................... $	4,800	$ 3,195	$ 7,995
Indirect expenses:			
Sales salaries expense........................ $	22,100	$13,260	$ 35,360
Rent expense	5,400	3,000	8,400
Bad debts expense	760	465	1,225
Insurance expense	400	300	700
Share of office expenses.....................	6,080	3,720	9,800
Total indirect expenses.................. $	34,740	$20,745	$ 55,485
Total expenses .... $	39,540	$23,940	$ 63,480
Net Income (Loss)................................ $	18,960	$ (540)	$ 18,420

As to the remainder of Department B's equipment, Department A will have
to make whatever use it can of it, since it has little or no resale value.

c. Two thirds of the insurance expense presently charged to Department B,
the portion on its inventory, will be eliminated when Department B is
discontinued.

d. Eliminating Department B will reduce total office expenses by 30%.

Required:
1. List in separate columns and total the amounts of Department B's escapable
and inescapable expenses.
2. Under the assumption that Department A's sales will not be affected by the
elimination of Department B, prepare an income statement showing what
the concern can expect to earn from the operation of Department A after
the elimination of Department B and with the subleasing of its equipment
and space.

Problem 22–5A

Tom Citrus marketed a million pounds of grapefruit from his citrus grove
last year, and he prepared the following statement to show the results:

Income from the Sale of Grapefruit
For Year Ended March 31, 19—

	Results by Grades			Combined
	No. 1	No. 2	No. 3	
Sales by grades:				
No. 1, 400,000 lbs. @ $0.055 per lb.............	$22,000			
No. 2, 400,000 lbs. @ $0.045 per lb.............		$18,000		
No. 3, 200,000 lbs. @ $0.01 per lb			$ 2,000	
Combined sales......................................				$42,000
Costs:				
Tree pruning and grove care @ $0.00756				
per lb..	$ 3,024	$ 3,024	$ 1,512	$ 7,560
Fruit picking, grading, and sorting @ $0.0126				
per lb..	5,040	5,040	2,520	12,600
Marketing @ $0.0034 per lb	1,360	1,360	680	3,400
Total costs..	$ 9,424	$ 9,424	$ 4,712	$23,560
Net Income or (Loss)	$12,576	$ 8,576	$ (2,712)	$18,440

Upon completing the statement, Mr. Citrus thought a wise course of action might be to leave the small No. 3 grapefruit on the trees to fall off and be plowed under when he cultivated between the trees, and thus avoid the loss from their sale. However, before doing so he consulted you.

When you examined the statement, you recognized the grove care, picking, grading, and sorting costs as joint costs that Mr. Citrus had allocated on a per pound basis. You asked about the marketing costs and learned that $3,200 of the $3,400 was incurred in placing the No. 1 and No. 2 fruit in boxes and delivering it to the warehouse of the fruit buyer. The cost per pound for this was the same for both grades. You also learned that the remaining $200 was for loading the No. 3 fruit on the trucks of a soft drink bottler who bought this grade in bulk at the citrus grove for use in making a soft drink.

Required:
Prepare an income statement that will reflect better the results of producing and marketing the grapefruit.

Decision problem 22-1, Lee, May, and Nash   Paul Lee inherited a small plot of land; and to develop it, he entered into a partnership with Roy May, an investor, and Ted Nash, a real estate operator. Lee invested his land in the partnership at its $45,000 fair value, May invested $45,000 in cash, and Nash invested $6,000 cash; and the partners agreed to share losses and gains equally. The partnership installed streets and water mains costing $51,000 and divided the land into 14 building lots. They priced Lots 1, 2, 3, and 4 for sale at $9,000 each; Lots 5, 6, 7, 8, 9, 10, 11, and 12 at $10,500 each; and Lots 13 and 14 at $12,000 each. The partners agreed that Nash could take Lot 14 at cost for his personal use. The remaining lots were sold, and the partnership dissolved. Determine the amount of partnership cash each partner should receive in the dissolution.

Decision problem 22–2, Tick-Tack Sales

Dale Hall asked his new bookkeeper to prepare a departmental income statement for his company, Tick-Tack Sales. Following is the statement the bookkeeper prepared:

TICK-TACK SALES
Departmental Income Statement
Year Ended December 31, 19—

	Tick Department	Tack Department	Combined
Sales	$80,000	$120,000	$200,000
Cost of goods sold	54,560	81,840	136,400
Gross profit on sales	$25,440	$ 38,160	$ 63,600
Warehousing expenses	$ 5,900	$ 5,900	$ 11,800
Selling expenses	10,200	11,200	21,400
General and administrative expenses	3,300	3,300	6,600
Total expenses	$19,400	$ 20,400	$ 39,800
Net Income	$ 6,040	$ 17,760	$ 23,800

Mr. Hall does not think the bookkeeper's statement reflects the profit situation in the company's two selling departments and he has asked you to redraft it with any supporting schedules or comments you think appropriate. Your investigation reveals the following:

1. The company sold 400 Ticks and 350 Tacks during the year. A Tack costs twice as much as a Tick, but the bookkeeper ignored all of this and apportioned cost of goods sold between the two departments on the basis of sales.

2. A Tick and a Tack are approximately the same weight and bulk. However because there are two styles of Ticks and three styles of Tacks, the company must carry a 50% greater number of Tacks than Ticks in its inventory.

3. The company occupies the building on the following basis:

	Area of Space	Value of Space
Warehouse	80%	60%
Tick sales office space	5%	10%
Tack sales office space	5%	10%
General office space	10%	20%

4. Warehousing expenses consisted of the following:

Wages expense	$ 6,200
Depreciation of building	4,000
Heating and lighting expenses	1,000
Depreciation of warehouse equipment	600
Total	$11,800

The bookkeeper charged all the building's depreciation plus all of the heating and lighting expenses to warehousing expenses.

5. Selling expenses as apportioned by the bookkeeper consisted of the following:

	Tick Department	Tack Department
Sales salaries	$ 8,000	$ 9,000
Advertising	2,000	2,000
Depreciation of office equipment	200	200
Totals	$10,200	$11,200

Sales salaries and depreciation of office equipment were charged to the two departments on the basis of actual amounts incurred. Advertising was apportioned equally by the bookkeeper. The company has an established advertising budget based on dollars of sales which it followed closely during the year.

6. General and administrative expenses consisted of the following:

Office salaries	$6,000
Depreciation of office equipment	400
Miscellaneous office expenses	200
Total	$6,600

Decision problem 22–3, Motor Sales Company

Motor Sales Company sells a standard model and a deluxe model of a motor that is manufactured for it. Statistics on last year's sales of the two models were as follows:

	Standard	Deluxe
Units sold	800	400
Selling price per unit	$200	$300
Cost per unit	$110	$155
Sales commission per unit	$ 20	$ 30
Indirect selling and administrative expenses	$ 50	$ 75

Indirect selling and administrative expenses totaled $70,000 and were allocated on a "joint cost" basis. In other words the standard model produced $160,000 of revenue and the deluxe model produced $120,000; consequently, the standard model was assigned $\frac{4}{7}$ of the $70,000 of indirect expenses and the deluxe model was assigned $\frac{3}{7}$. The shares assigned to the models were in each case divided by the units sold to get the $50 and $75 per unit for each model.

Management of Motor Sales Company is not certain which of three courses of action it should take. It can: (1) through advertising push the sales of the standard model, (2) through advertising push the sales of the deluxe model, or (3) do no additional advertising, in which case sales of each model will continue at present levels. The demand for the motor is fairly stable, and an increase in the number of units of one model sold will cause a proportionate decrease in the sales of the other model. However, through the expenditure of $5,000 for advertising, the company can shift the sale of 200 units of the standard model to the deluxe model, or vice versa, depending upon which model receives the advertising attention.

Should the company advertise; and if so, should it advertise the standard model or the deluxe model? Back your position with income statements.

23

Manufacturing accounting

■ In previous chapters consideration has been given to the accounting problems of service-type and merchandising concerns. In this chapter some problems of manufacturing enterprises are examined.

Manufacturing and merchandising concerns are alike in that both depend for revenue upon the sale of one or more commodities or products. However, they differ in that a merchandising company buys the goods it sells in the finished state in which they are sold, while a manufacturing concern buys raw materials which it manufactures into the finished products it sells. For example, a shoe store buys shoes and sells them in the same form in which they are purchased; but a manufacturer of shoes buys leather, cloth, glue, nails, and dye and turns these items into salable shoes.

Basic difference in accounting ■ The basic difference in accounting for manufacturing and merchandising concerns grows from the idea in the preceding paragraph — the idea that a merchant buys the goods he sells in their finished-ready-for-sale state, while a manufacturer must create what he sells from raw materials. As a result the merchant can easily determine the cost of the goods he has bought for sale by examining the debit balance of his Purchases account, but the manufacturer must combine the balances of a number of material, labour, and overhead accounts to determine the cost of the goods he has manufactured for sale.

697

To emphasize this difference, the cost of goods sold section from a merchandising concern's income statement is condensed and reproduced below beside that of a manufacturing company.

Merchandising Company

Cost of goods sold:
Beginning merchandise inventory $14,200.00
Cost of goods purchased 34,150.00
Goods available for sale $48,350.00
Ending merchandise inventory 12,100.00
    Cost of goods sold $36,250.00

Manufacturing Company

Cost of goods sold:
Beginning finished goods
  inventory .... $ 11,200.00
Cost of goods manufactured (see
  Manufacturing Statement) 170,500.00
Goods available for sale $181,700.00
Ending finished goods inventory 10,300.00
    Cost of goods sold $171,400.00

Notice in the costs of goods sold section from the manufacturing company's income statement that the inventories of goods for sale are called *finished goods inventories* rather than merchandise inventories. Notice too that the "Cost of goods purchased" element of the merchandising company becomes "Cost of goods manufactured (see Manufacturing Statement)" on the manufacturer's income statement. These differences result because the merchandising company buys its goods ready for sale, while the manufacturer creates its salable products from raw materials.

The words "see Manufacturing Statement" refer the income statement reader to a separate schedule called a manufacturing statement (see page 703) which shows the costs of manufacturing the products produced by a manufacturing company. The records and techniques used in accounting for these costs are the distinguishing characteristics of manufacturing accounting.

Systems of accounting in manufacturing concerns

■ The accounting system used by a manufacturing concern may be either a so-called general accounting system like the one described in this chapter or a cost accounting system. A general accounting system uses periodic physical inventories of raw materials, goods in process, and finished goods; and it has as its goal the determination of the total cost of all goods manufactured during each accounting period. Cost accounting systems differ in that they use perpetual inventories and have as their goal the determination of the unit cost of manufacturing a product or performing a service. Such systems are discussed in the next two chapters.

Elements of manufacturing costs

■ A manufacturer takes *raw materials* and by applying *direct labour* and *factory overhead* converts these materials into finished products. Raw materials, direct labour, and factory overhead are the "elements of manufacturing costs."

Raw materials

Raw materials are the commodities that enter directly into and become a part of a finished product. Such items as leather, dye, cloth, nails, and glue are raw materials of a shoe manufacturer. Raw materials are often called *direct materials*. Direct materials are materials the costs of which are chargeable directly to the product or products manufactured, and are distinguished from *indirect materials* or factory supplies which are such items as grease and oil for machinery, cleaning fluids, etc. Indirect materials are accounted for as factory overhead.

The raw materials of a manufacturer are called "raw materials," even though they may not necessarily be in their natural raw state. For example, leather is manufactured from hides, nails from steel, and cloth from cotton. Nevertheless, leather, nails, and cloth are the raw materials of a shoe manufacturer even though they are the finished products of previous manufacturers.

Direct labour

Direct labour is labour, the cost of which is chargeable directly to the product or products manufactured. It is often described as the labour of those people who work, either with machines or hand tools, directly on the materials converted into finished products. In manufacturing, direct labour is distinguished from *indirect labour*. Indirect labour is the labour of superintendents, foremen, millwrights, engineers, janitors, and others who do not work directly on the manufactured products. Indirect labour aids in production; often it makes production possible but it does not enter directly into the finished product. Indirect labour is accounted for as a factory overhead cost.

In a general accounting system, an account called *Direct Labour* is debited each payday for the wages of those workers who work directly on the product. Likewise, each payday, the wages of indirect workers are debited to one or more indirect labour accounts. Also, at the end of each period, the amounts of accrued direct and indirect labour are recorded in the direct and indirect labour accounts by means of adjusting entries. From this it can be seen that a manufacturing company's payroll accounting is similar to that of a merchandising concern. When a cost accounting system is not involved, no new techniques are required and only the new direct and indirect labour accounts distinguish the payroll accounting of a manufacturer from that of a merchant.

Factory overhead

Factory overhead, often called *manufacturing overhead* or *factory burden,* includes all manufacturing costs other than for direct materials and direct labour. Factory overhead may include:

Indirect labour.
Factory supplies.
Repairs to buildings and equipment.
Insurance on plant and equipment.
Taxes on plant and equipment.
Supervision.
Heat, lights, and power.

Depreciation of plant and equipment.
Patents written off.
Small tools written off.
Workmen's compensation insurance.
Payroll taxes on the wages of the
    factory workers.

Factory overhead does not include selling and administrative expenses. Selling and administrative expenses are not factory overhead because they are not incurred in order to produce the manufactured products. They could be called selling and administrative overhead, but this is not factory overhead.

All factory overhead costs are accumulated in overhead cost accounts which vary from company to company, with the exact accounts depending in each case upon the nature of the company and the information desired. For example, one account called "Expired Insurance on Plant Equipment" may be maintained, or an expired insurance account each for buildings and the different kinds of equipment may be used. But regardless of accounts, overhead costs are recorded in the same ways as are selling and administrative expenses. Some, such as indirect labour and light and power, are recorded in registers or journals as they are paid and are then posted to the accounts. Others, such as depreciation and expired insurance, reach the accounts through adjusting entries.

Accounts unique to a manufacturing company

■ Because of the nature of its operations, a manufacturing concern's ledger normally contains more accounts than that of a merchandising concern. However, some of the same accounts are found in the ledgers of both, for example, Cash, Accounts Receivable, Sales, and many selling and administrative expenses. Nevertheless, although there are accounts in common, many accounts are unique to a manufacturing company. For instance, accounts such as Machinery and Equipment, Accumulated Depreciation of Machinery and Equipment, Factory Supplies, Factory Supplies Used, Raw Materials Inventory, Raw Material Purchases, Goods in Process Inventory, Finished Goods Inventory, and Manufacturing Summary are normally found only in the ledgers of manufacturing concerns. Some of these accounts merit special attention.

Raw Material Purchases account

When a general accounting system is in use, the cost of all raw materials purchased is debited to an account called Raw Material Purchases. Often a special column is provided in the Voucher Register or other journal for the debits of the individual purchases, thus making it possible to periodically post these debits in one amount, the column total.

Raw Materials Inventory account

When a general accounting system is in use, the raw materials on hand at the end of each accounting period are determined by a physical inventory; and through a closing entry the cost of this inventory is debited to the Raw Materials Inventory account where it becomes a record of the materials on hand at the end of one period and the beginning of the next.

Goods in Process Inventory account

All manufacturing concerns except those in which the manufacturing process is instantaneous normally have on hand at any time partially processed products called *goods in process* or *work in process*. These are products in the process of being manufactured, products that have received a portion or all of their materials and have had some labour and overhead applied but that are not completed.

In a manufacturing concern using a general accounting system the amount of goods in process at the end of each accounting period is determined by a physical inventory; and through a closing entry the cost of this inventory is debited to the Goods in Process Inventory account where it becomes a record of the goods in process at the end of one period and the beginning of the next.

Finished Goods Inventory account

The finished goods of a manufacturer are the equivalent of a store's merchandise; they are products in their completed state ready for sale. Actually, the only difference is that a manufacturing concern creates its finished goods from raw materials, while a store buys its merchandise in a finished, ready-for-sale state.

In a general accounting system the amount of finished goods on hand at the end of each period is determined by a physical inventory; and through a closing entry the cost of this inventory is debited to the Finished Goods Inventory account as a record of the finished goods at the end of one period and the beginning of the next.

The three inventories — raw materials, goods in process, and finished goods — are current assets for balance sheet purposes.

Income statement of a manufacturing company

■ The income statement of a manufacturing company is similar to that of a merchandising concern. To see this, compare the income statement of Nelson Hardware Company, Illustration 5–1 on page 139, with that of Excel Manufacturing Company, Ltd., Illustration 23–1 on page 702. Notice that the revenue, selling, and general and administrative expense sections are very similar. However, when the cost of goods sold sections are compared, a difference is apparent. Here the item "Cost of goods manufactured" replaces the "purchases" element, and finished goods inventories take the place of merchandise inventories.

Observe in the cost of goods sold section of Excel Manufacturing Company's income statement that only the total cost of goods manufactured is shown. It would be possible to expand this section to show the detailed costs of the materials, direct labour, and overhead entering into the cost of goods manufactured. However, if this were done, the income statement would be long and unwieldy. Consequently, the common practice is to show only the total cost of goods manufactured on the income statement and to attach a supporting schedule showing the details. This supporting schedule is called a "schedule of the cost of goods manufactured" or a "manufacturing statement."

The Excel Manufacturing Company, Ltd.
Income Statement for Year Ended December 31, 19—

Revenue:			
Sales..			$310,000
Cost of goods sold:			
Finished goods inventory, January 1, 19—............		$ 11,200	
Cost of goods manufactured (see Manufacturing			
Statement)..		170,500	
Goods available for sale......................................		$181,700	
Finished goods inventory, December 31, 19—.......		10,300	
Cost of goods sold			171,400
Gross profit..			$138,600
Operating expenses:			
Selling expenses:			
Sales salaries expense	$18,000		
Advertising expense..	5,500		
Delivery wages expense	12,000		
Shipping supplies expense	250		
Delivery equipment insurance expense	300		
Depreciation expense, delivery equipment.........	2,100		
Total selling expenses..................................		$ 38,150	
General and administrative expenses:			
Office salaries expense....................................	$15,700		
Miscellaneous general expense........................	200		
Bad debts expense	1,550		
Office supplies expense...................................	100		
Depreciation expense, office equipment............	200		
Total general and administrative expenses.....		17,750	
Total operating expenses			55,900
Operating income...			$ 82,700
Financial expense:			
Mortgage interest expense			4,000
Income before income taxes			$ 78,700
Less income taxes			32,600
Net Income			$ 46,100
Net income per common share (20,000 shares			
outstanding)...			$2.31

Illustration
23–1

Manufacturing statement ■ The cost elements of manufacturing are raw materials, direct labour, and factory overhead; and a manufacturing statement is normally constructed in such a manner as to emphasize these elements. Notice in Illustration 23–2 that the first section of the statement shows the cost of raw materials used. Also observe the manner of presentation is the same as that used on the income statement of a merchandising company to show cost of goods purchased and sold.

The so-called second section shows the cost of direct labour used in production, and the third section shows factory overhead costs. If overhead accounts are not too numerous, the balance of each is often listed in this third section, as in Illustration 23–2. However, if overhead accounts are numerous, only the total of all may be shown; and in such

The Excel Manufacturing Company, Ltd.
Manufacturing Statement for Year Ended December 31, 19—

Raw materials:

Raw materials inventory, January 1, 19—		$ 8,000
Raw materials purchased $85,000		
Freight on raw materials purchased 1,500		
Delivered cost of raw materials purchased............	86,500	
Raw materials available for use..........................	$94,500	
Raw materials inventory, December 31, 19—	9,000	
Raw materials used		$ 85,500
Direct labour		60,000
Factory overhead costs:		
Indirect labour...	$ 9,000	
Supervision	6,000	
Power..	2,600	
Repairs and maintenance...................................	2,500	
Factory taxes...	1,900	
Factory supplies used.......................................	500	
Factory insurance expired.................................	1,200	
Small tools written off.......................................	200	
Depreciation of machinery and equipment............	3,500	
Depreciation of building....................................	1,800	
Patents written off..	800	
Total factory overhead costs...........................		30,000
Total manufacturing costs.............................		$175,500
Add: Goods in process inventory, January 1, 19—...		2,500
Total goods in process during the year...........		$178,000
Deduct: Goods in process inventory, December 31, 19—		7,500
Cost of Goods Manufactured................................		$170,500

Illustration
23–2

cases the total is supported by a separate attached schedule showing each cost.

In the last section the calculation of cost of goods manufactured is completed. Here the cost of the beginning goods in process inventory is added to the sum of the manufacturing costs to show the cost of all goods in process during the period. Then, the cost of the goods still in process at the end is subtracted to show cost of the goods manufactured.

The manufacturing statement is prepared from the Manufacturing Statement columns of a work sheet. The items that appear on the statement are summarized in these columns, and all that is required in constructing the statement is a rearrangement of the items into the proper statement order. Illustration 23–3 shows the manufacturing work sheet.

Work sheet for a manufacturing company

■ In examining Illustration 23–3, note first that there are no Adjusted Trial Balance columns. These columns are omitted because the experienced accountant commonly omits such columns from his work sheet to save time and effort. How a work sheet without Adjusted Trial Balance columns is prepared and how this saves time and effort were explained in Chapter 5.

The Excel Manufacturing Company, Ltd.
Manufacturing Work Sheet for Year Ended December 31, 19 —

Account Titles	Trial Balance Dr.	Trial Balance Cr.	Adjustments Dr.	Adjustments Cr.	Mfg. Statement Dr.	Mfg. Statement Cr.	Income Statement Dr.	Income Statement Cr.	Balance Sheet Dr.	Balance Sheet Cr.
Cash	11,000								11,000	
Accounts receivable	32,000								32,000	
Allowance for doubtful accounts		300		(a) 1,550						1,850
Raw materials inventory	8,000				8,000	9,000			9,000	
Goods in process inventory	2,500				2,500	7,500			7,500	
Finished goods inventory	11,200						11,200	10,300	10,300	
Office supplies	150			(b) 100					50	
Shipping supplies	300			(c) 250					50	
Factory supplies	750			(d) 500					250	
Prepaid insurance	1,800			(e) 1,500					300	
Small tools	1,300			(f) 200					1,100	
Delivery equipment	9,000								9,000	
Accumulated depreciation of delivery equipment		1,900		(g) 2,100						4,000
Office equipment	1,700								1,700	
Accumulated depreciation of office equipment		200		(h) 200						400
Machinery and equipment	72,000								72,000	
Accumulated depr. of machinery and equipment		3,000		(i) 3,500						6,500
Factory building	90,000								90,000	
Accumulated depreciation of factory building		1,500		(j) 1,800						3,300
Land	9,500								9,500	
Patents	12,000			(k) 800					11,200	
Accounts payable		14,000								14,000
Mortgage payable		50,000								50,000
Common stock		100,000								100,000
Retained earnings		3,660								3,660
Sales		310,000						310,000		
Raw material purchases	85,000				85,000					
Freight on raw materials	1,500				1,500					
Direct labour	59,600		(l) 400		60,000					
Indirect labour	8,940		(l) 60		9,000					

Account	Trial Balance Dr	Trial Balance Cr	Adjustments Dr	Adjustments Cr	Manufacturing Dr	Manufacturing Cr	Income Statement Dr	Income Statement Cr	Balance Sheet Dr	Balance Sheet Cr
Supervision	6,000				6,000					
Power expense	2,600				2,600					
Repairs and maintenance	2,500				2,500					
Factory taxes	1,900				1,900					
Sales salaries expense	18,000						18,000			
Advertising expense	5,500						5,500			
Delivery wages expense	11,920		(l) 80				12,000			
Office salaries expense	15,700						15,700			
Miscellaneous general expense	200						200			
Mortgage interest expense	2,000		(m) 2,000				4,000			
	484,560	484,560								
Bad debts expense			(a) 1,550				1,550			
Office supplies expense			(b) 100				100			
Shipping supplies expense			(c) 250				250			
Factory supplies used			(d) 500		500					
Factory insurance expired			(e) 1,200		1,200					
Delivery equipment insurance expense			300				300			
Small tools written off			(f) 200		200					
Depreciation expense, delivery equipment			(g) 2,100				2,100			
Depreciation expense, office equipment			(h) 200				200			
Depreciation of machinery and equipment			(i) 3,500		3,500					
Depreciation of building			(j) 1,800		1,800					
Patents written off			(k) 800		800					
Accrued wages payable				(l) 540						540
Mortgage interest payable				(m) 2,000						2,000
Income taxes expense			(n) 32,600				32,600			
Income taxes payable				(n) 32,600						32,600
			47,640	47,640	170,500	170,500				
					16,500					
Cost of goods manufactured to Income Statement columns						170,500	170,500			
					187,000	187,000	274,200	320,300	218,850	
Net Income							46,100			46,100
							320,300	320,300	264,950	264,950

Illustration
23-3

To understand the work sheet of Illustration 23–3, recall that a work sheet is a tool of the accountant on which he—

1. Achieves the effect of adjusting the accounts before entering the adjustments in a journal and posting them to the accounts.
2. Sorts the adjusted account balances into columns according to the financial statement upon which they appear.
3. Calculates and proves the mathematical accuracy of the net income.

With the foregoing in mind, the primary difference between the work sheet of a manufacturing company and that of a merchandising company is an additional set of columns. Insofar as the adjustments are concerned, they are made in the same way on both kinds of work sheets. Also, the mathematical accuracy of the net income is proved in the same way. However, since an additional accounting statement, the manufacturing statement, is prepared for a manufacturing company, the work sheet of such a company has an additional set of columns, the Manufacturing Statement columns, into which are sorted the items appearing on the manufacturing statement.

Preparing a manufacturing company's work sheet ■ A manufacturing company's work sheet is prepared in the same manner as that of a merchandising concern. First a trial balance of the ledger is entered in the Trial Balance columns in the usual manner. Next, information for the adjustments is assembled, and the adjustments are entered in the Adjustments columns just as for a merchandising company. The adjustments information for the work sheet shown in Illustration 23–3 is as follows:

a. Estimated bad debt losses $\frac{1}{2}$% of sales, or $1,550.
b. Office supplies used, $100.
c. Shipping supplies used, $250.
d. Factory supplies used, $500.
e. Expired insurance on factory, $1,200; and expired insurance on the delivery equipment, $300.
f. The small tools inventory shows $1,100 of usable small tools on hand.
g. Depreciation of delivery equipment, $2,100.
h. Depreciation of office equipment, $200.
i. Depreciation of factory machinery and equipment, $3,500.
j. Depreciation of factory building, $1,800.
k. Yearly write-off of one seventeenth of the cost of patents, $800.
l. Accrued wages: direct labour, $400; indirect labour, $60; delivery wages, $80. All other employees paid monthly on the last day of each month.
m. One-half year's interest accrued on the mortgage, $2,000.
n. State and federal income taxes expense, $32,600.

After the adjustments are completed, the amounts in the Trial Balance columns are combined with the amounts in the Adjustments columns and are sorted to the proper Manufacturing Statement, Income Statement, or Balance Sheet columns, according to the statement on which they appear.

No new techniques are required in the sorting, just two decisions for each item: First, does the item have a debit balance or a credit balance; and second, on which statement does it appear? The first decision is necessary because a debit item must be sorted to a Debit column and a credit item to a Credit column. As for the second, a work sheet is a tool for sorting items according to their statement appearance; and to properly sort the items it is only necessary to know that asset, liability, and owner equity items appear on the balance sheet and are sorted to the Balance Sheet columns. The finished goods inventory plus the revenue, selling, general and administrative, and financial expense items go on the income statement and are sorted to the Income Statement columns. And finally, the raw material, goods in process, direct labour, and factory overhead items appear on the manufacturing statement and are sorted to the Manufacturing Statement columns.

After the trial balance items with their adjustments are sorted to the proper statement columns, the ending inventory amounts are entered on the work sheet. The raw materials and goods in process inventories appear on the manufacturing statement. Therefore, the ending raw materials and goods in process inventory amounts are entered in the Manufacturing Statement credit and Balance Sheet debit columns. They must be entered in the Manufacturing Statement credit column in order to make the difference between the two columns equal cost of goods manufactured. Likewise, since these inventory amounts represent end-of-the-period assets, they must be entered in the Balance Sheet debit column with the other assets.

The ending finished goods inventory is the equivalent of an ending merchandise inventory and receives the same work sheet treatment. It is entered in the Income Statement credit column and the Balance Sheet debit column. It is entered in the Income Statement credit column so that the net income may be determined; and since it is a current asset, it must also be entered in the Balance Sheet debit column.

After the ending inventories are entered on the work sheet, the Manufacturing Statement columns are added and their difference determined. This difference is cost of the goods manufactured; and after it is determined, it is entered in the Manufacturing Statement credit column to make the two columns equal. Also, it is entered in the Income Statement debit column, the same column in which the balance of the Purchases account of a merchant is entered. After this the work sheet is completed in the usual manner.

Preparing statements ■ After completion, the manufacturing work sheet is used in preparing the statements and in making adjusting and closing entries. The manufacturing statement is prepared from the information in the work sheet's Manufacturing Statement columns, the income statement from the information in the Income Statement columns, and the balance sheet from information in the Balance Sheet columns. After this the adjusting and closing entries are entered in the journal and posted.

Adjusting entries ■ The adjusting entries of a manufacturing company are prepared in the same way as those of a merchandising concern. An adjusting entry is entered in the General Journal for each adjustment appearing in the work sheet Adjustments columns. No new techniques are required here.

Closing entries ■ The account balances that enter into the calculation of cost of goods manufactured show manufacturing costs for a particular accounting period and must be closed and cleared at the end of each period. Normally they are closed and cleared through a Manufacturing Summary account, which is in turn closed and cleared through the Income Summary account.

The entries to close and clear the manufacturing accounts of Excel Manufacturing Company are as follows:

Dec.	31	Manufacturing Summary	187,000.00	
		Raw Materials Inventory		8,000.00
		Goods in Process Inventory		2,500.00
		Raw Material Purchases		85,000.00
		Freight on Raw Materials.......................		1,500.00
		Direct Labour .....:...............................		60,000.00
		Indirect Labour		9,000.00
		Supervision...		6,000.00
		Power Expense.....................................		2,600.00
		Repairs and Maintenance		2,500.00
		Factory Taxes.......................................		1,900.00
		Factory Supplies Used........................../		500.00
		Factory Insurance Expired		1,200.00
		Small Tools Written Off		200.00
		Depr. of Machinery and Equipment.........		3,500.00
		Depreciation of Building........................		1,800.00
		Patents Written Off...............................		800.00
		To close those manufacturing accounts having debit balances.		
	31	Raw Materials Inventory	9,000.00	
		Goods in Process Inventory	7,500.00	
		Manufacturing Summary		16,500.00
		To set up the ending raw materials and goods in process inventories and to remove their balances from the Manufacturing Summary account.		

The entries are taken from the information in the Manufacturing Statement columns of the Illustration 23–3 work sheet. Compare the first entry with the information shown in the Manufacturing Statement debit column. Note how the debit to the Manufacturing Summary account is taken from the column total, and how each account having a balance in the column is credited to close and clear it. Also observe that the second entry has the effect of subtracting the ending raw materials and goods in process inventories from the manufacturing costs shown in the work sheet's debit column.

The effect of the two entries is to cause the Manufacturing Summary account to have a debit balance equal to the $170,500 cost of goods manufactured. This $170,500 balance is closed to the Income Summary account along with the other cost and expense accounts having balances in the Income Statement debit column. Observe the following entry which is used to close the accounts having balances in the Income Statement debit column of the Illustration 23–3 work sheet and especially note its last credit.

Dec.	31	Income Summary	274,200.00	
		Finished Goods Inventory		11,200.00
		Sales Salaries Expense		18,000.00
		Advertising Expense		5,500.00
		Delivery Wages Expense		12,000.00
		Office Salaries Expense		15,700.00
		Miscellaneous General Expense		200.00
		Mortgage Interest Expense		4,000.00
		Bad Debts Expense		1,550.00
		Office Supplies Expense		100.00
		Shipping Supplies Expense		250.00
		Delivery Equipment Insurance Expense		300.00
		Depreciation Expense, Delivery Equipment		2,100.00
		Depreciation Expense, Office Equipment		200.00
		Income Tax Expense		32,600.00
		Manufacturing Summary		170,500.00
		To close the income statement accounts having debit balances.		

After the foregoing entry, the remainder of the income statement accounts of Illustration 23–3 are closed as follows:

Dec.	31	Finished Goods Inventory	10,300.00	
		Sales	310,000.00	
		Income Summary		320,300.00
		To close the Sales account and to bring the ending finished goods inventory on the books.		
	31	Income Summary	46,100.00	
		Retained Earnings		46,100.00
		To close the Income Summary account.		

■ In a manufacturing company using a general accounting system, at the end of each period, an accounting value must be placed on the inventories of raw materials, goods in process, and finished goods. No particular problems are encountered in valuing raw materials because the items are in the same form in which they were purchased and a cost or market price may be applied. However, placing a valuation on goods in process and finished goods is generally not so easy because goods in process and finished goods consist of raw materials to which certain amounts of labour and overhead have been added. They are not in the same form in which they were purchased. Consequently, a price paid a previous producer cannot be used to measure their inventory amount. Instead, their inventory amount must be built up by adding together estimates of the raw materials, direct labour, and overhead costs applicable to each item.

Estimating raw material costs applicable to a goods in process or finished goods item is usually not too difficult. Likewise, from its percentage of completion, a responsible plant official can normally make a reasonably accurate estimate of the direct labour applicable to an item. However, estimating factory overhead costs presents more of a problem, which is often solved by assuming that factory overhead costs are closely related to direct labour costs, and this is often a fair assumption. Frequently there is a close relation between direct labour costs and such things as supervision, power, repairs, etc. Furthermore, when this relation is used to apply overhead costs, it is assumed that the relation of overhead costs to the direct labour costs in each goods in process and finished goods item is the same as the relation between total factory overhead costs and total direct labour costs for the accounting period.

For example, an examination of the manufacturing statement in Illustration 23–2 will show that Excel Manufacturing Company, Ltd.'s total direct labour costs were $60,000 and its overhead costs were $30,000. Or, an examination will show that during the year the company incurred in the production of all its products $2 of direct labour for each $1 of factory overhead costs. Or, during the year the company's overhead costs were 50% of direct labour cost.

Overhead Costs, $30,000 ÷ Direct Labour, $60,000 = 50%

Consequently, in estimating the overhead applicable to a goods in process or finished goods item, Excel Manufacturing Company may assume that this 50% overhead rate is applicable. It may assume that if in all its production the overhead costs were 50% of the direct labour costs, then in each goods in process and finished goods item this relationship also exists.

If Excel Manufacturing Company makes this assumption and its goods in process inventory consists of 1,000 units of Item X with each unit containing $3.75 of raw material and having $2.50 of applicable direct labour, then the goods in process inventory is valued as shown in Illustration 23–4.

Product	Estimated Raw Material Cost	Estimated Direct Labour Applicable	Overhead (50% of Direct Labour	Estimated Total Unit Cost	No. of Units	Estimated Inventory Cost
Item X	$3.75	$2.50	$1.25	$7.50	1,000	$7,500.00

Illustration
23–4

Excel Manufacturing Company may use the same procedure in placing an accounting value on the items of its finished goods inventory.

Questions for class discussion

1. How does the income statement of a manufacturing company differ from the income statement of a merchandising company?
2. What are the three elements of manufacturing costs?
3. What are (a) direct labour, (b) indirect labour, (c) direct material, (d) indirect material, and (e) factory overhead costs?
4. Name several items that are accounted for as factory overhead costs.
5. Name several accounts that are often found in the ledgers of both manufacturing and merchandising companies. Name several accounts that are found only in the ledgers of manufacturing companies.
6. What three new inventory accounts appear in the ledger of a manufacturing company?
7. How are the raw material inventories handled on the work sheet of a manufacturing company? How are the goods in process inventories handled? How are the finished goods inventories handled?
8. Which inventories of a manufacturing company receive the same work sheet treatment as the merchandise inventories of a merchandising company?
9. Which inventories of a manufacturing company appear on its manufacturing statement? Which appear on the income statement?
10. What accounts are summarized in the Manufacturing Summary account? What accounts are summarized in the Income Summary account?
11. What are the three manufacturing cost elements emphasized on the manufacturing statement?
12. What account balances are sorted into the Manufacturing Statement columns of the manufacturing work sheet? What account balances are sorted into the Income Statement columns? What account balances are sorted into the Balance Sheet columns?
13. Why is the cost of goods manufactured entered in the Manufacturing Statement credit column of a work sheet and again in the Income Statement debit columns?
14. May prices paid a previous manufacturer for items of raw materials determine the balance sheet amount for the items of the raw materials inventory? Why? May such prices also determine the balance sheet amounts for the goods in process and finished goods inventories? Why?
15. Standard Company used an overhead rate of 70% of direct labour cost to

apply overhead to the items of its goods in process inventory. If the manufacturing statement of the company showed total overhead costs of $84,700, how much direct labour did it show?

Class exercises The following items appeared in the Manufacturing Statement and Income Statement columns of Dale Company's year-end work sheet:

	Manufacturing Statement		Income Statement	
	Debit	Credit	Debit	Credit
Raw materials inventory.........................	11,000	12,000	....	....
Goods in process inventory	14,000	10,000	....	....
Finished goods inventory	....	....	15,000	16,000
Sales.....................................	....	....	....	225,000
Raw material purchases	45,000	....	....	....
Direct labour	50,000	....	....	....
Indirect labour	11,000	....	....	....
Power.....................................	6,000	....	....	....
Machinery repairs	1,000	....	....	....
Rent of factory building	9,000	....	....	....
Selling expenses controlling	....	....	42,000	....
Administrative expenses controlling	....	....	25,000	....
Income taxes expense.........................	....	....	9,000	....
	147,000	22,000	....	....
Cost of goods manufactured....................		125,000	125,000	....
	147,000	147,000	216,000	241,000
Net Income			25,000	....
			241,000	241,000

Exercise 23–1

From the information just given prepare a manufacturing statement for Dale Company.

Exercise 23–2

Under the assumption Dale Company has outstanding 20,000 shares of $10 par value common stock and no preferred stock, prepare an income statement for the company.

Exercise 23–3

Prepare compound closing entries for Dale Company.

Exercise 23–4

A company that uses the relation between its overhead and direct labour costs to apply overhead to its goods in process and finished goods inventories incurred the following costs during a year: materials, $75,000; direct labour, $60,000; and factory overhead costs, $90,000. (a) Determine the company's overhead rate. (b) Under the assumption the company's $10,000 ending goods in process inventory had $3,000 of direct labour costs, determine the inventory's material costs. (c) Under the assumption the company's $15,000 finished goods inventory had $5,000 of material costs, determine the inventory's labour costs and its overhead costs.

Exercise 23–5

The trial balance of Valley Products Company, Ltd. follows. To save time the trial balance amounts are in numbers of one or two digits.

VALLEY PRODUCTS COMPANY, LTD.
Trial Balance, December 31, 19 –

Cash	$ 2	
Accounts receivable	4	
Allowance for doubtful accounts		$ 1
Raw materials inventory	3	
Goods in process inventory	2	
Finished goods inventory	4	
Factory supplies	3	
Prepaid factory insurance	4	
Machinery	20	
Accumulated depreciation, machinery		6
Common stock		15
Retained earnings		8
Sales		76
Raw material purchases	17	
Direct labour	14	
Indirect labour	3	
Power	4	
Machinery repairs	2	
Rent of factory building	9	
Selling expenses controlling	8	
Administrative expenses controlling	7	
Totals	$106	$106

Required:
Prepare a work sheet form on ordinary notebook paper, copy the trial balance on the work sheet form, and complete the work sheet using the following information:

a. Ending inventories: raw materials, $2; goods in process, $4; finished goods, $3; and factory supplies, $2.
b. Allowance for doubtful accounts, an additional $1. (Debit Administrative Expenses Controlling.)
c. Factory insurance expired, $2.
d. Depreciation of machinery, $3.
e. Accrued payroll payable: direct labour, $4; and indirect labour, $2.

Problems   Problem 23-1

The following items appeared in the Manufacturing Statement and Income Statement columns of a work sheet prepared for Steel Products Company on December 31, 19—, the end of its annual accounting period.

	Manufacturing Statement		Income Statement	
	Debit	Credit	Debit	Credit
Raw materials inventory...	18,500	17,600	....	....
Goods in process inventory	12,200	15,400	....	....
Finished goods inventory	....	....	22,400	21,500
Sales...	....	....	....	282,200
Raw material purchases	94,400	....	....	....
Direct labour	53,900	....	....	....
Indirect labour	9,600	....	....	....
Factory rent..	6,000	....	....	....
Supervision...	12,000	....	....	....
Power...	4,800	....	....	....
Repairs to machinery..	3,200	....	....	....
Selling expenses controlling	....	....	28,700	....
Administrative expenses controlling	....	....	29,900	....
Factory supplies used	2,400	....	....	....
Factory insurance expired	1,200	....	....	....
Small tools written off..	600	....	....	....
Depreciation of machinery....................................	7,100	....	....	....
Patents written off...	800	....	....	....
Income taxes expense...	....	....	6,200	....
	226,700	33,000	....	....
Cost of goods manufactured..................................	....	193,700	193,700	....
	226,700	226,700	280,900	303,700
Net Income			22,800	....
			303,700	303,700

Required:
1. Prepare a manufacturing statement and an income statement for Steel Products Company. Assume the company has 15,000 shares of $10 par value common stock and no preferred stock outstanding.
2. Prepare compound closing entries for the company.

Problem 23-2

The work sheet prepared for Hilltop Company at the end of last year had the following items in its Manufacturing Statement columns:

| | Manufacturing Statement | |
	Debit	Credit
Raw materials inventory	12,500	11,900
Goods in process inventory	14,800	?
Raw materials purchased	58,200	
Direct labour	100,000	
Indirect labour	14,300	
Factory supervision	12,000	
Heat, light, and power	18,400	
Machinery repairs	4,500	
Rent of factory	7,800	
Property taxes	1,100	
Factory insurance expense	2,400	
Factory supplies used	6,100	
Depreciation expense, machinery	10,500	
Small tools written off	400	
Patents written off	2,500	
	265,500	?
Cost of goods manufactured		?
	265,500	265,500

The columns do not show the amount of the ending goods in process inventory and the cost of the goods manufactured. However, the company makes a single product; and on December 31, at the end of last year, there were 3,000 units of this product in the goods in process inventory, with each unit containing an estimated $1.40 of materials and having an estimated $2 of direct labour applied.

Required:
1. Calculate the relation between direct labour and factory overhead costs and use this relation to place an accounting value on the ending goods in process inventory.
2. After placing a value on the ending goods in process inventory, prepare a manufacturing statement for the company.
3. Prepare entries to close the manufacturing accounts and to summarize their balances in the Manufacturing Summary account.
4. Prepare an entry to close the Manufacturing Summary account.

Problem 23–3

The December 31, 19—, trial balance of Plastic Products Company, Ltd. appeared as follows:

PLASTICS PRODUCTS COMPANY, LTD.
Trial Balance, December 31, 19—

Cash	$ 12,300	
Accounts receivable	16,200	
Allowance for doubtful accounts		$ 200
Raw materials inventory	17,100	
Goods in process inventory	24,400	
Finished goods inventory	28,700	
Prepaid factory insurance	4,100	
Factory supplies	13,100	
Machinery	287,500	
Accumulated depreciation, machinery		78,400
Accounts payable		15,300
Common stock, $10 par value		150,000
Retained earnings		64,900
Sales		572,500
Raw material purchases	185,100	
Direct labour	79,500	
Indirect labour	36,600	
Heat, light, and power	13,600	
Machinery repairs	9,400	
Selling expenses controlling	81,200	
General expenses controlling	72,500	
Totals	$881,300	$881,300

The following inventory and adjustments information was available at the year-end:

a. Allowance for doubtful accounts to be increased to $1,200. (Debit General Expenses Controlling.)
b. An examination of policies showed $3,100 of factory insurance expired.
c. An inventory of factory supplies showed $3,400 of unused supplies on hand.
d. Estimated depreciation on factory machinery, $31,300.
e. Accrued direct labour, $500; and accrued indirect labour, $300.
f. Income taxes expense, $14,800.
g. Year-end inventories:
   (1) Raw materials, $16,700.
   (2) Goods in process consisted of 3,000 units of product with each unit containing an estimated $3.85 of materials and having $1.50 of direct labour applied.
   (3) Finished goods inventory consisted of 2,000 units of product with each unit containing an estimated $6.20 of materials and having an estimated $3 of direct labour applied.

Required:

1. Enter the trial balance on a work sheet form and make the adjustments from the information given. Then sort the items to the proper Manufacturing Statement, Income Statement, and Balance Sheet columns.
2. After the Direct Labour and factory overhead cost accounts have been adjusted and carried into the Manufacturing Statement columns, determine the relation between direct labour and overhead costs and use this relation

to determine the overhead applicable to each unit of goods in process and finished goods. After the amounts of overhead applicable to the units of goods in process and finished goods are determined, calculate the balance sheet amounts for these inventories, enter the amounts on the work sheet, and complete the work sheet.

3. From the work sheet prepare a manufacturing statement and an income statement.
4. Prepare compound closing entries.

Problem 23–4

The year-end trial balance of Lake Manufacturing Company carried these items:

LAKE MANUFACTURING COMPANY
Trial Balance, December 31, 19—

Cash	$ 10,800	
Raw materials inventory	12,300	
Goods in process inventory	14,700	
Finished goods inventory	13,200	
Prepaid factory insurance	3,400	
Factory supplies	7,200	
Machinery	165,700	
Accumulated depreciation, machinery		$ 48,400
Small tools	3,100	
Patents	7,300	
Common stock, $5 par value		100,000
Retained earnings		27,400
Sales		338,500
Raw material purchases	55,400	
Discounts on raw material purchases		1,100
Direct labour	89,400	
Indirect labour	16,900	
Factory supervision	18,500	
Heat, light, and power	16,700	
Machinery repairs	5,400	
Rent of factory	12,000	
Property taxes	3,200	
Selling expenses controlling	30,800	
Administrative expenses controlling	29,400	
Totals	$515,400	$515,400

Additional Information:
a. Expired factory insurance, $2,600.
b. Factory supplies used, $6,100.
c. Depreciation of factory machinery, $15,300.
d. Small tools written off, $600.
e. Patents written off, $1,500.
f. Accrued wages payable: (1) direct labour, $600; and (2) indirect labour, $200.
g. Income taxes expense, $10,500.
h. Ending inventories: (1) raw materials, $13,500; (2) goods in process con-

sisted of 3,000 units of product with each unit containing an estimated $1.05 of materials and having had $1.50 of direct labour applied; and (3) finished goods consisted of 2,000 units of product with each unit containing an estimated $1.64 of materials and having had an estimated $2.60 of direct labour applied.

Required:
1. Enter the trial balance on a work sheet form; make the adjustments from the information given; and then sort the items to the proper Manufacturing Statement, Income Statement, and Balance Sheet columns.
2. After the Direct Labour account and the factory overhead cost accounts have been adjusted and carried into the Manufacturing Statement columns, determine the relation between overhead costs and direct labour and use the relation to determine the overhead applicable to each unit of goods in process and finished goods. After the overhead applicable to each unit of goods in process and finished goods is determined, calculate the inventory amounts for the goods in process and finished goods inventories. Enter these inventory amounts on the work sheet and complete the work sheet.
3. From the work sheet prepare an income statement and a manufacturing statement.
4. Prepare compound closing entries.

Problem 23–5

The following information was taken from the records of a manufacturing concern:

Inventories	Beginning	Ending
Raw materials	$10,900	$11,400
Goods in process	14,800	12,900
Finished goods	16,100	19,300
Cost of goods sold	$226,900	
Direct labour	90,000	
Factory overhead costs	79,500	

Required:
On the basis of the information given determine for the accounting period:
1. Cost of goods manufactured.
2. Total manufacturing costs.
3. Cost of raw materials used.
4. Cost of raw materials purchased.
   (Hint: It may be helpful to set up the manufacturing statement and the cost of goods sold section of the income statement.)

Alternate problems

Problem 23–1A

The following items appeared in the Manufacturing Statement and Income Statement columns of a work sheet prepared for Hillside Manufacturing Company on December 31, 19–, the end of its annual accounting period.

	Manufacturing Statement		Income Statement	
	Debit	Credit	Debit	Credit
Raw materials inventory..	14,000	17,500	....	....
Goods in process inventory	6,500	5,000	....	....
Finished goods inventory	....	....	18,500	17,600
Sales...	....	....	....	308,500
Raw material purchases	102,500	....	....	....
Discounts on raw material purchases......................	....	5,500	....	....
Freight on raw materials	1,600	....	....	....
Direct labour	47,900	....	....	....
Indirect labour	7,500	....	....	....
Superintendence	10,400	....	....	....
Heat, lights, and power...	4,300	....	....	....
Maintenance and repairs	3,000	....	....	....
Factory taxes expense	4,800	....	....	....
Miscellaneous factory expenses............................	2,700	....	....	....
Selling expenses controlling	....	....	58,700	....
Administrative expenses controlling	....	....	37,200	....
Income taxes expense	....	....	6,800	....
Depreciation of factory building	1,200	....	....	....
Depreciation of machinery and equipment...............	4,800	....	....	....
	211,200	28,000	....	....
Cost of goods manufactured................................	....	183,200	183,200	....
	211,200	211,200	304,400	326,100
Net Income			21,700	
			326,100	326,100

Required:
1. From the information in the columns prepare an income statement and a manufacturing statement. Assume the company has outstanding 10,000 shares of $10 par value common stock and no preferred stock.
2. Prepare compound closing entries.

Problem 23–2A

The Manufacturing Statement columns from the work sheet prepared by Valley Products Company at the end of last year follow. The item amounts shown are after all adjustments were completed but before the ending work in process inventory was calculated and entered and before cost of goods manufactured was calculated.

Valley Products Company produces a single product. On December 31, at the end of last year, its goods in process inventory consisted of 4,000 units of the product with each unit containing an estimated $1.40 of materials and having an estimated $1 of direct labour applied.

	Manufacturing Statement	
	Debit	Credit
Raw materials inventory	14,200	12,800
Goods in process inventory	15,300	?
Raw material purchases	59,900	
Direct labour	90,000	
Indirect labour	13,800	
Factory supervision..	12,000	
Heat, light, and power	17,900	
Machinery repairs..	4,400	
Rent of factory...	7,200	
Property taxes...	800	
Factory insurance expense	2,200	
Factory supplies used...	6,300	
Depreciation of factory machinery..............................	9,900	
Small tools written off..	700	
Patents written off...	1,300	
	255,900	?
Cost of goods manufactured		?
	255,900	255,900

Required:
1. Calculate the relation between direct labour and factory overhead costs and use this relation to determine a cost for the ending goods in process inventory.
2. After placing a cost on the ending goods in process inventory, determine the cost of goods manufactured.
3. Prepare a manufacturing statement for Valley Products Company.
4. Prepare entries to close the manufacturing accounts and to summarize their balances in the Manufacturing Summary account.
5. Prepare an entry to close the Manufacturing Summary account.

Problem 23–4A

The December 31, 19 –, trial balance of Keno Products Company appears at the top of the next page and the following year-end adjustment and inventory information is available:
a. Expired factory insurance, $2,800.
b. Factory supplies used, $7,400.
c. Depreciation of factory machinery, $20,900.
d. Small tools written off, $700.
e. Patents written off, $2,500.
f. Accrued wages payable: (1) direct labour, $800; (2) indirect labour, $300; and (3) factory supervision, $200.
g. Income taxes expense, $14,500.
h. Ending inventories: (1) raw materials, $13,500; (2) goods in process consists of 4,000 units of product with each unit containing an estimated $1.25 of materials and having had an estimated $1 of direct labour applied; and (3)

KENO PRODUCTS COMPANY, LTD.
Trial Balance, December 31, 19—

Cash	$ 6,700	
Raw materials inventory	14,200	
Goods in process inventory	15,100	
Finished goods inventory	13,800	
Prepaid factory insurance	4,100	
Factory supplies	8,600	
Machinery	172,700	
Accumulated depreciation, machinery		$ 38,400
Small tools	3,800	
Patents	9,200	
Common stock, $5 par value		100,000
Retained earnings		28,700
Sales		355,600
Raw material purchases	62,400	
Discounts on raw material purchases		1,200
Direct labour	79,200	
Indirect labour	19,500	
Factory supervision	14,800	
Heat, light, and power	17,600	
Machinery repairs	5,500	
Rent of factory	12,000	
Property taxes	3,800	
Selling expenses controlling	32,100	
Administrative expenses controlling	28,800	
Totals	$523,900	$523,900

finished goods consists of 2,500 units of product with each unit containing an estimated $1.37 of raw materials and having had an estimated $1.80 of direct labour applied.

Required:
1. Enter the trial balance on a work sheet form and make the adjustments from the information given. Then sort the items to the proper Manufacturing Statement, Income Statement, and Balance Sheet columns.
2. After the Direct Labour and factory overhead cost accounts have been adjusted and carried into the Manufacturing Statement columns, determine the relation between direct labour and overhead costs and use this relation to determine the overhead applicable to each unit of goods in process and finished goods. After the amounts of overhead applicable to the units of goods in process and finished goods are determined, calculate the balance sheet amounts for these inventories, enter these inventory amounts on the work sheet and complete the work sheet.
3. From the work sheet prepare an income statement and a manufacturing statement.
4. Prepare compound closing entries.

Problem 23-5A

Mesa Company uses the relation between its overhead and direct labour costs to apply overhead to its goods in process and finished goods inventories. Last December 31, at the end of its annual accounting period, the concern's ending goods in process and finished goods inventories were assigned these costs:

	Goods in Process	Finished Goods
Materials	$ 2,200	$ 3,600
Labour	3,000	4,500
Overhead	?	5,400
Totals	$?	$13,500

This additional information was available from the concern's records:

Ending raw materials inventory	$ 8,400
Cost of goods manufactured during the year	181,300
Factory overhead costs for the year	71,400
Beginning of the year inventories:	
Raw materials	8,700
Goods in process	9,400

Required:
On the basis of the information given and any data that can be derived from it, prepare the concern's manufacturing statement for the past year.

Decision problem 23-1, Decker's Cabinet Shop

Several years ago Danny Decker took over the operation of his family's cabinet shop from his father. Once the shop specialized in manufacturing cabinets for homes, but of late years it has turned more and more to building boats to the specifications of its customers. However, this business is seasonal in nature, since few people order boats in October, November, December, and January. As a result, things are rather slow around the shop during these months.

Danny has tried to increase business during the slow months. However, most prospective customers who come into the shop during these months are shoppers; and when Danny quotes a price for a new boat, they commonly decide the price is too high and walk out. Danny thinks the trouble arises from his application of a rule established by his father when he ran the shop. The rule is that in pricing a job to a customer, "always set the price so as to make a 10% profit over and above all costs, and be sure that all costs are included."

Danny says that in pricing a job, the material and labour costs are easy to figure, but that overhead is another thing. His overhead consists of depreciation of building and machinery, heat, lights, power, taxes, and so on, which in total run to $600 per month whether he builds any boats or not. Furthermore, when he follows his father's rule, he has to charge more for a boat built during the slow months because the overhead is spread over fewer jobs. He readily admits that this seems to drive away business during the months he needs business most, but he finds it difficult to break his father's rule, for as he says, "Dad did alright in this business for many years."

Explain with assumed figures to illustrate your point why Danny charges more for a boat made in December than for one built in May, a very busy month. Suggest how Danny might solve his pricing problem and still follow his father's rule.

Decision Problem 23–2, Precision Tool Company

Precision Tool Company has been in business for three years, manufacturing a single product, a tool, which is sold to mail-order companies. Sales have increased substantially each year, but net income has not, and the company president has asked you to analyze the situation and tell him why.

The company's condensed income statements for the past three years show:

	1st Year	2d Year	3d Year
Sales	$228,000	$306,000	$366,000
Cost of goods sold:			
Finished goods inventory, January 1	$ 0	$ 6,000	$ 18,000
Cost of goods manufactured	128,000	187,000	216,000
Goods for sale	$128,000	$193,000	$234,000
Finished goods inventory, December 31	6,000	18,000	15,000
Cost of goods sold	$122,000	$175,000	$219,000
Gross profit from sales	$106,000	$131,000	$147,000
Selling and administrative expenses	83,600	107,100	122,000
Net Income	$ 22,400	$ 23,900	$ 25,000

Investigation disclosed the following additional information:

a. The company sold 7,600 units of its product during the first year in business, 10,200 during the second year, and 12,200 during the third year. All sales were at $30 per unit, and no discounts were granted.

b. There were 400 units in the finished goods inventory at the end of the first year, 1,200 at the end of the second year, and 1,000 at the end of the third year.

c. The units in the finished goods inventory were priced each year at 50% of their selling price, or at $15 per unit.

Prepare a report to the president which shows: (1) the number of units of product manufactured each year, (2) the cost each year to manufacture a unit of product, and (3) the selling and administrative expenses per unit of product sold each year. Also, (4) prepare an income statement showing the correct net income each year, using a first-in, first-out basis for pricing the finished goods inventory. And finally, (5) express an opinion as to why net income has not kept pace with the rising sales volume.

Decision
problem
23–3, Surf
Manufac-
turing
Company,
Ltd.

On January 1, 197A, Surf Manufacturing Company, Ltd. had outstanding 4,000 shares of common stock, issued at $10, and it had the following assets and liabilities:

Cash	$ 4,000
Accounts receivable	10,000
Raw materials inventory	4,000
Goods in process inventory	2,000
Finished goods inventory	3,000
Plant and equipment, net	32,000
Accounts payable	5,000

During 197A the company paid no dividends, although it earned a 197A net income (ignore income taxes) that increased its retained earnings by 50%. At the year-end the amounts of the company's accounts receivable, accounts payable, and common stock outstanding were the same as of the beginning of the year. However, its cash increased $5,000, its raw materials and goods in process inventories each increased 50%, and its finished goods inventory increased by one third during the year. The net amount of its plant and equipment decreased $4,000 due to depreciation, chargeable three fourths to factory overhead costs and one fourth to general and administrative expenses. The year's direct labour costs were $12,000 and factory overhead costs were 75% of that amount. Cost of finished goods sold was $40,000 and all sales were made at prices 50% above cost. Selling expenses were 10% and general and administrative expenses were 15% of sales.

Based on the information given and on amounts you can derive therefrom, prepare a manufacturing work sheet for the company.

24

Cost accounting, job order and process

In a general accounting system for a manufacturer, such as that described in the previous chapter, physical inventories are required at the end of each accounting period in order to determine cost of goods manufactured. Furthermore, cost of goods manufactured as determined under such a system is the cost of all goods that were manufactured during the period, and commonly no effort is made to determine unit costs. A cost accounting system differs in that it is based on perpetual inventories and its emphasis is on unit costs and the control of costs.

There are two common types of cost accounting systems: (1) job order cost systems and (2) process cost systems. However, of the two there are an infinite number of variations and combinations. A job order system is described first.

JOB ORDER COST ACCOUNTING

In cost accounting a *job* is a turbine, machine, or other product manufactured especially for and to the specifications of a customer. A job may also be a single construction project of a contractor. A *job lot* is a quantity of identical items, such as 500 typewriters, manufactured in one lot as a job or single order; and a *job order cost system* is one in which costs are assembled in terms of jobs or job lots of product.

As previously stated, a job cost system differs from a general accounting system in that its primary objective is the determination of the cost of each job or job lot of product as it is finished. A job cost system also differs in that all inventory accounts used in such a system are perpetual inventory accounts controlling subsidiary ledgers. For example, in a job cost system the purchase and use of all materials are recorded in a perpetual inventory account called Materials which controls a subsidiary ledger having a separate ledger card (Illustration 24–1) for each different kind of material used. Likewise, in a job cost system the Goods in Process and Finished Goods accounts are also perpetual inventory accounts controlling subsidiary ledgers.

In addition to perpetual inventory controlling accounts, job cost accounting is also distinguished by the flow of manufacturing costs from the Materials, Factory Payroll, and Overhead Costs accounts into and through the Goods in Process and Finished Goods accounts and on to the Cost of Goods Sold account. The flow is diagrammed in Illustration 24–2 on the next page. An examination of the diagram and a moment's thought will show that costs flow through the accounts in the same way materials, labour, and overhead are placed in production in the factory, move on to become finished goods, and finally are sold.

MATERIALS LEDGER CARD

Item _Whatsit clip_   Stock No. _C-347_   Location in Storeroom _Bin 137_

Maximum _400_   Minimum _150_   Number to Reorder _200_

	Received				Issued				Balance		
Date	Receiving Report No.	Units	Unit Price	Total Price	Requisition No.	Units	Unit Price	Total Price	Units	Unit Price	Total Price
3/1									180	1.00	180.00
3/5					4345	20	1.00	20.00	160	1.00	160.00
3/11					4416	10	1.00	10.00	150	1.00	150.00
3/12	C-114	200	1.00	200.00					350	1.00	350.00
3/25					4713	21	1.00	21.00	329	1.00	329.00

Illustration 24–1

Job cost sheets

■ The heart of a job cost system is a subsidiary ledger of *job cost sheets* called a *Job Cost Ledger*. The cost sheets are used to accumulate costs by jobs. A separate cost sheet is used for each job.

Observe in Illustration 24–3 how a job cost sheet is designed to accumulate costs. Although this accumulation is discussed in more detail later, it may be summarized as follows. When a job is begun, information as to the customer, job number, and job description is filled in on a blank cost sheet and the cost sheet is placed in the Job Cost Ledger.

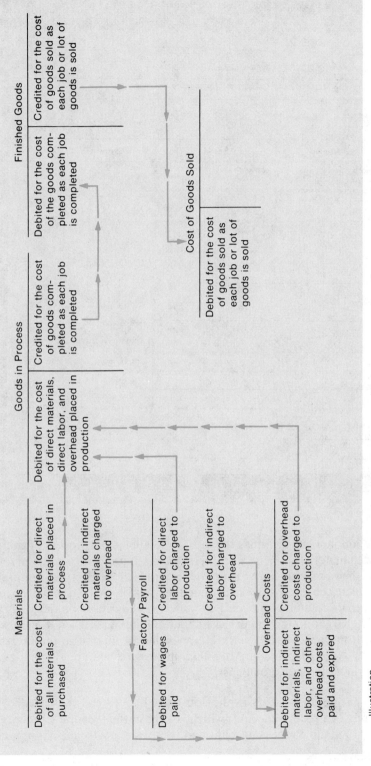

Materials

Debited for the cost of all materials purchased

Credited for direct materials placed in process

Credited for indirect materials charged to overhead

Factory Payroll

Debited for wages paid

Credited for direct labor charged to production

Credited for indirect labor charged to overhead

Overhead Costs

Debited for indirect materials, indirect labor, and other overhead costs paid and expired

Credited for overhead costs charged to production

Goods in Process

Debited for the cost of direct materials, direct labor, and overhead placed in production

Credited for the cost of goods completed as each job is completed

Finished Goods

Debited for the cost of the goods completed as each job is completed

Credited for the cost of goods sold as each job or lot of goods is sold

Cost of Goods Sold

Debited for the cost of goods sold as each job or lot of goods is sold

Illustration
24–2
Diagram showing the flow of costs in a job cost system

JOB COST SHEET

Customer's Name __Cone Lumber Company_____ Job No. _7452_
Address __Winnipeg, Manitoba__
Job Description __10 H.P. electric motor to customer's specifications__

Date
Promised __4/1__   Date
                          Started __3/23__   Date
                                                    Completed _3/29_

Date	Materials		Labour		Overhead Costs Applied		
	Requisition No.	Amount	Time Ticket No.	Amount	Date	Rate	Amount
19-- Mar. 23	4698	53.00	C-3422	6.00	3/29	150 per cent of the direct labour	$123.00
24			C-3478	16.00			
			C-3479	6.00			
25	4713	21.00	C-4002	16.00			
26			C-4015	16.00			
27			C-4032	12.00			
28			C-4044	10.00			

Summary of Costs

Materials _____ $ 74.00

Labour _____ 82.00

Overhead _____ 123.00

Total Cost
of the job _____ 279.00

	Total	74.00	Total	82.00

Remarks:
   Completed and shipped
   3/29

Illustration
24-3

The job number identifies the job and simplifies the process of charging it with materials, labour, and overhead. As materials are required for the job, they are transferred from the materials storeroom and are used to complete the job. At the same time their cost is charged to the job in the Materials column of the job's cost sheet. Labour used on the job is likewise charged to the job in the Labour column; and when the job is finished, the amount of overhead applicable is entered in the Overhead Costs Applied column. After this, the cost totals are summarized to determine the job's total cost.

The Goods in Process account ■ The job cost sheets in the Job Cost Ledger are controlled by the Goods in Process account, which is kept in the General Ledger. And, the Goods in Process account and its subsidiary ledger of cost sheets operate in the usual manner of controlling accounts and subsidiary ledgers. The material, labour, and overhead costs debited to each individual job on its cost sheet must be debited to the Goods in Process account either as individual amounts or in totals. Likewise all credits to jobs on their cost sheets must be credited individually or in totals to the Goods in Process account.

In addition to being a controlling account, the Goods in Process account is a perpetual inventory account operating somewhat as follows: At the beginning of a cost period the cost of any unfinished jobs in process is shown by its debit balance. Throughout the cost period materials, labour, and overhead are placed in production in the factory; and periodically their costs are debited to the account (note the last three debits in the Goods in Process account that follows). Also, throughout the period the cost of each job completed (the sum of the job's material, labour, and overhead costs) is credited to the account as each job is finished. As a result, the account is a perpetual inventory account the debit balance of which shows after all posting is completed; and without a physical inventory, the cost of the unfinished jobs still in process. For example, the following Goods in Process account shows a $12,785 March 31 ending inventory of unfinished jobs in process.

Goods in Process

Date		Explanation	Debit	Credit	Balance
Mar.	1	Balance, beginning inventory			2,850
	10	Job 7449 completed		7,920	(5,070)
	18	Job 7448 completed		9,655	(14,725)
	24	Job 7450 completed		8,316	(23,041)
	29	Job 7452 completed		279	(23,320)
	29	Job 7451 completed		6,295	(29,615)
	31	Materials used	17,150		(12,465)
	31	Labour applied	10,100		(2,365)
	31	Overhead applied	15,150		12,785

Accounting for materials under a job cost system ■ Under a job cost system all materials purchased are placed in a materials storeroom under the care of a storeroom keeper, and are issued to the factory only in exchange for properly prepared material requisitions (Illustration 24–4). The storeroom provides physical control over materials. The requisitions enhance the control and also provide a means of charging material costs to jobs or, in the case of indirect materials, to factory overhead costs. The requisitions are used as described in the next paragraphs.

When a material is needed in the factory, a material requisition is prepared and signed by a foreman, superintendent, or other responsible person. The requisition identifies the material and shows the number of

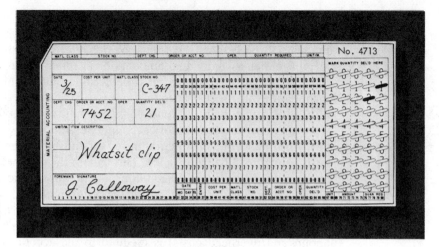

Illustration
24–4

the job or overhead account to which it is to be charged, and is given to the storeroom keeper in exchange for the material. The storeroom keeper forwards the requisition to the accounting department. Normally, requisitions are forwarded in batches, with an entire day's requisitions being a common batch.

Issuing units of material to the factory reduces the amount of that particular material in the storeroom. Consequently, when a material requisition reaches the accounting department, it is first recorded in the Issued column of the materials ledger card of the material issued. This reduces the number of units of that material shown to be on hand. Note the last entry in Illustration 24–1, which records the requisition of Illustration 24–4.

Materials issued to the factory may be used on jobs or for some overhead task, such as machinery repairs. Consequently, after being entered in the Issued columns of the proper materials ledger cards, a batch of requisitions is sorted by jobs and overhead accounts and charged to the proper jobs and overhead accounts. Materials used on jobs are charged to the jobs in the Materials columns of the job cost sheets. (Note the last entry in the Materials column on the cost sheet of Illustration 24–3 where the requisition of Illustration 24–4 is recorded.) Materials used for overhead tasks are charged to the proper overhead accounts in the Overhead Costs Ledger. A company using a job cost system commonly has an Overhead Costs controlling account in its General Ledger which controls a subsidiary Overhead Costs Ledger having an account for each overhead cost, such as Heating and Lighting or Machinery Repairs. Consequently, a requisition for light bulbs, for example, is charged to the Heating and Lighting account in the subsidiary Overhead Costs Ledger.

Material ledger cards, job cost sheets, and overhead cost accounts are all subsidiary ledger accounts controlled by accounts in the General Ledger. Consequently, in addition to the entries just described, entries must also be made in the controlling accounts. To make these entries, the requisitions charged to jobs and the requisitions charged to overhead accounts are accumulated until the end of a month or other cost period when they are separately totaled; and if, for example, the requisitions charged to jobs during the month total $17,150 and those charged to overhead accounts total $320, an entry like the following is made:

Mar.	31	Goods in Process	17,150.00	
		Overhead Costs...	320.00	
		Materials		17,470.00
		To record the materials used during March.		

The debit to Goods in Process in the illustrated entry is equal to the sum of the requisitions charged to jobs on the job cost sheets during March. The debit to Overhead Costs is equal to the sum of the requisitions charged to overhead accounts, and the credit to Materials is equal to the sum of all requisitions entered in the Issued columns of the material ledger cards during the month.

Accounting for labour in a job cost system ■ Time clocks, clock cards, and a Payroll Register similar to those described in an earlier chapter are commonly used in a factory to record the hours and cost of the work of each direct and indirect labour employee. Furthermore, without the complications of payroll taxes, income taxes, and other deductions, the entry to pay the employees is as follows:

Mar.	7	Factory Payroll...	2,900.00	
		Cash...		2,900.00
		To record the factory payroll and pay the employees.		

The entry just given is repeated at the end of each pay period; consequently, at the end of a month or other cost period the Factory Payroll account has a series of debits (see Illustration 24–6) like the debit of this entry, and the sum of these debits is the total amount paid the direct and indirect labour employees during the month.

The clock cards just mentioned are a record of hours worked each day by each employee, but they do not show how the employees spent their time or the specific jobs and overhead tasks on which they worked. Consequently, if the hours worked by each employee are to be charged to specific jobs and overhead accounts, another record called a *labour time ticket* must be prepared. Labour time tickets like the one shown in Illustration 24–5 tell how an employee spent his time while at work.

The time ticket of Illustration 24–5 is a "pen-and-ink" ticket and is suitable for use in a plant in which only a small number of such tickets

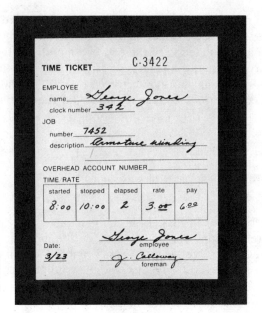

Illustration
24–5
**A labour
time ticket**

are prepared and recorded each day. In a plant in which many tickets are prepared, a time ticket that can be made into a punched card similar to Illustration 24–4 would be more suitable.

Labour time tickets serve as a basis for charging jobs and overhead accounts for an employee's wages. Throughout each day a labour time ticket is prepared each time an employee is changed from one job or overhead task to another. The tickets may be prepared by the worker, his foreman, or a clerk called a timekeeper. If the employee works on only one job all day, only one ticket is prepared. If he works on more than one job, a separate ticket is made for each. At the end of the day all the tickets of that day are sent to the accounting department.

In the accounting department the direct labour time tickets are charged to jobs on the job cost sheets (see the first entry in the Labour column of Illustration 24–3 where the ticket of Illustration 24–5 is recorded); and the indirect labour tickets are charged to overhead accounts in the Overhead Costs Ledger. The tickets are then accumulated until the end of the cost period when they are separately totaled; and if, for example, the direct labour tickets total $10,100 and the indirect labour tickets total $2,500, the following entry is made:

Mar.	31	Goods in Process...	10,100.00	
		Overhead Costs	2,500.00	
		Factory Payroll...		12,600.00
		To record the March time tickets.		

The first debit in the illustrated entry is the sum of all direct labour time tickets charged to jobs on the job cost sheets, and the second debit is the sum of all tickets charged to overhead accounts. The credit is the total of the month's labour time tickets, both direct and indirect. Notice in Illustration 24–6 that after this credit is posted, the Factory Payroll account has a $605 credit balance. This $605 is the accrued factory payroll payable at the month's end, and it is also the dollar amount of time tickets prepared and recorded during the days following the end of the March 28 pay period.

Factory Payroll				
Date	Explanation	Debit	Credit	Balance
Mar. 7	Weekly payroll payment	2,900		2,900
14	Weekly payroll payment	2,950		5,850
21	Weekly payroll payment	3,105		8,955
28	Weekly payroll payment	3,040		11,995
31	Labor cost summary		12,600	(605)

Illustration 24–6

Accounting for overhead in a job cost system

■ In a job cost system, if the cost of each job is to be determined at the time it is finished, it is necessary to associate with each job the costs of its materials, labour, and overhead. Requisitions and time tickets make possible a direct association of material and labour costs with jobs. However, overhead costs are incurred for the benefit of all jobs and cannot be related directly to any one. Consequently, to associate overhead with jobs it is necessary to relate overhead to, for example, direct labour costs and to apply overhead to jobs by means of a *predetermined overhead application rate.*

A predetermined overhead application rate based on direct labour cost is established by (1) estimating before a cost period begins the total overhead that will be incurred during the period; (2) estimating the cost of the direct labour that will be incurred during the period; then (3) calculating the ratio, expressed as a percentage, of the estimated overhead to the estimated direct labour cost. For example, if a cost accountant estimates that a factory will incur $180,000 of overhead during the year about to begin and that $120,000 of direct labour will be applied to production during the period, and these estimates are used to establish an overhead application rate, the rate is 150% and is calculated as follows:

$$\frac{\text{Next Year's Estimated Overhead Costs, \$180,000}}{\text{Next Year's Estimated Direct Labour Costs, \$120,000}} = 150\%$$

After a predetermined overhead application rate is established, it is used throughout the year to apply overhead to jobs as they are finished. Overhead is assigned to each job, and its cost is calculated as follows: (1) As each job is completed the cost of its materials is determined by adding the amounts in the Materials column of its cost sheet. Then (2) the cost of its labour is determined by adding the amounts in the Labour column. Next (3) the applicable overhead is calculated by multiplying the job's total labour cost by the predetermined overhead application rate and is entered in the Overhead Costs Applied column. Finally (4) the job's material, labour, and overhead costs are entered in the summary section of the cost sheet and totaled to determine the cost of the job.

The predetermined overhead application rate is also used to assign overhead to any jobs still in process at the cost period end. Then, the total overhead assigned to all jobs during the period is recorded in the accounts with an entry like this:

Mar.	31	Goods in Process...	15,150.00	
		Overhead Costs		15,150.00
		To record the overhead applied to jobs during March.		

The illustrated entry assumes that the overhead applied to all jobs during March totaled $15,150, and after it is posted the Overhead Costs account appears as in Illustration 24–7.

Overhead Costs

Date		Explanation	F	Debit	Credit	Balance
Mar.	31	Indirect materials	G24	320		320
	31	Indirect labour	G24	2,500		2,820
	31	Miscellaneous payments	D89	3,306		6,126
	31	Accrued and prepaid items	G24	9,056		15,182
	31	Applied			15,150	32

Illustration
24–7

In the Overhead Costs account of Illustration 24–7 the actual overhead costs incurred during March are represented by four debits. The first two need no explanation; the third represents the many payments for such things as water, telephone, and so on; while the fourth represents such things as depreciation, expired insurance, taxes, et cetera.

When overhead is applied to jobs on the basis of a predetermined overhead rate based upon direct labour costs as in this discussion, it is assumed that the overhead applicable to a particular job bears the same relation to the job's direct labour cost as the total estimated overhead of the factory bears to the total estimated direct labour costs. This assumption may not be proper in every case. However, when the ratio of overhead to direct labour cost is approximately the same for all jobs, an overhead rate based upon direct labour cost offers an easily calculated and fair basis for assigning overhead to jobs. In those cases in which the ratio of overhead to direct labour cost does not remain the same for all jobs, some other relationship must be used. Often overhead rates based upon the ratio of overhead to direct labour hours or overhead to machine-hours are used. However, a discussion of these is reserved for a course in cost accounting.

Overapplied and underapplied overhead

■ When overhead is applied to jobs by means of an overhead application rate based on estimates, the Overhead Costs account seldom, if ever, has a zero balance. At times actual overhead incurred exceeds overhead applied, and at other times overhead applied exceeds actual overhead incurred. When the account has a debit balance (overhead incurred in excess of overhead applied), the balance is known as *underapplied overhead;* and when it has a credit balance (overhead applied in excess of overhead incurred), the balance is called *overapplied overhead.* Usually the balance is small and fluctuates from debit to credit throughout a year. However, any balance in the account must be disposed of at the end of each year before a new accounting period begins.

If the year-end balance of the Overhead Costs account is material in amount, it is reasonable that it be disposed of by apportioning it among the goods still in process, the finished goods inventory, and cost of goods sold. This has the effect of restating the inventories and goods sold at "actual" cost. For example, assume that at the end of an accounting period, (1) a company's Overhead Costs account has a $1,000 debit balance (underapplied overhead), and (2) the company had charged the following amounts of overhead to jobs during the period: jobs still in process, $10,000; jobs finished but unsold, $20,000; and jobs finished and sold, $70,000. In such a situation the following entry apportions fairly the underapplied overhead among the jobs worked on during the period:

Dec.	31	Goods in Process..	100.00	
		Finished Goods..	200.00	
		Cost of Goods Sold......................................	700.00	
		Overhead Costs		1,000.00
		To clear the Overhead Costs account and charge the underapplied overhead to the work of the accounting period.		

Sometimes when the amount of over- or underapplied overhead is immaterial, all of it is closed to Cost of Goods Sold under the assumption that the major share would be charged there anyway and any extra exactness gained from prorating would not be worth the extra record keeping involved.

Recording the completion of a job

■ When a job is completed, its cost is transferred from the Goods in Process account to the Finished Goods account with an entry like the following which transfers the cost of the job the cost sheet of which appears on page 728:

Mar.	29	Finished Goods..	279.00	
		Goods in Process....................................		279.00
		To transfer the cost of Job No. 7452 to		
		Finished Goods.		

In addition to the entry, and at the same time it is made, the completed job's cost sheet is removed from the Job Cost Ledger, marked "completed," and filed away. This is in effect the equivalent of posting a credit to the Job Cost Ledger equal to the credit to the Goods in Process controlling account.

Recording cost of goods sold ■ When a cost system is in use, the cost to manufacture a job or job lot of product is known as soon as the goods are finished. Consequently, when goods are sold, since their cost is known, the cost can be recorded at the time of sale. For example, if goods costing $279 are sold for $450, the cost of the goods sold may be recorded with the sale as follows:

Mar.	29	Accounts Receivable—Cone Lumber Co...........	450.00	
		Cost of Goods Sold.......................................	279.00	
		Sales		450.00
		Finished Goods.....................................		279.00
		Sold for $450 goods costing $279.		

When cost of goods sold is recorded at the time of each sale, the balance of the Cost of Goods Sold account shows at the end of an accounting period the cost of goods sold during the period.

PROCESS COST ACCOUNTING

■ A *process* is a step in manufacturing a product, and a *process cost system* is one in which costs are assembled in terms of processes or manufacturing steps.

Process cost systems are found in companies producing cement, flour, or other products the production of which is characterized by a large volume of standardized units manufactured on a more or less continuous basis. In such companies responsibility for completing each step in the production of a product is assigned to a department. Costs are then assembled by departments, and the efficiency of each department is measured by the processing costs incurred in processing the units of product that flow through the department.

Assembling costs by departments ■ When costs are assembled by departments in a process cost system, a separate goods in process account is used for the costs of each department. For example, assume a company makes a product from metal that is cut to size in a cutting department, sent to a bending department to be bent into shape, and then on to a painting department to be painted.

Such a concern would collect costs in three goods in process accounts, one for each department, and costs would flow through the accounts as in Illustration 24–8.

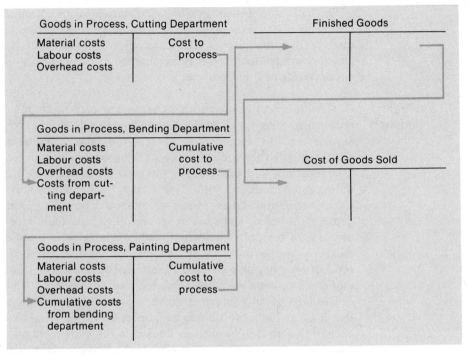

Illustration
24–8

Observe in Illustration 24–8 that each department's material, labour, and overhead costs are charged to the department's goods in process account. (It is assumed there were indirect materials charged to the bending department.) Observe too how costs are transferred from department to department, just as the product is transferred in the manufacturing procedure. The cost to cut the product in the cutting department is transferred to the bending department; and the sum of the costs in the first two departments is transferred to the third department; and finally the sum of the processing costs in all three departments, which is the cost to make the product, is transferred to finished goods.

Charging costs to departments ■ Since there are no jobs in a process cost system, accounting for material and labour costs in such a system is much simplified. Material requisitions may be used. However, a consumption report kept by the storeroom keeper and showing the materials issued to each department during a cost period is often substituted. Likewise, labour time tickets may be used; but since most employees spend all their working time in the same department, an end-of-the-period summary of the payroll records is usually all that is required in charging labour to the departments. And since there are no jobs, there is no need to distinguish between direct and indirect materials and direct and indirect labour. All that is required is that material and labour costs, both direct and indirect, be charged to the proper departments.

The lack of jobs also simplifies accounting for overhead in a process cost system. Since there are no jobs to charge with overhead on completion, predetermined overhead application rates are not required and actual overhead incurred may be charged directly to the goods in process accounts of the departments.

Equivalent finished units

■ A basic objective of a process cost system is the determination of unit processing costs for material, labour, and overhead in each processing department. This requires that (1) material, labour, and overhead costs be accumulated for each department for a cost period of, say, a month; (2) a record be kept of the number of units processed in each department during the period; and then (3) that costs be divided by units processed to determine unit costs. However, it should be observed that when a department begins and ends a cost period with partially processed units of product, the units completed in the department are not an accurate measure of the department's production. Rather, in such instances production must be measured in terms of *equivalent finished units* and unit costs become *equivalent finished unit costs*.

The idea of an equivalent finished unit is based on the assumption that it takes the same amount of labour, for instance, to one-half finish each of two units of product as it takes to fully complete one, or it takes the same amount of labour to one-third finish each of three units as to complete one. Equivalent finished units are discussed further in the Delta Processing Company illustration that follows.

Process cost accounting illustrated

■ The process cost system of Delta Processing Company, a company manufacturing a patented home remedy called Noxall, is used to illustrate process cost accounting.

The procedure for manufacturing Noxall is as follows: Material A is finely ground in Delta Processing Company's grinding department, after which it is transferred to the mixing department where Material B is added, and the resulting mixture is thoroughly mixed. The mixing process results in finished product, Noxall, which is transferred on completion to finished goods. All Material A placed in process in the grinding department is placed in process when the grinding process is first begun; but the Material B added in the mixing department is added evenly throughout its process. In other words, a product one-third mixed in the latter department has received one third of its Material B and a product three-fourths mixed has received three fourths. Labour and overhead are applied evenly throughout each department's process.

At the end of the April cost period, after entries recording materials, labour, and overhead were posted, the company's two goods in process accounts appeared as follows:

Goods in Process, Grinding Department

Date		Explanation	Debit	Credit	Balance
Apr.	1	Beginning inventory			4,250
	30	Materials	9,900		14,150
	30	Labour	5,700		19,850
	30	Overhead	4,275		24,125

Goods in Process, Mixing Department

Date		Explanation	Debit	Credit	Balance
Apr.	1	Beginning inventory			3,785
	30	Materials	2,040		5,825
	30	Labour	3,570		9,395
	30	Overhead	1,020		10,415

The production reports prepared by the company's two department foremen give the following information about inventories and goods started and finished in each department during the month:

	Grinding Department	Mixing Department
Units in the beginning inventories of goods in process	30,000	16,000
April 1 stage of completion of the beginning inventories of goods in process	$\frac{1}{3}$	$\frac{1}{4}$
Units started in process and finished during period	70,000	85,000
Total units finished and transferred to next department or to finished goods	100,000	101,000
Units in the ending inventories of goods in process.....................	20,000	15,000
Stage of completion of ending inventories of goods in process......	$\frac{1}{4}$	$\frac{1}{3}$

After receiving the production reports, the company's cost accountant prepared a process cost summary, Illustration 24–9, for the grinding department. A process cost summary is a report peculiar to a processing company; a separate one is prepared for each processing department and shows: (1) the costs charged to the department, (2) the department's equivalent unit processing costs, and (3) the costs applicable to the department's goods in process inventories and its goods started and finished.

Observe in Illustration 24–9 that a process cost summary has three sections. In the first, headed Costs Charged to the Department, are summarized the costs charged to the department. Information for this section comes from the department's goods in process account. Compare the first section of Illustration 24–9 with the goods in process account of the grinding department shown above.

The second section of a process cost summary shows the calculation of equivalent unit costs. The information for this section as to units involved and fractional units applicable to the inventories comes from the production report of the department foreman. Information as to material, labour, and overhead costs comes from the first section of the summary.

Notice in the second section of Illustration 24–9 that there are two separate equivalent unit calculations. Two calculations are required because material added to the product and labour and overhead added are not added in the same proportions and at the same stages in the processing procedure of this department. As previously stated, all material is added at the beginning of this department's process, and labour and overhead are added evenly throughout the process. Consequently, the number of equivalent units of material added is not the same as the number of equivalent units of labour and overhead added.

Observe in the calculation of equivalent finished units for materials that the beginning-of-the-month inventory is assigned no material. In the grinding department all material placed in process is placed there at the beginning of the process. The 30,000 beginning inventory units were begun during March and were one-third completed at the beginning of April. Consequently, these units received all their material during March when their processing was first begun.

Note also how the $9,900 cost of the material charged to the department in April is divided by 90,000 equivalent units of material to arrive at an $0.11 per equivalent unit cost for material consumed in this department.

Now move on to the calculation of equivalent finished units for labour and overhead and note that the beginning inventory units were each assigned two thirds of a unit of labour and overhead. If these units were one-third completed on April 1, then two thirds of the work done on these units was done in April. Beginning students often have difficulty at this point. In a situation such as this they are apt to assign only an additional one-third unit of labour and overhead when two thirds is required.

Before going further observe that the essence of the equivalent unit calculation for labour and overhead is that to do two thirds of the work on 30,000 units, all the work on 70,000 units, and one fourth the work on 20,000 units is the equivalent of doing all the work on 95,000 units. Then observe how the $5,700 of labour cost and $4,275 of overhead cost charged to the department are each divided by 95,000 to determine equivalent unit costs for labour and overhead.

When a department begins and ends a cost period with partially processed units of product, it is necessary to apportion the department's costs between the units that were in process in the department at the beginning of the period, the units started and finished during the period, and the ending inventory units. This division is necessary to determine the cost of the units completed in the department during the period; and the division and assignment of costs are shown in the third section of the process cost summary.

Notice in the third section of Illustration 24–9 how costs are assigned to the beginning inventory. The first amount assigned is the $4,250 beginning inventory costs. This amount represents the material, labour, and overhead costs used to one-third complete the inventory during

Delta Processing Company
Process Cost Summary, Grinding Department
For Month Ended April 30, 19—

COSTS CHARGED TO THE DEPARTMENT:

Material requisitioned...	$ 9,900
Labour charged...	5,700
Overhead costs incurred..	4,275
	$19,875
Goods in process at the beginning of the month..	4,250
Total Costs to Be Accounted for..	$24,125

EQUIVALENT UNIT PROCESSING COSTS:

Material:	Units Involved	Fraction of a Unit Added	Equivalent Units Added
Beginning inventory...	30,000	-0-	-0-
Units started and finished...	70,000	one	70,000
Ending inventory	20,000	one	20,000
			90,000

Equivalent unit processing cost for material: $9,900 ÷ 90,000 = $0.11

Labour and overhead:	Units Involved	Fraction of a Unit Added	Equivalent Units Added
Beginning inventory	30,000	⅔	20,000
Units started and finished	70,000	one	70,000
Ending inventory...	20,000	¼	5,000
			95,000

Equivalent unit processing cost for labour: $5,700 ÷ 95,000 = $0.06
Equivalent unit processing cost for overhead: $4,275 ÷ 95,000 = $0.045

COSTS APPLICABLE TO THE WORK OF THE DEPARTMENT:

Goods in process, one-third processed at the beginning of April:

Costs charged to the beginning inventory of goods in process during previous month..	$4,250	
Material added (all added during March)	-0-	
Labour applied (20,000 × $0.06)	1,200	
Overhead applied (20,000 × $0.045)...	900	
Cost to process..		$ 6,350

Goods started and finished in the department during April:

Material added (70,000 × $0.11)..	$7,700	
Labour applied (70,000 × $0.06)..	4,200	
Overhead applied (70,000 × $0.045)...	3,150	
Cost to process...		15,050
Total cost of the goods processed in the department and transferred to the mixing department (100,000 units at $0.214 each)		$21,400

Goods in process, one-fourth processed at the end of April:

Material added (20,000 × $0.11)..	$2,200	
Labour applied (5,000 × $0.06)	300	
Overhead applied (5,000 × $0.045)	225	
Cost to one-fourth process		2,725
Total Costs Accounted for...		$24,125

Illustration
24–9

March, the previous cost period. Normally, the second charge to a beginning inventory is for additional material assigned to it. However, in the grinding department no additional material costs are assigned the beginning inventory because these units received all of their material when their processing was first begun during the previous month. The second charge to the beginning inventory is for labour. The $1,200 portion of applicable labour costs is calculated by multiplying the number of equivalent finished units of labour used in completing the beginning inventory by the cost of an equivalent finished unit of labour (20,000 equivalent finished units at $0.06 each). The third charge to the beginning inventory is for overhead. The applicable $900 portion is determined by multiplying the equivalent finished units of overhead used in completing the beginning inventory by the cost of an equivalent finished unit of overhead (20,000 × $0.45).

After costs are assigned to the beginning inventory, the procedures used in their assignment are repeated for the units started and finished. Then the cost of the units completed and transferred to finished goods, in this case the cost of the 30,000 beginning inventory units plus the cost of the 70,000 units started and finished, is determined by adding the costs assigned to the two groups. In this situation the total is $21,400 or $0.214 per unit ($21,400 ÷ 100,000 units = $0.214 per unit).

Before going further, notice in the second section of the grinding department's process cost summary that the equivalent finished unit cost for materials is $0.11, for labour is $0.06, and for overhead is $0.045, a total of $0.215. Notice, however, in the third section of the summary that the unit cost of the 100,000 units finished and transferred is $0.214, which is less than $0.215. It is less because costs were less in the department during the previous month and the 30,000 beginning units were one-third processed at these lower costs.

The grinding department's process cost summary is completed by assigning costs to the ending inventory, and after it was completed the accountant prepared the following entry to transfer from the grinding department to the mixing department the cost of the 100,000 units processed in the department and transferred during April. Information for the entry as to the cost of the units transferred was taken from the third section of Illustration 24–9.

Apr.	30	Goods in Process, Mixing Department..............	21,400.00	
		Goods in Process, Grinding Department.....		21,400.00
		To transfer the cost of the 100,000 units of product transferred to the mixing department.		

Posting the entry had the effect on the accounts shown in Illustration 24–10. Observe that the effect is one of transferring and advancing costs from one department to the next just as the product is transferred and advanced in the manufacturing procedure.

Date		Explanation	Debit	Credit	Balance
Apr.	1	Beginning inventory			4,250
	30	Materials	9,900		14,150
	30	Labour	5,700		19,850
	30	Overhead	4,275		24,125
	30	Units to mixing department		21,400	2,725

Goods in Process, Mixing Department

Date		Explanation	Debit	Credit	Balance
Apr.	1	Beginning inventory			3,785
	30	Materials	2,040		5,825
	30	Labour	3,570		9,395
	30	Overhead	1,020		10,415
	30	Units from grinding department	21,400		31,815

Illustration
24–10

After posting the entry transferring to the mixing department the grinding department costs of the units transferred, the cost accountant prepared a process cost summary for the mixing department. Information required in its preparation was taken from the mixing department's goods in process account and production report. The summary appeared as in Illustration 24–11.

Two points in Illustration 24–11 require special attention. The first is the calculation of equivalent finished units. Since the materials, labour, and overhead added in the mixing department are all added evenly throughout the process of this department, only a single equivalent unit calculation is required. This differs from the grinding department, the previous department, where it will be recalled that two equivalent unit calculations were required. Two were required because material placed in process and the labour and overhead placed in process were not placed in process at the same stages in the processing procedure.

The second point needing special attention in the mixing department cost summary is the method of handling the grinding department costs transferred to this department. During April, 100,000 units of product with accumulated grinding department costs of $21,400 were transferred to the mixing department. Of these 100,000 units, 85,000 were started in process in the department, finished, and transferred to finished goods. The remaining 15,000 were still in process in the department at the end of the cost period.

Notice in the first section of Illustration 24–11 how the $21,400 of grinding department costs transferred to the mixing department are added to the other costs charged to the department. Compare the information in this first section with the mixing department's goods in process account as it is shown on page 739 and again in Illustration 24–10.

Delta Processing Company
Process Cost Summary, Mixing Department
For Month Ended April 30, 19—

COSTS CHARGED TO THE DEPARTMENT:

Materials requisitioned	$ 2,040
Labour charged	3,570
Overhead costs incurred..	1,020
Total processing costs...	$ 6,630
Goods in process at the beginning of the month...	3,785
Costs transferred from the grinding department (100,000 units at $0.214 each)................	21,400
Total Costs to Be Accounted for..	$31,815

EQUIVALENT UNIT PROCESSING COSTS:

Materials, labour, and overhead:	Units Involved	Fraction of a Unit Added	Equivalent Units Added
Beginning inventory	16,000	¾	12,000
Units started and finished	85,000	one	85,000
Ending inventory..	15,000	⅓	5,000
Total equivalent units			102,000

Equivalent unit processing cost for materials: $2,040 ÷ 102,000 = $0.02
Equivalent unit processing cost for labour: $3,570 ÷ 102,000 = $0.035
Equivalent unit processing cost for overhead: $1,020 ÷ 102,000 = $0.01

COSTS APPLICABLE TO THE WORK OF THE DEPARTMENT:

Goods in process, one-fourth completed at the beginning of April:

Costs charged to the beginning inventory of goods in process during previous month..	$ 3,785
Materials added (12,000 × $0.02)...	240
Labour applied (12,000 × $0.035)	420
Overhead applied (12,000 × $0.01)	120
Cost to process..	$ 4,565

Goods started and finished in the department during April:

Costs in the grinding department (85,000 × $0.214)	$18,190
Materials added (85,000 × $0.02)..	1,700
Labour applied (85,000 × $0.035)	2,975
Overhead applied (85,000 × $0.01)	850
Cost to process..	23,715
Total accumulated cost of goods transferred to finished goods (101,000 units at $0.28)	$28,280

Goods in process, one-third processed at the end of April:

Costs in the grinding department (15,000 × $0.214)	$ 3,210
Materials added (5,000 × $0.02)	100
Labour applied (5,000 × $0.035)	175
Overhead applied (5,000 × $0.01)..	50
Cost to one-third process	3,535
Total Costs Accounted for..	$31,815

Illustration
24–11

Notice again in the third section of the mixing department's process cost summary how the $21,400 of grinding department costs are apportioned between the 85,000 units started and finished and the 15,000 units still in process in the department. The 16,000 beginning goods in process units received none of this $21,400 charge because they were transferred from the grinding department during the previous month. Their grinding department costs are included in the $3,785 beginning inventory costs.

The third section of the mixing department's process cost summary shows that 101,000 units of product (16,000 beginning inventory units plus 85,000 started and finished) with accumulated costs of $28,280 were completed in the department during April and transferred to finished goods. The cost accountant used the following entry to transfer the accumulated cost of these 101,000 units from the mixing department's goods in process account to the finished Goods account.

Apr.	30	Finished Goods...	28,280.00	
		Goods in Process, Mixing Department........		28,280.00
		To transfer the accumulated grinding department and mixing department costs of the 101,000 units transferred to Finished Goods.		

Posting the entry had the effect shown in Illustration 24–12.

Goods in Process, Mixing Department

Date		Explanation	Debit	Credit	Balance
Apr.	1	Beginning inventory			3,785
	30	Materials	2,040		5,825
	30	Labour	3,570		9,395
	30	Overhead	1,020		10,415
	30	Units from grinding department	21,400		31,815
	30	Units to finished goods		28,280	3,535

Finished Goods

Date		Explanation	Debit	Credit	Balance
Apr.	30	Units from mixing department	28,280		28,280

Illustration 24–12

Questions for class discussion

1. What are the main two types of cost accounting systems? Which system generally fits best the needs of a manufacturer who (a) manufactures machinery to its customers' specifications, (b) manufactures adding machines in lots of 500, and (c) manufactures paint?

2. Give the cost accounting meaning of the following:
   a. Job order cost system.   e. Job cost sheet.
   b. Process cost system.   f. Labour time ticket.
   c. Job.   g. Materials requisition.
   d. Job lot.   h. Process cost summary.
3. What subsidiary ledger is controlled by (a) the Materials account and (b) the Goods in Process account?
4. How is the inventory of goods in process determined in a general accounting system like that described in Chapter 23? How may this inventory be determined in a job cost system?
5. What is the purpose of a job cost sheet? What is the name of the ledger containing the job cost sheets of the unfinished jobs in process? What account controls this ledger?
6. What business papers are the bases for the job cost sheet entries for (a) materials and (b) for labour?
7. Refer to the job cost sheet of Illustration 24–3. How was the amount of overhead costs charged to this job determined?
8. How is a predetermined overhead application rate established? Why is such a predetermined rate used to charge overhead to jobs?
9. Why does a company using a job cost system normally have either over-applied or underapplied overhead at the end of each accounting period?
10. At the end of a cost period the Overhead Costs controlling account has a debit balance. Does this represent overapplied or underapplied overhead?
11. What are the basic differences in the products and in the manufacturing procedures of a company to which a job cost system is applicable as opposed to a company to which a process cost system is applicable?
12. What is an equivalent finished unit of labour? Of materials?
13. What is the assumption on which the idea of an equivalent finished unit of, for instance, labour is based?
14. What is the production of a department measured in equivalent finished units if it began an accounting period with 8,000 units of product that were one-fourth completed at the beginning of the period, started and finished 50,000 units during the period, and ended the period with 6,000 units that were one-third processed at the period end?
15. The process cost summary of a department commonly has three sections. What is shown in each section?

Class exercises

Exercise 24–1

PART 1. In December, 197A, a cost accountant established his company's 197B overhead application rate based on direct labour cost. In setting the rate he estimated the company would incur $240,000 of overhead costs during 197B and it would apply $160,000 of direct labour to the products that would be manufactured during 197B. Determine the rate.

PART 2. During February, 197B, the company of Part 1 began and completed Job No. 874. Determine the job's cost under the assumption that on its completion the job's cost sheet showed the following materials and labour charged to it:

	JOB COST SHEET						
Customer's Name Hiltop Mine					Job No. 874		

Job Description   5 H.P. Solidifier

| Date | Materials | | Labour | | Overhead Costs Applied | | |
	Requisition Number	Amount	Time Ticket Number	Amount	Date	Rate	Amount
Feb. 2	1524	68.00	2116	12.00			
3	1527	47.00	2117	20.00			
4	1531	10.00	2122	16.00			

Exercise 24–2

In December, 197A, a cost accountant established the following overhead application rate for applying overhead to the jobs that would be completed by his company during 197B:

$$\frac{\text{Estimated Overhead Costs, \$152,000}}{\text{Estimated Direct Labour Costs, \$95,000}} = 160\%$$

At the end of 197B the company's accounting records showed that $158,000 of overhead costs had actually been incurred during 197B and $100,000 of direct labour, distributed as follows, had been applied to jobs during the year.

Direct labour on jobs completed and sold .... $ 80,000
Direct labour on jobs completed and in the finished goods inventory   15,000
Direct labour on jobs still in process......................................   5,000
Total $100,000

Required:
1. Set up an Overhead Costs T-account and enter on the proper sides the amounts of overhead costs incurred and applied. State whether overhead was overapplied or underapplied during the year.
2. Give the entry to close the Overhead Costs account and allocated its balance between jobs sold, jobs finished but unsold, and jobs in process.

Exercise 24–3

Zest Company uses a job cost system in which overhead is charged to jobs on the basis of direct labour cost, and at the end of a year the company's Goods in Process account showed the following

Goods in Process			
Materials	175,000	To finished goods	391,000
Labour	90,000		
Overhead	135,000		

Required:

1. Determine the overhead application rate used by the company.
2. Determine the cost of the labour and the cost of the overhead charged to the one job in process at the year-end under the assumption it had $4,000 of materials charged to it.

Exercise 24-4

During a cost period a department finished and transferred 25,000 units of product to finished goods, of which 5,000 units were in process in the department at the beginning of the cost period and 20,000 were begun and completed during the period. The 5,000 beginning inventory units were three-fifths completed when the period began. In addition to the transferred units, 6,000 additional units were in process in the department, one-third completed when the period ended.

Required:

1. Calculate the equivalent units of product completed in the department during the cost period.
2. Under the assumption that $12,000 of labour was used in processing the units worked on in the department during the period, and that labour is applied evenly throughout the process of the department, determine the cost of an equivalent unit of labour.
3. Determine the shares of the $12,000 of labour cost that should be charged to each of the inventories and to the units begun and completed during the period.

Exercise 24-5

A department completed 56,000 units of product during a cost period, of which 16,000 units were in process at the beginning of the period and 40,000 units were begun and completed during the period. The beginning inventory units were one-fourth processed when the period began. In addition to the completed units, 9,000 more units were in process in the department and were two-thirds processed when the period ended.

Required:

Calculate the equivalent units of material added to the product of the department under each of the following unrelated assumptions: *(a)* All the material added to the product of the department is added when its process is first begun. *(b)* The material added to the product of the department is added evenly throughout the process. *(c)* One half the material added in the department is added when the product is first begun and the other half is added when the product is three-fifths completed.

Problems **Problem 24-1**

A cost accountant estimated before a year began that his small company would incur during the ensuing year the direct labour of 18 men working 2,000 hours each at an average rate of $3.50 per hour. He also estimated the concern would incur the following overhead costs during the year.

Indirect labour	$ 28,800
Depreciation of factory building	18,500
Depreciation of machinery	32,600
Machinery repairs	5,400
Heat, lights, and power	12,700
Property taxes, factory	10,800
Factory supplies	4,600
Total	$113,400

At the end of the year for which the cost estimates were made the company's records showed that it had actually incurred $114,500 of overhead costs during the year and that it had completed five jobs and had begun the sixth. The completed jobs were assigned overhead on completion, and the in-process job was assigned overhead at the year-end. The jobs had the following direct labour costs:

Job No. 203 (sold and delivered)	$ 24,450
Job No. 204 (sold and delivered)	26,800
Job No. 205 (sold and delivered)	20,100
Job No. 206 (sold and delivered)	28,650
Job No. 207 (in finished goods inventory)	18,750
Job No. 208 (in process, unfinished)	6,250
Total	$125,000

Required:
Under the assumption the concern used a predetermined overhead application rate based on the costs accountant's estimates of overhead and direct labour costs in applying overhead to the six jobs, determine: (1) the predetermined overhead application rate used, (2) the total overhead applied to jobs during the year, and (3) the over- or underapplied overhead at the year-end. (4) Prepare a general journal entry to close the Overhead Costs account and to prorate its balance between goods in process, finished goods, and goods sold.

Problem 24–2

Cactus Manufacturing Company completed the following external and internal transactions during its first cost period:
a. Purchased materials on account, $21,000.
b. Paid the wages of factory employees, $18,650.
c. Paid miscellaneous overhead costs, $2,600.
d. Material requisitions were used during the cost period to charge materials to jobs. The requisitions were then accumulated until the end of the cost period when they were totaled and recorded with a general journal entry. (Instructions for the entry are given in item *j*.) An abstract of the requisitions showed the following amounts of materials charged to jobs. (Charge the materials to the jobs by making entries directly in the job T-accounts in the subsidiary Job Cost Ledger.)

```
Job No. 1.....................................  $  3,950
Job No. 2.....................................     1,950
Job No. 3.....................................     4,200
Job No. 4.....................................     4,450
Job No. 5.....................................       850
   Total......................................  $15,400
```

e. Labour time tickets were used to charge jobs with direct labour. The time tickets were then accumulated until the end of the cost period when they were totaled and recorded with a general journal entry. (Instructions for the entry are given in item *k.*) An abstract of the tickets showed the following amounts of labour charged to the several jobs. (Charge the labour to the several jobs by making entries directly in the job T-accounts in the Job Cost Ledger.)

```
Job No. 1.....................................  $  3,600
Job No. 2.....................................     2,100
Job No. 3.....................................     3,900
Job No. 4.....................................     4,200
Job No. 5.....................................       450
   Total......................................  $14,250
```

f. Job Nos. 1, 3, and 4 were completed and transferred to finished goods. A predetermined overhead application rate of 160% of direct labour cost was used to apply overhead to each job upon its completion. (Enter the overhead in the job T-accounts; mark the jobs "completed"; and make a general journal entry to transfer their costs to the Finished Goods account.)

g. Job Nos. 1 and 3 were sold on account for a total of $38,000.

h. At the end of the cost period, charged overhead to the uncompleted jobs at the rate of 160% of direct labour cost. (Enter the overhead in the job T-accounts.)

i. At the end of the cost period made an adjusting entry to record:

```
Depreciation of factory building.......................  $  3,500
Depreciation of machinery..............................     6,300
Expired factory insurance..............................     1,000
Accrued factory taxes payable..........................     1,800
   Total...............................................  $12,600
```

j. Separated the material requisitions into direct material requisitions and indirect material requisitions, totaled each kind, and made a general journal entry to record them. The requisition totals were:

```
Direct materials.............................................  $15,400
Indirect materials...........................................    3,000
   Total.....................................................  $18,400
```

k. Separated the labour time tickets into direct labour time tickets and indirect labour time tickets, totaled each kind, and made a general journal entry to record them. The ticket totals were:

Direct labour $14,250
Indirect labour 4,650
   Total $18,900

l. Determined the total overhead assigned to all jobs and made a general journal entry to record it.

Required:

1. Open the following general ledger T-account: Materials, Goods in Process, Finished Goods, Factory Payroll, Overhead Costs, and Cost of Goods Sold.
2. Open an additional T-account for each of the five jobs. Assume that each job's T-account is a job cost sheet in a subsidiary Job Cost Ledger.
3. Prepare general journal entries to record the applicable information of items *a, b, c, f, g, i, j, k,* and *l*. Post the portions of the entries affecting the general ledger accounts.
4. Enter the applicable information of items *d, e, f,* and *h* directly in the T-accounts that represent job cost sheets.
5. Present statistics to prove the balances of the Goods in Process and Finished Goods accounts.
6. List the general ledger accounts and tell what is represented by the balance of each.

Problem 24–3

If the working papers that accompany this text are not being used, omit this problem.

Valley Company manufactures to the special order of its customers a machine called a dripdrop. On April 1 of the current year the company had a $4,090 materials inventory but no inventories of goods in process or finished goods. However, on that date it began Job No. 1, a dripdrop for Big Company, and Job No. 2, a dripdrop for Little Company; and during April it completed the following summarized internal and external transactions:

1. Recorded invoices for the purchase on credit of 450 units of Material X and 50 units of Material Y. The invoices and receiving reports carried this information:

    Receiving Report No. 1, Raw Material X, 450 units at $5 each
    Receiving Report No. 2, Raw Material Y, 50 units at $10 each

    (Record the invoices with a single journal entry and post to the general ledger T-accounts, using the transaction numbers to identify the amounts in the accounts. Enter the receiving report information on the proper materials ledger cards.)

2. Requisitioned materials as follows:

    Requisition No. 1, for Job No. 1 .... 220 units of Material X
    Requisition No. 2, for Job No. 1 .... 60 units of Material Y
    Requisition No. 3, for Job No. 2 .... 176 units of Material X
    Requisition No. 4, for Job No. 2 .... 50 units of Material Y
    Requisition No. 5, for 20 units of machinery lubricant

(Enter the requisition amounts for direct materials on the materials ledger cards and on the job cost sheets. Enter the indirect material amount on the proper materials ledger card and debit it to the Indirect Materials account in the subsidiary Overhead Costs Ledger. Assume the requisitions are accumulated until the end of the month and will be recorded with a general journal entry. Instructions for this entry follow in the problem.)

3. Received time tickets from the timekeeping department as follows:
   Time tickets Nos. 1 through 60 for direct labour on Job No. 1, $1,000
   Time tickets Nos. 61 through 100 for direct labour on Job No. 2, $800
   Time tickets Nos. 101 through 120 for machinery repairs, $350
   (Charge the direct labour tickets to the proper jobs and charge the indirect labour time tickets to the Indirect Labour account in the Subsidiary Overhead Costs Ledger. Assume the time tickets are accumulated until the end of the month for recording with a general journal entry.)

4. Made the following cash disbursements during the month:
   Paid factory payrolls totaling $2,000.
   Paid for miscellaneous overhead items totaling $950.
   (Record the payments with general journal entries and post to the general ledger accounts. Enter the charge for miscellaneous overhead items in the Subsidiary Overhead Costs Ledger.)

5. Finished Job No. 1 and transferred it to the finished goods warehouse. *(The company charges overhead to each job by means of a predetermined overhead application rate based on direct labour costs. The rate is 75%. (1) Enter the overhead charge on the cost sheet of Job No. 1. (2) Complete the cost summary section of the cost sheet. (3) Mark "Finished" on the cost sheet. (4) Prepare and post a general journal entry to record completion of the job and its transfer to finished goods.)*

6. Prepared and posted a general journal entry to record both the cost of goods sold and the sale of Job No. 1 to Big Company for $4,700.

7. At the end of the cost period, charged overhead to Job No. 2 based on the amount of direct labour applied to the job thus far. *(Enter the applicable amount of overhead on the job's cost sheet.)*

8. Totaled the requisitions for direct materials, totaled the requisitions for indirect materials, and made and posted a general journal entry to record them.

9. Totaled the direct labour time tickets, totaled the indirect labour time tickets, and made and posted a general journal entry to record them.

10. Determined the amount of overhead applied to jobs and made and posted a general journal entry to record it.

Required:
1. Record the transactions as instructed in the narrative.
2. Complete the statements in the book of working papers by filling in the blanks.

Problem 24–4

A department that produces a product on a continuous basis incurred $9,520 of labour cost during the cost period just ended. During the period the department completed and transferred 27,500 units of its product to finished goods. Of these 27,500 units, 4,500 were in process in the department when the period began and 23,000 were begun and completed during the period. The 4,500 beginning inventory units were one-third finished when the period began. In addition to the transferred units, 8,000 other units were in process in the department and were one-fourth finished when the period ended.

Required:

Calculate (1) the equivalent units of labour applied to the product of the department during the cost period, (2) the cost of an equivalent unit of labour, and (3) the shares of the $9,520 of labour cost applicable to the beginning inventory, the units started and finished, and the ending inventory. Assume that labour is added to the product of the department evenly throughout its process.

Problem 24–5

Tiptop Company manufactures a product that is processed in two departments, the mixing department and the drying department. At the end of the May cost period the mixing department reported the following: beginning goods in process inventory, 5,000 units, three-fifths completed at the beginning of the period; units started and finished during the cost period, 13,000; ending inventory of goods in process, 4,000 units, one-fourth completed.

The company assumes that all materials, labour, and overhead applied to the product in the mixing department are applied evenly throughout the department's process; and after all material, labour, and overhead costs had been charged to the department, its goods in process account appeared as follows:

Goods in Process, Mixing Department

Date		Explanation	Debit	Credit	Balance
May	1	Balance			1,878.00
	31	Materials	3,520.00		5,398.00
	31	Labour	4,000.00		9,398.00
	31	Overhead	2,400.00		11,798.00

Required:

Prepare a process summary for the mixing department and draft the general journal entry to transfer to the drying department the cost of the product finished in the mixing department and transferred.

Problem 24–6

Iron Products Company manufactures a product that is processed in two departments, the casting department and the polishing department. The product is begun in the casting department and completed in the polishing department. All materials used in the product are added in the casting department, and labour and overhead are applied. The product is then complete insofar as the casting department is concerned and is transferred to the polishing department where more labour and overhead, but no additional materials, are added to complete the product, which is then transferred to finished goods.

At the end of the April cost period, after entries charging the polishing department with labour and overhead costs and the cost of the units transferred to it from the casting department were posted, the goods in process account of the polishing department appeared as follows:

Goods in Process, Polishing Department

Date		Explanation	Debit	Credit	Balance
Apr.	1	Balance (3,900 units ⅓ processed)			7,325.00
	30	Labour	4,650.00		11,975.00
	30	Overhead	12,450.00		24,425.00
	30	Cost of 14,400 units transferred from casting department	21,600.00		46,025.00

There were no units lost or spoiled in the polishing department during April and 15,900 units were completed in the department during the month and were transferred to finished goods, leaving 2,400 units in the department that were one-sixth processed at the month end.

Required:

1. Prepare a process cost summary for the department under the assumption that labour and overhead are added evenly throughout the department's process.
2. Prepare the entry to transfer to finished goods the cost of the 15,900 units finished in the department during April.

Alternate problems

Problem 24-1A

During December, 197A, a cost accountant established his company's 197B overhead application rate by estimating the company would assign 10 men to direct labour tasks in 197B and that each man would work 2,000 hours at $3.40 per hour during the year. At the same time he estimated the company would incur the following amounts of overhead costs during 197B:

Indirect labour	$34,500
Depreciation of factory building	10,300
Depreciation of machinery	18,000
Machinery repairs	3,200
Heat, lights, and power	6,900
Property taxes, factory	6,800
Factory supplies expense	1,900
Total	$81,600

At the end of 197B the accounting records showed the company had actually incurred $78,200 of overhead costs during the year while completing five jobs and beginning the sixth. The completed jobs were assigned overhead on completion, and the in-process job was assigned overhead at the year-end. The jobs had the following direct labour costs:

Job 207 (sold and delivered)............................ $11,900
Job 208 (sold and delivered)............................ 12,100
Job 209 (sold and delivered)............................ 13,300
Job 210 (sold and delivered)............................ 12,200
Job 211 (in finished goods inventory)................ 13,200
Job 212 (in process, unfinished) 3,300
    Total.. $66,000

Required:
1. Determine the overhead application rate established by the cost accountant under the assumption it was based on direct labour cost.
2. Determine the total overhead applied to jobs during the year and the amount of over- or underapplied overhead at the year-end.
3. Prepare the general journal entry to dispose of the over- or underapplied overhead by prorating it between goods in process, finished goods, and goods sold.

Problem 24–2A

Lakeside Company completed the following transactions, among others, during a cost period:
a. Purchased materials on credit, $12,200.
b. Paid factory wages, $11,800.
c. Paid miscellaneous factory overhead costs, $800.
d. Material requisitions were used during the cost period to charge materials to jobs. The requisitions were then accumulated until the end of the cost period when they were totaled and recorded with a general journal entry. (Instructions for the entry are given in item *j*.) An abstract of the requisitions showed the following materials charged to jobs. (Charge the materials to the jobs by making entries directly in the job T-accounts in the subsidiary Job Cost Ledger.)

Job No. 1 .... $2,500
Job No. 2 2,000
Job No. 3 2,400
Job No. 4 2,100
Job No. 5 800
    Total....................................... $9,800

e. Labour time tickets were used to charge jobs with direct labour. The time tickets were then accumulated until the end of the cost period when they were totaled and recorded with a general journal entry. (Instructions for the entry are given in item *k*.) An abstract of the tickets showed the following labour charged to the several jobs. (Charge the labour to the jobs by making entries directly in the job T-accounts in the Job Cost Ledger.)

Job No. 1....................................... $2,200
Job No. 2....................................... 1,600
Job No. 3....................................... 2,100
Job No. 4....................................... 1,900
Job No. 5....................................... 600
    Total....................................... $8,400

f. Job Nos. 1, 3, and 4 were completed and transferred to finished goods. A predetermined overhead application rate of 140% of direct labour cost was used to apply overhead to each job upon its completion. (Enter the overhead in the job T-accounts; mark the jobs "completed"; and make a general journal entry to transfer their cost to the Finished Goods account.)

g. Job Nos. 1 and 3 were sold on credit for a total of $22,500.

h. At the end of the cost period, charged overhead to the uncompleted jobs at the rate of 140% of direct labour cost. (Enter the overhead in the job T-accounts.)

i. At the end of the cost period, made an entry to record depreciation on the factory building, $1,500; depreciation on the machinery, $3,300; expired factory insurance, $400; and accrued factory taxes payable, $300.

j. Separated the material requisitions into direct material requisitions and indirect material requisitions, totaled each kind, and made a general journal entry to record them. The requisition totals were:

Direct materials	$ 9,800
Indirect materials	1,800
Total	$11,600

k. Separated the labour time tickets into direct labour time tickets and indirect labour time tickets, totaled each kind, and made a general journal entry to record them. The ticket totals were:

Direct labour	$ 8,400
Indirect labour	3,500
Total	$11,900

l. Determined the total overhead charged to all jobs and made a general journal entry to record it.

Required:

1. Open the following general ledger T-accounts: Materials, Goods in Process, Finished Goods, Factory Payroll, Overhead Costs, and Costs of Goods Sold.

2. Open an additional T-account for each of the five jobs. Assume that each job's T-account is a job cost sheet in a subsidiary Job Cost Ledger.

3. Prepare general journal entries to record the applicable information of items *a, b, c, f, g, i, j, k,* and *l.* Post the portions of the entries affecting the general ledger accounts.

4. Enter the applicable information of items *d, e, f,* and *h* directly in the T-accounts that represent job cost sheets.

5. Present statistics to prove the balances of the Goods in Process and Finished Goods accounts.

6. List the general ledger accounts and tell what is represented by the balance of each.

Problem 24–3A

If the working papers that accompany this text are not being used, omit this problem.

Top Job Shop manufactures to the special order of its customers a machine called a tiptop. On April 1 the company had a $4,090 materials inventory but no inventories of goods in process or finished goods. However, on that date it began Job No. 1, a tiptop for Big Company, and Job No. 2, a tiptop for Little Company. It then completed the following summarized internal and external transactions:

1. Recorded invoices for the purchase of 350 units of Material X and 260 units of Material Y on credit. The invoices and receiving reports carried this information:

    Receiving Report No. 1, Material X, 350 units at $5 each
    Receiving Report No. 2, Material Y, 260 units at $10 each

    (Record the invoices with a single journal entry and post to the general ledger T-accounts, using the transaction numbers to identify the amounts in the accounts. Enter the receiving report information on the proper materials ledger cards.)

2. Requisitioned materials as follows:

    Requisition No. 1, for Job 1...........................200 units of Material X
    Requisition No. 2, for Job 1...........................230 units of Material Y
    Requisition No. 3, for Job 2............................90 units of Material X
    Requisition No. 4, for Job 2...........................200 units of Material Y
    Requisition No. 5, for 10 units of machinery lubricant

    (Enter the requisition amounts for direct materials on the materials ledger cards and on the job cost sheets. Enter the indirect material amount on the proper materials ledger card and debit it to the Indirect Materials account in the subsidiary Overhead Costs Ledger. Assume the requisitions are accumulated until the end of the month and will be recorded with a general journal entry. Instructions for the entry follow in the problem.)

3. Received time tickets from the timekeeping department as follows:

    Time tickets Nos. 1 through 50 for direct labour on Job No. 1, $1,200
    Time tickets Nos. 51 through 90 for direct labour on Job No. 2, $1,000
    Time tickets Nos. 91 through 100 for machinery repairs, $375

    (Charge the direct labour time tickets to the proper jobs; charge the indirect labour time tickets to the Indirect Labour account in the Subsidiary Overhead Costs Ledger. Assume the tickets are accumulated until the end of the month for recording with a general journal entry.)

4. Made the following cash disbursements during the month:

    Paid factory payrolls totaling $2,350 during the April cost period.
    Paid for miscellaneous overhead items totaling $1,200.

    (Record the payments with general journal entries and post to the ledger accounts. Enter the charge for miscellaneous overhead items in the Subsidiary Overhead Costs Ledger.)

5. Finished Job No. 1 and transferred it to the finished goods warehouse.

    (Top Job Shop charges overhead to each job on completion by means of a predetermined overhead application rate based on direct labour costs. The rate is 70%. Enter the overhead charge (1) on the cost sheet of Job No. 1. (2) Complete the cost summary section of the cost sheet. (3) Mark "Finished" on the cost sheet. (4) Prepare and post a general journal entry to record completion of the job and its transfer to finished goods.)

6. Prepared and posted a general journal entry to record the sale on credit of Job No. 1 to Big Company for $8,500.

7. At the end of the April cost period, charged overhead to Job. No. 2 based

on the direct labour applied to the job in April. *(Enter the applicable amount of overhead on the job's cost sheet.)*

8. Totaled the requisitions for direct materials, totaled the requisitions for indirect materials, and made and posted a general journal entry to record them.

9. Totaled the direct labour time tickets, totaled the indirect labour time tickets, and made and posted a general journal entry to record them.

10. Determined the amount of overhead applied to jobs and made and posted a general journal entry to record it.

Required:

1. Record the transactions as instructed in the narrative.
2. Complete the statements in the book of working papers by filling in the blanks.

Problem 24–4A

A department in which labour is added evenly throughout its process incurred $18,500 of labour cost during a period in which it completed 52,000 units of product. Of these 52,000 units, 8,000 were in process in the department, three-fourths processed when the period began and 44,000 were begun and completed during the period. In addition to the completed units, 10,000 other units were in process in the department and were two-fifths processed at the period end.

Required:

Determine (1) the equivalent units of labour applied to the product of the department during the period, (2) the cost of an equivalent unit of labour, and (3) the shares of the $18,500 of labour cost that should be charged to the beginning inventory, the units started and finished, and the ending inventory.

Problem 24–5A

Sand Processing Company manufactures a simple product on a continuous basis in a single department. All materials are added in the manufacturing process when the process is first begun. Labour and overhead are added evenly throughout the process.

During the current April cost period the company completed and transferred to finished goods a total of 50,000 units of product. These consisted of 15,000 units that were in process at the beginning of the cost period and 35,000 units that were begun and finished during the period. The 15,000 beginning goods in process units were complete as to materials and one-fifth complete as to labour and overhead when the period began.

In addition to the completed units, 9,000 other units were in process at the end of the period, complete as to materials and one-third complete as to labour and overhead.

Since the company has but one processing department, it has only one Goods in Process account in its ledger. At the end of the period, after entries recording materials, labour, and overhead had been posted, the account appeared as follows:

Goods in Process

Date		Explanation	Debit	Credit	Balance
Apr.	1	Balance			6,474.00
	30	Materials	14,564.00		21,038.00
	30	Labour	13,800.00		34,838.00
	30	Overhead	10,850.00		45,688.00

Required:
Prepare a process cost summary and a general journal entry to transfer to finished goods the cost of the product completed by the company during April.

Decision problem 24–1, Paddock Company

Paddock Company manufactures a small electric tool that it sells to distributors who in turn sell to hardware stores. The company uses a job cost system to accumulate costs of job lots of the product. For the past several years it has sold an average of 40,000 of the tools annually at $15 each, using about 75% of its production capacity to produce them. It applies overhead to job lots manufactured on the basis of direct labour cost, and next year's rate is based on these estimates:

$$\frac{\text{Estimated Factory Overhead Costs, \$240,000}}{\text{Estimated Direct Labour Costs, \$120,000}} = 200\% \text{ Application Rate}$$

Next year's estimated production costs for the tool, assuming 40,000 units are produced, are $11 per unit, and consist of the following:

Materials	$ 2
Direct labour	3
Manufacturing overhead (200% rate)	6
Estimated cost per unit	$11

The company's sales manager is negotiating with a mail-order company for the sale of 10,000 of the tools, but the mail-order company's highest bid is $9.25 per unit with its own name on each unit. No changes in the tool are required to fit it to the mail-order company's specifications other than affixing the mail-order company's brand name to each unit, which will cost 10 cents per unit for additional materials.

The company president can see no point in accepting the order, for, as he says, "Why manufacture units and sell them, when you will lose money on every unit sold." The sales manager is not sure the new business should be rejected, and has asked you to make a further study of costs before a final decision is reached.

In your investigation of costs you find that next year's estimated manufacturing overhead consists of $200,000 of what is known as fixed overhead costs plus variable overhead costs of $1 per unit for 40,000 units, which together total $240,000. (Fixed overhead costs are such costs as depreciation of factory building, taxes, insurance, and the like. They receive their name from the fact that their total amounts do not change with a change in the number of units produced but remain fixed. Variable overhead costs are costs that vary with the number of units produced and are for such things as power and indirect materials.)

You also find that selling and administrative expenses consist of $100,000 of fixed expenses plus 50 cents per unit of variable selling and administrative expenses. Acceptance of the mail-order business will not affect fixed costs nor change present variable costs per unit, including material and direct labour costs per unit.

Make a report stating under what circumstances you think the new business should be accepted or rejected. Attach to your report a condensed columnar income statement that shows revenue, costs, and before-tax income from present business in its first two columns; the same information for the new business in its second set of columns; and the combined results of both the new and old business in the third set of columns. In preparing the statement, show as separate amounts the material, direct labour, fixed overhead, variable overhead, fixed selling and administrative costs, and variable selling and administrative costs for present business, for the new business, and combined.

Decision problem 24-2, Oswego Manufacturing Company

Oswego Manufacturing Company uses a job cost system in accounting for manufacturing costs, and following are a number of its general ledger accounts with the January 1 balances and some January postings shown. The postings are incomplete. Commonly only the debit or credit of a journal entry appears in the accounts, with the offsetting debits and credits being omitted. Also, the amounts shown represent total postings for the month and no date appears. However, this additional information is available: (1) The company charges jobs with overhead on the basis of direct labour cost, using a 75% overhead application rate. (2) The $13,000 debit in the Overhead Costs account represents the sum of all overhead costs for January other than indirect materials and indirect labour. (3) The accrued factory payroll on January 31 was $2,000.

Materials		
Jan. 1 Bal.	9,000	11,000
	14,000	

Factory Payroll		
21,000	Jan. 1 Bal.	1,000

Goods in Process		
Jan. 1 Bal.	5,000	44,000
Materials	10,000	
Labour	20,000	

Cost of Goods Sold	

Finished Goods		
Jan. 1 Bal.	8,000	45,000

Factory Overhead Costs	
13,000	

Copy the accounts on a sheet of paper, supply the missing debits and credits, and use key letters to tie together the debits and credits of the entries. Answer these questions: (1) What was the January 31 balance of the Finished Goods account? (2) How many dollars of factory payroll were paid during January? (3) What was the cost of goods sold during January? (4) How much overhead was actually incurred during the month? (5) How much overhead was charged to jobs during the month? (6) Was overhead overapplied or underapplied during the month?

Decision problem 24–3, Merrick Company

On May 17, 1976, a fire destroyed the plant, the inventories, and some of the accounting records of Merrick Company, and you have been asked to determine for insurance purposes the amounts of raw materials, goods in process, and finished goods destroyed. The company used a job order cost system, and you were able to obtain this additional information:

a. The company's December 31, 1975, balance sheet showed the following inventory amounts: materials, $12,000; goods in process, $15,000; and finished goods, $18,000. The balance sheet also showed a $2,000 liability for accrued factory wages payable.

b. The company's predetermined overhead application rate was 80% of direct labour cost.

c. Goods costing $75,000 were sold and delivered to customers between January 1 and May 17, 1976.

d. Materials costing $26,000 were purchased between January 1 and May 17, and $24,000 of direct and indirect materials were issued to the factory.

e. Factory wages totaling $29,000 were paid between January 1 and May 17, and on the latter date there were $1,000 of accrued factory wages payable.

f. The debits to the Overhead Costs account during the period before the fire totaled $19,000 of which $2,000 was for indirect materials and $3,000 was for indirect labour.

g. Goods costing $72,000 were finished and transferred to finished goods between January 1 and May 17.

h. It was decided that the May 17 balance of the Overhead Costs account should be apportioned between goods in process, finished goods, and cost of goods sold. Between January 1 and May 17 the company had charged the following amounts of overhead to jobs: to jobs sold, $14,000; to jobs finished but unsold, $4,000; and to jobs still in process on May 17, $2,000.

Determine the May 17 inventories of materials, goods in process, and finished goods. (T-accounts may be helpful in organizing the data.)

25

Budgeting; standard costs

■ A *budget* is a plan of future action expressed in monetary terms; and *budgeting* is the process of planning future action.

The primary reason for preparing a budget is to maximize profits; but the benefits of budgeting go beyond this as outlined in the following section.

Other benefits from budgeting

■ Investigation, study, and research

When a concern prepares a budget and plans, its actions are usually based upon thorough investigations, study, and research. Not only should this result in the best conceivable plans but it should also instill in executives the habit of basing decisions upon investigations and study.

Control

A budget aids in controlling business operations. It does this by influencing the actions of people. For example, when a department manager knows that his department's expenses will be compared with the planned expenses of a budget, he is influenced toward keeping the expenses at the planned level.

Coordination

Coordination requires that a business be operated as a whole rather than as a group of separate departments. When a budget plan is prepared, each department's objectives are determined in advance, and these objectives are coordinated; for example, the production department is scheduled to produce approximately the number of units the selling department can sell.

Communication

When a budget is prepared, the budget becomes a means of informing the organization not only of plans that have been approved by management but also of budgeted actions management wishes the organization to take during the budget period.

Motivation

When obtainable budgeted objectives are set, all persons responsible can normally be depended upon to make every effort to attain or exceed the objectives for which they are personally responsible.

The budget period ■ Budget periods normally coincide with accounting periods. This means that in most companies the budget period is one year in length. However, in addition to their annual budgets, many companies prepare long-range budgets setting forth major objectives for from 3 to 5 or 10 years in advance. Such long-range budgets are often used as the framework into which each annual budget is fitted.

Although most budgets are prepared for a year, yearly budgets are commonly broken down into quarterly or monthly budgets. Short-term budgets of a quarter or a month are useful yardsticks for measuring the degree of accomplishment toward the total results desired.

When an annual budget is broken down into monthly budgets, monthly reports like that of Illustration 25–1 are prepared to compare actual achievements with the budgeted plan.

The budget committee ■ The task of preparing a budget should not be made the responsibility of any one department; and the budget definitely should not be handed down from above as the "final word." Rather budget figures and budget estimates should be developed from the bottom up. For example, the sales department should have a hand in preparing sales estimates and the production department should be responsible for preparing its own expense budget. Otherwise production and salespeople may say the budget figures are meaningless, as they were prepared by front office personnel who know nothing of sales and production problems.

Nevertheless, the preparation of a budget needs central guidance, and this is commonly supplied by a budget committee of department heads or other high-level executives who are responsible for seeing that budget figures are realistically established and coordinated. If a department submits budget figures that do not reflect proper performance, the

Consolidated Stores, Ltd.
Income Statement with Variations from Budget
For Month Ended April 30, 19—

	Actual	Budget	Variations
Sales	$63,500	$60,000	$+ 3,500
Less: Sales returns and allowances	1,800	1,700	+ 100
Sales discounts	1,200	1,150	+ 50
Net sales	$60,500	$57,150	$+ 3,350
Cost of goods sold:			
Merchandise inventory, April 1, 19—	$42,000	$44,000	$− 2,000
Purchases, net	39,100	38,000	+ 1,100
Freight-in	1,250	1,200	+ 50
Goods for sale	$82,350	$83,200	$− 850
Merchandise inventory, April 30, 19—	41,000	44,100	− 3,100
Cost of goods sold	$41,350	$39,100	$+ 2,250
Gross profit	$19,150	$18,050	$+ 1,100
Operating expenses:			
Selling expenses:			
Sales salaries	$ 6,250	$ 6,000	$+ 250
Advertising expense	900	800	+ 100
Store supplies used	550	500	+ 50
Depreciation of store equipment	1,600	1,600	
Total selling expenses	$ 9,300	$ 8,900	$+ 400
General and administrative expenses:			
Office salaries	$ 2,000	$ 2,000	
Office supplies used	165	150	$+ 15
Rent	1,100	1,100	
Expired insurance	200	200	
Depreciation of office equipment	100	100	
Total general and administrative expenses	$ 3,565	$ 3,550	$+ 15
Total operating expenses	$12,865	$12,450	$+ 415
Income from Operations	$ 6,285	$ 5,600	$+ 685

Illustration
25–1

figures should be returned to the department with the budget committee's comments. The originating department then either adjusts the
figures or defends them. It should not change the figures just to please
the committee, since it is important that all parties agree that the figures
are reasonable and attainable.

Preparing the budget

■ A company's budget, often called the *master budget,* normally consists of a number of budgets; for example, it may be composed of a sales
budget, a production budget, numerous departmental expense budgets,
a plant and equipment or capital budget, and a cash budget.

Sales budget

The sales budget, an estimate of goods to be sold and revenue to be
derived from sales, is the usual starting point in the budgeting procedure,
since the plans of all departments are related to sales and expected
revenue. The sales budget commonly grows from a reconciliation of
forecasted business conditions, plant capacity, proposed selling expenses, such as advertising, and estimates of sales. As to sales estimates,

since people normally feel a greater responsibility for reaching goals they have had a hand in setting, traveling salesmen of a concern having such salesmen and department managers in a department store are asked to submit through their sales manager estimates of sales for their territories and departments. The final sales budget is then based on these estimates as reconciled for forecasted business conditions, selling expenses, et cetera.

Merchandising, production, and material purchases budgets

In a store, merchandise must be purchased before it is sold, and in a factory it must be produced. Thus, once sales estimates are completed it is necessary to plan merchandise purchases or product production.

MERCHANDISING BUDGET.   Monthly departmental sales forecasts are the usual starting point in building a store's merchandising budget. Illustration 25–2 shows such a budget for Department A of Consolidated Stores, Ltd. The sales figure in Illustration 25–2 is the budgeted

Consolidated Stores, Ltd.
Merchandising Budget for Department A, Month of February, 19—

Sales at planned selling prices (see sales budget)	$ 6,800
Budgeted purchases for February:	
Cost of goods to be sold during February (60% of $6,800)	$ 4,080
Planned February 28th inventory	8,000
Total merchandise required	$12,080
Inventory on February 1	7,600
Budgeted Purchases for February	$ 4,480

Illustration 25–2

February sales from the concern's previously prepared sales budget. Then since the markup in this department is 40% (based on sales), cost of goods sold is 60% of budgeted sales; and if planned inventories for the department are known, budgeted departmental purchases can be determined as in the illustration.

To produce a storewide merchandising budget, a budget similar to Illustration 25–2 is prepared for each department. Then all the departmental budgets are combined for a monthly merchandising budget for the entire store and the monthly budgets are combined again for the year's budget.

PRODUCTION AND MATERIAL PURCHASES BUDGETS.   The production budget for a manufacturing concern is prepared in much the same way as a store's merchandising budget. To begin, an estimate of the units of each product to be manufactured is made, often as in Illustration 25–3.

After the production budget and the number of units of each product to be manufactured are determined, the next step is to set up the material purchases budget. To do this a materials specification sheet showing kinds and quantities of materials needed for proposed production is

The Marine Production Company
Production Budget
Planned Quantity of Goods to Be Manufactured
For the Year Ending December 31, 197A

Units of product required to meet sales estimates	62,300
Planned inventory, December 31, 197A	8,600
Total units required	70,900
Units in inventory, January 1, 197A	8,100
Number of Units to Be Manufactured	62,800

Illustration
25-3

prepared. From this an estimate of materials to be purchased can be made as in Illustration 25-4 (assume in this illustration for sake of brevity that only one kind of material is needed and that two units of it are used to make each unit of finished goods).

The Marine Production Company
Material Purchases Budget
Planned Quantity and Cost of Raw Material to Be Purchased
For the Year Ending December 31, 197A

Required units of material for goods to be manufactured (62,800 × 2)	125,600
Planned inventory, December 31, 197A	21,200
Total units of material required	146,800
Units in January 1, 197A, material inventory	18,600
Units to be purchased	128,200
Estimated unit cost	× $2
Estimated Cost of Material to Be Purchased	$256,400

Illustration
25-4

After the material purchases budget is completed, labour costs and factory overhead are estimated. Then all estimates are assembled in a statement of budgeted cost of goods to be manufactured.

Expense budgets

As soon as a tentative sales estimate is made, it is communicated to department heads such as the sales manager and office manager who are asked to make expense estimates for their departments. The department heads normally base their estimates on the previous year's expenses, adjusted for increases or decreases in service expected of them, changes in wage scales, changes in supply costs, and other pertinent data. Their estimates must meet the approval of the budget committee or be increased or decreased; asking for estimates from department heads helps secure their cooperation in carrying out the final budget.

Plant and equipment budget

The plant and equipment or capital budget lists equipment to be scrapped and additional equipment to be purchased if the proposed production program is carried out. The purchase of additional equipment requires funds; and anticipating equipment additions in advance normally makes it easier to provide the funds. Also at times estimated production may exceed plant capacity. Budgeting makes it possible to anticipate this and either revise the production schedule or increase plant capacity. Planning plant and equipment purchases is called capital budgeting, and this is discussed in more detail in Chapter 27.

Cash budget

After tentative sales, expenses, production, and equipment budgets have been set, the cash budget is prepared. This budget is important. A company should have at all times enough cash to meet needs but not too much. Too much cash is undesirable because it often cannot be profitably invested. A cash budget requires management to forecast cash receipts and disbursements, and usually results in better cash management. Also, it enables management to arrange well in advance for loans to cover any anticipated inadequacies.

In preparing the cash budget, anticipated receipts are added to the beginning cash balance, and anticipated expenditures are deducted. Annual cash budgets are usually broken down into monthly budgets as in Illustration 25–5.

Consolidated Stores, Ltd.
Cash Budget for January, 19—

Cash balance, January 1, 19—............................		$32,500
Add estimated cash receipts:		
Cash sales...................................	$43,200	
Collections of accounts receivable...............	18,650	
Interest on investments................................	750	
Property rentals..	1,800	64,400
Available cash..		$96,900
Deduct estimated disbursements:		
Accounts payable...	$41,300	
Income taxes...	2,750	
Payrolls..	8,250	
Building repairs...	15,300	
Dividends..	4,000	
Miscellaneous items.....................................	1,200	72,800
Estimated Cash Balance, January 31, 19—.........		$24,100

Illustration
25–5

Master budget

After the sales, expense, production, equipment, and cash budgets are coordinated and completed, they are combined into a master budget. The master budget is then approved and transmitted to the organization as the approved objectives for the budget period.

■ Preparing and carrying out a budget involves all departments; consequently, it is not primarily an accounting function. However, the task of assembling data and translating it into financial terms often falls to the accounting department. Furthermore, since the accounting department is in charge of accounting records and is constantly dealing with actual transactions, it is well qualified to deal with budget data.

One budget task the accounting department is commonly called upon to perform is to prepare from the budget an estimated income statement for the budget year and an estimated balance sheet as it will appear at the end of the budget year if budget plans are carried out. This task is, in a sense, actually one of accounting for events before they happen.

■ Normally, when the accounting department is called on to prepare an estimated balance sheet and an estimated income statement as they will appear at the end of the budget period, it is called upon to do so a month or more before the budget period begins. For example, the accounting department may be given a copy of the budget during the last week of November and be requested to prepare estimated statements for the year beginning the following January 1.

During the last week in November, the accounting department does not know what the following December 31 post-closing or January 1 opening account balances will be. Consequently, its first task is to project the company's account balances ahead and arrive at the December 31 estimated post-closing trial balance for the current year.

After arriving at this estimated post-closing trial balance, it is commonly entered in the first two money columns of a work sheet. Next the budgeted transactions and adjustments are entered in the second pair of work sheet columns in the same manner as adjustments are entered on an ordinary work sheet. For example, if the budget calls for sales on account of $250,000, the name of the Sales account is entered on the work sheet in the Account Titles column below the names of the estimated trial balance accounts; and then Sales is credited and Accounts Receivable is debited for $250,000 in the second pair of money columns.

After all budgeted transactions and adjustments are entered on the work sheet, the estimated trial balance amounts in the first pair of money columns are combined with the budget amounts in the second pair of columns and are sorted to the proper Income Statement and Balance Sheet columns of the work sheet. After this, the estimated income statement and estimated balance sheet are prepared from the information in the Income Statement and Balance Sheet columns in the same manner as an ordinary income statement or balance sheet.

■ Some concerns prepare what are known as "fixed" budgets; others prepare so-called "variable" or "flexible" budgets.

The budgets discussed thus far have been of the fixed variety. When a fixed budget is prepared, the best information available is used to arrive at an estimate of the operating level expected during the budget year. All plans are then based on this one expected or "fixed" level of activity. A fixed budget, in other words, assumes a single level of activity, and cost and expense estimates are made for this one level only.

The weakness of a fixed budget is that it makes no provision for an operating level different from that planned; and there are often years in which for unforeseen reasons the actual operating level varies substantially from the budget plan. Furthermore, when this occurs, good management requires that costs and expenses be adjusted to fit the new unplanned activity level; and under a fixed budget, for lack of planning, these adjustments have to be made on a "best-guess" basis. True, these best guesses may prove satisfactory; but planning in advance for several activity levels should produce both better cost control and more precise guidance for management.

A variable budget differs from a fixed budget in that it provides cost and expense estimates for varying rates of operating activity. For example, a concern preparing a variable budget may estimate it will sell during the coming budget year, depending upon economic conditions, from 100,000 to 160,000 units of product. It then provides in its flexible budget, for instance, a set of cost and expense estimates for the 100,000-unit level, another set for the 110,000-unit level, another for 120,000 units, still another for 130,000, and so on up to 160,000 units. In other words, when a flexible budget is prepared, cost and expense estimates are made for each of the several production levels that may be experienced. Then, as the year progresses and the actual operating level becomes known, the budget costs and expenses for that level are compared with the actual costs and expenses. Any variations provide cost control data for managerial action.

STANDARD COSTS

■ In the previous chapter it was said that there are two basic types of cost systems, job order and process, but an infinite number of variations of the two. A *standard cost system,* one based on *standard* or *budgeted costs,* is such a variation.

The costs of a job or a process as discussed in the previous chapter were historical costs, historical in the sense that they had been incurred and were history by the time they were recorded. Such costs are useful; but to judge whether or not they are reasonable or what they should be, management needs a basis of comparison. Standard costs offer such a basis.

Standard costs are the costs that should be incurred under normal conditions in producing a given product or part or in performing a particular service. They are established by means of engineering and accounting studies made before the product is manufactured or the service performed; and once established, they are used to judge the reasonableness of the actual costs incurred when the product or service is produced. Standard costs are also used to place responsibilities when actual costs vary from standard.

Accountants speak of *standard material cost, standard labour cost,* and *standard overhead cost;* and this terminology is used in this chapter; however, it should be observed that standard material, labour, and overhead costs are really budgeted material, labour, and overhead costs.

Establishing standard costs

■ Great care and the combined efforts of people in accounting, engineering, personnel administration, and other management areas are required in establishing standard costs. Time and motion studies are made of each labour operation in a product's production or in performing a service to learn both the best way to perform the operation and the standard labour time required under normal conditions for performance. Exhaustive investigations are also made of the quantity, grade, and cost of each material required; and machines and other productive equipment are subject to detailed studies in an effort to achieve maximum efficiencies and to learn what costs should be.

However, regardless of care exercised in establishing standard costs and in revising them as conditions change, actual costs incurred in producing a given product or service are apt to vary from standard costs. When this occurs, the difference in total cost is likely to be a composite of several cost differences. For example, the quantity, or the price, or both the quantity and price of the material used may have varied from standard; and the labour time, or the labour price, or both the time and price of labour may have varied. Likewise, overhead costs may have varied.

Variances

■ When actual costs vary from standard costs, the differences are called *variances*. Variances may be favourable or unfavourable. A favourable variance is one in which actual cost is below standard cost, and an unfavourable variance is one in which actual cost is above standard.

When variances occur, they are isolated and studied for possible remedial action and to place responsibilities. For example, if the standard material cost for producing 2,000 units of Product A is $800 but material costing $840 was used in producing the units, the $40 variance may have resulted from paying a price higher than standard for the material, a greater quantity of material than standard may have been used, or there may have been some combination of these causes. The price paid for a material is a purchasing department responsibility; consequently, if the variance was caused by a price greater than standard, responsibility rests with the purchasing department. On the other hand, since the production department is usually responsible for the amount of material used, if a quantity greater than standard was used, responsibility normally rests with the production department. However, if more than a standard amount of material was used because the material was of a grade below standard, causing more than normal waste, responsibility is back on the purchasing department for buying a substandard grade.

■ As previously stated, when variances occur, they are isolated and studied for possible remedial action and to place responsibilities. For example, assume that XL Company has established the following standard costs per unit for its Product Z:

Material (1 pound per unit at $1 per pound) $1.00
Direct labour (1 hour per unit at $3 per hour)............... 3.00
Overhead ($2 per standard direct labour hour)............. 2.00
Total standard cost per unit $6.00

Material variances

Assume further that during May, XL Company completed 3,500 units of Product Z, using 3,600 pounds of material costing $1.05 per pound, or $3,780. Under these assumptions the actual and standard material costs for the 3,500 units are:

Actual cost: 3,600 pounds @ $1.05 per pound......... $3,780
Standard cost: 3,500 pounds @ $1.00 per pound......... 3,500
Excess of actual over standard cost..................... $ 280

Observe that the actual material cost for these units is $280 above their standard cost. This excess cost may be isolated as to causes in the following manner:

QUANTITY VARIANCE:
Actual units at the standard price.............. 3,600 lbs. @ $1.00   = $3,600
Standard units at the standard price.......... 3,500 lbs. @ $1.00   =   3,500
Variance (unfavourable)........................   100 lbs. @ $1.00   = $100

PRICE VARIANCE:
Actual units at the actual price.................. 3,600 lbs. @ $1.05   = $3,780
Actual units at the standard price.............. 3,600 lbs. @ $1.00   =   3,600
Variance (unfavourable)........................ 3,600 lbs. @ $0.05   =   180
Excess material cost $280

The analysis shows that $100 of the excess material cost resulted from using 100 more pounds than standard, and $180 resulted from a unit price $0.05 above standard. With this information management can go to the responsible individuals for explanations.

Labour variances

Labour cost in manufacturing a given part or in performing a service depends on a composite of the number of hours worked (quantity) and the wage rate paid (price). Therefore, when the labour cost for a task varies from standard, it too may be analyzed into a quantity variance and a price variance.

For example, the direct labour standard for the 3,500 units of Product Z is one hour per unit, or 3,500 hours at $3 per hour. If 3,400 hours costing $3.10 per hour were used in completing the units, the actual and standard labour costs for these units are:

```
Actual cost: 3,400 hours @ $3.10 per hour ............... $10,540
Standard cost: 3,500 hours @ $3.00 per hour ............. 10,500
    Excess of actual over standard cost .................... $    40
```

In this case actual cost is only $40 over standard, but isolating the variances involved reveals the following:

```
QUANTITY VARIANCE:
    Standard hours at standard price ............ 3,500 hrs. @ $3.00  =  $10,500
    Actual hours at standard price ............... 3,400 hrs. @ $3.00  =   10,200
        Variance (favourable) .........................   100 hrs. @ $3.00  =            $300

PRICE VARIANCE:
    Actual hours at actual price ................... 3,400 hrs. @ $3.10  =  $10,540
    Actual hours at standard price ............... 3,400 hrs. @ $3.00  =   10,200
        Variance (unfavourable) ...................... 3,400 hrs. @ $0.10  =              340
        Excess labour cost .........................                                    $  40
```

The analysis shows a favourable quantity variance of $300, which resulted from using 100 fewer direct labour hours than standard for the units produced. However, this favourable variance was more than offset by a wage rate $0.10 above standard.

When a factory or department has workers of various skill levels, it is the responsibility of the foreman or other supervisor to assign to each task a workman or workmen of no higher skill level than is required to accomplish the task. In this case an investigation could reveal that workers of a higher skill level were used in producing the 3,500 units of Product Z; hence, fewer labour hours were required for the work. However, because the workers were of higher grade, the wage rate paid them was higher than standard.

Charging overhead to production

■ When standard costs are used, factory overhead is charged to production by means of a predetermined standard overhead rate. The rate may be based on the relation of overhead to standard labour cost, standard labour hours, standard machine-hours, or some other measure of production. For example, XL Company charges its Product Z with $2 of overhead per standard direct labour hour; and since the direct labour standard for Product Z is one hour per unit, the 3,500 units manufactured in May were charged with $7,000 of overhead.

Before going on, recall that only 3,400 actual direct labour hours were used in producing these units. Then note again that overhead is charged to the units, not on the basis of actual labour hours but on the basis of standard labour hours. Standard labour hours are used because the amount of overhead charged to these units should not be less than standard simply because less than the standard (normal) amount of labour was used in their production. In other words, overhead should not vary from normal simply because labour varied from normal.

■ A variable or flexible factory overhead budget is the starting point in establishing reasonable standards for overhead costs. A flexible budget is necessary because the actual production level may vary from the expected level; and when this happens, certain costs vary with production, but others remain fixed. This may be seen by examining XL Company's flexible budget shown in Illustration 25–6.

In examining Illustration 25–6, note that the budgeted costs are classified as either fixed or variable. A *fixed cost* is one that remains the same in total at all production levels, and a *variable cost* is one that varies with and in proportion to each change in the production level. For example, unless there is some sort of escalator clause in the rent contract, the amount of rent that must be paid remains the same in total whether the factory is temporarily closed or is running on a one-, two-, or three-shift basis, and consequently rent is a fixed cost. On the other hand, power to run the machines increases or decreases as the production level increases or decreases, and is therefore a variable cost.

XL Company
Flexible Overhead Costs Budget
For Month Ended May 31, 19—

	Production Levels				
	60%	70%	80%	90%	100%
Production in units.............................	3,000	3,500	4,000	4,500	5,000
Standard direct labour hours	3,000	3,500	4,000	4,500	5,000
Budgeted factory overhead:					
Fixed costs:					
Building rent..............................	$1,000	$1,000	$1,000	$1,000	$1,000
Depreciation, machinery................	1,200	1,200	1,200	1,200	1,200
Supervisory salaries....................	1,800	1,800	1,800	1,800	1,800
Totals.....................................	$4,000	$4,000	$4,000	$4,000	$4,000
Variable costs:					
Indirect labour.............................	$1,200	$1,400	$1,600	$1,800	$2,000
Indirect materials.........................	900	1,050	1,200	1,350	1,500
Power and lights	600	700	800	900	1,000
Maintenance	300	350	400	450	500
Totals.....................................	$3,000	$3,500	$4,000	$4,500	$5,000
Total Factory Overhead...................	$7,000	$7,500	$8,000	$8,500	$9,000

Illustration
25–6

Observe in Illustration 25–6 that XL Company has established standard costs for five production levels, ranging from 60% to 100% of capacity. Such a range is established because when actual costs are known, they should be compared with the standards for the level actually achieved and not with the standards at some other level. For example, if the plant actually operated at 70% capacity during May, actual costs incurred at this 70% level should be compared with standard costs at this level and not with costs established for the 80% or 90% levels.

In setting overhead standards, after the flexible overhead budget is prepared, management must determine the expected operating level for the plant. This can be 100% of capacity; but it seldom is since errors in scheduling work, breakdowns, and, perhaps, the inability of the sales force to sell all the product produced commonly reduced the operating level to some point below full capacity.

After the flexible budget is set up and the expected operating level is determined, overhead costs at the expected level are related to, for example, labour hours at this level to establish the standard overhead rate. The rate thus established is then used to charge overhead to production. For example, assume XL Company decided that 80% of capacity is the expected operating level for its plant. The company then arrived at its $2 per direct labour hour overhead rate by dividing the budgeted $8,000 of overhead costs at the 80% level by the 4,000 standard direct labour hours required to produce the product manufactured at this level.

Overhead variances

■ As previously stated, when standard costs are used, overhead is applied to production on the basis of a predetermined overhead rate. Then at the end of a cost period the difference between overhead applied and overhead actually incurred is analyzed and variances are calculated to set out responsibilities for the difference.

Overhead variances are computed in several ways. A common way divides the difference between overhead applied and overhead incurred into (1) the *volume variance* and (2) the *controllable variance*.

Volume variance

The volume variance is the difference between (1) *the amount of overhead budgeted at the actual operating level achieved during the period* and (2) *the standard amount of overhead charged to production during the period*. For example, assume that during May XL Company actually operated at 70% of capacity, producing 3,500 units of Product Z, which were charged with overhead at the standard rate. Under this assumption the company's volume variance for May is:

VOLUME VARIANCE:
Budgeted overhead at 70% of capacity $7,500
Standard overhead charged to production (3,500
    standard labour hours at the $2 per hour) 7,000
    Variance (unfavourable) .... $ 500

To understand why this volume variance occurred, reexamine the flexible budget of Illustration 25–6 and observe that at the 80% level the $2 per hour overhead rate may be subdivided into $1 per hour for fixed overhead and $1 per hour for variable overhead. Furthermore, at the 80% (normal) level, the $1 for fixed overhead exactly covers the fixed overhead. However, when this $2 rate is used for the 70% level, and again subdivided, the $1 for fixed overhead will not cover all the fixed overhead because $4,000 is required for fixed overhead and 3,500 hours at $1 per hour equals only $3,500. In other words, at this 70% level the $2 per hour standard overhead rate did not absorb all the overhead incurred; it lacked $500, the amount of the volume variance. Or again, the volume variance resulted simply because the plant did not reach the expected operating level.

An unfavourable volume variance tells management that the plant did not reach its normal operating level; and when such a variance is large, management should investigate the cause or causes. Machine breakdowns, failure to schedule an even flow of work, and a lack of sales orders are common causes. The first two may be corrected in the factory, but the third requires either more orders from the sales force or a downward adjustment of the operating level considered to be normal.

Controllable variance

The controllable variance is the difference between (1) *overhead actually incurred and* (2) *the overhead budgeted at the operating level achieved.* For example, assume that XL Company incurred $7,650 of overhead during May; and since its plant operated at 70% of capacity during the month, its controllable overhead variance for May is:

CONTROLLABLE VARIANCE:
Actual overhead incurred $7,650
Overhead budgeted at operating level achieved........ 7,500
　　Variance (unfavourable)...................................... $ 150

The controllable overhead variance measures management's efficiency in adjusting controllable overhead costs (normally variable overhead) to the operating level achieved. In this case management failed by $150 to get overhead down to the amount budgeted for the 70% level.

Although the controllable overhead variance measures management's efficiency in adjusting overhead costs to the operating level achieved, an overhead variance report is a more effective means for showing just where management achieved or failed to achieve the budgeted expectations. Such a report for XL Company appears in Illustration 25–7.

Combining the volume and controllable variances

The volume and controllable variances may be combined to account for the difference between overhead actually incurred and overhead charged to production. For example, XL Company incurred $7,650 of overhead during May and charged $7,000 to production, and its

XL Company
Factory Overhead Variance Report
For Month Ended May 31, 19—

VOLUME VARIANCE:

Normal production level .... 80% of capacity.

Production level achieved.................................... 70% of capacity.

Volume variance.. $ 500 (unfavourable) .

CONTROLLABLE VARIANCE

	Budget	Actual	Favourable	Unfavourable
Fixed overhead costs:				
Building rent	$1,000	$1,000		
Depreciation, machinery	1,200	1,200		
Supervisory salaries	1,800	1,800		
Total fixed......................................	$4,000	$4,000		
Variable overhead costs:				
Indirect labour	$1,400	$1,525		$125
Indirect materials	1,050	1,025	$ 25	
Power and lights............................	700	750		50
Maintenance..................................	350	350		
Total variable.............................	$3,500	$3,650		
Total controllable variances...			$ 25	$175
Net Controllable Variance (Unfavourable)			150	
			$175	$175

Illustration
25–7

overhead variances may be combined as follows to account for the difference:

VOLUME VARIANCE:

Overhead budgeted at operating level achieved........................... $7,500

Standard overhead charged to production (3,500 standard
hours at $2 per hour) 7,000

Variance (unfavourable)... $500

CONTROLLABLE VARIANCE:

Actual overhead incurred $7,650

Overhead budgeted at operating level achieved........:................... 7,500

Variance (unfavourable)... 150

Excess of overhead incurred over overhead charged to
production... $650

Controlling a business through standard costs

■ Business operations are carried on by people, and control of a business is gained by controlling the actions of the people responsible for its revenues, costs, and expenses. When a budget is prepared and standard costs established, control is maintained by taking appropriate action when actual costs vary from standard or from the budget.

Reports like the ones shown in this chapter are a means of calling management's attention to these variations, and a review of the reports is essential to the successful operation of a budget program. However, in making the review, management should practice the control technique known as *management by exception*. Under this technique management gives its attention only to the variances in which actual costs are significantly different from standard and it ignores the cost situations in which performance is satisfactory. In other words, management concentrates its attention on the exceptional or irregular situations and pays little or no attention to the normal.

Standard costs in the accounts
■ Standard costs can be used solely in the preparation of management reports and need not be taken into the accounts. However, in most standard cost systems such costs are taken into the accounts to facilitate both the record keeping and the preparation of reports.

No effort will be made here to go into the record-keeping details of a standard cost system. This is reserved for a course in cost accounting. Nevertheless, when standard costs are taken into the accounts, entries like the following (the data for which are taken from the discussion of material variances on page 772) may be used to take the standard costs into the Goods in Process account and to set out in variance accounts any variances:

May	31	Goods in Process...	3,500.00	
		Material Quantity Variance.............................	100.00	
		Material Price Variance.................................	180.00	
		Materials		3,780.00
		To charge production with 3,600 pounds of material @ $1.05 per pound.		

Variances taken into the accounts are allowed to accumulate in the variance accounts until the end of an accounting period. If at that time the variance amounts are immaterial, they are closed to Cost of Goods Sold as an adjustment of the cost of goods sold. However, if the amounts are large, they may be prorated between Goods in Process, Finished Goods, and Cost of Goods Sold.

Questions for class discussion

1. What is a budget? What benefits result from preparing a budget?
2. What is the normal length of a budget period?
3. Why should each department be asked to prepare its own budget estimates?
4. What are the duties of the budget committee?
5. What is a sales budget? A departmental expense budget? A production budget? A capital budget? A cash budget? A master budget?
6. A manufacturing concern plans to begin a budget year with 1,700 units of its product on hand; it plans to sell 48,000 units during the year and to end the year with a 2,000-unit inventory. If production is to be at a uniform rate throughout the year, how many units should the concern plan to produce each month?

7. Differentiate between a fixed budget and a flexible or variable budget.
8. What is a standard cost? For what are standard costs used?
9. In standard cost accounting, what is a variance?
10. Why is a material variance isolated into a price variance and a quantity variance? Who is normally responsible for the price paid for a material? Who is normally responsible for the amount of material used in production?
11. What is a flexible overhead costs budget? Why is such a budget used in a standard cost system?
12. What is a fixed cost? What is a variable cost? When production volume in a factory increases, do fixed costs per unit increase, decrease, or remain unchanged? Why?
13. What may cause a plant to operate below capacity?
14. What is a volume variance? What is a controllable overhead variance?
15. What does an unfavourable volume variance indicate? What does a favourable controllable variance indicate?

Class exercises

Exercise 25–1

Alpha Department Store's sales budget for its Department Two calls for $8,500 of sales during March. The department is expected to begin March with a $6,000 inventory at cost and end the month with a $7,000 inventory. Cost of goods sold averages 60% of sales in the department.

Required:
Prepare a March purchases budget for the department.

Exercise 25–2

Beta Company manufactures and sells Product B. The company estimates it will have 1,800 units of the product in its April 1 finished goods inventory and that it will sell 12,500 units of the product during the year's second quarter. The company also believes it should begin the year's third quarter with 2,000 units of Product B in its inventory.

Required:
Prepare a production budget showing the number of units of Product B to be manufactured during the year's second quarter.

Exercise 25–3

A furniture manufacturer has just completed 1,000 identical tables using 9,800 board feet of lumber costing $3,626. The company's material standards for one unit of this table are 10 board feet of lumber at $0.35 per board foot.

Required:
Isolate the material price and material quantity variances in manufacturing the 1,000 tables.

Exercise 25–4

The manufacturer of Exercise 25–3 takes standard costs into its accounts. As a result, in charging material costs to Goods in Process, it also takes any variances into its accounts.

Required:

1. Under the assumption that the materials used in manufacturing the tables of Exercise 25–3 were charged to Goods in Process on March 8, give the entry to charge the materials and to take the variances into the accounts.
2. Under the further assumption that the variances of Exercise 25–3 were the only variances of the year and were considered immaterial, give the year-end entry to close the variance accounts.

Exercise 25–5

Following are the standard costs for one unit of a company's product:

Material (1 unit @ $5 per unit) .... $ 5
Direct labour (1 hour @ $3 per hour)............................. 3
Factory overhead (1 hour @ $2 per hour)........................ __2__
    Standard cost... $10

The $2 per direct labour hour overhead rate is based on a normal, 85% of capacity operating level and the following monthly flexible budget information:

	Operating Levels	
	80%	85%
Budgeted production in units...	8,000	8,500
Budgeted overhead:		
Fixed overhead..	$8,500	$8,500
Variable overhead	8,000	8,500

During the past month the company operated at 80% of capacity and produced 8,000 units of product with the following overhead costs:

Fixed overhead costs............................. $ 8,500
Variable overhead costs .... __8,100__
    Total overhead costs....................... $16,600

Required:
Isolate the overhead variance into a volume variance and a controllable variance.

Problems   **Problem 25–1**

Desert Company sells three products which it purchases in their finished ready-for-sale state, and it expects the following March 1 inventories for the products: Product A, 3,800 units; Product B, 3,250 units; and Product C, 5,600 units. The company's manager is disturbed because each product's expected March 1 inventory is excessive in relation to immediately expected sales. Consequently, he has set as a goal a month-end inventory for each product that is equal to one half the following month's expected sales. Expected sales in units for March, April, and May are as follows:

	Expected Sales in Units		
	March	April	May
Product A.............................	4,600	5,000	3,800
Product B.............................	2,800	3,400	3,600
Product C.............................	5,400	5,200	5,800

Required:
Prepare unit purchases budgets for the three products for each of March and April.

Problem 25–2

Jack Reed, the owner of Mesa Sales, approached his bank on April 1 for a $12,000, 90-day, 7% loan to be used as follows:

Pay past-due accounts payable	$ 4,500
Increase inventory (to be paid for in May).................	5,000
Increase the store's cash balance	2,500
Total..	$12,000

The bank's loan officer was interested in Mr. Reed's ability to repay the loan and asked him to forecast his company's June 30 cash position.
The company's April 1 current position is:

Cash on hand and in bank	$ 2,200
Accounts receivable	28,500
Merchandise inventory..	16,000
Total current assets	$46,700
Accounts payable ($4,500 past due)	20,300
Working capital..	$26,400

The company's budgeted sales, purchases, and cash expenditures for April, May, and June, other than for the payment of accounts payable, are as follows:

	April	*May*	*June*
Sales	$35,000	$34,000	$32,000
Purchases...	25,400	19,200	21,600
Payroll	3,000	3,000	3,000
Rent...	1,500	1,500	1,500
Other expenses	1,600	1,400	1,700
Personal withdrawals of owner	600	600	600

All of the company's sales are on credit, and past experience indicates 80% will be collected in the month following the sale, 15% in the next month, 4% in the next, and the remainder will not be collected. Application of this experience to the April 1 accounts receivable balance indicates $22,600 of the $28,500 will be collected during April, $4,000 during May, and $1,000 during June. The desired $5,000 inventory increase is included in the $25,400 of purchases budgeted by the store for April.

Required:
Prepare April, May, and June cash budgets for Mesa Sales. Assume the bank loan is made on April 1 and repaid on June 30, the inventory is increased $5,000 at once, the past-due accounts are paid from the loan proceeds, the remaining accounts are paid during April, and all merchandise purchased, including the inventory increase, is paid for during the month following its purchase.

Problem 25–3

A company has established the following standard costs for one unit of its product:

Material (3 gallons @ $5 per gallon)............................	$15.00
Direct labour (3 hours @ $3.50 per hour)...................	10.50
Overhead (3 hours @ $3 per hour)............................	9.00
Total standard cost..	$34.50

The $3 per direct labour hour overhead rate is based on a normal, 80% of capacity, operating level for the company's plant and the following flexible budget information for April:

	Operating Levels	
	80%	90%
Production in units..	800	900
Direct labour hours..	2,400	2,700
Fixed factory overhead...	$4,000	$4,000
Variable factory overhead	3,200	3,600

During April the company operated at 90% of capacity, producing 900 units of product having the following actual costs:

Material (2,650 gallons @ $5.10 per gallon)...............	$13,515
Direct labour (2,800 hours @ $3.40 per hour).............	9,520
Fixed factory overhead	4,000
Variable overhead	3,425

Required:
Isolate the material and labour variances into price and quantity variances and isolate the overhead variance into the volume and the controllable variances.

Problem 25–4

Western Company makes a single product for which it has established the following standard costs per unit:

Materials (20 lbs. @ $0.50 per lb.)............................	$10
Direct labour (4 hrs. @ $3 per hr.)............................	12
Factory overhead (4 hr. @ $3.25 per hr.)...................	13
Total standard cost..	$35

The $3.25 per direct labour hour overhead rate is based on a normal, 90% of capacity, operating level for the plant. The company's monthly flexible factory overhead budget shows the following:

	Operating Levels		
	80%	90%	100%
Production in units...	400	450	500
Standard direct labour hours	1,600	1,800	2,000
Budgeted factory overhead:			
Fixed costs:			
Rent	$ 800	$ 800	$ 800
Depreciation, machinery............................	1,400	1,400	1,400
Insurance and taxes..................................	200	200	200
Supervisory salaries.................................	1,200	1,200	1,200
Variable costs:			
Indirect materials	600	675	750
Indirect labour...	800	900	1,000
Power and lights	400	450	500
Maintenance...	200	225	250

During April the company operated at 80% of capacity and completed 400 units of its product, which were charged with the following standard costs:

Materials (8,000 lbs. @ $0.50 per lb.)........................ $ 4,000
Direct labour (1,600 hrs. @ $3 per hr.)...................... 4,800
Factory overhead (1,600 hrs. @ $3.25 per hr.)............ 5,200
Total.. $14,000

The actual April costs were:

Materials (8,100 lbs.)............................. $ 3,969
Direct labour (1,550 hrs.) 4,805
Rent 800
Depreciation, machinery........................ 1,400
Insurance and taxes.............................. 200
Supervisory salaries.............................. 1,200
Indirect materials 650
Indirect labour...................................... 775
Power and lights 380
Maintenance... 210
Total... $14,389

Required:
1. Isolate the material and labour variances into price and quantity variances.
2. Prepare a factory overhead variance report showing the volume and controllable variances.

Problem 25-5

Sunshine Company has established the following standard costs for one unit of its product:

Material (5 lbs. @ $0.75 per lb.) $3.75
Direct labour (1 hr. @ $3 per hr.) 3.00
Overhead (1 hr. @ $2.50 per hr.) 2.50
    Total standard cost $9.25

The $2.50 per direct labour hour overhead rate is based on a normal, 80% of capacity operating level, and at this level the company's monthly output is 2,000 units. However production does vary slightly, and each 1% variation results in a 20-unit increase or decrease in the production level. Following are the company's budgeted overhead costs at the 80% level for one month:

SUNSHINE COMPANY
Budgeted Monthly Factory Overhead at 80% Level

Fixed Costs:
    Depreciation expense, building .... $ 800
    Depreciation expense, machinery 1,000
    Taxes and insurance 200
    Supervision 1,000
      Total fixed costs $3,000
Variable Costs:
    Indirect materials .... $ 800
    Indirect labour 500
    Power 400
    Repairs and maintenance 300
      Total variable costs   2,000
Total Overhead Costs $5,000

During April of the current year the company operated at 75% of capacity, produced 1,900 units of product, and incurred the following actual costs:

Material (9,800 lbs.) .... $ 7,252
Direct labour (1,850 hrs.) 5,920
Depreciation expense, building 800
Depreciation expense, machinery 1,000
Taxes and insurance 200
Supervision 1,000
Indirect materials 725
Indirect labour 500
Power 385
Repairs and maintenance 260
    Total $18,042

Required:
1. Prepare a flexible overhead budget for the company showing the amount of each fixed and variable cost at the 75%, 80%, and 85% levels.

2. Isolate the material and labour variances into quantity and price variances and isolate the overhead variance into the volume variance and the controllable variance.
3. Prepare a factory overhead variance report showing the volume and controllable variances.

Alternate problems

Problem 25–1A

Tri-Products Company sells three products which it purchases in their finished ready-for-sale state. Expected sales for May, June, and July are:

	Expected Sales in Units		
	May	June	July
Product X..	5,200	6,800	5,400
Product Y..	7,200	7,000	6,600
Product Z..	3,800	3,600	4,400

The expected April 30 inventories for the products are: Product X, 5,000 units; Product Y, 7,500 units; Product Z, 4,500 units; and the company's manager is disturbed because each product's expected April 30 inventory is excessive in relation to immediately expected sales. Consequently, he has set as a goal a month-end inventory for each product that is equal to one half the following month's expected sales.

Required:
Prepare purchases budgets in units for the three products for each of May and June.

Problem 25–2A

Near the end of March of the current year Ted Zeppo, the owner of Zeppo Sales, approached his bank for a $10,000 loan to be made on May 1 and repaid 60 days thereafter with interest at 7½%. Mr. Zeppo planned to buy new store equipment costing $10,000 in April and needed the loan to pay for it in May. The bank's loan officer was interested in Mr. Zeppo's ability to repay the loan and asked him to forecast the June 30 cash position of his business.

Mr. Zeppo estimated the March 31 current position of his business would be as follows:

Cash on hand and in bank........................	$ 5,500
Accounts receivable...............................	46,400
Merchandise inventory............................	29,800
Total current assets	$81,700
Accounts payable...................................	31,400
Working capital.....................................	$50,300

He also estimated his second quarter sales, purchases, and cash expenses as follows:

	April	May	June
Sales...	$48,000	$50,000	$46,000
Purchases...................................	29,600	27,600	26,400
Payroll.......................................	4,500	4,500	4,500
Rent expense	2,000	2,000	2,000
Other cash expenses......................	2,800	2,600	3,000

All sales are on credit and past experience indicates that 80% is collected in the month following the sale, 15% in the next month, 4% in the next, and the remainder is not collected. Application of this experience to the March 31 accounts receivable balance indicates that $38,000 will be collected in April, $4,000 in May, and $1,000 in June.

Required:

Prepare April, May, and June cash budgets for Zeppo Sales. Assume the bank loan is made on May 1 and repaid on June 30, the store equipment is purchased in April and paid for in May, the March 31 accounts payable are paid in April, and all merchandise purchased is paid for during the month following its purchase.

Problem 25–3A

Zeal Company has established the following standard costs for one unit of its product:

Materials (2 units @ $1.60 per unit)...........................	$ 3.20
Direct labour (3 hrs. @ $3.25 per hr.).......................	9.75
Factory overhead (3 hrs. @ $1.50 per hr.).................	4.50
Total standard cost per unit	$17.45

The $1.50 per direct labour hour overhead rate is based on a normal, 96% of capacity operating level for the company's plant and the following flexible budget information for May:

	Operating Levels	
	80%	96%
Production in units...	5,000	6,000
Direct labour hours	15,000	18,000
Fixed factory overhead...	$ 9,000	$ 9,000
Variable factory overhead	15,000	18,000

During May the company operated at 80% of capacity and produced 5,000 units of product having the following actual costs:

Materials (10,500 units @ $1.55 per unit)...................	$16,275
Direct labour (14,800 hours @ $3.40 per hour)	50,320
Fixed factory overhead	9,000
Variable factory overhead.......................................	15,500

Required:

Isolate the material and labour variances into price and quantity variances and isolate the overhead variance into the volume variance and the controllable variance.

Problem 25–4A

Hydra Company manufactures a product for which it has established the following standard costs per unit:

Material (6 lbs. @ $2.50 per lb.).	$15.00
Direct labour (3 hrs. @ $3.50 per hr.)	10.50
Overhead (3 hrs. @ $3 per hr.)	9.00
Total standard cost	$34.50

The $3 per direct labour hour overhead rate is based on a normal, 90% of capacity, operating level for the company's plant and the following flexible budget information for one month's operations.

	Operating Levels		
	80%	90%	100%
Production in units	800	900	1,000
Standard direct labour hours	2,400	2,700	3,000
Budgeted factory overhead:			
Fixed costs:			
Depreciation, building	$1,200	$1,200	$1,200
Depreciation, machinery	1,500	1,500	1,500
Taxes and insurance	200	200	200
Supervisory salaries	1,600	1,600	1,600
Total fixed costs	$4,500	$4,500	$4,500
Variable costs:			
Indirect materials	$1,280	$1,440	$1,600
Indirect labour	1,200	1,350	1,500
Power	400	450	500
Maintenance	320	360	400
Total variable costs	$3,200	$3,600	$4,000
Total Factory Overhead	$7,700	$8,100	$8,500

During April the company operated at 80% of capacity and incurred the following actual costs in producing 800 units of its product:

Materials (4,700 lbs @ $2.55 per lb.)		$11,985
Direct labour (2,500 hrs. @ $3.40 per hr.)		8,500
Overhead costs:		
Depreciation expense, building	$1,200	
Depreciation expense, machinery	1,500	
Taxes and insurance	200	
Supervisory salaries	1,600	
Indirect materials	1,250	
Indirect labour	1,300	
Power	425	
Maintenance	300	7,775
Total		$28,260

Required:

1. Isolate the material and labour variances into price and quantity variances.
2. Prepare a factory overhead variance report showing the volume and controllable variances.

Problem 25–5A

Salish Company manufactures a product for which it has established the following standard costs per unit:

Material (2 lbs. @ $1.25 per lb.)	$2.50
Direct labour (½ hr. @ $3.40 per hr.)	1.70
Overhead (½ hr. @ $3 per hr.)	1.50
Total standard cost	$5.70

The $3 per direct labour hour overhead rate is based on a normal, 80% of capacity operating level, and at this level the company's monthly output is 4,000 units. However, production does vary slightly, and each 1% variation results in a 40-unit increase or decrease in the production level. Following are the company's budgeted overhead costs at the 80% level for one month.

SALISH COMPANY
Budgeted Monthly Factory Overhead at 80% Level

Fixed overhead costs:		
Depreciation expense, building	$1,100	
Depreciation expense, machinery	1,000	
Taxes and insurance	200	
Supervision	1,500	
Total fixed overhead costs		$3,800
Variable overhead costs:		
Indirect materials	$ 840	
Indirect labour	600	
Power	360	
Repairs and maintenance	400	
Total variable overhead costs		2,200
Total Overhead Costs		$6,000

During March of the current year the company operated at 90% of capacity, produced 4,400 units of product, and incurred the following actual costs:

Materials (8,600 lbs.)	$10,922
Direct labour (2,300 hrs.)	7,705
Depreciation expense, building	1,100
Depreciation expense, machinery	1,000
Taxes and insurance	200
Supervision	1,500
Indirect materials	950
Indirect labour	650
Power	385
Repairs and maintenance	475
	$24,887

Required:

1. Prepare a flexible overhead budget for the company showing the amount of each fixed and variable cost at the 70%, 80%, and 90% levels.
2. Isolate the material and labour variances into quantity and price variances and isolate the overhead variance into the volume variance and the controllable variance.
3. Prepare a factory overhead variance report showing the volume and controllable variances.

Decision problem 25–1, Husky Company

Joe Kirby has been an employee of Husky Company for the past five years, the last four of which he has worked in the stamping department. Seven months ago he was made foreman of the department, and since then has been able to end a long period of internal dissention, high employee turnover, and inefficient operation in the department. Under Joe's supervision the department's production has increased, employee morale has improved, absenteeism has dropped, and for the past two months the department has been beating its standard for the first time in years.

However, a few days ago Lee Nash, an employee in the department, suggested to Joe that the company install a new kind of controls on the department's machines similar to those developed by a competitor. The controls would cost $12,000 installed and would have an eight-year life and no salvage value. They should increase production 10%, reduce maintenance costs $500 per year, and do away with the labour of one man.

Joe's answer to Lee was, "Forget it. We are doing OK now; we don't need the extra production; and besides, jobs are hard to find and if we have to let someone go, who'll it be?"

Do you think standard costs had anything to do with Joe's answer to Lee? Explain. Do you agree with Joe's answer? Should Joe be the person to make a decision such as this? How can a company be sure that suggestions such as Lee's are not lost in the chain of command?

Decision problem 25–2, Ottawa Company

Ottawa Company manufactures Product A for which the demand is seasonal and which cannot be stored for long periods; consequently, the number of units manufactured varies with the season. In accounting for costs, the company charges actual costs incurred to a goods in process account maintained for the product, which it closes at the end of each quarter to Finished Goods. At the end of last year, which was an average year, the following cost report was prepared for the company manager:

OTTAWA COMPANY
Quarterly Report of Costs for Product A
Year Ended December 31, 19—

	1st Quarter	2d Quarter	3d Quarter	4th Quarter
Materials	$ 46,800	$ 54,250	$ 31,400	$ 23,700
Direct labour	140,100	162,400	94,000	70,800
Fixed factory overhead costs	70,000	70,000	70,000	70,000
Variable factory overhead costs	76,800	89,250	51,800	39,000
Total manufacturing costs	$333,700	$375,900	$247,200	$203,500
Production in units	60,000	70,000	40,000	30,000
Cost per unit	$5.56	$5.37	$6.18	$6.78

The manager asked you to explain why unit costs for the product varied from a low of $5.37 in the second quarter to a high of $6.78 in the last quarter, and he asked you to suggest a better way to accumulate or allocate costs. He feels he must have quarterly reports for purposes of control, so attach to your explanation a schedule showing what last year's material, labour, and overhead costs per unit would have been had your suggestion or suggestions been followed for the year.

Decision problem 25–3, York Company

York Company has established the following standard costs for one unit of a product it manufactures, called a whatsit:

Material (1 unit @ $3 per unit)........................... $3
Labour (½ hour @ $4 per hour)............................ 2
Overhead ($2 per standard direct labour hour)....... 1
        Standard cost $6

Machines 101 and 102 are used in manufacturing whatsits. The machines require skill and careful attention in their operation, since it is necessary to stop them during the manufacturing process and to measure and make adjustments in their settings in order to produce a satisfactory product. Furthermore, if the adjustments are not properly made, the material and the product are spoiled. The amount of material budgeted for one unit of product does not include any allowance for spoilage, since the two-whatsits-per-hour production rate allows ample time for making measurements and proper machine adjustments.

Last week Machine 101 was operated by an employee named Ted Lee and Machine 102 was operated by Roy May. Both employees are paid $4 per hour and both worked 40 hours last week. Following are statistics resulting from the operations of their machines:

	Machine 101 (Ted Lee)	Machine 102 (Roy May)
Units started in production.....................................	78	108
Good units completed	75	90
Units spoiled (no salvage value)............................	3	18

Which employee did the better job in operating his machine? Present analyses to back your opinion.

26

Cost-volume-profit analysis

■ Cost-volume-profit analysis is a means of predicting the effect of changes in costs and sales levels on the income of a business. In its simplest form it involves the determination of the sales level at which a company neither earns a profit nor incurs a loss, in other words, the point at which it breaks even. For this reason it is often called break-even analysis. However, the technique can be expanded to answer additional questions, such as: What sales volume is necessary to earn a desired net income? What net income will be earned if unit selling prices are reduced in order to increase sales volume? What net income will be earned if a new machine that will reduce unit labour costs is installed? What net income will be earned if we change the sales mix? When the technique is expanded to answer such additional questions, the descriptive phrase, cost-volume-profit analysis, is more appropriate than break-even analysis.

Cost behaviours ■ Conventional cost-volume-profit analyses require that costs be classified as either fixed or variable. However, when costs are examined, it is recognized that some are definitely fixed in nature, others are recognized to be variable, but still others are neither fixed nor completely variable.

791

Fixed costs

A fixed cost is one that remains the same at all levels of production, for example, rent expense. If the factory building is rented for, say, $1,000 per month, this cost remains the same whether the factory operates on a one-shift, two-shift, or an around-the-clock basis. Likewise, the cost is the same whether 100 units of product are produced in a month, 1,000 units are produced, or any other number up to the full capacity of the plant. However, it should be observed that while fixed costs remain the same in total at any level of production, fixed costs per unit of product decrease as volume increases. For example, if rent is $1,000 per month and two units of product are produced in a month, the rent cost per unit is $500; but if production is increased to 10 units per month, rent cost per unit decreases to $100. Likewise it decreases to $2 per unit if production is increased to 500 units per month.

When production volume is plotted on a graph, units of product are shown on the horizontal axis and dollars of cost are shown on the vertical axis. Fixed costs are then expressed as a horizontal line, since they remain the same in total at all levels of production. This is shown in the Illustration 26–1 graph where the fixed costs remain at $32,000 at all production levels from zero to 2,000 units of product.

Variable costs

A variable cost is one that varies with volume and in the same proportion, for example, the cost of the material that enters into a product. If material costing $20 is required in the production of one unit of product, material costs are $20 if one unit of product is manufactured, $40 if two units are manufactured, $60 if three units are manufactured, and so on up for any number of units. Variable costs appear on a graph as a straight line that climbs up the graph as the production volume increases, as in Illustration 26–1.

Other costs

Costs are not necessarily either fixed or variable. Some costs are semivariable. They go up with volume but not in the same proportion. Other costs go up in steps, for example, supervisory salaries. Supervisory salaries may be more or less fixed for any production volume from zero to the maximum that can be completed on a one-shift basis. Then if an additional shift must be added to increase production, a whole new group of supervisors must be hired and supervisory salaries go up by a lump-sum amount. They then remain fixed at this level until a third shift is added when they go up another lump sum. In addition to semivariable and "stair step" costs, there are costs that are curvilinear (curved line) in nature. They go up with volume, but when plotted on a graph, they must be plotted as a curved line. For example, people who work the second shift in a factory are generally not as productive as

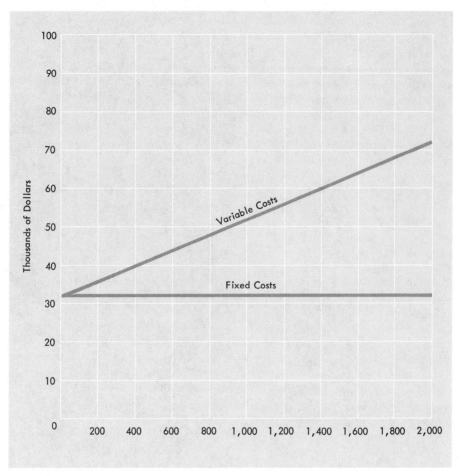

Illustration
26–1

those who work the regular or daytime shift, and people on the third or "graveyard" shift are usually even less productive. Consequently, labour costs will rise more rapidly than volume when such shifts are added. The plotting of curvilinear and "stair step" costs is shown in Illustration 26–2.

Cost as-sumptions ■ Conventional cost-volume-profit analysis is based on relationships that can be expressed as straight lines. The lines are then compared in order to answer the questions to which the analysis is applicable. Consequently, the reliability of the answers secured through application of the technique rests on three basic assumptions, which for any one analysis are:

1. The per unit selling price is constant. (The selling price per unit will remain the same at all production levels.)
2. Variable costs are truly variable.
3. Fixed costs are truly fixed.

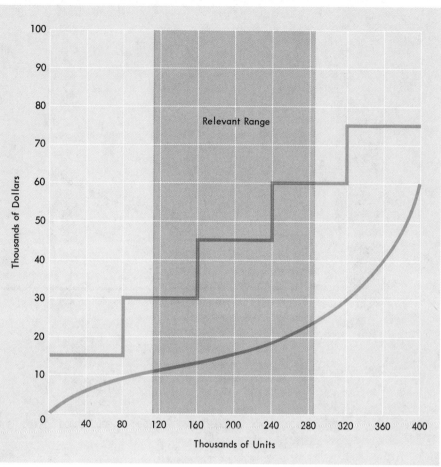

Illustration
26–2

When these assumptions are met, straight lines for costs and revenues result. However, the assumptions do not always reflect actuality, and the further from actuality one or more of the basic assumptions is in a given analysis, the less reliable are the results of the analysis. Nevertheless, two factors tend to make costs behave in straight-line approximations. First, variable costs that are not truly variable tend to offset each other when lumped together; and when lumped together, do approximate a straight line. Second, over the relevant range of operations the assumptions that costs are either fixed or variable and that their relations to volume may be plotted as straight lines are reasonably realistic. Exceptions are easily found, however. (The relevant range of operations, as plotted in Illustration 26–2, is the normal operating range for the business. It excludes the extremely high and low levels which are not apt to be encountered.)

With these exceptions in mind, it must be recognized that cost-volume-profit analysis yields approximate answers to questions concerning the interrelations of costs, volume, and profits. However, if it is recognized that the answers are approximations, cost-volume-profit analysis is a useful managerial tool.

Break-even point ■ A company's break-even point is the sales level at which it neither earns a profit nor incurs a loss. It may be expressed either in units of product or in dollars of sales. To illustrate its calculation, assume that Alpha Company sells for $100 per unit a single product having $70 of variable costs per unit sold. If the fixed costs involved in selling the product are $24,000, the company breaks even on the product as soon as it sells 800 units or as soon as its sales volume reaches $80,000. This break-even point may be determined as follows:

1. Each unit sold at $100 recovers its $70 variable costs and contributes $30 toward the fixed costs.
2. The fixed costs are $24,000; consequently, 800 units ($24,000 ÷ $30 = 800) must be sold to pay the fixed costs.
3. And 800 units at $100 each produce an $80,000 sales volume.

The $30 amount that the sales price of this product exceeds variable costs per unit is its *contribution margin per unit*. In other words, the contribution margin per unit is the amount that the sale of one unit contributes toward recovery of the fixed costs and then toward a profit.

Also, the contribution margin of a product expressed as a percentage of its sales price is its *contribution rate*. For instance, the contribution rate of the $100 product of this illustration is 30% ($30 ÷ $100 = 30%).

And with contribution margin and contribution rate defined, it is possible to set up the following formulas for calculating a break-even point in units and in dollars:

$$\text{Break-Even Point in Units} = \frac{\text{Fixed Costs}}{\text{Contribution Margin}}$$

$$\text{Break-Even Point in Dollars} = \frac{\text{Fixed Costs}}{\text{Contribution Rate}}$$

Application of the second formula to figures for the product of this illustration gives this result:

$$\text{Break-Even Point in Dollars} = \frac{\$24,000}{30\%} = \frac{\$24,000}{0.30} = \$80,000$$

Calculated either way, Alpha Company's break-even point may be proved with an income statement, as in Illustration 26–3. Observe in the illustration that revenue from sales exactly equals the sum of the fixed and variable costs at the break-even point. Recognizing this will prove helpful in understanding the material that follows in this chapter.

Break-even graph ■ A cost-volume-profit analysis may be shown graphically as in Illustration 26–4; and when presented in this form, the graph is commonly called a break-even graph or break-even chart. On such a graph

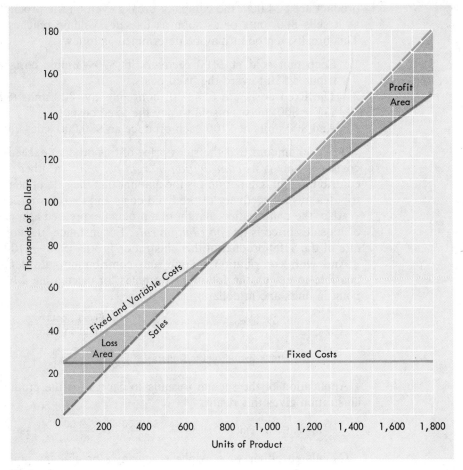

Alpha Company
Income Statement at the Break-Even Point

Sales (800 units @ $100 each)...		$80,000
Costs:		
Fixed costs	$24,000	
Variable costs (800 units @ $70 each)...........................	56,000	80,000
Net Income		$ -0-

Illustration
26–3

Illustration
26–4

the horizontal axis shows units sold, the vertical axis shows both dollars of sales and dollars of costs, and costs and revenues are plotted as straight lines. The illustrated graph shows the break-even point of Alpha Company. A break-even graph is prepared as follows:

1. The line representing fixed costs is plotted at the fixed cost level. Note that it is a horizontal line, since the fixed costs are the same at

all sales levels. Actually, the fixed costs line is not essential to the analysis; however, it contributes important information and is commonly plotted on a break-even chart.

2. Next the sales line is projected from the point of zero units and zero dollars of sales to the point of maximum sales shown on the graph. In choosing the maximum number of units to be shown, a better graph results if the number chosen is such that it will cause the break-even point to fall near the center of the graph.

3. Next the variable cost line is plotted. Note that it begins at the fixed cost level and, as a result, shows total costs at all production levels. At the zero sales level there are no variable costs, only fixed costs. However, at any level above zero sales all the fixed costs are present and so are the variable costs for that level. Consequently, beginning the variable cost line at the fixed cost level makes it show total costs. Also observe that the variable cost line bisects the sales line at the break-even point. It bisects at this point because at the break-even point the revenue from sales exactly equals the sum of the fixed and variable costs, in other words, the total costs.

In reading a break-even chart, the vertical distance between the sales line and the total cost line represents a loss to the left of the break-even point and a profit to the right of it. The amount of profit or loss at any given sales level can be determined from the graph by measuring the vertical distance between the sales line and the total expense line at the given level.

Sales required for a desired net income

■ A slight extension of the concept behind the break-even calculation will produce a formula that may be used in determining the sales level necessary to produce a desired net income. The formula is:

$$\text{Sales at Desired Income Level} = \frac{\text{Fixed Costs} + \text{Net Income} + \text{Income Taxes}}{\text{Contribution Rate}}$$

To illustrate the formula's use, assume that Alpha Company of the previous section, the company having $24,000 of fixed costs and a 30% contribution rate has set a $20,000 after-tax income goal for itself. Assume further that in order to have a $20,000 net income, the company must earn $28,500 and pay $8,500 in income taxes. Under these assumptions, $175,000 of sales are necessary to produce a $20,000 net income. This is calculated as follows:

$$\text{Sales at Desired Income Level} = \frac{\text{Fixed Costs} + \text{Net Income} + \text{Income Taxes}}{\text{Contribution Rate}}$$

$$\text{Sales at Desired Income Level} = \frac{\$24,000 + \$20,000 + \$8,500}{30\%}$$

$$\text{Sales at Desired Income Level} = \frac{\$52,500}{30\%} = \$175,000$$

In the formula just given the contribution rate was used as the divisor and the resulting answer was in dollars of sales. The contribution margin can also be used as the divisor; and when it is, the resulting answer is in units of product.

Margin of safety ■ The difference between a company's current sales and sales at its break-even point, when sales are above the break-even point, is known as its margin of safety. The margin of safety is the amount sales may decrease before a loss is incurred. It may be expressed in units of product, dollars, or as a percentage of sales. For example, if current sales are $100,000 and the break-even point is $80,000, the margin of safety is $20,000 or 20% of sales, calculated as follows:

$$\frac{\text{Sales} - \text{Break-Even Sales}}{\text{Sales}} = \text{Margin of Safety}$$

or

$$\frac{\$100,000 - \$80,000}{\$100,000} = 20\% \text{ Margin of Safety}$$

Income from a given sales level ■ Cost-volume-profit analysis goes beyond break-even analysis and can be used to answer other questions. For example, what income will result from a given sales level? To understand the analysis used in answering this question, recall the factors that enter into the calculation of income. When expressed in equation form, they are:

$$\text{Sales} - (\text{Fixed Costs} + \text{Variable Costs}) = \text{Income}$$

And like any mathematical equation, the factors can be transposed and made to read:

$$\text{Income} = \text{Sales} - (\text{Fixed Costs} + \text{Variable Costs})$$

In its last form the equation may be used to calculate the income that will result at a given sales level. For example, assume that Alpha Company of the previous illustrations wishes to know what income will result if its sales level can be increased to $200,000, which would be 2,000 units of its product at $100 per unit. To determine the answer, recall that the variable costs per unit of this product are $70 and note that the $70 is 0.7 of the product's selling price. Consequently, variable costs for 2,000 units of the product are 0.7 of the selling price of these units or are $140,000 ($200,000 × 0.7 = $140,000). Alpha Company's fixed costs are $24,000. Therefore, if these known factors are substituted in the equation for determining income, the equation will read:

$$\begin{aligned} \text{Income} &= \$200,000 - [\$24,000 + (0.7 \times \$200,000)] \\ \text{Income} &= \$200,000 - \$164,000 \\ \text{Income} &= \$36,000 \end{aligned}$$

The $36,000 is "before-tax" income; and as a result, if Alpha Company wishes to learn its after-tax income from the sale of 2,000 units of its product, it will have to apply the appropriate tax rates to the $36,000.

■ A company may wish to know what would happen to its break-even point if it reduced the selling price of its product in order to increase sales. Or it might wish to know what would happen if it installed a new machine that would increase its fixed costs, but which would reduce variable costs. These are two of several possible questions involving changes in selling prices and costs; and at first glance such changes seem to violate the basic assumptions on which cost-volume-profit analysis is based. However, this is not true. A constant selling price, truly variable costs, and truly fixed costs are assumed to hold for any analysis involving the assumed price and costs. However, changes may be made, and if made, the new price and new costs are assumed to remain constant for the analyses involving that price and those costs. The fact that changes can be made in the factors makes it possible to predict the effect of changes before the changes are actually made.

To illustrate the effect of changes, assume that Alpha Company is considering the installation of a new machine that will increase the fixed costs of producing and selling its product from $24,000 to $30,000. However, the machine will reduce the variable costs from $70 per unit of product to $60. The selling price of the product will remain unchanged at $100, and the company wishes to know its break-even point if the machine is installed. Examination of the costs shows that the installation will not only increase the company's fixed costs, but it will also change the contribution margin and contribution rate of the company's product. The new contribution margin will be $40 ($100 − $60 = $40), and the new contribution rate will be 40% ($40 ÷ $100 = 0.4 or 40%). Consequently, if the machine is installed, the company's new break-even point will be:

$$\text{Break-Even Point in Dollars} = \frac{\$30,000}{0.4} = \$75,000$$

In addition to their use in determining Alpha Company's break-even point, the new fixed costs and the new contribution rate may be used to determine the sales level needed to earn a desired net income, or to determine the expected income at a given sales level, or to answer other questions the company will want to answer before installing the new machine.

■ The break-even point for a company selling a number of products can be determined by using a hypothetical unit made up of units of each of the company's products in their expected sales mix. Such a hypothetical unit is really a composite unit and is treated in all analyses as though it were a single product. To illustrate the use of such a hypothetical unit, assume that Beta Company sells three products, A, B, and C, and it wishes to calculate its break-even point. Unit selling prices for the three products are: Product A, $5; Product B, $8 and Product C, $4. The sales mix or ratio in which the products are sold is 4:2:1, and the company's fixed costs are $48,000. Under these assumptions a composite unit selling price for the three products can be calculated as follows:

```
4 units of Product A   @   $5 per unit = $20
2 units of Product B   @   $8 per unit =  16
1 unit  of Product C   @   $4 per unit =   4
      Selling price of a composite unit   $40
```

Also, if the variable costs of selling the three products are Product A, $3.25; Product B, $4.50; and Product C, $2, the variable costs of a composite unit of the products are:

```
4 units of Product A   @   $3.25 per unit = $13
2 units of Product B   @   $4.50 per unit =   9
1 unit  of Product C   @   $2.00 per unit =   2
      Variable costs of a composite unit    $24
```

With the variable costs and selling price of a composite unit of the company's products calculated, the contribution margin for a composite unit may be determined by subtracting the variable costs of a composite unit from the selling price of such a unit, as follows:

$$\$40 \;-\; \$24 \;=\; \$16 \text{ Contribution Margin per Composite Unit}$$

The $16 contribution margin may then be used to determine the company's break-even point in composite units. The break-even point is:

$$\text{Break-Even Point in Composite Units} \;=\; \frac{\text{Fixed Costs}}{\text{Composite Contribution Margin}}$$

$$\text{Break-Even Point in Composite Units} \;=\; \frac{\$48,000}{\$16}$$

$$\text{Break-Even Point} \;=\; 3,000 \text{ composite units}$$

The company breaks even when it sells 3,000 composite units of its products. However, to determine the number of units of each product it must sell to break even, the number of units of each product in the composite unit must be multiplied by the number of composite units needed to break even, as follows:

```
Product A:   4 × 3,000 = 12,000 units
Product B:   2 × 3,000 =  6,000 units
Product C:   1 × 3,000 =  3,000 units
```

The accuracy of all these computations can be proved by preparing an income statement showing the company's revenues and costs at the break-even point. Such a statement is shown in Illustration 26–5.

A composite unit made up of units of each of a company's products in their expected sales mix may be used in answering cost-volume-profit questions in addition to the break-even point. In making all such analyses it is assumed that the product mix remains constant at all sales

Beta Company
Income Statement at the Break-Even Point

Sales:
Product A (12,000 units @ $5)		$ 60,000
Product B (6,000 units @ $8).............................		48,000
Product C (3,000 units @ $4).............................		12,000
Total revenue...		$120,000
Costs:		
Fixed costs...	$48,000	
Variable costs:		
Product A (12,000 units @ $3.25) $39,000		
Product B (6,000 units @ $4.50)........................ 27,000		
Product C (3,000 units @ $2.00)........................ 6,000		
Total variable costs	72,000	
Total costs..		120,000
Net Income...		$ -0-

Illustration
26–5

levels just as the other factors entering into an analysis are assumed to be constant. Nevertheless, this does not prevent changes in the assumed sales mix in order to learn what would happen if the mix were changed. However, problems involving changes in the sales mix require a recomputation of the composite unit selling price and composite unit variable costs for each change in the mix.

Evaluating the results ■ Cost-volume-profit analyses have their greatest use in predicting what will happen when changes are made in selling prices, product mix, and the various cost factors. However, in evaluating the results of such analyses, several points should be borne in mind. First, the analyses are used to predict future results. Therefore, the data put into the formulas and on the graphs are assumed or forecasted data. Consequently, the results of the analyses are no more reliable than the data used. Second, cost-volume-profit analyses as presented here are based on the assumption that in any one analysis selling price will remain constant, fixed costs are truly fixed, and variable costs are truly variable. This assumption does not always reflect reality. Therefore, at best the answers obtained through cost-volume-profit analyses are approximations. However, if this is recognized, cost-volume-profit analyses can be useful to management in making decisions.

The cost-volume-profit analyses presented in this chapter are based on the assumption that revenues and costs may be expressed as straight lines; and as pointed out, such an assumption does not always hold. Therefore, it should be noted that cost-volume-profit analyses based on curvilinear relationships are also possible. However, the use of curvilinear relationships takes some rather sophisticated mathematics, and a discussion is deferred to a more advanced text.

1. For what is cost-volume-profit analysis used?
2. What is a fixed cost? Name two fixed costs.
3. When there are fixed costs in manufacturing a product and the number of units manufactured is increased, do fixed costs per unit increase or decrease? Why?
4. What is a variable cost? Name two variable costs.
5. What is a semivariable cost?
6. What two factors tend to make it possible to classify costs as either fixed or variable.
7. What is the break-even point in the sale of a product?
8. A company sells a product for $80 per unit. The variable costs of producing and selling the product are $52 per unit. What is the product's contribution margin per unit? What is its contribution rate?
9. If the variable cost line is begun at the fixed cost level on a break-even graph, what does the line show?
10. When a break-even graph is prepared, why are the fixed costs plotted as a horizontal line?
11. What is a company's margin of safety?
12. When we speak of a company's sales mix, what is meant by sales mix?

Exercise 26–1

Alpha Company manufactures Product A which it sells for $75 per unit. The variable costs of manufacturing the product are $60 per unit, and the annual fixed costs incurred in manufacturing it are $35,640. Calculate the product's (1) contribution margin, (2) its contribution rate, (3) the break-even point for the product in units, and (4) the break-even point in dollars of sales.

Exercise 26–2

Prepare an income statement for Alpha Company's Product A (Exercise 26–1), showing sales, fixed costs, and variable costs at the break-even point.

Exercise 26–3

Assume that Alpha Company of Exercise 26–1 wishes to earn a $30,000 annual after-tax income from the sale of its Product A and that it must pay 50% of its income in income taxes. Calculate (1) the number of units of its Product A it must sell to earn a $30,000 after-tax income from the sale of the product. (2) Calculate the number of dollars of sales of Product A that are needed to earn a $30,000 after-tax income.

Exercise 26–4

The sales manager of Alpha Company (Exercise 26–1) thinks that within two years annual sales of the company's Product A will reach 8,000 units at $75 each. Calculate the company's (1) before-tax income from the sale of these units and (2) calculate its after-tax income from the sale of the units.

Exercise 26–5

Beta Company markets Products A and B which it sells in the ratio of five units of Product A at $2 each to each three units of Product B at $6 each. The variable costs of marketing Product A are $1.68 per unit, and the variable costs for Product B are $4.20 per unit. The annual fixed costs for marketing both products are $14,000. Calculate (1) the selling price of a composite unit of these products, (2) the variable costs per composite unit, (3) the break-even point in composite units, and (4) the number of units of each product that will be sold at the break-even point.

Problems   **Problem 26–1**

Zeppo Company manufactures a number of products, one of which, Product Z, sells for $400 per unit. The fixed costs of manufacturing Product Z are $62,400, and the variable costs are $280 per unit.

Required:
1. Calculate the company's break-even point in the sale of Product Z *(a)* in units and *(b)* in dollars of sales.
2. Prepare a break-even graph for Product Z. Use 1,000 as the maximum number of units on your graph.
3. Prepare an income statement showing sales, fixed costs, and variable costs for Product Z at the break-even point.
4. Determine the sales volume in dollars that the company must achieve to earn a $45,000 after-tax (50% rate) income from the sale of Product Z.
5. Determine the after-tax income the company will earn from a $600,000 sales level for Product Z.

Problem 26–2

Bongo Company buys its Product B in bulk and packages it for resale. Last year the company earned an unsatisfactory after-tax return from the sale of 20,000 packages of Product B at $5 per package. Last year's costs for the product were:

Fixed costs $38,500
Variable costs:
    Bulk Product B (sufficient for 20,000 packages)................ 55,000
    Packaging materials and other variable packaging costs...... 5,000
Income tax rate... 50%

The sales manager believes that if the selling price of the product is reduced 10% and a slight change is made in its packaging, the number of units sold will double. The packaging change will increase variable packaging costs 25% per unit, but doubling the units sold will gain a 5% reduction in the product's bulk price. The packaging and volume changes will not affect fixed costs.

Required:
1. Calculate the dollar break-even points for the product at the $5 sales price and at the $4.50 sales price.

2. Prepare a break-even graph for the sale of the product at each price. Use 40,000 as the maximum number of units on both graphs.
3. Prepare a condensed comparative income statement showing the results of selling the product at $5 per unit and the estimated results of selling it at $4.50 per unit.

Problem 26–3

Zest Company manufactured and sold 5,000 units of its Product Z last year with the following unsatisfactory results:

Sales...		$100,000
Costs:		
Fixed...	$22,000	
Variable	80,000	102,000
Loss from the Sale of Product Z..................		$ (2,000)

An investigation shows that if the company will install a new machine it can save sufficient piece-rate labour and spoiled materials to reduce the variable costs of manufacturing Product Z by 15%. The new machine will increase fixed costs $2,320 annually.

Required:
1. Calculate last year's break-even point for Product Z in dollars and in units.
2. Calculate the break-even point in dollars and in units under the assumption the new machine is installed.
3. Prepare a break-even graph for Product Z under the assumption the new machine is installed. Use 8,000 as the maximum number of units on your graph.
4. Prepare an income statement showing expected annual results from the sale of Product Z with the new machine installed, no change in selling price, and no change in the number of units sold. Assume a 50% income tax rate.
5. Calculate the sales level required to earn a $12,000 annual after-tax income from the sale of Product Z with no change in its selling price and the new machine installed. Prepare an income statement showing the results from the sale of Product Z at this level.

Problem 26–4

Mesa Company sells a number of products, among which are Products X and Y. Last year the company sold 10,000 units of each of these products at $100 per unit, earning $100,000 from the sale of each as the following condensed income statement shows:

	Product X	Product Y
Sales...	$1,000,000	$1,000,000
Costs:		
Fixed costs	$ 200,000	$ 600,000
Variable costs....................................	600,000	200,000
Total costs..	$ 800,000	$ 800,000
Income before taxes	$ 200,000	$ 200,000
Income taxes (50% rate).........................	100,000	100,000
Net Income..	$ 100,000	$ 100,000

Required:

1. Calculate the break-even point for each product in dollars.
2. Prepare a break-even graph for each product. Use 10,000 as the maximum number of units on each graph.
3. Prepare a condensed income statement showing in separate columns the net income the company will earn from the sale of each product under the assumption that without a change in selling prices, the number of units of each product sold declines 25%.
4. Prepare a second condensed income statement showing in separate columns the net income the company will earn if the number of units of each product sold increases 25% without a change in selling prices.

Problem 26–5

Best Company manufactures and sells three products, A, B, and C. Product A sells for $15 per unit, Product B sells for $10 per unit, and Product C sells for $8 per unit. Their sales mix is in the ratio of 4:2:5, and the variable costs of manufacturing and selling the products have been: Product A, $10; Product B, $6.50; and Product C, $5. The fixed costs of manufacturing and selling the three products are $151,200. Material X has been used in manufacturing both Products A and C; however, a new material has just come on the market, and if it is substituted for Material X, it will reduce the variable cost of manufacturing Product A by $1 and Product C by $0.40.

Required:

1. Determine the company's break-even point in dollars and the number of units of each product sold at the break-even point under the assumption Material X is used in manufacturing Products A and C. Show all pertinent calculations.
2. Determine the company's break-even point in dollars and the number of units of each product sold at the break-even point under the assumption the new material is used in manufacturing Products A and C. Show all pertinent calculations.

Alternate problems

Problem 26–1A

Among the products sold by Nash Company is Product N, which sells for $450 per unit. The fixed costs of selling Product N are $85,500, and the variable costs are $270 per unit.

Required:

1. Calculate the company's break-even point in the sale of Product N *(a)* in units and *(b)* in dollars of sales.
2. Prepare a break-even graph for Product N, using 1,000 as the maximum number of units on the graph.
3. Prepare an income statement showing sales, fixed costs, and variable costs for Product N at the break-even point.
4. Determine the sales volume in dollars required to achieve a $40,000 after-tax (50% rate) income from the sale of Product N.
5. Determine the after-tax income the company will earn from a $500,000 sales level for Product N.

Problem 26–2A

Last year Gale Company sold 40,000 units of its product at $5 per unit with the following results:

Sales		$200,000
Costs:		
Fixed	$60,000	
Variable:		
Material X (40,000 lbs. @ $2 per lb.)	80,000	
Other variable	40,000	180,000
Income before taxes		$ 20,000

A new material, Material Y, has recently come on the market; and if substituted for the Material X presently used in the product, material costs can be reduced from $2 per unit to $1 per unit. The substitution will have no effect on the product's quality; but it will give Gale Company a choice in pricing the product. (1) The company can maintain the present per unit price, sell the same number of units, and make a $1 per unit greater profit. Or (2) it can reduce the product's price $1 per unit, an amount equal to the material savings, and because of the lower price, increase the units sold by 40%. If the latter choice is made, the $60,000 of fixed costs will remain fixed and the "other variable" costs will vary with volume.

Required:
1. Calculate the break-even point in dollars for each alternative.
2. Prepare a break-even graph for each alternative. The company's capacity is 60,000 units, and this should be used as the upper limit on the graphs.
3. Prepare a comparative income statement showing sales, fixed costs, variable costs, and after-tax (50% rate) net income for each alternative.

Problem 26–3A

Last year Surf Company earned an unsatisfactory $2,610 after-tax income from the sale of 25,000 packages of its Product S at $4 each. The company buys Product S in bulk and packages it for resale. Following is condensed income statement information showing last year's results from the sale of the product:

Sales		$100,000
Bulk cost of Product S	$50,000	
Packaging material and other variable packing costs	10,000	
Fixed costs	34,780	94,780
Income before taxes		$ 5,220
Income taxes (50% rate)		2,610
Net Income from Sale of Product S		$ 2,610

It has been suggested that if the company will invest $5,000 in advertising and make a small change in the packaging of Product S, sales will increase 60%. The packaging change will increase variable packaging costs 10% per unit but will not affect other fixed and variable costs.

Required:

1. Calculate last year's break-even point for Product S in dollars.
2. Calculate the break-even point in dollars under the assumption the $5,000 is spent for advertising and the packaging change is made.
3. Prepare a break-even graph under the assumptions of Part 2. Use 50,000 as the maximum number of units on the graph.
4. Prepare an income statement showing the expected results under the assumption the $5,000 is spent for advertising, the packaging change is made, and sales increase by 60%.
5. Assume that instead of increasing 60% with the advertising and packaging change, sales increased to 50,000 units at $4 per unit. *(a)* Present calculations that show the amount of after-tax income that will be earned at this level. *(b)* Prepare an income statement showing sales, costs, and net income at this $200,000 sales level.

Problem 26–5A

West Company manufactures and sells Products X, Y, and Z in the ratio of three units of Product X to two units of Product Y to four units of Product Z. Product X sells for $10 per unit, Product Y sells for $6 per unit, and Product Z sells for $2 per unit. The variable costs of manufacturing and selling the products have been: Product X, $6; Product Y, $4; and Product Z, $1.50; and the fixed costs incurred in manufacturing and selling the three products are $126,000.

Material M has been used in manufacturing Products Y and Z; however, a new material has just come on the market, and if substituted for Material M, it will reduce the variable costs of Product Y by $0.50 per unit and Product Z by $0.25 per unit.

Required:

1. Determine the company's break-even point in dollars and the number of units of each product sold at the break-even point when Material M is used in manufacturing Products Y and Z. Show all pertinent calculations.
2. Determine the company's break-even point in dollars and the number of units of each product sold at the break-even point under the assumption the new material is substituted in manufacturing Products Y and Z. Show all pertinent calculations.

Decision problem 26–1, Simcoe Company

Simcoe Company operated at near capacity last year, producing and selling 200,000 gallons of its product with the following results:

Sales			$500,000
Manufacturing costs:			
Fixed	$100,000		
Variable	200,000	$300,000	
Selling and general expenses:			
Fixed	$ 70,000		
Variable	50,000	120,000	420,000
Income before taxes			$ 80,000

The company has an opportunity to enter into a five-year contract for the annual sale of 150,000 gallons of the product in the export market at $1.90 per gallon, FOB factory. Delivery on the contract would require a plant addition that would increase fixed manufacturing costs by 75% annually. The contract would not increase the totals of present fixed and variable selling and general expenses. Variable manufacturing costs would vary with volume.

Management is not certain it should enter into the contract, and it has asked you for your opinion, including the following:

1.   An estimated income statement for the first year following the plant addition, assuming no change in domestic sales.
2.   A comparison of break-even sales levels before the plant addition and after the contract expiration. Assume after-contract sales and expense levels, other than fixed manufacturing costs, will be at the same levels as last year.
3.   A statement showing net income after the contract expiration but at sales and expense levels of last year, other than fixed manufacturing costs.

Decision problem 26–2, Tri-Products Company

Tri-Products Company manufactures and sells Products A, B, and C. Last year's sales mix for the three products was in the ratio of 5:4:1, with combined sales totaling 10,000 units. Product A sells for $100 per unit and has a 20% contribution rate, Product B sells for $80 per unit and has a 30% contribution rate, and Product C sells for $60 per unit and has a 40% contribution rate. The fixed costs of manufacturing and selling the products total $139,000. The company estimates that sales of the three products will continue at the 10,000 unit level next year. However, the sales manager is of the opinion that if the company's advertising and sales efforts are slanted further toward Products B and C during the coming year, with no increases in the amounts of money expended, the sales mix of the three products can be changed to the ratio of 3:5:2.

Should the company change its sales mix through advertising and sales efforts? What effect will the change have on the composite contribution rate of the three products? What effect will it have on the company's break-even point? Back your answers with figures.

Decision problem 26–3, Calgary Company

Calgary Company earned $75,000 before taxes in 197A, and its income statement provided the following summarized information:

Sales		$600,000
Costs:		
Variable costs............................	$300,000	
Fixed costs................................	225,000	525,000
Income before taxes.........................		$ 75,000

The company operated at near capacity during 197A, and a 10% annual increase in the demand for its product is expected. As a result the company's management is trying to decide how to meet this demand. Two alternatives are being considered. The first calls for changes that will increase variable costs to 55% of the selling price of the company's product but will not change fixed costs. The second calls for a capital investment that will increase fixed costs 10% but will not affect variable costs.

Which alternative do you recommend? Back your recommendation with income statement information and any other data you consider relevant.

Analytical and review problem

Problem 26–1 A&R

While on vacation Miss McKenna, president of McKenna Works, took in a seminar on "Reporting to Top Management." One of the seminars was on the use of P/V charts which Miss McKenna thought would have applicability to her firm.

Upon returning, Miss McKenna summoned the controller, Mr. Pollice, to her office, told him of the seminar and asked for a report on how soon such a reporting procedure could be implemented at McKenna Works. The next day a memorandum arrived accompanied by a break-even chart (reproduced below) based on standard budgeted costs and representative of the cost breakdown, and the cost-volume-profit relationship under the current selling price and cost structure.

The president studied the chart and filed it away for reference at month-end.

On April 3, on arrival at work, the president found the March Income State-

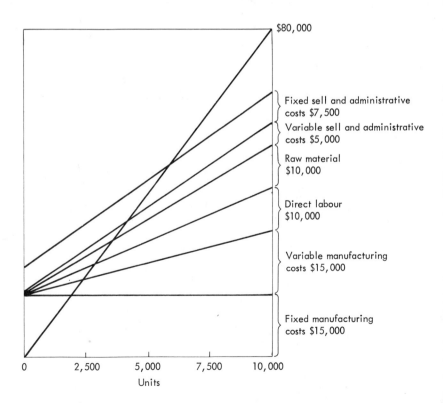

ment on her desk (reproduced below). It was not long before Mr. Pollice was on the carpet trying to explain the apparent discrepancy between the income statement and the break-even chart.

MCKENNA WORKS LIMITED
Income Statement
For the Month Ending March 31, 1976

Sales 7,000 units @ $8		$56,000
Cost of Sales at standard $5		35,000
		$21,000
Selling and Administrative Costs		11,000
"Normal" net income		$10,000
Variances:*		
Material price and usage .... $500 cr.		
Labour rate and efficiency .... 300 dr.		
Budget variance... 800 cr.		1,000
		$11,000

* The company uses standard absorption costing.

Miss McKenna was heard saying. "I don't know what kind of accounting you are practicing—I can't understand how when the break-even chart indicates that at 7,000 unit sales volume net income should be $5,500 and you show in the income statement an amount that is double—you expect me to have confidence in your reporting? You had better go back to your office and examine your figures and come back with an explanation—and it had better be good, short, ($\frac{1}{2}$ page) and to the point."

Required:

As Mr. Pollice's assistant he has asked you to prepare the report to reconcile the income statement and break-even chart net incomes.

27

Capital budgeting; managerial decisions

■ A business decision involves choosing between two or more courses of action, with the best choice normally being the one offering the highest return on the investment or the greatest cost savings. Business managers at times make such decisions intuitively and without trying to measure systematically the advantages and disadvantages of each possible choice. Often they make intuitive decisions because they are unaware of any other way to choose; but sometimes the available information is so sketchy or unreliable that systematic measurement is useless. Also, intangible factors such as convenience, prestige, and public opinion are at times more important than the factors that can be reduced to a quantitative basis. Nevertheless, in many situations it is possible to reduce the anticipated consequences of alternative choices to a quantitative basis and measure them systematically. This chapter will examine several.

Capital budgeting ■ Planning plant asset investments is called *capital budgeting*. The plans may involve new buildings, new machinery, or whole new projects; but in every case the objective is to earn a satisfactory return on the invested funds; and to accomplish this often requires some of the most crucial and difficult decisions faced by management. The decisions are difficult because they are commonly based on estimates projected well into a future that is at best uncertain; and they are crucial because (1) large sums of money are often involved; (2) funds are committed for long periods of time; and (3) once a decision is made and a project is begun, it may be difficult or impossible to reverse the effects of a poor decision.

Capital budgeting involves the preparation of cost and revenue estimates for all proposed projects, an examination of the merits of each, and a choice of those worthy of investment. It is a broad field, and this text must limit its discussion to three ways of comparing investment opportunities. They are the *payback period*, the *return on average investment*, and *discounted cash flows*.

Payback period

Generally an investment in a machine or other plant asset will produce a *net cash flow*, and the payback period for the investment is the time required to recover the investment through this net cash flow. For example, assume that Murray Company is considering several capital investments, among which is the purchase of a machine to be used in manufacturing a new product. The machine will cost $16,000, have an eight-year service life, and no salvage value. The company estimates that 10,000 units of the machine's product will be sold each year, and the sales will result in $1,500 of after-tax net income, calculated as follows:

Annual sales of new product...		$30,000
Deduct:		
Cost of materials, labour, and overhead other than depreciation on the new machine......................................	$15,500	
Depreciation on the new machine	2,000	
Additional selling and administrative expenses	9,500	27,000
Annual before-tax income...		$ 3,000
Income tax (assumed rate, 50%)..		1,500
Annual after-tax net income from new product sales..................		$ 1,500

Through annual sales of 10,000 units of the new product, Murray Company expects to gain $30,000 of revenue and $1,500 of net income. The net income will be available to pay back the new machine's cost; but in addition, since none of the funds that flow in from sales flow out for depreciation, so will the amount of the annual depreciation charge. The $1,500 of net income and the $2,000 depreciation charge total $3,500, and together are the *annual net cash flow* expected from the investment. Furthermore, this annual net cash flow will pay back the investment in the new machine in 4.6 years, calculated as follows:

$$\frac{\text{Cost of New Machine, \$16,000}}{\text{Annual Net Cash Flow, \$3,500}} = 4.6 \text{ Years to Recover Investment}$$

The answer just given is 4.6 years. Actually, when $16,000 is divided by $3,500, the result is just a little over 4.57; but 4.6 years is close enough for a decision. Remember that the calculation is based on estimated net income and estimated depreciation; consequently, it is pointless to carry the answer to several decimal places.

In choosing investment opportunities, a short payback period is a desirable factor because (1) the sooner an investment is recovered the sooner the funds are available for other uses and (2) a short payback period also means a short "bail-out period" if conditions should change. However, the payback period should never be the only factor considered, because it ignores the length of time revenue will continue to be earned after the end of the payback period. For example, one investment may pay back its cost in three years and cease to produce revenue at that point, while a second investment may require five years to pay back its cost but will continue to produce income for another 15 years.

Rate of return on average investment

The rate of return on the average investment in a machine is calculated by dividing the after-tax net income from the sale of the machine's product by the average investment in the machine. For example, Murray Company estimates it will earn a $1,500 after-tax net income from selling the product of the $16,000 machine it proposes to buy. As to average investment, each year depreciation will reduce the book value of the machine $2,000, and the company will recover this amount of its investment through the sale of the machine's product. Consequently, the company may assume it will have $16,000 invested in the machine during its first year, $14,000 during the second, $12,000 during the third, and so on for the machine's eight-year life. Or, in other words, the company may assume it will have an amount equal to the machine's book value invested each year. If it makes this assumption, then the average amount it will have invested during the eight-year life is the average of the machine's book values. This is $9,000 and may be calculated as follows:

Year	Beginning of the Year Book Value		
1.........................	$16,000		
2.........................	14,000		
3.........................	12,000		
4.........................	10,000	$\dfrac{\$72,000}{8}$	= $9,000 Average Book Value and Average Investment
5.........................	8,000		
6.........................	6,000		
7.........................	4,000		
8.........................	2,000		
Total......................	$72,000		

In the illustrated calculation the eight yearly book values were averaged to determine average investment. A shorter way to the same answer is to average the book values of the machine's first and last years in this manner:

$$\frac{\$16,000 + \$2,000}{2} = \$9,000$$

And since the answer is the same either way the calculation is made, the shorter calculation is preferable.

After average investment is determined, the rate of return on average investment is calculated, as previously stated, by dividing the estimated annual after-tax net income from the sale of the machine's product by average investment, as follows:

$$\$1,500 \div \$9,000 = 16\tfrac{2}{3}\% \text{ Return on Average Investment}$$

At this point students commonly want to know if $16\tfrac{2}{3}\%$ is a good investment return. The answer is that it is better than, say, 12%, but not as good as 18%; or in other words, a return is good or bad only when related to other returns. Also, factors other than return, such as risk, are always involved in investment decisions. However, when average investment returns are used in comparing and deciding between capital investments, the one having the least risk, the shortest payback period, and the highest return for the longest time is usually the best.

Rate of return on average investment is easy to calculate and understand, and as a result has long been used in selecting investment opportunities. Furthermore, when the opportunities produce uniform cash flows, it offers a fair basis for selection. However, a comparison of *discounted cash flows* with amounts to be invested offers a better means of selection.

An understanding of discounted cash flows requires an understanding of the concept of present value. This concept is explained in the Appendix, and the explanation should be reviewed at this point by any student who does not fully understand it.

Discounted cash flows

When a business invests in a new plant asset, it expects to secure from the investment a stream of future cash flows, and normally it will not invest unless the flows are sufficient to return the amount of the investment plus a satisfactory return on the investment. For example, will the cash flows from the investment in the machine being considered by Murray Company return the amount of the investment plus a satisfactory return? If Murray Company considers a 10% compound annual return a satisfactory return on its capital investments, it can answer this question with the calculations of Illustration 27–1.

To secure the machine of Illustration 27–1, Murray Company must invest $16,000. However, from the sale of the machine's product it will recapture $2,000 of its investment each year in the form of depreciation; and in addition it will earn a $1,500 annual net income. Or in other words, the company will receive a $3,500 net cash flow from the invest-

Analysis of Proposed Investment in Machine

Years Hence	Net Cash Flows	Present Value of $1 at 10%	Present Value of Net Cash Flows
1	$3,500	0.909	$ 3,181.50
2	3,500	0.826	2,891.00
3	3,500	0.751	2,628.50
4	3,500	0.683	2,390.50
5	3,500	0.621	2,173.50
6	3,500	0.565	1,977.50
7	3,500	0.513	1,795.50
8	3,500	0.467	1,634.50

Total present value............................... $18,672.50
Amount to be invested........................... 16,000.00
Positive Net Present Value..................... $ 2,672.50

Illustration
27–1

ment each year for eight years. These net cash flows, shown in the second column of Illustration 27–1, are multiplied by the amounts in the third column to determine their present values, which are shown in the last column. Observe that the total of these present values exceeds the amount of the required investment by $2,672.50. Consequently, if Murray Company considers a 10% compound return satisfactory, this machine will recover its required investment, plus a 10% compound return, and $2,672.50 in addition.

Generally, when the cash flows from an investment such as this, discounted at a satisfactory rate, have a present value in excess of the investment, the investment is a good one and is worthy of acceptance. Also, when several investment opportunities of the same size and risk are being compared, the one having the highest positive net present value is the best.

Shortening the calculation

In Illustration 27–1 the present values of $1 at 10% for each of the eight years involved are shown, and it is assumed that each year's cash flow is multiplied by the present value of $1 at 10% for that year to determine its present value. The present values of the eight cash flows are then added to determine their total, which is one way to determine total present value. However, since in this case the cash flows are uniform, there are two shorter ways. One shorter way is to add the eight yearly present values of $1 at 10% and to multiply $3,500 by the total. Another even shorter way is based on Table 2 in the Appendix. Table 2 shows the present value of $1 to be received periodically for a number of periods. In the case of the Murray Company machine, $3,500 is to be received annually for eight years. Consequently, to determine the present value of these annual receipts discounted at 10%, go down the 10% column of Table 2 to the amount opposite eight periods. It is 5.335.

Therefore, the present value of the eight annual $3,500 receipts is $3,500 multiplied by 5.335 or is $18,672.50.

Cash flows not uniform

Present value analysis has its greatest usefulness when cash flows are not uniform. For example, assume a company can choose one capital investment from among Projects A, B, and C. Each requires a $12,000 investment and will produce cash flows as follows:

Years Hence	Annual Cash Flows		
	Project A	Project B	Project C
1	$ 5,000	$ 8,000	$ 1,000
2	5,000	5,000	5,000
3	5,000	2,000	9,000
	$15,000	$15,000	$15,000

Note that all three projects produce the same total cash flow. However, the flows of Project A are uniform, those of Project B are greater in the earlier years, while those of Project C are greater in the later years. Consequently, when present values of the cash flows, discounted at 10%, are compared with the required investments, the statistics of Illustration 27–2 result.

	Years Hence	Present Values of Cash Flows Discounted at 10%		
		Project A	Project B	Project C
	1	$ 4,545	$ 7,272	$ 909
	2	4,130	4,130	4,130
	3	3,755	1,502	6,759
Total present values...........		$12,430	$12,904	$11,798
Required investments.........		12,000	12,000	12,000
Net Present Values		+$ 430	+$ 904	−$ 202

Illustration 27–2

Note that an investment in Project A has a $430 positive net present value, an investment in Project B a $904 positive net present value, and an investment in Project C a $202 negative net present value. Therefore, if a 10% return is required, an investment in Project C should be rejected, since the investment's net present value indicates it will not earn such a return. Furthermore, as between Projects A and B, other things being equal, Project B is the better investment, since its cash flows have the higher net present value.

Salvage value and accelerated depreciation

The $16,000 machine of the Murray Company example was assumed to have no salvage value at the end of its useful life. Often a machine is expected to have a salvage value, and in such cases the expected salvage value is treated as an additional cash flow to be received in the last year of the machine's life.

Also, in the Murray Company example, depreciation was deducted on a straight-line basis; but in actual practice, an accelerated depreciation method, such as the declining-balance method, is commonly used for tax purposes. Accelerated depreciation results in larger depreciation deductions in the early years of an asset's life and smaller deductions in the later years, which in turn result in smaller income tax liabilities in the early years and larger ones in later years. However, this does not change the basic nature of a present value analysis. It only results in larger cash flows in the early years and smaller ones in later years, which in turn normally make an investment more desirable.

Selecting the earnings rate

The selection of a satisfactory earnings rate for capital investments is always a matter for top-management decision. Formulas have been devised to aid management; but in many companies the choice of a satisfactory or required rate of return is largely subjective. Management simply decides that enough investment opportunities can be found that will earn, say, a 10% compound return, and this becomes the minimum below which the company refuses to make an investment of average risk.

Whatever the required rate, it is always higher than the rate at which money can be borrowed, since the return on a capital investment must include not only interest but also an additional allowance for risks involved. Therefore, when the rate at which money can be borrowed is around 6%, a required after-tax return of 10% compounded may be acceptable in industrial companies, with a lower rate for public utilities and a higher rate for companies in which investment opportunities are unusually good or the risks are high.

Replacing plant assets

In our dynamic economy, new and better machines are constantly coming on the market. As a result the decision to replace an existing machine with a new and better machine is common. Often the existing machine is in good condition and will produce the required product; but the new machine will do the job with a large savings in operating costs. In such a situation management must decide whether the after-tax savings in operating costs justifies the investment.

The amount of after-tax savings from the replacement of an existing machine with a new machine is complicated by the fact that depreciation on the new machine for tax purposes is based on the book value of the old machine plus the cash given in the exchange. There can be other complications too; consequently, a discussion of the replacement of plant assets is deferred to a more advanced course.

Accepting additional business

■ Costs obtained from a cost accounting system are average costs and also historical costs. They are useful in product pricing and in controlling operations, but in a decision to accept an additional volume of business they are not necessarily the relevant costs. In such a decision the relevant costs are the additional costs, commonly called the *incremental* or *differential costs*.

For example, a concern operating at its normal capacity, which is 80% of full capacity, has annually produced and sold approximately 100,000 units of product with the following results:

Sales (100,000 units @ $10)		$1,000,000
Materials (100,000 units @ $3.50)	$350,000	
Labour (100,000 units @ $2.20)	220,000	
Overhead (100,000 units @ $1.10)	110,000	
Selling expenses (100,000 units @ $1.40)	140,000	
Administrative expenses (100,000 units @ $0.80)	80,000	900,000
Operating income		$ 100,000

The concern's sales department reports it has an exporter who has offered to buy 10,000 units of product at $8.50 per unit. The sale to the exporter is several times larger than any previous sale made by the company; and since the units are being exported, the new business will have no effect on present business. Therefore, in order to determine whether the order should be accepted or rejected, management of the company ask that statistics be prepared to show the estimated net income or loss that would result from accepting the offer. It received the following figures based on the average costs previously given:

Sales (10,000 units @ $8.50)		$85,000
Materials (10,000 units @ $3.50)	$35,000	
Labour (10,000 units @ $2.20)	22,000	
Overhead (10,000 units @ $1.10)	11,000	
Selling expenses (10,000 units @ $1.40)	14,000	
Administrative expenses (10,000 units @ $0.80)	8,000	90,000
Operating Loss		$ (5,000)

If a decision were based on these average costs, the new business would likely be rejected. However, in this situation average costs are not relevant. The relevant costs are the added costs of accepting the new business. Consequently, before rejecting the order, the costs of the new business were examined more closely and the following additional information obtained: (1) Manufacturing 10,000 additional units of product would require materials and labour at $3.50 and $2.20 per unit just as with normal production. (2) However, the 10,000 units could be manufactured with overhead costs in addition to those already incurred of only $5,000 for power, packing, and handling labour. (3) Commissions and other selling expenses resulting from the sale would amount to $2,000 in addition to the selling expenses already incurred. And (4) $1,000 additional administrative expenses in the form of clerical work would be required if the order were accepted. Based on this added information, the statement of Illustration 27–3 showing the effect of the additional business on the company's normal business was prepared.

	Present Business	Additional Business	Present Plus the Additional Business
Sales............................	$1,000,000	$85,000	$1,085,000
Materials	$350,000	$35,000	$385,000
Labour..........................	220,000	22,000	242,000
Overhead......................	110,000	5,000	115,000
Selling expenses	140,000	2,000	142,000
Administrative expense	80,000	1,000	81,000
Total	900,000	65,000	965,000
Operating Income...	$ 100,000	$20,000	$ 120,000

Illustration
27–3

It is obvious from Illustration 27–3 that when present business is charged with all present costs and the additional business is charged only with its incremental or differential costs, accepting the additional business at $8.50 per unit will apparently result in $20,000 additional income before taxes.

Incremental or differential costs always apply to a particular situation at a particular time. For example, adding units to a given production volume might or might not increase depreciation expense. If the additional units require the purchase of more machines, depreciation expense is increased. Likewise, if present machines are used but the additional units shorten their life, more depreciation expense results. However, if present machines are used and their depreciation depends more on the passage of time or obsolescence rather than on use, additional depreciation expense might not result from the added units of product.

Buy or make ■ Incremental or differential costs are often a factor in a decision as to whether a given part or product should be bought or made. For example, a manufacturer has idle machines upon which he can make Part 417 of his product. This part is presently purchased at a $1.20 delivered cost per unit. The manufacturer estimates that to make Part 417 would cost $0.45 for materials, $0.50 for labour, and an amount of overhead. At this point a question arises as to how much overhead should be charged. If the normal overhead rate of the department in which the part would be manufactured is 100% of direct labour cost, and this amount is charged against Part 417, then the unit costs of making Part 417 would be $0.45 for materials, $0.50 for labour, and $0.50 for overhead, a total of $1.45. At this cost, the manufacturer would be better off to buy the part at $1.20 each.

However, on a short-run basis the manufacturer might be justified in ignoring the normal overhead rate and in charging Part 417 for only the added overhead costs resulting from its manufacture. Among these added overhead costs might be, for example, power to operate the machines that would otherwise be idle, depreciation on the machines if the part's manufacture resulted in additional depreciation, and any other overhead that would be added to that already incurred. Furthermore, if these added overhead items total less than $0.25 per unit, the manufacturer might be justified on a short-run basis in manufacturing the part. However, on a long-term basis, Part 417 should be charged a full share of all overhead.

Any amount of overhead less than $0.25 per unit results in a total cost for Part 417 that is less than the $1.20 per unit purchase price. Nevertheless, in making a final decision as to whether the part should be bought or made, the manufacturer should consider in addition to costs such things as quality, the reactions of customers and suppliers, and other intangible factors. When these additional factors are considered, small cost differences may become a minor factor.

Other costs
■ *Sunk costs, out-of-pocket costs,* and *opportunity costs* are additional costs encountered in managerial decisions.

A sunk cost is a cost resulting from a past irrevocable decision, and is sunk in the sense that it cannot be avoided. As a result, sunk costs are irrelevant in decisions affecting the future.

An out-of-pocket cost is a cost requiring a current outlay of funds. Material costs, supplies, heat, and power are examples. Generally, out-of-pocket costs can be avoided; consequently, they are relevant in decisions affecting the future.

Costs as discussed thus far have been outlays or expenditures made to obtain some benefit, usually goods or services. However, the concept of costs can be expanded to include *sacrifices made to gain some benefit.* For example, if a job that will pay a student $1,200 for working during the summer must be rejected in order to attend summer school, the $1,200 is an opportunity cost of attending summer school.

Obviously, opportunity costs are not costs in the accounting sense of the term and they are not entered in the accounting records; but they may be relevant in a decision involving rejected opportunities, such as in a decision to scrap or rebuild defective units of product, where both sunk and opportunity costs are commonly encountered.

■ Any costs incurred in manufacturing units of product that do not pass inspection are sunk costs and as such should not enter into a decision as to whether the units should be sold for scrap or be rebuilt to pass inspection. For example, a concern has 10,000 defective units of product that cost $1 per unit to manufacture. The units can be sold as they are for $0.40 each, or they can be rebuilt for $0.80 per unit, after which they can be sold for their full price of $1.50 per unit. Should the company rebuild the units or should it sell them in their present form? Obviously, the original manufacturing costs of $1 per unit are sunk costs and are irrelevant in the decision; so based on the information given, the comparative returns from scrapping or rebuilding are:

	As Scrap	Rebuilt
Sale of defective units	$4,000	$15,000
Less cost to rebuild		(8,000)
Net Return	$4,000	$ 7,000

From the information given, it appears that rebuilding is the better decision, and this is true if the rebuilding does not interfere with normal operations. However, suppose that to rebuild the defective units the company must forgo manufacturing 10,000 new units that will cost $1 per unit to manufacture and can be sold for $1.50 per unit. In this situation the comparative returns may be analyzed as follows:

	As Scrap	Rebuilt
Sale of defective units	$ 4,000	$15,000
Less cost to rebuild the defective units		(8,000)
Sale of new units	15,000	
Less cost to manufacture the new units	(10,000)	
Net Return	$ 9,000	$ 7,000

If the defective units are sold without rebuilding, then the new units can also be manufactured and sold, with a $9,000 return from the sale of both the new and old units, as shown in the first column of the analysis. Obviously this is better than forgoing the manufacture of the new units and rebuilding the defective units for a $7,000 net return.

The situation described here also may be analyzed on an opportunity cost basis as follows: If to rebuild the defective units the company must forgo manufacturing the new units, then the return on the sale of the new units is an opportunity cost of rebuilding the defective units. This opportunity cost is measured at $5,000 (revenue from sale of new units, $15,000, less their manufacturing costs, $10,000, equals the $5,000 benefit that will be sacrificed if the old units are rebuilt); and an opportunity cost analysis of the situation is as follows:

	As Scrap	Rebuilt
Sale of defective units	$4,000	$15,000
Less cost to rebuild the defective units		(8,000)
Less opportunity cost (return sacrificed by not manufacturing the new units)		(5,000)
Net Return	$4,000	$ 2,000

Observe that it does not matter whether this or the previous analysis is made, since either way there is a $2,000 difference in favour of scrapping the defective units.

Process or sell ■ Sunk costs, out-of-pocket costs, and opportunity costs are also encountered in a decision as to whether it is best to sell an intermediate product as it is or process it further and sell the product or products that result from the additional processing. For example, a company has 40,000 units of Product A that cost $0.75 per unit or a total of $30,000 to manufacture. The 40,000 units can be sold as they are for $50,000 or they can be processed further into Products X, Y, and Z at a cost of $2 per original Product A unit. The additional processing will produce the following numbers of each product, which can be sold at the unit prices indicated:

Product X	10,000 units @ $3
Product Y	22,000 units @ $5
Product Z	6,000 units @ $1
Lost through spoilage	2,000 units (no salvage value)
Total	40,000 units

The net advantage of processing the product further is $16,000, as shown in Illustration 27–4.

Revenue from further processing:		
Product X, 10,000 units @ $3	$ 30,000	
Product Y, 22,000 units @ $5	110,000	
Product Z, 6,000 units @ $1	6,000	
Total revenue		$146,000
Less:		
Additional processing costs, 40,000 units @ $2	$ 80,000	
Opportunity cost (revenue sacrificed by not selling the Product A units)	50,000	
Total		130,000
Net advantage of further processing		$ 16,000

Illustration 27–4

Note that the revenue available through the sale of the Product A units is an opportunity cost of further processing these units. Also notice that the $30,000 cost of manufacturing the 40,000 units of Product A does not appear in the Illustration 27–4 analysis. This cost is present regardless of which alternative is chosen; therefore it is irrelevant to the decision. However, the $30,000 does enter into a calculation of the net income from the alternatives. For example, if the company chooses to further process the Product A units, the gross return from the sale of Products X, Y, and Z may be calculated as follows:

Revenue from the sale of Products X, Y, and Z		$146,000
Less:		
Cost to manufacture the Product A units.............................	$30,000	
Cost to further process the Product A units.........................	80,000	110,000
Gross return from the sale of Products X, Y, and Z..................		$ 36,000

Deciding the sales mix ■ When a company sells a combination of products, ordinarily some of the products are more profitable than others, and normally management should concentrate its sales efforts on the more profitable products. However, if production facilities or other factors are limited, an increase in the production and sale of one product may require a reduction in the production and sale of another. In such a situation management's job is to determine the most profitable combination or sales mix for the products and concentrate its efforts in selling the products in this combination.

To determine the best sales mix for its products, management must have information as to the contribution margin of each product, the facilities required to produce and sell each product, and any limitations on these facilities. For example, assume that a company produces and sells two products, A and B. The same machines are used to produce both products, and the products have the following selling prices and variable costs per unit:

	Product A	Product B
Selling price...	$5.00	$7.50
Variable manufacturing costs.......................	3.50	5.50
Contribution margin.....................................	$1.50	$2.00

If the amount of production facilities required to produce each product is the same and there is an unlimited market for Product B, the company should devote all its facilities to Product B because of its larger contribution margin. However, if the company's facilities are limited to, say, 100,000 machine-hours of production per month and one machine-hour is required to produce each unit of Product A but two machine-hours are required for each unit of Product B, the answer differs. Under these circumstances, if the market for Product A is unlimited, the company should devote all its production to this product because it produces $1.50 of contribution margin per machine-hour, while Product B produces only $1 per machine-hour.

Actually, when there are no market or other limitations, a company should devote all its efforts to its most profitable product. It is only when there is a market or other limitation on the sale of the most profitable product that a need for a sales mix arises. For example, if in this instance one machine-hour of production facilities are needed to produce each unit of Product A and 100,000 machine-hours are available, 100,000 units of the product can be produced. However, if only 80,000 units can be sold, the company has 20,000 machine-hours that can be devoted to the production of Product B, and 20,000 machine-hours will produce 10,000 units of Product B. Consequently, the company's most profitable sales mix under these assumptions is 80,000 units of Product A and 10,000 units of Product B.

The assumptions in this section have been kept simple. More complicated factors and combinations of factors exist. However, a discussion of these is deferred to a more advanced course.

Questions for class discussion

1. What is capital budgeting? Why are capital budgeting decisions crucial to the business concern making the decisions?
2. A successful investment in a machine will produce a net cash flow. Of what does this consist?
3. If depreciation is an expense, explain why, when the sale of a machine's product produces a net income, the portion of the machine's cost recovered each year through the sale of its product includes both the net income from the product's sale and the year's depreciation on the machine.
4. Why is a short payback period on an investment desirable?
5. What is the average amount invested in a machine during its life if the machine cost $28,000, has an estimated five-year life, and an estimated $3,000 salvage value?
6. Is a 15% return on the average investment in a machine a good return?
7. Why is the present value of the expectation of receiving $100 a year hence less than $100? What is the present value of the expectation of receiving $100 one year hence, discounted at 12%?
8. What is indicated when the present value of the net cash flows from an investment in a machine, discounted at 12%, exceeds the amount of the investment? What is indicated when the present value of the net cash flows, discounted at 12%, is less than the amount of the investment?
9. What are the incremental costs of accepting an additional volume of business?
10. A company manufactures and sells 250,000 units of product in this country at $5 per unit. The product costs $3 per unit to manufacture. Can you describe a situation under which the company may be willing to sell an additional 25,000 units of the product abroad at $2.75 per unit?
11. What is a sunk cost? An out-of-pocket cost? An opportunity cost? Is an opportunity cost a cost in the accounting sense of the term?
12. Any costs that have been incurred in manufacturing a product are sunk costs. Why are such costs irrelevant in deciding whether to sell the product in its present condition or to make it into a new product through additional processing?

Exercise 27-1

Machine A cost $12,000 and has an estimated five-year life and no salvage value. Machine B cost $12,000 and has an estimated five-year life and a $2,000 salvage value. Under the assumption that the average investment in each machine is the average of its yearly book values, calculate the average investment in each machine.

Exercise 27-2

A company is planning to buy a new machine and produce a new product. The machine will cost $16,000, have a four-year life, and no salvage value, and will be depreciated on a straight-line basis. The company expects to sell 2,000 units of the machine's product each year with these results:

Sales		$60,000
Costs:		
Materials, labour, and overhead excluding depreciation on the new machine	$32,000	
Depreciation on the new machine	4,000	
Selling and administrative expenses	20,000	56,000
Income before taxes		$ 4,000
Income taxes		2,000
Net Income..		$ 2,000

Required:
Calculate (1) the payback period and (2) the return on the average investment in this machine.

Exercise 27-3

Under the assumption that due to the high risk involved, the company of Exercise 27-2 demands a 14% compound return from capital investments such as that described in Exercise 27-2, determine the total present value and net present value of the net cash flows, discounted at 14%, from the machine it plans to buy.

Exercise 27-4

A company can invest in each of three projects, A, B, and C. Each project requires a $10,000 investment and will produce cash flows as follows:

Years	Annual Cash Flows		
Hence	Project A	Project B	Project C
1	$ 4,000	$ 6,000	$ 2,000
2	4,000	4,000	4,000
3	4,000	2,000	6,000
	$12,000	$12,000	$12,000

Required:

Under the assumption the company requires a 10% compound return from its investments, determine in which of the projects it should invest.

Exercise 27–5

A company has 10,000 units of Product X that cost $1 per unit to manufacture. The 10,000 units can be sold for $15,000, or they can be further processed at a cost of $7,000 into Products Y and Z. The additional processing will produce 4,000 units of Product Y that can be sold for $2 each and 6,000 units of Product Z that can be sold for $2.25 each.

Required:

Prepare an analysis to show whether the Product X units should be further processed.

Problems

Problem 27–1

A company that sells a number of products is planning to add a new one to its line. It estimates it can sell 40,000 units of the new product annually at $5 per unit, but to manufacture the product will require new machinery costing $50,000 and having a five-year life and no salvage value. The new product will have a $2 per unit direct material cost and a $1 per unit direct labour cost. Manufacturing overhead chargeable to the new product, other than for depreciation on the new machinery, will be $25,000 annually; and $35,000 of additional selling and administrative expenses will be incurred annually in selling the product. The company's income tax rate is 50%.

Required:

Using straight-line depreciation, calculate (1) the payback period on the investment in new machinery, (2) the rate of return on the average investment, and (3) the net present value of the net cash flows discounted at 14%.

Problem 27–2

A company can invest in either of two projects, A or B. With straight-line depreciation, the projects will produce the following estimated annual results:

	Project A		Project B	
Sales..		$140,000		$150,000
Costs:				
Materials $35,000			$38,000	
Labour 28,000			32,000	
Manufacturing overhead including depreciation on new machinery...................... 40,000			42,000	
Selling and administrative expenses............................. 29,000		132,000	30,000	142,000
Income before taxes		$ 8,000		$ 8,000
Income taxes.............................		4,000		4,000
Net Income...............................		$ 4,000		$ 4,000

Project A will require a $50,000 investment in new machinery that will have a six-year life and a $2,000 salvage value. Project B will require a $50,000 investment in new machinery that will have a five-year life and no salvage value.

Required:
Calculate the payback period, the return on average investment, and the net present value of the net cash flows from each project discounted at 12%. State which project you think is the better investment and why.

Problem 27–3

A company is considering a $90,000 investment in machinery to produce a new product. The machinery is expected to have a five-year life and no salvage value, and sales of its product are expected to produce $34,000 of income before depreciation and income taxes. Since income taxes take 50% of the company's income, with depreciation calculated on a straight-line basis, this means an $8,000 annual after-tax income, calculated as follows:

Income before depreciation and income taxes............	$34,000
Depreciation ($90,000 ÷ 5 years)...........................	18,000
Income before taxes...	$16,000
Income taxes...	8,000
Net Income from Sale of Product...........................	$ 8,000

The company demands a 12% compound return on such investments, and its controller has calculated that the $90,000 investment will earn such a return. However, in presenting his figures to the company president, he pointed out that the desirability of the investment could be increased by depreciating the machinery on a declining-balance basis. The president wanted to know why an accounting method would improve the desirability of an investment in machinery.

Required:
1. Calculate the company's net income from the sale of the new product for each of the five years with depreciation calculated by the declining-balance method. (Use double the straight-line rate.)
2. With the machinery depreciated on a straight-line basis, calculate the net present value of the net cash flows discounted at 12%.
3. With the machinery depreciated on a declining-balance basis, calculate the net present value of the net cash flows discounted at 12%.
4. Explain why declining-balance depreciation improves the desirability of this investment.

Problem 27–4

Southwest Company annually manufactures and sells 10,000 units of one of its products at $25 per unit. The units cost $22.50 each to manufacture and sell, and in producing and selling the 10,000 units the company has the following costs and expenses:

Fixed costs and expenses:
Manufacturing overhead............................ $60,000
Selling expenses 15,000
Administrative expenses 25,000

Variable costs and expenses:
Materials ($3 per unit).............................. $30,000
Direct labour ($5 per unit)......................... 50,000
Manufacturing overhead ($2 per unit)........... 20,000
Selling expenses ($1.50 per unit) 15,000
Administrative expenses ($1 per unit)........... 10,000

An exporter has offered to buy 2,000 units of the product at $17.50 each to be sold abroad. The new business will not affect the company's present sales, its fixed costs and expenses, nor any of its per unit variable costs and expenses.

Required:
Prepare an income statement showing (1) in one set of columns the revenue, costs, expenses, and income before taxes from present business; (2) in a second set of columns the revenue, costs, expenses, and income before taxes from the sales to the exporter; and (3) in a third set of columns the combined results of both kinds of sales.

Problem 27–5

Last year Verde Company manufactured and sold 1,000 units of a machine called a dodad with the following results:

Sales (1,000 units @ $200)............................		$200,000
Costs and expenses:		
Variable:		
Materials...	$40,000	
Labour..	50,000	
Factory overhead...................................	30,000	
Selling and administrative expenses............	10,000	
Fixed:		
Factory overhead...................................	30,000	
Selling and administrative expenses............	20,000	180,000
Income before taxes.....................................		$ 20,000

A federal agency has asked for bids on 100 dodads almost identical to Verde Company's machine, the only difference being an extra part not presently installed on the Verde Company dodad. To install the extra part would require the purchase of a new machine costing $1,000, plus $1 per unit for additional material and $2 per unit for additional labour. The new machine would have no further use after the completion of the government contract, but it could be sold for $300. Sale of the additional units would not affect the company's fixed costs and expenses, but all variable costs and expenses, including variable selling and administrative expenses, would vary with volume.

Required:
1. List with their total the unit costs of the material, labour, and et cetera that would enter into the lowest unit price the company could bid on the special order without causing a reduction in income from normal business.
2. Under the assumption the company bid $170 per unit and was awarded the contract for the 100 special units, prepare an income statement showing (1) in one set of columns the revenues, costs, expenses, and income before taxes from present business; (2) in a second set of columns the revenue, costs, expenses, and income before taxes from the new business; and (3) in a third set of columns the combined results of both the old and new business.

Alternate Problems

Problem 27–1A

Multi-Products Company is considering a $60,000 investment in new machinery to produce a new product. The machinery will have a five-year life and no salvage value, and this additional information is available:

Estimated sales of new product...	$140,000
Estimated costs:	
Materials...	25,000
Labour...	40,000
Overhead excluding depreciation on new machinery...................	33,000
Selling and administrative expenses	20,000
Income taxes	50%

Required:
Using straight-line depreciation, calculate (1) the payback period on the investment in new machinery, (2) the rate of return on the average investment, and (3) the net present value of the net cash flows discounted at 12%.

Problem 27–2A

Alpha Company is considering an investment in one of two projects. Project One requires a $72,000 investment in new machinery having a six-year life and no salvage value. Project Two requires a $74,000 investment in new machinery having a five-year life and a $4,000 salvage value. The products of the projects differ; however, each will produce an estimated $6,000 after-tax net income for the life of the project.

Required:
Calculate the payback period, the return on average investment, and the net present value of the net cash flows from each project discounted at 12%. State which project you think is the better investment and why.

Problem 27–3A

Beta Company is considering a project that requires a $65,000 investment in machinery having a five-year life and a $5,000 salvage value. The project will annually produce $24,000 of income before depreciation on the new machinery and income taxes. The company's income taxes take 50% of its before-tax income; consequently, with depreciation calculated on a straight-line basis, the project will produce a $6.000 annual after-tax income calculated as follows:

Income before depreciation and income taxes............	$24,000
Depreciation [($65,000 − $5,000) ÷ 5]	12,000
Income before taxes...	$12,000
Income taxes	6,000
Net Income from the Project................................	$ 6,000

The company refuses to invest in a project that will not earn at least a 12% compound return, and it has been determined that this project will earn such a return. However, it has been pointed out that if the company will depreciate the machinery of the project on a declining-balance basis, the compound return from the investment can be materially increased.

Required:
1. Calculate the company's net income from the project for each of the five years with depreciation calculated on a declining-balance basis at double the straight-line rate.
2. With the machinery depreciated on a straight-line basis, calculate the net present value of the net cash flows discounted at 12%.
3. With the machinery depreciated on a declining-balance basis, calculate the net present value of the net cash flows discounted at 12%.
4. Explain why declining-balance depreciation increases the desirability of this investment.

Problem 27–4A

Jumbo Company manufactures and sells in this country a number of products, one of which is a machine that sells for $15 per unit. During a normal year the company manufactures and sells 10,000 units of this machine with these results:

Sales...		$150,000
Costs:		
Materials	$28,000	
Direct labour.....................................	30,000	
Manufacturing overhead.......................	20,000	
Selling expenses.................................	22,000	
Administrative expenses.......................	25,000	125,000
Income before taxes		$ 25,000

An exporter has offered to buy 1,000 of the machines at $11.50 each for sale abroad, but since the price is below normal cost, the company president does not think the offer should be accepted. However, an examination of a normal year's costs and their relation to the new business shows: (1) Material costs are 100% variable. (2) One third of the direct labour on the additional machines could be done during regular hours with additional employees at regular wage rates, but two thirds would have to be done at overtime rates 50% above regular rates. (3) Of a normal year's manufacturing overhead, one half remains fixed at any production level from zero to 12,000 units and one half varies with volume. (4) There would be no additional selling expenses resulting from the new business. (5) Accepting the new business would increase administrative expenses $1,200.

Required:

Prepare a comparative income statement showing in one set of columns the sales, costs, and income before taxes from normal business, in a second set of columns the sales, costs, and income from the new business, and in the third set of columns the combined results of both the old and new business.

Problem 27-5A

Duo Company's sales and costs for its two products last year were:

	Product A	*Product B*
Unit selling price	$20	$10
Variable costs per unit	$5	$5
Fixed costs	$100,000	$50,000
Units sold	10,000	20,000

Through sales effort the company can change its sales mix. However, sales of the two products are so interrelated that a percentage increase in the sales of one product causes an equal percentage decrease in the sales of the other, and vice versa.

Required:

1. State which of its products the company should push, and why.
2. Prepare a columnar statement showing last year's sales, fixed costs, variable costs, and income before taxes for Product A in the first pair of columns, the results for Product B in the second set of columns, and the combined results for both products in the third set of columns.
3. Prepare a like statement for the two products under the assumption that the sales of Product A are increased 20%, with a resulting 20% decrease in the sales of Product B.
4. Prepare a third statement under the assumption that the sales of Product A are decreased 20%, with a resulting 20% increase in the sales of Product B.

Decision problem 27-1, Huron Paper Company

Huron Paper Company operates a number of paper mills, one of which is in Sudbury. The Sudbury mill was once a profitable operation, but its plant and equipment are getting old and the immediate area no longer produces sufficient pulp logs to supply the mill's needs. Consequently, logs are being hauled from greater and greater distances, with a resulting increase in their cost, and the mill is now just breaking even.

Construction of a new mill is under consideration, to be located in an area with an ample supply of pulp, good water, and low-cost hydroelectric power. However, demand for the company's product is not sufficient to keep both the old and new mills in operation; therefore, if the new mill is built, the old mill will have to be abandoned.

The company's directors have asked you to analyze the situation and recommend whether or not the old mill should be abandoned and the new mill built. The following information is available:

LOSS FROM ABANDONING THE SUDBURY MILL. The land, buildings, and machinery of the Sudbury mill have a $3,700,000 book value. Very little of the machinery can be moved to the new mill. Most will have to be scrapped. Therefore, if the mill is abandoned, it is estimated that only $500,000 of the investment in the mill can be recovered through the sale of its land and buildings, the sale of scrap, and by moving some of its machinery to the new mill. The remaining $3,200,000 will be lost.

COST OF THE NEW MILL. The new mill will cost $10,000,000 and will have an estimated 20-year life. It will double the present 100,000-ton capacity of the Sudbury mill, and it is estimated the 200,000 tons of product produced in the new mill can be sold without a price reduction.

COMPARATIVE PRODUCTION COSTS. A comparison of the production costs per ton at the old mill with the estimated costs at the new mill shows the following:

	Old Mill	New Mill
Raw materials, labour, and plant expenses (exclusive of depreciation)	$65.00	$55.50
Depreciation	4.00	2.50
Total Costs per Ton	$69.00	$58.00

The higher per ton depreciation charge at the old mill results primarily from depreciation being allocated to fewer units of product.

Prepare a report analyzing the advantages and disadvantages of the move, including your recommendations. You may assume that sufficient pulp logs are available for the Sudbury mill to continue in operation long enough to recover the mill's full cost. However, due to the mill's high costs, operation will be at the break-even point. Present any pertinent analyses based on the data given.

Decision problem 27–2, Essex Company

Essex Company has operated for a number of years selling an average of 50,000 units of its product annually at $15 per unit. Its costs at this sales level are:

Direct materials	$250,000
Direct labour	150,000
Manufacturing overhead:	
Variable	60,000
Fixed	40,000
Selling and administrative expenses:	
Variable	50,000
Fixed	110,000
Income taxes	50%

At a 50,000-unit level the company does not utilize all of its plant capacity, but management thinks that by further processing the product, it can do so. If the product is further processed, it can be sold for $16.50 per unit. Further processing will increase fixed manufacturing overhead by $5,000 annually, and it will increase variable manufacturing costs per unit as follows:

Materials	$0.30
Direct labour	0.40
Variable manufacturing overhead	0.20
Total	$0.90

Selling the further processed product will not affect fixed selling and administrative expenses, but it will increase variable selling and administrative expenses 10%. Further processing is not expected to either increase or decrease the number of units sold.

Should the company further process the product? Back your opinion with a simple calculation and also a comparative income statement showing present results and the estimated results with the product further processed.

Decision problem 27–3, Norfolk Company

Norfolk Company sells an average of 50,000 units of its Product 2XY each year and earns a $1 per unit after-tax (50% rate) net income on each unit sold. The company assembles the product from components, some of which it buys and some of which it manufactures. One of the components is a gauge that the company manufactures on special equipment that has a $25,000 book value, a five-year remaining life, and is depreciated at the rate of $5,000 per year. The variable costs of manufacturing the gauge are:

Direct materials	$1.15
Direct labour	1.00
Variable overhead	0.25
Total variable costs	$2.40

The gauge can be purchased from a supplier at a $2.66 per unit delivered cost. If it is purchased, the special equipment used to manufacture it can be sold for cash at its book value (no profit or loss) and the cash can be invested in other projects that will pay a 10% compound after-tax return, which is the return the company demands on all its capital investments.

Should the company continue to manufacture the gauge, or should it sell the special equipment and buy the gauge? Back your answer with explanations and computations.

Analytical and review problem

Problem 27–1 A&R

Five investment opportunities of equal cost offer the following cash flow patterns:

Year	A	B	C	D	E
1	1,000	3,000	2,500	2,000	4.000
2	1,000	3,000	2,500	2,000	4,000
3	1,000	3,000	2,500	2,000	4.000
4	1.000	3,000	2,500	2,000	4,000
5	1,000	3,000	2,500	2,000	4,000
6	4,000	2,000	2,500	3,000	1,000
7	4,000	2,000	2,500	3,000	1,000
8	4,000	2,000	2,500	3,000	1,000
9	4,000	2,000	2,500	3,000	1,000
10	4,000	2,000	2,500	3,000	1,000
Total	$25,000	$25,000	$25,000	$25,000	$25,000

Rank the five alternatives in terms of desirability and give justification for your ranking.

28

Tax
considerations
in
business decisions

■ Not too many years ago, when tax rates were low, management could afford to ignore or dismiss as of minor importance the tax effects of a business decision; but today, when about half the income of a business must commonly be paid out in income taxes, this is no longer wise. Today, a successful management must constantly be alert to every possible tax savings, recognizing that it is often necessary to earn two "pre-tax dollars" in order to keep one "after-tax dollar," or that a dollar of income tax saved is commonly worth a two-dollar reduction in any other expense.

Tax planning ■ When a taxpayer plans his affairs in such a way as to incur the smallest possible tax liability, he is engaged in tax planning. Tax planning requires the application of tax laws to the alternate ways in which every transaction may be completed, and a choice in each case of the way that will result in the smallest tax liability.

Normally tax planning requires that a tax-saving opportunity be recognized at the time it arises. This is because although it is sometimes possible to take advantage of a previously overlooked tax saving, the common result of an overlooked opportunity is a lost opportunity.

Since effective tax planning requires an extensive knowledge of both tax laws and business procedures, it is not the purpose of this chapter to make expert tax planners of elementary accounting students. Rather, the purpose is to make students aware of the merits of effective tax planning, recognizing that for complete and effective planning, the average student, businessman, or citizen should seek the advice of a public accountant, tax consultant, or other qualified person.

Tax evasion and tax avoidance ■ In any discussion of taxes a clear distinction should be drawn between tax evasion and tax avoidance. Tax evasion is illegal and may result in heavy penalties; but tax avoidance is a perfectly legal and profitable activity.

Taxes are avoided by preventing a tax liability from coming into existence. This may be accomplished by any legal means, for example, by the way in which a transaction is completed, or the manner in which a business is organized, or by a wise selection from among the options provided in the Income Tax Act. It makes no difference how, so long as the means is legal and it prevents a tax liability from arising.

In contrast, tax evasion involves the fraudulent denial and concealment of an existing tax liability. For example, taxes are evaded when taxable income, such as interest, dividends, tips, fees, or profits from the sale of stocks, bonds, and other assets, is unreported. Taxes are also evaded when items not legally deductible from income are deducted. For example, taxes are evaded when the costs of operating the family automobile are deducted as a business expense, or when charitable contributions not allowed or not made are deducted. Insofar as this text is concerned, tax evasion is illegal and should be scrupulously avoided.

Provincial income taxes ■ All provinces levy income taxes. The provinces are free to impose whatever tax they choose, but to have the tax collected by the federal government, the provincial tax must be expressed as a percentage of the federal tax. Combined income tax rates, equal to the federal rates plus minimum provincial rates, are used throughout this chapter. Some provinces levy income taxes at rates higher than the minimums used in calculating the combined rates. However, other than noting the existence of provincial tax laws and that they increase the total tax burden and make tax planning even more important, the following discussion is limited to the federal income tax.

History and objectives of the federal income tax ■ The history of today's federal income tax legislation dates to 1917, when the Income War Tax Act was passed. This Act, with numerous amendments, remained in effect until the Income Tax Act of 1948 became law in 1949. Widespread recognition of defects in the income tax system led, in 1962, to the appointment of the Royal Commission on Taxation. The Commission's report was published in 1967 and made serious criticism of the existing law and proposed some fundamental changes.

The need for general reform was made clear and in 1969 the Government of Canada placed before Parliament, the Canadian people, and the provincial governments its major proposals for reform of the income tax structure. After considerable debate, on June 30, 1971, a Tax Reform Bill was presented to Parliament to replace the 1948 Act as of January, 1972. The 1972 Act with numerous amendments remains in effect today.

The original purpose of the federal income tax was to raise revenue, but over the years this original goal has been expanded to include the following and other nonrevenue objectives:

1. To achieve a fair distribution of the tax burden based upon ability to pay.
2. To promote steady economic growth and continuing prosperity.
3. To recognize modern social needs.
4. To interfere as little as possible with incentives to work and invest.
5. To promote investment in the economy in the direction that meets the demands of consumers and foreign markets.
6. To spur economic ventures that involve exceptional risks and promise exceptional rewards.
7. To promote widespread understanding of and voluntary compliance with tax laws, combined with enough detail to block opportunities for abuse.
8. To adopt a tax system that can and will be used by the provinces as well as Canada.

Also, just as the objectives have expanded over the years, so have the rates and the number of people required to pay taxes. In 1917 the minimum rate was 4% and maximum for individuals was 29%. This contrasts with the 1975 minimum (federal and provincial) 12% rate for individuals and maximum of nearly 67%. Likewise, the total number of tax returns filed has grown from a few thousand in 1917 to well over 8,000,000 last year.

Synopsis of
the federal
income tax

■ The following brief synopsis of the federal income tax is given at this point because it is necessary to know something about the federal income tax in order to appreciate its effect on business decisions.

Classes of taxpayers

Federal income tax law recognizes three classes of taxpayers: individuals, corporations, and trusts. Members of each class must file returns and pay taxes on taxable income.

A business operated as a single proprietorship or partnership is not treated as a separate taxable entity under the law. Rather, a single proprietor must report the income from his business on his individual return; and each partner in a partnership is required to include his share of partnership net income on his individual return. In other words, the income of a single proprietorship or partnership, whether withdrawn from the business or not, is taxed as the individual income of the single proprietor or partners.

The treatment given corporations under the law is different, however. A business operated as a corporation must file a return and pay taxes on its taxable income. Also, if a corporation pays out in dividends some or all of its "after-tax income," its stockholders must report these dividends as income on their individual returns. Because of this, it is commonly claimed that corporation income is taxed twice, once to the corporation and again to its stockholders.

The individual income tax

The amount of income tax an individual must pay each year depends upon his gross income, deductions, exemptions, and tax credits; and it is calculated as in Illustration 28–1.

Several items as outlined in Illustration 28–1 require additional explanation, for example:

GROSS INCOME. Income tax law defines gross income as *all income from whatever source derived, unless expressly excluded by law.* Gross income, therefore, includes income from operating a business, which is defined as "the profit therefrom for the year," and is the same as net income determined by the application of generally accepted accounting principles, unless a departure from such principles is provided by law. One important departure is for capital cost allowance deductions as explained later in this chapter. Gross income also includes gains from property sales, dividends, interest, rents, royalties, and compensation for services, such as salaries, wages, fees, commissions, bonuses, and tips. Actually, the answers to two questions are all that is required to determine whether an item should be included or excluded. The two questions are: (1) Is the item income? (2) Is it expressly excluded by law? If an item is income and not specifically excluded, it must be included.

Certain items are recognized as not being income, for example, gifts, inheritances, and in most cases the proceeds of life insurance policies paid upon the death of the insured. These are not income and are excluded. Other items such as the first $500 of fellowships, scholarships, and bursaries are specifically excluded. Also excluded are the gain on the sale of the taxpayer's principal residence, gains from gambling, windfall gains, and certain gains on the sale of personal property.

DEDUCTIONS TO ARRIVE AT NET INCOME. The nature of allowable deductions from gross income fall into three classifications:

1. Deductions which are a postponement of current period income to future periods. These include: Canada or Quebec pension plan contributions, registered pension plan contributions, and registered retirement savings plan contributions.

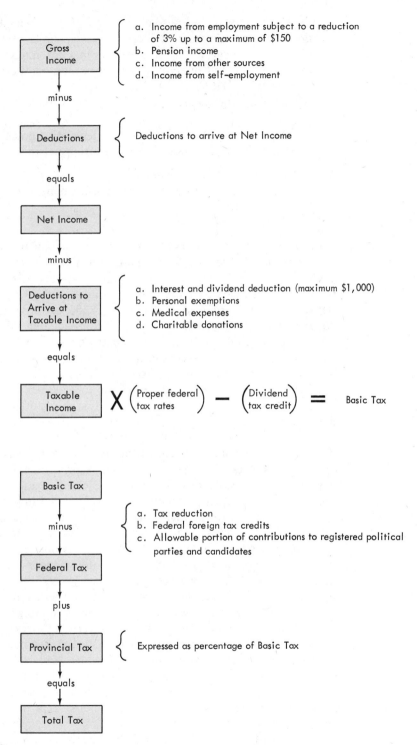

Gross Income

a. Income from employment subject to a reduction of 3% up to a maximum of $150
b. Pension income
c. Income from other sources
d. Income from self-employment

minus

Deductions

Deductions to arrive at Net Income

equals

Net Income

minus

Deductions to Arrive at Taxable Income

a. Interest and dividend deduction (maximum $1,000)
b. Personal exemptions
c. Medical expenses
d. Charitable donations

equals

Taxable Income

$$\text{Taxable Income} \times \left(\begin{array}{c}\text{Proper federal}\\ \text{tax rates}\end{array}\right) - \left(\begin{array}{c}\text{Dividend}\\ \text{tax credit}\end{array}\right) = \text{Basic Tax}$$

Basic Tax

minus

a. Tax reduction
b. Federal foreign tax credits
c. Allowable portion of contributions to registered political parties and candidates

Federal Tax

plus

Provincial Tax

Expressed as percentage of Basic Tax

equals

Total Tax

Illustration
28–1

2. Deductions for the purpose of enhancing future income, and deductions to maintain current income. An example of the former is tuition fees paid to an educational institution. Union and professional fees and unemployment insurance contributions are examples of the latter.
3. Adjustments for business losses of other years.

DEDUCTIONS FROM NET INCOME. By legislative grace an individual taxpayer is permitted certain deductions from net income. These are:

1. Personal exemption allowances.
2. Medical expenses of the taxpayer and his dependents.
3. Charitable donations.
4. Investment income allowance.

Commencing with the 1974 taxation year, personal exemptions are adjusted annually to include a cost-of-living allowance. The adjusted exemptions for 1975 include a basic deduction of $1,878 for single taxpayers (or married taxpayers filing as single) and $3,522 for married taxpayers filing as such. A deduction of $353 per child is allowed for children under 16 years of age and $646 for each dependent child over the age of 16 and for other dependents related to the taxpayer. An additional deduction of $1,174 is allowed taxpayers over 65 and individuals who are blind or infirm. Provision is also made for deduction of child-care expenses. This deduction is up to $500 per child with a limit of $2,000 per family and may not exceed two-thirds of income of parent making the claim.

A standard deduction of $100 is allowed every taxpayer for charitable donations and medical expenses. If more than $100 is claimed, supporting receipts must be included with the tax return. A maximum of 20% of net income may be claimed for donations in any taxation year.

INVESTMENT INCOME. To encourage saving and investment, to give partial recognition to the claim that in the case of dividends income is "taxed twice," and for other reasons the law provides for special treatment of investment income received from qualifying domestic corporations. Beginning in 1974, $1,000 of interest income was allowed to be excluded in determining taxable income. In 1975, the provision was extended to include dividend income. Thus, an investment income exemption not to exceed $1,000 is deducted in computing taxable income just as personal deductions are deducted from net income. In addition, qualifying dividends continue to receive special treatment; the law requires that dividends received must first be "grossed up" by $33\frac{1}{3}\%$ and included in income. However, 20% of the grossed up amount is allowed as a deduction in arriving at the "Basic Tax." Provincial income taxes, Quebec excepted, are calculated as a percentage of the federal basic tax.

The dividend tax credit and the $1,000 investment income allowance materially reduce the tax on dividends, particularly for taxpayers whose income falls in the low-income brackets. This can be seen in Illustration 28–2 where the effect of the special treatment of dividend income at three levels of taxable income is shown. A comparison of the amounts of dividend income remaining after federal taxes with the amounts of after-tax ordinary income that would remain at the same levels is also shown in the illustration. Note that when $1,500 of the dividend income falls in the 25% and 35% brackets the result is a negative amount of federal income tax that may be deducted from the tax on other income but cannot be refunded.

Dividend Income	25%	35%	47%
Dividend income	$1,500	$1,500	$1,500
Add 33⅓%	500	500	500
Grossed up dividend	$2,000	2,000	$2,000
Less: Investment income allowance	1,000	1,000	1,000
Taxable amount	$1,000	$1,000	$1,000
Federal income tax	$ 250	$ 350	$ 470
Less 20% dividend tax credit	400	400	400
Basic federal tax	($ 150)	($ 50)	$ 70
Dividend income	$1,500	$1,500	$1,500
Less: Federal income tax	(150)	(50)	70
After basic federal tax income	1,650	1,550	1,430
Ordinary Income:			
Ordinary income	$1,500	$1,500	$1,500
Federal income tax on $1,500	375	525	705
After basic federal tax income	$1,125	$ 975	$ 795

Illustration
28–2
Federal tax bracket

OTHER TAX CREDITS. *(a)* Tax reduction—if the "Basic Federal Tax" is less than $200, the reduction is the amount of "Basic Federal Tax"; if the "Basic Federal Tax" is between $200 and $2,500 the reduction is $200; if the "Basic Federal Tax" is over $2,500, the reduction is 8% of "Basic Federal Tax" with a maximum of $500. *(b)* Federal foreign tax credits—a percentage of taxes paid to certain foreign countries on income earned in those countries is allowed as a deduction. *(c)* Allowable federal political contribution tax credit—the allowable credit in 1975 is as follows: 75% of the first $100; 50% of the next $450; 33⅓% of amount in excess of $550 with maximum of $500, not to exceed "Net Federal Tax."

PREPAYMENTS. Individual taxpayers are required to pay income taxes on a pay-as-income-is-earned basis throughout each year. Then, before April 30, after the end of each year, every taxpayer must file a tax return reporting the amount of his income and the tax thereon. At that time he may claim a refund for any overpayment or he must pay any balance due. Penalties are assessed for a major underpayment.

The pay-as-you-earn basis works differently for employees and for those individuals whose sources of income are other than employment.

The procedure by which employers withhold income taxes from the salary, wages, or other remuneration such as commissions paid the taxpayer by an employer has been discussed in a previous chapter. Payment by those in self-employment and those individuals whose income is from sources other than employment needs further discussion.

Individual taxpayers, who earn the bulk of their income from sources other than employment, are required to pay their income taxes in quarterly installments based on the estimated income for the current taxation year. The estimate is based on one of two bases:

1. The taxpayer's ascertained income of the preceding year, or
2. A different amount based on known altered circumstances.

Using the estimated amount, the taxpayer computes his estimated tax obligation for the year, and remits one quarter of the latter amount to the Receiver General of Canada on or before each of March 31, June 30, September 30, and December 31.

Federal Tax				Provincial Tax	
These rates are to be applied to "Taxable Income"				These rates are to be applied to "Basic Federal Tax"	
Taxable Income	Tax			Province	Tax Rate
$ 587 or less	9%			Alberta 36.0%	
587 .... $	53 + 18% on next $		587	British Columbia 30.5	
1,174	158 + 19% " "		1,174	Manitoba 42.5	
2,348	382 + 20% " "		1,174	New Brunswick 41.5	
3,522	616 + 21% " "		2,348	Newfoundland 40.0	
5,870	1,109 + 23% " "		2,348	Nova Scotia 38.5	
8,218	1,649 + 25% " "		2,348	Ontario 30.5	
10,566	2,236 + 27% " "		2,348	Prince Edward Island 36.0	
12,914	2,870 + 31% " "		3,522	Saskatchewan 40.0	
16,436	3,962 + 35% " "		11,740		
28,176	8,071 + 39% " "		17,610		
45,786	14,939 + 43% " "		24,654		
70,440	25,540 + 47% on remainder				

Note: Quebec collects its share of personal income tax, calculation of which is not based on "Basic Federal Tax."

Illustration
28–3
**Schedule of 1975
income tax rates**

INCOME TAX RATES. Our income tax rates are progressive in nature. By this is meant that each additional segment or bracket of taxable income is subject to a higher rate than the preceding segment or bracket. This may be seen by examining Illustration 28–3 which shows the rates applied to taxable income.

It is generally recognized that our Canadian income tax rates are steeply progressive. Proponents claim that this is only fair, since the taxpayers most able to pay, those with higher incomes, are subject to higher rates. Opponents, on the other hand, claim the high rates stifle initiative. For example, a young executive earning $25,000 of taxable income per year, upon being offered a new job carrying additional responsibilities and a $5,000 salary increase, might turn the new job down, feeling the after-tax increase in pay insufficient to compensate for the extra responsibilities.

Whether or not our progressive income tax rates stifle initiative is probably open to debate. However, there is no question that the rates do cause high-income taxpayers to search for tax-saving opportunities.

Special tax treatment of capital gains and losses

From a tax-saving point of view, one of the most important features of our federal income tax laws is the special treatment given gains from capital asset sales and exchanges. The usual effect of this special treatment is a tax on net capital gains that is one half the tax on an equal amount of income from some other source, commonly called "ordinary income." For this reason, whenever possible, tax planners try to cause income to emerge in the form of capital gains rather than as ordinary income.

Capital gains may be realized on such capital assets as investment in stocks and bonds, personal property, and depreciable property used in a business. Realized capital gains are taxable under the following general rules:

1. One half of capital gains to be included in income and taxed at normal personal or corporate rates.
2. All taxpayers may offset one half of capital losses against one half of capital gains; individual taxpayers may also deduct up to $1,000 of capital losses from other income. The deduction may be made in the current year, the preceding year, or any number of subsequent years until losses are fully absorbed.
3. Gains are generally taxable and losses deductible when a taxpayer sells an asset, when he makes a gift of an asset, or at his death.
4. A gain realized by a taxpayer in selling his home is exempt from tax.
5. No gain realized on an item of personal property is taxed unless the asset's selling price is more than $1,000.

A capital gain on the sale of a capital asset occurs when the proceeds of the sale exceed the *basis* of the asset sold, and a loss occurs when the asset's basis exceeds the proceeds. The basis for a depreciable asset is usually cost. A depreciable asset sold at more than its book value but at cost or less than cost results in a portion or all of depreciation previously charged against the asset to be treated as ordinary income. A capital gain results if the depreciable asset is sold at more than cost and the gain is equal to proceeds less cost.

To illustrate the recognition of a capital gain on disposal of a depreciable asset, assume that an apartment building which cost $60,000 and on which $8,000 of depreciation has accumulated is sold for $72,000. The basis of the asset is its cost, $60,000; therefore, the capital gain is $12,000 ($72,000 − $60,000). The $8,000 difference between the cost of the asset, $60,000, and its book value, $52,000, is referred to as recaptured capital cost allowance (discussed later in this chapter) and is taxed as ordinary income.

The tax savings resulting from the special treatment of capital gains may be illustrated as follows. If a taxpayer has $1,400 of capital gains and $400 of capital losses, and other income that places these gains in a 35% tax bracket, he is required to include only $500 of gain in taxable income and to pay only a $175 ($500 × 35%) tax thereon. Consequently, his effective tax rate on the gains is 17.5% ($175 ÷ $1,000 = 17.5%) and is one half what it would be if the $1,000 were ordinary income.

Individual income tax computation

The Canadian income tax system is based on self-assessment and its success relies, to a marked extent, on the cooperation of the individual taxpayers. Every taxpayer is required to complete and file his yearly income tax return in which he must supply information as to income earned, deductions and exemptions claimed, and his calculation of income tax payable for the completed calendar year.

An individual taxpayer's tax computation, demonstrating the main features of income tax legislation is shown in Illustration 28–4. The computation is based on assumed data for a hypothetical taxpayer, resident in the province of Ontario, Mr. James Evans, a publisher's representative, married with two daughters ages two and four. Mrs. Evans teaches piano and their combined 1975 income and tax-related expenditures are:

Income:
Income from employment	$18,200.00
Dividend income from Canadian corporations	600.00
Interest on bonds and on bank account	320.00
Piano lesson income (Mrs. Evans)	1,600.00
Taxable benefit from personal use of employer's car	200.00
Gain on shares of stock that cost $2,800 and were sold for $3,750	950.00
Loss on shares of stock that cost $3,550 and were sold for $3,200	350.00

Expenditures:
Donations to church and charitable organizations	730.00
Contributions to a registered pension fund	1,200.00
Contributions to a registered retirement saving plan	1,300.00
Canada Pension Plan contribution	120.60
Unemployment insurance contribution	134.68
Contribution to registered political party	100.00

Mr. James Evans
Income Tax Computation

Gross income:
Employment income		$18,200.00	
Less: Maximum employment expense		150.00	$18,050.00
Dividend income (grossed up by one-third)			800.00
Interest			320.00
Taxable benefit from use of employer's car			200.00
Capital gains (one-half of the net gain)			300.00
Total gross income			$19,670.00

Deduct:
Canada Pension Plan contribution		$ 120.60	
Unemployment insurance contribution		134.68	
Contribution to registered pension plan		1,200.00	
Contribution to registered retirement saving plan		1,300.00	2,755.28
Net income			$16,914.72

Deduct:
Personal exemptions (see schedule below)		$ 2,970.00	
Interest and dividend allowance		1,000.00	
Charitable donations		730.00	4,700.00
Taxable income			$12,214.72

Federal tax:
Tax on $10,566.00		$ 2,236.00	
Tax on 1,648.72 @ 27%		445.15	
		$ 2,681.15	
Less: Dividend tax credit (20% of $800)		160.00	
Basic Federal Tax		$ 2,521.15	
Less: Tax reduction	$201.69		
Political contribution	75.00	$276.69	
Total federal tax			$2,244.46
Ontario provincial tax:			
$2,521.15 @ 30.5%			768.95
Total federal and provincial income tax			$3,013.41

Illustration 28–4

The personal exemptions claimed in Illustration 28–4 are calculated as follows:

Basic exemption			$1,878
Marital exemption:			
Basic marital exemption		$1,644	
Deduct: Income of wife	$1,600		
Less: Nontaxable portion	344	1,256	388
Exemption for dependent children:			
Two daughters under age of 16 years			704
Total personal exemptions			$2,970

The corporation income tax

For income tax purposes, the taxable income of a corporation organized for profit is calculated in much the same way as the taxable income of an individual. However, there are important differences, five of which follow:

a. Dividends received by a public corporation from another corporation are exempt from tax.

b. Dividends received by a private Canadian corporation from another Canadian corporation are subject to two sets of rules: one for dividends received from a subsidiary (more than 50% ownership) and the other for dividends from portfolio investments. Dividends from subsidiaries are exempt from tax. Dividends received by private corporations from nonsubsidiary corporations are subject to a special $33\frac{1}{3}\%$ tax which is fully refunded to the corporation as dividends are paid to shareholders. For every $3 of dividends paid, $1 of tax is refunded.

c. Corporations may deduct capital losses from capital gains, but not from other income; and like individual taxpayers they may carry losses back one year and forward until absorbed by capital gains.

d. Deductions for exemptions do not apply to a corporation, and a corporation does not have certain other deductions of an individual, such as for personal medical expenses.

e. In addition, the big difference between the corporation and the individual income tax is that the corporation tax rate is not progressive but consists of a general federal tax rate and a general provincial tax rate. In 1975, the federal tax rate was 47%, however subject to numerous adjustments, for example, the small business deduction and manufacturing and processing profits deduction. The provincial rates vary from province to province and in 1975 ranged from 10% to 13% of taxable income earned in the province. Because of the complexity of corporate taxation and variation in effective rates not only from province to province but from corporation to corporation, for purposes of this chapter, a 50% combined federal and provincial tax rate is assumed for all corporations except those qualifying for the small business deduction. A 25% tax rate is assumed for these.

Corporations also must pay income tax as income is earned. Payments are made in 12 monthly installments and are based on a corporation's actual income of the preceding fiscal year, or on the preceding year's income adjusted for known altered circumstances. The monthly payments commence on the last day of the third month of the fiscal year in which the income is earned and the final payment is due two months after the end of the fiscal year. For example, a corporation with a September 1 to August 31 fiscal year must make its first payment on the year's tax on November 30 and the final payment on the next October 31, and a corporation with a fiscal year beginning on January 1 must make its first payment on March 31 and the final payment on the last day of February of the following year.

■ Alternative decisions commonly have different tax effects. Following are several examples illustrating this.

Form of business organization

The difference between individual and corporation tax rates commonly affects one of the basic decisions a businessman must make; namely, that as to the legal form his business should take. Should it be a single proprietorship, partnership, or corporation? The following factors influence the decision:

a.   As previously stated, a corporation is a taxable entity. Its income is taxed at corporation rates, and any portion distributed in dividends is taxed again as individual income to its stockholders. On the other hand, the income of a single proprietorship or partnership, whether withdrawn or left in the business, is taxed only once, as individual income of the proprietor or partners.

b.   In addition, a corporation may pay salaries to stockholders who work for the corporation, and the sum of these salaries is a tax-deductible expense in arriving at the corporation's taxable income. In a partnership or a single proprietorship on the other hand, salaries of the partners or the proprietor are nothing more than allocations of income.

In arriving at a decision as to the legal form his business should take, an Ontario businessman, with the foregoing points in mind, must estimate how he will fare taxwise under each form, and select the best. For example, assume that a businessman is choosing between the single proprietorship and corporate forms, and that he estimates his business will have annual gross sales of $250,000, with cost of goods sold and operating expenses, other than his own salary as manager, of $218,000. Assume further that $12,000 per year is a fair salary for managing such a business and the owner plans to withdraw all profits from the business. Under these assumptions the businessman will fare taxwise as shown in Illustration 28–5.

Under the assumptions of Illustration 28–5, the businessman will incur $677 less tax under the corporate form than as a proprietorship. Since the difference is only $677 other considerations, such as ease of formation or lack of stockholder liability, become deciding factors. However, when funds for growth are considered, the picture may change.

Growth is commonly financed through retained earnings; and when it is, organizing a business as a corporation may prove advantageous, since income retained in a business organized as a corporation is not taxed as individual income to its stockholders, but the income of a single proprietorship is so taxed whether retained in the business or withdrawn. For instance, if the business of Illustration 28–5 is organized as a corporation and its $15,000 of earnings are retained in the business, the owner is required to pay individual income taxes on only his $12,000

Operating results under each form:		Proprietorship		Corporation
Estimated sales...		$250,000		$250,000
Cost of goods sold and operating expenses other				
than owner-manager's salary $218,000			$218,000	
Salary of owner-manager.. –0–		218,000	12,000	230,000
Before-tax income		$ 32,000		$ 20,000
Corporation income tax at 25%		–0–		5,000
Net Income...		$ 32,000		$ 15,000
Owner's after-tax income under each form:				
Single proprietorship net income..............................		$ 32,000		
Corporation salary				$ 12,000
Dividends...				15,000
Total individual income		$ 32,000		$ 27,000
Individual income tax (assuming deductions and				
exemptions amounting to $6,000 under both forms				
plus a 20% dividend tax credit under the corporation				
form)		9,538		$ 3,861
Owner's After-Tax Income..		$ 22,462		$ 23,139

Illustration
28–5

salary. This would reduce his individual tax burden under the corporate form from $3,861 to $1,486 (to the nearest even dollar), a difference of $2,375, which can be used by the business interest free.

When earnings are retained in a corporation to finance growth, the growth normally results in an increase in the price of the corporation's stock, and the owners of the stock may capture the retained earnings in the form of capital gains upon the sale of the stock. However, whether such gains ultimately result in a tax savings depends upon the tax bracket of the taxpayer at the time he realizes the capital gains, as is pointed out in the following section.

Dividends and growth

It was explained earlier in this chapter that it is normally to a taxpayer's advantage to have income emerge in the form of capital gains rather than as ordinary income. Furthermore, at a certain level of taxable income the effective tax rate on dividends is higher than the tax rate on capital gains so that it becomes advantageous to have a capital gain rather than a dividend. Observe in Illustration 28–6 that in the $16,436 to $28,176 taxable income bracket, the effective tax rate on dividends from Canadian corporations is higher than the effective capital gains tax rate. Also, the tax rate on dividends increases more rapidly than the tax rate on capital gains. For this reason it is at time to the advantage of the owner of an incorporated business to forgo dividends and at a later date, through the sale of the business, to take the profits of his business in the form of capital gains resulting from growth.

Taxable Income $	Federal Tax Rate %	Effective Federal Capital Gains Tax Rate %	Effective Federal Tax Rate on Dividends From Canadian Corporation* %
1,174 to 2,348 19		9.5	–
2,348 to 3,522 20		10.0	–
3,522 to 5,870 21		10.5	0.8
5,870 to 8,218 23		11.5	2.3
8,218 to 10,566 25		12.5	3.8
10,566 to 12,914 27		13.5	5.4
12,914 to 16,436 31		15.5	10.5
16,436 to 28,176 35		17.5	18.3
28,176 to 45,786 39		19.5	23.9
45,786 to 70,440 43		21.5	29.4
Over 70,440 47		23.5	depends on amount of dividends

*Based on assumption that the grossed up dividend is equal to the difference of the minimum and maximum of each range.

Illustration
28–6

Method of financing

When a corporation is in need of additional financing, it is often to its advantage to borrow the funds rather than to issue stock, since interest on debt is a tax-deductible expense but dividends are not. For example, assume that a corporation with a 50% tax rate needs $100,000 for an expansion, and that it can earn 15% on the $100,000, before interest and taxes. If the company secures the funds by issuing 7% preferred shares, it will earn $15,000 before taxes and $7,500 after taxes and the after-tax earnings will little more than cover the preferred dividends. However, if it borrows the $100,000 at 7%, the $7,000 of interest on the loan will be a tax-deductible expense and as a result the company will have only $8,000 of taxable earnings from the expansion. Furthermore, since the tax on $8,000 is 50% of that amount, the company will have $4,000 left for its common stockholders.

Although, due to taxes, it is commonly to the advantage of a limited company to borrow rather than to issue shares, other factors are often involved. For example, borrowed capital may be difficult to obtain, especially if the owners are supplying a very small portion of total financing. Also, borrowing exposes the corporation to greater risks than does raising capital through the sale of shares.

In addition to a choice between borrowing funds and issuing shares, taxes are also a factor in a decision as whether to buy or lease assets. Taxes enter into such decisions because a leasing arrangement may offer rental deductions in excess of depreciation and interest.

Timing transactions

Timing of transactions can be of importance in tax planning. For example, if a company has several security investments to be sold and some of the sales will result in losses and other in gains, sales should be balanced so that an excess of losses over gains does not result. This is because a corporation cannot deduct from other income amounts by which capital losses exceed capital gains. For individual taxpayers timing and matching security sales may not be as important, since individuals can deduct $1,000 annually of net capital losses from ordinary income.

Timing is also a factor in plant asset sales and purchases, because tax rules permit the deduction for tax purposes of a full year's depreciation on any plant asset on hand at the end of a year. Therefore, a company planning a plant asset purchase early in, say, 197B, should advance the purchase date to December 197A, so that it can take a full year's depreciation on the asset in 197A. Likewise, if a plant asset is to be sold near the end of a year, the sale should be held up until after the year-end, so that depreciation can be taken on the asset.

Net income and taxable income ■ The taxable income of a business commonly differs from its reported net income. It differs because (1) net income is determined by the application of generally accepted accounting principles, (2) while tax rules are used in determining taxable income, and (3) the rules differ from the generally accepted accounting principles on some points. For example:

a. The application of accounting principles requires that the full amount of any material gains from capital asset sales and exchanges be taken into reported net income, but for tax purposes only 50% of the net gains from such sales commonly enters into taxable income.

b. Accounting principles require an estimate of future costs, such as, for example, costs of making good on guarantees; and accounting principles require a deduction of such costs from revenue in the year the guaranteed goods are sold. However, tax rules do not permit the deduction of such costs until after the guarantor has to make good on his guarantee.

c. Reported net income also differs from taxable income because the taxpayer uses a method or procedure for accounting purposes that he feels fairly reflects periodic net income, but is required to use a different method or procedure for tax purposes. For example, the last-in, first-out inventory method of cost allocation is widely used for accounting purposes, but is not permitted for tax purposes. Likewise, many companies use straight-line depreciation for accounting purposes, but are required to use a different procedure, called capital cost allowances, for tax purposes.

Capital cost allowances ■ Depreciation accounting has been greatly influenced by income tax laws. The 1948 Income Tax Act replaced the complex body of rules that had developed for the purpose of limiting the amount of depreciation allowed for tax purposes. The Act defined and set a limit on amounts which could be deducted, for tax purposes, in respect to the cost of depreciable assets. These amounts are known as "capital cost allowances."

The capital cost allowances are identical in nature and purpose with the accountants' concept of depreciation and are based on the declining-balance method, discussed in Chapter 11. For tax purposes, the taxpayer may claim the maximum allowed or any part thereof in any year regardless of the depreciation method and the amounts he uses in the accounting records.

Although capital cost allowances are based on the declining-balance method, certain procedures have been set out by the Regulations of the Act. The more important of these are:

1. All depreciable assets are grouped into a comparatively small number of classes and a maximum rate allowed is prescribed for each group. The assets most commonly in use are set out below according to the class to which they belong, with the maximum rate of allowance for each such class.

    Class 3 (5%) Brick, cement, and stone buildings.
    Class 6 (10%) Frame, log, stucco, and corrugated iron buildings.
    Class 7 (15%) Ships, scows, canoes, and rowboats.
    Class 10 (30%) Automobiles, trucks, and tractors.
    Class 8 (20%) Machinery, equipment, and furniture.

2. The assets of a designated class are considered to form a separate pool of costs. The costs of asset additions are added to their respective pools of undepreciated capital cost. When assets are disposed of, the proceeds received from disposal are deducted from the proper pool. The balance of each pool of costs is also diminished by the accumulated capital cost allowances claimed. A capital cost allowance is claimed on the balance, referred to as the undepreciated capital cost, in the pool at the end of the fiscal year. Since capital cost allowances are computed on year-end balances, use of assets for only a part of the year is ignored. Thus, a full year's capital cost allowance is claimed on assets acquired during the year and no allowance is claimed on assets disposed of during the year.

3. "Losses" and "gains" on disposal of individual assets disappear into the pool of undepreciated capital costs except when an asset is sold for more than its capital cost. In this case, proceeds of disposal in excess of the capital cost of the asset are normally treated as a capital gain. Where the proceeds of disposal (excluding the capital gain, if any) exceed the undepreciated capital cost of the class immediately before the sale, the amount of the excess is treated as a "recapture" of capital cost allowances previously made. Such a recapture is considered as ordinary income. When all of the assets in a class are disposed of and the proceeds are less than the undepreciated capital cost of the class immediately before the sale, the pro-

ceeds less the undepreciated capital cost may be deducted in determining the year's taxable income.

Companies must, with few exceptions, use capital cost allowances for tax purposes, but commonly use straight-line depreciation in their accounting records. A problem arising from this practice is discussed in the next section.

**Taxes
and the
distortion
of net
income**

■ When one accounting procedure is required for tax purposes and a different procedure is used in the accounting records, a problem arises as to how much income tax expense should be deducted each year on the income statement. If the tax actually incurred in such situations is deducted, reported net income often varies from year to year due to the postponement and later payment of taxes. Consequently, in such cases, since stockholders may be misled by these variations, many accountants are of the opinion that income taxes should be allocated in such a way that any distortion resulting from postponing taxes is removed from the income statement.

To appreciate the problem involved here, assume that a corporation purchased a $1,000,000 helicopter to "taxi" passengers from the airport to the inner city. The helicopter is expected to produce a million and a half dollars of revenue in each of the succeeding five years and $600,000 of income before depreciation and taxes. Assume further that the company must pay income taxes at a 50% rate and that it plans to use straight-line depreciation in its records but, for tax purposes, to take the maximum capital cost allowance in each of the first four years of the helicopter's use plus sufficient capital cost allowance in the fifth year as to reduce the machine's undepreciated capital cost allowance to its salvage value. A helicopter is a Class 16 asset and the maximum capital cost allowance for such assets is 40%, and if the helicopter has a five-year life and a $100,000 salvage value, annual straight-line depreciation and capital cost allowances will be as follows:

Year	Straight-Line Depreciation	Capital Cost Allowances
1	$180,000	$400,000
2	180,000	240,000
3	180,000	144,000
4	180,000	86,400
5	180,000	29,600
	$900,000	$900,000

And since the company elects to take maximum capital cost allowances for tax purposes, it will be liable for $100,000 of income taxes on the first year's income, $180,000 on the second, $228,000 on the third, $256,800 on the fourth, and $285,200 on the fifth. The calculation of these taxes is shown in Illustration 28–7.

Annual Income Taxes	Year 1	Year 2	Year 3	Year 4	Year 5	Total
Income before depreciation and income taxes	$600,000	$600,000	$600,000	$600,000	$600,000	$3,000,000
Capital cost allowances	400,000	240,000	144,000	86,400	29,600	900,000
Taxable income	$200,000	$360,000	$456,000	$513,600	$570,400	$2,100,000
Annual Income Taxes (50% of Taxable Income)	$100,000	$180,000	$228,000	$256,800	$285,200	$1,050,000

Illustration
28–7

Furthermore, if the company were to deduct its actual tax liability each year in arriving at income to be reported to its stockholders, it would report the amounts shown in Illustration 28–8.

Income after Deducting Actual Tax Liabilities	Year 1	Year 2	Year 3	Year 4	Year 5	Total
Income before depreciation and income taxes	$600,000	$600,000	$600,000	$600,000	$600,000	$3,000,000
Depreciation (straight line)	180,000	180,000	180,000	180,000	180,000	900,000
Income before taxes	$420,000	$420,000	$420,000	$420,000	$420,000	$2,100,000
Income taxes (actual liability of each year)	100,000	180,000	228,000	256,800	285,200	1,050,000
Remaining Income	$320,000	$240,000	$192,000	$163,200	$134,800	$1,050,000

Illustration
28–8

Observe in Illustrations 28–7 and 28–8 that total depreciation, $900,000, and total capital cost allowances, $900,000, are the same. Also note that the total tax liability is the same in each case. Then note the distortion of the yearly income figures in Illustration 28–8, due to the postponement of taxes.

If this company should report successive annual income figures of $320,000, $240,000, $192,000, $163,200, and then $134,800, some of its stockholders might be misled as to the company's earnings trend. Consequently, in cases such as this many accountants think income taxes should be allocated so that the distortion caused by the postponement of taxes is removed from the income statement. These accountants advocate that—

When one accounting procedure is used in the accounting records and a different procedure is used for tax purposes, the tax expense deducted on the income statement should not be the actual tax liability, but the amount that would be payable if the procedure used in the records were also used in calculating the tax.

If the foregoing is applied in this case, the corporation will report to its stockholders in each of the four years the amounts of income shown in Illustration 28-9.

Net Income That Should Be Reported to Stockholders	Year 1	Year 2	Year 3	Year 4	Year 5	Total
Income before depreciation and income taxes	$600,000	$600,000	$600,000	$600,000	$600,000	$3,000,000
Depreciation (straight line)	180,000	180,000	180,000	180,000	180,000	900,000
Income before taxes	$420,000	$420,000	$420,000	$420,000	$420,000	$2,100,000
Income taxes (amounts based on straight-line depreciation)	210,000	210,000	210,000	210,000	210,000	1,050,000
Net Income	$210,000	$210,000	$210,000	$210,000	$210,000	$1,050,000

Illustration
28-9

In examining Illustration 28-9, recall that the company's tax liabilities are actually $100,000 for the first year, $180,000 for the second, $228,000 for the third, $256,800 for the fourth, and $285,200 for the fifth, a total $1,050,000. Then observe that when this $1,050,000 liability is allocated evenly over the five years, the distortion of the annual net incomes due to the postponement of taxes is removed from the published income statements.

Entries for the allocation of taxes ■ When income taxes are allocated as in Illustration 28-9, the tax liability of each year and the deferred taxes are recorded with a work sheet adjustment and an adjusting entry, after which the taxes are paid. The adjusting entries and the entries in general journal form for the payment of the taxes (without explanations) are as follows:

Year 1	Income Taxes Expense	210,000.00	
	Income Taxes Payable		100,000.00
	Deferred Income Taxes		110,000.00
Year 1	Income Taxes Payable	100,000.00	
	Cash		100,000.00
Year 2	Income Taxes Expense	210,000.00	
	Income Taxes Payable		180,000.00
	Deferred Income Taxes		30,000.00
Year 2	Income Taxes Payable	180,000.00	
	Cash		180,000.00
Year 3	Income Taxes Expense	210,000.00	
	Deferred Income Taxes	18,000.00	
	Income Taxes Payable		228,000.00
Year 3	Income Taxes Payable	228,000.00	
	Cash		228,000.00

Year 4	Income Taxes Expense	210,000.00	
	Deferred Income Taxes	46,800.00	
	Income Taxes Payable		256,800.00
Year 4	Income Taxes Payable	256,800.00	
	Cash		256,800.00
Year 5	Income Taxes Expense	210,000.00	
	Deferred Income Taxes	75,200.00	
	Income Taxes Payable		285,200.00
Year 5	Income Taxes Payable	285,200.00	
	Cash		285,200.00

In the entries the $210,000 debited to Income Taxes Expense each year is the amount that is deducted on the income statement in reporting annual net income. Also, the amount credited to Income Taxes Payable each year is the actual tax liability of that year.

Observe in the entries that since the actual tax liability in each of the first two years is less than the amount debited to Income Taxes Expense, the difference is credited to Deferred Income Taxes. Then note that in the last three years, since the actual liability each year is greater than the debit to Income Taxes Expense, the difference is debited to Deferred Income Taxes. Now observe in the following illustration of the company's Deferred Income Taxes account that the debits and credits exactly balance each other out over the five-year period:

Deferred Income Taxes

Year	Explanation	Debit	Credit	Balance
1			110,000.00	110,000.00
2			30,000.00	140,000.00
3		18,000.00		122,000.00
4		46,800.00		75,200.00
5		75,200.00		–0–

In passing it should be observed that many accountants believe the interests of government, business, and the public would be better served if there were more uniformity between taxable income and reported net income. However, since the federal income tax is designed to serve other purposes than raising revenue, it is apt to be some time before this is achieved.

Questions for class discussion

1. Jackson expects to have $500 of income in a 50% bracket; consequently, which should be more desirable to him: (a) a transaction that will reduce his income tax by $100 or (b) a transaction that will reduce an expense of his business by $150?

2. Why must a taxpayer normally take advantage of a tax-saving opportunity at the time it arises?

3. Distinguish between tax avoidance and tax evasion. Which is legal and desirable?
4. What are some of the nonrevenue objectives of the federal income tax?
5. What nonrevenue objective is gained by granting a lower tax rate to small corporations?
6. What questions must be answered in determining whether an item should be included or excluded from gross income for tax purposes?
7. Name several items that are not income for tax purposes.
8. What justification is given for permitting an individual to claim a dividend tax credit on dividends from domestic corporations?
9. What is a capital gain?
10. An individual has had capital asset transactions that have resulted in nothing but capital gains. What special tax treatment may be given these gains?
11. For tax purposes, what is "ordinary income"?
12. Why do tax planners try to have income emerge as a capital gain?
13. It is often a wise tax decision for the owner of an incorporated business to forgo the payment of dividends from the earnings of his business. Why?
14. Why does the taxable income of a business commonly differ from its net income?

Class exercises

Exercise 28–1

List the letters of the following items and write after each either the word included or excluded to tell whether the item should be included or excluded from gross income for income tax purposes.

a. A portable TV set having a $100 fair market value which was received as a door prize.
b. Tips received while working as a parking lot attendant.
c. Cash inherited from a deceased aunt.
d. Scholarship received from a university.
e. Unemployment insurance benefits.
f. Workmen's compensation insurance received as the result of an accident while working on a part-time job.
g. Gain on the sale of a personal automobile bought and rebuilt.
h. Dividends from stock in domestic corporations received by an individual.
i. Dividends on stock in domestic public corporations received by a corporation.
j. Interest on a savings account.

Exercise 28–2

During 1975 Ted Hall, who is married with two dependent children over 16 years of age, earned $9,200 as an employee of an electronics company. He had $1,390 of income tax, $133.68 of unemployment insurance, and $120.60 of Canada Pension Plan taxes withheld from his pay cheques. He also received $150 in dividends from a domestic corporation in which he owned stock. During the year Ted made a number of small charitable donations: however, he did not retain any receipts. Show the calculation of Ted's taxable income in the manner outlined in the chapter. Then using the rate schedule of Illustration 28–3, show the calculations of net income tax payable or refund due Ted. (Assume that Ted Hall resides in British Columbia.)

Exercise 28–3

A taxpayer who had no other capital gains sold for $7,500 a number of shares of stock he had purchased for $5,700. Use the rate schedule of Illustration 28–3 and determine the amount of federal income tax the taxpayer will have to pay on the gain from this transaction under each of the following unrelated assumptions:

a. The taxpayer had $16,436 of taxable income from other sources.
b. The taxpayer had $28,176 of taxable income from other sources.
c. The taxpayer had $70,440 of taxable income from other sources.

Repeat *(a), (b),* and *(c)* assuming that instead of the capital gain, the taxpayer received the amount of the gain in dividends.

Problems **Problem 28–1**

Ted Moss has operated Mesa Sales for a number of years with the following average annual results:

MESA SALES
Income Statement for an Average Year

Sales..		$280,000
Cost of goods sold	$165,000	
Operating expenses	85,000	250,000
Net Income		$ 30,000

Mr. Moss is unmarried and without dependents and has been operating Mesa Sales as a single proprietorship. He has been withdrawing $12,000 each year to pay his personal living expenses. His total deductions and personal exemptions amount to $2,250. He has no income other than from Mesa Sales.

Required:
1. Assume that Mr. Moss is considering the incorporation of his business beginning with the 1975 tax year and prepare a comparative income statement for the business showing its net income as a single proprietorship and as a corporation. Assume that if he incorporates, Mr. Moss will pay $12,000 per year to himself as a salary.
2. Use the rate schedule of Illustration 28–3 and determine the amount of federal income tax Mr. Moss will have to pay for himself and for his business under each of the following assumptions: *(a)* the business is not incorporated; *(b)* the business is incorporated, pays Mr. Moss a $12,000 annual salary as manager, and also pays him $12,000 per year in dividends; and *(c)* the business is incorporated, pays Mr. Moss a $12,000 salary, but does not pay any dividends.

Problem 28–2

Ted Pace is a practicing lawyer. Some of the information contained in his 1975 income tax return follows:

Income from law practice	$22,000
Dividend income from Canadian corporation	900
Interest income	420
Capital gains	200
Capital losses	800
Registered Retirement Saving Plan contributions	4,000
Canada Pension Plan contributions	241
Personal exemptions	3,874

Required:

Compute Mr. Pace's quarterly income tax payments for the current year. Assume that Mr. Pace's circumstances and expectations have not changed from the previous year. Show supporting computations. (Assume that Mr. Pace resides in Nova Scotia.)

Problem 28–3

PART 1. At the beginning of his taxation year, Dale Isley purchased an apartment building for $300,000. The building is of frame and stucco construction. Mr. Isley took maximum capital cost allowance for each year and resold the building four years after purchase.

Required:

For each of the following selling prices, determine the amount of profit or loss realized and state how the profit or loss affected Mr. Isley's taxable income: *(a)* $330,000; *(b)* $230,000; *(c)* $190,000.

PART 2. In 1974A, Mr. Dale Isley started a trucking business and purchased the following trucks: No. 1 for $12,800; No. 2 for $19,520; and No. 3 for $15,680. In 197B he purchased truck No. 4 for $17,600 and truck No. 5 for $18,400 and sold truck No. 1 for $8,800. No truck purchases or disposals took place in 197C.

Required:

Calculate the maximum capital cost allowance for the year 197C.

Problem 28–4

Early in January 197A, Deeplake Corporation installed a new machine in its plant that cost $240,000 and was estimated to have a four-year life and a $16,000 salvage value. The machine enabled the company to add a new product to its line that produces $160,000 of income annually before depreciation or capital cost allowance and income taxes. The company allocates income taxes in its reports to its stockholders, since it uses straight-line depreciation in its accounting records and for tax purposes, deducts the maximum capital cost allowance each year of an asset's life, until salvage value is reached.

Required:

1. Prepare a schedule showing 197A, 197B, 197C, 197D, and total net income for the four years after deducting maximum capital cost allowances and actual taxes. Assume a 50% income tax rate and that the maximum capital cost allowance rate of the asset of this problem is 50%.

2. Prepare a second schedule showing each year's net income and the four-year total after deducting straight-line depreciation and actual taxes.
3. Prepare a third schedule showing income reported to stockholders with straight-line depreciation and allocated taxes.
4. Set up a T-account for Deferred Income Tax and show therein the entries that result from allocating the income taxes.

Problem 28–1A

Richard Hall is married with no dependent children. He has no income other than from Valley Sales, a profitable single proprietorship business that Mr. Hall owns and which averages $350,000 annually in sales, with a 40% gross profit and $100,000 of operating expenses. Hall's total deductions and personal exemptions amount to $5,000. In the past, Mr. Hall has withdrawn $12,000 annually from the business for personal living expenses plus sufficient additional cash to pay the income tax on his return.

Mr. Hall thinks he can save taxes by reorganizing his business into a corporation beginning with the 1975 tax year. If the corporation is organized Mr. Hall will own all of the outstanding shares and the corporation will pay him a $15,000 per year salary for managing the business.

Required:
1. Prepare a comparative income statement for the business showing its net income as a single proprietorship and as a corporation.
2. Use the rate schedule of Illustration 28–3 and determine the amount of income taxes Hall will pay for himself and for the business under each of the following assumptions: *(a)* the business remains a single proprietorship; *(b)* the business is incorporated, pays Mr. Hall a $15,000 salary, but pays no dividends; *(c)* the business is incorporated, pays Mr. Hall a $15,000 salary, and pays $15,000 in dividends. (Assume that Mr. Hall resides in Ontario and if incorporated the company would qualify for the small corporation tax rate.)

Problem 28–2A

David Douglas is a practicing accountant. He is married with no dependent children. Some of the information contained in his last year's income tax return follows:

Income from the accounting practice	$16,500
Dividend income from Canadian corporations	300
Interest income	260
Capital gains	100
Capital losses	300
Wife's income	1,300
Registered Retirement Saving Plan contributions	3,300
Canada Pension Plan contributions	241
Donations	680

Required:
Compute the current year's quarterly payment that Mr. Douglas must make. Assume that the circumstances and expectation Mr. and Mrs. Douglas have

have not changed from the previous year. Show supporting computations. (Mr. Douglas resides in the province of Newfoundland.)

Problem 28–3A

PART 1. At the beginning of his taxation year, Lee Hall purchased an apartment building for $300,000. The building is of brick construction. Mr. Hall took maximum capital cost allowance for each year and resold the building three years after purchase.

Required:

For each of the following selling prices, determine the amount of profit or loss realized and state how the profit or loss affected Mr. Hall's taxable income: *(a)* $315,000; *(b)* $282,000; *(c)* $243,000.

PART 2. At the beginning of 197A the undepreciated capital cost allowance of Class 10 assets was $58,800. During 197A, additions to the class amounted to $39,200. In 197B, proceeds from disposal of Class 10 assets amounted to $12,600. No purchase or disposal transactions took place during 197C.

Required:

Calculate the maximum capital cost allowance on Class 10 assets for the year 197C.

Problem 28–4A

At a $350,000 cost, Green Hill Corporation installed a new machine in its plant early in January, 197A, so that it could add a new product to its line. It estimated the new machine would have a four-year life, a $28,000 salvage value, and its product would produce $315,000 of income each year before capital cost allowance or depreciation and income taxes at an assumed 50% rate. The company uses straight-line depreciation for its accounting records. It also allocates income taxes in its reports to stockholders, because for tax purposes, it deducts the maximum capital cost allowance each year of an asset's life until salvage value is reached.

Required:

1. Prepare a schedule showing 197A, 197B, 197C, 197D and total net income for the four years from the sale of the new product after deducting maximum capital cost allowances and actual income taxes. Assume that the maximum capital cost allowance rate of the asset of this problem is 50%.
2. Prepare a second schedule showing each year's income and total net income after deducting straight-line depreciation and actual income taxes.
3. Prepare a third schedule showing income reported to stockholders with straight-line depreciation and allocated income taxes.
4. Set up a T-account for Deferred Income Tax and show therein the entries that result from allocating the income taxes.

Decision problem 28–1, Koko Corporation

Jerry Hern and his wife own all the outstanding stock of Koko Corporation, a company Jerry organized several years ago and which is growing rapidly and needs additional capital. Ted Cole, a friend of the family, examined the following comparative income statement, which shows the corporation's net income for the past three years and which was prepared by its bookkeeper, and expressed a tentative willingness to invest the required capital by purchasing a portion of the corporation's unissued stock.

KOKO CORPORATION
Comparative Income Statement, 197A, 197B, 197C

	197A	197B	197C
Sales	$750,000	$825,000	$890,000
Costs and expenses other than depreciation			
and income taxes	$465,000	$500,000	$540,000
Depreciation expense	105,000	115,000	120,000
Income taxes	75,000	80,000	90,000
Total costs and expenses	$645,000	$695,000	$750,000
Net Income	$105,000	$130,000	$140,000

However, before making a final decision, Ted Cole asked permission for his own accountant to examine the accounting records of the corporation. Permission was granted, the examination was made, and the accountant prepared the following comparative income statement covering the same period of time.

KOKO CORPORATION
Comparative Income Statement. 197A, 197B, and 197C

	197A	197B	197C
Sales	$750,000	$825,000	$890,000
Costs and expenses other than depreciation	$465,000	$500,000	$540,000
Depreciation expense*	105,000	115,000	120,000
Total costs and expenses	$570,000	$615,000	$660,000
Income before income taxes	$180,000	$210,000	$230,000
Applicable income taxes	90,000	105,000	115,000
Net Income	$ 90,000	$105,000	$115,000

* The corporation deducted $135,000 of depreciation expense on its 197A tax return, $165,000 on its 197B return, and $170,000 on its 197C return.

Jerry Hern was surprised at the difference in annual net incomes reported on the two statements and immediately called for an explanation from the public accountant who set up the corporation's accounting system and who prepares the annual tax returns of the corporation and the Herns.

Explain why there is a difference between the net income figures on the two statements, and account for the difference in the net incomes. Prepare a statement that will explain the amounts shown on the corporation bookkeeper's statement. Assume a 50% income tax rate.

Analytical and review problems

Problem 28–1 A&R

Using the data given in the Chapter, determine the federal and provincial income taxes for Mr. James Evans under the following conditions:

a. Assume that Mr. Evans resides in *your* province.

b. Use current year's amounts for:
   1. Personal deductions.
   2. Canada Pension Plan.
   3. Unemployment Insurance.
c. Use current year's federal and provincial income tax rates.

Problem 28–2 A&R

On January 1, 19X1, Val D'or Limited bought, for $100,000 cash, machinery which, for income tax purposes is to be subjected to a capital cost allowance rate of 30% on the diminishing balance. For financial accounting purposes an 8-year life with $4,000 scrap value is to be used. Current and expected income tax rates are 50%. Val D'or has an annual income of $150,000 before considering depreciation of the machinery in question or income taxes.

Required:

Give journal entries (omit narrative but show supporting computation) at December 31, 19X1 and at December 19X4, to accrue Val D'or's income tax liability and to reflect tax allocation.

(CGA adapted)

Appendix

The concept of
present value

■ As a rule a business will not invest $1 today unless it expects to get back somewhat more than $1 at a later date, with the "somewhat more" being earnings or interest on the investment. Likewise, if a business makes an investment today that will return $1 a year from now, the $1 to be received a year hence has a *present value* that is somewhat less than $1. How much less depends upon how much the business expects to earn on its investments. If it expects to earn, say, a 10% annual return, the expectation of receiving $1 a year hence has a present value of $0.909. This can be verified as follows: $0.909 invested today to earn 10% annually will earn $0.0909 in one year, and when the $0.0909 earned is added to the $0.909 invested—

Investment	$0.909
Earnings	0.0909
Total	$0.9999

the investment plus the earnings equal $0.9999, which rounds to the $1 expected.

Likewise, the present value of $1 to be received two years hence is $0.826 if a 10% compound annual return is expected. This also can be verified as follows: $0.826 invested to earn 10% compounded annually will earn $0.0826 the first year it is invested, and when the $0.0826 earned is added to the $0.826 invested—

```
Investment ...................................... $0.826
First year earnings ......................... 0.0826
End-of-year-one amount................. $0.9086
```

the investment plus the first year's earnings total $0.9086. And during the second year this $0.9086 will earn $0.09086, which when added to the end-of-the-first-year amount—

```
End-of-year-one amount................. $0.9086
Second year earnings..................... 0.09086
End-of-year-two amount................. $0.99946
```

equals $0.99946, which rounds to the $1 expected at the end of the second year.

Present value tables

The present value of $1 to be received any number of years in the future can be calculated by using the formula, $1/(1 + i)^n$, with i being the interest rate and n the number of years to the expected receipt. However, the formula need not be used, since tables showing present values computed with the formula at various interest rates are readily available. Table 1, with its amounts rounded to either three or four decimal places, is such a table. (Three or four decimal places would not be sufficiently accurate for some uses, but will suffice here.)

Present Value of $1 at Compound Interest

Periods Hence	3%	3½%	4%	6%	7%	8%	10%	12%	14%	15%
1	0.9709	0.9662	0.9615	0.943	0.935	0.926	0.909	0.893	0.877	0.870
2	0.9426	0.9335	0.9246	0.890	0.873	0.857	0.826	0.797	0.769	0.756
3	0.9151	0.9019	0.8890	0.840	0.816	0.794	0.751	0.712	0.675	0.658
4	0.8885	0.8714	0.8548	0.792	0.763	0.735	0.683	0.636	0.592	0.572
5	0.8626	0.8420	0.8219	0.747	0.713	0.681	0.621	0.567	0.519	0.497
6	0.8375	0.8135	0.7903	0.705	0.666	0.630	0.565	0.507	0.456	0.432
7	0.8131	0.7860	0.7599	0.665	0.623	0.584	0.513	0.452	0.400	0.376
8	0.7894	0.7594	0.7307	0.627	0.582	0.540	0.467	0.404	0.351	0.327
9	0.7664	0.7337	0.7026	0.592	0.544	0.500	0.424	0.361	0.308	0.284
10	0.7441	0.7089	0.6756	0.558	0.508	0.463	0.386	0.322	0.270	0.247
11	0.7224	0.6849	0.6496	0.572	0.475	0.429	0.351	0.287	0.237	0.215
12	0.7014	0.6618	0.6246	0.497	0.444	0.397	0.319	0.257	0.208	0.187
13	0.6810	0.6394	0.6006	0.469	0.415	0.368	0.290	0.229	0.182	0.163
14	0.6611	0.6178	0.5775	0.442	0.388	0.341	0.263	0.205	0.160	0.141
15	0.6419	0.5969	0.5553	0.417	0.362	0.315	0.239	0.183	0.140	0.123
16	0.6232	0.5767	0.5339	0.394	0.339	0.292	0.218	0.163	0.123	0.107
17	0.6050	0.5572	0.5134	0.371	0.317	0.270	0.198	0.146	0.108	0.093
18	0.5874	0.5384	0.4936	0.350	0.296	0.250	0.180	0.130	0.095	0.081
19	0.5703	0.5202	0.4746	0.331	0.277	0.232	0.164	0.116	0.083	0.070
20	0.5537	0.5026	0.4564	0.312	0.258	0.215	0.149	0.104	0.073	0.061

Table 1

Observe in Table 1 that the first amount in the 10% column is the 0.909 used in the previous section to introduce the concept of present value. The 0.909 in the 10% column means that the expectation of receiving $1 a year hence when discounted for one period, in this case one year, at 10%, has a present value of $0.909. Then note that the second amount in the 10% column is the $0.826 previously used, which means that the expectation of receiving $1 two years hence, discounted at 10%, has a present value of $0.826.

Using present values in investment decisions

Whether or not an investment is a wise one depends upon a number of factors, including the risks involved and whether or not the expected returns justify the risks. Normally the risks are judged and a rate of return is demanded that will justify the anticipated risks. The expected returns are then discounted at this rate to determine whether or not the investment will earn the required return. For example, a company has an opportunity to invest $20,000 in a project, the risks of which it feels justify a 12% compound return. The investment will return $10,000 at the end of the first year, $9,000 at the end of the second year, $8,000 at the end of the third year, and nothing thereafter. Will the project return the original investment plus the 12% demanded? The calculations in Illustration A–1 indicate that it will. In Illustration A–1 the expected returns in the second column are multiplied by the amounts in the third column to determine the present values in the last column; and since the total of the present values exceeds the required investment by $1,799, the project will return the $20,000 investment, plus a 12% return thereon, and $1,799 extra.

Years Hence	Expected Returns	Present Value of $1 at 12%	Present Value of Expected Returns
1	$10,000	0.893	$ 8,930
2	9,000	0.797	7,173
3	8,000	0.712	5,696
Total present value of the returns............................			$21,799
Less investment required			20,000
Excess over 12% demanded			$ 1,799

Illustration A–1

In Illustration A–1 the present value of each year's return was separately calculated, after which the present values were added to determine their total. Separately calculating the present value of each of several returns from an investment is necessary when the returns are unequal, as in this example. However, in cases where the periodic returns are equal, there are shorter ways of calculating the sum of their present values. For instance, suppose a $3,500 investment will return $1,000 at the end of each year in its five-year life, and an investor wants to know the present value of these returns discounted at 12%. In this case the periodic returns are equal, and a short way to determine their total present value at 12% is to add the present values of $1 at 12% for periods one through five (from Table 1), as follows—

$$
\begin{array}{r}
0.893 \\
0.797 \\
0.712 \\
0.636 \\
\underline{0.567} \\
\underline{\underline{3.605}}
\end{array}
$$

and then to multiply $1,000 by the total. The $3,605 result ($1,000 × 3.605 = $3,605) is the same as would be obtained by calculating the present value of each year's return and adding the present values. However, although the result is the same either way, the method demonstrated here requires four fewer multiplications.

Present value of $1 received periodically for a number of periods

Table 2 is based on the idea demonstrated in the previous paragraph, the idea that the present value of a series of equal returns to be received at periodic intervals is nothing more than the sum of the present values of the individual returns. Note the amount on the table's fifth line in the 12% column. It is the same 3.605 amount arrived at in the previous

Present Value of $1 Received Periodically for a Number of Periods

Periods Hence	3%	3½%	4%	6%	7%	8%	10%	12%	14%	15%
1	0.971	0.966	0.962	0.943	0.935	0.926	0.909	0.893	0.877	0.870
2	1.914	1.900	1.886	1.833	1.808	1.783	1.736	1.690	1.647	1.626
3	2.829	2.802	2.775	2.673	2.624	2.577	2.487	2.402	2.322	2.283
4	3.717	3.672	3.630	3.465	3.387	3.312	3.170	3.037	2.914	2.855
5	4.580	4.515	4.452	4.212	4.100	3.993	3.791	3.605	3.433	3.352
6	5.417	5.329	5.242	4.917	4.767	4.623	4.355	4.111	3.889	3.784
7	6.230	6.115	6.002	5.582	5.389	5.206	4.868	4.564	4.288	4.160
8	7.020	6.874	6.733	6.210	5.971	5.747	5.335	4.968	4.639	4.487
9	7.786	7.608	7.435	6.802	6.515	6.247	5.759	5.328	4.946	4.772
10	8.530	8.317	8.111	7.360	7.024	6.710	6.145	5.650	5.216	5.019
11	9.253	9.002	8.761	7.887	7.499	7.139	6.495	5.988	5.453	5.234
12	9.954	9.663	9.385	8.384	7.943	7.536	6.814	6.194	5.660	5.421
13	10.635	10.303	9.986	8.853	8.358	7.904	7.103	6.424	5.842	5.583
14	11.296	10.921	10.563	9.295	8.746	8.244	7.367	6.628	6.002	5.724
15	11.938	11.517	11.118	9.712	9.108	8.560	7.606	6.811	6.142	5.847
16	12.561	12.094	11.652	10.106	9.447	8.851	7.824	6.974	6.265	5.954
17	13.166	12.651	12.166	10.477	9.763	9.122	8.022	7.120	6.373	6.047
18	13.754	13.190	12.659	10.828	10.059	9.372	8.201	7.250	6.467	6.128
19	14.324	13.710	13.134	11.158	10.336	9.604	8.365	7.366	6.550	6.198
20	14.878	14.212	13.590	11.470	10.594	9.818	8.514	7.469	6.623	6.259

Table 2

section by adding the first five present values of $1 at 12%. All the amounts shown in Table 2 could be arrived at by adding amounts found in Table 1. However, there would be some slight variations due to rounding.

When available, Table 2 is used to determine the present value of a series of equal amounts to be received at periodic future intervals. For example, what is the present value of a series of ten $1,000 amounts, with one $1,000 amount to be received at the end of each of 10 successive years, discounted at 8%? To determine the answer, go down the 8% column to the amount opposite 10 periods (years in this case). It is 6.710, and $6.71 is the present value of $1 to be received annually at the ends of each of 10 years, discounted at 8%. Therefore, the present value of the ten $1,000 amounts is 1,000 times $6.71 or is $6,710.

Discount periods less than a year in length

In the examples thus far the discount periods have been measured in intervals one year in length. Often discount periods are based on intervals shorter than a year. For instance, although interest rates on corporation bonds are usually quoted on an annual basis, the interest on such bonds is normally paid semiannually. As a result, a calculation involving the present value of the interest to be received on such bonds must be based on interest periods six months in length.

To illustrate a calculation based on six-month interest periods, assume an investor wants to know the present value of the interest he will receive over a period of five years on some corporation bonds. The bonds have a $10,000 par value and interest is paid on them every six months at a 7% annual rate. Since interest at a 7% annual rate is at the rate of $3\frac{1}{2}$% per six-month interest period, the investor will receive $10,000 times $3\frac{1}{2}$% or $350 in interest on these bonds at the end of each six-month interest period. In five years there are ten such periods. Therefore, if these ten receipts of $350 each are to be discounted at the interest rate of the bonds, to determine their present value, go down the $3\frac{1}{2}$% column of Table 2 to the amount opposite ten periods. It is 8.317, and the present value of the ten $350 semiannual receipts is 8.317 times $350 or is $2,910.95.

Index

A

Accelerated depreciation, 337
Account
  balance of, 27
  balance-column form, 95
  Capital, 30
  code numbers, 150
  contra, 65
  determining the balance of, 41
  normal balance of, 96
  numbers in posting, 45
  opposite from normal balance,
    96
  T-account form, 26
  two-column form, 41
  Withdrawals, 30
Accountancy as a profession, 2
Accountant
  tax services of, 3
  work of, 2
Accounting
  accrual basis of, 73
  for bad debts, 254
  and bookkeeping distinguished,
    5
  cash basis of, 73
  for cash sales, 244
  changes, 423, 537

Accounting—Cont.
  concepts, 413
    business entity concept, 8,
      413
    going-concern concept, 9,
      340, 413
    periodicity concept, 415
    stable-dollar concept, 414
  corporation, 473
  for corporation income taxes,
    516, 845
  cost, 4, 725, 770
  cycle, 114
  departmental, 665
  equation, 9
  general, 4
  governmental, 4
  machines, 184
  manufacturing, 697
  mechanics of double entry, 32
  for a merchandising concern,
    131
  methods, changes in, 423
  for natural resources, 368
  for no-par stock, 503
  for notes and interest, 275
  partnership, 435

Accounting—*Cont.*
  for payrolls, 389
  periods, 61, 114
  for plant and equipment, 331
  principles, 416
    basis of authority for, 412
    business entity concept, 8, 413
    conservatism, 311, 423
    consistency, 309, 421
    cost principle, 8, 416
    full-disclosure principle, 422
    going-concern concept, 9, 340, 413
    matching principle, 73, 417
    materiality, 366, 424
    nature of, 412
    need for, 411
    objectivity principle, 421
    periodicity concept, 415
    and the public accountant, 424
    stable-dollar concept, 414
  private, 4
  public, 3
  responsibility, 665, 679
  statements, 5
  why study, 2
Accounts, 26
  adjusting the, 61
  arrangement in the ledger, 72
  balance-column, 95
  closing the, 103
  contra, 65
  controlling, 171
  nominal, 114
  payable, 7, 29
    controlling account, 178
    ledger, 178
    schedule of, 182
  real, 114
  receivable, 7, 28
    aging, 259
    direct write-off of, 260
    ledger, 171
    schedule of, 182
    turnover, 265
  temporary proprietorship, 114
  uncollectible, 254
Accrual basis of accounting, 73
Accrued
  bond interest, 569
  expenses, 66, 73
  interest on notes receivable, 294
  items, disposing of, 73
  revenues, 68, 74
Accruing payroll taxes, 403
Accumulated depreciation on the balance sheet, 66, 339
Acid-test ratio, 609

Adjusted trial balance, 69
  columns, dispensing with, 146
  columns on the work sheet, 101
  statements, from, 69
Adjustment process, 72
Adjustments
  need for, 61
  normal corrections and, 535
Agency, mutual, 436
Agent, transfer, 473
Aging accounts receivable, 259
Allocating
  depreciation, 335
  expenses, 670
  income taxes, 854
Allowance for bad debts: *see* Allowance for doubtful accounts
Allowance for depreciation; *see* Accumulated depreciation on the balance sheet
Allowance for doubtful accounts, 255
American Accounting Association, 412
American Institute of Certified Public Accountants, 75, 413
  Internal Control, 214
Analysis of financial statements, 601
Analyzing entries, statement of changes in financial position, 629
Applications of funds; *see* Uses of funds
Appropriations of retained earnings, 530
Arrangement of accounts in the ledger, 72
Assets
  circulating, 630
  classification of, 75
  current, 75
  defined, 7
  fixed; *see* Plant asset
  intangible, 76, 369
  plant, 83, 331, 361
  quick, 609
  wasting, 368
Audit, purposes of, 3, 425
Auditing, 3, 425
Average investment in a plant asset, 813

B

Bad debt, writing off, 257, 260
Bad debts, 254
  aging accounts receivable, 259
  allowance method of accounting for, 255
  on the balance sheet, 256

Bad debts—*Cont.*
  direct write-off of a, 260
  estimating, 255, 259
  recoveries, 258, 261
Balance
  of an account, 27
  of an account, computing, 41
  red ink, 96
  trial, 40
Balance-column account, 95
Balance sheet, 6, 74
  account form, 79
  classified, 75
  common-size, 605
  comparative, 538, 602, 606
  consolidated, 542, 544
  corporation, 581
  equation, 9
  items, arrangement of, 79
  report form, 79
  single-step, 538
Bank discount, 282
Bank loans, 281
Betterments, 368
Bonds
  accrued interest on, 576
  amortizing discount on, 572
  amortizing premium on, 575
  borrowing money with, 566
  callable, 577
  characteristics of, 566
  contract interest rate, 570
  convertible, 578
  coupon, 566
  discount on, 570
  interest-method of amortizing discounts and premiums, 572
  interest rates, 570
  as investments, 582
  issuing, 568
  market rate of interest on, 570
  premium on, 574
  price quotations, 578
  redemption of, 577
  registered, 566
  sale of by investors, 577
  serial, 566
  sinking fund, 578
  sold at a discount, 570
  sold between interest dates, 569
  sold at a premium, 574
  why issued, 567
Book of final entry, 42
Book of original entry, 42
Book value of
  plant assets, 336
  stock, 484
Break-even
  analysis, 791
  graph, 795

Break-even —*Cont.*
point, 795
point, multi-product, 799
Budget
capital, 767, 811
cash, 768
committee, 764
expense, 767
fixed and variable, 769
flexible, 769
master, 765
material purchases, 766
merchandising, 766
period, 764
plant and equipment, 767
preparing a, 765
reports, 764
sales, 765
Budgeting, 5, 763
benefits of, 763
Burden, factory, 699
Business entity concept, 8, 409
Business papers, 26
for purchases, 216
Buy or make decisions, 819

C

Callable bonds, 577
Canada Business Corporations
Act, 499, 504
Canada Pension Plan, 392
Canceled cheques, 250
Capital
account, 30
budgeting, 811
discounted cash flows in, 814
payback period, 812
rate of return on average investment, 813
use of present values in, 814
contributions of owners and creditors, 612
cost allowance, 850
expenditures, 368
gains, 843
and revenue expenditures, 368
Cash
accounting for, 243
and accrual basis of accounting, 73, 644
basis of revenue recognition, 417
budget, 768
from current operations, 643
defined, 28
Disbursements Journal, 178
discounts, 133, 229
dividends, 480
over and short, 249
Receipts Journal, 173
registers, 244, 669

Cash flow, 643
Cash flow statement, 643
Cash flows, discounted, 814
Certificate of protest; *see* Notice of protest
CGA, 2, 562, 809
Changes in accounting methods, 423, 536
CICA, 2, 305, 309, 311, 333, 374, 412, 415, 423, 505, 529, 535, 544, 545, 548, 549, 583, 614, 629, 630, 632
Cheque Register, 181, 228
Cheques, canceled, 250
Classified balance sheet, 74
Clock card, 395
Closing entries
the accounts after, 107
for expense accounts, 105
and the Income Summary account, 107
and the inventory account, 145
of a manufacturing concern, 708
and revenue accounts, 103
why made, 100
for the Withdrawals account, 107
Code numbers, account, 150
Columnar journals, 170
Common-size statements, 605
Comparative statements, 601
Composite units of product, 800
Computers, 186
Concept of present value, 863
bond interest, 570
capital budgeting, 814
Concepts; *see* Accounting, principles
Conservatism, 311, 423
Consistency, 309, 421
Consolidated balance sheet, 539
Consolidations, 539
dividends of subsidiary, 546
earnings of subsidiary, 545
goodwill from, 544
minority interest in, 542
principles of, 539
purchase versus pooling of interests, 548
Contingent liabilities, 285, 423, 502
Contra account, 65
Contributed capital, 474
and dividends, 512
on the statements, 512
Contribution margin, 795
Contribution to overhead, 677
Contribution rate, 795
Controllable costs, 678

Controllable variances, 776
Controlling accounts, 171
accounts payable, 178
accounts receivable, 178
in cost accounting, 726
in plant asset records, 344
rule for posting to, 176
Controlling a business with standard costs, 777
Convertible bonds, 578
Copyrights, 371
Corporation
accounting, 473
advantages of a, 465
balance sheet, 581
bylaws, 468
charter, 467
disadvantages of a, 467
income taxes, 467, 516, 847
insiders, 418
management of a, 469
minimum legal capital of, 499
organization costs, 469
organizing a, 467
outsiders, 418
registrar, 473
retained earnings, 474, 529
separate legal entity of, 466
stockholders' rights, 481
transfer agent, 473
Corporations, consolidations, 539
Correcting entries, 45
Corrections, normal, 535
Cost
accounting
job order, 725
process, 736
standard, 770
behaviours, 793
centres, 666
departure from, 287, 397
of goods sold, 134, 305
or replacement, the lower, 310
of merchandise purchased, 136
principle, 8, 416
Cost-volume-profit analysis, 791
assumptions on which based, 793
Costs
differential, 818
fixed, 794
incremental, 818
joint, 680
measuring and matching, 420
opportunity, 820
out-of-pocket, 820
semivariable, 792
stair step, 791
sunk, 820
transportation, 152
variable, 792

Credit
    and debit, 31
    memoranda, 147
    period, 133
    terms, 133
Crossfooting, 176
Cumulative preferred stock, 482
Current assets, 75
Current ratio, 608
Cycle, accounting, 114

D

Data processing, 169
    electronic, 186
    mechanical, 184
Days' sales uncollected, 610
Death of a partner, 447
Debentures, 566
Debit and credit, 31
Debit memoranda, 147
Declining-balance depreciation,
    336
Deed of trust, 566
Deferred revenue; see Unearned
    revenue
Deficit, 476
Department, unprofitable, elimi-
    nating, 676
Departmental analysis sheets, 667
Departmental contribution to
    overhead, 677
Departmental expense allocation
    sheet, 675
Departmentalization, basis of,
    666
Depreciation, 64
    accelerated, 337
    allocating, 335
    on balance sheet, 339
    declining-balance, 336
    nature of, 333
    for partial years, 343
    revising rates, 364
    straight-line, 335
    sum-of-the-years'-digits, 337
    units-of-production, 335
Differential costs, 822
Direct expense, 670
Direct labour, 699
Direct materials, 698
Direct write-off of bad debts, 260
Discarding plant assets, 314
Discount
    bank, 282
    bond, 570
    cash, 133, 229
    liability, 286, 502
    lost, 230
    on notes payable, 282, 292
    on notes receivable, 284, 294
    period, cash, 133
    period, note, 285

Discount — Cont.
    on stock, 502
    trade, 151
Discounted cash flows, 814
Discounts
    filing invoices to take, 136
    on purchases, 136
    on sales, 133
Disposing of accrued items, 73
Disposing of appropriations of re-
    tained earnings, 532
Dividends
    in arrears, 483
    cash, 480
    from contributed capital, 512
    dates involved, 480
    declaring, 480
    and growth, 852
    policy, 480
    recording, 480
    restricted by outstanding bonds,
        582
    restricted by treasury stock
        purchases, 506
    in stock, 513
Dollar signs, use of, 46
Donations, of outsiders, 512
Donations, of stockholders, 510
Double-entry accounting, 32
Drawing account, 30

E

Earnings rate, selecting, 817
Earnings per share, 536, 614
Electric bookkeeping machines,
    668
Electronic data processing, 186
Eliminating an unprofitable de-
    partment, 676
Employee's earnings record, 401
Employer's payroll taxes, 402
Entries
    adjusting, 62
    closing, 102
    reversing, 293
Equities, 7
Errors
    correcting, 45
    inventory, 312
Estimated statements, 769
Estimating bad debts, 255
Estimating inventories, 315
Events subsequent to date of
    statements, 423
Exchanging plant assets, 362
Expense allocation sheet, 674
Expense budget, 767
Expenses
    accrued, 66
    allocating, 670
    bases for allocating, 672
    controllable, 678

Expenses — Cont.
    differential, 818
    direct, 670
    escapable, 676
    fixed, 794
    general and administrative, 140
    incremental, 818
    indirect, 670
    inescapable, 676
    matching with revenues, 73,
        419
    mechanics of allocating, 674
    opportunity, 820
    out-of-pocket, 820
    prepaid, 62, 75
    selling, 139
    sunk, 820
    variable, 792
Extraordinary gains and losses,
    534, 641
Extraordinary repairs, 367

F

Factory burden, 699
Factory overhead, 699
Federal income tax exemptions,
    391, 840
Federal income taxes
    corporation, 845
    employees', 391
    individual, 838
Financial statements, analysis of,
    601
Finished goods inventory
    account, 701
First-in, first-out, 307
Fixed assets; see Plant assets
Fixed costs, 792
Fixed and variable budgets, 769
Flow of funds, flow of cash, 629
FOB destination, 152
FOB shipping point, 152
Freight-in, 137
Full-disclosure principle, 422
Funds
    flow of, 629
    nature, 630
    sources, 630
    uses, 632
Funds statement; see Statement
    of changes in financial posi-
    tion

G

Gains and losses
    capital, 843
    on exchange of plant assets, 341
    extraordinary, 534
General and administrative ex-
    penses, 139
General Journal, 42

Going-concern concept, 9, 340, 413
Goods in Process account, 728
Goods in Process Inventory account, 701
Goodwill, 372, 544, 548
Gross income, for tax purposes, 838
Gross profit method of estimating inventories, 318
Gross profit from sales, 132
Gross profits, departmental, 666
Gross sales, 132

H

Heading
  balance sheet, 6
  income statement, 5
History and objectives of the federal income tax, 836
Holder in due course, 290

I

Income
  accumulated; see Retained earnings
  allocated to partners, 438
  retained; see Retained earnings
Income statement
  classification of items on, 139
  common-size, 607
  comparative, 538, 603
  departmental, 670
  manufacturing concern, 700
  merchandising concern, 139
  multiple-step, 539
  single-step, 538
Income tax
  allocation of, 852
  avoidance, 836
  capital gains, 843
  classes of taxpayers, 857
  corporation, 845
  credits, 841
  effect of financing methods on, 849
  effects of alternate decisions on, 847
  evasion, 836
  gross income, 838
  history and objectives, 836
  individual, 837
  prepayments, 841
  rates, corporation, 846
  rates, individual, 842
  synopsis of, 837
  timing transactions, 849
Incremental costs, 818
Indirect expenses, 670
Indirect labour, 699
Indirect materials, 699
Individual earnings record, 401

Insiders, corporation, 418
Intangible assets
  amortization of, 373
  copyrights, 371
  goodwill, 372, 544, 548
  leasehold improvements, 371
  leaseholds, 371
  patents, 370
  research and development costs, 370
  trademarks and names, 373
Interest
  accrued, 290, 294
  bond, 570
  calculating, 277
  partnership, nature of, 440
  tables, 278
Interim statements, 317
Internal auditing, 5, 216
Internal control, 213
  cash, 243
  cash disbursements, 222, 245
  cash discounts, 229
  cash in the mail, 244
  cash sales, 244
  principles of, 213
  purchases, 216
Inventories
  and cost of goods sold, 305
  departure from cost in, 312
  estimating, 315
  finished goods, 701
  first-in, first-out, 307
  goods in process, 701
  gross profit method of estimating, 318
  items included in, 309
  last-in, first-out, 308
  merchandise, 135
  periodic, 134, 314
  perpetual, 134, 314
  physical, 146
  raw material, 700
  retail method of estimating, 315
  turnover, 611
Inventory
  assigning a cost to, 306
  cost, elements of, 309
  cost or replacement, the lower, 310
  errors, 312
  losses, 138, 316
  summary sheets, 147
  systems, 134, 314
  taking a physical, 146
  tickets, 146
Investment income, 840
Investments
  on the balance sheet, 75, 586
  stocks and bonds as, 582
  temporary and long-term, 585

Invoice, 219
  approval form, 221
  checking the, 221
  filing to take discount, 136
  recording at net amount, 230
Invoices as a Sales Journal, 183
Issued stock, 506

J

Job, 725
Job Cost Ledger, 726
Job cost sheets, 726
Job lot, 725
Job order cost accounting, 725
Joint cost, 680
Journal
  Cash Disbursements, 178
  Cash Receipts, 173
  Cheque Register, 181, 228
  columnar, 170
  General, 42
  need for, 42
  Purchases, 178
  Purchases, multicolumn, 183
  Sales, 170
  Sales Returns and Allowances, 177
  Voucher Register, 226

K–L

Key letters on work sheet, 100
Labour
  direct, 699
  indirect, 699
  time ticket, 731
  variance, 772
Land, 77, 332
Last-in, first-out inventories, 308
Leasehold improvements, 371
Leaseholds, 371
Ledger
  Accounts Payable, 178
  Accounts Receivable, 171
  arrangement of accounts in, 72
  General, 171
  Job Cost, 726
  Plant Asset, 344
  subsidiary, 170
Leverage, 484
Liabilities
  contingent, 285, 423
  current, 77
  long-term, 77, 565, 631
Liability
  lack of stockholder, 466
  unlimited, of partner, 436
Lifo inventories, 308
Limited life, partnership, 436
Liquidation, partnership, 447
Long-term investments, 75, 586

M

Maker of a note, 275
Management advisory services, 3
Managerial decisions, 811
Manufacturing
  accounting, 697
  statement, 702
  systems of accounting, 698
Margin of safety, 800
Markups and markdowns, 317
Master budget, 768
Matching principle, 73, 417
Matching revenues and expenses, 73, 417
Material
  direct, 699
  indirect, 699
  in job order cost accounting, 729
  ledger card, 726
  requisition, 729
Material purchases budget, 766
Material variances, 772
Materiality, principle of, 310, 424
Maturity date of a note, 276
Maturity value, 288
Mechanical data processing, 184
Mechanics of double-entry accounting, 32
Merchandise inventory, 135, 305
Merchandise turnover, 611
Merchandising budget, 766
Minority interest, 542
Mortgage, 30, 565
Mutual agency, 436

N

Natural business year, 115
Natural resources, 368
Net present value, 816
Net worth, 78
Nominal accounts, 114
Noncumulative preferred stock, 482
No-par stock, 503
Normal balance of accounts, 96
Normal corrections and adjustments, 535
Notes payable, 280
Notes receivable, 283
  collecting an out-of-town, 290
  discounted, 284
  dishonoured, 284, 287
Notice of protest, 287
NSF cheques, 253

O

Objectivity principle, 421
Obsolescence, 334
Opportunity cost, 820
Ordinary repairs, 366
Organization costs, 469

Out-of-pocket costs, 820
Outsiders, corporation, 418
Outstanding cheques, 251
Outstanding stock, 506
Overhead
  accounting for, 699, 733, 773
  application rate, 733
  contribution to, 677
  factory, 699
  in a job cost system, 733
  over- and underapplied, 735
  variances, 775
Overhead Costs Ledger, 730
Owner equity, 8
  accounts, 30
  on the balance sheet, 78
  increasing the, 13

P

Par value stock, 484, 499
Parent company, 539
Participating preferred stock, 482
Partnership
  accounting, 435
  advantages and disadvantages of, 437
  allocating earnings, 438
  characteristics of, 435
  death of a partner, 447
  liquidation, 447
  nature of earnings, 438
  salaries and interest, 440
  sale of an interest in, 442
  withdrawal of a partner, 443
Patents, 370
Payback period, 812
Payee of a note, 275
Paying the employees, 399
Payroll
  accounting, 389
  bank account, 401
  cheque, 400
  Register, 395
  taxes
    accruing, 403
    of the employer, 402
    paying the, 403
Percentage-of-completion basis for revenue recognition, 419
Periodic inventories, 134, 146
Periodicity concept, 415
Periods in the accounts, 46
Perpetual inventories, 134, 313
Petty cash fund, 245
Petty Cash Record, 247
Physical inventories, 146
Pin-punched price tags, 668
Plant assets
  average investment in, 813
  balance sheet values, 340
  capital budgeting, 811
  cost of, 332

Plant assets—*Cont.*
  discarding, 341
  exchanging, 362
  natural resources, 368
  productive life of, 334
  records, 344
  repairs and replacements, 366
  salvage value, 335
  service life, 334
Plant and equipment budget, 767
Pledged assets to long-term debt, 612
Post-closing trial balance, 113
Posting, 44
  Cash Disbursements Journal, 181
  Cash Receipts Journal, 175
  General Journal, 44
  Purchases Journal, 178
  reference numbers, 45
  rule for controlling accounts, 176
  Sales Journal, 171
  Voucher Register, 227
Predetermined overhead application rate, 733
Preemptive right of stockholders, 481
Preferred stock, 481
Premium, on bonds, 574
Premium, on stock, 500
Prepaid expenses, 75
Present value
  and bond interest rates, 570
  and capital budgeting, 814
  concept, 863
  tables, 864, 866
  using in investment decisions, 865
Price-earnings ratio, 614
Price level changes, 414, 615
Price tags, pin-punched, 668
Price variance, 772
Prior period adjustments, 537
Proceeds of a note, 285
Process cost accounting, 736
Process cost summary, 739
Process or sell decisions, 826
Production basis of revenue recognition, 419
Production budget, 766
Productive life, plant asset, 334
Profit centre, 766
Profit-volume analysis, 791
Program, computer, 188
Promissory note, 275
Protest fee, 287
Protesting a note, 287
Provincial income taxes, 836
Proxy, 470
Public accounting, 3
Punched cards, 668

Punched paper tape, 669
Purchase order, 218
Purchase requisition, 217
Purchases
  controlling, 216
  discounts, 136
  returns and allowances, 137
Purchases of assets used in the
  business, 193
Purchases Journal, 178
  multicolumn, 193

Q–R

Quantity variance, 772
Quick assets, 609
Ratio
  acid-test, 609
  current, 608
  pledged assets to debt, 612
Raw materials, 698
Raw Materials Inventory
  account, 700
Real accounts, 114
Receiving report, 220
Reconciling the bank balance, 250
Redemption of bonds, 577
Registered bonds, 566
Registers; see Journal
Repairs and replacements, 366
Research and development costs,
  370
Responsibility accounting, 665,
  679
Retail method of estimating inventories, 315
Retained earnings, 529
  appropriations, 530
  capitalized in a stock dividend,
    514
  and dividends, 529
  restricted by treasury stock
    purchase, 506
  statement, 533
Retirement of stock, 509
Return on
  assets employed, 613
  plant asset investments, 813
  stockholders' equity, 614
Returned purchases, 137
Returned sales, 133
Revenue
  accrued, 68, 74
  defined, 68
  expenditures, 368
  matching with expenses, 73,
    419
  recognition, 417
  from sales, 132
  unearned, 67, 77
Reversing entries, 293
Revising depreciation rates, 364
RIA, 2

Rights of stockholders, 481
Rule, posting, for controlling ac-
  counts and subsidiary ledg-
  ers, 176
Rule-of-thumb standards, 611
Rules of debit and credit, 31

S

Salaries, allocation of, 673
Salaries, partnership, 440
Sale of a partnership interest, 442
Sales
  to achieve desired income, 797
  allowances, 133
  basis of revenue recognition,
    417
  budget, 765
  discounts, 133
  invoices as a Sales Journal, 183
  Journal, 171
  mix, 801, 827
  returns and allowances, 133
  Returns and Allowances Jour-
    nal, 177
  taxes, 182
Salvage value of plant assets, 335
Schedule of accounts payable,
  182
Schedule of accounts receivable,
  259
Scrap or rebuild defective units,
  825
Scrap value, 335
Selling expenses, 139
Service life, plant asset, 334
Single-step income statement, 538
Sinking fund, bond, 578
Small tools, 361
Sources of funds, 630
Specific invoice prices for inventory, 307
Split up of stock, 515
Standard costs
  in the accounts, 778
  controlling a business with, 777
  establishing, 771
  establishing overhead
    standards, 774
Standards of comparison, 611
Statement of changes in financial
  position, 629, 632
  preparing a, 629, 633
  working paper for, 636
Statement of partner's capital,
  442
Statements
  analyzing, 601
  common-size, 605
  comparative, 536, 601, 605
  consolidated, 539
  interim, 315
  preparing from work sheet, 102

Stock
  authorization of, 476
  book value, 484
  Certificate Book, 472
  certificates, 471
  common, 481
  discounts, 502
  dividends in, 513
  dividends on balance sheet, 515
  exchanging for assets other than
    cash, 477
  liquidation value, 486
  market value, 486
  no-par value, 503
  par value, 484, 499
  preferred, 481
  preferred, why issue, 483
  premiums, 500
  redemption value, 486
  retirement of, 509
  selling for cash, 477
  selling through subscriptions,
    477
  splits, 515
  stated value, 503
  treasury, 504
  values, 484
Stockholder donations, 510
Stockholders, rights of, 481
Stocks and bonds as investments,
  582
Straight-line depreciation, 335
Subscribed stock on the balance
  sheet, 479
Subscriptions to stock, 477
Subsidiary, corporation, 539
Subsidiary ledgers, 170
  proving balances in, 182
  rule for posting to, 176
Sum-of-the-years'-digits depreciation, 337
Sunk costs, 820

T

T-accounts, 26
Tax
  considerations in decisions, 835
  evasion and avoidance, 836
  planning, 835
Taxes
  and distortion of net income,
    852
  income, 835
  payroll, 390, 392, 402
  sales, 182
Taxpayers, classes of, 841
Temporary proprietorship
  accounts, 114
Terms, credit, 133
Terms, transportation, 152
Ticket, inventory, 146
Timekeeping, 395

Times fixed interest charges
earned, 613
Trade discounts, 151
Trade marks and names, 373
Transfer agent, 473
Transportation costs, 152
Transportation terms, 152
Treasury stock, 504
on the balance sheet, 506
reissuance of, 507
Trend percentages, 604
Trial balance
adjusted, 69
preparing, 40
proof offered by, 40
Trustee, sinking fund, 579
Trustee of bondholders, 566
Turnover
accounts receivable, 609
merchandise inventory, 611

U

Uncollectible accounts, 254
Underapplied overhead, 735
Underwriter, 566
Unearned revenue, 67, 77
Unemployment insurance, 389
Union contracts, 393
Units-of-production depreciation,
335
Unlimited liability, partnership,
436

Unpaid vouchers file, 228
Uses of funds, 632

V

Variable budgets, 769, 774
Variable costs, 792
Variances, 771
isolating, 772
labour, 772
material, 772
overhead, 775
volume, 775
Vendee and vendor, 219
Volume-profit analysis, 791
Volume variance, 775
Voucher, 222
recording a, 226
Register, 226
system, 222
system Cheque Register, 228
system and control, 222
Vouchers, unpaid file, 228

W–Z

Wage bracket withholding table,
394
Wages, accrued, 66
Wages, allocation of, 672
Wages and Hours Law, 393
Wages, hours, and union con-
tracts, 394

Wasting assets, 368
Weighted average inventories,
307
Weighted average invoice prices,
307
Withdrawals, 30
Withholding employees' income
taxes, 391
Work of an accountant, 3
Work sheet, 98, 140, 702
and adjusting entries, 102
and closing entries, 102, 144,
707
and financial statements, 102
illustrated, 99, 141, 703
manufacturing, 703
merchandising, 140
need for, 97
preparing a, 98
sorting items on, 101
Working capital, 607
analyzing changes in, 640
Working paper for a statement of
changes in working capital,
636
Working papers, 114, 636
Workmen's compensation, 393
Writing off a bad debt, 257,
260
Year, natural business, 115
Zeros in the accounts, 46

This book has been set in 10 point Times Roman, leaded 2 points. Chapter numbers are 48 point Helvetica Medium and chapter titles are 24 point Helvetica Small. The size of the type page is 32$\frac{1}{2}$ by 49$\frac{1}{2}$ picas.